Fodor's 97

Scandinavia

" "When it comes to information on regional history, what to see and do, and shopping, these guides are exhaustive."

—*USAir Magazine*

"Usable, sophisticated restaurant coverage, with an emphasis on good value."
—Andy Birsh, *Gourmet Magazine* columnist

"Valuable because of their comprehensiveness."
—*Minneapolis Star-Tribune*

"Fodor's always delivers high quality...thoughtfully presented...thorough."

—*Houston Post*

"An excellent choice for those who want everything under one cover."

—*Washington Post* "

Fodor's Travel Publications, Inc.
New York • Toronto • London • Sydney • Auckland
http://www.fodors.com/

Fodor's Scandinavia

Editors: Amy McConnell and Rebecca Miller

Contributors: Robert Andrews, Judy Blumenberg, David Brown, Audra Epstein, Catherine Hill-Herndon, Karina Porcelli, Kathryn Sampson, Heidi Sarna, Helayne Schiff, Mary Ellen Schultz, M. T. Schwartzman (Gold Guide editor), Dinah Spritzer

Creative Director: Fabrizio La Rocca

Associate Art Director: Guido Caroti

Photo Researcher: Jolie Novak

Cartographer: David Lindroth

Cover Photograph: Peter Guttman

Text Design: Between the Covers

Copyright

Special Sales

Fodor's Travel Publications are available at special discounts for bulk purchases for sales promotions or premiums. Special editions, including personalized covers, excerpts of existing guides, and corporate imprints, can be created in large quantities for special needs. For more information, contact your local bookseller or write to Special Markets, Fodor's Travel Publications, 201 East 50th Street, New York, NY 10022. Inquiries from Canada should be directed to your local Canadian bookseller or sent to Random House of Canada, Ltd., Marketing Department, 1265 Aerowood Drive, Mississauga, Ontario L4W 1B9. Inquiries from the United Kingdom should be sent to Fodor's Travel Publications, 20 Vauxhall Bridge Road, London, England SW1V 2SA.

PRINTED IN THE UNITED STATES OF AMERICA

10 9 8 7 6 5 4 3 2 1

CONTENTS

ON THE ROAD WITH FODOR'S

WE'RE ALWAYS THRILLED to get letters from readers, especially one like this:

It took us an hour to decide what book to buy and we now know we picked the best one. Your book was wonderful, easy to follow, very accurate, and good on pointing out eating places, informal as well as formal. When we saw other people using your book, we would look at each other and smile.

Our editors and writers are deeply committed to making every Fodor's guide "the best one"—not only accurate but always charming, brimming with sound recommendations and solid ideas, right on the mark in describing restaurants and hotels, and full of fascinating facts that make you view what you've traveled to see in a rich new light.

About Our Writers

Our success in achieving our goals—and in helping to make your trip the best of all possible vacations—is a credit to the hard work of our extraordinary writers and editors.

Michael J. Kissane is a freelance journalist and translator who has been living in Iceland for more than 13 years. His main interests are nature and travel; his degree in wildlife biology has him sampling trout streams whenever possible.

A native Texan, **Shelley Panill** moved to Norway, became fluent in Norwegian, and still managed to write. In addition to interviewing scores of Norwegians, including Liv Ullmann, Shelley has covered topics ranging from whaling to travel to the Nobel Peace Prize. She writes regularly for *The European* (London) and United Press International (UPI).

Karina Porcelli is a freelance writer who divides her time between Copenhagen and Washington, D.C.

Kathryn M. Sampson was born traveling, in a U.S. Army airplane in Japan. She credits her mother, Clare, for setting an example as an educated, adventurous, resilient tourist. While enjoying the comforts of Stockholm, Kathryn is currently working on an account of her African train trip from Abidjan to Ouagadougou.

Amanda Wunder studied history at the University of Helsinki for 9 months. She is currently working on a doctorate in European history.

New This Year

This year we've reformatted our guides to make them easier to use. Each chapter of *Scandinavia '97* begins with brand-new recommended itineraries to help you decide what to see in the time you have; a section called When to Tour points out the optimal time of day, day of the week, and season for your journey. You may also notice our fresh graphics, new in 1996. More readable and more helpful than ever? We think so—and we hope you do, too.

On the Web

Also check out Fodor's Web site (http://www.fodors.com/), where you'll find travel information on major destinations around the world and an ever-changing array of travel-savvy interactive features.

How to Use This Book

Organization

Up front is the **Gold Guide.** Its first section, **Important Contacts A to Z,** gives addresses and telephone numbers of organizations and companies that offer destination-related services and detailed information and publications. **Smart Travel Tips A to Z,** the Gold Guide's second section, gives specific information on how to accomplish what you need to in Scandinavia as well as tips on savvy traveling. Both sections are in alphabetical order by topic.

Chapters in *Scandinavia '97* are arranged alphabetically by country. Each one begins with a synopsis of the country's pleasures and pastimes, followed by an exploring section with recommended itineraries and tips on when to visit. Chapters are then broken into major regions and cities, with recommended walking or driving tours. Within each region, towns are covered in logical geographical order, while attractive stretches of road and minor points of interest between them are indicated by the designation *En Route;* all restaurants and lodgings are grouped together within town sections. Within each city, sights are covered alphabetically. Throughout the book, Off the Beaten Path sights appear after the sights or towns from which they are most easily accessible. The Essentials section at the end of each region or city covers getting there, getting around, and helpful contacts and resources. A countrywide A to Z section—an expanded version of Essentials appears at the end of each chapter.

Icons and Symbols

★   Our special recommendations
✕   Restaurant
🏠   Lodging establishment
✕🏠 Lodging establishment whose restaurant warrants a detour
⛺   Campgrounds
🐤   Good for kids (rubber duckie)
☞   Sends you to another section of the guide for more information
✉   Address
☎   Telephone number
FAX Fax number
🕐   Opening and closing times
💷   Admission prices (those we give apply only to adults; substantially reduced fees are almost always available for children, students, and senior citizens)

Numbers in white and black circles—②and ❷, for example—that appear on the maps, in the margins, and within the tours correspond to one another.

Dining and Lodging

The restaurants and lodgings we list are the cream of the crop in each price range. Price charts appear in the Pleasures and Pastimes section that follows each chapter introduction.

Hotel Facilities

We always list the facilities that are available—but we don't specify whether they cost extra: When pricing accommodations, always ask what's included. Breakfast is almost always included in the price of Scandinavian hotels.

Restaurant Reservations and Dress Codes

Reservations are always a good idea; we note only when they're essential or when they are not accepted. Book as far ahead as you can, and reconfirm when you get to town. Unless otherwise noted, the restaurants listed are open daily for lunch and dinner. Most are closed for Christmas, and many close for the entire month of December. We mention dress only when men are required to wear a jacket or a jacket and tie. Look for an overview of local habits under Dining in the Pleasures and Pastimes section that follows each chapter introduction.

Credit Cards

The following abbreviations are used: **AE,** American Express; **DC,** Diners Club; **MC,** MasterCard; and **V,** Visa.

Please Write to Us

You can use this book in the confidence that all prices and opening times are based on information supplied to us at press time; Fodor's cannot accept responsibility for any errors. Time inevitably brings changes, so always confirm information when it matters—especially if you're making a detour to visit a specific place. In addition, when making reservations be sure to mention if you have a disability or are traveling with children, if you prefer a private bath or a certain type of bed, or if you have specific dietary needs or any other concerns.

Were the restaurants we recommended as described? Did our hotel picks exceed your expectations? Did you find a museum we recommended a waste of time? If you have complaints, we'll look into them and revise our entries when the facts warrant it. If you've discovered a special place that we haven't included, we'll pass the information along to our correspondents and have them check it out. So send your feedback, positive *and* negative, to the Scandinavia Editor at 201 East 50th Street, New York, New York 10022—and have a wonderful trip!

Karen Cure
Editorial Director

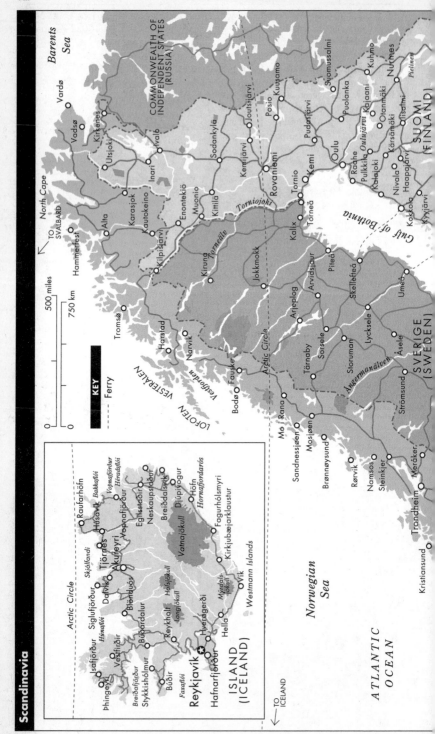

Scandinavia

Barents Sea

COMMONWEALTH OF INDEPENDENT STATES (RUSSIA)

Vardø
Vadsø
Kirkenes
Utsjoki
Ivalo
Sodankylä
Kentjärvi
Joutsijärvi
Posio
Kuusamo
Syömussalmi
Kuhmo
Nurmes

SUOMI (FINLAND)

Pelinen

TO SVALBARD
North Cape
Hammerfest
Alta
Karasjok
Kautokeino
Enontekiö
Muonio
Kittilä
Rovaniemi
Kemijärvi
Puolanka
Otanmäki
Ilisalmi
Kajaani
Pulkkila Oulujärvi
Raahe
Oulu
Kemi
Tornio
Torneå
Kalix
Kälviä
Kokkola
Kälsämäki
Haapajärvi
Nivala
Kyyjärvi

Torniojoki

Kilpisjärvi
Kiruna
Jokkmokk
Gulf of Bothnia

Tromsø
Harstad
Narvik
Arctic Circle
Arjeplog
Arvidsjaur
Piteå
Skellefteå
Umeå

VESTERÅLEN
Vestfjorden
LOFOTEN
Bodø
Fauske
Mo i Rana
Tärnaby
Sorsele
Storuman
Lycksele
Åsele

KEY
------ Ferry

500 miles
750 km

SVERIGE (SWEDEN)

Ångermanälven

Sandnessjøen
Mosjøen
Brønnøysund
Rørvik
Namsos
Steinkjer
Strömsund
Östersund
Meråker

Trondheim
Kristiansund

Arctic Circle
Raufarhöfn
Bakkaflói
Vopnafjörður
Héraðslói
Húsavík
Skjálfandi
Tjörnes
Akureyri
Egilsstaðir
Neskaupstaður
Breiðdalsvík
Vopnafjörður
Djúpivogur
Höfn
Hornafjarðarós
Siglufjörður
Dalvík
Fagurhólsmýri
Vatnajökull
Ísafjörður
Himaflói
Blönduós
Búðardalur
Reykholt
Hólsjökull
Langjökull
Kirkjubæjarklaustur
Þingeyri
Vestfirðir
Stykkishólmur
Breiðafjörður
Hvalfjörður
Hvetagerði
Myrdalsjökull
Vík
Fasaflói
Búðir
Hella
Westmann Islands

Reykjavík
Hafnarfjörður

ISLAND (ICELAND)

Norwegian Sea

ATLANTIC OCEAN

TO ICELAND

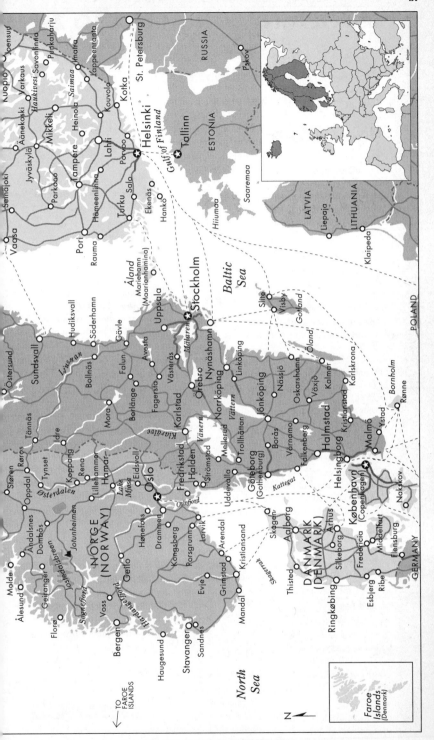

THE GOLD GUIDE / IMPORTANT CONTACTS

IMPORTANT CONTACTS A TO Z

An Alphabetical Listing of Publications, Organizations, and Companies That Will Help You Before, During, and After Your Trip

A

AIR TRAVEL

The major gateways to Scandinavia include Iceland's **Kevlavik International Airport**, 48 kilometers (30 miles) outside of Reykjavík (☎ 011–354–425–1/0200); Denmark's **Kastrup International Airport** in Copenhagen (☎ 011–45–31/541701); Sweden's **Arlanda International Airport** in Stockholm (☎ 011–46–8/767–6100); Norway's **Fornebu Airport** in Oslo (☎ 011–47–224/97598); and Finland's **Vantaa International Airport** in Helsinki (☎ 011–358–060/08100).

FLYING TIME

Flying time from New York to Reykjavík is 5½ hours; to Copenhagen, 7¾ hours; to Stockholm, 8 hours; to Oslo, 7½; to Helsinki, 8 hours. From Los Angeles to Copenhagen, flying time is 9¾ hours; to Helsinki, 11¼ hours.

CARRIERS

To COPENHAGEN➤ Contact **Scandinavian Airlines (SAS)** (☎ 800/221–2350), **Delta** (☎ 800/221–1212), and **Finnair** (☎ 800/950–5000).

To REYKJAVÍK➤ Contact **Scandinavian Airlines (SAS)** (☎ 800/221–2350), **Finnair** (☎ 800/950–5000), and **Icelandair** (☎ 800/223–5500).

To OSLO➤ Contact **Scandinavian Airlines (SAS)** (☎ 800/221–2350), **Delta** (☎ 800/221–1212), and **Finnair** (☎ 800/950–5000).

To STOCKHOLM➤ Contact **Scandinavian Airlines (SAS)** (☎ 800/221–2350), **American Airlines** (☎ 800/433–7300), **Delta** (☎ 800/221–1212), and **Finnair** (☎ 800/950–5000).

IN THE U.K.

Carriers serving Scandinavia from the United Kingdom include **SAS** (☎ 0171/734–4020, FAX 0171/465–0537), which flies to Bergen, Copenhagen, Göteborg, Oslo, Stavanger, and Stockholm; **British Airways** (☎ 0181/897–4000; outside London, 0345/222–111), serving Bergen, Copenhagen, Göteborg, Helsinki, Oslo, Stavanger, and Stockholm; **Maersk Air** (☎ 0171/333–0066), which flies between London and Copenhagen; **Aer Lingus** (☎ 0181/899–4747; in Ireland, 01/844–4777); **Icelandair** (☎ 0171/388–5599); and **Trans Swede** (☎ 01293/568–812).

COMPLAINTS

To register complaints about charter and scheduled airlines, contact the U.S. Department of Transportation's **Aviation Consumer Protection Division** (✉ C-75, Washington, DC 20590, ☎ 202/366–2220). Complaints about lost baggage or ticketing problems and safety concerns may also be logged with the **Federal Aviation Administration (FAA) Consumer Hotline** (☎ 800/322–7873).

CONSOLIDATORS

For the names of reputable air-ticket consolidators, contact the **United States Air Consolidators Association** (✉ 925 L St., Suite 220, Sacramento, CA 95814, ☎ 916/441–4166, FAX 916/441–3520). For discount air-ticketing agencies, *see* Discounts & Deals, *below*.

PUBLICATIONS

For general information about charter carriers, ask for the Department of Transportation's free brochure **"Plane Talk: Public Charter Flights"** (✉ Aviation Consumer Protection Division, C-75, Washington, DC 20590, ☎ 202/366–2220). The Department of Transportation also publishes a 58-page booklet, **"Fly Rights,"** available from the Consumer Information Center (✉ Supt. of Documents, Dept. 136C, Pueblo, CO 81009; $1.75).

B

BETTER BUSINESS BUREAU

For local contacts in the hometown of a tour operator you may be considering, consult the **Council of Better Business Bureaus** (⌧ 4200 Wilson Blvd., Suite 800, Arlington, VA 22203, ☎ 703/276–0100, ℻ 703/525–8277).

Bus tours can be effective for smaller regions within Norway, Sweden, Finland, and Denmark, but all have excellent train systems, which offer much greater coverage in less time than buses. Detailed information on bus routes is available through local tourist offices (☞ A to Z section in the chapter of your destination).

C

The major car-rental companies represented in Scandinavia are **Alamo** (☎ 800/327–9633; in the U.K., 0800/272–2000), **Avis** (☎ 800/331–1084; in Canada, 800/879–2847), **Budget** (☎ 800/527–0700; in the U.K., 0800/181181), **Dollar** (☎ 800/800–4000; in the U.K., where it is known as Eurodollar, 0990/565656), **Hertz** (☎ 800/654–3001; in Canada, 800/263–0600; in the U.K., 0345/555888), and **National InterRent** (sometimes known as Europcar InterRent outside North America; ☎ 800/227–3876; in the U.K., 0345/222–525). In Copenhagen, rates begin at $86 a day and $231 a week. In Stockholm, rates begin at $111 a day and $384 a week. In Oslo, rates begin at $122 a day and $264 a week. Prices do not include tax,

which ranges from 23% to 25%.

RENTAL WHOLESALERS

Contact **Auto Europe** (☎ 207/828–2525 or 800/223–5555), **Europe by Car** (☎ 800/223–1516; in CA, 800/252–9401), or the **Kemwel Group** (☎ 914/835–5555 or 800/678–0678).

FLYING

Look into **"Flying with Baby"** (⌧ Third Street Press, Box 261250, Littleton, CO 80163, ☎ 303/595–5959; $4.95 includes shipping), cowritten by a flight attendant. **"Kids and Teens in Flight,"** free from the U.S. Department of Transportation's Aviation Consumer Protection Division (⌧ C-75, Washington, DC 20590, ☎ 202/366–2220), offers tips on children flying alone. Every two years the February issue of *Family Travel Times* (☞ Know-How, *below*) details children's services on three dozen airlines. **"Flying Alone, Handy Advice for Kids Traveling Solo"** is available free from the American Automobile Association (AAA) (send stamped, self-addressed, legal-size envelope: ⌧ Flying Alone, Mail Stop 800, 1000 AAA Dr., Heathrow, FL 32746).

KNOW-HOW

Family Travel Times, published quarterly by Travel with Your Children (⌧ TWYCH, 40 5th Ave., New York, NY 10011, ☎ 212/477–

5524; $40 per year), covers destinations, types of vacations, and modes of travel.

TOUR OPERATORS

Contact **Rascals in Paradise** (⌧ 650 5th St., Suite 505, San Francisco, CA 94107, ☎ 415/978–9800 or 800/872–7225).

IN THE U.S.

The **U.S. Customs Service** (⌧ Box 7407, Washington, DC 20044, ☎ 202/927–6724) can answer questions on duty-free limits and publishes a helpful brochure, "Know Before You Go." For information on registering foreign-made articles, call 202/927–0540 or write U.S. Customs Service, Resource Management, 1301 Constitution Ave. NW, Washington, DC 20229.

COMPLAINTS➤ Note the inspector's badge number and write to the commissioner's office (⌧ 1301 Constitution Ave. NW, Washington, DC 20229).

CANADIANS

Contact **Revenue Canada** (⌧ 2265 St. Laurent Blvd. S, Ottawa, Ontario K1G 4K3, ☎ 613/993–0534) for a copy of the free brochure **"I Declare/Je Déclare"** and for details on duty-free limits. For recorded information (within Canada only), call 800/461–9999.

U.K. CITIZENS

HM Customs and Excise (⌧ Dorset House, Stamford St., London SE1 9NG, ☎ 0171/

202–4227) can answer questions about U.K. customs regulations and publishes a free pamphlet, **"A Guide for Travellers,"** detailing standard procedures and import rules.

D
DISABILITIES & ACCESSIBILITY

COMPLAINTS

To register complaints under the provisions of the Americans with Disabilities Act, contact the U.S. Department of Justice's **Disability Rights Section** (⊠ Box 66738, Washington, DC 20035, ☎ 202/514–0301 or 800/514–0301, FAX 202/307–1198, TTY 202/514–0383 or 800/514–0383). For airline-related problems, contact the U.S. Department of Transportation's **Aviation Consumer Protection Division** (☞ Air Travel, *above*). For complaints about surface transportation, contact the Department of Transportation's **Civil Rights Office** (⊠ 400 7th St. SW, Room 10215, Washington, DC 20590, ☎ 202/366–4648).

LODGING

The **Best Western** chain (☎ 800/528–1234) offers properties with wheelchair-accessible rooms in Helsinki, Oslo, and Stockholm and just outside Copenhagen. If wheelchair-accessible rooms are not available, ground-floor rooms are provided.

ORGANIZATIONS

TRAVELERS WITH HEARING IMPAIRMENTS➤ The **American Academy of Otolaryngology** (⊠ 1 Prince St., Alexandria,

VA 22314, ☎ 703/836–4444, FAX 703/683–5100, TTY 703/519–1585) publishes a brochure, "Travel Tips for Hearing Impaired People."

TRAVELERS WITH MOBILITY PROBLEMS➤ Contact the **Information Center for Individuals with Disabilities** (⊠ Box 256, Boston, MA 02117, ☎ 617/450–9888; in MA, 800/462–5015; TTY 617/424–6855); **Mobility International USA** (⊠ Box 10767, Eugene, OR 97440, ☎ and TTY 541/343–1284, FAX 541/343–6812), the U.S. branch of a Belgium-based organization (☞ *below*) with affiliates in 30 countries; **MossRehab Hospital Travel Information Service** (☎ 215/456–9600, TTY 215/456–9602), a telephone information resource for travelers with physical disabilities; the **Society for the Advancement of Travel for the Handicapped** (⊠ 347 5th Ave., Suite 610, New York, NY 10016, ☎ 212/447–7284, FAX 212/725–8253; membership $45); and **Travelin' Talk** (⊠ Box 3534, Clarksville, TN 37043, ☎ 615/552–6670, FAX 615/552–1182), which provides local contacts worldwide for travelers with disabilities.

TRAVELERS WITH VISION IMPAIRMENTS➤ Contact the **American Council of the Blind** (⊠ 1155 15th St. NW, Suite 720, Washington, DC 20005, ☎ 202/467–5081, FAX 202/467–5085) for a list of travelers' resources or the **American Foundation for the Blind** (⊠ 11 Penn Plaza, Suite 300, New York, NY 10001, ☎

212/502–7600 or 800/232–5463, TTY 212/502–7662), which provides general advice and publishes **Access to Art** ($19.95), a directory of museums that accommodate travelers with vision impairments.

IN THE U.K.

Contact the **Royal Association for Disability and Rehabilitation** (⊠ RADAR, 12 City Forum, 250 City Rd., London EC1V 8AF, ☎ 0171/250–3222) or **Mobility International** (⊠ rue de Manchester 25, B-1080 Brussels, Belgium, ☎ 00–322–410–6297, FAX 00–322–410–6874), an international travel-information clearinghouse for people with disabilities.

PUBLICATIONS

Several publications for travelers with disabilities are available from the **Consumer Information Center** (⊠ Box 100, Pueblo, CO 81009, ☎ 719/948–3334). Call or write for its free catalog of current titles. The Society for the Advancement of Travel for the Handicapped (☞ Organizations, *above*) publishes the quarterly magazine **"Access to Travel"** ($13 for 1-year subscription).

The 500-page **Travelin' Talk Directory** (⊠ Box 3534, Clarksville, TN 37043, ☎ 615/552–6670, FAX 615/552–1182; $35) lists people and organizations who help travelers with disabilities. For travel agents worldwide, consult the **Directory of Travel Agencies for the Disabled** (⊠ Twin Peaks Press, Box 129, Vancouver, WA 98666, ☎

360/694–2462 or 800/637–2256, FAX 360/696–3210; $19.95 plus $3 shipping).

TRAVEL AGENCIES & TOUR OPERATORS

The Americans with Disabilities Act requires that all travel firms serve the needs of all travelers. That said, you should note that some agencies and operators specialize in making travel arrangements for individuals and groups with disabilities, among them **Access Adventures** (⊠ 206 Chestnut Ridge Rd., Rochester, NY 14624, ☎ 716/889–9096), run by a former physical-rehab counselor.

TRAVELERS WITH MOBILITY PROBLEMS➣ Contact **Accessible Journeys** (⊠ 35 W. Sellers Ave., Ridley Park, PA 19078, ☎ 610/521–0339 or 800/846–4537, FAX 610/521–6959), an escorted-tour operator exclusively for travelers with mobility impairments; **Flying Wheels Travel** (⊠ 143 W. Bridge St., Box 382, Owatonna, MN 55060, ☎ 507/451–5005 or 800/535–6790), a travel agency specializing in European cruises and tours; **Hinsdale Travel Service** (⊠ 201 E. Ogden Ave., Suite 100, Hinsdale, IL 60521, ☎ 708/325–1335), a travel agency that benefits from the advice of wheelchair traveler Janice Perkins; and **Wheelchair Journeys** (⊠ 16979 Redmond Way, Redmond, WA 98052, ☎ 206/885–2210 or 800/313–4751), which can handle arrangements worldwide.

TRAVELERS WITH DEVELOPMENTAL DISABILITIES➣ Contact the nonprofit **New Directions** (⊠ 5276 Hollister Ave., Suite 207, Santa Barbara, CA 93111, ☎ 805/967–2841).

TRAVEL GEAR

The **Magellan's** catalog (☎ 800/962–4943, FAX 805/568–5406) includes a section devoted to products designed for travelers with disabilities.

DISCOUNTS & DEALS

AIRFARES

For the lowest airfares to Scandinavia, call ☎ 800/FLY–4–LESS.

CLUBS

Contact **Entertainment Travel Editions** (⊠ Box 1068, Trumbull, CT 06611, ☎ 800/445–4137; $28–$53, depending on destination), **Great American Traveler** (⊠ Box 27965, Salt Lake City, UT 84127, ☎ 800/548–2812; $49.95 per year), **Moment's Notice Discount Travel Club** (⊠ 7301 New Utrecht Ave., Brooklyn, NY 11204, ☎ 718/234–6295; $25 per year, single or family), **Privilege Card** (⊠ 3391 Peachtree Rd. NE, Suite 110, Atlanta, GA 30326, ☎ 404/262–0222 or 800/236–9732; $74.95 per year), **Travelers Advantage** (⊠ CUC Travel Service, 49 Music Square W, Nashville, TN 37203, ☎ 800/548–1116 or 800/648–4037; $49 per year, single or family), or **Worldwide Discount Travel Club** (⊠ 1674 Meridian Ave., Miami Beach, FL 33139, ☎ 305/534–2082; $50 per year for family, $40 single).

HOTEL ROOMS

For hotel room rates guaranteed in U.S. dollars, call **Steigenberger Reservation Service** (☎ 800/223–5652).

PASSES

☞ Train Travel, *below.*

STUDENTS

Members of Hostelling International–American Youth Hostels (☞ Students, *below*) are eligible for discounts on car rentals, admissions to attractions, and other selected travel expenses.

PUBLICATIONS

Consult *The Frugal Globetrotter,* by Bruce Northam (⊠ Fulcrum Publishing, 350 Indiana St., Suite 350, Golden, CO 80401, ☎ 800/992–2908; $16.95 plus $4 shipping). For publications that tell how to find the lowest prices on plane tickets, *see* Air Travel, *above.*

Also see Fodor's *Affordable Europe* (available in bookstores, or ☎ 800/533–6478; $18.50).

F

FERRIES

The main ferry operators running within Scandinavian waters are **Larvik Line** (⊠ Hoffsveien 15, Skøyen, Box 265, N–0212 Oslo, Norway, ☎ 47/22–52–55–00, FAX 47/22–52–15–40), **Color Line** (⊠ Box 30, DK–9850 Hirsthals, Denmark, ☎ 45/99–56–19–66, FAX 45/98–94–50–92; Hjortneskaia, Box 1422 Vika, N–0115 Oslo, Norway, ☎ 47/22–94–

44–00, FAX 47/22–83–
07–71; c/o Bergen
Line, Inc., 505 5th
Ave., New York,
NY 10017, ☎ 800/
323–7436, FAX 212/
983–1275; Tyne Com-
mission Quay, North
Shields NE29 6EA,
Newcastle, England,
☎ 0191/296–1313,
FAX 091/296–1540),
and **ScandLines** (✉
Box 1, DK–3000 Hels-
ingør, Denmark, ☎ 45/
49–26–26–83, FAX 45/
49–26–11–24; Knut-
punkten 44, S–252 78
Helsingborg, Sweden,
☎ 46/42–186100,
FAX 46/42–187410).

The chief operator
between England and
many points within
Scandinavia is **DFDS/
Scandinavian Seaways**
(✉ Sankt Annae Plads
30, DK–1295 Copen-
hagen, Denmark,
☎ 45/33–42–30–00,
FAX 45/33–42–30–69;
DFDS Travel Centre,
15 Hanover St., Lon-
don W1R 9HG, ☎
0171/409–6060, FAX
0171/409–6035; DFDS
Seaways USA Inc.,
6555 NW 9th Ave.,
Suite 207, Fort Laud-
erdale, FL 33309,
☎ 800/533–3756,
FAX 305/491–7958;
Box 8895, Scandia-
hamnen, S–402 72
Göteborg, Sweden,
☎ 46/8–650650), with
ships connecting Har-
wich and Newcastle
to Göteborg and
Amsterdam.

Connections from
Denmark to Norway
and Sweden are avail-
able through DFDS
and the **Stena Line**
(✉ Trafikhamnen,
DK–9900 Frederik-
shavn, Denmark,
☎ 45/96–20–02–00,
FAX 45/96–20–02–81;
Jernbanetorget 2,

N–0154 Oslo 1,
Norway, ☎ 47/22–33–
50–00, FAX 47/22–41–
44–40; Scandinavia AB,
S–405 19 Göteborg,
Sweden, ☎ 46/31–
775–0000, FAX 46/31–
858595).

You can sail along the
magnificent west coast
of Norway with the
Fjord Line (✉ Slotts-
gatan 1, N–5003
Bergen, Norway, ☎ 47/
55–32–37–70, FAX 47/
55–32–38–15).

Connections to the
Faroe Islands from
Norway and Denmark
are available through
the **Smyril Line** (DFDS—
☞ *above*—or J. Bronks-
goøta 37, Box 370,
FR–110 Tórshavn,
Faroe Islands, ☎ 298/
15–900, FAX 298/15–
707; Bergen, Norway,
☎ 47/55–32–09–70,
FAX 47/55–96–02–72).

The **Silja Line** (✉
Kungsgatan 2, S–111
43 Stockholm, Sweden,
☎ 46/8–22–21–40,
FAX 46/8–667–8681; c/o
Scandinavian Seaways,
Parkeston Quay Scand.
House, Harwich,
England, ☎ 44/255–
240–240, FAX 44/255–
240–268) offers
luxurious cruises to
Finland, with depar-
tures from Stockholm
to Åbo, Helsingfors,
Helsinki and Turku,
and a crossing from
Umeå to Vaasa.

Travel by car often
necessitates travel by
ferry. Some well-known
vehicle and passenger
ferries run between
Dragør, Denmark (just
south of Copenhagen),
and Limhamn, Sweden
(just south of Malmö);
between Helsingør,
Denmark, and Helsing-
borg, Sweden; and
between Copenhagen

and Göteborg, Sweden.
On the Dragør/
Limhamn ferry (Scand-
Lines), taking a car one-
way costs SKr395
(about $60 or £39). An
easy trip runs between
Copenhagen and Göte-
borg on **Stena Line** (in
Sweden, ☎ 031/75–
00–00). The Helsingør/
Helsingborg ferry
(ScandLines also) takes
only 25 minutes; taking
a car along one-way
costs SKr330 (about
$50 or £33). Fares for
round-trip are cheaper,
and on weekends the
Öresund Runt pass (for
crossing between
Dragoør and Limhamn
one way and Helsing-
borg and Helsingoør
the other way) costs
only SKr495 (about
$75 or £49).

G

GAY & LESBIAN TRAVEL

ORGANIZATIONS

The **International Gay
Travel Association** (✉
Box 4974, Key West,
FL 33041, ☎ 800/448–
8550, FAX 305/296–
6633), a consortium of
more than 1,000 travel
companies, can supply
names of gay-friendly
travel agents, tour
operators, and accom-
modations.

PUBLICATIONS

The premier interna-
tional travel magazine
for gays and lesbians is
Our World (✉ 1104 N.
Nova Rd., Suite 251,
Daytona Beach, FL
32117, ☎ 904/441–
5367, FAX 904/441–
5604; $35 for 10
issues). The 16-page
monthly *"Out & About"*
(☎ 212/645–6922 or
800/929–2268, FAX 800/
929–2215; $49 for 10

issues and quarterly calendar) covers gay-friendly resorts, hotels, cruise lines, and airlines.

TOUR OPERATORS

Toto Tours (✉ 1326 W. Albion Ave., Suite 3W, Chicago, IL 60626, ☎ 312/274–8686 or 800/565–1241, FAX 312/274–8695) offers group tours to worldwide destinations.

TRAVEL AGENCIES

The largest agencies serving gay travelers are **Advance Travel** (✉ 10700 Northwest Fwy., Suite 160, Houston, TX 77092, ☎ 713/682–2002 or 800/292–0500), **Islanders/Kennedy Travel** (✉ 183 W. 10th St., New York, NY 10014, ☎ 212/242–3222 or 800/988–1181), **Now Voyager** (✉ 4406 18th St., San Francisco, CA 94114, ☎ 415/626–1169 or 800/255–6951), and **Yellowbrick Road** (✉ 1500 W. Balmoral Ave., Chicago, IL 60640, ☎ 312/561–1800 or 800/642–2488). **Skylink Women's Travel** (✉ 2460 W. 3rd St., Suite 215, Santa Rosa, CA 95401, ☎ 707/570–0105 or 800/225–5759) serves lesbian travelers.

H
HEALTH

FINDING A DOCTOR

For its members, the **International Association for Medical Assistance to Travellers** (✉ IAMAT, membership free; 417 Center St., Lewiston, NY 14092, ☎ 716/754–4883; 40 Regal Rd., Guelph, Ontario N1K 1B5, ☎ 519/836–

0102; 1287 St. Clair Ave. W, Toronto, Ontario M6E 1B8, ☎ 416/652–0137; 57 Voirets, 1212 Grand-Lancy, Geneva, Switzerland, no phone) publishes a worldwide directory of English-speaking physicians meeting IAMAT standards.

MEDICAL ASSISTANCE COMPANIES

The following companies are concerned primarily with emergency medical assistance, although they may provide some insurance as part of their coverage. For a list of full-service travel insurance companies, *see* Insurance, *below.*

Contact **International SOS Assistance** (✉ Box 11568, Philadelphia, PA 19116, ☎ 215/244–1500 or 800/523–8930; Box 466, Pl. Bonaventure, Montréal, Québec H5A 1C1, ☎ 514/874–7674 or 800/363–0263; 7 Old Lodge Pl., St. Margarets, Twickenham TW1 1RQ, England, ☎ 0181/744–0033), **Medex Assistance Corporation** (✉ Box 5375, Timonium, MD 21094-5375, ☎ 410/453–6300 or 800/537–2029), **Traveler's Emergency Network** (✉ 3100 Tower Blvd., Suite 3100A, Durham, NC 27702, ☎ 919/490–6065 or 800/275–4836, FAX 919/493–8262), **TravMed** (✉ Box 5375, Timonium, MD 21094, ☎ 410/453–6380 or 800/732–5309), or **Worldwide Assistance Services** (✉ 1133 15th St. NW, Suite 400, Washington, DC 20005, ☎ 202/331–1609 or 800/821–2828, FAX 202/828–5896).

I
INSURANCE

IN CANADA

Contact **Mutual of Omaha** (✉ Travel Division, 500 University Ave., Toronto, Ontario M5G 1V8, ☎ 800/465–0267 in Canada or 416/598–4083).

IN THE U.S.

Travel insurance covering baggage, health, and trip cancellation or interruptions is available from **Access America** (✉ 6600 W. Broad St., Richmond, VA 23230, ☎ 804/285–3300 or 800/334–7525), **Carefree Travel Insurance** (✉ Box 9366, 100 Garden City Plaza, Garden City, NY 11530, ☎ 516/294–0220 or 800/323–3149), **Near Travel Services** (✉ Box 1339, Calumet City, IL 60409, ☎ 708/868–6700 or 800/654–6700), **Tele-Trip** (✉ Mutual of Omaha Plaza, Box 31716, Omaha, NE 68131, ☎ 800/228–9792), **Travel Guard International** (✉ 1145 Clark St., Stevens Point, WI 54481, ☎ 715/345–0505 or 800/826–1300), **Travel Insured International** (✉ Box 280568, East Hartford, CT 06128, ☎ 203/528–7663 or 800/243–3174), and **Wallach & Company** (✉ 107 W. Federal St., Box 480, Middleburg, VA 22117, ☎ 540/687–3166 or 800/237–6615).

IN THE U.K.

The **Association of British Insurers** (✉ 51 Gresham St., London EC2V 7HQ, ☎ 0171/600–3333) gives advice by phone and publishes the free pamphlet

"Holiday Insurance and Motoring Abroad," which sets out typical policy provisions and costs.

L
LODGING

For information on hotel consolidators, *see* Discounts, *above.*

APARTMENT & VILLA RENTAL

Among the companies to contact are **Europa-Let** (⌂ 92 N. Main St., Ashland, OR 97520, ☎ 541/482–5806 or 800/462–4486, FAX 541/482–0660) and **Property Rentals International** (⌂ 1008 Mansfield Crossing Rd., Richmond, VA 23236, ☎ 804/378–6054 or 800/220–3332, FAX 804/379–2073).

HOME EXCHANGE

Some of the principal clearinghouses are **HomeLink International/Vacation Exchange Club** (⌂ Box 650, Key West, FL 33041, ☎ 305/294–1448 or 800/638–3841, FAX 305/294–1148; $78 per year), which sends members five annual directories, with a listing in one, plus updates; and **Intervac International** (⌂ Box 590504, San Francisco, CA 94159, ☎ 415/435–3497, FAX 415/435–7440; $65 per year), which publishes four annual directories.

M
MONEY

ATMS

For specific foreign **Cirrus** locations, call ☎ 800/424–7787; for foreign **Plus** locations, consult the Plus directory at your local bank.

CURRENCY EXCHANGE

If your bank doesn't exchange currency, contact **Thomas Cook Currency Services** (☎ 800/287–7362 for locations). **Ruesch International** (☎ 800/424–2923 for locations) can also provide you with foreign banknotes before you leave home and publishes a number of useful brochures, including a "Foreign Currency Guide" and "Foreign Exchange Tips."

WIRING FUNDS

Funds can be wired via **MoneyGram**ˢᴹ (for locations and information in the U.S. and Canada, ☎ 800/926–9400) or **Western Union** (for agent locations or to send money using MasterCard or Visa, ☎ 800/325–6000; in Canada, 800/321–2923; in the U.K., 0800/833833; or visit the Western Union office at the nearest major post office).

P
PACKING

For strategies on packing light, get a copy of **The Packing Book,** by Judith Gilford (⌂ Ten Speed Press, Box 7123, Berkeley, CA 94707, ☎ 510/559–1600 or 800/841–2665, FAX 510/524–4588; $7.95 plus $3.50 shipping).

PASSPORTS & VISAS

IN THE U.S.

For fees, documentation requirements, and other information, call the State Department's **Office of Passport Ser-**

vices information line (☎ 202/647–0518).

CANADIANS

For fees, documentation requirements, and other information, call the Ministry of Foreign Affairs and International Trade's **Passport Office** (☎ 819/994–3500 or 800/567–6868).

U.K. CITIZENS

For fees, documentation requirements, and to request an emergency passport, call the **London Passport Office** (☎ 0990/210410).

PHOTO HELP

The **Kodak Information Center** (☎ 800/242–2424) answers consumer questions about film and photography. The *Kodak Guide to Shooting Great Travel Pictures* (available in bookstores; or contact Fodor's Travel Publications, ☎ 800/533–6478; $16.50 plus $4 shipping) explains how to take expert travel photographs.

S
SAFETY

"Trouble-Free Travel," from the AAA, is a booklet of tips for protecting yourself and your belongings when away from home. Send a stamped, self-addressed, legal-size envelope to Trouble-Free Travel (⌂ Mail Stop 75, 1000 AAA Dr., Heathrow, FL 32746).

SENIOR CITIZENS

EDUCATIONAL TRAVEL

The nonprofit **Elderhostel** (⌂ 75 Federal St., 3rd Floor, Boston, MA 02110, ☎ 617/426–7788), for people 55 and older, has offered inexpensive study programs since 1975. Courses cover everything from marine science to Greek mythology and cowboy poetry. Costs for two- to three-week international trips—including room, board, and transportation from the United States—range from $1,800 to $4,500.

Interhostel (✉ University of New Hampshire, 6 Garrison Ave., Durham, NH 03824, ☎ 603/862–1147 or 800/733–9753), for travelers 50 and older, has two- to three-week trips; most last two weeks and cost $2,000–$3,500, including airfare.

ORGANIZATIONS

Contact the **American Association of Retired Persons** (✉ AARP, 601 E St. NW, Washington, DC 20049, ☎ 202/434–2277; annual dues $8 per person or couple). Its Purchase Privilege Program secures discounts for members on lodging, car rentals, and sightseeing.

Additional sources for discounts on lodgings, car rentals, and other travel expenses, as well as helpful magazines and newsletters, are the **National Council of Senior Citizens** (✉ 1331 F St. NW, Washington, DC 20004, ☎ 202/347–8800; annual membership $12) and Sears's **Mature Outlook** (✉ Box 10448, Des Moines, IA 50306, ☎ 800/336–6330; annual membership $14.95).

GROUPS

The major tour operators specializing in

student travel are **Contiki Holidays** (✉ 300 Plaza Alicante, Suite 900, Garden Grove, CA 92640, ☎ 714/740–0808 or 800/266–8454) and **AESU Travel** (✉ 2 Hamill Rd., Suite 248, Baltimore, MD 21210-1807, ☎ 410/323–4416 or 800/638–7640).

HOSTELING

In the United States, contact **Hostelling International–American Youth Hostels** (✉ 733 15th St. NW, Suite 840, Washington, DC 20005, ☎ 202/783–6161, FAX 202/783–6171); in Canada, **Hostelling International–Canada** (✉ 205 Catherine St., Suite 400, Ottawa, Ontario K2P 1C3, ☎ 613/237–7884); and in the United Kingdom, the **Youth Hostel Association of England and Wales** (✉ Trevelyan House, 8 St. Stephen's Hill, St. Albans, Hertfordshire AL1 2DY, ☎ 01727/855215 or 01727/845047). Membership (in the U.S., $25; in Canada, C$26.75; in the U.K., £9.30) gives you access to 5,000 hostels in 77 countries that charge $5–$40 per person per night.

ORGANIZATIONS

A major contact is the **Council on International Educational Exchange** (✉ mail orders only: CIEE, 205 E. 42nd St., 16th Floor, New York, NY 10017, ☎ 212/822–2600, info@ciee. org). The **Educational Travel Centre** (✉ 438 N. Frances St., Madison, WI 53703, ☎ 608/256–5551 or 800/747–5551, FAX 608/256–2042) offers rail passes

and low-cost airline tickets, mostly for flights that depart from Chicago.

In Canada, also contact **Travel Cuts** (✉ 187 College St., Toronto, Ontario M5T 1P7, ☎ 416/979–2406 or 800/667–2887).

PUBLICATIONS

Check out the **Berkeley Guide to Europe** (available in bookstores; or contact Fodor's Travel Publications, ☎ 800/533–6478; $18.95 plus $4 shipping).

T

The country code for Denmark is 45; for Finland, 348; for Iceland, 354; for Norway, 47; and for Sweden, 46. For local access numbers abroad, contact **AT&T USADirect** (☎ 800/874–4000), **MCI** Call USA (☎ 800/444–4444), or **Sprint** Express (☎ 800/793–1153).

Among the companies that sell tours and packages to Scandinavia, the following are nationally known, have a proven reputation, and offer plenty of options.

GROUP TOURS

Super-Deluxe➤ **Abercrombie & Kent** (✉ 1520 Kensington Rd., Oak Brook, IL 60521-2141, ☎ 708/954–2944 or 800/323–7308, FAX 708/954–3324) and **Travcoa** (✉ Box 2630, 2350 S.E. Bristol St., Newport Beach, CA 92660, ☎ 714/476–2800 or 800/992–2003, FAX 714/476–2538).

Deluxe➤ **Globus** (✉ 5301 S. Federal Circle,

Littleton, CO 80123, ☏ 303/797–2800 or 800/221–0090, FAX 303/795–0962), **Maupintour** (✉ Box 807, 1515 St. Andrews Dr., Lawrence, KS 66047, ☏ 913/843–1211 or 800/255–4266, FAX 913/843–8351), and **Tauck Tours** (✉ Box 5027, 276 Post Rd. W, Westport, CT 06881, ☏ 203/226–6911 or 800/468–2825, FAX 203/221–6828).

FIRST-CLASS➤ **Bennett Tours** (✉ 270 Madison Ave., New York, NY 10016-0658, ☏ 212/532–5060 or 800/221–2420, FAX 212/779–8944), **Brendan Tours** (✉ 15137 Califa St., Van Nuys, CA 91411, ☏ 818/785–9696 or 800/421–8446, FAX 818/902–9876), **Caravan Tours** (✉ 401 N. Michigan Ave., Chicago, IL 60611, ☏ 312/321–9800 or 800/227–2826), **Delta Dream Vacations** (☏ 800/872–7786), **Finnair** (☏ 800/950–5000), **Insight International Tours** (✉ 745 Atlantic Ave., Boston, MA 02111, ☏ 617/482–2000 or 800/582–8380), **Scantours** (✉ 1535 6th St., No. 205, Santa Monica, CA 90401-2533, ☏ 310/451–0911 or 800/223–7226, FAX 310/395–2013), and **Trafalgar Tours** (✉ 11 E. 26th St., New York, NY 10010, ☏ 212/689–8977 or 800/854–0103, FAX 800/457–6644).

BUDGET➤ **Cosmos** (☞ Globus, *above*).

PACKAGES

Independent vacation packages are available from all the group-tour operators listed above. Also contact **Icelandair** (☏ 800/757–3876) and

DER Tours (✉ 11933 Wilshire Blvd., Los Angeles, CA 90025, ☏ 310/479–4140 or 800/782–2424).

FROM THE U.K.

Contact **Scandinavian Travel Service** (✉ 29A Nork Way, Banstead, Surrey SM7 1PB, ☏ 01737/212500) and **Scantours** (✉ 21–24 Cockspur St., London SW1Y 5DA, ☏ 0171/839–2927).

THEME TRIPS

ADVENTURE➤ For Scandinavian adventures, from dogsledding to bicycling to cruising the fjords, contact **Borton Overseas** (✉ 1621 E. 79th St., Bloomington, MN 55425, ☏ 612/883–0704 or 800/843–0602, FAX 612/883–0221). For a host of adventures, call **Scandinavian Special Interest Network** (✉ 38 Valley View Trail, Sparta, NJ 07871, ☏ 201/729–8961, FAX 201/729–6565.

BICYCLING➤ Bike trips in Scandinavia are available from **Backroads** (✉ 1516 5th St., Berkeley, CA 94710-1740, ☏ 510/527–1555 or 800/462–2848, FAX 510-527-1444) and **Euro-Bike Tours** (✉ Box 990, De Kalb, IL 60115, ☏ 800/321–6060, FAX 815/758–8851).

CRUISING➤ For a cruise of Scandinavia's fjords, contact **Bergen Line** (✉ 405 Park Ave., New York, NY 10022, ☏ 212/319–1300 or 800/323–7436, FAX 212/319–1390), **EuroCruises** (✉ 303 W. 13th St., New York, NY 10014, ☏ 212/691–2099 or 800/688–3876), and **Swan Hellenic/Classical**

Cruises & Tours (✉ 132 E. 70th St., New York, NY 10021, ☏ 800/252–7745, FAX 212/774–1545).

FISHING➤ For fly-fishing packages contact **Scandinavian Special Interest Network** (☞ Adventure, *above*).

FOLK ART AND CRAFTS➤ For a journey into the wonderful arts and crafts of Scandinavia, contact **Borton Overseas** (☞ Adventure, *above*) and **Scandinavian Special Interest Network** (☞ Adventure, *above*).

GENEALOGY➤ Travelers of Scandinavian descent looking for their roots should contact **Brekke Tours** (✉ 802 N. 43rd St., Suite D, Grand Forks, ND 58203, ☏ 701/772–8999 or 800/437–5302), **KITT Holidays** (✉ 2 Appletree Sq., No. 150, 8011-34th Ave. S, Minneapolis, MN 55425, ☏ 612/854–8005 or 800/262–8728), or **Scan Travel Center** (✉ 66 Edgewood Ave., Larchmont, NY 10538, ☏ 914/834–3944 or 800/759–7226, FAX 914/834–7528).

HIKING/WALKING➤ For a challenging trek across Scandinavia's fjords and mountains try **Above the Clouds Trekking** (✉ Box 398, Worcester, MA 01602, ☏ 508/799–4499 or 800/233–4499, FAX 508/797–4779) and **Backroads** (☞ Bicycling, *above*).

HORSEBACK RIDING➤ **FITS Equestrian** (✉ 685 Lateen Rd., Solvang, CA 93463, ☏ 805/688–9494 or 800/666–3487, FAX 805/688–2943) can put you in the saddle in Scandinavia.

MUSIC➤ **Dailey-Thorp Travel** (⊠ 330 W. 58th St., No. 610, New York, NY 10019-1817, ☎ 212/307–1555 or 800/998–4677, FAX 212/974–1420) specializes in classical music and opera programs.

ORGANIZATIONS

The **National Tour Association** (⊠ NTA, 546 E. Main St., Lexington, KY 40508, ☎ 606/226–4444 or 800/755–8687) and the **United States Tour Operators Association** (⊠ USTOA, 211 E. 51st St., Suite 12B, New York, NY 10022, ☎ 212/750–7371) can provide lists of members and information on booking tours.

PUBLICATIONS

Contact the USTOA (☞ Organizations, *above*) for its **"Smart Traveler's Planning Kit."** Pamphlets in the kit include the "Worldwide Tour and Vacation Package Finder," "How to Select a Tour or Vacation Package," and information on the organization's consumer protection plan. Also get a copy of the Better Business Bureau's **"Tips on Travel Packages"** (⊠ Publication 24-195, 4200 Wilson Blvd., Arlington, VA 22203; $2).

TRAIN TRAVEL

DISCOUNT PASSES

Scandinavia rail passes are sold by travel agents as well as **Rail Europe** (⊠ 226–230 Westchester Ave., White Plains, NY 10604, ☎ 914/682–5172 or 800/438–7245; 2087 Dundas

East, Suite 105, Mississauga, Ontario L4X 1M2, ☎ 416/602–4195).

Eurail and EuroPasses are available through travel agents and **Rail Europe** (⊠ 226-230 Westchester Ave., White Plains, NY 10604, ☎ 914/682–5172 or 800/438–7245; 2087 Dundas East, Suite 105, Mississauga, Ontario L4X 1M2, ☎ 416/602–4195), **DER Tours** (⊠ Box 1606, Des Plaines, IL 60017, ☎ 800/782–2424, FAX 800/282–7474), or **CIT Tours Corp.** (⊠ 342 Madison Ave., Suite 207, New York, NY 10173, ☎ 212/697–2100 or 800/248–8687, or 800/248–7245 in western U.S.).

TRAVEL GEAR

For travel apparel, appliances, personal-care items, and other travel necessities, get a free catalog from **Magellan's** (☎ 800/962–4943, FAX 805/568–5406), **Orvis Travel** (☎ 800/541–3541, FAX 703/343–7053), or **TravelSmith** (☎ 800/950–1600, FAX 415/455–0554).

ELECTRICAL CONVERTERS

Send a self-addressed, stamped envelope to the **Franzus Company** (⊠ Customer Service, Dept. B50, Murtha Industrial Park, Box 142, Beacon Falls, CT 06403, ☎ 203/723–6664) for a copy of the free brochure "Foreign Electricity Is No Deep, Dark Secret."

TRAVEL AGENCIES

For names of reputable agencies in your area,

contact the **American Society of Travel Agents** (⊠ ASTA, 1101 King St., Suite 200, Alexandria, VA 22314, ☎ 703/739–2782), the **Association of Canadian Travel Agents** (⊠ Suite 201, 1729 Bank St., Ottawa, Ontario K1V 7Z5, ☎ 613/521–0474, FAX 613/521–0805), or the **Association of British Travel Agents** (⊠ 55–57 Newman St., London W1P 4AH, ☎ 0171/637–2444, FAX 0171/637–0713).

U
U.S.
GOVERNMENT
TRAVEL BRIEFINGS

The U.S. Department of State's American Citizens Services office (⊠ Room 4811, Washington, DC 20520; enclose SASE) issues **Consular Information Sheets** on all foreign countries. These cover issues such as crime, security, political climate, and health risks and list embassy locations, entry requirements, currency regulations, in addition to providing other useful information. For the latest information, stop in at any U.S. passport office, consulate, or embassy; call the interactive hot line (☎ 202/647–5225, FAX 202/647–3000); or, with your PC's modem, tap into the department's computer bulletin board (☎ 202/647–9225).

V
VISITOR
INFORMATION

The **Scandinavian Tourist Board,** in the United States and Canada, will accept phone and mail requests: ✉ 655 3rd Ave., New York, NY 10017, ☎ 212/949–2333, FAX 212/983–5260.

In the United Kingdom contact the individual country's tourist boards: **Danish Tourist Board** (✉ 55 Sloan St., London SW1X 9SY, ☎ 071/259–5959, FAX 071/259–5955), **Finnish Tourist Board** (✉ 30–35 Pall Mall, London SW1Y 5LP, ☎ 0171/839–4048, FAX 0171/321–0696), **Iceland Tourist Information Bureau** (✉ 172 Tottenham Court Rd.,

London WP1 9LG, ☎ 0171/388–5599, FAX 0171/387–5711), **Norwegian Tourist Board** (✉ 5 Lower Regent St., London SW1Y 4LR, ☎ 0171/839–6255, FAX 0171/839–6014), and the **Swedish Travel and Tourism Council** (✉ 73 Welbeck St., London W1M 8AN, ☎ 0171/935–9784, FAX 0171/935–5853).

W
WEATHER

For current conditions and forecasts, plus the local time and helpful

travel tips, call the **Weather Channel Connection** (☎ 900/932–8437; 95¢ per minute) from a touch-tone phone.

The *International Traveler's Weather Guide* (✉ Weather Press, Box 660606, Sacramento, CA 95866, ☎ 916/974–0201 or 800/972–0201; $10.95 includes shipping), written by two meteorologists, provides month-by-month information on temperature, humidity, and precipitation in more than 175 cities worldwide.

SMART TRAVEL TIPS A TO Z

Basic Information on Traveling in Scandinavia and Savvy Tips to Make Your Trip a Breeze

A

AIR TRAVEL

If time is an issue, **look for nonstop flights,** which require no change of plane. If possible, **avoid connecting flights,** which stop at least once and can involve a change of plane, even though the flight number remains the same; if the first leg is late, the second waits.

For better service, **fly smaller or regional carriers,** which often have higher passenger satisfaction ratings. Sometimes they have such in-flight amenities as leather seats or greater legroom, and they often have better food.

CUTTING COSTS

Scan the Sunday travel section of most newspapers for deals.

MAJOR AIRLINES➤ The least-expensive airfares from the major airlines are priced for round-trip travel and are subject to restrictions. Usually, you must **book in advance and buy the ticket within 24 hours** to get cheaper fares, and you may have to **stay over a Saturday night.** The lowest fare is subject to availability, and only a small percentage of the plane's total seats are sold at that price. It's smart to **call a number of airlines, and when you are quoted a good price, book it on the spot**—the

same fare may not be available on the same flight the next day. Airlines generally allow you to change your return date for a $25 to $50 fee. If you don't use your ticket, you can apply the cost toward the purchase of a new ticket, again for a small charge. However, most low-fare tickets are nonrefundable. To get the lowest airfare, **check different routings.** If your destination has more than one gateway, **compare prices to different airports.**

FROM THE U.K.➤ To save money on flights, **look into an APEX or Super-PEX** APEX tickets must be booked in advance and have certain restrictions. Super-PEX tickets can be purchased right at the airport.

CONSOLIDATORS➤ Consolidators buy tickets for scheduled flights at reduced rates from the airlines, then sell them at prices below the lowest available from the airlines directly—usually without advance restrictions. Sometimes you can even get your money back if you need to return the ticket. Carefully read the fine print detailing penalties for changes and cancellations. If you doubt the reliability of a consolidator, **confirm your reservation with the airline.**

ALOFT

AIRLINE FOOD➤ If you hate airline food, **ask for special meals when booking.** These can be vegetarian, low-cholesterol, or kosher, for example; commonly prepared to order in smaller quantities than standard fare, they can be tastier.

JET LAG➤ To avoid this syndrome, which occurs when travel disrupts your body's natural cycles, try to maintain a normal routine. At night, **get some sleep.** By day, move about the cabin to **stretch your legs, eat light meals, and drink water—not alcohol.**

SMOKING➤ Smoking is not allowed on flights of six hours or less within the continental United States. Smoking is also prohibited on flights within Canada. For U.S. flights longer than six hours or international flights, **contact your carrier regarding its smoking policy.** Some carriers have prohibited smoking throughout their system; others allow smoking only on certain routes or even certain departures of that route.

WITHIN SCANDINAVIA

Scandinavia is larger than it looks on a map, and many native travelers choose to fly between the capital cities, using trains and buses for domestic travel.

THE GOLD GUIDE / SMART TRAVEL TIPS

If you are traveling from south to north in Norway, Sweden, or Finland, flying is a necessity: Stavanger in southern Norway is as close to Rome, Italy, as it is to the northern tip of Norway.

For international travelers, one or two stopovers can often be purchased more cheaply along with an international ticket. With SAS, the least expensive tickets (Jackpot) are round-trip, must include a Saturday night, and can be bought only within Scandinavia from 7 to 14 days ahead. Ask about low rates for hotels and car rental in connection with Jackpot tickets. Weekend Jackpot tickets can be bought right up to flight time. SAS also gives couples traveling together a discount off some tickets and significant discounts on SAS hotels and car rentals. Low-priced round-trip weekend excursions from one Scandinavian capital to another (minimum three-day stay) can be bought one day in advance from SAS.

C

CAMERAS, CAMCORDERS, & COMPUTERS

IN TRANSIT

Always keep your film, tape, or disks out of the sun; never put these on the dashboard of a car. Carry an extra supply of batteries, and **be prepared to turn on your camera, camcorder, or laptop computer for security**

personnel to prove that it's real.

X-RAYS

Always **ask for hand inspection at security.** Such requests are virtually always honored at U.S. airports and are usually accommodated abroad. Photographic film becomes clouded after successive exposure to airport X-ray machines. Videotape and computer disks are not damaged by X-rays, but **keep your tapes and disks away from metal detectors.**

CUSTOMS

Before departing, **register your foreign-made camera or laptop with U.S. Customs.** If your equipment is U.S.-made, call the consulate of the country you'll be visiting to find out whether it should be registered with local customs upon arrival.

CAR RENTAL

CUTTING COSTS

To get the best deal, **book through a travel agent who is willing to shop around.** Ask your agent to **look for fly-drive packages,** which also save you money, and **ask if local taxes are included** in the rental or fly-drive price. These can be as high as 20% in some destinations. Don't forget to find out about required deposits, cancellation penalties, drop-off charges, and the cost of any required insurance coverage.

Also **ask your travel agent about a company's customer-service record.** How has it responded to late plane arrivals and vehicle

mishaps? Are there often lines at the rental counter, and—if you're traveling during a holiday period—does a confirmed reservation guarantee you a car?

Always **find out what equipment is standard** at your destination before specifying what you want; automatic transmission and air-conditioning are usually optional—and very expensive.

Be sure to **look into wholesalers**—companies that do not own their own fleets but rent in bulk from those that do and often offer better rates than traditional car-rental operations. Prices are best during off-peak periods; rentals booked through wholesalers must be paid for before you leave the United States.

INSURANCE

When driving a rented car, you are generally responsible for any damage to or loss of the rental vehicle. Before you rent, **see what coverage you already have** under the terms of your personal auto insurance policy and credit cards.

If you do not have auto insurance or an umbrella insurance policy that covers damage to third parties, **consider purchasing CDW or LDW.**

Find out if your credit card or personal auto insurance will cover the loss of stolen vehicles, since collision policies that car-rental companies sell for European rentals typically do not.

REQUIREMENTS

Ask about age requirements: Several countries require drivers to be over 20 years old, but some car-rental companies require that drivers be at least 25. In Scandinavia your own driver's license is acceptable for a limited time; check with the country's tourist board before you go. **Consider an International Driver's Permit,** available from the American or Canadian Automobile Association or, in the United Kingdom, from the AA or RAC.

SURCHARGES

Before you pick up a car in one city and leave it in another, **ask about drop-off charges or one-way service fees,** which can be substantial. Note, too, that some rental agencies charge extra if you return the car before the time specified on your contract. To avoid a hefty refueling fee, **fill the tank just before you turn in the car**—but be aware that gas stations near the rental outlet may overcharge.

CHILDREN & TRAVEL

In Scandinavia children are to be seen *and* heard and are genuinely welcome in most public places.

When traveling with children, **plan ahead** and **involve your youngsters** as you outline your trip. When packing, **include a supply of things to keep them busy** en route (☞ Children & Travel *in* Important Contacts A to Z). On sightseeing days, try to **schedule** activities of special interest to your children, like a trip to a zoo or a playground. If you **plan your itinerary around seasonal festivals,** you'll never lack for things to do. In addition, **check local newspapers for special events** mounted by public libraries, museums, and parks.

BABY-SITTING

For recommended local sitters, **check with your hotel desk.**

DISCOUNTS

Children are entitled to discount tickets (often as much as 50% off) on buses, trains, and ferries throughout Scandinavia, as well as reductions on special City Cards. Children under 18 pay half-price and children under 2 pay 10% on SAS and Linjeflyg round-trips. The only restriction on this discount is that the family travel together and return to the originating city in Scandinavia at least two days later. With the ScanRail Pass—good for rail journeys throughout Scandinavia—children under 4 (on lap) travel free; those 4–11 pay half-fare and those 12–25 pay 75% of the adult fare.

DRIVING

If you are renting a car, don't forget to **arrange for a car seat when you reserve.** Sometimes they're free.

FLYING

As a general rule, infants under two not occupying a seat fly at greatly reduced fares and occasionally for free. If your children are two or older **ask about special children's fares.** Age limits for these fares vary among carriers. Rules also vary regarding unaccompanied minors, so again, check with your airline.

BAGGAGE➤ In general, the adult baggage allowance applies to children paying half or more of the adult fare. If you are traveling with an infant, **ask about carry-on allowances** before departure. In general, for infants charged 10% of the adult fare you are allowed one carry-on bag and a collapsible stroller, which may have to be checked; you may be limited to less if the flight is full.

SAFETY SEATS➤ According to the FAA, it's a good idea to **use safety seats aloft** for children weighing less than 40 pounds. Airline policies vary. U.S. carriers allow FAA-approved models but usually require that you buy a ticket, even if your child would otherwise ride free, since the seats must be strapped into regular seats. However, some U.S. and foreign-flag airlines may require you to hold your baby during takeoff and landing—defeating the seats' purpose. Other foreign carriers may not allow infant seats at all, or may charge a child rather than an infant fare for their use.

FACILITIES➤ When making your reservation, **request children's meals or freestanding bassinets** if you need them; the latter are available only to those seated at the bulkhead,

THE GOLD GUIDE / SMART TRAVEL TIPS

where there's enough legroom. If you don't need a bassinet, **think twice before requesting bulkhead seats**—the only storage space for in-flight necessities is in inconveniently distant overhead bins.

LODGING

Most hotels allow children under a certain age to stay in their parents' room at no extra charge; others charge them as extra adults. Be sure to **ask about the cutoff age.**

Many youth hostels offer special facilities (including multiple-bed rooms and separate kitchens) for families with children. Family hostels also provide an excellent opportunity for children to meet youngsters from other countries. Contact the AYH (☞ Students *in* Important Contacts A to Z).

CUSTOMS & DUTIES

To speed your clearance through customs, **keep receipts for all your purchases abroad** and **be ready to show the inspector what you've bought.** If you feel that you've been incorrectly or unfairly charged a duty, you can **appeal assessments in dispute.** First ask to see a supervisor. If you are still unsatisfied, **write to the port director** at your point of entry, sending your customs receipt and any other appropriate documentation. The address will be listed on your receipt. If you still don't get satisfaction, you can take your case to customs headquarters in Washington.

ON ARRIVAL

Limits on what you can bring in duty-free vary from country to country. **Check with individual country tourist boards for limits on alcohol, cigarettes, and other items.** Also be careful to check before bringing food of any kind into Iceland.

IN THE U.S.

You may bring home $400 worth of foreign goods duty-free if you've been out of the country for at least 48 hours and haven't already used the $400 allowance, or any part of it, in the past 30 days.

Travelers 21 or older may bring back 1 liter of alcohol duty-free, provided the beverage laws of the state through which they reenter the United States allow it. In addition, regardless of their age, they are allowed 100 non-Cuban cigars and 200 cigarettes. Antiques, which the U.S. Customs Service defines as objects more than 100 years old, are duty-free. Original works of art done entirely by hand are also duty-free. These include, but are not limited to, paintings, drawings, and sculptures.

Duty-free, travelers may mail packages valued at up to $200 to themselves and up to $100 to others, with a limit of one parcel per addressee per day (and no alcohol or tobacco products or perfume valued at more than $5); on the outside, the package must be labeled as being either for personal use or an unsolicited gift, and a

list of its contents and their retail value must be attached. Mailed items do not affect your duty-free allowance on your return.

IN CANADA

If you've been out of Canada for at least seven days, you may bring in C$500 worth of goods duty-free. If you've been away for fewer than seven days but for more than 48 hours, the duty-free allowance drops to C$200; if your trip lasts between 24 and 48 hours, the allowance is C$50. You cannot pool allowances with family members. Goods claimed under the C$500 exemption may follow you by mail; those claimed under the lesser exemptions must accompany you.

Alcohol and tobacco products may be included in the seven-day and 48-hour exemptions but not in the 24-hour exemption. If you meet the age requirements of the province or territory through which you reenter Canada, you may bring in, duty-free, 1.14 liters (40 imperial ounces) of wine or liquor *or* 24 12-ounce cans or bottles of beer or ale. If you are 16 or older, you may bring in, duty-free, 200 cigarettes, 50 cigars or cigarillos, and 400 tobacco sticks or 400 grams of manufactured tobacco. Alcohol and tobacco must accompany you on your return.

An unlimited number of gifts with a value of up to C$60 each may be mailed to Canada duty-free. These do not affect your duty-free allowance on your return. Label the package "Unsolicited Gift—Value Under $60." Alcohol and tobacco are excluded.

IN THE U.K.

If your journey was wholly within European Union (EU) countries, you no longer need to pass through customs when you return to the United Kingdom. If you plan to bring back large quantities of alcohol or tobacco, check in advance on EU limits.

From countries outside the EU, including Iceland, Norway, and Sweden, you may import, duty-free, 200 cigarettes, 100 cigarillos, 50 cigars, or 250 grams of tobacco; 1 liter of spirits or 2 liters of fortified or sparkling wine or liqueurs; 2 liters of still table wine; 60 milliliters of perfume; 250 milliliters of toilet water; plus £136 worth of other goods, including gifts and souvenirs.

D

DINING

Although restaurants in Scandinavia's major cities offer the full range of dining experiences, eating out in any of the smaller towns will probably be limited to traditional local fare, or imported fast-food joints such as McDonald's and Pizza Hut. Local food can be very good, especially in the seafood and game categories, but bear in mind that northern climes beget exceptionally hearty, and heavy, meals. Sausage appears in a thousand forms, likewise potatoes. Some

particular northern tastes can seem very different, such as the fondness for pickled and fermented fish—to be sampled carefully at first—and a universal obsession with sweet pastries, ice cream, and chocolate. Other novelties for the visitor might be the use of fruit in main dishes and soups, or sour milk on breakfast cereal, or preserved fish paste as a spread for crackers, or the prevalence of crackers and complete absence of sliced bread. The Swedish *smörgåsbord* and its Scandinavian cousins are often the traveling diner's best bet, since they include fresh fish and vegetables alongside meat and starches; they are also among the lower-priced menu choices.

Restaurant meals are a big-ticket item throughout Scandinavia, but there are ways to keep the cost of eating down. Take full advantage of the large, buffet breakfast usually included in the cost of a hotel room. At lunch, look for the "menu" that offers a set two- or three-course meal for a set price, or limit yourself to a hearty appetizer. At dinner, pay careful attention to the price of wine and drinks, since the high tax on alcohol raises these costs considerably. For more information on affordable eating, *see* Costs under Money and Expenses, *below*.

DISABILITIES & ACCESSIBILITY

Facilities for travelers with disabilities in Scandinavia are gener-

ally good, and most of the major tourist offices offer special booklets and brochures on travel and accommodations.

When discussing accessibility with an operator or reservationist, **ask hard questions.** Are there any stairs, inside *or* out? Are there grab bars next to the toilet *and* in the shower/tub? How wide is the doorway to the room? To the bathroom? For the most extensive facilities, meeting the latest legal specifications, **opt for newer accommodations,** which more often have been designed with access in mind. Older properties or ships must usually be retrofitted and may offer more limited facilities as a result. Be sure to **discuss your needs before booking.**

DISCOUNTS & DEALS

You shouldn't have to pay for a discount. In fact, you may already be eligible for all kinds of savings. Here are some time-honored strategies for getting the best deal.

LOOK IN YOUR WALLET

When you **use your credit card to make travel purchases,** you may get free travel-accident insurance, collision damage insurance, or medical or legal assistance, depending on the card and bank that issued it. Visa and MasterCard provide one or more of these services, so **get a copy of your card's travel benefits.** If you are a member of the AAA or an oil-company-sponsored road-assistance plan, always **ask hotel or car-rental reservationists for auto-club discounts.** Some clubs offer additional discounts on tours, cruises, or admission to attractions. And don't forget that auto-club membership entitles you to free maps and trip-planning services.

SENIORS CITIZENS & STUDENTS

As a senior-citizen traveler, you may be eligible for special rates, but you should **mention your senior-citizen or student status up front.** If you're a student or under 26, **carry an official ID card** (☞ Senior-Citizen Discounts *and* Students on the Road, *below*) for discounts.

DIAL FOR DOLLARS

To save money, **look into "1-800" discount reservations services,** which often have lower rates. These services use their buying power to get a better price on hotels, airline tickets, and sometimes even car rentals. When booking a room, always **call the hotel's local toll-free number** (if one is available) rather than the central reservations number—you'll often get a better price. Ask the reservationist about special packages or corporate rates, which are usually available even if you're not traveling on business.

JOIN A CLUB?

Discount clubs can be a legitimate source of savings, but you must use the participating hotels and visit the participating attractions in order to realize any benefits. Remember, too, that you have to pay a fee to join, so **determine if you'll save enough to warrant your membership fee.** Before booking with a club, **make sure the hotel or other supplier isn't offering a better deal.**

GET A GUARANTEE

When shopping for the best deal on hotels and car rentals, **look for guaranteed exchange rates,** which protect you against a falling dollar. With your rate locked in, you won't pay more even if the price goes up in the local currency.

DRIVING

Excellent, well-marked roads make driving a great way to explore Scandinavia—but beware that gasoline costs about $1.00 per liter of lead-free gas, roughly four times the typical U.S. price. Ferry costs are steep, and reservations are vital. Tolls on some major roads add to the expense, as do the high fees for city parking; tickets for illegal parking are painfully costly.

Also be aware that there are relatively low legal blood-alcohol limits and tough penalties for driving while intoxicated in Scandinavia. Penalties include suspension of the driver's license and fines or imprisonment and are enforced by random police roadblocks in urban areas on weekends. In addition, an accident involving a driver with an illegal blood-alcohol level usually voids all insur-

ance agreements, so the driver becomes responsible for his own medical bills and damage to the cars.

In a few remote areas, especially in Iceland and northern Norway, Sweden, and Finland, road conditions can be unpredictable, and careful planning is required for safety's sake. It is wise to **use a four-wheel-drive vehicle** and to **travel with at least one other car** in these areas.

Keep your headlights on at all times; this is required by law in most of Scandinavia. Also by Scandinavian law, everyone, even babies, must **wear seat belts.**

F

FERRIES

Taking a ferry isn't only fun, it's often necessary in Scandinavia. Many companies arrange package trips (☞ Tour Operators *in* Important Contacts A to Z), some offering a rental car and hotel accommodations as part of the deal.

Ferry crossings often last overnight. The trip between Copenhagen and Oslo, for example, takes approximately 16 hours, most lines leaving at about 5 PM and arriving about 9 the next morning. The direct cruise between Stockholm and Helsinki takes 12 hours, usually leaving at about 6 PM and arriving the next morning at 9. The shortest ferry route runs between Helsingør, Denmark, and Helsingborg, Sweden; it takes only 25 minutes.

I

INSURANCE

Travel insurance can protect your monetary investment, replace your luggage and its contents, or provide for medical coverage should you fall ill during your trip. Most tour operators, travel agents, and insurance agents sell specialized health-and-accident, flight, trip-cancellation, and luggage insurance as well as comprehensive policies with some or all of these coverages. Comprehensive policies may also reimburse you for delays due to weather—an important consideration if you're traveling during the winter months. Some health-insurance policies do not cover preexisting conditions, but waivers may be available in specific cases. Coverage is sold by the companies listed in Important Contacts A to Z; these companies act as the policy's administrators. The actual insurance is usually underwritten by a well-known name, such as the Travelers or Continental Insurance.

Before you make any purchase, **review your existing health and homeowner's policies** to find out whether they cover expenses incurred while traveling.

BAGGAGE

Airline liability for baggage is limited to $1,250 per person on domestic flights. On international flights, it amounts to $9.07 per pound or $20 per kilogram for checked baggage (roughly $640 per 70-pound bag) and $400 per passenger for unchecked baggage. Insurance for losses exceeding the terms of your airline ticket can be bought directly from the airline at check-in for about $10 per $1,000 of coverage; note that it excludes a rather extensive list of items, shown on your airline ticket.

COMPREHENSIVE

Comprehensive insurance policies include all the coverages described above, plus some that may not be available in more specific policies. If you have purchased an expensive vacation, especially one that involves travel abroad, comprehensive insurance is a must; **look for policies that include trip delay insurance,** which will protect you in the event that weather problems cause you to miss your flight, tour, or cruise. A few insurers will also sell you a waiver for preexisting medical conditions. Some of the companies that offer both these features are Access America, Carefree Travel, Travel Insured International, and TravelGuard (☞ Insurance *in* Important Contacts A to Z).

FLIGHT

You should **think twice before buying flight insurance.** Often purchased as a last-minute impulse at the airport, it pays a lump sum when a plane crashes, either to a beneficiary if the insured dies or sometimes to a surviving passenger who loses his or her eyesight or a limb. Supplementing the airlines' coverage described in the limits-of-liability paragraphs on your ticket, it's expensive and basically unnecessary. Charging an airline ticket to a major credit card often automatically provides you with coverage that may also extend to travel by bus, train, and ship.

HEALTH

Medicare generally does not cover health care costs outside the United States; nor do many privately issued policies. If your own health insurance policy does not cover you outside the United States, **consider buying supplemental medical coverage.** It can reimburse you for $1,000–$150,000 worth of medical and/or dental expenses incurred as a result of an accident or illness during a trip. These policies also may include a personal-accident, or death-and-dismemberment, provision, which pays a lump sum ranging from $15,000 to $500,000 to your beneficiaries if you die or to you if you lose one or more limbs or your eyesight, and a medical-assistance provision, which may either reimburse you for the cost of referrals, evacuation, or repatriation and other services, or automatically enroll you as a member of a particular medical-assistance company (☞ Health Issues *in* Important Contacts A to Z).

U.K. TRAVELERS

You can buy an annual travel insurance policy valid for most vacations during the year in

THE GOLD GUIDE / SMART TRAVEL TIPS

which it's purchased. If you are pregnant or have a preexisting medical condition, make sure you're covered before buying such a policy.

TRIP

Without insurance, you will lose all or most of your money if you cancel your trip, regardless of the reason. Especially if your airline ticket, cruise, or package tour is nonrefundable and cannot be changed, it's essential that you **buy trip-cancellation-and-interruption insurance.** When considering how much coverage you need, look for a policy that will cover the cost of your trip plus the nondiscounted price of a one-way airline ticket should you need to return home early. Read the fine print carefully, especially sections that define "family member" and "preexisting medical conditions." Also **consider default or bankruptcy insurance,** which protects you against a supplier's failure to deliver. Be aware, however, that if you buy such a policy from a travel agency, tour operator, airline, or cruise line, it may not cover default by the firm in question.

L

LANGUAGE

Despite the fact that four of the five Scandinavian tongues are in the Germanic family of languages, it is a myth that someone who speaks German can understand Danish, Icelandic, Swedish, and Norwegian. Fortu-

nately, English is widely spoken in Scandinavia. German is the most common third language. Outside major cities, English becomes rarer, and it's a good idea to **take along a dictionary or phrase book.** Even here, however, anyone under the age of 50 is likely to have studied English in school.

Danish, Norwegian, and Swedish are similar, and fluent speakers can generally understand each other. A foreigner will most often be struck by the lilting rhythm of spoken Swedish, which takes a bit of getting used to for Danes and Norwegians, who often choose to speak English with Swedes.

Characters special to these three languages are the Danish "ø" and the Swedish "ö," pronounced a bit like a very short "er", similar to the French "eu"; "æ" or "ä," which sounds like the "a" in "ape" but with a glottal stop, or the "a" in "cat," depending on the region, and the "å" (also written "aa"), which sounds like the "o" in "ghost." The important thing about these characters isn't that you pronounce them correctly—foreigners usually can't—but that you know to look for them in the phone book at the very end. Mr. Søren Åstrup, for example, will be found after "Z." Æ or Ä and Ø or Ö follow.

Icelandic, because of its island isolation, is the language closest to what the Vikings spoke

1,000 years ago. Although Norwegian, Danish, and Swedish have clearly evolved away from the roots common to all four languages, Icelandic retains a surprising amount of its ancient heritage, and Icelanders want to keep it that way: A governmental committee in Iceland has the express task of coming up with Icelandic versions of new words such as *computer.* Two characters are unique to Icelandic and Faroese: the "Þ," which is pronounced like the "th" in "thing"; and the "ð," which is pronounced like the "th" in "the."

Finnish is a non-Germanic language more closely related to Hungarian than to the other Scandinavian languages. A visitor isn't likely to recognize anything on the average newspaper's front page. A linguistic cousin to Finnish is still spoken by the Sami (Lapps), who inhabit the northernmost parts of Norway, Sweden, Finland, and Russia.

LODGING

In the larger cities, lodging ranges from first-class business hotels run by SAS, Sheraton, and Scandic to good-quality tourist-class hotels, such as RESO, Best Western, Scandic Budget, and Sweden Hotels, to a wide variety of single-entrepreneur hotels. In the countryside, look for independently run inns and motels. In Denmark they're called *kroer;* in Norway, *fjellstuer* or *pensjonat;*

in Finland, *kienvari;* and elsewhere, guest houses. Before you leave home, **ask your travel agent about discounts** (☞ Hotels, *below*), including summer hotel checks for Best Western, Scandic, and Inter Nor hotels, a summer Fjord pass in Norway, and enormous year-round rebates at SAS hotels for travelers over 65. All EuroClass (business class) passengers can get discounts of at least 10% at SAS hotels when they book through SAS.

Two things about hotels usually surprise North Americans: the relatively limited dimensions of Scandinavian beds and the generous size of Scandinavian breakfasts. Scandinavian double beds are often about 60 inches wide or slightly less, close in size to the U.S. queen size. King-size beds (72 inches wide) are difficult to find and, if available, require special reservations.

Older hotels may have some rooms described as "double," which in fact have one double bed plus one foldout sofa big enough for two people. This arrangement is occasionally called a combi-room but is being phased out.

Many older hotels, particularly the country inns and independently run smaller hotels in the cities, do not have private bathrooms. Ask ahead if this is important to you.

Scandinavian breakfasts resemble what many people would call lunch, usually including breads, cheeses, marmalade, hams, lunch meats, eggs, juice, cereal, milk, and coffee. Generally, the farther north you go, the larger the breakfasts become. Breakfast is often included in the price of the hotel, except in Finland and in deluxe establishments elsewhere.

Make reservations whenever possible. Even countryside inns, which usually have space, are sometimes packed with vacationing Europeans.

Ask about high and low seasons when making reservations, since different countries define their tourist seasons differently. Some hotels lower prices during tourist season, whereas others raise them during the same period.

APARTMENT & VILLA RENTAL

If you want a home base that's roomy enough for a family and comes with cooking facilities, **consider taking a furnished rental.** This can also save you money, but not always—some rentals are luxury properties (economical only when your party is large). Home-exchange directories list rentals—often second homes owned by prospective house swappers—and some services search for a house or apartment for you (even a castle if that's your fancy) and handle the paperwork. Some send an illustrated catalog; others send photographs only of specific properties, sometimes at a charge; up-front registration fees may apply.

HOME EXCHANGE

If you would like to find a house, an apartment, or some other type of vacation property to exchange for your own while on holiday, **become a member of a home-exchange organization,** which will send you its updated listings of available exchanges for a year and will include your own listing in at least one of them. Arrangements for the actual exchange are made by the two parties involved, not by the organization.

HOTELS

All five Scandinavian countries offer Inn Checks, or prepaid hotel vouchers, for accommodations ranging from first-class hotels to country cottages. These vouchers, which must be purchased from travel agents or from the Scandinavian Tourist Board (☞ Visitor Information *in* Important Contacts A to Z) before departure, are sold individually and in packets for as many nights as needed and offer savings of up to 50%. Most countries also offer summer bargains for foreign tourists. For further information about Scandinavian hotel vouchers, contact the Scandinavian Tourist Board.

M
MEDICAL ASSISTANCE

No one plans to get sick while traveling, but it happens, so **consider** signing up with a medical assistance company. These outfits provide referrals, emergency evacuation or repatriation, 24-hour telephone hot lines for medical consultation, cash for emergencies, and other personal and legal assistance. They also dispatch medical personnel and arrange for the relay of medical records.

MONEY

In this book currencies are abbreviated DKr (Danish kroner), FM (Finnish mark), IKr (Icelandic kroner), NKr (Norwegian kroner), and SKr (Swedish kronor). In individual countries you may see prices indicated with Kr only, and you may see exchange rates in banks quoted for DKK, FIM, ISK, NOK, and SEK, respectively. Currency-exchange rates at press time are listed in the Country Essentials sections at the end of each chapter, but **since rates fluctuate daily, you should check them at the time of your departure.**

ATMS

CASH ADVANCES➤ Before leaving home, **make sure that your credit cards have been programmed for ATM use** in Scandinavia. Note that Discover cards are rarely accepted overseas. Local bank cards often do not work overseas either; **ask your bank about a Visa debit card,** which works like a bank card but can be used at any ATM displaying a Visa logo.

TRANSACTION FEES➤ Although fees charged for ATM transactions

may be higher abroad than at home, Cirrus and Plus exchange rates are excellent, because they are based on wholesale rates offered only by major banks.

COSTS

Costs are high in Denmark, Norway, and Sweden, higher still in Finland, and highest in Iceland, where so many things must be imported. Basic sample prices are listed in the Country A to Z section at the end of each chapter. Throughout the region, be aware that sales taxes can be very high, but foreigners can get some refunds by shopping at tax-free stores (☞ VAT, *below*). City cards can save you transportation and entrance fees in many of the larger cities.

You can **reduce the cost of food by planning.** Breakfast is often included in your hotel bill; if not, you may wish to buy fruit, sweet rolls, and a beverage for a picnic breakfast. Electrical devices for hot coffee or tea should be bought abroad, though, to conform to the local current. **Opt for a restaurant lunch instead of dinner,** since the latter tends to be significantly more expensive. Instead of beer or wine, **drink tap water**—liquor can cost four times the price of the same brand in a store—but do specify tap water, as the term "water" can refer to soft drinks and bottled water, which are also expensive. Throughout Scandinavia, the tip is included in the cost of your meal.

In most of Scandinavia, liquor and strong beer (over 3% alcohol) can be purchased only in state-owned shops, at very high prices, during weekday business hours, usually 9:30 to 6. A 70- or 75-centiliter bottle of whiskey in Sweden, for example, can easily cost SKr250 (about $35). Denmark takes a less restrictive approach, with liquor and beer available in the smallest of grocery stores, open weekdays and Saturday morning, but Danish prices, too, are high. (When you visit relatives in Scandinavia, a bottle of liquor or fine wine bought duty-free on the trip over is often a much-appreciated gift.)

EXCHANGING CURRENCY

For the most favorable rates, **change money at banks.** You won't do as well at exchange booths in airports or rail and bus stations, in hotels, in restaurants, or in stores, although you may find their hours more convenient. To avoid lines at airport exchange booths, **get a small amount of the local currency before you leave home.**

TAXES

Information on taxes, including VAT (value-added) taxes, can be found in the Country A to Z section at the end of each chapter.

VAT➤ One way to beat high prices is to **take advantage of tax-free shopping.** Throughout Scandinavia, you can make major purchases free of tax if you have a foreign passport. Ask about tax-free shopping when you make a purchase for $50 (about £32) or more. When your purchases exceed a specified limit (which varies from country to country), you receive a special export receipt. Keep the parcels intact and take them out of the country within 30 days of purchase. When you leave, you can obtain a refund of the tax in cash from a special office at the airport, or, upon arriving home, you can send your receipts to an office in the country of purchase to receive your refund by mail. Be aware that limits for EU tourists are higher than for those coming from outside the EU. In Sweden, for non-EU tourists, the refund is about 15%; in Finland, 12% to 16% for purchases over FM200; in Norway, 23% for purchases over NKr308; in Denmark, 18% for purchases over DKr600; in Iceland, 15% for purchases over IKr5,000.

TRAVELER'S CHECKS

Whether or not to buy traveler's checks depends on where you are headed; **take cash to rural areas and small towns, traveler's checks to cities.** The most widely recognized checks are issued by American Express, Citicorp, Thomas Cook, and Visa. These are sold by major commercial banks for 1%–3% of the checks' face value—it pays to **shop around.** Both American Express and Thomas Cook issue checks that can be countersigned and used

by either you or your traveling companion. So you won't be left with excess foreign currency, **buy a few checks in small denominations** to cash toward the end of your trip. Before leaving home, **contact your issuer for information on where to cash your checks** without incurring a transaction fee. Record the numbers of all your checks, and keep this listing in a separate place, crossing off the numbers of checks you have cashed.

WIRING MONEY

For a fee of 3%–10%, depending on the amount of the transaction, you can have money sent to you from home through Money-Gram^SM or Western Union (☞ Money Matters *in* Important Contacts A to Z). The transferred funds and the service fee can be charged to a Master-Card or Visa account.

P

PACKING FOR SCANDINAVIA

Bring a folding umbrella and a lightweight raincoat, as it is common for the sky to be clear at 9 AM, rainy at 11 AM, and clear again in time for lunch. **Pack casual clothes,** as Scandinavians tend to dress more casually than their Continental brethren. If you have trouble sleeping when it is light or are sensitive to strong sun, **bring an eye mask and dark sunglasses;** the sun rises as early as 4 AM in some areas, and the far-northern latitude causes it to slant at angles unseen elsewhere on the globe. **Bring bug**

repellent if you plan to venture away from the capital cities; large mosquitoes can be a real nuisance on summer evenings in Denmark as well as in the far-northern reaches of Norway and Sweden. Bring an extra pair of eyeglasses or contact lenses in your carry-on luggage, and if you have a health problem, **pack enough medication** to last the trip or have your doctor write you a prescription using the drug's generic name. **Do not put prescription drugs or valuables in luggage to be checked,** and carry medications in the original packaging to avoid problems with customs officials. Also, don't forget the addresses of offices that handle refunds of lost traveler's checks.

ELECTRICITY

To use your U.S.-purchased electric-powered equipment, **bring a converter and an adapter.** The electrical current in Scandinavia is 220 volts, 50 cycles alternating current (AC); wall outlets take Continental-type plugs, with two round prongs.

If your appliances are dual-voltage, you'll need only an adapter. Hotels sometimes have 110-volt outlets for low-wattage appliances near the sink, marked FOR SHAVERS ONLY; don't use them for high-wattage appliances like blow-dryers. If your laptop computer is older, carry a converter; new laptops operate equally well on 110 and 220 volts, so you need only an adapter.

LUGGAGE

Ask about airline baggage allowances in advance, since they often vary depending on the airline, the route, and the class of your ticket. In general, on domestic flights and on international flights between the United States and foreign destinations, you are entitled to check two bags. A third piece may be brought on board, but it must fit easily under the seat in front of you or in the overhead compartment. In the United States, the FAA gives airlines broad latitude regarding carry-on allowances, and they tend to tailor them to different aircraft and operational conditions. Charges for excess, oversize, or overweight pieces vary.

If you are flying between two foreign destinations, note that baggage allowances may be determined not by piece but by weight—generally 88 pounds (40 kilograms) in first class, 66 pounds (30 kilograms) in business class, and 44 pounds (20 kilograms) in economy. If your flight between two cities abroad connects with your transatlantic or transpacific flight, the piece method still applies.

SAFEGUARDING YOUR LUGGAGE➤ Before leaving home, **itemize your bags' contents** and their worth, and label them with your name, address, and phone number. (If you use your home address, cover it so that potential thieves can't see it readily.) Inside each bag, **pack a copy of your itinerary.** At check-in, **make sure that each bag is correctly tagged** with the destination airport's three-letter code. If your bags arrive damaged—or fail to arrive at all—file a written report with the airline before leaving the airport.

PASSPORTS & VISAS

If you don't already have one, **get a passport.** It is advisable that you **leave one photocopy of your passport's data page** with someone at home and keep another with you, separated from your passport, while traveling. If you lose your passport, promptly call the nearest embassy or consulate and the local police; having the data-page information can speed replacement.

U.S. CITIZENS

All U.S. citizens, even infants, need only a valid passport to enter any Scandinavian country for stays of up to three months. Application forms for both first-time and renewal passports are available at any of the 13 U.S. Passport Agency offices and at some post offices and courthouses. Passports are usually mailed within four weeks; allow five weeks or more in spring and summer.

CANADIANS

You need only a valid passport to enter any Scandinavian country for stays of up to three months. Passport application forms are available at 28 regional passport offices, as well as post offices and travel agencies. Whether for a first or a renewal passport, you must apply in person. Children under 16 may be included on a parent's passport but must have their own to travel alone. Passports are valid for five years and are usually mailed within two to three weeks of application.

U.K. CITIZENS

Citizens of the United Kingdom need only a valid passport to enter any Scandinavian country for stays of up to three months. Applications for new and renewal passports are available from main post offices and at the passport offices in Belfast, Glasgow, Liverpool, London, Newport, and Peterborough. You may apply in person at all passport offices, or by mail to all except the London office. Children under 16 may travel on an accompanying parent's passport. All passports are valid for 10 years. Allow a month for processing.

S

SENIOR-CITIZEN DISCOUNTS

To qualify for age-related discounts, **mention your senior-citizen status up front** when booking hotel reservations, not when checking out, and before you're seated in restaurants, not when paying the bill. Note that discounts may be limited to certain menus, days, or hours. When renting a car, **ask about promotional car-rental discounts**—they can net even lower costs than your senior-citizen discount.

TRAIN TRAVEL

Travelers over 60 can buy a **SeniorRail Card** for DKr150 (about $27) in Scandinavia. It gives 30% discounts on train travel in 21 European countries for a whole year from purchase.

Prices in Scandinavia are never low, but quality is high, and specialties are sometimes less expensive here than elsewhere. Swedish crystal, Icelandic sweaters, Danish Lego blocks and furniture, Norwegian furs, and Finnish fabrics—these are just a few of the items to look for. Keep an eye out for sales, called *udsalg* in Danish, *rea* in Swedish, and *ale* in Finnish.

To save money, **look into deals available through student-oriented travel agencies.** To qualify, you'll need to have a bona fide student ID card. Members of international student groups are also eligible (☞ Students *in* Important Contacts A to Z).

T

LONG-DISTANCE

Avoid making long-distance calls from your hotel room, since many hotels charge up to 400% more than the calling card rate. Some hotels also block the access codes of long-distance carriers, so

travel with more than one company's calling card—one of them might work. If the hotel operator claims that you cannot use any phone card, ask to be connected to an international operator, who will help you access your phone card. You can also dial the international operator yourself. If none of this works, try calling your phone company collect in the United States. If collect calls are also blocked, call from a pay phone in the hotel lobby. Before you go, **find out the local access codes** for your destinations.

A package or tour to Scandinavia can make your vacation less expensive and more hassle-free. Firms that sell tours and packages reserve airline seats, hotel rooms, and rental cars in bulk and pass some of the savings on to you. In addition, the best operators have local representatives available to help you at your destination.

A GOOD DEAL?

The more your package or tour includes, the better you can predict the ultimate cost of your vacation. Make sure you know exactly what is covered, and **beware of hidden costs.** Are taxes, tips, and service charges included? Transfers and baggage handling? Entertainment and excursions? These can add up.

Most packages and tours are rated deluxe, first-class superior, first class, tourist, or budget.

The key difference is usually accommodations. If the package or tour you are considering is priced lower than in your wildest dreams, **be skeptical.** Also, **make sure your travel agent knows the accommodations** and other services. Ask about the hotel's location, room size, beds, and whether it has a pool, room service, or programs for children, if you care about these. Has your agent been there in person or sent others you can contact?

BUYER, BEWARE

Each year a number of consumers are stranded or lose their money when operators—even very large ones with excellent reputations—go out of business. To avoid becoming one of them, take the time to **check out the operator**—find out how long the company has been in business and ask several agents about its reputation. Next, **don't book unless the firm has a consumer-protection program.** Members of the USTOA and the NTA are required to set aside funds for the sole purpose of covering your payments and travel arrangements in case of default. Non-member operators may instead carry insurance; look for the details in the operator's brochure—and for the name of an underwriter with a solid reputation. Note: When it comes to tour operators, **don't trust escrow accounts.** Although there are laws governing those of charter-flight operators, no governmental body prevents tour operators from raiding the till.

Next, **contact your local Better Business Bureau and the attorney general's offices** in both your own state and the operator's; have any complaints been filed? Finally, **pay with a major credit card.** Then you can cancel payment, provided that you can document your complaint. Always **consider trip-cancellation insurance** (☞ Insurance, *above*).

BIG VS. SMALL➤ **Consider the value of lower prices versus personalized service.** Operators that handle several hundred thousand travelers per year can use their purchasing power to give you a good price, and their high volume may also indicate financial stability. But some small companies provide more personalized service; because they tend to specialize, they may also be more knowledgeable about a given area.

USING AN AGENT

Travel agents are excellent resources. In fact, large operators accept bookings made only through travel agents. But it's good to **collect brochures from several agencies** because some agents' suggestions may be skewed by promotional relationships with tour and package firms that reward them for volume sales. If you have a special interest, **find an agent with expertise in that area;** ASTA can provide leads in the United States. (Don't rely solely on your agent, though; agents may be unaware of small-niche operators, and some special-interest travel companies only sell direct.)

SINGLE TRAVELERS

Prices are usually quoted per person, based on two sharing a room. If traveling solo, you may be required to pay the full double-occupancy rate. Some operators eliminate this surcharge if you agree to be matched up with a roommate of the same sex, even if one is not found by departure time.

TRAIN TRAVEL

DISCOUNT PASSES

Scandinavia is one of 17 countries in which you can **use Eurail-Passes,** which provide unlimited first-class rail travel, in all of the participating countries, for the duration of the pass. If you plan to rack up the miles, get a standard pass. These are available for 15 days ($522), 21 days ($678), one month ($838), two months ($1,148), and three months ($1,468).

In addition to standard EurailPasses, **ask about special rail-pass plans.** Among these are the Eurail Youthpass (for those under age 26), the Eurail Saverpass (which gives a discount for two or more people traveling together), a Eurail Flexipass (which allows a certain number of travel days within a set period), the Euraildrive Pass, and the Europass Drive (which combines travel by train and rental car).

Whichever pass you choose, remember that you must **purchase your pass before you leave** for Europe.

Many travelers assume that rail passes guarantee them seats on the trains they wish to ride. Not so. You need to **book seats ahead even if you are using a rail pass;** seat reservations are required on some European trains, particularly high-speed trains, and are a good idea on trains that may be crowded—particularly in summer on popular routes. You will also need a reservation if you purchase sleeping accommodations.

TRAVEL GEAR

Travel catalogs specialize in useful items that can **save space when packing** and make life on the road more convenient. Compact alarm clocks, travel irons, travel wallets, and personal-care kits are among the most common items you'll find. They also carry dual-voltage appliances, currency converters, and foreign-language phrase books. Some catalogs even carry miniature coffeemakers and water purifiers.

U

U.S. GOVERNMENT

The U.S. government can be an excellent source of travel information. Some of this is free, and some is available for a nominal charge. When planning your trip, **find out what government materials are available.** For just a couple of dollars, you can get a variety of publications from the Consumer Information Center in Pueblo, Colorado. Free consumer information also is available from individual government agencies, such as the Department of Transportation or the U.S. Customs Service. For specific titles, see the appropriate publications entry in Important Contacts A to Z.

W
WHEN TO GO

The Scandinavian tourist season peaks in June, July, and August, when daytime temperatures are often in the 70s (21°C to 26°C) and sometimes rise into the 80s (27°C to 32°C). Detailed temperature charts are included in individual country chapters. In general, the weather is not overly warm, and a brisk breeze and brief rainstorms are possible anytime. Nights can be chilly, even in summer.

Visit in summer if you want to experience the delightfully long summer days. In June, the sun rises in Copenhagen at 4 AM and sets at 11 PM and daylight lasts even longer farther north, making it possible to extend your sightseeing into the balmy evenings. Many attractions extend their hours during the summer, and many shut down altogether when summer ends. Fall, spring, and even winter are pleasant, despite the area's reputation for gloom. The days become shorter quickly, but the sun casts a golden light one does not see farther south. On dark days, fires and candlelight will warm you indoors.

The Gulf Stream warms Denmark, the western coast of Norway, and Iceland, making winters in these areas similar to those in London. Even the harbor of Narvik, far to the north in Norway, remains ice-free year-round. Away from the protection of the Gulf Stream, however, northern Norway, Sweden, and Finland experience very cold, clear weather that attracts skiers; even Stockholm's harbor, well south in Sweden but facing the Baltic Sea, freezes over completely.

CLIMATE

The following are average daily maximum and minimum temperatures for major Scandinavian cities.

COPENHAGEN

Jan.	36F	2C	May	61F	16C	Sept.	64F	18C
	28	− 2		46	8		52	11
Feb.	36F	2C	June	66F	19C	Oct.	54F	12C
	27	− 3		52	11		45	7
Mar.	41F	5C	July	72F	22C	Nov.	45F	7C
	30	− 1		57	14		37	3
Apr.	52F	11C	Aug.	70F	21C	Dec.	39F	4C
	37	3		57	14		34	1

✓ **HELSINKI**

Jan.	30F	− 1C	May	64F	18C	Sept.	53F	11C
	26	− 3		49	9		39	4
Feb.	34F	1C	June	60F	16C	Oct.	46F	8C
	24	− 4		48	9		36	2
Mar.	36F	2C	July	68F	20C	Nov.	32F	0C
	26	− 3		55	13		26	− 3
Apr.	46F	8C	Aug.	64F	18C	Dec.	32F	0C
	32	0		53	12		24	− 4

REYKJAVÍK

Month	°F	°C	Month	°F	°C	Month	°F	°C
Jan.	36F	2C	May	50F	10C	Sept.	52F	11C
	28	− 2		39	4		43	6
Feb.	37F	3C	June	54F	12C	Oct.	45F	7C
	28	− 2		45	7		37	3
Mar.	39F	4C	July	57F	14C	Nov.	39F	4C
	30	− 1		48	9		32	0
Apr.	43F	6C	Aug.	57F	14C	Dec.	36F	2C
	34	1		46	8		28	− 2

OSLO

Month	°F	°C	Month	°F	°C	Month	°F	°C
Jan.	28F	− 2C	May	61F	16C	Sept.	60F	16C
	19	− 7		43	6		46	8
Feb.	30F	− 1C	June	68F	20C	Oct.	48F	9C
	19	− 7		50	10		38	3
Mar.	39F	4C	July	72F	22C	Nov.	38F	3C
	25	− 4		55	13		31	− 1
Apr.	50F	10C	Aug.	70F	21C	Dec.	32F	0C
	34	1		54	12		25	− 4

STOCKHOLM

Month	°F	°C	Month	°F	°C	Month	°F	°C
√ Jan.	30F	−1C	May	57F	14C	Sept.	59F	15C
	23	−5		43	6		48	9
Feb.	30F	−1C	June	66F	19C	Oct.	48F	9C
	23	−5		52	11		41	5
Mar.	37F	3C	July	72F	22C	Nov.	41F	5C
	25	−4		57	14		34	1
Apr.	46F	8C	Aug.	68F	20C	Dec.	36F	2C
	34	1		55	13		28	−2

1 Destination: Scandinavia

FAIRY TALES AND FJORDS

THE ISLANDS OF STOCKHOLM mirrored in the water, the ships and Little Mermaid of Copenhagen, Oslo and its majestic fjord, the bay and peninsulas of Helsinki, Reykjavík with its busy deep-blue harbor: the capitals of Scandinavia are unthinkable without the water that surrounds and sustains them.

What is true of the capitals is equally true of the countries. Denmark consists of one peninsula and more than 400 islands, half of them inhabited. Finland and Sweden used to dispute which country was really "the land of a thousand lakes." Finland settled it, after counting almost 190,000. An island summer in the archipelago is part of every Stockholmer's childhood memory. The mail packets of Norway's Hurtigruten sail north from Bergen along the fjord-indented coast and turn around at Kirkenes on the Russian border, 2,000 kilometers (1,242 miles) later. Iceland is so dependent on the surrounding sea that it has been known to take on the British navy to protect its fishing limits.

Water has never separated the Scandinavian nations. In the early days it was far easier to cross a stretch of water than it was to penetrate dense and trackless forests. It was their mastery of shipbuilding that enabled the Vikings to rule the waves 1,000 years ago. Their ocean-going ships could be beached, and this gave them the advantage of surprise.

Viking exploration and conquests ranged from North America to the Black Sea and from Greenland to Mallorca. These voyagers developed the angular Runic alphabet, ideal for carving in stone. In Sweden alone, more than 2,000 runic stones still stand, in memory of Vikings who fell in far-away battles. The Vikings also devised a complex mythology and created literature of such realism and immediacy that even today the Icelandic sagas can be read with admiration and enjoyment.

You might think that, with so much in common, the Scandinavians would keep peace among themselves, but this was not to be. By the 11th century the passion that had inflamed the Vikings was spent, and Christianity defeated the old beliefs. The Swedes departed on a dubious crusade to conquer the Finns and annex their land. The Norwegians, having colonized Iceland, squabbled among themselves and disappeared as a nation for 500 years. By the 16th century, Scandinavia was divided between Denmark and Sweden, bound together by mutual antagonism. The two countries were at war with one another for a total of 134 years, and the conflict was perpetuated by history books written from nationalistic points of view.

What happened in the distant past has acquired the status of myth and deeply influenced the Scandinavians' self-image. Modern history has left more obvious marks. Allegiances and dependencies were reshuffled early in the 19th century, as a consequence of the Napoleonic Wars, which transformed the European landscape. Sweden lost Finland, which spent the next 100 years as a czarist province. Norway declared its independence from Denmark but was thrust into a union with Sweden.

Scandinavian cultures thrived throughout these years. Artist Akseli Gallen-Kallela painted the scenes of a mythological past that Jean Sibelius fashioned into tone poems. Norway experienced a cultural renaissance, led by artists such as Edvard Grieg, Henrik Ibsen, and Edvard Munch. From Denmark came philosopher Søren Kierkegaard, writer Hans Christian Andersen, and the composer Carl Nielsen. Sweden produced the painters Anders Zorn and Carl Larsson and dramatist August Strindberg.

Large-scale emigration to the United States (including a million Swedes) peaked during the latter half of the century, only decades before new industries transformed the old farming economy.

In the early years of this century the Norwegians finally became masters in their own house. This could not have happened without strong nationalist sentiment, and it is to the credit of both Norway and Sweden that the divorce was amicable. The Russian revolution brought civil war to Finland, followed by independence, for the first time in that nation's history. Finland was attacked again in 1939, by Stalin's forces, and was eventually defeated but never occupied. Denmark and Norway, attacked by Germany in 1940, were not spared that fate. After the war had ended, Iceland declared its independence from Denmark.

Denmark, Norway, and Iceland are members of NATO. Denmark is also a paid-up member of the European Union. Sweden and Finland also joined the EU in January 1995. Norwegians, however, turned down the government's proposal for EU membership in a referendum in 1994, and did not join with its neighbors.

Scandinavians, like the British, often talk of Europe as though they are not part of it. They see themselves as different. They dream of the *joie de vivre* that they believe all southerners enjoy, but maintain that the moral fiber and know-how of the Scandinavians are superior to anything you find south of the border.

It used to be said that sick-leave levels were so high in Sweden that there were more sick people in a factory than in a hospital. Scandinavians in all five countries have become so used to high levels of social services that the political coloration of the government seems to matter less, as long as the services are delivered. This requirement is not easily squared with the vociferous demand for lower taxes, but compromises are being made. In Sweden, for example, the government and labor unions recently agreed to make the first day of sick leave an unpaid day, virtually evaporating the absenteeism that led to the old factory–hospital joke.

More than the rest of Europe, Scandinavia has been influenced by the American lifestyle and its ethos of professionalism. This coexists, sometimes precariously, with the "socialism with a human face" that has influenced these societies for the past 50 years or more. Among the measures introduced recently is Sweden's 12-month maternity-paternity leave, which requires fathers to take at least 30 days for themselves: An idea that was decried as madness has done wonders for marriage and fatherhood.

The English language, too, has influenced the Scandinavians, who are not bound by a native language. Iceland was colonized from Norway, but present-day Icelandic is incomprehensible to other Scandinavians. Finnish, like Hungarian, is one of the enigmatic Finno-Ugric languages. Danish, a language rich in glottal stops, is not understood by many Swedes, and Danish TV programs have to be subtitled. Norwegian, in pronunciation and vocabulary halfway between the two, sometimes serves as an intra-Scandinavian mode of communication. But get a group of Scandinavians together and what are they most likely to speak? English.

THERE IS STILL MUCH TRUTH in the myth of the taciturn Scandinavian. A story tells of the two Danes, two Norwegians, and two Swedes who were marooned on a desert island. When a rescue party arrived six months later, they found that the two Danes had started a cooperative and that the two Norwegians had founded a local chapter of the patriotic society Sons of Norway. The two Swedes were waiting to be introduced.

Stereotypes about national characteristics abound among Scandinavians. Danes believe the saving grace of humor will take the sting out of most of life's vicissitudes. The Finns attribute their survival to their *sisu,* or true grit. Icelanders are known as a nation of hard workers, singers, and drinkers, who think there is always a way for things to get fixed. The Norwegians find virtue in being, like Ibsen's Peer Gynt, *sig selv nok,* which means self-reliant in all things. The Swedes, the most introspective of the lot, take pride in their reliability and admit to "Royal Swedish envy" as their principal vice.

The strain of melancholy that runs through the Scandinavian character becomes pronounced in the lonely north. In Finland, the most popular dance—one in which dance halls specialize to the exclusion of all others—is the tango, precisely because it is so sad. But there's no need to look only to Argentine imports: Virtually all Scandinavian folk music, even when rhythms are rapid and gay, is in a minor key.

Perhaps this tendency to melancholia is natural in a region where solitude abounds. In northern Scandinavia the woods close in, pine and spruce mingling with white-trunked birches, with a clearing or a field žhere and there. Farther north the hegemony of the forest becomes complete, challenged only by the lakes. On a clear night, from an aircraft, the moonlight is reflected in so many lakes that it seems to cut a shining path to the horizon.

But the forest is not as silent and lonely as you might think. Walk along a Scandinavian country road on an evening in early summer, and you will hear the barking of roe deer at your approach and the forlorn hooting of loons from the lakes. You will see stately moose coming out of the woods to graze in the fields. Juniper bushes cast long, eerie shadows, and on a hilltop skeletal pines are silhouetted against a still clear sky. No wonder that in ages past popular imagination peopled these forests with sprites and trolls and giants.

Having a summer home is not a great luxury in Scandinavia. On Friday afternoons there are traffic jams in Oslo, as the Norwegians escape to their cabins in the mountainous interior. In Stockholm the waterways are clogged with motorboats heading for summer cottages in the archipelago. The Finns and Icelanders, less urbanized than their neighbors, almost always have a village or isolated farmstead they consider their real home.

Modern Scandinavia is largely a secular society, but woods and lakes hold a special mystique. A midnight boat ride on an island-studded lake, with the moon suspended just above the treetops, is very close to a religious experience for the people of the north, as their souls fill with a tremendous wistfulness and a sense of simultaneous sadness and joy.

—Eric Sjogren

Eric Sjogren, a Swedish travel writer based in Brussels, is a frequent contributor to the New York Times *and other publications.*

WHAT'S WHERE

Denmark

The Kingdom of Denmark dapples the Baltic Sea in an archipelago of some 450 islands and the arc of one peninsula. Measuring 43,069 square kilometers (17,028 square miles), with a population of 5 million, it is the geographical link between Scandinavia and Europe.

The island of Sjælland, the largest of the Danish isles, is the most popular tourist destination. Here you'll find Copenhagen, Scandinavia's largest city (population 1.5 million), Denmark's capital, and the seat of the oldest kingdom in the world. If there's such as a thing as a cozy city, this is it: Bicycles spin alongside cars in the narrow streets, and a handful of skyscrapers are tucked away amid cafés, museums, and quaint old homes. To the north of the city are royal castles (including Helsingør's Kronberg of *Hamlet* fame) and ritzy beach towns. To the west, Roskilde holds relics of medieval Denmark. And to the west and south, rural towns and farms edge up to beach communities and fine white beaches, often surrounded by forests.

Fyn (Funen), the smaller of the country's two main islands, is the site of Denmark's third-largest city, Odense, the birthplace of Hans Christian Andersen. It's no wonder this area inspired many fairy tales: Seven hundred miles of coastline and lush stretches of vegetable and flower gardens are punctuated by manor houses, beech glades, castles, swan ponds, and thatched houses.

Jylland, Denmark's western peninsula, shares its southern border with Germany. At the northern tip lies Skagen, a luminous, dune-covered point, and just below it are Århus and Aalborg, respectively Denmark's second- and fourth-largest cities. The heart of the peninsula, mostly lakeland and beech forests, is dotted with castles and parklands and is home to the famed Legoland. Along the east coast, deep fjords are rimmed by forests. The south holds marshlands, gabled houses, and Ribe, Denmark's oldest town.

Finally, there's the island of Bornholm, 177 kilometers (110 miles) southeast of Sjælland, with a temperate climate that distinguishes it from the rest of Denmark. Bornholm's natural beauty and winsomely rustic towns have earned it the title of Pearl of the Baltic.

Finland ✓

Finland is one of the world's northernmost countries, with its entire Lapland region located above the Arctic Circle. It's a country of beautiful scenery and strong, spirited citizens. Sweden and Russia fought over the land for centuries, but the Finns themselves are neither Scandinavian nor Slavic. Helsinki, the capital since 1812, is a meeting ground for eastern and western Europe. Built on peninsulas and islands along the Baltic coast, the city's streets curve around bays, and bridges arch across to nearby islands. Stunning architecture abounds, from 19th-century neoclassical buildings to sleek, modern high-rises. Helsinki is the country's cultural hub and home to one-sixth of the nation's population.

In the southwest lies Turku, the former capital. Founded more than 750 years ago, the city was the main gateway through which cultural influences reached Finland over the centuries. It remains a busy harbor, from which you can sail for the rugged and fascinating autonomous Åland Islands. Encompassing some 6,500 of the more than 30,000 islands that form the magnificent archipelago along Finland's coastline, the Ålands were long the subject of a territorial dispute between Finland and Sweden. The islands are home to many families that fish or run small farms, and the rural settlements form an intriguing contrast with the striking coastal scenery.

Eastern and central Finland are dimpled with nearly 200,000 lakes, most fringed with tiny cabins (the lake cabin is a Finnish vacation institution). Amid the many delightful small towns of the Lakelands, the larger Savonlinna is hugged by gigantic Lake Saimaa and is worth a visit for its waterbound scenery and cultural life. Opera, drama, ballet, and instrumental performances fill the month of July at the Savonlinna Opera festival.

Lapland, north of the Arctic Circle, is an area of unspoiled wilderness. Summer is a time of round-the-clock daylight, whereas the winter landscape is lit only by reflections on the snow. As it has become more accessible, the area has developed comfortable hotels and modern amenities, but nature is the star attraction—reindeer (there are more than 300,000 here), great forests, gin-clear streams, and the midnight sun's reflection on a lake's dark water.

Iceland

Iceland is the westernmost outpost of Europe, 800 kilometers (500 miles) from the nearest European landfall in Scotland, and more than 80% of its 103,000 square kilometers (40,000 miles) remains uninhabited. The capital city of Reykjavík is home to half the island's 250,000 citizens. Set on a fjord, against the backdrop of Mt. Esja, the city's concrete houses with their red, blue, and green roofs create a vibrant tableau. The thriving arts scene here includes theater, ballet, symphonies, museums, and private galleries. An hour's drive from Reykjavík is Þingvellir, a national park and a symbol of the nation's heritage. In AD 930, settler Grímur Geitskór chose it as the meeting site of the Icelandic general congress. In the north, Akureyri, Iceland's second-largest city, offers several museums and the Lystigarðurinn (Arctic Botanical Gardens). The east coast's Hallormsstaður Forestry Reserve offers camping spots in the country's largest forest. Throughout the island, waterfalls and fjords are sites of stunning natural beauty.

Norway

Norway, roughly 155,000 square miles, is about the same size as California. Approximately 30% of this long, narrow country is covered with clear lakes, lush forests, and rugged mountains. Western Norway, bordered by the Norwegian Sea and the Atlantic Ocean, is the fabled land of the fjords—few places on earth can match the power and splendor of this land. The magnificent Sognefjord, the longest inlet in western Norway, is only one of many fjords found here, including the Hardangerfjord, the Geirangerfjord, the Lysefjord, and the Nordfjord.

Bergen, often hailed as the "Fjord Capital of Norway," is the second-largest city in the country. The cobblestone streets, the well-preserved buildings at the Bryggen, and the seven mountains that surround the city all add to its storybook charm.

Eastern Norway, bordered by Sweden (and Finland and Russia to the north), has rolling hills, abundant valleys, and fresh lakes—much more subdued than the landscape of the west. Near Gudbrandsdalen (Gudbrands Valley) you'll find Lillehammer, the site of the 1994 Winter Olympics. Almost directly south, rising from the shores of the Oslofjord, is the capital of Norway—Oslo. With a population of about a half million, Oslo is a friendly, manageable city.

If you follow the coast south, you'll come to Kristiansand, one of Sørlandet's (the Southland's) leading cities. Sørlandet is known for its long stretches of unspoiled, uncrowded beach. Stavanger, farther west, is one of the most cosmopolitan cities in Scandinavia—its oil and gas industry draws people from around the globe.

Halfway between Oslo and Bergen lies Hardangervidda (Hardanger plateau), Norway's largest national park. At the foot of the plateau is Geilo, one of the country's most popular ski resorts. Almost directly north is the bustling city of Trondheim.

From here, a thin expanse of land stretches up to the Nordkapp (North Cape). Known as the Land of the Midnight Sun (the display of the northern lights in the winter is pretty amazing, too), this area has exquisite views: glaciers, fjords, and rocky coasts. Narvik, a major Arctic port, is the gateway to the Lofoten Islands, where puffins and penguins can be seen. Even farther north is one of Norway's major universities, Tromsø, which is the lifeline to settlements and research centers at the North Pole. At the very top of Norway is the county of Finnmark, where many Sami (native Laplanders) live. Access to the area is primarily through Hammerfest, Europe's northernmost city, where the sun is not visible from November 21 to January 21, but is uninterrupted May 17 through July 29.

Sweden

In Sweden, streamlined, ultramodern cities give way to lush forests and timbered farmhouses, and modern western European democracy coexists with strong affection for a monarchy. With 277,970 square kilometers (173,731 square miles) for only 8.6 million residents, almost all have room to live as they choose.

Stockholm, one of Europe's most beautiful capitals, is built on 14 small islands. Bustling, skyscraper-lined boulevards are a short walk from twisting medieval streets in this modern yet pastoral city. South of the city, in Småland province, are isolated villages whose names are bywords when it comes to fine crystal glassware: Kosta, Orrefors, Boda, and Strømbergshyttan. Skåne, the country's southernmost province, is an area of fertile plains, sand beaches, scores of castles and manor houses, thriving farms, medieval churches, and summer resorts.

Sweden's second-largest city, Göteborg, is on the west coast. A Viking port in the 11th century, today the city is home to the Scandinavium indoor arena; Nordstan, one of Europe's largest indoor shopping malls; and Liseberg, Scandinavia's largest amusement park. A cruise on the Göta Canal provides a picturesque coast-to-coast journey through the Swedish countryside.

Dalarna, the central region of Sweden, is considered the most typically Swedish of all the country's 24 provinces, a place of forests, mountains, and red-painted wooden farmhouses and cottages by the shores of pristine, sun-dappled lakes. The north of Sweden, Norrland, is a place of wide-open spaces. Golden eagles soar above snowcapped crags; huge salmon fight their way up wild, tumbling rivers; rare orchids bloom in Arctic heathland; and wild rhododendrons splash the land with color.

NEW AND NOTEWORTHY

Denmark

The year 1997 is the 150th anniversary of the venerable Carlsberg Brewery, one of the largest supporters of the arts in Denmark. Celebrations will include festive beer-based events as well as cultural exhibits highlighting Carlsberg-supported institutions such as the Ny Carlsberg Glyptotek, Royal Copenhagen Porcelain, and even Tivoli.

The billion-dollar expansion and renovation of Copenhagen Airport will be completed in stages until 2000, when it will include Terminal 2 (linking international and domestic terminals), a train station with check-in facilities, and general refurbishing. In the meantime, you need not worry about travel delays. The construction is being done at night and in segments for minimal disruption.

The Great Belt, Europe's other channel tunnel linking the island of Fyn to Zealand, is due to be ready for train traffic by mid-1997, and auto traffic by mid-1998. When completed, it will be the world's longest offshore suspension bridge.

Finland ✓

As expected, Finland joined the European Union (EU) on January 1, 1995, after a referendum in October, 1994. Finland's EU membership marks a formal end to the country's postwar policy of neutrality. The commitment to strengthening political and economic ties to Western Europe means that Finland has become more competitive and accessible to tourists. One of the direct impacts of EU membership has been a drop in food prices, of 5% to 10%.

Finland held parliamentary elections in March 1995. The new government is presided over by Prime Minister Paavo Lipponen, who is a Social Democrat. His government is an unusual five-party coalition, which includes the Social Democratic party and the conservative Coalition party, plus the Greens, the Leftist Alliance, and the Swedish People's Party. Finland is emerging from a devastating recession, but its unemployment rate is still one of the highest in Europe.

Iceland

As the number of tourists to Iceland continues to grow—the industry is now second only to fishing as a source of foreign revenue—the need to foster it year-round has come more to the attention of politicians and professionals. A severe recession in the early 1990s led to lower prices, and efforts have been made to keep them down. Iceland now offers a greater selection than ever of affordable accommodations, including farmhouses, guest houses, and camping holidays; restaurants have also tried to hold the line. When considering costs in Iceland, bear in mind not only its remote, island location, but also a hefty tax system that supports an impressive contemporary society.

More than ever before, Europe's most sparsely populated country is seeking to preserve its natural resources and attractions, such as its fragile wild highlands. At the same time, the country's lowland road system is being improved to provide better safety and to reduce erosion caused by rural traffic.

In 1996, Iceland's new president, Óafur Ragnar Grímsson, succeeded Vigdís Finnbogadóttir, who declined to run for a fifth term. Finnbogadóttir had been president since 1980, when she was the first woman in the world to be democratically elected head of state. Her replacement, Grímsson, was previously a member of the Parliament and a cabinet minister, as well as Chairman of the People's Alliance party, Alþýðubandalagið. How much power he will have remains to be seen—presidents traditionally do not exert much political influence in Iceland—but politically influential or not, Grímsson will take the nation into the new millenium.

Norway

Despite gloomy predictions, Norway still has not suffered any aftershocks from its rejection of the EU. The heated debate about joining the EU ended in November 1994 when Norway narrowly rejected membership. Despite the decisions of its close neighbors, Sweden and Finland, in favor of the EU, the country has remained steadfast in its refusal to join, rendering it a Eurosceptics' mecca. Unemployment in the country remains low and morale is high. However, the country is still struggling to define its relationship with the outside world, despite its high profile as an international peacemaker.

Tourists' money will go a bit farther in 1997, due to a slight decline in visitors to Norway and a resulting increase in competition. Tourists can expect to reap the benefits of lower prices when it comes to accommodation and food. Prices for Norwegian arts and crafts remain steep, however.

Trondheim celebrates its 1,000th anniversary in 1997: Events throughout the year will commemorate the city's history since its founding by King Olav Tryggvason. Some highlights are the Nordic Ski Championships, a festival week with concerts and parades, and the Cutty Sark Tall Ship Race. Coincidentally, American sociologists recently named Trondheim one of the world's most livable cities, thanks to its low buildings, wide streets, clean air, and modern offerings.

In 1996, at an international conference directed by the Worldwide Fund for Nature (WWF) and the Norwegian Polar Research Institute, the vote to establish guidelines for tourists visiting the vulnerable arctic environments of Norway was unanimous. One company in Svalbard went as far to say that tourists should be required to pass a test before "being let loose" in the arctic landscape. General rules to protect the fragile environs against mass tourism should be in effect sometime this year.

Sweden ✓

Sweden joined the EU in January, 1995, even though popular approval of membership among Swedes was far from unanimous. The anticipated drop in consumer prices has not materialized, although there is a slightly greater variety of imports available. With the dollar weakening against the krona over the past three years, Sweden has become a relatively expensive country to visit. Hotel and restaurant costs are high, as are most museum admission prices. However, thanks to government subsidies of theater, art, and music institutions, entertainment remains a relative bargain.

Sweden's travel industry, historically geared mostly toward Swedes and other Scandinavians, has in recent years been making a bigger push to market Sweden to international visitors. English-language printed material is increasingly available in museums, tourist offices, and other information centers, and Stockholm is advertising its year-round attractions instead of focusing only on its usual sun- and water-worshiping activities.

Plans for a physical link between Sweden and the Continent are similarly controversial: Construction of the 18-kilometer (11-mile) rail-and-road bridge over the Öresund, the sound separating Sweden and Denmark, was due to begin in 1993. At press time (December, 1996), following lengthy environmental assessments, the Swedish Parliament had given final approval to the project, but environmental activists were still strongly opposed and were likely to create further delays.

FODOR'S CHOICE

Dining

Denmark

★**Kong Hans, Copenhagen.** Franco-Danish cuisine, from foie gras with raspberry-vinegar sauce to warm oysters with salmon roe, is served in a subterranean setting with whitewashed walls and vaulted ceilings. *$$$$*

★**Café St. Jacques.** Though the chef and owners come from some of the finest restaurants in town, this unassuming little place manages to maintain its casual, friendly ambience—and some of the most creative seasonal cuisine around. *$$*

Finland ✓

★**Alexander Nevski, Helsinki.** Czarist-era dishes are the specialty at this Russian restaurant—try the roast bear in a pot. *$$$$*

★**Kynsilaukka, Helsinki.** Three young owner-chefs produce tasty cuisine that favors garlic; there's even garlic beer. *$$*

Iceland

★**Við Tjörnina, Reykjavík.** Some claim the food here is the best in the country. Unusual ingredients are the secret. *$$$*

Norway

★**Bagatelle, Oslo.** One of the best restaurants in Europe features the Franco-Norwegian cuisine of internationally known owner-chef Eyvind Hellstrøm. *$$$$*

★**Refsnes Gods.** Chef Oddmund Haarsaker adds a French touch to traditional Norwegian seafood for what some call the best fare in Norway. *$$$*

Sweden ✓

★**Ulriksdals Wärsdhus, Stockholm.** The lunchtime smörgåsbord is renowned at this restaurant in an 1868 country inn. *$$$$*

★**The Place, Göteborg.** Sample delicious and exotic dishes, from smoked breast of pigeon to beef tartar with caviar. *$$$*

★**Örtagården, Stockholm.** This delightful vegetarian, no-smoking restaurant is above the Östermalmstorg food market. *$$*

Lodging

Denmark

★**D'Angleterre, Copenhagen.** This grande dame has hosted everyone from royalty to rock stars. $$$$

★**Skovshoved, Copenhagen.** Licensed since 1660, this lovely art-filled inn is nestled amid fishing cottages on the harbor, 8 kilometers (5 miles) from the city. $$$

★**Vandrehjem (Family and Youth Hostels), anywhere in Denmark.** More than 100 excellent youth hostels welcome travelers of all ages. $

Finland ✓

★**Rivoli Jardin, Helsinki.** This town-house hotel is small and personal, with excellent service and an ideal location just two short blocks from the Esplanade Gardens. $$$$

Iceland

★**Holt, Reykjavík.** Luxuriously appointed rooms are a bit small, but the excellent service, gourmet restaurant, and central location more than compensate. $$$

Norway

★**Kvikne's Hotel, Balestrand.** This huge wooden gingerbread house at the edge of the Sognefjord has been a landmark since 1915. $$

★**Hotel Admiral.** Right on the water across the harbor from Bryggen, this dockside warehouse dates from 1906 but was converted to a hotel in 1987. $$–$$$

Sweden ✓

★**Lady Hamilton, Stockholm.** The quirks of this modern hotel in a 15th-century building include a medieval well where you can now take a dip. $$$$

★**Mäster Johan Hotel, Malmö.** The unpretentious exterior of this Best Western hotel disguises a plush and meticulously crafted interior. $$$$

Castles and Churches

Denmark

★**Christianborg Slot, Copenhagen.** The queen still receives guests in this 12th-century castle.

★**Kronborg Slot, Helsingør, Sjælland.** William Shakespeare never saw this fantastic castle, but that didn't stop him from using it as the setting for *Hamlet*.

★**Rosenborg Slot, Copenhagen.** The only castle that is still passed down from monarch to monarch, Rosenborg Slot is home to the crown jewels.

Finland ✓

★**Temppeliaukion Kirkko (Temple Square Church), Helsinki.** A copper dome is the only part of this modern church visible from above ground, since the church itself is carved into the rock cliffs below.

★**Uspenskin Kirkko (Uspenski Cathedral), Helsinki.** Glistening onion domes top this Russian Orthodox cathedral, built in 1868 in the Byzantine-Slavonic style.

Iceland

★**Hótel Borg.** The art deco rooms and modern conveniences here are among the country's finest. $$$

Norway

Akershus Slott, Oslo. Parts of this historic fortress, on the brow of the fjord, date to the 1300s.

★**Ambassadeur.** Built in 1889 as an apartment hotel, this still has a turn-of-the-century feel, and a staff that will meet your every need. $$$–$$$$

Sweden ✓

★**Drottningholms Slott (Queen's Island Castle), Stockholm.** This is one of the most delightful European palaces, embracing all that was best in the art of living practiced by mid-18th-century royalty.

★**Kalmar Slott, Småland.** The "Key to the Realm" during the Vasa era, this Renaissance palace commands the site of an 800-year-old fortress on the Baltic shore.

★**Kungliga Slottet (Royal Palace), Stockholm.** In this magnificent granite edifice, you can tour the State Apartments, the Royal Armory, and the Treasury, where the crown jewels are kept.

Museums

Denmark

★**Louisiana Modern Art Museum, Copenhagen.** A half-hour drive from the city is this home to a world-class collection of art from Warhol to Picasso.

⭐ **National Museet, Copenhagen.** Brilliantly renovated, and regarded as one of the best national museums in Europe, this museum houses exhibits that chronicle Danish cultural history.

Finland

⭐ **Seurasaaren Ulkomuseo (Seurasaari Outdoor Museum), Helsinki.** Old farmhouses and barns were brought from all over Finland to create this museum of Finnish rural architecture.

⭐ **Ortodoksinen Kirkkomuseo (Orthodox Church Museum), Kuopio.** Religious art from Karelia's monasteries was brought to Kuopio after World War II, creating a rare collection of Orthodox art in this small town in the Lakelands.

Iceland

⭐ **Arbæjarsafn (Open-Air Municipal Museum), Reykjavik.** Tour this village of 18th- and 19th-century houses, furnished with period reproductions and displaying household utensils and tools.

Norway

⭐ **Munchmuseet (Munch Museum), Oslo.** Edvard Munch, one of Scandinavia's leading artists, bequeathed thousands of his works to Oslo when he died in 1944.

⭐ **Norsk Folkemuseum (Norwegian Folk Museum), Bygdøy, Oslo.** Some 140 structures from all over the country have been reconstructed on the museum grounds.

Sweden

⭐ **Skansen, Stockholm.** Farmhouses, windmills, barns, and churches are just some of the buildings brought from around the country for preservation at this museum.

⭐ **Vasa Museet, Stockholm.** Visit the *Vasa,* a warship SW that sank on its maiden voyage in 1628, was raised nearly intact in 1961, and now resides in its own museum.

⭐ **Zorn Museet, Mora.** Many fine paintings by Anders Zorn (1860–1920), Sweden's leading Impressionist painter, are displayed in this museum next to the beautiful house he built in his hometown.

Special Moments

Denmark

Walking through Tivoli at dusk

Watching a bonfire on Skt. Hansaften (the longest day of the year)

Finland

Cloudberry-picking in Lapland in August

Iceland

Bobbing among glacial ice floes in Jökulsárlón lagoon

Watching the Northern Lights in December from Þingvellir

Norway

Eating dinner in a Sami tent, with your reindeer parked outside

People-watching along Oslo's Karl Johans Gate during the 17th of May (Constitution Day) celebrations

Admiring the monumental sculptures in Oslo's Vigeland Park

Sweden

Dogsledding in Norrland

Watching a Lucia procession at Christmastime

Sailing in the Stockholm archipelago

GREAT ITINERARIES

The itineraries that follow suggest ways in which Scandinavian destinations can be combined and give an idea of reasonable (minimum) amounts of time needed in various destinations. Elements from different itineraries can be combined to create an itinerary that suits your interests.

Sand, Surf, and Ships, Scandinavia Style

Scandinavia is defined by water. Glaciers, rivers, and sea tides determine the geography; oceans shape the history and culture. Tiny Denmark, for example, would probably not exist as a country today, except that it sticks up like a cork in the bottleneck entrance to the Baltic Sea, making it strategically important for great shipping and trading countries such as England, which has both attacked and defended the country over trading issues during the past 400 years. What better way, then, to see the land of the Vikings than by water?

Duration

Two weeks

The Main Route

Three nights: Denmark. Fly to Copenhagen. Explore the city and its waterways: Nyhavn's tall ships and myriad restaurants; Christianshavn, with its encircling moat and canals reflecting colorful old buildings, including the beautiful Royal Naval Museum; and the canal-ringed palace of Christiansborg, where you can visit the Danish Parliament and the royal reception rooms. Enjoy the twinkling lights and happy atmosphere of Tivoli from May to September. Take a harbor cruise, passing the Little Mermaid perched on her rock. Sun on the beaches north of town or sail the Øresund—maybe even all the way around Sjælland. You'll love the museum castle of Frederiksborg, set in its lake an hour north of Copenhagen, and the Karen Blixen Museum at Rungstedlund. Continue by air to Stockholm.

Six nights: Sweden. Beautiful Stockholm comprises 14 islands surrounded by sparkling water, clean enough for fishing and swimming even in the city center. You can take ferries all around town and out into the enchantingly lovely archipelago, with its 24,000 islands. Don't miss the picturesque Old Town, the new museum for the salvaged 17th-century warship *Vasa*, or Skansen, the world's oldest open-air museum.

From Stockholm, take the train across Sweden to Göteborg, where you can explore the west-coast beaches warmed by the Gulf Stream. Try sea fishing or windsurfing, and visit the 17th-century fortress of Elfsborg, guarding the harbor entrance. Take a ferry to Oslo.

Five nights: Norway. In Oslo, visit the Viking Ship and *Kon-Tiki* museums and the fabulous Frogner sculpture park. The Bergen Railway will carry you across the roof of Norway in 6½ dramatic hours. If you can spare an extra day, stop in Myrdal for a side trip on the Flåm Railway and a short cruise on the beautiful Aurland Fjord before continuing to Bergen. Here you'll enjoy Bryggen, a collection of reconstructed houses dating from the Hansa period in the 14th century, the famous fish market, and the funicular. Marvel at the magnificent, ever-changing Norwegian coastline aboard a steamship to Trondheim, from which you can fly to Oslo or Copenhagen, then home.

Information

See Chapters 2, 4, 5, and 6.

If you already know Copenhagen and Stockholm, consider visiting the beautiful islands of Bornholm (the Danish pearl of the Baltic) and/or Gotland (Sweden). Bornholm boasts lovely scenery and beaches that are perfect for surfing and sailing; excellent golf courses; one of the largest castle ruins in Scandinavia; and some charming architecture, including the famous round churches from the 12th and 13th centuries. You can reach it by ferry from Copenhagen or from Ystad, in southern Sweden, bringing your car if you like. Contact **Bornholmtrafikken** (✉ Kvaesthusbroen 2, DK-1252 Copenhagen, Denmark, ☎ 45/33–13–18–66, ℻ 45/33–93–18–66). Gotland is the largest island in the Baltic, with peaceful little towns and fishing villages, and a picturesque capital, Visby, with a medieval flavor and a well-preserved city wall from the 14th and 15th centuries. "Medieval Week" in early August is celebrated with mummers, knights and tourneys, and lots of other special attractions. Ferries sail from Stockholm and several other Swedish ports. For information, contact **Gotlands Turistforening** (✉ Hamngatan 4, Box 1403, S–621 25 Visby, ☎ 46/498–247065, ℻ 46/498–278940).

Scandinavian Mountains

For those who like snow-clad mountains, Scandinavia has plenty to offer: glacier climbing, reindeer and dogsledding, cross-country skiing, and just plain old hiking amid gorgeous surroundings.

Duration

Two weeks

Five nights: Norway. Fly to Oslo and then on to Bodø or another destination in northern Norway. Some of the country's most striking ranges are the Lofoton and Vesterålen mountains, near Bodø, along with the Lyngen Peninsula in Troms. Begin with a four-day hiking tour or a glacier walk guided by **Den Norske Turistforening** (DNT, Norwegian Mountain Touring Association) (⊠ Postboks 1963 Vika, N–0125 Oslo 1, ☎ 22/832550 or 22/838040). From Bodø, fly to Narvik; then take the train to Kiruna, Sweden, the largest town in Swedish Lapland.

Five nights: Sweden. Welcome to the Arctic Circle, the land of the midnight sun, where the sun stays above the horizon 24 hours during the summer solstice. In Kiruna, join a three-day white-water-canoeing trip. Take a rest, rent a car, and visit the beaver colonies at Ramsele and the fine collection of Sami art in Jokkmokk. Drive to Gällivare, where the Sami celebrate their annual church festivals. Drive or take the train to Rovaniemi, Finland, about 323 kilometers (200 miles) from Kiruna, a five- or six-hour drive. Watch out for deer and other animals on the road.

Four nights: Finland. Rovaniemi is an end point for the Road of the Four Winds, or, simply, the Arctic Road, which runs 1,000 kilometers (620 miles) north from Helsinki. In summer, look for the salmon-fishing competition, reindeer herding, gold panning, logging, and the Russian Orthodox Skolt Lappish festivals that are held throughout the region. Fly from Rovaniemi to Helsinki and then home.

See Chapters 3, 5, and 6.

Tracing the Vikings

Traces can still be found of the seafaring warriors who, from the 8th through the 11th century, traded with, settled in, or raided the part of the world that became known as Western Europe, Iceland, Greenland, Labrador, Newfoundland, and Russia. The Vikings' 1,000-year-old remains are scattered throughout Scandinavia and provide a fascinating record of their culture.

10 days

Three nights: Denmark. Begin in Copenhagen with a visit to the Danish National Museum, which has many Viking exhibits labeled in English; one discusses how the Vikings could navigate their ships across vast oceans at a time when most people believed the world was flat. Take the train to the Viking Ship Hall in Roskilde (less than an hour west of Copenhagen), where five ships, found in the Roskilde Fjord and dating from around AD 1000, have been restored. At the nearby Lejre Forsøgscenter (Lejre Archaeological Research Center), you can see how the Vikings lived. On the way back, visit Trelleborg in western Sjælland, where you'll find the remains of a staging area for troops led by Knud (Canute), who in 1016 became king of England, Denmark, Norway, and part of Sweden. In May, you can enjoy a colorful Viking pageant in the lovely park at Frederikssund.

Rent a car or take a train and stay overnight in Vejle, on the large peninsula of Jylland; then head for Jelling, where two Viking kings—Gorm the Old and his son, Harald Bluetooth, Knud's great-grandfather—reigned. They left two large burial mounds and two runestones, dating from around AD 950. In June, attend a performance of the Viking play *The Stoneship* on Fårup Sø.

If you have more time, you can visit many other Viking sites in Denmark: Ribe, Denmark's oldest town and site of a Viking village open-air museum; Hedeby; Høje, where graves are marked by 4-foot-tall stones placed in the pattern of a ship; Moesgård museum near Århus; Fyrkat, a 10th-century ring fortress near Hobro; Lindholm; Mammen; Aggersborg; and Viborg. Return to Copenhagen and fly to Oslo, Norway.

Three nights: Norway. Go straight to the Oslo Viking Ship Hall, where you'll see the finest single collection of excavated and preserved Viking ships, once used as burial sepulchres for nobles. Families can entertain the children at VikingLandet, a new Oslo amusement park that offers Viking-era adventures. The next day, in Oslo's Historical Museum, you'll find beautiful jewelry from the 9th century: gold necklaces, silver ornaments, and "gripping beasts," whimsical monsters fashioned from amber and other materials. Fly to Stockholm.

Four nights: Sweden. In the State Historical Museum you'll find swords, saddlery, and wonderful Viking gold jewelry, including amulets in the shape of a hammer, the symbol of Thor, the thunder god. At Gamla Uppsala (Old Uppsala), an easy drive north of Stockholm, there are burial grounds for three 6th-century Viking monarchs. In summer take the ferry to the island of Gotland in time for the Folk Sports Olympiad to see games the way they were played in the distant past. One contest, known as *varpa*, is won by tossing a stone nearest a stake. Another, *stångstörtning*, involves the tossing of 16-foot poles. In the Gotland Historical Museum, you'll find valuables that were buried with the Vikings, including Arabic, Byzantine, German, Bohemian, Hungarian, and Anglo-Saxon coins that reflect the warriors' wanderings. Return to Stockholm and then home.

Information

See Chapters 2, 5, and 6.

Architecture and Handicrafts

Scandinavian furniture, architecture, and handicrafts are world renowned.

Duration

11 days

The Main Route

Three nights: Denmark. Strolling through Copenhagen, you'll be amazed by the number of beautiful buildings, punctuated by green copper spires and tinkling fountains. Don't miss the 15th-century Church of the Holy Ghost and the Baroque Church of Our Saviour. Brick Renaissance buildings from the reign of King Christian IV include the Stock Exchange, surmounted by a spire of twisting dragontails; the exquisite Rosenborg Castle in its flowery park, housing the crown jewels and royal art and furniture, including the famous life-size silver lions; and the Round Tower, Copenhagen's first observatory, from which you'll see the old town spread out like a map. Enjoy charming Gråbrødretorv and the colorful old buildings reflected in the canals of Nyhavn and Christianshavn. Monumental are Christiansborg Palace, housing the Par-liament and royal reception rooms, and Amalienborg Palace, home of the royal family. Examples of modern monumentality are the exciting new planetarium and the golden brick mass of Gruntvig's Church. An hour north of Copenhagen, visit the museum castles of Frederiksborg in Hillerød and Kronborg (Hamlet's castle) in Helsingør.

Danish applied art is famed for fine design and high quality. In Copenhagen, visit Illum's Bolighus, a mecca for all kinds of home furnishings, and have a gourmet lunch at Paustian, where fine contemporary furniture and accessories are displayed in a building by the Danish architect Jørn Utzon (of Sydney Opera House fame). Enjoy the porcelain showrooms of Royal Copenhagen and Bing & Grøndahl. Watch exquisite glass being blown at the Holmegård Glass factory, about an hour south of town. Visit the Georg Jensen Museum and the Kunstindustrimuseet, with its Rococo buildings and fine exhibits of European and Asian handicrafts. Historical walking tours in English are held daily and are the best introduction to the city's architecture. Take the overnight train or fly to Stockholm.

Two nights: Sweden. Stroll around Stockholm's old town (Gamla Stan) for views of the magnificent 700-year-old cathedral and the 608-room Royal Palace. From the tower of the beautiful modern Town Hall, with its handmade brickwork and golden mosaics, gaze over Stockholm's 14 islands and glittering, clean waters. Visit the Skansen open-air museum's collection of 150 regional buildings and handicraft shops, ending with dinner, a concert, or outdoor entertainment. The National Museum has a fine collection of Scandinavian applied arts, while the Nordic Museum documents examples of daily life from the past 500 years. The Vasa Museum is noteworthy for its new building as well as for the fabulous warship, recently raised from where it sank on its maiden voyage in 1628. Slightly outside the city, visit the Ulriksdal Castle and park and the Carl Milles Sculpture Garden in Lidingö. If you can spend an extra day, take a ferry or drive to Gripsholm Castle or Drottningholm, the royal residence in its lovely park. Alternatively, drive to Insjöen to visit Sätergläntan, a center for courses in traditional handicrafts; or take a train to Växjö and see the Glass Museum, a collection of startling Swedish designs in crystal. From Stockholm, take the overnight ferry to Helsinki.

Five nights: Finland. The Museum of Applied Arts will give you an overview of the development of Finnish architecture and design, and the Helsinki Information Center offers exhibitions, films, and slide shows. See the fine neoclassical Senate Square and the Art Nouveau buildings at Eira and Katajanokka, as well as Eliel Saarinen's Helsinki railway station from 1914. Don't miss Finlandiatalo, the concert hall designed by Finland's greatest architect, Alvar Aalto; the Temppeliaukio Church, hollowed out from rock with only its dome showing; or the magnificent sculpture commemorating the composer Jean Sibelius. The Gallen-Kallela Museum is a studio-castle in the National Romantic style built on a rocky peninsula, designed by the artist for his paintings, drawings, sculpture, textiles, and furniture. Check with the University of Industrial Arts in Helsinki, the largest of its kind in Scandinavia, on its current exhibits, often held in collaboration with Design Forum Finland. Fine china and pottery are displayed at the Arabia Museum and traditional folk handicrafts at the Virkki Museum of Handicrafts. Visit the Artek factory, which features furniture by Alvar Aalto, and the Marimekko and Vuokko textile factories. Rent a car to visit the Finnish Glass Museum, 50 kilometers (31 miles) north of Helsinki in Riihimäki, with permanent exhibits on glassmaking and exhibitions of old Finnish glassware and crystal as well as works by contemporary designers. Stop by the Hvitträsk, a turn-of-the-century studio designed by and for three Finnish architects as a laboratory for their aesthetic principles.

Take a ferry to Suomenlinna Island fortress, partly built by Russians, where you will find the Nordic Art Center. Also stop in at the garden city of Käpylä, a residential area built in the 1920s in a unique neoclassical style reminiscent of traditional Finnish wood architecture. If you have time, drive or take a bus along the King's Road, west to Lovisa or east to Turku. This historic road affords spectacular coastal views and is studded with buildings and monuments of interest.

Information

See Chapters 2, 3, and 6.

FESTIVALS AND SEASONAL EVENTS

Denmark

New Year's Eve: Fireworks at the Town Hall Square are set off by local revelers.

March: The **Ice Sculpture Festival** takes place in Nuuk, Greenland; the **Nuuk Marathon** draws a hardy crowd of runners.

April: In Greenland, the **Arctic Circle Race** begins in Kangangerlussuaq and ends in Sisimiut.

April 16: The Queen's Birthday is celebrated with the royal guard in full ceremonial dress as the royal family appears before the public on the balcony of Amalienborg Castle.

May: Copenhagen Carnival includes boat parades in Nyhavn and costumed revelers in the streets.

May–August: The **Tivoli Gardens** in Copenhagen open with rides, concerts, and entertainment. Special activities and concerts are planned for the 145th anniversary of the Tivoli Guard.

May–September: Legoland, a park constructed of 35 million Lego blocks, opens in Billund, Jylland.

June: The **Around Fyn Regatta** starts in Kerteminde. The **Round Zealand Regatta,** one of the largest yachting events in the world, starts and ends in Helsingør. The **Aalborg Jazz Festival** fills the city with four days of indoor and outdoor concerts, many of them free. The **Viking Festival** in Frederikssund includes open-air performances of a Viking play.

On **Midsummer's Night,** Danes celebrate the longest day of the year with bonfires and picnics.

June 21: Greenland National Day celebrates the anniversary of Home Rule.

June–July: The **Roskilde Festival,** the largest rock concert in northern Europe, attracts dozens of bands and 75,000 fans.

July: The **Copenhagen Jazz Festival** gathers international and Scandinavian jazz greats for a week of concerts, many of them free.

July 4: The **Fourth of July** celebration in Rebild Park, near Aalborg, sets off the only American Independence Day festivities outside the United States.

Mid-July: The **Århus Jazz Festival** gathers European and other world-renowned names, with indoor and outdoor concerts.

August: Between the 7th and 10th, the **Cutty Sark Tall Ship Race** brings more than 100 ships to the Copenhagen harbor.

Mid-August: The annual **Copenhagen Water Festival** celebrates the city's ties to the sea with concerts, exhibits, and plenty of outdoor activities.

September: The **Århus Festival,** Denmark's most comprehensive fête, fills the city with concerts, sports, and theater.

Finland

January: The **Arctic Rally** gets into gear yearly in Rovaniemi, Lapland.

February: Shrove Tuesday Celebrations, throughout Finland, include skiing, skating, and tobogganing events; **Finlandia Ski** is a 75-kilometer (47-mile) Hämeenlinna–Lahti ski event.

March: The **Tar Skiing Race** in Oulu is the oldest cross-country ski trek (75 kilometers [47 miles]) in the country, and the **Porokuninkuusajot Reindeer Races** are run in Inari at the end of the month. The **Lady Day church festival** in Enontekiö includes reindeer racing and lassoing competitions.

The **Tampere International Short Film Festival** features some of the best film in its category in Finland's third-largest city.

April: April Jazz/Espoo features foreign and Finnish performers in a Helsinki suburb; Rovaniemi is host to **Lapland's Ski-Orienteering Days.**

May: Vapunaatto and Vappu (May Day Eve and May Day) celebrations occur nationwide and include picnicking and drinking; **Kainuu Jazz** means four days of listening to native and foreign musicians jamming in Kajaani.

June: The **Kuopio Music and Dance Festival** is on stage in Kuopio, while the **Naantali Music Festival** soothes the ears of chamber-music lovers; **Joensuu Festival** stages a wide variety of musical events, from classical to modern, many held on an open-air stage; **Juhannus** (Midsummer Eve and Day) is celebrated nationwide with bonfires and all-night boat cruises. The **Hanko Regatta** is a popular open-sea sailing competition.

July: The **Savonlinna Opera Festival,** on a grand scale and a month long, is a festival of international opera staged at Olavinlinna Castle, Savonlinna; **Pori Jazz,** Finland's premier international jazz festival, is set in Pori; the **Kuhmo Chamber Music Festival** is a week of chamber music in eastern Finland; and the **Kaustinen Folk Music Festival** is based in Kaustinen, western Finland. The **Ruisrock Festival,** held in Turku's Ruissalo Recreational Park, is Finland's oldest and largest rock festival.

August: The **Turku Music Festival** has Baroque to contemporary performances; the **Tampere International Theater Festival** includes plays staged by Finnish and foreign troupes; the **Helsinki Festival** means two weeks of dance, music, drama, and children's shows in the capital and its environs; the world's top drivers test their skills in Jyväskylä at the **Thousand Lakes Rally** for a grueling three days.

October: The **Baltic Herring Festival** is the premier fishermen's fish market, for one weekend on the quayside in Helsinki.

November: Tampere Jazz, a modern jazz event, holds court in Tampere; the **Children's Festival** in Helsinki consists of performance art of all kinds; for an entire week children's films from around the world are

shown at the **Oulu International Children's Film Festival; Kaamos Jazz** is a festival of jazz in Lapland's winter twilight, at Saariselkä/Tankavaara, near Ivalo.

December: Independence Day (December 6) means a parade to the candlelit Senate Square in Helsinki; **Lucia Day** is celebrated in Helsinki on December 13 with a concert at Finlandiatalo; ✓**New Year's celebrations** vary, but the fireworks can be seen every year from Senate Square in Helsinki.

Iceland

January 19–mid-February: Traditional Icelandic foods and drinks are served at Þorri Banquets around the country.

March 23–31: Fjord cruises, jazz concerts, and dances accompany a week of skiing at the **Ski Festival** in Safjörður.

June 1: Many coastal towns celebrate **Sjómannadagur** (Seamen's Day); in Reykjavík there are rowing and swimming competitions, speeches, and an awards ceremony.

June 17: Iceland National Day is a nationwide party, with parades and outdoor dancing downtown in Reykjavík, Akureyri, and other towns.

Late June: The Arctic Open Golf Tournament is held, in the midnight sun, on the 18-hole golf course at Akureyri.

June–July: Just south of Reykjavík in Hafnarfjörður, the **International Viking Festival** celebrates the country's Viking heritage with a Viking village, living-history demonstrations, battle

enactments, and a Viking-ship sailing competition.

July–August: The **Skálholt Music Festival,** at the south's Skálholt Cathedral, includes concerts of Baroque and contemporary music every weekend.

August 3–5: Bank Holiday Weekend draws large crowds for outdoor celebrations throughout the country.

August 3–5: Þjóðhátíð 1874 (National Festival) is celebrated in Vestmannaeyjar (the Westmann Islands).

Mid-August: Icelandic and European musicians give performances during the **Kirkjubæjarklaustur Chamber Music Festival.**

August: Reykjavík Marathon sends world-class distance runners on their annual race around the city.

Norway

January: In Tromsø, the **Northern Lights Festival** celebrates the return of daylight with performances by notable Norwegian and international musicians.

February: Lillehammer's **Winter Festival** is a cultural affair including music, theater, and art exhibitions. The **Røros Fair** in the town of Roros (designated as Cultural Heritage Landmark by UNESCO) has been an annual tradition since 1854.

February 20–March 2: The **Nordic World Ski Championships** in Trondheim is the biggest event celebrating Trondheim's 1,000th-year anniversary.

March: Europe's largest dogsledding competition,

the **Finnmark Race,** follows old mail routes across Finnmarksvidda. The **Birkebeiner Race** commemorates a centuries-old cross-country ski race from Lillehammer to Rena. At the **Voss Jazz Festival,** European and American jazz and folk artists appear at Voss, a major ski resort in western Norway.

March–April: The **Karasjok Easter Festival** features a variety of concerts, theater performances, art exhibits, snowmobile rallies, and reindeer races.

May 17: Constitution Day brings out every Norwegian flag and crowds of marchers for parades and celebrations throughout the country.

May: The **Grete Waitz Race** is a 5-kilometer (3-mile), women-only street marathon in Oslo. The festivities of the annual **Bergen International Festival,** customarily opened by the king, include dance, music, and theater performances.

May 30–June 8: Trondheim's 1,000-year anniversary is in full swing during the city's **Festival Week.**

June 23: Midsummer Night, called *Sankt Hans Afton,* is celebrated nationwide with bonfires, fireworks, and outdoor dancing. Meet fellow Norwegian Americans and Norwegians at the annual **Emigration Festival** in Stavanger.

July: The plays, exhibitions, concerts, and historic walking tours of the **Kristin Festival** pay tribute to *Kristin Lavransdatter,* the Nobel prizewinning novel by

Sigrid Undset; they are held at Jorund Farm, the site of Liv Ullmann's movie based on the same novel. More than 400 jazz musicians participate in the extremely popular **Molde International Jazz Festival.**

July 23–26: Boats and crews of the **Cutty Sark Regatta** will be in Trondheim.

August: You'll find none other than folk music, folk dancing, and folk songs at the **Telemark International Folk Music Festival** in the town of Bo in Telemark. The **Peer Gynt Festival** in Lillehammer brings art exhibits, processions with national costumes, and open-air theater performances of Henrik Ibsen's *Peer Gynt*—as well as Edvard Grieg's music. The **Oslo Chamber Music Festival** draws participants from around the world.

Late August: The **Norwegian Food Festival** presents the Norwegian Championship in cooking, seminars, and lectures.

September: The **Oslo Marathon** stretches 42 kilometers (26 miles) through the streets of Oslo.

December 10: The **Nobel Peace Prize** is awarded in Oslo—by invitation only.

Sweden

January 13: Knut signals the end of Christmas festivities and "plundering" of the Christmas tree: Trinkets are removed from the tree, edible ornaments eaten, and the tree itself thrown out.

February (first Thursday, Friday, and Saturday): A **market** held in the small town of Jokkmokk, above

the Arctic Circle, features both traditional Lapp artifacts and plenty of reindeer.

Shrove Tuesday: Special buns called *semlor* are eaten; lightly flavored with cardamom, filled with almond paste and whipped cream, they are traditionally placed in a dish of warm milk and topped with cinnamon.

March (first Sunday): The **Vasaloppet ski race** is 88 kilometers (55 miles) from Sälen to Mora in Dalarna, and attracts entrants from all over the world.

Maundy Thursday: Small girls dress up as witches and hand out "Easter letters" for small change. *Påskris,* twigs tipped with brightly dyed feathers, decorate homes. ···

April 30: For the **Feast of Valborg,** bonfires are lit to celebrate the end of winter. The liveliest celebrations involve the students of the university cities of Uppsala, 60 kilometers (37 miles) north of Stockholm, and Lund, 16 kilometers (10 miles) north of Malmö.

May 1: Labor Day marches and rallies are held nationwide.

June 6: National Day is celebrated, with parades, speeches, and band concerts nationwide.

June: Midsummer's Eve and Day celebrations are held on the Friday evening and Saturday that fall between June 20 and 26. Swedes decorate their homes with flower garlands, raise maypoles, and dance around them to folk music.

August 4–13: Stockholm Water Festival celebrates the city's clean water environment with watersports performances, a fireworks competition, and many other events all over town.

August (second Wednesday): Crayfish are considered a delicacy in Sweden, and on this day, the **Crayfish premiere,** friends gather to eat them at outdoor parties.

November 11: St. Martin's Day is celebrated primarily in the southern province of Skåne. Roast goose is served, accompanied by *svartsoppa,* a bisque made of goose blood and spices.

December: For each of the four weeks of **Advent,** leading up to Christmas, a candle is lit in a four-pronged candelabra.

December 10: Nobel Day sees the presentation of the Nobel prizes by King Carl XVI Gustaf at a glittering banquet held in the Stockholm City Hall.

December 13: On **Santa Lucia Day** young girls are selected to be "Lucias"; they wear candles (today usually electric substitutes) in their hair and sing hymns with their handmaidens and "star

boys" at ceremonies around the country.

December 24: Christmas Eve is the principal day of Christmas celebration. Traditional Christmas dishes include ham, rice porridge, and *lutfisk* (ling that is dried and then boiled).

December 31: New Year's Eve is the Swedes' occasion to shoot off an astounding array of fireworks. Every household has its own supply, and otherwise quiet neighborhood streets are full of midnight merrymakers.

2 Denmark

With its highest mountain standing at a mere 135 meters and its most-visited attraction an amusement park, it's no wonder Denmark is so often described as hyggelig—*cozy, warm, and welcoming. A tiny land made up of 450 islands and the arc of one long peninsula, Hans Christian Andersen's home has the fairy tale quality you'd expect: Half-timber villages cozy up to provincial towns, and footsteps—not traffic—mark the tempo.*

By Karina
Porcelli

THE KINGDOM OF DENMARK dapples the Baltic Sea in an archipelago of some 450 islands and the arc of one peninsula. Measuring 43,069 square kilometers (17,028 square miles) and with a population of 5 million, it is the geographical link between Scandinavia and Europe. Half-timber villages and well-groomed agriculture cozy up to provincial towns and a handful of cities, where footsteps, not traffic, mark the tempo. Mothers safely park baby carriages outside bakeries while outdoor cafés fill with cappuccino-sippers, and lanky Danes pedal to work in lanes thick with bicycle traffic. Clearly this is a land where the process of life is the greatest reward.

Many visitors pinch themselves in disbelief and make long lists of resolutions to emulate the Danes. Their lifestyle is certainly enviable. Many of the qualities that have pressure-cooked life in other Western countries have not yet touched this land. Long one of the world's most liberal countries, Denmark has a highly developed social-welfare system. Hefty taxes are the subject of grumbles and jokes, but Danes remain proud of their state-funded medical and educational systems and high standard of living. They enjoy life with monthlong vacations, 7½-hour workdays, and overall security.

Educated, patriotic, and keenly aware of their tiny international stance, most Danes travel extensively and have a balanced perspective of their nation's benefits and shortfalls. As in many other provincial states, egalitarianism is often a constraint for the ambitious. In Denmark, the *Jante* law, which refers to a literary principle penned in the early 20th century by Axel Sandemose, essentially means "Don't think you're anything special"—and works as an insidious cultural barrier to talent and aspiration. On the other hand, free education and state support give refugees, immigrants, and the underprivileged an opportunity to begin new, often prosperous lives.

The history of the tiny country stretches back 250,000 years, when Jylland (Jutland) was inhabited by nomadic hunters, but it wasn't until AD 500 that a tribe from Sweden, called the Danes, migrated south and christened the land Denmark.

The Viking expansion that followed, based on the country's strategic position in the north, saw struggles for control of the North Sea with England and Western Europe, for the Skagerrak (the strait between Denmark and Norway) with Norway and Sweden, and for the Baltic with Germany, Poland, and Russia. With high-speed ships and fine-tuned warriors, intrepid navies navigated to Europe and Canada, invading and often pillaging, until, under King Knud (Canute) the Great (995–1035), they captured England.

After the British conquest, Viking supremacy declined as feudal Europe learned to defend itself. Internally, the pagan way of life was threatened by the expansion of Christianity, which was introduced under Harald Bluetooth, who in AD 980 "baptized" the country, essentially to avoid war with Germany. For the next several hundred years, the country tried to maintain its Baltic power under the influence of the German Hanseatic League. Under the leadership of Valdemar IV (1340–1375), Sweden, Norway, Iceland, Greenland, and the Faroe Islands became a part of Denmark. Sweden broke away by the mid-15th century and battled Denmark for much of the next several hundred years, whereas Norway remained under Danish rule until 1814 and Iceland until 1943. Greenland and the Faroe Islands are still self-governing Danish provinces.

Denmark

North Sea

Skagerrak

TO GREENLAND
TO FAROE ISLANDS

Skagen

Hirtshals
Frederikshavn
Hjørring
Sæby

Brønderslev

Hanstholm

Thisted
Lim-fjord
Limfjord
Aalborg

Nykøbing

Hadsund

Lemvig
Skive
Struer
Viborg
Holstebro
Jylland
Randers

Ringkøbing
Herning
Silkeborg

Skanderborg
Århus
Ebeltoft

Horsens
Samsø

Grindsted
Vejle
Billund

Skjern
Fredericia

Esbjerg
Holsted
Middelfart
Kolding
Odense
Kerteminde

Fanø
Assens
Fyn
Ribe
Vojens
Nyborg
Rømø
Haderslev
Fåborg
Skærbæk
Åbenrå
Lillebælt

Tønder
Als
Svendborg
Troense
Tranekær
Sønderborg
Rudkøbing
Ærøskøbing
Marstal
Ærø
Langeland

Læsø

Aalborg Bugt

Kattegat

Anholt

Grenå

SWEDEN

Tisvildeleje
Hornbaek
Nykøbing
Helsingør
Frederikssund
Hillerød
Kalundborg
Holbæk
Jyderup
Roskilde
Copenhagen
Slagelse
Ringsted
Amager
Korsør
Køge
Køge Bugt
Næstved
St. Heddinge
Karrebæksminde
Vordingborg
Stege
Nakskov
Møn
Nykøbing
Falster
Rødby
Maribo
Lolland
Nysted

Samsøbælt

Store-bælt

Sjælland

Ostsee

TO BORNHOLM

SWEDEN
Baltic Sea

Bornholm

Rønne

GERMANY

N

0   50 miles
0   75 km

Denmark prospered again in the 16th century, thanks to the Sound Dues, a levy charged to ships crossing the Øresund, the slender waterway between Denmark and Sweden. Under King Christian IV, a construction boom crowned the land with what remain architectural gems, but his fantasy spires and castles, compounded with the Thirty Years' War in the 17th century, led to state bankruptcy.

By the 18th century, absolute monarchy had given way to representative democracy, and culture flourished. Then, in a fatal mistake, Denmark sided with France and refused to surrender its navy to the English during the Napoleonic Wars. In a less than valiant episode of British history, Lord Nelson turned his famous blind eye to the destruction and bombed Copenhagen to bits. The defeated King Frederik VI handed Norway to Sweden. Denmark's days of glory were over.

Though Denmark was unaligned during World War II, the Nazis invaded in 1940. Against them, the Danes used the only weapons they had: a cold shoulder and massive underground resistance. After the war, Denmark focused inward, refining its welfare system and concentrating on its main industries of agriculture, shipping, and financial and technical services. It is an outspoken member of the European Union (EU), championing environmental responsibility and supporting development in emerging economies. It was one of the only countries to forgive a considerable amount of Third World debt during the World Summit in Copenhagen in 1995.

Expensive as it is, Denmark is in many ways less pricey than the rest of Scandinavia. At the height of summer, when businesses shut down (usually for all of July), conference hotels often lower prices and offer weekend specials. Denmark is also the only Nordic country with relaxed drinking laws and moderate beer and wine prices, an attraction that induces other Scandinavians to hop over for splurge weekends.

Copenhagen fidgets with its modern identity, trying to integrate its role as a Scandinavian-European link and cozy capital. The center of Danish politics, culture, and finance, it copes through balance and a sense of humor with a taste for the absurd. Stroll the streets and you'll pass classical architecture painted in candy colors, businessmen clad in jeans and T-shirts, and, on sunny days, ebullient Danes stripping down on beaches and in parks.

Copenhagen is the attention-getter, but it would be a shame to miss the surrounding countryside of Sjælland (Zealand). Less than an hour away, the land is checkered with fields and half-timber cottages. Roskilde, to the east, has a 12th-century cathedral, while in the north, Helsingør is crowned with the Kronborg Castle of *Hamlet* fame. Beaches, some chic, some deserted, are powdered by fine white sand.

Fyn (Funen) has rightly earned its storybook reputation by making cuteness a local passion. The city of Odense, Hans Christian Andersen's birthplace, is cobbled with crooked old streets and lilliputian cottages. Jylland's landscape is the most severe, with Ice Age–chiseled fjords and hills (which the Danes sheepishly call mountains). Nonetheless, its provincial towns have timbered neighborhoods, while the cities of Århus and Aalborg offer museums and nightlife rivaling Copenhagen's.

The best way to discover Denmark is to strike up a conversation with a Dane. Affable and hospitable, they'll probably approach you before you get the chance. They have a wonderful word, *hyggelig,* which defies definition but comes close to meaning a cozy and charming hospitality. A summertime beach picnic can be as hyggelig as tea on a cold winter's night. The only requirement is the company of a Dane.

Pleasures and Pastimes

Beaches

In this country of islands, coastline, and water, beaches come in many breeds. In Sjælland, a series of chic strands stretches along *Strandvejen*—the old beach road—pinned down by a string of lovely old seaside towns; here is where young people go to strut and preen. Fyn's gentle, golden beaches are less a showplace than a quiet getaway for a largely northern European crowd. The windswept peninsula of Jylland has the country's longest, most expansive, and most dramatic beaches—at the tip of the peninsula you can even see the line in the waves where the Kattegat meets the Skaggerak Sea.

Bicycling

Without a doubt, Denmark is one of the world's best places for cycling. Three-quarters of the population have bicycles, and more than half make use of them, on roads that effectively coordinate public transportation and cycle traffic. In Copenhagen, the bike routes along the city's swan-filled central lakes and café-studded streets give you an insider's sense of the sights, smells, and sounds of the city. The countrysides are also lined with paths, especially Jylland and the island of Bornholm.

Boating and Sailing

Well-marked channels and nearby anchorages make sailing and boating easy and popular along the whole of the 7,300-kilometer (4,500-mile) coastline. Waters range from the open seas of the Kattegat and the Baltic to Smålandshavet (between Sjælland and Lolland Falster) and the calm Limsfjord in Jylland. In Copenhagen, scores of marinas bristling with crisp, white sails and the historic harbors of Christianshavn and Nyhavn are lined with old wooden houseboats, motorboats, yachts, and their colorful crews. This is not a pastime reserved just for the well heeled: Tousle-haired parents and babes, partying youths, and leathery pensionists tend to their boats and picnics, lending the marinas a festive, community spirit.

Boat rentals are available in most areas. Canoe and kayak rentals are also available for exploring the country's calm streams. For details, contact the Danish Tourist Board.

Danish Design

Danish design has earned an international reputation for form and function, and any visitor will have a hard time resisting the boutiques and crafts shops. The best sales are after Christmas until February. Best buys are glassware, stainless steel, pottery, ceramics, and fur. Danish antiques and silver are also much cheaper than in the United States. For major purchases—Bang & Olufsen products, for example—check prices stateside first so you can spot a good price. The best selection of shops and department stores is in Copenhagen, though crafts shops are also located in the pedestrian streets of most smaller towns.

Dining

From the hearty meals of Denmark's seafaring heritage to the inspired creations of a new generation of chefs, Danish cuisine combines the best of tradition and novelty. Though the country has long looked to the French as a beacon of gastronomy, there has recently been a proud return to the Danish kitchen, emphasizing fresh, local ingredients. Sample fresh fish and seafood from the Baltic, free-range chickens from the island of Bornholm, beef and pork from the peninsula of Jutland, and more exotic delicacies such as reindeer, caribou, seal meat, and even whale from Greenland. Denmark's famed dairy products, including sweet butter and milk, as well as a burgeoning organic foods industry, all contribute to the freshness of the modern Danish kitchen.

Lunchtime is reserved for *smørrebrød*. The best restaurants that serve these open-face sandwiches are modest, family-run places, with a focus on generous portions (though never excessive) and artful presentation. Certainly, diners who face tender mounds of roast beef topped with pickles or baby shrimp marching across a slice of French bread are experiencing a slice of authentic Danish culture.

One thing that has not changed is top-notch liquid refreshment that is available at virtually all restaurants. Slowly the ubiquitous Carlsberg and Tuborg are being accompanied by other international brews, but you can't do better than to stick with the Danish brands. Those who like harder stuff should try the famous *snaps*, the aquavit traditionally drunk with cold food. The Danes are also great drinkers of fine wines, and surprisingly, the prices are among the most reasonable in Europe.

As with many things Danish, form is as important as content: Friends and family gather together early, usually between 6 and 7:30, at a table set with cut flowers, cloth napkins, a crisp tablecloth and candlelight, to savor a meal. Everything—even the open-face sandwiches—is eaten this way, slowly, enjoyably, with a knife and fork.

Meal prices vary little between town and country. Though approximate ratings are given below, remember that careful ordering can get you a moderate meal at a very expensive restaurant. Prices are per person and include a first course, entrée, and dessert, plus taxes and tip, but not wine.

CATEGORY	COPENHAGEN	OTHER AREAS
$$$$	over DKr400	over DKr350
$$$	DKr200–DKr400	DKr200–DKr350
$$	DKr120–DKr200	DKr100–DKr200
$	under DKr120	under DKr100

Lodging

Accommodations in Denmark range from spare to resplendent. Luxury hotels in the city or countryside offer rooms of a high standard, and in a manor-house hotel you may find yourself sleeping in a four-poster bed. Even inexpensive hotels are well designed with good materials and good, firm beds—and the country's 100 youth and family hostels and 500-plus campgrounds are among the world's finest.

Farmhouses and *kroer* (old stagecoach inns) offer a terrific alternative to more traditional hotels. Perhaps the best way to see how the Danes live and work, farm stays allow you to share meals with the family and perhaps even help with the chores. If you prefer more independent arrangements, you can rent a summer home in the countryside.

Prices are for two people in a double room and include service and taxes and usually breakfast.

CATEGORY	COPENHAGEN	OTHER AREAS
$$$$	over DKr1,100	over DKr850
$$$	DKr800–DKr1,100	DKr650–DKr850
$$	DKr670–DKr800	DKr450–DKr650
$	under DKr670	under DKr450

Exploring Denmark

Denmark is divided into three regions: the two major islands of Sjælland and Fyn, and the peninsula of Jutland. To the east, Sjælland is Denmark's largest and most populated island, with Copenhagen as its focal point. Denmark's second largest island, Fyn, is a pastoral, undulating land of farms and summer-house beach villages, with Odense as its one major town. To the west, the relatively vast peninsula of Jutland connects Denmark to the European continent; here are the towns of Arhus and Aalborg.

Numbers in the text correspond to numbers in the margin and on the maps.

Great Itineraries

IF YOU HAVE 3 DAYS

Take at least two days to explore and enjoy ⊞ **Copenhagen** ①–㉞, Denmark's heart and Scandinavia's biggest city. The last day, head north of the city, first to **Rungsted** ㉟ to see Karen Blixen's manor-house and the lush garden surrounding it, then to the Louisiana Museum of Modern Art in **Humlebæk** ㊱, and its equally stunning grounds.

IF YOU HAVE 5 DAYS

After two days and nights in ⊞ **Copenhagen** ①–㉞, head north to **Rungsted** ㉟ and **Humlebæk** ㊱; then spend the night in ⊞ **Helsingør** ㊲. The next day, visit the castles of Helsingør and **Hillerød** ㊴, and then venture west to medieval **Roskilde** ㊶. Day five, enjoy the dramatic nature and history of **Møn** ㊹ and a tour of the villages and beaches of Lolland/Falster, before returning to Copenhagen. An alternative last-day tour is to head west, to Hans Christian Andersen's birthplace of **Odense** ㊿, on the island of Funen.

IF YOU HAVE 7 DAYS

A week will allow you to explore the island of Funen and the peninsula of Jutland. Be sure to rent a car for the latter—it's the quickest way to make it from the historic cities ⊞ **Århus** ㋕ and ⊞ **Aalborg** ㋘ to the blond beaches of **Skagen** ㋙, with time left over to meander through a couple of smaller villages and spin through the countryside. With good planning, you'll be able to fit in a short, organized trip to Greenland or the Faroe Islands, especially if you "piggyback" a weekend tour onto a transatlantic trip through Icelandair, which as of press time (December 1996) was the only airline organizing such trips. Naturally, you could devote at least a week to exploring either the Faroe Islands or Greenland, or for that matter, much longer.

When to Tour Denmark

Summertime, when the lingering sun brings out the best in the climate and the Danes, is undoubtedly the best time to visit. The weather is relatively consistent around the country, though Bornholm tends to stay warmer and sunnier longer than elsewhere. July is a busy tourist month; it also happens to be the traditional, national industrial holiday month, when most Danes flee to their summer homes, or often, abroad. Summer is also the season of music festivals such as the jazz fests in Copenhagen and Aalborg in June, and Århus in July.

Though winter is dark and rainy, it is a great time to visit museums, libraries, and the countless atmospheric meeting places in which the Danes take refuge. The weeks preceding Christmas are a prime time to experience Tivoli without the crowds.

COPENHAGEN

Copenhagen (København in Danish) has no glittering skylines, few killer views, and only a handful of meager skyscrapers. Traffic is manageable, events are organized, and the pace is utterly human. Even at the height of the busy summer there is always a quiet café or a lakeside bench available.

In the streets, bicycles spin alongside smooth auto traffic. In the early morning in the pedestrian streets of the city's core, Strøget, the air is redolent of freshly baked bread and soap-scrubbed storefronts. If there's such a thing as a cozy city, this is it.

Extremely livable and relatively calm, Copenhagen is not a microcosm of Denmark, but rather a cosmopolitan city with an identity of its own. Denmark's political, cultural, and financial capital, it is inhabited by 1.5 million Danes, a fifth of the population, as well as a growing immigrant community. Filled with museums, restaurants, cafés, and lively nightlife, it has its greatest resource in its spirited inhabitants. Imaginative and unconventional, the affable Copenhageners exude an egalitarian philosophy that embraces nearly all lifestyles and leanings.

The town was a fishing colony until 1157, when Valdemar the Great gave it to Bishop Absalon, who built a castle on what is now Christianborg. It grew as a center on the Baltic trade route and became known as *købmændenes havn* (merchants' harbor) and eventually København. In the 15th century it became the royal residence and the capital of Norway and Sweden. A hundred years later, Christian IV, a Renaissance king obsessed with fine architecture, began a building boom that crowned the city with towers and castles, many of which still exist. They are almost all that remain of the city's 800-year history; much of Copenhagen was destroyed during two major fires in the 18th century and Lord Nelson's bombings during the Napoleonic Wars.

Despite a tumultuous history, Copenhagen survives as the liveliest Scandinavian capital. With its backdrop of copper towers and crooked rooftops, the venerable city is humored by playful street musicians and performers, soothed by one of the highest standards of living in the world, and spangled by the thousand lights and gardens of Tivoli.

Exploring Copenhagen

The sights of Copenhagen rarely jump out at you; its elegant spires and cobbled streets are best sought out on foot, and lingered over. This calm belies the fact that Copenhagen is Scandinavia's largest and most densely populated capital, and one of its oldest towns. It is not divided like most other cities into single-purpose districts; instead it is a multilayered capital where people work, play, shop, and live throughout its central core.

With its tangle of one-way streets, and excellent bus- and train system, Copenhagen is most efficiently and pleasantly negotiated by foot. A good way to explore it is to use Rådhus Pladsen as a starting point for three walks: first winding north from the Town Hall Square to the Citadel; next focusing on the area around the Royal Palace; finally ending around Strøget and down Vesterbrogade.

The city is surrounded by water, be it sea or canal; it is built on two islands—Sjælland and Amager—and connected by bridges and drawbridges. The maritime atmosphere is indelible, especially around Nyhavn and Christianshavn. Leave enough time in your tours to linger and enjoy the views of life from the sidewalk cafés in the shady squares.

Town Hall Square to the Citadel

In 1728, and again in 1795, fires broke out in central Copenhagen with devastating effect. Disaster struck again in 1801, when Lord Nelson bombed the city—*after* the Danes had surrendered and *after* he was ordered to stop, he pretended not to see by turning his famed blind eye to the command. These events still shape modern Copenhagen, which was rebuilt with wide, curved-corner streets—which made it easier for fire trucks to turn—and large, four-sided apartment buildings centered with courtyards. Arguably the liveliest portion of the city, it's packed with shops, restaurants, businesses, and apartment buildings, as well as the crowning architectural achievements of Christian IV—all of it aswarm with Danes and visitors.

Copenhagen's central spine consists of the five consecutive pedestrian strands known as Strøget and the surrounding tangle of roads and court-yards. Less than a mile square, it is best explored on foot. Across the capital's main harbor is the smaller, 17th-century Christianshavn. In the early 1600s, this area was mostly a series of shallows between land, which were eventually dammed. King Christian IV offered these patches of partially flooded land for free, with additional tax benefits, to any-one who could fill them in and construct sturdy buildings for trade, commerce, and housing for the shipbuilding workers, as well as for defense against sea attacks. Today its colorful boats and postcard mar-itime atmosphere make it one of the toniest parts of town.

A GOOD WALK

The city's heart is the **Rådhus Pladsen** (City Hall Square), which in-cludes the Baroque-style **Rådhus** ① (City Hall) and its clock-tower. On the right side of the square is the **Lurblæserne** ② (Lur Blower Column), a well-known landmark and meeting point for most area tours. If you continue to the square's northeastern corner and turn right, you will be in Frederiksberggade, the first of the five pedestrian streets that make up **Strøget** ③, Copenhagen's shopping district. Walk past the cafés and trendy boutiques to the double square of Gammeltorv (Old Square) and Nytorv (New Square), which are lined with street vendors selling inexpensive jewelry.

Down Rådhusstræde toward Frederiksholms Kanal, the **National Museet** ④ (National Museum) contains an amazing collection of Viking artifacts. Cross Frederiksholms Kanal to Christiansborg Slotsplads, a small atoll divided by the canal and dominated by the burly **Chris-tiansborg Slot** ⑤ (Christiansborg Castle), whose complex includes the Folketinget (Parliament House), the Kongelige Repræsantationlokaler (Royal Reception Chambers), and the Højesteret (Supreme Court). Also on the island, north of the castle, is **Thorvaldsens Museum** ⑥, devoted to the works of one of Denmark's most important sculptors, Bertel Thor-valdsen. On the south end of Slotsholmen is the three-story Ro-manesque-style **Kongelige Bibliotek** ⑦ (Royal Library), edged by carefully tended gardens and tree-lined avenues. Back on the south face of Christiansborg are the **Teatermuseum** ⑧ (Theater Museum) and the **Kongelige Stald** (Royal Stables), two side attractions that convey a sense of what royal life used to be.

On the street that bears its name is the **Tøjhusmuseet** ⑨ (Royal Dan-ish Arsenal Museum), and a few steps away is the architecturally mar-velous **Børsen** ⑩ (Stock Exchange). Directly south of Børsen, near Højbro Plads, a delightful row of houses borders the northern edge of Slotsholmen. Across from Børsen is **Holmens Kirke** (Islet's Church), famed for the naval heroes buried within. To the east of Holmens Kirke, across the drawbridge (Knippelsbro) that connects Slotsholmen with **Chris-tianshavn,** is one of the oldest parts of Copenhagen. Farther north, the former shipyard of Holmen is a cultural zone of expansive venues and several departments of the Copenhagen University.

From nearly anywhere in the area, you can see the green-and-gold spire of **Vor Frelsers Kirke** ⑪ (Our Savior's Church). Across the Knippels Torve-gade Bridge, straight down the street about a mile, is Amagertorv, one of Strøget's five streets. On the right is **W.Ø. Larsens Tobacco Museum,**

28

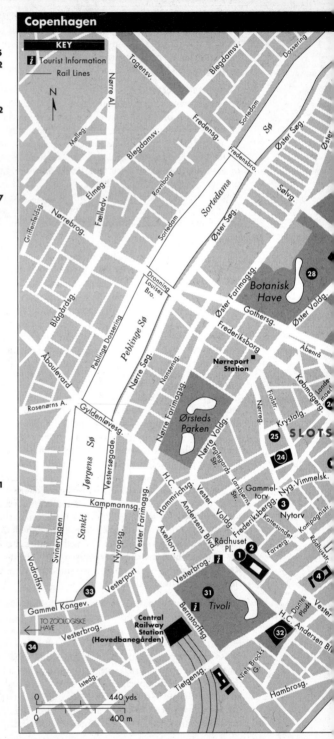

Copenhagen

KEY

🛈 Tourist Information
— Rail Lines

while farther down the street on the left is the 18th-century **Helligånds Kirken** ⑫, (Church of the Holy Ghost), one of the city's oldest places of worship. On Østergade, the easternmost of the streets that make up Strøget, the massive spire of **Nikolaj Kirke** ⑬ (Nicholas Church) looks many sizes too large for the tiny cobbled streets below.

TIMING

To see only the museums and sights, block out about 45 minutes for each, depending on your interests. Typically, Christiansborg and the ruins, and the National Museum, take at least an hour and a half each—more for Viking fans.

The hundreds of shops along Strøget are enticing, so plan extra shopping and café time—at least as much as your wallet can afford. Depending on your interests, most sights and museums can see be seen in about an hour, though you'll need more time to see an IMAX film at the Tycho Brahe Planetarium.

It's hard to imagine why so many Copenhagen sights keep such peculiar, and often short, hours. This is exacerbated by telephone hours that are often even shorter. Especially during the fall and winter seasons, it's a good idea to call and confirm opening times. This is especially true for churches, which may be closed to the public during mass, weddings, and other private affairs.

SIGHTS TO SEE

⑩ **Børsen.** Allegedly the oldest stock exchange still in use, this masterpiece of fantasy and architecture is topped by a spire of three intertwined dragons' tails—said to have been twisted by its builder, King Christian IV. Built between 1619 and 1640, it was originally used as a sort of medieval mall, filled with shopping stalls that a French diplomat described as having "everything decorative and practical for all male and female purposes." With its steep roofs, tiny windows, and gables, the building is one of Copenhagen's treasures. ☉ *Not open to the public.*

★ ⑤ **Christiansborg Slot.** Surrounded by canals on three sides, the massive granite Christiansborg Castle is where the queen officially receives guests; from 1441 until the fire of 1795, it was used as the royal residence. Though the first two castles on the site were burned, Christiansborg remains an impressive Baroque compound, even by European standards: It includes the **Folketinget** (Parliament House), the **Kongelige Repræsantationlokaler** (Royal Reception Chambers, where you'll be asked to don slippers to protect the floors); and the **Højesteret** (Supreme Court), located on the site of the city's first fortress and built by Bishop Absalon in 1167.

While the castle was being built at the turn of the century, the National Museum excavated the **ruins** lying beneath it. Now this dark, subterranean maze contains fascinating models and architectural relics.

Before you leave the area, wander around **Højbro Plads** and the delightful row of houses that border the northern edge of Slotsholmen. The quays in front of them were long used for Copenhagen's fish market, though today a lone early morning fisherwoman hawking fresh fish, marinated herring, and slithering eel is the only person who carries on the tradition. ⊠ *Christiansborg,* ☎ *33/92–64–92. Folketinget,* ☎ *33/37–55–00.* ⊠ *Ruins DKr15; reception chambers DKr28; Folketinget free.* ☉ *Ruins: daily 9:30–3:30; closed Mon. and Sat., Oct.–May.* ☉ *Reception chambers (guided tours only): May and Sept., Tues.–Sun., with English tour at 11 and 3; June–Aug., Tues.–Sun. 11, 1, and 3; Oct.–Dec. and*

Feb.–Apr., Tues., Thurs., and Sun. 11 and 3. Closed Jan. ⊙ *Folketinget: Mon.–Sat., tours hourly (except noon) 10–4.*

Christianshavn. This tangle of cobbled avenues, antique street lamps, and Left Bank atmosphere constitutes one of the oldest neighborhoods in the city—even the old system of earthworks, the best preserved of Copenhagen's original fortification walls—still exists. Now gentrified, the area harbors restaurants, cafés, and boutiques, and its ramparts are now edged with green areas and walking paths, making it the perfect neighborhood for an afternoon or evening amble.

OFF THE
BEATEN PATH

CHRISTIANIA – If you are nostalgic for the '60s counterculture, head to this anarchists' commune at the corner of Prinsessegade and Badsmandsstræde, on Christianshavn. Founded in 1971 when students occupied army barracks, it is now a peaceful community of people who choose not to conform to Copenhagen's rules but who run a number of successful businesses, including a bike shop, a bakery, a rock club, and a communal bathhouse. Giant wall cartoons preach drugs and peace, but the inhabitants are less fond of cameras and picture-taking—which they forbid within the compound.

HOLMEN – Previously isolated (indeed closed) from central Copenhagen, and just north of Christianhavn, this former shipyard is where ships and ammunition were produced until a few years ago. It was formally opened as the sight of the 1995 U.N. Summit on Human Development and played an important role as a cultural area during Copenhagen's 1996 reign as the Cultural Capital of Europe. Today, its several cultural venues include the city's biggest performance space— the Torpedo Hall (where torpedoes were actually produced)—and several educational buildings, among them the Danish Art Academy's Architecture School, the National Theater School, the Rhythmic Music Conservatory, and the Danish Film School, all of which continue to present special activities.

⓬ **Helligånds Kirken.** On the Amagertorv section of Strøget, the 18th-century Church of the Holy Ghost was founded as an abbey of the Holy Ghost and remains one of the city's oldest places of worship. Its choir contains a font by the sculptor Thorvaldsen, and more modern art is contained within the large exhibition room—once a hospital—that faces Strøget. ⊠ *Niels Hemmingsengade 5,* ☎ *33/12–95–55.* 🖾 *Free.* ⊙ *Weekdays noon–4.*

Holmens Kirke. The Islet's church is the burial place of two of the country's most revered naval heroes—Niels Juel, who crushed the Swedish fleet at Køge in 1677, and Peder Tordenskjold, who defeated Charles XII of Sweden during the Great Northern War in the early 18th century. ⊠ *Holmens Kanal,* ☎ *33/13–61–78.* 🖾 *Free.* ⊙ *May 15–Sept. 15, weekdays 9–2, Sat. 9–noon; Sept. 16–May 14, Mon.–Sat. 9–noon.*

❼ **Kongelige Bibliotek.** The Royal Library houses more than 2 million volumes—the country's largest collection of books, newspapers, and manuscripts. Inside, you can peruse records of the Viking journeys to America and Greenland, as well as original manuscripts by Hans Christian Andersen and Karen Blixen (Isak Dinesen). Afterward, leave time to ramble around the statue of philosopher Søren Kierkegaard (1813–55), the formal gardens, and the tree-lined avenues that surround the scholarly building. In September 1998, the library will be expanded with a massive granite block-like annex placed between the current building and the waterfront. ⊠ *Christians Brygge 8,* ☎ *33/93– 01–11.* 🖾 *Free.* ⊙ *Weekdays 9–7, Sat. 10–7.*

(C) **Kongelige Stald.** Early in the day, between 9 and noon, time stands still on these Royal Stable grounds, when riders elegantly clad in breeches and jackets exercise the horses. On display are vehicles, including coaches and carriages, as well as harnesses, used by the Danish monarchy from 1778 to the present. ⊠ *Christiansborg Ridebane 18,* ☎ *33/40−26−76.* ☑ *DKr10.* ☉ *Nov.–Apr., weekends 2–4; May–Oct., Fri.–Sun. 2–4.*

➋ **Lurblæserne.** Perhaps the most picturesque structure in the Radhus Pladsen, the Lur Blower Column is topped by two Vikings blowing an ancient trumpet called the *lur.* The 1914 sculptor took a great deal of artistic license—the lur dates from the Bronze Age, 1500 BC, whereas the Vikings lived a mere 1,000 years ago. This is one of the most important landmarks in the city, often used as a starting and meeting point for city tours.

★ (C) ➍ **National Museet.** Peaked by massive overhead windows, the brilliantly renovated National Museet (National Museum) is regarded as one of the best national museums in Europe. Originally built as a royal residence in the 18th century, the structure became a museum in the 1930s and now houses extensive collections that chronicle Danish cultural history from prehistoric to modern times, including one of the largest collections of Stone Age tools in the world, as well as Egyptian, Greek, and Roman antiquities. A children's museum with a Viking ship, castles from the Middle Ages, and other touchable exhibits, closes one hour before the rest of the museum. ⊠ *Frederiksholms Kanal 12,* ☎ *33/13−44−11.* ☑ *DKr30.* ☉ *Tues.–Sun. 10–5.*

⓭ **Nikolaj Kirke.** Though the green spire of the imposing Nicholas Church—named for the patron saint of seafarers—appears as old as the surrounding medieval streets, it is actually relatively young. The current building was finished in 1914; the previous structure, which dated from the 13th century, was destroyed by the 1728 fire. Today the church is an art gallery and exhibition center that often shows more experimental work. ⊠ *Nikolaiplads,* ☎ *33/93−16−26.* ☑ *Changing admission for special exhibitions.* ☉ *Daily noon—5.*

NEED A
BREAK?   **Café Nikolaj** (⊠ Nikolaiplads, ☎ 33/93–16–26), inside Nikolaj Kirke, is a reliable, inexpensive café with good Danish pastries and light meals. It's open noon to 3 for lunch and until 5 for cakes and drinks.

➊ **Rådhuset.** The mock-Renaissance building dominating what many Danes consider Copenhagen's most impressive square is the Rådhus (City Hall), completed in 1905. Architect Martin Nyrop's creation was popular from the start, perhaps because he envisioned that it should give "gaiety to everyday life and spontaneous pleasure to all . . ."; accordingly, a statue of Copenhagen's 12th-century founder, Bishop Absalon, sits atop the main entrance.

Besides serving as an important ceremonial meeting place for Danish VIPs, the intricately decorated Rådhus contains the first World Clock, a multidialed, superaccurate astronomical timepiece, with a 570,000-year calendar, that took inventor Jens Olsen 27 years to complete before it was put into action in 1955. If you're feeling energetic, take a guided tour up the 350-foot bell tower for the panoramic, but not particularly inspiring, view.

The Radhus Pladsen (City Hall Square) is the hub of Copenhagen's commercial district. The modern glass and gray-steel **bus terminal** flanking its northwest side and completed in 1996 has French granite floors, pear-tree-wood shelving, and underground marble bathrooms. The

DKr15-million ($2.8-million) creation proved to be so architecturally contentious—more for its placement than for its design—that there was serious discussion of moving it.

Before you leave the square, look up to see one of the city's most charming sculptures. Diagonally across the Rådhus Pladsen, atop a corner office building, you'll see a **neon thermometer and a gilded barometer**: On sunny days a golden sculpture of a girl on a bicycle appears; on rainy days there's a girl with an umbrella. The bronze sculpture was created by the Danish artist E. Utzon Frank in 1936. ⊠ *Rådhus Pladsen,* ☎ *33/66–25–82.* ☒ *Tour DKr20, tower DKr10.* ⊙ *Mon.–Wed. and Fri. 9:30–3, Thurs. 9:30–4, Sat. 9:30–1. Tours in English weekdays at 3, Sat. at 10. Tower tours Mon.–Sat. at noon.*

★ ❸　**Strøget.** Though it is referred to as one street, the city's pedestrian spine, which is pronounced *Stroy*-et, is actually a series of five streets. Strøget is where Copenhagen shops, and by mid-morning, particularly on Saturdays, it is congested with people, baby-prams and street performers. Past the trendy, sometimes flashy-and-trashy boutiques of **Frederiksberggade** is the double square of **Gammeltorv** (Old Square) and **Nytorv** (New Square), which during summer is often crowded with street vendors selling cheap jewelry.

In 1728 and again in 1795, much of Strøget was heavily damaged by fire. When rebuilding, the city fathers straightened and widened the streets. Today, between the swanky boutiques and newer architecture, you can still see buildings from this reconstruction period, as well as a few that survived the fires.

In addition to shoppers, Strøget attracts strollers by the hundreds. Outside the windows of posh fur and porcelain shops, and bustling cafés and restaurants, the sidewalks have the festive air of a street fair.

❽　**Teatermuseum.** The Theater Museum is inside the Royal Court Theater of 1766, which King Christian VII built as the first court theater in Scandinavia. Bone up on theater and ballet history, and then wander around the boxes, stage, and dressing rooms. ⊠ *Christiansborg Ridebane 18,* ☎ *33/11–51–76.* ☒ *DKr20.* ⊙ *Wed. 2–4, Sun. noon–4.*

❻　**Thorvaldsens Museum.** The 19th-century artist Bertel Thorvaldsen (1770–1844), perhaps Denmark's greatest sculptor, is buried at the center of this museum in a simple, ivy-covered tomb. Greatly influenced by the statues and reliefs of classical antiquity, he is recognized as one of the world's greatest neoclassical artists and completed many commissions all over Europe. The museum, which was once a coachhouse to Christiansborg, now houses Thorvaldsen's interpretations of classical and mythological figures, as well as an extensive collection of paintings and drawings by other artists that Thorvaldsen assembled while living, for most of his life, in Rome. The outside frieze by Jørgen Sonne depicts the sculptor's triumphant return to Copenhagen after years abroad. ⊠ *Porthusgade 2,* ☎ *33/32–15–32.* ☒ *Free; DKr20 for special exhibitions.* ⊙ *Tues.–Sun. 10–5.*

❾　**Tøjhusmuseet.** Along the street that bears its name, the Tøjhusmuseet (Royal Danish Arsenal Museum) is housed in one of the oldest buildings in central Copenhagen. The Renaissance structure, built by King Christian IV, contains impressive displays of uniforms, weapons, and armor in an arched hall 200 yards long. ⊠ *Tøjhusgade 3,* ☎ *33/11–60–37.* ☒ *DKr20.* ⊙ *Tues.–Sun. 10–4.*

⓫　**Vor Frelsers Kirke.** Dominating the area around Christianshavn is the green-and-gold spire of Our Savior's Church, a Gothic structure built in 1696. Local legend has it that the staircase encircling it was built curling the wrong way around, so that when its architect reached the top and realized what he'd done, he jumped. ⊠ *Skt. Annægade,* ☎ *31/57–27–98.* 🎫 *Tower: DKr20.* ⊙ *Mar. 15–May, Mon.–Sat. 9–3:30, Sun. noon–3:30; June–Aug., Mon.–Sat. 9–4:30, Sun. noon–4:30; Sept.–Mar. 14, Mon.–Sat. 10–1:30, Sun. noon–1:30. Closed to tourists during services and special functions; call ahead. Tower closed Nov.–mid-Apr. and during inclement weather.*

W.Ø. Larsens Tobakmuseet. Looking like a storefront window from the outside, the Tobacco Museum in fact has a full-fledged collection of pipes made in every conceivable shape from every conceivable material. Look for the tiny pipe that's no bigger than an embroidery needle. There are also paintings, drawings, and an amazing collection of smoking accoutrements. ⊠ *Amagertorv 9,* ☎ *33/12–20–50.* 🎫 *Church free.* ⊙ *Weekdays 9:30–5.*

Around the Royal Palace

North of Kongens Nytorv, the city becomes a fidgety grid of wider boulevards and parks that point toward upscale Østerbro—an area wreathed by buildings and manors commissioned by wealthy merchants and bluebloods. In the mid-1700s, King Frederik V donated parcels of this land to anyone who committed to build on it the designs of architect Niels Eigtved (who also designed the Royal Theater). The jewel of this crown remains Amalienborg, where four noblemen built Rococo mansions.

A GOOD WALK

At the end of Strøget, **Kongens Nytorv** ⑭ (the King's New Square) is flanked on its south side by the **Kongelige Teater** ⑮ (Danish Royal Theater), and backed by **Charlottenborg,** which contains the Danish Academy of Fine Art. The street leading southeast from Kongens Nytorv is **Nyhavn** ⑯ (New Harbor), a onetime sailors' haunt and now a popular waterfront hub of restaurants, cafés, and boutiques. The end of the harbor is the departure point for the high-speed craft to Malmö; on the other side, Kvævthusbroen (at the end of Skt. Annæ Plads) is the quay for boats to Oslo and Bornholm.

Left of the harbor front is the grand square called Skt. Annæ Plads. Perpendicular to the square is Amaliegade, whose wooden colonnade borders the cobbled square of **Amalienborg** ⑰, the royal residence, flanked on the harbor side by a pleasant garden. Across the square, it's a step to Bredgade, where the Baroque **Marmorkirken** ⑱ (Marble Church) flaunts its Norwegian marble structure. Farther on is the **Kunstindustrimuseet** ⑲ (Museum of Decorative Art), a Rococo building with a fine collection of handicrafts and art. Back on Store Kongensgade, turn right onto Esplanaden and you'll arrive at the enormously informative **Frihedsmuseet** ⑳ (Liberty Museum), located on the aptly named Churchill Park. At the park's entrance stands the English church, St. Albans and, in the center, the **Kastellet** ㉑ (Citadel), a reminder of the city's grim military history. At its perimeter is Langelinie, a waterfront promenade with a view of Denmark's best-known pin-up, **Den Lille Havfrue** ㉒ (the Little Mermaid). Back toward Esplanaden, you'll pass the **Gefion Springvandet** ㉓ (Gefion Fountain) as you head back toward the center of town.

TIMING

Save the Royal Theatre, the Liberty Museum, and the Museum of Decorative Arts, this tour largely consists of parks, gardens, canals and the exteriors of other sights. Pace it according to the weather—if it's nice, linger in the parks, especially along Kastellet and Amalienhaven, and plan on a long lunch at Nyhavn. Set aside a full day for everything. The Kunstindustrimuseet merits about an hour, more if you plan on perusing the design books in the museum's well-stocked library. The Frihedsmuseet may require more time: Its evocative portrait of Danish life during World War II intrigues even the most history-weary teens and may keep you spellbound for hours.

SIGHTS TO SEE

⓱ Amalienborg. The four identical Rococo buildings occupying this square have housed the royals since 1784. The Christian VIII palace across from the Queen's residence houses the **Amalienborg Museum**, which displays the second division of the Royal Collection (the first is at Rosenborg Slot) and chronicles royal lifestyles between 1863 and 1947. Here you can view the study of King Christian IX (1818–1906) and the drawing room of his wife, Queen Louise. Their rooms are packed with family gifts and regal baubles, ranging from tacky knickknacks to Fabergé treasures, including a table clock made of nephrite and rubies, and a small costume collection.

In the center of the square is a magnificent statue of King Frederik V by the French sculptor Jacques François Joseph Saly. One of the finest equestrian statues in the world, it reputedly cost as much as all the buildings combined. Every day at noon, the Royal Guard and band march from Rosenborg Slot through the city for the changing of the guard. On Queen Margrethe's birthday, April 16, at noon, crowds of Danes gather to cheer their monarch, who stands and waves from her balcony. On Amalienborg's harbor side are the trees, gardens, and fountains of **Amelienhaven, Amalia's Gardens.** ⊠ *Amalienborg Museum,* ☎ *33/12–21–86.* 🎟 *DKr35.* ⊙ *Mar.–Oct., daily 11–4; Nov.–Feb., Tues.–Sun. 11–4.*

Charlottenborg. This Dutch Baroque–style castle was built by Frederik III's half brother in 1670 as a residential palace with a large garden, but since 1754 it has housed the faculty and students of the Danish Academy of Fine Art. On the western side of Kongens Nytorv, you'll see the stately white New Georgian facade of the 200-year-old **D'Angleterre,** the grande dame of Copenhagen hotels, which was massively renovated in 1995. ⊠ *Nyhavn 2,* ☎ *33/13–40–22.* 🎟 *DKr20.* ⊙ *Fri.–Wed. 10–5, Thurs. 10–7.*

㉒ Den Lille Havfrue. On the Langelinie promenade, *The Little Mermaid* is the somewhat overrated 1913 statue commemorating Hans Christian Andersen's lovelorn creation, and the subject of hundreds of travel posters. Donated to the city by Carl Jacobsen, the son of the founder of Carlsberg Breweries, the innocent waif has also been the subject of some cruel practical jokes, including decapitation and the loss of an arm, but she is currently in one piece. Especially on sunny Sundays, the Langelinie promenade is thronged with Danes and visitors who come to see the statue.

★ ⓴ Frihedsmuseet. Flanked by a homemade tank the Danes used to spread the news of the Nazi surrender after World War II, the museum gives an evocative, sometimes moving picture of the heroic Danish resistance movement, which managed to save 7,000 Jews from the Nazis by hiding them, then smuggling them to Sweden. The museum also displays everyday objects, as well as radios often operated by members of the country's amateur radio operators club. ⊠ *Churchillparken,* ☎ *33/13–77–14.* 🎟 *Free.* ⊙ *Sept. 16–Apr., Tues.–Sat. 11–3, Sun. 11–4; May–Sept. 15, Tues.–Sat. 10–4, Sun. 10–5.*

㉓ Gefion Springvandet. Not far from *The Little Mermaid,* the Gefion Fountain illustrates yet another dramatic myth, that of the goddess Gefion, who was promised as much of Sweden as she could carve in a night.

The story goes that she changed her sons to oxen and carved out the island of Sjælland.

NEED A
BREAK?

The **Langelinie Pavillonen** (⌗ Langelinie, ☎ 33/12–12–14) serves a steady flow of tourists with substantial, rather pricey French-Danish specialties such as smoked salmon and tournedos of beef. Aside from this you'll find nothing but a few ice cream vendors; the nearest cafés are either back on Østerbrogade or toward the center of the city.

㉑ Kastellet. At Churchill Park's entrance stands the English church, St. Albans. From there, walk north on the main path and you'll reach the Citadel, whose smooth, peaceful walking paths, marina, and greenery belie its fierce past as a city fortification. Built in the aftermath of the Swedish siege of the city on February 10, 1659, its double moats were among the improvements that were made to the city's defense. The Citadel served as the city's main fortress into the 18th century, but in a grim reversal during World War II, the Germans used it as their headquarters during their occupation. ⌗ *Free.* ☉ *Daily, 6 AM–sunset.*

⑮ Kongelige Teater. The stoic, pillared and gallery-fronted Danish Royal Theater is the country's preeminent venue for music, ballet, and drama. Its two stages and sumptuous red-velvet interiors host the Danish opera and ballet, as well as the theater. The Danish Royal Ballet remains one of the world's great companies, with a repertoire ranging from classical to modern works.

The current building was opened in 1874, though the annex, known as the Nesting Box, was not inaugurated until 1931. The front of the building is flanked by statues of Danish poet Adam Oehlenschläger and by author Ludvig Holberg, whose works remain the core of Danish theater. Born in Bergen, Norway, in 1684, Holberg came to Denmark as a student, and stayed for the rest of his life. Often compared to Molière, he wrote 32 of his comedies in a "poetic frenzy" between 1722 and 1728, and, legend has it, he complained the entire time of interminable headaches. A frugal man, he published the works himself, made an enormous fortune, and invested in real estate. Perhaps the theater is taking his cue: An annex to the theater designed by Norwegian architect Sverre Fehn is under construction next door, on the east side of the theater. With an estimated budget of DKr620 million—roughly $115 million—it will be constructed of pale concrete, marble, and oak, and will transform Tordenskjoldsgade into a covered shopping promenade. It is scheduled for completion in 2001. ⌗ *Tordenskjoldsgade 3,* ☎ *33/14–10–02.* ☉ *Not open for tours.*

★ ⑭ Kongens Nytorv. The King's New Square is dominated by a mounted statue of Christian V, made in 1688 by the French sculptor Lamoureux, who conspicuously depicted the king as a Roman emperor. Every year, at the end of June, graduating high school students wearing white caps arrive in horse-drawn carriages and dance beneath the furrowed brow of the sober statue.

NEED A
BREAK?

Dozens of restaurants and cafés line Nyhavn. Among the best is **Cap Horn** (⌗ Nyhavn 21, ☎ 33/12–85–04), where moderately priced hearty and light Danish specialties are served in a dining room that's designed to look like a cozy, art-filled ship's galley.

⑲ Kunstindustrimuseet. Originally built in the 18th century as a royal hospital, the fine Rococo-style Museum of Decorative Art today houses a large selection of European and Asian handicrafts, as well as ceramics, silverware, and tapestry—in addition to special changing exhibitions that often focus on contemporary design. The museum's excellent library is stocked with design books and magazines, and there's also a small café. If you need some fresh air, tour the neat, mustard-colored enclave of **Nyboder,** a perfectly laid-out compound of flat, long, former sailors' homes built by Christian IV. Like Nyhavn, this salty sailors' area was seedy and boisterous at the beginning of the 1970s, but today has become one of Copenhagen's more fashionable neighborhoods. ⊠ *Bredgade 68,* ☎ *33/14–94–52.* 🖼 *DKr35 (additional fee for some special exhibits).* ⊙ *Permanent collection, Tues.–Sun. 1–4; changing exhibits, Tues.–Sat. 10–4, Sun. 1–4.*

⑱ Marmorkirken. Officially called the Frederikskirke but referred to as the Marble Church, this ponderous Baroque structure is made of precious Norwegian marble; begun in 1749, it lay unfinished due to budget restraints from 1770 to 1874 before it was finally completed and consecrated in 1894. Perched around the exterior are 16 statues of various religious leaders from Moses to Luther, and below them stand sculptures of outstanding Danish ministers and bishops. Before you leave the area, walk past the exotic gilded onion domes of the **Russiske Ortodoks Kirke** (Russian Orthodox Church). ⊠ *Bredgade,* ☎ *33/15–37–63.* 🖼 *Free.* ⊙ *Daily 11–2.*

★ ⑯ Nyhavn. This harbor-front neighborhood—translated as New Harbor—was actually built 300 years ago to attract traffic and commerce to the center of the city. Today the area swarms with action, especially on sunny days, when locals and visitors gather in its waterfront cafés. Until 1970, the area was a favorite haunt of sailors. Though restaurants, boutiques, and antiques stores now outnumber the tattoo parlors, many old buildings have been well preserved and give the harbor its authentic 18th-century maritime atmosphere; there is even a fleet of old-time sailing ships that you can view from the quay. Hans Christian Andersen lived at various times in the houses at numbers 18, 20, and 67.

Down Vesterbrogade

At the south of the city are the vibrant working-class and immigrant neighborhoods of Vesterbro, where you'll find a good selection of inexpensive ethnic restaurants and shops. There's more in the café-, restaurant-, club-, and shop-filled areas of Nørrebrogade and Skt. Hans Torv, both in Nørrebro.

Both Vesterbro and Nørrebro were built up in the 1850s, largely because the city center itself had become so densely populated with people moving in from the provinces. By the 1880s, many of the buildings that now line these neighborhoods were being hastily thrown up as housing for area laborers. Typically decorated with a row of pedimental windows and a portal entrance, they contain one- to three-room apartments. In the past few years, a massive urban renewal program has renovated many of these flats, but to this day many share hall toilets, have no showers, and are heated only by kerosene ovens.

A GOOD WALK

From Langelinie, take the train from Østerport Station to Nørreport Station and walk down Fiolstræde to **Vor Frue Kirke** ㉔ (Church of Our Lady), which crowns the area with one very tall copper spire and four shorter ones—a set of peaks that mark it as Copenhagen's principal place of worship. North again on Fiolstræde is the main building of **Københavns Universitet** ㉕ (Copenhagen University). Past the university on the corner of Krystalgade is the arklike **Københavns Synagoge** (Copenhagen Synagogue), designed by the noted contemporary architect Gustav Friederich Hetsch.

Fiolstræde ends at the Nørreport train station on Nørrevoldgade. Perpendicular to it is Frederiksborggade, which leads into the neighborhood of Nørrebro to the north; to the south after the Kultorvet (Coal Square), Frederiksborggade turns into the pedestrian street Købmagergade. From anywhere in the area, you can see the stout **Rundetårn** ㉖ (Round Tower): It stands as one of Copenhagen's most beloved landmarks, with an observatory from which you can view the heavens above. Straight down from the Round Tower on Landemærket, Gothersgade gives way to **Rosenborg Slot** ㉗ (Rosenborg Castle), whose picturesque Dutch Renaissance design stands out against the vivid green of the well-tended Kongens Haven (King's Garden). For a more concentrated dose of plants and living things, cross Øster Voldgade from the palace to the 25-acre **Botanisk Have** ㉘ (Botanical Garden).

Leave the garden through the north exit to reach the **Statens Museum for Kunst** ㉙ (National Art Gallery), whose vast collection is especially strong on Matisse. An adjacent building houses the **Hirschsprungske Samling** ㉚ (Hirschsprung Collection), with 19th-century Danish art.

Back at the Nørreport station, you can catch a train back to Copenhagen's main station. When you exit on Vesterbrogade, make a right and you'll see the city's best-known attraction, **Tivoli** ㉛, perhaps the only amusement park in the world located in the center of a capital city. At the southern end of the gardens, on Hans Christian Andersen Boulevard, the neoclassical **Ny Carlsberg Glyptotek** ㉜ (New Carlsberg Museum) contains one of the most impressive collections of antiquities and sculpture in northern Europe. Tucked between St. Jørgens Lake and the main arteries of Vestersøgade and Gammel Kongevej is the **Tycho Brahe Planetarium** ㉝, which has a permanent space exhibition as well as an Omnimax Theater.

Continue down Vesterbrogade into **Vesterbro,** Copenhagen's equivalent of New York's Lower East Side. Parallel to it is Istegade, Copenhagen's half-hearted red-light district, where mom-and-pop kiosks and ethnic restaurants stand side by side with seedy porn shops and shady outfits aiming to satisfy all proclivities. Though it is relatively safe, you may want to avoid the area for a late-night stroll.

Farther down Vesterbrogade is **Københavns Bymuseum** ㉞ (Copenhagen City Museum), whose entrance is flanked by a miniature model of medieval Copenhagen.

TIMING

All of the sights on this tour are relatively close together and can be seen in one day. Tivoli offers charms throughout the day, both in the sunshine and after the sun sets. Visit in the late afternoon, and stay until midnight, when the park is illuminated only by colored electrical bulbs and the flash of fireworks.

SIGHTS TO SEE

㉘ **Botanisk Have.** The lush Botanical Gardens include 25 acres of trees, flowers, ponds, sculptures, and a rather spectacular *Palmehuset* (Palm House), containing tropical and subtropical plants. There's also an observatory and a geological museum. Take time to explore the gardens and watch the pensionists feed the birds. Some have been coming here so long that the birds actually alight on their fingers. ✉ *Gothersgade 128*, ☎ *33/12–74–60.* ☜ *Free.* ☾ *Gardens daily 8:30–4. Palm House daily 10–3.*

OFF THE BEATEN PATH **ARBEJDERMUSEET** – The Workers Museum chronicles the history of the working class from 1870 to the present, with evocative life-size "day-in-the-life-of" exhibits, including reconstructions of a city street and tram and an original apartment once belonging to a brewery worker, his wife, and eight children. Changing exhibits focusing on Danish as well as international issues are often excellent. The museum also has a 19th-century-style restaurant serving old-fashioned Danish specialties, and a '50s-style coffee shop. ⊠ *Rømersgade 22,* ☎ *33/13–01-52.* ⌨ *DKr25.* ۞ *Tues.–Fri. 10–3, weekends 11–4.*

......

㉚ Hirschsprungske Samling. The Hirschsprung Collection of 19th-century Danish art showcases works from the country's golden age—especially the late-19th-century paintings of the Skagen School, whose luminous works capture the play of light and water so characteristic of the Danish countryside. ⊠ *Stockholmsgade 20,* ☎ *31/42–03–36.* ⌨ *DKr20.* ۞ *Mon. and Thurs.–Sun. 11–4, Wed. 11–9.*

㉞ Københavns Bymuseum. In the heart of Vesterbro, Copenhagen's surprisingly interesting City Museum is housed in a 17th-century building flanked by a meticulously maintained model of medieval Copenhagen. Inside, an evocative collection chronicles the city's history. There is also a memorial room for philosopher Søren Kierkegaard (whose last name means cemetery), the father of existentialism. ⊠ *Vesterbrogade 59,* ☎ *31/21–07–72.* ⌨ *Free.* ۞ *May–Sept., Tues.–Sun. 10–4; Oct.–Apr., Tues.–Sun. 1–4.*

㉕ Københavns Universitet. The country's leading school for higher learning, Copenhagen University was constructed in the 19th century on the site of the medieval bishops' palace. The nearby **Sømods Bolcher** (⊠ Nørregade 36, ☎ 33/12–60–46) is a must for children and candy lovers: Its old-fashioned hard candy is pulled and cut by hand. ⊠ *Nørregade 10,* ☎ *35/32–26–26.*

★ **㉜ Ny Carlsberg Glyptotek.** Among Copenhagen's most important museums—thanks to its exquisite collection of antiquities as well as its Gauguins and Rodins, the neoclassical New Carlsberg Museum was donated to the city in 1888 by Carl Jacobsen—son of the founder of the Carlsberg Breweries—and has been maintained by the Carlsberg Foundation ever since. Surrounding its lush indoor garden, a series of nooks and chambers houses the vast collection of works by Gauguin, Degas, and other Impressionists, as well as an extensive assemblage of Egyptian, Greek, Roman, and French sculpture—along with the best collection of Etruscan art outside Italy and Europe's finest collection of Roman portraits. The museum's new wing was especially constructed to house its excellent Impressionist collection. ⊠ *Dantes Plads 7,* ☎ *33/41–81–41.* ⌨ *DKr15 (free Wed. and Sun.).* ۞ *Sept.–Apr., Tues.–Sat. noon–3, Sun. 10–4; May–Aug., Tues.–Sun. 10–4.*

★ **㉗ Rosenborg Slot.** The Dutch Renaissance Rosenborg Castle contains ballrooms, halls, and reception chambers, but for all of its grandeur, there's an intimacy that makes you think the king might return any minute. Part of this has to do with the thousands of objects displayed, including beer glasses, gilded clocks, golden swords, family portraits, a pearl-studded saddle, and gem-encrusted tables—not to mention an adjacent treasury containing the royal jewels. The castle's setting is equally welcoming: It's smack in the middle of the **King's Garden,** amid lawns, park benches, and shady walking paths.

King Christian IV built the Rosenborg Castle as a summer residence but loved it so much that he ended up living, and dying, there. It remained the royal residence until the early 19th century, when it became a museum. In 1849, when the absolute monarchy was abolished, the royal castles became state property, except for Rosenborg, which is still passed down from monarch to monarch. Once a year, during the fall holiday, the castle stays open until midnight, and visitors are invited to explore its darkened interior with bicycle lights. ⊠ *Øster Voldgade 4A,* ☎ *33/15–32–86.* 🎟 *DKr40.* ☉ *Castle late-Oct.–Apr., Tues., Fri., and Sun. 11–2; treasury Tues.–Sun. 11–3; both May, Sept.–Oct. daily 11–3; June–Aug., daily 10–4.*

★ ㉖ **Rundetårn.** The stout Round Tower is one of the most unusual, and certainly most charming, buildings in the city. Instead of climbing stairs, visitors scale a smooth, 600-foot spiral ramp upon which, legend has it, Peter the Great of Russia rode a horse alongside his wife, Catherine, who took a carriage. The building was constructed as an observatory in 1642 by Christian IV and is still maintained as the oldest such structure in Europe. It includes an art gallery with changing exhibits and, at its top, a panoramic view of the twisted streets and crooked roofs of Copenhagen. An observatory and telescope are open to the public October through mid-March, Tuesday and Wednesday nights from 7 to 10; an astronomer is on hand to answer questions. Occasional concerts are also held within its massive stone walls. ⊠ *Købmagergade 52A,* ☎ *33/93–66–60.* 🎟 *DKr15.* ☉ *Sept.–May, Mon.–Sat. 10–5, Sun. noon–4; June–Aug., Mon.–Sat. 10–8, Sun. noon–8. Observatory and telescope, mid-Oct.–mid-Mar., Tues.–Wed. 7–10.*

㉙ **Statens Museum for Kunst.** The National Art Gallery is flanked by a sculpture garden filled with classical, modern, and whimsical works. The collections range from golden age and modern Danish art to works by Rubens, Dürer, and the Impressionists, as well as other European masters. Particularly fine are the museum's 20 Matisses. Changing exhibits often focus on very contemporary art. ⊠ *Sølvgade 48–50,* ☎ *33/91–21–26.* 🎟 *DKr20–DKr40 (depending on the exhibit).* ☉ *Tues. and Thurs.–Sun. 10–4:30, Wed. 10–9.*

★ ✋ ㉛ **Tivoli.** Copenhagen's best-known attraction, conveniently located next to its main train station, attracts an astounding number of visitors: In its comparatively short season, from May to September, more than 4 million people come through its gates. Tivoli is more sophisticated than a mere funfair: Among its attractions are a pantomime theater, an open-air stage, elegant restaurants (24 in all), and frequent classical, jazz, and rock concerts. There are also fantastic flower displays both in the lush gardens and floating on the swan-filled ponds. On Wednesday and Saturday nights elaborate fireworks displays are presented, and every day the Tivoli Guard, a youth version of the Queen's Royal Guard, performs maneuvers. Try to see Tivoli at least once by night, when 100,000 colored lanterns illuminate the Chinese pagoda and the main fountain. The park was established in the 1840s, when Danish architect George Carstensen persuaded a worried King Christian VIII to let him build an amusement park on the edge of the city's fortifications, rationalizing that "when people amuse themselves, they forget politics." ⊠ *Vesterbrogade 3,* ☎ *33/15–10–01.* 🎟 *Mon.–Sat. 11–1, DKr30; 1–9:30, DKr44; 9:30–midnight, DKr20; Sun. 11–9:30, DKr30; 9:30–midnight, DKr20.* ☉ *Late-Apr.–mid-Sept., daily 10 AM–midnight.*

··

OFF THE
BEATEN PATH

ARKEN – The Ark is the metropolitan area's newest modern art museum, having opened in March 1996. A mirage-like construction designed in the metaphor of a ship by young architect Søren Robert Lund, it has received as much attention for its arresting metal and white concrete architecture as it has for its contents. Set against the flat coast 20 kilometers (12½ miles) south of Copenhagen, it contains a massive sculpture room, exhibits of both modern Danish and international art, and space for more experimental installations. There are also plans to hold dance, theater, film, as well as multimedia shows. To get here you must take the train to the Ishøj station, and then connect to a shuttle bus. ⊠ *Skovvej 42*, ☎ *43/42–02–22*. 🖭 *DKr45*. ◷ *Tues.–Sun., 10–5*.

🟢 **Tycho Brahe Planetarium.** This modern, cylindrical planetarium, which appears to be sliced at an angle, has astronomy exhibits and an **Omnimax Theater** that takes visitors on a visual journey up through space and down under the seas. Changing films range in topic from the Rolling Stones to the Kuwait fires of the gulf war. The Omnimax Theater is not recommended for children under seven, since they may be frightened by the overwhelming visual effects. ⊠ *Gammel Kongevej 10*, ☎ *33/12–12–24*. 🖭 *Planetarium DKr65. Gardens DKr55*. ◷ *Show times vary. Gardens weekdays 9–5, weekends 9–6*.

Vesterbro. This neighborhood at the southern end of Vesterbrogade is Copenhagen's equivalent of New York's Lower East Side. Populated by many of the city's immigrants, students, and union workers, it's a great place to find ethnic groceries, discount shops, and inexpensive international restaurants.

🟢 **Vor Frue Kirke.** Serving as Copenhagen's cathedral since 1924, the Church of Our Lady occupies a site that has drawn worshipers since the 13th century, when Bishop Absalon built a chapel here. Today's church is actually a reconstruction: The original church was destroyed during the Napoleonic Wars. Five towers top the neoclassical structure, making the church a distinctive landmark. Inside you can see Thorvaldsen's marble sculptures of Christ and the 12 Apostles, and his Moses and David in bronze. ⊠ *Nørregade, Frue Plads*, ☎ *33/15–10–78*. 🖭 *Free*. ◷ *Mon.–Sat. 9–5*.

OFF THE
BEATEN PATH
ZOOLOGISKE HAVE – The park-bound Zoological Gardens boasts more than 2,000 animals; a small petting zoo and playground with cows, horses, rabbits, goats, and hens; and an indoor rainforest buzzing with butterflies, sloths, alligators, and other tropical creatures. Many of the animals are fed in the early afternoon, including the sea lions, lions, and elephants; call to ask about feeding times. ⊠ *Roskildevej 32*, ☎ *36/30–25–55*. 🖭 *DKr55*. ◷ *Weekdays 9–5, weekends 9–6*.

Dining

Food is one of the great pleasures of a stay in Copenhagen, a city with more than 2,000 restaurants. Traditional Danish fare spans all price categories: You can order a light lunch of traditional *smørrebrød* (sandwiches), munch alfresco from a street-side *pølser* (sausage) cart, or dine out on Limfjord oysters and local plaice. Even the most upscale restaurants have moderate-price fixed menus, but the cost of wine will increase your total enormously. Happily, the local Tuborg and Carlsberg beers complement the traditional fare better than wine does. Though few Danish restaurants require reservations, it's best to call ahead if you want to avoid a wait.

The Danes are Francophiles when it comes to fine dining, and many restaurants are fond of combining fresh, local ingredients with French preparation. The city's more affordable ethnic restaurants are concentrated in Vesterbro, Nørrebro, and the side streets off Strøget.

$$$$ ✕ **Gyldne Fortun's Fiskekældere.** Among the city's finest seafood restaurants, this "fish cellar" is brightly decorated with seashell-shaded halogen lamps and aquariums. Across the street from Christiansborg (the Parliament), it is popular with politicians as well as businesspeo-

ple. Try the fillets of Scandinavian sole poached in white wine, stuffed with salmon mousseline, glazed with hollandaise, and served with prawns. ⊠ *Ved Stranden 18,* ☎ *33/12–20–11. Reservations essential. AE, DC, MC, V. No lunch weekends.*

$$$$ ✕ **Kong Hans.** Five centuries ago this was a Nordic vineyard, but now
★ it's one of Scandinavia's finest restaurants. Chef Daniel Letz's French-inspired cuisine uses the freshest local and French ingredients; the setting is subterranean and mysterious, with whitewashed walls and vaulted ceilings. Try the foie gras with raspberry-vinegar sauce or the warm oysters with salmon roe. ⊠ *Vingårdstræde 6,* ☎ *33/11–68–68. Jacket required. AE, DC, MC, V. No lunch. Closed July.*

$$$$ ✕ **Krogs.** This elegant canal-front restaurant commands a loyal clientele—both foreign and local. Mirrored ceilings and pale-green walls adorned with paintings of old Copenhagen create an understated ambience. The menu (printed in five languages) includes such specialties as poached Norwegian salmon served with spinach, cranberries, and saffron. ⊠ *Gammel Strand 38,* ☎ *33/15–89–15. Jacket required. Reservations essential. AE, DC, MC, V.*

$$$$ ✕ **Skt. Gertrudes Kloster.** The history of this medieval monastery goes back 700 years, and from the beginning its vaulted stone interiors have welcomed tradesmen and wayfarers. The dining room is bedecked with hundreds of icons, and the only light is provided by 2,000 candles. The French menu is extensive, with such specials as fresh fillet of halibut steamed in oyster sauce and l'Alsace duck breast in sherry vinaigrette. ⊠ *32 Hauser Plads,* ☎ *33/14–66–30. Reservations essential. Jacket and tie. AE, DC, MC, V. No lunch.*

$$$ ✕ **Els.** When it opened in 1853, the intimate Els was the place to be seen before the theater, and the painted Muses on the walls still watch diners rush to make an eight o'clock curtain. Antique wooden columns complement the period furniture, including tables inlaid with Royal Copenhagen tile work. Chef Pierre Gravelund changes his nouvelle Danish-French four-course menu every two weeks, always incorporating game, fish, and market produce. ⊠ *Store Strandestræde 3,* ☎ *33/14–13–41. Jacket required. AE, DC, MC, V.*

$$$ ✕ **Kommandanten.** Fancifully decorated by master florist Tage Andersen,
★ with brushed iron and copper furniture, down pillows, and foliage-flanked lights, this is among the city's most chic dinner spots, attracting well-heeled businesspeople and local celebrities. The adventuresome international fare includes rabbit with bouillon-cooked lentils, herbs, and bacon, and marinated salmon with oysters and parsley. ⊠ *Ny Adelgade 7,* ☎ *33/12–09–90. Jacket required. AE, DC, MC, V. No lunch Sun. Closed Sat.*

$$$ ✕ **L'Alsace.** Set in the cobbled courtyard of Pistolstræde and hung with
★ paintings by Danish surrealist Wilhelm Freddie, this restaurant is peaceful and quiet, attracting such diverse diners as Queen Margrethe, Elton John, and Pope Paul II. The hand-drawn menu lists oysters from Brittany, terrine de foie gras, and choucroûte à la Strasbourgeoise (a hearty mélange of cold cabbage, homemade sausage, and pork). Try the superb fresh-fruit tarts and cakes for dessert, and ask to sit in the patio overlooking the courtyard. ⊠ *Ny Østergade 9,* ☎ *33/14–57–43. AE, DC, MC, V. Closed Sun.*

$$$ ✕ **Pakhuskælderen.** Part of the Nyhavn 71 hotel, this intimate restaurant attracts a mix of business and holiday guests. Chef Thomas Durluv's specialties include orange-poached monkfish jaws (ugly but delicious!) served with French spinach and almond sauce, as well as baked salmon in a puff-pastry net served on a coriander-and-champagne sauce. The Danish lunch special usually includes a herring starter, followed by a light plate, a drink, and dessert. The restaurant's thick white walls and raw timbers lend it a mood of antiquity. ⊠ *Nyhavn 71,* ☎ *33/11–85–85. Reservations essential. AE, DC, MC, V. Closed July.*

$$$ ✕ **Wiinblad.** This restaurant doubles as a gallery inspired by, and in tribute to, the work of contemporary Danish artist Bjørn Wiinblad. Almost everything—tiles, wall partitions, plaques, candlesticks, vases, and even some tables—has been made by the great Dane, and the effect is bright, cheerful, and very elegant. The eatery offers an ample breakfast buffet, lunch, tea, and grilled specialties for dinner. Try the pickled herring served with new potatoes and topped with sour cream, or breast of duck in cranberry cream sauce. ⊠ *Hotel D'Angleterre, Kongens Nytorv 34,* ☎ *33/12–80–95. AE, DC, MC, V.*

$$ ✕ **Copenhagen Corner.** Diners here are treated to a superb view of the Rådhus Pladsen, as well as to a terrific smørrebrød, both of which compensate for the often harried staff. Specialties include fried veal with bouillon gravy and fried potatoes; entrecôte in garlic and bordelaise sauce, served with creamed potatoes; and a herring plate with three types of spiced and marinated herring and boiled potatoes. ⊠ *Rådhus Pladsen,* ☎ *33/91–45–45. AE, DC, MC, V.*

$$ ✕ **El Meson.** Guests at Copenhagen's best Spanish restaurant are seated at smoothly worn wooden tables in a dimly lit dining room hung with earthen crockery. The wait staff is knowledgeable and serves generous portions of beef spiced with spearmint, lamb with honey sauce, or paella valenciano—made with rice, chicken, ham, shrimp, lobster, squid, green beans, and peas—for two. ⊠ *Hausers Plads 12 (behind Kultorvet),* ☎ *33/11–91–31. AE, DC, MC, V. No lunch. Closed Sun.*

$$ ✕ **Havfruen.** A life-size wooden mermaid swings from the ceiling in this small, rustic fish restaurant in Nyhavn. Natives love the cozy, maritime-bistro air and come for the daily changing French and Danish menu, which is heavy on cream sauces, fresh salmon, turbot, and cod. ⊠ *Nyhavn 39,* ☎ *33/11–11–38. DC, MC, V.*

$$ ✕ **Ida Davidsen.** Five generations old, this world-renowned lunch spot is synonymous with smørrebrød. Dimly lit, with worn wooden tables and news clippings of famous visitors, it's usually packed. Creative sandwiches include the H. C. Andersen, with liver pâté, bacon, and tomatoes, and the airplane clipper—steak tartare shaped like a plane and topped with caviar, smoked salmon, and egg yolk. There's also a terrific smoked duck that Ida's husband, Adam, smokes himself. ⊠ *Store Kongensgade 70,* ☎ *33/91–36–55. Reservations essential. DC, MC, V. No dinner. Closed weekends and July.*

$$ ✕ **Peder Oxe.** Situated on a 17th-century square, this lively, countrified bistro has rustic tables and 15th-century Portuguese tiles. All entrées, which include grilled steaks and fish—and the best fancy burgers in town—come with an excellent self-service salad bar. Damask-covered tables are set with heavy cutlery and opened bottles of hearty Pyrénées wine. A clever call-light for the waitress is above each table. ⊠ *Gråbrødretorv 11,* ☎ *33/11–00–77. D, MC, V.*

$$ ✕ **Restaurant Le St. Jacques.** This tiny restaurant barely accommodates
★ a dozen tables, but as soon as the sun shines, diners spill out of its icon-filled dining room, to sit at tables facing busy Østerbrogade. The chef and owners come from some of the finest restaurants in town, but claim they started this place in order to slow down the pace and enjoy the company of their customers. The fare changes according to what is available at the market, but expect fabulous concoctions—smoked salmon with crushed eggplant, Canadian scallops with leeks and salmon roe in a beurre blanc sauce, sole with basil sauce and reduced balsamico glaze, and a savory poussin with sweetbreads scooped into phyllo pastry atop a bed of polenta and lentils. Close tables, and chitchat with the owners give this a true café atmosphere. ⊠ *Skt. Jacobs Plads 1,* ☎ *31/42–77–07. Reservations essential. DC, MC, V.*

44

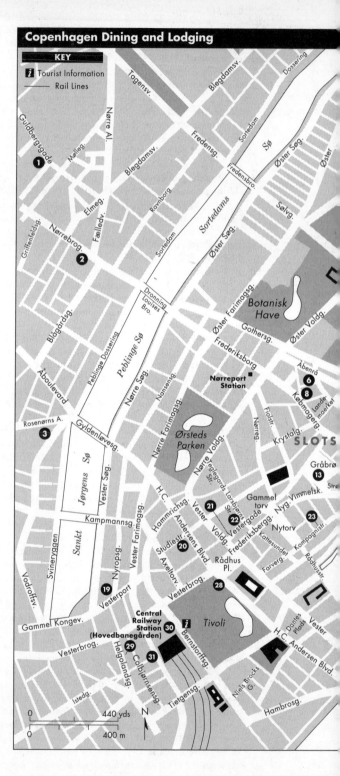

Copenhagen Dining and Lodging

KEY

i Tourist Information
— Rail Lines

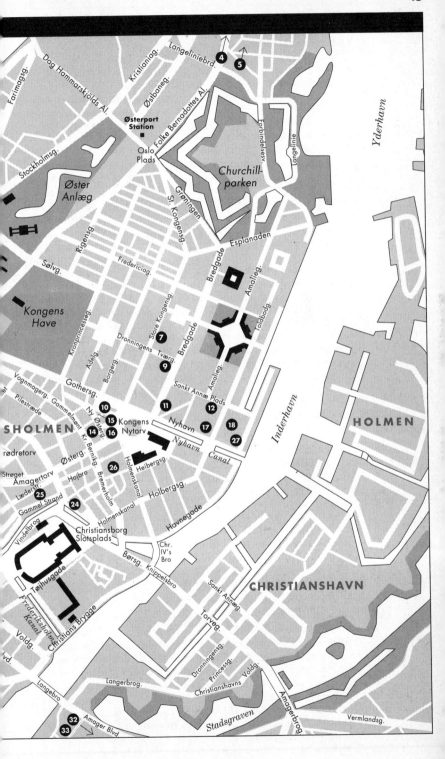

Farimagsg.

Dag Hammarskjölds Al.

Kristianiag.

Langeliniebr. **4** **5**

Østbaneg.

Folke Bernadottes Al.

Stockholmsg.

**Østerport
Station**

Oslo
Plads

Forbindelsesv.

Langelinie

**Øster
Anlæg**

Grønningen

St. Kongensg.

Rigensg.

*Churchill-
parken*

Yderhavn

Sølvg.

Fredericiag.

Esplanaden

Bredgade

Amalieg.

**Kongens
Have**

Store Kongensg.

Kronprincesseg.

Dronningens Tværg.

Adelg.

Borgerg.

7

9

Bredgade

Amalieg.

Toldbodg.

Gothersg.

Sankt Annæ Plads

Vognmagerg. Gammelmønt

Ny Østerg.

Pilestræde

10

15 Kongens

11

14 **16** Nytorv

12

Nyhavn

17

18

Inderhavn

HOLMEN

SHOLMEN

Kr. Bernikg.

Nyhavn

Canal

27

rødretorv

Østerg.

Amagertorv

Højbro

Bremerholm

Heibergsg.

Strøget

Læderstr.

25

Gammel Strand

24

Holmenskanal

26

Holbergsg.

Havnegade

Vindelbro

Holmens kanal

*Christiansborg
Slotsplads*

Chr.
IV's
Bro

CHRISTIANSHAVN

Tøjhusgade

Børsg. Knippelsbro

Sankt Annæg.

Frederiksholms Kanal

Christians Brygge

Vold.

Langebro

Langerbrog.

Torveg.

Dronningensg.

Princessg.

Christianshavns Voldg.

Amagerbrog.

vd.

32

33 Amager Blvd

Stadsgraven

Vermlandsg.

$$ ✕ **Victor.** Excellent people-watching and good bistro fare are the calling cards at this French-style corner café. It's best during weekend lunches, when young and old gather for such specialties as rib roast, homemade pâté, and smoked salmon and cheese platters. Come here for one of the best brunches in town. The menu becomes pricier after 6 PM. ✉ *Ny Østergade 8,* ☎ *33/13–36–13. AE, DC, MC, V.*

$ ✕ **Flyvefisken.** Silvery stenciled fish swim along blue-and-yellow walls in this funky Thai eatery, one of the city's more experimental restaurants. The fare is on the spicy side, and includes chicken with cashew nuts, and herring shark in basil sauce. ✉ *Lars Bjørnstræde 18,* ☎ *33/14–95–15. DC, MC, V. Closed Sun.*

$ ✕ **Kasmir.** This quiet, carpet-shrouded Indian restaurant is a favorite with locals, who come for the unusual vegetarian and fish menu. Specialties include tandoori-fried salmon, a hearty lentil soup, and the basic side dishes—such as *bhajis* (fried vegetables in tomato sauce), *raita* (yogurt and cucumbers), and *nan* (thick round bread). ✉ *Nørrebrogade 35,* ☎ *35/37–54–71. AE, MC, V.*

$ ✕ **Quattro Fontane.** On a corner west of the lakes, one of Copenhagen's best Italian restaurants is a busy, noisy, two-story affair, packed tight with marble-topped tables and a steady flow of young Danes. Served by chatty Italian waiters, the homemade food includes cheese or beef ravioli or cannelloni, linguine with clam sauce, and thick pizza. ✉ *Guldbergsgade 3,* ☎ *31/39–39–31. No credit cards.*

$ ✕ **Riz Raz.** On a corner off Strøget, this Middle Eastern restaurant hops
★ with young locals, families, couples, and anyone who appreciates good value and spicy fare. The inexpensive all-you-can-eat buffet is heaped with lentils, tomatoes, potatoes, olives, hummus, warm pita bread, *kufte* (Middle Eastern meatballs), yogurt and cucumbers, pickled vegetables, bean salads, and occasionally pizza. ✉ *Kompagnistræde 20,* ☎ *33/15–05–75. Reservations essential. DC, MC, V.*

Lodging

Copenhagen is well served by a wide range of hotels, but overall, they are among Europe's most expensive. The hotels around the seedy red-light district of Istedgade (which looks more dangerous than it is) are the least expensive. During summer, reservations are recommended, but should you arrive without one, try the hotel booking desk in the tourist office. They can give you a same-day, last-minute price (if available) for about DKr200–DKr250 for a single hotel room. This service will also locate rooms in private homes, with rates starting at about DKr160 for a single. Young travelers should head for **Huset** (✉ Rådhusstræde 13, ☎ 33/15–65–18); after hours, check the bulletin board outside for suggestions on accommodations. Breakfast is included in the room rate at the following hotels unless otherwise indicated.

$$$$ ▥ **D'Angleterre.** The grande dame of Copenhagen has a new group of
★ owners and a swimming pool and night club. Still the city's finest hotel, D'Angleterre welcomes royalty and rock stars in palatial surroundings: An imposing New Georgian facade leads into an English-style sitting room. Standard guest rooms are furnished in pastels, with overstuffed chairs and modern and antique furniture. The spit-and-polish staff accommodates every wish. Breakfast is not included in the rates. ✉ *Kongens Nytorv 34, DK–1050 KBH K,* ☎ *33/12–00–95,* ℻ *33/12–11–18. 130 rooms, 28 suites. 2 restaurants, bar, room service, pool, concierge, meeting rooms, nightclub, parking (fee). AE, DC, MC, V.*

$$$$ ▥ **Nyhavn 71.** In a 200-year-old warehouse, this quiet and slightly fraying hotel is a good choice for privacy-seekers. It overlooks the old ships of Nyhavn, and its maritime interiors have been preserved with their original thick plaster walls and exposed brick. The rooms are tiny but

cozy, with warm woolen spreads, dark woods, soft leather furniture, and crisscrossing timbers. Breakfast is not included in the rates. ⊠ *Nyhavn 71, DK–1051 KBH K,* ☎ *33/11–85–85,* 𝔽𝔸𝕏 *33/93–15–85. 82 rooms, 6 suites. Restaurant, bar, room service, concierge, meeting rooms, free parking. AE, DC, MC, V.*

$$$$ ⊞ **SAS Scandinavia.** Near the airport, this is one of northern Europe's largest hotels, and Copenhagen's token skyscraper. An immense lobby, with cool, recessed lighting and streamlined furniture, gives access to the city's first (and only) casino. Guest rooms are large and somewhat institutional but offer every modern convenience, making this a good choice if you prefer convenience to character. Breakfast is not included in the rates. ⊠ *Amager Blvd. 70, DK–2300 KBH S,* ☎ *33/11–24–23,* 𝔽𝔸𝕏 *31/57–01–93. 542 rooms, 52 suites. 4 restaurants, bar, room service, pool, health club, casino, concierge, meeting rooms, free parking. AE, DC, MC, V.*

$$$ ⊞ **Kong Frederik.** North of Rådhus Pladsen and a two-minute walk from Strøget, this intimate hotel has the same British style as its sister hotel, the D'Angleterre. The difference is the sun-drenched Queen's Restaurant, where a hearty morning buffet is served (not included in rates) in addition to lunch and dinner. The rooms are elegant, with Asian vases, mauve carpets, and blue spreads. Ask for a top room, with a view of the city's towers. ⊠ *Vester Voldgade 25, DK–1552 KBH V,* ☎ *33/12–59–02,* 𝔽𝔸𝕏 *33/93–59–01. 110 rooms, 13 suites. Restaurant, bar, room service, meeting rooms, free parking. AE, MC, V.*

$$$ ⊞ **Neptun.** This elegant, centrally situated hotel was bought years ago with the intention of making it the bohemian gathering place of Copenhagen, but proprietress Bente Noyens has also made it practical. The lobby and lounge are light, with slender furnishings and peach schemes, and guest rooms have a tasteful modern decor. Next door there's a regional Danish restaurant. ⊠ *Skt. Annæ Plads 14–20, DK–1250 KBH K,* ☎ *33/13–89–00,* 𝔽𝔸𝕏 *33/14–12–50. (In the U.S., call Best Western, 800/528–1234.) 133 rooms, 13 suites. Restaurant, room service, meeting rooms, free parking. AE, DC, MC, V.*

$$$ ⊞ **The Phoenix.** This luxury hotel has automatic glass doors, crystal chandeliers, and gilt touches everywhere. The staff is multilingual and adept at accommodating both a business and a tourist clientele. The suites and business-class rooms boast faux antiques and 18-carat gold bathroom fixtures, whereas the standard rooms are very small, measuring barely 9 by 15 feet. Although it's convenient to central-city attractions, the hotel gets a certain amount of street noise, so light sleepers should ask for rooms above the second floor. ⊠ *Bredgade 37, DK–1260 KBH K,* ☎ *33/95–95–00,* 𝔽𝔸𝕏 *33/33–98–33. 212 rooms, 7 suites. Restaurant, pub (closed Sun.), meeting room. AE, DC, MC, V.*

$$$ ⊞ **Plaza.** With its convenient location and plush homey atmosphere, this hotel attracts the likes of Tina Turner and Keith Richards. Close to Tivoli and the main station, the building opens with a stately lobby and the adjacent Russian restaurant (with perhaps the best vodka selection in town), Alexander Nevski. The older rooms are scattered with antiques; newer ones are furnished in a more modern style. ⊠ *Bernstorffsgade 4, DK–1577 KBH V,* ☎ *33/14–92–62,* 𝔽𝔸𝕏 *33/93–93–62. 93 rooms, 6 suites. Restaurant, bar, room service, concierge, meeting rooms, parking (fee). AE, DC, MC, V.*

$$$ ⊞ **Sheraton.** Near the Tycho Brahe Planetarium and Lake District, this 18-story hotel offers impeccable service and standard Sheraton-style decor. The lobby is modern and vast, with dim lighting, plants, and leather sofas, and the rooms are generous and bright, done up in mint and peach and furnished with modern, gray wooden furniture. ⊠ *Vester Søgade 6, DK–1601 KBH V,* ☎ *33/14–35–35,* 𝔽𝔸𝕏 *33/32–12–23. 471 rooms, 35 suites. 2 restaurants, piano bar, no-smoking floor,*

room service, massage, sauna, concierge, meeting rooms, free parking. AE, DC, MC, V.

$$$ ⊞ **Skovshoved.** This delightful, art-filled inn is 8 kilometers (5 miles)
★ north of town, near a few old fishing cottages beside the yacht harbor. Licensed since 1660, it has retained its provincial charm. Its larger rooms overlook the sea, whereas smaller ones rim the courtyard; all have both modern and antique furnishings. ✉ *Strandvejen 267, DK–2920 Charlottelund,* ☎ *31/64–00–28,* ℻ *31/64–06–72. 20 rooms. Restaurant, bar, meeting room. AE, DC, MC, V.*

$$ ⊞ **Ascot.** Beautifully renovated, this charming downtown hotel's two outstanding features are a wrought-iron staircase and an excellent breakfast buffet. The lobby is classically decorated with marble and columns, but the guest rooms and apartments are cozy, with modern furniture and bright colors; some have kitchenettes. ✉ *Studiestræde 61, DK–1554 KBH V,* ☎ *33/12–60–00,* ℻ *33/14–60–40. 143 rooms, 30 apartments. Restaurant, bar, exercise room, meeting rooms, free parking. AE, DC, MC, V.*

$$ ⊞ **Copenhagen Admiral.** A five-minute stroll from Nyhavn, overlooking old Copenhagen and Amalienborg, the monolithic Admiral was once a grain warehouse but now affords travelers no-nonsense accommodations. With massive stone walls, broken by rows of tiny windows, it's one of the less expensive top hotels, cutting frills and prices. Its guest rooms are spare, with jutting beams and modern prints. ✉ *Toldbodgade 24–28, DK–1253 KBH K,* ☎ *33/11–82–82,* ℻ *33/32–55–42. 365 rooms, 52 suites. Restaurant, bar, sauna, nightclub, meeting rooms, free parking. AE, DC, MC, V.*

$$ ⊞ **Triton.** Despite its seedy surroundings, this streamlined hotel attracts a cosmopolitan clientele thanks to a central location in Vesterbro. The large rooms, in blond wood and warm tones, all include modern bathrooms and state-of-the-art fixtures. The buffet breakfast is exceptionally generous, the staff friendly. There are also family rooms, with a bedroom and a dining-sitting area with a foldout couch. ✉ *Helgolandsgade 7–11, DK–1653 KBH V,* ☎ *31/31–32–66,* ℻ *31/31–69–70. 123 rooms, 2 suites, 4 family rooms. Bar, meeting room. AE, DC, MC, V.*

$ ⊞ **Amager Hostel.** This simple lodging is 4½ kilometers (3 miles) outside out of town, close to the airport. Before 5 PM on weekdays, take Bus 46 from the main station directly to the hostel. After 5, from Rådhus Pladsen or the main station, take Bus 10 to Mozartplads, and change to Bus 37. Ask the driver to signal your stop. The hostel is spread over nine interconnecting buildings, all laid out on one floor. International Youth Hostel members—including student backpackers as well as families—use the communal kitchen, or buy breakfast and dinner from the restaurant. The hostel is also wheelchair-accessible, which makes it popular with guests with special needs. ✉ *Vejlands All 200–2300 KBH S,* ☎ *32/52–29–08,* ℻ *32/52–27–08. 64 rooms with 2 beds, 80 family rooms with 5 beds, 4 large communal bathrooms. Restaurant, TV room. No credit cards.*

$ ⊞ **Cab–Inn Scandinavia.** This bright hotel is just west of the lakes and Vesterport Station. Its impeccably maintained rooms are distinctly small but are designed with superefficiency to include ample showers, stowaway and bunk beds, and even electric water kettles. The hotel is popular with business travelers in winter and kroner-pinching backpackers and families in summer. Its sister hotel, the Cab-Inn Copenhagen (☎ *31/21–04–00,* ℻ *31/21–74–09*) is just around the corner, at Danasvej 32–34. ✉ *Vodroffsvej 55–57, DK–1900 Frederiksberg C,* ☎ *35/36–11–11,* ℻ *35/36–11–14. 201 rooms. Breakfast room, snack bar, exercise room, meeting rooms. AE, DC, MC, V.*

$ ▣ **Missionhotellet Nebo.** Though it's between the main train station and Istedgade's seediest porn shops, this budget hotel is still prim, comfortable, and well maintained by a friendly staff. Its dormlike guest rooms are furnished with industrial carpeting, polished pine furniture, and gray-stripe duvet covers. There are baths, showers, and toilets at the center of each hallway, and downstairs there's a breakfast restaurant with a tiny courtyard. ⊠ *Istedgade 6, DK–1650 KBH V,* ☎ *31/21–12–17,* ▣ *31/23–47–74. 96 rooms, 40 with bath. AE, DC, MC, V.*

Nightlife and the Arts

Nightlife

Most nightlife is concentrated in the area in and around Strøget, though there are student and "left" cafés and bars in Nørrebro and more upscale spots in Østerbro. Many restaurants, cafés, bars, and clubs stay open after midnight, a few until 5 AM. Copenhagen used to be famous for jazz, but unfortunately that has changed in recent years, with many of the best clubs closing down. However, you'll find nightspots catering to almost all musical tastes, from bop to ballroom music—and for the younger crowd, house, rap, and techno—in trendy clubs soundtracked by local DJs. The area around Nikolaj Kirke boasts the highest concentration of trendy discos and dance spots, with cover prices averaging DKr40.

BARS AND LOUNGES

The nightclub **Fellini** (⊠ beneath the SAS Royal Hotel, 1 Hammerichsgade, ☎ 33/93–32–39) has a dance floor and plays all sorts of music while catering especially to international businessmen, who are more than happy to pay for the outrageously expensive booze. **Peder Oxe's** basement (⊠ Gråbrødretorv 11, ☎ 33/11–11–93) is casual and young, though nearly impossible to squeeze into on weekends. The **Library,** in the Plaza Hotel (⊠ 4 Bernstorffsgade, ☎ 33/14–92–62), is an elegant spot for a quiet drink. The more than 270-year-old **Hviids Vinstue** (⊠ Kongens Nytorv 19, ☎ 33/15–10–64) attracts all kinds, young and old, single and coupled, for a glass of wine or cognac. **Vin & Ølgod** (⊠ Skindergade 45, ☎ 33/13–26–25) draws a diverse crowd for singing, beer drinking, and linking of arms for old-fashioned dancing to corny swing bands.

CAFÉS

Café life appeared in Copenhagen in the '70s and quickly became a compulsory part of its urban existence. The cheapest sit-down eateries in town, with a cappuccino and sandwich often costing less than DKr40, cafés are lively and relaxed at night, and the crowd is always an interesting mix. **Café Sommersko** (⊠ Kronprinsensgade 6, ☎ 33/14–81–89) is the granddaddy, with a surprisingly varied and exotic menu (try the delicious french fries with pesto) and an eclectic crowd. **Krasnapolsky** (⊠ Vestergade 10, ☎ 33/32–88–00) packs a young, hip, and excruciatingly well-dressed audience at night, a more mixed group for its quiet afternoons. **Café Dan Turrell** (⊠ Skt. Regnegade 3, ☎ 33/14–10–47), another old café, is as mixed as Sommersko and a favorite with students and intellectuals. **Victors Café** (⊠ Ny Østergade 8, ☎ 33/13–36–13) is all brass and dark wood, lovely for a light lunch. At the very chic **Europa** (⊠ Amagertorv 1, ☎ 33/14–28–09), people-watching and coffee far surpass the fare. At the juncture of Købmagergade and Strøget is the art nouveau–style **Café Norden** (⊠ Østergade 61, ☎ 33/11–77–91), where substantial sandwiches and cappuccinos make up for minimal table space. On Nørrebro's main square, Skt. Hanstorv, the all-in-one rock club–restaurant–café **Rust** (⊠ Guldbergsgade 8, ☎ 35/37-72-83) is packed all the time. Hearty, fresh dishes are served inside, and there's grill food outside on the terrace. In the evenings, **Sebastopol** (⊠ Guldbergsgade 2, ☎ 35/36–30–02) is as trendy as Rust, packed with well-dressed locals; weekend mornings, sample the ample brunch, which often includes eggs, bacon, gorgonzola cheese, and bread.

CASINOS

The **Casino Copenhagen** at the SAS Scandinavia (⊠ Amager Boulevarden 70, ☎ 33/11–51–15) has American and French roulette, blackjack, baccarat, and slot machines. Admission is DKr60 (you must show a photo ID), and the casino is open 2 PM to 4 AM.

DISCOS AND DANCING

Most discos open at 11 PM, have a cover charge (about DKr40), and pile on steep drink prices. Among the most enduring clubs is **Woodstock** (⊠ Vestergade 12, ☎ 33/11–20–71), where a mixed audience grooves to music of the '60s. **Rosie McGees** (⊠ Vesterbrogade 2A, ☎ 33/32–19–23) is a very popular English-style pub with Mexican food and dancing. The fashionable **Park Café** (⊠ Østerbrogade 79, ☎ 35/26–63–42:), which was renovated in 1996 with a new dance floor and a refurbished café, is one of the most popular discos in town. There's an old-world café with live music downstairs, a disco upstairs, and a movie theater next door. **Absalon** (⊠ Frederiksberggade 38, ☎ 33/16–16–99), which happens to be popular with men in uniforms (policemen and soldiers, among them), is a lively club with live music in the basement and a disco above. The **Hard Rock Café** (⊠ Vesterbrogade 3, ☎ 33/12–43–33), just next door to Tivoli, is as commercially formulaic as its other global clones. **Søpavillionen** (⊠ Gyldenløvesgade 24, ☎ 33/15–12–24), between St. Jørgen's and Peblinge lakes, glows white on the outside; within there's pop and disco on Friday and Saturday nights for an older crowd. At the **Røde Pimpernel** (⊠ Hans Christian Andersen Blvd. 7, ☎ 33/12–20–32), an adult audience gathers for dancing to live orchestras, trios, and old-time music. **Sabor Latino** (⊠ Vester Voldgade 85, ☎ 33/11–97–66) is the U.N. of discos, with an international crowd dancing to salsa and other Latin rhythms.

GAY BARS

The **Amigo Bar** (⊠ Schønbergsgade 4, ☎ 31/21–49–15) serves light meals and is popular with men of all ages. Much larger than the Amigo Bar is the mammoth **Club Amigo** (⊠ Studiestræde 31A, ☎ 33/15–33–32), which includes a sauna, solarium, and cinema as well as two discos, After Dark and Metro. The dark, casual **Cosy Bar** (⊠ Studiestræde 24, ☎ 33/12–74–27) is the place to go at the end of the night (it usually stays open until 8 AM). **Sebastian Bar Café** (⊠ Hyskenstræde 10, ☎ 33/32–22–79) is relaxed for a drink or a coffee, and is among the best cafés in town. **Central Hjørnen** (⊠ Kattesundet 18, ☎ 33/11–85–49) is a small bar that's been around for about 70 years. **Masken** (⊠ Studiestræde 33, ☎ 33/91–67–80) is a relaxed bar welcoming both men and women. **Babooshka** (⊠ Turesensgade 6, ☎ 33/15–05–36) is a cozy lesbian café that welcomes men. **Hotel Jørgensen** (⊠ Rømersgade 11, DK–1362, ☎ 33/13–81–86, FAX 33/13–97–43) is a gay-friendly hotel where both men and women tend to congregate. **Hotel Windsor** (⊠ Frederiksborgade 30, ☎ 33/11–08–30, FAX 33/11–63–87) is another gay-friendly hotel.

For more information, call or visit the **Lesbiske og Bøsser Landsforening** (⊠ Lesbian and Gay Association; Teglgaardstræde 13, 1452 KBH K, ☎ 33/13–19–48), which has a library, and more than 45 years of experience. Check the local free paper *Xpansion* for listings of nightlife events and clubs.

JAZZ CLUBS

Hard times have thinned Copenhagen's once-thriving jazz scene. Among the clubs still open, most headline local names, though European and international artists also perform, especially in July, when the Copenhagen Jazz Festival spills over into the clubs. **La Fontaine** (⊠ Kompagnistræde 11, ☎ 33/11–60–98) is Copenhagen's quintessential jazz dive, with sagging curtains, impenetrable smoke, crusty lounge lizards, and the random barmaid nymph. **Copenhagen Jazz House** (⊠ Niels Hemmingsensgade 10, ☎ 33/15–26–00) is infinitely more upscale than La Fontaine, attracting European and some international names to its chic, modern bar-like ambience. **Jazzhus Slukefter** (⊠ Vesterbrogade 3, ☎ 33/11–11–13) is Tivoli's jazz club, and attracts some of the biggest names in the world.

ROCK CLUBS

Copenhagen has a good selection of rock clubs, most of which cost less than DKr40. Almost all are filled with young, fashionable crowds. They tend to open and go out of business with some frequency, but you can get free entertainment newspapers and flyers advertising gigs at almost any café. **Cafe'en Funk** (⊠ Blegdamsvej 2, ☎ 31/35–17–41) plays jazz, rock, and folk. The **Pumpehuset** (⊠ Studiestræde 52, ☎ 33/93–19–60) is the place for soul and rock. For good old-fashioned rock and roll, head to **Lades Kælder** (⊠ Kattesundet 6, ☎ 33/14–00–67), a local hangout just off Strøget.

The Arts

The most complete English calendar of events is included in the tourist magazine **Copenhagen This Week** and includes musical and theatrical events as well as films and exhibitions. Copenhagen's main theater and concert season runs from September through May, and tickets can be obtained either directly from theaters and concert halls or from ticket agencies. **Billetnet** (☎ 35/28–91–83) is the post-office box office, and has tickets for almost everything in town. Billetnet's owner, **ARTE** (⊠ Hvidkildevej 64, ☎ 38/88–49–00), is another good source for tickets. Keep in mind that same-day purchases at the box office ARTE (⊠ near the Nørreport train station, Fiolstræde side, no phone) will give you half off. Tivoli's **Billetcenter** (⊠ Vesterbrogade 3, ☎ 33/15–10–12) issues tickets for its own events.

FILM

Films open in Copenhagen a few months to a year after their U.S. premieres. Nonetheless, the Danes are avid viewers, willing to pay DKr60 per ticket, wait in lines for premieres, and read subtitles. Monday nights are traditionally half-price, but tickets go fast (other weeknights also offer discounts). Call the theater for reservations, and pick up tickets (which include a seat number) an hour before the movie. Most theaters have a café, so it's not hard to sit back and people-watch before the show. Among the city's alternative venues is **Vester Vov Vov** (⊠ Absalonsgade 5, ☎ 31/24–42–00) in Vesterbro, where you can precede second-run films with a light meal, beer, or coffee in the café. The **Grand** (⊠ Mikkel Bryggersgade 8, ☎ 33/15–16–11) shows new foreign and arty films, and is located just next door to its sister café.

OPERA, BALLET, AND THEATER

Tickets at the **Kongelige Teater** (⊠ Royal Theater, ☎ 33/14–10–02) are reasonably priced at DKr70–DKr400; the season is October to May. It is home to the Royal Danish Ballet, one of the premier companies in the world. Not as famous, but also accomplished, are the Royal Danish Opera and the Royal Danish Orchestra, the latter of which performs in all productions. Plays are exclusively in Danish. For information and reservations, call the theater. Beginning at the end of July, you can order tickets for the following season by writing to the theater (⊠ The Royal Theater, Attn. Ticket Office, Box 2185, DK–1017 KBH). For English-language theater, call either the professional London Toast Theater (☎ 33/33–80–25) or the amateur Copenhagen Theater Circle (☎ 31/62–86–20).

Outdoor Activities and Sports

Beaches

North of Copenhagen along the old beach road, **Strandvejen,** there's a string of lovely old seaside towns and beaches. The **Bellevue Beach** (across the street from Klampenborg Station) is packed with locals and also has cafés, kiosks, and surfboard rentals. **Charlottelund Fort** (⊠ Bus 6 from Rådhusplads) is a bit more private, but you'll have to pay (about DKr10) to swim off the pier. The beaches along the tony town of **Vedbæk,** 18 kilometers (11 miles) north of Copenhagen, are not very crowded.

Bicycling

Copenhagen is a cyclist's city. Bike rentals (DKr100–DKr200 deposit and DKr30–DKr60 per day) are available throughout the city, and most roads have bike lanes. Follow all traffic signs and signals; bicycle lights must be used at night. For more information, contact the **Dansk Cyclist Forbund** (⊠ Danish Cyclist Federation, Rømersgade 7, ☎ 33/32–31–21).

Golf

Some clubs do not accept reservations; call for specific details. Keep in mind that virtually all clubs in Denmark require that you are a member of another club for admittance. Handicap requirements vary widely, so call to check.

One of Denmark's best courses (where international tournaments are played) is the 18-hole **Rungsted Golf Klub** (⊠ Vestre Stationsvej 16, ☎ 42/86–34–44). It requires a 30 handicap for all players on weekdays; on weekends and holidays there's a 24 handicap for men and a 29 handicap for women. The 18-hole **Københavns Golf Klub** (⊠ Dyrehaven 2, ☎ 31/63–04–83) is said to be Scandinavia's oldest. Greens fees range from DKr180 to DKr300, and you must reserve at least five days in advance—further ahead in the summer.

Health and Fitness Clubs

A day pass for weights and aerobics at the **Fitness Club** is DKr65 (⊠ Vesterbrogade at Scala, ☎ 33/32–10–02). **Form og Figur** (Form and Figure) offers one-hour aerobics classes for DKr50 at the SAS Globetrotter Hotel in Amager (⊠ Engvej 171, ☎ 31/55–00–70), and weights, treadmill, and stationary bikes for DKr75 at the SAS Scandinavia Hotel (⊠ Amager Blvd. 70, ☎ 31/54–28–88) and Øbro-Hallen (⊠ Ved Idrætsparken 1, ☎ 35/26–79–39).

Horseback Riding

You can ride at the Dyrehavebakken (Deer Forest Hills) in Lyngby at the **Fortunens Ponyudlejning** (⊠ VedFortunen 33, ☎ 45/87–60–58). A 50-minute session, where both experienced and inexperienced riders go out with a guide, costs about DKr85.

Jogging

The 6-kilometer (4-mile) loop around the three swan-filled lakes just west of the center of the city—St. Jorgens, Peblinge, and Sortedams—is a runner's heaven. There are also paths at the Rosenborg Have; the Frederiksberg Garden (near Frederiksberg Station, at the corner of Frederiksberg Allé and Pile Allé); and the Dyrehaven, north of the city near Klampenborg.

Spectator Sports

Danish soccer fans call themselves *Rolegans* (which loosely translates as well-behaved fans), as opposed to hooligans, and idolize the national team's soccer players as superstars. When the rivalry is most intense (especially against Sweden and Norway), fans don face paint, wear head-to-toe red-and-white, incessantly wave the *Dannebrog* (Danish flag), and have a good time whether or not they win. The biggest stadium in town for national and international games is **Parken** (⊠ P. H. Lings Allé 2, ☎ 35/43–31–31). Tickets (DKr150 for slightly obstructed, DKr250–DKr300 for unobstructed) can be bought at any post office.

Swimming

Swimming is very popular, and pools are crowded but well maintained. Separate bath tickets can also be purchased. Admission to local pools (DKr20–DKr50) includes a locker key, but you'll have to bring your own towel. Most pools are 25 meters long.

The beautiful **Frederiksberg Svømmehal** (⊠ Helgesvej 29, ☎ 38/88–00–71) still maintains its old art deco decor with sculptures and decorative tiles. **Øbro Hallen** (⊠ Ved Idrætsparken 3, ☎ 31/42–30–65) is in the large sports compound north of the center. The pool is lined with sculptures, and there is a 10-meter diving tower; massage is also available. **Vesterbro Svømmehal** (⊠ Angelgade 4, ☎ 31/22–05–00) is a modern concrete facility, but many enjoy swimming next to the large glass windows. The 50-meter **Lyngby Svømmehal** (⊠ Lundoftevej 53, ☎ 45/87–44–56) is one of metropolitan Copenhagen's newest pools, with a separate diving pool.

Tennis

Courts fees for guests are very high, often including court rental (DKr75 per person) and a separate nonmembers' user fee (as high as DKr130). If you are still interested, courts are available at some sports centers, but keep in mind that they are open to guests before 1 PM only. **Københavns Boldklub** (⊠ PeterBangs Vej 147, ☎ 38/71–41–50) is in Frederiksberg, a neighborhood just west of central Copenhagen. **Hellerup Idræts Klub** (⊠ Hartmannsvej 37, ☎ 31/62–14–28) is about 5 kilometers (3 miles) north of town. **Skovshoved Idræts Forening** (⊠ Krørsvej 5A, ☎ 31/64–23–83) is along the old beach road about 10 kilometers (6 miles) north of town.

Shopping

Copenhagen seems to have been designed with shoppers in mind. Small, easy to explore on foot, and conveniently crammed with boutiques and specialty stores, the city's core is a showcase for world-famous Danish design and craftsmanship. The best buys are such luxury items as crystal, porcelain, silver, and furs. Look for sales (*tilbud* or *udsalg* in Danish) and check antiques and secondhand shops for classics at cut-rate prices.

Although prices are inflated by a hefty 25% Value Added Tax (Danes call it MOMS), non-EU citizens can receive about a 20% refund. For more details and a list of all tax-free shops, ask at the tourist board for a copy of the *Tax-Free Shopping Guide*.

Department Stores

Illum (⊠ Østergade 52, ☎ 33/14–40–02), not to be confused with Illums Bolighus (☞ Design, *below*), is a well-stocked department store with a lovely rooftop café and excellent basement grocery. **Magasin** (⊠

Kongens Nytorv 13, ☎ 33/11–44–33), the largest department store
in Scandinavia, occupies nearly an entire block and includes another
top-quality basement marketplace. **Daells** (✉ Fiolstræde, ☎ 33/12–
78–25) is not a high-end department store, but if you find yourself yearn-
ing for basic Danish goods, like wool underwear and frying pans, this
is the place to find them at relatively reasonable prices.

Shopping Districts/Streets/Malls

The pedestrian-only **Strøget** and adjacent Købmagergade are *the* shopping streets, but wander down the smaller streets for lower-priced, off-
beat stores. You'll find the most exclusive shops at the end of Strøget,
around Kongens Nytorv, and on Ny Adelgade, Grønnegade, and Pis-
tolstræde, but remember that taxes and transportation costs push designer prices up in Denmark. **Scala,** the city's glittering café- and
boutique-studded mall, is across the street from Tivoli and has a trendy
selection of clothing stores. Farther south in the city, on **Vesterbrogade,**
you'll find discount stores—especially leather and clothing shops.

Specialty Stores

ANTIQUES

For silver, porcelain, and crystal, the well-stocked shops on **Bredgade**
are upscale and expensive. On Strøget, **Royal Copenhagen Porcelain**
(✉ Amagertorv 6, ☎ 33/13–71–81) carries old and new china, porcelain patterns, and figurines, as well as seconds. **Kaabers Antikvariat**
(✉ Skindergade 34, ☎ 33/15–41–77) is an emporium for old and rare
books, prints, and maps. If you're looking for silver, Christmas plates,
or porcelain, head to **H. Danielsens** (✉ Læderstræde 11, ☎ 33/13–
02–74). **Danborg Gold and Silver** (✉ Holbergsgade 17, ☎ 33/32–93–
94) is one of the best places for estate jewelry and silver flatwear. For
furniture, **Ravnsborggade** has dozens of stores that carry traditional
pine, oak, and mahogany furniture, in addition to such smaller items
as lamps and tableware. (Some of them sell tax-free and can arrange
shipping.)

AUDIO EQUIPMENT

For high-tech design and acoustics, **Bang & Olufsen** (✉ Østergade 3,
☎ 33/15–04–22) is so renowned that its products are in the permanent design collection of New York's Museum of Modern Art. (Check
prices at home first to make sure you are getting a deal.) You'll find
B&O and other international names at **Fredgaard** (✉ Nørre Voldgade
17, ☎ 33/13–82–45), near Nørreport Station.

CLOTHING

Retail clothing tends to be expensive and trendy, so stick to the best
stores—where you can be sure of the quality. **Brødrene Andersen** (✉
Østergade 7–9, ☎ 33/15–15–77) sells Hugo Boss, Hermes, and
Pringle sweaters for men. **Jens Sørensen** (✉ Vester Voldgade 5, ☎ 33/12–
26–02) is where you'll find fine men's and women's clothing and outerwear, and a Burberry collection. **Petitgas Chapeaux** (✉ Købmagergade
5, ☎ 33/13–62–70) is a venerable old shop for old-fashioned men's
hats. The **Company Store** (✉ Frederiksberggade 24, ☎ 33/11–35–55)
is for trendy, youthful styles, typified by the Danish Matinique label.
If you are interested in the newest Danish designs, keep your eyes open
for cooperatives and designer-owned stores. Among the most inventive handmade women's clothing shops is **Met Mari** (✉ Vestergade 11,
☎ 33/15–87–25). Thick, traditional, patterned and solid Scandinavian sweaters are available at the **Sweater Market** (✉ Frederiksberggade 15, ☎ 33/15–27–73), but remember that the higher-quality
hand-made sweaters are more expensive than the machine-made models. **Artium** (✉ Vesterbrogade 1, ☎ 33/12–34–88) offers a beautiful

array of colorful, Scandinavian-designed sweaters and clothes along-side useful and artful household gifts.

CRYSTAL AND PORCELAIN

Minus the VAT, such Danish classics as Holmegaard crystal and Royal Copenhagen porcelain are less expensive than they are back home. Signed art glass is always more expensive, but be on the lookout for seconds as well as secondhand and unsigned pieces. Tucked in a lovely court-yard is the elegant shop **Hinz/Kjær Glasdesign** (⊠ Østergade 24, ☎ 33/32–83–82), where the work of this American-Danish couple in-cludes bright glasses, bowls, and other functional art. **Chicago** (⊠ Vimmelskaftet 47 on Strøget, ☎ 33/12–30–31) shows off a wide va-riety of Scandinavian art and functional glass. **Skandinavisk Glas** (⊠ Ny Østergade 4, ☎ 33/13–80–95) has a large selection of Danish and international glass and a helpful, informative staff. **Holmegaards Glass** (⊠ Østergade 15, ☎ 33/12–44–77) has a Strøget location, as well as a factory 97 kilometers (60 miles) south of Copenhagen, near the town of Næstved (☎ 55/54–62–00), that is smaller than the shop in Copenhagen but has a larger selection of seconds, discounted 20% to 50%. (The store on Østergade also has a limited selection of seconds.) The **Royal Copenhagen** shop (⊠ Amagertorv 6, ☎ 33/13–71–81) has firsts and seconds. For a look at the goods at their source, try the **Royal Copenhagen Factory** (⊠ Smallegade 45, ☎ 31/86–48–48).

DESIGN

Part gallery, part department store, **Illums Bolighus** (⊠ Amagertorv 6, ☎ 33/14–19–41) shows off cutting-edge Danish and international de-sign—art glass, porcelain, silverware, carpets, and loads of grown-up toys. **Lysberg, Hansen and Therp** (⊠ Bredgade 3, ☎ 33/14–47–87), one of the most prestigious interior-design firms in Denmark, has sump-tuous showrooms done up in traditional and modern styles, as well as an exquisite gift shop with silk, silver, and leather accessories. **Interieur** (⊠ Gothersgade 91, ☎ 33/13–15–56) displays fresh Danish style as well as chic kitchenware. Master florist **Tage Andersen** (⊠ Ny Adel-gade 12, ☎ 33/93–09–13) has a fantasy-infused gallery-shop filled with one-of-a-kind gifts and arrangements where browsers (who generally don't purchase the pricey items) are charged a DKr40 admission.

FUR

Denmark, the world's biggest producer of ranched minks, is the place to go for quality furs. Furs are ranked into four grades: Saga Royal, Saga, Quality 1, and Quality 2. Copenhagen's finest furrier, dealing only in Saga Royal quality, and purveyor to the royal family, is **Birger Chris-tensen** (⊠ Østergade 38, ☎ 33/11–55–55), which presents a new col-lection yearly from its in-house design team. Expect to spend about 20% less than in the United States for same-quality furs ($5,000–$10,000 for mink, $3,000 for a fur-lined coat). Birger Christensen is also among the preeminent fashion houses in town, carrying Donna Karan, Chanel, Prada, Kenzo, Jil Sander and Yves Saint Laurent. **A.C. Bang** (⊠ Øster-gade 27, ☎ 33/15–17–26) carries less expensive furs. **Otto D. Mad-sen** (⊠ Vesterbrogade 1, ☎ 33/13–41–10) is not as chichi as some of Copenhagen's furriers, but has inexpensive prices.

SILVER

Check the silver standard of a piece by its stamp. Three towers and "925S" (which means 925 parts out of 1,000) mark sterling. Two tow-ers are used for silver plate. The "826S" stamp was used until the 1920s. Even with shipping charges, you can expect to save 50% from Amer-ican prices when buying Danish silver (especially used) at the source. For one of the most recognized names in international silver, visit **Georg Jensen** (⊠ Amagertorv 4, ☎ 33/11–40–80), an elegant, austere shop aglitter with velvet-cushioned sterling. **Peter Krog** (✉ 4 Bredgade, ☎ 33/12–45–55) stocks collectors' items in silver, primarily Georg Jensen place settings, compotes, and jewelry. **Ketti Hartogsohn** (✉ Palægade 8, ☎ 33/15–53–98) carries all sorts of silver knickknacks and settings. The **English Silver House** (✉ Pilestræde 4, ☎ 33/14–83–81) is an emporium of used estate silver. The city's largest (and brightest) silver store is **Sølvkælderen** (✉ Kompagnistræde 1, ☎ 33/13–36–34), with an endless selection of tea services, place settings, and jewelry.

Street Markets

Check with the tourist board or the tourist magazine *Copenhagen This Week* for flea markets. Bargaining is expected. For a good overview of antiques and junk, visit the flea market at **Israels Plads** (✉ near Nørreport Station), open May–October, Saturday 8–2. It is run by more than 100 professional dealers, and prices are steep, but there are loads of classic Danish porcelain, silver, jewelry, and crystal, plus books, prints, postcards, and more. Slightly smaller than the Israels Plads market, and with lower prices and more junk, is the market behind ✉ **Frederiksberg Rådhus** (summer Saturday mornings). The junk-and-flea market that takes place Saturdays in summer and stretches from Nørrebros Runddel down the road along the Assistens Kirkegårn (cemetery) claims to be one of the longest in the world.

Copenhagen A to Z

Arriving and Departing

BY CAR

The E–66 highway, via bridges and ferry routes, connects Fredericia (on Jylland) with Middelfart (on Fyn), a distance of 16 kilometers (10 miles), and farther on to Copenhagen, another 180 kilometers (120 miles) east. Farther north, from Århus (in Jylland), there is direct ferry service to Kalundborg (on Sjælland). From there, Route 23 leads to Roskilde, about 72 kilometers (45 miles) east. Take Route 21 east and follow the signs to Copenhagen, another 40 kilometers (25 miles). Make reservations for the ferry in advance through **DSB** (☎ 33/14–88–80).

BY FERRY

From Sweden there are frequent ferry connections to Copenhagen, including several daily ships from Malmö, Limhamn, Landskrona, and Helsingborg. There is also a high-speed craft from Malmö.

BY PLANE

Copenhagen's **Kastrup Airport,** 10 kilometers (6 miles) southeast of downtown, is the gateway to Scandinavia. In addition to international flights, domestic routes are served by SAS (☎ 32/33–68–48). Among the many airlines that serve Kastrup are British Airways (☎ 33/14–60–00), Icelandair (☎ 33/12–33–88), and Delta (☎ 33/11–56–56).

Though the 10-kilometer (6-mile) drive from the airport to downtown is quick and easy, there's public transportation as well. **SAS coach buses** leave the international arrivals terminal every 15 minutes, from 5:42 AM to 9:45 PM, cost DKr32, and take 25 minutes to reach Copenhagen's main train station on Vesterbrogade. Another SAS coach from Christianborg, on Slotsholmsgade, to the airport runs every 15 minutes between 8:30 AM and noon, and every half-hour from noon to 6 PM. **HT** city buses depart from the international arrivals terminal every 15 minutes, from 4:30 AM (Sunday 5:30) to 11:52 PM, but take a long, circuitous route. Take Bus 250S for the Rådhus Pladsen and transfer. Tickets (one way) cost DKr15.

If you'd rather take a **taxi,** the 20-minute ride downtown costs from DKr75 to DKr120. Lines form at the international arrivals terminal. In the unlikely event there is no taxi available, call ☎ 31/35–35–35.

BY TRAIN

Copenhagen's **Hovedbanegården** (central station) is the hub of the DSB network, and is virtually connected to most major cities in Europe. Intercity trains leave every hour, usually on the hour, from 6 AM to 10 PM for principal towns in Fyn and Jylland. Find out more from **DSB Information** (☎ 33/14–17–01). You can make reservations at the central station, at most other stations, and through travel agents.

Getting Around

Copenhagen is small, with most sights within its square-mile center. Wear comfortable shoes and explore it on foot. Or follow the example of the Danes and rent a bike. For the footsore, an efficient transit system is available.

BY BICYCLE

Bikes are delightfully well suited to Copenhagen's flat terrain and are popular among Danes as well as visitors. Bike rental costs DKr25–DKr60 a day, with a deposit of DKr100–DKr200. Contact Københavns Cyclebørs (⊠ Track 12, Copenhagen main train station, ☎ 33/14–07–17), Danwheel-Rent-a-Bike (⊠ Colbjørnsensgade 3, ☎ 31/21–22–27), or Urania Cykler (⊠ Gammel Kongevej 1, ☎ 31/21–80–88).

BY BUS AND BY TRAIN

The **Copenhagen Card** offers unlimited travel on buses and suburban trains, admission to more than 40 museums and sights around Sjælland, and a reduction on the ferry crossing to Sweden. You can buy the card, which costs DKr140 (24 hours), DKr230 (48 hours), or DKr295 (72 hours)—half-price for children—at tourist offices and hotels and from travel agents.

Trains and buses operate from 5 AM (Sunday 6 AM) to midnight. After that, night buses run every half hour from 1 AM to 4:30 AM from the main bus station at Rådhus Pladsen to most areas of the city and surroundings. Trains and buses operate on the same ticket system and divide Copenhagen and surrounding areas into three zones. Tickets are validated on a time basis: On the basic ticket, which costs DKr10 per hour, you can travel anywhere in the zone in which you started. A discount *klip kort,* good for 10 rides, costs DKr75 and must be stamped in the automatic ticket machines on buses or at stations. Get zone details from the 24-hour information service (☎ 36/45–45–45 for buses, 33/14–17–01 for S trains).

BY CAR

If you are planning on seeing the sights of central Copenhagen, a car is not convenient. Parking spaces are at a premium and, when available, are expensive. A maze of one-way streets, relatively aggressive drivers, and bicycle lanes make it even more complicated. If you are going to drive, choose a small car that's easy to parallel park, bring a lot of small change to feed the meters, and be very aware of the cyclists on your right-hand side: They always have the right-of-way.

BY TAXI

The shiny computer-metered Mercedes and Volvo cabs are not cheap. The base charge is DKr15, plus DKr8–DKr10 per kilometer. A cab is available when it displays the sign FRI (free); it can be hailed or picked up in front of the main train station or at taxi stands, or by calling ☎ 31/35–35–35.

Contacts and Resources

CAR RENTALS

All major international car rental agencies are represented in Copenhagen; most are located near the Vesterport Station. Try Europcar (⊠ Kastrup Airport, ☎ 32/50–30–90) or Pitzner Auto (⊠ Kastrup Airport, ☎ 32/50–90–65).

CURRENCY EXCHANGE

Almost all banks (including the Danske Bank at the airport) exchange money. Most hotels cash traveler's checks and exchange major foreign currencies, but they charge a substantial fee and give a lower rate. After normal banking hours, Den Danske Bank exchange is open at the **main railway station,** daily June to August 7 AM–10 PM, and daily September to May, 7 AM–9 PM. **American Express** (⊠ Amagertorv 18, ☎ 33/12–23–01) is open weekdays 9–5 and Saturday 9–noon. In the center of Copenhagen are the four locations of the **Danish Change** (⊠ Vesterbrogade 9A; Østergade 61; Vimmelskaftet 47; Frederiksberggade 5; ☎ 33/93–04–18), which is open April to October, daily 10–8, November to March, daily 10–6. **Tivoli** (⊠ Vesterbrogade 3, ☎ 33/15–10–01) also exchanges money; it is open May to September, daily noon–11 PM.

DOCTORS AND DENTISTS

Emergency dentists (⊠ 14 Oslo Plads, no ☎), near Østerport Station, are available weekdays 8 PM–9:30 PM and weekends and holidays 10 AM–noon. Only cash is accepted as payment.

After normal business hours, **emergency doctors** make house calls in the central city. Call ☎ 38/88–60–41. Fees are payable in cash only; night fees are approximately DKr300–400.

EMBASSIES AND CONSULATES

U.S. Embassy (⊠ Dag Hammarskjölds Allé 24, ☎ 31/42–31–44). **Canadian Embassy** (⊠ Kristen Bernikows Gade 1, ☎ 33/12–22–99. **U.K. Embassy** (⊠ Kastesvej 36–40, ☎ 35/26–46–00).

EMERGENCIES

Police, fire, and **ambulance,** (☎ 112). **Auto Rescue/Falck** (☎ 31/14–22–22). **Rigshospitalet** (⊠ Blegdamsvej 9, ☎ 35/45–35–45). **Frederiksberg Hospital** (⊠ Nordre Fasanvej 57, ☎ 38/34–77–11).

ENGLISH-LANGUAGE BOOKSTORES

Steve's Books and Records (⊠ Ved Stranden 10, ☎ 33/11–94–60) has new and used English books. **Boghallen** (⊠ Rådhus Pladsen 37, ☎ 33/11–85–11, ext. 309), the bookstore of the Politiken publishing house, offers a good selection of English-language books. At **Arnold Busck** (⊠ Kobmagergade 49, ☎ 33/12–24–53), you'll find an excellent English-language department, along with a textbook section, a small selection of CDs, and lots of comic books.

GUIDED TOURS

The Copenhagen Tourist Board monitors all tours and has brochures and information. Most tours run through the summer until September. Only the Grand Tour of Copenhagen is year-round. In any case, it's always a good idea to call first to confirm availability. For tour information call **Copenhagen Excursions** (☎ 31/54–06–06).

Walking Tours. All tours begin at Lurblæserne (Lur Blower Column), in front of the Palace Hotel at the Rådhus Pladsen, and reservations are not necessary. Walking tours begin in front of the Tourist Information Office (⊠ Bernstorffsgade 1, ☎ 33/11-13-25) at 10:30 and 2 daily (call to confirm); the 2-hour tour takes in the exteriors of most of the city's major sights. **The Royal Tour of Copenhagen** (2¾ hours) covers the exhibitions at Christiansborg and Rosenborg, and visits

Amalienborg Square. **The Grand Tour of Copenhagen** (2½ hours) includes Tivoli, the Carlsberg Glyptotek, Christiansborg Palace, Børsen, the Royal Theater, Nyhavn, Amalienborg Palace, the Gefion Fountain, the Grundtvig Church, and Rosenborg Castle. The **City Tour** (1½ hours) is more general, passing the Carlsberg Glyptotek, Christiansborg Palace, Thorvaldsen's Museum, the National Museum, Børsen, the Royal Theater, Rosenborg, the National Art Gallery, the Botanical Gardens, Amalienborg, the Gefion Fountain, and *The Little Mermaid*.

Boat Tours. The **Harbor and Canal Tour** (1 hour) leaves from Gammel Strand and the east side of Kongens Nytorv from May to mid-September. Contact Canal Tours (☎ 33/13–31–05) or the Tourist Board. The **City and Harbor Tour** (2½ hours) includes a short bus trip through town and sails from the Fish Market on Holmens Canal through several more waterways, ending near Strøget.

Commercial Tours. Tours of the **Carlsberg Brewery**—which include a look into the draft and horse stalls—meet at the Elephant Gate (⊠ Ny Carlsbergvej 140, ☎ 33/27–13–14) weekdays at 11 and 2. **The Royal Porcelain Factory** (⊠ Smallegade 45, ☎ 31/86–48–48) has tours that end at its shop on weekdays at 9, 10, and 11 from mid-September until April, and weekdays at 9, 10, 11, 1, and 2 from May through mid–September.

LATE-NIGHT PHARMACIES

Steno Apotek (⊠ Vesterbrogade 6C, ☎ 33/14–82–66) and Sønderbro Apotek (⊠ Amangerbrogade 158, ☎ 31/58–01–40) are open 24 hours a day.

TRAVEL AGENCIES

Leading travel agencies include American Express (⊠ Amagertorv 18, ☎ 33/12–23–01), Carlsen Wagons-Lits (⊠ Ved Vesterport 6, ☎ 33/14–27–47), and Skibby Rejser (⊠ Vandkunsten 10, ☎ 33/32–85–00). For **student and budget travel,** try Kilroy Travels Denmark (⊠ Skindergade 28, ☎ 33/11–00–44). For **charter packages,** stick with Spies (⊠ Nyropsgade 41, ☎ 33/32–15–00) or Tjæreborg (⊠ Nyropsgade 41, ☎ 33/11–41–00).

VISITOR INFORMATION

The main tourist information office is **Danmarks Turistråd** (⊠ Danish Tourist Board, Bernstorffsgade 1, ☎ 33/11–13–25). It is open in May, weekdays 9–5, Saturday 9–2, and Sunday 9–1; June through mid-September, daily 9–6; and mid-September through April, weekdays 9–5 and Saturday 9–noon. Youth information in Copenhagen is available at **Use-It** (⊠ Huset, Rådhusstræde 13, ☎ 33/15–65–18).

SIDE TRIPS FROM COPENHAGEN

Eksperimentarium

8 km (6 mi) north of Copenhagen.

In the beachside town of Hellerup is the user-friendly Eksperimentarium (Experimentarium), where more than 200 exhibitions are clustered in various Discovery Islands, each exploring a different facet of science, technology, and natural phenomena. A dozen hands- and body-on exhibits allow visitors to take skeleton-revealing bike rides, measure their lung capacity, stir up magnetic goop, play ball on a jet stream, gyrate to gyroscopes, and to experience topics from movie history to the human face, up close and hands on. Take Bus 6 from Rådhus Plads. ⊠ *Tuborg Havnevej,* ☎ *39/27–33–33.* ☞ *DKr69.* ☉ *Mon., Wed., and Fri. 9–6; Tues. and Thurs. 9–9; weekends 11–6.*

Louisiana

35 km (22 mi) north of Copenhagen (via the E4 highway or the coastal road, Strandvejen; or take the Helsingør train to the Humlebæk station and walk to the right 10 min).

A world-class collection of modern art is housed in this museum on the "Danish Riviera," the north Sjælland coast. Even if you can't tell a Rauschenberg from a Rembrandt, you should make the 30-minute trip to see its elegant rambling structure, surrounded by a large park. Inside, Warhols vie for space with Giacomettis and Picassos; added attractions include contemporary exhibits as well as concerts and films. In the summer, Danes bring their children to picnic in the sculpture garden and on the banks of the sound. ⊠ *Gammel Strandvej 13, Humlebæk,* ☎ *49/19–07–19.* ⊡ *DKr48.* ⊙ *Mon., Tues., and Thurs.–Sun. 10–5, Wed. 10–10.*

Dragør

22 km (14 mi) of Copenhagen (take Bus 30 or 33 from Rådhuspladsen).

On the island of Amager, less than an hour from Copenhagen, the quaint fishing town of Dragør (pronounced *drah*-wer) feels far away in distance and time. The town's history is separated from the rest of Copenhagen's because it was settled by Dutch farmers in the 16th century. The community was ordered by King Christian II to provide fresh produce and flowers for the royal court. Still meticulously maintained, it has neat rows of white, terra-cotta-roofed houses trimmed with wandering ivy, roses, and the occasional waddling goose. According to local legend, the former town hall's chimney was built with a twist so that meetings couldn't be overheard.

The **Dragør Museum** (⊠ Strandlinien 4, ☎ 32/53–41–06), located in one of the oldest houses in town, contains a collection of furniture, costumes, drawings, and model ships. Admission is DKr20; it's open Tuesday–Friday 2–5, weekends noon–6. A ticket to the Dragør Museum also affords entrance to the nearby **Mølsted Museum** (⊠ Dr. Dichs Plads 4, ☎ 32/53–41–06), which displays paintings by the famous local artist Christian Mølsted. If you're still energetic, swing by the **Amager Museum** (⊠ Hovedgade 4 and 12, ☎ 32/53–93–07), which details the Dutch colony. It's open Tuesday through Sunday noon to 4; admission is DKr20.

Frilandsmuseet

16 km (10 mi) north of Copenhagen.

Just north of Copenhagen is Lyngby, whose main draw is the Frilandsmuseet, an open-air museum. About 50 farmhouses and cottages representing various periods of Danish history have been painstakingly dismantled, moved, reconstructed, and filled with period furniture and tools. The museum is surrounded by trees and gardens; bring lunch and plan to spend the day. To get here, take the S-train to the Sorgenfri Station, then walk right and follow the signs. ⊠ *Frilandsmuseet. 100 Kongevejen, Lyngby,* ☎ *45/85–02–92.* ⊡ *DKr30.* ⊙ *Mid-Apr.–Sept., Tues.–Sun. 10–5; third wk in Oct., 10–4.*

Museet for Moderne Kunst

20 km (12) south of Copenhagen (take the S-train in the direction of either Hundige, Solrød Strand, or Køge to Ishøj Station, then pick up bus 128 to the museum.

Architect Søren Robert Lund was just 25 when he was awarded the commission for this forward-looking museum, which he designed in metal and white concrete set against the flat coast south of Copenhagen. The museum opened in March 1996 to great acclaim, both for its architecture and its collection. Its massive sculpture room exhibits both modern Danish and international art, as well as experimental works. Dance, theater, film, and multimedia exhibits are additional attractions. ⊠ *Skovvej 42,* ☎ *43/42–02–22.* ⊡ *DKr45.* ☉ *Tues.–Sun., 10–5.*

SJÆLLAND AND ITS ISLANDS

The goddess Gefion is said to have carved Sjælland (Zealand) from Sweden. If she did, she must have sliced the north deep with a fjord, while she chopped the south to pieces and left the sides bowing west. Though the coasts are deeply serrated, Gefion's myth is more dramatic than the flat, fertile land of rich meadows and beech stands.

Slightly larger than the state of Delaware, Sjælland is the largest of the Danish islands. From Copenhagen, almost any point on it can be reached in an hour and a half, making it the most traveled portion of the country—and it is especially easy to explore by traveling from town to town by road, as outlined within the following tours. To the north of the capital, the ritzy beach towns line up between Hellerup and Humlebæk. Helsingør's Kronborg, which Shakespeare immortalized in *Hamlet,* and Hillerød's stronghold of Frederiksborg, considered one of the most magnificent Renaissance castles in Europe, also lie to the north. To the west of Copenhagen is Roskilde, medieval Denmark's most important town, with an eclectic cathedral that was northern Europe's spiritual center 1,000 years ago.

West and south, rural towns and farms edge up to beach communities and fine white beaches, often surrounded by forests. Beaches with summer cottages, white dunes, and calm waters surround Gilleleje and the neighboring town of Hornbæk. The beach in Tisvildeleje, farther west, is quieter and close to woods. Even more unspoiled are the Lilliputian islands around southern Sjælland, virtually unchanged over the past century.

Most of Sjælland can be explored in day trips from Copenhagen. The exceptions are the northwestern beaches around the Sejerø Bugt (Sejerø Bay) and those south of Møn, all of which require at least a night's stay and a day's loll.

Outdoor Activities and Sports

Because the landscape is so flat, Sjælland is excellent for undemanding cycling. Most roads have cycle lanes, and tourist boards are stocked with maps detailing local routes.

With plenty of lakes, rivers, and coastline, Sjælland also has good fishing: A license, which costs DKr100, can be purchased from any post office, and is required to fish along Sjælland's coast. Elsewhere, inland and on the ocean, check with the local tourist office for license requirements, which vary from one area to another. Remember, it is illegal to fish within 1,650 feet of the mouth of a stream.

About 15 kilometers (10 miles) north of Copenhagen, especially in the Lynby area, several calm lakes and rivers are perfect for canoeing: the Mølleå (Mølle River) and the Bagsværd, Lyngby, and Furesø (Bagsværd, Lyngby, and Fur lakes). **Frederiksdal Kanoudlejning** (⊠ Nybrovej, Lyngby, ☎ 45/85–67–70) offers hourly, daily, and package canoe tours and rentals throughout the region. For trips on the tranquil Suså

Sjælland and Its Islands

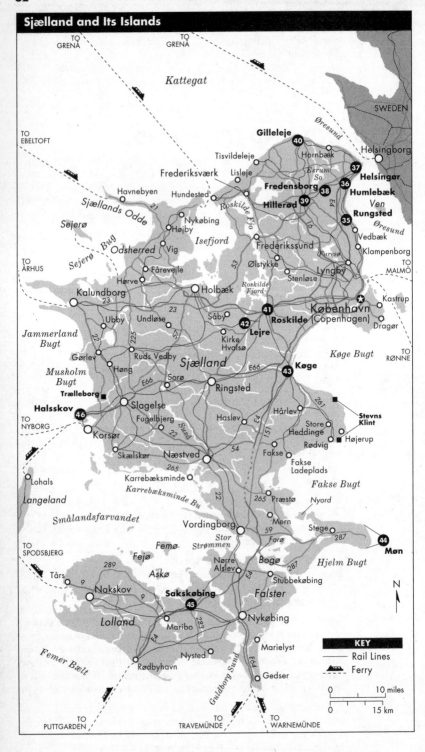

TO GRENÅ

TO GRENÅ

Kattegat

SWEDEN

TO EBELTOFT

Øresund

Gilleleje **40**

Helsingborg

Tisvildeleje

Hornbæk

Helsingør **37**

Frederiksværk

Lisleje

Esrum So

36 **Helsingør**

Havnebyen

Hundested

Fredensborg **38**

Humlebæk

Sjællands Odde

Hillerød **39**

Ven

Rungsted

Roskilde Fjo

35

Sejerø

Nykøbing

Højby

Vedbæk

Øresund

Sejerø

Odsherred

Vig

Isefjord

Frederikssund

Furesø

Klampenborg

Bugt

Ølstykke

TO ÅRHUS

Fåreveile

53

Stenløse

Lyngby

TO MALMÖ

Hørve

Roskilde Fjord

Kalundborg

Holbæk

41

Kastrup

23

23

Såby

København
(Copenhagen)

Jammerland Bugt

Ubby

Undløse

42

Dragør

225

Lejre

57

Kirke Hvalsø

Køge Bugt

TO RØNNE

Gørlev

Ruds Vedby

Sjælland

E66

43 **Køge**

Musholm Bugt

Høng

Sorø

E66

Trælleborg

Slagelse

Ringsted

Hårlev

Stevns Klint

Halskov

46

Fugelbjerg

Haslev

151

Store Heddinge

TO NYBORG

Korsør

22

Suså

E4

Rødvig

Højerup

Skælskør

Næstved

54

Fakse

Fakse Ladeplads

265

Karrebæksminde

Fakse Bugt

Karrebæksminde Bu

22

265

Præstø

Nyord

Smålandsfarvandet

Vordingborg

Mern

Stege

287

44 **Møn**

TO SPODSBJERG

Femø

Stor Strømmen

59

Forø

Bogø

Hjelm Bugt

Langeland

Fejø

Nørre Alslev

287

N

Tårs

289

Askø

E4

Stubbekøbing

9

Nakskov

9

Sakskøbing

Falster

45

Nykøbing

Lolland

Maribo

283

Marielyst

Nysted

E4

Rødbyhavn

Gedser

Femer Bælt

Guldborg Sund

E55

TO PUTTGARDEN

TO TRAVEMÜNDE

TO WARNEMÜNDE

KEY

— Rail Lines

🚢 Ferry

0 _____ 10 miles

0 _____ 15 km

(Sus River) in South Sjælland, call **Susåen Kanoudlejning** regarding canoe rental (☎ 53/64–61–44).

Shopping

Keep in mind that shopping in this area can be considerably cheaper than in Copenhagen. Take time to meander through the pedestrian streets that run through the center of most towns, and ask about flea markets, which traditionally take place Saturday mornings.

Rungsted

⑤ *21 km (13 mi) north of Copenhagen.*

Between Copenhagen and Helsingør is **Rungstedlund,** the elegant, airy former manor of Baroness Karen Blixen. The author of *Out of Africa* and several accounts of aristocratic Danish life, Blixen wrote under the pen name Isak Dinesen. The manor house, where she lived as a child and to which she returned in 1931, is open as a museum and displays manuscripts, photographs, and memorabilia documenting her years in Africa and Denmark. Leave time to wander around the gardens. ⊠ *Rungstedlund,* ☎ *42/57–10–57.* 🎫 *DKr30 (for combined train and admission tickets, call DSB,* ☎ *33/14–17–01).* ⊙ *May–Sept., daily 10–5; Oct.–Apr., Wed.–Fri. 1–4, weekends 11–4.*

Dining

$$ ✕ **Strandmollekroen.** Stop at this 200-year-old beachfront inn, lo-
★ cated in Klampenborg, as you drive north from Copenhagen to Rungsted. It's burnished with deep-green walls and filled with antiques and hunting trophies, but the best views are of the Øresund from the back dining room. The fare is seafood and steaks served elegantly. For a bit of everything, try the seafood platter, with lobster, crab claws, and Greenland shrimp. ⊠ *Strandvejen 808,* ☎ *31/63–01–04. AE, DC, MC, V.*

Shopping

The **Danish Amber Gallery** (⊠ Skodsborgparken 21, Skodsborg, ☎ 45/80–71–62), 18 kilometers (11 miles) north of Copenhagen and 7 kilometers (4 miles) south of Rungsted, has a good selection of jewelry and a workshop.

Humlebæk

⑥ *10 km (6 mi) north of Rungsted; 30 km (19 mi) north of Copenhagen.*

This elegant seaside town is home of the must-see **Louisiana** museum, which is as famed for its stunning location and architecture as it is for its collection. Housed in a pearly 19th-century villa surrounded by dramatic views of the Øresund waters, the permanent collection includes modern American paintings and Danish paintings from the COBRA (a trend in northern European painting that took its name from its active locations: Copenhagen, Brussels, Amsterdam) and Deconstructionism movements. Be sure to see the haunting collection of Giacomettis backdropped by picture windows overlooking the sound. The new children's wing has pyramid-shape chalkboards, kid-proof computers, and weekend activities under the guidance of an artist or museum coordinator. ⊠ *Gammel Strandvej 13,* ☎ *49/19–07–19.* 🎫 *DKr48 (for combined train and admission tickets, call DSB,* ☎ *33/14–17–01).* ⊙ *Thurs.–Tues. 10–5, Wed. 10–10.*

Helsingør

⑦ *19 km (12 mi) north of Humlebæk; 47 km (29 mi) north of Copenhagen.*

At the northeastern tip of the island is Helsingør, the departure point for ferries to the Swedish town of Helsingborg, and the site of **Kronborg Slot.** William Shakespeare based *Hamlet* on Danish mythology's Amleth, and used this castle as the setting even though he had never seen it. Built in the late 16th century, it's 600 years younger than the Elsinore we imagine from the tragedy; it was built as a Renaissance tollbooth. From its cannon-studded bastions, forces collected Erik of Pomerania's much-hated Sound Dues, a tariff charged to all ships crossing the sliver of water between Denmark and Sweden. Well worth seeing are the 200-foot-long dining hall and the dungeons, where there is a brooding statue of Holger Danske. According to legend, the Viking chief sleeps, but will awaken to defend Denmark when it is in danger. (The largest Danish resistance group during World War II called itself Holger Danske after its fearless forefather.) ⊠ *Helsingør,* ☎ *49/21–30–78.* ⊠ *DKr30.* ☉ *May–Sept., daily 10:30–5; Oct. and Apr., Tues.–Sun. 11–4; Nov.–Mar., Tues.–Sun. 11–3.*

Thanks to the hefty tolls collected by Erik of Pomerania, Helsingør prospered. Stroll past the carefully restored medieval merchants' and ferrymen's houses in the middle of town. On the corner of Stengade and Skt. Annæ Gade near the harbor, you'll come to **Skt. Olai's Kirke,** the country's largest parish church and worth a peek for its elaborately carved wooden altar. ⊠ *St. Olai Gade 51,* ☎ *49/21–00–98 between 9 and noon only.* ⊠ *Free.* ☉ *May 15–Sept. 14, daily noon–3, with tours at 2; rest of yr, daily noon–2.*

Next door to Skt. Olai's Kirke is the 15th-century **Carmelite Kloster** (Carmelite Convent), one of the best-preserved examples of medieval architecture in Scandinavia. After the Reformation it was used as a hospital, and by 1630 it had become a poorhouse. ⊠ *Skt. Anna Gade 38,* ☎ *49/21–17–74.* ⊠ *DKr10.* ☉ *Tour daily at 2; call ahead to confirm.*

If you want to know more about Helsingør, head to the modest **By Museum** (Town Museum), which has exhibits of 19th-century handicrafts, dolls, and a model of the town. ⊠ *Skt. Annæ Gade 36,* ☎ *49/21–00–98.* ⊠ *DKr10.* ☉ *Daily noon–4.*

OFF THE BEATEN PATH

MARIENLYST SLOT – One kilometer (½ mi) north of Helsingør is the Louis XVI–style Marienlyst Castle. Built in 1587, it provided King Frederik II with a garden, as well as a delicate change of scenery from the militant Kronborg. Today the gardens have been replanted, and the interiors contain paintings by north Sjælland artists, as well as a gallery with changing arts and crafts exhibitions. ⊠ *Marienlyst Allé,* ☎ *49/21–16–27.* ⊠ *DKr20.* ☉ *Daily noon–5.*

Dining and Lodging

$$$ ✕☑ **Hotel Hamlet.** A few minutes from the harbor, this overly renovated hotel has lost some of its charm but makes an attempt at character with raw timbers and deep-green walls. The rooms are furnished in rose schemes and dark wood, all comfortable, if nondescript. Downstairs, the Ophelia Restaurant serves traditional Danish seafood, steaks, and open-face sandwiches. ⊠ *Bramstrædet 5, DK–3000,* ☎ *49/21–28–02,* 𝖥𝖠𝖷 *49/26–01–30. 36 rooms. Restaurant, bar, meeting room. AE, DC, MC, V. Closed Dec. 24–Jan. 1.*

Outdoor Activities and Sports

The **Helsingør Golf Klub** has 18 holes (⊠ Gamle Hellebækvej, Helsingør, ☎ 49/21–29–70), with a weekday handicap of 36 for men and women, and a weekend handicap of 24 for men and 36 for women. It's a beautiful, parklike course, with trees, and, on clear days, views across the sound to Sweden.

Nightlife and the Arts

Some summers, **Kronborg Castle** is the site of outdoor performances of *Hamlet* by internationally renowned theater groups. The schedule varies from year to year, so check with the tourist board.

In the center of town, **New York, New York** (⊠ Hovedvagtsstræde 2, ☎ 49/26–42–21) draws the young to disco.

Fredensborg

38 *15 km (9 mi) southwest of Helsingør; 33 km (20 mi) northwest of Copenhagen.*

Commanding this town is the **Fredensborg Slot** (Castle of Peace), built by Frederik IV to commemorate the 1720 peace treaty with Sweden. The Castle of Peace was originally inspired by French and Italian castles, with a towering domed hall in the center; however, 18th-century reconstructions conceal the original design and instead serve as a review of domestic architecture. The castle became a favorite of Frederik V, who lined the gardens with marble sculptures of ordinary people. It is now the summer residence of the royal family; interiors are closed except during July. In 1996, a newly constructed Orangerie (hothouse) opened. The neatly trimmed park around the palace, connecting with Lake Esrum, is a lovely spot for a stroll. ☎ *42/28–00–25.* ☉ *Palace, July, daily 1–5; park, year-round.*

Dining and Lodging

$$$$ ✕⊞ **Hotel Store Kro.** Built by King Frederik IV, this magnificent Renaissance annex to Fredensborg Castle is the archetypal stately inn. In-
★ side it's appointed with European antiques and paintings, while outside glass gazebos and classical statues overlook a lovely garden. The rooms are equally sumptuous, with delicately patterned wallpapers and antiques. The romantic restaurant, specializing in French fare, has a fireplace and a grand piano. ⊠ *Slotsgade 6, DK–3480,* ☎ *42/28–00–47,* ℻ *42/28–45–61. 49 rooms. Restaurant, bar, room service, sauna, meeting rooms, free parking. AE, DC, MC, V.*

$$$$ ✕⊞ **Marienlyst.** This hotel is full of flashy neon, bolts of drapery, and
★ glass. A large casino and endless lounges provide entertainment, but when guests tire of gambling, there's a huge second-floor "Swinging Pool," with a water slide, swim-up bar, and sauna. The rooms are all plush and pastel, with every convenience. ⊠ *Nordre Strandvej 2, DK–3000,* ☎ *49/21–40–00,* ℻ *49/21–49–00. 220 rooms, 11 suites. 2 restaurants, 2 bars, room service, indoor pool, sauna, casino, nightclub, meeting rooms. AE, DC, MC, V.*

Hillerød

39 *10 km (6 mi) south of Fredensborg; 41 km (26 mi) northwest of Copenhagen.*

Hillerød's **Frederiksborg Slot** (castle) was acquired and rebuilt by Frederik II, but the fortress was demolished by his son, king-cum-architect Christian IV, who rebuilt it as one of Scandinavia's most magnificent castles. With three wings and a low entrance portal, the moated Dutch-Renaissance structure covers three islets and is peaked with dozens of gables, spires, and turrets. The interiors include a two-story marble gallery known as the Great Hall. Audaciously festooned with drapery, paintings, and reliefs, it sits on top of the vaulted chapel, where monarchs were crowned for 200 years. Devastated by a fire in 1859, the castle was reconstructed with the support of the Carlsberg Foundation, and it now includes a museum of Danish history. ☎ *42/26–04–39.* ▣

DKr30. ⊙ Apr. and Oct., daily 10–4; May–Sept., daily 10–5; Nov.–Mar., daily 11–3.

Dining

$ ✕ **Slotsherrenskro.** Under the shadow of the Frederiksborg Castle, this busy family restaurant is in what used to be the castle stables. Antique on the outside, it's bright orange inside, with prints and paintings of royalty and the castle. Popular with visitors to the castle, the Danish menu ranges from quick open-face sandwiches to savory stews, soups, and steaks. ⊠ *Slotherrens Kro,* ☎ *42/26–75–16. DC, MC, V. No dinner Thurs., Nov.–Mar.*

Gilleleje

40   *25 km (16 mi) northwest of Hillerød, 55 km (35 mi) northwest of Copenhagen.*

Gilleleje is at the very top of Sjælland. Once a small fishing community, it experiences a population explosion every summer, when northern Europeans take to its woods and fine, sandy beaches. It was a favorite getaway of philosopher Søren Kierkegaard, who wrote: "I often stood there and reflected over my past life. The force of the sea and the struggle of the elements made me realize how unimportant I was." The less existential will go for a swim and visit the philosopher's monument on a nearby hill. The old part of town, with its thatched and colorfully painted houses, is good for a walk.

Odsherred

34 km (21 mi) west of Gilleleje; 80 km (50 mi) northwest of Copenhagen (via Roskilde).

This hammer-shape peninsula is curved by the Sejerø Bugt (bay) and dotted with hundreds of **burial mounds.** Getting here involves driving to Hundested, then taking the 25-minute ferry ride to Røvig.

If you are a devotee of ecclesiastical art, make a pilgrimage to explore the frescoes of the Romanesque-Gothic-Renaissance **Højby kirke** (Højby Church) in the town of Højby, near Nykøbing Sjælland.

In the town of FåAresvejle is the Gothic **Fårevejle kirke,** with the earl of Bothwell's chapel.

Sjællands Odde (Zealand's Tongue), the tiny strip of land north of the Sejerø Bay, offers slightly marshy but private beach strands. Inside the bay, the beaches are once again smooth and blond.

Roskilde

41   *101 km (63 mi) northeast of Odsherred, 32 km (20 mi) west of Copenhagen (on Rte. 156).*

Roskilde is Sjælland's second-largest town and one of its oldest. During a weekend at the end of June, it's filled with the rock music of the **Roskilde Festival,** said to be the largest outdoor concert in northern Europe, attracting 75,000 people.

Roskilde was the royal residence in the 10th century and became the spiritual capital of Denmark and northern Europe in 1170, when Bishop Absalon built the **Roskilde Domkirke** (Roskilde Cathedral) on the site of a church erected 200 years earlier by Harald Bluetooth. Overwhelming the center of town, the current structure took more than 300 years to complete and thus provides a one-stop crash course in Danish architecture. Inside are an ornate Dutch altarpiece and the sarcophagi, ranging from opulent to modest, of 38 Danish monarchs. Predictably, Christian IV is interred in a magnificent chapel with a massive painting of himself in combat and a bronze sculpture by Thorvaldsen. In modest contrast is the newest addition, the simple brick chapel of King Frederik IX, who died in 1972, outside the church. On the interior south wall above the entrance is a 16th-century clock that depicts St. George charging a dragon, which hisses and howls, echoing throughout the church and causing Peter Døver, "the Deafener," to sound the hour. A squeamish Kirsten Kiemer, "the Chimer," shakes her head in fright but manages to strike the quarters. ⊠ *Domkirkestræde 10,* ☎ *42/35–27–00.* 🎫 *DKr6.* ☉ *Hours vary; call ahead.*

Less than a kilometer (½ mile) north of the cathedral, on the fjord, is the **Vikingeskibshallen** (Viking Ship Museum), a modern museum that contains five Viking ships sunk in the fjord 1,000 years ago to block the passage of enemy ships. They were discovered in 1957. The painstaking recovery involved building a watertight dam and then draining the water from that section of the fjord. The splinters of wreckage were then preserved and reassembled in an ongoing process. A deep-sea trader, a warship, a ferry, a merchant ship, and a fierce 92½-foot man-of-war attest to the Vikings' sophisticated and aesthetic boat-making skills. ⊠ *Strandengen,* ☎ *42/35–65–55.* 🎫 *DKr30.* ☉ *Apr.–Oct., daily 9– 5; Nov.–Mar., daily 10–4.*

Dining and Lodging

$$ ✕ **Spise Loftet.** Its name means Eating Loft, and its menu is mix-and-
★ match: appetizer, entrée, dessert, and salad bar for DKr120. Choices range from vegetable quiche and steaks to Calvados or apple pie for dessert. The double-decker interior has two tables downstairs and a dozen upstairs beneath a gleaming white cathedral ceiling. ⊠ *Algade 42,* ☎ *42/35–15–46. AE, DC, MC, V.* ☉ *Fri. and Sat. only.*

$$ ✕🏨 **Hotel Prindsen.** Centrally located in downtown Roskilde, this convenient hotel, built 100 years ago, is popular with business guests. Renovations have given it an elegant dark-wood lobby and nondescript rooms that are nonetheless homey and comfortable. Downstairs, the restaurant La Bøf serves up grill and fish fare, and next door there's a cozy bar. ⊠ *Algade 13,* ☎ *42/35–80–10,* 🆁🆇 *42/35–81–10. 38 rooms. Restaurant, bar, meeting room. AE, DC, MC, V.*

$ 🏨 **Roskilde Vandrehjem Hørgården.** In front of a grassy yard, this youth hostel is perfect for families and budget travelers. In a former schoolhouse 2 kilometers (1¼ miles) east of the Roskilde Domkirke, everything looks straight out of third grade, and the rooms, with bunks, look like camp. ⊠ *Hørhusene 61, DK–4000,* ☎ *42/35–21–84,* 🆁🆇 *46/32– 66–90. 21 rooms with 4 beds each, 8 showers. Kitchen. No credit cards.* ☉ *May–Sept.; call at other times for possible openings.*

Nightlife and the Arts

The young head to **Gimle** (⊠ Ringstedgade 30, ☎ 42/35–12–13) for live rock on the weekends. **Kloster Kælderen** (⊠ Store Gråbrødrestræde 23, ☎ 42/37–20–33) is a beer basement with a 20- to 30-something crowd. The **Bryggerhesten** (⊠ Algade 15, ☎ 42/35–01–03), which means "the draft horse," is where adults have a late supper and beer in cozy surroundings. During the summer **Mullerudi** (⊠ Djalma Lunds Gord 7, ☎ 42/37–03–25) is an arty spot with indoor and outdoor seating and live jazz.

Outdoor Activities and Sports

Roskilde has an 18-hole **golf course** (⊠ Kongemarken 34, ☎ 42/37–01–80) with views of the twin-peaked Roskilde Cathedral, and an encircling forest.

Shopping

Between Roskilde and Holbæk is **Kirke Sonnerup Kunst-håndværk** (⊠ Art Handicrafts, Englerupvej 62, Såby, ☎ 46/49–25–77), which has a good selection of pottery, glass, clothing, and woodwork produced by more than 50 Danish artists.

Lejre

42 *10 km (6 mi) west of Roskilde, 40 km (25 mi) west of Copenhagen.*

The **Lejre Forsøgscenter** (Lejre Archaeological Research Center) is a 50-acre compound composed of a reconstructed village dating from the Iron Age and two 19th-century farmhouses. During the summer they are inhabited by a handful of hardy Danish families. Under the observation of researchers, these people go about their daily routine—grinding grain, herding goats—providing a clearer picture of ancient ways of life. In Bodalen (Fire Valley), visitors (especially children) can grind corn, file an ax, and sail in a dugout canoe. ⊠ *Slangæleen,* ☎ *46/48–08–78.* ☞ *DKr45.* ☉ *May–Sept., daily 10–5.*

Køge

43 *20 km (13 mi) southwest of Lejre, 40 km (25 mi) southeast of Copenhagen.*

The well-preserved medieval town of Køge is known for its historic witch hunts. In the centrally located **Køge Museum,** a 17th-century merchant's house, you will see souvenirs from Hans Christian Andersen, costumes, local artifacts, an executioner's sword, and a 13th-century stone font. A story is told that the font had to be removed from the town church after a crippled woman committed an unsavory act into it, hoping her bizarre behavior would cure her. Also on exhibit are 16th-century silver coins from a buried treasure of more than 2,000 coins found in the courtyard of Langkildes Gård. ⊠ *Nørregade 4,* ☎ *53/65–02–62.* ☞ *DKr15.* ☉ *Sept.–May, weekdays 2–5, weekends 1–5; June–Aug., daily 10–5.*

The old part of Køge is filled with 300 half-timber houses, all protected by the National Trust; it's a lovely area for a stroll. At the end of Kirkestræde, the 15th-century **Skt. Nikolai Kirke** (St. Nicholas Church) was once a lighthouse; its floor is covered with more than 100 tombs of Køge VIPs. Carved angels line the church's walls, but most have had their noses struck off—a favorite pastime of drunken Swedish soldiers in the 1700s. ⊠ *Kirkestræde,* ☎ *53/65–13–59.* ☞ *Free.* ☉ *Sept.–May, weekdays 10–noon; June–Aug., weekdays 10–4. Tower tours end July–mid-Aug., weekdays 11, noon, and 1.*

If you have time, visit the **Køge Kunst Museet** (Køge Art Museum), which has changing exhibitions and an extensive permanent collection of sketches, sculpture, and other modern Danish art. ⊠ *Nørregade 29,* ☎ *53/66–24–14.* ☞ *DKr15. Free with admission ticket from the Køge Museum* (☞ above). ☉ *Tues.–Sun. 11–5.*

En Route Twenty-four kilometers (15 miles) south of Køge near Rødvig, the chalk cliffs called Stevns Klint are worth a stop because of the 13th-century **Højerup Kirke** (church) built above them. As the cliffs eroded, first the cemetery, then the choir toppled into the sea. In recent years the church has been restored and the cliffs below bolstered by masonry to prevent further damage. ⊠ *Højerup Church, Stevns Klint, no* ☎ . ✉ *DKr5.* ⊙ *Apr.–Sept., daily 11–5.*

Møn

🟤 *85 km (52 mi) south of Stevns Klint, 130 km (81 mi) south of Copenhagen.*

The island of Møn is pocked throughout with nearly 100 Neolithic burial mounds, but it is most famous for its dramatic chalk cliffs, the **Møns Klint,** which are three times as large as Stevns Klint, to the north. Rimmed by a beech forest, the milky-white 75-million-year-old bluffs plunge 400 feet to a small, craggy beach—accessible by a path and more than 500 steps. Wear good walking shoes, and take care; though a park ranger checks the area for loose rocks, the cliffs crumble suddenly. Once there, Danish families usually spend their time hunting for blanched fossils of cuttlefish, sea urchins, and other sea life. The cliffs are an important navigational marker for ships, defining south Sjælland's otherwise flat topography.

You can walk to a delightful folly of the 18th century, **Liselund Slot** (not to be confused with a hotel of the same name), which is 4 kilometers (2½ miles) north of the cliffs. Antoine de la Calmette, the island's sheriff and a royal chamberlain, took his inspiration from Marie Antoinette's *Hameau* (Hamlet) at Versailles and built the structure in 1792 for his beloved wife. The thatched palace, complete with English gardens, combines a Norwegian country facade with elegant Pompeian interiors. In this lovely setting, Hans Christian Andersen wrote his fairy tale *The Tinder Box.* The palace has been open to the public since 1938. Tours are given in Danish and German. ☎ *55/81–21–78.* ✉ *DKr20.* ⊙ *Tours May–Oct., Tues.—Fri. Mon.–10:30, 11, 1:30, and 2; Sat.— Sun. 10:30, 11, 1:30, 2, 4, and 4:30.*

Møn's capital, **Stege,** received its town charter in 1268. Take time to explore its medieval churches, including Elmelunde, Keldby, and Fanefjord, all famous for their naive frescoes. Thought to have been completed by a collaborative group of artisans, the whimsical paintings include pedagogic and biblical doodlings.

Dining and Lodging

$$ ✕⌂ **Liselund Ny Slot.** Set in a grand old manor on an isolated estate, ★ this modern hotel offers stately accommodations minus stodginess. The square staircase and painted ceilings have been preserved, while the renovated rooms are fresh and simple, with wicker and pastel schemes, half of them overlooking a swan-filled pond and the forest. Downstairs there's a restaurant serving Danish cuisine. ⊠ *Liselund Ny Slot, DK–4791 Børre,* ☎ *55/81–20–81,* ⅿ *55/81–21–91. 25 rooms, 1 suite. Restaurant, meeting rooms. AE, DC, MC, V.*

Falster

3 km (2 mi) south of Bøgo; 24 km (15 mi) south of Møn; 99 km (62 mi) south of Copenhagen.

Accessible by way of the striking Farø Bridge or the parallel Storstrømsbroen (Big Current Bridge) from Vordingborg, Falster is shaped like a tiny South America and has excellent blond **beaches** to rival those of its tropical twin. Among the best are the southeastern Marielyst and southernmost Gedser. Almost everywhere on the island you'll find cafés, facilities, and water-sports rentals. Falster is also one of the country's major producers of sugar beets.

Dining and Lodging

$$$ ✕ **Czarens Hus.** This stylish old inn dates back more than 200 years, when it was a guest house and supply store for area farmers and merchants. Deep-green walls, gold trim, and chandeliers provide a background for antique furnishings. The specialty of the house is Continental Danish cuisine, which translates as creative beef and fish dishes, often served with cream sauces. Try the *Zar Beuf* (calf tenderloin in a mushroom-and-onion cream sauce). ✉ *Langgade 2,* ☎ 54/85–28–29. *Jacket required. AE, DC, MC, V.*

$$$ ✕ **Steenhus.** Done up in bright pastels, this central and very popular restaurant is touted as one of the best in the area. The menu includes traditional Danish dishes, such as schnitzel and fresh fish, as well as more daring Danish specialties, such as duck with raspberry and chanterelle-mushroom sauce. It's dimly lit, with high-back striped booths and benches and dark wood. ✉ *Torvet,* ☎ 54/85–82–82. *DC, MC, V. Closed Dec. 24–Jan. 2.*

$$ ✕▥ **Hotel Falster.** This sleek and efficient hotel accommodates conference guests as well as vacationers, with an ambience that's comfortable and businesslike. Rustic brick walls and Danish antiques mix with sleek Danish-design lamps and sculpture. Rooms are comfortably done with dark wood and modular furniture. ✉ *Skovalleen, Nykøbing Falster, DK-4800,* ☎ 54/85–93–93, ℻ 54/82–21–99. *70 rooms. Restaurant, bar, meeting room. AE, DC, MC, V.*

Outdoor Activities and Sports

The 18-hole **Sydsjælland Golf Klub** is on Falster (✉ Præstolandevej 39, Mogenstrup, ☎ 53/76–15–55). Over 25 years old, the park course is lined with a number of small lakes.

Sakskøbing

❹❺ *19 km (12 mi) west of Nykøbing Falster.*

The history of Lolland dates back more than 1,000 years, to a man named Saxe, who sat at the mouth of the fjord and collected a toll. He later cleared the surrounding land and leased it. It became known as Saxtorp and eventually Sakskøbing, the island's capital. Though most people head straight for the beaches, the area has a few sights, including an excellent car museum in the central 13th-century **Ålholm Slot** (castle), with more than 150 vehicles and a water tower with a smiling face. The town is accessible by bridge from Nykøbing Falster. ✉ *Parkvej 7, Nysted,* ☎ 53/87–15–09. ▦ *Car museum DKr50; castle DKr50. Combination ticket DKr90.* ☉ *Car museum June–Aug., daily 11–5; Sept.–May, weekends 11–4. Castle June–Aug., daily 11–5; Sept.–May, weekends 11–4.*

☾ The **Knuthenborg Safari Park** on Lolland, just 8 kilometers (5 miles) west of Sakskøbing, has a drive-through range where you can rubberneck at tigers, zebras, rhinoceroses, and giraffes, and pet camels, goats, and ponies. Besides seeing 20 species of animals, children can also play in Miniworld, which has a jungle gym, a minitrain, and other rides. ✉ *Knuthenborg Safaripark, DK-4930 Maribo,* ☎ 53/88–80–89. ▦ *DKr70.* ☉ *May–Sept. 15.*

☾ On the island of Lolland, the **Middelaldercentret** (Center for the Middle Ages) is a reconstructed medieval village. Especially geared toward children, the center invites school classes to dress up in period costumes and experience life from a millennium ago. Day guests can participate in activities that change weekly—from cooking to medieval knife making to animal herding and, on weekends, folk dances and other cultural happenings. ⊠ *Nykøbing Falster, 90 min south of Copenhagen,* ☎ *54/86–19–34.* 🖼 *DKr35.* ☉ *May–mid-Sept., Tues.–Sat., 10–4, Sun. 10–5.*

Dining and Lodging

$$ ✕🖼 **Lalandia.** This massive water-park hotel has an indoor pool, a beach-side view, and lots of happy families. Located on the southern coast of Lolland, about 27 km (16 miles) southwest of Sakskøbing, the modern white apartments, with full kitchen and bath, accommodate up to eight people. There are three family-style restaurants—a steak house, an Italian buffet, and a pizzeria. ⊠ *Røbdy Havn, DK–4970 Rødby,* ☎ *54/60–42–00,* 🅵🅰🆇 *54/60–41–44. 636 apartments. 3 restaurants, bar, indoor pool, sauna, 9-hole golf course, 5 tennis courts, health club, playground, meeting rooms. AE, DC, MC, V.*

$ ✕🖼 **Hotel Saxkjøbing.** Behind its yellow half-timber facade, this comfortable hotel is short on character and frills, but the rooms are bright, sunny, and modern, if very simply furnished. In the center of town, the hotel is convenient to everything. Its family-style restaurant serves pizzas, steaks, and salads. ⊠ *Torvet 9, Saxkjøbing, DK–4990,* ☎ *53/89–40–39,* 🅵🅰🆇 *53/89–53–50. 30 rooms, 20 with bath. Restaurant, bar, meeting room. AE, DC, MC.*

En Route Disneyland Paris may be floundering, but **BonBon Land,** in the tiny southern Sjælland town of Holme Olstrup between Rønnede and Næstved, attracts thousands of children and their parents every day. In fact, it ranks among the most visited attractions in the country, especially popular with the Danes themselves. Filled with rides and friendly costumed grown-ups, the park is an old-fashioned playland, with a few eating and drinking establishments thrown in for adults. ☎ *53/76–26–00 or 53/76–33–00.* 🖼 *DKr84, DKr95 during the high season.* ☉ *Early May–mid-June and early Aug.–mid-Sept., daily 10–7; mid-June–early Aug., daily 10–9.*

Halsskov

46 *95 km (60 mi) northwest of Falster, 110 km (69 mi) southwest of Copenhagen.*

Europe's second-longest tunnel-bridge (18 kilometers/11 miles) will soon link Halsskov, on west Sjælland, to Nyborg, on east Fyn. Rail traffic is scheduled to commence on the West bridge and tunnel in June, 1997; auto traffic will commence in 1998, on the east and west bridge. The **Storebælt Udstillings Center** (Great Belt Exhibition Center), detailing the work, includes videos and models and makes for an informative stop while you're waiting for a ferry. ⊠ *Halsskov Odde,* ☎ *58/35–01–00.* 🖼 *DKr35.* ☉ *Oct.–Apr., Tues.–Sun. 10–5; May–Sept., daily 10–8.*

Outoor Activities and Sports

Just 15 kilometers (10 miles) east of Slagelse and 30 kilometers (19 miles) east of Halsskov is the Suså (Sus River), where you can arrange hourly, day- and weeklong trips. Call **Susåen Kanoudlejning** regarding canoe rentals (☎ *53/64–61–44*).

The 18-hole **Korsør Course** (⊠ Ørnumvej 8, Korsør, ☎ *53/57–18–36*) is in Korsør, less than 3 kilometers (2 miles) south of Halsskov.

Shopping

In Næstved, 49 kilometers (31 miles) southeast of Halsskov, the **Holmegaards Glassværker** (Glass Workshop) (Glassværksvej 52, Fensmark, ☎ *55/54–62–00*) sells seconds of glasses, lamps, and occasionally art glass, with savings of up to 50% off the wholesale cost.

OFF THE
BEATEN PATH

TRÆLLEBORG – Viking enthusiasts will want to head 18 kilometers (11 miles) east from Halsskov to Slagelse to see its excavated Viking encampment with a reconstructed army shelter. No longer content to rely on farmer warriors, the Viking hierarchy designed the geometrically exact camp within a circular, moated rampart, thought to be of Asian inspiration. The 16 barracks, of which there is one model, could accommodate 1,300 men. ⌧ *Trælleborg Allé*, ☎ *53/54–95–06.* ⌧ *DKr15.* ⊙ *Apr.–Sept., daily 10–6.*

Sjælland and Its Islands A to Z

Arriving and Departing

BY CAR

There are several **DSB** car ferries from Germany. They connect Kiel to Bagenkop, on the island of Langeland (from there, drive north to Spodsbjerg and take another ferry to Lolland, which is connected to Falster and Sjælland by bridges); Puttgarden to Rødbyhavn on Lolland; and Travemünde and Warnemünde to Gedser on Falster. Sjælland is connected to Fyn, which is connected to Jylland, by bridges and frequent ferries. If you are driving from Sweden, take a car ferry from either Helsingborg to Helsingør or Limhamn to Dragør. Or sail directly to Copenhagen (☞ Arriving and Departing by Car, in Copenhagen Essentials, *above*). In Denmark, call DSB (☎ 33/14–88–80); in Sweden, call DSB Sweden (☎ 46/31–80–57–00).

BY PLANE

Copenhagen's **Kastrup Airport** is Sjælland's only airport (☞ Arriving and Departing by Plane in Copenhagen Essentials, *above*).

BY TRAIN

Most train routes to Sjælland, whether international or domestic, are directed to Copenhagen. Routes to north and south Sjælland almost always require a transfer at Copenhagen's main station. For timetables, call **DSB** (☎ 33/14–17–01).

Getting Around

BY CAR

Highways and country roads throughout Sjælland are excellent, and traffic—even around Copenhagen—is manageable most of the time. As elsewhere in Denmark, be careful to give right-of-way to the bikes driving to the right of the traffic.

BY PUBLIC TRANSPORTATION

The **Copenhagen Card,** which affords free train and bus transport, as well as admission to museums and sights, is valid within the HT-bus and rail system, which extends north to Helsingør, west to Roskilde, and south to Køge (☞ Getting Around in Copenhagen Essentials, *above*). Every town in Sjælland has a central train station, usually within walking distance of hotels and sights. (For long distances, buses are not convenient.) The only part of the island not connected to the DSB network is the sliver of northwestern peninsula known as Sjællands Odde (Zealand's Tongue). Trains leave from Holbæk to Højby, where you can bus to the tip of the point. For information, call the private railway company **Odsherrede** (☎ 53/41–00–03). Two vintage trains (dating from the 1880s) run from Helsingør and Hillerød (☎ 48/30–00–30 or 42/12–00–98) to Gilleleje.

Contacts and Resources

EMERGENCIES

Police, fire, or **ambulance** (☎ 112). **Helsingør Hospital** (⌧ Esrumvej 145, ☎ 48/29–29–29). **Roskilde Hospital** (⌧ Roskilde Amtssygehus,

Køgevej 7, ☎ 46/32–32–00). **Helsingør Pharmacy** (✉ Axeltorvs, Groskenstræde 2A, ☎ 49/21–12–23). **Stengades Pharmacy,** (✉ Stengade 46, ☎ 49/21–86–00). **Roskilde Pharmacy** (✉ Dom Apoteket, Algade 8, ☎ 42/35–40–16). **Svane Apoteket** (✉ Skomagergade 12, ☎ 42/35–83–00).

Check with the local tourism boards for general sightseeing tours in the larger towns or for self-guided walking tours. Most tours of Sjælland begin in Copenhagen. For information, call Vikingbus (☎ 31/57–26–00) or Copenhagen Excursion (☎ 31/54–06–06). The Roskilde **Vikingland Tour** (6 hours) includes the market and cathedral, Christian IV's Chapel, and the Viking Ship Museum. The **Afternoon Hamlet Tour** (4½ hours) includes Frederiksborg Castle and the exterior of Fredenborg Palace. The **Castle Tour of North Zealand** (7 hours) visits Frederiksborg Castle and the outside of Fredenborg Palace, and stops at Kronborg Castle.

The turn-of-the-century *Saga Fjord* (Viking Ship Museum) (✉ Vikingeskibshallen, ☎ 42/35–35–75) gives tours of the waters of the Roskildefjord from April through September; meals are served on board. Schedules vary.

Helsingør (✉ Havnepladsen 3, ☎ 49/21–13–33). **Hillerød** (✉ Slotsgade 52, ☎ 42/26–28–52). **Køge** (✉ Vestergade 1, ☎ 53/65–58–00). **Lolland** (✉ Østergårdgade 7, Nykøbing Falster), ☎ 54/85–13–03). **Roskilde** (✉ Fondens Bro 3, ☎ 42/35–27–00). **Sakskøbing** (in summer, ✉ Torvegade 4, ☎ 53/89–56–30; in winter, ☎ 53/89–45–72). **Stege** and **Møn** (✉ Storegade 2, Stege, ☎ 55/81–44–11).

FYN AND THE CENTRAL ISLANDS

Christened the Garden of Denmark by its most famous son, Hans Christian Andersen, Fyn (Funen) is the smaller of the country's two major islands. A patchwork of vegetable fields and flower gardens, the flat-as-a-board countryside is relieved by beech glades and swan ponds. Manor houses and castles pop up from the countryside like magnificent mirages. Some of northern Europe's best-preserved castles are here: the 12th-century Nyborg Slot, travel pinup Egeskov Slot, and the lavish Valdemars Slot. The fairy-tale cliché often attached to Denmark really does spring from this provincial isle, where the only faint pulse emanates from Odense, its capital. Trimmed with thatched houses and green parks, the city makes the most of the Andersen legacy but surprises with a rich arts community at the Brandts Klædefabrik, a former textile factory turned museum compound.

The towns described in this tour are organized in the order you would visit them when traveling from one to the next by road. It's even quick and easy to reach the smaller islands of Langeland and Tåsinge—both are connected to Fyn by bridges. Slightly more isolated is Ærø, where the town of Ærøskøbing, with its painted half-timber houses and winding streets, seems caught in a delightful time warp.

Nightlife and the Arts
Castle concerts are held throughout the summer at Egeskov, Nyborg, and Valdemar castles and the rarely opened Krengenrup manor house near Assens. Check with the local tourism office for schedules.

Outdoor Activities and Sports
Flat and smooth, Fyn is perfect for biking. Packages with bike rental, hotel accommodations, and half-board for the entire region are avail-

Fyn and the Central Islands

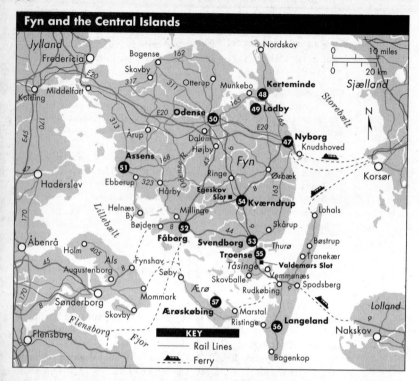

able from **Hotel Svendborg** (✉ Centrumpladsen, 5700 Svendborg, ☎ 62/21–17–00). For maps and tips, contact the local tourist offices.

Shopping

Wednesday and Saturday are market days in towns across Fyn throughout the summer. Often held in the central square, these morning markets offer fresh produce, flowers, and cheeses. Check with the local tourist office for details.

Nyborg

47 *75 km (47 mi) west of Copenhagen, including ferry passage across the Great Belt; 30 km (19 mi) southeast of Odense.*

Most visitors begin their tour of Fyn in Nyborg, a 13th-century town that was Denmark's capital during the Middle Ages. The city's major landmark, the moated 12th-century **Nyborg Slot** (castle), was the seat of the Danehof, the Danish parliament from 1200 to 1413. It was here that King Erik Klipping signed the country's first constitution, the Great Charter, in 1282. Besides geometric wall murals and an armory collection, the castle houses changing art exhibits. ✉ *Slots-pladsen,* ☎ *65/31–02–07.* ⊡ *DKr20.* ☉ *Mar.–May and Sept.–Oct., Tues.–Sun. 10–3; June–Aug., daily 10–5.*

Cross Gammel Torv and walk down the street to the **Nyborg Museum,** housed in a half-timber merchant's house from 1601, for a picture of 17th-century life. Besides furnished rooms, there's a small brewery. ✉ *Slotspladsen 11,* ☎ *65/31–02–07.* ⊡ *Dkr10.* ☉ *Mar.–May, Tues.–Sun. 10–3; June–Aug., daily 10–5; Sept.–Oct., Tues.–Sun. 10–3.*

Dining and Lodging

$$ ✕ **Danehofkroen.** Outside Nyborg Slot, this family-run restaurant does a brisk lunch business, serving traditional Danish meals to tourists who enjoy a view of the castle and its tree-lined moat. The menu is meat-and-potatoes, with such dishes as *flæskesteg* (sliced pork served with the crisp rind). ⊠ *Slotsplads,* ☎ *65/31–02–02. Reservations essential. No credit cards. Closed Mon.*

$$$$ ✕⊞ **Hesselet.** This modern hotel looks like a brick slab outside, a refined Anglo-Asian sanctuary inside. The guest rooms are furnished with cushy, modern furniture, and most have a splendid view of the Storebælt (Great Belt). ⊠ *Christianslundsvej 119, 5800 Nyborg,* ☎ *65/31–30–29,* FAX *65/31–29–58. 46 rooms, 4 suites. Restaurant, room service, indoor pool, sauna, meeting rooms. AE, DC, MC, V.*

Shopping
Many of Fyn's manor houses and castles now double as antiques emporiums. The largest is at **Hindemae** (⊠ near Rte. 315, 12 km/7 mi west of Nyborg, Exit 46 or 47 in Ullerslee, ☎ 65/35–22–05). A modest selection of antiques is for sale at **Hønnerup Hougård** (⊠ Hougårdsvej 6, Hønnerup, 40 km/25 mi northwest of Nyborg, Exit 55 to Route 161 toward Middelfart; follow the signs to Hønnerup; ☎ 64/49–13–00).

Kerteminde

48 *21 km (13 mi) north of Nyborg, 20 km (13 mi) northeast of Odense.*

Kerteminde is an important fishing village and picturesque summer resort. On Langegade, walk past the neat half-timber houses to Møllebakken and the museum of the Danish painter **Johannes Larsen** (1867–1961). Across from a crimson strawberry patch and a 100-year-old windmill, the artist built a modest country cottage that has been perfectly preserved, right down to the teacups. In front, there's a sculpture of a woman by Kai Nielsen. Local legend has it that one night, after a particularly wild party in Copenhagen, its legs were broken off. An ambulance was called, and once it arrived, the enraged driver demanded that the artists pay a fine. A chagrined Larsen paid, and in return kept the wounded sculpture. ⊠ *Møllebakken,* ☎ *65/32–37–27.* ⊡ *DKr30.* ☉ *Mar.–May and Sept.–Oct., Tues.–Sun. 10–4; Nov.–Feb., Wed. and Sun. noon–4; June–Aug., daily 10–5.*

Dining
$$ ✕ **Rudolph Mathis.** This busy harborside restaurant is topped by two chimneys venting open grills that broil popular fish dishes, such as catfish with butter, fennel, and Pernod sauce, and grilled turbot in green-pepper-and-lime sauce. ⊠ *Dosserengen 13,* ☎ *65/32–32–33. AE, DC, MC, V. Closed Mon. Jan.–Mar., Sun. Oct. and Dec.*

Shopping
Just a few miles north of Kerteminde is **Bjørnholt Keramik** (⊠ Risingevej 12, Munkebo, ☎ 65/97–40–90), where you can watch ceramics in the making.

Ladby

49 *4 km (2½ mi) south of Kerteminde, 16 km (10 mi) east of Odense.*

The village of Ladby is best known as the home of the 1,100-year-old remains of the **Ladbyskibet.** This Viking chieftain's ship burial is complete with hunting dogs and horses for his trip to Valhalla—the afterlife. ⊠ *Vikingevej 12,* ☎ *65/32–16–67.* ⊡ *DKr20.* ☉ *Mar.–mid-May, daily 10–4; mid-May–mid-Sept., daily 10–6; mid-Sept.–Oct., daily 10–4; Nov.–Feb., weekends 11-3.*

Odense

 20 km (12 mi) southwest of Ladby on Route 165, 144 km (90 mi) west of Copenhagen.

It's no coincidence that Odense, the capital of Fyn and third largest city in Denmark, is reminiscent of a storybook village—much of its charm is built upon the legend of its most famous son, author Hans Christian Andersen.

Begin at the flourishing Kongens Have (King's Garden) and 18th-century Odense Castle, now a government building, and walk east on Stationsvej to Thomas B. Thriges Gade and Hans Jensens Stræde, where the **Hans Christian Andersen Hus** (Hans Christian Andersen House) stands in a neighborhood of half-timber houses and cobbled streets. Inside, the storyteller's life is chronicled through his photographs, drawings, letters, and personal belongings. There's also a library with Andersen's works in more than 100 languages, where you can listen to fairy tales on tape. ⊠ *Hans Jensenstraede 37-45,* ☎ *66/13–13–72.* ▣ *DKr25.* ☉ *Sept.–May, daily 10–4; June–Aug., daily 9–6.*

At the end of Hans Jensens Stræde is the sleek **Carl Nielsen Museum,** which has multimedia exhibits of the life and work of Denmark's most famous composer (1865–1931) and of his wife, the sculptor Anne Marie Carl-Nielsen. ⊠ *Claus-Bergs Gade 11,* ☎ *66/13–13–72, ext. 4671.* ▣ *DKr15.* ☉ *Daily 10–4.*

Take a left on Claus-Bergs Gade to **Møntergården,** Odense's museum of urban history, which occupies four 17th-century row houses in a shady, cobbled courtyard. Exhibits range from interiors of the Middle Ages to Denmark's Nazi occupation to an impressive coin collection. ⊠ *Overgade 48–50,* ☎ *66/13–13–72.* ▣ *DKr15.* ☉ *Daily 10–4.*

Toward the pedestrian zone of St. Knuds Kirkestræde, just in front of the Andersen Park, is the stately **St. Knuds Kirke,** built from the 13th to the 15th century, the only purely Gothic cathedral in Denmark. Inside there's an intricate wooden altar covered with gold leaf, carved by German sculptor Claus Berg. Beneath the sepulchre are the bones of St. (King) Knud, who was killed during a farmers' uprising in 1086, and his brother.

On Munkemøllestræde, the diminutive **H. C. Andersens Barndomshjem** (H. C. Andersen's Childhood Home) is where the young boy and his parents lived in a room barely 5 feet by 6 feet. ⊠ *Hans Jensens Stræde 37-45,* ☎ *66/13–13–72.* ☉ *Jun.–Aug., daily 9–6, Sept.–May, daily 10–4.*

Filosofgangen is the embarkation point for the Odense River Cruises (☎ *65/95–79–96*). Here you can catch a boat (May–mid-Aug., daily 10, 11, 1, 2, 3, and 5, returning 35 minutes later) downriver to the Fruens Bøge (the Lady's Beech Forest) and then walk down Erik Bøghs Sti (Erik Bøgh's footpath) to **Den Fynske Landsby** (the Fyn Village). Among the country's largest open-air museums, it includes 25 farm buildings and workshops, a vicarage, a water mill, and a theater, which in summer stages adaptations of Andersen's tales. Afterward, cruise back to the town center or catch Bus 21 or 22, and walk down the boutique- and café-lined pedestrian street, which in summer is abuzz with street performers, musicians, and brass bands. ⊠ *Sejerskovvej,* ☎ *66/13–13–72.* ▣ *DKr20.* ☉ *Apr.–May and Sept.–Oct., daily 10–4; June–Aug., daily 10–7:30; Nov.–Mar., Sun. and holidays 10–4.*

North of the river and parallel to Kongensgade is the artist compound of **Brandt's Klædefabrik.** A former textile factory, the four-story building now houses the Museet for Fotokunst (the Museum of Photographic

Art), Danmarks Grafiske Museum (the Danish Graphics Museum), the Dansk Presse Museum (the Danish Press Museum), and Kunsthallen (an art gallery). Exhibits vary widely from national to international offerings, but the photography museum and the art gallery especially show experimental work. ⊠ *Brandt's Passage 37,* ☎ *66/13–78–97.* ⊠ *Photography museum DKr20; graphics museum DKr20; press museum DKr5; art gallery DKr25; combined ticket DKr40.* ☉ *Sept.–June, Tues.–Sun. 10–5; July and Aug., daily 10–5.*

Take Bus 91 from the railway center on Jernbanegade 10 kilometers (6 miles) south of Odense to **Hollufgård,** a former 16th-century manor that now houses the city's archaeological department. Although the house itself remains closed, its grounds contain a completely renovated former barn and adjacent buildings that display special exhibits, including the archaeological find of the month, as well as ecology displays. Nearby are a sculpture center, where you can see an artist at work, and a sculpture garden. ⊠ *Hestehaven 201,* ☎ *66/13–13–72.* ⊠ *DKr25.* ☉ *Nov.–Apr., Sun. and Danish holidays 11–4; Apr.–Oct., Tues.–Sun. 10–5.*

Dining and Lodging

$$$ ✕ **Marie Louise.** Near the pedestrian street, this elegant whitewashed dining room glitters with crystal and silver. The daily Franco-Danish menu typically offers such specialties as salmon scallop with bordelaise sauce and grilled veal with lobster-cream sauce. Business and holiday diners are sometimes treated to gratis extras—such as quail's egg appetizers or after-dinner drinks. ⊠ *Lottrups Gaard, Vestergade 70–72,* ☎ *66/17–92–95. Jacket and tie. AE, DC, MC, V. Closed Sun.*

$$$ ✕ **Under Lindetræt.** Once a bakery, this award-winning restaurant is now done up in linen and lace and frequented by well-heeled tourists. Classic French cuisine, such as medallions of beef with lemon-mushroom sauce and poached smoked salmon with green herbs, is served in a private parlor atmosphere, in the glow of low-hanging lamps and a fireplace. ⊠ *Ramsherred 2,* ☎ *66/12–92–86. Jacket required. DC, MC, V.*

$$ ✕ **Den Gamle Kro.** Built within the courtyards of several 17th-century homes, this popular restaurant has walls of ancient stone sliced by a sliding glass roof. The Franco-Danish menu includes fillet of sole stuffed with salmon mousse, and chateaubriand with garlic potatoes, but there's also inexpensive smørrebrød. ⊠ *Overgade 23,* ☎ *66/12–14–33. DC, MC, V.*

$$ ✕ **Frank A.** Guarded by a larger-than-life-size wooden bulldog named
★ Tobias, this merry meeting place is dominated by high-kitsch curios and paintings and an enormous collection of bric-a-brac. Friendly waiters serve drinks and French-inspired Danish dishes, such as ham schnitzel with creamed potatoes and pepper steak flambé, to a mostly local crowd. ⊠ *Jernbanegade 4,* ☎ *66/12–27–57. DC, MC, V.*

$$ ✕ **Restaurant Provence.** A few minutes from the pedestrian street, this intimate black-and-white dining room puts a modern twist on Provençal cuisine, with such dishes as venison in blackberry sauce and tender duck breast cooked in sherry. ⊠ *Dogstræde 31,* ☎ *66/12–12–96. DC, MC, V.*

$ ✕ **Den Grimme Ælling.** The name of this restaurant means the Ugly
★ Duckling, but inside it's simply homey, with pine furnishings and family-style interiors. It's also extremely popular with tourists and locals alike, thanks to an all-you-can-eat buffet heaped with cold and warm dishes. ⊠ *Hans Jensens Stræde 1,* ☎ *65/91–70–30. DC, MC.*

$ ✕ **Målet.** A lively crowd calls this sports club its neighborhood bar; after the steaming plates of schnitzel served in a dozen ways, soccer is the chief delight of the house. ⊠ *Jernbanegade 17,* ☎ *66/17–82–41. Reservations not accepted. No credit cards.*

$$$ ⊞ **Grand Hotel.** A century old, with renovated fin-de-siècle charm, this imposing four-story, brick-front hotel greets guests with old-fashioned luxury. The original stone floors and chandeliers lead to a wide staircase and upstairs guest rooms that are modern, with plush furnishings and sleek marble bathrooms. ⊠ *Jernabanegade 18, 5000 Odense C,* ☎ *66/11–71–71,* FAX *66/14–11–71. 134 rooms, 13 suites. Room service, sauna. AE, DC, MC, V.*

$ ⊞ **Hotel Ydes.** This bright, colorful hotel is a good bet for students and budget-conscious travelers tired of barracks-type accommodations. The plain, white hospital-style rooms are spotless and comfortable. ⊠ *Hans Tausensgade 11, 5000 Odense C,* ☎ *66/12–11–31. 30 rooms, 24 with bath. Café. MC, V.*

Nightlife and the Arts

In summer the thespians of the **Odense Street Theater** parade through the streets, dramatizing the tales of the town's most famous son, Hans Christian Andersen. **Den Fynske Landsby** has regular Andersen plays from mid-July to mid-August. Call the Odense tourist office for show times.

Odense's central Arcade is an entertainment mall, with bars, restaurants, and live music ranging from corny sing-alongs to hard rock. For a quiet evening, stop by **Café Biografen** (⊠ Brandt's Passage, ☎ 66/13–16–16) for a cup of espresso or a beer, a light snack, and the atmosphere of an old movie house. Or settle in to see one of the wide variety of films screened here.

Fyn's sole casino is in the slick glass atrium of the **SAS Hans Christian Andersen Hotel** (⊠ Claus Bergs Gade 7, Odense, ☎ 66/14–78–00), where you can gamble at blackjack, roulette, and baccarat.

At the **All Night Boogie Dance Café** (⊠ Nørregade 21, ☎ 66/14–00–39), a laid-back crowd grooves to pop, disco, and '60s music.

The **Atlantic Night Club** (⊠ Overgade 45, ☎ 65/91–05–27) is chic, with revolving mirror balls and strobe lights.

The Cotton Club (⊠ Pantheonsgade 5C, ☎ 66/12–55–25), with its crowd of grizzly old-timers and earnest youths, is a venue for traditional jazz.

Dexter's (⊠ Vindergade 65, ☎ 66/13–68–88) has all kinds of jazz—from Dixieland to fusion.

Outdoor Activities and Sports

The **Odense Eventyr Golfklub** (☎ 66/17–11–44) is 4 kilometers (2½ miles) southwest of Odense, and was built in 1993. The 27-hole **Odense Golf Klub** (☎ 65/95–90–00), 6 kilometers (4 miles) southeast of Odense, was built in 1980 and is relatively flat, with some trees and woods. The nine-hole driving range and putting greens (☎ 65/96–80–08) in **Blommenlyst** are 12 kilometers (7 miles) from Odense, west toward Middlefart.

Shopping

Uromageren Hus (The Mobile Maker's House) (⊠ Ravnsherred 4, ☎ 66/12–70–44) is just across from the H. C. Andersen Museum. Inside, handmade mobiles range from simple paper hangings to intricate ceramic balloons.

Assens

51 *38 km (24 mi) south of Odense (take Rte. 168; then drive south on the Strandvej [Beach Road] off Rte. 323 in the town of Å).*

★ Near the quiet town of Assens is one of the most extraordinary private gardens in Denmark: Tove Sylvest's sprawling **Seven Gardens.** A privately owned botanical United Nations, the gardens represent the flora of seven European countries, including many plants rare to Denmark. ⊠ Å *Strandvej 62, Ebberup,* ☎ *64/74–12–85.* ⌧ DKr40. ☉ *May–Oct., daily 10–5.*

Children will appreciate a detour 18 kilometers (11 miles) northeast to Fyn's **Terrarium,** where they can examine all kinds of slippery and slithery creatures, including snakes, iguanas, alligators, and the nearly extinct blue frog. ⊠ *Kirkehelle 5, Vissenbjerg,* ☎ *64/47–18–50.* ⌧ *DKr30.* ☉ *May–Aug., daily 10–6; Sept.–Apr., daily 10–4.*

Fåborg

52 *30 km (18 mi) south of Odense (via Rte. 43).*

This is a lovely 12th-century town whose surrounding beaches are invaded by sun-seeking Germans and Danes in summer. Four times a day you can hear the dulcet chiming of a carillon, the island's largest. In the center of town is the controversial *Ymerbrønden* sculpture by Kai Nielsen, depicting a naked man drinking from an emaciated cow while it licks a baby.

The 18th-century **Den Gamle Gård** (Old Merchant's House), of 1725, chronicles the local history of Fåborg through furnished interiors as well as exhibits of glass and textiles. ⊠ *Holkegade 1,* ☎ *62/61–33–38.* ⌧ *DKr20.* ☉ *May–Sept., daily 10:30–4:30.*

The **Fåborg Museum for Fynsk Malerkunst** (Fyn Painting Museum) has a good collection of turn-of-the-century paintings and sculpture by the Fyn Painters, a school of artists whose work captures the dusky light of the Scandinavian sun. ⊠ *Grønnegade 75,* ☎ *62/61–06–45.* ⌧ *DKr25.* ☉ *Apr.–May and Sept.–Oct., daily 10–4; Nov.–Mar., daily 11–3; June–Aug., daily 10–5.*

Dining and Lodging

$ ✕ **Vester Skerninge Kro.** Midway between Fåborg and Svendborg, this traditional inn is cluttered and comfortable. Pine tables are polished from years of serving hot stews and homemade *mediste pølse* (mild grilled sausage) and *æggkage* (fluffy omelet made with cream, smoked bacon, chives, and tomatoes). ⊠ *Krovej 9, Vester Skerninge,* ☎ *62/24–10–04. No credit cards. Closed Tues.*

$$$$ ✕⌂ **Falsled Kro.** Once a smuggler's hideaway, the 500-year-old Falsled Kro is now one of Denmark's most elegant inns. A favorite among well-heeled Europeans, it has appointed its cottages sumptuously with European antiques and stone fireplaces. The restaurant combines French and Danish cuisines, using ingredients from its garden and markets in Lyon. ⊠ *Assensvej 513, DK–5642 Millinge,* ☎ *62/68–11–11,* ⌧ *62/68–11–62. 14 rooms, 3 apartments. Restaurant, room service, 3-hole golf course, horseback riding, boating, helipad. AE, DC, MC, V. Closed mid-Dec.–Feb.*

$$$$ ✕⌂ **Steensgaard Herregårdspension.** A long avenue of beeches leads to this 700-year-old moated manor house, 7 kilometers (4½ miles) northwest of Fåborg. The rooms are elegant, with antiques, four-poster beds, and yards of silk damask. The fine restaurant serves wild game from the manor's own reserve. ⊠ *Steensgaard 4, 5642 Millinge,* ☎

62/61–94–90, ⒡ᴬˣ 62/61–78–61. *15 rooms, 13 with bath. Restaurant, tennis court, horseback riding, helipad. AE, DC, MC, V. Closed Jan.*

Svendborg

⓼ *25 km (15½ mi) east of Fåborg (via Rte. 44 east), 44 km (28 mi) south of Odense.*

Svendborg is Fyn's second-largest town, and one of the country's most important—not to mention happy—cruise harbors. It celebrates its eight-century-old maritime traditions every July, when old Danish wooden ships congregate in the harbor for the circular Fyn rundt, or regatta. Play your cards right, and you might hitch aboard and shuttle between towns. Contact the tourist board or any agreeable captain. With many charter-boat options and good marinas, Svendborg is an excellent base from which to explore the hundreds of islands of the South Fyn Archipelago.

In Svendborg center is Torvet—the town's market square. To the left on Fruestræde is the black-and-yellow Anne Hvides Gård, the oldest secular structure in Svendborg and one of the four branches of **Svendborgs Omegns Museum** (Svendborg County Museum). This evocative exhibit includes 18th- and 19th-century interiors and glass and silver collections. ⊠ *Fruestræde 3,* ☏ *62/21–02–61.* ⚏ *DKr20.* ☺ *May–mid-June, daily 10–4; mid-June–Oct., daily 10–5; Nov.–Apr., daily 1–4. Closed weekends Jan.–Feb.*

Take a left on Teatergade and cross Skolegade to Bagergade (Baker's Street), which is lined with some of Svendborg's oldest half-timber houses. On the left, at the corner of Grubbemøllevej and Svinget, is the **Viebæltegård,** the headquarters of the Svendborg County Museum, a former poorhouse. You can wander through dining halls, washrooms, and the "tipsy clink," where inebriated citizens were left to sober up as recently as 1974. ⊠ *Grubbemøllevej 13,* ☏ *62/21–02–61.* ⚏ *DKr20. Combined admission to Anne Hvides and Svendborg Omegns museums DKr25.* ☺ *May–mid-June, daily 10–4; mid-June–Oct., daily 10–5; Nov.–Apr., daily 1–4. Closed weekends Jan.–Feb.*

Dining and Lodging

$$ ✕ **Sandig.** This austere white eatery near the harbor is spartan, but
★ food, not decor, is owner-chef-waiter-dishwasher Volkert Sandig's priority. His daily-changing French-Danish menu includes inventive fish and beef specialties. Try cod served with mussel and garlic sauce or roast veal with mushroom ragout. ⊠ *Kullinggade 1b, Svendborg,* ☏ *62/22–92–11. DC, MC, V. Closed daily 2–6 and Sun.*

$ ✕ **Ærø.** A dim hodgepodge of ship parts and maritime doodads, this harborside restaurant is peopled by brusque waitresses and serious local trenchermen. The menu is staunchly old-fashioned, featuring *frikadeller* (fried meatballs), fried *rødspætte* (plaice) with hollandaise sauce, and dozens of smørrebrød options. ⊠ *Brøgade 1 ved, Ærøfærgen,* ☏ *62/21–07–60. DC, MC, V. Closed Sun.*

$$ ✕🖬 **Margrethesminde.** The Fyn equivalent of a bed-and-breakfast, this manor house is 16 kilometers (10 miles) west of Svendborg. Owners Marlene Philip and Henrik Nielsen have furnished the sunny house with bright colors and modern furnishings, and serve their guests a generous breakfast, ranging from Danish pastries or dark bread and cheese to bacon and eggs. The guest rooms overlook the surrounding countryside. ⊠ *Fåborgvej 154, 5762 Vester Skerninge,* ☏ *62/24–10–44,* ⒡ᴬˣ *62/24–10–62. 2 double rooms (1 with bath), 2 single rooms. Bicycles. MC.*

Nightlife and the Arts

A diverse crowd congregates at **Bortløbne Banje** (⊠ Klosterplads 7, ☎ 62/22–31–21) to hear live rock and blues. **Chess** (⊠ Vestergade 7, ☎ 62/22–17–16) is popular with a young crowd that comes for the live bands. **Crazy Daizy** (⊠ Frederiksgade 6, ☎ 62/21–67–60) attracts a casual, over-21 crowd to dance to oldies and rock. Svendborg doesn't have a permanent jazz club, but the **Orangi** (⊠ Jessens Mole, ☎ 62/22–82–92), an old sailing ship that's moored in the harbor, is a popular summer restaurant with live jazz.

Kværndrup

54 *15 km (9 mi) north of Svendborg, 28 km (18 mi) south of Odense.*

Over this town presides the moated Renaissance **★Egeskov Slot,** one of the best-preserved island-castles in Europe. Peaked with copper spires and surrounded by Renaissance, Baroque, English, and peasant gardens, the castle has an antique-vehicle museum and the world's largest maze, designed by the Danish scientist-turned-poet Piet Hein. The castle is a still a private home, though visitors can see a few of the rooms, including the great hall, the hunting room, and the Riborg Room, where the daughter of the house was locked up from 1599 to 1604 after giving birth to a son out of wedlock. ⊠ *Kværndrup,* ☎ *62/27–10–16.* ⌑ *Castle and museum DKr100.* ☉ *Castle May–June and Aug.–Sept., daily 10–5; July, daily 10–8. Museum May and Sept., daily 10–5; June and Aug., daily 9–6; July, daily 9–8.*

Troense

55 *3 km (2 mi) south of Svendborg (via the Svendborg Sound Bridge), 43 km (27 mi) south of Odense.*

The island of Tåsinge is known for its local 19th-century drama involving Elvira Madigan (recall the movie?) and her married Swedish lover, Sixten Sparre. Preferring heavenly union to earthly separation, they shot themselves and are now buried on the island's central Landet churchyard. It's a tradition for brides to throw their bouquets on the lovers' grave.

Troense is Tåsinge's main town, and one of the country's best-preserved maritime villages, with half-timber buildings opening through hand-carved doors. South of town is **★Valdemars Slot,** dating from 1610, one of Denmark's oldest privately owned castles. Visitors can wander at will through almost all the sumptuously furnished rooms (everything is under electronic surveillance), the libraries, and the candle-lit church. There's also an X-rated 19th-century cigar box that shouldn't be missed. ⊠ *Troense,* ☎ *62/22–61–06 or 62/22–50–04.* ⌑ *DKr45.* ☉ *May and Sept.–Oct., daily 10–5; June–Aug., daily 10–6.*

Dining

$$$$ ✕ **Restaurant Valdemars Slot.** Beneath the castle, this domed restaurant is ankle-deep in pink carpet and aglow with candlelight. Fresh ingredients from France and Germany and wild game from the castle's preserve are the staples of the ever-changing menu. Venison with cream sauce and duck breast à l'orange are typical of the French-inspired cuisine. A less expensive annex, Den Grå Dame, serves traditional Danish food. ⊠ *Slotsalleen 100, Troense,* ☎ *62/22–59–00. Jacket and tie. AE, DC. Closed Mon.*

Shopping

For delicate hand-blown glass, visit **Glasmagerne** (⊠ Vemmenæsvej 10, Tåsinge, ☎ 62/54–14–94).

Langeland

 16 km (10 mi) southeast of Troense, 64 km (40 mi) southwest of Odense.

Accessible by a causeway bridge from Tåsinge and also by a one-hour ferry ride from Fåborg, Langeland is the largest island of the southern archipelago, rich in relics, with smooth, tawny beaches. Bird-watching is excellent on the southern half of the island, where migratory flocks roost before setting off on their cross-Baltic journey. To the south are Ristinge and Bagenkop, two towns with good beaches; at Bagenkop you can catch the ferry to Kiel, Germany.

Outdoor Activities and Sports

Langeland has particularly rich waters for fishing, with cod, salmon, flounder, and gar. For package tours, contact **Ole Dehn** (⊠ Søndergade 22, Lohals, DK–5953 Tranekær, ☎ 62/55–17–00).

Ærøskøbing

★ *30 km (19 mi) south of Svendborg; 74 km (46 mi) south of Odense, plus a one-hour ferry ride, either from Svendborg or Langeland.*

The island of Ærø, where country roads wend through fertile fields, is aptly called the Jewel of the Archipelago. About 27 kilometers (16 miles) southeast of Søby on the island's north coast, the storybook town of Ærøskøbing is the port for ferries from Fåborg. Established as a market town in the 13th century, it did not flourish until it became a sailing center during the 1700s. At night when the street lights illuminate the cobbled streets, it is as though time has stood still.

Ferries provide the only access to the island. The ferry from Svendborg to Ærøskøbing takes 1 hour, 15 minutes. In addition, there's a one-hour ferry from Fåborg to Søby, a town on the northwest end of the island; and a shorter one from Rudkøbing—on the island of Langeland—to Marstal, on the eastern end of Ærø.

Down the main central road in Ærøskøbing, take a left onto Smegade to visit one of Denmark's most arresting shrines to obsession. History is recorded in miniature at the **Flaskeskibssamlingen** (Bottle Ship Collection), thanks to a former ship's cook known as Peter Bottle, who painstakingly built nearly 2,000 bottle ships in his day. The combination of his life's work and the enthusiastic letters he received from fans and disciples around the world make for a surprisingly moving collection. ⊠ *Smegade 22, Ærøskøbing,* ☎ *62/52–29–51.* ⊠ *DKr15.* ☉ *July–mid-Aug., daily 10–5; rest of yr, daily 10–4.*

Dining and Lodging

$$ ✕⌂ **Ærøhus.** A half-timber building with a steep red roof, the Ærøhus looks like a rustic cottage on the outside, an old, but overly renovated aunt's house on the inside. Hanging pots and slanted walls characterize the public areas, and pine furniture and cheerful duvets keep the guest rooms simple and bright. The garden's five cottages have small terraces. ⊠ *Vestergade 38, DK–5970,* ☎ *62/52–10–03,* FAX *62/52–21–23. 30 rooms, 17 with bath; 5 cottages. Restaurant. AE, V. Closed Dec. 27–Jan. 20.*

Fyn and the Central Islands A to Z

Arriving and Departing

BY CAR

From Copenhagen, take the E20 west to Halsskov, near Korsør, and drive aboard the Great Belt ferry, which costs about DKr300 per car, with up to five passengers and a reservation. For ferry reservations, call **DSB** (☎ 33/14–88–00). The ferry departs daily every 40 minutes. You'll arrive in Knudshoved, near Nyborg, which is a half hour from either Odense or Svendborg. At press time (December 1996), there still were no definite plans regarding costs for passage on the Great Belt Bridge.

BY PLANE
Odense Airport (☎ 65/95–50–72), 11 kilometers (7 miles) north of Odense, is served by Mærsk Air (☎ 65/95–53–55) and Muk Air (☎ 65/95–50–20 or 98/19–03–88), which make eight daily flights between Copenhagen and Odense. The 25-minute hop costs about DKr1,300. You can make reservations with the airlines themselves or through SAS (☎ 32/32–00–00). Metered **airport taxis** charge about DKr140 for the 15-minute drive downtown. A **Mærsk Airbus** meets each flight and stops at the Grand Hotel, Hans Christian Andersen Hotel, and the main railway station. The fare is about DKr60.

BY TRAIN
Trains from Copenhagen's main station depart for the three-hour trip to Odense's train station hourly, every day. Stations in both towns are central, close to hotels and sights. The one-way fare is about DKr150. A reservation costs an additional DKr30 (☎ 33/14–17–01).

Getting Around
BY BICYCLE
With their level terrain and short distances, Fyn and the central islands are perfect for cycling. You can rent bikes at Cykel Biksen (⊠ Nedergade 14–16, Odense, ☎ 66/12–40–98) or Fåborg Sportshandel (⊠ Havnegade 40, Fåborg, ☎ 62/61–28–22).

BY BUS AND TRAIN
Large towns are served by intercity trains. The Nyborg–Odense–Middelfart and the Odense–Svendborg routes are among the two most important. The only other public transportation is by bus. Timetables are posted at all bus stops and central stations. Passengers buy tickets on board and pay according to the distance traveled (☎ 66/11–71–11). For central Odense, the **Odense Eventyrpas** (Adventure Pass), available at the tourism office, affords admission to sights and museums and free city bus and train transport. The cost for a two-day pass is DKr90; for a one-day pass, DKr50.

BY CAR
The highways of Fyn are excellent, and small roads meander beautifully on two lanes through the countryside. Traffic is light except during the height of summer, in highly populated beach areas.

Contacts and Resources
EMERGENCIES
Police, fire, or **ambulance** (☎ 112). **Odense Hospital,** (⊠ J. B. Winsløws Vej, ☎ 66/11–33–33). Emergency **Doctor** between 4 PM and 7 AM, (☎ 65/90–60–10). **Other Emergencies,** call Falck (☎ 66/11–22–22). **Ørnen Apoteket** (⊠ Vestergade 80, Odense, ☎ 66/12–29–70).

GUIDED TOURS
Few towns offer organized tours, but check the local tourist offices for step-by-step walking brochures. The 2½-hour **Odense Walking Tour** departs from the tourist office during July and early August at 11 AM every Tuesday, Wednesday, and Thursday. It includes the exteriors of the Hans Christian Andersen sights and the cathedral. Full-day **Hans Christian Andersen** tours to Odense depart from Copenhagen's Rådhus Pladsen mid-May–mid-September, Sunday at 8:30 AM, and cost DKr460. (Six out of 11 hours are spent in transit.) Call ☎ 31/54–06–06 for reservations.

VISITOR INFORMATION

Most city tourism offices are open weekdays 10–4 during the fall and winter, weekdays 9–5 and Saturdays 10–noon in spring and summer. **Odense Tourist Office** (✉ City Hall, ☎ 66/12–75–20) has information for all of Fyn, including the helpful "Tourist Information on Fyn" brochure. Additional tourist offices include **Kerteminde** (✉ Strandgade 1, ☎ 65/32–11–21), **South Fyn Tourist Board** (✉ Centrumpladsen, Svendborg, ☎ 62/21–09–80), **Nyborg** (✉ Torvet 9, ☎ 65/31–02–80), **Ærøskøbing** (✉ Torvet, ☎ 62/52–13–00).

JYLLAND

Jylland (Jutland), Denmark's western peninsula, is the only part of the country that's naturally connected to mainland Europe; its southern boundary is the frontier with Germany. In contrast to the smooth, post-card-perfect land of Fyn and Sjælland, this Ice Age–chiseled peninsula is bisected at the north by the craggy Limfjord and spiked below by the Danish "mountains." Himmelbjerget, the zenith of this modest range, peaks at 438 feet; farther south, the Yding Skovhøj plateau rises 568 feet—modest hills just about anywhere else.

The first inhabitants of Denmark were hunters who lived in southern Jylland 250,000 years ago. You can see flint tools and artifacts from this period locked away in museums, but the land holds more stirring relics from a later epoch: After 1,000 years, Viking burial mounds and stones still swell the land, some in protected areas, others lying in farmers' fields, tended by grazing sheep.

The windswept landscapes filmed in *Babette's Feast,* the movie version of the Karen Blixen (Isak Dinesen) novel, trace the west coast northward to Skagen, a luminous, dune-covered point (geographically similar to the Outer Banks of North Carolina). To the east, facing Fyn, Jylland is cut by deep fjords rimmed with forests. The center is dotted with castles, parklands, and the famed Legoland. Ribe, Denmark's oldest town, lies to the south and west; Århus and Aalborg, respectively Denmark's second- and fourth-largest cities, face east and have nightlife and sights to rival Copenhagen's.

Nearly three times the size of the rest of Denmark, with long distances between towns, the peninsula of Jylland can easily take at least several days, even weeks, to explore. If you are pressed for time, concentrate on a single tour or a couple of cities. Delightful as they are, the islands are suitable only for those with plenty of time, as many require an overnight stay. The following tour focuses on chunks of the peninsula and is organized as you would explore them with a car.

Outdoor Activities and Sports

Canoe rentals (about DKr180 per day) are available in the lake district, Limfjord, and almost all lakes and rivers. One- to three-day package tours throughout the region are available with either camping or hostel accommodations. For more information, contact the local tourist boards.

The lake district is a great place for fishing and angling. License requirements vary and package tours are also available; contact any local tourist office for details.

Kolding

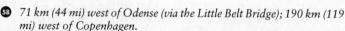

58 *71 km (44 mi) west of Odense (via the Little Belt Bridge); 190 km (119 mi) west of Copenhagen.*

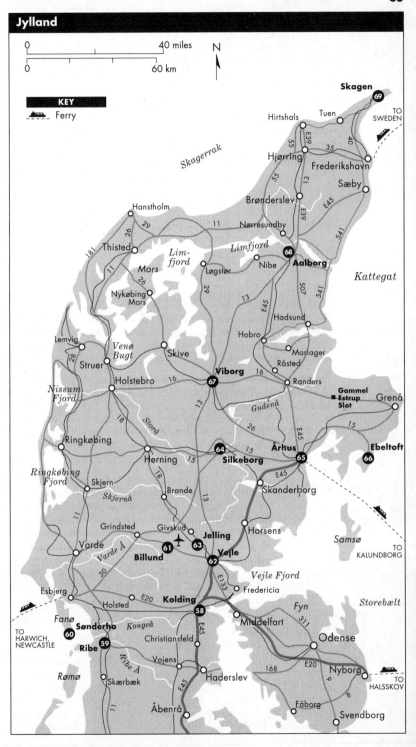

Jylland

0   40 miles   N
0   60 km

KEY
Ferry

Skagen 69
TO SWEDEN
Hirtshals   Tuen
Hjørring
Frederikshavn
Sæby
E39
55
55
35
40
E1
E39
Brønderslev
Hanstholm
Nørresundby
E45
541
29
11
Thisted
Lim-fjord
Limfjord
68 Aalborg
Løgstør   Nibe
Kattegat
26
181
11
Mors
29
507
541
26
Nykøbing Mors
13
E45
Hadsund
Lemvig
Venø Bugt
Skive
Hobro
Mariager
Råsted
Struer
Viborg 67
16
Randers
Gammel Estrup Slot
Grenå
28
Holstebro
16
13
Nissum Fjord
Storå
Gudenå
26
15
Ringkøbing
18
Silkeborg
Århus 65
E45
Ebeltoft
Ringkøbing Fjord
Herning
64
15
15
66
18
Skanderborg
Skjern
Brande
E45
Samsø
Skjernå
13
TO KALUNDBORG
Grindsted
Givskud
Jelling 63
Horsens
11
61
62 Vejle
Varde
Varde Å
Billund
Vejle Fjord
30
E133
Esbjerg
E20
Kolding
Fredericia
Storebælt
Holsted
58
Fyn
Middelfart
Fanø
Sønderho 60
Kongeå
311
Odense
TO HARWICH, NEWCASTLE
Ribe 59
Christiansfeld
E45
E20
Nyborg
Rømø
Vojens
168
Skærbæk
Haderslev
Fåborg
8
TO HALSSKOV
11
Åbenrå
Svendborg
Ribe Å
Skagerrak

Here is the well-preserved **Koldinghus,** a massive stonework structure that was a fortress and then a royal residence during the Middle Ages and is a historical museum today. In the winter of 1808, during the Napoleonic Wars, Spanish soldiers set fire to most of it while trying to stay warm. ⊠ *Rådhusstræde,* ☎ *75/50–15–00, ext. 5400.* ⊠ *DKr30.* ☉ *Daily 10–5.*

Dining and Lodging

$$$ ✕⊞ **Hotel Koldingfjord.** An impressive neoclassical building, this vast
★ hotel has mahogany floors and pyramid skylights. It's five minutes from town and faces the Kolding Fjord and 50 acres of countryside. The rooms vary in size (with 39 in a separate annex), but all have mahogany beds, bright prints, and views of fjord or forest. There's also an excellent French-Danish restaurant. Breakfast is included in the rates. ⊠ *Fjordvej 154, DK–6000 Strandhuse,* ☎ *75/51–00–00,* ⅋⅋ *75/51–00–51. 115 rooms, 8 suites. Restaurant, bar, indoor pool, sauna, 2 tennis courts, health club. AE, DC, MC, V. Closed Dec. 21–Jan. 1.*

★ Ribe

⑤⑨ *60 km (36 mi) southwest of Kolding, 150 km (103 mi) southwest of Århus.*

In the southeastern corner of Jylland, Ribe is well worth the detour: It's the country's oldest town, with a medieval center preserved by the Danish National Trust. From May to mid-September, a night watchman circles the town, telling of its history and singing traditional songs. Visitors who wish to accompany him gather at the main square at 10 PM.

The **Ribe Domkirke** (Cathedral) stands on the site of one of Denmark's earliest churches, built around AD 860. The present structure dates from the 12th century, with a 14th-century bell tower. Note the Cat Head Door, said to be for the exclusive use of the devil. ⊠ *Torvet,* ☎ *75/42–06–19.* ⊠ *DKr5.* ☉ *May, Mon.–Sat. 10–5, Sun. noon–5; June–Aug., Mon.–Sat. 10–6, Sun. noon–6; Sept., Mon.–Sat. 10–5, Sun. noon–5; Oct.–Apr., Mon.–Sat. 11–3, Sun. noon–3.*

Ribe's newest attraction is the **Ribes Vikinger** (Museum for the Viking Period and the Middle Ages), which is divided into several sections. The Viking Center is an outdoor exhibit detailing how the Vikings lived day-to-day, including their homes, food, and crafts—all demonstrated by real people. Another section of the museum chronicles Viking history with conventional exhibits of household goods, tools, and clothing. In addition, there's a multimedia room, with an interactive computer screen (more than 4 feet wide) where you can search for more Viking information in the form of text, pictures, and videos. ⊠ *Odinsplads,* ☎ *75/42–22–22.* ⊠ *DKr30.* ☉ *Nov.–Mar., Tues.–Sun., 10–5; Apr.–June and Sept.–Oct., daily 10–4; July–Aug., daily 10–5.*

Dining and Lodging

$ ✕ **Sælhunden.** This 300-year-old canal-side tavern barely accommodates a dozen tables, but its cozy atmosphere makes it popular with wayfarers and locals. Its name means "male seal"; the only seal mementos left are a few skins and pictures, but you can still order a "seal's special" of cold shrimp, sautéed potatoes, and scrambled eggs or—an old Danish favorite—fat strips of bacon served with cream gravy and boiled potatoes. ⊠ *Skibbroen 13,* ☎ *75/42–09–46. Reservations not accepted. DC, MC, V. Closed for dinner after 8:45.*

$$$ ✕⊞ **Hotel Dagmar.** In Ribe's quaint center, this cozy half-timber hotel
★ encapsulates the charm of the 16th century—with stained-glass windows, sloping wooden floors, and carved chairs. The lavish rooms are

all appointed with antique canopy beds, fat armchairs, and chaise longues. The fine French restaurant serves such specialties as fillet of salmon in sorrel cream sauce. ⊠ *Torvet 1, DK–6760,* ☎ *75/42–00–33,* ℻ *75/42–36–52. 48 rooms. Restaurant, bar, meeting rooms, free parking. AE, DC, MC, V. Closed Dec. 24–Jan. 1.*

$ 🏠 **Ribe Family and Youth Hostel.** In the center of town, this plain, red-brick hostelry is run by helpful wardens Jens Philipsen and Gudrun Rishede. Six- and four-bed family rooms are arranged in clusters of two, each with its own private bath and toilet in a small hallway. There are also eight new four-bed rooms with completely private facilities. They are functional and childproof, with pine bunks and industrial carpeting. ⊠ *Ribehallen, Skt. Pedersgade 16,* ☎ *75/42–06–20,* ℻ *75/42–42–88. 152 beds, in 34 family rooms. Cafeteria, kitchen. No credit cards. Closed Dec.–Jan.*

Sønderho

🙄 *30 km (19 mi) northwest of Ribe, plus 12-min ferry from Esbjerg; 153 km (96 mi) southwest of Århus, plus 12-min ferry from Esbjerg.*

During the 19th century, the tiny island of **Fanø** had an enormous ship-building industry and a fleet second only to Copenhagen's. The shipping industry deteriorated, but the proud maritime heritage remains.

From Fanø's ferry port in Nordby, take a bus south to Sønderho. Along the tiny winding lanes are thatched cottages decorated with ships' relics, figureheads, painted doors, and brass lanterns. You may even see people wearing the traditional costumes, especially on *Sønder-hodag,* a town fest held on the third Sunday in July.

Dining and Lodging

$$ ✕🏠 **Sønderho Kro.** Just 13 kilometers (8 miles) from Fanø's main town
★   of Nordby, this 270-year-old thatched inn is one of Jylland's finest, its charm preserved with a beamed foyer, painted doors, and timbered ceilings. The rooms are gussied up with four-poster beds, elegant tapestries, and gauzy curtains. The Franco-Danish restaurant serves excellent seafood on its old tables. ⊠ *Kropladsen 11, DK–6720, Sønderho,* ☎ *75/16–40–09. 6 rooms, 2 suites. Restaurant. AE, DC, MC, V. Closed weekdays Nov.–Jan., and Feb.*

Billund

🙄 *101 km (63 mi) southwest of Århus.*

★   Billund's only claim to fame is **Legoland,** an amusement park in which everything is constructed from 35 million plastic Lego bricks. Among its incredible structures are scaled-down versions of cities and villages, working harbors and airports, a Statue of Liberty, a statue of Sitting Bull, Mount Rushmore, a safari park, and a Pirate Land. There are also exhibits of toys from pre-Lego days, the most exquisite of which is Titania's Palace, a sumptuous dollhouse built in 1907 by Sir Neville Wilkinson for his daughter. The Lego empire is expanding: The company's goal is to open one park globally every three years, but Danes maintain that theirs, the original, will always be the best. ⊠ *Billund,* ☎ *75/33–13–33.* ▣ *DKr100 adults, DKr90 children.* ☉ *Apr.–Sept., daily 10–8.*

Vejle

🙄 *40 km (25 mi) east of Billund, 73 km (46 mi) southwest of Århus.*

On the east coast, Vejle is beautifully positioned on a fjord, amid forest-clad hills. You can hear the time of day chiming on the old **Dominican**

monastery clock; the clock remains, but the monastery long ago gave way to the town's imposing 19th-century city hall.

In the center of town, at Kirke Torvet, is **Skt. Nicolai Kirke** (St. Nicholas Church). In the left arm of the cross-shape church, lying in a glass Empire-style coffin, is the body of a bog woman, found preserved in a peat marsh in 1835, that dates to 500 BC. The church walls contain the skulls of 23 thieves executed in the 17th century. ✉ Kirke Torvet, ☎ 75/82–41–39. ⏲ May–Sept., weekdays 9–5, Sat. 9–noon, Sun. 9–11:30.

Dining and Lodging

$$$$ ✕🏨 **Munkebjerg Hotel.** Seven kilometers (4½ miles) southeast of town, surrounded by a thick beech forest and majestic views of the Vejle Fjord, this elegant hotel attracts guests who prefer privacy. The rooms overlook the forest and are furnished in blond pine and soft green, and the lobby is rustic. There are also two top-notch French-Danish restaurants and a swank casino. ✉ *Munkebjergvej 125, DK–7100,* ☎ *75/72–35–00,* FAX *75/72–08–86. 145 rooms, 2 suites. 2 restaurants, room service, indoor pool, sauna, tennis court, health club, casino, convention center, helipad. AE, DC, MC, V. Closed Dec. 20–28.*

Nightlife

The casino at the **Munkebjerg Hotel** (✉ Munkebjergvej 125, Vejle, ☎ 75/72–35–00) has blackjack, roulette, baccarat, and slot machines.

Jelling

(63) *10 km (6 mi) northeast of Vejle (via Rte. 18), 83 km (52 mi) southeast of Århus.*

In Jelling, two 10th-century burial mounds mark the seat of King Gorm and his wife, Thyra. Between the mounds are two **Runestener** (runic stones), one of which is Denmark's certificate of baptism, showing the oldest known figure of Christ in Scandinavia. The inscription explains that the stone was erected by Gorm's son, King Harald Bluetooth, who brought Christianity to the Danes in AD 960.

The most scenic way to get to Jelling is via the **vintage steam train** that runs from Vejle every Sunday in July and the first Sunday in August.

Silkeborg

(64) *60 km (38 mi) north of Jelling; 43 km (27 mi) west of Århus.*

At the banks of the River Gudena begins Jylland's lake district. Stretching from Silkeborg in the west to Skanderborg in the east, this area contains some of Denmark's loveliest scenery and most of its meager mountains, including the 438-foot **Himmelbjerget,** at Julsø (Lake Jul). You can climb the narrow paths through the heather and trees to the top, where an 80-foot tower stands sentinel, placed there on Constitution Day in 1875 in memory of King Frederik VII.

The best way to explore the lake district is by water, as the Gudena winds its way some 160 kilometers (100 miles) through lakes and wooded hillsides down to the sea. Take one of the excursion boats or, better still, the world's last coal-fired paddle steamer, ***Hjejlen***, which runs in the summer and is based in Silkeborg. Since 1861 it has paddled its way through narrow stretches of fjord, where the treetops meet overhead, to the foot of the Himmelbjerget. ✉ *Havnen, Silkeborg,* ☎ *86/82–07–66 (reservations).* 🎫 *Round-trip tickets DKr39–DKr76. Departs Silkeborg Harbor 10 and 1:45 Sun. in June, daily mid-June–July.*

★ Silkeborg's main attractions are housed in the **Kulturhistoriske Museum** (Museum of Cultural History): the 2,200-year-old Tollund Man and

Elling Girl, two bog people preserved by natural ingredients in the soil and water. Discovered in 1950, the Tollund Man remains the best-preserved human face from the Iron Age. He was killed by strangulation—the noose remains around his neck—with a day's worth of stubble that can still be seen on his hauntingly serene face. ⊠ *Hovedgådsvej,* ☎ *86/82–15–78.* ☒ *DKr20.* ⊙ *Apr. 15–Oct. 23, daily 10–5; Oct. 24–Apr. 14, Wed. and weekends noon–4.*

Dining

$$ ✕ **Spisehuset Christian VIII.** Cut off from Silkeborg's center by a highway, this tiny crooked building seems transported from another time. Inside it's elegant and busy, with an international group of diners occupying the dozen cramped tables. The inventive menu includes tournedos of New Guinea fowl with mushrooms, and such fish specialties as smoked salmon in snail-and-cream sauce and poached turbot with scallops and spring onions. ⊠ *Christian VIII Vej 54,* ☎ *86/82–25–62. AE, DC, MC, V. Closed Sun.*

Århus

㊞ *40 km (24 mi) east of Silkeborg.*

Århus is Denmark's second-largest city, and, with its funky arts and college community, one of its most pleasant. The town is liveliest during the 10-day **Århus Festival** in September, which combines everything from concerts, theater, and exhibitions to beer tents and sports. In addition, the **Århus International Jazz Festival** in early or mid-July gathers international and local greats. In July, the **Viking Moot** draws aficionados to the beach below the Museum of Prehistory at Moesgård. Activities and exhibits include market booths, ancient defense techniques, and rides on Viking ships.

A good starting point is the **Rådhus,** probably the most unusual city hall in Denmark. Built in 1941 by noted architects Arne Jacobsen and Erik Møller, the pale Norwegian-marble block building is controversial but cuts a startling figure when illuminated in the evening. ⊠ *Park Allé,* ☎ *86/12–16–00.* ☒ *City hall DKr10; tower DKr5. Guided tours only in Danish mid-June–early Sept., weekdays at 11; tower tours weekdays at noon and 4.*

★ Not to be missed is the town's open-air museum, known as **Gamle By** (Old Town), made up of 70 half-timber houses, a mill, and a millstream, all carefully moved from locations throughout Jylland and meticulously re-created, inside and out. ⊠ *Viborgvej,* ☎ *86/12–31–88.* ☒ *DKr50.* ⊙ *Jan.–Mar. and Nov., daily 11–3; Apr. and Oct., daily 10–4; May and Sept., daily 9–5; June–Aug., daily 9–6; Dec., Mon.–Sat. 10–3, Sun. 10–4.*

In a 250-acre forest in a park south of Århus is the indoor-outdoor **Moesgård Forhistorisk Museum** (Prehistoric Museum), with exhibits on ethnography and archaeology, including the famed Grauballe Man, a 2,000-year-old corpse so well bog-preserved that scientists could determine his last meal. Also, take the Forhistoriskvej (Prehistoric Trail) through the forest, which leads past Stone- and Bronze-Age displays to reconstructed houses from Viking times. ⊠ *Moesgård Allé,* ☎ *86/27–24–33.* ☒ *DKr30.* ⊙ *Jan.–Apr. and mid-Sept.–Dec., Tues.–Sun. 10–4; May–mid-Sept., Tues.–Sun. 10–5.*

☺ If you are visiting Århus with children, visit its provincial **Tivoli,** with rides, music, and lovely gardens. ⊠ *Skovbrynet,* ☎ *86/14–73–00.* ☒ *DKr30.* ⊙ *Mid-Apr.–May, daily 1–9; May–mid-June, daily 1–10; mid-June–mid-Aug., daily 1–11.*

Be sure to ask about the **Århus Pass,** which affords free passage on buses, and admission to museums and sights as well as tours. A two-day pass is DKr110 and a seven-day is DKr155.

Dining and Lodging

$ ✕ **Rio Grande.** Full of the standard-issue blankets, straw hats, and bright colors that characterize Mexican restaurants all over the world, Rio Grande is a favorite with youngsters, families, and even businesspeople. Heaping plates of tacos, enchiladas, and chili are a good value—and tasty, too. ⊠ *Vestergade 39,* ☎ *86/19–06–96. AE, MC, V.*

$$$ ✕⊞ **Royal Hotel.** In operation since 1838, Århus's grand hotel has welcomed such greats as Arthur Rubinstein and Marian Anderson. Well-heeled guests are welcomed into a stately lobby appointed with Chesterfield sofas, modern paintings, and a winding staircase that leads to the rooms above. The plush rooms vary in style and decor, but all have rich drapery, velour and brocade furniture, and marble bathrooms. ⊠ *Store Torv 4, DK–8100 Århus C,* ☎ *86/12–00–11,* FAX *86/76–04–04. 105 rooms, 7 suites. Restaurant, bar, sauna, casino, business services. AE, DC, MC, V.*

$ ⊞ **Youth Hostel Pavilionen.** As in all Danish youth and family hostels, the rooms here are clean, bright, and functional. The secluded setting in the woods near the fjord is downright beautiful. Unfortunately, the hostel can get a bit noisy. ⊠ *Marienlunsdvej 10,* ☎ *86/16–72–98,* FAX *86/10–255–60. 32 rooms, 11 with private shower, 4 shared showers and toilets. Cafeteria (breakfast only), kitchen. AE, MC, V. Closed mid-Dec.–mid-Jan.*

Nightlife and the Arts

There's no better time to visit Århus than during the 10-day **Århus Festival Week** in September, when jazz, classical, and rock concerts are nonstop, in addition to drama, theater, and dance.

BARS, LOUNGES, AND DISCOS

The **Café Mozart** (⊠ Vesterport 10, ☎ 86/18–55–63) plays classical music and serves homemade organic Middle Eastern and other ethnic specialties, including what it claims is the world's biggest pita bread. Despite its groovy name, the **Beach Club** in the Hotel Marselis (⊠ Strandvejen 25, ☎ 86/14–44–11) attracts all ages for classical music, but as the night goes on, the beat gets more danceable, with rock and disco. **Down Town** (⊠ Store Torv 4, ☎ 86/13–95–77) is relegated almost exclusively to youngsters. **David Crockett** (⊠ Frederiksgade 72, ☎ 86/12–77–55) offers a mix of styles (including an English pub, circus bar, cowboy saloon, and two discos) where over-20-year-olds go to have casual fun and dance to music from the '70s to the present. **Blitz** (⊠ Klostergade 34, ☎ 86/19–10–99) is one of more trendy and alternative spots in Århus, cranking out techno-pop tunes.

CASINOS

The **Royal Hotel** (⊠ Store Torv 4, ☎ 86/12–00–11) is the city's casino with blackjack, roulette, baccarat, and slot machines.

JAZZ CLUBS

For jazz, head to **Bent J's** (⊠ Nørre Allé 66, ☎ 86/12–04–92), a small club with free-admission jam sessions three times a week and occasional big-name concerts. **Glazz Huset** (⊠ Åboulevarden 35, ☎ 86/12–13–12) is Århus's big jazz club, attracting some international stars.

Ebeltoft

⑥⑥ *45 km (28 mi) east of Århus.*

If you have time, drive northeast to the tip of what Danes call Jylland's nose, Ebeltoft, a town of crooked streets, sloping row houses, and local crafts shops. Danish efficiency is showcased beside the ferry, at the **Vindmølleparken,** one of the largest windmill parks in the world, where 16 wind-powered mills on a curved spit of land generate electricity for 600 families. ⊠ *Færgehaven,* ☎ *86/34–12–44.* ☞ *Free.* ⊙ *Daily.*

You can't miss the **Frigate Jylland,** which is dry-docked on the town's main harbor. The renovation of the three-masted tall ship was financed by Danish shipping magnate Mærsk McKinney Møller, and it's a testament to Denmark's maritime yore: Wander through to examine the bridge, gun deck, galley, captain's room, and perhaps most impressive of all, the 10½-ton pure copper and pewter screw, and voluptuous Pomeranian pine figurehead. ⊠ *Strandvejen 4,* ☎ *86/34–10–99.* ☞ *DKr40.* ⊙ *Daily 10–4.*

Also on the Ebeltoft harbor is the **Glasmuseum** (Glass Museum). Its small, light, and airy interior is the perfect setting for its glass collection, which ranges from the mysterious symbol-imbedded monoliths of Swedish glass sage Bertil Vallien to the luminous gold pavilions of Japanese artist Kyohei Fujita. The museum, once a customs and excise house, overlooks the Ebeltoft Bay, and includes a glass workshop where international students come to study their craft. There's also a shop, where functional pieces, art, and books are for sale. ⊠ *Strandvejen 8,* ☎ *86/34–17–99.* ☞ *DKr40.* ⊙ *Mid-May–mid-Oct., daily 10–5; mid-Sept.–mid-May daily 1–4.*

Viborg

⑥⑦ *60 km (36 mi) west of Randers, 66 km (41 mi) northeast of Århus.*

Viborg dates to at least the 8th century, when it was a trading post and a place of pagan sacrifice. Later it became a center of Christianity, with monasteries and an episcopal residence. The 1,000-year-old **Hærvejen,** the old military road that starts near here, was once Denmark's most important connection with the outside world—though today it lives on as a bicycle path. Legend has it that in the 11th century King Canute set out from Viborg to conquer England; he succeeded, of course, and ruled from 1016 to 1035. Today you can buy reproductions of a silver coin minted by the king, embossed with the inscription "Knud, Englands Kong" (Canute, King of England).

Built in 1130, Viborg's **Domkirke** (Cathedral) was once the largest granite church in the world. Today only the crypt remains of the original building; the structure was restored and reopened in 1876. The dazzling early 20th-century biblical frescoes are by Danish painter Joakim Skovgard. ⊠ *Mogensgade,* ☎ *86/62–10–60.* ☞ *Free.* ⊙ *June–Aug., Mon.–Sat. 10–4; Sun. noon–5; Sept. and Apr.–May, Mon.–Sat. 11–4, Sun. noon–4; Oct.–Mar., Mon.–Sat. 11–3, Sun. noon–3.*

Aalborg

⑥⑧ *80 km (50 mi) north of Viborg; 112 km (70 mi) north of Århus.*

The gentle waters of the Limfjord sever Jylland completely. Clamped to its narrowest point is Aalborg, Denmark's fourth-largest community, which celebrated its 1,300th birthday with a year of festivities in 1992—and once and for all cementing the town's party reputation. The gateway between north and south Jylland, the city is a charming combination of new and old: twisting lanes filled with medieval houses and, nearby, broad modern boulevards.

Among Aalborg's sights, the local favorite is the magnificent 17th-cen-
★ tury **Jens Bang Stenhus** (Jens Bang's Stone House), built by a wealthy
merchant. Chagrined that he was never made a town council member,
the cantankerous Bang avenged himself by caricaturing his political enemies in gargoyles all over the building and then adding his own face,
its tongue sticking out at town hall. A five-story building dating from
1624, it has a vaulted stone beer-and-wine cellar that is one of the most
atmospheric in the country. ⊠ *Østerä 9.*

On Gammel Torv, the Baroque **Budolfi Kirke** (Cathedral) is dedicated
to the English saint Botolph. The church, which was originally made
of wood, has been rebuilt several times in its 800-year history and is
now made of stone. It includes a copy of the original tower of the Rådhus (City Hall) in Copenhagen, which was taken down about a century ago. The money for the construction was donated to the church
by a generous local merchant and his sister, both of whom, locals say,
had no other family upon which to lavish their wealth.

Next to Budolfi Kirke is the 15th-century **Helligandsklosteret** (Monastery
of the Holy Ghost). One of Denmark's best-preserved monasteries—
and perhaps the only one that admitted both nuns and monks—it is
now a home for the elderly; unfortunately, it is generally not open to
the public. During World War II the monastery was the meeting place
for the Churchill Club, a group of Aalborg schoolboys who became
world-famous for their sabotage of the Nazis, even after the enemy
thought they were locked up. ☎ *98/12–02–05.*

In the center of the old town is **Jomfru Ane Gade,** named, as the story
goes, for an aristocratic maiden who was accused of being a witch, then
beheaded. Now the street's fame is second only to that of Copenhagen's
Strøget. Despite the flashing neon and booming music of about 30 discos, bars, clubs, and eateries, the street attracts a thick stream of mixed
pedestrian traffic, and appeals to all ages.

The only Fourth of July celebrations outside the United States annually blast off in nearby **Rebild Park,** a salute to the United States for
welcoming some 300,000 Danish immigrants. The tradition dates
back to 1912.

Just north of Aalborg at Nørresundby (still considered a part of greater
Aalborg) is **Lindholm Høje,** a Viking and Iron Age burial ground where
stones placed in the shape of a ship enclose many of the site's 682 graves
and sheep often outnumber tourists. At its entrance there's a museum
that chronicles Viking civilization and recent excavations. ⊠ *Hvorupvej,*
☎ *98/17–55–22.* 🖾 *Museum DKr20; burial-ground free.* ☉ *Easter–mid-
Oct., daily 10–5; rest of yr, daily 10–4.*

Dining and Lodging

$$ ✕ **Dufy.** Light and bright on an old cobbled street, these are among
the most popular eateries in town. Downstairs, bistro-style Cafeen has
a French-style ambience, with marble-topped tables, engraved mirrors,
and windows overlooking Jomfru Ane Gade, while upstairs, Dufy is
more elegant and quieter. The French menu is the same in both, in-
cluding lobster-and-cognac soup for two, sliced roast duck with Wal-
dorf salad, and beef fillet. ⊠ *Jomfru Ane Gade 8,* ☎ *98/16–34–44.
DC, MC, V.*

$$ ✕ **Spisehuset Kniveog Gaffel.** In a 400-year-old building parallel to Jum-
★ fru Ane Gade, this busy restaurant is crammed with oak tables, crazy
slanting floors, and candlelight, while a year-round courtyard is a veritable greenhouse. Young waitresses negotiate the mayhem to deliver
inch-thick steaks, the house specialty. ⊠ *Maren Turisgade 10,* ☎ *98/
16–69–72. DC, MC, V. Closed Sun.*

$ ✕ **Duus Vinkælder.** This amazing cellar is part alchemist's dungeon, part neighborhood bar. Though most people come for a drink before or after dinner, you can also get a light bite. During the summer the menu is mostly smørrebrød, but during the winter, grilled specialties include *pølser* (sausages), *frikadeller* (oblong Danish meatballs), *biksemad* (a meat-and-potato hash), and the restaurant's special liver pâté. ⊠ *Østerä 9*, ☎ *98/12–50–56. DC, V. Closed Sun.*

$$$$ ✕🔲 **Helnan Phønix.** Centrally located in a sumptuous old mansion, this hotel is popular with international and business guests. The rooms are luxuriously furnished with plump chairs and polished, dark-wood furniture; in some the original raw beams are still intact. The Brigadier serves excellent French and Danish food. ⊠ *Vesterbro 77, DK–9000,* ☎ *98/12–00–11,* 𝔽𝔸𝕏 *98/16–31–66. 185 rooms, 120 with bath and shower, 57 with shower; 3 suites. Restaurant, bar, café, room service, sauna, meeting room. AE, DC, MC, V.*

Nightlife and the Arts
Duus Vinkælder (⊠ Østerä 9, ☎ 98/12–50–56), the atmospheric wine cellar of the Jens Bang Stenhus, is extremely popular, and certainly is one of the most characteristic beer and wine cellars in all of Denmark. **Gaslight** (⊠ Jomfrue Ane Gade 23, ☎ 98/10–17–50) plays rock and grinding dance music to a young crowd. **Rendez-Vous** (⊠ Jomfrue Ane Gade 5, ☎ 98/16–88–80) has an upstairs dance floor packed with 18- to 25-year-olds dancing to standard disco. **Ambassadeur** (⊠ Vesterbro 76, ☎ 98/12–62–22), with four dance restaurants and live music, is popular with a mature audience.

The city's sole casino is at the **Limsfjordshotellet** (⊠ Ved Stranden 14–16, ☎ 98/16–43–33) with blackjack and more.

Aalborg doesn't have a regular jazz club, but local musicians get together at least once a week for **jam sessions.** Ask the tourist board for details. If you're there in the fall or winter, head to the harbor-side **Kompasset** (⊠ Vesterbådehavn, ☎ 98/13–75–00), where live jazz is paired with a Saturday-afternoon lunch buffet.

Skagen

69 *88 km (55 mi) north of Aalborg, 212 kilomters (132 miles) north of Århus.*

At the windswept northern tip of Jylland is Skagen (pronounced *skane*), a very popular summer beach area for well-heeled Danes, where, historically, the long beaches and luminous light have inspired painters and writers alike. The 19th-century Danish artist Holger Drachmann (1846–1908) and his friends, including the very popular P. S. Kroyer, founded the Skagen School of painting, which captured the special quality of northern light; you can see their efforts on display in the **Skagen Museum.** ⊠ 4 Brøndumsvej 4, ☎ 98/44–64–44. 🖼 DKr30. ☉ Apr. and Oct., Tues.–Sun. 11–4; May and Sept., daily 10–5; June–Aug., daily 10–6; Nov.–Mar., Wed.–Fri. 1–4, Sat. 11–4, Sun. 11–3.

Danes say that in Skagen you can "stand one foot in the Kattegat, the strait between Sweden and eastern Jylland, the other in the Skagerrak, the strait between western Denmark and Norway." The point is so thrashed by storms and clashing waters that the 18th-century **Tilsandede Kirke** (Sand-Buried Church), 2 kilometers (1¼ miles) south of town, is completely covered by dunes.

Even more famed than the Buried Church is the west coast's dramatic
★ **Råbjerg Mile,** a protected migrating dune that moves about 33 feet a
year and is accessible on foot from the Kandestederne.

Dining and Lodging

$$$ ✕⊡ **Brøndums Hotel.** A few minutes from the beach, this 150-year-
★ old gabled inn is furnished with antiques and Skagen School paintings.
The 21 guest rooms in the main building, which are beginning to show
their age, are without TVs or phones. Their old-fashioned decor in-
cludes wicker chairs, Oriental rugs, and pine four-poster beds. The 25
annex rooms are more modern. The hotel has a fine Danish-French
restaurant with a lavish cold table. ⊠ *Anchersvej 3, DK–9990,* ☎ *98/44–
15–55,* ⅏ *98/45–15–20. 46 rooms, 12 with bath. Restaurant, meet-
ing rooms. AE, DC, MC, V. Closed Dec. 24–Jan. 1.*

Jylland A to Z

Arriving and Departing

BY CAR AND FERRY

More than 25 ferry routes connect the peninsula to the rest of Den-
mark (including the Faroe Islands), as well as England, Norway and
Sweden, with additional connections to Kiel and Puttgarden, Ger-
many, the Baltics, Poland, and Russia. Most travelers however, drive
north from Germany, or arrive from the islands of Sjælland or Fyn.
The ferry prices, which can get steep, vary according to how many are
traveling and the size of the vehicle. For most ferries, you can get in-
formation and make reservations by calling FDM, the Danish auto-
mobile association (☎ 35/43–02–00).

From Copenhagen or elsewhere on Sjælland, you can drive the 110 kilo-
meters (69 miles) across the island, then cross the Storebælt (Big Belt)
aboard either the Halsskov-Knudshoved (1 hour) or the Korsør-Ny-
borg (1 hour, 15 minutes) ferry. You then drive the 85 kilometers (53
miles) across Fyn and cross from Middelfart to Frederecia, Jylland over
the Lillebæltsbro (Little Belt Bridge). More choices abound here, since
two bridges link Middelfart to Fredericia. The older, lower bridge (2
kilometer/1¼ mile) follows Route 161, while the newer suspension bridge
(1 kilometer/½ mile) on E20 is faster. For direct Sjælland to Jylland pas-
sage, you can take the ferry between Sjælland's Odde and Ebeltoft (1
hour, 40 minutes), or a car-ferry hydrofoil (1 hour, 25 minutes) between
Århus and Kalundborg. The conventional DSB ferry (3 hours, 15 min-
utes) is larger and slower, but more akin to a cruise ship. Also from
Kalundborg, you can sail to Juelsminde (3 hours), 74 kilometers (46
miles) south of Århus.

Other major routes include those of **Scandinavian Seaways** (☎ in Es-
bjerg, 75/12–48–00; in Copenhagen, 33/15–63–00) which links Har-
wich and Newcastle to Esbjerg in the southwest. There are ferries
from Göteborg (3¼ hours), on Sweden's west coast and Oslo, Norway
(10 hours), to Frederikshavn in the northeast. Call **Stena Line** (☎
96/20–02–00) for both.

Ferries from Hundested, Sjælland, to Grena in east Jylland take 2½ hours;
those from Kalundborg to Århus take 3 hours. For information, call
DSB (☎ 33/14–17–01). **Scandinavian Seaways** (☎ in Esbjerg, 75/12–
48–00; in Copenhagen, 33/15–63–00) links Harwich and Newcastle
to Esbjerg in the southwest. There are ferries from Göteborg (3¼ hours),
on Sweden's west coast and Oslo, Norway (10 hours), to Frederikshavn
in the northeast. Call **Stena Line** (☎ 96/20–02–00) for both.

Billund Airport, 2 kilometers (1¼ miles) southwest of downtown, receives flights from London, Stockholm, Brussels, Amsterdam, and Frankfurt on Mærsk Air (☎ 75/33–28–44) and on the Norwegian carrier Braathens from Oslo. Sunair (☎ 75/33–16–11) serves Billund, Århus, Oslo, Stockholm, and Göteborg. Several domestic airports, including Aalborg, Århus, and Esbjerg, are served by Mærsk and SAS (75/16–03–33), both of which have good connections to Copenhagen. Cimber Air (☎ 74/42–22–77) links Sønderborg, just north of the German border with Copenhagen.

BY TRAIN
DSB (☎ 33/14–17–01) makes hourly runs between Copenhagen and Fredericia. The 3½-hour trip includes train passage aboard the ferry, which crosses the Store Bælt between Korsør, on west Sjælland, and Nyborg, on east Fyn.

Getting Around
BY BICYCLE
Jylland has scores of bike paths, and many auto routes also have cycle lanes. Keep in mind that distances are much longer here than elsewhere in the country, and that even these humble hills are a challenge for children and novice cyclists. Consider prearranged package holidays, which range from island day trips to eight-day excursions. Among the offices that can help with bike tips are the tourist boards in Viborg and Silkeborg and in Vejen (☎ 75/36–26–96), or the **County of North Jylland** tourist office (✉ Niels Bohrsvej, Box 8300, DK–9220 Aalborg, ☎ 96/35–10–00).

Bike rentals are available in most towns from the tourism board, which can also supply maps and brochures. In the west, the **Vestkyst-stien** (west-coast path) goes from Skagen in the north to Bulbjerg in the south. On the east, the **Vendsyssel-stien** (winding path) goes from Frederikshavn to the mouth of the Limfjord. The Stkyst-stien (east-coast path) follows and leads to the south of the Limfjord. In the south, much of the 1,000-year-old **Hærvejen** (Old Military Road) has been converted into a network of picturesque cycling lanes. It's signposted for all 240 kilometers (145 miles) through the center of Jylland, from Padborg in the south to Viborg in the north.

BY BUS
Intercity buses are punctual but slower than trains. Passengers can buy tickets on the bus and pay according to destination. For schedules and fares, call **DSB** weekdays (☎ 86/12–67–03). For intercity travel, schedules are posted at all bus stops and fares are usually under DKr10.

BY CAR
Although train and bus connections are excellent, sights and towns are widely dispersed, so Jylland is best explored by car. Whether you decide to take speedy, modern highways or winding old roads, traffic is virtually nonexistent.

BY TRAIN
For long trips, the **DSB** (☎ 86/13–17–00) trains are fast and efficient, with superb views of the countryside. Smaller towns do not have innercity trains, so you'll have to switch to buses once you arrive.

Contacts and Resources
EMERGENCIES
Emergency **Doctor,** in Aalborg (☎ 98/13–62–11), in Århus (☎ 86/20–10–22). **Ambulance, fire,** or **police** (☎ 112). **Århus Pharmacy** (✉ Løve

Apoteket, Store Torv 5, ☎ 86/12–00–22). **Aalborg Pharmacy** (✉ Budolfi Apotek, corner of Vesterbro and Algade, ☎ 98/12–06–77).

GUIDED TOURS

Guided tours are few and far between, but check with the local tourism offices for tips and reservations. Some carry brochures that describe walking tours. The **Århus Round the City** tour (2½ hours) begins at the tourist office and includes Den Gamle By, the Domkirke, the concert hall, the university, and the harbor. **Aalborg's City Tour** (2 hours) departs from Adelgade and includes most of the town museums, the Budolfi Cathedral, Monastery of the Holy Ghost, Town Hall, the Jens Bang Stenhus, and Jomfru Ane Gade. A **Legoland Tour** departs from Copenhagen at 8 AM on Tuesday and weekends and costs DKr350. Call ☎ 31/54–06–06 for reservations.

VISITOR INFORMATION

Tourism offices are open weekdays 10–4, Saturday 9–noon in winter and 9–6 weekdays and Saturday in the summer. **Aalborg** (✉ Østerå 8, ☎ 98/12–60–22). **Århus** (✉ Rådhuset, ☎ 86/12–16–00). **Billund** (✉ c/o Legoland A/S, Åstvej, ☎ 75/33–19–26). **Randers** (✉ Erik Menveds Plads 1, ☎ 86/42–44–77). **Ribe** (✉ Torvet 3–5, ☎ 75/42–15–00). **Silkeborg** (✉ Godthåbsvej 4, ☎ 86/82–19–11). **Viborg** (✉ Nytorv 5, ☎ 86/61–16–66).

Be sure and ask about the **Jutland Pass** coupon booklet (DKr75), available from tourist offices and Statoil gas stations throughout Jylland (though Scandic Hotels and the Stena Line Ferries between Denmark and Sweden often distribute it free of charge). It's packed with nearly 200 coupons, affording restaurant, museum, and sightseeing deals.

BORNHOLM

Called the Pearl of the Baltic for its natural beauty and winsomely rustic towns, Bornholm, 177 kilometers (110 miles) southeast of Sjælland, is geographically unlike the rest of Denmark. A temperate climate has made this 588-square-kilometer (436-square-mile) jumble of granite bluffs, clay soil, and rift valleys an extravagance of nature. Rich plantations of fir bristle beside wide dunes and vast heather fields; lush gardens teem with fig, cherry, chestnut, mulberry, and blue-blooming Chinese Emperor trees; and meadows sprout 12 varieties of orchids. Denmark's third-largest forest, the Almindingen, crowns the center; the southern tip is ringed with some of Europe's whitest beaches.

During the Iron and Bronze ages, Bornholm was inhabited by seafaring and farming cultures that dotted the land with their burial dolmens and engravings. From the Middle Ages to the 18th century, the Danes battled the Swedes for ownership of the island, protecting it with strongholds and fortified churches, many of which still loom over the landscape.

Today Bornholmers continue to draw their livelihood from the land and sea—and increasingly from tourism. The towns bristle with chalk-white chimneys, the harbors are abob with painted fishing boats, and in spring and summer the fields blaze with amber mustard and grain.

Certainly, few people come to Bornholm to stay indoors. Long, silky beaches, rolling hills and troll-inspiring forests make this a summer haven for walking, hiking, and swimming—particularly for families, many of whom take their summer vacations by packing provisions and children onto a pair of bikes, and winding throughout the island.

Bornholm is famous throughout Scandinavia for its craftspeople, especially its glassblowers and ceramicists, whose work is often pricier in Copenhagen and Stockholm. In the center of each town (especially Gudhjem and Svaneke), you'll find crafts shops and *værksteder* (workshops). When you're on the road, watch for *keramik* (ceramics) signs, which direct you to artists selling from home.

Outdoor Activities and Sports

FISHING

Cod, salmon, and herring fishing are excellent in season, though better from a boat than from shore. Licenses cost DKr25 per day, DKr75 per week, and DKr100 per year. Contact the tourist board for details and information on charter trips. Among the handful of charter companies is **Peter Prüssing** (⊠ Gudhjem, ☎ 56/48–54–63), who arranges trips between Gudhjem and Snogebæk.

HIKING

In contrast to the rest of Denmark, Bornholm is hilly and rugged. Marked trails crisscross the island, including three 4-kilometer (2½-mile) hikes through the Almindingen Forest and several more through its Ekkodalon (Echo Valley). The northern coastline is beautiful but a rocky and more strenuous walk. Ask for a map, routes, and tips from any tourism office. The *Bornholm Green Guide,* available in shops and tourism offices, offers suggestions for walking and hiking tours.

SWIMMING

Beach worshipers thrive in Bornholm. The swimming and sunning are best south, between Pedersker and Snogebæk, where the dunes are tall and the beaches wide. As elsewhere in Denmark, topless bathing is common and nude bathing is tolerated.

Rønne

⑦ *190 km (120 mi) southeast of Copenhagen (7 hrs by ferry).*

Borhholm's capital, port, and largest town is Rønne, a good starting point for exploring northward or eastward. East of Nørrekås Harbor on Laksegade, you'll find an enchanting area of rose-clad 17th- and 18th-century houses, among them the tile-roof **Erichsens Gård** (farm). The home of the wealthy Erichsen family, whose daughter married the Danish poet Holger Drachmann, it is preserved with paintings by Danish artist Kristian Zahrtmann, period furnishings, and a lovely garden. ⊠ Laksegade 7, ☎ 56/95–87–35. ☐ DKr15. ☉ May–mid-Oct., Mon.–Sat. 10–5, Sun. 1–5.

Just off Store Torv (the main square) is the **Bornholm Museum,** which features local geologic and archaeological exhibits in addition to more than 4,500 pieces of ceramics and glass. The museum also displays 25 18th-century *Bornholmure* (Bornholm Clocks), which are as characteristic of the island as smoked herring. In 1744, a Dutch ship was wrecked on Bornholm, and the English grandfather clocks it carried became the models for the island's clocks. ⊠ Skt. Mortensgade 29, ☎ 56/95–07–35. ☐ DKr20. ☉ Apr.–Oct., Mon.–Sat. 10–5, Sun. 1–5; Nov.–Apr., Tues., Thurs., and Sun. 2–5.

Dining and Lodging

$$ ✕ **Rådhuskroen.** With exposed timbers, comfortable armchairs, and close-set tables, this restaurant provides a softly lit change from Rønne's busy streets. The menu is Bornholm Continental, with such specialties as poached Baltic salmon with salmon roe and lobster sauce and grilled fillet of rosefish (redfish) with curry sauce. Beef choices include pepper steak with wine and cream sauce. ⊠ Nørregade 2, ☎ 56/95–00–69. AE, D, MC, V.

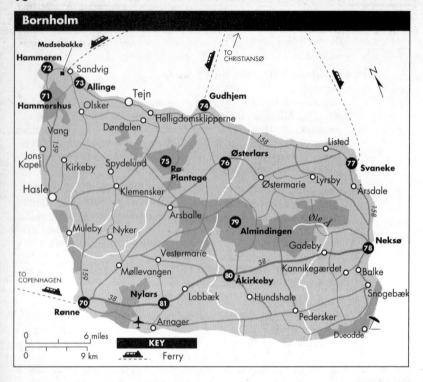

Bornholm

$$$ ✕🏨 **Fredensborg.** The island's standard for luxury is set at this hotel, situated on a curve of forest near a small beach. The glass and tile lobby is spare and sunny, the staff pleasant and eager. The dozen ample apartments have full kitchens, and guest rooms are done in pastel schemes, with modern furniture and balconies overlooking the sea. The rustic restaurant, De Fem Ståuerne, serves traditional Danish food. ✉ *Strandvejen 116, DK–3700,* ☎ *56/95–44–44,* FAX *56/95–03–14. 72 rooms, 12 apartments. Restaurant, bar, room service, hot tub, sauna, tennis court, meeting rooms. AE, DC, MC, V.*

$$$ ✕🏨 **Hotel Griffen.** Just off a busy street and the Rønne harbor, this is one of Bornholm's largest and most modern hotels. It's three stories tall, with plenty of windows and views of the sea on one side and Rønne on the other. The rooms, done in deep-brown tones, have every modern convenience. ✉ *Kredsen 1, DK–3700,* ☎ *56/95–51–11,* FAX *56/95–52–97. 140 rooms, 2 suites. Restaurant, bar, room service, indoor pool, sauna, dance club, meeting rooms. AE, DC, MC, V. Closed mid-Dec.–Jan. 7.*

⚠ **Galløkken Camping** (✉ Strandvejen 4, DK–3700 Rønne, ☎ 56/95–23–20) is just a short walk from the Rønne center, near an old military museum. The grounds are open, but trees surround the perimeter. There are good shower and cooking facilities.

Nightlife and the Arts

Bornholm's nightlife is limited to a handful of discos and clubs in Rønne. **Sølvknappen** (✉ Store Torv, ☎ 56/95–48–01) is a moderate-size disco frequented by young locals. **Vise Vesth Huset** (✉ Brøddegade 24, ☎ 56/48–50–80) is popular for light meals and live folk music.

Outdoor Activities and Sports

The **Bornholm Golf Club** near Rønne (☎ 56/95–68–54) is an 18-hole park course in a natural setting with plenty of wildlife and fauna—the brochure even boasts that you can enjoy nightingales and wild orchids along the course. There's also a restaurant and pro shop.

Shopping

A Bornholmur is a type of grandfather clock handmade on the island. Antique versions cost from DKr5,000 to DKr9,000 and more. New clocks modeled from museum originals are custom-made by **Bornholmerure** (⊠ Torneværksvej 26, Rønne, ☎ 56/95–31–08). The clocks often have round faces but can be rectangular as well and are completely hand-painted. On the hour, the modern clocks sound the hour with music—which ranges from Mozart and Verdi to Sondheim and Andrew Lloyd Webber. A handmade custom clock can cost as much as DKr25,000 ($3,840).

You can pick up unusual gifts and one-of-a-kind clothing made of hand-printed textiles at **Bente Hammer** (⊠ Nyker Hovedgade 32, Rønne, ☎ 56/96–33–35).

There is a large **vegetable and fruit market** on Wednesday and Saturday mornings in Store Torv, the main square in Rønne.

En Route   Fourteen kilometers (8½ miles) north of Rønne is the bluff known as **Jons Kapel.** A medieval legend has it that a monk, Brother Jon, lived in a cave and used these treacherous sea cliffs as a pulpit for his impassioned sermons. Wear rubber-sole hiking boots to climb the stairs that lead to the pulpit, where the agile friar stood atop the dramatic 72-foot-high cliffs that loom over the crashing waves.

Hammershus★

71 *8 km (5 mi) north of Jons Kapel, 30 km (19 mi) north of Rønne.*

The ruins of the fortress of Hammershus constitute northern Europe's largest stronghold. The hulking fortress was begun in 1255 by the archbishop of Lund (Sweden), and became the object of centuries of struggle between Denmark and Sweden. In 1658 Danes under Jens Kofoed killed its Swedish governor, and the castle was given back to Denmark. Used until 1743, it became a ruin when it was quarried for stone to fortify Christiansø and that island's buildings. The government finally intervened in 1822, and the site is now a mass of snaggletoothed walls and towers atop a grassy knoll. During restoration work in 1967, 22 gold German guilders were found. Occasionally, concerts and other performances are held at the ruins. *No phone.* ⌨ *Free.*

Nightlife and the Arts

They don't happen nearly enough, but check with the local tourism office to see if any special events are planned at or near Hammershus: The ruins add a spectacular dimension to classical music and the performing arts.

Hammeren

72 *5 km (3 mi) north of Hammershus, 36 km (23 mi) north of Rønne.*

Despite constant Baltic winds, rare plants and trees grow on the warm, granite-scattered Hammeren (the Hammer), including radiant anemones. The knuckle of land jutting from the island's northern tip is nearly separated from the island by a deep rift valley and the Hammer Sø (Hammer Lake). Look across the water south of the tip to the stone formation known as the Camel Heads.

En Route   A little more than 3 kilometers (2 miles) southeast of Hammeren, **Madsebakke** is the largest collection of Bronze Age rock carvings in Denmark. They are presumed to be ceremonial carvings, which ancient fishermen and farmers hoped would bring good weather and bountiful crops. The most interesting of them depicts 11 ships, including one with a sun wheel.

Allinge

73 *3 km (2 mi) east of Madsebakke, 21 km (13 mi) north of Rønne.*

In Allinge and its twin town Sandvig, you'll find centuries-old neighborhoods and, particularly in Allinge, half-timber houses and herring smokehouses sprouting tall chimneys. Just south is a wood the islanders call the **Trolleskoven** (Troll Forest). Legend says trolls live in the woods, and when they "brew" fog, they escape the heat in the kitchen and go out looking for trouble. The most mischievous is the littlest troll, Krølle Bølle.

Dining and Lodging

$$ ★ ✕🏨 **Strandhotellet.** Romantic old-world charm is the draw at this venerable hotel. On a corner across from the harbor, it has a white arched entry into a stone-and-whitewashed lobby. The rooms are furnished in plain beech furniture with woolen covers and pastel colors. ✉ *Strandpromenaden 7, Sandvig, DK–3770,* ☎ *56/48–03–14,* FAX *56/48–02–09. 50 rooms, 1 suite. Restaurant, bar, sauna, steam room, health club. AE, DC, MC, V. Closed mid-Oct.–mid-Apr.*

⚠ **Sandvig Familie Camping** (✉ Sandlinien 5, DK–3770 Allinge, ☎ 56/48–04–47 or 56/48–00–01) renovated its large kitchen and bathing facilities in 1996. It is pleasantly located close to the beach, so that most of its sites enjoy a view of the water.

Shopping

Kampeløkken (✉ Havnegade 45, Allinge, ☎ 56/48–17–66) gallery shop stocks the work of 24 potters and four glassblowers.

En Route Eight kilometers (5 miles) southeast of Allinge along the coastal path, you'll come upon the grottoes and granite cliffs of the **Helligdomsklipperne** (Cliffs of Sanctuary), which contain a well-known rock formation best seen from the boats that ply the nearby waters in summer. In the Middle Ages, people used to visit these waters, believing that they had holy, healing powers—hence the name.

Just southeast of the Helligdomsklipperne, a pastoral coastal path leads to the tiny, preserved **Døndalen Forest.** Its fertile soil bears a surprising array of Mediterranean vegetation, including fig and cherry trees. During rainy periods there's a waterfall at the bottom of the dale.

Gudhjem

★ **74** *18 km (11 mi) east of Allinge, 33 km (21 mi) northeast of Rønne.*

Especially at the height of summer, Gudhjem (God's Home) is perhaps the most tourist-packed town on Bornholm—and the reason is obvious. Tiny half-timber houses and gift shops with lace curtains and clay roofs line steep stone streets that loop around the harbor. The island's first smokehouses still produce alder-smoked golden herring.

Walk down Brøddegade, which turns into Melstedvej; here you'll find ★ ☾ the **Landsbrugs Museum** (Agricultural Museum) and Mestedgaard, a working farm with cows, horses, sheep, pigs, geese, and wandering kittens. The farm includes the well-kept house and garden of a 19th-century farm family. Notice the surprisingly bright colors used on the interior of the house, and leave time to visit the old shops, where you can buy locally produced woolen sweaters, wooden spoons, and even homemade mustard. ⊠ *Melstedvej 25,* ☎ *56/48–55–98.* ⊠ *DKr20.* ☉ *Mid-May–mid-Oct., Tues.–Sun. 10–5.*

OFF THE
BEATEN PATH **BORNHOLM KUNST MUSEUM –** Follow the main road, Hellidomsvej, out of town in the direction of Allinge/Sandvig, and you'll come to Bornholm's art museum, an excellent example of the Danes' ability to integrate art, architecture and natural surroundings. Built by the architectural firm of Fogh and Foelner, the white-painted brick, granite and sandstone building is centered by a thin stream of "holy," trickling water that exits the building and leads the visitor to a walkway and overlook above the Helligdomsklipperne (Cliffs of Sanctuary; ☞ *above*). Throughout, the walls of the museum are punched out by picture windows overlooking nearby grazing cows and the crashing Baltic: a natural accompaniment to the art. Most of the works are by Bornholmers, including a body of Modernist work by Olaf Høst, Karl Esaksen and Olaf Rude, who recognized a particular ability in Bornholm's sea-surrounded light to bring out the poignancy in abstract scenes of local life. The museum also displays some sculpture and glass, as well as a survey of more historical paintings. Check out the restaurant and shop. ⊠ *Hellidomsvej 95,* ☎ *56/48-43-86.* ⊠ *DKr30.* ☉ *Apr.–Oct., daily 10–5; Nov.–Mar, Tues., Thur., Sun. 1-5.*

Lodging

$ ⌂ **Skt. Jørgens Gård Vandrehjem.** In a half-timber 100-year-old former manor house, this hostel in the middle of Gudhjem offers single- to eight-bed rooms with standard Danish hostel style: pine bunks and industrial carpeting. ⊠ *Gudhjem Vandrehjem, DK–3760,* ☎ *56/48–50–35,* FAX *56/48–56–35. 52 rooms, 26 with bath. Restaurant, 6 kitchens. No credit cards.*

Shopping

Baltic Sea Glass (⊠ Melstedvej 47, Gudhjem, ☎ 56/48–56–41), on the main road just on the outskirts of town, offers high-quality, bright, imaginative decanters, glasses, candlesticks, and one-of-a-kind pieces, including an old-fashioned fly-catcher. In town, see the delicate porcelain bowls of **Per Rehfeldt** (⊠ Kastenievej 8, ☎ 56/48–54–13). Unique, hand-thrown ceramic work is available from and by **Julia Manitius** (⊠ Holkavej 12, ☎ 56/48–55–99).

OFF THE
BEATEN PATH **CHRISTIANSØ –** A 45-minute boat ride northeast from Gudhjem will bring you to the historic island of Christiansø. Though it was originally a bastion, the Storetårn (Big Tower) and Lilletårn (Little Tower) are all that remain of the fort, which was built in 1684 and dismantled in 1855. The barracks, street, and gardens, for which the earth was transported in boats, have hardly changed since that time and remain under the jurisdiction of the defense ministry, making this a tiny tax-free haven for its 100 inhabitants. Nearby, the rocky, uninhabited island of **Græsholmen** is an inaccessible bird sanctuary—the only place in Denmark where the razorbill and guillemot breed.

Rø Plantage

🕖 *6 km (4 mi) south of Gudhjem, 24 km (15 mi) northeast of Rønne.*

Rø Plantation is a new but dense forest that serves as a quiet foil to the hubbub of Gudhjem. A century ago it was a heather-covered grazing area, but after stone dikes were erected to keep the cattle out, spruce, pine, larch, and birch were cultivated. The cool refuge now consists largely of saplings and new growth—the result of devastating storms in the late '50s and '60s.

Outdoor Activities and Sports

Rø Golfbane (⊠ Spellingevej 3, ☎ 56/48–40–50) has won various European and Scandinavian awards for its natural beauty—and challenges. It is set close to the coastal cliffs, and enjoys views of the sea. It has a pro shop and restaurant.

Østerlars

⑦⑥ *5 km (3 mi) southeast of Rø Plantage, 22 km (14 mi) northeast of Rønne.*

The standout attraction here is the **Østerlars Kirke.** The largest of the island's four round churches, it was built in about 1150; extensions, including the buttresses, were added later. Constructed from boulders and slabs of limestone, the whitewashed church was part spiritual sanctuary, part fortification, affording protection from enemy armies and pirates. Inside is the island's only painted tympanum, with a faded image of a cross and decorative foliage. Several Gothic wall paintings—including depictions of the Annunciation and Nativity—have survived from the 1300s. ⊠ *Gudhjemsvej 28,* ☎ *56/49–82–64.* 🖾 *DKr4.* ☉ *Apr.–mid-Oct., Mon.–Sat. 9–5.*

Svaneke

⑦⑦ *21 km (13 mi) east of Østerlars, 49 km (31 mi) northeast of Rønne.*

The coastal town of Svaneke, Denmark's easternmost settlement, is an enchanting hamlet of 17th- and 18th-century houses, winding cobbled streets, and a harbor that was sliced from the rocky earth. Once a fishing village, it is now immaculately preserved and home to a thriving artists' community.

Dining and Lodging

$$ ✕🖫 **Siemsens Gaard.** Built in a 400-year-old merchant house, this U-shape hotel with a gravel-courtyard café overlooks the harbor. Inside it's cushy with Chesterfield sofas beneath severe black-and-white prints and antiques. The rooms differ, but all are done up in stripped pine and soft colors. The bright, modern restaurant serves Franco-Danish food, with a menu of 125 options—from club sandwiches to smoked Baltic salmon to smørrebrød. ⊠ *Havnebryggen 9, DK–3740,* ☎ *56/ 49–61–49,* 🅵🅰🆇 *56/49–61–03. 50 rooms. Restaurant, café, sauna, health club. AE, DC, MC, V.*

$$ 🖫 **Hotel Østersøen.** Across from the harbor, this newly renovated
★ hotel has a provincial facade and a Key West courtyard with palm trees and a swimming pool. Industrial carpets and century-old beams line the modern lobby, and the stark apartments (rented by the week) are furnished with leather sofas, swanky teak dinette sets, and streamlined furniture. The hotel is well suited for families and couples traveling in pairs. ⊠ *Havnebryggen 5, DK–3740,* ☎ *56/49–60–20,* 🅵🅰🆇 *56/49–72– 79. 21 apartments. Outdoor pool, business services. AE, DC.*

Shopping

Stroll through the ateliers and boutiques in the central Glastorvet in Svaneke. Among them is the studio of **Pernille Bülow,** one of Denmark's most famous glassblowers. Her work is sold in Copenhagen's best design shops. Even if you buy directly from her studio (⊠ Glastorvet, Brænderigænget 8, ☎ 56/49–66–72), don't expect bargains—though you may be lucky to find seconds—but do expect colorful, experimental work. **Askepot** (⊠ Postgade 5, Svaneke, ☎ 53/99–70–42), whose name means Cinderella, sells handmade **leather** hats, jackets, shoes, bags, belts, and wallets.

Neksø

78 *9 km (5½ mi) south of Svaneke, 48 km (30 mi) northeast of Rønne.*

Neksø (or Nexø) is a typical island town, bustling with visitors and locals who shop and live around its busy harbor, which is lined with fishing boats from throughout the Baltics and Eastern Europe. Though it looks like a typical 17th-century town, it was rebuilt almost completely after World War II, when the Russians bombed it to dislodge stubborn German troops who refused to surrender—three days after the rest of Denmark had been liberated. The Russians lingered on the island until April 1946.

Wander down to the harbor to find, in a mustard-yellow building, the **Neksø Museum,** which has a fine collection of fishing and local history exhibits. The museum also houses photographs and memorabilia of Danish author Martin Andersen Hansen (1909–55), who changed his last name to Nexø after his beloved town. A complicated and vehement socialist, he wrote, among other works, *Pelle the Conqueror,* which is set in Bornholm at the turn of the century, when Swedish immigrants were exploited by Danish landowners. The story was turned into an Academy Award–winning film. ⊠ *Havnen,* ☎ 56/49–25–56. 🔳 *DKr10.* ⊘ *May–Oct., Tues.–Sun. 10–4.*

Outdoor Activities and Sports

GOLF

The 18-hole **Nexø Golf Club** (☎ 56/48₋89–87) is close to the island's best sandy, rock-free beaches.

WINDSURFING

The best windsurfing beaches are on the southern sandy coast, where the winds are strong and the beaches sandy (the shores are rockier north of Neksø). **Windsurfing ved Balke Strand** (☎ 56/95–00–77), 4 kilometers (2½ miles) south of Neksø, offers classes and board rentals.

Shopping

For exquisite **woodwork** see Bernard Romain (⊠ Rønnevej 54, Neksø, ☎ 56/48–86–66).

Almindingen

79 *23 km (14 mi) west of Neksø, 27 km (17 mi) northeast of Rønne.*

The lush Almindingen, Denmark's third-largest forest, is filled with ponds, lakes, evergreens, well-marked trails, and blooms with lily of the valley in spring. Within it, the oak-lined **Ekkodalen** (Echo Valley)—where children love to hear their shouts resound—is networked with trails leading to smooth rock faces that soar 72 feet high. At the northern edge, near the road to Østermarie, stood one of Bornholm's most famous sights until 1995: seven evergreens growing from a single trunk. The tree fell that year, but pass by, and you might see the remains of its curious trunk.

Outdoor Activities and Sports

Check with the tourist board for a map delineating three 4-kilometer (2½-mile) hikes through the Almindingen Forest and several more through its Echo Valley. The *Bornholm Green Guide,* available in shops and tourism offices, offers walking and hiking routes.

Åkirkeby

80 *5 km (3 mi) south of Almindingen, 24 km (15 mi) east of Rønne.*

Åkirkeby is the oldest town on the island, with a municipal charter from 1346. The town's church, the **Åkirke,** is Bornholm's oldest and largest, dating from the mid-13th century. Though it is not a round church, both walls and tower were well suited for defense. The altarpiece and pulpit are Dutch Renaissance from about 1600, but the carved sandstone font is as old as the church itself. ⊠ *Torvet,* ☎ *56/97–41–03.* ⌑ *DKr5.* ⊙ *Mon.–Sat. 10–4.*

Nylars

⑧¹ *8 km (5 mi) west of Åkirkeby, 9 km (6 mi) east of Rønne.*

Like the Østerlars church, the round **Nylars Kirke** dates from 1150. The chalk paintings from the Old Testament on its central pillar are the oldest on the island, possibly dating from 1250. Even older are the runic stones on the church's porch. Both are of Viking origin. ⊠ *Kirkevej,* ☎ *56/97–20–13.* ⌑ *Suggested donation DKr3.* ⊙ *Mid-May–mid-Sept., Mon.–Sat. 9–5.*

Bornholm A to Z

Arriving and Departing

BY BUS

A Gråhund (Greyhound) No. 866 bus from Copenhagen's main station travels to Dragør, boards a ferry to Limhamn, and then continues to Ystad, where it connects with a ferry to Rønne. Buses depart twice daily, once in the morning and again in late afternoon. Call **Bornholm Bussen** (☎ 44/68–44–00).

BY CAR FERRY AND HYDROFOIL

The **Bornholmstrafikken** car ferry from Copenhagen's Kvæsthusbro Harbor (near Nyhavn) departs at 11:30 PM year-round and from June through July daily (except Wednesday) at 8:30 AM. The trip takes seven hours. To avoid delays, make reservations. Comfortable sleeping bunks in a massive hall are also available for an extra cost.

The Nordbornholms Turistbureau (North Bornholm Tourist Board, ☎ 56/48–00-01) is the agent for a summer ferry that links Neu Mukran (3½ hours) and Sassnitz (3½ hours) on the island of Rügen in Germany; **Bornholmstrafikken** (☎ 56/95–18–66), a competing company, offers passage aboard the ferry to Neu Mukran (3½ hours), which is just 5 kilometers (3 miles) from Sassnitz. Prices vary according to the number of people traveling and the size of the vehicle. There is also a boat between Swinoujście, Poland and Rønne (seven hours); call **Polferries** (☎ +48/936–5174) in Poland. A hydrofoil from Nyhavn goes to Malmö, Sweden, where it connects with a bus to Ystad and a ferry to Rønne. The four-hour voyage runs twice daily, usually in the morning and again in the late afternoon. Call **Flyve Bådene** (☎ 33/12–80–88).

BY PLANE

The airport is 5 kilometers (3 miles) south of Rønne at the island's southwestern tip. Maersk Air (☎ 56/95–11–11) makes several daily flights only from Copenhagen. Lufthansa (☎ 33/37–73–33) flies from Berlin and Hamburg; Eurowings (☎ 49/231–924–5306) from Dortmund and Osnabrück.

Getting Around

BY BICYCLE

Biking is eminently feasible and pleasant on Bornholm, thanks to a network of more than 200 kilometers (125 miles) of cycle roads, including an old railway converted to a cross-island path. Rentals of sturdy two-speeds and tandems are available for about DKr50 a day at more than 20 different establishments all over the island—near the ferry, at the airport, and in Allinge, Gudhjem, Hasle, Pedersker (near Åkirkeby), Rønne, Svaneke, and most other towns. Try Bornholms Cykeludlejning (⊠ Nordre Kystevej 5, ☎ 56/95–13–59) or Cykel-Centret (⊠ Søndergade 7, ☎ 56/95–06–04), both in Rønne.

BY BUS

Though bus service is certainly not as frequent as in major cities, there are regular connections between towns. Schedules are posted at all stations, and you can usually pick one up on board. The fare is DKr8 per zone, or you can buy a *klip-kort* (punch ticket) of 10 *klips* for DKr64 (☎ 56/95–21–21). A 24-hour bus pass costs DKr100. Children 5–11 pay half-price.

BY CAR

There are excellent roads on the island, but be alert for cyclists and occasional wandering cows.

Contacts and Resources

EMERGENCIES

Ambulance, accident, or **fire** (☎ 112). **Bornholm's Central Hospital** (⊠ Sygehusvej, Rønne, ☎ 56/95–11–65). **Rønne Apotek** (⊠ Store Torvegade 12, Rønne, ☎ 56/95–01–30).

GUIDED TOURS

The **Bornholmrund** (Round Bornholm) bus tour (8½ hours), beginning at 9:30 Tuesday and Thursday, includes Rønne, Hammershus, Allinge, Gudhjem, Østerlars Church, Svaneke, Nexø, Balka, Åkirkeby, and the Almindingen Forest. To make reservations, call the Bornholm Tourist Center. An aerial tour in a Cessna or Piper plane (20–45 min.) covers either the entire coast or the northern tip. Call **Klippefly** (☎ 56/95–35–73 or 56/48–42–01). From mid-June to mid-September, boats to the Helligdomsklipperne (Sanctuary Cliffs) leave Gudhjem at 10:30, 1:30, and 2:30, with extra sailings mid-June to mid-August. Call **Thor Båd** (☎ 56/48–51–65). Boats to Christiansø depart from Svaneke at 10 AM daily year-round; May to September daily at 10:20 from Gudhjem, and at 1 from Allinge; between mid-June and August, an additional boat leaves Gudhjem weekdays at 9:40 and 12:15. Call **Christiansø Farten** (☎ 56/48–51–76) for additional information.

The **BAT** (Bornholm Municipality Traffic Company, ☎ 56/95–21–21) offers some amazingly progressive summer tours. All are offered Tuesday through Friday, from the end of June until early August. All begin at the red bus terminal at Snellemark 30 in Rønne at 10 AM and cost DKr100. (You can also buy a 24-hour bus card for DKr100, or a five- or seven-day card for DKr350, good for both the regional buses and the tours.) Tour prices do not include some DKr5–DKr10 admissions or lunch at a herring smokehouse. The five-hour **Kunst og håndværk** (Arts and Crafts) tour includes stops at glass, pottery, textile, and silver studios. During the summer, different studios are visited each day. The **Grønne Bus** (Green Bus) visits sights that illustrate the ways in which the island's exquisite flora and fauna are being preserved. **Bondegårdsbussen** (Farm Bus) visits chicken, cow, and pig farms, as well as a "free-range" pig farm, to show the differences in practice and attitude between conventional and progressive farming. The **Veteranbus** (Veteran Bus), a circa World War II Bedford, connects some of Bornholm's oldest industries, including a clock maker, a water mill, and Denmark's last windmill used for making flour.

VISITOR INFORMATION

Bornholm's Information Center, ⊠ Ndr. Kystvej 3, Rønne, ☎ 56/95–95–00. Local tourist offices: **Allinge** (⊠ Kirkegade 4, ☎ 56/48–00–

01). **Åkirkeby** (✉ Torvet 2, ☎ 56/97–45–20). **Gudhjem** (✉ Åbogade 9, ☎ 56/48–52–10. **Hasle** (✉ Havnegade 1, ☎ 56/96–44–81). **Nexø,** (✉ Åsen 4, ☎ 56/49–32–00). **Svaneke** (✉ Storegade 24, ☎ 56/49–63–50).

GREENLAND

When Eric the Red discovered Greenland (Kalaallit Nunaat in Greenlandic, Grønland in Danish) a thousand years ago, his Norsemen thought they had reached the edge of the world. After it, there was only *Ginnungagap,* the endless abyss.

Greenland still commands awe from the handful of visitors who venture off the usual Scandinavian path to explore the world's largest island. Measuring more than 1.3 million square kilometers (840,000 square miles), it's larger than Italy, France, Great Britain, unified Germany, and Spain combined. The coastal regions are sparsely populated with 55,000 Danes and Inuit—the indigenous people, whose roots can be traced to the native inhabitants of Canada's Arctic, and further back to the people of High Alaska. More than 80% of the land is eternally frozen beneath an ice cap that, at its deepest, reaches a thickness of 3 kilometers (2 miles). If it melted, sea levels around the world would rise nearly 20 feet.

With so few tourists (less than 15,000 annually, almost all on preset package tours), Greenland remains one of the world's least developed regions. By its nature, the region is far more difficult to explore than dwarfed mother Denmark. Travel is possible only by helicopter or coastal boat, since there are few roads and no railroads. However, the southern and western towns, which are trimmed with building-block red-and-green houses and well-used harbors, have adequate hotels, airfields and helicopter pads, and some summertime ferry service. Man-made luxuries are few, but the rewards of nature are savagely beautiful. Below the Arctic Circle, the draws include Norse ruins, Ice Age–gouged mountains, and jagged fjords. Farther north, dogsleds whip over icy plains, and ferries glide past icebergs as big as city blocks.

Greenland's first inhabitants probably arrived some 4,000 years ago from what is today Canada. Various Inuit peoples continued to migrate to and roam across the island, but current Greenlanders are descendants of a particular Canadian Inuit culture that arrived around AD 1000. Greenland's recorded history began at about the same time, in AD 982, when Eric and his Norse settlers claimed the land, but after 400 years of colonization they mysteriously disappeared. During this period Denmark and Norway were joined under the Danish crown, a union that muddled ownership of Greenland until 1933, when the International High Court awarded Denmark complete sovereignty. (Because of this dual heritage, almost every town has a Greenlandic and a Danish name.) Geographically isolated and increasingly politically independent, Greenlanders are intent on redefining their ethnic identity in a modern world. They refer to themselves as Inuit, in solidarity with native peoples of Canada, Alaska, and the former Soviet Union, and speak their own language in addition to Danish.

In 1978 Denmark granted Greenland home rule, vesting its tiny *Landsting* (parliament) in the capital Nuuk/Godthåb with power over internal affairs. Though Denmark continues to devolve power, it still administers foreign policy and provides large doses of financial aid to bolster an economy based on fishing, animal husbandry, construction, and, increasingly, tourism.

Since most travelers follow preset routes, the following towns and sights are arranged south to north in geographic order and not necessarily in the order they would be visited. Though our tour describes perhaps only one major museum or sight per village, certainly there is much more to see in Greenland's changeable nature: Venture along the wooden stairs and boardwalks that connect most private homes and provide inner-village walking paths; sit beneath the expanse of an iceberg and listen to it moan; awake at 3 AM to take a stroll through the sunshine. There is no private property in Greenland—nature is free for all to enjoy, and in Greenlandic fashion, it is best savored slowly. Those who love this island do not move through it at a clip: It's more gratifying to let it move you.

Outdoor Activities and Sports

Hiking in Greenland is unlimited. Keep in mind, however, that it's wiser to join an organized hike with an experienced guide than to attempt a solo expedition, since it's not uncommon for rescue crews to have to go out in search of lost hikers. Organized excursions are available in Nuuk/Godthåb and Narsarsuak for about DKr150 for a half day, DKr300 for a full day. The tourist offices of Qaqortoq/Julianehåb and Sisimiut/Holsteinsborg arrange hikes upon request and charge according to the number of participants. For the most popular hiking areas in Greenland, new topographic maps at 1:50,000 are available. In these areas, experienced hikers can find their way without a guide. To cross the polar ice cap or to enter Greenland's national parkland—which is the size of Great Britain and France combined—you must obtain a license. Contact the **Danish Polar Center** (✉ Strandgade 100H, DK–1401 KBH K, ☎ 32/88–01–00, FAX 32/88–01–01).

The right to hunt in Greenland is reserved for residents; however, visitors can buy fishing licenses (DKr200) from the local police, major hotels, and tourism offices. Hunting laws in Greenland have changed in recent years, so you may be allowed to hunt as a member of an organized tour. Call the local tourist board for details.

Narsarsuaq

82 *4 hrs, 50 min from Copenhagen by plane.*

Narsarsuaq, meaning Great Plain in English, is a name that aptly describes the wide, smooth land that harbors one of Greenland's largest civilian airports. The town is accessible from Copenhagen, Reykjavík, and Kangerlussuaq only by plane, but to Nuuk/Godthåb by plane and boat—though the latter are booked months in advance.

Not far from the edge of town, visitors can take a 10-kilometer (6-mile) boat ride from the Narsarsuaq harbor to an area where icebergs have broken off from a nearby glacier. There they are invited to collect glacial ice for the cocktails served on board.

Also near Narsarsuaq is the point locals call **Hospitalsdalen** (Hospital Valley), a controversial area named for an alleged American hospital where Korean War wounded were said to have been hidden away so as not to weaken morale back home. Though most history books deny the story, many locals swear it's true.

Qaqortoq/Julianehåb

83 *6 hours by ferry from Narsarsuaq.*

With a population of 3,600, this is the largest town in southern Greenland and one of the loveliest. In the town square you'll see the island's only fountain, surrounded by half-timber and brightly colored houses.

Greenland

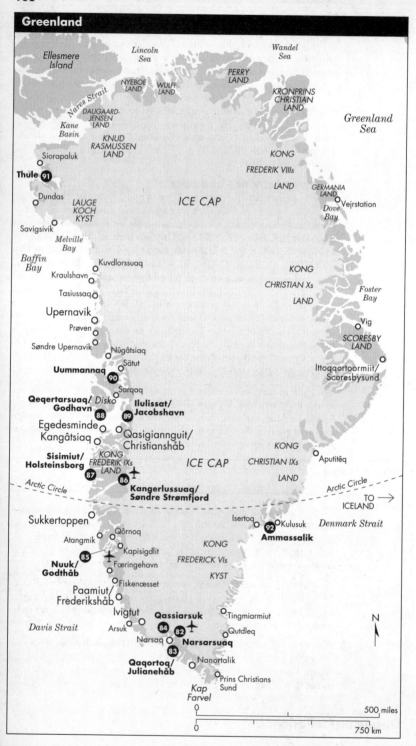

Ellesmere Island

Lincoln Sea

Wandel Sea

NYEBOE LAND

WULFF LAND

PERRY LAND

KRONPRINS CHRISTIAN LAND

Nares Strait

DAUGAARD-JENSEN LAND

Kane Basin

KNUD RASMUSSEN LAND

Greenland Sea

Siorapaluk

Thule 91

Dundas

LAUGE KOCH KYST

ICE CAP

KONG FREDERIK VIIIs LAND

GERMANIA LAND

Vejrstation

Dove Bay

Savigsivik

Melville Bay

Baffin Bay

Kuvdlorssuaq

Kraulshavn

Tasiussaq

Upernavik

Prøven

Søndre Upernavik

Nûgâtsiaq

Sätut

Uummannaq

90

Sarqaq

KONG CHRISTIAN Xs LAND

Foster Bay

Vig

SCORESBY LAND

Ittoqqortoormiit/ Scoresbysund

Qeqertarsuaq/ Godhavn

Disko

88

89

Ilulissat/ Jacobshavn

Egedesminde

Kangâtsiaq

Qasigiannguit/ Christianshåb

Sisimiut/ Holsteinsborg

KONG FREDERIK IXs LAND

87

86

ICE CAP

KONG CHRISTIAN IXs LAND

Aputitêq

Arctic Circle

Kangerlussuaq/ Søndre Strømfjord

Arctic Circle

TO ICELAND →

Sukkertoppen

Atangmik

Qôrnoq

Kapisigdlit

Nuuk/ Godthåb

85

Føringehavn

Fiskenæsset

Isertoq

Kulusuk

92

Ammassalik

Denmark Strait

KONG FREDERIK VIs KYST

Paamiut/ Frederikshåb

Ivigtut

Davis Strait

Arsuk

Qassiarsuk

84

82

Tingmiarmiut

Qutdleq

Narsaq

Narsarsuaq

83

Qaqortoq/ Julianehåb

Nanortalik

Prins Christians Sund

Kap Farvel

N

0   500 miles

0   750 km

Though the oldest building in town is the cooper shop, which dates from 1797, the most interesting is the smithy, from 1871, which now houses the **Julianehåb Museum.** Inside are handmade hunting tools, kayaks, Inuit clothing, and a furnished sod house you can enter. A traditional dwelling, it remained cozy and warm even during the harsh winter. ☜ *Free.* ⊙ *Weekdays 11–4.*

Dining and Lodging

$$ ✕🏠 **Hotel Qaqortoq.** Built in 1987, this hotel is among the more modern on the huge island. Its glass-and-white facade atop a hill overlooks the surrounding fjord and the picturesque center of town. The rooms are simple but comfortable, all with private bath, TV, and phone. ⊠ *Box 155, DK–3920,* ☎ *299/3–82–82,* 𝐅𝐀𝐗 *299/3–72–34. 21 rooms. Restaurant, billiards, bar. DC, MC, V.*

OFF THE BEATEN PATH

HVALSEY CHURCH – A nice half-day excursion from Qaqortoq is the 14½-kilometer (9-mile) sailboat ride to the well-preserved ruins of Hvalsey Church, site of a large and well-attended Norse wedding in 1408—the community's last recorded activity before it mysteriously disappeared. As the church is close to a rocky beach, the hardy can opt for a frigid dip.

Qassiarsuk

84 *30 min by boat from Narsarsuaq.*

The main focus of the tiny village of Qassiarsuk is the breeding of sheep. Though there are few modern facilities in town, the **Norse ruins** are fascinating and include, for example, the Brattahlíð—1,000-year-old ruins of Eric the Red's farm.

The remains of **Tjodhilde Kirke** are especially intriguing: This was touted as the first Christian church on the North American continent (Greenland is geographically considered part of North America and politically thought to be part of Europe). It was from this point that Eric the Red's son, Leif Ericsson, began the expedition in AD 1000 that took him to Vinland, somewhere on the coast of North America. The first Greenlandic Ting (outdoor parliament), fashioned after those in Iceland, was also held here at about the same time.

Nuuk/Godthåb

85 *1 hr, 25 min from Narsarsuaq by small plane (15 hrs by ferry); 7 hrs by plane from Ottowa.*

Nuuk/Godthåb, the capital of Greenland, is beautifully situated on a peninsula between two fjords. It was founded in 1728 by the Norwegian missionary Hans Egede; his harborside home is now the private residence of the island's home-rule premier.

The centrally located **Landsmuseet** (National Museum) has a good permanent display that includes kayaks, costumes, and hunting weapons, an art exhibit, and the five 15th-century mummies of Qilakitsoq, one of Greenland's archaeological treasures. Among the most striking are a woman and child so well preserved that even their 500-year-old clothes are in pristine condition. ⊠ *Hans Egede Vej 8,* ☎ *22611.* ☜ *Free.* ⊙ *Tues.–Sun. 1–4.*

Dining and Lodging

$$$$ ✕🏠 **Hotel Hans Egede.** This hotel is the largest in Greenland. The rooms are plain and functional but have such extras as minibars, TVs, VCRs, and phones. The sixth-floor Sky Top Restaurant, known for its lovely view of the fjords and its inventive nouveau Greenlandic menu, pre-

pares local fish using French methods. ⊠ *Box 289, DK–3900,* ☎
299/2–42–22, FAX *299/2–44–87. 108 rooms. Restaurant, pub, dance
club, meeting rooms. DC, MC, V.*

Kangerlussuaq/Søndre Strømfjord

86 *1 hr from Nuuk/Godthåb by plane; 4 hrs, 20 min by plane from
Copenhagen.*

Kangerlussuaq/Søndre Strømfjord is at the head of one of the longest
and deepest fjords in the world. The airport, Greenland's most vital,
lies just 25 kilometers (15½ miles) from the ice cap. Until World War
II, nobody lived here permanently, but Greenlanders came in the spring
to hunt reindeer. During the war, the U.S. Air Force chose its dry, stable climate for an air base, called Bluie West Eight. The military moved
out in the fall of 1992, selling all the facilities to the local government
for the sum of $1.

Sisimiut/Holsteinsborg

87 *40 min from Kangerlussuaq/Søndre Strømfjord by helicopter.*

Sisimiut/Holsteinsborg, on the Davis Strait, is a hilltop town full of Dan-
ish-style wooden houses—a local luxury, as all wood is imported. A
favorite area for dogsledging, it is also the southernmost boundary for
walrus hunting; the walrus, though extremely rare, is a popular game
animal because of its valuable tusks. The Greenlandic name Sisimiut
means Burrow People.

Qeqertarsuaq/Godhavn

88 *1 hr, 20 min from Illulissat by helicopter (8 hrs, 30 min by coastal boat;
reserve far in advance).*

In the Disko Bugt (Bay) is the island of Qeqertarsuaq/Disko, where the
main town is Qeqertarsuaq/Godhavn. Until 1950 this was the capital
of northern Greenland; Nuuk/Godthåb served as the southern capital.
The task was divided because it was too difficult to rule the entire island from one town. Accessible by helicopter and ship, Godhavn is often
booked to capacity by European tourists who come for the organized
dogsledging trips. This is the only area in Greenland with summertime
dogsledging.

Ilulissat/Jakobshavn

89 *45 min from Kangerlussuaq/Søndre Strømfjord by plane.*

In the center of Disko Bay is Ilulissat/Jakobshavn, which lies 300 kilometers (185 miles) north of the Arctic Circle. At the tip of its fjord is
the Northern Hemisphere's most productive glacier, calving 20 million
tons of floes each day—the equivalent, according to the Greenland tourist
board, of the amount of water New York City uses in a year. For a
humbling experience, take one of the helicopter tours that circle the
glacier. A violent landscape of floating ice giants and dazzling panoramas, it's been inhabited by the Inuit for as long as 4,000 years. The
town was founded in 1741 by a Danish merchant, Jakob Severin.
Today the largest industry is shrimping, though in the winter dogsled-
ders fish for halibut along the fjord.

Visit the **Knud Rasmussens Fødehjem** (boyhood home of Knud Rasmussen): This Danish-Greenlandic explorer (1879–1933) initiated the
seven Thule expeditions, which enlarged the knowledge of Arctic geography and Inuit culture. At the museum you can follow his explo-

rations through photographs, equipment, and clothing. ⌧ *DKr20.* ☉ *Daily 10–4.*

Dining and Lodging

$$$ ✕🏨 **Hotel Arctic.** This modern hotel, divided into two low-lying red buildings, is in the mountains on the edge of town, and provides views of the ice fjord and the mountains. Rooms are simple, with bathroom, phone, radio, and TV; try to reserve one with a view of the harbor. The main dining room has panoramic views of the iceberg-filled harbor and serves fine beef and fish dishes. ⌧ *Box 1501, DK–3952,* ☎ *299/4–41–53,* 🗚 *299/4–39–24. 40 rooms. Restaurant, sauna, billiards, meeting rooms. AE, DC, MC.*

$$$ ✕🏨 **Hotel Hvide Falk.** The compact rooms in this centrally located, moderate-size, two-story building are furnished with TVs and small desks, and have magnificent views of the icebergs and the Disko Mountains. The restaurant, which specializes in seafood—especially herring, cod, and salmon—looks out over the bay abob with icebergs. ⌧ *Box 20, DK–3952,* ☎ *299/4–33–43,* 🗚 *299/4–35–08. 27 rooms. Restaurant. DC.*

Uummannaq

⑩ *55 min from Ilulissat/Jakobshavn by helicopter.*

The inhabitants of the town of Uummannaq, on the island of the same name, maintain Greenlandic traditions in step with modern European life. Ranging from hunters to linguists, they are as apt to drive dogsleds as they are four-wheel drives. The town is situated beneath the magnificent hues and double humps of the granite Uummannaq Mountain, 3,855 feet high. Because the village is also perched on uneven stone cliffs, housing largely consists of brightly painted, freestanding cottages rather than the ugly Danish barracks that line some of the larger towns.

The **Uummannaq Museum** gives a good overview of life on the island, with photographs and costumes of local hunters and displays on the now-defunct mines of the area. Exhibits also detail the doomed 1930 expedition of German explorer Alfred Wegener, and there is also a bit on the Qilakitsoq mummies (☞ Nuuk/Godthåb, above), which were found in a nearby cave in 1977. ⌧ *Uummannaq Museum,* ☎ *4–81–04.* 🖭 *Free.* ☉ *Weekdays 8–4.*

The **Uummannaq Church,** which dates from 1937, is the only stone church in Greenland and is made from local granite. Next door to it are three sod huts, typical Inuit dwellings until just a couple of decades ago.

Though there is plenty of **dogsledging** north of the Arctic Circle, the trips that set out from Uummannaq are the most authentic, since local hunters drive, and also the most gentle, since the terrain here is especially smooth. Visitors sit comfortably on fur-lined sledges that tear across the frozen fjord in the hands of experienced Inuit drivers. Trips can be arranged at the Hotel Uummannaq and range from a few hours to several days of racing through the terrifying beauty of the landscape and sleeping in the shadows of towering icebergs.

Dining and Lodging

$$ ✕🏨 **Uummannaq Hotel.** This natty harborside hotel and brand-new extension offer bright, compact rooms with white, Danish-designed furniture, as well as a fine restaurant that serves local specialties, including polar bear, caribou, seal, and plenty of fish. ⌧ *Box 202, DK–3961,* ☎ *4–85–18,* 🗚 *4–82–62. 22 rooms, 10 in a nearby annex. Restaurant, bar. AE, MC, V.*

Thule

91 *2 hrs, 40 min from Uummannaq by passenger-cargo plane; 1 hr, 45 min by plane from Kangerlussuaq/Søndre Strømfjord.*

The northern reaches of Greenland are sparsely populated, with few hotels. The American air base at Thule, used for monitoring the Northern Hemisphere, is difficult to visit, but check with the Danish Foreign Ministry in Copenhagen (☎ 33/92–00–00) or the Royal Danish Embassy in Washington, DC.

Ammassalik

92 *2 hrs from Reykjavík by plane, connecting via helicopter from Kulusuk.*

Much of the east coast is empty. The only accessible towns are Ammassalik and Kulusuk, a tiny village slightly farther northeast. Both towns welcome most of Greenland's visitors, day-trippers from Iceland. Though tours (which are arranged through Icelandair) are usually short—often just day trips—they are very well organized, offering an accurate (and relatively affordable) peek at Greenlandic culture and the natural splendor of the Arctic.

Dining and Lodging

$$ ✕⊡ **Hotel Angmagssalik.** Perched on a mountain, with a lovely view of the town and harbor, this hotel is decorated with a simple wood interior, both in the guest rooms and common areas. ⊠ *Box 117, DK–3900,* ☎ *1–82–93,* ⅂⅃ᴬˣ *1–83–93. 30 rooms, 18 with private shower and toilet. Restaurant, bar. AE, DC, MC, V.*

Greenland A to Z

Arriving and Departing

The main airport in Greenland is Kangangerlussuaq/Søndre Strømfjord. International flights also arrive to a lesser frequency into Narsarsuaq for those who are destined for south Greenland. Kulusuk is the main airport for the east coast. Nuuk and Ilulissat also serve as domestic airports.

Helicopters and small planes connect small towns. Because of Greenland's highly variable weather, delays are frequent. As with all arrangements in Greenland, confirm all flights, connections, and details with your local travel agent or airline representative before you leave home. Trying to fax or call the local airlines in Greenland is not a sensible option.

The most common points of departure for Greenland are Denmark and Iceland. If you're going by way of **Iceland,** Icelandair has flights from New York, Baltimore, Fort Lauderdale, and Orlando to Keflavík, Iceland, daily in summer, and Greenlandair (Grønlandsfly in Danish) makes one flight a week between Keflavík and Narsarsuaq, year-round. It's more expensive to go by way of **Copenhagen,** with SAS, which flies six times a week to Kangangerlussuaq/Søndre Strømfjord. Connections are also available through **Canada,** where you can catch an early morning flight from Ottawa to Frobisher Bay on Baffin Island, then cross the Davis Strait to Strømfjord/Kangangerlussuaq or Nuuk/Godthåb on Firstair.

Getting Around

BY BOAT

The most beautiful passage between towns is by water. Every town has a harbor, where private boats can be hired for connections or excursions. Some coastal boats ply the waters of the west coast, making frequent stops, but space is limited and booked months in advance by locals. Again, reserve early. Boat voyages, including luxury cruises, are also available from Canada's Frobisher Bay, Norway's *Svalbard* (archipelago), and Iceland. Contact **KNI Service** (⌧ Box 608, DK–3900 Nuuk, ☏ 2–52–11, ℻ 2–32–11) or Greenland Travel in Copenhagen (☏ 33/13–10–11).

BY HELICOPTER AND PLANE

Greenlandair is the only airline licensed for domestic flights on the island. Its modest fleet of helicopters and small planes is booked year-round, so make reservations well in advance.

Contacts and Resources

EMERGENCIES

Every community has its own fire, ambulance, and police numbers and dentist and doctor, all of which you may reach through your hotel. The best way to handle emergencies is to avoid danger in the first place. Don't take risks, ask for advice, and give your travel agent and hotel your itinerary so that they can reach you in case of emergencies—or if you don't show up when you're due.

Hospital. Sana (Dronning Ingrids) Hospital, ⌧ *DK–3900 Nuuk*, ☏ *2–11–01.*

GUIDED TOURS

On-the-spot excursions are available in most towns and range from about DKr250 for a half-day to DKr600 for a full day, more for dogsledging, boat, and helicopter trips. Because transportation and accommodations are limited, have all details of your trip—connections, accommodations, sightseeing, and meals—arranged by an **experienced travel agent**, tour organizer, or airline. (It's also helpful to bring a copy of your tour contract and all confirmations.) Tour packages range from one- to four-day east-coast excursions from Reykjavík by Icelandair to monthlong nature expeditions, which can include sailing, hiking, hunting, dogsledging (February to May), whale safaris, and iceberg-watching. In the U.S. contact **Bennett of Scandinavia** (⌧ 270 Madison Ave., New York, NY 10016, ☏ 800/221–2420), **Eurocruises** (⌧ 303 W. 13th St., New York, NY 10014, ☏ 800/688–3876), **Icelandair** (⌧ Symphony Woods, 5950 Symphony Woods Rd., Columbia, MD 21044, ☏ 800/223–5500), **Quark Expeditions** (⌧ 980 Post Rd., Darien, CT 06820, ☏ 203/656–0499), **Scanam** (⌧ 933 Hwy. 23, Pompton Plains, NJ 07444, ☏ 800/545–2204), **Scantours Inc.** (⌧ 1535 6th St., Suite 209, Santa Monica, CA 90401, ☏ 800/223–7226), or **Travcoa** (⌧ 4000 McArthur Blvd. E, Suite 650, Newport Beach, CA 92660, ☏ 714/476–2800). In Canada, contact **Pedersen World Tours** (⌧ 15 Wertheim Ct., Suite 402, Richmond Hill, Ontario L4B 3H7, ☏ 416/882–5470). In Denmark, contact **Arctic Adventure** (⌧ Reventlowsgade 30, DK–1651 KBH V, ☏ 33/25–32–21). **Greenland Travel** (☞ Visitor Information, below) also operates out of Denmark.

LATE-NIGHT PHARMACIES

If you are taking medication, bring enough to last throughout your visit. In emergencies, the local hospital can fill prescriptions.

VISITOR INFORMATION

There is a tourism office in almost every town, but brochures, maps, and specific information may be limited. Call ahead for an exact street address (a 299 access code must be dialed before all phone numbers when calling from outside Greenland). **Ammassalik** (⌧ Box 120, DK–3913 Ammassalik, ☏ 1–82–77, ℻ 1–80–77). **Ilulissat/Jakobshavn** (⌧ Box 272, DK–3952 Ilulissat, ☏ 4–43–22, ℻ 4–39–33.) **Kangerlussuaq/Søndre Strømfjord** (⌧ Box 49, DK–3910, Kangerlussuaq, ☎ 1–10–98, FAX 1–14–98). **Nuuk/Godthåb** (✉ Box 199, DK–3900 Nuuk, ☎ 2–27–00, FAX 2–27–10). **South Greenland Tourism** (✉ Box 128, DK–3920 Qaqortoq, ☎ 3–84–44, FAX 3–84–95). **Qasigiannguit/Christianhåb** (✉ Hotel Igdlo, Box 160, DK–3951 Qasigiannguit, ☎ 4–50–81, FAX 4–55–24). **Qeqertarsuaq/Godhavn** (✉ Box 113, DK–3953 Qeqertarsuaq, ☎ 4–71–96, FAX 4–71–98). **Sisimiut/ Holsteinsborg** (✉ Box 65, DK–3911 Sisimiut, ☎ 1–48–48, FAX 1–56– 22). **Uummannaq** (✉ c/o Hotel Uummannaq, Box 202, DK–3961 Uummannaq, ☎ 4–85–18, FAX 4–82–62). In Copenhagen, **Greenland Travel** (✉ Gammel Mønt 12, ☎ 33/13–10–11) has a helpful and knowledgeable staff. **Greenland Tourism** (✉ Pilestræde 52, ☎ 33/13–69– 75) is another reliable Copenhagen-based operation.

THE FAROE ISLANDS

The 18 Faroe Islands (Føroyar in Faroese; Færøerne in Danish) lift up out of the North Atlantic in an extended knuckle of a volcanic archipelago. All but one are inhabited, by 43,700 people and 70,000 sheep. The native Færøese live by fishing, fish farming, and shepherding, and carefully maintain their refreshingly civilized pace of life.

Situated 300 kilometers (188 miles) northwest of Scotland, 430 kilometers (270 miles) southeast of Iceland, and 1,300 kilometers (812 miles) northwest of Denmark, the fjord-chiseled islands support little vegetation besides a bristle of short grasses and moss. The climate is oceanic: humid, changeable, and stormy, with surprisingly mild temperatures— 52°F in the summer, and 40°F in the winter—and a heavy annual rainfall of 63 inches.

Of their 1,399 square kilometers (540 square miles), 6% is fertile, the rest rough pasture—an Eden for 70 breeding and 120 migratory species of birds, among them thousands of gannets, auks, and puffins. Beneath azure skies and rugged, mossy mountains, villages of colorful thatched houses cling to hillsides while large trawlers and small fishing boats stream in and out of their harbors. Religious and proud, the Faroese have built churches in nearly every settlement.

Catholic monks from Ireland were the first to settle the islands, but they died out and were replaced by Norwegian Vikings, who settled the land in about AD 800. It was here that the *Løgting* (parliament) met for the first time in AD 900 in Tórshavn—where it still meets. Under the Danish crown, the islands have had a home-rule government since 1948, with their own flag and language.

The roots of the Faroese language are in Old West Norse. Most people speak English, but a Danish dictionary can be helpful to the visitor; Danish is the second language.

It's difficult for visitors to understand the isolation or the practical relationship the Faroese have with the natural world. Dubious outsiders, for example, accuse locals of cruelty during the traditional pilot-whale harvests. An essential foodstuff, the sea mammals are killed in limited numbers in order to reduce the islands' dependence on imported meat. The profit factor is eliminated: Whale meat is not sold—it's given away to the townspeople in equal portions on a per capita basis. The hunt is also an important social bond involving both the young and the old.

In 1993 the islands plunged into a severe depression, with unemployment, formerly an unknown phenomenon, surging from below 3% to more than 20%. The hard times are the result of a changing global fishing industry coupled with overdevelopment of the local infra-

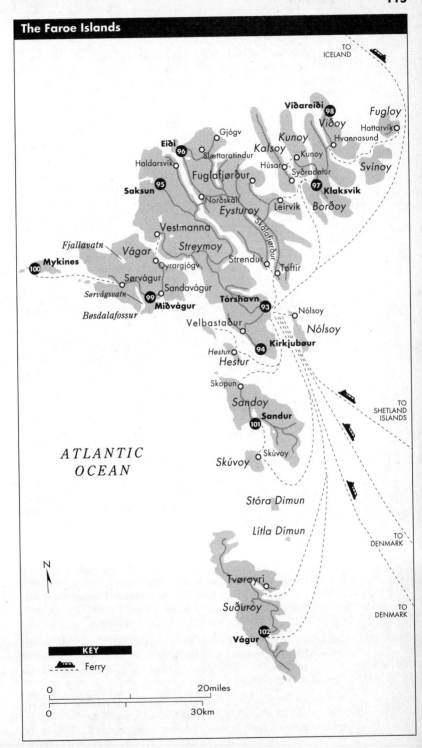

The Faroe Islands

TO ICELAND

Viðareiði 98

Fugloy

Viðoy

Hattarvík

Gjógv

Kunoy

Eiði 96

Slættaratindur

Kalsoy

Hvannasund

Haldarsvík

Kunoy

Svínoy

Fuglafjørður

Húsar

Syðradalur

Saksun 95

97 Klaksvík

Norðskáli

Eysturoy

Leirvík

Borðoy

Fjallavatn

Vestmanna

Streymoy

Vágar

Skálafjørður

Mykines 100

Oyrargjógv

Strendur

Tóftir

Sørvágur

Sandavágur

Sørvágsvatn

99 Miðvágur

Tórshavn 93

Nólsoy

Bøsdalafossur

Velbastaður

Nólsoy

Hestur

94 Kirkjubøur

Hestur

Skopun

TO SHETLAND ISLANDS

Sandoy

Sandur

101

Skúvoy

ATLANTIC OCEAN

Skúvoy

Stóra Dimun

Lítla Dímun

TO DENMARK

N

Tvøroyri

Suðuroy

TO DENMARK

Vágur 102

KEY

Ferry

0   20miles

0   30km

structure that left island coffers empty. Islanders are increasingly compelled to eye tourism as a salvation.

The following tour is organized in a way you might see the islands, using Tórshavn on the island of Streymoy as a base, and spending one night in Klaksvík on the island of Borðoy. The very efficient bus and connecting boat service is the best way to travel between towns (☞ Faroe Islands Essentials, *below*).

Tórshavn

㊗ *1,343 km (839 mi) northeast of Copenhagen (2 hrs, 15 min by plane).*

Most visitors who arrive on the Faroe Islands by plane begin their explorations on the largest and most traveled island of Streymoy, which, though carved by sheer cliffs and waterfalls, has good roads and tunnels. On the northern end of the island are bird sanctuaries and a NATO base. On its southeastern flank is one of the world's tiniest capitals, Tórshavn, named for the Viking god Thor. Centrally located among the islands, Tórshavn has a population of 16,000. A Viking parliament was founded here in about AD 1000, but it did not have any real legislative power until 1948. St. Olav's Day, July 29, is named for the Norwegian king who brought Christianity to the islands. Celebrations include rowing competitions and group dances in the form of a chain—a sort of North Atlantic ring dance.

The rugged **Tinganes** is a small peninsula between the east and west bays that was the site of both the old trading post and the meetings of the local parliament (tinganes means "assembly place"). Here you can see several buildings, including some of the town's oldest, dating from the 17th and 18th centuries, and some old warehouses, which today house the government offices. At the end of the docks is **Skansin,** a fort built in 1580 by Magnus Heinason to protect the town against pirate attacks. After many reconstructions, it reached its present shape in 1790 and was used as the Faroe headquarters of the British Navy during World War II. Two guns from that period remain.

Down from the Tinganes is Old Main Street, which is lined with small 19th-century houses and crossed by twisting streets. In the same direction, you'll come to the slate **Havnar Kirkja** (Tórshavn's Church), rebuilt many times in its 200-year history. Inside is a model of a ship salvaged from an 18th-century wreck, its bell and an altar piece dating from 1647.

There are very few trees on the islands. **Tórshavn Park,** a walk up Hoyviksvegur, used to be the pride of the town—it was a rare cultivated oasis of green trees in a land where storms and strong winds flatten tall vegetation. Planted around the turn of the century, the park thrived until 1988, when a storm virtually destroyed it.

Just off R. C. Effersøes Gøta is the **Kongaminnið** (King's Memorial) on Norðrari Ringvegur, a basalt obelisk commemorating the visit of King Christian IX in 1874. Standing atop a hill, it commands a good view of the old town.

At the northern tip of Tórshavn is the modern **Norðurlandahúsið** (Nordic Culture House), built in 1983, which hosts an international jazz festival in mid-August as well as theater and concerts throughout the year. ⊠ *Norðrari Ringvegur,* ☎ *298/17900. Call for event schedules.*

Dining and Lodging

$$$ ✕▥ **Hotel Föroyar.** Five minutes from the center of Tórshavn, this hotel has a view of the Old Town. The rooms all have TVs, refrigerators, and

phones, and there's a good restaurant with island specialties. ⊠ *Oyggjarvegur,* ☎ *17500,* FAX *16019. 216 beds. Restaurant. AE, DC, MC.*

$$$ ✕🏨 **Hotel Hafnia.** Close to the pedestrian streets of town, this modern business hotel offers a good buffet and big-city ambience. The rooms vary in size, but all are comfortably appointed with TVs, telephones, desks, and private showers. The restaurant serves Faroese seafood, including local cod and flounder. ⊠ *Áarvegur 4,* ☎ *11270,* FAX *15250. 76 beds. Restaurant. AE, DC, MC.*

$$ 🏨 **Skansin Guesthouse.** Hard times have forced owner Frantz Restorff to close part of his guest house, but the rest of it, where he and his wife live, remains open to guests, who will experience typical Faroese hospitality within the modesty and personality of this private home. Filled with their belongings—a watercolor of a family-owned island, family photos, a collection of old records—the house is familiar and cozy. The Restorffs serve a generous breakfast (included in the room rate) and offer expert advice and assistance in planning activities. Guests have use of the kitchen. ⊠ *Jekaragøta 8, Box 57, FR–110 Tórshavn,* ☎ *12242,* FAX *10657. 22 beds. No credit cards.*

$$ 🏨 **Youth Hostel Tórshavn.** Open as a hotel from July to September, this summer-only hotel is a school during the winter. ⊠ *Vesturgøta 15,* ☎ *18900,* FAX *15707. 100 beds. AE, DC, MC.*

$ 🏨 **Tórshavnar Sjómansheim.** Centrally located in the middle of Tórshavn, this modest hotel caters to those who need only a bed to be happy; rooms are clean and basic, with dark hand-me-down furniture. The restaurant serves one special of the day, ranging from beef stew to—if there is a catch—whale. ⊠ *Tórsgøta 4,* ☎ *13515,* FAX *13286. 55 beds. Restaurant. No credit cards.*

OFF THE
BEATEN PATH

BOAT TRIP FROM VESTMANNA – You can take a bus from Tórshavn to Vestmanna (40 km/25 mi north of Tórshavn), where a boat takes you through narrow channels from which you can see sheep grazing atop sheer cliffs; in the spring the sheep are hoisted up the 700 meters (2,310 feet) with ropes, and in the fall they are caught and brought back down—apparently this process makes them taste better. Double-check the bus schedule before you leave, as it's easy to get stranded out here. Contact the Tórshavn tourist office for more details.

Kirkjubøur

⑨④ *13 km (8 mi) south of Tórshavn.*

From Tórshavn, a bus takes you to the outskirts of Kirkjubøur, from which you will have to walk a mile—through fields populated with ponies and sheep—to the tiny town (ask the tourist office in Tórshavn for detailed directions), which has a population of 60. The townsfolk live in black houses with red window frames and green grass roofs perched on hillsides around the tiny, often fog-shrouded harbor. At the southern tip of the island, the town was the Faroes' spiritual and cultural center from 1269 to 1308.

A particularly ambitious priest, Bishop Erland, built a cathedral in the town in the 13th century—there is some controversy over whether or not it was ever completed—and the ruins of the Gothic **Magnus Cathedral** still stand. Inside the church is a large stone tablet engraved with an image of Christ on the cross, flanked by the Virgin Mary and Mary Magdalene, and an inscription to St. Magnus and St. Thorlak. During restoration work in 1905, the tablet was removed to reveal well-

preserved relics of the saints. In 1538, after the Reformation, the episcopal see was dissolved and with it the town's power.

Just next door to the Magnus Cathedral is the restored **St. Olav's Church,** which dates from 1111 and is now the only church from that time still in use. Most of its sculptures have been removed to Copen-hagen, leaving little to see, but there's a hole in the north wall that once allowed lepers standing outside to watch the mass and receive the Eu-charist. The altarpiece is the work of the most famous painter of the islands, Sámal Mikines.

Near the church is a farmhouse, the **Roykstovan.** Legend has it that the lumber for the building came drifting to the town, neatly numbered and bundled, from the Sogne Fjord in Norway. Inside are the tradi-tional Faroese one-main-room living quarters and a dozen other rooms. It's been in the same family for the last 16 generations, and it is here that foreign dignitaries are welcomed to the town.

Saksun

⑨⑤ *30 km (18 mi) northwest of Tórshavn.*

Among the fjords that slice the northern end of Streymoy is the tiny town of Saksun, one of the most popular excursions on the island. Set around a pastoral lake in the midst of a deep valley are scattered sod-roof houses with lovely views. The town also swarms with great skuas, large brown seabirds prone to low dives. As you unwittingly near their nests, you will certainly notice their cantankerous presence.

Eiðli

⑨⑥ *52 km (32 mi) north of Tórshavn.*

The island of Eysturoy, just east of Streymoy, is connected to the latter by bridge and buses. The center of activity is the town of Eiði, which lies to the northwest in a spectacular landscape. Looking northwest, you can see two 250-foot cliffs, a part of local mythology: One night an Ice-landic giant and his wife came to carry the islands to Iceland, but she dropped them, giving the islands their cracked geography. Once the sun rose, the giants were petrified and transformed into the bluffs.

Due east of Eiðli is the islands' highest point, the 2,910-foot **Slæt-taratindur** mountain. The shores of the southern **Skálafjørður,** the longest fjord in the archipelago, are where the majority of the island's 10,500 people live.

Dining and Lodging

$$ ✕▥ **Hotel Eiði.** Perched on a hilltop in a village near the sea, about an hour by bus from Tórshavn, this slightly dated hotel is small and clean, with TVs and refrigerators in all rooms. ⊠ *FR–470 Eiði,* ☎ *298/23456,* ℻ *298/23200. 28 beds. Restaurant. DC, MC, V.*

$ ▥ **Gjáargarður.** This youth hostel, built in traditional Faroese style, has a prime position on the north end of the island, near the ocean and the mountains. ⊠ *FR–476,* ☎ *23171,* ℻ *23505. 100 beds. No credit cards.*

Klaksvík

⑨⑦ *35 km (22 mi) northeast of Tórshavn.*

The island of Borðoy is accessible by boat from eastern Eysturoy. On its southwest coast, nearly divided by two fjords, Klaksvík is the Faroes' second-largest town and most important fishing harbor (its fleet of sophisticated boats harvests cod, haddock, herring, and other fish).

Within this scattering of islands, Borðoy, Viðoy, and Kunoy are connected by causeways. The other three islands, Fugloy, Svinoy, and Kalsoy, are accessible by passenger boat or helicopter.

Within Klaksvík, the baptismal font in the **Christianskirkjan** (Christian's Church) is a piece of carved granite thought to have been used in pagan rituals in Denmark 4,000 years ago. Suspended from the church roof is a 24-foot boat used by a former vicar to visit nearby towns; the boat—common in Danish churches—is a symbol that God is watching over the village fishermen.

Lodging

$$ 🏨 **Klaksvíkar Sjómansheim.** Sheep graze on the front lawn of this big, white hotel; the back overlooks the colorful harbor. The staff is cheery and helpful, and rooms—request one with a harbor view—offer no-frills comfort; showers and toilets are located in the hallways, but sinks are in the rooms. The restaurant serves generous portions of the homemade special of the day. ⊠ *Vikavegur 39, FR–700 Klaksvík,* ☎ *55333. 34 rooms. No credit cards.*

$ 🏨 **Youth Hostel and Guest House Ibuð.** This youth and family hostel, the only one on the northern islands, is in a former hotel, built in 1945. It is near a ferry slip and surrounded by hiking trails. ⊠ *Garðavegur 31, FR–700 Klaksvík,* ☎ *55403 or 57555. 28 youth hostel beds, 8 guest house beds. No credit cards.*

Viðareiði

98 *18 km (11 mi) north of Klaksvík.*

The island of Viðoy is among the wildest and most beautiful of the islands, with mountains of 2,800 feet and sheer cliffs plunging into extremely rough, unnavigable waters. Amazingly, 600 people live here, many in the town of Viðareiði. Cape Enniberg, at its northernmost tip, is 2,460 feet high; it's the world's highest cape rising directly from the sea. From the town of Viðareiði you can take a boat tour (call Tora Tourist Travel) to see many seabirds nesting on cliff walls, including kittiwakes and puffins—endearing little black-and-white birds with enormous orange beaks. The Faroese have a remarkable relationship with the puffins, harvesting them by the thousands for food and yet not endangering their numbers.

Lodging

$ 🏨 **Hotel Norð.** In a small town of 300 inhabitants on the northern end of the island, this simple business hotel has beautiful surroundings and great bird-watching. ⊠ *FR–750 Viðareiði,* ☎ *51061,* 📠 *51144. 20 beds. No credit cards. Closed Oct.–May.*

Miðvágur

99 *18 km (11 mi) west of Tórshavn.*

Vágar, the third-largest island, takes its name from its fjords, and it is cut by three of them, as well as by the Fjallavatn and Sørvágsvatn lakes, the last of which is fed by the Bøsdalafossur, a 100-foot waterfall. The main town here is Miðvágur, an excellent perch for auk- and gannet-watching.

Dining and Lodging

✕🏨 **Hotel Vágar.** A standard small hotel, this one is modern. ⊠ *FR–380 Sørvágur,* ☎ *32955,* 📠 *32310. 50 beds. Restaurant. AE, DC, MC.*

Mykines

 48 km (30 mi) west of Miðvágar (1 hr, 15 min by boat; 15 min by he-licopter).

It's rough sailing to the tiny atoll of Mykines and only manageable when weather permits. In the town of the same name, population 15, the few dwellings are roofed with sod. The town was sited here to be close to the **Mykineshólmur,** an islet swarming with thousands of puffins, which are harvested for food. You can get here by traversing the island north-ward on foot about 2 kilometers (1¼ miles) from the boat landing in Søvágur.

Sandur

 25 km (16 mi) south of Tórshavn, 16 km (10 mi) south of Klaksvík.

Sandoy, the fifth-largest island, lies to the south. Relatively fertile, it's named for the sandy white beaches of the town of Sandur, on its bay. Sheep graze on green hills, and the lakes north and west of town swell with auks, purple sandpipers, and great skuas. This is great walking or cycling country (bike rentals are available in town).

Vágur

 64 km (40 mi) south of Tórshavn.

The southernmost island, Suðuroy, is milder than the others, with cul-tivated green fields at its center and mountains along the coast. Fer-ries from Tórshavn dock either in Vágur or the quieter village of Tvøroyri.

Lodging

$$ 🏨 **Hotel Tvøroyri.** In the middle of town, this old hotel has simple, clean rooms and minimal service. ✉ *FR–800 Tvøroyri,* ☎ *71171,* 𝔽𝔸𝕏 *72171. 21 beds. AE.*

$ 🏨 **Hotel Bakkin.** This plain lodging is usually booked by fishermen and local workers. ✉ *FR–900 Vágur,* ☎ *73961. 18 beds. No credit cards.*

Faroe Islands A to Z

Arriving and Departing

BY FERRY

There is frequent ferry service to all islands, with the most remote areas served by helicopter as well. Once a week in summer there are car fer-ries from Esbjerg (33 hours) to Tórshavn. Call **DFDS** (☎ 33/11–22–55). Year-round ferries depart from Hirtshals, Jylland on Friday and arrive in Tórshavn on Monday (48 hours), and there are regular con-nections to and from Aberdeen. Call **Faroeship** (☎ 39/29–26–88) for more information.

BY PLANE

SL Visitor Cards are sold at airports (☞ Getting Around, *below*). De-lays due to heavy fog are common. **From Copenhagen** there are daily connections to the western island of Vágar that take about two hours. From there, count another 2½ hours to get to Tórshavn by bus and ferry. For reservations on either Danair or Atlantic Airways, call SAS (☎ 32/32–68–68) in Copenhagen or Flogfelag Føroya (☎ 298/32755) in the Faroe Islands. Maersk Air (☎ 32/31–45–45 in Copenhagen; ☎ 298/11025 in Tórshavn) flies year-round between Copenhagen and Billund, on Jutland, and the Faroe Islands, with other connections avail-able from Amsterdam, Brussels, Frankfurt, London, Paris and Stock-holm. Two weekly flights are also available from **Reykjavik** (☎

91–25100) on Icelandair, which also flies once a week, in the summer, from Glasgow to the Faroes and on to Iceland.

Getting Around

BY BUS, FERRY, AND HELICOPTER

The main islands are connected by regular ferries; smaller ones are linked by mailboat and helicopter. The **SL Visitor Card** is a good value for exploring the islands; it affords free passage on all SL (the local transportation company) buses and ferries. Be sure to buy the card at the airport (or from your travel agent) to pay for the trip to Tórshavn. It costs DKr385 for four days, DKr600 for seven days, DKr900 for 14 days; it's half-price for children under 13, free for those under 7 years old. For ferries, call **Strandfaraskip Landsins,** Tórshavn (☎ 298/14550, FAX 298/16000). **Helicopter Service** is in Vagar (☎ 298/33410). In towns, and between islands that are connected by bridges, there is regular bus service. For schedules and reservations, call **Bygdaleiðir** in Tórshavn (☎ 298/14550).

BY CAR

Driving laws are the same as in Denmark. Car rentals are available in Tórshavn and at Vagar Airport. A network of two-lane asphalt roads has been built between towns, using tunnels and bridges. The roads are best on the nine main islands. Speed limits are 50 kilometers per hour (30 miles per hour) in urban areas, 80 kph (50 mph) outside. Once outside towns, beware of untethered animals. The islanders are extremely strict about drunk driving.

Contacts and Resources

EMERGENCIES

Ambulance, fire, police (☎ 000). **Tórshavn Pharmacy** (✉ by SMS shopping center, ☎ 298/11100) . **Klaksvík Pharmacy** (✉ Klaksvíksvegur, ☎ 298/55055), or **Tvøroyri Pharmacy** (☎ 298/71076).

GUIDED TOURS

In addition to the local tours offered by many hotels, two main tour operators on the islands, Kunningarstovan (✉ Vaglid, Tórshavn, ☎ 298/15788) and Tora Tourist Travel (✉ N. Finsensgøta, Tórshavn, ☎ 298/15505), offer angling, city, and bird-watching tours. Among these are boat tours of Nolsoy and Hestur (Kunningarstovan), which leave from Tórshavn harbor and include coastal sailing through the Kapilsund strait and along Hestur's west coast to see puffins and other seabirds. The 3-hour trips are aboard the 50-year-old wooden schooner *Nordlys* (*Northern Light*), and guests may even get a chance to do some fishing. Tora Tourist Travel organizes a tour to Gjógv, the northernmost village on Eysturoy (5 hours), including a view of mountains and a local village, and the Vestmanna Birdcliffs Tour (6 hours), which includes a look at bird colonies and nearby caves.

VISITOR INFORMATION

The helpful brochure "Around the Faroe Islands," published by the tourist board, is available at local tourist offices. In Copenhagen, call the **Faroese Government Office** (✉ Højbroplads 7, ☎ 33/14–08–66). Within the Faroe Islands, try the following: **Klaksvík Tourist Information** (✉ N. Palsgøta, FR–700 Klaksvík, ☎ 298/56939). **Aldan Tourist Information** (✉ Reyngøta 17, FR–100 Tórshavn, ☎ 298/19391). The **Danish Tourist Board** (branches in Denmark and abroad) can also supply information.

DENMARK A TO Z

Arriving and Departing

From North America

BY PLANE

From New York, flights to Copenhagen take 7 hours, 40 minutes. From Chicago they take 8 hours, 15 minutes. From Los Angeles the flight time is 10 hours, 55 minutes.

Copenhagen's **Kastrup Airport,** the hub of Scandinavian air travel, is 10 kilometers (6 miles) from the capital's center. **Scandinavian Airlines System** (SAS; ☎ 800/221–2350), the main carrier, makes nonstop flights from Chicago, Newark, and Seattle. **British Airways** (☎ 800/247–9297) offers connecting flights via London from Atlanta, Boston, Chicago, Dallas, Detroit, Los Angeles, Miami, New York, Orlando, Philadelphia, Pittsburgh, San Francisco, Seattle, and Washington, D.C. **Icelandair** (☎ 800/223–5500) makes connecting flights via Reykjavík from Baltimore, Fort Lauderdale, New York, and Orlando. **Delta** (☎ 800/221–1212) has direct service from Atlanta and New York, connecting to 217 cities in North America.

From the United Kingdom

BY BUS

Not particularly comfortable or fast, bus travel is inexpensive. **Eurolines** (⊠ 23 Crawley, Luton, Bedfordshire LU1 1HX, ☎ 0158/240–4511; Copenhagen office, ☎ 33/25–95–11) travels from London's Victoria Station on Saturday at 9:30 PM and arrives in Copenhagen 24 hours later.

BY CAR AND FERRY

Scandinavian Seaways Ferries (DFDS) (⊠ Scandinavia House, Parkeston Quay, Harwich, Essex CO12 4QG, England, ☎ 01255/24–02–40; in Denmark, ☎ 33/11–22–55) sail from Harwich to Esbjerg (20 hours) on Jylland's west coast and from Newcastle to Esbjerg (21 hours). Schedules in both summer and winter are very irregular. There are many discounts, including 20% for senior citizens and the disabled, and 50% for children between the ages of 4 and 16.

The only part of Denmark that is connected to the European continent is Jylland, via the E45 highway from Germany. The E20 highway then leads to Middelfart on Fyn and east to Knudshoved. From there a ferry crosses to Korsør on Sjælland and E20 leads east to Copenhagen. Another option is to take the three-hour car ferry from Århus directly to Kalundborg in western Sjælland. From there, Route 23 leads to Copenhagen. Make reservations for the ferry in advance through the **Danish State Railway (DSB,** ☎ 33/14–88–80). (*Note:* During the busy summer months, passengers without reservations for their vehicles can wait hours.) The eventual completion of the Storebælt Bridge, connecting Fyn and Sjælland, should speed up rail connections and auto traffic.

BY PLANE

From London to Copenhagen the flight takes 1 hour, 55 minutes.

British Airways (⊠ 156 Regent St., London W1, ☎ 0181/897–4000) flies nonstop from Heathrow, Gatwick, Birmingham, and Manchester. **SAS Scandinavian Airlines** (⊠ SAS House, 52–53 Conduit St., London W1R 0AY, ☎ 0171/734–6777) flies nonstop from Heathrow, Manchester, and Glasgow and also from London to Århus. **Brymon European Airways** (⊠ Plymouth City Airport, Croenhill, Plymouth PL6 8BW, ☎ 0121/782–0711) flies nonstop from Birmingham. **Aer Lingus** (⊠ 67 Deans Gate, Manchester, ☎ 0161/832–5771) flies direct from

Manchester. **Maersk Air** (⊠ Terminal House, 52 Grosvenor Gardens, London, SW1, ☎ 0171/333-0066) flies nonstop from Gatwick to Billund and Copenhagen.

BY TRAIN

Trains within Europe are well connected to Denmark, with Copenhagen serving as the main hub; however, it's often little cheaper than flying, especially if you make your arrangements from the United States. Eurorail and Eurail Saverpasses, which can be purchased only in the United States, are accepted by the Danish State Railway and on some ferries operated by DSB. From London, the crossing (23 hours, including ferry) can be arranged through the British Rail European Travel Center (⊠ Victoria Station, London, ☎ 0171/834–2345), Eurotrain (⊠ 52 Grosvenor Gardens, London SW1, ☎ 0171/730–3402) and Wasteels (⊠ 121 Wilton Rd., London SW1, ☎ 0171/834–7066).

The **ScanRail** pass, which affords unlimited train travel throughout Denmark, Finland, Norway, and Sweden and restricted ferry passage in and beyond Scandinavia, comes in various denominations: 5 days of travel within 15 days ($222 first class, $176 second class); 10 days within a month ($346 first class, $278 second class); or 1 month ($504 first class, $404 second class). In the U.S., call RailEurope (☎ 800/438–7245) or **DER** (☎ 800/782–2424), which also offers a 21-day pass for $400 (first class) or $320 (second class). Buy your tickets in the U.S.: Though they are available in Denmark, they are more expensive. Various discounts are offered to holders of the pass by hotel chains and other organizations; ask DER, RailEurope, or your travel agent for details.

Getting Around

By Car

Roads here are good and largely traffic-free (except for the manageable traffic around Copenhagen); you can reach most islands by toll bridges.

Major international **car rental** agencies are represented throughout Denmark. Smaller companies include: Europcar (⊠ Kastrup Airport, ☎ 32/50–30–90) and Pitzner Auto (⊠ Kastrup Airport, ☎ 32/50–90–65). In Copenhagen, most car-rental agencies are located near the Vesterport Station.

RULES OF THE ROAD

Drivers need a valid driver's license, and if you're using your own car, it must have a certificate of registration and national plates. A triangular hazard-warning sign is compulsory in every car and is provided with rentals. No matter where you sit in a car, you must wear a seat belt, and cars must have low beams on at all times. Motorcyclists must wear helmets and use low-beam lights as well.

Drive on the right and give way to traffic—*especially to cyclists*—on the right. A red-and-white YIELD sign or a line of white triangles across the road means you must yield to traffic on the road you are entering. Do not turn right on red unless there is a green arrow indicating that this is allowed. Speed limits are 50 kilometers per hour (30 miles per hour) in built-up areas; 100 kph (60 mph) on highways; and 80 kph (50 mph) on other roads. If you are towing a trailer, you must not exceed 70 kph (40 mph). Speeding and, especially, drinking and driving are treated severely, even if no damage is caused. Americans and foreign tourists must pay fines on the spot.

BREAKDOWNS

Before leaving home, consult your insurance company. Members of organizations affiliated with Alliance International de Tourisme (AIT) can get technical and legal advice from the Danish Motoring Organization (FDM) (✉ Firskovvej 32, 2800 Lyngby, ☎ 45/93–08–00), open 10–4 weekdays. All highways have emergency phones, and you can call the rental company for help. If you cannot drive your car to a garage for repairs, the rescue corps Falck (☎ 33/14–22–22) can help anywhere, anytime. In most cases they do charge for assistance.

GASOLINE

Gasoline costs about DKr6.60 per liter.

PARKING

You can usually park on the right-hand side of the road, though not on main roads and highways. Signs reading PARKERING/STANDSNING FORBUNDT mean no parking or stopping, though you are allowed a three-minute grace period for loading and unloading. In town, parking discs are used where there are no automatic ticket-vending machines. Get discs from gas stations, post offices, police stations, or tourist offices, and set them to show your time of arrival. For most downtown parking, you must buy a ticket from an automatic vending machine and display it on the dash. Parking costs about DKr9 or more per hour in town, DKr7 elsewhere.

By Plane

Copenhagen's **Kastrup Airport** is the hub of all domestic routes. Most other airports are located in areas that serve several cities. Flight times within the country are all less than one hour. Denmark's major carriers are SAS (☎ 32/32–68–68), Danair (☎ 31/51–50–55), and Maersk Air (☎ 32/45–35–35).

Intra-Scandinavian travel is usually expensive. If you want to economize, look into the **Visit Scandinavia Fare.** One coupon costs about $80; six are about $480, for unlimited air travel in Denmark, Sweden, Norway, and Finland. It is sold only in the United States. Coupons can be used year-round for a maximum of three months and must be purchased in conjunction with transatlantic flights.

By Public Transportation

Traveling by bus or train is easy because DSB and a few private companies cover the country with a dense network of services, supplemented by buses in remote areas. Hourly intercity trains connect the main towns in Jylland and Fyn with Copenhagen and Sjælland, using high-speed diesels, called IC-3, on the most important stretches. All these trains make one-hour ferry crossings of the Great Belt, the waterway separating Fyn and Sjælland. You can reserve seats on intercity trains, and you *must* have a reservation if you plan to cross the Great Belt. Buy tickets at stations for trains, buses, and connecting ferry crossings. Bus tickets are usually sold on the bus. Children under 5 travel free, and those between 5 and 12 travel for half-price. Ask about discounts for senior citizens and groups of three or more. The ScanRail Pass, for travel anywhere within Scandinavia (Denmark, Sweden, Norway, and Finland), and the Interail and Eurail passes are also valid on all DSB trains, as well as some ferry crossings. Call the DSB Travel Office (☎ 33/14–17–01 or 42/52–92–22) for additional information.

Contacts and Resources

Language

Most Danes, except those in rural areas, speak English well. Bring a phrase book if you plan to visit the countryside or the small islands.

Lodging

CAMPING

If you wish to camp in one of Denmark's 500-plus approved campsites, you'll need an International Camping Carnet or Danish Camping Pass (available at any campsite and valid for one year). For details on camping and discounts for groups and families, contact **Campingrådet** (✉ Hesseløgade 16, DK–2100 Copenhagen Ø, ☎ 39/27–88–44).

FARM VACATIONS

There's a minimum stay of three nights for most farm stays. Bed-and-breakfast costs DKr175; half-board, around DKr245. Lunch and dinner can often be purchased for DKr25 to DKr35, and full board can be arranged. Children under 4 get 75% off; 4–11 get 50%. Contact the **Horsens Tourist Office** (✉ Søndergade 26, DK–8700 Horsens, Jylland, ☎ 70/10-41-90, FAX 75/60–21–90).

HOTELS

Make your reservations well in advance, especially in resort areas near the coasts, to avoid having to overnight last-minute in costly hotels. Many places offer summer reductions to compensate for the slowdown in business traveling and conferences.

Many Danes prefer a shower to a bath, so if you particularly want a bath, ask for it, but be prepared to pay more. Taxes are usually included in prices, but check when making a reservation. As time goes on, it appears that an increasing number of hotels are eliminating breakfast from their room rates; even if it is not included, breakfast is usually well worth its price.

The very friendly staff at the **hotel booking desk** (☎ 33/12–28–80) in the main tourist office (✉ Bernstorffsgade 1, DK–1577 Copenhagen V) can help find rooms in hotels, hostels, and private homes, or even at campsites. Prices range from budget upward. Prebooking in private homes and hotels must be done two months in advance, but last-minute (as in same-day) hotel rooms can also be found and will save you 50% off the normal price.

INNS

Contact **Dansk Kroferie** (✉ Vejlevej 16, DK–8700 Horsens, ☎ 75/64–87–00) to order a free catalog of bed-and-breakfast inns, but choose carefully: The organization includes some chain hotels that would be hard-pressed to demonstrate a modicum of inn-related charm. The price of an inn covers one overnight stay in a room with bath, breakfast included. Note that some establishments tack an additional DKr125 surcharge onto the price of a double. You can save money by investing in **Inn Checks,** valid at 87 inns. Each check costs DKr375 per person or DKr575 per couple. **Family checks** (DKr650–DKr725) are also available.

RENTALS

A simple house with room for four will cost from DKr2,500 per week upward. Contact **DanCenter** (✉ Falkoner Allé 7, DK–2000 Frederiksberg, ☎ 31/19–09–00).

YOUTH AND FAMILY HOSTELS

If you have an International Youth Hostels Association card (obtainable before you leave home), the average cost is DKr65 to DKr85 per person. Without the card, there's a surcharge of DKr22. The hostels fill up quickly in summer, so make your reservations early. Most hostels are particularly sympathetic to students and will usually find them at least a place on the floor. Bring your own linens or sleep sheet, though these can usually be rented at the hostel. Sleeping bags are not allowed.

Contact **Landsforeningen Danmarks Vandrehjem** (✉ Vesterbrogade 39, DK–1620, Copenhagen V, ☎ 31/31–36–12, FAX 31/31–36–26). It charges for information, but you can get a free brochure, "Camping/Youth and Family Hostels," from the Danish Tourist Board.

Mail

POSTAL RATES

Airmail letters and postcards to the United States cost DKr5 for 20 grams. Letters and postcards to the United Kingdom and EU countries cost DKr3.75. You can buy stamps at post offices or from shops selling postcards.

RECEIVING MAIL

You can arrange to have your mail sent general delivery, marked *Poste Restante,* to any post office, hotel, or inn. The address for the main post office in Copenhagen is Tietgensgade 37, DK–1704 KBH. If you do not have an address, **American Express** (✉ Amagertorv 18, DK–1461 KBH K, ☎ 33/12–23–01) will also receive and hold cardholders' mail.

Money and Expenses

CURRENCY

The monetary unit in Denmark is the krone (DKr), which is divided into 100 øre. At press time (December 1996), the krone stood at 5.7 to the dollar, 8.9 to the pound sterling, and 4.1 to the Canadian dollar. Most major credit cards are accepted in Denmark, American Express less frequently than others, and Carte Blanche rarely. Traveler's checks can be exchanged in banks and at many hotels, restaurants, and shops.

SAMPLE PRICES

Denmark's economy is stable, and inflation remains reasonably low. Although lower than Norway's and Sweden's, the Danish cost of living is nonetheless high, especially for such luxuries as cigarettes and alcohol. Prices are highest in Copenhagen, lower elsewhere in the country. Some sample prices: cup of coffee, DKr14–DKr20; bottle of beer, DKr15–DKr25; soda, DKr10–DKr15; ham sandwich, DKr25–DKr40; 1-mile taxi ride, DKr35–DKr50, depending on traffic.

TAXES

All hotel, restaurant, and departure taxes and VAT (what the Danes call MOMS) are automatically included in prices. VAT is 25%; non-EU citizens can obtain an 18% refund. The more than 1,500 shops that participate in the tax-free scheme have a white TAX FREE sticker on their windows. Purchases must be at least DKr300 per store and must be sealed and unused in Denmark. At the shop, you'll be asked to fill out a form and show your passport. The form can then be turned in at any airport or ferry customs desk, where you can choose a check or charge-card credit. Keep all your receipts and tags; occasionally, customs authorities do ask to see purchases, so pack them where they will be accessible.

TIPPING

The egalitarian Danes do not expect to be tipped. Service is included in bills for hotels, bars, and restaurants. Taxi drivers round up the fare to the next krone but expect no tip. The exception is hotel porters, who receive about DKr5 per bag.

Opening and Closing Times

MUSEUMS

A number of Copenhagen's museums hold confounding hours, so always call first to confirm. As a rule, however, most museums are open 10 to 3 or 11 to 4 and are closed on Monday. In winter, opening hours are shorter, and some museums close for the season. Check the local papers or ask at tourist offices for current schedules.

SHOPS

Though many Danish stores are expanding their hours, sometimes even staying open on Sundays, most shops still keep the traditional hours: weekdays 10 to 5:30, until 7 on Thursday and Friday, until 1 or 2 on Saturday—though the larger department stores stay open until 5. Everything except bakeries, kiosks, flower shops, and a handful of grocers are closed on Sunday, and most bakeries take Monday off. The first and last Saturday of the month are Long Saturdays, when even the smaller shops, especially in large cities, stay open until 4 or 5. Grocery stores stay open until 8 PM on weekdays, and kiosks until much later.

BANKS

Banks in Copenhagen are open weekdays 9:30 to 4 and Thursdays until 6. Several *bureaux de change,* including the ones at Copenhagen's central station and airport, stay open until 10 PM. Outside Copenhagen, banking hours vary.

Outdoor Activities and Sports

BIKING

Bicycles can be sent as baggage between most train stations and can also be carried onto most trains and ferries; contact **DSB** (☎ 33/14–17–01) for information. All cabs must be able to take bikes and are equipped with racks (they add a modest fee).

Most towns have rentals, but check with local tourism offices for referrals. For more information, contact the **Danish Cyclist Federation** (✉ Rømersgade 7, DK–1362 KBH K, ☎ 33/32–31–21). The Danish Tourist Board also publishes bicycle maps and brochures.

BikeDenmark, a Copenhagen-based outfitter, combines the flexibility of individual tours with the security of an organized outing. Choose from four preplanned seven-day tours, which include bikes, maps, two fine meals per day, charming hotel accommodations, and hotel-to-hotel baggage transfers. To book in the United States, contact Borton Oversees (✉ 5516 Lyndale Ave. S, Minneapolis, MN 55419, ☎ 800/843–0602), Nordique Tours (✉ 5250 W. Century Blvd., Suite 626, Los Angeles, CA 90045, ☎ 800/995–7997), or Scanam World Tours (✉ 933 Rte. 23, Pompton Plains, NJ 07444, ☎ 800/545–2204).

FISHING AND ANGLING

Licenses are required for fishing along the coasts; requirements vary from one area to another for fishing in lakes, streams, and the ocean. Licenses generally cost around DKr100 and can be purchased from any post office. Remember—it is illegal to fish within 1,650 feet of the mouth of a stream.

Telephones

Telephone exchanges throughout Denmark were changed over the past couple of years. If you hear a recorded message or three loud beeps, chances are the number you are trying to reach has been changed. KTAS information (☎ 118) can always find current numbers.

LOCAL CALLS

Phones accept 1-, 5-, 10-, and 20-kroner coins. Pick up the receiver, dial the number, always including the area code, and wait until the party answers; then deposit the coins. You have roughly a minute per krone, so you can make another call on the same payment if your time has not run out. When it does, you will hear a beep and your call will be disconnected unless you deposit another coin. Dial the eight-digit number for calls anywhere within the country. For calls to the Faroe Islands (☎ 298) and Greenland (☎ 299), dial ☎ 00, then the three-digit code, then the five-digit number.

INTERNATIONAL CALLS

Dial ☎ 00, then the country code (1 for the United States and Canada, 44 for Great Britain), the area code, and the number. It's very expensive to telephone or fax from hotels, although the regional phone companies offer a discount after 7:30 PM. It's more economical to make calls from either the Copenhagen main rail station or the airports.

OPERATORS AND INFORMATION

Most operators speak English. For national directory assistance, dial ☎ 118; for an international operator, dial ☎ 113; for a directory-assisted international call, dial ☎ 115. To reach an AT&T direct operator in the United States, for collect, person-to-person, or credit-card calls, dial ☎ 80–01–0010.

Visitor Information

Danish Tourist Board ⊠ *655 3rd Ave., New York, NY 10017,* ☎ *212/ 949–2333.*

Danish Contact Center ⊠ *c/o Helen Bergstrøm, Box 636, Streetsville, Mississauga, Ontario L5M 2C2,* ☎ *416/820–8984.*

Danish Tourist Board ⊠ *55 Sloane St., London SW1 XSY,* ☎ *0171/259– 5957.*

3 Finland

Nature dictates life in this Nordic land, where winter brings perpetual darkness and summer, perpetual light. Gin-clear streams run through vast forests lit by the midnight sun, and reindeer roam free. Even the arts mimic nature: Witness the soaring monuments of Alvar Aalto, evocative of Finland's expansive forests—and the music of Jean Sibelius, which can swing from a somber nocturne to a joyful crescendo, like a streak of sunlight in the woods.

IF YOU LIKE MAJESTIC OPEN SPACES, fine architecture, and civilized living, Finland is for you. The music of Jean Sibelius, Finland's most famous son, tells you what to expect from this Nordic landscape. Both can swing from the somber nocturne of midwinter darkness to the tremolo of sunlight slanting through pine and birch, or from the crescendo of a blazing sunset to the pianissimo of the next day's dawn. The architecture of Alvar Aalto and the Saarinens, Eliel and son Eero, visible in many U.S. cities, also bespeaks the Finnish affinity with nature, with soaring spaces evocative of Finland's moss-floored forests. Eliel and his family moved to the United States in 1923 and became American citizens—but it was to a lonely Finnish seashore that Saarinen had his ashes returned.

Updated by Amanda Wunder

Until 1917, Finland was under the domination of its nearest neighbors, Sweden and Russia, who fought over it for centuries. After more than 600 years under the Swedish crown and 100 under the Russian czars, the country inevitably bears many traces of the two cultures, including a small (6%) but influential Swedish-speaking population and a scattering of Russian Orthodox churches.

But the Finns themselves are neither Scandinavian nor Slavic. They are descended from wandering tribes who probably came from west of Russia's Ural Mountains and settled on the swampy shores of the Gulf of Finland before the Christian era. The Finnish tongue belongs to the Finno-Ugric language group; it is related to Estonian and, very distantly, to Hungarian.

There is a tough, resilient quality to the Finn. Finland is one of the very few countries that shared a border with the Soviet Union in 1939 and retained their independence. Indeed, no country has fought the Soviets to a standstill as the Finns did in the grueling 105-day Winter War of 1939–40. This resilience stems from the turbulence of the country's past and from the people's determination to work the land and survive the long, brutal winters. The Finn lives in a constant state of confrontation—against the weather and the land. Finns are stubborn, patriotic, and self-sufficient, yet not aggressively nationalistic. On the contrary, rather than boasting of past battles, Finns are proud of finding ways to live in peace with their neighbors. They are trying to cling to their country's independence and their personal freedom even as they begin their membership in the European Union (EU), which they joined in January of 1995.

The average Finn volunteers little information, but that's due to reserve, not indifference. Make the first approach and you may have a friend for life. Finns like their silent spaces, though, and won't appreciate back-slapping familiarity—least of all in the sauna, still regarded by many as a spiritual as well as a cleansing experience.

Pleasures and Pastimes

Boating
Finns love all kinds of boating, and there are good facilities for guests' boats in most ports. Southwest Finland is a sailor's paradise, and the town marinas will welcome you and provide a full range of services. Hanko, the southernmost town in Finland, has the country's largest marina.

Cafés
That more coffee is consumed per capita in Finland than in any other country is evidenced by the staggering number of cafés throughout the

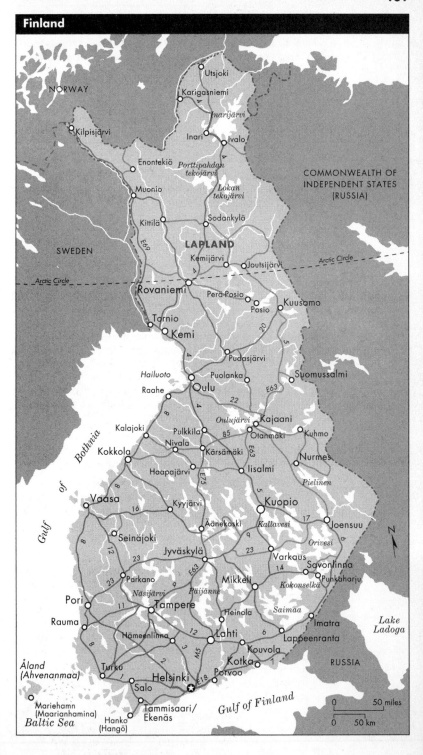

Finland

NORWAY

Utsjoki

Karigasniemi

Inarijärvi

Kilpisjärvi

Inari Ivalo

Enontekiö *Porttipahdan
tekojärvi*

COMMONWEALTH OF
INDEPENDENT STATES
(RUSSIA)

Muonio *Lokan
tekojärvi*

Kittilä Sodankylä

LAPLAND

E63

Kemijärvi Joutsijärvi

Arctic Circle

Arctic Circle

Rovaniemi Perä-Posio Kuusamo

Tornio Posio

Kemi 20

Pudasjärvi 5

Hailuoto Puolanka Suomussalmi

Raahe Oulu 22 E63

8 4 *Oulujärvi* Kajaani

Kalajoki Pulkkila 85 Kuhmo

Nivala Otanmäki E63

Kokkola Kärsämäki

Haapajärvi Iisalmi Nurmes

E75 *Pielinen*

Vaasa Kyyjärvi 5 Kuopio

16 Äänekoski *Kallavesi* 17 Joensuu

Seinäjoki 9 *Orivesi*

8 12 23 23 Varkaus

Jyväskylä E63 14 Savonlinna

23 Parkano 9 Mikkeli *Kokonselkä* Punkaharju

Näsijärvi *Päijänne*

Pori 11 Tampere *Saimaa*

Rauma Heinola Imatra

Hämeenlinna 12 Lahti 6 Lappeenranta

8 3 M5

Åland Turku 2 Kotka RUSSIA

(Ahvenanmaa) Salo Helsinki Porvoo E18

Mariehamn Tammisaari/
(Maarianhamina) Ekenäs

Baltic Sea Hanko
(Hangö) *Gulf of Finland*

SWEDEN

Bothnia

of

Gulf

*Lake
Ladoga*

N

0 50 miles

0 50 km

country. Particularly in Helsinki, patrons of cafés downtown and around the waterfront spill outside onto the streets. In addition to coffee, Finnish cafés serve a variety of baked goods: *Munkki* (doughnuts), *pulla* (sweetbread), and other confections are consumed with vigor by both young and old.

Dining

Finnish food is known for freshness rather than variety, although recent years have seen major improvements in restaurant cuisine. Ironically, the hardest meal to find is the authentic Finnish meal—products from the forest, lakes, and sea. It is far easier to find pizza, which Finns prefer with many toppings.

However, search and you will find the stunning meals Finns make with game—pheasant, reindeer, hare, and grouse—accompanied by wildberry compotes and exotic mushroom sauces. The chanterelle grows wild in Finland, as do dozens of other edible mushrooms, such as the tasty morel.

Other specialties are *poronkäristys* (reindeer casserole), *lihapullat* (meatballs in sauce), *uunijuusto* (oven cheese), and *hiilillä paistetut silakat* (charcoal-grilled Baltic herring). *Voileipäpöytä,* the Finnish cousin to smoørgåsbord, is a cold table served at breakfast or lunch where you are free to take as little or as much food as you like.

Fish is popular, of course, especially smoked fish. Crayfish season begins on July 21. Finnish baked goods are renowned. *Mämmi,* a dessert made of wheat flour, malt, and orange peels and served with cream and sugar, is served at Easter. More nourishing are *karjalan piirakka,* thin, oval wheat-bread pirogi filled with rice or mashed potatoes and served warm with a mixture of egg and butter. *Kalakuk ko* is generally seen in Savolax and consists of wheat bread with small pieces of meat and onions baked inside the dough, served warm with melted butter.

Hearty meat dishes include *karjalan paisti,* in which pork, lamb, and beef are mixed and baked for many hours. *Maksalaatikko* is a dish that combines liver, rice, and raisins, served with melted butter.

Helsinki and other cities offer a decent variety of foreign restaurants, the dominant ones being Russian and Chinese. Home-cooked meals tend to be beef or pork accompanied by potatoes. Yogurt and other dairy products are extremely good. The Finns like to make pizza at home. Pancakes with filling, homemade bread, and sweet buns are other at-home favorites.

The prices of alcohol are legendary. A "cheap" bottle of wine (all wine is imported, though some is domestically bottled) will cost FM 100 in a restaurant. The Finns make good beer, with a large brew costing around FM 20. Cocktails usually start at about FM 25. Spirits and liqueurs are pricey, too, but you'll fare a little better at **Alko,** the state liquor monopoly, open Monday–Thursday 10–5, Friday 10–6, Saturday 9–2. Some Alko stores are also open until 8 on Friday and 6 on Saturday.

Jacket and tie are required in most of the restaurants in the $$$$ category and many in the $$$ category. In all other establishments casual but neat dress is the norm.

CATEGORY	HELSINKI*	OTHER AREAS*
$$$$	over FM 200	over FM 170
$$$	FM 150–FM 200	FM 140–FM 170
$$	FM 80–FM 150	FM 80–FM 140
$	under FM 80	under FM 80

per person for a three-course meal, excluding drinks

Fishing

The fish-rich waters of the Baltic archipelago and innumerable inland lakes and streams assure that you will never run out of fishing opportunities. The waters of the Ålands are especially rich with pike, whitefish, salmon, and perch, and ice fishing makes this a year-round sport.

Lodging

From do-it-yourself campgrounds to pampering spas, lodging in the South Coast and Ålands takes advantage of the summer weather and scenery. The towns of southern, coastal Finland really come to life in the nightless months of summer, and cabins for rent abound. Rent a cabin amid the beautiful coastal scenery, and enjoy a true vacation. Another option is to take advantage of the spas in the region, where the spa tradition has flourished since the 18th century.

Every class of lodging exists in Finland, from five-star urban hotels to rustic cabins on lake shores and in the forest. Cleanliness is the rule, as is modern decor and plumbing. The standard setup includes a bathroom in each room with toilet and shower; only exceptions to this standard (for example full bathroom with bathtub or shared bath) are mentioned in reviews in this chapter.

The price categories below are based on weekday rates. Greater discounts are available on weekends and in summer months, especially between midsummer and July 31, when prices are usually 30% to 50% lower.

CATEGORY	HELSINKI*	OTHER AREAS*
$$$$	over FM 900	over FM 700
$$$	FM 600–FM 900	FM 550–FM 700
$$	FM 400–FM 600	FM 400–FM 550
$	under FM 400	under FM 400

All prices are for a standard double room, including service charge and taxes.

Saunas

An authentic Finnish sauna is an obligatory experience, and it's not hard to find: There are 1.4 million saunas in this country of 5 million people. The traditional Finnish sauna—which involves relaxing on wooden benches, occasionally pouring water onto hot coals and swatting your neighbor's back with birch branches—is an integral part of cabin life, so be sure not to miss it. In the cities, almost every hotel has at least one sauna. For information, call the **Finnish Sauna Society** (☎ 09/678–677).

Shopping

Finland is known for design. Helsinki has the widest selection of goods—from Arabia ceramics to Iittala glass to Marimekko clothing and textiles—and also the highest prices. Most large manufacturers and design firms set standard prices throughout the country. Furs, called *turkki* in Finnish, are a good buy. You might also want to take home some of the delicious smoked or marinated fish found here—available vacuum-packed at Helsinki Airport.

Wilderness Expeditions

There are countless opportunities for exploring the forests and fells, rapids and waterfalls, mountains and gorges of Lapland. Intrepid explorers can probe the deepest areas of the national forests on skis or by snowmobile, take a photo safari to capture the matchless landscape forever, canoe down the clear rivers filled with salmon and trout, hunt for mushrooms in the mushroom forests, or pick cloudberries and lingonberries in the bogs.

Exploring Finland

Finland's capital, Helsinki, commands the southern coast and shelters more than one-tenth of the country's population. Older towns are located in the southwest, where the culture of the South Coast and the Åland Islands has an unmistakably Swedish influence. Northern Finland—Finnish Lapland—straddles the Arctic Circle and is the most sparsely populated part of the country. Finland's central region is dominated by the Lakelands, the country's vacation belt.

Numbers in the text correspond to numbers in the margin and points of interest on the maps.

Great Itineraries

Keep in mind that Finland is a large country, and while train service between towns is quite good, some trips can take an entire day. To make the most of your time, take advantage of Finnair's efficient domestic air service between Helsinki and destinations farther afield, such as Savonlinna and Rovaniemi.

IF YOU HAVE 2 DAYS

You'll have plenty of time to take in all the sites of ⛛ **Helsinki** ①–㉗, but not enough to venture outside the capital city area. Since Helsinki is fairly small and its major attractions are within walking distance of one another, it's easy to see all the architectural high points and at least one of the city's excellent museums in one day. On the second day, you might take a harbor tour and visit the fortress island Suomenlinna, or take a side trip to **Espoo, Porvoo,** or **Vantaa,** or to the **Gallen-Kallela Estate** in Tarvaspää.

IF YOU HAVE 5 DAYS

After spending one or two nights in ⛛ **Helsinki** ①–㉗, head to the destination of your choice: Lapland, the South Coast and Ålands, or the Lakelands. Another option is to spend four nights in Helsinki, venturing out for easy, fun day trips to nearby towns: The cultural center **Turku** ㉛; **Tampere** ㊹, with its amusement park; and the castle town **Hämeenlinna** ㊺ are all less than two hours away by train.

IF YOU HAVE 10 DAYS

Ten days allows the tireless traveler time to explore much of Finland. If your goal is to see all the different regions, one option is to spend your first night in ⛛ **Helsinki** ①–㉗, then take a train from Helsinki to ⛛ **Turku** ㉛ on the southwest coast on the following day. Using Turku as a base, take a side trip to see the fancy homes and beaches of **Hanko** ㉚, the historic wooden town of **Rauma** ㉜, or the medieval pilgrimage village, **Naantali** ㉝. From Turku you can fly to ⛛ **Rovaniemi** ㉟, the gateway to Finnish Lapland. Use Rovaniemi as a base to explore Lapland, going as deep into the wilderness as you desire; then take a train or a plane to ⛛ **Savonlinna** ㊶ in western Finland, home of Finland's greatest castle. Take a scenic boat ride through the heart of Finland from Savonlinna to ⛛ **Kuopio** ㊸, where you'll see the Russian Orthodox tradition flourishing in the city's monastery. From Kuopio, you can fly back to Helsinki.

When to Tour Finland

Finland's tourist season commences in June, when the growing daylight hours herald the opening of summer restaurants and outdoor museums, and the commencement of boat tours and cruises. Summer is by far the best time to visit Helsinki, the Lakelands, and the South Coast and Åland Islands, which come out of hibernation to enjoy the long, bright, but not overly hot summer days. A special draw in the Lakelands is the Savonlinna Opera Festival, held in late July or early August.

For a real treat, visit Lapland—home of Santa Claus—in December. Operating on a different schedule altogether, the tourist season in the north focuses on winter events, when the snow is deep and the Northern Lights bright. Summer weather in Lapland offers a different repertoire to the traveler, when the snow and ice of the north give way to flowing rivers and greenery.

HELSINKI

Helsinki is a city of the sea, built on peninsulas and islands along the Baltic coast. Streets and avenues curve around bays, bridges arch across to nearby islands, and ferries reach out to islands farther offshore.

Having grown dramatically since World War II, Helsinki now absorbs about one-sixth of Finland's population. The city covers a total of 433 square miles and includes 315 islands. However, most of its sights, hotels, and restaurants cluster on one peninsula, forming a compact hub of special interest for the traveler.

Helsinki is a relatively young city compared with other European capitals. In the 16th century, King Gustav Vasa of Sweden decided to woo trade from the Estonian city of Tallinn and thus challenge the Hanseatic League's monopoly on Baltic trade. Accordingly, he commanded the people of four Finnish towns to pack up their belongings and relocate at the rapids on the River Vantaa. The new town, founded on June 12, 1550, was named Helsinki.

For three centuries, Helsinki (Helsingfors in Swedish) had its ups and downs as a trading town. Turku, to the west, remained Finland's capital and intellectual center. Ironically, Helsinki's fortunes improved when Finland fell under Russian rule as an Autonomous Grand Duchy. Czar Alexander I wanted Finland's political center closer to Russia and, in 1812, selected Helsinki as the new capital. Shortly afterward, Turku suffered a disastrous fire, forcing the university to move to Helsinki. From then on, Helsinki's future was secure.

Just before the czar's proclamation, a fire destroyed many of Helsinki's traditional wooden structures, precipitating the construction of new buildings suitable for a nation's capital. The German-born architect Carl Ludvig Engel was commissioned to rebuild the city, and as a result, Helsinki has some of the purest neoclassical architecture in the world. Add to this foundation the modern buildings designed by talented Finnish architects and the result is a European capital city that is as architecturally eye-catching as it is distinct from other Scandinavian and European capitals.

Exploring Helsinki

Helsinki's charms are both natural and man-made: Its numerous parks and seaside walkways weave in and around a stunning variety of architectural styles that combine the influence of Stockholm and St. Petersburg with the local inspiration of 20th-century Finnish design. The attentive observer is bound to discover endless delightful details—a grimacing gargoyle; a foursome of male sculptures supporting the weight of a balcony on their shoulders; a building painted in striking colors, with contrasting flowers in the windows.

The city center is compact and easily explored on foot, with the main tourist sights grouped in several clusters, and the nearby islands are easily accessible by ferry. Southeast Helsinki, along the water, is a residential neighborhood that's home to the government embassies as well

136

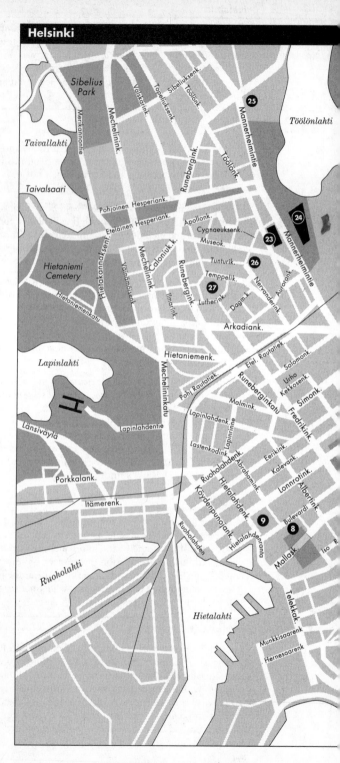

Helsinki

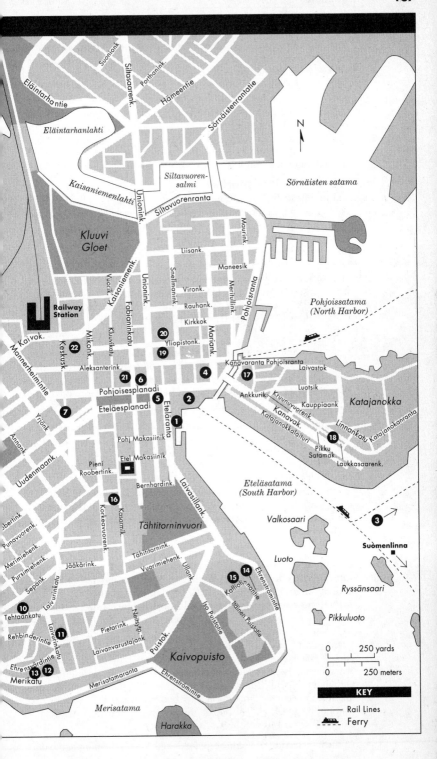

as several museums and galleries and a sprawling park, Kaivopuisto. On a clear day you can look off the southeast coast of mainland Helsinki and see Suomenlinna, a group of islands that once served as a defensive bulwark and now form a historically rich tourist destination with art museums and gardens to explore. A small landmass, called Katajanokka, juts out from the eastern side of the mainland; it harbors the Russian Orthodox Cathedral, ferry terminals, and old renovated brink warehouses that now hold restaurants and shops. Just west of Katajanokka, Senate Square and its Lutheran Cathedral mark the beginning of the city center, which extends westward along Aleksanterinkatu. In western Helsinki, Bulevardi is lined with cafés, secondhand bookstores, and businesses.

From Market to Market

The orange tents of the Kauppatori (Market Square) brighten even the cold snowy winter months with fresh flowers, fish, handicrafts, and produce; during warmer weather, the market fills with shoppers and browsers who stop for the ubiquitous coffee and munkki. The outdoor market overlooks the seaborne traffic of the South Harbor. From here you can take the local ferry service to Korkeasaari Island, home of the Helsinki Zoo, or begin a walking tour that will take you through the neighborhoods of Helsinki, from the harbor through the shopping district of the city center, ending with a walk down the tree-lined Bulevardi to the indoor Hietalahden Tori (Hietalahti Market).

A GOOD WALK

Begin your journey at the indoor redbrick market square, **Vanha Kauppahalli** ①, along the South Harbor. From here you can see the orange tents of the outdoor market, the **Kauppatori** ②. Helsinki's zoo, **Korkeasaari Elaintarha** ③, is accessible by a daily ferry from the South Harbor, just east of the market, or by metro.

Helsinki's first public monument, the **Obeliski Keisarinnan kivi** (Czarina's Stone), stands in the Market Square along Pohjoisesplanadi. Across the street from the market, the series of beautiful old buildings along Pohjoisesplanadi includes the pale-blue Kaupungintalo and, at the easternmost end of the street, the well-guarded **Presidentinlinna** ④. Leaving the view of the waterfront with its ferries and sightseeing boats behind, walk back west along Pohjoisesplanadi and cross the street to the square of the **Havis Amanda** ⑤ statue and fountain. You can stop at the **City Tourist Office** ⑥ for information and maps.

From the City Tourist Office, continue walking west on Pohjoisesplanadi until the street terminates at Mannerheimintie. A few yards west of the City Tourist Office, you'll see the Art Nouveau **Jugendsali** (⊠ Pohjoisesplanadi 19, ☎ 09/169–2277): Originally designed as a bank in 1906, it now serves as a cultural information office and a temporary exhibition hall for Finnish photography. After walking past the Arabia ceramics and the Marimekko clothing stores, you'll see the elephantine Gröngvistin Talo (Grönqvist's block) on your left across the park: Designed by architect Theodor Höijer and built in 1903, this was Scandinavia's largest apartment building at the time. Before hitting Mannerheimintie, you'll pass the Akateeminen Kirjakauppa and Stockmann's, respectively Finland's largest bookstore and department store (☞ Shopping, *below*). The bookstore was designed by Alvar Aalto, Finland's most famous architect.

At the intersection of Pohjoisesplanadi and Mannerheimintie, the distinctive round **Svenska Teatern** ⑦ is sure to catch your eye. Turn left on Mannerheimintie, cross the street, and take a right onto broad, tree-shaded Bulevardi, passing Vanha Kirkkopuisto (Old Church Park), usually called Ruttopuisto (Plague Park) for the 18th-century plague victims buried there. Continue southwest on Bulevardi until you reach the **Sinebrychoffin Taidemuseo** ⑧, a former mansion surrounded by a beautiful park. The **Hietalahden Tori** ⑨ is just across the street and slightly southeast of the museum, with an indoor food market and a flea market outside.

TIMING

Head out early if you wish to see both markets in action, since they close around 2 PM. It will take about 45 minutes to walk this route from Kauppatori to Hietalahti. Note that the Sinebrychoff Museum of Foreign Art is closed on Tuesdays. For a side trip to the zoo, the ferry to Korkeasaari Island takes less than a half hour, but allow time to wait for the ferry both coming and going.

SIGHTS TO SEE

⑥ **City Tourist Office.** Originally built in 1816 as a private house for a Russian businessman, this structure was rebuilt—with the exception of the facade—in 1968; it underwent significant renovation and enlargement in spring of 1996. The helpful staff provide brochures and listings of local events. ⊠ *Pohjoisesplanadi 19,* ☎ *90/169–3757 or 90/174–088.* ☉ *May–Sept., weekdays 8:30–6, weekends 10–3; Oct.–Apr., weekdays 8:30–4, closed weekends.*

⑤ **Havis Amanda.** Helsinki is "the Daughter of the Baltic," and this fountain's brass centerpiece, a young lady perched on rocks and surrounded by dolphins, embodies that title. The Havis Amanda fountain was commissioned by the city fathers as a symbol of Helsinki; sculptor Ville Vallgren completed her in 1908 using a Parisian girl as his model. Partying university students annually crown the Havis Amanda with their white caps on the eve of Vappu, the May 1 holiday. ⊠ *Eteläesplanadi and Eteläranta.*

⑨ **Hietalahden Tori** (Hietalahti Market). The brick market hall is crammed with vendors selling fish, flowers, produce, and meat, while a simultaneous outdoor flea market has tables piled with the detritus of countless Helsinki attics and cellars. Shoppers can stop amid the action for coffee, doughnuts, and meat pies. This market is especially popular with Helsinki's Russian community. ⊠ *Bulevardi and Hietalahdenkatu.* ☉ *Mon.–Sat. 7–2; mid-May–Aug., also weekdays 3–8.*

② **Kauppatori** (Market Square). This year-round outdoor market is one of Helsinki's most charming institutions. Wooden stands with orange and gold awnings bustle in the mornings when everyone—tourists and locals alike—comes to shop, browse, or sit and enjoy coffee and conversation. Buy a freshly caught perch for the evening's dinner, a bouquet of bright flowers for a friend, or a fur pelt or hat. In summer the fruit and vegetable stalls are replaced with an arts-and-crafts market in the evening. ⊠ *Eteläranta and Pohjoisesplanadi.* ☉ *Mon.–Sat. 7–2; summer, also Mon.–Sat. 3:30–8.*

③ **Korkeasaari Elaintarha** (Helsinki Zoo). Korkeasaari Island is home to one of the world's most northernmost zoos, where snow leopards and reindeer enjoy the cold Finnish climate. The zoo is entirely within the limits of this small island, but the winding paths make the zoo seem much larger than it actually is. Outdoor play equipment is an added attraction for children. The ferry departs approximately every 30 minutes from the South Harbor. The trip takes less than a half hour; arrival and departure times are posted at the harbor. Alternatively, you can take the metro to the Kulosaari stop, cross under the tracks, and then follow the signs 20 minutes to the zoo. ⊠ *Korkeasaari Island,* ☎

09/19981. 🖼 *FM 20.* ☉ *Jan.–Feb., daily 10–4; Mar.–Apr., daily 10–
6; May–Sept., daily 10–8; Oct.–Dec., daily 10–4.*

Obeliski Keisarinnan kivi. This obelisk with a double-headed golden
eagle, the symbol of Imperial Russia, was erected in 1835, toppled during the Russian Revolution in 1917 and fully restored in 1972.

❹ Presidentinlinna (President's Palace). This stately building has a long
history that mirrors the history of Finland itself: Originally built as a
private residence for a German businessman, it was redesigned in 1843
as a palace for the czars; then it served as the official residence of Finland's presidents from 1919 to 1993. Today it houses President Martti
Ahtisaari's offices and is the scene of official receptions. The most interesting part of the house is said to be its hall of mirrors, but the uni-
formed guards will prevent you from entering and finding out. ⊠
Pohjoisesplanadi 1.

❽ Sinebrychoffin Taidemuseo (Sinebrychoff Museum of Foreign Art).
The Sinebrychoffs were a wealthy Russian family that started a brew-
ing company and lived in this splendid mansion with wildly opulent
furniture. The Sinebrychoff home and collection of foreign art are
now a public museum that houses a staid collection of Dutch and Swedish
17th- and 18th-century portraits, a lively collection of landscapes,
miniatures, and porcelain, and the mansion's original decorative furniture. The yellow-and-white neo-Renaissance mansion, built in 1840,
looks over the once-private **Sinebrychoffin Park** and its tower. In summer, outdoor concerts are occasionally held in the park. ⊠ *Bulevardi
40,* ☎ *09/1733–6360.* 🖼 *FM 10; FM 25 for special exhibitions.* ☉
Mon., Thurs., and Fri. 9–5; Wed. 9–9; weekends 11–5.

❼ Svenska Teatern (Swedish Theater). A full-time Swedish-language theater continues to flourish in this 19th-century structure. The round theater has been rebuilt many times since the original was built in 1827,
but the red and gold auditorium inside dates from the 19th century. The
first wooden theater, considered too vulnerable to fire, was replaced by
a stone building in 1866. Ironically, the "safer" stone building was itself nearly destroyed by a fire. The theater was renovated in 1936 by a
team of architects that included Eero Saarinen and Jarl Eklund, and the
current whitewashed round theater is eye-catching for its shape and for
the dignified simplicity of its design. The Swedish Theater has its own
company, which performs plays in Swedish year-round. ⊠ *Pohjoisesplanadi 2,* ☎ *09/170–238.* ☉ *Box office daily noon–performance time.*

NEED A   The **Aalto Café** (⊠ Pohjoisesplanadi 39, ☎ 09/121–446) on the Aca-
BREAK?   demic Bookstore's mezzanine is a pleasant lunch or snack stop where
                you can peer down at the tranquil hordes of book browsers.

❶ Vanha Kauppahalli (Old Market Hall). From piles of colorful fish roe
to marinated Greek olives, the old brick market hall on the waterfront
is a treasury of delicacies. The vendors set up permanent stalls with
decorative carved woodwork. ⊠ *Eteläranta, along the South Harbor.*
☉ *Weekdays 8–5, Sat. 8–2.*

Residential and Seaside Helsinki

Bordered by the sea, the south side of Helsinki is filled with parks and
elegant residences. A walking tour through the neighborhood can
begin at the Mikael Agricola Church—whose spire is visible from afar
on a clear day—and continue past a few charming early 20th-century
dwellings, along the waterfront, and into the winding paths of
Kaivopuisto, which lead into the elegant embassy neighborhood. From
this seaside area, it's a short jaunt to yet another fine park, Tähti-

torninvuori, and finally to the Museum of Finnish Architecture, near the city center.

A GOOD WALK

Begin at the sharp-spired **Mikael Agricolan Kirkko** ⑩ in the small park, Tehtaanpuisto. Cross Tehtaankatu and walk south down Laivurinkatu past Eiran Sairaala (Eira Hospital) (✉ Laivurinkatu 29), with its witch-hat towers and triangular garret windows. Continue south on Laivurinkatu, passing the Art Nouveau **Villa Johanna** ⑪ on your left. An open view of the Baltic will be just ahead. At the end of the street is the **Taideteollisuusmuseo** ⑫, (Museum of Applied Arts with an impressive collection of applied arts: Stop in for a visit or turn right on Merikatu. After passing the beautiful **Villa Ensi** ⑬, you'll arrive at the eternal flame of the Merenkulkijoiden Muistomerkki (Seafarers' Torch), commissioned by the city as a tribute to Finnish sailors and a symbol of hope for their safe return.

Turn east to walk along Merisatamanranta, the seaside promenade. Out at sea is a handful of the thousands of islands that make up the Gulf of Finland Archipelago. During the winter months, Finns walk across the frozen sea to the nearby islands, with dogs and even baby buggies. On the land side, the facades of the Eira and Kaivopuisto districts' grandest buildings form a parade of architectural splendor. One tradition that remains, even in this upscale neighborhood, is rug-washing in the sea—an incredibly arduous task. You may be astounded to see people leave their rugs to dry in the sea air without fear of theft.

Turn away from the water and walk north on Iso Puistotie to **Kaivopuisto,** a shady oasis surrounded by opulent private residences and embassies; plan on spending half an hour wandering along its pleasant paths. From the park, follow the eastward loop of Kalliolinnantie through the embassy district to the **Mannerheim Museo** ⑭. On the same street, the tiny **Cygnaeuksen Galleria** ⑮ displays works of Finnish painters, sculptors, and folk artists. Follow Itäinen Puistotie to Tehtaankatu 1, where you'll see the enormous fenced-in Russian Embassy complex; then walk up Ullankatu to **Tähtitorninvuori,** a peaceful park with a view. For those seriously interested in architecture, the **Suomen Rakennus-taiteen Museo** ⑯ is just west of the observatory; follow any of the small streets that go west, and turn right on Kasarmikatu.

TIMING

It takes a little over one hour to walk this route, beginning at the Agricola Church and ending at the Museum of Finnish Architecture. Although the Seafarer's Torch is best seen at night, you may wish to make the walk during the day to take in the subtle beauty of the elegant residences in the area.

SIGHTS TO SEE

❶ **Cygnaeuksen Galleria** (Cygnaeus Gallery). This tiny gallery, housed in a cottage with a tower that overlooks the harbor, is the perfect setting for works by various Finnish painters, sculptors, and folk artists. This was once the summer home of Fredrik Cygnaeus (1807–81), a poet and historian who generously left his cottage and all the art inside to the Finnish public. ✉ *Kalliolinnantie 8,* ☎ *09/656–928.* ☞ *FM 10.* ☉ *Thurs.–Sun. 11–4, Wed. 11–7.*

Kaivopuisto (Well Park). This large, shady, path-filled park was once the site of a popular spa that drew people from St. Petersburg, Tallinn, and all of Scandinavia until its popularity faded during the Crimean War. All the spa structures were eventually destroyed except one, the **Kaivohuone,** now a renowned and refined bar-restaurant (☞ Nightlife and the Arts, *below*). Across from the entrance of Kaivohuone, take

Kaivohuoneenrinne through the park past a grand Empire-style villa built by Albert Edelfelt, father of the famous Finnish painter who bore the same name. Built in 1839, it is the oldest preserved villa in the park.

⓮ **Mannerheim Museo** (Mannerheim Museum). Gustaf Mannerheim (1867–1951) was a complex character who wore many hats: He served as a high-level official in the Russian czar's guard, he was a trained anthropologist who explored Asia, and he is revered as a great general who fought for Finland's freedom and later became the new country's president. The Mannerheim Museo is set in the great Finnish military leader's well-preserved family home and exhibits his letters and personal effects. The museum also includes collections European furniture, Asian art, and military medals and weaponry. ⊠ *Kalliolinnantie 14,* ☎ *09/635–443.* ☑ *FM 30: includes guided tour.* ☉ *Fri.–Sun., 11–4; Mon.–Thurs. by appointment.*

⓾ **Mikael Agricolan Kirkko** (Mikael Agricola Church). Built in 1935 by Lars Sonck, this church is named for the Finnish religious reformer who is considered to be the father of written Finnish. Mikael Agricola (circa 1510–1557) wrote the first Finnish children's speller, the *Abckiria* (published around 1543), and translated the New Testament into Finnish (published in 1548). The church's sharp spire and tall brick steeple are visible from **Tehtaanpuisto,** a small neighboring park. The inside of the church is quite bare, and no visitors are allowed except during Sunday services. ⊠ *Tehtaankatu 23A,* ☎ *09/633–654. Services Sun. from 10 AM; check outside for additional times.*

⓰ **Suomen Rakennustaiteen Museo** (Museum of Finnish Architecture). Stop by the architecture museum to pick up a list of buildings by Alvar Aalto in Helsinki, the most famous of which is Finlandiatalo (☞ Töölö, *below*). Though the permanent exhibits of this museum are far from comprehensive, specialists will want to visit the extensive library and bookstore. ⊠ *Kasarmikatu 24,* ☎ *09/661–918.* ☑ *FM 20.* ☉ *Tues. and Thurs.–Sun. 10–4, Wed. 10–7.*

Tähtitorninvuori. Named for the astronomical observatory within its borders (the observatory belongs to the astronomy department of Helsinki University and is closed to the public), this park has sculptures, winding walkways, and a great view of the South Harbor below.

⓬ **Taideteollisuusmuseo** (Museum of Applied Arts). Finland is famous for the accomplishments of its modern designers, and the best of Finnish design can be seen here in permanent and temporary displays of furnishings, jewelry, ceramics, and more. The Museum of Applied Arts hosts temporary exhibits of international design as well. ⊠ *Laivurinkatu 3,* ☎ *09/622–0540.* ☑ *FM 20.* ☉ *June–Aug., daily 11–5; Sept.–May, Tues. and Thurs.–Sun. 11–5, Wed. 11–8.*

NEED A BREAK? The **Café Ursula** (⊠ Ehrenströmintie 3, ☎ 09/652–817) is a favorite among locals for coffee, ice cream, pastries, and light lunches.

⓭ **Villa Ensi.** This pale ocher Art Nouveau villa, now a private apartment building, was designed by Selim A. Lindqvist and named after his wife, Johanna, and daughter, Ensi. The two bronze statues in front—*Au Revoir* and *La Joie de la Maternité* by J. Sören-Ring—date from 1910. ⊠ *Merikatu 23.*

⓫ **Villa Johanna.** Though this stunning Art Nouveau villa (circa 1906) is now privately owned by the Post Office Bank of Finland, which uses the villa for corporate dinners and events, it's still worth a look from the outside. Look for the carved roaring serpent above the front door. ⊠ *Laivurinkatu 25.*

Katajanokka and Senate Square

The Katajanokka is separated from the mainland by a canal and begins just east of the market square. A charming residential quarter as well as a busy cargo and passenger-ship port, this area is home to Helsinki's most famous sights, from the dazzling Uspenski Cathedral to the elegant Lutheran Cathedral that dominates Senate Square. The National Gallery is also nearby.

A GOOD WALK

The first sight on Katajanokka is the onion-domed **Uspenskin Katedraali** ⑰ on Kanavakatu. From the cathedral, walk down Kanavakatu, turn left on Ankkurikatu, and then right on Laukkasaarenkatu, where a sign will point out the **Wanha Satama** ⑱, a nice place for shopping or having a drink. From there, head back southwest a short distance to the seafront and cross one of the two short bridges back over to Market Square.

From Market Square, take any street north to **Senaatintori** ⑲. The north side of the square is dominated by the **Tuomiokirkko** ⑳; the pale yellow Valtionneuvosto (Council of State) and the main building of Helsingin Yliopisto (Helsinki University) flank the east and west sides, respectively. The main university library is just north of the main building on Unioninkatu. At the south end of the square, old merchants' homes are currently occupied by stores, restaurants, and the Kiseleff Bazaar Hall (☞ Shopping, *below*).

Walk one block west to Fabianinkatu, where the **Pörssitalo** ㉑ is on the west side of the street. Turn around and walk 1½ blocks north on Fabianinkatu; then turn left on Yliopistonkatu. You'll run into the side of the **Valtion Taidemuseo** ㉒; to enter the museum, turn right on Mikonkatu and then immediately left on Kaivokatu.

TIMING

Allow 30 to 45 minutes to walk from the Uspenski Cathedral to the National Gallery following this route. Be sure to check the opening hours of both cathedrals before you leave—both of them close on religious holidays.

SIGHTS TO SEE

㉑ **Pörssitalo** (Stock Exchange). Although the trading is fully automated, the beautiful interior of the Stock Exchange, with its bullet-shaped chandeliers, is worth seeing. The Pörssitalo was designed by Lars Sonck and built in 1911. ⊠ *Fabianinkatu 14,* ☎ *09/650–133.* ⊙ *Weekdays 8–5.*

★ ⑲ **Senaatintori** (Senate Square). This is the heart of neoclassical Helsinki, and the harmony of the three buildings flanking Senaatintori exemplifies one of the purest styles of European architecture. The square and the surrounding buildings were designed by the German architect Carl Ludvig Engel. On the square's west side is one of the main buildings of **Helsingin Yliopisto** (Helsinki University), and up the hill is the university library. On the east side is the **Valtionneuvosto** (Council of State), completed in 1822 and once the seat of the Autonomous Grand Duchy of Finland's Imperial Senate. At the lower end of the square are former merchants' homes now occupied by stores and restaurants.

⑳ **Tuomiokirkko** (Lutheran Cathedral of Finland). The Lutheran Cathedral dominates Senaatintori, with steep steps and green domes. Completed in 1852, it was designed, as was most of the area, by the famous architect Carl Ludvig Engel, who also designed much of Tallinn and St. Petersburg. Wander through the tasteful blue-gray interior, with its white moldings and the statues of German reformers Martin Luther and Philipp Melancthon as well as the famous Finnish bishop Mikael Agricola. Concerts are frequently held inside the church, and the crypt at the rear is the site of frequent historic and architectural exhibitions and bazaars. ⊠ *Yliopistonkatu 7.* ⊘ *May–Sept., weekdays 9–7, Sat. 9–6, Sun. noon–6; Oct.–Apr., weekdays 10–4, Sat. 10–6, Sun. noon–6.*

NEED A
BREAK?

Café Engel (⊠ Aleksanterinkatu 15, ☎ 09/652–776), named for the architect Carl Ludvig Engel, serves coffee and berry cheesecake right on Senate Square.

★ ⑰ **Uspenskin Katedraali** (Uspenski Cathedral). Perched atop a small rocky cliff over the North Harbor, the main cathedral of the Russian Orthodox religion in Finland is distinguished by its brilliant gold onion domes—but its imposing redbrick edifice, decorated by 19th-century Russian artists, is no less distinctive. The cathedral was built and dedicated in 1868 in the Byzantine-Slavonic style and remains the biggest Orthodox church in Scandinavia. ⊠ *Kanavakatu 1,* ☎ *09/634–267.* ⊘ *May–Sept., Tues. 9:30–6, Wed.–Fri. 9:30–4, Sat. 9–noon, Sun. noon–3; Oct.–Apr., Tues. and Thurs. 9–2, Wed. noon–6, Fri. noon–6, Sun. noon–2.*

NEED A
BREAK?

On the north flank of Katajanokka, near the end of Katajanokan Pohjois-ranta, you'll see the **Katajanokan Casino** (⊠ Laivastokatu 1, ☎ 09/622–2772), built in 1911 as a warehouse; it later became a naval officers' casino, and today it's a seaside restaurant. Set on its own headland, the casino has a summer terrace from which you can gaze across the North Harbor to the Kruunuhaka district while sipping a cold beer.

㉒ **Valtion Taidemuseo** (Finnish National Gallery). The best of Finnish art reposes in the Valtion Taidemuseo. This splendid neoclassical building actually houses two museums: the **Ateneum**, with Finnish art from the 18th century to the 1960s, and the **Museum of Contemporary Art**, with national and contemporary art from the 1960s to the present. The gallery features major European works, but the outstanding attraction is the Finnish art, particularly the works of Akseli Gallen-Kallela, which were inspired by the national epic *Kalevala*. The rustic portraits by Albert Edelfelt are enchanting, and many contemporary Finnish artists are well represented. ⊠ *Kaivokatu 2–4,* ☎ *09/173–361.* ▣ *FM 20.* ⊘ *Tues. and Fri. 9–6, Wed. and Thurs. 9–8, weekends 11–5.*

OFF THE
BEATEN PATH

LINNANMÄKI – Helsinki's best-known amusement park can be reached by Trams 3B and 3T from in front of the railway station. ⊠ *Tivolikuja 1,* ☎ 09/773-9400. ▣ *FM 15.* ⊘ *Late Apr.–mid-May, weekends, hrs vary; May–mid-June, weekdays 4–10, Sat. 1–10, Sun. 1–9; mid-June–mid-Aug., daily 1–10; mid-Aug.–first wk in Sept., hrs vary.*

⑱ **Wanha Satama** (Old Harbor). Though it appears from the outside to be nothing more than an old brick warehouse, this is actually a small shopping center with several food stores, restaurants, and cafés; there's even an art gallery in the left-hand (north) wing. (*Note:* The "W" in Wanha is pronounced as a "V.") ⊠ *Kanavakatu and Pikku Sata-makatu.*

Suomenlinna

A former island fortress now taken over by resident artists, Suomenlinna (Finland's Castle) (☎ 09/66–341) is a quirky, perennially popular collection of museums, parks, and gardens. In 1748 the Finnish army helped build the impregnable fortress, long referred to as the Gibraltar of the North; since then it has expanded into a series of interlinked islands. Although Suomenlinna has never been taken by assault, its occupants did surrender twice without a fight—once to the Russians in 1809 and again to the British in 1855 during the Crimean War. Today Suomenlinna makes a lovely excursion from Helsinki, particularly in early summer, when the island is engulfed in a mauve-and-purple mist of lilacs, the trees introduced from Versailles by the Finnish architect Ehrensvärd.

There are no street names on the island, so be sure to get a map (FM 7) from the Helsinki City Tourist Office before you go or buy one at the Tourist Information kiosk on the island. From June 1 to August 31, guided English-language tours leave from the information kiosk daily at 12:30 and 2:30. To book a group tour, call ☎ 09/668–154.

A GOOD WALK

Suomenlinna is easily reached by public ferry (FM 9) or round-trip private boat tour (FM 20), both of which leave from Helsinki's Market Square. Although its fortification occupied six islands, its main attractions are now concentrated on two, Susisaari and Kustaanmiekka. When you land at Suomenlinna, you will be facing the **Pohjoismaisen Taidekeskuksen Galleria,** whose exhibits of Nordic art are usually worth a look. Go through the archway of the center and proceed uphill to the **Suomenlinna Kirkko,** the local church-lighthouse. Walk past the church and the pastel-colored private wooden homes to the **Ehrensvärd Museo,** a historical museum. The Tourist Information kiosk is nearby, alongside Tykistölahti Bay; it is open May 5 through August 31, daily 10–5. Walk along the eastern coast of Susisaari until you reach the submarine **Vesikko**. From there, walk south and cross over to Kustaanmiekka, where you can visit the **Rannikkotykistömuseo** to learn everything you ever wanted to know about arms and artillery.

TIMING

The ferry ride from the South Harbor to Suomenlinna takes about a half hour. Plan to spend an afternoon on the islands; you'll need about four hours to explore the fortress and museums. If possible, try to plan your visit to the Kustaanmiekka around lunchtime so that after investigating its ramparts and visiting its museums you can spend your lunch hour at its fine restaurant, Walhalla (☞ *below*).

SIGHTS TO SEE

Ehrensvärd Museo (Ehrensvärd Museum). Augustin Ehrensvärd directed the fortification of the islands of Suomenlinna from 1748 until 1772, the year of his death. This historical museum named for the military architect exhibits a model-ship collection and officers' quarters dating from the 18th century. Ehrensvärd's tomb is also here. ⊠ *Susisaari, Suomenlinna,* ☎ *09/668–154.* ▣ *FM 10.* ☉ *Jan. 2–May 7, weekends 11–5; May 8–Aug. 31, daily 10–5; Sept. 1–30, daily 10–5; Oct. 1–Nov. 30, weekends 11–4:30.*

Pohjoismaisen Taidekeskuksen Galleria (Nordic Arts Center). Changing exhibitions of contemporary works include sculpture, video art, painting, and more. ⊠ *Susisaari, Suomenlinna (at ferry dock),* ☎ *09/668–148.* ▣ *Free.* ☉ *Tues.–Sun. 11–6. Closed between exhibits; call ahead for details.*

Rannikkotykistömuseo (Coastal Guard Artillery Museum). Arms from World Wars I and II are on display here in a vaulted arsenal. ⊠ *Kustaanmiekka, Suomenlinna,* ☎ *09/161–5295.* ▣ *FM 10.* ☉ *May 8–Aug. 31, daily 10–5; Sept. 1–30, daily 11–5.*

Suomenlinna Kirkko (Suomenlinna Church). This dual-function church-lighthouse was built in 1854 as an Orthodox church and has since

become Lutheran. The church is open to the public on Sunday from
noon to 4.

Vesikko. Jump aboard this submarine, which was built in Turku in
1931–33 and served in World War II. ⌑ *FM 10.* ☉ *May 13–Sept., daily
11–4.*

Töölö

Most of Helsinki's major cultural buildings—the opera house, concert
hall, and national museum—are located within a short distance of each
other around the perimeter of the lake called Töölönlahti. The lake itself is lovely in all seasons, and the walking and biking paths are well
trodden by locals. The winding streets just east of Mannerheimintie
enfold the Temppeliaukio Kirkko (Temple Square Church), whose un-
exceptional facade covers its amazing cavernous interior. Also nearby,
the Sibelius park cuts a large swath out of the neighborhood and borders the sea.

A GOOD WALK

Begin your sightseeing in the lakeside area of Mannerheimintie by the
equestrian statue of Marshal Mannerheim, directly behind the main
post office. Walk northwest on Mannerheimintie, passing the red granite Parliament House on your way to the **Suomen Kansallismuseo** ㉓,
Finland's national museum, on the left. If the building looks familiar
to you, it probably is; its spired outline was the backdrop for televised
reports on the 1990 U.S.–Soviet summit. When you leave the museum,
cross Mannerheimintie to **Finlandiatalo** ㉔, the Alvar Aalto–designed
concert hall. Behind the hall lies the inlet bay of Töölönlahti. If you
walk along the well-used paths that follow the contour of the lake, you'll
soon come to the **Suomen Kansallisooppera** ㉕, Helsinki's opera house.

From the opera house, walk southeast on Mannerheimintie until you
see Cygnaeuksenkatu on your right; turn right and then take a left on
Nervanderinkatu, where you'll reach the **Helsingin Taidehalli** ㉖, with
its fine collection of Finnish art. A few steps farther, take the small street
directly across from the art hall to the modern **Temppeliaukio Kirkko** ㉗,
a church carved into rock cliffs. If you still have energy, cross
Runeberginkatu and walk west on Samonkatu until you reach Mechelininkatu. Walk a ways north on Mechelininkatu, and Sibelius park
will appear on your left. Here you'll find the magnificent **Sibelius-monumentti** (Sibelius Monument).

TIMING

Allow 30 to 45 minutes to follow this tour as far as the Temppeliaukio
Kirkko; from there it's a 15-minute walk to the Sibelius park and
monument. Be sure to check the Temppeliaukio Kirkko's hours, which
are slightly erratic.

SIGHTS TO SEE

㉔ **Finlandiatalo** (Finlandia Hall). This white, winged concert hall was one
of Alvar Aalto's last creations. Its appearance is especially impressive
on foggy days or at night. If you can't make it to a concert here, try
to take a guided tour. ⌑ *Karamzininkatu 4,* ☎ *09/40241.* ⌑ *Tickets
FM 40–FM 80. Concerts usually held Wed. and Thurs. nights.*

㉖ **Helsingin Taidehalli** (Helsinki Art Hall). Here you'll see the best of contemporary Finnish art, including painting, sculpture, architecture, and
industrial art and design. ⌑ *Nervanderinkatu 3,* ☎ *09/444–135.* ⌑
Varies according to exhibition but is usually FM 20. ☉ *June–July, weekdays 11–5, Sun. noon–4; Aug.–May, Tues.–Sat. 11–6, Sun. noon–5.*

Sibelius-monumentti (Sibelius Monument). What could be a better
tribute to Finland's great composer than this soaring silver sculpture

of organ pipes? The monument itself is worth the walk, but you'll also enjoy the setting of **Sibeliuksen puisto** (Sibelius Park) next to the water. ⊠ *Sibeliuksen puisto, Mechelininkatu.*

㉕ **Suomen Kansallisooppera** (Finnish National Opera). Grand gilded operas, classical ballets, and booming concerts all take place in Helsinki's splendid opera house, a striking example of modern Scandinavian architecture that opened its doors in 1993. All events at the National Opera draw crowds, so buy your tickets early. ⊠ *Helsinginkatu 58,* ☎ *box office 09/4030–2211.* 🎫 *FM 25. Guided tours by appointment only (*☎ *09/4030–2350).*

OFF THE
BEATEN PATH

SEURASAAREN ULKOMUSEO – On an island about 3 kilometers (2 miles) northwest of the city center, the Seurasaari Outdoor Museum was founded in 1909 to preserve rural Finnish architecture; the old farmhouses and barns that were brought to Seurasaari come from all over Finland. Many are rough-hewn log buildings dating from the 17th century; these were of primary inspiration to architects of the late 19th-century national revivalist movement in Finland. All exhibits are marked by signposts along the trails; be sure not to miss the church boat and the gabled church. Seurasaari Island is connected to land by a pedestrian bridge and is a restful place for walking throughout the year, with its forest trails and ocean views. You can walk there in about 40 minutes from the opera house by following Mannerheimintie northeast, then turning left onto Linnankoskenkatu. From here, follow the coast and signposts. Alternatively, take Bus 24, which you can board downtown in front of the Swedish theater at the west end of Pohjoisesplanadi. ⊠ *Seurasaari,* ☎ *09/484-712 or 09/484-562.* 🎫 *Museum FM 10.* ☉ *Mid-May–mid-Sept.*

TAMMINIEMI – The grand house overlooking Seurasaari from the mainland is Tamminiemi, where the late Finnish president Urho Kekkonen lived from 1956 to 1986. Originally known as Villa Nissen, Tamminiemi was built in 1904. Inside are the scores of gifts presented to Finland's longest-serving president by leaders from around the world. His study is the most fascinating room, with its gift from the United States of a cupboard full of *National Geographic* maps of the world. To assure an English-speaking guide, phone ahead (you cannot visit unguided). All large groups should call ahead. When you've seen the house, stop for pastries and Russian-style tea at **Tamminiemintien Kahvila** (⊠ Tamminiemintie 8, ☎ 09/481–003). To get here from the opera house, follow Mannerheimintie northeast, then turn left onto Linnankoskenkatu. From here, follow the coast and signposts. Alternatively, take Bus 24, which you can board downtown in front of the Swedish theater at the west end of Pohjoisesplanadi. ⊠ *Seurasaarentie 15, 00250,* ☎ *09/480-684.* 🎫 *FM 15.* ☉ *Sept.–June, Tues.–Sun. 11–5, Thurs. 11–7; July–Aug., Fri.–Wed. 11–5, Thurs. 11–7.*

㉓ **Suomen Kansallismuseo** (National Museum). The museum's exhibits take you from Finnish prehistory through medieval church art to contemporary Sami culture. The frescoes that decorate the vaulted ceiling are Akseli Gallen-Kallela's vibrant illustrations of the *Kalevala,* Finland's national epic. Temporary exhibits usually focus on different cultures from around the world. A charming turn-of-the-century–style café serves homemade pastries and freshly brewed coffee on the first floor. ⊠ *Mannerheimintie 34,* ☎ *09/405–0470.* 🎫 *FM 15.* ☉ *Sept.–May, Tues. 11–8, Wed.–Sun. 11–4; June–Aug., Tues. 11–8, Wed.–Sun. 11–5.*

★ ㉗ **Temppeliaukio Kirkko** (Temple Square Church). Topped with a copper dome, the church looks like a half-buried spaceship from the outside. In truth, it's really a modern Lutheran church carved into the rock cliffs below. The sun shines in from above, illuminating the stunning interior with its birch pews, modern pipe organ, and cavernous walls. Ecumenical and Lutheran services in various languages are held throughout the week. ⊠ *Lutherinkatu 3,* ☎ *09/494–698.* ⊙ *Daily 11–8; closed Tues. 1–2 and during concerts and services.*

Dining

Helsinki is home to some of Finland's best eating establishments. Although the Russian restaurants are the star attraction, try to seek out Finnish specialties such as game—pheasant, reindeer, hare, and grouse—accompanied by wild-berry compotes and exotic mushroom sauces.

Most restaurants close on major national holidays—only a few hotel restaurants stay open for Christmas. Many of the more expensive establishments close on weekends.

$$$$ ✕ **Alexander Nevski.** Helsinki is reputed to have the best Russian restau-
   ★ rants in the Nordic region, and the Nevski is foremost among them. It sets high standards in the preparation of czarist-era dishes, with an emphasis on game. Try the breast of willow grouse baked in a clay pot, traditional roe-filled blintzes, or borscht. Among the more extraordinary offerings is roast bear in a pot, which must be ordered in advance. Set at the edge of the harbor and marketplace, Nevski has all the trappings you'd expect to find in a czar's dining hall—heavy draperies, glistening samovars, potted palms, and crisp linen tablecloths. ⊠ *Pohjoisesplanadi 17,* ☎ *09/639–610. AE, DC, MC, V.*

$$$$ ✕ **Amadeus.** The elegant decor in this old town house between Sen-
   ★ ate Square and the South Harbor matches the czarist architecture of the neighborhood. The game, reindeer, and mushroom dishes have made it a favorite of Helsinki gourmets. The two dining rooms are tinted in soft browns and pinks. As an appetizer, try the slightly salted salmon with vegetable tartare, and as a main course, one of the many game dishes. ⊠ *Sofiankatu 4,* ☎ *09/626–676. AE, DC, MC, V. Closed Sun.*

$$$$ ✕ **Galateia.** The white grand piano and paintings of languid mermaids lend a classy, serene ambience to Helsinki's best seafood restaurant. From the top floor of the Hotel Inter-Continental, Galateia offers a nighttime panorama that takes in the city lights and an illuminated Finlandia Hall reflected in Töölö Bay. Fresh Continental-style seafood is served, along with caviar and roe specialties. If you are in Helsinki during the crayfish season, this is one of the best places to sample it. Attentive and knowledgeable waiters offer an impressive selection of appropriate wines. ⊠ *Mannerheimintie 46 (Inter-Continental),* ☎ *09/405–5900 or 09/40551. AE, DC, MC, V. Closed weekends. No lunch.*

$$$$ ✕ **Havis Amanda.** Across the street from the Havis Amanda statue, its namesake restaurant specializes in seafood dishes. Several different fixed menus are available for both lunch and dinner. Try the flamed cloudberry crêpes with ice cream for dessert. ⊠ *Unioninkatu 23,* ☎ *09/666–882. AE, DC, MC, V. Closed Sun.*

$$$$ ✕ **Pamir.** Located on the second floor of the Strand Inter-Continental
   ★ Hotel, this intimate restaurant may not offer terrific views of the adjacent waterfront, but good service and fine fare make up for it. Pamir's accent is on Finnish game and fish dishes. Renowned chef Pertti Lipäinen, who used to be with the Palace Gourmet, prepares specialties that include reindeer liver, smoked fillet of reindeer, stuffed hare, fillet of duck, and rainbow trout. ⊠ *John Stenbergin ranta 4,* ☎ *09/39351. AE, DC, MC, V. Closed weekends. No lunch.*

$$$$ ✕ **Restaurant Palace.** This outstanding hotel restaurant has a magnificent view of the South Harbor. Chef Markus Maulavirta's specialty is

French and Finnish fare, including such creations as jellied roe of vendance (a type of whitefish) with sour-cream–dill sauce, or reindeer fillet and tongue with rowanberry sauce. ⊠ *Eteläranta 10 (Palace Hotel),* ☎ *09/134–561. AE, DC, MC, V. Closed weekends. No lunch in July.*

$$$$ ✕ **Savoy.** With its airy, Alvar Aalto–designed, functionalist dining room overlooking the Esplanade gardens, the Savoy is a frequent choice for business lunches and was also Finnish statesman Marshal Karl Gustaf Mannerheim's favorite; he is rumored to have introduced the *Vorschmack* (minced lamb and anchovies) recipe. The Savoy's menu includes the ubiquitous reindeer fillet served with cumin potatoes, as well as such old-fashioned Finnish home-cooked dishes as meatballs, grilled herring, and *läski soosi* (fried fatty pork in brown sauce). ⊠ *Eteläesplanadi 14,* ☎ *09/176–571.*

$$$ ✕ **Bellevue.** The spare lines of Bellevue belie its real age—it has been around since 1917, serving imaginative dishes inspired by Russian cuisine of yore and Finnish country fare. In a room with pale table linens, wood-and-plush seats, and tremendous modern paintings, you can sample the innovative meat dishes and blinis for which the Bellevue is famous. As an appetizer, try the salted cucumbers topped with sour cream and honey, or *shashlik*—lamb fillet served with mushroom rice. The plush interior of this elegant town house has many shining samovars, but only some of them are functional; each table has lighted candles. Appropriately, the restaurant is tucked behind the Russian Orthodox Uspenski Cathedral. ⊠ *Rahapajankatu 3,* ☎ *09/179–560. AE, DC, MC, V. No lunch weekends and in July.*

$$$ ✕ **Kosmos.** Just a short walk from Stockmann's, this cozy restaurant has become a lunchtime favorite among businesspeople who work nearby. In the evenings the restaurant is frequented by artists and journalists. Its high ceilings and understated decor give it a Scandinavian atmosphere of simplicity and efficiency. Among the specialties are sweetbreads with curry, cream, and port sauce, and mutton chops stuffed with ground veal and olives and served with garlic potatoes. ⊠ *Kalevankatu 3,* ☎ *09/607–603. AE, DC, MC, V. Closed weekends.*

$$$ ✕ **Piekka Finnish Restaurant.** Designed in birchwood from floor to ceil-
★ ing, and decorated with stuffed animal heads, glass birds, copper coffeepots, and handwoven table linens in rich blues, Piekka provides the perfect setting for Finland's national cuisine. The menu includes delicately prepared reindeer and other game and seasonal fish dishes. Honey-seasoned birch sap is a specialty of the house. ⊠ *Sibeliuksenkatu 2,* ☎ *09/493–591. AE, DC, MC, V.*

$$$ ✕ **Ritarisali.** The very hearty French cuisine here emphasizes locally caught seafood. Large windows shed light on immaculate, embossed white table linens, wood paneling, warm creamy-orange walls, and parquet floors with Oriental rugs. ⊠ *Kalevankatu 5 (Hotel Torni),* ☎ *09/131–131. AE, DC, MC, V. Closed weekends.*

$$$ ✕ **Sipuli.** Sipuli stands at the foot of the Russian Orthodox Uspenski Cathedral and gets its name from the golden onionlike cupolas that adorn the famous structure. In this brick warehouse building dating from the 19th century, the redbrick walls and dark-wood panels are enhanced by a skylight that offers a spectacular view of the cathedral. For starters try the escargots in sherry and Gorgonzola sauce, and for the main course the smoked fillet of pike perch with salmon mousse and gravy sauce, or noisettes of reindeer topped with game sauce. ⊠ *Kanavaranta 3,* ☎ *09/179–900. AE, DC, MC, V. Closed weekends. No lunch.*

$$$ ✕ **Troikka.** The Troikka takes you back to czarist times in decor—samovars, icons, portraits of Russian writers—and music, and offers exceptionally good Russian food and friendly service. Try the *zhakuska,* an assortment of Russian appetizers including such delicacies as Baltic

150

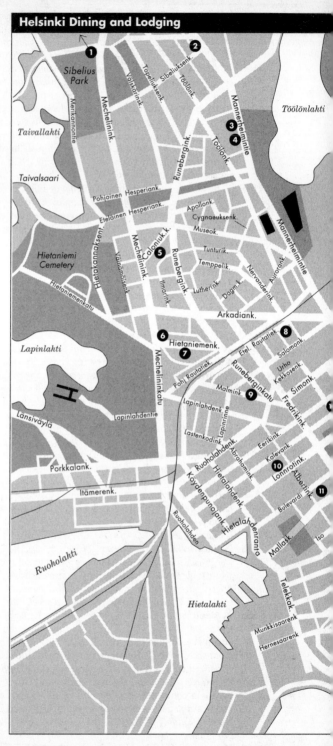

Helsinki Dining and Lodging

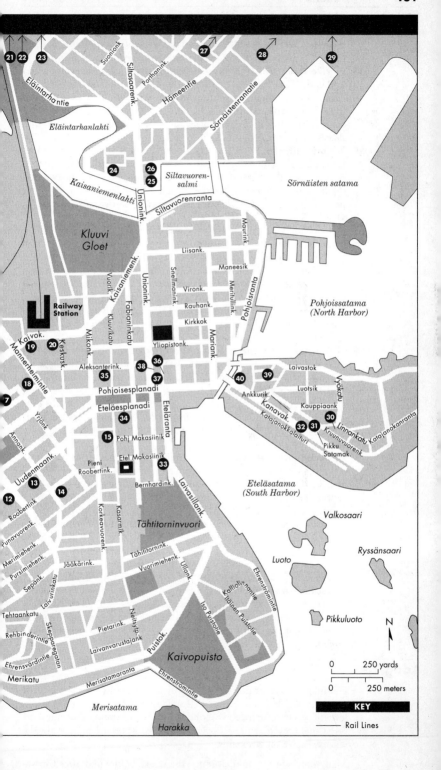

㉑ ㉒ ㉓

㉗ ㉘ ㉙

*Eläintarha*ntie

Suoniok. *Porthanink.* *Siltasaarenk.*

Hämeentie

Sörnäistenrantatie

Eläintarhanlahti

Kaisaniemenlahti

㉔

㉖ ㉕

Siltavuoren-salmi

Unionk. *Siltavuorenranta*

Sörnäisten satama

Kluuvi Gloet

Liisank.

Maurink.

Maneesik.

Snellmanink. *Unionk.* *Fabianinkatu* *Kaisaniemenk.* *Vuorik.* *Kluvikatu*

Railway Station

Vironk.

Rauhank.

Kirkkok.

Meritullink. *Pohjoisranta*

Pohjoissatama (North Harbor)

⑲ ⑳

Kaivok. *Keskusk.* *Mikonk.*

Aleksanterink.

Yliopistonk.

Mariank.

⑱

Mannerheimintie

㊳ ㊱

Laivastok

⑦

㉟

Pohjoisesplanadi

㊲

㊴ ㊴ ㊴

㊴ ㊴

Luotsik.

Vyokatu

Ankkurik.

⑳

Yrjonk.

Eteläesplanadi

Eteläranta

㉞

Kanavak.

Katajanokkalaituri

Kauppiaank.

Katajanokanranta

Annank.

⑮ *Pohj Makasiink.*

㉜ ㉛ ㉚

Linnankatu

Kruunuvuorenk.

⑫ ⑬ ⑭

Etel Makasiink.

㉝

Uudenmaank.

Roobertink.

Pieni Roobertink.

Bernhardink.

Pikku Satamak.

Punavuorenk. *Merimiehenk.* *Pursimiehenk.* *Sepänk.*

Korkeavuorenk.

Kasarmik.

Laivasillank.

Eteläsatama (South Harbor)

Tähtitorninvuori

Valkosaari

Ryssänsaari

Tähtitornink.

Luoto

Jääkärink.

Vuorimiehenk.

Ullank.

Laiv urinkatu

Tehtaankatu

Pietarink.

Neitsytp.

Ehrenströmintie

Kalliolinnantie

Iläinen Puistotie

Pikkuluoto

Rehbinderintie *Skepparegatan*

Laivanvarustajank.

Iso Puistotie

N

Ehrensvärdintie

Merikatu

Merisatamaranta

Puistok.

Kaivopuisto

Ehrenströmintie

| 0 | | 250 yards |
| 0 | | 250 meters |

KEY

—— Rail Lines

Merisatama

Harakka

herring, homemade poultry pâté, wild mushrooms, and marinated garlic. Other Troikka specialties include Siberian *pelmens* (small meat pastries), beef Stroganoff, and cutlet Kiev. ⊠ *Caloniuksenkatu 3,* ☎ *09/445–229. AE, DC, MC, V. Closed Sun., and weekends in July.*

$$$ ✕ **Villa Thai.** Near Helsinki's shopping district, this restaurant offers authentic Thai food in traditional surroundings. The staff dress in Thai silks, and diners can chose between Western and Thai-style seating. The prawn curry with coconut milk and pineapple is a house specialty. Live music in the evenings adds extra atmosphere. ⊠ *Bulevardi 28,* ☎ *09/680–2778. AE, DC, MC, V.*

$$ ✕ **Café Raffaello.** In the heart of Helsinki's Wall Street, this cozy Italian restaurant with redbrick walls, parquet floors, and decorative frescoes is reputed for friendly service, reasonable prices, and tasty pasta, salad, and meat dishes; try the grilled Cajun beefsteak with garlic potatoes or the mint chicken breast with rice. ⊠ *Aleksanterinkatu 46,* ☎ *09/653–930. AE, DC, MC, V.*

$$ ✕ **Kynsilaukka.** This is one of Helsinki's most imaginative restau-
★   rants. Dominated by garlic (there's even garlic beer), the food is fresh and beautifully presented and is often served by the three young owner-chefs themselves. The seafood bouillabaisse is superb, as are the cold marinated reindeer, the garlic cream soup, and the lamb pot. For dessert, the pancakes with cloudberry sauce and ice cream are a must. All portions are served in two sizes. The decor is rustic and comfortable. The set lunch menu is a good buy. ⊠ *Fredrikinkatu 22,* ☎ *09/651–939. AE, DC, MC, V.*

$$ ✕ **Omenapuu.** Generous windows overlook the downtown bustle at this restaurant on the second floor of a large office building in the heart of a busy shopping district. The fare is Finnish and international; periodic theme weeks feature various assortments of game, vegetables, and fish. Live piano music adds to the pleasant atmosphere in the mirrored, red-carpeted room. Take the outside elevator located in front of the shopping mall up to the second floor. ⊠ *Keskuskatu 6, 2nd floor,* ☎ *09/630–205. AE, DC, MC, V.*

$ ✕ **China.** One of the city's oldest Chinese restaurants, this place specializes in Cantonese fare. Apart from an extensive variety of beef, pork, and chicken dishes, there's an unusual pike perch with sweet-and-sour sauce. The Peking duck is recommended but must be ordered two days in advance. ⊠ *Annankatu 25,* ☎ *09/640–258. AE, DC, MC, V.*

$ ✕ **Pikku Satama.** This casual eatery in Katajanokka's Wanha Satama (a renovated brick warehouse complex) serves a variety of food—pizza, baked potatoes with various toppings, and hot dishes—in an informal but impressive setting. Both lunch and dinner specials are served. ⊠ *Pikku Satamakatu 3,* ☎ *09/174–093. AE, DC, MC, V. Closed Sun.*

$ ✕ **Ravintola Mechelin.** Helsinki's catering school operates this brasserie-style restaurant decorated in pine. In summer the emphasis is on Finnish food, particularly salmon and reindeer. Low prices and a good location—just west of Mannerheimintie—make it a favorite. ⊠ *Perhonkatu 11,* ☎ *09/4056–2118. AE, DC, MC, V.*

Lodging

Helsinki's hotels are notoriously expensive, and most cater to the business traveler. The standards of cleanliness are high, though, and the level of service usually corresponds to the price. Standard rooms tend to be small, even at more expensive hotels. Rates are almost always less expensive on weekends.

Many hotels in Helsinki close for the weeks before and after Christmas, and some close for Easter and Midsummer. Schedules vary from year to year, so call in advance.

$$$$ ☆ **Inter-Continental Helsinki.** One of the most popular hotels in Helsinki,
★ this local institution is modern, centrally located hotel, and particularly popular with American business travelers. Decor in the rather small
rooms is pleasant and light—oatmeal and light green carpets, subtle
floral-print bedspreads and curtains. Services for business travelers are
excellent; there's a business center that offers secretarial services and
has a photocopy machine, and 30 of the hotel rooms are equipped with
fax machines. Galateia (☞ Dining, *above*) offers good seafood and a
wonderful view. ⊠ *Mannerheimintie 46, 00260,* ☎ *09/40551,* FAX
*09/405–5255. 552 rooms, 12 suites. 2 restaurants, bar, café, no-smok-
ing rooms, room service, indoor pool, beauty salon, saunas, meeting
rooms. AE, DC, MC, V.*

$$$$ ☆ **Kalastajatorppa.** In the plush western Munkkiniemi neighborhood,
this hotel catered to U.S. presidents Ronald Reagan in 1988 and George
Bush in 1990 and 1992. A 15- to 25-minute ride by taxi from the city
center, the hotel has also been a favorite of international artists seeking anonymity. The best rooms are in the seaside annex, but all are large
and airy, decorated in fresh pastel colors with clear pine and birchwood
paneling. Rooms in the main building may be equipped with bath and
terrace or with showers only; prices vary accordingly. ⊠ *Kalastaja-
torpantie 1, 00330,* ☎ *09/458–152 or 09/45811,* FAX *09/458–1668.
235 rooms, 8 suites. 2 restaurants, 2 bars, no-smoking rooms, 2 indoor pools, saunas, beach, nightclub, meeting rooms. AE, DC, MC,
V. Sometimes closed Dec. 25.*

$$$$ ☆ **Palace.** Built for the 1952 Olympic games, this small hotel is on the
9th and 10th floors of a waterfront commercial building with a splendid view of the South Harbor. Its faithful clientele, which is largely British,
American, and Swedish, appreciates the personal service that comes
with its small size and such intimate touches as daily afternoon tea.
The decor is nondescript, except for the wood paneling and plush carpet, and amenities in the guest rooms are few. The hotel's restaurants
(especially the Palace Gourmet, ☞ Dining, *above*) are among Helsinki's
best. All rooms were renovated in 1991. ⊠ *Eteläranta 10, 00130,* ☎
09/134–561, FAX *09/654–786. 50 rooms, 14 junior suites, 2 suites. 2
restaurants, bar, café, room service, sauna. AE, DC, MC, V. Closed
Dec. 25.*

$$$$ ☆ **Radisson SAS Hotel Helsinki.** Opened in the summer of 1991, this
hotel was conceived and built to serve the business traveler. It's set in
a residential section of the central city, right on the metro line. Two
floors are made up of Royal SAS Club rooms, including several suites
and conference areas. The decor varies with the rooms; some are elegant Scandinavian (light colors and wood), others are Asian (warm colors and silk bedcovers), and some are Italian (modern with primary
colors). If you want more space and privacy, try the art deco–style business-class rooms on the top floor. The Johan Ludvig restaurant specializes in grilled meats; Ströget is cheaper and offers pasta, salads, and
hamburgers. There's an SAS check-in counter and service center in the
lobby. ⊠ *Runeberginkatu 2, 00100,* ☎ *09/69580,* FAX *09/6958–7100.
260 rooms, 7 suites. 2 restaurants, bar, room service, saunas, health
club, meeting rooms. AE, DC, MC, V.*

$$$$ ☆ **Ramada Presidentti.** In the heart of Helsinki, this hotel is spacious,
quiet, and has well-lighted rooms, with a wide range of facilities. Its
main restaurant, Four Seasons, serves tasty buffet meals. Gamblers take
note: Finland's first international casino was inaugurated here in 1991.
⊠ *Eteläinen Rautatiekatu 4, 00100,* ☎ *09/6911,* FAX *09/694–7886. 460
rooms with bath and 35 with shower. 2 restaurants, 2 coffee shops,
no-smoking rooms, indoor pool, massage, sauna, casino, nightclub, meeting rooms. AE, DC, MC, V.*

$$$$ ◨ **Sokos Hotel Hesperia.** Close to the city center, the Hesperia is modern with a Finnish flair. The marble-floored lobby's convenient semi-circle of service booths includes a hairdresser and barbershop, a car-rental service, and a gift shop. The relatively spacious contemporary rooms are well equipped but unmemorable except for those with king-size beds—a rarity in Helsinki hotels. Some rooms overlook Töölö Bay and the main avenue, Mannerheimintie; back rooms face a quieter street. ⊠ *Mannerheimintie 50, 00260,* ☎ *09/43101,* ℻ *09/431–0995. 383 rooms, 4 suites. Restaurant, bar, café, minibars, no-smoking rooms, room service, indoor pool, saunas, health club, helipad. AE, DC, MC, V. Closed Dec. 25.*

$$$$ ◨ **Strand Inter-Continental.** From the tastefully furnished rooftop
★ saunas and the large, crisply decorated rooms to the bathrooms with heated floors and the car-wash service in the basement garage, this recently opened hotel leaves you wanting for nothing—except maybe some wealthy donor to help you pay the bill. The hotel's distinctive use of granite and Finnish marble in the central lobby is accentuated by a soaring atrium. Choose from a lobby bar and two restaurants—the superb Pamir (haute-cuisine seafood, steak, or game; ☞ Dining, *above*) or the Atrium Plaza (light meals). Though it is in a traditionally socialist, working-class neighborhood, the location is central, and the waterfront vistas are a pleasure. An entire floor is reserved for nonsmokers, and five of the eight suites have panoramic views of the sea. ⊠ *John Stenbergin ranta 4, 00530,* ☎ *09/39351,* ℻ *09/393–5255. 200 rooms, 10 suites. 2 restaurants, bar, room service, indoor pool, saunas. AE, DC, MC, V. Closed Dec. 25.*

$$$$ ◨ **Torni.** The original part of this hotel was built in 1903, and its towers and internal details still reflect some of the more fanciful touches of Helsinki's Jugendstil period, although a new functionalist-style section was added in 1931. The original section has striking views of Helsinki from the higher floors—the Torni is one of the city's tallest buildings—and some of the rooms have large windows. Old-section rooms on the courtyard are recommended; some have high ceilings with original carved-wood details and wooden writing desks; many also have little alcoves and other pleasing design oddities. A conference room at the top of the tower has art exhibitions that change monthly. ⊠ *Yrjönkatu 26, 00100,* ☎ *09/131–131,* ℻ *09/131–1361. 154 rooms with bath or shower, 9 suites. 2 restaurants, 3 bars, room service, saunas, room service, meeting rooms. AE, DC, MC, V. Closed Dec. 25.*

$$$ ◨ **Airport Hotel Rantasipi.** This fully equipped, modern accommoda-
★ tion satisfies Helsinki's need for an airport hotel that meets the highest international standards. Convenient for layovers, the hotel borders the airport commercial zone and has the best conference facilities near the airport. A standard room includes a large sofa and usually a king-size bed and has such soft touches as paisley bedspreads and wicker furniture; all rooms are soundproof and air-conditioned. ⊠ *Robert Hubertintie 4, 01510 Vantaa,* ☎ *09/87051,* ℻ *09/822–846. 300 rooms, 4 suites. 2 restaurants, piano bar, minibars, no-smoking rooms, indoor pool, convention center. AE, DC, MC, V.*

$$$ ◨ **Grand Marina.** Housed inside an early 19th-century customs warehouse in the plush Katajanokka Island neighborhood, the Grand Marina has one of the best convention centers in Finland, accommodating up to 1,500 people. Its good location, friendly service, ample modern facilities, and reasonable prices have made this hotel a favorite among tourists. Ask for a room with a view of South Harbor. ⊠ *Katajanokanlaituri 7, 00160,* ☎ *09/16661,* ℻ *09/664–764. 462 rooms with shower or bath. 5 restaurants, bar, pub, saunas. AE, DC, MC, V.*

$$$ ⊞ **Lord Hotel.** Off on a quiet side street, this small luxury hotel distin-
★ guishes itself with a rare combination of character, consistency, and ser-
vice. The front section is a handsome stone castle, built in 1903, whose
wood-beamed, medieval-style rooms have been converted into restau-
rants, lounges, a cavernous banquet hall, conference rooms, a sauna lounge,
and an airy breakfast room. A walkway across an inner court brings you
to the modern building housing the guest rooms. Each of the rooms ex-
hibits fine attention to detail: The desks and lighting are excellent; the
contemporary-style furnishings, in soothing pastel blue and gray tones,
comfortable; and the storage space ample. There are discounts on week-
ends and in summer. ⊠ *Lönnrotinkatu 29, 00180,* ☎ *09/615–815,* FAX
*09/680–1315. 48 rooms with shower or bath, 1 suite (17 rooms are
equipped with a hot tub). Restaurant, bar, saunas, meeting rooms, free
parking. AE, DC, MC, V. Sometimes closed Dec. 25.*

$$$ ⊞ **Rivoli Jardin.** This central town house is just two short blocks off
★ the Esplanade Gardens, with small rooms overlooking a quiet court-
yard. Standard doubles have twin beds, though queen-size beds are also
available. The hotel is small and places emphasis on personal service.
Breakfast—included in the room rate—is served at the hotel's Winter
Garden next to the lobby bar. ⊠ *Kasarmikatu 40, 00130,* ☎ *09/177–
880,* FAX *09/656–988. 53 rooms, 1 suite. Restaurant, bar, sauna. AE,
DC, MC, V. Closed Dec. 25.*

$$$ ⊞ **Seurahuone Socis.** This Viennese-style town house was built in
1914 and has a loyal clientele won over by its ageless charm and cos-
mopolitan atmosphere. Well-worn elegance pervades all areas, from
the grand main stairway and the chandeliered Art Nouveau café to the
ornate, skylit Socis pub. The traditionally furnished rooms in the old
section (renovated in 1992) have brass beds, high ceilings, chandeliers,
and teak cabinets; the new section has sleek, modern rooms, so spec-
ify your preference. Many of the rooms, even the modern ones, are fur-
nished with Victorian antiques. More spacious "superior" rooms are
more expensive. As the hotel faces the railway station and houses a
popular disco in addition to a café and a pub, the lobby and public
area are among the busiest in town. ⊠ *Kaivokatu 12, 00100,* ☎
09/69141, FAX *09/691–4010. 118 rooms, 5 suites. Restaurant, bar,
café, pub, saunas. AE, DC, MC, V. Sometimes closed Dec. 25.*

$$ ⊞ **Anna.** Pleasantly situated in a central, residential neighborhood, the
Anna is in a seven-story apartment building dating from the 1930s.
Room fittings are modern, however, with light, comfortable furniture.
The room price includes a buffet breakfast. ⊠ *Annankatu 1, 00120,*
☎ *09/648–011,* FAX *09/602–664. 60 rooms, 1 suite. Brasserie, no-smok-
ing floor, sauna. AE, DC, MC, V. Closed Dec. 25 and Jan. 1.*

$$ ⊞ **Anton.** The furnishings in this hotel's rooms are much like those you'd
find in a typical Finnish home: simple, clean lines; a plethora of wood
tones; duvets in bright, primary colors. In a traditional Helsinki
working-class neighborhood and near the center and the Market
Square, the Anton is also conveniently close to the airport bus stop and
the Hakaniemi metro stop. ⊠ *Paasivuorenkatu 1, 00530,* ☎ *09/750–
311,* FAX *09/701–4527. 32 rooms, 3 suites. AE, DC, MC, V. Closed
Dec. 25.*

$$ ⊞ **Arthur.** Owned by the Helsinki YMCA, the Arthur is centrally located, unpretentious, and comfortable, and it has a restaurant. ⊠
Vuorikatu 19, 00100, ☎ *09/173–441,* FAX *09/626–880. 143 rooms with
shower or bath. Restaurant, sauna. AE, DC, MC, V.*

$$ ⊞ **Aurora.** Built in 1970 and renovated from 1989 to 1991, this red-
brick hotel has small modern rooms decorated in pale blues, greens,
and peach; larger rooms have brown wood paneling. A 10-minute bus
ride from the city center, it's also just across from the Linnanmäki Amuse-
ment Park and has therefore become a favorite of families. ⊠

Helsinginkatu 50, 00530, ☎ *09/717–400,* FAX *09/714–240. 70 rooms with shower or bath. Restaurant, pool, sauna, spa, squash. AE, DC, MC, V. Closed Dec. 25.*

$$ ☷ **Hotel Pilotti.** In a quiet suburban setting within five minutes' drive of the airport, the Pilotti is also about 5 kilometers (3 miles) from Heureka (the Finnish Science Center). Built in 1989, it is modern inside and out; each compact room has a large, round porthole-style window. ☒ *Veromäentie 1, 01510 Vantaa,* ☎ *09/870–2100,* FAX *09/870–2109. 112 rooms, 4 suites. Restaurant, pub, sauna, meeting rooms. AE, DC, MC, V.*

$$ ☷ **Marttahotelli.** This convenient establishment is small and cozy, with simply decorated, fresh, white rooms. The hotel was fully renovated in 1989. ☒ *Uudenmaankatu 24, 00120,* ☎ *09/646–211,* FAX *09/680–1266. 40 rooms with shower, 5 with bath. Sauna. AE, DC, MC, V. Closed Dec. 25, Midsummer, and sometimes Easter.*

$$ ☷ **Merihotelli.** Next to Hakaniemi Market Square, Merihotelli is only a 10-minute walk from the heart of Helsinki. The smallish guest rooms are decorated in shades of pale blue, and the ambience is serene. ☒ *John Stenbergin ranta 6, 00530,* ☎ *09/69121,* FAX *09/691–2214. 87 rooms with shower. Café, bar. AE, DC, MC, V. Closed Dec. 25.*

$$ ☷ **Olympia.** There's a fine ambience in the public areas of this hotel, with their stone floors, wood-paneled walls, and sturdy furniture. By contrast, the rooms are light, with white walls and blue-green textiles and upholstery. The hotel dates from 1962; the most recent redecoration was in 1990. ☒ *Läntinen Brahenkatu 2, 00510,* ☎ *09/69151,* FAX *09/691–5219. 98 rooms, 1 suite. 2 restaurants, no-smoking rooms, sauna, nightclub. AE, DC, MC, V. Sometimes closed Dec. 25.*

$ ☷ **Finn Apartments.** Situated on a side street north of Hakaniemi Square, 10 minutes by tram from the city center, this apartment hotel offers clean, reasonably priced rooms. One option for guests, many of whom are businesspeople, is a private studio apartment with kitchenette and bathroom; an even less expensive choice is an unpretentious, light-colored economy room. The cheapest rooms must be shared with another guest. ☒ *Franzeninkatu 26, 00530,* ☎ *09/773–1661,* FAX *09/701–6889. 100 rooms. Café, saunas, coin laundry. AE, DC, MC, V.*

$ ☷ **Hostel Academica.** Fully renovated in 1992, this summer hotel is made up of what are, during the rest of the year, university students' apartments. Each floor has a small lounge; the rooms are sturdy, modern, and have their own small kitchens. Family rooms and extra beds are also available, and there are special family rates. Guests can eat reduced-price meals at the nearby Perho restaurant. The central location is good for shopping and transport. ☒ *Hietaniemenkatu 14, 00100,* ☎ *09/402–0206,* FAX *09/441–201. 115 rooms with shower and kitchenette. Pool, sauna, tennis court, coin laundry. AE, DC, MC, V. Closed Sept. 2–May.*

$ ☷ **Omapohja.** Dating from 1906, this inn, which occupies a mint-green Jugendstil building, used to be a base for actors performing at the state theater next door. The rooms are cozily old-fashioned, with wood-paneled walls and handwoven bedspreads; they also have tremendous windows. ☒ *Itäinen Teatterikuja 3, 00100,* ☎ *09/666–211. 15 rooms, 3 with shower. MC, V. Closed Dec. 25.*

$ ☷ **Skatta.** Set in the quiet Katajanokka Island neighborhood 2 kilometers (1¼ miles) from the railway station, this modest hotel began as a home for sailors at the turn of the century and was converted into a hotel in 1960. The brownish-red rooms offer good views of the South Harbor. ☒ *Linnankatu 3, 00160,* ☎ *09/659–233,* FAX *09/631–352. 23 rooms with shower and kitchenette. Sauna, exercise room. AE, DC, MC, V. Sometimes closed Dec. 25 and Easter.*

$ ⊞ **Vantaa Hostel.** As hostels go, this is one of the cleanest and brightest you'll ever find. It was built in 1980 and enlarged in 1989; the old wing is cheaper than the rooms in the new extension. ⊠ *Valkoisenlähteentie 52, 01300 Vantaa,* ☎ *09/839–3310,* ⨳ *09/839–4366. 6 rooms with shared bath and shower, 24 rooms with shower. Closed Dec. 25.*

Nightlife and the Arts

Nightlife

At night, street life in restrained Helsinki consists mainly of youths hanging out in the city's downtown parks. The range of clubs is limited to quiet places for a chat or discos and hotel nightclubs with loud music. Cover charges average FM 15–FM 50.

The Helsinki City Tourist Office has a "Clubs and Music Bars" listing of music nights and cover-charge details for various venues.

BARS AND LOUNGES

A stylish crowd mingles in whimsical postmodern surroundings at the new **Cincin Bar** (⊠ Arctia Hotel Marski, Mannerheimintie 10, ☎ 09/68–061). **Kappeli** (⊠ Eteläesplanadi 1, ☎ 09/179–242) is the first Finnish restaurant to brew its own beer. Its leaded windows offer an excellent view of the Havis Amanda statue. The **Socis Pub** (⊠ Kaivokatu 12, ☎ 09/691–4004) at the Seurahuone Hotel has a turn-of-the-century European ambience. **Säkkipilli** (⊠ Kalevankatu 2, ☎ 09/605–607) is an English-style pub. **Raffaello** (⊠ Aleksanterinkatu 46, ☎ 09/653–930) is a new bar that attracts a young crowd of professionals who work in the Helsinki financial district. For a taste of Ireland, visit one of Helsinki's most popular pubs, **O'Malley's** (⊠ Hotel Torni, Yrjönkatu 28, ☎ 09/131–131).

Vanha Ylioppilastalo (⊠ Mannerheimintie 3, ☎ 09/1311–4224) attracts students with live music, usually on weekends—blues, folk, and jazz. **Cantina West** (⊠ Kasarmikatu 23, ☎ 09/622–1500) is a lively spot for enjoying imported country, country-rock, and Tex-Mex music.

CASINOS

Casino Ray (⊠ Eteläinen Rautatie 4, ☎ 09/694–2900), which opened in 1991, offers roulette, blackjack, and slot machines on the third floor of the Ramada Presidentti Hotel.

GAY AND LESBIAN BARS

Gay Disco Triangle, at Botnia Club (⊠ Museokatu 10, ☎ 09/446–940) has gay nights every Monday; for details, contact the gay switchboard, SETA (Wed.–Fri. and Sun. 6–9 PM, ☎ 09/135–8305). **Blue Boy** (⊠ Eerinkatu 14, ☎ 09/608–826) is a popular gay bar. **Don't Tell Mama** (⊠ Annankatu 32, ☎ 09/694–1122) is also for men only. **New Faces** (⊠ Lönnrotinkatu 29, ☎ 09/719–257) is a lesbian nightspot.

JAZZ CLUBS

Helsinki's newest and most popular jazz club, **Storyville** (⊠ Museokatu 8, ☎ 09/408–007), offers live jazz every night. **Jumo Jazzclub** (⊠ Keskuskatu 6, ☎ 09/171–585), conveniently located in the railway-station tunnel, has pleasant jazz evenings, usually on Tuesday, Wednesday, and Friday. **Hot Tomato Jazz Club** (⊠ Annankatu 6, ☎ 09/680–1701) has live jazz Tuesday to Sunday 8 PM–3AM.

NIGHTCLUBS

The **Hesperia Hotel Nightclub** (⊠ Mannerheimintie 50, ☎ 09/43101), Helsinki's largest and most famous club, occasionally hosts big-name acts. Enjoy gorgeous city views and the cabaret-style floor shows at the ninth-floor **Sky Bar** (⊠ Hotel Vaakuna, Asemaaukio 2, ☎ 09/131–

181). **Fizz** is a popular bar and nightclub at the Arctia Hotel Marski (⊠ Mannerheimintie 10, ☎ 09/68061). For a night of dancing, head downtown to **Fennia** (⊠ Mikonkatu 17, ☎ 09/666–355). **Kaivohuone** (⊠ Kaivohuone Kaivopuisto, ☎ 09/177–881) is an old spa structure in beautiful Kaivopuisto.

Friday and Saturday nights at **Botnia Club** (⊠ Museokatu 10, ☎ 09/446–940) are strictly disco. The university-owned **Tavastia Club** (⊠ Urho Kekkosenkatu 4–6, ☎ 09/694–3066) is one of the best clubs for top Finnish talent as well as some solid imports.

The Arts

For a list of events, pick up *Helsinki This Week,* available in hotels and tourist offices. For tickets, contact **Lippupalvelu** (⊠ Mannerheimintie 5, in the Bio-Bio cinema arcade, ☎ 09/9700–4700 or 09/664–466). **Tiketti** (⊠ Yrjönkatu 29C, ☎ 09/9700–4204) is the other main ticket agency.

In summer, plays and music are performed at many outdoor theaters, including Keskuspuisto, Suomenlinna, Mustikkamaa, and the Seurasaari Islands, and also at the Rowing Stadium. **The Helsinki Festival,** a performance and visual-arts celebration set in venues around the city, is held yearly in early autumn.

CONCERTS

Finlandiatalo (Finlandia Hall) (⊠ Karamzininkatu 4, ☎ 09/40241), the home of the Helsinki Philharmonic, hosts many visiting world-class orchestras. Finland has produced many fine conductors, and because many of them are based abroad—Esa-Pekka Salonen, Jukka-Pekka Saraste, and Paavo Berglund, for example—their homecomings are lavishly fêted. Concerts are generally held from September through May on Wednesday and Thursday evenings. The splendid **Suomen Kansallisooppera,** the Finnish National Opera (⊠ Helsinginkatu 58, ☎ 09/4030–2211), is in a waterside park by Töölönlahti. Original Finnish opera is often performed here, in addition to international favorites. The rock-hewn **Temppeliaukio Kirkko** (⊠ Lutherinkatu 3, ☎ 09/494–698) is a favorite venue for choral and chamber music. The **Sibelius Academy** (⊠ Pohjois Rautatiekatu 9, ☎ 09/405–441) hosts frequent performances, usually by students.

FILM

There are about 50 cinemas in Helsinki. Foreign films have Finnish and Swedish subtitles. Movie listings are in most daily papers and are also posted at the kiosk near the eastern entrance of the main train station. Most cinemas have assigned seats. Tickets cost FM 35–FM 45.

THEATER

Though the recession has forced the state to cut back on its generous financing, private support of the arts continues to be strong—especially for the theaters, the best-known of which are the National Theater, City Theater, Swedish Theater, and the Lilla Teatern. However, unless you are fluent in Finnish or Swedish, you'll have a difficult time understanding the performances. Check *Helsinki This Week* for a listing of current performances.

Outdoor Activities and Sports

Bicycling

Helsinki and environs make for good biking because there is a decent network of trails, many running through parks, forests, and fields. The free area sporting map (Ulkoilukartta) gives details of all trails. Daily rentals are available from **Green Bike** (⊠ Mannerheimintie 13, 00100 Helsinki, ☎ 050/550–1020).

Golf

For full information on golf in Helsinki and environs, contact the **Finnish Golf Union** (⊠ Radiokatu 20, 00240 Helsinki, ☎ 09/158–2244). There are 9- and 18-hole and par-3 (FM 60–FM 70) courses in Helsinki and surroundings, with greens fees from FM 160 to FM 250.

Swimming

The best beaches in Helsinki are Pihlajasaari, Mustikkamaa, Uunisaari. The beach at **Hietaniemi** is especially popular with young people. Among Helsinki's indoor swimming pools and saunas, the oldest and one of the most famous is **Yrjönkatu Uimahalli** (⊠ Yrjönkatu 21B, ☎ 09/60981), where swimming is in the nude.

Tennis

There are some 6 tennis centers and 31 clubs in Helsinki. For specifics, contact the **Finnish Tennis Association** (⊠ Myllypuro Tennis Center, Varikkotie 4, 00900 Helsinki, ☎ 09/338–122). It's best to bring your own equipment, although rentals are available.

Shopping

Helsinki's shopping facilities are constantly improving. Although many international stores are still absent, there are several malls and shopping districts where you can shop thoroughly and in comfort. Stores are generally open weekdays 9–6 and Saturday 9–1. The Forum and Stockmann's are open weekdays 9–8 and Saturday 9–6.

Kiosks remain open late and on weekends; they sell such basics as milk, juice, and tissues. Stores in Asematunneli, the train-station tunnel, are open weekdays 10–10 and weekends noon–10.

Department Stores

Stockmann's (⊠ Aleksanterinkatu 52, ☎ 09/1211) is Helsinki's premier department store. **Aleksi 13** (⊠ Aleksanterinkatu 13, ☎ 09/131–441) is less expensive than Stockmann's.

Shopping Districts

Pohjoisesplanadi, on the north side of the Esplanade, has most of Helsinki's trademark design stores—including Arabia, Marimekko, and Aarikka—and a wide array of other goods.

Senaatintori, on the south side of Senate Square, has a host of souvenir and crafts stores (open weekdays 10–6, Sat. 10–3), with several antiques shops and secondhand bookstores on the adjoining streets. Next to Senate Square is the **Kiseleff Bazaar Hall,** an attractive shopping gallery.

There are many smaller boutiques in the streets **west of Mannerheimintie,** Fredrikinkatu and Annankatu, for example. There is one pedestrian shopping street a few blocks south of the Esplanade, on **Iso Roobertinkatu;** stores here are conventional, but the atmosphere is more relaxed than it is around Mannerheimintie and the Esplanade.

Shopping Malls

All of Helsinki's shopping malls have a good mix of stores plus several cafés and restaurants. **Forum** (⊠ Mannerheimintie 20) is a large shopping complex. **Kaivopiha** (⊠ Kaivokatu 10) is across from the train station. **Kluuvi** shopping center (⊠ Aleksanterinkatu 9–Kluuvikatu 5) is a major mall. The large **Itäksekus** shopping complex in east Helsinki can be reached by metro.

Specialty Stores

ANTIQUES

Many shops sell china, furniture, and art. China, cut glass, and old farm furniture are other popular products; the last is harder to find. The **Kruunuhaka** area (north of Senate Square) is the best bet for antiques. Try **Antik Oskar** (⌧ Rauhankatu 7, ☎ 09/135–7410), **Antiikkiliike Karl Fredrik** (⌧ Mariankatu 13, ☎ 09/630–014), **Punavuoren Antiikki** (⌧ Mariankatu 14, ☎ 09/662–682), and **Atlas Antiques** (⌧ Rauhankatu 8, ☎ 09/628–186), if you are interested in coins, banknotes, medals, and silver. Also try the **Punavuori district,** between Eerikinkatu and Tehtaankatu; many shops here also sell secondhand books (there's usually a small selection in English).

CERAMICS AND ACCESSORIES

Firms like **Hackman Shop Arabia** (which also sells Iittala and Nuutajärvi) (⌧ Pohjoisesplanadi 25, ☎ 09/170–055), **Pentik** (⌧ Pohjoisesplanadi 27C, ☎ 09/625–558), and **Aarikka** (⌧ Pohjoisesplanadi 25–27, ☎ 09/652–277) offer ceramics, leather, accessories, and wooden toys. The **Arabia factory** (⌧ Hämeentie 135), at the end of the Tram 6 line, exhibits older designs.

CLOTHING

Bright, modern, unusual clothes for men, women, and children in quality fabrics are sold at **Marimekko** (⌧ Pohjoisesplanadi 31, ☎ 09/177–944; Eteläesplanadi 14, ☎ 09/170–724), and the **Forum** shopping mall (⌧ Mannerheimintie 20, ☎ 09/694–1498), on the Esplanade in Helsinki (additional outlets are located in other cities). Though the products are costly, they're worth a look even if you don't plan to spend.

JEWELRY

Kaunis Koru (⌧ Aleksanterinkatu 28, ☎ 09/626–850; Pohjoisesplanadi 31, ☎ 09/666–161) and **Lapponia Jewelry** (⌧ Mäkelänkatu 60A, ☎ 09/146–4600) produce avant-garde silver and gold designs, while **Kalevala Koru** (⌧ Unioninkatu 25, ☎ 09/171–520) bases its designs on traditional motifs dating back as far as the Iron Age.

SAUNA SUPPLIES

For genuine Finnish sauna supplies like wooden buckets, bath brushes, and birch-scented soap, visit the **Sauna Shop** in the Kiseleff Bazaar (⌧ Aleksanterinkatu 28) or the fourth floor of Stockmann's (⌧ Aleksanterinkatu 52, ☎ 09/1211).

Street Markets

Helsinki's main street markets specialize in food, but all have some clothing (new and used) and household products. **Hietalahden Tori** has an indoor market with fresh food products, and an outdoor market with an ever-changing assortment of used items. **Hakaniemi** has everything from Eastern spices to used clothing. The **Market Square** sells some furs in addition to its standard products. Hours are Monday–Saturday 7–2; in summer they reopen from 3:30 to 8. Almost adjacent to the Market Square is the **Old Market Hall** (open weekdays 8–5, Sat. 8–2), where you can browse and shop for anything from flowers to vegetables, meat, and fish. **Hietalahti's flea market** is open Monday–Saturday 7–2; in summer it reopens from 3 to 8.

Helsinki A to Z

Arriving and Departing

BY PLANE

All domestic and international flights to Helsinki use Helsinki-Vantaa International Airport, 20 kilometers (14 miles) north of the city.

Helsinki is served by most major European airlines, as well as several East European carriers. European airlines include **SAS** (⊠ Keskuskatu 7A, ☎ 09/2280–82222), **Lufthansa** (⊠ Yrjönkatu 29A, ☎ 09/694–9900), **SwissAir** (⊠ Mikonkatu 7, ☎ 09/175–300), **British Airways** (⊠ Aleksanterinkatu 21A, ☎ 09/650–677), and **Air France** (⊠ Pohjoisesplanadi 27C, ☎ 09/625–862). North American service is available from **Delta** (⊠ Salomonkatu 17B, ☎ 09/694–2422).

Between the Airport and Downtown. A local bus, the No. 615, runs three to four times an hour between the airport and the main railway station. The fare is FM 15, and the trip takes about 40 minutes. Local Bus 614 runs three times a day between the airport and the main bus station; the trip takes approximately 40 minutes and the fare is FM 15. Finnair buses carry travelers to and from the railway station (Finnair's city terminal) two to four times an hour, with a stop at the Inter-Continental hotel. Request stops along the route from the airport to the city are also made. Travel time from the Inter-Continental hotel is about 30 minutes and about 35 minutes from the main railway station; the fare is FM 24.

A limousine ride into central Helsinki will cost about FM 600; contact **International Limousine System** (⊠ Alkutie 32H, 00660, ☎ 09/744–577 or 049/421–801).

There is a taxi stop at the arrivals building. A cab ride into central Helsinki will cost between FM 100 and FM 140. Driving time is 20 to 35 minutes, depending upon the time of day. Check to see if your hotel has a shuttle service, although this is not common here. **Airport Taxi Service** (☎ 09/2200–2500; ☞ FM 60, FM 90 for two passengers, FM 110 for three) operates shuttles between the city and the airport. Reserve two hours before flight departure; for flights departing before 7 AM, reserve before 8 PM.

Getting Around

The center of Helsinki is compact and best explored on foot. However, the City Tourist Office provides a free Helsinki route map that shows all public transportation. The **Helsinki Card** gives unlimited travel on city public transportation as well as free entry to many museums, a free sightseeing tour, and a variety of other discounts. It's available for one, two, or three days (FM 105, FM 135, FM 165) and can be bought at most hotels or at the City Tourist Office.

BY BOAT

All boat tours depart from the Market Square. The easiest way to choose one is to go to the square in the morning and read the information boards describing the tours. The City Tourist Office has the most current information. Most tours run in the summer only. You can go as far afield as Porvoo (☞ Side Trips, *below*) or take a short jaunt to the zoo.

A ferry to the Suomenlinna fortress island runs about twice an hour, depending on the time of day. The ferry to the zoo island, Korkeasaari, also departs from Market Square.

BY BUS, METRO, AND TRAM

The bus and tram networks are extensive, and service is frequent. The main bus station in downtown Helsinki is Linja-autoasema (⊠ Simonkatu 3, ☎ 09/682–701). Be sure to pick up a route map at the tourist office—many stops do not have them. If you have a one-trip ticket, or *Kertalippu* (FM 9), or a 10-trip ticket, or *Kymmenen matkan kortti* (FM 75), available at R-Kiosks, you must validate it yourself. Single-trip tram tickets (FM 7, no transfer; FM 9, one transfer allowed) are available on board. The metro system is small but has fast and frequent service from around 5:25 AM to 11:20 PM Monday through Saturday and infrequent service on Sunday; the cost is the same as for buses and trams.

BY CAR

Ring Roads One and Three are the two major highways that encircle the city. Mannerheimintie and Hämeentie are the major trunk roads out of Helsinki. Mannerheimintie feeds into Highway E79, which travels west and takes you to the Ring Roads. Hämeentie leads you to Highway E4 as well as Roads 4 and 7. From either route, you will find directions for Road 137 to the airport. For specific route information, contact the **Automobile and Touring Club of Finland** (⊠ Autoliitto ry, Hämeentie 105 A, PL 35, 00550 Helsinki, ☎ 09/774–761) or the City Tourist Office.

BY TAXI

There are numerous taxi stands; central stands are at Railway Square on the west side of the station, the main bus station, and in the Esplanade. Taxis can also be flagged, but this can sometimes be difficult, since many are on radio call.

BY TRAIN

Helsinki's suburbs as well as most of the rest of southern, western, and central Finland are well served by trains. Travel on trains within the Helsinki city limits costs the same as all public transport, FM 9 or less if you use the 10-trip tickets (☞ *above*). A 10-trip **Helsinki Area Ticket,** or *Seutulippu,* for FM 125 also provides a small discount for travel back and forth to adjacent areas such as Espoo and Vantaa.

Contacts and Resources

DENTISTS

Töölö Dental Care Center (⊠ Runeberginkatu 47 A, ☎ 09/431–4500), weekdays 8–3.

DOCTORS

Dial 10023 for doctor referrals.

EMBASSIES

U.S. Embassy, Itäinen Puistotie 14A, 00140 Helsinki, ☎ 09/171–931. **Canadian Embassy,** Pohjoisesplanadi 25B, 00100 Helsinki, ☎ 09/171–141. **U.K. Embassy,** Itäinen Puistotie 17, 00140 Helsinki, ☎ 09/2286–5100.

EMERGENCIES

The general emergency number is 112; call it for any emergency situation. Coins are not needed to make this call on pay phones.

Police. Dial 112.

Ambulance. Dial 112. Specify whether the situation seems life-threatening so that medical attendants can begin immediate treatment in the ambulance.

Töölön Sairaala (⊠ Töölönkatu 40, ☎ 09/4711) is a centrally located hospital (about 2 kilometers/1¼ mile from city center) with a 24-hour emergency room and first-aid service.

ENGLISH-LANGUAGE BOOKSTORES

Akateeminen Kirjakauppa (⊠ Academic Bookstore, ⊠ Pohjoisesplanadi 39, ☎ 09/12141) is the largest English-language bookstore; it's also the most expensive. Like the Academic Bookstore, **Suomalainen Kirjakauppa** (The Finnish Bookstore) (⊠ Aleksanterinkatu 23, ☎ 09/651–855) sells English-language books, newspapers, and magazines.

Bus tours are a good way to get oriented in Helsinki. There is a 1½-hour bus tour of central Helsinki sights that comes free with the Helsinki Card; otherwise the cost is FM 70. The tour leaves from Railway Square (Asema-aukio) daily at 11 AM and 1:30 PM May–September, Sunday at 11 AM October–April. It also departs from Olympia Terminal (⊠ South Harbor, Eteläsatama) daily at 9:45 AM May–September and from the Havis Amanda (⊠ Market Square, Kauppatori) daily at 10:30 AM, 12:30 PM, and 2:30 PM May–September. For more information, contact **Suomen Turistiauto** (☎ 09/588-5166).

A year-round two-hour tour leaves from the Olympic Harbor daily at 9:30 AM. The cost is FM 90 for adults and FM 45 for children under 12, not including lunch. For more information, call **Ageba Travel** (☎ 09/669–193). From April through October, Ageba also has a daily 2½-hour tour at 11 AM from the Olympic Harbor costing FM 100, excluding lunch.

Orientation Tours. The Helsinki City Tourist Office distributes a pamphlet called "Helsinki Sightseeing : 3T," which describes points of interest along the 3T tram's downtown route. The tram ride provides a good orientation to the city for the price of a regular fare (FM 7). You can get on board in front of the railway station on Kaivokatu for the 60-minute round-trip.

Personal Guides. Helsingin Matkailuyhdistys (Helsinki Tourist Association) (⊠ Lönnrotinkatu 7, 00120, ☎ 09/645–22) is a guide-booking center that will arrange personal tour guides.

Walking Tours. The city tourist office has an excellent brochure, "See Helsinki on Foot," with six walks covering most points of interest.

Yliopiston Apteekki (⊠ Mannerheimintie 96, ☎ 09/415–778) is open daily 24 hours.

Banks are open weekdays 9–9:15 to 4–5. Many offices and embassies close at 3 PM June–August. Stores are open weekdays 9–6 and Saturday 9–1 or 2 and are closed on Sunday. Some stores in malls remain open until 8 PM on weekdays and until 4 on Saturday. In the Asematunneli (train station tunnel), stores are open weekdays 10–10 and weekends noon–10.

The **Helsinki City Tourist Office** (⊠ Pohjoisesplanadi 19, 00100 Helsinki, ☎ 09/169–3757) is open May 2–September 30, weekdays 8:30–6, weekends 10–3; October 1–April 30, weekdays 8:30–4. The **Finnish Tourist Board's Information Office** (⊠ Eteläesplanadi 4, 00130 Helsinki, ☎ 09/4030–1211 or 09/4030–1300), covering all of Finland, is open June–August, weekdays 8:30–5, Saturdays 10–2; September–May, weekdays 8:30–4.

Suomen Matkatoimisto (Finland Travel Bureau) (⊠ Kaivokatu 10 A, PL 319, 00100 Helsinki, ☎ 09/18261) is the country's main travel agency. The Finland Travel Bureau's affiliate in the United Kingdom is **Norvista** (⊠ 227 Regent Street, W1R 8PD London, ☎ 0171/409–7334). **Finnway Inc.** (⊠ 228 E. 45th St., 14th Floor, New York, NY 10017, ☎ 212/818–1198) is the United States' affiliate of the Finland Travel Bureau.

SIDE TRIPS FROM HELSINKI

The Helsinki environs are full of attractions, most of them no more than a half-hour bus or train ride from the city center. From the idyllic former home of Finland's national artist to the utopian garden city of Tapiola in Espoo, the options abound.

Gallen-Kallela Estate

Set at the edge of the sea and surrounded by towering, wind-bent pines, the turreted brick-and-stucco **Gallen-Kallela Estate** was the self-designed studio and home of the Finnish Romantic painter Akseli Gallen-Kallela. Gallen-Kallela (1865–1931) lived in the mansion on and off from its completion in 1913 until his death. Inside, the tremendous open rooms of the painter's former work spaces make the perfect exhibition hall for his paintings. Also displayed are some of his posters and sketches of the ceiling murals he made for the Paris Art Exhibition at the turn of the 20th century. There is a café on the grounds. To get to the estate, take Tram 4 from in front of the City Sokos department store on Mannerheimintie. From the Munkkiniemi stop transfer to Bus 33, or walk the 2 kilometers (1¼ miles) through the woods. ⊠ *Gallen-Kallelantie 27, Tarvaspää,* ☎ *09/513–388.* ☜ *FM 35.* ⊙ *May 15–Aug. 31, Mon.–Thurs. 10–8, Fri.–Sun. 10–5; rest of yr, Tues.–Sat. 10–4, Sun. 10–5.*

Espoo

30 km (19 mi) west of Helsinki.

The garden city of Tapiola, one of Finland's architectural highlights, is in Espoo, Helsinki's next-door neighbor. Designed by Alvar Aalto, the urban landscape of alternating high and low residential buildings, fountains, gardens, and swimming pools blends into the natural surroundings. Guides and sightseeing tours are available from the **Espoo Visitor and Convention Bureau** (⊠ Keskustorni, 13th Floor, 02100 Espoo, ☎ 09/460–311). The Helsinki Area Ticket (☞ Helsinki Essentials, *above*) provides discount fares to Espoo.

Porvoo

50 km (31 mi) east of Helsinki.

Porvoo is a living record of the past, with its old stone streets and painted wooden houses that line the riverbank. There are a number of artisan boutiques around the old Town Hall Square, and you'll want to be sure to take a stroll into the Old Quarter to see the multicolored old wooden houses. Visit the 15th-century stone-and-wood cathedral, **Porvoon Tuomiokirkko,** where the diet of the first duchy of Finland was held in the 1800s. The **Walter Runebergin Veistoskokoelma** (Walter Runeberg Sculpture Collection) (⊠ Aleksanterinkatu 3–5, ☎ 019/581–330) is a lovely sculpture collection. The **Porvoo Museo** (⊠ Välikatu 11, ☎ 019/524–8042) captures the region's social and cultural history through exhibits on daily life and household objects. Next door to the Porvoo Museo, the **Edelfelt-Vallgren Museo** (⊠ Välikatu 11, ☎ 019/524–8042) exhibits Edelfelt's art.

Near Porvoo in Haikko, you can visit the **Albert Edelfeltin Atelje,** the painter's studio of Albert Edelfelt. Also near Porvoo is the **Savilinna Taide- ja Käsityökeskus** (Savilinna Arts and Handicrafts Center) (⊠ Suomenkyläntie 32, ☎ 019/583–483), a ceramics workshop where you can watch ceramics artists at work, participate in classes, view art exhibits, and visit the gift shop and café. Contact the **Porvoo City Tourist**

Office (✉ Rauhankatu 20, 06100 Porvoo, ☎ 019/580–145) for details on all local sights. A branch at old Town Hall Square is open June–August 15.

Part of the fun of visiting Porvoo is the journey to get there, especially when you go by boat (there are also bus and road connections). In summer (mid-June–mid-Aug.), there are daily cruise departures from Helsinki's South Harbor (average round-trip cost is FM 135; travel time depends on the boat; the *J. L. Runeberg* takes 3½ hours, the *Queen* 2½ hours each way). You will be taken westward through dozens of islands before landing at Porvoo, which is small enough to be covered on foot. Contact **Porvoon Sataman Info** (Porvoo Harbor Information) at ☎ 019/584–727.

Vantaa

20 km (12 mi) north of Helsinki.

Although it is not a remarkable city, Vantaa, the municipality just north of Helsinki proper (and home to the international airport) has some notable attractions that are well worth seeing, plus a welcome surplus of open green space, and trails for biking, hiking, and jogging. Don't miss the 15th-century **Helsingin Pitajan Kirkko** (Parish Church Village; Kirkkoaukio).

Vantaa is a good place to keep in mind as a base if your trip to Helsinki coincides with a convention and you can't find accommodations there: It's close to the airport and easily reached by public transport; and the Helsinki Area Ticket (☞ Helsinki Essentials, *above*) includes Vantaa.

ⓒ The **Heureka Suomalainen Tiedekeskus** (Heureka Finnish Science Center) has interactive exhibits on topics as diverse as energy, language, and papermaking. There is also a cafeteria, a park, and a planetarium with taped commentary available in English. ✉ *Tiedepuisto 1, Tikkurila, Vantaa,* ☎ *09/85799.* ☜ *FM 75.* ☉ *Mon.–Wed. 10–6, Thurs. 10–8, Fri.–Sun. 10–6.*

Near the Myyrmäki train station on the Helsinki–Martinlaakso suburban line (M train) is the **Myyrmäki Kirkko** (✉ Uomatie 1, Myyrmäki Vantaa), an evocative example of Finnish contemporary church architecture. It has brilliant white walls, columns of tall windows, and vivid tapestries that mark events in the Lutheran calendar.

Other Vantaa attractions are the **Viherpaja, Japanese, and Cactus Gardens.** ✉ *Meiramitie 1,* ☎ *09/822–628.* ☜ *Japanese Garden FM 5; other gardens free.* ☉ *June–Aug., weekdays 8–6, weekends 9–2; Sept.–May, weekdays 8–7, weekends 9–5.*

The **Suomen Ilmailumuseo** (Finnish Aviation Museum) has 50 military and civilian aircraft on display. ✉ *Tietotie 3,* ☎ *09/821–870.* ☜ *FM 20.* ☉ *Daily noon–6.*

Contact the **Vantaa Tourist Office** (✉ Unikkotie 2, Tikkurila, 01300 Vantaa, ☎ 09/83–3134) for more information.

SOUTH COAST AND ÅLANDS

Those with a weakness for islands will be thrilled to see their magical world stretching along Finland's coastline. There, in the Gulf of Finland and the Baltic, more than 30,000 islands form a magnificent archipelago. The rugged and fascinating Åland Islands group lies westward from Turku, forming an autonomous province of its own. Turku, the former capital, was the main gateway through which cultural influences reached Finland over the centuries.

A trip to Turku via Hanko and Tammisaari will give you a taste of Finland at its most historic and scenic. Many of Finland's oldest towns lie in this southwest region of the country, having been chartered by Swedish kings—hence the predominance of the Swedish language here.

The southwest is a region of flat, often mist-soaked rural farmlands. The larger villages are highly scenic with their traditional wooden houses, but except in the summer, when the cultural life of the region briefly comes alive, the southwest is pastoral and quiet.

It's easy to explore this region by rail, bus, or car, then to hop on a ferry bound for the Ålands, halfway between Finland and Sweden. Drive along the southern coast on your way to Turku, the regional capital, stopping at the charming coastal towns along the way. Or take a train from Helsinki to Turku, catching buses from Turku to other parts of the region.

Snappertuna

㉘ *124 km (77 mi) southeast of Turku; 75 km (47 mi) southwest of Helsinki.*

Snappertuna is a small farming town with a proud hilltop church, a charming homestead museum, and the handsome restored ruin of **Raaseporin Linna** (Raseborg Castle), set in a small dale. The castle is believed to date from the 12th century. One 16th-century siege left the castle damaged, but restorations have given it a new face. In summer, concerts, dramas, and old-time market fairs are staged here. ☎ *019/234–015.* ✆ *FM 5.* ☉ *May 1–Aug. 31, daily 10–8. Guided tours arranged by Tammisaari tourist office May 15–Aug. 15.*

En Route   En route to Tammisaari, you'll want to take the kids to the amusement park in Karjaa, where **Lystiland** (Amusement Land) includes a miniature train tour on an enchanted forest path. ✉ *Vanha Turuntie,* ☎ *019/236 450.* ✆ *FM 30.* ☉ *June–Aug. 15, daily noon–7.*

Tammisaari

㉙ *16 km (10 mi) south of Snappertuna; 109 km (68 mi) southwest of Turku.*

Tammisaari (Ekenäs) has a colorful Old Quarter, 18th- and 19th-century buildings, and a lively marina. The scenery is dazzling in summer, when the sun glints off the water and marine traffic is at its peak. The **Tammisaaren Museo** (Tammisaari Museum) is the provincial museum of western Uusimaa and provides a taste of the region's culture and history. ✉ *Kustaa Vaasan katu 13,* ☎ *019/263–3161.* ✆ *FM 10.* ☉ *May 20–July, Tues.–Sun. 11–4; Aug.–May 19, Tues.–Thurs. 6 PM–8PM.*

Dining and Lodging

$$ ✕▥ **Ekenäs Stadshotell and Restaurant.** This modern, airy hotel is set amid fine lawns and gardens. The rooms, each with its own balcony, have wide picture windows and comfortable modern furnishings, all in pale and neutral colors. The location, near the sea and the old town, is right in the heart of Tammisaari. The restaurant offers Continental food and Swedish-Finnish seafood specialties prepared by a veteran chef. ✉ *Pohjoinen Rantakatu 1, 10600 Tammisaari,* ☎ *019/241–3131,* FAX *019/246–1550. 16 rooms, 2 suites. Restaurant, 3 bars, pub, room service, indoor pool, dance club. AE, DC, MC, V.*

The South Coast and Ålands

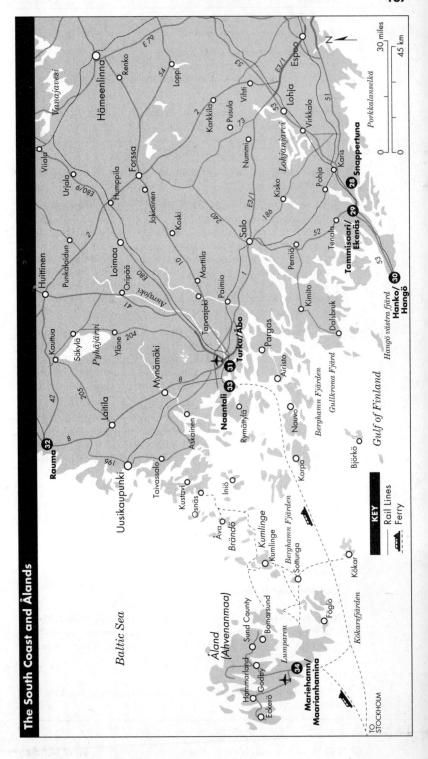

Nightlife and the Arts
The **Scandinavian Guitar Festival** comes to Tammisaari in August.

Outdoor Activities and Sports
BOATING

A variety of boats can be rented from the local tourist office.

TENNIS

There are public tennis courts on Tammisaari. Contact the local tourist office for details.

Hanko

㉚ *37 km (23 mi) southwest of Tammisaari; 141 km (88 mi) southeast of Turku.*

In the coastal town of Hanko (Hangö), you'll find long stretches of sandy beach—about 30 kilometers, or 21 miles' worth in total—some sandy and some with sea-smoothed boulders, and some of the largest and most fanciful private homes in Finland, their porches edged with gingerbread iron- and woodwork, with crazy towers sprouting from their roofs. Favorite pastimes here are beachside strolls, bike rides along well-kept paths, and, best of all, long walks along the main avenue past the great wooden houses with their wraparound porches. Hanko is also a popular sailing center, with Finland's largest guest harbor.

In addition to creature comforts, this customs port has a rich history. Fortified in the 18th century, the Hanko defenses were destroyed by the Russians in 1854, during the Crimean War. Later it became a popular spa town for Russians, then the port from which more than 300,000 Finns emigrated to North America between 1880 and 1930.

☾ Through the telescope of **Vesitorni** (Hanko's Watch Tower), you can follow the comings and goings of the town's marine traffic and get a grand view of some of the very small islands sprinkled around the peninsula's edges. ⊠ *Vartiovuori*, ☎ *019/280–3411.* ⌨ *FM 5.* ☾ *May 15– June 11, daily 11–3; June 12–Aug. 12, daily 11–7; Aug. 13–Aug. 27, daily 11–3.*

Lodging
$ ⚐ **Camping Silversand.** There are various facilities at this large campground near the water, including eight-person cabins and full hookups for trailers, as well as trailers and tents for rent. ⊠ *Hopeahietikko, 10960 Hanko,* ☎ *019/248–5500 (off-season, 09/716–422),* ☒ *019/713–713. Cafeteria, store, cooking facilities, sauna, showers, bathrooms.* ☾ *May 2–Aug. 13.*

Outdoor Activities and Sports
BOATING

A variety of boats can be rented at the guest harbor Info-Point in Hanko, or through the local tourist office. The annual **Hanko Regatta** takes place on a weekend at the end of June or beginning of July and is popular among young people and families.

TENNIS

For information about Hanko's public tennis courts, contact the local tourist office.

Turku

㉛ *140 km (87 mi) northwest of Hanko, 166 km (102 mi) west of Helsinki.*

Founded at the beginning of the 13th century, Turku is the nation's oldest city and was the original capital of newborn Finland; its early importance in the history of Finland has earned Turku the title of "the cradle of Finnish culture." Turku has a long history as a commercial and intellectual center (the city's name means "trading post"); once the site of the first Finnish university, it has two major universities, the Finnish University of Turku and the Swedish-speaking Åo Akademi. With a population of more than 160,000, Turku is now the fifth-largest city in Finland and has commercial significance in its year-round harbor.

The 700-year-old **Turun Tuomiokirkko** (Turku Cathedral) remains the seat of the archbishop of Finland. Although it was partially gutted by fire in 1827, the cathedral has been completely restored. In the choir are R. W. Ekman's frescoes portraying Bishop Henry (an Englishman) baptizing the then-heathen Finns and Mikael Agricola offering the Finnish translation of the New Testament to Gustav Vasa of Sweden. The cathedral also houses a museum, which includes a collection of medieval church vestments, silver chalices, and wooden sculptures. ⊠ *Turun Tuomiokirkko,* ☎ *02/251–0651.* ☜ *Free.* ☉ *Apr. 16–Sept. 15, daily 9–8, rest of yr, daily 9–7.*

Where the Aura flows into the sea stands **Turun Linna** (Turku Castle), one of the city's most important historical monuments. The oldest part of the fortress was built at the end of the 13th century, and the newer part dates from the 16th century. The castle was damaged by bombing in 1941, and its restoration was completed in 1961. Many of its seemingly infinite rooms hold rather incongruous exhibits: Next to a display on medieval life (featuring a dead rat to illustrate the Black Death) is a roomful of 1920s flapper costumes. The vaulted chambers themselves give you a sense of the domestic lives of the Swedish royals. There is a good gift shop and a pleasant café on the castle grounds. ⊠ *Linnankatu 80,* ☎ *02/262–0300.* ☜ *FM 20.* ☉ *Apr. 16–Sept. 15, daily 10–6; rest of yr, Mon. 2–7, Tues.–Sun. 10–3.*

The **Turun Taidemuseo** (Turku Art Museum) holds some of Finland's most famous paintings, including Akseli Gallen-Kallela's oft-reproduced "Defense of the Sampo" (1896). In addition to works by Gallen-Kallela, there's a broad selection of turn-of-the-century Finnish art and modern multimedia works. ⊠ *Aurakatu 26, Puolanpuisto,* ☎ *02/233–0954.* ☜ *About FM 30 (admission depends on current exhibits).* ☉ *Apr. 1–Sept. 30, Tues., Fri., and Sat. 10–4, Wed. and Thurs. 10–7, Sun. 11–6; rest of yr, Tues.–Sat. 10–4, Sun. 11–6.*

NEED A BREAK?
The **Hamburg Börs Hotel** (⊠ Kauppiaskatu 6, ☎ 02/637–381) has a pleasant German-style tavern for drinks or meals; it's next to the market square.

Dining and Lodging

$$$ ✕ **Calamare.** In the heart of the city at the Hotel Marina Palace, this restaurant has maintained a high standard for its fish and meat dishes; try the Delicacy Plate, a tasty dish with Baltic herring, roe in mustard sauce, shrimp, fillet of beef, egg, and marinated mushrooms. Calamare has impressive views of the Auajoki River and a Mediterranean atmosphere with Roman-style statues and palm trees. ⊠ *Linnankatu 32,* ☎ *02/336–2126. AE, DC, MC, V.*

$$$ ✕ **Julia.** French country fare is the specialty in this informal and cozy restaurant where you can enjoy a tasty meal by the warmth of a fireplace. ⊠ *Eerikinkatu 4,* ☎ *02/336–3251. AE, DC, MC, V. Closed Sun.*

$$ ✕ **Suomalainen Pohja.** Next to the attractive Turku Art Museum and a stone's throw from the market square, this restaurant has large windows that offer a splendid view of an adjacent park. Seafood, poultry, and game dishes have earned a good reputation here; try the fillet of reindeer with sautéed potatoes or the cold smoked rainbow trout with asparagus. ⊠ *Aurakatu 24,* ☎ *02/251–2000. AE, DC, MC, V. Closed weekends.*

$$$$ 🏨 **Park Hotel.** Built in 1904 in the art nouveau style for a British executive who ran the local shipyard, the castlelike Park Hotel is one of Finland's most unusual lodgings. Its rooms have high ceilings and are decorated with antique furniture. Just two blocks from the main market square, it's in the heart of Turku. ⊠ *Rauhankatu 1, 20100 Turku,* ☎ *02/251–9666,* FAX *02/251–9696. 21 rooms. Restaurant, minibars, sauna. AE, DC, MC, V.*

Nightlife and the Arts

Turku seems a staid town at first glance, but there is a lively artistic community here. It is most active during the August Music Festival (☞ Festivals and Seasonal Events *in* Chapter 1) and the Ruisrock Festival in July.

Outdoor Activities and Sports

For details on Turku's public tennis courts, contact the local tourist office.

Rauma

32 *92 km (50 mi) northwest of Turku.*

The third-oldest city in Finland, Rauma is widely known for its tradition of lace making and its annual Lace Week, held every year at the end of July. In addition, the city is known for the beauty of its old wooden houses, painted in its original distinctive 18th- and 19th-century colors. The colors are so extraordinary, in fact, that no house can be repainted until the Old Rauma Association approves the color. UNESCO has designated Rauma's Gamla (Old Town) a World Heritage Site. You can take a bus to Rauma from Turku in 1½ hours. For information and bus schedules, contact the Rauma City Tourist Office (☞ Visitor Information, *below*).

Naantali

33 *17 km (10½ mi) west of Turku.*

Built around a convent of the Order of Saint Birgitta in the 15th century, the coastal village of Naantali is an aging medieval town, a former pilgrimage destination, an artists' colony, and a modern resort all rolled into one. Many of its buildings date from the 17th century, following a massive rebuilding after the Great Fire of 1628. There are also a number of 18th- and 19th-century buildings, which form the basis of the Old Town—a settlement by the water's edge. These shingled wooden buildings were originally built as private residences, and many remain so, although a few now house small galleries.

Naantali's extremely narrow cobblestone lanes gave rise to a very odd law. During periods when economic conditions were poor, Naantalians earned their keep by knitting socks and exporting them by the tens of thousands. Men, women, and children all knitted so feverishly that the town council forbade groups of more than six from meeting in narrow lanes with their knitting—and causing road obstructions.

A major attraction in the village is **Kultaranta,** the summer residence for Finland's presidents, with its more than 3,500 rosebushes. Guided tours can be arranged through the Naantali tourist board year-round.

⊠ *Luonnonmaasaari. Call the Naantali tourist board to check opening times, which vary greatly.*

The convent **Naantalin Luostarikirkko** (Naantali's Vallis Gratiae) was founded in 1443 and completed in 1462. The convent, which housed both monks and nuns, operated under the aegis of the Catholic church until it was dissolved by the Reformation in the 16th century. The buildings fell into disrepair and were restored from 1963 to 1965. The church is all that remains of the convent. ⊠ *Nunnakatu, Naantali,* ☎ *02/850–109.* 🎫 *Free for nonguided visits.* ☉ *Daily May–Aug.; Sun. afternoons Sept.–Apr. Group tours available; call the Naantali tourist office for opening hours and details).*

NEED A
BREAK? Near Naantali's marina, a footbridge leads to **Kailo Island,** a popular summer activity center with a theater, beach, sports and picnic facilities, and a snack bar.

☺ On Kailo Island in Naantali, **Moomin World** theme park brings to life all the famous characters of this famous Scandinavian fairy tale written by a Finnish woman, Tore Jansson. The tale emphasizes family, respect for the environment, and new adventures. ⊠ *Kailo Island, PL 48, 21101 Naantali,* ☎ *02/435–6111.* 🎫 *FM 75 (includes boat trip to Viski Island).* ☉ *June 15–Aug. 15, daily 10–8.*

Dining and Lodging

$$ ✕ **Tavastin Kilta.** This summer restaurant has a view of the boat harbor. Broiled steaks and fish, plus some vegetarian dishes, are served in an Old World bishop's dining room, a nautical bar, or a tapas bar decorated in 19th-century style—choose your fancy. Lemon pastries are a dessert specialty. ⊠ *Mannerheiminkatu 1,* ☎ *02/435–1066. AE, DC, MC, V.*

$$–$$$$ 🏨 **Naantali Kylpylä Spa.** The emphasis here is on pampering, with foot massages, shiatsu physical therapy, mud packs, and spa-water and algae baths. Activities include gymnastics and a special seven-day fasting program offered twice a year under medical supervision. All kinds of health packages can be arranged, including health-rehabilitation programs. It is set on a peninsula in a grandiose building that replaced the original spa on the site. ⊠ *Matkailijantie 2, 21100,* ☎ *02/44550,* 📠 *02/445–5621. 229 rooms. Pools, beauty salon, massage, Turkish bath. AE, DC, MC, V.*

Nightlife and the Arts

The **Naantali Music Festival** offers chamber music at the beginning of June (☞ Festivals and Seasonal Events *in* Chapter 1).

Outdoor Activities and Sports

Naantali has several bathing areas. Contact the local tourist board.

Shopping

In Naantali you'll find the workshop of a famous Finnish contemporary jewelry designer, **Karl Laine** (⊠ Mannerheiminkatu 10B, ☎ 02/751–648). His use of brass and gold and his combinations of starkly geometric and richly clustered metals, sometimes studded with tiny precious stones, are singular in their creativeness.

Mariehamn and the Åland Islands

❸❹ *155 km (93 mi) west of Turku.*

The Ålands, a collection of small rocky islands, are inhabited in large part by families that fish or run small farms. Their connection with the sea is inevitable, and their tradition of being at sea is revered. Some of the greatest grain ships sailing the seas were built by the Gustav Eriksson family in Mariehamn.

In all, the Ålands are composed of more than 6,500 islands and skerries; virtually all the inhabitants are Swedish-speaking and very proud of their largely autonomous status. Nearly half the population lives in the tiny capital of Mariehamn (Maarianhamina), the hub of Åland life and the main port, on the main island of Åland.

The **Museifartyget Pommern** (**Pommern** Museum Ship), situated in Mariehamn West Harbor at the center of town, is one of the last existing grain ships in the world. Once owned by the sailing fleet of the Mariehamn shipping magnate Gustaf Erikson, the ship carried wheat between Australia and England from 1923 to 1939. ☎ 018/531–421. ✉ FM 15. ⊙ May–Aug., daily 9–5; July, daily 9–7; Sept.–Oct., daily 10–4.

NEED A
BREAK?

Stop for a snack and a seaside view at the ÅSS **Segelpaviljongen** marina restaurant (✉ Strandpromenaden, ☎ 018/19141), just down the quay from the Museifartyget *Pommern*.

In prehistoric times the islands were, relatively speaking, heavily populated, as is shown by traces of no fewer than 10,000 ancient settlements, graves, and strongholds. A visit to **Sund County** will take you back to the earliest days of life on the islands, with its remains from prehistoric times and the Middle Ages. **Kastelholm** is a medieval castle built by the Swedes to strengthen their presence on Åland. ✉ Kastelholm, ☎ 018/43812. ✉ FM 20. ⊙ Guided tours May–June, daily 10–5, July 9:30–8, Aug.–Sept. 10–5.

Jan Karlsgården Friluftsmuseum (Jan Karl Garden Outdoor Museum) is a very popular open-air museum, with buildings and sheds from the 18th century that portray farming life on the island 200 years ago. ✉ Kastelholm, ☎ 018/43812. ✉ FM 10. ⊙ May–June and Aug.–Sept., daily 9:30–5; July, daily 9:30–8.

About 8 kilometers (5 miles) from the village of Kastelholm in Sund are the scattered ruins of **Bomarsund Fort,** a huge naval fortress built by the Russians in the early 19th century and only half finished when it was destroyed by Anglo-French forces during the Crimean War.

Spend a few days in the outdoors, staying in **Hammarland,** located north of Mariehamn, near Eckerö. This makes a perfect getaway in the Ålands, with snug, wooden cabins in the timeless style of Finnish summer cottages, including the genuine wood-fired Finnish sauna.

Dining and Lodging

$$ 🏠 **Björklidens Stugby.** The cabins are small, but the draw here is really the outdoors. Enjoy the free rowboats, grassy lawns, and trees with swings. It is 25 kilometers (17 miles) from Mariehamn. ✉ 22240 Hammarland, ☎ 018/37800, FAX 018/37801. 15 cabins. Beach, TV room, outdoor grill, fishing, playground, washing machines. No credit cards. Closed late Nov.–Mar.

$$–$$$ ✕🏠 **Arkipelag.** In the heart of Mariehamn, the bayside Arkipelag Hotel is known for its fine marina and lively disco-bar. The rooms are modern and comfortable, with huge picture windows, and the restaurants, set in long, wood-paneled rooms with wide windows overlooking an ocean inlet, serve fresh Åland seafood. Try the crayfish when it's in season. In the terrace restaurant, the fresh shrimp sandwiches with dill mayonnaise are a treat. ✉ Strandgatan 31, 22100 Mariehamn, ☎ 018/24020,

FAX *018/24384. 78 rooms, 8 suites. 2 restaurants, bar, indoor-outdoor pool, sauna, casino, nightclub, meeting rooms. DC, MC, V.*

Outdoor Activities and Sports

BICYCLING

Most towns have bikes for rent from about FM 35 per day (FM 150 per week). The fine scenery and the terrain, alternately dead flat and gently rolling, make for ideal cycling. The roads are not busy once you leave the highway. **The Suomen Retkeilymajajärjestö** (Finnish Youth Hostel Association) (✉ Yrjönkatu 38B, 00100 Helsinki, ☎ 09/694–0377) has bicycle trips varying in length from four days to two weeks (with overnight stops at hostels if you wish). For Åland bicycle routes and tour packages, contact **Ålandsresor Ab** (✉ PB 62, 22101 Mariehamn, ☎ 018/28040) or **Viking Line** (✉ Storagatan 2, 22100 Mariehamn, ☎ 018/26011).

BOATING

A variety of boats can be rented through the local tourist office. These are marvelous sailing waters for experienced mariners.

FISHING

Many fishing packages are available in the Ålands. Try **Ålandsresor** (✉ Torggatan 2, 22100 Mariehamn, ☎ 018/28040). **Viking Line** (✉ Storagatan 2, 22100 Mariehamn, ☎ 018/26011) also offers packages for anglers.

TENNIS

Mariehamn and Hammarland have public tennis courts. Contact the local tourist office for details.

South Coast and Ålands A to Z

Arriving and Departing

BY BUS

There is good bus service connecting the capital to the southwest from Helsinki's long-distance bus station, just west of the train station off Mannerheimintie. Contact **Matkahuolto** (✉ Simonkatu 3, 00200 Helsinki, ☎ 09/682–701) for information.

BY CAR

The Helsinki–Turku trip is 165 kilometers (100 miles) on Route E3; signs on E3 will tell you where to turn off for the south-coast towns of Tammisaari and Hanko. Most of southwestern Finland is well served by public transport, so a car is not necessary.

BY FERRY

Åland is most cheaply reached by boat from Turku and Naantali. Call **Silja Line** in Turku (☎ 02/652–6244), Mariehamn (☎ 018/16711), Tampere (☎ 03/216–2000), or Helsinki (☎ 09/180–4422); or call **Viking Line** in Turku (☎ 02/63311), Mariehamn (☎ 018/26011), Tampere (☎ 03/249–0111), or Helsinki (☎ 09/12351). Tickets can also be purchased at the harbor.

BY PLANE

The region's airports are at Mariehamn and Turku. Both have connections to Helsinki and Stockholm, with service by Finnair and its charter company KarAir.

BY TRAIN

Trains leave Helsinki for Turku several times a day; however, for most smaller towns, you must stop at stations along the Helsinki–Turku route and change to a local bus. Bus fares are usually a bit cheaper than train fares.

Contacts and Resources

EMERGENCIES

The nationwide emergency number is **112;** it can be used to call police and ambulance services. A major medical center in the region is the **Turun Yliopistollinen Keskusairaala** (University of Turku Central Hospital) (⊠ Kiinamyllynkatu 4–8, Turku, ☎ 02/261–1611). For dentists, call the **Turun Hammaslääkärikeskus** (Turku Dental Center) (⊠ Hämeenkatu 2, Turku, ☎ 02/233–3778).

GUIDED TOURS

Ageba Special Travel Service (⊠ Pohjoisranta 4, Helsinki, ☎ 09/661–123) arranges a variety of tours in the region.

The 100-kilometer (65-mile) Seven Churches tour from Turku, taking in the area's major medieval churches and a country manor house, lasts about seven hours and is arranged (for groups of 25 or more only) through **Varsinais-Suomen Matkailuyhdistys** (⊠ Läntinen Rantakatu 13, 20100 Turku, ☎ 02/251–7333).

The Tammisaari tourist office offers a variety of boat **Archipelago Tours** that last from 1½ to 7 hours. The tours, which take place on a restaurant boat and visit the national park, cost from about FM 70 to FM 100 per person depending on the length of the cruise. Take a 3-hour steamship cruise between Turku and Naantali, enjoying a smørgåsbord lunch or gourmet dinner while drifting around the archipelago (FM 65–FM95); contact the Naantali tourist office or the **Steamship Company s/s Ukkopekka** (⊠ Linnankatu 38, 20100 Turku, ☎ 02/233–0123).

VISITOR INFORMATION

Main tourist offices: **Åland** (⊠ Storagatan 11, 22100 Mariehamn, ☎ 018/27310). **Hanko** (⊠ Bulevardi 10, 10900, ☎ 019/280–3411). **Naantali** (⊠ Kaivotori 2, 21100, ☎ 02/435–0850). **Tammisaari** (Ekenäs) (⊠ Raatihuoneentori, 10600, ☎ 019/263–2100). **Turku** (⊠ Aurakatu 4, 20100, ☎ 02/233–6366).

LAPLAND

Lapland is often called Europe's last wilderness, a region of endless forests, fells, and great silences. Settlers in Finnish Lapland walked gently and left the landscape almost unspoiled. Now easily accessible by plane, train, or bus, this Arctic outpost offers comfortable hotels and modern amenities, yet you won't have to go very far to find yourself in an almost primordial setting.

The oldest traces of human habitation in Finland have been found in Lapland, and hordes of Danish, English, and even Arabian coins indicate the existence of trade activities many centuries ago. Only about 4,500 Sami (natives of Lapland) still live here; the remainder of the province's population of 200,000 is Finnish. Until the 1930s, Lapland was still largely unexploited, and any trip to the region was an expedition. Lapland's isolation ended when the Canadian-owned Petsamo Nickel Company completed the great road that connects Rovaniemi with the Arctic Sea, now known as the Arctic Highway. Building activities increased along this route, the land was turned and sown, and a few hotels were built to cater to an increasing number of visitors.

The Sami population makes up a small minority in the northern regions of Finland, Norway, Sweden, and Russia. Though modern influences have changed many aspects of their traditional way of life, the inquisitive and respectful visitor will discover a thriving Sami culture. Sami handicrafts make use of natural resources, reflected in skilled woodwork, bonework, and items made of reindeer pelts. The Lady Day church festival in Enontekiö in March is a particularly colorful event, attended by many Sami in their most brilliant dress and usually featuring reindeer racing or lassoing competitions.

Summer in Lapland has the blessing of round-the-clock daylight, and beautiful weather typically accompanies the nightless days. In early fall the colors are so fabulous that the Finns have a special word for it: *ruskaa*. If you can take the intense but dry cold, winter in Lapland is full of fascinating experiences, from the Northern Lights to reindeer roundups. Depending on how far north of the Arctic Circle you travel, the sun might not rise for several weeks around midwinter. But it is never pitch-black; light reflects from the invisible sun below the horizon even during midday, and there is luminosity from the ever-present snow.

But Finns cherish the outdoors no matter what the light. Here it is the wilderness that's the draw. For although the cities have fine facilities and cultural events, it is the lonely fells with the occasional profile of a reindeer herd crossing, the gin-clear forest streams, and the bright trail of the midnight sun reflected on a lake's blackest waters that leave the most indelible impressions.

Be sure while you're here to sample such local foods as cloudberries, lingonberries, fresh salmon, and reindeer (served smoked and sautéed, in meatballs and steaks). Restaurants serve hearty soups, crusty rye bread, delicious baked Lappish cheese, and dark brewed coffee in wooden cups with meals—you won't leave hungry.

Handicrafts

You'll find unique souvenirs in Lapland, and you may learn to love the traditional Lapp handicrafts, which are both functional and attractive. Keep an eye out for the camping knives with beautifully carved bone or wooden handles, colorful weaving and embroidered mittens and gloves, felt shoes, and birch-bark baskets and rucksacks.

Outdoor Activities and Sports

Winter sports reign here, from the quirky ice golfing to the traditional cross-country skiing. Vuokatti, Ylläs, Saariselkä, and Kiilopää are Lapland's leading downhill and cross-country ski centers. Try the Levi resort in western Lapland (⊠ Levin Matkailu, 99100 Kittilä, ☎ 016/643–466), Pyhätunturi in southern Lapland (⊠ Hotelli Pyhätunturi, 98530 Pyhätunturi, ☎ 016/812 081), Saariselkä in eastern Lapland (⊠ Pohjois-Lapin Matkaialu, 99800 Ivalo, 016/662–521), and Ruka (⊠ Rukakeskus, 93620 Rukatunturi, ☎ 08/868–1231), on the eastern border, just below Lapland.

In summer, canoeing opportunities are unlimited, ranging from canoe trips on Lake Inari to forays over the rapids of the Ivalojoki River. Summer golf takes on such unusual guises as midnight-sun golf and Green Zone Tornio-Haparanda Golf—you'll play nine holes in Finland and the other nine in Sweden (Meri-Lapin Golfklubi, ☎ 016/431–8711).

Rovaniemi

㉟ *832 km (516 mi) north of Helsinki.*

The best place to start your tour of Lapland is Rovaniemi, where the Ounas and Kemi rivers meet almost on the Arctic Circle. Often called the Gateway to Lapland, Rovaniemi is in fact the administrative hub and communications center of the province.

If you're expecting an Arctic shantytown, you're in for a surprise. After Rovaniemi was all but razed by the retreating German army in 1944, Alvar Aalto directed the rebuilding and devised an unusual street layout: From the air, the layout mimics the shape of reindeer antlers! During rebuilding, the population rose from 8,000 to more than 34,000—so be prepared for a contemporary city, university town, and cultural center on the edge of the wilderness.

One of the town's architectural wonders is **Lappia-Talo** (Lappia House), the Aalto-designed concert and congress center that houses the world's most northernmost professional theater. ⊠ *Hallituskatu 11,* ☎ *016/322–2944.*

One of the best ways to tune in to the culture of Finland's far north is to visit the **Arktikum** (Arctic Research Center). The Arktikum houses the Museum of the Province of Lapland, whose riveting exhibit on Sami life tells the full story of their survival. ⊠ *Pohjoisranta 4,* ☎ *016/317–840.* ☎ *FM 45.* ☉ *May–Aug., daily 10–6; Sept.–Apr., Tues.–Sun. 10–6.*

Rovaniemi's real claim to fame is that Santa Claus lives in its suburbs at **Joulupukin Pajakylä** (Santa Claus Village). Lapps in native dress and reindeer hauling sleighs enhance its feeling of authenticity. (This is likely to be the only place where your children will be able to pet a reindeer—the ones you'll see in the wild are shy.) Here gifts can be bought in midsummer for shipping at any time of year, and postcards can be mailed from the special Arctic Circle post office. There's also a complete souvenir shopping complex, plus the impressive sight of the mountains of mail that pour in from children all over the world. Yes, he answers every letter! ⊠ *Santa Claus Village, 96930 Arctic Circle,* ☎ FAX *016/356–2096; Santa's Post Office,* ☎ *016/356–2157.* ☎ *Free.* ☉ *June–Aug., daily 8–8; Sept.–Nov., daily 10–5; Dec., daily 9–7; Jan.–May, daily 10–5. Closed when Santa is abroad on Dec. 25.*

NEED A
BREAK?

Along the 3-kilometer (2-mile) hike to Ounasvaara Hill for midnight-sun viewing from on high, stop at the **Sky Hotel Ounasvaara** (⊠ 96400 Rovaniemi, ☎ 016/335–3311) for coffee and pastries at the café.

Dining and Lodging

$$ ✕ **Fransmanni.** This restaurant, with a nice view of the Kemijoki River, specializes in different types of international, Finnish, and Lapp casserole dishes. Try the pepper beef casserole with its tasty cream sauce. Service is friendly. ⊠ *Vaakuna Hotel, Koskikatu 4,* ☎ *016/332–211. AE, DC, MC, V.*

$$ ✕ **Ounasvaaran Pirtit.** This is one of Rovaniemi's best restaurants, specializing in traditional Finnish and Lapp food. Try the sautéed salmon with cream and boiled potatoes or sautéed reindeer with mashed potatoes. If possible, call ahead to order. ⊠ *Antinmukka 4,* ☎ *016/369–056. Reservations required. AE, DC, MC, V.*

$$$ ✕🏠 **Hotelli Lapponia.** Opened in 1992, this modern hotel is in the heart of Rovaniemi. Light blue, gray, and brown color schemes decorate the rooms, some of which have individual saunas or hot tubs. ⊠ *Koskikatu 23, 96200,* ☎ *016/33661,* FAX *016/313–770. 167 rooms, 9 with sauna, 8 with hot tub. 5 restaurants, bar, pub, no-smoking rooms, nightclub. AE, DC, MC, V.*

$$–$$$ ✕🏠 **Hotel Pohjanhovi.** Stretched along the shore of the Kemijoki River, this hotel combines modern amenities with quick access to the fells. The rooms are large, with low ceilings and big windows. The decor varies from white-walled rooms with autumn-toned upholstery and wood trim to black walls with light upholstery—for those who have trouble sleeping during the days of the midnight sun. ⊠ *Pohjanpuistikko 2, 96200,* ☎ *016/33711,* FAX *016/313–997. 216 rooms, 4 suites. Restau-*

Lapland

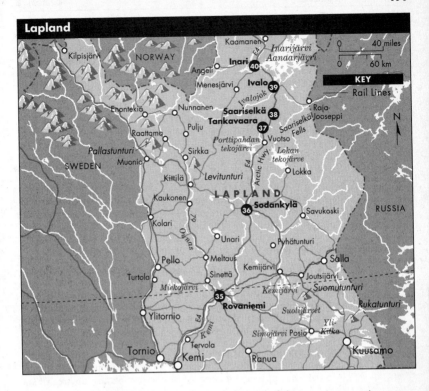

rant, bar, café, saunas, squash, boating, fishing, casino, meeting rooms. AE, DC, MC, V.

$$ ✕▥ **Hotel Rudolf.** Set in the center of Rovaniemi, the Rudolf has bright, homey rooms with parquet floors and soft, subtle lighting; the furniture is modern. Don't expect anything extraordinary from the restaurant, which normally caters to groups. The short menu lists such basics as onion steak with fried potatoes, and reindeer pepper steak with creamed potatoes. ⊠ *Koskikatu 41, 96100,* ☎ *016/342–3222,* 🆉 *106/342–3226. 41 rooms. Restaurant, indoor pool, saunas, meeting room. AE, DC, MC, V.*

$$ ✕▥ **Sky Hotel Ounasvaara.** On a hilltop 3 kilometers (2 miles) from the center of town, Sky Hotel is the top choice in Rovaniemi for views, hiking, and skiing, both slalom and cross-country—especially for those with a car. First-floor rooms were renovated in 1992. Some rooms have bathtubs—a rarity—and many have saunas. Especially large rooms with kitchenettes are available for families. The restaurant, Panorama, has large windows that provide pleasant views; sample dishes à la carte, such as barbecued whitefish, reindeer casserole, fried snow grouse, and desserts such as Lapland cheese with Arctic cloudberries, and lingonberry parfait. ⊠ *96400 Rovaniemi,* ☎ *016/335–3311,* 🆉 *016/318–789. 69 rooms, 47 with saunas. Restaurant, saunas, hiking, cross-country skiing, downhill skiing. AE, DC, MC, V.*

$$ ✕▥ **Sokos HotelVaakuna.** Opened in January 1992, the Vaakuna is a recent addition to the hotel scene in Rovaniemi. The lobby has comfortable armchairs and marble floors; rooms are small and painted in pastel shades. There are two restaurants: Fransmanni (☞ *above*) and Rosso, which serves Italian pastas and pizzas. ⊠ *Koskikatu 4, 96200 Rovaniemi,* ☎ *016/332–211,* 🆉 *016/332–2199. 159 rooms with shower. 2 restaurants, pub, saunas, exercise room, nightclub. AE, DC, MC, V.*

$–$$ ✕🏨 **Hotelli Oppipoika.** Attached to one of Finland's premier hotelier and restaurateur schools, this is a hotel where good service and fine cuisine are guaranteed. The modern rooms have pressed birch paneling and are well lighted. ⊠ *Korkalonkatu 33, 96200 Rovaniemi,* ☎ *016/338–8111,* 🖷 *016/346–969. 40 rooms. Restaurant, no-smoking rooms, indoor pool, saunas, exercise room, meeting room. AE, DC, MC, V.*

Outdoor Activities and Sports

Karttakeskus (⊠ Hallituskatu 1–3C, 96100 Rovaniemi, ☎ 016/329–4111) provides maps of marked trails in Lapland.

OFF THE
BEATEN PATH

SALLA REINDEER FARM – In the winter, visitors can obtain a reindeer driver's license (FM 30 adults, FM 20 children) and feed the animals at the Salla Reindeer Farm, 150 kilometers (93 miles) east of Rovaniemi. ⊠ *PL 7, 98901 Salla,* ☎ *016/37771.*

Sodankylä and the Fells

36 *130 km (81 mi) north of Rovaniemi (via Rte. 4 or 5).*

The Sodankylä region is one of the oldest Sami settlements, and today it is one of the most densely populated areas of Finnish Lapland. In the town of Sodankylä there is a Northern Lights Observatory (for professionals only) and an ancient wooden church.

Lapland is dominated by great moor-like expanses called fells. The modern tourist center of Luosto, 25 kilometers (16 miles) south of Sodankylä, is in the heart of the fell district of southern Lapland—an area of superb hiking, mountain cycling, orienteering, and skiing. If you don't have a car, a daily bus makes the 60-kilometer (37-mile) trip from Kemijärvi to Luosto. Kemijarvi is 87 kilometers (54 miles) north of Rovaniemi and can be reached via local train.

Lodging

$$ 🏨 **Arctia Hotel Luosto.** Situated amid the fells southeast of Sodankylä, this small-scale hotel is modern and comfortable. It is built in a unique *kelo* (dead wood) timber style. Each cabin has a fireplace, sauna, and kitchenette. ⊠ *Luostotunturi, 99550 Aska,* ☎ *016/624–400,* 🖷 *016/624–410. 54 cabins, 5 hotel rooms. Restaurant, saunas, boating, cross-country skiing, snowmobiling. AE, DC, MC, V.*

Tankavaara

37 *105 km (65 mi) north of Sodankylä; 130 km (81 mi) north of Luosto; 225 km (140 mi) north of Rovaniemi.*

The town of Tankavaara is the most accessible and the best-developed of several gold-panning areas. The **Kultamuseo** (Gold Museum) tells the century-old story of Lapland's hardy fortune seekers. Real prospectors will show you how to pan gold dust and tiny nuggets from the silt of an icy stream. ⊠ *Kultakylä, 99695 Tankavaara,* ☎ *016/626–158.* 🎫 *Summer, FM 55; winter, FM 25.* ☼ *June–Aug. 15, daily 9–6; Aug. 16–Oct., daily 9–5; Nov.–May, daily 10–4. Summer admission includes gold washing.*

Dining and Lodging

$$ ✕ **Wanha Waskoolimies.** In the tradition of the old gold prospectors, this rustic restaurant consists of three rooms hewn from logs. Daily specials such as "Fish in the Gold Pan" and "Prospector's Beef" will give you a taste of simple but high-quality Lapland fare; the restaurant has received the Lappi à la Carte gourmet citation. ⊠ *Tankavaaran Kultakylän,* ☎ *016/626–158. DC, V.*

$ ✕⊡ **Hotel Korundi.** In a quiet setting just off the Arctic Highway, this hotel has cozy, contemporary rooms for two to five people, each with its own fireplace. You can try your luck at panning for gold here, or visit the Gold Museum, which traces the history of prospecting in Lapland. The restaurant is in a separate building. ⊠ *99695 Tankavaara,* ☎ *016/626–158,* ℻ *016/626–261. 8 rooms, 7 with fireplace. Saunas, hiking, bicycles, cross-country skiing. AE, DC, MC, V.*

Saariselkä

③⑧ *40 km (25 mi) north of Tankavaara; 135 km (84 mi) north of Sodankylä; 265 km (165 mi) north of Rovaniemi.*

You could hike and ski for days in this area without seeing another soul. Saariselkä has a variety of accommodations and makes a central base from which to set off on a trip into the true wilderness. There are marked trails through forests and over fells, where little has changed since the last Ice Age. More than 1,556 kilometers (965 miles) of this magnificent area has been named the **Uhrokekkosen Kansallispüisto** (Urho Kekkonen National Park). The park guide center is at Tankavaara.

Dining and Lodging

$–$$$$ ✕⊡ **Saariselkä Spa.** Completed in 1990, this hotel is known for its luxurious spa center. The glass-domed swimming area is crammed with foliage, fountains, water slides, wave machines, and a hot tub; the solarium, saunas, and Turkish baths are adjacent. The guest rooms' decor includes pressed blond and dark wood, slate-blue carpet, and bedspreads in muted blues, purples, and pinks. Moderately priced cabin accommodations are also available. Note that the breakfast and spa facilities are included in prices. Children 7–14 stay at half-price; children under 7 stay free. The bus stops at the hotel. ⊠ *99830 Saariselkä,* ☎ *016/668–555,* ℻ *016/668–328. 37 rooms, 36 apartment cabins. Restaurant, miniature golf (Sept.–May), tennis court, badminton, exercise room, paddle tennis, squash, volleyball, meeting rooms. AE, DC, MC, V.*

$$$ ✕⊡ **Hotelli Riekonkieppi.** The piney comfort of the rooms and the quietude of the setting make this a good Lapland base. Eight wood buildings with 12 to 16 rooms each make it especially popular with families. The restaurant has a cozy fireplace, pine furniture, and a small exhibition of Sami jewelry. Its regional and Continental menu is strong on reindeer and fish. ⊠ *Raitopolku 2, 9983 Saariselkä,* ☎ *016/668–601,* ℻ *016/668–602. 104 rooms. Restaurant, 2 pools, saunas, squash. AE, DC, MC, V. Closed May.*

$$$–$$$$ ⊡ **Riekonlinna.** Run by Reikonkieppi Hotel, Riekonlinna is the latest and best-equipped addition to the developing tourist complex on the fringes of the wilderness fells. The pinewood and blue-textile decor of this contemporary Lappish hotel, built in 1987 and renovated in 1990, goes well with its natural setting. All of the modern rooms have a balcony. It has a meeting center, a multisport complex, and it is only 30 minutes from Ivalo Airport. The restaurant serves fresh local specialties, including reindeer, salmon, and snow grouse. The hotel's location provides excellent cross-country and downhill skiing possibilities; snowmobiling and reindeer safaris are also offered. ⊠ *Lutontie, Saariselkä, 99839,* ☎ *016/668–601,* ℻ *016/668–602. 124 rooms with shower, 2 suites. Restaurant, 2 pools, massage, saunas, 2 tennis courts, squash, boating. AE, DC, MC, V.*

Outdoor Activities and Sports

Lapland's waters are exceptionally clean and good for swimming. Many hotels have pools, and **Saariselkä Spa** at Saariselkä features an indoor water world.

Ivalo

❸❾ *40 km (25 mi) north of Saariselkä; 193 km (116 mi) north of Rovaniemi.*

The village of Ivalo is the main center for northern Lapland. With its first-class hotel, airport, and many modern amenities, it offers little to the tourist in search of a wilderness experience, but the huge island-studded expanses of **Inarijärvi** (Lake Inari), north of Ivalo, offer virtually limitless boating, fishing, hiking, and hunting opportunities.

🖑 **Tunturikeskus Kiilopää** (⊠ 99800 Ivalo, ☎ 016/667–101) has a multiactivity center for children, including snow-castle building, centrifuge sledding, ski tracks, and reindeer and dogsled trips; there are summer activities, too.

A seven-hour trip up the Lemmenjoki River from Ivalo can be arranged by **Lemmenjoen Lomamajat** (⊠ Lemmenjoki, ☎ 016/57135).

Dining and Lodging

$–$$$$ ✕🖬 **Tunturikeskus Kiilopää.** This "Fell Center" is in the midst of a hikers' and cross-country skiers' paradise in the Urho Kekkonen National Park district, 45 kilometers (30 miles) south of Ivalo Airport. Accommodations are in beautifully crafted log cabins, apartments, or individual hotel rooms, all made of wood and stone; apartments have picture windows and fireplaces. The casual restaurant serves reindeer and other game entrées. ⊠ *99800 Ivalo,* ☎ *016/667–101,* FAX *016/667–121. 8 cabins, 8 apartments, 34 rooms with shower, 9 youth hostel rooms. Restaurant, no-smoking rooms, cross-country skiing, ski shop. AE, DC, MC, V.*

$$ ✕🖬 **Ivalo.** Modern and well equipped for business travelers and families, this hotel is 1 kilometer (½ mile) from Ivalo, right on the Ivalojoki River. The lobby has marble floors, and there's a brick fireplace in the lounge. The rooms are spacious and modern, with burlap woven wallpaper, oatmeal carpets, and lots of blond birchwood trimming; ask for a room by the river. The restaurant offers local and Continental fare, as well as delicious "Lappi à la Carte" meals. ⊠ *Ivalontie 34, 99800 Ivalo,* ☎ *016/688–111,* FAX *016/661–905. 94 rooms. 2 restaurants, pool, saunas, boating, recreation room, baby-sitting. AE, DC, MC, V.*

$ ✕🖬 **Kultahippu.** In the heart of Ivalo, along the Ivalojoki River, Kultahippu claims to have the northernmost nightclub in Finland. Guest rooms are cozy, with simple birchwood furnishing; larger rooms—with sauna—are available for families. The restaurant serves traditional Lapp meals à la carte. ⊠ *Petsamontie 1, 99800 Ivalo,* ☎ *016/661–825,* FAX *016/662–510. 30 rooms with bath, 7 with sauna. Restaurant, hot tub, sauna, beach. AE, DC, MC, V.*

Inari

❹⓿ *40 km (24 mi) northwest of Ivalo; 333 km (207 mi) north of Rovaniemi.*

It is a beautiful drive northwest from Ivalo, along the lakeshore, to Inari, home of the *Sámi Parlamenta* (Sami Parliament). The **Saamelaismuseo** (Sami Museum), on the village outskirts, covers all facets of Sami culture. ⊠ *Inari,* ☎ *016/671–014.* 🖷 *FM 20.* 🕘 *June–Aug. 10, daily 8–10; Aug. 11–31, daily 8–8; Sept. 1–20, weekdays 9–3:30. Call ahead for winter hrs (*☎ *016/51014).*

OFF THE
BEATEN PATH

INARIN POROFARMI – This working reindeer farm 14 kilometers (9 miles) southeast of Inari is where racing reindeer are trained. You can drive a reindeer sled or be pulled on skis by the magical beasts. ✉ *Kaksama-järvi, Inari,* ☎ *016/56512.*

Dining and Lodging

$$ ✕🏨 **Inari Kultahovi.** This cozy inn, renovated in 1987, is located on the wooded banks of the swiftly flowing Juutuajoki Rapids. The no-frills rooms (doubles only) are small, with handwoven rugs and birch-wood furniture. In summer you'll need a reservation to get a table at Kultahovi's restaurant; the specialties are salmon and reindeer, but try the tasty whitefish caught from nearby Lake Inari. ✉ *99870 Inari,* ☎ *016/671–221,* 🟫 *016/671–250. 29 rooms with shower. Restaurant, saunas. DC, MC, V. Closed Dec. 25.*

Outdoor Activities and Sports

Lapptreks (✉ 99870 Inari, ☎ 016/58567) offers a combined canoe-ing, hiking, and gold-panning trip.

Lapland A to Z

Arriving and Departing

The best base for exploring is Rovaniemi, which connects with Helsinki and the south by road, rail, and air links; there is even a car-train from Helsinki.

BY BUS

Bus service into the region revolves around Rovaniemi; from there you can switch to local buses.

BY CAR

If you are driving north, follow Arctic Highway No. 4 (national high-way) to Kuopio–Oulu–Rovaniemi, or go via the west coast to Oulu, then to Rovaniemi. From Rovaniemi, the national highway continues straight up to Lake Inari via Ivalo. The roads are generally good, but some in the extreme north may be rough.

BY PLANE

The airports serving Lapland are at Enontekiö, Ivalo, Kemi, Kittilä, Kuusamo, Oulu, Rovaniemi, and Sodankylä. Finnair serves all these airports with flights from Helsinki, though not all flights are nonstop. You can also fly to the north from most of southwestern Finland's larger cities and from the lakes region.

BY TRAIN

Train service will get you to Rovaniemi and Kemijärvi. From there you must make connections with other forms of transport.

Getting Around

BY BUS

Buses leave five times daily from Rovaniemi to Inari (five hours) and five times a day to Ivalo (four hours). You can take countryside taxis to your final destination; taxi stands are at most bus stations.

BY CAR

The Arctic Highway will take you north from Rovaniemi at the Arc-tic Circle to Inari, just below the 69th parallel. If you'd rather not rent a car, however, all but the most remote towns are accessible by bus, train, or plane.

BY PLANE

There is service every day but Sunday between Rovaniemi and Ivalo. You can also fly between Oulu or Rovaniemi to Ivalo, Enontekiö, Kemi, and Sodankylä, all on Finnair domestic services (Air Botnia). Finnair also has daily flights directly from Helsinki to Kuusamo. There are seasonal schedules.

Contacts and Resources

EMERGENCIES

The nationwide emergency number is **112;** it can be used for police and ambulance services. Lapland's leading hospital is **Lapin Keskussairaala** (Lapland Central Hospital) (✉ Ounasrinteentie 22, Rovaniemi, ☎ 016/3281). Dentists can be reached at **Hammashoitola Viisaudenhammas** (✉ Koskikatu 9 B, Rovaniemi, ☎ 016/347–620).

GUIDED TOURS

Guided tours in towns are arranged through city tourist offices. Tours to Lapland can be purchased through **Area Travel** (✉ Mikonkatu 2, 00100 Helsinki, ☎ 09/818–383).

A great variety of specialty tours cater to both general and special interests, from white-water rafting to nature-photography tours. The national tourist board's "Lappi à la Carte" booklet suggests gourmet trails through the north. From Rovaniemi, the tourist board has a 2½-hour evening Arctic Circle tour.

Finnair arranges many tours from Helsinki, including ski trips for three or seven days; the Arctic Safari to Lapland (one day, one night); the Husky Safari (three days, two nights); and the Santa Claus Flight to Rovaniemi (one day, one night). Reservations and itinerary details are available from **Finnair** (✉ Mannerheimintie 102, 00250 Helsinki, ☎ 09/81881, ℻ 09/818–8360). **Lapptreks** (✉ 99870 Inari, ☎ 016/58567) arranges reindeer, canoe, and snowmobile safaris; ski treks; and fishing trips. **Lapland Travel Ltd.** (✉ Koskikatu 1, 96100 Rovaniemi, ☎ 016/346–052) offers fly-fishing and combined canoe-and-fishing trips.

Finland Travel Bureau (✉ Kaivokatu 10A, 00100 Helsinki, ☎ 09/18261) offers a winter Polar Safari Adventure Tour (four days, three nights). From Inari, Feelings Unlimited runs two-hour Lake Inari tours that leave from the Sami Museum and visit a Sami stone altar and burial island. Reservations are available from **Raimo Mustkangas** (✉ Inari, July–Sept., ☎ 016/671–352; Rovaniemi, year-round, ☎ 049/396–841).

For independent travelers, the **Finnish Youth Hostel Association** (✉ Yrjönkatu 38B, 00100 Helsinki, ☎ 09/694–0377, ℻ 09/693–1349) can suggest various itineraries, including cycling "safaris" through Lapland. The association will also recommend accommodations in various hostels, cabins, and campgrounds.

VISITOR INFORMATION

Ivalo (✉ Ivalontie 12, 99800, ☎ 016/662–521). **Kemijärvi** (✉ Kuumaniemenkatu 2 A, 98100, ☎ 016/813–777). **Kuusamo** (✉ Torangintaival 2, 93600, ☎ 08/850–2910). **Oulu** (✉ Torikatu 10, 90100, ☎ 08/314–1294). **Rovaniemi** (✉ Koskikatu 1, 96200, ☎ 016/346–270). **Saariselkä** (✉ Saariselkätie, PL 22, 99831, ☎ 016/668–122). **Salla** (✉ PL 59, 98901 Salla, ☎ 016/832–141). **Sodankylä** (✉ Sodankylä Matkailu Oy, Jäämerentie 9, 99600, ☎ 016/613–474).

THE LAKELANDS

Nearly 200,000 lakes dimple Finland's gentle topography, according to recent counts. Nearly every lake, big or small, is fringed with tiny cabins. The lake cabin is a Finnish institution, and until the recent advent of cheap package tours abroad, nearly every Finnish family vacationed in the same way—in its cabin on a lake.

In general, the larger towns of this region are much less appealing than the smaller lake locales. But Savonlinna stands out among the towns, not only for its stunning, waterbound views—it is hugged by gigantic Lake Saimaa—but for its cultural life. The monthlong Savonlinna Opera Festival in July is one of Finland's greatest. The quality of the opera, ballet, drama, and instrumental performance here during the annual festival weeks is world-class. Most events are staged at the 14th-century Olavinlinna Castle, splendidly positioned just offshore.

Savonlinna is the eponymous home of Finland's greatest castle. To the west, the smaller Hämeenlinna has its own lakeside castle. There are small medieval churches scattered through the Lakelands, the most famous of which is the stone church in Hattula, whose interior is a gallery of medieval painted scenes.

For centuries the lakeland region was a much-contested buffer zone between the warring empires of Sweden and Russia. After visiting the people of the Lakelands, you should have a basic understanding of the Finnish word *sisu* (guts), a quality that has kept Finns independent.

Savonlinna is the best-placed town in the Lakelands and can make a convenient base from which to begin exploring the region. Rail service is good in the Lakelands, and all the places on this tour are accessible by train from Helsinki. (The train ride from Helsinki to Tampere takes about two hours.) While Savonlinna is an easy starting-point in this region, Tampere and Hämeenlinna are only short train rides from Helsinki, and they can make good daylong excursions from the capital city.

The Land of a Thousand Lakes is also the perfect setting for a long or short boat cruise. Travel from one town to the next by boat, enjoy a lake cruise with dinner, or simply take a relaxing sightseeing cruise.

Outdoor Activities and Sports

The **Finlandia Canoe Relay** takes place in mid-June. Stretching over a grueling seven days, the 400- to 500-kilometer (250- to 310-mile) relay is a real test of endurance. For information on where the race will kick off, contact the Finnish Canoe Association.

There are numerous windsurfing centers on the shores of Lakes Saimaa and Paijanne. For details, contact the **Finnish Windsurfing Association** (☞ Sports *in* Finland A to Z, *below*).

Shopping

Many Lakelands towns have textile workshops or factories, called *Tekstiilitehdas* or *Tekstiilimyymälä*, featuring woven wall hangings and rya rugs (*ryijy* in Finnish). The Lakelands region is the birthplace of famous Finnish glassware, and you'll find the Iittala Glass Centre just outside of Hämeenlinna. The soil here yields a rich clay, and ceramics works selling dishes and pottery are ubiquitous.

Traditional outdoor markets are held throughout the region, usually on Saturdays. Most sell produce, and you'll find the wild mushrooms and berries that are so abundant in this region. The various preserves—jams, compotes, and sauces included—are all delicacies and make good gifts; Finns eat them with thin pancakes. In the autumn you'll find slightly larger markets when towns have their September fairs. These vestiges of harvest festivals are now mostly excuses to hold fun fairs and consume coffee and doughnuts.

Savonlinna

④ *335 km (208 mi) northeast of Helsinki.*

One of the larger Lakelands towns, Savonlinna is best known for having the finest castle in all of Finland. The town takes advantage of this stunning attraction by holding major events, such as the annual opera festival, in the castle courtyard. The center of Savonlinna is a series of islands linked by bridges. First, stop in at the tourist office for information; then cross the bridge east to the open-air market that flourishes alongside the main passenger quay. It's from here that you can catch the boat to Kuopio and Lappeenranta. In days when waterborne traffic was the major form of transportation, Savonlinna was the central hub of the passenger fleet serving Saimaa, the largest lake system in Europe. Now the lake traffic is dominated by cruise and sightseeing boats, but the quayside still bustles with arrivals and departures every summer morning and evening.

A 10-minute stroll from the quay to the southeast brings you to Savonlinna's most famous sight, the castle **Olavinlinna.** First built in 1475 to protect Finland's eastern border, the castle retains its medieval character and is one of Scandinavia's best-preserved historic monuments. Still surrounded by water that once bolstered its defensive strength, the fortress rises majestically out of the lake. Every July the **Savonlinna Opera Festival** (☎ 015/514–700 or 015/21866) is held in the castle's courtyard, offering a spellbinding combination of music and setting. You will need to make reservations well in advance for both tickets and hotel rooms, as Savonlinna becomes a mecca for music lovers. Contact the Savonlinna Tourist Service (☞ Visitor Information, *below*) for a current festival schedule and ticket information. The festival also includes arts and crafts exhibits around town. ⊠ *Olavinlinna,* ☎ *015/531–164.* 🎟 *FM 20; includes guided tour on the hr.* ☉ *June–Aug., daily 10–5; Sept.–May, daily 10–3.*

Near Olavinlinna, two 19th-century steam schooners, **SS Salama, SS Mikko,** and **SS Savonlinna** house an excellent museum on the history of lake traffic, including the fascinating floating timber trains that are still a common sight on Saimaa today. 🎟 *FM 15.* ☉ *Aug.–June, Tues.–Sun. 11–5; July, Tues.–Sun. 10–8.*

OFF THE
BEATEN PATH

VISULAHDEN MATKAILUKESKUS – In Mikkeli, 5 kilometers (3 miles) from Savonlinna, the Visulahti Tourist Center includes a waxworks, an old car museum, and an amusement park.

Dining and Lodging

$$$ ✕ **Rauhalinna.** This romantic turn-of-the-century timber villa was built by a general in the Imperial Russian Army. From town it's 16 kilometers (10 miles) by road, 40 minutes by boat. Both food and atmosphere are Old Russian, but some Finnish specialties are also available. Popular dishes include fish *solyanka,* a rainbow trout soup; and fried pork chops with a sour cream sauce, fried onions, pickled cucumbers, and sweet peppers. ⊠ *Lehtiniemi,* ☎ *015/523–119, for special bookings in winter* ☎ *015/57500. Reservations required during festival season. AE, DC, MC, V.* ☉ *June 4–Aug. 16.*

$$ ✕ **Majakka.** Founded in 1969, Majakka is centrally located and has an intimate atmosphere with booths, two aquariums, and plenty of plants. Some tables offer nice views of the adjacent park and the Haukivesi Lake harbor. Try the pepper steak topped with a pepper-and-cream sauce. ⊠ *Satamakatu 11,* ☎ *015/21456. Reservations required during festival season. AE, DC, MC, V.*

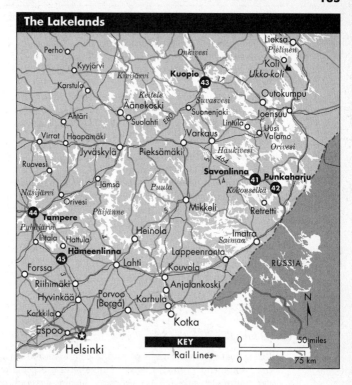

The Lakelands

$$ ✕ **Paviljonki.** Just 1 kilometer (½ mile) from the city center is Paviljonki, the restaurant of the Savonlinna restaurant school. Large windows offer views of the lake. The menu is short; try the noisettes of wild boar with an apple cognac sauce and potato blinis. The restaurant closes early (8 PM) and has a lunch buffet. ✉ *Rajalahdenkatu 4,* ☎ *015/520–960. DC, MC, V.*

$$ ✕ **Ravintola Hopeasalmi.** Right on the market square is a 100-year-old steamboat that has been converted into a restaurant and bar. The restaurant specializes in generous portions of local fish; the *muikku* (whitefish) is fried with rye, salt, and pepper and served with mashed potatoes. ✉ *Kauppatori,* ☎ *015/21701. DC, MC, V. Closed mid-Sept.–Apr.*

$$ ✕ **Snellman.** This small, 1920s-style mansion is in the center of town. Meals are served against a quiet background of classical music. Among the specialties of the house are cold-salted salmon and steak with morel sauce. ✉ *Olavinkatu 31,* ☎ *015/273–104. AE, DC, MC, V.*

$$$–$$$$ ⚐ **Seurahuone.** This old town house is near the market and passenger harbor. A new extension opened in 1989 to satisfy the growing number of tourists that visit the city during summer. Rooms are small but modern; be sure to ask for one that overlooks the picturesque harbor. ✉ *Kauppatori 4–6, 57130,* ☎ *015/5731,* ℻ *015/273–918. 84 rooms. 6 restaurants, bar, saunas, dance club, nightclub. AE, DC, MC, V.*

$$$ ⚐ **Casino Spa.** Built in the 1960s and renovated in 1986, the Casino Spa has a restful lakeside location on an island linked to the center of town by a pedestrian bridge. Rooms are basic with brown cork floors, white walls, and simple furnishings; all except one have a balcony. ✉ *Kylpylaitoksentie, Kasinonsaari, 57130,* ☎ *015/57500,* ℻ *015/272–524. 80 rooms. Restaurant, pool, saunas, spa, boating. AE, DC, MC, V.*

$–$$ 🏨 **Vuorilinna Holiday Hotel.** The simple white rooms of this modern
student dorm become hotel rooms in summer. Guests may use the facilities, including the restaurant, of the nearby Casino Spa hotel. ⊠ *Kasi-
nonsaari, 57130,* ☎ *015/57500,* 🖷 *015/272–524. 225 rooms, with
shared showers, toilets, and kitchenettes. AE, DC, MC, V. Closed
Sept.–May.*

$ 🏨 **Family Hotel Hospits.** In the heart of Savonlinna overlooking Saimaa
Lake, this YMCA hotel has small, unpretentious rooms. ⊠ *Linnankatu
20, 57130,* ☎ *015/515–661,* 🖷 *015/515–120. 22 rooms. Breakfast
room, sauna. AE, DC, MC, V.*

Outdoor Activities and Sports
Saimaa Sailing Oy (⊠ Valtakatu 37 B 18, 53100 Lappeenranta, ☎
05/411–8560) is the biggest boat-rental firm in the Lakeland region.
Sailboats and motorboats can be rented on a daily or weekly basis. The
base is the handsome, historic coastal town of Lappeenranta, 155
kilometers (96 miles) southeast of Savonlinna.

OFF THE   **OLD MINE OF OUTUKUMPU** – This child-friendly complex 187 kilometers
BEATEN PATH   (116 miles) north of Savonlinna consists of an amusement park, a mining
               museum, and a mineral exhibition. ⊠ *Kiisukatu 6,* ☎ *013/554-795.*

Punkaharju

④② *35 km (22 mi) east of Savonlinna.*

Rising out of the water and separating the Puruvesi and Pihlajavesi lakes,
the 8-kilometer (5-mile) ridge of Punkaharju is a geographical wonder that predates the Ice Age. At times the pine-covered rocks narrow
to only 25 feet, yet the ridge still manages to accommodate a road and
train tracks.

Ⓒ Just south of Punkaharju is the **Taidekeskus Retretti** (Retretti Art Center). One of the most popular excursions from Savonlinna, Retretti is
accessible via a two-hour boat ride or a 30-minute, 29-kilometer (18-
mile) bus trip. It consists of a modern art complex of unique design
and includes a new cavern section built into the Punkaharju ridge. It's
also a magnificent setting for concerts in summer and the site of more
than 40 different indoor and outdoor scheduled summertime activities. ☎ *015/644–253* 🖷 *FM 65.* ☉ *May 24–June 21 and Aug., daily
10–6; June 22–July, daily 10–7.*

Near Retretti is the **Punkaharju National Hotel** (⊠ Punkaharju 2, ☎
015/644–251). The building was constructed as a gamekeeper's lodge
for Czar Nicholas I in 1845, but it has been enlarged and restored and
is now a restful spot for a meal or an overnight visit.

Lodging
$$ 🏨 **Punkaharju Valtion Hotelli.** A manor house with small rooms dec-
orated in the old Finnish country style, this hotel is a half hour's drive
from Savonlinna. It was fully renovated in 1994. ⊠ *58450 Punkaharju,*
☎ *015/739–611,* 🖷 *015/441–784. 24 rooms. Restaurant, saunas, 2
tennis courts, beach. DC, MC, V.*

Kuopio

④③ *220 km (137 mi) northwest of Punkaharju; 185 km (115 mi) north-
west of Savonlinna.*

You'll internalize the meaning of Finland's proximity to Eastern Eu-
rope in Kuopio, with its Russian Orthodox monastery and museum.

The boat from Savonlinna arrives at Kuopio's passenger harbor, where a small evening market holds forth daily from 3 to 10.

Kuopio's tourist office is close to the **Tori** (marketplace). Called *mualiman napa* ("the belly-button of the world"), Kuopio's market square should be one of your first stops, for it is one of the most colorful outdoor markets in Finland. ☉ *Apr.–Sept., weekdays 7–5, Sat. 7–2; Oct.–Mar., weekdays 7–2.*

The **Ortodoksinen Kirkkomuseo** (Orthodox Church Museum) has one of the most interesting and unusual collections of its kind. When Karelia (the eastern province of Finland) was ceded to the Soviet Union after World War II, religious art was taken out of the monasteries and brought to Kuopio. The collection is eclectic and, of its type, one of the rarest in the world. ✉ *Karjalankatu 1, Kuopio,* ☎ *017/261–8818.* ☒ *FM 15.* ☉ *May–Aug., Tues.–Sun. 10–4; Sept.–Apr., weekdays noon–3, weekends noon–5.*

Visitors who are fascinated by the treasures in the museum will want to visit the Orthodox convent of Lintula and the **Valamon Luostari** (Valamo Monastery). A major center for Russian Orthodox religious and cultural life in Finland, the monastery hosts daily services. Precious 18th-century icons and sacred objects are housed in the main church and in the icon conservation center. The Orthodox library is the most extensive in Finland and is open to visitors. There is a café-restaurant on the grounds, and hotel and hostel accommodations are available at the monastery. ✉ *Uusi Valamo,* ☎ *017/570–111 (017/570–1501 for hotel reservations).* ☒ *Guided tours FM 20.* ☉ *Mar.–Sept., daily 7 AM–9 PM; Oct.–Feb., daily 8 AM–9 PM.*

The **Lintulan Luostari** (Lintula Convent) can be reached by boat from Valamo, or you can visit both the convent and the monastery by boat on scenic day excursions from Kuopio. *Tickets available from the Kuopio Tourist Service,* ✉ *Haapaniemenkatu 17,* ☎ *017/182–584.* ☉ *Convent June 13–Aug. Bus tours June–Aug., Sat. at 10 AM.* ☒ *FM 210. Boat cruises June 25–Aug., Tues.–Sun.* ☒ *FM 240.*

Puijon Näkötorni (Puijo Tower) is best visited at sunset, when the lakes shimmer with reflected light. The slender tower is 3 kilometers (2 miles) northwest of Kuopio. It has two observation decks and is crowned by a revolving restaurant with marvelous views. ☎ *017/209–103.* ☒ *Summer, FM 15; Oct.–Apr., free.* ☉ *May 2–Sept., daily 11–11; Oct.–Apr., daily 11–10.*

Dining and Lodging

$$ ✕ **Musta Lammas.** Near the passenger harbor, Musta Lammas is located in the basement of a brewery founded in 1862; it has been attractively adapted from its beer-cellar days, retaining the original redbrick walls and beer barrels. The specialty here is the smoked muikku—a kind of whitefish—with sour cream and mashed potatoes. ✉ *Satamakatu 4,* ☎ *017/262–3494. AE, DC, MC, V. Closed Sun. No lunch.*

$$ ✕ **Sampo Vapaasatama.** Situated in the town center, Sampo was founded in 1931, but its Scandinavian furniture dates from the 1950s. High ceilings and large chandeliers give it an elegant look. Try the muikku smoked, fried, grilled, or in a stew with pork, potatoes, and onions. ✉ *Kauppakatu 13,* ☎ *017/261–4677. AE, DC, MC, V.*

$$$ ▥ **Arctia Hotel Kuopio.** Completed in 1987, the Arctia is the newest and most modern of the local hotels. Rooms are spacious by European standards, with large beds and generous towels. It's on the lakefront and also close to the center of town. ✉ *Satamakatu 1, 70100,* ☎

017/195–111, FAX *017/195–170. 141 rooms. Pool, sauna, hot tub, boating. AE, DC, MC, V.*

$$ 🏨 **Hotel Spa Rauhalahti.** About 5 kilometers (3 miles) from the town center, Rauhalahti is set near the lakeshore and has no-frills rooms and cabins. A number of amenities cater to sports lovers and families. The hotel has three restaurants, including the tavern-style Vanha Apteekkari—a local favorite. ⊠ *Katiskaniementie 8, 70700,* ☎ *017/473–111,* FAX *017/473–470. 106 rooms, 13 apartments, 20 hostel rooms. Pool, hot tub, saunas, spa, tennis court, exercise room, horseback riding, squash, boating. AE, DC, MC, V.*

$$ 🏨 **Iso-Valkeinen Hotel.** On the lakeshore only 5 kilometers (3 miles) from the town center, this hotel has large, quiet rooms in six one-story buildings. Several rooms have balconies with views of the nearby lake. ⊠ *Päiväranta, 70420,* ☎ *017/539–6100,* FAX *017/539–6555. 100 rooms with shower. 2 restaurants, pool, saunas, miniature golf, tennis court, beach, boating, fishing, nightclub. AE, DC, MC, V.*

Outdoor Activities and Sports

Karelia Golf (⊠ 80780 Kontioniemi, ☎ 013/732–411) is one of Finland's best 18-hole golf courses.

Tampere

④ *293 km (182 mi) southwest of Kuopio; 174 km (108 mi) northwest of Helsinki.*

The country's third-largest city, Tampere is an industrial center with a difference. From about the year 1000, this was a base from which traders and hunters set out on their expeditions to northern Finland; it was not until 1779 that a Swedish king, Gustav III, founded the city itself. In 1828 a Scotsman named James Finlayson came to the infant city and established a factory for spinning cotton. This was the beginning of "big business" in Finland. The Finlayson firm is today one of the country's major industrial enterprises.

Artful siting is the secret of this factory town. An isthmus little more than half a mile wide at its narrowest point separates the lakes Näsijärvi and Pyhäjärvi, and at one spot the **Tammerkoski Rapids** provide an outlet for the waters of one to cascade through to the other. Called the Mother of Tampere, these rapids once provided the electrical power on which the town's livelihood depended. Their natural beauty has been preserved in spite of the factories on either bank, and the well-designed public buildings grouped around them enhance their general effect.

Adding to Tampere's natural beauty is the **Hämeensilta Bridge,** with its four statues by the well-known Finnish sculptor Wäinö Aaltonen, in the heart of town. Close to the bridge, near the high-rise Sokos Hotel Ilves, are some old factory buildings that have been restored as shops and boutiques.

At Verkatehtaankatu 2, the city **tourist office** offers helpful service and sells a 24-hour Tourist Ticket (FM 25), which allows unlimited travel on city transportation.

☸ A 1½-kilometer (1-mile) walk west, then north from the heart of Tampere brings you to the **Särkänniemen Huvikeskus** (Särkäniemi Recreation Center), a major recreation complex for both children and adults. Its many attractions include an amusement park, a children's zoo, a planetarium, and a well-planned aquarium with a separate dolphinarium.

Within Särkäniemi, the **Sara Hildénin Taidemuseo** (Sara Hildśn Art Museum) (☎ 03/214–3134) is a striking example of Finnish architecture, with the works of modern Finnish and international artists, including

Chagall, Klee, Miró, and Picasso. The museum is open daily from 11 to 6. Admission is FM 15.

Särkäniemi's profile is punctuated by the 550-foot **Näsinneulan Näkötorni** (Näsinneula Observatory Tower), Finland's tallest observation tower and the dominant feature of the Tampere skyline. The top of the tower holds an observatory and a revolving restaurant. The views are magnificent, commanding the lake, forest, and town—the contrast between the industrial maze of Tampere at your feet and the serenity of the lakes stretching out to meet the horizon is unforgettable. The tower is open daily form June through August from 10 to 10, and from September through May from 10 to 4. Admission is FM 12. ⊠ *Särkänniemen,* ☎ *03/248–8111. ☑ Särkänniemen Passport (dolphinarium and 3 other attractions, excluding amusement park rides) FM 75. ☉ Check locally for museum hours and exhibits; children's zoo May–Aug., daily 10–6 or 8; other attractions May–Aug., daily 10–10.*

While in western Tampere, be sure to visit one of the city's best museums, the **Amurin Työläiskorttelimuseo** (Amuri Museum of Workers' Housing). Its 30-plus wooden houses, sauna, bakery, and haberdashery date from the 1880s to the 1970s and are so well done that you half expect the original inhabitants to return at any minute. ⊠ *Makasiininkatu 12,* ☎ *03/214–1633. ☑ FM 15. ☉ Mid- May–mid-Sept., Tues.–Sat. 9–5, Sun. 11–5.*

It was in Tampere that Lenin and Stalin first met, and this fateful occasion is commemorated with displays of photos and mementos in the **Lenin Museo** (Lenin Museum). ⊠ *Hämeenpuisto 28, 3rd Floor,* ☎ *03/212–7313. ☑ FM 15. ☉ Weekdays 9–5, weekends 11–4.*

At the foot of the Pyynikki ridge is the **Pyynikin Kesäteatteri** (Pyynikki Open Air Theater), with a revolving auditorium that can be moved, even with a full load of spectators, to face any one of the sets. ⊠ *Pyynikin Kesäteatteri,* ☎ *03/216–0300.*

On the east side of town is the modern **Kalevan Kirkko** (Kaleva Church). What may appear from the outside to be a grain elevator is in fact, as seen from the interior, a soaring monument to space and light. ☉ *May–Aug., daily 10–5; Sept.–Apr., daily 11–3.*

Most buildings in Tampere, including the cathedral, are comparatively modern. The **Tuomiokirkko** (Cathedral) was built in 1907 and houses some of the best-known masterpieces of Finnish art, including Magnus Encknell's fresco *The Resurrection* and Hugo Simberg's *Wounded Angel* and *Garden of Death*. ☉ *May–Aug., daily 10–6; Sept.–Apr., daily 11–3.*

OFF THE
BEATEN PATH
HAIHARAN NUKKE-JA PUKUMUSEO – Only 3 kilometers (2 miles) southwest of the city center, the Haihara Doll and Costume Museum exhibits thousands of dolls from all over the world dating from the 12th to the 20th century. Costumes are mainly Finnish from the 19th century. ⊠ *Hatanpää kartano, Hatanpään puistokuja 1,* ☎ *03/222-6261. ☑ FM 20. ☉ Apr.–Sept., Tues.–Sat. 10–5, Sun. noon–5; Oct.–Mar., Wed.–Sun. noon–5.*

Dining and Lodging

$$$ ✕ **Tiiliholvi.** This former bank vault has been turned into a romantic cellar restaurant with Jugendstil furniture, redbrick walls, and stained-glass decorations. Try the willow grouse Stroganoff or sour-cream mutton with hash potatoes. The chocolate cake is a good choice for dessert. ⊠ *Kauppakatu 10,* ☎ *03/212–1220. AE, DC, MC, V.*

$$ ✕ Astor. The most recent appearance on the Tampere scene has a moderately priced brasserie section and a more expensive restaurant. Parquet floors, soft yellow and red walls, and candlelight lend a touch of elegance. Try the reindeer fillet with cranberry sauce or the willow grouse. ⊠ *Aleksis Kivenkatu 26,* ☎ *03/213–3522. Reservations essential. DC, MC, V.*

$$ ✕ Bodega Salud. The Salud has a well-earned reputation for Spanish specialties, though it also offers such unconventional dishes as grilled alligator and stewed kangaroo. The decor is unconventional, too, with stuffed animals—birds, turtles, bulls' heads, and cow pelts. ⊠ *Otavalankatu 10,* ☎ *03/223–5996. AE, DC, MC, V.*

$$ ✕ Silakka. The name of this restaurant translates into the main gastronomic theme: Baltic herring. The buffet—a must—offers four cold and three warm Baltic herring dishes, salmon soup, and six salads. Other specialties include flambéed salmon topped with a cream chanterelle sauce, and fried perch with a cream morel sauce. On the second floor of the Koskikeskus shopping mall, Silakka has a casual, unpretentious atmosphere. ⊠ *Hatanpään valtatie 1, Koskikeskus,* ☎ *03/214–9740. DC, MC, V.*

$$ ▥ Cumulus Koskikatu. This centrally located hotel overlooks the tamed rapids of Tammerkoski. Rooms are fresh and modern; for an extra FM 40 you can enjoy a view of the rapids. The Finnair terminal is in the same building. ⊠ *Koskikatu 5, 33100,* ☎ *03/242–4399,* ⅢЖ *03/242–4399. 227 rooms with shower. Restaurant, bar, pool, saunas, nightclub. AE, DC, MC, V.*

$$ ▥ Sokos Hotel Ilves. Soaring above a newly gentrified area of old warehouses near the city center, this 18-story hotel is Tampere's tallest building. All rooms above the sixth floor have spectacular views of the city and Pyhäjärvi and Näsijärvi lakes. ⊠ *Hatanpään valtatie 1, 33100,* ☎ *03/262–6262,* ⅢЖ *03/262–6263. 336 rooms. 4 restaurants, no-smoking rooms, pool, hot tub, saunas, exercise room, nightclub. AE, DC, MC, V.*

$ ▥ Domus Summer Hotel. About 3 kilometers (2 miles) from the center of town, in the Kaleva district, this hotel is a student dormitory that rents rooms during the summer. All rooms are equipped with refrigerators and hot plates; a room with a shower costs an extra FM 50. This is a good option for cost-conscious families. ⊠ *Pellervonkatu 9, 33540,* ☎ *03/255–0000,* ⅢЖ *03/222–5409. 147 rooms, 80 with shower. Pool, saunas, dance club. MC, V. Closed Sept.–May.*

OFF THE
BEATEN PATH
RUNOILIJAN TIE – One of the most popular excursions from Tampere is the Runoilijan Tie (Poet's Way) boat tour along Lake Näsijärvi. The boat passes through the agricultural parish of Ruovesi, where J. L. Runeberg, Finland's national poet, used to live. Shortly before the boat docks at Virrat, you'll pass through the straits of Visuvesi, where many artists and writers spend their summers. ⊠ *Finnish Silverline and Poet's Way, Verkatehtaankatu 2, 33100 Tampere,* ☎ *03/212–4804.* ▨ *FM 310 round-trip.*

ÄHTÄRI – Not far north of Virrat is Ähtäri, where Finland's first wildlife park has been established in a beautiful setting, with a holiday village, a good hotel, and recreation facilities.

Hämeenlinna

㊺ *78 km (48 mi) southeast of Tampere; 98 km (61 mi) north of Helsinki (via Hwy. 12).*

The big castle and small museums of Hämeenlinna make this town a good place for a day trip. It's also a good point from which to visit nearby gems such as the **Iittalan Lasikeskus** (Iittala Glass Centre). The magnificent glass is produced by top designers, and the seconds are bargains you won't find elsewhere. ⊠ *14500 Iittala,* ☎ *03/535–6230.* 🖳 *FM 10 (FM 7 in winter).* ☉ *Museum May–Aug., daily 10–6; Sept.–Apr., weekdays 10–5, weekends 10–6. Factory shop May–Aug., daily 10– 8; Sept.–Apr., daily 10–6.*

Hämeenlinna's secondary school has educated many famous Finns, among them composer Jean Sibelius (1865–1957). The only surviving timber house in the town center is the **Sibeliuksen syntymäkoti** (Sibelius birthplace), a modest dwelling built in 1834. The museum staff will play your favorite Sibelius CD as you tour the rooms, one of which contains the harmonium Sibelius played as a child. ⊠ *Hallituskatu 11.* 🖳 *FM 10.* ☉ *May–Aug., daily 10–4; Sept.–Apr., daily noon–4.*

Swedish crusaders began construction on **Hämeen Linna** (Häme Castle) in the 13th century to strengthen and defend the Swedish position in the region. What began as a fortified camp evolved over the centuries into a large castle of stone and brick. In modern times, the castle, one of Finland's oldest, has served as a granary and a prison, and it is now restored and open to the public for tours and exhibitions. The castle sits on the lakeshore, 1 kilometer (½ mile) north of Hämeenlinna's town center. Guided tours in English take place every hour in the summer and are available every hour in winter by appointment only. ⊠ *Kustaa III:n katu 6,* ☎ *03/675–6820.* 🖳 *FM 15; includes guided tour.* ☉ *May–Aug. 14, daily 10–6; rest of yr, daily 10–4.*

OFF THE BEATEN PATH

HATTULAN KIRKO – Six kilometers (3½ miles) north of Hämeenlinna is Hattula, whose Church of the Holy Cross is the most famous of Finland's medieval churches. Its interior is a fresco gallery of biblical scenes whose vicious little devils and soulful saints are as vivid as when they were first painted around 1510. ⊠ *Hattula,* ☎ *03/672-3383 during opening hrs; 03/637-2477 at all other times.* 🖳 *FM 15.* ☉ *May 14– Aug. 14, daily 11-5; open at other times by appointment.*

Dining and Lodging

$$ ✗ **Huviretki.** In the heart of the city at the Cumulus Hotel is Huviretki, the city's most popular restaurant. Specialties include "vineyard lamb," a fillet of lamb with garlic potatoes, zucchini, mushrooms, tomatoes, and garlic cloves; salmon and crayfish with a Gouda cheese sauce; and pepper steak with a cream-pepper sauce and french fries. There's a wide range of salads and meat dishes. ⊠ *Raathuneenkatu 16–18,* ☎ *03/64881. AE, DC, MC, V.*

$$ ✗ **Piiparkakkutalo.** Located in a renovated old-timber building, Piiparkakkutalo specializes in meat dishes; try the chateaubriand with cream cognac sauce and blue-cheese potatoes. ⊠ *Kirkkorinne 2,* ☎ *03/612-1606. AE, DC, MC, V.*

$$$ 🏨 **Rantasipi Aulanko.** One of Finland's top hotels sits on the lakeshore
★   in a beautifully landscaped park 6½ kilometers (4 miles) from town. Built in 1938, it was completely renovated in 1989. All rooms have wall-to-wall carpeting and overlook the golf course, park, or lake. ⊠ *13210 Hämeenlinna,* ☎ *03/658–801,* 🖷 *03/658–1922. 245 rooms. Restaurant, indoor pool, massage, saunas, 18-hole golf course, tennis court, horseback riding, boating, nightclub. AE, DC, MC, V.*

Outdoor Activities and Sports

GOLF

Hotel Vaakuna (⊠ Possentie 7, 13200 Hämeenlinna, ☎ 03/5831) has an 18-hole lakeside golf course.

SKIING

Find out about ski events, including the February Hämeenlinna–Lahti Finlandia Race, from the **Finlandia Ski Race Office** (⊠ Urheilukeskus, 15110 Lahti, ☎ 03/734–9811). The March Salpausselkä Ski Games and jumping events are also in Lahti.

En Route If you're driving between Helsinki and Hämeenlinna along Highway 12, around Riihimäki you'll see signs for the **Suomen Lasimuseo** (Finnish Glass Museum). Follow them! It's an outstanding display of the history of glass from early Egyptian times to the present, beautifully arranged in an old glass factory. ⊠ *Tehtaankatu 21, Riihimäki,* ☎ *019/741–494.* ▣ *FM 15.* ☉ *Apr.–Sept., daily 10–6; Oct.–Dec. and Feb.–Mar., Tues.–Sun. 10–6.*

Lakelands A to Z

Arriving and Departing

BY BUS

Buses are the best form of public transport into the region, with frequent connections to lake destinations from most major towns. It is a six-hour ride from Helsinki to Savonlinna.

BY CAR

The region is vast, so the route you choose will depend on your destination. Consult the Finnish Automobile Association or tourist boards for route advice.

BY PLANE

Airports in the Lakelands are at Tampere, Mikkeli, Jyväskylä, Varkaus, Lappeenranta, Savonlinna, Kuopio, and Joensuu. Flight time to the Savonlinna area from Helsinki is 40 minutes. All the airports are served by Finnair's domestic service, including the KarAir charter company.

The Joensuu–Kuopio–Lahti–Tampere road belt will transport you quickly from one major point to the next, but if you are going to be taking a lake vacation you will usually finish your journey on small roads. The last stretch to the *mökki* (cabin) may be unpaved. You will need a detailed map to find most mökkis, which tend to be tucked away in well-hidden spots.

BY TRAIN

Trains run from Helsinki to Lahti, Mikkeli, Imatra, Lappeenranta, Joensuu, and Jyväskylä. There is sleeping-car service to Joensuu and Kuopio and, in summer only, to Savonlinna. The trip from Helsinki to Savonlinna takes 5½ hours.

Contacts and Resources

EMERGENCIES

The nationwide emergency number is **112;** it can be used to call police and ambulance services. A major hospital is **Tampere Keskussairaala** (Tampere Central Hospital) (⊠ Teiskontie 35, Tampere, ☎ 03/247–5111). For dental care call **Hammaslääkäri Päivystys** (☎ 049/625–555), weekdays 9–8, weekends 11–3.

GUIDED TOURS

A program of **Friendly Finland Tours,** available trough travel agencies in Finland and abroad, offers escorted packages that include stops in the Lakelands. The three-day "Saimaa Lake Tour" and the seven-day "Scenic Tour" both start in Helsinki. Brochures are available from the **Finland Travel Bureau** (☎ 09/18261) and its overseas offices (☞ Helsinki Essentials, *above*).

Boat Tours. Avid canoeists should contact the Finnish Canoe Association. Almost all of its 67 clubs arrange guided tours; canoes are rented at about FM 100 per day. **Lintusalon Melontakeskus** (✉ 52200 Puumala, ☎ 05/88759) arranges numerous lakeland canoe tours.

Ikaalinen Tourist Service (✉ Valtakatu 7, 39500, ☎ 03/450–1221) runs white-water trips and canoe safaris in the region. **Lieksan Matkailu Oy** (✉ Pielisentie 7, 81700 Lieksa, ☎ 013/520–2400) is another river-trip outfitter. **Mike's Canoe and Paddling Service** (✉ Mikan Kanotti-ja Melontapalvelu and Haukankatu 27, 50190 Mikkeli, ☎ 049/840–362 for both addresses) designs tailor-made canoe tours.

Many sailing schools operate in the lakes region, with courses for sailors of all levels. Contact the **Finnish Yachting Association** (✉ Radiokatu 20, Helsinki, ☎ 09/158–2110) or **Naviconsult Sailing** (✉ 06830 Kullonkylä, ☎ 049/840–312 or019/22532) for details.

Guided fishing tours are offered by **Heinola Matkailupalvelu** (✉ Torikatu 8, 18100 Heinola, ☎ 03/158–444).

Cruises. There are dozens of boat-tour companies operating in the Lakelands; contact the Finnish Tourist Board Head Office or local tourist offices in the region for a complete list as well as details of routes. Also try **Western Lakeland Silverline and Poets' Way Tour** (✉ Verkatehtaankatu 2, 33100 Tampere, ☎ 03/124–803). **Western Lakeland and Lake Päijänne Tour** (✉ Lake Päijänne Cruises, Pellonpää, 40820 Haapaniemi, ☎ 014/618–885 or 014/263–447). **Saimaa Lakeland** (✉ Roll Cruises of Finland Ltd., Matkustajasatama, Kauppakatu 1, 70100 Kuopio, ☎ 017/262–6744).

VISITOR INFORMATION
Heinola (✉ Torikatu 8, 18100, ☎ 03/158–444). **Hämeenlinna** (✉ Sibeliuksenkatu 5A, 13100, ☎ 03/621–2388). **Imatra** (✉ Liikekeskus Mansikkapaikka, PL 22, 55121, ☎ 05/681–2500). **Joensuu/North Karelia** (✉ Koskikatu 1, 80100, ☎ 013/167–5300). **Jyväskylä** (✉ Asemakatu 6, 40100, ☎ 014/624–211). **Kuopio** (✉ Haapaniemenkatu 17, 70110, ☎ 017/182–584). **Lahti** (✉ Torikatu 3B, PL 175, 15111, ☎ 03/81817). **Lappeenranta** (✉ Linja-autoasema, PL113, 53101, ☎ 05/616–2600). **Mikkeli** (✉ Hallituskatu 3A, 50100, ☎ 015/151–444). **Savonlinna** (✉ Puistokatu 1, 57100, ☎ 015/273–492). **Tampere** (✉ Verkatehtaankatu 2, PL 87, 33100, ☎ 03/212–6652).

FINLAND A TO Z

Arriving and Departing

By Plane
FROM NORTH AMERICA
All international flights arrive at Helsinki-Vantaa International Airport, 20 kilometers (12 miles) north of the city center. For arrival and departure information, call ☎ 9600/8100 (24 hours).

Finnair (☎ 800/950–5000) offers domestic and international flights, with daily direct service from New York. **Delta** (☎ 800/241–4141) has direct service from New York. **British Airways** (☎ 800/247–9297), **Lufthansa** (☎ 800/645–3880), and **Scandinavian Airlines System** (SAS) (☎ 800/221–2350) also fly to Helsinki.

Flying time from New York to Helsinki is about 8 hours, 9 hours for the return trip.

Finnair, British Airways, and some charter companies fly from London to Helsinki. Ask the Finnish National Tourist Board for names of companies specializing in travel packages to Finland. Finnair in the United Kingdom is located at 14 Clifford Street, London W1X 1RD (☎ 0171/629–4349).

Flying time from London to Helsinki is 2 hours, 45 minutes.

By Ship
DFDS Scandinavian Seaways (✉ Scandinavia House, Parkeston Quay, Harwich, Essex, ☎ 255/240–234) sails from Harwich to Göteborg, Sweden, with overland (bus or train) transfer to Stockholm; from there, Silja and Viking Line ships cross to the Finnish Åland Islands, Turku, and Helsinki. Traveling time is about two days (☞ Getting Around by Ferry, *below*).

Getting Around

By Bicycle
Finland is a wonderful place for bicycling, with its easy terrain, light traffic, and wide network of bicycle paths. You can get bike-route maps for most major cities. In Helsinki, cycling is a great way to see the main peninsula as well as some of the surrounding islands, linked by bridges. Rentals average FM 40–FM 60 per day. **Suomen Retkeilymajajärjestö** (Finnish Youth Hostel Association) (✉ Yrjönkatu 38B, 00100 Helsinki, ☎ 09/694–0377, ℻ 09/693–1349) offers a free brochure with information on long-distance cycling trips and hostels. Bicycle rentals are available from **Green Bike** (✉ Mannerheimintie 13, 00100 Helsinki, ☎ 050/550–1020).

By Bus
The Finnish bus network, **Matkahuolto** (✉ Linja-autoasema, Simonkatu 3, 00200 Helsinki, ☎ 09/682–701), is extensive and the fares are reasonable. You can also travel by bus between Finland and Norway, Sweden, or Russia. Full-time students can purchase a discount card for FM 30 that translates into a 50% discount on longer trips. Senior citizens will get good discounts with the **65 Card** for FM 32; it's available at Matkahuolto offices. Adults in groups of three or more are entitled to a 25% discount.

A **Coach Holiday Ticket** (FM 340) is good for up to 1,000 kilometers (620 miles) of travel for two weeks.

By Car
Driving is pleasant on Finland's relatively uncongested roads. At press time (December 1996) gasoline cost FM 4.90 per liter. Driving is on the right-hand side of the road. You must always use low-beam headlights outside built-up areas. Seat belts are compulsory for everyone. You must yield to cars coming from the right at most intersections where roads are of equal size. There are strict drinking-and-driving laws.

Speed limits range from 40 to 80 and sometimes 100 kph (25 to 50 and sometimes 65 mph), depending on road size and proximity to settled areas. Late autumn and spring are the most hazardous times to drive. Roads are often icy in autumn (*kelivaroitus* is the slippery road warning), and the spring thaw can make for *kelirikko* (heaves). The **Automobile Touring Club of Finland** (✉ Autoliitto ry, Hämeentie 105 A, 00550 Helsinki, ☎ 09/774–761) has a wealth of information, including where to rent studded tires, which are mandatory—except for foreign-registered cars—from December through February.

Foreigners involved in road accidents should immediately notify the **Finnish Motor Insurers' Bureau** (⊠ Liikennevakuutuskeskus, Bulevardi 28, 00120 Helsinki, ☎ 09/680–401) as well as the police.

CAR RENTALS

Car rental in Finland is not cheap, but a group rental might make it worthwhile. Be on the lookout for weekend and summer discounts. It is cheaper to rent directly from the United States before coming to Finland. Some Finnish service stations also offer car rentals at reduced rates. Regular daily rates range from FM 250 to FM 550 (US$60–$130), and per-kilometer surcharges from FM 2 to FM 7 (48¢–$1.70). Car rentals are normally 30% cheaper on weekends. Insurance is sold by the rental agencies. Some centrally located agencies are **Avis** (⊠ Pohjoinen Rautatiekatu 17, Helsinki, ☎ 09/441–155; airport office, ☎ 09/822–833 or 9800/2828), **Budget** (⊠ Hotel Inter-Continental, ☎ 09/497–477; airport office, ☎ 09/870–1606 or 9800/2535), **Hertz** (⊠ Mannerheimintie 44, ☎ 09/446–910; airport office, ☎ 09/821–052 or 9800/2012), and **Europcar Interrent** (⊠ John Stenbergin ranta 6, ☎ 09/758–3354; airport office, ☎ 09/826–677 or 9800/2154).

By Ferry

Finland is one of the world's major shipbuilding nations, and the ferries that cruise the Baltic to the Finnish Åland Islands and Sweden seem more like luxury liners. The boat operators make so much money selling duty-free alcohol, perfume, and chocolate that they spare no expense on facilities, which include saunas, children's playrooms, casinos, a host of bars and cafés, and often superb restaurants.

All classes of sleeping accommodations are available on board the journeys from Stockholm to Turku (about 11 hours) and from Stockholm to Helsinki (about 15 hours). Two other connections are Vaasa–Sundsvall and Umeå (Sweden), Kokkola–Skellefteå (Sweden), Helsinki–Travemünde (Germany), and Helsinki–Tallinn (Estonia).

In Helsinki, the Silja terminal for ships arriving from Stockholm is at Olympialaituri (Olympic Harbor), on the west side of the South Harbor. The Viking Line terminal for ships arriving from Stockholm is at Katajanokkanlaituri (Katajanokka Harbor), on the east side of the South Harbor. Both Silja (⊠ Mannerheimintie 2, ☎ 9800/74552) and Viking (⊠ Mannerheimintie 12, ☎ 09/123–577) have downtown agencies where brochures, information, and tickets are available.

By Plane

Finland's flagship air carrier, Finnair, runs an extensive domestic service that includes the charter companies KarAir and Finnaviation. Domestic flights are relatively cheap, and as some planes have a set number of discount seats allotted, it's best to reserve early. Finnair's "Finnish Holiday Tickets" provide 10 one-way coupons good for 30 days of travel within Finland. At press time (December 1996), the price for these coupons was FM 2,065 (US$500). For information, contact **Finnair** (⊠ Helsinki-Vantaa Airport, Tietotie 11, 01530 Vantaa, ☎ 09/818–800).

By Taxi

Taxis travel everywhere in Finland. The meter starts at FM 30, with surcharges at certain times and on certain days. In cities people generally go to one of the numerous taxi stands and take the first available taxi. You can hail a cab, but most are on radio call. The main phone number for taxi service is 700–700. Many taxi drivers take credit cards.

Tipping is unnecessary; if you want to leave something, round up to the nearest FM 5–FM 10. A receipt is a *kuitti*.

By Train

The Finnish State Railways, or VR, serve southern Finland well, but connections in the central and northern sections are scarcer and are supplemented by buses. Helsinki is the main junction, with Riihimäki to the north a major hub. You can get as far north as Rovaniemi and Kemijärvi by rail, but to penetrate farther into Lapland, you'll need to rely on buses, domestic flights, or local taxis.

First- and second-class seats are available on all express trains. Children ages 6–16 travel half-fare, and there is a 20% reduction when three or more people travel together. You must make a seat reservation on special fast trains (FM 15–FM 70). For FM 50, senior citizens (over 65) can buy a special pass entitling them to 50% discounts on train fares. Car and passenger trains leave daily for northern Finland. Passenger trains leave Helsinki twice daily for St. Petersburg (8 hours) and once daily on an overnighter to Moscow (15 hours). Travel to Russia requires a visa. To get to northern Sweden or Norway, you must combine train–bus or train–boat travel.

Inquiries on train travel can be made to the Finnish State Railways at the main railroad station in Helsinki or to the **Information Service** (⊠ Vilhonkatu 13, PL 488, 00101 Helsinki, ☎ 09/010–0121).

RAIL PASSES

The **Finnrail Pass** gives unlimited first- or second-class travel within a set time; the 3-day pass costs FM 505 (FM 760 for first-class), the 5-day pass FM 685 (FM 1,030), and the 10-day pass FM 945 (FM 1,420). Children pay half-fare. These passes can be bought in the United States and Canada by calling Rail Europe (☎ 800/438–7245); in the United Kingdom from Norvista (previously Finlandia Travel, ☎ 071/409–7334); and from the Finnish State Railways, or VR (☎ 09/100127).

The **ScanRail Pass** offers unlimited travel in Scandinavia for 21 days. The **InterRail Pass** is for travelers under 26 who are not residents of Scandinavia. The more general **EurailPass** is good for train travel throughout all of Europe. The **Eurail Youth Pass** entitles those under 26 to travel throughout Europe. The **Rail Europe Senior Card** is for men and women older than 60.

Contacts and Resources

Language

Finnish, the principal language, is a Finno-Ugric tongue related to Estonian with distant links to Hungarian. The country's second official language is Swedish, although only about 6% of the population speaks it. In the south, most towns have Finnish and Swedish names; if the Swedish name is listed first, it indicates more Swedish than Finnish speakers live in that area. The third language is Sami, the language of the Laplanders. English is spoken in most cities and resorts.

Late-Night Pharmacies

Late-night pharmacies are found only in large towns. Look under *Aptekki* in the phone book; listings include pharmacy hours.

Lodging

The **Hotel Booking Center** (⊠ Rautatieasema, 00100, ☎ 09/171–133) in Helsinki, at the railway station, will make reservations only in Helsinki and surroundings for FM 12 (telephone reservations are free). **Suomen Hotellivaraukset** (⊠ Nervanderinkatu 5 D 40, 00100 Helsinki,

☎ 09/499–155) will make reservations anywhere in Finland at no cost. **Best Western Hotels Finland** (✉ Merimiehenkatu 29 A, 00150 Helsinki, ☎ 09/655–855) is a reliable national hotel chain. **Arctia Hotel Partners** (✉ Ankkurikatu 1, 00160 Helsinki, ☎ 09/696–901) is another national hotel chain.

Lomarengas (✉ Malminkaari 23C, 00700 Helsinki, ☎ 09/3516–1321; Eteläesplanadi 4, 00130 Helsinki, ☎ 09/170–611) has lists of reasonably priced bed-and-breakfasts, holiday cottages, farm accommodations, and car-rental services. It also arranges stays at a range of facilities, including *mökki* (cabin) holidays. **Suomen 4H-liitto** (✉ Abrahaminkatu 7, 00180 Helsinki, ☎ 09/642–233) arranges farm vacations.

CAMPING

Finland is prime camping territory because of the great wealth of open space. If you camp outside authorized areas and in a settled area, you must get the landowner's permission, and you cannot camp closer than 300 feet to anyone's house. You may also swim anywhere that is not clearly marked as private property. Finncamping Cheque (FM 70) is a coupon system for campers. For more information, contact the **Finnish Travel Association** (✉ Camping Department, Mikonkatu 25, PL 776, 00101 Helsinki, ☎ 09/170–868). The group also sells the National Camping Card, a useful ID card. The annually updated list of campsites, including classifications and English-language summary, is sold at large bookstores and R-kiosks. A free brochure listing 200 campsites in Finland is available from city tourist offices.

SUMMER DORMITORIES

During the summer season (June–August) many university residence halls in Finland open their doors to visitors. Prices (usually from FM 173 per night in Helsinki and FM 124 elsewhere in Finland) are much lower than those in ordinary hotels, and meals are generally available. Ask the Finnish Tourist Board or the Finnish Youth Hostel Association (✉ Yrjönkatu 38B, 00100 Helsinki, ☎ 09/694–0377) for its brochure on budget accommodations.

Mail

Post offices are open weekdays 9–5; stamps, express mail, registered mail, and insured mail service are available. There is no Saturday delivery. Airmail letters and postcards to destinations outside Europe cost FM 3.40; letters and postcards to other Scandinavian countries, the Baltics, and within Finland, FM 2.40; to the rest of Europe, FM 3.20. You may receive letters care of Poste Restante anywhere in Finland; the Poste Restante address in the capital is Mannerheimintie 11F, 00100 Helsinki, at the side of the rail station. It is open weekdays 8 AM–9 PM, Saturday 9–6, and Sunday 11–9. You can also post mail 24 hours a day at Finland Post's Express Service (✉ Läkkisepäntie 11, 00620 Helsinki, ☎ 9800/70784), 8–5.

Money and Expenses

The unit of currency is the Finnmark (FM), also abbreviated as FIM and FMK. The Finnmark is divided into 100 pennies (penniä) in denominations of 10- and 50-penniä and 5- and 10-mark coins. Bills begin with the FM 20 note and progress to FM 50, 100, 500, and 1,000. At press time (December 1996) the exchange rate was FM 4.26 to the U.S. dollar, FM 6.55 to the pound sterling, and FM 3.13 to the Canadian dollar. There are exchange bureaus in all bank branches; some post offices, which also function as banks (Postipankki); major hotels; and at Helsinki-Vantaa Airport. Some large harbor terminals also have exchange bureaus, and international ferries have exchange desks. Banks give the best exchange rates, however. Extended exchange and banking hours at Kansallis-Osake-Pankki (KOP) bank booths at the airport are 6:30 AM–11 PM daily. The Postipankki bank booth is open daily 6:30 AM–8:30 PM.

SAMPLE PRICES

The devaluations of its currency in November 1991 and September 1992 brought Finland's notoriously high prices down to more reasonable levels. If you opt for campsites or cabin rentals rather than hotel rooms and shop for meals carefully, you can cut costs considerably. Helsinki is Finland's most expensive city for lodging. Food costs tend to be standardized across the country, however.

Some sample prices: cup of coffee, FM 7; soda, FM 10–FM 13; Continental breakfast in hotel, FM 32–FM 75; bottle of beer, FM 15–FM 20; 1-mile taxi ride, around FM 30.

TAXES

There is a 22% sales tax on most consumer goods. Nonresidents can recover 12% to 16% by going through the "tax-free for tourists" procedure: When you ask for your tax rebate, you'll get a tax-free voucher and your goods in a sealed bag. Present the voucher and unopened bag at tax-free cashiers when leaving Finland or when departing the EU. These are located at most major airports, on board most long-distance ferries, and at major overland crossings into Norway and Russia. Refunds are available only in Finnish marks. For a high fee, the tax refund can also be sent to your home country.

TIPPING

Tipping is not the norm in Finland, but it is not unheard of, so use your own discretion. Finns normally do not tip cab drivers, but if they do they round up to the nearest FM 5. Give FM 5 to train or hotel porters if you wish. Coat-check fees are usually posted, and tips above this amount are not expected. For all other services, no tip or FM 5 is acceptable.

Outdoor Activities and Sports

For general information, contact the **Finnish Sports Association,** the umbrella organization for the many specific sports associations (⌧ Radiokatu 20, 00240 Helsinki, ☎ 09/1581).

BICYCLING

Route maps are available from local tourist offices and from the Finnish Youth Hostel Association. Pick up a copy of "Finland for Cyclists," an informative booklet available at the Finnish Tourist Board (⌧ Eteläesplanadi 4, 00130 Helsinki, ☎ 09/4030–1300).

BOATING

Contact the **Finnish Yachting Association** (⌧ Radiokatu 20, 00240, Helsinki, ☎ 09/158–2110) or the **Finnish Motorboating Association** (⌧ Radiokatu 20, 00240 Helsinki, ☎ 09/158–2561).

CANOEING

Contact the **Finnish Canoe Association** (⌧ Olympic Stadium, 00250 Helsinki, ☎ 09/494–965).

FISHING

A fishing license (FM 30–FM 200) can be obtained from any post office and is valid for one year. In addition to this general fishing license, a regional fishing permit must also be obtained. The **Finnish Forest and Parks Service** (⌧ Vernissäkatu 4, 01300 Vantaa, ☎ 09/857–841) will provide a brochure listing 100 fishing spots and guidance, too. Pick up a copy of "Finland for Anglers," an informative booklet available at the Finnish Tourist Board.

GOLF

Contact the **Finnish Golf Union** (✉ Radiokatu 20, 00240 Helsinki, ☎ 09/158–2244).

HIKING

Pick up the informative "Finland for Hikers" booklet at the Finnish Tourist Board. If you want to hike on state-owned land in eastern and northern Finland, write to the **Finnish Forest and Parks Service** (✉ Vernissäkatu 4, 01300 Vantaa, ☎ 09/857–841). For organized hiking tours for families with children, as well as beginners, contact **Suomen Latury** (✉ Fabianinkatu 7, 00130 Helsinki, ☎ 09/170–8101). Maps of marked trails throughout Finland can be ordered through **Karttakeskus Pasila** (✉ Opastinsilta 12, 00520 Helsinki, ☎ 09/154–521).

ORIENTEERING

Contact the **Finnish Orienteering Association** (✉ Radiokatu 20, 00240 Helsinki, ☎ 09/158–2453).

SAILING

Some of Finland's most popular inland sailing races are the Hanko Regatta, the Helsinki Regatta, the Rauma Sea Race, and the Päijäinne Regatta. Contact the **Finnish Yachting Association** (☞ *above*) for details.

Sailing vacation packages are organized by **Midnight Sun Charter Ltd.** (✉ PL 126, 00161 Helsinki, ☎ 09/622–2470, 𝖥𝖠𝖷 09/622–2394).

SKIING

Contact **Suomen Latu** (✉ Fabianinkatu 7, 00130 Helsinki, ☎ 09/170–101) for information about ski centers and resorts nationwide. Finnair offers fly–ski packages to the north.

WATERSKIING

Contact the **Finnish Water-Ski Association** (✉ Opintie 2, 20200 Harjevalta, ☎ 02/740–600).

WINDSURFING

Contact the **Finnish Windsurfing Association** (✉ c/o the Finnish Yachting Association, Radiokatu 20, Helsinki, ☎ 09/158–2110).

Telephones

INTERNATIONAL CALLS

You can call overseas at the post and telegraph office, in the "Lennätin" section, where you also may send faxes, telegrams, and telexes. In Helsinki, at Mannerheimintie 11B, the section is open weekdays 9–9, Saturdays 10–4. The "Finland Direct" pamphlet tells you how to reach an operator in your own country for collect or credit-card calls. Use any booth that has a green light, and pay the cashier when you finish. You can also ask for a clerk to arrange a collect call; when it is ready, the clerk will direct you to a booth. The access code for AT&T USADirect calls is 9800/10010. The MCI access code is 9800/10280. Sprint's is 9800/10284.

The front of the phone book has overseas calling directions and rates. You must begin all direct overseas calls with 990 plus country code (1 for the United States/Canada, 44 for Great Britain). Finnish operators can be reached by dialing 020–208 for overseas information or for placing collect calls.

LOCAL CALLS

Finland is gradually moving to the phone-card system, and some phones only accept the *Tele Kortti,* available at post offices, R-kiosks, and some grocery stores in increments of FM 30, 50, 100, and 150. Public phones charge FM 2 and take coins of up to FM 5. Kiosks often have phones. Airport and hotel phones take credit cards. Ringing tones vary but are distinguishable from busy signals, which are always rapid. Most pay telephones have picture instructions illustrating how they operate.

Calls within Finland can be made from any phone. Remember that if you are dialing out of the immediate area you must dial 0 first, followed by the one- to two-digit region code (example: 0–9 for Helsinki), then the number. Drop the 0 when calling Finland from abroad. Finland's country code is 358. Note that local phone numbers can have four to eight digits.

OPERATORS AND INFORMATION

For an operator in the United States, dial 9800/10010; in Canada, dial 9800/10011; and in the United Kingdom, dial 9800/10440. Other important numbers are as follows: 112, general emergency; 10040, news in English; 100–151, wake-up call; 118, Helsinki information; 118, information elsewhere in Finland; 020–208, international information.

Visitor Information

Finnish Tourist Board Head Office (✉ Suomen Matkailun edistämiskeskus, Eteläesplanadi 4, PL 625, 00101 Helsinki, ☎ 09/4030–1211 or 09/4030–1300).

Finnish Tourist Board, 655 3rd Ave., New York, NY 10017, ☎ 212/949–2333; 1900 Avenue of the Stars, Suite 1070, Los Angeles, CA 90067, ☎ 310/277–5226.

Finnish Tourist Board, 66–68 Haymarket, London SW1Y 4RF, ☎ 0171/839–4048.

4 Iceland

On the highway from Keflavík International Airport into Iceland's capital, Reykjavík, the traveler is met by an eerie moonscape under a mystical sub-Arctic sky. The low terrain is barely covered by its thin scalp of luminescent green moss. Here and there columns of steam rise from hot spots in the lava fields. Although trees are few and far between, an occasional scrawny shrub clings to a rock outcropping. The very air smells different—clean and crisp—and it's so clear here you can see for miles.

Updated by
Michael J.
Kissane and
Bernard
Scudder

WELCOME TO ICELAND, one of the most dramatic natural spectacles on this planet. It is a land of dazzling white glaciers and black sands, blue hot springs, rugged lava fields, and green, green valleys. This North Atlantic island offers insight into the ferocious powers of nature, ranging from the still-warm lavas of the 1973 Vestmannaeyjar volcanic eruption and that of Mt. Hekla in 1991 to the chilling splendor of the Vatnajökull Glacier. Generally the country is barren, with hardly a tree to be seen, but its few birches, wildflowers, and delicate vegetation are all the more lovely in contrast. Contrary to the country's forbidding name, the climate is surprisingly mild.

Located so far north—part of the country touches the Arctic Circle—Iceland has the usual Scandinavian long hours of darkness in winter. This may be why Icelanders are such good chess players (Iceland played host to the memorable Fischer-Spassky chess match of 1972). These long nights may also explain why, per capita, more books are written, printed, bought, and read in Iceland than anywhere else in the world. The birth rate is unusually high for Europe, too!

Another reason for its near-universal literacy may be Iceland's long tradition of participatory democracy, dating from AD 930, when the first parliament met at Þingvellir. Today it's a modern Nordic (most would find the term "Scandinavian" too limited) society with a well-developed social welfare system. Women have a unique measure of equality, in that they retain their surname on marriage. Children are given a surname created from their father's first name, so that Magnús, son of Svein, becomes Magnús Sveinsson; Guðrún, daughter of Pétur, becomes Guðrún Pétursdóttir. Guðrún keeps her maiden name even after she marries, since naturally enough she remains her father's daughter rather than becoming her father-in-law's son. Her children will take a patronymic from their father's first name. Perhaps there is no connection, but it is interesting to note that in 1980 Iceland also voted in as president the first woman head of state to take office in a democratic election anywhere in the world, Vigdís Finnbogadóttir. After four four-year terms in office, she did not seek reelection in 1996, and a new president was chosen.

Iceland was settled by Vikings, with some Celtic elements, more than a thousand years ago (the first Norse settlers arrived in AD 874, but there is some evidence that Irish monks landed even earlier). Life in the settlement period and Viking era is described in the sagas that were written in Iceland some three hundred years later, in the 13th century. Icelanders today still speak a language that has changed remarkably little from the ancient Viking tongue in which the sagas were written. The Norse settlers brought to the island sturdy horses, robust cattle, and Celtic slaves, which is why you'll see so many redheads here today. Perhaps Irish tales of the supernatural spawned Iceland's traditional lore of the *huldufólk,* or "hidden people," said to reside in splendor in rocks and crags. Even today some roads and construction projects may be changed to accommodate elfin homes. Look for a sharp, inexplicable bend in the road with a rock beside it, and the chances are you'll be peeping into an elf's private residence.

Iceland is the westernmost outpost of Europe, 800 kilometers (500 miles) from the nearest European landfall (in Scotland) and nearly 1,600 kilometers (1,000 miles) from Copenhagen, which was its administrative capital during Danish rule from 1380 to 1918. In the middle of the North Atlantic, where the warm Gulf Stream from the south confronts

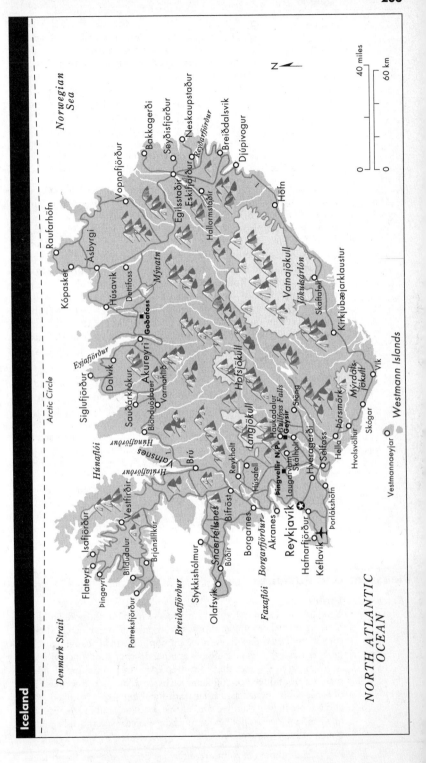

Iceland

Denmark Strait

Norwegian Sea

Arctic Circle

N

40 miles

60 km

Raufarhöfn

Bakkagerði

Seyðisfjörður

Neskaupstaður

Reyðarfjörður

Breiðdalsvik

Djúpivogur

Vopnafjörður

Egilsstaðir

Eskifjörður

Hallormstaðir

Höfn

Ásbyrgi

Kópasker

Húsavik

Dettifoss

Mývatn

Goðafoss

Vatnajökull

Jökulsárlón

Skaftafell

Kirkjubæjarklaustur

Eyjafjörður

Akureyri

Dalvik

Varmahlíð

Siglufjörður

Sauðárkrókur

Blönduós

Hofsjökull

Vik

Mýrdals-jökull

Þórsmörk

Skógar

Westmann Islands

Húnaflói

Húnafjörður

Vatnsnes

Hrútafjörður

Brú

Reykholt

Langjökull

Haukadalur

Gullfoss Falls

Geysir

Stöng

Hella

Hvolsvöllur

Sellfoss

Hveragerði

Skálholt

Þingvellir N.P.

Laugarvatn

Húsafell

Vestfirðir

Flateyri

Ísafjörður

Þingeyri

Bíldudalur

Brjánslækur

Patreksfjörður

Breiðafjörður

Stykkishólmur

Búðir

Ólafsvik

Snæfellsnes

Bifröst

Borgarnes

Borgarfjörður

Akranes

Faxaflói

Reykjavik

Hafnarfjörður

Keflavik

Þorlákshöfn

Vestmannaeyjar

NORTH ATLANTIC OCEAN

the icy Arctic currents from the north, it also straddles the mid-Atlantic ridge, where the edges of two tectonic plates, the North American and the European, meet. As the plates slowly move apart, they create the volcanic activity by which Iceland is still being formed. (There has been an eruption in Iceland on an average of every five years during the past few centuries, the latest being that of Mt. Hekla in January 1991.) Beneath the snowy glaciers and rugged lava are fires that heat hot springs and geysers all over the island, and the resourceful Icelanders have harnessed this thermal energy to heat their homes, power industry, and warm their outdoor swimming pools year-round. Swift rivers produce abundant hydroelectricity, another pollution-free and renewable energy resource.

More than 80% of the island's 103,000 square kilometers (40,000 square miles) remains uninhabited. Ice caps cover 11% of the country, more than 50% is barren, and 6% consists of lakes and rivers. Less than 2% of the land in Iceland is cultivated, although another 23% is grazing land of varying quality. Surrounded by the sea, the Icelanders have become great fishermen, and fish remains the cornerstone of the Icelandic economy. Seafood exports pay for the imported foodstuffs and other goods that today's Icelanders require, all of which could not be produced economically in such a small society (population 267,000). Partly because so much has to be imported, and partly due to valued-added taxes on most goods and services, prices are steep in Iceland. Hotel and restaurant prices are relatively high, but you can always find a number of inexpensive alternatives for lodging, food, and travel—provided you look.

While the cosmopolitan capital, Reykjavík, is a good place to start your visit, any traveler who wants to know Iceland should venture out into the countryside, where rainbow-arched waterfalls cleave mountains with great spiked ridges and snowcapped peaks. Climb mountains, ford rivers, watch birds, catch trout or salmon, even tend sheep and cattle at a typical Icelandic farm. Although the majority of visitors opt to see the country in the warmest months of June, July, and August, a growing minority choose the winter season, when attractions include downhill and cross-country skiing, snowmobiling, and tours by specially equipped 4-by-4 added vehicles across the snow-blanketed landscape. Unless you use a wet suit, the ocean here is always too cold for swimming, but the country is full of hot springs and naturally heated pools where Icelanders from all walks of life—from cabinet ministers on down—congregate for a soak or a swim year-round.

Pleasures and Pastimes

Dining

You have not eaten in Iceland until you've tried the seafood: haddock, halibut, lobster, prawns, scallops, sole, monkfish, ocean perch, shrimp, turbot, *tindabikkja* (starry ray), salmon, and trout caught in clear mountain rivers. Icelandic lamb is another delicacy, its distinct wild taste resulting from the fact that the sheep roam free in the grasslands of the interior and feed on highland herbs. In addition to succulent cuts of fresh lamb, menus also offer traditional *hangikjöt* (smoked lamb) and a more lightly flavored alternative, London lamb. Game, such as duck and reindeer, is popular at more expensive restaurants. Local beef is also of high quality.

Part of the culinary revolution of the last decade included a proliferation of new domestic cheeses, many modeled on European specialty cheeses. Gouda remains number one, but there are many excellent types, including *Búri, Flóa Camembert, Dala-Brie,* and blue cheese. *Skyr,* a delicious yogurtlike food made from skim milk, is especially good with fresh fruit; one of its by-products is a cool drink called *mysa* (whey).

The menu in Iceland used to be very simple—boiled meats and fishes. Now many restaurants offer innovative cuisine, and the best restaurants keep up with the latest culinary trends worldwide. Most menus consist of a marriage of the best in traditional Scandinavian cooking and classic French cuisine.

These days, though, the food spectrum in Reykjavík is even broader. In addition to an array of Asian and Italian eateries, you'll find cafés featuring Mexican, east Indian, and even Lebanese dishes. Ethnic and specialty restaurants are thriving in Iceland. You'll also find several successful vegetarian restaurants. Many of these ethnic eateries, in addition to countless new coffee shops, are found in old midtown Reykjavík.

Most restaurants are licensed to serve the full range of alcoholic beverages—local or imported beer, wines of various origins, cognac, and spirits. Wines, however, are very expensive. Like other Scandinavian countries, Iceland is renowned for its ales and spirits, the most famous being *brennivín*. Its nickname, "black death," alludes not only to the black labels on its bottles but also to the physical effects of drinking too much of it. Brennivín is associated with the midwinter celebrations of Þorrablót, when it is drunk ice-cold and undiluted; more commonly, it is drunk mixed with cola. Icelandic vodkas, such as *Eldurís* and *Icy,* are also of high quality.

The following chart defines the price categories used in the restaurant reviews in this chapter.

CATEGORY	COST*
$$$$	over IKr3,500
$$$	IKr2,500–IKr3,500
$$	IKr1,500–IKr2,500
$	under IKr1,500

per person for a three-course meal, including taxes and service charge and excluding wine

Lodging

Farm holidays are an increasingly popular mode of lodging in Iceland, even among Icelanders themselves. This is a fun way to get to know the country and its people and to explore the magnificent natural surroundings. You can choose from about 110 locations around Iceland, half of them real, working farms (☞ Lodging *in* Iceland A to Z, *below*). Know ahead of time what each farm offers, for they vary widely: You might stay in a separate cottage, in a bed in the farmhouse, or in a sleeping bag in an outbuilding. Some farms have cooking facilities for guests, while others serve full meals if requested. Make reservations well in advance of your visit.

Hotels in Reykjavík and larger towns generally offer the amenities typical of all good hotels: hair dryer, trouser press, telephone, and satellite TV in every room. Many travelers, however, find the simple guest houses adequate, whereas others prefer a bed-and-breakfast at a private home. You will find that even the most basic facilities are clean and hygienic.

The following chart defines the price categories used in the hotel reviews in this chapter. Breakfast is usually included in the price, but inquire to be certain.

CATEGORY	COST*
$$$$	over IKr12,000
$$$	IKr9,000–IKr12,000
$$	IKr6,000–IKr9,000
$	under IKr6,000

All prices are for a standard double room with bath.

Outdoor Activities and Sports

FISHING

The countryside abounds with rivers and lakes where you can catch salmon, sea trout, brown trout, or char. The trout season normally runs April through October 20. Permits can be bought on the spot for a number of lakes and rivers; prices vary from a couple of hundred kronas up to several thousand per day, depending upon the quality of the fishing.

The normal salmon season runs from early June to the end of September. At most rivers, guides and accommodations are provided. (Cabin, cottage, or lodge accommodations are included in the higher rates.) Fishing at the most popular (and expensive) rivers must be booked at least a year in advance (☞ Outdoor Activities and Sports *in* Iceland A to Z, *below*), and you pay $810–$2,000 per fishing rod per day, not including travel. For other rivers you are encouraged to make reservations at least two months in advance and expect to pay $150–$1,000 per rod per day. However, it is often possible to buy salmon-fishing permits during the summer at tackle shops or angling clubs. Fees for salmon rivers are essentially for rental of the stream as much as for a license to fish. Usually there is no catch limit, and only a certain number of fishermen are allowed on each section or "beat."

HIKING

Much of Iceland's wilderness offers breathtaking scenery for hikers, with unparalleled solitude and beauty, especially in the highlands. Vast, surreal volcanic mountain panoramas are crowned by huge glaciers. Wide panoramic vistas punctuated by steamy plumes from hot springs or laced with pristine streams and waterfalls are a photographer's dream. In late summer, hikers may find wild blueberries, crowberries, or bramble berries a special bonus for their efforts.

HORSEBACK RIDING

The Icelandic horse is a purebred descendant of its ancestors from the Viking age, small but strong, exceptionally surefooted, intelligent, and easy to handle. This horse has a particularly interesting stepping style called the *tölt,* or "running walk," which yields an extraordinarily smooth ride. This gait is actually so smooth that a popular demonstration has the rider carrying a tray of drinks at full speed without spilling a drop! Horse lovers from around the world often make a special point of trying these amazing five-speed steeds for themselves. A number of firms offer a variety of tours, from short 1-day trips to 12-day treks, for more experienced riders, across various regions.

SKIING

The winter season begins in January, when the days become longer, and usually lasts through April. There are about 90 ski lifts around the country, and at the larger resorts both alpine and cross-country skiing trails are available. Those less-expert on the slopes can take comfort in the scarcity of trees. You can ride higher up the slopes in style on Jeep tours from late winter through summer.

SNOWMOBILING

This is an exhilarating way for people aged 18 to 80 to experience Iceland's amazing white wonderland. Unlike elsewhere, this glacial grandeur occurs at just over 3,000 feet, so it is only the scenery and the excitement that leave you breathless, not the altitude. You can be on Europe's largest glaciers within two hours of Reykjavík. Supervised tours available from late winter through most of summer include instruction in use of a snowmobile, helmets, and snowsuits. Leaders and end-guides see to it that everybody stays safely on track and that nobody gets left behind.

SWIMMING

Almost every sizable community in Iceland has at least one public outdoor swimming pool. Since most are generally heated by thermal springs, they are usually enjoyed year-round, serving as a magnet for vibrant activity. Locals from all walks of life have been known to form diverse, adult groups that routinely start their day swimming some laps, socializing, and soaking in a hot pot. Not only does this combination of exercise and warm relaxation have health benefits, but it provides a pleasant atmosphere for an effective community grape-vine—you never know with whom you may be swimming. It's only logical that swimming is a required course in schools and this too, may explain why it is the nation's most common sports activity. During summer months with the long daylight, pools are often open until 8 PM.

The most famous pool in the country is about 40 minutes from Reykjavík. The warm, pastel-blue water of this pool, called the Blue Lagoon, has mineral content reputed to be therapeutic.

Pools in the larger towns usually have water slides and kiddie areas. The modern Árbær pool, on the outskirts of Reykjavík has indoor and outdoor sections, a water slide, a whirlpool, saunas, and enclosures for nude sunbathing.

Shopping

The classic gift to bring home from Iceland is the Icelandic sweater, hand-knit in traditional designs; no two sweaters are alike. The thick, soft Icelandic yarn makes a warm fabric that also breathes easily, just right for keeping sailors snug throughout long days at sea. The natural lanolin of the sheep is left in the yarn, which lightly mats its fibers for extra protection from cold and damp.

Pickled herring and smoked salmon are the main fish delicacies. Choose between gravlax (dill-cured salmon), sliced smoked salmon, or whole fillets of smoked salmon or trout. Herring bits come marinated in wine, garlic, and other sauces. You may also want to pick up a small jar of Icelandic lumpfish caviar, or some *harðfiskur* (dried fish), which is best eaten in small bits (and some say a clothespin on the nose). Icelandic lamb is another delicacy; you can buy it frozen or smoked.

Like other Scandinavian countries, Iceland produces local ales and spirits, the most famous being *brennivín*, an 80-proof liquor similar to aquavit. All alcoholic beverages, including imported beer and table wine, are sold exclusively at state-run liquor stores (ÁTVR), which are few and far between. These stores are open weekdays 9–6 and do not take credit cards. Though prices here are high, they are considerably less than in restaurants.

Jewelry is a popular souvenir of Iceland. For upwards of IKr1000 you can buy silver replicas of Viking brooches, rings, necklaces, and religious symbols such as the *Þórshamar* (Thor's hammer), runic letters, and pagan magical letters. A number of silversmiths also design beautiful modern jewelry with Icelandic stones, such as agate, jasper, and black obsidian, as well as other precious stones.

Exploring Iceland

Iceland almost defies division into separate regions with its inlets and bays, thorough lacework of rivers, and complex coastline of fjords all crowned by an unpopulated highland of glaciers and barrens. A certain amount of over-simplification is involved in dividing the country into four compass directions, but since the Icelandic national emblem depicts four legendary symbols—one for each corner of the country—the number is not totally arbitrary.

The West is an expansive section of rugged fjords and lush valleys, starting just north of Reykjavík and extending all the way up to the extreme northwest. The North is a region of long, sometimes broad, valleys and finger-like peninsulas, reaching toward the Arctic Circle. The East has fertile farmlands and the country's largest forest, as well as its share of fjords. The latter, though shorter, are nonetheless attractive. Iceland's South stretches from the lowest eastern fjords, essentially all the way west to the capital's outskirts. It encompasses rich piedmont farmland and wide, sandy coastal and glacial plains. Powerful rivers drain the area, which is dotted with impressive waterfalls. Here you'll find the National Parks of Skaftafell and Þingvellir, as well as the nation's highest peak, Hvannadalshnúkur.

Great Itineraries

With only a few days on your hands, you can experience a fair number of Iceland's major attractions. You can take organized day-trips from Reykjavík (☞ Guided Tours *in* Reykjavík A to Z, *below*) or explore the surrounding area yourself with a rental car. Ask travel agents or tour operators about special offers that allow you to fly one way and take a bus the other. You can theoretically drive the Ring Road skirting the coast around the whole of Iceland in two days, but that pace qualifies as rally driving, and you won't see much. Realistically, you should allow at least a week to travel the Ring Road, which includes roadside sightseeing, overnighting, and just relaxing in the tranquil environment that unfolds the moment you leave Reykjavík. Side jaunts add significant time, as secondary roads are often not paved. When traveling outside Reykjavík, always allow plenty of time to make it back for departing flights.

IF YOU HAVE 4 DAYS

Start by taking a leisurely tour of 🎢 **Reykjavík.** The mix of the old and new in the capital's midtown is highlighted by the difference between the **Alþingishús** (Parliament House) from the 1800s and the **Ráðhús** (Reykjavík City Hall), less than a decade old. At the **Stjórnarráð** (Government House), ask yourself how many countries have their executive offices in a former jail as this country does! The city's outdoor sculpture is as eclectic as its architecture. Colorful rooftops abound, and ornate gingerbreading can be spotted on the better-kept older buildings. The open-air **Árbær Folk Museum** on the outskirts of town is an ideal place to view the evolution of Icelandic lifestyles. From here it's a short walk to the **Árbær pool,** where you can swim indoors or out. Another family favorite is the pool at **Laugardal Park,** where you'll find a **Botanical Garden** and **Farm Animal Park.** Those who prefer a wider, less urban scope, should opt for the "**Golden Circle**" approach on their first day, and take in spectacular **Gullfoss** waterfall, the **Geysir** hot springs area, and **Þingvellir National Park.**

On day two, check the weather report. Depending on conditions, you could take a flight for a day in the 🎢 **Westmann Islands** and see how the islanders have turned the 1973 eruption of **Heimaey** to their advantage. A cruise around the island takes you to bird cliffs, and you may even spot seals or whales. On the third day, spend a leisurely morning in Heimaey, and head back to Reykjavík to take in any missed sights.

If it's sunny in the west on your second day, another alternative is to head for **Snæfellsnes peninsula.** The 9:30 AM **Akraborg ferry** takes you and your vehicle across to Akranes for a leisurely start. Look for dolphins arching along the way and comical puffin birds splashing clear of the ship. Driving north to **Borgarnes** and west out on the peninsula takes you to **Buðir** for lunch, and a stroll on the beach. Start to circle the mystic mountain whose profile changes by the minute, peek in at the small harbor of **Arnarstapa,** and on the peninsula's north, go from **Ólafsvík** on to ⊞ **Stykkishólmur.** If there's time, a cruise among the islets of **Breiðifjörður** will give both a visual and gourmet taste of the life at sea, as fresh shellfish is taken aboard for sampling. On the third day, depart **Stykkishólmur,** cross the Snæfellsnes arm, going south from here to close the loop. Don't worry about making the last ferry at 5 PM from Akranes, because the drive around Hvalsfjörður (Whale Fjord) back to the capital takes you through beautiful country on a good, paved road.

On your last day, be otherwise packed for your flight home, and stop at the surreal **Blue Lagoon,** not far from Grindavík, for a late morning–early afternoon experience that leaves you refreshed and only 20 minutes from the airport for an afternoon flight connection.

IF YOU HAVE 6 DAYS

To the first three days of the tour above, add a morning flight to **Akureyri** on day four. Take a rental car and visit the numerous historical houses here, such as **Matthíasarhús, Nonnahús, Laxdalshús,** and **Davíðshús.** After lunch, take some time at the **Lystigarðurinn** (Arctic Botanic Gardens). Next drive east to the Lake Mývatn area, taking in **Goðafoss** (Waterfall of the Gods) and maybe even **Dettifoss** along the way. Base yourself at ⊞ **Mývatn** and enjoy the rest of day four and a good part of day five in the area, visiting **Dimmuborgir** lava formations, **Námaskarð** sulphur springs, and many shoreline birding areas. Return to ⊞ Akureyri for the fifth night, possibly taking in a trio of fascinating churches at **Saubær, Grund,** and **Möðruvellir.** On day six, leave the north on a morning flight back to Reykjavík, and if time permits, duck in for a quick dip in the **Blue Lagoon,** to relax and reflect on your visit.

IF YOU HAVE 10 DAYS

Having first made reservations for you and your vehicle on the car ferry *Baldur* for day two, follow the Snæfellsnes itinerary from the four-day tour above as far as ⊞ Stykkishólmur and spend the first night there, perhaps taking an evening cruise of the **Brieðarfjörður islands.** On day two take the *Balur* ferry to Brjánslæk, where you disembark and take a rather rough gravel road 1½–2 hours west toward the village of ⊞ **Patreksfjörður** and the incredible bird cliffs at **Látrabjarg.** Overnight in Patreksfjörður and return back along the rugged Barðarstönd coast toward the main part of the country and the inland area of ⊞ **Hrútafjörður,** for night three.

Day four starts with the **Vatnsnes Circle,** where the peculiar, huge **Hvítserkur** stands offshore. Back on Route 1, turn north at **Varmahlíð** and visit the major classic farmstead **Glaumbæ,** and go through **Sauðárkrókur** to the ancient **cathedral at Hólar.** Once back on the Ring Road, end the day in ⊞ **Akureyri.** This major northern community has many attractions to see on day five, including four well-preserved classic houses of significant Icelandic figures: **Matthíasarhús, Nonnahús, Laxdalshús,** and **Davíðshús.** Three interesting churches, **Saubær, Grund,** and **Möðruvellir,** are also regional landmarks worth seeing while based in Akureyri.

Day six leads you east past **Goðafoss** (Waterfall of the Gods) and **Dettifoss,** Europe's most powerful waterfalls, to the aviary crossroads at **Lake Mývatn.** By all means spend at least one night in this area, and on day seven visit the false-craters, the eerie shapes at **Dimmuborgir,** and the bubbling sulphur muds of **Námaskarð.** Day seven is a lucky day for bird-watchers, because nowhere else in Europe is there a greater variety of waterfowl. Spend the night near the lake in ⊞ **Reykjahlíð.** Exhilarated by this natural wonderland, head three hours east to ⊞ **Egilsstaðir** for the eighth night. A nice outing from here is to the large forestry station at Hallormstaðir.

Rest well in Egilsstaðir, since day nine is a long haul around the entire southeast corner of Iceland. You'll see the southeastern fjords, the south end of Europe's largest glacier **Vatnajökull,** the town of **Höfn,** glacier lagoons, and **Skaftafell National Park.** The Ring Road takes you over wide lava flows and broad sandy plains to the town of ⊞ **Vík.** The sea arch of **Dyrhólaey** is just east of town, with its beautiful black beach. Overnight in Vík, and depart early the next morning, about 9 AM, for **Reykjavik.** Along the way you'll pass the stunning waterfalls of **Skogarfoss** and **Seljalandsfoss,** beneath the glacier Eyjafjallajökull. If you have an afternoon departure from Keflavík on this same day, you'll have to be satisfied with a Ring Road glimpse of **Mt. Hekla** to the north of **Hella.** After **Selfoss,** you come to **Hveragerði** and climb up the plateau along the home stretch to the capital area.

When to Tour Iceland

Don't let its name fool you—Iceland is a year-round destination. If you want to go fishing, ride Icelandic horses, or be enchanted by the midnight sun, May through August is the time to visit. Long days of summer may soon have you behaving like a local, stretching your schedule into the wee hours of the morning. Fall defies prediction. It can be a crisp time of berry picking and beautiful colors on the heaths, or of challenging gales, when it's best to join a friend for a cup of coffee and philosophical discussion in a cozy café. Fall and winter evenings bring a surprising assortment of cultural performances, both modern and classic. Nature provides its share of drama with the spellbinding Northern Lights, which are seen most often on cold, clear nights. First-time viewers are sure to be mesmerized by the magical iridescence of huge plumes and curtains of yellow-green to magenta, arching as if alive across the evening sky. On New Year's Eve, Icelanders attempt to outdo the lights by shooting off millions of dollars worth of fireworks. It is hard to imagine a more amazing display than seeing the Northern Lights and fireworks together during a time when there is barely six hours of daylight.

REYKJAVÍK

The sprawling city of Reykjavík is the nation's nerve center, the seat of government, home to almost half of the island's population, and the main point of contact with the outside world. It's a relaxed, casual city where people enjoy having fun, even (or especially) during the dark days of winter.

Set on a bay overlooked by proud Mt. Esja, with its ever-changing hues, Reykjavík presents a colorful sight, its concrete houses painted in light colors and topped by vibrant red, blue, and green roofs.

Any part of town can be reached by city bus, but take a walk around to get an idea of the present and the past. In the Old Town, classic wooden buildings rub shoulders with modern timber and concrete structures. Many once-neglected old houses in the Grjótaþorp and Þingholt districts have been lovingly restored to their former glory. Others have fallen prey to bulldozers or been moved to the Árbær Folk Museum.

Reykjavík's name comes from the Icelandic words for smoke or steam, *reykur,* and for bay, *vík.* In AD 874, Norseman Ingólfur Arnarson saw Iceland rising out of the misty sea and came ashore at a bay eerily shrouded with plumes of steam from nearby hot springs. Today most of the houses in Reykjavík are heated by near-boiling water from the hot springs. Hot water is pumped 27 kilometers (16 miles) from Nesjavellir into the city. Natural heating means that there is little air pollution, so that even though Reykjavík's name means literally Smoky Bay, there's no smoke around. You may notice, however, that the hot water brings a slight sulfur smell to the bathroom.

On the top of Öskjuhlíð, the hill overlooking Reykjavík Airport, up to 24,000 cubic meters of hot water is stored in six vast tanks. Between the tanks and atop them is the Perlan (Pearl), its silvery glass dome visible from all over the city. Opened in 1991, it was built as a monument to Iceland's invaluable geothermal water supplies. Inside you can view art exhibits and see stagings of musical events. The theme of hot water is emphasized by a fountain that spouts every few minutes like a geyser. Above the tanks a circular viewing platform offers panoramic vistas, together with telescopes and multilingual recorded commentaries, plus a coffee bar and an ice cream parlor. The crowning glory is a revolving restaurant under the glass dome; it's pricey, but the view is second to none.

In contrast to the almost treeless countryside, Reykjavík has many tall Icelandic birches, rowans, and willows, as well as imported pines and spruces. At Tjörnin Lake, near the city center, you can observe many of the 17 species of duck that nest in the country.

Reykjavík is the logical starting point for any visit to Iceland. Prices for hotel rooms, restaurant meals, and short tours are easily on a par with those of Amsterdam, Copenhagen, London, and Paris, although you can walk around its historic areas and visit its museums free of charge or for a modest fee.

Exploring Reykjavík

Historic Downtown

Numbers in the text correspond to numbers in the margin and on the map.

A GOOD WALK
What better guiding presence on a tour of historic Reykjavík than the man who started it all, one of the first settlers of Iceland and Reykjavík's founder, Ingólfur Arnarson. Overlooking the old city center and harbor is a grassy knoll known as Arnarhóll, topped by a statue of Ingólfur Arnarson. From here there's a fine panorama of Reykjavík's architectural mélange: 18th-century stone houses, 19th-century small wooden houses, office blocks from the '30s and '40s, and to the north, the black, futuristic Seðlabanki (Central Bank). You'll see Ingólfur facing you from his knoll if you take any of the cross-town buses that stop at Lækjartorg plaza.

Behind him on his left, on Hverfisgata, is the classic white **Landsbókasafnið** ① (Old National Library), with its crests paying tribute to giants of Icelandic literature. Next to it the **Þjóðeikhúsið** ② (National Theater) is basalt black, with its interior also reflecting the natural influence of polygonal lava columns. Back down from these buildings to Lækjargata, just left of Hverfisgata, is the **Stjórnarráð** ③ (Govern-

212

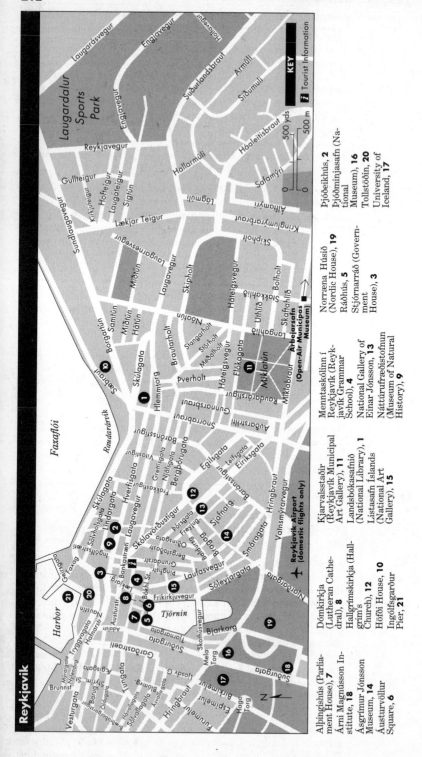

Reykjavik

KEY

i Tourist Information

500 yds

500 m

Laugardalur Sports Park

Faxaflói

Harbor

Tjörnin

Reykjavik Airport (domestic flights only)

Árbæjarsafn (Open-Air Municipal Museum)

N

Alþingishús (Parliament House), **7**
Árni Magnússon Institute, **18**
Ásgrímur Jónsson Museum, **14**
Austurvöllur Square, **6**

Dómkirkja (Lutheran Cathedral), **8**
Hallgrímskirkja (Hallgrím's Church), **12**
Höfði House, **10**
Ingólfsgarður Pier, **21**

Kjarvalsstaðir (Reykjavik Municipal Art Gallery), **11**
Landsbókasafnið (National Library), **1**
Listasafn Íslands (National Art Gallery), **15**

Menntaskólinn í Reykjavík (Reykjavik Grammar School), **4**
National Gallery of Einar Jónsson, **13**
Náttúrufræðistofnun (Museum of Natural History), **9**

Norræna Húsið (Nordic House), **19**
Ráðhús, **5**
Stjórnarráð (Government House), **3**

Þjóðleikhús, **2**
Þjóðminjasafn (National Museum), **16**
Tollstöðin, **20**
University of Iceland, **17**

ment House), which contains the offices of the prime minister. Across Bankastræti and continuing along the hill above Lækjargata and the oversize pavement chessboard on the same side stands the historic mid-19th–century Bernhöftstorfa row of distinct two-story wooden houses, two of which are now restaurants. The building closest to the park is **Menntaskólinn í Reykjavík** ④ (Reykjavík Grammar School).

Next, Lækjargata bends a bit as you go south, and it ends at one corner of the **Tjörnin Lake.** Lækjargata, as its name, "Brook Street," suggests, once linked the lake and the shore. Today it is the busy main artery linking the city center with main roads out to residential parts of town. Overlooking Tjörnin Lake is the modern **Ráðhús** ⑤ (City Hall) on the corner of Vonarstræti and Tjarnargata.

Sometimes known as the heart of the city, Austurvöllur—the area between Tjörnin Lake and the harbor—is where Reykjavík all started. From the lake, follow Templarasund a little over a block north to **Austurvöllur Square** ⑥, which is dominated by a statue of Jón Sigurðsson (1811–79), who led Iceland's fight for independence from Denmark. Sigurðsson looks approvingly at the 19th-century **Alþingishús** ⑦ (Parliament House), which is on Kirkjustræti. Next to the Parliament is the **Dómkirkjan** ⑧ (Lutheran Church) on the corner of Templarasund and Kirkjustræti. From the square toward the harbor runs Pósthússtræti, taking its name from the main post office, which stands on the corner of **Austurstræti.** Lækjartorg plaza is less than a minute away, and here you can end your tour with a coffee at any of several nearby cafés. Ice cream is also available from kiosks. On sunny days the benches along the sidewalks at Austurvöllur Square and the grass itself are a great place to lounge around. However, if you still have some time left, this is a good place to depart for the **Árbæjarsafn** (Open-Air Municipal Museum). From Austurstræti, you can catch a bus to the suburbs to see this re-created Icelandic village. However, if you don't want to leave the city, you can take a detour to the **Náttúrufræðistofnun** ⑨ (Museum of Natural History) and the **Höfði House** ⑩. The museum is near the bus station at Hlemmur, and the Höfði House is just a little farther on, about a fifteen minute walk northeast, from the museum.

SIGHTS TO SEE

★ ❼ **Alþingishús** (Parliament House). One of Iceland's oldest stone buildings, it was built in 1880–1. Iceland's Alþing Parliament held its first session in AD 930 and hence is the oldest continually functional representative parliament in the world. When it's in session (October–May), you can view the proceedings from the visitors' gallery here. Depending on the urgency of the agenda, any number of Iceland's 63 parliament members, who represent a spectrum of five political parties, may be present. Rarely are all of the current 11 ministers, who oversee 15 ministries, on hand together. ⊠ *Austurvellir Square,* ☎ *563–0631.*

Austurstræti. Once closed to cars, this street starts at the junction of Lækjargata and Bankastræti (Bankastræti actually turns into Austurstræti). Austurstræti is now generally open to auto traffic coming downhill from Bankastræti. It should be obvious if the street is closed to traffic, but to be sure, check the sign over the metallic entry arch. If it reads OPI, auto traffic is allowed; if the sign reads LOKA, motorized traffic is prohibited. On select weekends when the street is closed, an impromptu market sometimes develops with vendors selling anything from sweaters to foods and souvenirs.

....

OFF THE
BEATEN PATH

Árbæjarsafn (Open-Air Municipal Museum) – Twenty minutes from midtown Reykjavík you can visit lost centuries—and it's well worth the trip. The "village" here is filled with 18th- and 19th-century houses furnished in old-fashioned style, displaying authentic household utensils and tools for cottage industries. The museum hums with life on summer weekends, when a variety of educational events are organized. You'll see demonstrations of old-fashioned farm activities or taste piping-hot *lummur* (chewy pancakes) from a peat-fired farmhouse stove. Take Bus 10 from Hlemmur station (or 100 from Austurstræti) to the museum. ✉ *Ártúnsblettur,* ☎ *577–1111.* 🎫 *IKr300.* ☉ *June–Aug., Tues.–Sun. 10–6.*

⑥ Austurvöllur Square (East Field). East Field is a peculiar name for a west central square. The reason—it's just east of the presumed spot where first settler Ingólfur Arnarson built his farm, today near the corner of what is now Aðalstræti.

★ **⑧ Dómkirkja** (Lutheran Cathedral). Historically, a place of worship has existed on this site since AD 1200. The current structure—a small, charming church, built 1788–96—is Iceland's cathedral representing the state religion, Lutheranism. It was here that sovereignty and independence were first blessed and endorsed by the church. Iceland's national anthem, actually a hymn, was first sung here in 1874. Since 1845 every session of the Alþing has begun in the fall with all members and cabinet ministers attending a service held here. Among the treasured items here is a baptismal font carved and given by the famous 19th-century master sculptor Bertel Thorvaldsen, who was half Icelandic. ✉ *Austurvellir Square,* ☎ *551–2113.* ☉ *Mon., Tues., Thurs., Fri. 9–5; Wed. 10–5, unless in use for services.*

⑩ Höfði House. Standing solitary, unadorned, and defiantly open to the sea on Borgartún is this historic building. Some say this is where the Cold War began to thaw when Mikhail Gorbachev and Ronald Reagan met at the Reykjavík Summit of 1986. A massive, impressive building, Höfði was built in 1909 as a residence for the French consul. Subsequent owners included the eccentric writer Einar Benediktsson and the British Consul during the early part of WWII. Winston Churchill once stayed here during a wartime visit. Apparently, he wasn't bothered at the time, but the British Consul repeatedly noticed a very haunting presence, which was consistent with legend, and moved out. Eventually, the British sold the house and it became city property. It now serves as a venue for special city business and is decorated with some of the city's art holdings. ✉ *Near the junction of Borgartún and Nótún.*

❶ Landsbókasafnið (Old National Library). Crests on the facade of this impressive building name significant Icelandic literary figures. Erected between 1906 and 1908, the building is now closed and books have been moved to the new **Þjóðarbókhlaðan** (National and University Library), west of the National Museum (☞ Museums and the University, *below*). ✉ *The first building on Hverfisgata at old midtown.*

OFF THE
BEATEN PATH   **Laugardalur Park** - Besides a large swimming pool at this recreational area, there are picnic and barbecuing facilities available, as well as a ♺ **Farmyard Animal Zoo,** which includes goats, cows, horses, seals, and fish. A **Family Park** has a variety of rides and games, such as "crazy bikes"—a driving school complete with miniature traffic lights—and a scale model of a Viking ship. Also in the park is the **Grasagarður** (Botanical Garden) (☎ 553–8870, 🖷 568–1278), with its extensive outdoor collection of native and exotic plants. Coffee and baked items are available in summer at the cozy conservatory. On the edge of Laugardalur Park, opposite the traffic circle at its entrance, is the **Ásmundur Sveinsson Sculpture Museum** (☎ 553–2155), facing Scandic Hótel Esja. To get to the park, take Bus 2 or 5 east or in summer, a Museum Bus runs

hourly from Lækjatorg Plaza to numerous cultural sites, including the park. ✉ *Farmyard Animal Zoo*, ☎ *53–7700.* ▦ *IKr300.* ☉ *Zoo and park summer, daily 10–7; zoo only winter, Mon.–Tues. and Thurs.–Fri. 1–5, weekends 10–6.*

Laugavegur. This has traditionally been the city's main shopping street, although it now meets stiff competition from the Kringlan shopping mall uptown (☞ Shopping, *below*). It takes about 20 minutes to walk down at a leisurely pace, unless, of course, you stop to peruse the high-fashion clothing stores, jewelry and record shops, bookstores, bars, coffeeshops, and restaurants that you pass on the way.

❹ **Menntaskólinn í Reykjavík** (Reykjavík Grammar School). Iceland's oldest educational establishment celebrated 150 years of operation in 1996. Its graduates have from the early days dominated the country's political and social life. Former president Vigdís Finnbogadóttir and numerous cabinet ministers, including Iceland's current prime minister, Davíð Oddsson, are graduates, as were classmates film producer Hrafn Gunnlaugson and well-known author Þórarinn Eldjarn. ✉ *Corner of Amtmannsstígur and Lækjargata.*

❾ **Náttúrufræðistofnun** (Museum of Natural History). Exhibits focus on Icelandic natural history and geology. Among the exhibits is one of the last great auks. It's small as museums go, and the interesting exhibits take only a little time to go through. ✉ *Hverfisgata 116,* ☎ *562–9822.* ▦ *Free.* ☉ *Tues., Thurs., and weekends 1:30–4.*

★ ❷ **Þjóðleikhús** (National Theater). This basalt-black building, just next door to the Landsbókasafnið, was designed by architect Guðjón Samúelsson. Construction started in 1928 but was interrupted for lack of funds during the depression. Before opening in 1950, it was occupied by British troops in WWII. The concrete interior ceiling was an amazing architectural accomplishment of its day. It mimics polygonal basalt columns frequently encountered in Icelandic nature. Except during the biennial Reykjavík Arts Festival, summer is the off-season for the theater. Otherwise it is the venue of a diverse schedule of cultural events, fall to spring. Theatrical works are usually performed in Icelandic, but musicals and operettas are sometimes given in original languages. ✉ *Hverfisgata 19,* ☎ *551–1200.*

❺ **Ráðhús** (City Hall). Modern architecture and nature meet at this building overlooking **Tjörnin Lake**—notice the moss growing on the stone walls. Inside is a tourist information desk and a cozy coffee bar. A three-dimensional model of Iceland is usually on display in the gallery, which hosts various temporary exhibitions. The natural pond attracts birds—and bird-lovers—year-round (one corner of the pond does not freeze) and is also popular with ice-skaters in winter. ✉ *Bounded by Fríkirkjuvegi, Vonarstræti, and Tjarnargata.*

❸ **Stjórnarráð** (Government House). This low white building constructed in the 18th century as a prison today houses the office of the prime minister. ✉ *At Lækjatorg plaza.*

Museums and the University

Art lovers can have a busy time in what is still called Reykjavík's "eastern" quarter (even though it is now geographically in the west and center, as the city expands to the east). This tour will give you a good look at some of Iceland's finest art, both paintings and sculpture.

A GOOD WALK

Start at **Kjarvalsstaðir** ⑪ (Reykjavík Municipal Art Museum), which is reachable by Buses 1, 111, and 114 from downtown. From here, set your bearings on the 210-foot stair-stepped gray-stone tower of **Hall-grímskirkja** ⑫ (Hallgrimur's Church). It is about a 10-minute walk from the art museum. Starting along Flókagata, take a left at Snorrabraut and then a right onto Egilsgata. The church tower offers the city's highest vantage point, with a fantastic panoramic view of the city. After this lofty experience, exit the church and spend some time at the **National Gallery of Einar Jónsson** ⑬, which faces the church across Eiríksgata at the corner with Njarðargata. Sculpture aficionados will enjoy the monumental works that explore a wide range of religious and mythical subjects. After this rather profound display of sculpture, walk four short blocks down Njarðargata and left on Bergsstaðstr:ae:ti to visit the **Ásgrímur Jónsson Museum** ⑭ to see how a well-loved neo-impressionist painter responded to national inspiration.

On Njarðargata go downhill toward the park to Sóeyjargata, where you will turn right, following along the Tjörnin Lake. As you pass the music tower and a bridge dividing the lake, Sóeyjargata becomes Fríkirkjuvegur. You'll see a statue of the Berlin bear and across from him Bertel Thorvaldsen's *Adonis*. He guards the corner of the grounds to the ornate building of Reykjavík's Youth and Recreational Council.

Next to this is the **Listasafn Íslands** ⑮ (National Gallery). Next, leave between the National Gallery and the pleasant, corrugated-iron-covered Fríkirkja (Free Lutheran Church) next door, to go back to Fríkirkjuvegur, which you should follow to the left and over the bridge on Skothúvegur, which divides the lake. At the end of Skothúvegur, you will pass the old Reykjavík cemetery on your right and a traffic circle on your left.

On the south side is the gray concrete building of the **Þjóðminjasafn** ⑯ (National Museum), where you can see Viking artifacts, national costumes, weaving, and more.

The National Museum is on the campus of the **University of Iceland** ⑰, founded 1911. Leave the museum by walking between its main entrance side and the Félagsstofnun Stúdenta (Student Union), which has an excellent international bookshop. Continue south along a tree-lined walk to the main university building.

Head south, directly in front of the main building, above the crescent, and along the tree-lined walk. Once you pass the Löberg Law Building, you will come to Oddi, the Social Sciences Building on your left, and to your right is the Árnargarður Humanities Building. On the ground floor of this building is the **Árni Magnússon Institute** ⑱. It's a must for all visitors interested in the sagas, or ancient literature. After seeing the manuscripts, casual cultural browsers around the university campus may like to look in on a good selection from the University Art Collection, some of which is displayed on the second and third floor of Oddi. A good spot to end your tour is with coffee and cake at the white-and-blue **Norræna Húsið** ⑲ (Nordic House) cultural center on the east edge of campus.

SIGHTS TO SEE

⑱ **Árni Magnússon Institute.** Here you'll see priceless original vellum manuscripts of many of the sagas. These are kept under carefully controlled conditions on the ground floor of the Árnagarður Humanities Building. ⊠ *Suðurgata.* ☎ *552–5540.* ▣ *Free.* ☉ *Mid-June–Aug., Mon.–Sat. 2–4; other times by appointment.*

⑭ **Ásgrímur Jónsson Museum.** Except for rotating exhibits of the artist's extraordinary works in oils and watercolors, Ásgrímur Jónsson's house is left as it was when he died at the age of 82 in 1958. ⊠ *Bergstaðas-*

træti 74, ☎ *551–3644.* 🎫 *Free.* ☉ *June–Aug., Tues.–Sun. 1:30–4; Sept.–Nov. and Feb.–May, weekends 1:30–4.*

⑫ Hallgrímskirkja (Hallgrimur's Church). Completed in 1986 after more than 40 years of construction, the church is named for the 17th-century hymn writer Hallgrímur Pétursson and has a stylized concrete facade recalling both organ pipes and the distinctive columnar basalt formations you can see in certain sightseeing spots out in the country. Depending on timing, you may luck into hearing a performance or practice on the church's huge pipe organ. In front of Hallgrímskirkja is a **statue of Leifur Eiríksson,** the Icelander who discovered America 500 years before Columbus did. (Leif's father was Eric the Red, who discovered Greenland.) The statue, by American sculptor Stirling Calder, was presented to Iceland by the United States in 1930 to mark the millennium of the Alþing parliament. ⊠ *At the top of Skólavörðurstígur,* ☎ *551–0745.* 🎫 *Tower IKr200.* ☉ *May–Sept., daily 9–6; Oct.–Apr., daily 10–6.*

⑪ Kjarvalsstaðir (Reykjavík Municipal Art Museum). This museum is named in honor of Jóhannes Kjarval (1885–1972), the nation's best-loved painter. Kjarval's distinctive lava landscapes and mystical beings, along with various exhibitions of works by contemporary Icelandic and international artists, are displayed here. ⊠ *Flókagata,* ☎ *552–6131.* 🎫 *IKr300.* ☉ *Daily 10–6.*

⑮ Listasafn Íslands (National Gallery). Originally built as an icehouse, this was Reykjavík's hottest nightspot in the '60s. So hot was it, in fact, that it was gutted by fire in 1971. Now it has been adapted and extended as a temple to art. Here you'll find works from impressive collections of 20th-century Icelandic art, including old masters such as Kjarval and Gunnlaugur Scheving, as well as examples of 19th-century Danish art. In addition, the gallery stages international exhibitions, often from Nordic or Baltic countries, or from foreign collections of Icelandic paintings. A pleasant coffee shop with a view of the lake may be a good place to stop and have something to eat or drink. ⊠ *Fríkirkjuvegur 7,* ☎ *562–1000.* 🎫 *IKr200.* ☉ *Jan.–late Dec., Tues.–Sun. noon–6.*

⑬ National Gallery of Einar Jónsson. Looking like a fortress, this gallery is devoted to a pioneer of Icelandic sculpture, Einar Jónsson (1874–1954). There is a sculpture garden open at all times. The figure of Christ in Hallgrímskirkja is by Jónsson, and several of his unmistakable statues can be found around Reykjavík. ⊠ *Njarðargata,* ☎ *551–3797.* 🎫 *IKr200.* ☉ *June–mid-Sept., Tues.–Sun. 1:30–4; late Sept.–Nov. and Feb.–May, weekends only.*

⑲ Norræna Húsið (Nordic House). The white-and-blue cultural center was designed by Finnish architect Alvar Aalto. It includes a library, lecture-concert room, and a gallery in the basement. Scandinavian lectures and other Nordic events take place here. A university chamber concert series and other recitals are often held upstairs. ⊠ *At the corner of Sturlugata and Sæmundurgata,* ☎ *551–7030.* ☉ *Daily 2–7.*

NEED A
BREAK?

Looking for more than food for thought? The **Nordic House** cafeteria offers a tempting selection of sandwiches and cakes. Its bright atmosphere is a favorite haunt of the university intelligentsia.

⑰ University of Iceland. On the large crescent-shape lawn in front of the main university building is a **statue of Sæmundur Fróði,** a symbol of the value of book learning. Legend has it that after studying abroad, Sæmundur made a pact with the devil to get himself home, promising his soul if he arrived without getting wet. The devil changed into a seal to carry him home. Just as they arrived, Sæmundur hit the seal on the head with his Psalter, got his coattails wet, and escaped with his soul. ✉ *Across from Hringbraut Street and diagonally southwest from the park lake.*

16 **Þjóðminjasafn** (National Museum). Viking treasures and artifacts, silver work, wood carvings, and some unusual whalebone carvings are on display as well as historical textile, jewelry, and crafts items. There are also agricultural and maritime history exhibits. If you're feeling hungry, stop for some refreshment in the coffee shop. ✉ *Suðurgata 41,* ☎ *552–8888.* ☞ *IKr200.* ☉ *Mid-May–mid-Sept., Tues.–Sun. 11–5; rest of yr, Tues., Thurs., and weekends noon–5.*

The Harborfront

A GOOD WALK

Reykjavík's harborfront is the ideal place to see the bustling activity of Iceland's major export industry. From the old midtown, it's an easy three-block stroll north from Lækjagata Plaza to the harbor, where fish is the name of the game. Amble along the pier at Ægisgarður, which branches north off Geirsgata, and notice the freighters and colorful fishing and pleasure boats of all sizes as they come and go. Mt. Esja, the guardian mountain of Reykjavík, provides a scenic background, changing its color at the whim of the sun.

You may come across Icelandic youngsters learning their country's most important trade early, with their fishing lines dangling off the quayside. On weekends, a fish market at Miðgarður, just off Geirsgata, offers delicacies fresh from the boats.

The harborfront extends all the way along downtown Reykjavík. Walking a quick two blocks inland as you return toward Lækjagata Plaza brings you to the **Tollstöðin** ⑳ (Customs House). A walk around to the inland side on Tryggvagata reveals Iceland's largest mosaic mural, a harbor scene by Gerður Helgadóttir.

Looping back to the waterfront and curving southwest brings you to **Ingólfsgarður pier** ㉑, closest to Lækjatorg Plaza. Here you may spot one or more of Iceland's Coast Guard vessels docked for service. If you continue walking east along the shoreline, you'll pass the green, dual-pointed sculpture, *Partnership,* a gift to Iceland from a former U.S. ambassador and his wife. Even more dramatic, a few hundred yards farther along the shore is *Sólfar,* a modern tribute and stunning homage to Viking seafarers who first sailed into this harbor 1,100 years ago. It points proudly offshore toward Mt. Esja. The design for this brilliant stainless-steel sculpture won first prize in an art competition in conjunction with Reykjavík's bicentennial.

In good weather the verdant nearby island of **Viðey** is well worth a visit: Do not miss Áfangar, Richard Serra's landscape art arrangement of basalt pillars on the island's northern side.

SIGHTS TO SEE

㉑ **Ingólfsgarður pier.** A berth for Coast Guard vessels, there is a distinctive yellow beacon pylon at the end of this pier. A handful of ships, which tenaciously stood up to the British Navy during the Cod War, still vigorously enforce offshore fishing limits. The Coast Guard is the closest thing Iceland has to a national military. A full-size replica of a Viking ship (the Gokstad ship) was christened the *Íslandingur* (*Icelander*) in 1996. The port authorities set up an exhibition marquee in summer and arrange cruises and guided tours of the harbor on Wednesdays. For details call ☎ 551–5800. ✉ *Just off Faxagata.*

⑳ **Tollstööin** (Customs House). A bureaucratic necessity, especially for an island nation, it's nicely decorated with an impressive mural. ⊠ *Tryggvagata 19.*

Viðey. An unspoiled island in Kollafjörður, this is a wonderful place for a walk and a picnic. If you're a bird-watcher, definitely make the trip—it's a paradise for nesting birds. Here you can also see a little church and the 18th-century governor's residence, Viðey House, now an upscale restaurant. The island is accessible only by ferry (☎ 568–1085 or 562–1632) from its own pier. Buses 4, 8, and 9 stop nearby at the modern Sundahöfn freight harbor.

Dining

$$$$ ✕ **Gallery Restaurant.** Icelandic art covers the walls of this restaurant at the Hotel Holt, and the bar features drawings by Jóhannes Kjarval. Within walking distance of downtown, it has long been in the forefront of Icelandic restaurants, with impeccable service and mouthwatering wild game and seafood dishes. Favorites include gravlax and reindeer. The wine list and whiskey selection are famed for breadth—and price. ⊠ *Hotel Holt, Bergstaðastræti 37,* ☎ *552–5700. AE, DC, MC, V.*

$$$$ ✕ **Grillið.** Near the university campus atop the Saga Hotel, this quiet, cozy restaurant has a spectacular view of the capital and the surrounding hinterlands. Specialties include glazed scallops in blue-cheese sauce and crisp-broiled duck Brigarade. ⊠ *Hagatorg circle,* ☎ *552–5033. AE, DC, MC, V. No lunch.*

$$$$ ✕ **Jónatan Livingstone Mávur.** In fine gourmet tradition, everything here
★ is lovingly prepared by the chef, so don't be in any hurry. Start with one of the exquisite appetizers, such as three types of caviar. For an entrée, try the lamb that veritably melts in your mouth. Inventive sorbet desserts—from rhubarb to mango to sorrel—are just part of this restaurant's magic. ⊠ *Tryggvagata 4–6,* ☎ *551–5520. MC, V.*

$$$$ ✕ **Perlan.** This rotating restaurant atop Reykjavík's hot-water distribution tanks on Öskjuhlíð Hill is the city's trendiest eating place, with the most spectacular views in town (one revolution takes about two hours). The menu is international, with an emphasis on quality Icelandic ingredients, such as succulent lamb and seafood. Fresh is the word here. A special seafood menu changes from day to day, offering the best and freshest fish available. ⊠ *Öskjuhlíð,* ☎ *562–0203. AE, DC, MC, V. No lunch.*

$$$ ✕ **Astro.** By day, this spot is a café. Weeknights you'll find a restaurant that serves up savory Mediterranean- and Asian-influenced dishes. On weekend nights the story is altogether different—the place pulses with a life of its own as it turns into a dance spot, attracting some of Reykjavík's glitterati in an atmosphere described more as a "party house" than a nightclub. ⊠ *Austurstræti 22,* ☎ *552–9222. MC, V.*

$$$ ✕ **Óðinsvé.** Just east of downtown, this cozy restaurant is on the first floor of the Óðinsvé Hotel. Decorated in pastel colors, half the dining area is under a covered porch. The chefs cook in a Scandinavian-French style, with an emphasis on seafood. Choice appetizers include the fish chowder. Try the grilled lamb or butter-fried trout with almonds and shrimp for the main course; the best dessert is hot apple strudel. ⊠ *Óðinstorg,* ☎ *552–5090. AE, DC, MC, V.*

$$$ ✕ **Pasta Basta.** This small restaurant has four seating options: an area with intimate booths on the lower level; a small, bright conservatory at ground level; an open-air, canvas-covered patio (if the weather's good); and if it's really good, they lift the tent-top back, leaving you to sit under the large silver rowan tree, which they managed to spare when the place was converted. Crayons are provided so the kids can draw on the paper table cloth if they get fidgety. The fare is mostly Italian with some

Mediterranean flair. You may also want to visit the **La Dolcé Vita** bar upstairs. ⊠ *Klapparstíg 38,* ☎ *561–3131. MC, V. No lunch on winter weekends.*

$$$ ✕ **Við Tjörnina.** This restaurant on the second floor of a typical, cor-
★ rugated-iron-clad early-20th-century house is often claimed to be the best in Iceland. The owner, epicure Rúnar Marvinsson, runs the kitchen himself, turning out imaginative cuisine using unusual ingredients. Scallops in tomato-curry sauce is a good appetizer choice; *tindabikkja* (starry ray) with grapes, capers, and Pernod is an unforgettable entrée. Lunchtime can be a bargain, with a dish of the day for IKr1,000. The old-fashioned decor here remains true to the house, with a hand-carved bar and chairs, embroidered tablecloths, and crocheted drapes. ⊠ *Templarasund 3,* ☎ *551–8666. AE, MC, V.*

$$ ✕ **Carpe Diem.** Attached to Hotel Lind, this restaurant is sparsely dec-orated in a pleasantly peculiar way with mechanical paraphernalia. Lunch dishes include huge sandwiches or pasta with soup. Dinner entrées are equally hearty. ⊠ *Rauðarárstíg 18,* ☎ *552–4555. AE, MC, V.*

$$ ✕ **Hornið.** This welcoming bistro is light and airy with lots of natural wood, potted plants, and cast-iron bistro tables. The emphasis is on pizzas and pasta, but there's also a selection of meat and fish dishes; try the lamb pepper steak with mushrooms cooked in garlic. It's open all day for full meals or snacks; there's a variety of delicious cakes to go with the obligatory espresso. ⊠ *Hafnarstræti 15,* ☎ *551–3340. AE, DC, MC, V.*

$$ ✕ **Potturinn og pannan.** Here you'll get bang for your buck. One of the city's best buys, this restaurant is only a 10- to 15-minute walk from the uptown hotels. There's an American-style open salad bar and plenty of fresh-baked whole-grain bread to choose from. Excellent meat and fish dishes are served here. Try the marinated lamb served with green-pepper sauce. Meal prices include soup, bread, and coffee. Tiled floors, copper light fixtures, and tables with benches create a simple yet pleas-ant setting. Service is speedy and efficient, but it's a popular spot, so you may have a wait during peak lunch and dinner hours. An inexpensive children's menu and a play corner for the youngest diners make this a popular place for families. ⊠ *Brautarholt 22 (entered from Nóatún),* ☎ *551–1690. Reservations not accepted. AE, DC, MC, V.*

$$ ✕ **Þrír Frakkar hjá Úlfari.** This fine little charming restaurant with yel-lowish walls, wood paneling, and wrought-iron tables is in a residen-tial area not far from downtown. The menu highlights first-rate seafood, including succulent whale. Try the vegetable broth as an appetizer, but-ter-fried trout or the Portuguese-style bacalao (codfish stewed or fried with vegetables) as a main course, and apple pie for dessert. ⊠ *Bal-dursgata 14,* ☎ *552–3939. AE, DC, MC, V.*

$ ✕ **Bæjarins beztu.** The most famous, most popular fast-food eatery in Iceland may easily escape you. Facing the harbor, set in a parking lot at the corner of Tryggvagata and Pósthússtræti, this is the home of the original Icelandic hot dog; one person serves about a thousand hot dogs a day out the window of a tiny hut—watch how fast his or her hands move. Ask for *ayn-ah-mud-lou* (pronounced quickly in monotone with stress on "mud"), which means "one with everything": mustard, tomato sauce, *rémoulade* (mayonnaise with finely chopped pickles), and chopped raw and fried onions. Eat standing up or at one of the small outdoor tables. It's open from 10 AM until midnight. ⊠ *Tryg-gvagata and Pósthússtræti, no phone. No credit cards.*

Cafés

Try **Kaffi Reykjavík** (⊠ Vesturgata 2, ☎ 562–5530) in a picturesque 19th-century wooden building, with a veranda where you can sit in the sun; **Fógetinn** (⊠ Aðalstræti 10, ☎ 551–6323), an intimate spot with low ceilings; or arty **Cafe Solon Islandus** (⊠ Bankastræti 7a, ☎ 551–2666), where you can see some modern art, eat a snack, and have a perfect view of the cultural avant-garde. Also try **Tíu Dropar** coffeehouse (⊠ Laugavegur 27), which serves a tantalizing selection of homemade cakes and a variety of coffees.

Lodging

Hotels are located all around Reykjavík, with the Borg, Holt, and Óðinsvé hotels closest to downtown. Everything from modern, first-class Scandinavian-style hotels to inexpensive bed-and-breakfasts is available. Inquire at the desk whether your hotel offers complimentary admission tickets to the closest swimming pool.

There are many guest houses and bed-and-breakfasts around town that offer basic accommodations at relatively low prices. These accommodations can be booked in advance through your travel agent. The **Tourist Information Center** (⊠ Bankastræti 2, ☎ 562–3045, FAX 562–3057) has registers of guest houses (from about IKr3,000–IKr5,000 a night) and B&B accommodations (about IKr2,200–IKr3,600) in and around Reykjavík. The **Salvation Army** (⊠ Kirkjustræti 2, ☎ 561–3203) charges IKr3,000 for a double room without bath or breakfast. The **Reykjavík Youth Hostel** (⊠ Sundlaugavegur 34, ☎ 553–8110, FAX 588–9201) has 108 beds, without breakfast, for around IKr1,250 per night.

$$$$ 🏨 **Grand Hotel Reykjavik.** Formerly a Holiday Inn, this hotel was renovated in 1995 and resurrected to its new status. The rooms are good-size by European standards. The hotel offers free access to Laugardalur Park, including its pool. ⊠ *Sigtún 38,* ☎ *568–9000,* FAX *568–0675. 100 rooms, 3 suites. Restaurant, bar, lobby lounge, convention center. AE, DC, MC, V.*

$$$$ 🏨 **Hótel Borg.** Reykjavík's oldest hotel, built in 1930, has been refur-
★ bished to its original Art Deco glory. All rooms have satellite TV, VCR, and CD player; a direct fax to your room is provided on request. The rooms, which are truly luxurious, aim to combine good, old-fashioned quality with modern comfort. Tasteful prints, some antique, adorn the walls of the elegantly decorated rooms, which have fluffy down comforters covering the beds. The hotel is in the heart of the city, overlooking Austurvöllur and close to Parliament House. Breakfast here is great with home-baked breads, cheeses, cold cuts, fruit, and more. ⊠ *Pósthússtræti 11,* ☎ *551–1440,* FAX *551–1420. 32 rooms, 5 suites. Restaurant, bar. AE, DC, MC, V.*

$$$$ 🏨 **Hótel Holt.** Excellent service and a gourmet restaurant make this quietly elegant hotel a favorite among business travelers. Though the rooms are comparatively small by modern standards, many are decorated with works by leading Icelandic artists. The location is in a pleasant neighborhood close to the center of town. ⊠ *Bergstaðastræti 37,* ☎ *552–5700,* FAX *562–3025. 42 rooms, 12 suites. Restaurant, bar, lobby lounge, meeting room. AE, DC, MC, V.*

$$$$ 🏨 **Hotel Reykjavík.** Built in 1993, this hotel, within a few blocks of Reykjavík's Kjarvalsstaðir Municipal Art Museum and the Hlemmur bus station, is operated by the same management as the Grand Hotel. The hotel has two good ethnic restaurants: the Korean **Café Kim** and the Lebanese **Marhaba.** ⊠ *Rauðarárstígur 39,* ☎ *562–6250,* FAX *562–6350. 53 rooms, 7 suites. AE, DC, MC, V.*

$$$$ 🏨 **Hótel Saga.** Just off the university campus, this hotel is a 15-minute walk from most museums, shops, and restaurants. All rooms are above the fourth floor and have spectacular views. ⊠ *Hagatorg,* ☎ *552–9900,* FAX *562–3980. 216 rooms with bath, 8 suites. Restaurant, 6 bars, grill,* *no-smoking rooms, sauna, health club, nightclub, meeting rooms, travel services. AE, DC, MC, V.*

$$$$ 🏨 **Scandic Hótel Loftleiðir.** This hotel offers a wide range of amenities but is in a rather remote location. The advantage, however, is nearby Öskjuhlíð Hill, where you can take pleasant walks among the trees and shrubs, enjoy the superb view, and stroll up to Perlan for ice cream. Rooms are decorated in modern Scandinavian style, with pine furniture and pastel fabrics. You can get here by taking bus route 1. ✉ *Reykjavík Airport,* ☎ *505–0900,* FAX *505–0905. 220 rooms, 1 apartment suite. Restaurant, bar, pool, sauna, convention center, travel services. AE, DC, MC, V.*

$$$ 🏨 **Hótel Ísland.** This chunky, seven-story, postmodern silver-and-blue hotel is close to the Laugardalur park and recreation area. The light and airy rooms are decorated in peach-and-brown pastel floral prints, with dark wood and smooth, curved shapes. The views over the bay and Mt. Esja are terrific. ✉ *Ármúli 9,* ☎ *568–8999,* FAX *568– 9957. 119 rooms, 3 suites. Restaurant, bar, kitchenettes (5 rooms only), nightclub. AE, DC, MC, V.*

$$$ 🏨 **Hótel Lind.** This quietly unpretentious place is uptown, a block south of the Hlemmur bus station. Rooms are freshly decorated in shades of red and blue. The clientele is largely Icelanders from the countryside attending conferences or cultural events in Reykjavík. ✉ *Rauðarárstígur 18,* ☎ *562–3350,* FAX *562–3351. 44 rooms. Restaurant, bar, meeting rooms. AE, DC, MC, V.*

$$ 🏨 **City Hotel.** This small hotel stands on a quiet, centrally located residential street. Rooms are done in light colors, with furnishings of pale wood. ✉ *Ránargata 4a,* ☎ *511–1155,* FAX *552–9040. 31 rooms with bath or shower. Restaurant. AE, DC, MC, V.*

$$ 🏨 **Hotel Leifur Eiríksson.** Right across the street from the hilltop church of Hallgrímskirkja, this plain but pleasant hotel is conveniently situated within a short walk of most of Reykjavík's major attractions. Rooms are decorated in floral prints; some have balconies. ✉ *Skólavörðustígur 45,* ☎ *562–0800,* FAX *562–0804. 29 rooms with shower. Restaurant, bar. AE, DC, MC, V.*

$ 🏨 **Hotel Garður.** This student residence on the university campus offers basic but comfortable accommodations from June through August during summer vacation. Rooms are plainly furnished and have washbasins. ✉ *Hringbraut,* ☎ *511–5900,* FAX *483–4775 (bookings through Hótel Örk,* ☎ *483–4700). 44 rooms. AE, DC, MC, V.*

$ 🏨 **Smárar Guest House.** This guest house near the main bus terminal provides simple, clean accommodations. The rooms have washbasins. Guests have access to a fully equipped kitchen. ✉ *Snorrabraut 61,* ☎ *562–3330,* FAX *551–8945. 15 rooms. AE, DC, MC, V.*

Nightlife and the Arts

A wide variety of artistic activity can be found all over Reykjavík for most of the year, although the performing arts scene tends to quiet down somewhat in summer, except on even-numbered years, when the Reykjavík Arts Festival occurs in June. This event has featured performers ranging from Luciano Pavarotti to David Bowie. Something interesting is always going on in the field of the visual arts.

Consult the bimonthly *Around Reykjavík,* and the biweekly *What's on in Reykjavík,* both available at hotels, for events of interest. Most hotels offer satellite TV channels from Europe and the United States, in addition to State TV and three commercial channels, which all broadcast a large amount of outside material (mainly American) in original languages with subtitles.

Nightlife

Nightlife in Reykjavík essentially means two types of establishments: nightspots offering dancing with live music where an entrance fee is charged, and pubs, where entrance is free. Nightspots usually enforce some basic dress rules, so men should wear a jacket and tie and women should avoid wearing jeans. Pubs make no such demands. Some pubs, however, also have small dance floors and often charge an entrance fee if a live band is playing. Both pubs and nightspots charge high prices for drinks. The minimum age for entering such licensed premises is 18, for buying alcohol, 20.

The fashionable place to see and be seen is **Café Solon Islandus** where live music—everything from blues to classical—goes on into the wee hours on weekends. The latest arrival on the Reykjavík social scene is **Kaffi Reykjavík,** a spacious coffee bar–pub–restaurant (☞ Cafés, *above*). **Hótel Ísland** (✉ Ármúli 9, ☎ 568–7111), the largest restaurant and dance hall in Iceland, swallows more than a thousand guests at a time and offers nightclub shows and reviews.

The Arts

FILM

The eight movie houses around the capital have up to six screens each and for the most part show recent English-language films (with Icelandic subtitles). In summer, recent Icelandic films are screened with English subtitles for tourists. For listings, see the daily newspaper *Morgunblaðið*. The **Háskólabíó** (University Cinema, ☎ 552–2140) is on Hagatorg circle, near the university.

FOLKLORE

Traditional folklore in English, based on the Icelandic sagas and folktales, is offered in summer by the **Light Nights** actors' show at Tjarnargata 12 (opposite City Hall) and sometimes at other venues. Another group performs in English daily at 4 PM in summer at the Kaffileikhús (✉ Hlaðvarpinn, Vesturgata 3, ☎ 551–9055).

MUSIC

Visiting musicians play everything from classical to jazz, opera to rock. The **Icelandic Opera** (☎ 551–1475), a resident company, performs in winter at its home on Ingólfsstræti. The **Nordic House** (☎ 551–7030), **Sigurjón Ólafsson Sculpture Museum** (☎ 553–2906), **Gerðuberg Cultural Centre** (☎ 557–9166) and such churches as **Langholtskirkja** (☎ 553–5750) and **Hallgrímskirkja** (☎ 551–0745) are popular venues for classical concerts. The **Iceland Symphony Orchestra** (☎ 562–2255) plays regularly during the winter, usually alternate Thursday and Saturday evenings, at the University Cinemas.

THEATER

In winter, the **National Theater** (✉ Hverfisgata, ☎ 551–1200) and **City Theater** (✉ Listabraut, ☎ 568–0680) stage plays by Icelandic writers, such as Nobel Prize winner Halldór Laxness, as well as works by such diverse dramatists as Henrik Ibsen, Tennessee Williams, and Rodgers and Hammerstein.

Outdoor Activities and Sports

Fishing

In Reykjavík, contact the **Angling Club of Reykjavík** (✉ Háaleitisbraut 68, ☎ 568–6050) or the **Federation of Icelandic River Owners** (✉ Bolholt 6, ☎ 553–1510). Reykjavík tackle shops include **Veiðihúsið** (✉ Nóatún 17, ☎ 561–4085) and **Vesturröst** (✉ Laugavegur 178, ☎ 551–6770).

Golf

At the southern tip of Seltjarnarnes, the westernmost part of the Reykjavík area, **Golfklúbbur Ness** (✉ Suðurnes, ☎ 561–1930) has a well-kept 9-hole course with a great view in all directions. **Golfklúbbur Reykjavíkur** (✉ Grafarholti, ☎ 568–2215) is the granddaddy of them all, a challenging 18-hole course just east of Reykjavík.

Handball

Team handball, a national obsession and a big crowd-puller, is *the* winter sport in Iceland. For fast, furious, and exciting matches between Iceland's leading teams, as well as thrilling confrontations with some of the world's best handball nations, contact the **Handball Federation** (☎ 568–5422).

Horseback Riding

Two stables in the Reykjavík area rent horses by the hour or by the day. **Laxnes Horse Farm** (✉ Mosfellsdalur, ☎ 566–6179, or 562–1011 at Reykjavík Excursions) offers 3-hour riding tours for IKr3,000, including guides and transportation to and from Reykjavík. **Icelandic Riding Tours** (✉ Bæjarhraun 2, Hafnarfjörður, ☎ 565–3044) offers 2- to 7-hour rides for IKr2,000–IKr7,000, which also includes guides and transportation from Reykjavík hotels.

Jogging

In the crisp, clean air of the Reykjavík area, jogging is a pleasure on the wide sidewalks and in the parks. Favorite routes are around **Tjörnin Lake**, in **Laugardalur Park**, **Miklatún Park**, and Öskjuhlíð. For distance runners, there is the **Reykjavík Marathon** in August.

Skating

The artificial skating rink in **Laugardalur**, adjacent to the Botanical Gardens and Farm Zoo, rents skates and is open October–April.

Skiing

In wintertime, try the downhill and cross-country skiing at the **Bláfjöll** (☎ 561–8400) and **Skálafell** (☎ 566–6095) areas outside Reykjavík. Both have ski lifts, are within a 30-minute drive of the capital, and can be reached by BSÍ bus (☎ 552–2300).

Soccer

This favorite sport is played in summer before thousands of fans. A number of Icelandic soccer players are with professional soccer teams in Europe, and most come home to participate in international matches. The most important matches are played at **Laugardalsvöllur Stadium** (☎ 553–3527; take Bus 2 or 5 going east). Buy tickets at the box office just before the game, or inquire at downtown bookstores for advance sales.

Swimming

There are 11 swimming pools in the greater Reykjavík area, some with saunas. Rules of hygiene are strictly enforced—you must shower thoroughly, without a swimsuit, before entering the pool. The pools of **Vesturbær** at Hofsvallagata (Bus 4) and **Laugardalur** (Bus 2 or 5 going east) are favorite summer haunts. Both are open weekdays 7 AM–9:30 PM, weekends 8–7:30. A locker and access to the swimming pool cost IKr150, and you must bring or rent a towel. Use of the sauna is extra. Swimwear can be rented. *Note:* Swimming pools are one of the few places in Iceland where you should be on your guard against petty theft. If you are wearing snazzy running shoes, lock them up in a locker.

Shopping

The main shopping streets downtown are on and around **Austurstræti**, **Aðalstræti**, **Hafnarstræti Bankastræti**, **Laugavegur**, and **Skólavörðustigur**.

The **Kringlan Mall** is on the east side of town at the intersection of Miklabraut and Kringlumýrarbraut; take Bus 3 or 6 from Lækjartorg, or Bus 8 or 9 from Hlemmur. You'll also find crafts workshops and galleries all around town.

Specialty Stores

ART GALLERIES

Gallery Borg (⊠ Adalstræti 6, ☎ 552–4215 or 552–4211) displays the latest works by contemporary Icelandic artists.

Gallery Fold (⊠ Laugavegur 118d, entrance from Raaudarárstíur, ☎ 551–0400) has a large selection of prints, drawings, paintings, and sculpture by contemporary Icelandic artists, as well as some older Icelandic art.

Listhús (⊠ Engjateigur 17–19), opposite the Scandic Hotel Esja, is a complex of art stores and ateliers where you will find Icelandic arts and crafts. **Snegla** (⊠ Grettisgata 7, ☎ 562–0426) is operated by a group of accomplished women artists who work in many different media.

COINS AND STAMPS

Hjá Magna (⊠ Laugavegur 15, ☎ 552–3011) offers a wide selection. Due to the limited size of the issues involved, a number of Icelandic stamps and coins are considered valuable items.

Postphil (⊠ Ármúli 25, Box 8445, 128 Reykjavík; take Bus 11 from Hlemmur station). The post office has a special philatelic service with subscription schemes for new issues.

CRAFTS

Long the staple purchase of visitors, woolens include both traditional hand-knit sweaters (a good sweater is priced at about IKr6,500 to IKr8,000) and stylish, multicolored new designs. Lava ceramics, sheepskin rugs, and Viking-inspired jewelry are also popular souvenirs. **Álafoss** (⊠ Posthússtræti 13, ☎ 551–3404) sells primarily woolens but also stocks other souvenirs. **Handprjónasambandið** (⊠ Skólavörð 19, ☎ 552–1890), the Handknitting Association, has its own outlet, selling, of course, only handknits. **Islandia** (⊠ Kringlan mall, ☎ 568–9960) offers a range of woolens, giftware, and souvenirs.

Íslenskur Heimilisiönaður (⊠ Hafnarstræti 3, ☎ 551–1785), the Icelandic Handcrafts Center, offers knitted and woven woolen goods, as well as materials and kits for those who wish to try knitting or tapestry for themselves, and handmade gifts of glass, pottery, and precious metals. **Rammagerðin** (⊠ Hafnarstræti 19, ☎ 551–1122; ⊠ Scandic Hotel Loftleiðir, ☎ 552–5460; ⊠ Scandic Hotel Esja, ☎ 568–1124) stocks a large variety of hand- and machine-knitted woolen goods, as well as a range of hand-made souvenirs.

Street Markets

In summertime **Lækjartorg** sometimes fills with the stands of outdoor merchants offering anything from woolens, records, and books to vegetables, fruit, and bread. On weekends (and occasional weekdays) the lively and colorful **Kolaport** flea market (☎ 562–5030, FAX 562–5099) is open in an old ground-floor warehouse by the harborside (look for the big banner), where you may find almost anything on sale and almost certainly something you fancy.

Reykjavík A to Z

Arriving and Departing

BY PLANE

Keflavík Airport (☎ 425–0600), 50 kilometers (30 miles) southwest of the capital, hosts all international flights. For reservations and information in Reykjavík, contact **Icelandair** (☎ 505–0300) or **SAS** (☎ 562–2211).

Reykjavík Airport (☎ 569–4100) is the central hub of domestic air travel in Iceland. For reservations and information, contact **Icelandair** (☎ 505–0200), **Íslandsflug** (☎ 561–6060), or **Ernir** (☎ 562–4200).

Between the Airport and Downtown. The **Reykjavík FlyBus** (☎ 562–1011) leaves Keflavík (from directly outside the terminal building) and arrives in Reykjavík at the Scandic Loftleiðir Hotel at Reykjavík Airport. From there you can take a taxi or municipal bus to your destination. Buses are scheduled in connection with each flight arrival and departure. For departures catch the FlyBus at the Saga, Esja, and Scandic Loftleiðir hotels and the Grand Hotel Reykjavík. The FlyBus also leaves the youth hostel in Laugardalur at 5 AM daily June–August. The fare is IKr500 per person. The ride takes 40–50 minutes.

From Reykjavík Airport, the municipal (**SVR**) Bus 5 leaves from the Icelandair terminal on the western side of the airport. Other airlines operate from the east terminal (behind the Loftleiðir Hotel), which is served by Bus 17.

A taxi from the airport to Reykjavík is a little faster than the FlyBus and will cost IKr4,500, though if you share it with others you can split the cost. Taxi companies include **Aðalstöðin** (☎ 421–1515 or 425–2525) and **Ökuleiðir** (☎ 421–4141). From Reykjavík Airport a taxi to your hotel will cost around IKr600; there are direct phones to taxi companies in the arrivals hall.

Getting Around

The best way to see Reykjavík is on foot. Many of the interesting sights are in the city center, within easy walking distance of one another. There is no subway system.

BY BUS

The municipal bus (**SVR**) system (☎ 551–2700) is extensive, cheap, and reliable. Buses run from 7 AM to midnight or 1 AM. On most routes, buses run every 20 minutes during the day and every half hour evenings and weekends. Bus stops are marked by signposts with an "SVR" on top or by a bus shelter with a posted list of routes to outlying communities in the greater Reykjavík area. At press time, the flat fare within Reykjavík was IKr120, payable to the driver upon boarding. You can buy strips of tickets at a lower price from the drivers or at the main terminals. The fare allows you to travel any distance in town; if you have to change buses, ask for *skiptimiða* (*skiff*-tee-mee-tha), a transfer ticket that you give the second bus driver. The SVR system connects with AV, the bus system in the Kópavogur, Garðabær, and Hafnarfjörður municipalities south of Reykjavík. Buses marked with the "AV" logo (which actually looks more like a stylized, slanting "N") travel circuits about once an hour. If you plan an extended stay in the Reykjavík area, it may be worthwhile to buy a monthly season ticket, the Green Card, valid on all SVR and AV routes. A recent innovation in the bus system is a summertime Museum Bus, which makes four hourly cycles daily, departing Lækjatorg Plaza and making 16 stops at cultural sites. A ticket costs IKr400 and is good for unlimited travel for three days. Also, Tourist Cards, available from the Tourist Information Center (☞ Contacts and Resources, *below*), entitle the holder to unlimited bus travel in the city. *Note:* At press time a new bus schedule was being implemented, so check for current routes and rates.

BY CAR

The excellent bus system and quick, inexpensive taxis make automobiles unnecessary for getting around town, doubly so considering how expensive car rentals and gasoline are. Gas stations are usually open 7:30 AM–11 PM. Most have self-service pumps that accept IKr500, and IKr1,000 notes. Among the car rentals in Reykjavík are **Icelandair/Hertz** (☎ 505–0600, FAX 505–0650), **Geysir** (☎ 568–8888, FAX 581–3102), **Avis** (☎ 562–4433, FAX 562–3590), and **Europcar** (☎ 568–6915). **Gamla bílaleigan** (☎ 588–4010, FAX 551–4014) rents slightly older cars at lower prices.

BY TAXI

Most cabs are late-model fully equipped passenger sedans, including many Mercedes. They have small TAXI signs on top and can be hailed anywhere on the street; the LAUS sign indicates that the cab is available. There are taxi stands in a few locations around the city, but it is common to order a taxi by phone. Normally you will have to wait only a few minutes, except in the early hours of Saturday and Sunday mornings (about 3 AM), when all the nightspots in town close simultaneously. All cars are radio-equipped and respond to calls within minutes. Some taxis accept major credit cards, but you must state that you want to pay with a credit card when requesting the taxi. Fares are regulated by meter; rides around Reykjavík run between IKr500 and IKr800. Call **BSR** (☎ 561–0000), **Bæjarleiðir** (☎ 553–3500), or **Hreyfill** (☎ 588–5522). There is no tipping.

Contacts and Resources

BOOKSTORES

Eymundsson (✉ Austurstræti 18, ☎ 551–1130; also opposite Hlemmur bus station and at the Kringlan mall) carries foreign books as well as foreign newspapers and magazines, but these may be several days old. **Mál og menning** (✉ Laugavegur 18, ☎ 552– 4240; ✉ Síðumúli 7–9, ☎ 568–8577), one of the largest bookstores in the city, has an extensive foreign section. **Bóksala stúdenta** (Students Union Building, ✉ Hringbraut, next to Gamli Garður on the university campus, ☎ 561–5961) stocks a large selection of books in foreign languages.

DOCTORS AND DENTISTS

Six health centers with officially appointed family doctors receive patients on short notice 8–5 weekdays. Call the **Reykjavík Health Center** (☎ 552–2400) or look under *Heilsugæslustöð* in the phone book; at other times, call **Læknavakt** (Duty Doctors, ☎ 552–1230).

EMERGENCIES

The emergency ward at **Sjúkrahús Reykjavíkur city hospital** (☎ 569–6600) is open 24 hours a day.

GUIDED TOURS

Kynnisferðir (Reykjavík Excursions), owned by a consortium of travel companies, is the main tour operator in and out of Reykjavík. Kynnisferðir has offices at the Scandic Loftleiðir Hotel (☎ 562–1011) and at Bankastræti 2 (☎ 562–4422), adjacent to the Tourist Information Center. "Reykjavík City-Sightseeing" is a daily 2½-hour tour that provides useful orientation for newcomers; it includes museums and art galleries, shopping centers, and the like.

Many travel agencies offer English-speaking personal guides for tours of the city and outlying areas. Contact **Úrval-Útsýn Travel** (✉ Lágmúli 4, ☎ 569–9300, FAX 568– 5033) or **Samvinn Travel** (✉ Austurstræti 17, ☎ 569–1010, FAX 552–7796). The **Association of Travel Guides** (✉ Suðurlandsbraut 30, 108 Reykjavík, ☎ 588–8670) can provide qualified guides who work in a variety of languages and have different specialties.

LATE-NIGHT PHARMACIES

Reykjavík pharmacies take turns staying open around the clock. Signs indicating which establishment has the night watch (*næturvakt*) are posted in all pharmacies, and details are also published in newspapers. For information, call ☎ 551–8888.

OPENING AND CLOSING TIMES

Even though many Reykjavík citizens like to stay up late, most of the capital closes down early on weekdays, and Sunday remains largely a sabbatical day. **Bars, discotheques,** and **dance clubs** stay open until 1 AM Monday–Thursday and 3 AM Friday and Saturday. **Bus service** stops between midnight and 1 AM, but **taxis** run around the clock.

Post offices are open weekdays 8:30–4:30. The main post office at Ármúli 25 and the post office in the Kringlan mall remain open until 6 on weekdays, and the post office at the BSÍ bus terminal is also open 9–1 on Saturday. **Museums and galleries** are generally open Tuesday–Saturday 11–4 and Sunday 2–6. Monday is the usual closing day. **Shops** are open weekdays 9–6. A growing number of stores, especially food stores, open on Saturday and Sunday, though for shorter hours. Many smaller food stores are open daily until 10 or 11 PM. Bakeries, souvenir shops, florists, and kiosks are open daily.

VISITOR INFORMATION

The Reykjavík **Tourist Information Center** (✉ Bankastræti 2, ☎ 562–3045, FAX 562–4749), a few yards up the street from Lækjartorg Square, is open June–August weekdays 8:30–6, Saturday 8:30–2, and Sunday 10–2; September–May it's open weekdays 9–5, Saturday 10–2. The **Icelandic Tourist Board**'s headquarters next door (Gimli, ✉ Lækjargata 3, ☎ 552–7488, FAX 562–4749) is open June, July, and August, weekdays 8–4; the rest of the year, 9–5.

You can also contact the **U.S. Embassy** (✉ Laufásvegur 21, ☎ 562–9100), **British Embassy** (✉ Laufásvegur 49, ☎ 551–5883), or **Canadian Consulate** (✉ Suðurlandsbraut 10, ☎ 568–0820).

SIDE TRIPS FROM REYKJAVÍK

Hafnarfjörður

10 km (6 mi) south of Reykjavík. Take an AV (metro area) bus 140 or 141 from Lækjatorg Plaza or Hlemmur Station.

The harbor here in Hafnarfjörður, which means "harbor fjord", was an important commercial port centuries before Reykjavík, and today there's still healthy competition between the two. Stop in at the Tourist Information Center on Vesturgata, where you can get a map of the town's sights. Next to the information center is a **Maritime Museum** and a **Folk Museum.** Just off the harbor is the red-roofed **Hafnarborg Art Center.** If you're feeling peckish, stop in the **Fjörukráin Restaurant** a couple of hundred yards south on Strandgata where the food and staff's costumes are Viking inspired.

Blue Lagoon

★ *15 km (10 mi) from Keflavík Airport and 50 km (31 mi) from Reykjavík (turn off toward the village of Grindavík). Buses run from the BSÍ bus terminal in Reykjavík to the Blue Lagoon twice daily and three times a day in July and August.*

For a unique swimming experience, visit this man-made wonder. Superheated water is pumped up from 2 kilometers (1¼ miles) beneath the earth's surface to power a geothermal energy plant; the run-off water collects in the lava to form a warm, salty, mineral-rich lagoon. The atmosphere here is nearly eerie with fog-like clouds above the lagoon and the large stacks of the power plant in the background. Facilities at the lagoon have been upgraded, and there are separate areas for therapeutic and recreational use. If you've forgotten your bathing suit, you can rent one here. ✉ *Blue Lagoon (Svartsengi power plant)*, ☎ 426–8800, ✉ IKr350.

GOLDEN CIRCLE

If you make only one foray outside Reykjavík, take this popular trip to the lakes, waterfalls, and hot springs just inland from the capital. You'll begin at Þingvellir, the ancient seat of the world's first parliament; then you'll see the original Geysir hot spring (hence the term *geyser*); and, last, stop at Gullfoss, the "Golden Waterfall."

Þingvellir

About 50 kilometers (30 miles) northeast of Reykjavík. First via the Ring Rd. about 9 kilometers (6 miles) until just past the town of Moss-fellsbær, where you turn right on Rte. 36 for the remaining distance.

After an hour's drive from Reykjavík, along Route 36 across the Mos-fellsheiði heath, the broad lava plain of Þingvellir suddenly opens in front of you. This has been the nation's most hallowed place since AD 930, when the settler Grímur Geitskór chose it as the site for the world's oldest parliament, the Icelandic *Alþingi* (General Assembly). In July of each year delegates from all over the country camped at Þingvellir for two weeks, meeting to pass laws and render judicial sentences. Iceland remained a sovereign nation-state, ruled solely by the people without a personal sovereign or central government, until 1262, when it came under the Norwegian crown; even then, the Alþingi continued to meet at Þingvellir until 1798, when it was dissolved by Iceland's Danish rulers. In AD 1000 the Alþingi decided that Iceland should become a Christian country, but the old heathen gods continued to be worshiped in private. These Viking gods remain part of everyday English: Týr (as in Tuesday), Óðinn (as in Wednesday), Þór (as in Thursday), and the goddess Frigg (as in Friday).

Þingvellir, at the northern end of Þingvallavatn, Iceland's largest lake, is a national park and remains a potent symbol of the Icelandic heritage. Many national celebrations are held here. Besides its historic interest, Þingvellir holds a special appeal for naturalists: It is the geologic meeting point of two continents. At Almannagjá, on the west side of the plain, is the easternmost edge of the American tectonic plate, which is otherwise submerged in the Atlantic Ocean. Over on the plain's east side, at the Heiðargjá Gorge, you are at the westernmost edge of the Eurasian plate. In the 9,000 years since the Þingvellir lava field was formed, the tectonic plates have moved 231 feet apart. And they are still moving, at a rate of about a half an inch a year.

You can drive straight to the central plain once you enter the park, or walk there after turning right along the short road at the sign for **Al-mannagjá** (Everyman's Gorge). From the rim, there is a fabulous view from the orientation marker.

A path down into Almannagjá from the top of the gorge overlooking Þingvellir leads straight to the high rock wall of **Lögberg** (Law Rock), where the person chosen as guardian of the laws would recite them from memory. At the far end of the gorge is the **Öxarárfoss** (Öxará

Waterfall). Beautiful, peaceful picnic spots are just beyond it. Just below the waterfall in a deep stretch of the river lies the forbidding **Drekkingarhylur** pool, where it is said unfaithful wives were drowned.

Across the plain from Lögberg stand the church and **Þingvallabær,** the gabled manor house of Þingvellir, where the government of Iceland often hosts visiting heads of state. The **Nikulásargjá Gorge,** which is reached by a footbridge, is better know these days as **Peningagjá** (Money Gorge) because it's customary to fling a coin into the gorge's icy-cold water and make a wish. Don't even dream of climbing down to wade here—even though it looks shallow, it's more than 30 feet deep!

Dining and Lodging

$$ ✕🔲 **Valhöll.** This small, comfortable, first-class hotel has an excellent location right by the lake. Rooms are decorated in pastel colors and floral-print furnishings. The welcoming restaurant has both intimate seating and more open space for larger groups. Fresh trout from Þingvellir Lake is served smoked or broiled. For a coffee break you might try the delicious *pönnukökur* (crepes filled with whipped cream and jam). ⌧ *Þingvellir National Park,* ☎ *482–2622,* 𝔽𝔸𝕏 *483–4775. 30 rooms. Restaurant. MC, V. Closed Oct.–Apr.*

Outdoor Activities and Sports

BOATING

At Þingvellir you can rent boats for rowing on Þingvallavatn (the rental facility is on the river by the Valhöll Hotel). Take extraordinary safety precautions: The shoreline drops off precipitously and the water is ice-cold.

FISHING

Trout and char are plentiful in Þingvallavatn. Obtain fishing permits at the Valhöll Hotel at Þingvellir.

HORSEBACK RIDING

A number of stables offer guided trail rides in this area. Call the **Laxnes Pony Farm** (☎ 566–6179) on Route 36 to Þingvellir.

En Route Follow Route 36 for 7 kilometers (4 miles) east of the Þingvellir plain to Route 365, which climbs 16 kilometers (10 miles) across the moor. If you keep a close lookout, halfway along this road to the left under a high bluff is the large opening of a shallow cave in which a handful of people lived in the early 20th century.

Laugarvatn

About 20 km (12 mi) east of Þingvellir along Routes 36 and 365.

Laugarvatn means Warm Springs Lake, and true to its name, Laugarvatn is a lake warm enough for bathing. Its water is naturally heated by hot springs that are at the northern end of the lake. A cluster of buildings here house a school in winter and Edda hotels in summer. Drive around them to a bathhouse at the lake's edge where you can rent towels and take showers year-round. The entrance fee also covers a natural steam bath in an adjoining hut, where you actually sit atop a hissing hot spring.

Lodging

$ 🔲 **Edda Hússtjórnarskóli.** This comfortable hotel and restaurant combination is right on the lake. ⌧ *Laugarvatn,* ☎ *486–1154. 27 rooms. Restaurant, bar. MC, V. Closed Sept.–mid-June.*

$ 🔲 **Edda Menntaskóli.** This neighbor of the Edda Húsmæðraskóli also has a lakeside location, although accommodations are a little less plush. ⌧ *Laugarvatn,* ☎ *486– 1118. 88 rooms, some with shared bath. Restaurant, bar. MC, V. Closed Sept.–mid-June.*

Outdoor Activities and Sports

BOATING

Rowboats and sailboards can be rented on Laugarvatn Lake. At Sví-
navatn in Grímsnes you can rent Jet Skis (☎ 486–4437) for an exhilarating run on the lake.

HORSEBACK RIDING

Contact **Íshestar** (Icelandic Riding Tours) at Miðdalur near Laugarvatn
(☎ 486–1169).

Haukadalur

*From the town of Laugarvatn take the short spur, Rte. 364, to Rte.
37. If you are not already on Rte. 37, continue northeast for 25 km
(16 mi) to the junction with Rte. 35. Go not quite 10 km (6 mi) northeast on this route, and you'll see the Geysir Restaurant and Hotel by
the roadside—but by then you'll probably have seen steam rising as a
hot spring spouts into the air to guide you.*

The Geysir geothermal field in Haukadalur, home of the **Geysir** and
Strokkur geysers, is one of Iceland's classic tourist spots.

The famous Geysir hot spring used to gush a column of scalding water
130 to 200 feet into the air, but the old geyser has now gone into re-
tirement. Strokkur is a more reliable performer, having been drilled open
in 1964 after a quiet period of 70 years; it spouts up boiling water as
high as 100 feet at five-minute intervals. In the same area there are small
boreholes from which steam rises, as well as beautiful pools of blue
water. Don't crowd Strokkur, and always be careful when approach-
ing hot springs or mud baths—the ground may be treacherous, suddenly giving way beneath you.

Dining and Lodging

$ ✕⚏ **Hótel Geysir.** Beside the famous Geysir and Strokkur springs, this
hotel is decorated in an exuberant Viking style: Replica medieval
carved decorations such as dragon heads adorn public spaces. As hotels go, it is small and basic, but there's a large restaurant. The menu
includes various Icelandic specialties, such as salmon, rye bread baked
in the heat of geothermal springs, and *skyr* (milk curd) with cream.
There is a veranda where you can sit and enjoy the sun. ✉ *Haukadalur,*
☎ *486–8915,* ⅲ *486–8715. 15 rooms with shared baths. Restaurant,
bar, pool. MC, V. Closed Sept.–May.*

Gulfoss

About 6 km (4 mi) east along Route 35 from Geysir.

The thundering Gullfoss (Golden Falls) is the nation's most admired waterfall. Measuring 105 feet high, Gullfoss is a double cascade in the Hvítá
River, turning at right angles in mid-drop. Gullfoss enters a dramatic
chasm, which nonetheless has its gentle sides. On the western bank of
the river, where the steep walls begin to slant more, is a beautiful hidden spot a short, steep climb from the road. Called **Pjaxi,** from the Latin
pax (meaning "peace"), this is a restful nook of grassy knolls, natural
springs, clear streams, and birch trees—an ideal spot for a picnic.

Outdoor Activities and Sports

HORSEBACK RIDING

Horses can be hired for rides at **Brattholt** farm (☎ 486–8941), adjacent to Gullfoss.

WHITE-WATER RAFTING

An exciting way to see the Hvitá River canyon below Gullfoss Falls is at water level by rubber dinghy. Waterproof clothing and life jackets are supplied for an hour's thrilling journey down the churning glacial river. Call **Hvítárferðir** (⊠ Háagerði 41, Reykjavík, ☎ 568–2504).

Skálholt

From Gullfoss, follow the southbound Rte. 35 for 36 km (22 mi); then turn left onto Rte. 31 for another 3½ km (2 mi) to the right-hand turnoff.

Skálholt Cathedral makes an interesting stop on the way back from the Gullfoss falls to Reykjavík. This ancient place of worship was established in 1056, soon after Iceland converted to Christianity. A stone near the entry drive is believed to be where the last Catholic bishop, Jón Arason, and his son (celibacy was difficult to enforce so far from Rome) lost their heads when the Lutheran faith was ultimately enforced in 1550. The exquisitely simple building, consecrated in 1963, is the 11th church to be built on this site. Beneath it lies an ancient crypt. Skálholt, the seat of the southern bishopric, was the main center of learning and religion in Iceland until the 18th century. The modern memorial church at Skálholt houses many relics from the past. Works by two of Iceland's most important modern artists adorn the cathedral: a unique mosaic altarpiece by Nína Tryggvadòttir and stained-glass windows by Gerður Helgadòttir. Each summer the cathedral hosts the **Skálholt Music Festival,** which brings together musicians from Iceland and abroad who perform Baroque music on original instruments.

En Route   The return route from Skálholt to Reykjavík rolls through one of the most prosperous agricultural regions in Iceland. Drive 10 kilometers (6 miles) from the cathedral along Route 31 and then turn right to go south on Route 30; after 21 kilometers (13 miles), Route 30 ends at the Ring Road and you take a right onto Route 1 and head west toward Reykjavík. It's about 73 kilometers (44 miles) back to the capital, but if you have time, stop halfway along in Hveragerði.

Hveragerði

40 km (25 mi) from Reykjavík.

Hveragerði is home to a horticultural school, a large number of greenhouses heated by hot springs, and a fine swimming pool. The state's greenhouse research facility, where flowers and crops are grown with natural steam in large hot houses, is up the hill from the town's center. One of the country's most unabashed tourist spots, **Eden,** is a discrete distance from the Ring Road, with an exotic display of tropical plants, souvenir items, and a snack bar. The rather garish, large roadside building of fiberglass panels is all that's left of a failed amusement park.

Dining and Lodging

$$$ ╳▦ **Hótel Örk.** The greenhouses, mud pools, and hot springs of Hveragarði are a couple of blocks away from this white-concrete, blue-roofed hotel. Rooms and public spaces have mahogany furniture, original Icelandic art on the walls, and plenty of potted plants. Meals served in the ground-floor restaurant may include lobster soup with a touch of champagne, Icelandic lamb and vegetable soup, leg of lamb roasted with Icelandic herbs, or fresh ocean fish from the nearby town of Þorlákshöfn. ▦ *Breiðamörk 1,* ☎ *483–4700,* 𝔽𝔸𝕏 *483–4775. 81 rooms. Restaurant, pool, sauna, spa, golf course, tennis court. AE, MC, V.*

$ 🏠 **Ból.** This youth hostel in Hveragerði, open May through August, has 26 beds. ⊠ *Hveramörk 14, 810 Hveragerði,* ☎ *483–4198 or 483–4588.*

Outdoor Activities and Sports

SWIMMING

The region has numerous swimming pools, located wherever there is plenty of natural hot water. Contact the swimming pool in Hveragerði at ☎ 483–4113.

Golden Circle A to Z

Arriving and Departing

BY BUS

It is possible to explore this area by BSÍ bus, but you must allow plenty of time and perhaps stay overnight en route. **BSÍ Travel** (☎ 552–2300) serves Þingvellir twice daily (June–mid-Sept.) and Gullfoss/Geysir twice daily (June 15–Aug.).

BY CAR

This circuit should take seven or eight hours by car, allowing time for stops at the various sights. At the farthest point, Gullfoss, you'll only be 125 kilometers (78 miles) from Reykjavík, and most of the drive is along paved main roads.

Contacts and Resources

EMERGENCIES

In Hveragerði the **police** can be reached at ☎ 483–1154.

GUIDED TOURS

Kynnisferðir (Reykjavík Excursions, ☎ 562–1011 or 568–8922) offers an eight-hour guided Golden Circle tour May–September, daily at 9 AM, and October–April, daily except Tuesday and Thursday.

VISITOR INFORMATION

General information is available in Reykjavík at the **Tourist Information Center** or the **Icelandic Tourist Board** (☞ Visitor Information *in* Reykjavík, *above*). In Hveragerði, contact the **South Coast Travel Service and Information Center** (⊠ Breiðumörk 10, ☎ 483–4280).

THE WEST AND THE WESTERN FJORDS

If you imagine the map of Iceland as the shape of a beast, two rugged western peninsulas—Snæfellsnes and Vestfirðir—would be its proudly rearing head, jaws open wide around the huge bay of Breiðafjörður. The North Atlantic, just off this coast, is one of the country's prime fishing grounds. Busy fishing villages abound in Vestfirðir (the Western Fjords), but there are also tall mountains, remote cliffs thick with seabirds, and deep fjords carved out of basaltic rock. Inland in the extreme northwest corner, abandoned farmsteads and vestiges of ancient habitation are signs of the toll taken by isolation and forces of nature.

In the southern reaches, just north of the town of Borgarnes, the Ring Road bends to the northeast, giving the traveler a choice. You can follow Route 54, which branches northwest, leading along the southern reaches of the Snæfellsnes Peninsula, which is crowned by the majestic Snæfells Glacier. Or you can choose to follow the Ring Road to the east. Here you'll enter a world rich in natural beauty and steeped in the history of the sagas. In order best to enjoy the area, you should plan to give the east and west options a day each.

Borgarnes

The starting point for this regional tour is 116 km (72 mi) from Reyk-javík along the Ring Road. (The Reykjavík–Akranes ferry is a convenient shortcut.)

Borgarnes is the only coastal town in Iceland of any size that does *not* rely on fishing for its livelihood. Trade, commerce, and light industry are the mainstays of this community. If you're coming from the south, a new bridge, barely a decade old, has considerably shortened the Ring Road approach to town. It is now no longer necessary to drive around Borgarfjörður fjörd.

Dining and Lodging

$$ ✕🏨 **Hótel Borgarnes.** One of the biggest and most popular hotels on the west coast, this establishment offers both a cafeteria and an elegant restaurant. ✉ *Egilsgata 12–16,* ☎ *437–1119,* 🅵🅰🆇 *437–1443. 75 rooms. Restaurant, cafeteria. AE, DC, MC, V.*

$ 🏨 **Kleppjárnsreykir.** This youth hostel has 14 beds. ✉ *Runnar, Bló-maskálinn, Kleppjárnsreykir, 311 Borgarnes,* ☎ *435–1262 or 435–1185,* 🅵🅰🆇 *435–1437.*

Outdoor Activities and Sports

HORSEBACK RIDING

To rent horses for exploring the Borgarfjörður area, call **Jafnaskarð** farm (☎ 435–0028 or 437–7033) or **Varmaland Summer Hotel** (☎ 435–1303).

SWIMMING

You can swim at the pool in Borgarnes (✉ Skallagrímsgata, ☎ 437–0027).

En Route To explore the area inland from Borgarfjörður, drive northeast from Borgarnes on the Ring Road 11 kilometers (7 miles) until you come to Route 53 leading eastward. Turn right onto Route 53 and cross the one-lane bridge over the cloudy glacial Hvítá River. Take the first left turn onto Route 52 and in 10 minutes you'll arrive at the **Laxfoss** (Salmon Falls) on the Grímsá River, where salmon leap the rapids in summer. Continue across the Grímsá north on Route 50 a little more than 10 kilometers (6 miles) until you come to the **Kleppjárnsreykir** horticultural center, with its many greenhouses heated by thermal water from the region's hot springs.

Reykholt

Head northeast on Rte. 50 past Kleppjárnsreykir about 1 km (½ mi); then turn east onto Rte. 518 and follow for 8 km (5 mi).

Reykholt is the home of scholar-historian Snorri Sturluson (1178–1241). Author of the prose work *Edda,* a textbook of poetics, and the *Heimskringla,* a history of Norway's kings, Snorri was also a wealthy chieftain and political schemer. He was murdered in Reykholt in 1241 on the orders of the Norwegian king. A hot bathing pool believed to date from Snorri's time can be seen here, as well as part of the underground passage that once led from Snorri's homestead to the pool. An institute for Old Norse study, named after Snorri Sturluson, is here, as is an area secondary school.

Dining and Lodging

$ ✕🏨 **Edda Hotel.** This comfortable, modern building is a secondary school in winter and a hotel in summer. ✉ *Reykholt,* ☎ *435–1260. 48 rooms. Restaurant, bar. MC, V. Closed Sept.–mid-June.*

En Route   Continue for about 30 minutes on Route 518 to the colorful **Hraun-fossar** (Lava Falls). A multitude of natural springs under a birch-covered lava field above the Hvítá River creates a waterfall hundreds of feet wide, seemingly appearing out of nowhere across the bank from you. A little farther up the Hvíta, 10 minutes' walking distance from **Hraunfossar,** is the **Barnafossar** (Children's Falls), which carves strange figures out of the rock. Tradition says that two children lost their lives when a natural stone bridge over the churning maelstrom gave way. Today a trusty footbridge gives safe access to the opposite bank.

Húsafell Park is about 4 kilometers (2.4 miles) up the Route 518 eastward. This somewhat sheltered wooded area is a popular summer camping site, with its birch trees, swimming pool, and chalets. A gasoline station is here and a restaurant serves visitors June through August.

Bifröst

From Húsafell, return west past Reykholt, along Rtes. 518, 523, and some 50 km (30 mi) to the Ring Road, and go north about 13 km (8 mi) to Bifröst.

About 1½ kilometers (1 mile) north of Bifröst just off the Ring Road is the **Grábrók** volcanic cone, which you can easily scale for a panoramic view of the area. Grábrók's lava field, covered with moss, grass, and birches, has many quiet spots for a picnic. Eight kilometers (5 miles) north is the distinctive pyramid-shape **Mt. Baula,** a pastel-colored rhyolite mountain. In the 19th century, Icelanders enjoyed telling gullible foreign travelers fantastic stories of the beautiful green meadows and forests populated by dwarfs shepherding herds of fat sheep at Baula's summit.

Lodging

$$ 🏨 **Hótel Bifröst.** Low white school buildings with red roofs house this summer hotel beside the Ring Road in Borgarfjörður. ✉ *Hreðavatn,* ☎ *435–0000 or 435–0005,* 📠 *435–0020. 26 rooms, 8 with bath. Restaurant, bar, horseback riding. MC, V.*

Snæfellsnes Peninsula

The southern shore of this peninsula begins about 40 km (25 mi) northwest of Borgarnes; if you're heading south from Bifröst, it's about 30 km (18 mi) to the turnoff onto the peninsula from the Ring Road.

Begin the journey north from the crossroads with Route 54. As you drive farther west on the peninsula, you'll pass through the Staðarsveit district, with its beautiful mountain range. Many small lakes abound with water flowers, and there are myriad sparkling springs. At **Lýsuhóll,** a few minutes north of Route 54, you can bathe in the warm water of a naturally carbonated swimming pool. About 10 kilometers (6 miles) farther west is the **Búðahraun** lava field, composed of rough, slaggy apalhraun lava. Its surface makes walking difficult, but it's more hospitable to vegetation than are most other Icelandic landscapes; flowers, shrubs, herbs, and berries grow abundantly here.

Búðir

102 km (61 mi) from Borganes.

This tiny shoreline establishment has ancient origins as an inlet mooring for fishermen in the days of sails and rowing. If you look carefully, you may find centuries-old relics of the fishermen's shelters. An unpretentious church from 1850, a successor to the first chapel on this site in 1703, has maintained its original appearance. The lava surrounding this site has unique flora, including a rare subspecies of the buttercups,

called Goldilocks, or Ranuculus auricomus islandicus among scholars.
The area is protected as a registered nature preserve.

Dining and Lodging

$$ ✕🔲 **Hótel Búðir.** Under the magical Snæfellsjökull and close to a golden
beach, this hotel has an excellent restaurant, which serves such deli-
cacies as plaice with wild herbs, goose, ptarmigan, and cormorant. One-
day tours are available by air from Reykjavík to Búðir, including a riding
tour or boat trip followed by a meal. ✉ *Snæfellsnes, 311 Borgarnes,*
☎ *435–6700,* 𝖥𝖠𝖷 *435–6701. 25 rooms, 5 with bath. Restaurant,
boating, fishing, travel services. AE, DC, MC, V. Closed Oct.–Nov.*

En Route From Búðir, take a left turn onto the coastal route 574 for a 61-kilo-
meter (36-mile) drive circling the tip of the peninsula clockwise. On
your right you'll see the majestic Snæfells Glacier, **Snæfellsjökull,** which,
like that on Fujiyama in Japan, caps a volcano. The glacier was fea-
tured in Jules Verne's novel *Journey to the Center of the Earth* as the
spot where the explorers enter the depths of the world.

The coastal drive will take you past many small, beautiful villages. One
such is **Arnarstapi,** where the roof of a shore cave has fallen in, leav-
ing a high arch for cliff birds to loop through to and from their nests.
Hellnar is also a quaint spot. About an hour's walk from the road at
the western tip of the peninsula lie the **Svörtuloft Cliffs,** home to mul-
titudes of seabirds in nesting season.

Ólafsvík

*Either 61 km (36 mi) clockwise around the peninsula on Rte. 574 or
14 km (7 mi) across the Fróðárheiði cutoff from Búðir.*

This small village perched on shore under the north shoulder of Snæfell-
sjökull has the surprising distinction of being Iceland's oldest licensed
trading center. Commerce has taken place officially in Ólafsvík since 1687.

Outdoor Activities and Sports

At Ólafsvík you can stop at the Tourist Information Center (☎ 436–
1543) to arrange snowmobile tours or a hike to the top of the glacier.
The main highway (now numbered Route 57) begins again at Ólafsvík
and follows the north coast to Stykkishólmur.

SWIMMING

The local Ólafsvík pool (✉ Ennisbraut 9, ☎ 436–1199) is open to
the public.

Stykkishólmur

67 km (42 mi) east of Ólafsvík.

Stykkishólmur is an active port community with an excellent natural
harbor. Offshore fishing is a vital activity, even supporting a local scal-
lop fishery. A pair of classic timber houses from the 1800s give a clue
to the distinguished past. One, from 1828, bears the name of Árni Thor-
lacius, an early merchant who is noteworthy for establishing the na-
tion's oldest weather station, in 1845. The large building near the water
is a hospital that was built in 1936 by the Order of the Fransicans and
has been staffed since by its sisters.

A ferry sails twice daily from here to the extremely sparsely populated
islands of the Breiðafjörður. The island **Flatey,** where the ferry stops
over on the way to the Western Fjords, is worth a visit. The now
sleepy vacation village was an important center of commerce and
learning during the 19th century; many delightful old houses still stand
today, and the bird life is remarkable.

Dining and Lodging

$$ ✕▥ **Hótel Stykkishólmur.** This hotel makes a convenient jumping-off point for excursions to the islands of Breiðafjörður and for the ferry to the Western Fjords. It includes a good restaurant; the menu emphasizes seafood but also includes lamb, pork, and pasta, as well as pizza and hamburgers. ✉ *Vatnási,* ☎ *438–1330,* 🅵🅰🆇 *438–1579. 33 rooms. Restaurant, 9-hole golf course. DC, MC, V.*

$$ ▥ **Hótel Eyjaferðir.** This is a comfortable, utilitarian, family-run hotel in a quiet spot. ✉ *Aðalgata 8,* ☎ *438–1450. 14 rooms, some with private bath. MC, V.*

$ ▥ **Youth Hostel.** There are 50 beds here. ✉ *Höfðagata 1, 340 Stykkishólmur,* ☎ *438–1095,* 🅵🅰🆇 *438–1579.*

Outdoor Activities and Sports

SWIMMING

For information about the pool in Stykkishólmur, call ☎ 438–1272.

Ísafjörður

From Stykkishólmur, follow Rte. 57 70 km (50 mi) to Route 60. Alternately, from the Ring Road, pick up Rte. 60 about 10 km (6 mi) past Bifröst and drive 35 km (27 mi) to the intersection with Rte. 57. From there it's a long drive north—about 340 km (211 mi).

Ísafjörður is the uncrowned capital of the Vestfirðir (Western Fjords). Ísafjörður itself is one of the most important fishing villages in Iceland, but for visitors it functions mainly as a jumping-off point for tours of Hornstrandir, the splendid, peaceful but desolate land north of the 66th parallel, uninhabited since the 1950s. Geologically the oldest part of Iceland, Vestfirðir offers spectacular views of mountains, fjords, and sheer cliffs. Hikers and mountaineers may want to hire guides to explore this unspoiled region, and anglers come here to catch trout in the rivers and lakes. The northernmost cliffs of **Hornbjarg** and **Hælavíkurbjarg** are home to large bird colonies.

Dining and Lodging

$$ ✕▥ **Hótel Ísafjörður.** This is a good family hotel in the heart of town. No two rooms are alike, but all have old-fashioned furnishings and floral fabrics. The restaurant serves tasty seafood dishes, including grilled scallops in pesto sauce. Sightseeing tours and boat trips are offered in summer. ✉ *Silfurtorgi 2,* ☎ *456–4111,* 🅵🅰🆇 *456–4767. 32 rooms. Restaurant. AE, MC, V.*

Outdoor Activities and Sports

BICYCLING

Bikes can be rented from the **Hotel Ísafjörður** (☎ 456–4111).

SWIMMING

You can swim in the local Ísafjörður pool (✉ *Austurvegur 9,* ☎ 456–3200).

Patreksfjörður

190 km (114 miles) south of Ísafjörður, or 345 km (207 mi) from Borgarnes. If starting at Borgarnes, first take the Ring Road north, then follow Rte. 60 north to Vatnsfjörður, then take 62 west. A less arduous approach is to take the ferry from Stykkishólmur. After a brief stop at the isle of Flatey, the ferry stops at Brjánslæk. From here it's 54 km (32 mi) to Patreksfjörður.

One of the Western Fjords' many curious fishing villages, this one is named for the patron saint of Ireland. Houses here seem to crowd every available flat spot, right up to the sea. The harbor, built in 1946, was formed by deepening and opening a brackish lake to the sea.

The region's largest bird colony, with millions of residents, is at Látrabjarg, 60 kilometers (36 miles) from Patreksfjörður. The immense vertical cliff, more than 218 yards high, runs along the south shore of the Western Fjords. In years past, egg collectors dangled over the edges to gather eggs, which were an essential source of protein. This is Iceland's westernmost tip, and the waters offshore are treacherous to sailors. The skill of egg collectors proved heroic in 1947 in what has to qualify as one of maritime history's most incredible rescues. With mind-boggling agility, local Icelanders rappelled down the treacherous cliff and shot a lifeline out to the stranded trawler *Dhoon*. Then, using a seat harness, every single crew member of the ship was hauled up to safety on the top of the cliff—in the near-total darkness of December, no less.

Lodging

🏠 **Youth Hostel.** Open year-round, this hostel has eight beds. ⊠ *Afahús, Aðalstræti 65, 450 Patreksfjörður,* ☎ *456–1280 or 456–1275.*

The West and the Western Fjords A to Z

Arriving and Departing

BY BOAT

The **Akranes** car ferry, *Akraborg* (☎ 551–6050), sails three or four times daily year-round between Reykjavík and Akranes. In summer the *Baldur* car ferry (☎ 438–1120 or 456–2020) links Stykkishólmur, on the Snæfellsnes Peninsula, with Brjánslækur, on the southern coast of the Western Fjords, calling at Flatey Island. *Baldur* leaves Stykkishólmur at 10 AM and 4:30 PM in summer.

From Ísafjörður, you can travel by the **Fagranes** ferry (☎ 456–3155 or 456–4655) around the Western Fjords.

BY BUS

BSÍ Travel (Reykjavík Airport, ☎ 552–2300) runs frequent daily service to most towns in the region. It's a two-hour trip to Borgarnes, four hours to Stykkishólmur. Bus travel is not the most convenient way to visit the Western Fjords; service to Ísafjörður runs a couple of days a week in summer only, and it's a 12-hour trip.

BY CAR

From Reykjavík and the north, you reach the west via the Ring Road (Route 1). Route 54 branches off to the Snæfellsnes Peninsula; Routes 60 and 68 branch off to the Western Fjords. Those renting cars to drive to the Western Fjords are advised not to select the smallest sized cars, as roads can be rough, requiring good ground clearance underneath.

BY PLANE

Air travel is the best way to visit the Western Fjords. You can fly to Ísafjörður on **Icelandair** (☎ 505–0200) and **Ernir Air** (☎ 552–4200 or 456–4200), and from there via Ernir Air to Bíldudalur, Flateyri, Ingjaldssandur, Patreksfjörður, Reykjanes, Suðureyri, and Þingeyri.

Contacts and Resources

EMERGENCIES

For local **police** in Borgarnes call ☎ 437–1166, in Ísafjörður call ☎ 456–4222, and in Stykkishólmur call ☎ 488–1008.

GUIDED TOURS

The **Iceland Tourist Bureau** (☎ 562–3300) operates a 12-hour day trip from Reykjavík to the Western Fjords, with a flight to Ísafjörður and then sightseeing by bus. The tour departs daily June–August.

Vesturferðir (✉ Torfnes, Ísafjörður, ☎ 456–5111, 🖷 456–4767) runs tours around the Western Fjords.

Sightseeing tours of Breiðafjörður, with its innumerable islands and varied bird life, operate from **Stykkishólmur;** contact Eyjaferðir (☎ 438–1450). One-day sightseeing tours of the Western Fjords run in the summers from Ísafjörður (☎ 456–3155 or 456–4655).

VISITOR INFORMATION

In **Akranes,** the Tourist Information Center (✉ Skólabraut 31, ☎ 431–3327) is open 1–3. In **Borgarnes,** the Hyrnan (by the bridge, ☎ 437–2108 or 437–1208) provides information. In **Ísafjörður,** the Tourist Bureau (write: ✉ Box 277, Ísafjörður; office: ✉ Hafnarstræti 8, ☎ 456–5121, 🖷 456–5122) is open 9–noon and 1–5. In **Ólafsvík,** the Tourist Information Office (✉ Gamla pakkhúsið, ☎ 436–1543) is in a renovated 18th-century warehouse.

THE NORTH

From the Hrútafjörður (Rams' Fjord), which gouges deeply into the western end of the coast, to Vopnafjörður in the east, Iceland's north is a land created by the interplay of fire and ice. Inland, you can find the largest lava fields on earth, some with plants and mosses, others barren. Yet valleys sheltered by the mountains are lush with vegetation and rich in color, and the deeply indented coast offers magnificent views north toward the Arctic, especially spectacular under the summer's midnight sun.

The commercial and cultural center of Akureyri is Iceland's second-largest town; from there it's a pleasant drive to Lake Mývatn, where bird-watchers can spot vast numbers of waterfowl and hikers can explore weird lava formations. The weather is more stable here than in the south, and it's unusually mild around Mývatn, making it a pleasant outdoor destination.

Brú

27 km (16 mi) west of Hvammstangi, which is the nearest town just off the Ring Road.

If you're driving the full Ring Road route, you'll enter the north at Brú, snuggled at the inland end of the long Hrútafjörður. It is a tiny settlement, bordering on two regional districts where a post and telegraph station were established in 1950. A local folk museum offers a glimpse into the area's past.

Dining and Lodging

$$ ✕🏨 **Staðarskáli í Hrútafirði.** On Hrútafjörður, just east of Brú, this neat and clean accommodation offers good cooking—especially the grilled lamb—at reasonable prices. ✉ *Hrútarfirði, IS-500 Staðarhreppur,* ☎ *451–1150,* 🖷 *451–1107. 36 rooms, 18 with shower. Restaurant, meeting rooms.*

$ 🏨 **Edda Hotel.** The restaurant at this summer hotel is open all day. ✉ *Reykjum, IS-500 Brú,* ☎ *451–0004. 50 rooms. Restaurant, bar, pool, meeting rooms. AE, DC, V. Closed Sept.–mid-June. MC, V.*

$ 🏨 **Youth Hostel.** There are 30 beds here. ✉ *Sæberg Reykir, Hrútafjörður, 500 Brú,* ☎ *451–0015,* 🖷 *451–0034.*

Outdoor Activities and Sports

BICYCLING

Bikes can be rented at **Staðarskáli** (✉ Hrútafjörður, ☎ 451–1150).

HÚNAFLÓI (Polar Bear Cub Bay) – From Staðarskáli, follow the Ring Road east. You will be taking what locals call the Vatnsnes Circle around the peninsula of the same name. The loop itself totals about 83 kilometers (50 miles) along Routes 72 and 711. As you get farther out on the peninsula's west side, keep a lookout for seals and shore-bird activity, or maybe even spouting whales. Although the bay is called Húnaflói (Polar Bear Cub Bay), the reference is believed to be purely legendary. Eventually, the road magically becomes Route 711, and you turn around the tip of the peninsula and head south. As you near the mainland, look to the east for Hvíserkur, a bizarre, dinosaur-shape off-shore rock formation. It is as if an escapee from the Jurassic era became petrified as it drank from the sea!

Varmahlíð

136 km (82 mi) east of Brú and 94 km (56 mi) west of Akureyri at the crossroads of the Ring Road and Rte. 75 north to Sauðárkrókur. If you're coming from Rte. 711, it meets the Ring Road again, and here you should turn left and head east toward Blönduós and Varmahlíð.

The inland village of Varmahlíð is a rural service center with its own local abundant geothermal heating sources. In addition to a bank, hotel, general store, and gas station, a small natural history museum is here.

South of town you'll come to **Víðimýri,** where you can visit a turf-roofed **Víðimýrarkirkja** church, built in 1834. It has been faithfully restored and lovingly maintained and still serves the local parishioners to this day. The late president of Iceland, Kristján Eldjarn, who was a world authority of Nordic antiquities, once called it one of the most sublimely built and beautiful remnants of Icelandic architecture.

Glaumbær

Returning north, cross the Ring Road and head north on Rte. 75 about 10 km (6 mi) north of Varmahlíð.

The **Glaumbær Folk Museum** is in a turf-roofed farmhouse that originally belonged to affluent farmers. The museum gives a glimpse of 18th- and 19th-century living conditions in rural Iceland. In the 11th century, Glaumbær was the home of Guðríður Þorbjarnardottir and Þorfinnur Karlsefni, two of the Icelanders who attempted to settle in America after it was discovered by Leifur Eiríksson. Their son, Snorri, was probably the first European to be born in the New World. ☎ 453–6173. ▧ IKr120. ☉ *June–Aug., daily 10–noon and 1–7.*

Dining and Lodging

$$ ✕▧ **Hótel Varmahlíð.** A nice hotel, it is in the crossroad community of the same name. Some rooms here have access for people with disabilities. The staff can arrange golfing, fishing, or horseback riding for visitors. ⊠ *Varmahlíð,* ☎ *453–8170 or 453–8190,* ▣ *453–8870. 38 rooms, 15 with shower. Restaurant. MC, V.*

Sauðárkrókur

17 km (11 mi) north on Rte. 75 from Glaumbær.

Sauðárkrókur is a large coastal town with many services and amenities. In summer, boat trips from Sauðárkrókur to Drangey and Málmey islands provide striking views. On the eastern side of Skagafjörður, off Route 75, is the 18th-century stone cathedral of **Hólar,** which contains beautiful and priceless religious artifacts.

Lodging

$$ 🏨 **Hótel Áning.** This good-size hotel has a licensed restaurant. Hiking, horseback riding, and boat tours can be arranged from here. ✉ Sæmundarhlíð, ☎ 453–6717 or 453-5940, FAX 453–6087. 65 rooms with shower. Restaurant, meeting rooms. MC, V.

Akureyri

95 km (57 mi) east along the Ring Road from the junction with Rte. 75 south of Sauðákrókur.

Though not as cosmopolitan as Reykjavík, Akureyri, called the Capital of the North, is a lively place. A century ago, the farmers in the prosperous agricultural area surrounding Akureyri established KEA, a cooperative enterprise to combat the Danish businesses that dominated the area's economic life. Today KEA still runs most of the stores and industries in Akureyri.

Lying by the 64-kilometer-long (40-mile-long) Eyjafjörður, Akureyri is sheltered from the ocean winds and embraced by mountains on three sides. Late 19th-century wooden houses give the city center a sense of history, while the twin spires of a modern Lutheran church, rising on a green hill near the waterfront, provide a focal point. The church is named for Akureyri native Matthías Jochumsson, the poet who wrote Iceland's national anthem in 1874.

From the church it's a short walk from the town center on Eyrarlandsvegur to the **Lystigarðurinn** (Arctic Botanic Gardens), which have been planted with more than 400 species of Icelandic flora, including some rare Arctic plants, and foreign plants. **Matthíasarhús,** (✉ Eyrarlandsvegur 3), the house where Jochumsson once lived, is now open as a museum, daily 2–4. Akureyri has two other museums honoring Icelandic writers: **Davíðshús** (✉ Bjarkastígur 6), the home of poet Davíð Stefánsson, open weekdays 3–5, and **Nonnahús** (✉ Aðalstræti 54b), the boyhood home of children's writer and Jesuit priest Jón Sveinsson, open daily 2–4:30.

The **Náttúrugripasafnið** (Natural History Museum) displays specimens of all the bird species that nest in Iceland. ✉ Hafnarstræti 81, ☎ 462–2983. 🎫 IKr100. ☉ June and mid-Aug.–mid-Sept., Sun.–Fri. 1–4; July–mid-Aug., Sun.–Fri. 10–5; mid-Sept.–June, Sun. 1–3.

The **Minjasafnið** (Folk Museum) has a large collection of local relics and works of art, old farm tools, and fishing equipment. ✉ Aðalgata 58, ☎ 462–4162. 🎫 IKr150. ☉ Daily 1:30–5.

Laxdalshús (Laxdal House), which dates from the 18th century, is the oldest house in Akureyri. Beautifully restored, it is open to the public in summer. ✉ Hafnarstræti 11.

During June and July, make a point of taking an evening drive north from Akureyri along Route 82. The midnight sun creates breathtaking views along the coast of **Eyjafjörður.** Better still, take a cruise on the fjord: A ferry plies to and from the island of Hrísey in the waters of Eyjafjörður and out to Grímsey Island, 40 kilometers (25 miles) offshore, which straddles the Arctic Circle. Contact **Nonni Travel** (✉ Brekkugata 3, Akureyri, ☎ 461–1841, FAX 461–1843).

The **Arctic Open Golf Tournament** is held each year at Akureyri (the most northerly 18-hole course in the world) around the longest day of the year (in the midnight sun, needless to say!). For details, contact the Akureyri Golf Club (☎ 462–2974, FAX 461–1755) or the Iceland Tourist Bureau (☎ 562–3300, FAX 562–5895).

From Akureyri you can see to the south the pyramid-shape rhyolite mountain **Súlur** and, beyond it, **Kerling,** the highest peak in Eyjafjörður.

Dining and Lodging

$$$$ ✕ **Fiðlarinn.** The view is fabulous from this rooftop restaurant and bar overlooking Akureyri Harbor and Eyjafjörður. Danish haute cuisine is featured; try the lobster tails in champagne-cream sauce or roast reindeer with game sauce and apple salad. ⊠ *Skipagata 14,* ☎ *462–7100. AE, DC, MC, V.*

$$$ ✕ **Höfðaberg.** Part of the KEA Hotel (☞ Lodging, *below*), this fine restaurant has modern Scandinavian decor. The cuisine is Icelandic; good choices include the steamed halibut in white wine sauce and the mustard-glazed lamb with Icelandic mountain herbs. ⊠ *Hafnarstræti 87–89,* ☎ *462–2200. AE, DC, MC, V.*

$$$ ✕🏨 **Hótel KEA.** Mauve-and-maroon decor with dark-wood trim characterizes this property, which is on a par with many of the capital's hotels. In addition to the Höfðaberg restaurant, there is an inexpensive cafeteria on the ground floor. On weekends the KEA is one of the city's main dancing spots. ⊠ *Hafnarstræti 87–89,* ☎ *462–2200,* Ⅿ𝔸𝕏 *461–2285. 71 rooms with bath, 1 suite. Restaurant, bar, lobby lounge, meeting rooms. AE, DC, MC, V.*

$$$ 🏨 **Hótel Norðurland.** Rooms here are decorated with floral prints and Danish modern furniture. All have satellite TV. On the ground floor is the separately run Pizza 67 restaurant. ⊠ *Geislagata 7,* ☎ *462–2600,* Ⅿ𝔸𝕏 *462–7962. 28 rooms, 18 with bath. Restaurant, bar, minibars. AE, DC, MC, V.*

$ 🏨 **Youth Hostel.** There are 32 beds here. ⊠ *Stórholt 1, 600 Akureyri,* ☎ *462–3657.*

Outdoor Activities and Sports

GOLF

Enjoy golf at the world's northernmost 18-hole course, at Jaðar, on the outskirts of Akureyri. For information on the **Arctic Open Golf Tournament,** *see above.* There are also golf courses in **Ólafsfjörður** and **Sauðárkrókur.**

HIKING

Úrval-Útsýn (⊠ Ráðhústorg 3, ☎ 462–5000) and **Nonni Travel** (⊠ Brekkugata 3, ☎ 462–7922) run mountain hiking tours from Akureyri. Also contact **Ferðafélag Akureyrar** (⊠ Touring Club of Akureyri, Strandgata 23, 600 Akureyri, ☎ 462–2720).

HORSEBACK RIDING

In Akureyri, contact **Pólarhestar** (⊠ Grýtubakki 11, ☎ 463–3179).

SWIMMING

Akureyri has an excellent open-air pool (⊠ Þingvallastræti 13, ☎ 462–3260).

Shopping

As Iceland's second-largest city, Akureyri offers better shopping than most other towns outside of Reykjavík. Woolens, ceramics, and other gift items are available at **París** (⊠ Hafnarstræti 96, ☎ 462–7744). The **Folda** factory shop (⊠ Gleráreyrar, ☎ 462–1900) offers woolens and sheepskin rugs at discount prices.

OFF THE BEATEN PATH   **SIGLUFJÖRÐUR** – In the mid-1960s, this town was alive with prosperity from the area's abundance of herring, the silver of the sea. When the "Klondike era" ended with the collapse of the herring stock in 1968, the fleet turned to other fish types and Siglufjörður settled down. Today, though, the herring era has been reborn with the recovery of the herring stock. Demonstrations on the pier show just how little time it takes to dress and salt herring and fill the barrels. Each summer the "Herring Adventure," held the first weekend in August, turns the entire harbor into a festival of living history. Afterward, join in the merrymaking with music and dancing. If you miss the action, there is the Síldarminnjasafn (Herring Years Memorabilia Museum), on Snorragata, where herring exhibits, pictures, and paraphernalia, including wooden barrel lids with various "brandings," are on display. To get to this colorful port community, travel 192 kilometers (115 miles) north of Akureyri on Route 82, and then follow Route 76.

Grund

15 km (9 mi) along Rte. 821 from Akureyri.

Grund is an ancient farmstead, once home to some of the clansmen of the bloody Sturlungar feuds of the 13th century. Don't miss the attractive turn-of-the-century church, which, since 1978, has been on the historical registry. This impressive edifice was built in 1905 entirely at the personal expense of Magnú Sigurðsson, a farmer at Grund. It breaks tradition from the east–west orientation of most churches and is instead built on a north–south line. Behind the altar in its north end is a painting of the resurrection, dating from the 19th century.

Saurbær

13 km (8 mi) south on Rte. 821 from Grund.

Here you'll find a church built in the 1850s from wood and turf; it's typical of Icelandic dwellings through the centuries. Be prepared for, well, sheepish looks from locals if you ask what the name Saurbær means.

En Route From the Saurbær pullout, turn left back onto Route 821. After about 1½ kilometers (1 mile), take a right over the Eyjafjarðará River to Route 829, which runs north parallel to Route 821. Within a few hundred yards after turning north you'll reach the historic **Möðruvellir farm.** The church at Möðruvellir has an English alabaster altarpiece dating from the 15th century. From here it is 25 kilometers (16 miles) north to the Ring Road.

If you drive east from Akureyri on the Ring Road, passing farms left and right, you'll soon cross the **Vaðlaheiði** (Marsh Heath) and enter the **Fnjóskadalur** (Tree-Stump Valley), formed by glaciers only a few thousand years ago. Go a few hundred yards past Route 833, which leads south into the western part of the valley, and turn right onto the next road, which takes you to the **Vaglaskógur** (Log Forest), one of the largest forests in this relatively treeless country. Vaglaskógur was probably even larger originally, but through the centuries, trees were taken for building material and firewood. Its tallest birches reach some 40 feet.

Goðafoss

From the Saurbær pullout, turn left back onto Rte. 821 and travel 28 km (17 mi) north to the Ring Road. Proceed east about 22 km (13 mi). Directly from Akureyri, Goðafoss is about 50 km (30 mi).

The beautiful Goðafoss (Waterfall of the Gods) is in the Skjálfandi River. The name Goðafoss derives from a historic event in AD 1000 when Þorgeir Ljósvetningagoði, ordered by the Icelandic Parliament to choose between paganism and Christianity, threw his pagan icons into the waterfall. Just before you reach Goðafoss, you'll pass the **Ljósavatn church**

and farm where Þorgeir lived a millennium ago. Although the farm is long gone, you can visit the church, which houses, among other relics, some interesting runic stones recently unearthed. There are plans for a new church and memorial to be built here before the year 2000, the millennial anniversary of Iceland's conversion to Christianity.

Mývatn

About 100 km (62 mi) along the Ring Road east of Akureyri.

This exquisite natural area deserves at least a day's exploration. It is an area influenced by active geology; a recent fissure eruption occurred here in 1984. The area's "false craters" were formed when hot lava of ancient eruptions ran over marshland, causing steam jets to spout up, forming small cones. Lake Mývatn is an aqueous gem set amid mountains and lava fields. Fed by cold springs in the lake bottom and from warm springs in the northeastern corner, the shallow lake, 15 square miles in area yet only 3 to 13 feet deep, teems with life—fish, birds, and insects, including the swarming midges for which the lake is named.

Waterfowl migrate long distances to breed at Mývatn, where the duck population numbers up to 150,000 in summer. Indeed, the lake has Europe's greatest variety of nesting ducks, including some, like the Harlequin duck and Barrow's Goldeneye, which are found nowhere else in Europe. Dozens of other kinds of waders, upland birds, and birds of prey nest here as well. This sanctuary draws bird-watchers from all over the world on pilgrimages to add to their "life lists." Be sure to stay on established trails and pathways, as nests can be anywhere.

Turning off the Ring Road at Route 848, you'll pass **Skútustaðir,** a village on the lake's southern shore. Proceed along the eastern shore to the 396-meter-high (1,300-foot-high) **Hverfjall** ash cone, a few hundred yards from the road. Several paths lead to the top, where you can take in a sweeping view of the lake and surroundings. The outer walls of this volcanic crater are steep, but the ascent is easy. The walk around the top of the crater is about 4,300 feet. Southwest of Hverfjall is the **Dimmuborgir** (Dark Castles) lava field, a labyrinth of tall formations where you can choose between short and longer signposted routes through the eerie landscape. Among its mysterious arches, gates, and caves, the best-known is the **Kirkja** (Church), resembling a Gothic chapel (it's marked by a sign, lest you miss it). Don't wander off the paths, as Dimmuborgir is a highly sensitive environment.

Proceeding a few kilometers south from Mývatn on the Ring Road, you'll pass a factory that processes diatomite (tiny skeletons of algae) sucked from the bottom of the lake, where they have been deposited through the centuries. Diatomite is used in filters and is an important local export. The diatomite factory at Mývatn is highly controversial; conservationists fear that it may endanger the ecosystem of the lake, yet it provides welcome employment for some of the local population. Research is now under way, and the plant may be closed down within a few years.

Dining and Lodging

$$ 🏨 **Hotel Reykjahlíð.** This small, family-run hotel has a prime lakeside location, with great views. All rooms were refurbished in 1995. ✉ *Reykjahlíð Mývatnssveit,* ☎ *464–4142,* 📠 *464–4336. 9 rooms. AE, MC, V.*

$ 🏨 **Youth Hostel.** This hostel near Mývatn has 50 beds. ✉ *Bárðardalur, 645 Fosshóll,* ☎ *464–3108,* 📠 *464–3318.*

$$$ ✕⊞ **Hotel Reynihlíð.** This popular hotel has rooms decorated in pastel colors and a helpful general information service for tourists. The restaurant serves entrées such as fresh lake trout, and rhubarb pie for dessert. ⊠ *Reykjahlíð Mývatnssveit,* ☎ *464–4170,* FAX *464–4371. 41 rooms. Restaurant, bar, horseback riding, bicycles. AE, DC, MC, V.*

Outdoor Activities and Sports

BICYCLING

The **Hótel Reynihlíð** (⊠ Mývatnssveit, ☎ 464–4170) in Mývatn rents bicycles for exploring the area around the lake.

BOATING

At Mývatn, **Eldá Travel** (☎ 464–4220) provides boats for rental for those who want to explore the lake.

FISHING

Angling permits can be obtained from **Hotel Reynihlíð** (☎ 464–4103). For fly fishing on the famous Laxá River, contact **Eldá travel service** (☎ 464–4220 fishing June–Aug.).

HORSEBACK RIDING

The **Hotel Reynihlíð** (☎ 464–4170) in Mývatn offers pony treks around the lake. Near Hrútafjörður, **Arinbjörn Jóhannsson** (☎ 451–2938) in Brekkulækur also organizes horseback treks.

En Route In the **Námaskarð Mountain Ridge,** on the eastern side of the Ring Road, are bubbling mud and purple sulfur, boiling like a witch's cauldron in the strange red and yellow valleys. Hike around this fascinating area, but remember to step carefully. Though the sulphurous vapors may smell like rotten eggs, the brimstone fumes are generally harmless.

Húsavík

Rte. 87 branches off the Ring Road to Húsavík. From Akureyri, the drive is 90 km (56 mi).

This attractive port is on the north coast. From there take Route 85 north along the coast to Tjörnes, ending up inland at the lush nature reserve of **Ásbyrgi** (Shelter of the Gods). The forest here is surrounded by steep cliffs on all sides except the north, making it a peaceful shelter from the wind. Legend says this horseshoe-shape canyon was formed by the giant hoof of Sleipnir, the eight-footed horse of Óðinn.

Contiguous with Ásbyrgi is the wild and magnificent **Jökulsárgljúfur National Park,** the rugged canyon of the glacial Jökulsá River. At the southernmost point of the park, on Route 864, see Europe's most powerful waterfall, **Dettifoss,** where 212 tons of water cascade each second over a 145-foot drop. Farther inland at **Kverkfjöll,** hot springs rise at the edge of the Vatnajökull Glacier, creating spectacular ice caves. Tours operate from Húsavík; contact BSH (⊠ Garðabraut 7, Box 115, Húsavík, ☎ 464–2200, FAX 464–2201).

Dining and Lodging

$$$ ✕⊞ **Hotel Húsavík.** Popular with skiers, most of the rooms at this solid hotel were refurbished in 1994. There's a good restaurant serving seafood, including delicious smoked salmon pâté and several halibut and trout entrées. ⊠ *Ketilsbraut 22,* ☎ *464–1220,* FAX *464–2161. 34 rooms. Restaurant, bar, cafeteria. AE, DC, MC, V.*

The North A to Z

Arriving and Departing

BY BUS

BSÍ Travel (☎ 552–2300) runs daily bus service from Reykjavík to the north. It's 4½ hours to Blönduós and 6½ hours to Akureyri. Bus service from Akureyri takes less than 1½ hours to Húsavík and two hours to Mývatn.

The **Akureyri Bus Company** (✉ Gránufélagsgata 4, ☎ 462–3510; at bus terminal, ☎ 462–4442) operates scheduled trips around the region, including a tour by bus and ferry to Hrísey Island, home of Galloway cattle, and to Grímsey Island on the Arctic Circle.

BY CAR

It's a 432-kilometer (268-mile) drive from Reykjavík to Akureyri along the Ring Road (Route 1), a full day's journey. Branch off on Route 75 to Sauðárkrókur, or on Route 85 to Húsavík.

BY PLANE

Icelandair (☎ 505–0200) flies to Akureyri, Sauðárkrókur, and Húsavík. The flight to Akureyri takes about an hour. **Norlandair** and Icelandair (☎ 462–2000) share offices and operate flights from Akureyri to Grímsey, Húsavík, Kópasker, Ólafsfjörður, Raufarhöfn, Siglufjörður, Þórshöfn, and Vopnafjörður. The **Mýflug** air charter company (☎ 464–4107, FAX 464–4341) flies daily direct from Reykjavík to Mývatn, from June to August. In Reykjavík, this service is handled by Íslandsflug (☎ 561–6060).

Contacts and Resources

EMERGENCIES

To reach the local **police** in Akureyri, call ☎ 462–3222.

GUIDED TOURS

The **Iceland Tourist Bureau** (☎ 462–5855) operates a 12-hour day trip from Reykjavík to Akureyri and Lake Mývatn by plane to Akureyri and then by bus to Mývatn. The tour departs daily June through mid-September.

Úrval-Útsýn (✉ Ráðhústorg 3, ☎ 462–5000) and **Nonni Travel** (✉ Brekkugata 3, ☎ 461–1841, FAX 461–1843) run tours from Akureyri to Mývatn, historic sites, and the islands off the north coast.

VISITOR INFORMATION

In **Akureyri,** contact the Tourist Information Center (✉ Coach Terminal, Hafnarstræti 82, ☎ 462–7733); it is open June through August, weekdays 8:30–7 PM. In **Húsavík,** Húsavík Travel (✉ Stórigarður 7, ☎ 464–2100) is open weekdays 9–noon and 1–5.

THE EAST

In 1974, when the final bridge across the treacherous glacial rivers and shifting sands south of the Vatnajökull Glacier was completed, the eastern side of the island finally became accessible from Reykjavík. It is still a long journey by car, but as you approach the area from the south, you can watch ice floes gliding toward the sea while the great skuas, predatory seabirds, swoop across black volcanic beaches.

The east coast has a number of busy fishing towns and villages, and it seems as if each has its own private fjord. Farming thrives along the area's major valleys, which enjoy very pleasant summers. The Ring Road ties the inland hub of Egilsstaðir with the coastal communities in the southern part of the east. Secondary roads are spokes linking communities not on the Ring Road.

Egilsstaðir

273 km (164 mi) from Akureyri and 700 km (420 mi) from Reykjavík.

This town, on the shore of Lake Lögurinn and straddling the Ring Road, is the hub of the Eastern Fjords. Egilsstaðir is at the northern end of the long, narrow lake called **Lögurinn.** A fascinating addition to the town in 1996 was a new museum that houses impressive artifacts found in the area. The most dramatic is a Viking chieftain's grave site and its lavish relics, believed to be nearly 1,000 years old.

Although the town itself has no other particular sights to see, an easy 25-kilometer (15-mile) drive from town along the lake's southern shore, first on the Ring Road and then onto Route 931, will take you to the ★ beautiful **Hallormsstaður Forestry Reserve,** which contains the country's largest forest; more than 40 varieties of trees grow here, mostly aspen, spruce, birch, and larch. This is one of Iceland's most accessible paradises—don't miss it! The Atlavík campground on the lake south of Hallormsstaðaskógur is a popular vacation spot, and the lake is reputed to be home to a worm-like serpent that lies on a treasure chest.

In the highlands west of Lögurinn you may be able to spot Icelandic reindeer. Though not native to the island (they were originally brought from Norway in the 18th century), the reindeer have thrived to the point that they damage tree saplings and farm growth, so controlled hunting is allowed. Game managers have allowed the sale of licenses to hunt some 600 animals annually.

OFF THE
BEATEN PATH

EIÐAR – Just north of Egilsstaðir on the Borgarfjörður Road, open-air dramatic and musical entertainment is scheduled weekly in summer. It is in Icelandic, but English summaries are available, and you don't have to understand the language to learn folk dances! Contact Philip Vogler (⊠ Dalskógar 12, 700 Egilsstaðir, ☎ 471–1673, ⓕ 471–2190) for information.

Dining and Lodging

$$$ ✕☷ **Hótel Valaskjálf.** Large and practical, this hotel has a restaurant and a cafeteria. The owners also run a summer hotel in the Egilsstaðir secondary school, with both beds and sleeping-bag spaces. ⊠ *Skógarlönd, 700 Egilsstaðir,* ☎ *471–1500,* ⓕ *471–1501. 21 rooms. AE, MC, V.*

$ ✕☷ **Edda Hotel.** This smallish hotel is in a beautiful setting in Hallormsstaður; the natural harmony of forest, lake, and quiet bays is a real attraction. The Edda has a good restaurant. ⊠ *Hallormsstað 707,* ☎ *471–1705. 20 rooms with shared bath. Restaurant, bar, pool. AE, DC, V. Closed Sept.–mid-June.*

$ ☷ **Youth Hostel.** This hostel, open May through September, has 23 beds. ⊠ *Tunguhreppur, 701 Egilsstaðir,* ☎ *471–3010,* ⓕ *471–3009.*

Outdoor Activities and Sports

BICYCLING

Bikes can be rented at the campsite in Egilsstaðir (☎ 471–2320).

SWIMMING

There is a swimming pool in Egilsstaðir (☎ 471–1467).

Seyðisfjörður

25 km (16 mi) east of Egilsstaðir.

This seaside village has been incorporated for just over 100 years. Modern visitors may find it hard to believe that it was one of Iceland's major trade ports in the 19th century. In those days, tall sailing frigates crowded the fjord. Nowadays, the ferry Norröna arrives regularly during summers, dispatching tourists and their vehicles from Europe. Seyðisfjörður has a number of beautiful Norwegian-style wood houses and buildings dating from the 1800s.

Dining and Lodging

$$ ✕🏨 **Hótel Snæfell.** Red carpets and beige furnishings decorate this old, wooden house turned hotel. The restaurant, with glass walls overlooking the dramatic fjord, serves up tasty fare; entrée specials include starry ray and, for dessert, chocolate cake. ✉ *Austurvegur 3, Seyðisfjörður,* ☎ *472–1460,* 🗏 *472–1570. 9 rooms. Restaurant, bar, horseback riding, fishing. AE, MC, V.*

$ 🏨 **Youth Hostel.** There are 28 beds here. ✉ *Ránargata 9, 710 Seyðisfjörður,* ☎ *472–1410,* 🗏 *472–1486.*

Bakkagerði

71 km (44 mi) north and east on Rte. 94 from Egilsstaðir.

Bakkagerði is by Borgarfjörður (not to be confused with its larger namesake in the west). The Borgarfjörður Road, though bumpy, is entirely safe, but don't be in a hurry. Savor the swooping descent from the Vatnsskarð mountain pass and the spectacular coast road along Njarðvíkurskriður. In a land of stunning mountain scenery, Borgarfjörður (east) is a natural masterpiece, where the changing tones in the landscape have to be seen to be believed. The painter Jóhannes Kjarval lived here, and as can be seen in his paintings, the countryside made a deep impression on him.

Lodging

$ 🏨 **Youth Hostel.** Open May through September, this hostel has 17 beds. ✉ *Hreppsskrifstofan, 685 Bakkafjörður,* ☎ *473–1686,* 🗏 *473–1668.*

Neskaupstaður

71 km (43 mi) east of Egilsstaðir, this town is reached by first driving south along Rte. 92 and curving east through Eskifjörður, then traveling north over Iceland's highest pass, completing a U-shape length on Route 92.

This is the largest town on the east coast, and trading began here in 1882. It was a thriving place during the "herring boom," and fishing is still a mainstay. Minor industry and services are set here in a tranquil location under rugged mountainsides. Among the local attractions is a natural history museum.

Lodging

$$ 🏨 **Hótel Egilsbúð.** One of the town's major accommodations also provides space for those with sleeping bags. ✉ *Egilsbraut 1, 740 Neskaupstaður,* ☎ *477–1321,* 🗏 *477–1322. 21 rooms, 5 in winter. AE, MC, V.*

Outdoor Activities and Sports

FISHING

Angling permits for the river Norðfjarðurá are available at **Tröllanaust** (✉ Melgata 11, ☎ 477–1444).

SEA CRUISES

Cruises on the Norðfjörður fjörd with sea angling as an option are available by calling ☎ 477–1321 or 853–1718.

The Neskaupstaður pool (⊠ Miðstræti 15, ☎ 477–1243) is open to the public.

Eskifjörður

Either backtrack 23 km (14 mi) from Neskaustaður on Rte. 92 over the breathtaking 701-m (2,300-ft) pass at Oddskarð, or go 48 km (29 mi) from Egilsstaðir.

This charming fishing village has, among other things, a freezing plant, which has murals by Iceland's Catalan artist Baltazar. Eskifjörður is on the beautiful Hólmanes Cape, which is noted for a wide variety of flora and bird life, and the southern part is now a protected area. The town's landmark mountain, Hólmatindur, is 230 feet, and, though stunning in appearance, it shades the town from the sun from late September to April. If you have time, you may want to check out the East Iceland Maritime Museum.

Lodging

$ 🏨 **Hotel Askja.** This cozy, old-fashioned year-round hotel offers rooms with a shared bathroom. ⊠ *Hólvegur 4, IS-735 Eskifjörður,* ☎ *476– 1261.7 rooms. Restaurant, bar. AE, MC, V.*

$ 🏨 **Hótel Buðareyri.** The accommodations here are simple. ⊠ *IS-730 Reyðarfjörður,* ☎ *474–1378. 6 rooms with shared bath. Restaurant, bar. AE, MC, V.*

$ 🏨 **Youth Hostel.** There are 25 beds here. ⊠ *Búðargata 4, 730 Reyðarfjörður,* ☎ *474–1447, 𝕱𝕬𝕏 474–1454.*

Outdoor Activities and Sports

Angling permits for the river Eskifja:rðurá are available by calling the town council at ☎ 476–1170.

Here you can swim in Eskifjörður's local pool (⊠ Lambeyrarbraut 14, ☎ 476–1238).

En Route If you drive south along Route 93 from Eskifjörður, you'll skirt **Reyðarfjörður,** the largest of the eastern fjords, 30 kilometers (18 miles) long and 7 kilometers (4.2 miles) wide. The sheltered harbor made the town of the same name an important commerce center. This was true even more so after Reyðarfjörður was linked to the Fagridalur Valley road in the early 1900s. Iceland's only museum of World War II memorabilia (☎ 474–1245) is found here, where some troops were stationed during the war. It's open afternoons only, June through August.

Breiðdalsvik

83 km (50 mi) south of Egilsstaðir along the Ring Road or, more circuitously, about 74 km (45 mi) along Rte. 96 from Reyðarfjörður.

Here's a tiny village of a few hundred kindred souls. This hamlet, which hugs the shore on its own small inlet, began to grow after the development of a harbor deep enough for most ships. The earliest commercial records for Breiðdalsvík date from 1883.

Dining and Lodging

$ ✕🏨 **Hótel Bláfell.** Only a few years old, this small hotel has a rustic yet cozy exterior. The interior is bright, and there's an award-winning restaurant with a menu emphasizing seafood and lamb. In summer, the hotel offers chalets in the nearby countryside. Fishing permits are available for the area. ⊠ *Sólvellir 14, 760 Breiðdalsvík,* ☎ *475–6770,* ℻ *475–6668. 15 rooms, 7 with private bath. Restaurant, bar. AE, MC, V.*

Djúpivogur

144 km (87 mi) south of Egilsstaðir on the Ring Road.

A fishing village has existed on this site since about 1600, and some of the oldest buildings in town date from the days of Danish merchant control from 1788 to 1920. A nearby basalt mountain, **Búlandstindur,** rises to 6,130 feet and, perhaps because of its pyramidal shape, is considered to be a focus of mystical energy.

Dining and Lodging

$ ✗🏠 **Hótel Framtíð.** This small, wood-frame hotel is right by the harbor. In the dining room, home-style food is served in a friendly atmosphere. Try the wolffish cooked in honey with apple and curry, pan-fried redfish with mushrooms and brandy sauce, or roast puffin from nearby Papey Island. For dessert there's homemade ice cream with fruit and caramel sauce. There is camping with a laundry facility available nearby. ⊠ *Vogalandi 4, IS-165 Djúpivogur,* ☎ *478–8887,* ℻ *478–8187. 22 rooms with shared bath. Restaurant, bar, sauna, bicycles. AE, MC, V.*

$ 🏠 **Youth Hostel.** Open May through September, this hostel has 20 beds. ⊠ *Berunes, Berufjörður, 765 Djúpivogur,* ☎ *478–8988,* ℻ *478–8988.*

En Route To continue along the Ring Road, drive south from Egilsstaðir 150 kilometers (93 miles) to the rugged stretch of coast indented by the inlets of **Álftafjörður** (Swan Fjord) and **Hamarsfjörður.** Surrounded by majestic mountains, these shallow waters host myriad swans, ducks, and other birds that migrate here from Europe in the spring and summer.

Höfn

103 km (62 mi) south of Djúpavogur on the Ring Road.

Höfn is slowly being closed off from the ocean by silt washed by glacial rivers into the fjord. Spread out on a low-lying headland at the mouth of the fjord, Höfn offers a fine view of the awesome **Vatnajökull Glacier,** which is not only Iceland's largest but is equal in size to all the glaciers on the European mainland put together. From Höfn you can arrange tours of the glacier.

OFF THE   **JÖKULSÁRLÓN** (Glacial River Lagoon) – About 50 kilometers (31 miles)
BEATEN PATH west of Höfn, you can see large chunks of the glacier tumble and float around in a spectacular ice show. Boat trips on the lagoon are operated throughout the summer. For details call Fjölnir Torfason (☎ 478–1065). Light meals and refreshments are available at a small coffeehouse at the lagoon. On the **Breiðamerkur sands** west of the lagoon is the largest North Atlantic colony of skua, large predatory seabirds that unhesitatingly "dive-bomb" intruders in the nesting season.

Dining and Lodging

$$$ ✗🏠 **Hótel Höfn.** This modern hotel is clean and comfortable. There's a separate annex with an additional 30 rooms. You can grab a bite at the fast-food-style restaurant, or opt for the more formal restaurant, where lobster and reindeer are the specialties; there's also a nightly seafood buffet. ⊠ *Víkurbraut 780, Höfn, Hornafjörður,* ☎ *478–1240,* ℻ *478–1996. 70 rooms, 28 with private bath. 2 restaurants, bar. AE, MC, V.*

$ 🛏 **Youth Hostel.** This hostel, open May through September, has 27 beds. ✉ *Nýibær, Hafnarbraut 8, 780 Höfn,* ☎ *478–1736.*

$ 🛏 **Youth Hostel.** Open May through September, this hostel near Höfn has 45 beds. ✉ *Stafafell, Lón, 781 Höfn,* ☎ *478–1717,* ℻ *478–1785.*

Outdoor Activities and Sports

SWIMMING

The Höfn swimming pool (✉ Hafnarbraut, ☎ 478–1157) is open to the public.

WHALE-WATCHING

Whale-watching trips are available from Höfn (☎ 478–1701, ℻ 478–1901).

Skaftafell

50 km (31 mi) west of Jökulsárlón.

Bordering on Vatnajökull is Skaftafell, the largest of Iceland's three national parks. The surrounding glacier shelters Skaftafell from winds, creating a verdant oasis, and farther up is the highest mountain in Iceland, **Hvannadalshnúkur,** rising 6,950 feet. The famous **Svartifoss** (Black Falls) tumbles over a cliff whose sides resemble the pipes of a great organ. In the park you can walk for days on beautiful trails through a rare combination of green forest, clear water, waterfalls, sands, mountains, and glaciers. Do not miss **Sel,** a restored gabled farmhouse high up on the slope. Guided walks in the national park are organized daily.

Lodging

$ 🛏 **Hotel Skaftafell.** This guest house is a stone's throw from Skaftafell National Park, and transportation can be arranged to and from its attractions. The restaurant specializes in fish dishes and offers a seafood buffet for summer diners. Sleeping-bag accommodations are available. ✉ *Skaftafell, 781 Höfn,* ☎ *478–1945,* ℻ *478–1846. 21 rooms. Restaurant, bar, snack bar. MC, V.*

The East A to Z

Arriving and Departing

BY BOAT

The **Norröna** car ferry from Norway or Denmark, via the Faroe Islands, arrives in Seyðisfjörður. Contact Norröna Travel (✉ Laugavegur 3, 101 Reykjavík, ☎ 562–6362, ℻ 552–9450) or Austfar (✉ 710 Seyðisfjörður, ☎ 472–1111, ℻ 472–1105).

BY BUS

The east is so far from Reykjavík that bus travel is recommended only if you are making the entire circuit. From Akureyri the six-hour trip to Egilsstaðir runs daily in summer, three times a week the rest of the year. From Egilsstaðir there's frequent service around the region; it takes about five hours to get to Höfn.

BY CAR

The region is accessible by car on the Ring Road (Highway 1). The drive from Reykjavík, along the south coast, to Egilsstaðir is about 700 kilometers (434 miles), and from Akureyri 273 kilometers (170 miles).

BY PLANE

Icelandair (☎ 471–1210) and **Eastair** (☎ 471–1122) operate scheduled flights from Reykjavík to Egilsstaðir. From there, connections are to Bakkafjörður, Borgarfjörður, Breiðdalsvík, Fáskrúðsfjörður, Hornafjörður, Norðfjörður, and Vopnafjörður. **Íslandsflug** (☎ 561–6060) flies to Neskaupstaður and Egilsstaðir.

Contacts and Resources

EMERGENCIES

In **Egilsstaðir**, the **police** are at ☎ 471–1223; in **Eskifjörður**, ☎ 476–1106; in **Breiðdalsvík**, ☎ 475–1280; in **Bakkageröi**, ☎ 473–1400; in **Neskaupstaður**, ☎ 477–1332; in **Seyðisfjörður**, ☎ 472–1334; in **Djúpivogur**, ☎ 475–1280; in **Höfn**, ☎ 478–1282.

GUIDED TOURS

The **Iceland Tourist Bureau** (☎ 562–3300) operates a day trip from Reykjavík to Höfn by plane, with a snowmobile tour of the Vatnajökull Glacier and a boat tour on the Jökulsárlón Lagoon. The tour runs daily mid-June–August. Glacier tours are operated from many different locations around the Vatnajökull Glacier: from Eskifjörður by **Tanni** (☎ 476–1399, FAX 476–1599) and from Höfn by **Jöklaferðir** (☎ 478–1000, FAX 478–1901).

Sightseeing cruises of the fjords (with or without fishing along the way) operate from various coastal villages. **Fjarðaferðir** of Neskaupstaður (☎ 477–1321, FAX 477–1322) offers sea trips of Norðfjörður and neighboring Mjóifjörður.

VISITOR INFORMATION

In **Egilsstaðir**, the Tourist Information Office is at the campsite (☎ 471–2320). In **Seyðisfjörður**, the Austfar Travel Agency (✉ Fjarðargata 8, ☎ 472–1111) is open weekdays 9–noon and 1–5. In **Höfn**, the Tourist Information Center at the campsite (☎ 478–1701) is open July–August, daily 8–11 and 5–11.

THE SOUTH

The power of volcanoes is all too evident on this final leg of the Ring Road tour. At Kirkjubæjarklaustur you can still see scars of the great Laki eruption of 1783. At Stöng you can visit excavated ruins of a farmstead buried in 1104 by the eruption of Mt. Hekla, which was known throughout medieval Europe as the abode of the damned; Hekla is still active, having erupted most recently in 1991. Off the coast, the Vestmannaeyjar (Westmann Islands) are still being formed by volcanic activity, and a 1973 eruption almost wiped out all habitation. The south also includes Þórsmörk (Thor's Wood), a popular nature reserve.

Kirkjubæjarklaustur

272 km (163 mi) east of Reykjavík along the Ring Road.

This village is the site of an old convent active from the 12th century to the Reformation. Each August, Kirkjubæjarklaustur hosts a three-day international chamber music festival; contact the Community Center (☞ Visitor Information, *below*) for information. Just west of here is the **Laki volcano,** with more than 100 craters dotting the landscape. To get here, turn right on the highland road leading north. The great lava field of the south coast was created by this volcano in a single eruption, in 1783–84. The worst in Iceland's history, it wiped out about 70% of the country's livestock and a fifth of the population. Jón Steingrímsson, then the priest at Kirkjubæjarklaustur, is said to have stopped the advance of the lava by prayer. About 30 kilometers (19 miles) east of Kirkjubæjarklaustur, don't miss the little chapel at **Núpsstaður,** one of a handful of extant turf churches. This well-preserved building has remained almost unchanged since the 17th century.

Lodging

$ 🏨 **Edda Hotel.** One of three year-round Edda Hotels, this facility is in a modern building. Sleeping-bag accommodations are available.

✉ *Kirkjubæjarklaustur,* ☎ *487– 4799,* FAX *487–1996. 73 rooms, 57 with shower. Restaurant, pool. AE, MC, V.*

Outdoor Activities and Sports

BOATING

Boats can be rented for a cruise on Lake Hæðargarðsvatn near Kirkjubæjarklaustur (☎ 487–4723).

En Route   Travel west from Kirkjubæjarklaustur 25 kilometers (15 miles) on Route 1, turn right onto Route 208, and continue for 20 kilometers (12 miles) on the mountain road Route F22 to **Eldgjá,** a 32-kilometer-long (20-mile-long) volcanic rift. Historic records suggest that it erupted in AD 934 with a ferocity similar to that of the Laki eruption.

Vík

80 km (48 mi) west of Kirkjubæjarklaustur.

Proceeding west along the Ring Road from Kirkjubæjarklaustur, you'll cross the Mýrdalssandur Desert and arrive at the coastal village of Vík, with its vast population of Arctic terns. From Vík, sea trips are made by amphibious vehicle: There is no harbor, so the vehicles simply drive from the sandy beach into the sea. You can go angling, whale-watching, or sightseeing to nearby Dyrhólæy. Contact Adventure Tours (☎ 487–1334, FAX 487–1330). Twelve kilometers (7 miles) past Vík, turn left toward the ocean to reach the southernmost point of the country, the **Dyrhólaey Promontory,** with its lighthouse. The ocean has worn the black basalt rock here into the shape of an arch, 394 feet high; ships can sail through it in calm weather. This headland is also a bird sanctuary, so expect it to be closed during the nesting period in early summer.

Lodging

$ 🏨 **Hótel Vík.** Open year-round, here there are 20 rooms, some with private bath. ✉ *Klettsvegur,* ☎ *487–1480 or 487–1230,* FAX *487–1418.*

$ 🏨 **Youth Hostel.** There are 25 beds at this hostel, open May through mid-September. ✉ *Reynisbrekka Mýdalur, 870 Vík,* ☎ *487–1106,* FAX *487–1303.*

Outdoor Activities and Sports

BICYCLING

Bikes can be rented at the **Ársalir Guesthouse** (✉ Austuvegur 7, Vík, ☎ 487–1400).

SNOWMOBILING

Snowmobiling is possible in summer on the Mýrdalsjökull Glacier, overlooking Vík through **Snjósleðaferðir** (✉ Dugguvogur 10, 104 Reykjavík, ☎ 568–2310, FAX 581– 3102).

Shopping

In the small town of Vík, there are factory outlets selling woolen goods: **Katla** (✉ Víkurbraut 16, ☎ 487–1170) and **Vikurprjón** (✉ Smiðjuvegur 15, ☎ 487–1250).

Skógar

32 km (19 miles) west of Vík.

Here at the tiny settlement of Skógar, you can visit one of Iceland's best folk museums (☎ 487–8845). Old houses are preserved in their original state, and there is a vast collection of household items from the surrounding area. Among the mementos of this region's past is one of the tiny, frail boats in which local fishermen once navigated the treacherous coast. The museum is open May through mid-September, daily 9–noon and 1–6, or by appointment.

Lodging

⊞ **Edda Hotel.** Close to the Skógafoss waterfall, this hotel is beautifully located, with views of the sea and the mountains and glaciers. It
has a restaurant that serves a supper buffet. Sleeping-bag accommodations are available. ⊠ *Skógum,* ☎ *487–8870,* 𝐅𝐀𝐗 *562–5895. 34
rooms with shared bath. AE, MC, V. Closed Sept.–mid-June.*

En Route Just a couple of hundred yards west of Skógar, just off the Ring Road
is the impressive **Skógafoss,** a waterfall that's more than 197 feet high.
If you drive 30 kilometers (19 miles) further west along the Ring Road
from Skógar, follow the turnoff to **Seljalandsfoss,** another waterfall,
which will be on the right. This graceful ribbon-like waterfall drops
from an overhanging lava cliff and looks as if it belongs in Hawaii. If
you step carefully, you can walk behind it, but be prepared to get wet.

Þórsmörk

*30 km (19 miles) along the Ring Road from Skógar to the turnoff on
your right.*

You'll come to the powerful **Markarfljót River.** Route 249 on its east
bank leads 15 kilometers (9 miles) east across some treacherous streams
into the **Þórsmörk** (Thor's Wood) nature reserve, a popular vacation
area bounded on its eastern and southern sides by the Eyjafjalla and
Mýrdals glaciers. This route is passable only to 4x4 Jeeps and large vehicles, preferably traveling together. Þórsmörk, nestled in a valley surrounded by mountain peaks, enjoys exceptionally calm and often sunny
weather, making it a veritable haven of birch trees and other Icelandic
flora. There are many excellent trekking routes (☞ Hiking, *below*), such
as a day's trip over the **Fimmvörðuháls Mountain pass** (a compass is a
necessity) down to Skógar, or a three-day hike into the interior to visit
Landmannalaugar, where hot and cold springs punctuate a landscape
rich in pastel, yellow, brown, and red rhyolite hills carved by glacial rivers.

The road on the west bank of the Markarfljót leads 10 kilometers (6
miles) north into saga country, to the site of **Hlíðarendi,** the farm where
Gunnar Hámundarson, one of the heroes of *Njál's Saga*—the single
greatest classic work of Icelandic saga literature written around the 12th
century—lived and died. Exiled by the Alþing parliament for murder-
ing Þorgeir Oddkelsson, he refused to leave "these beautiful slopes."

In the lowlands to the southwest of the Markarfljót (turn off the Ring
Road, toward shore, and then onto Route 252 and drive 20 kilometers
[12 miles]) to another famous place from *Njál's Saga:* **Bergþórshvoll,**
where Njál's enemies surrounded his farmhouse and burned it to the
ground, killing all, but one—Kári, Njál's son-in-law, survived from beneath a collapsed roof under cover of smoke from the burning house.

Hvolsvöllur

*54 km (33 mi) west of Skógar along the Ring Road, and 39 km (24
mi) from Þórsmörk Preserve.*

This small community is a relatively recent establishment, settled in
1932. Hvolsvöllur is now a busy service center for the fertile farm country surrounding it. A major meat-processing operation has moved here
from the capital, infusing new vigor into the area. Hvolsvöllur is a good
base, if you are interested in *Njál's Saga* or the glacial scenery.

Lodging

$$ ⊞ **Hótel Hvolsvöllur.** This hotel in Hvolsvöllur offers basic rooms. ⊠
Hlíðarvegur 7, ☎ *487–8187,* 𝐅𝐀𝐗 *487–8391. 28 rooms. Restaurant,
bar. AE, MC, V.*

$ 🛏 **Youth Hostel.** There are 15 beds at this hostel open mid-April through mid-October. ✉ *Fljótsdalur, Fljótshlíð, 861 Hvolsvöllur,* ☎ *487–8498.*

Outdoor Activities and Sports

HIKING

Both main Icelandic touring clubs, **Ferðafélag Islands** (✉ Mörkin 6, 108 Reykjavík, ☎ 568–2533, FAX 568–2535) and **Útivist** (✉ Hallveigarstígur 1, Reykjavík, ☎ 551–4606, FAX 561–4606) maintain large cabins with sleeping-bag accommodations in Þórsmörk; many long-distance hikes are organized from there.

Hella

12 km (about 7 mi) west of Hvolsvöllur on the Ring Road and 51 km (31 mi) from Þórsmörk; 93 km (58 mi) traveling west to Reykjavík.

About 10 kilometers (6 miles) west of Hella, turn right onto Route 26 and drive 40 kilometers (25 miles) or so until you see, on your right, the tallest peak in the region—the famous **Hekla volcano,** which has erupted nearly 20 times in recorded history and remains active. In the Middle Ages, Hekla was known throughout Western Europe as the abode of the damned. Some 25 kilometers (16 miles) farther, Route 26 intersects Route 32; turn left and go 15 kilometers (9 miles) to the right turn for **Stöng,** an ancient settlement on the west bank of the Þjórsá River, Iceland's longest. The original farm here dates back almost 900 years; it was buried in 1104 when Hekla erupted, but you can visit the excavated ruins. A complete replica has been built, using the same materials the settlers used, south of Stöng at Búrfell on Route 32.

Lodging

$ 🛏 **Youth Hostel.** This hostel has 50 beds. ✉ *Leirubakki (near Selfoss) Landssveit, 851 Hella,* ☎ *487–6591,* FAX *487–6591.*

Selfoss

36 km (22 mi) west of Hella on the Ring Road.

This bustling town on the shores of the turbulent Ölfusá River is the largest in southern Iceland. Selfoss came into being in the 1930s and is a major agricultural community with the country's largest dairy plant.

Lodging

🛏 **Hótel Selfoss.** This hotel in Selfoss has a restaurant and bar. ✉ *Eyarvegur 7, IS-800 Selfoss,* ☎ *482–2500,* FAX *482–2524. 28 rooms. AE, MC, V.*

Outdoor Activities and Sports

BICYCLING

Bikes can be rented at **Vallholt 21** (✉ Selfoss, ☎ 482–2714).

GOLF

The Svarfhólsvöllur course, in Selfoss, is on the banks of the Ölfusá River.

SWIMMING

There is a swimming pool in Selfoss (✉ Bankavegur, ☎ 482–1227).

Shopping

The **Vöryhús KA** (✉ Ring Rd., ☎ 482–1000) is the area's largest supermarket, and the department store has a wide selection of goods.

En Route At Hveragerði, take a left turn onto Route 38 and drive 20 kilometers (12 miles) to **Þorlákshöfn**—the gateway to Vestmannaeyjar, the Westmann Islands.

Vestmannaeyjar (Westmann Islands)

A 3 ¼-hour journey south from Þorlákshöfn on the passenger-car ferry **Herjólfur** *brings you to the Vestmannaeyjar. Domestic airlines take about an hour.*

Hjörleifur, sworn brother of Reykjavík settler Ingólfur Arnarson, settled in Heimay (the only inhabited island of Westmann archipelago) with 5 Irish slaves—called Westmen. The slaves soon after murdered their master and fled to the offshore islands. Ingólfur avenged his brother by driving most of the slaves off the cliffs of the islands and killing them. This tiny cluster of 15 islands off the south coast was named in honor of the Irish slaves—the Westmen.

The islands were formed by volcanic eruptions only 5,000 to 10,000 years ago, and there is still much volcanic activity here. **Surtsey,** the latest addition, was formed in November 1963 with an eruption that lasted 3½ years. In 1973 a five-month-long eruption on **Heimaey** wiped out part of the town of Vestmannaeyjar. The island's entire population of about 5,000 was forced to flee in fishing boats, with only a few hours' notice. A few years later, however, the people of Vestmannaeyjar had removed tons of black lava dust from their streets and rebuilt everything. The lava, still hot, is used for heat by the resourceful islanders.

The main industry here is fishing, but another local occupation (nowadays more a sport than a job) is more unusual: egg hunting. Egg pickers dangle from ropes over the sheer black volcanic cliffs to collect eggs from the nests of seabirds. The islands are rich in birds, especially puffins, which are used for food.

Sightseeing cruises run around Vestmannaeyjar, offering views of dramatic sea caves and neighboring islands. Sightseeing flights over Surtsey and the rest of the Westmann Islands can be arranged from Reykjavík or from Heimaey. Heimaey has one of Iceland's best natural history museums, with an excellent aquarium where you can see some of the peculiar creatures of the deep.

On the first weekend of August, islanders celebrate the 1874 grant of Icelandic sovereignty with a huge festival in the town of Vestmannaeyjar, on Heimaey. The population moves into a tent city in the **Herjólfsdalur** (Herjolf's Valley) a short distance west of town for an extended weekend of bonfires, dance, and song.

Lodging

$$ 🏨 **Hotel Bræðraborg.** Like most places on the island, this hotel is not far from the harbor. Island excursions can be arranged for guests. ⊠ *Herjólfsgata 4,* ☎ *481–1515,* FAX *481-2922. 30 rooms, some with private bath.*

$ 🏨 **Youth Hostel.** Open May through mid-September, this hostel has 35 beds. ⊠ *Faxastígur 38, 900 Vestmannæyjar,* ☎ *481–2915,* FAX *481–1497.*

🏕 **Camping** is available at Herjólfsdalur, except when locals take over the spot on the first weekend in August for their holiday. Call ☎ 481–1088 or 481–1471 for information.

Outdoor Activities and Sports

GOLF
An 18-hole golf course (⊠ Hamarsvegur, ☎ 481–2363) is on the main Westmann island, Heimaey.

SWIMMING
The local swimming pool is at the sports center on Illugagata (☎ 481–2401 or 481–2402).

The South A to Z

Arriving and Departing

BY BUS

BSÍ has daily service from Reykjavík, stopping in Hella, Hvolsvöllur, Selfoss, Vík, and Þorlakshöfn. The journey to Vík takes less than four hours; to Þorlakshöfn or Selfoss, one hour.

BY CAR

Kirkjubæjarklaustur is 272 kilometers (169 miles) east of Reykjavík on the Ring Road. West from Höfn, it is 201 kilometers (125 miles) to Kirkjubæjarklaustur.

BY FERRY

The passenger and car ferry **Herjólfur** (☎ 481–2800 or 483–3413) sails daily to Vestmannaeyjar from Þorlákshöfn. There are immediate bus connections to Reykjavík from the Westmann Islands ferry at Þorlák-shöfn; the trip takes about 90 minutes.

BY PLANE

Icelandair (☎ 569–0200) and **Íslandsflug** (☎ 561–6060) fly daily from Reykjavík Airport to the Vestmannaeyjar (Westmann Islands); flight time is about 30 minutes.

Contacts and Resources

EMERGENCIES

Police stations in **Kirkjubæjarklaustur,** ☎ 487–4694; in **Hvolsvöllur,** ☎ 487–8434; in **Selfoss,** ☎ 482–1154; in the **Vestmannaeyjar,** ☎ 481–1666; in **Vík,** ☎ 487–1176.

GUIDED TOURS

The **Iceland Tourist Bureau** (☎ 562–3300) operates a 10-hour day trip from Reykjavík to the Vestmannaeyjar by plane, running daily all year. Arrangements can also be made for a 3-hour sightseeing flight over Heimaey in the islands. **Austurleið** bus company (✉ Austurvegi 1, Hvolsvöllur, ☎ 487–8197) operates tours to Þórsmörk, Skaftafell, the Eastern Fjords, and the interior.

VISITOR INFORMATION

In **Kirkjubæjarklaustur,** the Community Center (✉ Klausturvegur 10, ☎ 487–4620) is open mid-June–mid-August, daily 10–4. In **Vík,** the Camping Site (☎ 487–1345) and Víkurskáli (☎ 487–1230) will provide information. In **Selfoss,** information is provided at Tryggvaskáli (✉ next to bridge over Ölfusá River, ☎ 482–1704).

ICELAND A TO Z

Arriving and Departing

By Plane

All international flights originate from and arrive at **Keflavík Airport** (☎ 425–0600) in the southwestern corner of Iceland, 50 kilometers (30 miles) south of Reykjavík. On arrival you may spot some military aircraft, for Keflavík is also a NATO military installation, manned by the U.S. Navy. However, the Leifur Eiríksson terminal is completely separate from the base.

FROM NORTH AMERICA

Icelandair (✉ 610 5th Ave., New York, NY 10020, ☎ 800/223–5500) operates regular direct flights daily from New York City's JFK airport; service from Baltimore flies daily; service from Orlando runs twice a week in winter, once a week in summer; weekly flights operate out of Fort Lauderdale. As of spring 1996, flights leave from

Boston four times per week and from Hallifax, Nova Scotia, twice weekly.
The flight from New York to Keflavík takes 5½ hours.

Icelandair and **SAS** both operate between mainland Scandinavia and
Iceland. Hitherto in competition, the two airlines now coordinate services. For information on services, contact Icelandair in Copenhagen
(☎ 33/12–33–88), Stockholm (☎ 08/310240), or Oslo (☎ 67–53–
21–35), or SAS in Copenhagen (☎ 33/15–48–77) or Reykjavík (☎
562–2211).

Icelandair (✉ 172 Tottenham Court Rd., 3rd Floor, London W1P
9LG, ☎ 0171/388–5599) flies daily from London's Heathrow Airport
to Keflavík. There are two flights a week from Glasgow, and once a
week Icelandair flies from Glasgow via the Faroe Islands to Iceland.
The full round-trip fare from London in summer 1996 was £852
(APEX fare £310). The flight from London takes three hours.

Iceland is a good destination to combine with a trip to continental Europe. The full round-trip fare from New York to Iceland in August 1996
was $1,556 midweek (APEX fare $938), but the full round-trip fare
from New York to Luxembourg, Icelandair's main European gateway,
cost $2,114 midweek and allowed a stopover in Iceland for up to one
week. If you stop over in Iceland for three days or less, the round-trip
to Luxembourg would cost $698 midweek (weekend fares are slightly
higher). Various special discount offers, including great weekend fares,
may be available at different times, for limited-validity and prebooked
seats, so check on your options.

By Ship
It is possible to sail to Iceland on the car-and-passenger ferry *Norröna,*
operated by **Smyril Line** (✉ Box 370, 3800 Tórshavn, Faroe Islands,
☎ 1/5900, FAX 1/5707; Engelgarden, Nye Bryggen, N-5023 Bergen, Norway, ☎ 5/320970, FAX 5/960272; Norröna Travel, Laugavegur 3, 101
Reykjavík, Iceland, ☎ 562–6362, FAX 552–9450).

The Norröna plies between the Faroes, Esbjerg in Denmark, Bergen
in Norway, and Seyðisfjörður on the east coast of Iceland. Depending
upon your point of departure and your destination, the trip may involve a stopover of some days in the Faroes. Special offers for accommodations may be available through Smyril Line, and special
fly-cruise arrangements are available through Smyril Line and Icelandair. You can also sail between Iceland and Europe by freight vessel. **Eimskip,** Iceland's largest shipping company, offers limited passenger
accommodations (plus the option of taking your own car along) on
container vessels. You can sail from Immingham (England), Hamburg
(Germany), Antwerp (Belgium), or Rotterdam (Netherlands) to Reykjavík. Information and bookings are available from **Úrval-Útsýn Travel**
(✉ Lágmúli 4, 108 Reykjavík, ☎ 569–9300).

Getting Around
By Boat
There is daily scheduled ferry service year-round between Reykjavík
and Akranes on the ferry **Akraborg** (☎ 551–6050) and between Þorlákshöfn, on the southern coast, and Vestmannaeyjar (the Westmann
Islands) on the ferry **Herjólfur** (☎ 483–3413, FAX 551–2991). The **Baldur** car ferry (☎ 438–1120 or 456–2020, FAX 438–1093) sails twice
daily in summer from Stykkishólmur, on the Snæfellsnes Peninsula, across
Breiðafjörður Bay to Brjánslækur in the Western Fjords.

By Bus

An extensive network of buses serves most parts of Iceland; services are intermittent in the winter season, and some routes are operated only in summer. Fares range from IKr1,000 for a round-trip to Þingvellir to IKr6,500 for a round-trip to Akureyri. The bus network is operated from **Bifreiðastöð Íslands** (BSÍ, ⌧ Vatnsmýrarvegur 10, ☏ 552–2300, FAX 552–9973); its terminal is located on the northern rim of Reykjavík Airport.

If you want to explore the island extensively, it's a good idea to buy the **Omnibus Passport,** which covers travel on all scheduled bus routes, with unlimited stopovers. A seven-day pass costs about $210, a two-week pass $302, a three-week pass $395, and a four-week pass $440. The **Full Circle Passport,** which costs $195, is valid for a circular trip on the Ring Road mid-July to mid-September; you can take as long as you like to complete the journey as long as you keep heading in the same direction on the circuit (detours into the interior must be paid for separately).

The **Air/Bus Rover** ticket offered by Icelandair and BSÍ allows you to fly one-way to any domestic Icelandair destination and by bus in the other direction, so you can save some time and still have a chance to explore the countryside. Prices start at $129 for Reykjavík-Akureyri. The price rises to $212 if you take the mountain bus route by way of Sprengisandur instead of the Ring Road.

Holders of BSÍ Passport tickets are entitled to various discounts, for instance at campsites, Edda hotels, and on ferries. Mountain bikes can be rented from BSÍ at prices from $17 for a day to $305 for four weeks.

By Car

The Ring Road, which generally hugs the coastline, stretches almost 1,400 kilometers (900 miles) around Iceland. Although 80% of the road is paved, a long stretch across the Möîrudalsöræfi highlands in the east is still gravel. Much of Iceland's secondary road system is unpaved. Take great care on these roads, as driving on loose gravel surface takes some getting used to and is not for the timid motorist. Do not expect to travel fast.

Be cautious when driving in the interior in Iceland. The terrain can be treacherous, and many roads can be traversed only in four-wheel-drive vehicles; always drive in the company of at least one other car. Unbridged rivers, which must be forded, constitute a real hazard and should never be crossed without the advice of an experienced Iceland highland driver. Most mountain roads are closed by snow in winter and do not open again until mid-June or early July, when the road surface has dried out after the spring thaw. Before driving any distance in rural Iceland, be sure to pick up the brochure "Driving in Iceland" from any Tourist Information Center. This offers informative tips and advice about driving the country's back roads.

Service stations are spaced no more than half a day's drive apart, on both main roads and side roads. Service stations in the Reykjavík area are open Monday through Saturday 7:30 AM–8 PM; opening hours outside Reykjavík vary, but gas stations are often open until 11:30 PM. For information on road conditions and the availability of gas off the beaten track, call **Vegagerð Ríkisins** (Public Roads Administration) (⌧ Borgartún 5–7, Reykjavík, ☏ 563–1500).

Traffic outside Reykjavík is generally light, but roads have only one lane going in each direction, so stay within the speed limit: 70 kph (45 mph) on the open road, 50 kph (30 mph) in urban areas. Drivers are

required by law to use headlights at all times. Seat belts are required
for the driver and all passengers.

By Plane

Because so much of Iceland's central region is uninhabited, domestic
air transport has been well developed to link the coastal towns. It isn't
particularly cheap—round-trip fares range from IKr8,200 to
IKr15,600—but there are various discounts available. The longest domestic flight takes just over an hour.

In summer, **Icelandair** (☎ 505–0200) schedules daily or frequent
flights from Reykjavík to most of the large towns, such as Akureyri,
Egilsstaðir, Húsavík, Höfn, Ísafjörður, and Vestmannaeyjar. Icelandair
provides bus connections between airports outside Reykjavík and
nearby towns and villages.

Íslandsflug (☎ 561–6060) flies daily to Vestmannaeyjar, Egilsstaðir,
and Bíldudalur and also flies regularly to Flateyri, Siglufjörður, Neskaupstaður, Hólmavík, and Gjögur. **Norlandair** (☎ 461–2100) serves the
north from Akureyri, **Eastair** (☎ 471–1122) serves the east with charters out of Egilsstaðir, and **Ernir Air** (☎ 552–4200) serves the Western
Fjords from Ísafjörður. APEX tickets are available on domestic flights
if booked two days in advance. These offer savings of 50% on the full
airfare (e.g., round-trip Reykjavík to Akureyri IKr6,300 instead of
IKr12,600).

The **Fly As You Please Holiday Ticket** is valid for unlimited travel on
all Icelandair domestic routes for 12 days. Sold exclusively in advance
to Icelandair international passengers, it cost $435 in summer 1996.
The **Four-Sector Iceland Air Pass** is valid for a month and can be used
on any four sectors flown by Icelandair and Norlandair. This pass must
also be booked before arrival in Iceland and costs $290. Several other
types of Air Pass, covering different combinations of sectors, are also
available. The **Mini-Iceland Air Pass,** valid on two sectors, costs $170.

Contacts and Resources

Car Rentals

Renting a car in Iceland is expensive; it may well be worth arranging
a car in advance through your travel agent, who may be able to offer
a better deal. A typical price for a compact car is around Ikr6,000 per
day, with 100 kilometers (62 miles) free, plus IKr31 per kilometer. A
four-wheel-drive vehicle for rougher roads will cost about IKr12,000
per day, with 100 kilometers (62 miles) included, plus IKr60 per kilometer. These prices do not include collision damage waiver. There are
many car-rental agencies in Iceland, so it is worth shopping around for
the best buy. You must also pay for the gasoline, which is very expensive,
IKr67 to IKr75 per liter depending on octane rating. If you plan to explore the interior, make sure you rent a four-wheel-drive vehicle.

Avis (☎ 425–0760) and **Hertz/Icelandair** (☎ 569–0200) operate offices in the Leifur Eiríksson Terminal at Keflavík Airport.

Dining

More than 50 restaurants around the country participate in a tourist-
menu scheme: A meal of soup or starter, fish or meat dish, and coffee
costs IKr800–IKr1,000 for lunch or IKr1,100–IKr1,700 for dinner,
with discounts for children (children under five eat free). Participating restaurants display a TOURIST MENU sticker in their windows, and
a leaflet listing all participating restaurants is available free from the
Icelandic Hotel and Restaurant Association (✉ Hafnarstræti 20, 101
Reykjavík, ☎ 552–7410 or 562–1410, FAX 552–7478). Details of

restaurants all over the country and the services they offer are given in another booklet, "Dining and Wining," available free from the association.

Emergencies

Dial ☎ **112** in an emergency; it is a nationwide number.

Guided Tours

Inclusive guided tours are offered by a number of travel agencies in Iceland, the largest of which are **Samvinn Travel** (✉ Austurstræti 12, Reykjavík, ☎ 569–1010, FAX 569–1095), **Úrval-Útsýn Travel** (✉ Lágmúli 4, Reykjavík, ☎ 569–9300, FAX 567– 0202), and the **Iceland Tourist Bureau** (✉ Skógarhlíð 18, Reykjavík, ☎ 562–3300, FAX 562–5895). Most operators offer a range of tours by bus; some itineraries include air travel. Many agencies also offer the possibility of combining an Icelandic holiday with a tour of Greenland.

For the fit and active, hiking, biking, or horse-riding tours are also available. In these cases, accommodations will usually be in tents, guesthouses, or mountain huts. Guided hiking tours of the interior are organized by the **Touring Club of Iceland** (✉ Mörkin 6, ☎ 568–2533, FAX 568–2535). A variety of smaller travel agencies also offer tours, some of them quite specialized. For information, contact the **Icelandic Tourist Board** (✉ Gimli, Lækjargata 3, Reykjavík, ☎ 552–7488, FAX 562–4749).

Language

The official language is Icelandic, a highly inflected Germanic tongue brought to the country by the early Viking settlers. Since it has only slightly changed over the centuries, modern Icelanders can read the ancient manuscripts of the sagas without difficulty. English and Danish are widely spoken and understood, while many Icelanders also speak other Scandinavian languages or German, and some speak French.

The Icelandic alphabet contains two unique letters—þ, pronounced like the *th* in thin, and ð, pronounced like the *th* in leather.

Lodging

CAMPGROUNDS

Organized campgrounds are available throughout the country. Some are on private property, others are owned and operated by local communities, and still others are in protected areas supervised by the Nature Conservation Council. For a comprehensive listing of campgrounds, write or call the **Association of Leisure Site Owners** (c/o the Tourist Information Center, ✉ Bankastræti 2, 101 Reykjavík, ☎ 562–3045, FAX 562–4749). On the road, look for signs reading Tjaldstæði bönnuð (camping prohibited) or Tjaldstæði (camping allowed), or a simple tent symbol. Most campgrounds charge about IKr200 per person per night, plus IKr200 for the tent. Campsites in national parks are more expensive.

It is forbidden to use scrubwood for fuel; bring paraffin or gas stoves for cooking. Camping equipment can be rented in Reykjavík at **Tjaldaleigan Rent-a-Tent** (☎ 551–3072).

FARM HOLIDAYS

Write to **Icelandic Farm Holidays** (✉ Bændahöllinni við Hagatorg, 107 Reykjavík, ☎ 562–3640, FAX 551–9200) for a booklet describing all farms and their facilities. A double room without breakfast costs IKr1,950–IKr2,950 per night; sleeping-bag accommodations without breakfast costs IKr800–IKr1,250 per night. Summer cottages can be rented by the week; a six-bed cottage costs IKr32,500–IKr39,000 during peak season.

The **Icelandic Hotel and Restaurant Association** (☞ Dining, *above*) publishes a brochure each year with details of hotels and guest houses throughout the country. In addition to the **Edda** summer hotels, are two other local hotel "chains", the year-round **Rainbow** hotels (☎ 562–0160, FAX 562–0150) and the **Lykil (Key)** hotels (☎ 483–4700, FAX 483–4775), which also includes a university dormitory. The **Gist-Ís** organization (☎ 564–3090, FAX 564–3091) publishes a brochure on budget accommodations. During the summer season, hotels and even youth hostels may be fully booked, so make reservations well in advance.

You can also stay at any of more than 30 mountain huts located throughout the country and owned by **Ferðafélag Íslands** (the Touring Club of Iceland) (☎ 568–2533, FAX 568–2535). During summer season it is necessary to book space in these in advance. Depending on location, huts accommodate from 12 to 120 and are rated in two categories: **A**-class huts have running water and gas for cooking during summers, in addition to bunk beds and mattresses; **B**-class huts are basic shelters with bunk beds and mattresses.

Rental fees are discounted to Touring Club Members. A-class huts are IKr1,150 per person per night for nonmembers, IKr750 for members; B-class huts are IKr800 per person per night for nonmembers, IKr550 for members.

Eighteen boarding schools around the country, which would otherwise stand empty during the long summer vacation, open up as Edda summer hotels, offering both accommodations with made-up beds and more basic sleeping-bag facilities. A double room costs IKr4,550, a single IKr3,400. You can sleep on a mattress in your own sleeping bag for IKr850 to IKr1,350 per night depending on facilities. Most Edda hotels have restaurants offering good home-style cooking or better. Three Edda hotels in the south are open year-round: at Flúðir, toward the interior; at Hvolsvöllur; and at Vík. For information and bookings, contact the **Iceland Tourist Bureau** (⊠ Skógarhlíð 18, 101 Reykjavík, ☎ 562–3300, FAX 562– 5895).

At Iceland's 31 youth hostels, accommodations are inexpensive: about IKr1,250 per night, or IKr1,000 for members of the Youth Hostel Association. You get a bed, access to a kitchen and toilet, a pillow, and a blanket. Breakfast costs IKr500. Some hostels are crowded during the summer, so call ahead. Hostels outside Reykjavík permit you to use your own sleeping bag. For information, write to **Farfugladeild Reykjavíkur** (⊠ Sundlaugavegi 34, 105 Reykjavík, ☎ 553–8110, FAX 567–9201).

Mail

Stamps for postcards to Europe cost IKr30, for airmail letters IKr35. Stamps for postcards and airmail letters to the United States cost IKr65. Mail to and from northern Europe and Scandinavia usually takes two to three days. Other services are slower. All post offices also have fax machines for public use.

Money and Expenses

The unit of currency in Iceland is the króna (IKr). Icelandic notes come in denominations of IKr 500, 1,000, 2,000, and 5,000. Coins are IKr1, 5, 10, 50, and 100. The króna is divided into 100 *aurar,* which are as good as worthless. You can bring in any amount of foreign currency and exchange it in any Icelandic bank. However, don't bother trying to exchange currency before your departure, because Icelandic money is virtually unavailable at foreign banks. Also, Icelandic money can be difficult to exchange back home, so exchange any last krónas you are carrying at the departure terminal in Keflavík.

At press time (summer 1996) the exchange rate of the króna hovered around IKr67 to the U.S. dollar, IKr104 to the pound sterling, and IKr50 to the Canadian dollar.

SAMPLE PRICES

Iceland is an expensive destination, but the effect can often be softened by shopping around. For instance, a cup of coffee costs IKr100 at a cafeteria but IKr150 at a fine restaurant. An imported German beer or Icelandic brew costs IKr150–IKr200 (in six-packs only) at the state monopoly store (ÁTVR) but IKr600 at a bar. A can of soda costs IKr100 at the grocery, IKr150 at a restaurant or bar. A ready-made sandwich at the grocery store costs IKr160–IKr200, and at a bakery you can buy a roll and butter for about IKr70. A short taxi ride within Reykjavík costs IKr600. Hotels and restaurants cost up to 50% more in Reykjavík than elsewhere in the country.

TAXES

A 24.5% *virðisaukaskattur* (value-added tax, or VAT), commonly called VSK, applies to most goods and services. Usually the VAT is included in a price; if not, that fact must be stated explicitly. Foreign visitors can claim a partial refund on the VAT, which accounts for 19.68% of the purchase price of most goods and services. Fifteen percent of the purchase price for goods is refunded, providing you buy a minimum of IKr5,000 at one time. Souvenir stores issue "tax-free checks" that allow foreign visitors to collect the VAT rebates directly in the duty-free store when departing from Keflavík Airport. To qualify, keep your purchases in tax-free packages (except woolens), and show them to customs officers at the departure gate along with a passport and the tax-free check. If you depart the country from somewhere other than Keflavík, have customs authorities stamp your tax-free check, then mail the stamped check within three months to Iceland Tax-Free Shopping, Box 1200, 235 Keflavík, Iceland. You will be reimbursed in U.S. dollars at the current exchange rate.

Opening and Closing Times

All **banks** in Iceland are open weekdays 9:15–4. A few branches in major towns are also open Thursday 5–6. **Post offices** in most towns are open weekdays only from 8:30 or 9 AM to 4:30 or 5PM. **Lunch** is generally served from noon to 2, and **dinner** is between 6 and 9. Many of the more exclusive restaurants open only in the evenings. Outside Reykjavík it is generally possible to find **food stores** that remain open seven days a week.

Outdoor Activities and Sports

FISHING

The Icelandic Fishing Guide and a special fishing voucher book available from **Icelandic Farm Holidays** (✉ Bændahöllin við Hagatorg, 107 Reykjavík, ☎ 562–3640 or 551–9200) can be used in 50 river and lake locations around the country. Fishing-rod rental can often be arranged at some of these spots. If you wish to bring your own fishing tackle, it must be disinfected either at home (certificate needed) or by customs at Keflavík Airport.

Sea angling is becoming popular in Iceland as a leisure sport. Fishing cruises can be organized from many of the country's fishing towns and villages. For further information, contact the **Tourist Information Center** (✉ Bankastræti 2, ☎ 562–3044, FAX 562–4749). Several weekend deep-sea fishing competitions are held each year, a few are: at Whitsun in **Vest-manneyjar** (contact Elínborg Bernódusdóttir, ☎ 481–1279 or 481–1118); in June in **Reykjavík** (contact Birkir Þór Guðmundsson, ☎ 553–0734); in July at **Ísafjörður** (contact Kolbrún Halldórsdóttir, ☎ 456–3069); in August at **Akureyri** (contact Júlíus Snorrason, ☎ 462–1173).

GOLF

There are about 50 golf courses in Iceland. Most are primitive 9-hole courses, but there are six good 18-hole courses. The Arctic Open, played at the Akuryeri Golf course during the midnight sun in June, is one of the world's most unique tournaments. Greens fees range from IKr800 for par-three courses to IKr2,600 for 18-hole minimums. For information on golfing opportunities in Iceland, contact the **Golf Association** (☎ 568–6686, FAX 568–6086).

HIKING

Many organized tours from Reykjavík and other towns include some days of hiking. You can also join special hiking tours that are popular among Icelanders, arranged by the touring clubs. Contact **Ferðafélag Íslands** (Touring Club of Iceland) (⌧ Mörkin 6, 108 Reykjavík, ☎ 568–2533, FAX 568–2535) and **Útivist** (Touring Club Útivist) (⌧ Hallveigarstígur 1, 101 Reykjavík, ☎ 551–4606, FAX 561–4606). For serious exploring or hiking, you can obtain good up-to-date maps from **Landmælingar Íslands** (the Icelandic Geodetic Survey) (⌧ Laugavegi 178, 105 Reykjavík, ☎ 568–0999).

Be aware of the considerable dangers of hiking alone. Lava can be treacherous, with razor-sharp edges that can cut through clothes and skin. Footing can be tricky, as moss layers often hide uneven terrain. Do not stray too close to hot springs and sulfur springs, as the ground surrounding them may suddenly give way, leaving you standing in boiling water or mud. When hiking across country, follow paths made by sheep if footpaths are not available. When admiring the delicate flora, soft mosses, and lichen, remember that in preserves and national parks, it is illegal to pick flowers or take rock samples. Remeber that at sub-Arctic latitudes, it takes centuries for even the most common flowers to become established on this terrain. It's advisable to dress in layers, with a windproof outer shell, and have sturdy broken-in hiking shoes. When you are camping, tents should be firmly anchored against possible winds. Don't venture away from frequented areas unless you have researched the territory in advance and have a detailed map. Finally, always let someone know of your hiking plans, and avoid hiking alone.

HORSEBACK RIDING

Many equestrian events are held around the country during the summer months, from local races and contests to major regional championships. Contact **Landssamband Hestamannafélaga** (Equestrian Federation) (⌧ Bændahöllin, Hagatorg, 101 Reykjavík, ☎ 552–9899) for details of forthcoming horse events. There is even the international association FEIF for those in 20 countries who own or admire the Icelandic horse.

SKIING

In summer, the **Kerlingarfjöll Ski School** west of the Hofsjökull Glacier runs five- to six-day courses; you can also get lift tickets without taking lessons, and there are accommodations and food at the school. Contact **Úrval-Útsýn Travel Agency** (⌧ Lágmúli 4, 108 Reykjavík, ☎ 569–9300).

SNOWMOBILING

A company with varied glacier destinations is **ADD-ICE** (☎ 588–5555, FAX 588–5554). One popular excursion visits the glacial tongue, Sólheimarjökull, part of the larger Mýrdalsjökull glacier in the south. Contact **Snjósleðaferðir** (✉ Dugguvogi 10, IS-104 Reykjavík, ☎ 568–2310, FAX 581–3102). *See also* Guided Tours, *above.*

SWIMMING

Almost every sizable community in Iceland has at least one public outdoor swimming pool. Since most are generally heated by thermal springs, they can be enjoyed year-round. Inquire at the tourist office or a local hotel for the nearest pool.

Telephones

Iceland's country code is 354.

INTERNATIONAL CALLS

You can dial direct, starting with 00 followed by the country code and local number. An international calling card is a convenient mode of payment. Avoid charging overseas calls to your hotel bills, as the surcharge can double the cost of the call. Card phones are becoming more common: 100-unit phone cards (IKr500) can be purchased at all post offices and some other outlets. Dial ☎ 09 for an overseas operator (or ☎ 08 for overseas directory assistance).

LOCAL CALLS

Names are listed alphabetically in the telephone book by first name as a result of the patronymic system (men add -*son* to their father's first name, women add -*dóttir*). Jobs or professions are often listed together with names and addresses.

Pay phones are usually located indoors in post offices, hotels, or at transportation terminals. They accept IKr5, IKr10, or IKr50 coins, which are placed in the slot before dialing. The dial tone is continuous. A 10-minute call between regions costs between IKr50 and IKr75.

OPERATOR INFORMATION

For long-distance calls within Iceland, dial ☎ 02 for the operator or ☎ 03 for directory assistance.

Tipping

Tipping is not conventional in Iceland and may even be frowned upon. Service charges of 15% to 20% are included in prices when applicable.

Visitor Information

Icelandic Tourist Board (✉ 655 3rd Ave., New York, NY 10017, ☎ 212/949–2333, FAX 212/983–5260).

In the United Kingdom, **Icelandair** (✉ 172 Tottenham Court Rd., 3rd Floor, London W1P 9LG, ☎ 0171/388–5599, FAX 0171/387–5711) distributes information on behalf of the Iceland Tourist Board.

5 Norway

Knuckled by snow-topped mountains and serrated by Gulf Stream–warmed fjords, Norway has an abundance of magnificent views. No matter how or where you approach, if you fly above the clean ivory mountains of Tromsø in the winter, or tear by in a heart-stopping train north of Voss in the spring, getting there is often as eye-popping as arriving.

JUST NORTH OF LILLEHAMMER lives a Norwegian family on the banks of the Mjøsa Lake. Every year they pack their bags and drive to their holiday retreat, where they bask in the warmth of the long, northern sun for four full weeks—then they pack up and drive the 100 yards back home again.

By Melody
Favish and
Karina Porcelli

Updated by
Shelley Pannill
and William F.
Vazquez

Although most Norwegians vacation a bit farther from home, their sentiments—attachment to, pride in, and reverence for their great outdoors—remain the same as the feelings of those who only journey across the street. Whether in the verdant dales of the interior, the brooding mountains of the north, or the carved fjords and archipelagoes of the coast, their ubiquitous *hytter* (cabins or cottages) dot even the most violent landscapes. It's a question of perspective: To a Norwegian, it's not a matter of whether or not to enjoy the land but how to enjoy it at this very moment.

In any kind of weather, blasting or balmy, inordinate numbers are out of doors, to fish, bike, ski, hike, and, intentionally or not, strike the pose many foreigners regard as larger-than-life Norwegian: ruddy-faced, athletic, reindeer-sweatered. And all—from cherubic children to decorous senior citizens—are bundled up for just one more swoosh down the slopes, one more walk through the forest.

Although it's a modern, highly industrialized nation, vast areas of the country (up to 95%) remain forested or fallow; and Norwegians intend to keep them that way—in part by making it extremely difficult for foreigners, who may feel differently about the land, to purchase property.

When discussing the size of their country, Norwegians like to say that if Oslo remained fixed and the northern part of the country were swung south, it would reach all the way to Rome. Perched at the very top of the globe, this northern land is long and rangy, 2,750 kilometers (1,700 miles) in length, with only 4 million people scattered over it—making it the least densely populated land in Europe except for Iceland.

Thanks to the Gulf Stream, the coastal regions enjoy a moderate, temperate climate in winter, keeping the country green, while the interior has a more typical northern climate. Of course, throughout the land, winter temperatures can dip far below zero, but that doesn't thwart the activities of the Norwegians. As one North Caper put it, "We don't have good weather or bad weather, only a lot of weather."

Norwegians are justifiably proud of their native land and of their ability to survive the elements and foreign invasions. The first people to appear on the land were reindeer hunters and fisherfolk who were migrating north, following the path of the retreating ice. By the Bronze Age, settlements began to appear, and, as rock carvings show (and modern school children are proud to announce), the first Norwegians began to ski—purely as a form of locomotion—some 4,000 years ago.

The Viking Age has perhaps left the most indelible mark on the country. The Vikings' travels and conquests took them to Iceland, England, Ireland (they founded Dublin in the 840s), and North America. Though they were famed as plunderers, their craftsmanship and fearlessness are revered by modern Norwegians, who place ancient Viking ships in museums, cast copies of thousand-year-old silver designs into jewelry, and adventure across the seas in sailboats to prove the abilities of their forefathers.

Harald I, better known as Harald the Fairhaired, swore he would not cut his hair until he united Norway, and in the 9th century he succeeded in doing both. But a millennium passed between that great era and Norwegian independence. Between the Middle Ages and 1905, Norway remained under the rule of either Denmark or Sweden, even after the constitution was written in 1814.

The 19th century saw the establishment of the Norwegian identity and a blossoming of culture. This romantic period produced some of the nation's most famous individuals, among them composer Edvard Grieg, dramatist Henrik Ibsen, expressionist painter Edvard Munch, polar explorer Roald Amundsen, and explorer-humanitarian Fridtjof Nansen. Vestiges of nationalist lyricism spangle the buildings of the era with Viking dragonheads and scrollwork, all of which symbolize the rebirth of the Viking spirit.

Faithful to their democratic nature, Norwegians held a referendum to choose a king in 1905, when independence from Sweden became reality. Prince Carl of Denmark became King Haakon VII. His baby's name was changed from Alexander to Olav, and he, and later his son, presided over the kingdom for more than 85 years. When King Olav V died in January 1991, the normally reserved Norwegians stood in line for hours to write in the condolence book at the Royal Palace. Rather than simply sign their names, they wrote personal letters of devotion to the man they called the "people's king." Thousands set candles in the snow outside the palace, transforming the winter darkness into a cathedral of ice and flame.

Harald V, Olav's son, is now king, with continuity assured by his own young-adult son, Crown Prince Haakon. Norwegians continue to salute the royal family with flag-waving and parades on May 17, Constitution Day, a spirited holiday of independence that transforms Oslo's main boulevard, Karl Johans Gate, into a massive street party as people of all ages, many in national costume, make a beeline to the palace.

During both world wars, Norway tried to maintain neutrality. World War I brought not only casualties and a considerable loss to the country's merchant fleet but also financial gain through the repurchase of major companies, sovereignty over Svalbard (the islands near the North Pole), and the reaffirmation of Norway's prominence in international shipping. At the onset of World War II, Norway once again proclaimed neutrality and appeared more concerned with Allied minelaying on the west coast than with national security. A country of mostly fisherfolk, lumber workers, and farmers, it was just beginning to realize its industrial potential when the Nazis invaded. Five years of German occupation and a burn-and-retreat strategy in the north finally left the nation ravaged. True to form, however, the people who had been evacuated returned to the embers of the north to rebuild their homes and villages.

In 1968 oil was discovered in the North Sea, and Norway was transformed from a fishing and shipping outpost to a highly developed industrial nation. Though still committed to a far-reaching social system, Norway developed in the next 20 years into a wealthy country, with a per capita income and standard of living among the world's highest, as well as long life expectancy.

Stand on a street corner with a map, and a curious Norwegian will show you the way. Visit a neighborhood, and within moments you'll be the talk of the town. As a native of Bergen quipped, "Next to skiing, gossip is a national sport." With one foot in modern, liberal Scandinavia and the other in the provincial and often self-righteous countryside, Norway, unlike its Nordic siblings, is clinging steadfastly to its separate and distinct identity within Europe. Famous for its social restrictiveness—smoking is frowned upon, liquor may not be served before 3 PM (and never on Sunday), and violence, even among cartoon characters, is closely monitored—Norway is determined to repel outside interference, so much so that a national referendum in November 1994 chose to reject membership in the European Union for the second time. The next few years will show if prosperous Norway will pay an economic price for its proud assertion of independence.

Pleasures and Pastimes

Beaches

Many Norwegians enjoy beaches in the summer, but low water temperatures, from 14°C to 18°C (57°F to 65°F), are enough to deter all but the most hardy visitors from getting into the water. The beaches around Mandal in the south and Jaeren's Ogna, Brusand, and Bore, closer to Stavanger, are the country's best, with fine white sand. However, all along the Oslo Fjord are good beaches too. The western fjords are warmer and calmer than the open beaches of the south—although they have rock, and not sand, beaches—and inland freshwater lakes are chillier still than Gulf Stream–warmed fjords. Topless bathing is common, and there are nude beaches all along the coast.

Dining

Eating is a cultural element of Norwegian society. The Norwegians pride themselves on gracious entertaining and lavish dinner parties using their finest silver and glassware. Dining out in Norway is expensive, so many weekend nights are spent at the houses of friends and relatives enjoying long, candlelit dinners with lively conversation and oftentimes countless glasses of wine. (The BYOB—Bring Your Own Bottle—policy in Norway is common, since alcohol prices are so high.) Recently, as Norwegians spend more time in the office and less time at home, eating at restaurants has become more popular, especially in cities like Oslo and Stavanger. In these larger areas, the dining scene is thriving. Until lately, fine restaurants were invariably French, and fine food usually meant meat. Now, in addition to the old reliable restaurants that serve traditional Norwegian dishes, you'll find spots that serve everything from tapas to Thai cuisine.

Norwegians are beginning to feel competition from foreign foods, though, and are taking greater pride in their native cuisine. Today seafood and game have replaced beef and veal. Fish, from common cod and skate to the noble salmon, have a prominent place in the new Norwegian kitchen, and local capelin roe, golden caviar, is served instead of the imported variety. Norwegian lamb, full of flavor, is now in the spotlight, and game, from birds to moose, is prepared with sauces made from the wild berries that are part of their diet. These dishes are often accompanied by root vegetables.

Desserts, too, often feature fruit and berries. Norwegian strawberries and raspberries ripen in the long, early summer days and are sweeter and more intense than those grown farther south. Red and black currants are also used. Two berries native to Norway are *tyttebær* (lingonberries), which taste similar to cranberries but are much smaller, and *multer* (cloudberries), which look like orange raspberries but have an indescribable taste. These wild berries grow above the tree line and are a real delicacy. Multe are often served as *multekrem* (in whipped cream) as a dessert, whereas tyttebær preserves often accompany traditional meat dishes.

For centuries, Norwegians regarded food as fuel, and their dining habits still bear traces of this. *Frokost* (breakfast) is a fairly big meal, usually with a selection of crusty bread, jams, herring, cold meat, and cheese. *Geitost* (a sweet, caramel-flavored whey cheese made wholly or in part from goats' milk) and Norvegia (a Norwegian Gouda-type cheese) are on virtually every table. They are eaten in thin slices, cut with a cheese plane or slicer, a Norwegian invention, on buttered wheat or rye bread.

Lunsj (lunch) is simple and usually consists of *smørbrød* (open-faced sandwiches). Most businesses have only a 30-minute lunch break, so unless there's a company cafeteria, most people bring their lunch from home. Big lunchtime buffet tables, *koldtbord,* where one can sample most of Norway's special dishes all at once, are primarily for special occasions and visitors.

Middag (dinner), the only hot meal of the day, is early—from 1 to 4 in the country, 3 to 7 in the city—so many cafeterias serving home-style food close by 6 or 7 in the evening. In Oslo it's possible to get dinner as late as midnight at certain dining establishments, especially in summertime. You'll probably find that most restaurants in Oslo usually stop serving dinner around 10 PM.

Traditional, home-style Norwegian food is stick-to-the-ribs fare, served in generous portions and blanketed with gravy. One of the most popular meals is *kjøttkaker* (meat cakes), which resemble small Salisbury steaks, served with boiled potatoes, stewed cabbage, and brown gravy. Almost as popular are *medisterkaker* (mild pork sausage patties), served with brown gravy and caraway-seasoned sauerkraut, and *reinsdyrkaker* (reindeer meatballs), served with cream sauce and lingonberry jam. Other typical meat dishes include *fårikål,* a great-tasting lamb and cabbage stew, and *steik* (roast meat), always served well done. Fish dishes include poached *torsk* (cod) or *laks* (salmon), served with a creamy sauce called Sandefjord butter; *seibiff,* fried pollack and onions; and *fiskegrateng,* something between a fish soufflé and a casserole, usually served with carrot slaw.

Norway is known for several eccentric, often pungent fish dishes, but these are not representative—both *rakørret* and *raklaks* (fermented trout and salmon) and *lutefisk* (dried cod soaked in lye and then boiled) are acquired tastes, even for natives. These dishes are often served at holidays, accompanied by the national drink, *akevitt* (sometimes spelled aquavit), a schnapps-like liquor that is made from potatoes and caraway seeds.

Traditional desserts include the ubiquitous *karamellpudding* (crème caramel) and *rømmegrøt* (sour-cream porridge served with cinnamon sugar) and a glass of *saft* (raspberry juice). The latter, a typical farm dish, tastes very much like warm cheesecake batter—delicious. It's often served with *fenalår* (dried leg of mutton) and *lefsekling,* a thin tortilla made with sour cream and potatoes, buttered and coated with sugar. Christmastime brings with it a delectable array of light, sweet, and buttery pastries. The *bløtkake* (layered cream cake with custard, fruit, and marzipan) is a favorite for Christmas and special occasions but can be purchased in bakeries year-round.

CATEGORY	COST
$$$$	over NKr450
$$$	NKr300–NKr450
$$	NKr150–NKr300
$	under NKr150

per person for a three-course meal, including tax and 12½% service charge

Fishing

Whether it's fly-fishing for salmon or trout in western rivers or deep-sea fishing off the northern coast, Norway has all kinds of angling possibilities.

Hiking

Seemingly, one of the most common expressions in the Norwegian language is *gå på tur,* or go for a walk. Every city has surrounding trails where Norwegians usually spend a good part of their weekends hiking and strolling. Many of the trails have cabins where guests can rest, eat, and even spend the night. Den Norske Turistforening (☞ Bicycling *in* Norway A to Z, *below*) and affiliated organizations administer cabins and tourist facilities in the central and northern mountainous areas of the country and will arrange group hikes.

Lodging

Norway is a land of hard beds and hearty breakfasts. Hotel standards are high, and even the simplest youth hostels provide good mattresses with fluffy down comforters and clean showers or baths. Breakfast, usually served buffet style, is almost always included in the room price at hotels, whereas hostels often charge extra for the morning meal.

Norway has several hotel chains. SAS, which is a division of the airline, has a number of luxury hotels designed for the business traveler. Many are above the Arctic Circle and are the "only game in town." Rica and Reso hotels, also luxury chains, have expanded extensively in the past few years. Best Western, Rainbow, and Choice Hotels International are moderate chains, found in most major towns. The most interesting and distinctive hotel chain is Home Hotels (Swedish owned), which has successfully converted existing historic buildings into modern functional establishments in the middle price range. All Home Hotels provide an evening meal, jogging suits, free beer, and other amenities designed to appeal to the single, usually business, traveler. As far as value for money is concerned, they are Norway's best buy. The Farmer's Association operates simple hotels in most towns and cities. These reasonably priced accommodations usually have "-heimen" as part of the name, such as Bondeheimen in Oslo. The same organization also runs cafeterias serving traditional Norwegian food, usually called Kaffistova. All of these hotels and restaurants are alcohol-free.

At times it seems as though the SAS and Rica hotel chains are the only ones in northern Norway, and often that is true. These are always top-rate, usually the most expensive hotels in town, with the best restaurant and the most extensive facilities. Rustic cabins and campsites are also available everywhere, as well as some independent hotels.

In the Lofoten and Vesterålen islands, *rorbuer,* fishing cottages that have been converted into lodgings or modern versions of these simple dwellings, are the most popular form of accommodation. These rustic quayside cabins, with minikitchens, bunk beds, living rooms, and showers, are reasonably priced, and they give a unique experience of the region. *Sjøhus* (sea houses) are larger, usually two- or three-storied buildings similar to rorbuer.

Norway has 90 youth hostels, but in an effort to appeal to vacationers of all ages, the name has been changed to *vandrehjem* (travelers' homes). Norwegian hostels are among the best in the world, squeaky clean and with excellent facilities. Rooms sleep from two to six, and many have private showers. You don't have to be a member, but members get reductions, so it's worth joining. Membership can be arranged at any vandrerhjem, or you can buy a coupon book good for seven nights, which includes the membership fee. Linens are usually rented per night, so it's a good idea to bring your own—if you haven't, you can buy a *lakenpose* (sheet sleeping bag) at specialty stores, or one at the vandrerhjem (☞ Lodging *in* Norway A to Z, *below*).

Norway has more than 900 inspected and classified campsites, many with showers, bathrooms, and hookups for electricity. Most also have cabins or chalets to rent by the night or longer.

PRICE CATEGORY	MAJOR CITIES*	OTHER AREAS*
$$$$	over NKr1,300	over NKr1,000
$$$	NKr1,000–NKr1,300	NKr850–NKr1,000
$$	NKr800–NKr1,000	NKr650–NKr850
$	under NKr800	under NKr650

*All prices are for a standard double room, including service and 23% VAT.

Orienteering

One of Norway's most popular mass-participation sports is based on running or hiking over territory with a map and compass to find control points marked on a map. Special cards can be purchased at sports shops to be punched at control points found during a season. It's an enjoyable, inexpensive family sport, and gear can be purchased at any sports shop.

Shopping

Almost no one leaves Norway without buying a hand-knit sweater. Although the prices for these sweaters may seem high, the quality is outstanding. The classic knitting designs, with snowflakes and reindeer, are still bestsellers and can be bought at most *Husfliden* (homecraft) outlets and specialty stores, while more modern sweaters, made of combinations of brightly colored yarns, can be purchased from yarn shops. If you knit or needlepoint, you may want to take home some yarn or embroidery kits.

Given the Norwegians' affection for the outdoors, an abundance of high-quality sportsgear and outerwear is available. Good buys include Helly-Hansen rain gear, insulated boots, and the *supertrøye,* a gossamer-thin, insulated undershirt.

Handicraft lovers will marvel at Norway's goods. You'll find hand-made pewter and wrought-iron candlesticks, hand-dipped candles, hand-blown glass, and hand-turned wood bowls, spoons, and platters made of birch roots, decorated with rosemaling (intricate painted or carved floral folk-art designs). Although your visit may be in June, this is a great place to stock up on your Christmas goods. All Husfliden stores and many gift shops sell Christmas ornaments handmade from straw and wood shavings. *Juleduk* (Christmas tablecloths) with typical Norwegian themes are for sale year-round at embroidery shops. Other, more off-beat, items include *ostehøvler* (cheese slicers) and *kransekakeformer,* graduated forms for making almond ring cakes. If you're looking for Norwegian recipes, you may want to seek out Arne Brimi's cookbook—*A Taste of Norwegian Nature.* It's sold in most bookstores.

Silver is a good buy in Norway, especially with the value-added tax refund (☞ Taxes *in* Norway A to Z, *below*). Norwegian silver companies produce a wide range of patterns. At 830 parts to 1,000, compared with 925 parts in sterling, Norwegian silver is stronger than English or American, and the price is very competitive.

Unfortunately, Norwegian rustic antiques may not be exported. Even the simplest corner shelf or dish rack valued at $50 is considered a national treasure if it is known to be more than 100 years old. However, you'll find that there are some really good replicas of old Norwegian farm furniture available.

Skiing

The ski is Norway's contribution to the world of sports. In 1994 the Winter Olympics were held in Lillehammer, which, along with other Norwegian resorts, regularly hosts World Cup competitions and world skiing championships. In addition to downhill and cross-country, the 100-year-old Telemark style is enjoying a revival across the country. It involves a characteristic deep-knee bend in the turns and traditional garb, including heavy boots attached to the skis only at the toe. Cross-country skiing is a great way to see Norway's nature; it requires only basic equipment, and rentals are readily available. Most every city has lit trails for evening skiing. Norway's skiing season lasts from November to Easter. But winter's not the only time for skiing in Norway—you may want to try summer skiing on a glacier, which can be quite a novelty.

Exploring Norway

Norway is long and narrow, bordered by Sweden to the east, and jagged coastline to the west. The west coast is carved by deep, dramatic fjords, and small coastal villages dot the shores in between. Bergen, the country's second largest city, is touted as the capital of the West Coast.

Norway's official capital, Oslo, is in the east, only a few hours from the Swedish border. The coast, from Oslo around the southern tip of the country up to Stavanger, is filled with wide beaches and seaside communties. North of here, in Norway's central interior, the country is blanketed with mountains that sculpt the landscape, creating dramatic valleys and plateaus. Moving north, the land becomes wild and untouched. Outside of the north's two main cities, Trondheim and Tromsø, the land seems to stretch for miles, which it actually does—into the Arctic Circle and up to the Russian border. We describe each of these regions in its own section below.

Numbers in the text correspond to numbers in the margin and on the maps.

Great Itineraries

What sets Norway apart from other European countries is not so much its cultural tradition or its internationally renowned museums as its spectacular natural beauty. What other world capital has subway service to the forest, or lakes and hiking trails within city limits as Oslo does? Although it takes only a few days to briefly explore Oslo and its environs, a full week or more would allow for more leisurely explorations of Norway's stunning countryside, including its fjords, plateaus, mountains, and valleys.

IF YOU HAVE 5 DAYS

Oslo, Norway's capital, makes a good starting point since most flights to Norway arrive here. Spend your first two days exploring ⊞ **Oslo** ①– ㉘. Take it easy the first day and explore the downtown area—meander on Karl Johans Gate, see Akershus Castle and the Kvadraturen, and walk through Vigelands (Frogner) Park. On day two, head out to Bygdøy and visit the area's museums—the Vikingskiphuset is a must; the Bygdøy area will take nearly a full day. On the third day, depart for Bergen by train. This 6-hour trip across Norway's interior allows you to see some of the country's specacatular scenery, including **Hardangervidda.** When you get to ⊞ **Bergen** ㉞–㊾, check into your hotel and head to Bryggen—where you'll see some of the city's oldest, and best-preserved buildings—for dinner. Spend your fourth day explorging Bergen. If you have time, head out to Bergen's environs to see Troldhaugen, which was composer Edvard Grieg's house for 22 years. Spend

Norway

TO
SVALBARD

North Cape

Vardø

Vadsø

Kirkenes

Hammerfest

Alta

Karasjok

Kautokeino

*ATLANTIC
OCEAN*

Tromsø

FINLAND

Harstad

Narvik

*Norwegian
Sea*

Bodø   Fauske

Arctic Circle

Mo i Rana

Sandnessjøen   Mosjøen

Brønnøysund

SWEDEN

Gulf of Bothnia

Rørvik

Namsos

Steinkjer

Trondheim   Meråker

Støren

Kristiansund   Røros

Molde   Oppdal

Ålesund   Åndalsnes   Tynset

Geiranger   Dombås

Nordfjord   Otta   Koppang

Florø   Jostedalsbreen

Sognefjorden   Lillehammer   Rena

Voss   Geilo   Hamar

Bergen   Hønefoss   Eidsvoll

Baltic Sea

Drammen   Oslo

Haugesund   Kongsberg   Fredrikstad

Larvik   Halden

Stavanger   Porsgrunn

Sandnes   Arendal

Evje

Grimstad

Mandal   Kristiansand

Skagerrak

Kattegat

N

0   200 miles

0   300 km

your last night in Bergen, and on the fifth day, fly back to Oslo to catch your flight home.

IF YOU HAVE 10 DAYS

Spend your first four days following the tour above. On the fifth day, however, take the day trip, **Norway in a Nutshell** (☞ Guided Tours *in* Bergen A to Z, *below*), which is a bus-train-boat tour that takes you through some of the western fjord country. Spend your fifth night in Bergen, and on your sixth day, fly to 🏛 **Tromsø** ⑦⑧, which is north of the Arctic Circle. Spend the rest of the day touring Tromsø. Overnight here, and on your seventh day, rent a car and head for 🏛 **Alta** ⑦⑨. If you arrive early enough, visit the Alta Museum. Spend the night in Alta, and on the eighth day, continue your voyage, driving further on to 🏛 **Hammerfest** ⑧⓪, the world's northernmost town. Overnight in Hammerfest, and the next day, take an excursion up the the treeless tundra of the **Nordkapp** ⑧② (North Cape). Return to Hammerfest, and on your last day, return back to Oslo by plane via Alta. Then, from Fornebu airport in Oslo, bid *ha det* (good-bye) to Norway and head home.

When to Tour Norway

To experience the endless days of the Midnight Sun, the best time to visit Norway is mid-May to late July. Hotels, museums, and sights are open and transportation is beefed up. If you decide to travel in May, try to be in Norway on the 17th, or *Syttende Mai*, Norway's Constitution Day, when flag-waving Norwegians bedecked in national costumes, or *bunader,* fill the streets.

Autumn weather is quite unpredictable. The days can be cool and crisp, or wet and bone-chillingly cold. However, the Gulf Stream, which flows along the Norwegian coast, keeps the weather surprisingly mild for such a high latitude.

Norway in winter is a wonderland of snow-covered mountains glowing under the northern lights, and few tourists are around to get in your way (although many tourist sights are closed). The days may seem perpetually dark, and November through February can seem especially dreary. If it's skiing you're interested in, plan your trip for March or April, as there's usually still plenty of snow left. Take note that during Eastertime, many Norwegians head for the mountains so it's hard to get accommodations, and cities are literally shut down—even grocery stores close.

OSLO

Although it is one of the world's largest capital cities in area, Oslo has only 480,000 inhabitants. Nevertheless, in recent years the city has taken off: Shops are open later; cafés and restaurants are crowded at all hours; and theaters play to full houses every night of the week.

Even without nightlife, Oslo has a lot to offer—parks, water, trees, hiking and skiing trails (2,600 kilometers [1,600 miles] in greater Oslo), and above all, spectacular views. Starting at the docks opposite City Hall, right at the edge of the Oslo Fjord, the city sprawls up the sides of the mountains that surround it, providing panoramic vistas from almost any vantage point but no definable downtown skyline. A recent building spree has added a number of modern towers, particularly in the area around the Central Railway Station, which clash painfully with the neoclassical architecture in the rest of the city.

Oslo has been Norway's center of commerce for about 500 years, and most major Norwegian companies are based in the capital. The sea has always been Norway's lifeline to the rest of the world: The Oslo Fjord teems with activity, from summer sailors and shrimpers to merchant ships and passenger ferries heading for Denmark and Germany.

Oslo is an old city, dating from the mid-11th century. The city has actually burned down 14 times since its creation, and was all but destroyed by a fire in 1624, when it was redesigned and renamed Christiania by Denmark's royal builder, King Christian IV. During the mid-19th century, and under the influence of the Swedish king, Karl Johan, who ruled the newly united Kingdom of Norway and Sweden, the grand ax—named after himself—was constructed. A definite product of the European city planning trends, Karl Johans Gate has been at the center of city life ever since. An act of Parliament finally changed the city's name back to Oslo, its original Viking name, in 1925.

Exploring Oslo

Karl Johans Gate, starting at Oslo Sentralstasjon (Oslo Central Station, also called Oslo S Station) and ending at the Royal Palace, forms the backbone of downtown Oslo. Many of Oslo's museums and historic buildings lie between the parallel streets of Grensen and Rådhusgata. Just north of the center of town is a historic area with a medieval church and old buildings. West of downtown is Frogner, the residential area closest to town, with embassies, fine restaurants, antiques shops, galleries, and the Vigeland sculpture park. Farther west is the Bygdøy Peninsula, with five museums and a castle. Northwest of town is Holmenkollen, with beautiful houses, a famous ski jump, and a restaurant. On the east side, where many new immigrants live, are the Munch Museum and the botanical gardens.

Downtown: The Royal Palace to City Hall

Although the city is huge (454 square kilometers [175 square miles]), downtown Oslo is compact, with shops, museums, historic sights, restaurants, and clubs concentrated in a small, walkable center—brightly illuminated at night.

A GOOD WALK

Oslo's main promenade, Karl Johans Gate, runs from **Slottet** ① through town. Walk down the incline, and to your left you will see three yellow buildings of the old **Universitet** ②—today they are used only by the law school. Murals painted by Edvard Munch decorate the interior walls of these buildings. Around the corner from the university on Universitetsgata is the **Nasjonalgalleriet** ③, which contains hundreds of Norwegian, Scandinavian, and European works, including Munch's famous painting *The Scream*. Back-to-back with the National Gallery, across a parking lot, is a big cream-brick Art Nouveau–style building housing the **Historisk Museum** ④, whose collection of Viking artifacts is impressive. Continue along Frederiksgate to the university and cross Karl Johans Gate to the **Nationaltheatret** ⑤ and Studenterlunden Park. This impressive building is not only the national theater, but a popular meeting place—many buses stop out front, and the T-bane is right beside it.

Walk past the Lille Grensen shopping area and once again cross Karl Johans Gate to see **Stortinget** ⑥, the Norwegian Parliament. Then go back to Stortingsgata. From here, turn left on Universitetsgata, and walk through a cul-de-sac–type area toward the water to reach the redbrick **Rådhuset** ⑦, a familiar landmark with its two block towers, dedicated during Oslo's 900th-year jubilee celebrations in 1950. After visiting Rådhuset, end your tour with an øl (beer) or mineral water at one of the many outdoor cafés at **Aker Brygge** (☞ Dining, *below*).

TIMING

The walk alone should take no more than two hours, even if you take time to wander around in Royal Palace park. If you happen to be at the Royal Palace midday, you might catch the changing of the guard, which happens every day at 1:30. When you are planning your tour, take note that many museums are closed on Mondays.

SIGHTS TO SEE

4 **Historisk Museum (Historical Museum).** Intricately carved *stave kirke* (wood church) portals and other Viking and medieval artifacts are on display here. There's an exhibition about the great polar explorer Roald Amundsen, the first man to reach the South Pole, as well as Asian and African ethnographic exhibits. ✉ *Frederiksgt. 2,* ☎ *22/85–99–12.* ✆ *Free.* ☉ *Mid-May–mid-Sept., Tues.–Sun. 11–3; rest of yr, Tues.–Sun. noon–3.*

3 **Nasjonalgalleriet (The National Gallery).** Many Scandinavian impressionists, who have recently been discovered by the rest of the world, are represented here in Norway's official art museum. Some impressive fjord and moonlight scenes by Norwegian artists such as Christian Krogh and J.C. Dahl fill the walls of the 19th- and early-20th-century Norwegian rooms. The gallery also has an extensive Munch collection. It was from here that Munch's *The Scream* was stolen during the 1994 Winter Olympics. It was recovered and is back, with added security. ✉ *Universitetsgt. 13,* ☎ *22/20–04–04.* ✆ *Free.* ☉ *Mon., Wed., Fri., and Sat. 10–4; Thurs. 10–8; Sun. 11–3.*

5 **Nationaltheatret (The National Theater).** In front of this neoclassical theater, built in 1899, are statues of Norway's great playwrights, Bjørnstjerne Bjørnson (who wrote the words to the national anthem and won a Nobel Prize for his plays) and Henrik Ibsen, author of *A Doll's House, Hedda Gabler,* and *The Wild Duck.* Most performances are in Norwegian, so you may just want to take a guided tour of the interior. ✉ *Stortingsgt. 15,* ☎ *22/41–27–10.*

★ **7** **Rådhuset (City Hall).** The redbrick exterior of Oslo's City Hall may seem dull compared with the marble-floored interior, whose murals and frescoes are bursting with color. Many sculptures outside, as well as murals inside, reflect the artistic climate in Norway in the 1930s—socialist modernism in its highest form. Much of the adornment depicts not only daily life but also Viking gods and Norwegian literary figures. This may be the only City Hall in the world with a sculpture of a prostitute; it's on the east side of the building facing the fjord. The Nobel Peace Prize as been handed out in the Main Hall since 1990. ✉ *Rådhuspl.,* ☎ *22/86–16–00.* ✆ *Free.* ☉ *May–Aug., Mon.–Sat. 9–5, Sun. noon–4; Sept.–Apr., Mon.–Sat. 9–3:30, Sun. noon–4. Guided tours year-round, weekdays 10, noon, and 2.*

★ **1** **Slottet (The Royal Palace).** The neoclassical palace, completed in 1848, is closed to visitors, but the garden is open to the public. An equestrian statue of Karl Johan, king of Sweden and Norway from 1818 to 1844, stands in the square in front of the palace.

6 **Stortinget (The Norwegian Parliament).** Built in the middle of the 19th century, this classical building is perched on the top of a small hill. At night, the steps here become a great spot for people-watching. When Parliament is in session, the public gallery is open to curious onlookers. ✉ *Karl Johans Gt. 22,* ☎ *22/31–30–50.* ✆ *Free. Guided tours in July and Aug.*

2 **Universitetet (The University).** The great hall of the center building is decorated with murals by Edvard Munch, such as *The Sun,* whose pen-

Oslo

KEY

🛈 Tourist Information
Rail Lines

Frogner Park

BYGDØY

Frognerkilen

Langvikbukta

Aker Brygge

U.S. Emb...

0 ——— 1 mile
0 ——— 1 km

N

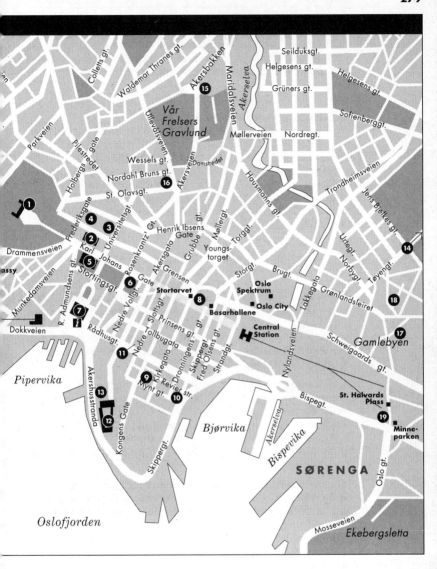

etrating rays over a fjord give a whole new meaning to the notion of daylight. It was the site of the Nobel Peace Prize award ceremony until 1989. The hall still receives other notable visitors, such as Salman Rushdie, who showed up almost unannounced in 1995. If you can't make it during hours of a reading or concert, you might be able to arrange a visit by phoning. ⊠ *Aulaen, Karl Johans Gt. 47,* ☎ *22/85–97–11* 🖪 *Free.* ☉ *July, weekdays 10:45–2.*

Kvadraturen and Akershus Castle

The Kvadraturen is the oldest part of Oslo still standing. In 1624, after the town of Oslo burnt down for the 14th time, King Christian IV renamed the city Christiania and moved it from the area that is today south of Oslo S Station, called Gamlebyen (☞ *below*), and rebuilt it adjacent to the Akershus fortress. The king decreed that houses were to be built in stone or brick instead of wood—in order to prevent future fires. He also built a stone wall around the newly rebuilt city to protect it from his enemies, the Swedes.

A GOOD WALK

The Kvadraturen area, which includes Akershus Slott, is bound on the east side of the fortress by Skippergata and on the north side by Karl Johans Gate between Oslo Domkirke and Stortorvet. The boundary follows Øvre Vollgata around to the other side of the fortress. Kvadraturen translates roughly as "square township," which refers to the area's geometrically ordered streets. Be aware that the streets around Skippergata and Myntgata are known as a mini red-light district, so you may see some unsavory characters. The area, however, is not dangerous, especially if you go during daylight.

Start at **Stortorvet,** Oslo's main square. On the right of the square is **Oslo Domkirke** ⑧, completed in 1697. Take a look inside—artists have been contributing to the cathedral's richly decorated interior since the 18th century. Behind the cathedral is a semicircular arcade called Kirkeristen, or **Basarhallene,** housing many small artisans' shops. The building, constructed in the middle of the 19th century, was inspired by medieval architecture.

From the cathedral, follow Kirkegata left past Karl Johan to the **Museet for Samtidskunst** ⑨, which is housed in the 1902 Bank of Norway building. Take some time to view the museum's contemporary works, especially the ones by Norwegian artists. From the museum, take the side street Revierstredet to Dronningensgate, where you'll come across a building that does not seem to fit in with its 17th-century neighbors. Designed and built in the early 1990s, this brick and steel office building houses the **Astrup Fearnley Museet for Moderne Kunst** ⑩. This stop is an absolute must for modern-art lovers.

Take Dronningensgate back to Rådhusgata and turn left. As you go up the street, notice the 17th-century building at 11 Rådhusgata. It houses the celebrated restaurant **Statholdergården** (☞ Dining, *below*). This was the home of the "statholder," the official representative from Copenhagen when Norway was under Danish rule.

Continue on Rådhusgata until you reach the corner of Nedre Slottsgate. The yellow building you see was the old city hall; now it's the 141-year-old **Gamle Rådhus** restaurant. This structure, first built in 1641, has also served as a courthouse, prison, and wine cellar. It became a restaurant in 1856. The revered dining spot closed down in 1996 after an unexplained fire, but the management hopes to reopen it late in 1997 (☞ Dining, *below*). Upstairs is the **Teatermuseet** ⑪. Diagonally across Rådhusgata in the two 17th-century buildings are an art gallery and an artsy café. The building that houses **Kafé Celcius** was one of the first buildings erected in Christian IV's town. The building has had myriad functions, starting as a schoolhouse and eventually serving as a military hospital and the living quarters of a mayor. If you look inside, you'll see a central fireplace that harks back to a time when it must have been a kitchen. The drooping ceilings are supported by wooden beams, and the floors are slate. It may be hard to resist not stepping inside this trendy café for something sweet (*varm sjokolade,* or hot chocolate, and a piece of pie).

Turn left on Akersgata and walk alongside the grassy hill to the entrance of **Akershus Slott og Festning** ⑫, the central element of Christian IV's Kvadraturen. It's a slight climb, but the views from the top are worth it. The castle became the German headquarters during the occupation of Norway in World War II, and many members of the Resistance were executed on the castle grounds. Their memorial has been erected at the site, across the bridge at the harbor end of the castle precinct. In a building next to the castle, at the top of the hill, is the **Norges Hjemmefront Museum** ⑬.

Walk back to Rådhusgata to see another interesting building, **Skogbrand Insurance** (Rådhusgt. 23B). Architects Jan Digerud and Jon Lundberg have won awards for their innovative 1985 vertical addition to this 1917 building. Once you have your fill of history and architecture, you can get in touch with something a bit more corporeal at the **Emanuel Vigeland Museum,** which displays artistic erotica created by the brother of the celebrated sculptor Gustav Vigeland. To get here, turn right on any of the streets along Rådhusgata back to Karl Johans and take T-bane (T-bane is short for *tunnelbane,* which is an underground railway, or subway) line 1 from National Theatret station direction Frognerseteren and get off at Slemdal.

TIMING

The walk alone should take at least three hours. Combined with museum visits and breaks, the itinerary could take up more than half a day. Akershus Festning will take at least half an hour. Many museums are closed Mondays. Astrup Fearnley is open afternoons only; and the Teatermuseet is open only a few days a week—plan your tour accordingly. Try to do this tour during daylight hours, catching late-afternoon sun from atop the Akershus grounds. Also note that the T-bane ride to the Emanuel Vigeland Museet in Slemdal takes about 15 minutes and that the museum is open only a few hours on Sunday afternoons.

SIGHTS TO SEE

⑫ **Akershus Slott og Festning (Akerhus Castle and Fortress).** The oldest part of the castle was built around 1300 and includes an "escape-proof" room built four centuries later for a thief named Ole Pedersen Høyland. In fact he broke out of this cell, robbed the Bank of Norway, was caught, and brought back to jail. With no possibility of a second escape, he killed himself here. Today some of the building is used for state occasions, but a few rooms, including the chapel, are open to the public. ⊠ *Akershus Slott, Festningspl.,* ☎ *22/41–25–21.* ☞ *Grounds and concerts free; castle NKr20.* ☉ *Grounds daily 6 AM–9 PM; concerts, mid-May–mid-Oct., Sun. at 2; castle May–mid-Sept., Mon.–Sat. 10–4. Guided tours May–Sept., Mon.–Sat. 11, 1, and 3; Sun. 1 and 3.*

⑩ **Astrup Fearnley Museet for Moderne Kunst (Astrup Fearnley Museum for Modern Art).** Shiny marble floors and white and gray walls (whose colors may change with the exhibitions) provide a neutral and elegant background for a series of fascinating and often disturbing works. Several works by the German artist Anselm Kiefer are part of the museum's permanent collection. Spacious exhibition rooms lead to a glassed-in sculpture garden with Niki de St. Phalle's sparrow and several other oversize, 20th-century figures. The major exhibition planned for spring 1997 includes works by Giacometti. ⊠ *Dronningens Gt. 4,* ☎ *22/93–60–60.* 🎫 *Nkr30.* ☉ *Tues., Wed., and Fri.–Sun. noon–4; Thurs. noon–7. Guided tours weekends at 1.*

EMANUEL VIGELANDS MUSEET – Although he never gained the fame of his brother Gustav, the creator of Vigeland Park, the younger Emanuel is an artist of some notoriety. His alternately saucy, natural, and downright erotic frescoes make even the sexually liberated Norwegians blush. To get here, take T-bane line 1 direction Frognerseteren and get off at Slemdal, one of Oslo's hillside residential neighborhoods. ⊠ *Grimelundsvn. 8,* ☎ *22/14-93-42.* 🎫 *Free.* ☉ *Sun. noon–3.*

❾ Museet for Samtidskunst (The Museum of Contemporary Art). The building, a good example of Norwegian Art Nouveau architecture, houses a fine collection of international and Norwegian contemporary works in small rooms. ⊠ *Bankpl. 4,* ☎ *22/33–58–20.* 🎫 *Free.* ☉ *Tues.–Wed., Fri. 10–5, Thurs. 10–8, Sat. 11–4, Sun. 11–5.*

⑬ Norges Hjemmefront Museum (Norwegian Resistance Museum). Winding hallways take you through a series of audiovisual displays documenting events that took place during the German occupation (1940–45). ⊠ *Norges Hjemmefrontmuseum, Akershus Festning,* ☎ *22/40–31–38.* 🎫 *NKr15.* ☉ *Mid-Apr.–mid-June and Sept., Mon.–Sat. 10–4, Sun. 11–4; mid-June –Aug., Mon.–Sat. 10–5, Sun. 11–5; Oct.–mid-Apr., Mon.–Sat. 10–3, Sun. 11–4.*

❽ Oslo Domkirke (Oslo Cathedral). In the 19th century, the fire department operated a fire lookout point from the bell tower here, which you can visit today. This dark brown brick structure has been Oslo's main church since the 17th century. Inside is an intricately carved Baroque pulpit and a five-story organ. ⊠ *Stortorvet 1,* ☎ *22/41–27–93.* 🎫 *Free.* ☉ *June–Aug., weekdays 10–3, Sat. 10–1; Sept.–May, weekdays 10–3.*

☺ ⑪ Teatermuseet (Theater Museum). The first public theater performance in Oslo took place here. Today, a collection of old pictures and costumes are on display. During open houses, children can try on costumes and have makeup applied. ⊠ *Nedre Slottsgt. 1,* ☎ *22/41–81–47.* 🎫 *NKr15.* ☉ *Wed., Thurs. 11–3, Sun. noon–4.*

Pascal (⊠ Tollbugt. 11, ☎ 22/42-11-19), an old-fashioned Norwegian *konditori,* serves enormous croissants and pastries with French coffee. Look for the little angels baking bread—they're painted on the ceiling.

East, North, and South of Downtown: Munch Museum, Damstredet, and Gamlebyen

The Munch Museum is east of the city center in Tøyen, an area where Edvard Munch spent many of his years in Oslo. The Tøyen district has a much different feel than Oslo's cushy west side—it's simpler and more industrial. West of Tøyen, just north of the city center, is the quiet, old-fashioned district of Damstredet, its quaint streets lined with artisans' shops. If you're a die-hard history buff, you'll probably enjoy the last half of this tour through Gamlebyen. However, if this is your first time in Oslo and you have a limited amount of time, you may want to end your tour at the Kunstindustrimuseet. Gamlebyen, south of the city center, is somewhat off the beaten track, and although the area is interesting, some of the ruins are barely discernible.

Start by taking any T-bane from the city center to Tøyen, where **Munchmuseet** ⑭ sits on a hill near the **Botanisk Hage,** a quiet oasis of plants and flowers. Munch's family lived in a house in the neighborhood during part of his life. After visiting the museum, head back toward the city center. Take the T-bane toward Sentrum and get off at Stortinget.

Head down Karl Johans Gate and take a right onto Akersgata. Follow it past the offices of **Aftenposten,** Norway's leading daily paper, which displays the day's headlines in the window. As you head up the hill, you will see a huge rotund building, **Deichmanske Bibliotek,** the city's library. When you reach St. Olavs Church, veer gently to the right on Akersveien. You may want to take a detour down **Damstredet** when you come to it—it's one of the city's oldest streets. Afterward, continue back along Akersveien. **Vår Frelsers Gravlund** (Our Saviour's Graveyard), where you can seek out the gravestones of many famous Norwegians who are buried here, including Ibsen and Munch, will be on your left. At the graveyard's northeastern corner is **Gamle Aker Kirke** ⑮, the city's only remaining medieval church.

On the other side of the cemetery, follow Ullevålsveien down the hill to the corner of St. Olavs Gate and Akersgata, where you'll find the **Kunstindustrimuseet** ⑯. The museum has a superb furniture collection and an entire floor of Norwegian decorative art.

If history and archaeology interest you, visit **Gamlebyen** ⑰, the old town, on the south side of Oslo S Station. South of here on Oslo Gate is St. Halvards Plass. During the 13th century, the area near St. Halvards Plass was the city's ecclesiastical center. Still intact are the foundations of **St. Halvards Kirke** ⑱, dating from the early 12th century. Some other ruins, including Korskirke and Olavs Kloster, lie in **Minneparken.** Nearby on Bispegata is **Oslo Ladegård** ⑲, a restored Baroque-style mansion that sits on the site and foundations of a 13th-century Bishop's Palace. Government construction of the Gardemoebanen (commuter railway) to the new Oslo Airport at Gardemoen has inspired many archaeologists and city historians to mobilize in an effort to preserve the ruins area. Plans are in the works for a Medieval Culture Park at nearby Sørenga.

The oldest traces of human habitation in Oslo are the 5,000-year-old carvings on the runic stones near **Ekebergsletta Park.** They are across the road from the park on Karlsborgveien and are marked by a sign reading FORTIDSMINNE. To reach the park, walk south on Oslo Gate until it becomes Mosseveien. The park will be on your right. Here is a good spot to rest your feet and end your tour.

TIMING
The Munchmuseet will take up most of the morning, especially if you take a guided tour. Don't plan your tour for a Monday because the Munchmuseet and Kunstindustrimuseet are closed. The second half of the tour, from Gamlebyen to Ekebergsletta, is a perfect way to spend a summer Sunday afternoon. Things are quiet, and locals tend to stroll around this area when the weather is nice.

SIGHTS TO SEE
⑮ **Gamle Aker Kirke (Old Aker Church).** Oslo's medieval stone basilica has undergone many changes since it was constructed around 1100. ⊠ *Akersvn. 26,* ☎ *22/69–35–82.* ☜ *Free.* ☉ *Mon.–Sat. noon–2, Sun. 9–1.*

⑰ **Gamlebyen (The Old City).** This area contains the last remains of medieval Oslo. Because of repeated fires, Christian IV moved Oslo from this site (after the fire of 1624) to a safer area near Akershus Festning (Akershus Fort). Today it's the largest homogenous archaeological site found in any capital city in Scandinavia. To get here, go back to Stortorvet and take *trikk* (as the Norwegians fondly call the streetcars) 18 marked "Ljabru" from Stortorvet to St. Halvards Plass (you can also take trikk 19 from Nationaltheatret). Contact Oslo Byantikvar (☎ 22/20–85–80) for information on guided tours of the area, or for a self-guided tour, ask the Norway Information Center where you can get a copy of *Guide to Gamlebyen* by Morten Krogstad and Erik Schia.

⑯ Kunstindustrimuseet (Museum of Applied Art). Clothes worthy of any fairy tale, including Queen Maud's jewel-encrusted, wasp-waist coronation gown from 1904, are displayed here in the museum's Royal Norwegian Costume Gallery. Extensive collections of industrial designs and arts and crafts include more than 35,000 objects. ⊠ *St. Olavs Gt. 1,* ☎ *22/20–35–78.* ⊡ *NKr20.* ⊙ *Tues.–Fri. 11–3, weekends noon–4.*

Minneparken. Oslo was founded by Harald Hårdråde ("Hard Ruler") in 1048, and the earliest settlements were near what is now Bispegata, a few blocks behind Oslo S Station. Ruins are all that are left of the city's former spiritual center: the **Korskirke** (Cross Church; ⊠ Egedes Gate 2), a small stone church dating from the end of the 13th century; and **Olavs Kloster** (Olav's Cloister; ⊠ St. Halvards Plass 3), built around 1240 by Dominican monks (⊠ Entrance at Oslo Gt. and Bispegt). Call the Oslo Bymuseum (☎ 22/42–06–45) for guided tours.

★ ⑭ Munchmuseet (Munch Museum). Edvard Munch, one of Scandinavia's leading artists, bequeathed an enormous collection of his work (about 1,100 paintings, 4,500 drawings, and 18,000 graphic works) to the city when he died in 1944. It languished in warehouses for nearly 20 years, until the city built a museum to house it in 1963. For much of his life Munch was a troubled man, and his major works, dating from the 1890s, with such titles as *The Scream* and *Vampire,* reveal his angst, but he was not without humor. His extraordinary talent as a graphic artist emerges in the print room, with its displays of lithograph stones and woodblocks. ⊠ *Tøyengt. 53,* ☎ *22/67–37–74.* ⊡ *NKr40.* ⊙ *June–Sept., daily 10–6; mid-Sept.–May, Tues.–Sat. 10–4, Thurs. and Sun. 10–6.*

⑲ Oslo Ladegård. The original building, a 13th-century Bispegård (Bishop's Palace), burned down in the 1624 fire, but its old vaulted cellar was not destroyed. The building was restored and rebuilt in 1725; it now belongs to the city council and contains scale models of 16th- to 18th-century Oslo. ⊠ *St. Halvards Pl., Oslogt. 13,* ☎ *22/19–44–68.* ⊡ *NKr20.* ⊙ *May–Sept.; guided tours on Wed. at 6, Sun. at 1.*

⑰ St. Halvards Kirke (St. Halvard's Church). This medieval church, named for the patron saint of Oslo, remained the city's cathedral until 1660. St. Halvard became the city's patron saint when his murdered body was found floating in the Drammensfjord, despite the presence of a heavy stone around his neck. He had been trying to save a pregnant woman from three violent pursuers when they caught and murdered him along with her. Stones from its walls were used to build Akershus Slott. ⊠ *Minneparken, entrance at Oslogt. and Bispegt.*

Frogner, Majorsturen, and Holmenkollen

One of the city's most stylish neighborhoods, Frogner combines old-world Scandinavian elegance with contemporary European chic. Most of the pastel-and-white buildings in the area were constructed in the early years of this century. Many have interesting wrought-iron work and beautiful sculptural detail. Terribly hip boutiques and galleries co-exist with embassies and ambassadors' residences on the streets near

In case you want to see the world.

At American Express, we're here to make your journey a smooth one. So we have over 1,700 travel service locations in over 120 countries ready to help. What else would you expect from the world's largest travel agency?

do more ®

AMERICAN
EXPRESS

Travel

http://www.americanexpress.com/travel

In case you want to be welcomed there.

We're here to see that you're always welcomed at establishments everywhere. That's why millions of people carry the American Express® Card – for peace of mind, confidence, and security, around the world or just around the corner.

do more

Cards

In case you're running low.

We're here to help with more than 118,000 Express Cash locations around the world. In order to enroll, just call American Express before you start your vacation.

do more

Express Cash

And just in case.

We're here with American Express® Travelers Cheques and Cheques *for Two.*® They're the safest way to carry money on your vacation and the surest way to get a refund, practically anywhere, anytime.

Another way we help you...

do more ®

Travelers Cheques

and around Bygdøy Allé. Holmenkollen, the hill past Frogner Park, features miles of ski trails—and more beautiful homes of the affluent.

A GOOD WALK

Catch the No. 12 "Majorstuen" trikk from Nationaltheatret on the Drammensveien side of the Royal Palace. You can also take the No. 15 from Aker Brygge.

Opposite the southwestern end of the palace grounds is the triangular **U.S. Embassy,** designed by Finnish-American architect Eero Saarinen and built in 1959. Look to the right at the corner of Drammensveien and Parkveien for a glimpse of the venerable **Nobel Institute.** Since 1905 these stately yellow buildings have been the lieu of seclusion where the five-member Nobel Committee decides who will win the Nobel Peace Prize. The 15,000-volume library is open to the public.

Stay on the trikk and ride to Frogner Park or walk the seven short blocks. To walk, follow Balders Gate to Arno Bergs Plass, with its central fountain. Turn left on Gyldenløves Gate (Street of the Golden Lion) until you reach Kirkeveien. Turn right, past the Dutch Embassy, and cross the street at the light, which is next to the trikk stop. Frogner Park, also called Vigelandspark interchangeably, is just ahead.

Walk through the front gates of the park and toward the monolith ahead: you are entering **Vigelandsparken** ⑳. There's nothing anywhere else in the world quite like this stunning sculpture garden designed by one of Norway's greatest artists; who is, ironically, virtually unknown to the rest of the world. Across from the park, you can study the method to his madness at **Vigelandsmuseet** ㉑.

After you leave the park, continue on Kirkeveien to the Majorstuen underground station. Here you have two options: You can take a walk down Bogstadveien, look at the shops, and explore the Majorstuen area and then take the Holmenkollen line of the T-bane to Frognerseteren; or you can skip the stroll down Bogstadveien and head right up to Holmenkollen. The train ride up the mountain is beautiful. If you have brought your children, you may want to make a detour at the first T-bane stop, Frøen, and visit the **Barnekunstmuseet.** In summer, the museum provides materials kids can use to create art.

Continue on the T-bane to the end of the line. This is Frognerseteren— the top of Holmenkollen—where city dwellers disappear to on winter weekends. The view of the city here is spectacular. The **Tryvannstårnet** ㉒ has an even better panoramic view of Oslo. Downhill is **Holmenkollbakken** ㉓, where Norway's most intrepid skiers prove themselves every February during the Holemenkollen Ski Festival.

TIMING

You will need a whole day for both neighborhoods since there is some travel time involved. The trikk ride from the city center to Frogner Park is about 15 minutes; the T-bane to Frognerseteren is about 20. You're no longer in the compact city center, so distances between sights are greater. The walk from Frognerseteren is about 15 minutes and is indicated with signposts. Try to save Holmenkollen with its magnificent views for a clear day. Summer times for museums and lookout points are extended because the days are so long. In the spring, though, go before the sun starts to set.

This is a good tour for Monday, since the museums mentioned are open, unlike most others in Oslo. If you want to see Norwegians before the age of two on skis, a winter Sunday in Frognerseteren is your best bet. Frognerpark has some skiers and sledders, and families flock to Holmenkollen for Sunday ski school.

SIGHTS TO SEE

Barnekunsimuseet (Children's Art Museum). The museum was the brainchild of Rafael Goldin, a Russian immigrant who has collected children's drawings from more than 150 countries. ⊠ *Lille Frøensvn. 4,* ☎ *22/46–85–73.* 🖼 *NKr30.* ☉ *Late June–mid-Aug., Tues.–Thurs. and Sun. 11–4; early Sept.–mid-Dec. and late Jan.–mid-June, Tues.–Thurs. 9:30–2, Sun. 11–4.*

★ ㉓ **Holmenkollbakken (Holmenkollen Ski Museum and Ski Jump).** Oslo's ski jump holds a special place in the hearts of Norwegians, who contend they invented the sport. The 1892 jump was rebuilt for the 1952 Winter Olympics and is still used for international competitions. At the base of the jump, turn right, past the statue of the late King Olav V on skis, to enter the museum. It displays equipment from the Fritjof Nansen and Roald Amundsen polar voyages and a model of a ski maker's workshop, in addition to a collection of skis, the oldest dating from pre-Viking times. You can also climb (or ride the elevator) to the top of the jump tower. It's intimidating enough with a firm grip on the rail, but on skis and snow, it's mind-boggling. ⊠ *Kongevn. 5,* ☎ *22/92–32–00.* 🖼 *NKr50.* ☉ *July–Aug., daily 9 AM–10 PM; June, daily 9–8; Apr.–May and Sept., daily 10–5; Oct.–Mar., 10–4.*

㉒ **Tryvannstårnet (Tryvann's Tower).** The view from Oslo's TV tower encompasses 36,000 square feet of hills, forests, cities, and several bodies of water. You can see as far as the Swedish border to the east and nearly as far as Moss to the south. ⊠ *Voksenkollen,* ☎ *22/14–67–11.* 🖼 *NKr30.* ☉ *May and Sept., daily 10–5; June, daily 10–7; July, daily 9 AM–10 PM; Aug., daily 9–8; Oct.–Apr., weekdays 10–3, weekends 11–4.*

㉑ **Vigelandsmuseet.** This small museum displays many of the plaster models for the Vigeland Park sculptures, the artist's woodcuts and drawings, and mementos of his life. ⊠ *Nobelsgt. 32,* ☎ *22/44–11–36.* 🖼 *NKr20.* ☉ *May–Sept., Tues.–Sat. 10–6, Sun. noon–7; Oct.–Apr., Tues.–Sat. noon–4, Sun. noon–6.*

★ ⑳ **Vigelandsparken (Frogner Park).** This park, formally called Frogner Park, contains over 50 copper statues by sculptor Gustav Vigeland, hence the moniker Vigelandspark. Vigeland began his career as a woodcarver, and his talent was quickly appreciated and supported by the townspeople of Oslo. In 1921 they provided him with a free house and studio, in exchange for which he began to chip away at his life's work, which he would ultimately donate to the city. He worked through World War II and the German occupation, and after the war the work was unveiled, to the combined enchantment and horror of the townsfolk. Included was the 470-ton monolith that is now the highlight of the park, as well as hundreds of writhing, fighting, and loving sculptures representing the varied forms and stages of human life. The figures are nude, but they're more monumental than erotic—bullet-headed, muscular men and healthy, solid women with flowing hair. Look for the park's most beloved sculpture—an enraged baby boy stamping his foot and scrunching his face in fury. Known as *Sinnataggen* (The Really Angry One), this ball of rage has been filmed, parodied, painted red, and even stolen from the park.

The grassy grounds of Vigelandspark are a living part of the city—people walk dogs on the green and bathe chubby babies in the fountains, and they jog, ski, and sunbathe throughout. The park complex also includes the City Museum, a swimming pool (☞ Outdoor Activities and Sports, *below*) an ice rink and skating museum (☎ 22/43–49–20), several playgrounds, and an outdoor restaurant, Herregårdskroen, where you can have anything from a buffet lunch to a three-course dinner. ✉ *Middlethunsgt.* ✉ *Park entrance free.*

Bygdøy

Oslo's most important historic sights are concentrated on Bygdøy Peninsula, as are several beaches, jogging paths, and the royal family's summer residence.

A GOOD WALK

The most pleasant way to get to Bygdøy, from May to September, is to catch a ferry from the Rådhuset. Times vary, so check with Nortra (☞ Visitor Information *in* Oslo A to Z, *below*) for schedules. Another alternative is to take Bus 30, marked "Bygdøy," from Stortingsgata at Nationaltheatret along Drammensveien to Bygdøy Allé, a wide avenue lined with chestnut trees. The bus passes Frogner Church and several embassies on its way to Olav Kyrres Plass, where it turns left, and soon left again, onto the peninsula. If you see some horses on the left, they come from the king's stables (the dark red building with the monogram); the royal family's current summer residence, actually just a big white frame house, is on the right. Get off at the next stop, Norsk Folkemuseum. The pink castle nestled in the trees is **Oscarshall Slott** ㉔, once a royal summer palace.

Next is the **Norsk Folkemuseum** ㉕, which consists of some 150 structures from all over the country that have been reconstructed on site. Around the corner to the right is the **Vikingskiphuset** ㉖, one of Norway's most famous attractions, which houses some of the best-preserved remains of the Viking era found yet.

Follow signs on the road to the **Fram-Museet** ㉗, an A-frame structure in the shape of a traditional Viking boathouse, which houses the famed *Fram* polar ship as well as artifacts from various expeditions. Across the parking lot from the Fram-Museet is the older **Kon-Tiki Museum** ㉘ with Thor Heyerdahl's famous raft, along with the papyrus boat *Ra II.* You can get a ferry back to the City Hall docks from the dock in front of the Fram-Museet. Before heading back to Oslo, you may want to have a snack at **Lanternen Kro,** which overlooks the entire harbor.

If your kids are squirming to break out of the museum circuit, entertain the thought of a trip to **VikingLandet.** This is Norway's newest attraction park—it stages the more peaceful aspects of the Vikings' existence, from farming to burial mounds. You can combine the excursion with a trip to **TusenFryd,** an amusement park next door.

TIMING

Block out a day for Bygdøy. You could spend at least half a day at the Folkemuseum alone. Note that the museums on Bygdøy tend to close earlier than its counterparts that close Mondays.

The HMK trip to VikingLandet is an afternoon trip, so count on spending half a day. It takes between 10 and 20 minutes to reach the park from downtown Oslo by bus. If you decide to go on your own from Oslo S Station, you might want to spend the whole day playing in both parks.

SIGHTS TO SEE

★ ⊙ ㉗ **Fram-Museet.** The *Fram* polar ship takes up almost every inch of this museum, which was constructed around it. Matter-of-fact displays of life on board ship vividly depict the history of polar exploration. The *Fram* was constructed in 1892 by Scottish-Norwegian shipbuilder Colin Archer. Fridtjof Nansen led the first *Fram* expedition, across the ice surrounding the North Pole; the ship's most famous voyage took Roald Amundsen to Antarctica, the first leg of his successful expedition to the South Pole in 1911. Visitors board the ship by gangplank and are allowed to walk all over the vessel. ✉ *Bygdøynes,* ☎ *22/43–83–70.* 🎫 *NKr20.* ☉ *June–Aug., daily 9–5:45; May and Sept., daily 10–4:45; Mar.– Apr. and Oct.–Nov., weekdays 11–2:45, weekends 11–3:45; Dec.–Feb., weekends 11–3:45.*

★ ☾ ㉘ **Kon-Tiki Museum.** The museum celebrates Norway's most famous 20th-century explorer. Thor Heyerdahl continued the Norwegian tradition of exploration in his 1947 voyage from Peru to Polynesia on the *Kon-Tiki,* a balsa raft, to confirm his theory that the first Polynesians originally came from Peru. The *Kon-Tiki,* now showing its age, is suspended on a plastic sea. The *Ra II* sailed from Morocco to the Caribbean in 1970. ✉ *Bygdøynesvn. 36,* ☎ *22/43–80–50.* 🎫 *NKr 25.* ☉ *Apr.–May and Sept., daily 10:30–5; June–Aug., daily 9:30–5:45; Oct.–Mar., daily 10:30–4.*

★ ☾ ㉕ **Norsk Folkemuseum (Norway's Folk Museum).** You'll get a bird's-eye view of the entire country with imaginative exhibitions, 153 authentic houses, and tour guides in traditional garb. The **Gol Stavkirke (Gol Stave Church),** constructed around 1200, is one of the most important buildings here. In summer and on weekends year-round, guides in the buildings demonstrate various home crafts, such as weaving tapestries, sewing national costumes, and baking flatbread. Indoor collections in the main building include toys, dolls and dollhouses, a Sami (Lapp) collection, national costumes, and Ibsen's actual study. On one side of this museum is a reconstructed 19th-century village, with shops and houses. Among its exhibits are a pharmaceutical museum and a dentist's office, complete with turn-of-the-century braces— a real mouthful of springs and bands. The museum puts on a summer calendar of special events, including daily activities from folk dancing to concerts with instruments from the museum's collection. ✉ *Museumsvn. 10,* ☎ *22/12–37–00.* 🎫 *NKr 50.* ☉ *May and Sept. daily 10–5; June–Aug., daily 9–6; Oct.–Apr., weekdays 11–3, Sun. 11–4.*

㉔ **Oscarshall Slott.** This eccentric neo-Gothic palace built in 1852 for King Oscar I served as a site for picnics and other summer pursuits. It now houses Norwegian art, including works by Tidemand and Gude. ✉ *Oscarshallvn.,* ☎ *22/43–77–49.* 🎫 *NKr15.* ☉ *Mid-May–mid-Sept., Tues., Thurs., and Sun. noon–4.*

☾ **VikingLandet.** Norway's first and only theme park on the Viking Age takes you back 1,000 years to experience daily life as a Viking. You encounter Viking warriors and nobles throughout the park, which is built on the idea of an early Viking community's farms and market places. You can combine the trip with a visit to **Norgesparken Tusenfryd,** Oslo's amusement park. There are carnival rides, such as a merry-go-round, a Ferris wheel, and a roller coaster with a loop, and a water slide. There's a separate entrance fee, but both parks are under the same management. HMK provides an afternoon bus excursion from Norway Information Center (☞ Guided Tours *in* Oslo A to Z, *below*). There's also a free shuttle bus that departs from the south side of Oslo S Station. ✉ *Both parks: Vinterbro,* ☎ *64/94–63–63.* 🎫 *Combined ticket NKr110.* ☉ *May–mid-June and late Aug.–Sept., weekends noon–6; early June, weekdays 10:30–3; late June–mid-Aug., daily noon–6.*

★ ㉖ **Vikingskiphuset.** Norway's claim to fame centers on its incorrigible Viking explorers, and this museum celebrates their fascinating culture. The building resembles a cathedral on the outside, and inside the feeling of reverence is very real. It's hard to believe that the three ships on display, all found buried along the Oslo Fjord, are nearly 1,200 years old. Viking elites wanted to make sure their dead were well equipped for life after death, so they buried them in long ships with all the neccessities, which sometimes included a servant. The discoverers of the *Oseberg* even found wood, leather, and woolen textiles intact. Burial ships often reflected the social status of the person buried. The richly carved *Oseberg*, thought to have been the burial chamber for Queen Åse, is the most decorative, whereas the *Gokstad* is a functional longboat, devoid of ornament. The small *Tune* has been left unrestored. Items found with the ships, including sleds with intricately carved decoration, tools, household goods, and a tapestry, are also on view. ⊠ *Huk Aveny 35,* ☎ *22/43–83–79.* ▭ *NKr30.* ☉ *May–Aug., daily 9–6; Sept., daily 11–5; Apr. and Oct., daily 11–4; Nov.–Mar., daily 11–3.*

Dining

Food was once an afterthought in Oslo, but not anymore. The city's chefs are winning contests worldwide. Norwegian cuisine, based on products from the country's pristine waters and lush farmland, is now firmly in the culinary spotlight. Menus change daily, weekly, or according to the season in many of Oslo's finer restaurants.

In Oslo, bad food is expensive and good food doesn't necessarily cost more—it's just a matter of knowing where to go. If you visit Oslo in summer, head for **Aker Brygge,** the wharf turned shopping area. Hundreds of café goers vie for the sun and the view at the fjord-side outdoor tables. Most restaurants here offer a summer menu that is considerably less expensive than the regular one. Aker Brygge is also a good place to buy shrimp, an activity that heralds the coming of summer for many locals. If you don't want to buy them fresh off the boat, order them at one of the floating restaurants. Generally they come on a baguette or in a big bowl with mayonnaise or Thousand Island dressing on the side.

A good place to get a meal that won't cost more than your hotel room is the food court at **Paléet Shopping Center,** which is open daily 10–8. A bit pricier, and a lot snazzier than the fast-food bonanzas of most American malls, this food court has a variety of stands with international fare, ranging from Danish and Greek to Italian and even American (although the burgers are served with red wine).

Many of the less-expensive restaurants listed below are simply cafés, bars, and even sometimes discotheques. These types of establishments are becoming increasingly popular as restaurants as Oslo's twentysomething generation decides it likes to eat out. (Because of high prices, eating out is a huge luxury for most Norwegians.) Meals at these cheaper spots invariably include pasta dishes, shellfish, pizzas, and salads rather than steaks, lobsters, and lamb chops. For a more exhaustive list of Oslo cafés, pick up a copy of *Café Guiden,* a glossy publication describing more than 100 spots in detail. It is available in most nightclubs, bars, and cafés. Note that some restaurants are closed on Sundays.

Downtown: Royal Palace to the Parliament

$$$$
★
✕ **D'Artagnan.** Diplomas, certificates, and prizes from all over the world line the walls of this downtown *restaurant gastronomique.* Owner Freddie Nielsen, one of Norway's most celebrated restaurateurs, received both his education and inspiration in France, but do not expect nouvelle cuisine here. Only the famished should embark upon the seven-course Grand Menu. The saffron-poached pike with asparagus is a good way to start a meal, and the boned fillet of salmon with dill lobster-cream sauce is attractive and flavorful. The veal is so tender you can

cut it with your fork. The dessert cart is loaded with jars of fruit preserved in liqueurs, which are served with sorbets and ice creams. ⊠ *Øvre Slottsgt. 16,* ☎ *22/41–50–62. AE, DC, MC, V. Closed weekends, Jan.–Aug., and all of July. No lunch.*

$$$ ✕ **Babette's Gjestehus.** This tiny restaurant is hidden in the shopping arcade by City Hall. Chef Ortwin Kulmus and his friendly staff know how to make their guests feel welcome—bright blue walls, starched white tablecloths, and lace curtains against paned windows also contribute to the rustic, homey feel. The food is Scandinavian with a French touch. Try the garlic-marinated rack of lamb in rosemary sauce or pan-fried breast of duck with creamed spring cabbage. Dishes vary according to season but are always well prepared. ⊠ *Rådhuspassasjen, Roald Amundsensgt. 6,* ☎ *22/41–64–64. Reservations essential. AE, DC, MC, V. Closed Sun. No lunch.*

$$$ ✕ **Theatercafeen.** This Oslo institution, on the ground floor of the Hotel
★ Continental, is *the* place to see and be seen. Built in 1900, the last Viennese-style café in northern Europe retains its Art Nouveau character. The menu is small and jumbled, with starters and main dishes interspersed; the only hint of the serving size is the price column. Pastry chef Robert Bruun's *konfektkake* (a rich chocolate cake) and apple tart served with homemade ice cream are reasons enough to visit. ⊠ *Stortingsgt. 24–26,* ☎ *22/82–40–50. AE, DC, MC, V.*

$$ ✕ **Dinner.** Though its name is not the best for a restaurant specializ-
★ ing in Szechuan-style cuisine, this is the place for Chinese food, both spicy and not so pungent. The mango pudding for dessert is wonderful. Don't bother with the other Chinese restaurants. ⊠ *Stortingsgt. 22,* ☎ *22/42–68–90. AE, DC, MC, V. No lunch.*

$$ ✕ **A Touch of France.** Just downstairs from D'Artagnan, Freddie Nielsen's clean, inviting wine bistro is straight out of Paris. The French ambience is further accented by the waiters' long, white aprons, the Art Nouveau decor, old French posters, and closely packed tables. The tempting menu includes a steaming hot bouillabaisse. A Touch of France is home to Norway's only rôtisserie. ⊠ *Øvre Slottsgt. 16,* ☎ *22/42–56–97. AE, DC, MC, V.*

$ ✕ **Brasserie 45.** Overlooking the fountain on Karl Johans Gate, this trendy brasserie serves a solid meal in a rather elegant Scandinavian setting, complete with candlelight, red walls, and shiny wooden floors. The idea is simple: 45 dishes for 45 kroner each. There are both meat and fish dishes, often garnished with a tasty "Brasserie 45 sauce," a tomato sweet-and-sour sauce and potatoes or pasta. The portions are small, but a three-course meal at NKr 135 is still a bargain in Oslo. ⊠ *Karl Johans Gt. 45 (upstairs),* ☎ *22/41–34–00. AE, DC, MC, V.*

$ ✕ **Café Sjakk Matt.** This trendy spot between Vika and Karl Johan is one of the many bars that serve food as well—although they've made it a specialty. However, you do have to order at the bar. A variety of pita sandwiches and melts, ratatouille, quiche, and the house specialty, lasagna, are some of what's on the menu. Hot dishes usually come with salad and nutty Norwegian bread. The place has a modern Scandinavian feel: dozens of candles, potted plants, and shiny floors. ⊠ *Haakon VII's Gt. 5,* ☎ *22/83–41–56. AE, DC, MC, V.*

$ ✕ **Den Grimme Ælling.** Dane Bjarne Hvid Pedersen's *smørbrød* are the best buy in town: lots of meat, fish, or cheese on a small piece of bread. This popular Copenhagen restaurant in the food court at Paleet also has daily dinner specials, such as homemade *hakkebøf* (Danish Salisbury steak) with gravy, onions, and potatoes. ⊠ *Paleet, Karl Johans Gt. 41B,* ☎ *22/42–47–83. No credit cards.*

$ ✕ **Kaffistova.** Norwegian country cooking is served, cafeteria style, at this downtown restaurant. Everyday specials include soup and a selection of entrées, including a vegetarian dish. *Kjøttkaker* (meat cakes) served with creamed cabbage is a Norwegian staple, and the steamed salmon with Sandefjord butter is as good here as in places where it costs three times as much. Low-alcohol beer is the strongest drink served. ⊠ *Rosenkrantz' Gt. 8,* ☎ *22/42–99–74. AE, DC, MC, V.*

$ ✗ **Vegeta.** Next to the Nationaltheatret bus and trikk station, this no-smoking restaurant is a popular spot for hot and cold vegetarian meals and salads. The all-you-can-eat specials offer top value. ✗ *Munkedamsvn. 3B,* ☎ *22/83–40–20. Reservations not accepted. No credit cards.*

Kvadraturen and Aker Brygge

$$$$ ✗ **Statholdergaarden.** Award-winning chef Bent Stiansen is currently the shining star of Norwegian haute cuisine. As a result, it is hard to get a table here—especially around Christmastime—so plan early. The four-course gastronomic menu changes daily. You can also order directly from the à la carte menu. Try one of the imaginative appetizers, such as smoked duck breast with fried goat cheese and pine nut salad. Specialties include salmon mousse and other fish delicacies. This restaurant, in a building that dates back to 1640, is in the heart of Oslo's oldest standing neighborhood. The main dining room has an ornate ceiling from 1740 and is decorated with chandeliers and Baroque chairs. ⊠ *Rådhusgt. 11,* ☎ *22/41–88–00. Reservations essential. Jacket and tie. AE, DC, MC, V. Closed Sun., 3 weeks in July.*

$$$ ✗ **Engebret Café.** This somber, old-fashioned restaurant at Bankplassen was a haunt for bohemian literati at the turn of the century. Today it draws tourists, especially in summer, for casual fare and drinks at the outdoor café. The more formal dinner menu includes traditional Norwegian staples, such as reindeer and salmon. Food critics give these two dishes rave reviews year after year. This is a good spot for refreshment after visiting the Contemporary Art Museum; try to get an outdoor table and listen to the museum's fountain trickle away in the distance. ⊠ *Bankplassen 1,* ☎ *22/33–66–94. AE, DC, MC, V.*

$$–$$$ ✗ **Lofoten Fiskerestaurant.** With all windows overlooking the water at Aker Brygge, this is Oslo's quintessential fish restaurant. All types of fish, from salmon to cod to monkfish, are served fresh and cooked in a variety of sauces, from house bouillabaisse to classic wine or safoslo specfron sauce. The clientele is well heeled, and the elegant wood-paneled interior brings to mind a vintage Scandinavian cruise ship. Try to get an outdoor table in summer: You take advantage of a cheaper menu as well as late-evening sunlight on the fjord. Service can be slow on busy evenings, but it's definitely worth the wait. ⊠ *Stranden 75, Aker Brygge,* ☎ *22/83–08–08. AE, DC, MC, V. Closed Sun.*

$$ ✗ **Det Gamle Raadhus.** This restaurant in the former city hall is famous for its *lutefisk,* a Scandinavian specialty made from dried fish that has been soaked in lye and then poached. However, the menu here does allow ample choice for the less daring. This is Oslo's oldest restaurant—it celebrated its 350th birthday in 1991. Unfortunately the restaurant suffered extensive fire damage in 1996, and had just closed at presstime, but was scheduled to reopen in 1997. Call 22/41–44–41 to be certain. ⊠ *Nedre Slottsgt. 1,* ☎ *22/42–01–07. AE, DC, MC, V. Closed Sun.*

$$ ✗ **Maud's.** In the same building as the Norway Information Center, this restaurant would logically attract tourists. However, it seems to attract more locals. The regional Norwegian dishes are so traditional that they seem exotic to some Norwegian city folk who left the nest long ago. Specialties include potato dumplings and myriad fish and meat dishes served with none other than potatoes boiled to perfection. Lunch plates and open-faced sandwiches are reasonably priced, as are

Oslo Dining and Lodging

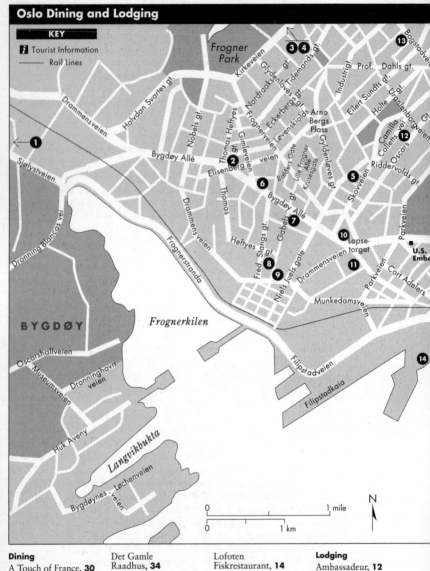

KEY

🛈 Tourist Information

—— Rail Lines

Dining

A Touch of France, **30**
Ambassadeur, **12**
Babette's
Gjestehus, **18**
Bagatelle, **10**
Brasserie 45, **24**
Café Sjakk Matt, **15**
Clodion Art Café, **2**
Coco Chalet, **33**
De Fem Stuer, **3**
Den Grimme
Ælling, **25**

Det Gamle
Raadhus, **34**
Dinner, **17**
Dionysos Taverna, **39**
Engebret Café, **36**
Feinschmecker, **6**
Frognerseteren, **4**
Hos Thea, **9**
Kaffistova, **31**
Kastanjen, **7**
Klosteret, **40**

Lofoten
Fiskrestaurant, **14**
Markveien Mat og
Vinhus, **41**
Maud's, **16**
Palace Grill, **11**
Restaurant
Le Canard, **5**
Statholdergaarden, **35**
Theatercafeen, **19**
Vegeta, **22**

Lodging

Ambassadeur, **12**
Bristol, **27**
Gabelshus, **8**
Grand Hotel, **32**
Haraldsheim, **42**
Holmenkollen Park
Hotel Rica, **3**
Hotell
Bondeheimen, **31**
Hotel Continental, **19**
Hotel Karl Johan, **26**
Munch, **29**

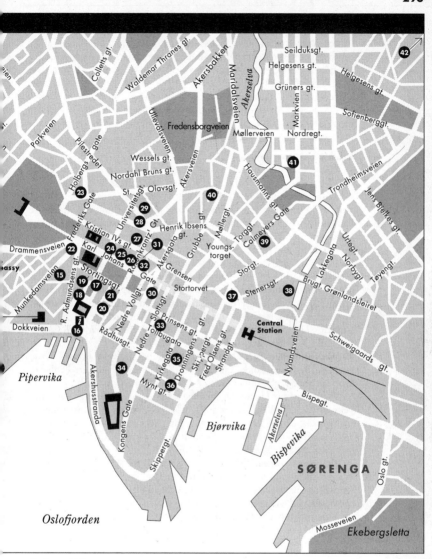

Radisson SAS
Park Royal, **1**

Radisson SAS
Scandinavia Hotel, **23**

Rainbow Cecil, **21**

Rainbow
Gyldenløve, **13**

Rainbow Hotel
Stefan, **28**

Reso Oslo Plaza, **38**

Rica Victoria, **20**

Royal Christiania, **37**

the "everyday meals," served from 1 to 7. ✉ *Vestbaneplassen. 1,* ☎ *22/83-72-28. AE, DC, MC, V. Closed Sun.*

$ ✕ **Coco Chalet.** Best known for its homemade cakes and pies, Coco Chalet is moving into the world of affordable haute cuisine. The Asian-inspired menu features a delectable chicken breast with vegetables julienne. The dining room of this restaurant in Oslo's oldest neighborhood feels somewhat like a haunted mansion: White tablecloths bedeck the tables at all hours of the day, spooky candelabras sit on the mantle, and the mostly female staff wears black uniforms with white aprons and collars. ✉ *Øvre Slottsgt. 8,* ☎ *22/33-32-66. AE, DC, MC, V.*

East of Downtown

$$$ ✕ **Klosteret.** This popular east-side eatery's name means "the cloisters." Its not-so-medieval dining room is downstairs in a spacious cellar with a rounded brick ceiling. Wacky iron candelabras sprouting from red walls like thorny branches and stark steel-backed chairs are somehow in perfect harmony with the gold-bedecked saints and Christ childs that adorn the walls. The hand-woven menus are sheathed in monastic hymnal pages and offer a variety of meat and fish, as well as a daily vegetarian dish. The scallops Oriental served with vegetables julienne is a heavenly appetizer. Main courses are often served atop a bed of sautéed leafy greens, which makes for an innovative presentation as well as a refreshing change from traditional Norwegian *kinakål,* a white lettuce-cabbage usually substituted for greens. Take a taxi. ✉ *Fredensborgvn. 13,* ☎ *22/20-66-90. AE, DC, MC, V. Closed Sun. and 3-4 weeks in July.*

$$$ ✕ **Markveien Mat og Vinhus.** This arty "food and wine house" in the heart of the Grunerløkka district serves fresh French-inspired cuisine. One favorite is the honey duck à l'orange, served in spring. The atmosphere is relaxed and the clientele is bohemian. Paintings cover the yellow walls, and the tables are black and somber. As most touristy spots in Oslo lie in the *Vest* (west), a trip to the *Øst* (east) will give you a chance to see how the other side lives. ✉ *Torvbakkgt. 12 (entrance on Markvn. 57),* ☎ *22/37-22-97. AE, DC, MC, V. Closed Sun.*

$$ ✕ **Dionysos Taverna.** Nicola Murati gives his guests a warm welcome
★ in this unpretentious little Greek restaurant. The hors d'oeuvre platter, which includes stuffed vine leaves, meatballs, feta cheese, tzatziki, tomatoes, and cucumbers, is a meal in itself. The souvlaki and moussaka are authentically prepared, as are the more unusual casserole dishes. A bouzouki duo provides live music on Thursday, Friday, and Saturday. ✉ *Calmeyersgt. 11,* ☎ *22/60-78-64. AE, MC, V. No lunch.*

Frogner and Majorstuen

$$$$ ✕ **Bagatelle.** One of Oslo's best restaurant is a short walk from down-
★ town. Paintings by contemporary Norwegian artists accent the otherwise subdued interior, but the food is the true show here. Internationally known chef-owner Eyvind Hellstrøm's cuisine is modern Norwegian with French overtones. His grilled scallops with a saffron-parsley sauce and the marinated salmon tartare with an herbed crème fraîche are extraordinary. Bagatelle has a wine cellar to match its food. ✉ *Bygdøy Allé 3,* ☎ *22/44-63-97. Jacket and tie. AE, DC, MC, V. Closed Sun. No lunch.*

$$$$ ✕ **Feinschmecker.** The name is German, but the food is modern Scandinavian. The atmosphere is friendly and intimate, with green rattan chairs, yellow tablecloths, and floral draperies. Owners Lars Erik Underthun, one of Oslo's foremost chefs, and Bengt Wilson, one of Scandinavia's leading food photographers, make sure the food looks as good as it tastes. The roast rack of lamb with crunchy fried sweetbreads on tagliatelle and the chocolate-caramel teardrop with passion-fruit sauce are two choices on the menu, which makes for fascinating reading. ✉

Balchensgt. 5, ☎ 22/44–17–77. Reservations essential. AE, DC, MC, V. Closed Sun., last 3 weeks of July. No lunch.

$$$ ✕ **Ambassadeur.** This cozy restaurant serving modern Scandinavian food is in the cellar of the Ambassadeur Hotel. Dark colors and Baroque-style paintings of food create a plush, cocoonlike ambience. The food itself stands in contrast to the decor—it's light, in both concept and color. The seafood salad with plump mussels and shrimp in light vinaigrette is a winner, and the scallops in lemon beurre blanc are delicate and subtle. The bar, one of Oslo's best, is comfortable and well stocked. ⊠ *Hotel Ambassadeur, Camilla Collets vei 15, ☎ 22/44–18–35. AE, DC, MC, V. Closed weekends and July. No lunch.*

$$$ ✕ **Hos Thea.** An old-fashioned–looking gem with blue-and-beige decor,
★ this restaurant has only 36 seats. It's at the beginning of Embassy Row, a short distance from downtown. Owner Sergio Barcilon, originally from Spain, is one of the pioneers of the new Scandinavian cooking. The small menu offers four or five choices in each category, but every dish is superbly prepared, from the venison in a sauce of mixed berries to the sherbets and fruitcake. Noise and smoke levels can be high late in the evening. ⊠ *Gabelsgt. 11, entrance on Drammensvn., ☎ 22/44–68–74. Reservations essential. AE, DC, MC, V. No lunch.*

$$$ ✕ **Palace Grill.** This tiny dining spot across from the Royal Palace has won its way into the ranks of the hip on the Oslo restaurant scene. You can sip a beer in the adjoining cowboy rock-and-roll bar while you wait for one of about eight tables. Don't let the "grill" part confuse you: It may be relaxed, but it's far from fast food. The Norwegian ingredients of the French-inspired menu, which is written on a hanging chalkboard, change daily. If you've had your fill of reindeer in Norway, you can still take a glimpse at the exotic sauces. Try the chicken leg with eggplant and sweet green shallot sauce if it's on the menu. ⊠ *Solligt. 2 (just off Dramensveien), ☎ 22/56–14–02. Reservations not accepted. AE, DC, MC, V. Closed Sun. and one month in summer.*

$$$ ✕ **Restaurant Le Canard.** Undoubtedly one of Oslo's plushest locales, this oasis in Frogner is brimming with eclectic antiques, Oriental rugs, chandeliers, and Baroque paintings. It is housed in a looming brick mansion with spires and wrought-iron decorations that was built at the turn of the century. The main dining room is spread throughout the first floor's rooms and color-coded salons; upstairs is reserved for private parties. In summer you can dine on the lawn in the garden. The specialty is, of course, duck, from beef with duck-liver in Madeira sauce to sautéed breast of duck with horseradish and cognac sauce. The wine cellar holds more than 2,000 bottles. ⊠ *Pres. Harbitzgt. 4, ☎ 22/55–65–65. AE, DC, MC, V. Closed Sun. No lunch in winter.*

$$ ✕ **Kastanjen.** This casual Frogner bistro is the kind every neighbor-
★ hood needs. The style of food is new traditional—modern interpretations of classic Norwegian dishes. The three-course meal is good value for the money, but check out the "dish of the day," at an unbeatable price. ✕ *Bygdøy Allé 18, ☎ 22/43–44–67. AE, DC, MC, V. Closed Sun., 2 wks in July.*

$ ✕ **Clodion Art Café.** A bright blue facade and cartoons of the suns, stars, and moon adorn the entrance to this trendy Frogner café. Meals here are light but always tasty: Try the spicy shrimp brochette with rice for a nice change from usual café fare. Go for aesthetic reasons instead and your hunger for creativity will be sated. Not an inch of the place is left unpainted, and the curvy, colorful couches–often procured at flea markets or art galleries—will make you want to stay all day. ⊠ *Bygdøy Allé 63, entrance on Thomas Heftyes Gt., ☎ 22/44–97–26. MC, V, DC.*

Holmenkollen

$$$$ ✕ **De Fem Stuer.** Near the famous Holmenkollen ski jump, in the his-
★   toric Holmenkollen Park Hotel, this restaurant has first-rate views and
       food. Chef Frank Halvorsen's modern Norwegian dishes have strong
       classic roots. Well worth trying is the three-course "A Taste of Norway,"
       with salmon, reindeer, and cloudberries. ⊠ *Holmenkollen Park Hotel,
       Kongevn. 26,* ☎ *22/92–27–34. Jacket and tie. AE, DC, MC, V.*

$$ ✕ **Frognerseteren.** Just above the Holmenkollen ski jump, this restau-
       rant, specializing in fish, reindeer, and venison, looks down on the en-
       tire city. Be sure not to miss the house specialty—scrumptious apple
       cake. The upstairs room has the same view as the more expensive
       panoramic veranda, and there is also an outdoor café. Take the Hol-
       menkollbanen to the end station and then follow the signs downhill
       to the restaurant. ⊠ *Hollmenkollvn. 200,* ☎ *22/14–37–36. AE, DC,
       MC, V.*

Lodging

Most hotels are centrally located, a short walk from Karl Johans Gate,
and often between the Royal Palace and the central railway station.
The newest hotels are in the area around Oslo S Station, at the bot-
tom end of Karl Johan. For a quiet stay, choose a hotel in Frogner, the
elegant residential neighborhood just minutes from downtown.

Lodging in the capital is expensive. Prices for downtown accommo-
dations are high, even for bed-and-breakfasts, although just about all
hotels have weekend, holiday, and summer rates (25% to 50% re-
ductions). Taxes and service charges, unless otherwise noted, are in-
cluded. Breakfast is usually included also, but be sure to ask before
booking your room.

You can cut your lodging costs considerably—and get more for your
money than with summer or weekend rates—by buying an Oslo Pack-
age in advance. This combines an Oslo Card (☞ Getting Around *in*
Oslo A to Z, *below*) with discounted room rates at almost all of Oslo's
better hotels. Contact local agents of the Scandinavian Tourist Board
for more information and reservations. In the U.S. or Canada, call
Scanam World Tours (☎ 201/835–7070, ℻ 201/835–3030); in the
U.K., **Norwegian State Railways** (☎ 0171/930–6666, ℻ 0171/321–
0624); and in Australia, the **Mansions Travel Service** (☎ 61/7–229–
5631, ℻ 61/7–221–9731).

Oslo usually has enough hotel rooms to go around, but it's always a
good idea to reserve a room at least for the first night of your stay, es-
pecially if you will be arriving late. Otherwise, the hotel accommoda-
tions office at Oslo S Station is open from 8 AM to 11 PM and can book
you in anything from a luxury hotel to a room in a private home for
a fee of NKr20. Usually there are last-minute discount rooms, and you
must pay for the room up front.

If you are interested in renting an apartment, contact **B&B Oslo Apart-
ments** (Stasjonsvn. 13, Blommenholm, 1300 Sandvika, ☎ 67/54–06–
80, ℻ 67/54–09–70), which is open weekdays 8:30–4. Most are
located in Bærum, 15 to 20 minutes from downtown Oslo, and about
20 are in Skøyen, a grassy suburban area, closer in to both the airport
and the center. All addresses provided by the group are no more than
a 10-minute walk from public transport.

Downtown: Royal Palace to the Parliament

$$$$ ▥ **Grand Hotel.** Right in the center of town on Karl Johans Gate, the
★   Grand has been Oslo's premier hotel since it opened in 1874. Ibsen
       used to start his mornings with a brisk walk followed by a stiff drink

at the Grand Café in the company of journalists. Munch was also a regular guest, and since his time the Grand has hosted many famous people and all recipients of the Nobel Peace Prize. Many Norwegians check in on Constitution Day, May 17, in order to have a room overlooking the parades. The lobby only hints at the style and flair of the rooms. Even standard rooms are large, looking more like guest quarters in an elegant house than hotel rooms. Those in the new wing are smaller, cheaper, and not as nice. The hotel's restaurant, Julius Fritzner, is considered one of Oslo's most elegant dining establishments. ⊠ *Karl Johans Gt. 31, 0159,* ☎ *22/42–93–90,* FAX *22/42–12–25. 289 rooms, 37 suites. 3 restaurants, 3 bars, indoor pool, sauna, health club, meeting rooms. AE, DC, MC, V.*

$$$$ ⊞ **Hotel Continental.** An elegant turn-of-the-century facade has put the
★ Continental on Norway's historic-preservation list. Its location—across from Nationaltheatret and next door to a high concentration of cafés, clubs, and cinemas—is perfect for both vacationers and business travelers. The Brockmann family, owners since 1900, have succeeded in combining the rich elegance of the Old World with modern, comfortable living. Munch graphics from the family's own collection adorn the walls. Antique furniture and shiny white porcelain fixtures add a distinctive touch to the rooms. Theatercafeen (☞ Dining, *above*) is a landmark, and the newest addition, Lipp, a restaurant-café-bar-nightclub, is among Oslo's "in" places. Dagligstuen (The Sitting Room) is a wonderful place in which to start or end the evening with an appetizer or nightcap. ⊠ *Stortingsgt. 24–26, 0161,* ☎ *22/82–40–00,* FAX *22/42–96–89. 158 rooms, 12 suites. 3 restaurants, 2 bars, nightclub. AE, DC, MC, V.*

$$$$ ⊞ **Radisson SAS Scandinavia Hotel.** Oslo's established business hotel, built in 1974, has some competition but can still hold its own: There's a business-class airline check-in in the lobby, and the lower-level shopping arcade has stylish clothing and leather-goods shops. The simple, elegant rooms come in four different styles: art deco, Italian, Asian, and predictably, for a hotel run by an airline, high-tech "business class." The SAS is across the street from the palace grounds downtown is a few blocks downhill. ⊠ *Holbergs Gt. 30, 0166,* ☎ *22/11–30–00,* FAX *22/11–30–17. 494 rooms, 3 large suites. 2 restaurants, 2 bars, pool, health club, nightclub, dance club, business center. AE, DC, MC, V.*

$$$ ⊞ **Bristol.** The Bristol caters to people who want a dignified hotel in the center of town. The immense lobby-lounge was decorated in the 1920s with an intricate Moorish theme and feels more like Fez than Scandinavia. Nevertheless, it is a tribute to style, and the piano bar is Oslo's most comfortable. The rooms do not necessarily reflect the lobby's lushness: Small and comfortable, they have all the amenities of modern Scandinavia and are simply decorated with Scandinavian or Regency-style furniture. ⊠ *Kristian IV's Gt. 7, 0164,* ☎ *22/82–60–00,* FAX *22/82–60–01. 141 rooms, 4 suites. 2 restaurants, 2 bars, nightclub, convention center. AE, DC, MC, V.*

$$$ ⊞ **Hotel Karl Johan.** The hundred-year-old Karl Johan, once known as the Nobel, is elegant. The lobby's hardwood floors are shiny and covered with Oriental rugs and velvety navy carpet; fabrics are gold and navy striped, and Old English caricatures adorn the off-white walls. Every room has a different Norwegian treasure, but the feel is sophisticated, not rustic. One look at the wrought-iron railing and art deco stained-glass windows that line the circular staircase will make you feel you're in 19th-century Paris. Its location, next door to the Grand, couldn't be better, and the hotel claims to have a set of regulars who prefer it to its overshadowing neighbor. If you're sensitive to noise, ask for a room away from Rosenkrantz' Gate, where bar hoppers and nightclubbers boogie until the wee hours. ⊠ *Karl Johans Gt. 33 , 0162,* ☎

22/42–74–80, FAX *22/42–05–19. 74 rooms, 12 suites. Restaurant, bar. AE, DC, MC, V.*

$$$ 🖪 **Rainbow Hotel Stefan.** This hotel makes every aspect of a stay here a positive experience, from hot drinks for late arrivals to breakfast tables complete with juice boxes and plastic bags for packing a lunch (request this service in advance). The top-floor lounge has books and magazines in English. The Stefan's kitchen is famous for creating the best buffet lunch in town. ⊠ *Rosenkrantz' Gt. 1, 0159,* ☎ *22/42–92– 50,* FAX *22/33–70–22. 138 rooms. Restaurant, library, meeting rooms. AE, DC, MC, V.*

$$$ 🖪 **Rica Victoria.** This modern business hotel occupies one of the city center's taller buildings, giving some top-floor rooms glimpses of Oslo's rooftops. The rooms, built around a center atrium, are elegant and very stylish, furnished with Biedermeier reproductions, brass lamps, and paisley-print textiles in bold reds and dark blues. Rooms with windows on the atrium may be claustrophobic for some but colorful and fun for others. ⊠ *Rosenkrantz' Gt. 13, 0160,* ☎ *22/42–99–40,* FAX *22/41–06– 44. 197 rooms, 4 suites. Restaurant, bar. AE, DC, MC, V.*

$$ 🖪 **Hotell Bondeheimen.** Founded in 1913 for country folk visiting the city, Bondeheimen, which means "farmers' home," still gives discounts to members of Norwegian agricultural associations. The interior, renovated in 1995, is simple and down-to-earth, furnished with all the makings of a contemporary Norwegian country home. Cube-shape cushioned chairs, sofas, and solid tables are made of pine, and fabrics and carpets are dyed in farmers' colors: green, blue, yellow, and red. Modern Norwegian graphics hang on the walls, and brand-new bathrooms have rustic swigs of hay on the walls. The lobby has a small library of books on Norway, even some in English. Bondeheimen is affiliated with the country kitchen Kaffistova (☞ *Dining, above*), which serves no alcohol. It is a good choice for families, but if you are looking for country quiet, ask for a room in back. ⊠ *Rosenkrantz' Gt. 8 (entrance on Kristian IV's Gate), 0159,* ☎ *22/42–95–30,* FAX *22/41–94–37. 76 rooms. Cafeteria, sauna, library, meeting room. AE, DC, MC, V.*

$$ 🖪 **Rainbow Cecil.** This modern hotel, one block from Parliament, is
★   down the road from several other, more expensive hotels and is closer to the main drag than most. The second floor opens onto a plant-filled atrium, the hotel's activity center. In the morning it's a breakfast room, with one of Oslo's best buffets, but in the afternoon it becomes a lounge, serving coffee, juice, and fresh fruit, with newspapers available in many languages. Many rooms face the atrium for the sake of peace and quiet, but others have a view of the Stortinget and its many passersby (in these you'll get a better feel for the city). The hotel provides umbrellas for rainy days and claims to have the best air-conditioning in the city for those rare—but beloved—summer heat waves. Special, less-expensive double rooms for the budget-conscious have a fold-out couch. ⊠ *Stortingsgt. 8, 0130,* ☎ *22/42–70–00,* FAX *22/42–26–70. 112 rooms, 2 suites. AE, DC, MC, V.*

East of Downtown

$ 🖪 **Haraldsheim.** Oslo's hilltop youth hostel is one of Europe's largest. Most of the rooms have four beds, and those in the new wing have showers. Bring your own sheets or rent them there. It is 6 kilometers (almost 3 miles) from the city center—take trikk 10 or 11 (marked "Kjelsås") to Sinsen. Nonmembers of the International Youth Hostel organization and those over 25 pay a surcharge. ⊠ *Haraldsheimvn. 4, 0409,* ☎ *22/15–50–43,* FAX *22/22–10–25. 264 beds. V.*

$ 🖪 **Munch.** This modern bed-and-breakfast, about a 10-minute walk from Karl Johans Gate, is unpretentious, well run, clean, and functional. The decent-size rooms are painted in pastels or blue with floral curtains. The lobby, with Chinese rugs and leather couches, contrasts with the rest of the hotel. ⊠ *Munchsgt. 5, 0165,* ☎ *22/42–42–75,* FAX *22/20–64–69. 180 rooms. Breakfast room. AE, DC, MC, V.*

Frogner, Majorstuen, and Holmenkollen

$$$$ 🏨 **Holmenkollen Park Hotel Rica.** The magnificent 1894 building in the national romantic style commands an unequaled panorama of the city in a quiet and natural setting. It is worth a visit even if you don't lodge there, perhaps for a meal at its legendary restaurant, De Fem Stuer (☞ Dining, *above*). The rather ordinary guest rooms are in a newer structure behind it. The ice-covered snowflake sculpture in the lobby is appropriate for a hotel that's a stone's throw from Holmenkollen ski jump. Ski and walking trails are just outside. ⊠ *Kongevn. 26, 0390,* ☎ *22/92–20–00,* FAX *22/14–61–92. 221 rooms. 2 restaurants, bar, pool, sauna, nightclub, cross-country skiing, convention center. AE, DC, MC, V.*

$$$–$$$$ 🏨 **Ambassadeur.** Hidden behind a pale pink facade with wrought-iron
★ balconies in a stylish residential area near the Royal Palace, the Ambassadeur is a 10- or 15-minute walk from both downtown and Frogner Park. Originally built in 1889 as an apartment hotel, it still has a turn-of-the-century feel. The owner has hand-picked antiques, china tea sets, and tapestries for the small downstairs salon. The rooms are also individually furnished according to themes. "Roma" rooms have canopy beds draped in pale taffeta and maps of old Rome on the walls. "Peer Gynt" rooms have Scandinavian landscape paintings and a Norwegian farmhouse feel. If it's a special occasion, request the pricey "Osa" suite. The painted wooden furniture, carved canopy bed, and exquisite printed fabrics could easily be on display at the Norwegian Folk Museum. All authentic, they belonged to a fiddler, the room's namesake, and were donated by the family when he died (his photograph is on the wall). The hotel's small, professional staff doesn't bother with titles because everyone does whatever task presents itself, from laundering a shirt on short notice to delivering room service. (☞ Ambassadeur *in* Dining, *above*.) ⊠ *Camilla Colletts vei 15, 0258,* ☎ *22/44–18–35,* FAX *22/44–47–91. 41 rooms, 8 suites. Restaurant, bar, indoor pool, sauna, meeting room. AE, DC, MC, V.*

$$ 🏨 **Gabelshus.** With only a discreet sign above the door, this ivy-covered brick house in a posh residential area is one of Oslo's most personal hotels. It's been owned by the same family for almost 50 years. The lounges are filled with antiques, some in the national romantic style, but the rooms are plain. It's a short walk to several of Oslo's best restaurants and a short trikk ride to the center of town. The Ritz Hotel, across the parking lot, is owned by the same family and takes the overflow. ⊠ *Gabels Gt. 16, 0272,* ☎ *22/55–22–60,* FAX *22/44–27–30. 50 rooms (plus 42 rooms in Ritz). Restaurant. AE, DC, MC, V.*

$ 🏨 **Rainbow Gyldenløve.** Nestled among the many shops and cafés on Bogstadveien, this hotel is one of the city's most reasonable. It is within walking distance of Vigeland Park, and the trikk stops just outside the door. Reproductions of city scenes from old Christiania (Oslo) hang in every room. 🏨 *Bogstadvn. 20, 0355,* ☎ *22/60–10–90,* FAX *22/60–33–90. 169 rooms. Coffee shop. AE, DC, MC, V.*

Near Fornebu Airport and Oslo S Station

$$$$ 🏨 **Reso Oslo Plaza.** Northern Europe's largest hotel is a three-minute walk from Karl Johans Gate and just across from Oslo's central train station. A snazzy 33-story skyscraper in a city that has few, Oslo Plaza has become a part of the city's skyline. It is favored by business travelers, who tend toward the pricier deluxe suites in the tower, where the views of Oslo are worth the price. Below the 27th floor, the standard rooms are decorated in red and blue tones and have ample marble baths. At press time, the hotel had just begun the lengthy process of redoing the top floors, which had a Japanese restaurant and popular nightclub. ⊠ *Sonja Henies Pl. 3, 0134,* ☎ *22/17–10–00,* FAX *22/17–73–00. 662 rooms, 20 suites. 3 restaurants, 2 bars, indoor pool, health club, nightclub, convention center. AE, DC, MC, V.*

$$$$ 🏨 **Royal Christiania.** It started out as bare-bones housing for 1952
★ Olympians. The original plain exterior has been retained, but inside it's a whole new luxury hotel, built around a central seven-story atrium. The emphasis here is on discreet comfort—the large rooms are decorated with soft-colored love seats and armchairs. The restaurant, La Trattoria, serves up delicious, traditional Italian fare. ⊠ *Biskop Gunnerus' Gt. 3, 0106,* ☎ *22/42–94–10,* FAX *22/42–46–22. 451 rooms, 73 suites. 3 restaurants, 3 bars, health club, indoor pool, nightclub, convention center. AE, DC, MC, V.*

$$$ 🏨 **Radisson SAS Park Royal.** Oslo Fornebu Airport's only hotel is somewhat anonymous, with long, narrow corridors and standard American-style hotel rooms. There are excellent business facilities, including a business-class airline check-in, and the airport bus stops right outside. ⊠ *Fornebuparken, Box 185, 1324 Lysaker,* ☎ *67/12–02–20,* FAX *67/12–00–11. 254 rooms, 14 suites. Restaurant, bar, tennis court, health club, business services. AE, DC, MC, V.*

Nightlife and the Arts

Nightlife

For the past few years Oslo has strived to be the nightlife capital of Scandinavia, while local government factions have talked about toughening laws on noise pollution and drinking. At any time of the day or night, people are out on Karl Johan, and many clubs and restaurants in the central area stay open until the wee hours. Still, strict zoning laws have prohibited the sale of anything harder than "light" beer after 2:30 AM, which means many nightclubs close their doors earlier than one would expect.

Night-lifers can pick up a copy of the free monthly paper *Natt og Dag* at almost any café, bar, or hip-looking shop. It lists rock, pop, and jazz venues and contains an "øl barometer," listing the city's cheapest and most expensive places for a beer—a necessary column in a city where a draft, on the average, costs NKr33. The listings are in Norwegian, but some ads are in English.

Many bars and nightclubs in Oslo have a minimum age, which will often give you a sense of who goes there. A minimum age of 18 will generally draw high schoolers, whereas 24 will draw young professionals.

BARS AND LOUNGES

Barbeint (⊠ Drammensvn. 20, ☎ 22/44–59–47) is an ultrahip spot where students, media folk, and local celebrities from the fashionable Frogner district convene on their way in from or out on the town. Avant-garde art adorns the walls, and the loud, cutting-edge music ranges from funk-metal and rock to rap. The trendiest twentysomethings imbibe the night away at **Beach Club** (⊠ Aker Brygge, ☎ 22/83–83–82), a kitschy American hamburger joint with life-size stuffed fish on the walls and diner-style tables and booths. If you're more partial to lounging than drinking, try the English-style bar at the **Bristol Hotel** (⊠ Kristian IV's Gt. 7, ☎ 22/41–58–40). **Børsen: Café Stock Exchange** (⊠ Nedre Vollgt. 19, enter on Stortingsgt., ☎ 22/33–08–00) caters to the cyber crowd and the upwardly mobile. The former can surf the net on one of several monitors that overlook a starry-skied dance floor while the latter speculate on beer prices, which fluctuate according to supply and demand. For variety, get an outdoor table at **Lorry** (✉ Parkvn. 12, ☎ 22/69–69–04), just over from the Royal Palace. Filled with a cast of grizzled old artists, the place advertises 204 brews, but don't be surprised if not all of them are in stock. For the serious beer connoisseur, **Oslo Mikrobryggeriet** (✉ Bogstadvn. 6, ☎ 22/56–97–76) brews six or seven varieties of beer, including the increasingly popular Oslo Pils, on the premises. **Studenten Bryggeri** (✉ Karl Johans Gt. 45, ☎ 22/42–56–80), another microbrewery, is often packed with students and loud music as well.

CAFÉS

Many cafés are open for cappuccino and quiet conversation practically around the clock, and they're the cheapest eateries as well (☞ Dining, *above*). **The Broker Café** (✉ Bogstadvn. 27, ☎ 22/69–36–47) in Majorstuen has great pasta and salads and old, comfortable sofas on which to drink or dine. **Café Bacchus** (✉ Dronningensgt. 27, ☎ 22/42–45–49), in the old railroad offices by Oslo Domkirke, is tiny but serves a mean brownie. A wrought-iron winding staircase leads up to more tables in a loft called "heaven," and background music is classical during the day, jazz into the night. Downtown, **Nichol & Son** (✉ Olavs Gt. 1, ☎ 22/83–19–60), a must for Jack Nicholson fans, is an ambient spot to relax with a newspaper. In the trendy area around Frogner and Homansbyen, try **Onkel Oswald** (✉ Hegdehaugsvn. 34, ☎ 22/69–05–35) for a burger or sandwich. The Spanish-inspired **Tapas** (✉ Hegdehausvn. 22, ☎ 22/60–38–28) serves bowls of café au lait in the morning and aperitif-size chunks of potatoes, chorizo, and cheese later on. The decor is colorful and stark, and the music ranges from rhumba to jazz.

DISCOS AND NIGHTCLUBS

Most discos open late, and the beat doesn't really start until around midnight. There's usually a minimum age, and the cover charge is around NKr50. Oslo's beautiful people congregate at the elegant **Barock** (✉ Universitetsgt. 26, ☎ 22/42–44–20). **Cosmopolite** (✉ Industrigt. 36, ☎ 22/69–16–63) has a big dance floor and music from all over the world, especially Latin America. **Kristiania** (✉ Kristian IV's Gt. 12, ☎ 22/42–56–60), another hot spot, has a live jazz club, a disco, and a bar filling up its three art-bedecked floors. **Lipp** (✉ Olav V's Gt. 2, ☎ 22/41–44–00) is extremely popular as a restaurant, nightclub, and bar. Most of the big hotels have discos that appeal to the over-30 crowd. **Smuget** (✉ Rosenkrantz Gt. 22, ☎ 22/42–52–62) is an institution: Live rock and blues every night except Sunday bring crowds who then flock to the in-house discotheque. Thursday is student disco night at **Snorre-Kompagniet** (✉ Rosenkrantz' Gt. 11, ☎ 22/33–52–60), where the hip-hopping clientele is often still teenaged.

GAY BARS

For information about gay and lesbian activities in Oslo, you can read *Blikk,* the gay newsletter, or call **LLH** (Landsforening for Lesbisk of Homofil Frigjøring, ☎ 22/36–19–48), the nationwide gay and lesbian liberation association. The union operates **Lille Metropol** (✉ St. Olavs Pl. 2, ☎ 22/20–19–48), which has a mixed crowd and organizes dance nights on the weekends. **Andy Capp Pub** (✉ Fr. Nansens Pl. 4, ☎ 22/41–41–65) draws an older crowd of mostly men, and it reeks of old smoke. **Den Sorte Enke** (The Black Widow, ✉ Karl Johans Gt. 10, ☎ 22/33–23–01), Oslo's self-designated "gay-house," attracts a crowd of mainly younger men to dance the night away. **London Bar og Pub** (✉ C. J. Hambros Pl. 5, ☎ 22/41–41–26) is packed on weekends with an over-30s crowd. **Potpurriet** (✉ Øvre Vollgt. 13, ☎ 22/41–14–40) organizes well-attended women's dance nights on the last Friday of each month but is very popular with gays and lesbians alike.

JAZZ CLUBS

Norwegians love jazz. Every August, the **Oslo Jazz Festival** (⊠ Toll-bugt. 28, ☎ 22/42–91–20) brings in major international artists and attracts big crowds. Festivities commence with a Dixie-style parade, but all types of jazz are present and explained in free leaflets and newsletters everywhere. **Gamle Christiania** (⊠ Grensen 1, ☎ 22/42–74–93) is the home of the New Orleans Jazz Workshop. **Herr Nilsen** (⊠ C.J. Hambros Pl. 5, ☎ 22/33–54–05) features some of Norway's most celebrated jazz artists in a Manhattanesque setting with brick walls and winding sofas. There is live music three days a week and a jazz café on Saturday afternoons. **Oslo Jazzhus** (⊠ Stockholmsgt. 12, ☎ 22/38–59–63) is in an out-of-the-way location and is open only Thursday through Saturday, but the music is worth the journey. **Rebekka West** (⊠ Kristian IV's Gt. 7, ☎ 22/41–51–08) is Oslo's no-frills jazz joint, whose Sunday-night jam sessions are legendary. **Stortorvets Gjæstgiveri** (⊠ Grensen 1, ☎ 22/42–88–63) often presents New Orleans–style and ragtime bands and is known for its swinging dance nights.

ROCK CLUBS

At Oslo's numerous rock clubs, the cover charges are low, the crowds young and boisterous, and the music loud. If your taste leans toward reggae and calypso, try the **Afro International Night Club** (⊠ Brenner-ivn. 5, ☎ 22/36–07–53), which has frequent Caribbean evenings. **Blue Monk** (⊠ St. Olavs Gt. 23, ☎ 22/20–22–90) has live music on Wednesdays, Fridays, and Saturdays—and the beer is surprisingly cheap. In the basement you'll find the boisterous Sub Pub, which airs punk and '80s classics. **Rockefeller** (⊠ Torggt. 16, ☎ 22/20–32–32) presents a good mix of musical styles, from avant-garde to salsa. Thursday is student disco night. **Sentrum Scene** (⊠ Arbeidersamfunnets Pl. 2, ☎ 22/20–60–40) claims to be Scandinavia's largest live-music venue. It certainly attracts big names including Warren Zevon, Lenny Kravitz, and the Neville Brothers.

The Arts

The monthly tourist information brochure *What's on in Oslo* lists cultural events in Norwegian, as does *Aftenposten,* Oslo's (and Norway's) leading newspaper, in its evening "Oslo Puls" section. The Wednesday edition of *Dagbladet,* Oslo's daily liberal tabloid, also gives an exhaustive preview of the week's events. Tickets to virtually all performances in Norway, from classical or rock concerts to hockey games, can be purchased at any post office. You can also call **Billet Service** (☎ 810–33–133) and pick up tickets at the post office later.

Nationaltheatret (⊠ Stortingsgt. 15, ☎ 22/41–27–10) performances are in Norwegian: Bring along a copy of the play in translation, and you're all set. **Det Norske Teater** (⊠ Kristian IV's Gt. 8, ☎ 22/42–43–44) is a showcase for pieces in Nynorsk, musicals, and guest artists from abroad.

The **Norwegian Philharmonic Orchestra,** under the direction of Mariss Janssons, is among Europe's leading ensembles. Its house, **Konserthuset** (⊠ Munkedamsvn. 14, ☎ 22/83–32–00), was built in 1977 in marble, metal, and rosewood. **Den Norske Opera** (⊠ Storgt. 23, ☎ 22/42–94–75 for information; 22/42–77–24 to order tickets between 10 and 6) and the ballet perform at Youngstorvet. The breathtaking **Gamle Logen** (⊠ Grev Wedels Pl. 2, ☎ 22/33–54–70), Norway's oldest concert hall, often sponsors classical music series, especially piano music.

For a thoroughly Norwegian cultural experience, check out the **Norwegian Masters** (☎ 22/43–34–70), who play character monologues from Ibsen's *Peer Gynt* against a backdrop of Munch paintings and to the music of the beloved Grieg, who originally wrote music to accompany the Norwegian fable. The performance takes place in English, and its venue changes from year to year.

All **films** are shown in the original language with subtitles, except for some children's films, which are dubbed. You can buy tickets to any film showing at the box office of any of Oslo's cinemas, and you can reserve tickets by calling any cinema and leaving your phone number. Tickets cost NKr 50 and are discounted some days in summer. If you like alternative and classic films, try **Cinemateket** (⊠ Dronningensgt. 16, ☎ 22/47–45–05), the city's only independent cinema.

Art galleries are cropping up all over town as a generation of young artists comes of age. While much official Norwegian art is folk art, some of the newer artists take a more postmodern approach to their craft. Pick up a copy of *Listen,* a brochure that lists all current exhibitions.

Outdoor Activities and Sports

Surrounding Oslo's compact center is a variety of lovely and unspoiled landscapes, including forests, farmland, and, of course, the fjord. Just 15 minutes north of the city center by tram is the **Oslomarka,** where locals ski in winter and hike in summer. The area is dotted with 27 small *hytter* (cottages), which are often available free of charge for backpackers on foot or on ski. These can be reserved through the **Norske Turistforening** (⊠ Stortingsgt. 28, ☎ 22/83–25–50), which has maps of the *marka* (fields and land), surrounding Oslo as well. The **Oslo Archipelago** is also a favorite with sunbathing urbanites, who hop ferries to their favorite isles.

Aerobics

If you need a fitness fix, you can visit one of the many health studios around the city. Most have a "klippekort" system, which means you buy 10 hours' worth of fitness and they "klip," or punch, your card with each entry. The ever-popular **Trim Tram** (⊠ Stranden 55, Aker Brygge, ☎ 22/83–66–50) offers myriad low- and high-intensity aerobics and step classes at reasonable rates. **Friskis & Svettis** (⊠ Munkedamsvn. 17–18, ☎ 22/83–25–40) holds free aerobics classes on the green in Frogner Park. From mid-May to mid-August you can watch or join the hundreds of health-conscious Osloites huffing and puffing and rolling in the dirt. Call for times and intensity levels.

Beaches

Beaches are scattered throughout the archipelago, although swimming is forbidden on some because of water contamination. Nevertheless, sun-loving Scandinavians pack every patch of sand during the long summer days to make up for lack of light in winter. The most popular beach is Paradisbukta at Huk (on the Bygdøy peninsula), which devotes one portion of the beach to nude bathers and the other to "clothed." To get there, follow signs along Huk Aveny from the Folk- and Viking Ship museums. You can also take Bus 30A, marked "Bygdøy," to its final stop.

Bicycling

Oslo is a bike-friendly city. There are many marked paths in and around town meant for bicycles and pedestrians, and cyclists are allowed to use sidewalks. (Note, however, that cars do not have to stop for bicycles the way they do for pedestrians at crosswalks.) One great ride starts at Aker Brygge and takes you along the harbor to the Bygdøy peninsula, where you can visit the museums or cut across the fields next to the royal family's summer house. Ask locals how to get to Huk, the peninsula's popular beach (☞ Beaches, *above*).

Den Rustne Eike (The Rusty Spoke) (⊠ Vestbanepl. 2, ☎ 22/83–72–
31), just a few doors down from the Norway Information Center, rents
bikes and equipment, including helmets. The store also offers five different sightseeing tours and has maps of the area for those braving it
on their own. If you feel like roughing the terrain of the Hollmenkollen
marka (woods), you can rent mountain bikes from **Tomm Murstad Skiservice** in the summer (⊠ Tryvannsvn. 2, ☎ 22/14–41–24). Just take T-
bane 1 to Frognerseteren and get off at the Voksenkollen station.
Syklistenes Landsforening (National Organization of Cyclists) (⊠
Stortingsgt. 23C, ☎ 22/41–50–80) sells books and maps for cycling
holidays in Norway and abroad and gives friendly, free advice. During summer months you can take your bike on a weekend express T-
bane (the "bike train") nonstop from Majorstuen to Frognerseteren
for twice the price of a regular ticket.

Fishing

A national fishing license (NKr90, available in post offices) and a local
fee (NKr100 from local sports shops) are required in order to fish in
the Oslo Fjord and the surrounding lakes. You can also fish throughout the Nordmarka woods area in a canoe rented from **Tomm Murstad**
(☞ Bicycling, *above*). Ice fishing is popular in winter, but you'll have
a hard time finding an ice drill—truly, you may want to bring one
from home.

Golf

Oslo's international-level golf course, **Oslo Golfklubb** (⊠ Bogstad,
0740 Oslo 7, ☎ 22/50–44–02) is private, and heavily booked, but
will admit members of other golf clubs if space is available. There is
also one 18-hole course. Visitors must have a handicap certificate of
24 or lower for men, 32 or lower for women, and the space is open to
visitors during the week before 2 PM and weekends after 2 PM. Fees
range from NKr250 to NKr300.

Hiking and Jogging

Head for the woods surrounding Oslo, the **marka,** for jogging or
walking; there are thousands of kilometers of trails, hundreds of them
lit. Frogner Park has many paths, and you can jog or hike along the
Aker River, but a few unsavory types may be about late at night or
early in the morning. Or you can take the Sognsvann trikk to the end
of the line and walk or jog along the Sognsvann stream. For walks or
jogs closer to town, explore the stately residential area around Drammensveien west of the Royal Palace, which has paths leading to Bygdøy.
The Norske Turistforening (☞ *above*) has many maps of trails around
Oslo and can recommend individual routes.

Running

Grete Waitz and Ingrid Kristiansen have put Norway on the marathon
runners' map in recent years. The first national marathon championships
were held in Norway in 1897, and the Oslo Marathon always attracts
a large following. **Norges Friidretts Forbund** (⊠ Karl Johans Gt. 2, 0104
Oslo, ☎ 22/42–03–03) has information about local clubs and competitions.

Skiing

The **Skiforeningen** (⊠ Kongevn. 5, 0390 Oslo 3, ☎ 22/92–32–00)
provides national snow-condition reports and can provide tips on the
multitude of cross-country trails. They also offer cross-country classes
for young children (3- to 7-year-olds), downhill for older children (7-
to 12-year-olds), and both, in addition to Telemark-style and racing
techniques, for adults.

Among the floodlit trails in the Oslomarka are the **Bogstad** (3.5 kilometers [2.1 miles], marked for the disabled and blind), the **Lillomarka** (about 25 kilometers [15.6 miles]), and the **Østmarken** (33 kilometers [20.6 miles]).

For downhill, which usually lasts from mid-December to March, there are 15 local city slopes as well as organized trips to several outside slopes, including **Norefjell** (☎ 32/14–94–00), 100 kilometers (66 miles) north of the city, are also available.

You can rent both downhill and cross-country skis (as well as other sports equipment) from **Tomm Murstad Skiservice** (✉ Tryvannsvn. 2, ☎ 22/14–41–24) at the Tryvann T-bane station. This is a good starting point for skiing; although there are but few downhill slopes in this area, a plethora of cross-country trails for every level of competence exist.

Swimming
Tøyenbadet (✉ Helgesensgt. 90, ☎ 22/67–18–87) and **Frogner Park** (☎ 22/44–74–29) have large outdoor swimming pools that are open from May 18 through August 20, depending on the weather (weekdays 7–5:45, weekends 10–5:30). Tø also has an indoor pool open year-round (Mon., Fri. 10–7; Tues., Thurs. 7–7; Wed., 11–7; weekends 10–2:30). All pools cost NKr36. Pools are free with the Oslo Card (☞ Getting Around, *below*).

Shopping

Oslo is the best place for buying anything Norwegian. Prices of handmade articles, such as knitwear, are controlled, making comparison shopping unnecessary. Otherwise shops have both sales and specials—look for the words *salg* and *tilbud*. Sales of seasonal merchandise, combined with the value-added tax refund, can save you more than half the original price. Norwegians do like au courant skiwear, so there are plenty of bargains in last season's winter sportswear.

Stores are generally open from 9 to 5 during the week, but they often close by 3 on Saturdays. Shopping malls and department stores are open later, until 8 during the week and 6 on weekends. Shops also stay open late Thursdays as well as on the first Saturday of the month, known as *super lørdag* (super Saturday) to enthusiastic shoppers. Only during the holiday season are stores open Sunday.

Several shopping districts stand out. From the city center, you can wander up the tree-lined Bygdøy Allé and poke around the fashionable **Frogner** area, which is brimming with modern and antique furniture stores, interior design shops, gourmet food shops, art galleries, haute couture, and a solid majority of Oslo's beautiful people. Stores of every ilk are crammed into the downtown area around **Karl Johans Gate,** where many shoppers flock. The concentration of department stores is especially high in this part of town. **Majorstuen** starts at the T-bane station with the same name and proceeds down Bogstadveien to the Royal Palace. Once you're off the main shopping street, a tiny smattering of independent shops and galleries cater to needs as obscure as your next safari hunt. **Vikaterrassen,** near Aker Brygge (☞ *below*), is a pleasant shopping street with small, exclusive stores. Its glass and concrete facade sits directly underneath a more magnificent building that houses Norway's Ministry of Foreign Affairs.

Department Stores
Christiania GlasMagasin (✉ Stortorvet 9, ☎ 22/90–89–00) is an amalgamation of shops under one roof rather than a true department

store, but it has a much more extensive selection of merchandise than most department stores in town. The best buys are glass and porcelain. Christmas decorations reflecting Norway's rural heritage are easily packed. There is also a wide selection of pewter ware. **Steen & Strøm** (⊠ Kongens Gt. 23, ☎ 22/41–68–00), one of Oslo's first department stores, offers the usual: cosmetics, clothing, books, accessories. It also has a well-stocked outdoors floor.

Shopping Centers

Aker Brygge, Norway's first major shopping center, is right on the water across from the Tourist Information Office at Vestbanen. Shops are open until 8 most days, and some even on Sundays. **Oslo City** (⊠ Stenersgt. 1E, ☎ 22/44–44–44), at the other end of downtown, with access to the street from Oslo S Station, is the largest indoor mall, but the shops are run-of-the-mill, and the food is mostly fast. The elegant **Paleet** (⊠ Karl Johans Gt. 39–41, between Universitetsgt. and Rosenkrantz' Gt., ☎ 22/41–70–86) opens up into a grand atrium lined with supports of various shades of black and gray marble. The main floor houses a good bookstore and some high-end clothing shops and the basement houses a food court.

Specialty Stores

ANTIQUES

Norwegian rustic antiques cannot be taken out of the country, but just about anything else can with no problem. The Frogner district is dotted with antiques shops, especially Skovveien and Thomas Heftyes Gate between Bygdøy Allé and Frogner Plass. Deeper in the heart of the Majorstua district, Industrigate is famous for its good selection of shops. **Blomqvist Kunsthandel** (⊠ Tordenskiolds Gt. 5, ☎ 22/41–26–31) has a good selection of small items and paintings, with auctions six times a year. The rare volumes at **Damms Antiqvariat** (⊠ Tollbugt. 25, ☎ 22/41–04–02) will catch the eye of any antiquarian book buff, with books in English as well as Norwegian, which could be harder to find back home. **Esaias Solberg** (⊠ Dronningens Gt. 27, ☎ 22/42–41–08), behind Oslo Cathedral, has exceptional small antiques. **Kaare Berntsen** (⊠ Universitetsgt. 12, ☎ 22/20–34–29) sells paintings, furniture, and small items, all very exclusive and priced accordingly. **Marsjandisen** (⊠ Paléet, ☎ 22/42–71–68), nestled in the slickest of shopping centers, carries "merchandise" ranging from discontinued Hadeland glasses to letter openers and authentic war-era postcards, pins, and buttons. **West Sølv og Mynt** (⊠ Niels Juels Gt. 27, ☎ 22/55–75–83) has the largest selection of silver, both old and antique, in town.

BOOKS

Bjørn Ringstrøms Antikvariat (⊠ Ullevålsvn. 1, ☎ 22/20–78–05), across the street from the Museum of Applied Art, has a wide selection of used books and records. **Erik Qvist** (⊠ Drammensvn. 16, ☎ 22/44–52–69), across from the Royal Palace, has an extensive English-language selection. **Pocketboka** (⊠ Ole Vigs Gt. 25, ☎ 22/69–00–18) at Majorstuen sells used paperbacks. **Tanum Libris** (⊠ Karl Johans Gt. 37–41, ☎ 22/41–11–00) has scores of English-language books, ranging from travel guides to contemporary fiction.

EMBROIDERY

Husfliden (☞ Handicrafts, *below*) sells embroidery kits, including do-it-yourself *bunader* (national costumes), and traditional yarn shops also sell embroidery. **Randi Mangen** (⊠ Jacob Aalls Gt. 17, ☎ 22/60–50–59), near Majorstuen, sells only embroidery.

FOOD

Buy a smoked salmon or trout for a special treat. Most grocery stores sell vacuum-packed fish. **W. Køltzow,** at Aker Brygge (⊠ Stranden 3, ☎ 22/83–00–70), specializes in fish and can pack smoked and marinated salmon for export.

FUR

Look for the Saga label for the best-quality farmed Arctic fox and mink. Other popular skins include Persian lamb, beaver, mink, and musquash. **Hansson** (⊠ Kirkevn. 54, ☎ 22/69–64–20), near Majorstuen has an excellent selection of furs. **Studio H. Olesen** (⊠ Karl Johans Gt. 31, enter at Rosenkrantz' Gt., ☎ 22/33–37–50) has the most exclusive designs.

FURNITURE

Norway is well known for both rustic furniture and orthopedic yet well-designed chairs. **Tannum** (⊠ Stortingsgt. 28, ☎ 22/83–42–95) is a good starting point. Drammensveien and Bygdøy Allé have a wide selection of interior-design stores.

GLASS, CERAMICS, AND PEWTER

Abelson Brukskunst (⊠ Skovvn. 27, ☎ 22/55–55–94), behind the Royal Palace, is crammed with the best modern designs. The shops at **Basarhallene** behind the cathedral also sell glass and ceramics. If there's no time to visit a glass factory (☞ Sidetrips, *below*), department stores are the best option: **Christiania GlasMagasin** (⊠ Stortorvet 9, ☎ 22/90–89–00) stocks both European and Norwegian glass designs. **Lie Antikk & Kunsthandverk** (⊠ Hegdehausveien 27, ☎ 22/60–98–61) is a tiny shop at the bottom of Bogstadveien that sells hundreds of glass figurines and colorful wine glasses and claims to have the city's best collection of blown glass. **Norway Designs** (⊠ Stortingsgt. 28, ☎ 22/83–11–00) specializes in glass crafted by Norwegian and Scandinavian folk artists and jewelers.

HANDICRAFTS

Basarhallene, the arcade behind the cathedral, is also worth a browse for handicrafts made in Norway. **Format Kunsthandverk** (⊠ Vestbanepl. 1, ☎ 22/83–73–12) has beautiful, yet pricey, individual pieces (but you can buy a postcard to show your friends back home). **Heimen Husflid AS** (⊠ Rosenkrantz' Gt. 8, ☎ 22/41–40–50, enter at Kristian IVs Gt.) has small souvenir items and a specialized department for Norwegian national costumes. **Husfliden** (⊠ Møllergt. 4, ☎ 22/42–10–75) has an even larger selection, including pewter, ceramics, knits, handwoven textiles, furniture, handmade felt boots and slippers, hand-sewn loafers, sweaters, national costumes, wrought-iron accessories, Christmas ornaments, and wooden kitchen accessories with such obscure and ancient forms even your Norwegian grandmother wouldn't figure out what they were used for—all made in Norway.

JEWELRY

Gold and precious stones are no bargain, but silver and enamel jewelry, along with reproductions of Viking pieces, are. Some silver pieces are made with Norwegian stones, particularly pink thulite. **David-Andersen** (⊠ Karl Johans Gt. 20, ☎ 22/41–69–55; Oslo City, ☎ 22/17–09–34) is Norway's best-known goldsmith, with stunning silver and gold designs. **ExpoArte** (⊠ Drammensvn. 40, ☎ 22/55–93–90), also a gallery, specializes in custom pieces and displays work of avant-garde Scandinavian jewelers. **Heyerdahl** (⊠ Roald Amundsensgt. 6, ☎ 22/41–59–18), near City Hall, is a good jeweler.

KNITWEAR AND CLOTHING

Norway is famous for its handmade, multicolored ski sweaters, and even mass-produced models are of top quality. The prices are regulated, so

buy what you like when you see it. **Husfliden** (☞ Handicrafts, *above*)
stocks handmade sweaters in the traditional style. **Maurtua** (✉ Fr.
Nansens Pl. 9, ☎ 22/41–31–64), near City Hall, has a huge selection
of sweaters and blanket coats. **Oslo Sweater Shop** (✉ SAS Scandinavia
Hotel, Tullinsgt. 5, ☎ 22/11–29–22) has one of the city's widest selections. **Rein og Rose** (✉ Ruseløkkvn. 3, ☎ 22/83–21–39), in the Vikat-
erassen strip, has extremely friendly salespeople and a good selection
of knitwear, yarn, and textiles. **Siril** (✉ Rosenkrantz' Gt. 23, ☎ 22/41–
01–80), near City Hall, is a small shop with attentive staff. **William
Schmidt** (✉ Karl Johans Gt. 41, ☎ 22/42–02–88), founded in 1853,
is Oslo's oldest shop specializing in sweaters and souvenirs.

SPORTSWEAR

Look for the ever-popular Helly-Hansen brand. The company makes
everything from insulated underwear to rainwear, snow gear, and great
insulated mittens. **Sportshuset** (✉ Ullevålsvn. 11, ☎ 22/20–11–21;
✉ Frognervn. 9C, ☎ 22/55–29–57) has the best prices. **Gresvig** (✉
Storgt. 20, ☎ 22/17–39–80) is a little more expensive but has a good
selection. **Sigmund Ruud** (✉ Kirkevn. 57, ☎ 22/69–43–90) also has
a comprehensive stock of quality sportswear.

WATCHES

For some reason, Swiss watches are much cheaper in Norway than in
many other countries. **Bjerke** (✉ Karl Johans Gt. 31, ☎ 22/42–20–
44; Prinsensgt. 21, ☎ 22/42–60–50) has the largest selection in town.

Street Markets

Although some discerning locals wonder where it procures its wares,
the best flea market is on Saturday at **Vestkanttorvet,** near Frogner Park
at Amaldus Nilsens Plass at the intersection of Professor Dahlsgate and
Eckerberg Gate. Check the local paper for weekend garage sales, or
loppemarkeder, held in schools.

Oslo A to Z

Arriving and Departing

BY BOAT

Several ferry lines connect Oslo with the United Kingdom, Denmark,
Sweden, and Germany. **Color Line** (☎ 22/22–94–45–70) sails to Kiel,
Germany, and to Hirtshals, Denmark; **DFDS Scandinavian Seaways** (☎
22/41–90–90) to Copenhagen via Helsingborg, Sweden; and **Stena Line**
(☎ 22/33–50–00) to Frederikshavn, Denmark.

BY BUS

The main bus station, **Bussterminalen** (☎ 22/17–01–66), is under Galleri Oslo, across from the Oslo S Station. You can buy local bus tickets at the terminal or on the bus. Tickets for long-distance routes on
Nor-Way Bussekspress (☎ 22/17–52–90, FAX 22/17–59–22) can be
purchased here or at travel agencies. For local traffic information, call
Trafikanten (☎ 22/17–70–30 or 177).

BY CAR

Route E18 connects Oslo with Göteborg, Sweden (by ferry between
Sandefjord and Strömstad, Sweden); Copenhagen, Denmark (by ferry
between Kristiansand and Hirtshals, Denmark); and Stockholm directly
overland. The land route from Oslo to Göteborg is the E6. All streets
and roads leading into Oslo have toll booths a certain distance from
the city center, forming an "electronic ring." The toll is NKr12 and
was implemented to reduce pollution downtown. If you have the cor-
rect amount in change, drive through one of the lanes marked "Mynt."
If you don't, or if you need a receipt, use the "Manuell" lane.

Oslo Fornebu Airport, 20 minutes southwest of the city, has international and domestic services. Nevertheless, the walks between international arrivals, baggage claim, and passport control are long.

SAS (☎ 810/03–300) is the main carrier, with both international and domestic flights. **Braathens SAFE** (☎ 67/59–70–00) and **Widerøe** (☎ 22/73–66–00) are the main domestic carriers.

Other major airlines serving Fornebu include **British Airways** (☎ 22/82–20–00), **Air France** (☎ 22/83–56–30), **Delta Air Lines** (☎ 22/41–56–00), **Finnair** (☎ 67/53–11–97), **Icelandair** (☎ 22/42–39–75), **KLM** (☎ 67/58–38–00), and **Lufthansa** (☎ 67/58–27–30).

Gardermoen Airport, 50 kilometers (30 miles) north of Oslo is slated to become Oslo's main airport by October 1998.

Between the Airport and Downtown: Oslo Fornebu Airport is a 15- to 20-minute ride from the center of Oslo at off-peak hours. At rush hour (7:30–9 AM from the airport and 3:30–5 PM to the airport), the trip can take more than twice as long. None of the downtown hotels provide free shuttle service, although some outside the city do.

Flybussen (☎ 67/59–62–20; NKr35; *to Oslo* weekdays and Sun. 7:30 AM–11:30 PM, Sat. 7:30 AM–11:00 PM; *to Fornebu* weekdays, 6 AM–9:40 PM, Sat. 6 AM–7:40 PM, Sun. 6 AM–9:50 PM) departs from its terminal under Galleri Oslo shopping center every 10–15 minutes and reaches Fornebu approximately 20 minutes later. Another bus departs from the SAS Scandinavia Hotel. Between the two buses, there are stops at the central train station as well as at Stortinget, Nationaltheatret, and near Aker Brygge. Another alternative is Suburban Bus 31, marked "Snarøya," which stops outside the Arrivals terminal. On the trip into town it stops on the main road opposite the entrance to the airport. You can catch this bus at both the central railway station, Jernbanetorget, or at Nationaltheatret. The cost is NKr20.

There is a taxi line to the right of the Arrivals exit. The fare to town is about NKr130. All taxi reservations should be made through the **Oslo Taxi Central** (☎ 22/38–80–90; dial 1 for direct reservation) no less than 20 minutes before pickup time.

Long-distance trains arrive at and leave from **Oslo S Station** (☎ 22/17–14–00), whereas most suburban commuter trains use **Nationaltheatret** or **Oslo S.** Commuter cars reserved for monthly pass holders are marked with a large black "M" on a yellow circle. Trains marked "IC," or InterCity, offer such upgraded services as breakfast and "office cars" with phones and power outlets, for an added fee.

Getting Around

Tickets on all public transportation within Oslo cost NKr18 without transfer, whereas tickets that cross communal boundaries have different rates. It pays to buy a pass or a multiple travel card, which includes transfers. A one-day "Tourist Ticket" pass costs NKr40, and a seven-day pass costs NKr120. A "Flexikort," purchased at post offices, tourist information offices, T-bane stations, and on some routes, is good for 10 trips with free transfer within one hour and costs NKr100. Oslo Sporveier operates most modes of transport in the city, including tram, bus, underground, train, and boat. **Trafikanten** (✉ Jernbanetorget, ☎ 22/17–70–30 or 177), the information office for public transportation, is open weekdays 7 AM–11 PM, weekends 8 AM–11 PM.

The **Oslo Card** offers unlimited travel on all public transport in greater Oslo as well as free admission to museums, sightseeing attractions, and the race track, as well as discounts at various stores and cinemas (May–July). A one-day Oslo Card costs NKr130, a two-day card NKr200, and a three-day card NKr240. It can be purchased at tourist information offices, hotels, and central post offices. The Oslo Package, available through the same office, combines a four-day Oslo Card with a discount on accommodations (☞ Lodging, *above*).

Most public transportation starts running by 5:30 AM, with the last run just after midnight. On weekends there is night service on certain routes.

BY BUS

About 20 bus lines, including six night buses on weekends, serve the city. Most stop at **Jernbanetorget** opposite Oslo S Station. Tickets can be purchased from the driver.

BY CAR

Oslo Card holders can park for free in city-run street spots or reduced rates in lots run by the city (P-lots), but pay careful attention to time limits and be sure to ask at the information office exactly where the card is valid. Parking is very difficult in the city—many places have one-hour limits and can cost up to NKr17 per hour. Instead of individual parking meters in P-lots, you'll find one machine that dispenses validated parking tickets to display in your car windshield. Travelers with disabilities with valid parking permits from their home country are allowed to park free and with no time limit in spaces reserved for the handicapped.

If you plan to do any amount of driving in Oslo, buy a copy of the *Stor Oslo* map, available at bookstores and gasoline stations. It may be a small city, but one-way streets and few exit ramps on the expressway make it very easy to get lost.

BY FERRY

A ferry to **Hovedøya** and other islands in the harbor basin leaves from **Vippetangen,** behind Akershus Castle (take Bus 29 from Jernbanetorget or walk along the harbor from Aker Brygge). These are great spots for picnics and short hikes. From April through September, ferries run between **Rådhusbrygge 3,** in front of City Hall, and **Bygdøy,** the western peninsula, where many of Oslo's major museums are located. There is also ferry service from **Aker Brygge** to popular summer beach towns along the fjord's coast, including **Drøbak** (☞ East of the Oslo Fjord, *below*).

BY STREETCAR/TRIKK

Eight trikk lines serve the city. All stop at **Jernbanetorget** opposite Oslo S Station. Tickets can be purchased from the driver.

BY SUBWAY/T-BANE

Oslo has seven T-bane lines, which converge at **Stortinget** station. The four eastern lines all stop at **Tøyen** before branching off, whereas the four western lines run through **Majorstuen** before emerging above ground for the rest of their routes to the northwestern suburbs. Tickets can be purchased at the stations. Get a free map, "Sporveiens hovedkart," of Oslo's extensive public transportation system at post offices, Trafikanten, and most centrally located stations. It is undoubtedly the best public transport map of Oslo for tourists.

BY TAXI

All city taxis are connected with the central dispatching office (☎ 22/38–80–90), which can take up to 30 minutes to send one during peak hours. Cabs can be ordered from 20 minutes to 24 hours in advance. Special transport, including vans and cabs equipped for people with disabilities, can be ordered (☎ 22/38–80–90; then dial 1 for direct reservations, 2 for advance reservations, 3 for information, and 4 if you have special needs). Taxi stands are located all over town, usually alongside Narvesen kiosks, and are listed in the telephone directory under "Taxi" or "Drosjer."

It is possible to hail a cab on the street, but cabs are not allowed to pick up passengers within 100 yards of a stand. It is not unheard of to wait for more than an hour at a taxi stand in the wee hours of the morning, after everyone has left the bars. A cab with its roof light on is available. Rates start at NKr18 for hailed or rank cabs, NKr55 for ordered taxis, depending upon the time of day.

Contacts and Resources

CHANGING MONEY
After normal banking hours, money can be changed at a few places. The bank at **Oslo S Station** is open June–September, daily 8 AM–11 PM; October–May, weekdays 8 AM–7:30 PM, Saturday 10–5. The bank at **Oslo Fornebu Airport** is open weekdays 6:30 AM–9 PM, Saturday 7–5, Sunday 7 AM–8 PM. All post offices exchange money. **Oslo Central Post Office** (⌧ Dronningensgt. 15) is open weekdays 8–6, Saturday 9–3.

DENTISTS
Oslo Kommunale Tannlegevakt (⌧ Kolstadgt. 18, ☎ 22/67–30–00) at Tøyen Senter is open evenings and weekends for emergencies. **Oslo Private Tannlegevakt** (⌧ Hansteens Gt. 3, ☎ 22/44–46–36), near the American Embassy, is a private clinic open seven days a week.

DOCTORS
Volvat Medisinske Senter (⌧ Borgenvn. 2A, ☎ 22/95–75–00) is Norway's largest private clinic, near the Borgen or Majorstuen T-bane stations, not far from Frogner Park. It is open weekdays from 8 AM to 10 PM, weekends 10 to 10. **Oslo Akutten** (⌧ N. Vollgt. 8, ☎ 22/41–24–40) is an emergency clinic downtown, near Stortinget. **Centrum Legesenter** (⌧ Fritjof Nansens Pl., ☎ 22/41–41–20) is a small, friendly clinic across from City Hall.

EMBASSIES
U.S. Embassy, Drammensvn. 18, ☎ 22/44–85–50. **Canadian Embassy,** Oscars Gt. 20, ☎ 22/46–69–55. **U.K. Embassy,** Thomas Heftyes Gt. 8, ☎ 22/55–24–00.

EMERGENCIES
Police: ☎ 112 or 22/66–90–50. **Fire:** ☎ 110 or 22/11–44–55. **Ambulance:** ☎ 113 or 22/11–70–80. **Car Rescue:** ☎ 22/23–20–85. **Emergency Rooms: Oslo Legevakt** (⌧ Storgt. 40, ☎ 22/11–70–70), the city's public and thus less expensive, but slower, hospital, is near the Oslo S Station and is open 24 hours. **Volvat Medisinske Senter** (⌧ Borgenvn. 2A, ☎ 22/95–75–00) operates an emergency clinic from 8 AM to 10 PM during the week, 10 to 10 on weekends.

GUIDED TOURS
Tickets for all tours are available from Tourist Information at Vestbanen (☞ Visitor Information, *below*) and at the Oslo S Station. Tickets for bus tours can be purchased on the buses. All tours, except HMK's Oslo Highlights tour (☞ *below*), operate during summer only.

Dogsled Tours: For a fast and exciting experience, tour the marka by dogsled. Both lunch and evening tours are available. Contact **Norske Sledehundturer** (⌧ Einar Kristen Aas, 1514 Moss, ☎ 69/27–56–40, FAX 69/27–37–86).
Forest Tours: Tourist Information at Vestbanen can arrange four- to eight-hour motor safaris through the forests surrounding Oslo (☎ 22/83–00–50).

Orientation: HMK Sightseeing (⊠ Hegdehaugsvn. 4, ☎ 22/20–82–06) offers several bus tours in and around Oslo. Tours leave from the Norway Information Center at Vestbanen; combination boat-bus tours depart from Rådhusbrygge 3, the wharf in front of City Hall. **Båtservice Sightseeing** (⊠ Rådhusbryggen 3, ☎ 22/20–07–1 5) has a bus tour, five cruises, and one combination tour.

Personal Guides: Tourist Information at Vestbanen can provide an authorized city guide for your own private tour. **OsloTaxi** (⊠ Trondheimsvn. 100, ☎ 22/38–80–70) also gives private tours.

Sailing: Norway Yacht Charter (⊠ H. Heyerdahls Gt. 1, ☎ 22/42–64–98) arranges sailing or yacht tours and dinner cruises for groups of 5 people to 600.

Sleigh Rides: You can ride an old-fashioned sleigh through Oslomarka, the wooded area surrounding the city. **Vangen Skistue** (⊠ Laila and Jon Hamre, Fjell, 1404 Siggerud, ☎ 64/86–54–81) will arrange this for you. In summertime, they switch from sleighs to horses.

Street Train: Starting at noon and continuing at 45-minute intervals until 10 PM, the Oslo Train, which looks like a chain of dune buggies, leaves Aker Brygge for a 30-minute ride around the town center. The train runs daily in summer. Ask at the Norway Information Center (☞ Visitor Information, *below*) for departure times.

Walking: Organized walking tours are listed in *What's on in Oslo,* available from Tourist Information and at most hotels.

LATE-NIGHT PHARMACIES

Jernbanetorgets Apotek (⊠ Jernbanetorget 4B, ☎ 22/41–24–82), across from Oslo S Station, is open 24 hours. **Sfinxen Apotek** (⊠ Bogstadvn. 51, ☎ 22/46–34–44), near Frogner Park, is open weekdays from 8:30 AM to 9 PM, Saturdays from 8:30 AM to 8 PM, and Sundays from 5 PM to 8 PM.

TRAVEL AGENCIES

Winge Reisebureau (⊠ Karl Johans Gt. 33/35, ☎ 22/00–45–90) is the agent for American Express—here you can cash travelers' checks. An **American Express** office is near the Rådhuset (⊠ Fritjof Nansens pl. 6, ☎ 22/98–37–35). **Bennett Reisebureau** (⊠ Linstowsgt. 6, ☎ 22/69–71–00) is a business travel agency. **Kilroy Travels Norway** (⊠ Universitetssenteret, Blindern, ☎ 22/85–32–40; or Nedre Slottsgt. 23, ☎ 22/42–01–20) distributes ISIC cards for students and GO cards for people under 25.

VISITOR INFORMATION

The main tourist office, the **Norway Information Center** (☎ 82/06–01–00; there is an extra charge to call this number), is in the old Vestbanen railway station. The hours are as follows: spring and fall 9–6; summer 9–8; winter 9–4. The office at the main railway station, **Sentralstasjonen** (⊠ Jernbanetorget, ☎ 22/17–11–24) is open daily 8 AM–11 PM; during winter the office takes a break from 3 PM to 4:30 PM. Look for the big, round blue-and-green signs marked with a white "i". Information about the rest of the country can be obtained from **NORTRA** (⊠ Nortravel Marketing, Postboks 2893, Solli, 0230 Oslo, ☎ 22/92–52–00, FAX 22/56–05–05).

SIDE TRIPS FROM OSLO

Henie-Onstad Kunstsenter and Bærums Verk

❶ The **Henie-Onstad Kunstsenter** (Henie-Onstad Art Center) is just a short jaunt from Oslo, about 12 kilometers (7 miles) southwest of the city on E18. This modern art center resulted from a union between Norway's famous skater Sonja Henie and Norwegian shipping magnate Niels Onstad. Henie had a shrewd head for money and marriage, and her third, to Onstad, resulted in the Center. They put together a fine collection of early-20th-century art, with important works by Leger, Munch, Picasso, Bonnard, and Matisse. Henie died in 1969, but she still skates her way through many a late-night movie. The three-time Olympic gold-medal winner was the first to realize the potential of the ice show, and her technical assistant, Frank Zamboni, has been immortalized in skating rinks around the world by the ice-finishing machine he developed just for her, the Zamboni. Buses 151, 152, and 251 from Oslo S Station stop near the entrance to the Henie-Onstad Center grounds. ⊠ *1311 Høvikodden*, ☎ *67/54–30–50.* ⌷ *NKr40.* ☉ *Mon. 9–5, Tues.–Fri. 9–9; also June–Aug., weekends 11–7, Sept. and May, weekends 11–5.*

② One of Oslo's fashionable suburbs, Bærum is about 20 minutes from the city. The area is mostly residential, but along the banks of the Lomma River you'll find charming **Bærums Verk.** In the 1960s, the owners of the Bærums Verk iron foundry fixed up their old industrial farm and made it into a historical site. Created in the 17th century after iron ore was discovered in the region, the ironworks of Bærum quickly became the country's primary iron source. Anna Krefting, a woman who ran the works during the 18th century, believed that workers who spent their days and nights in the foundry should live there as well and be protected by it. The ironworks of Bærum thus became a village in its own right.

As you explore the beautifully restored village, you'll first notice the cramped wooden cottages lining **Verksgata** where the workers once lived. Notice that the doors are in the back of the buildings; this in was in case a fire from the works spread through the main street. Crafts makers now lease space in the former living quarters. Here you can purchase wares from a doll maker, a glass blower, a carpenter, a chocolatier, and an embroiderer.

Cross the Lomma River to the entrance of the **Ovnmuseet** (Stove Museum), which displays centuries-old cast-iron stoves in the basement of the iron foundry's enormous smelter. Bærums Verk stoves were exported for centuries and still serve as antique fireplaces in many Oslo homes and service establishments. From Oslo, follow E16 in the direction of Hønefoss. Veer north on Route 168, following signs to Bærums Verk Senteret until you reach the tourist information office. ⊠ *Verksgt. 8B, Boks 39, 1353 Bærum*, ☎ *67/13–00–18 (information office).* ☉ *Verksgata weekdays 10–6, Sat. 10–3; some shops open Sun. Stove Museum weekends noon–3. Other times on request.*

NEED A BREAK? | Stop in at **Pannekake Huset** (The Pancake House: ⊠ Verksgt. 9, ☎ 67/ 15-07-02) for sweet or salty Dutch-style crepes and a cherry beer or hot chocolate. It's open Tuesday–Sunday afternoons only.

Dining

$$$ ✕ **Værtshuset Bærums Verk.** A must on any itinerary that includes the
★ neighboring iron works, this is Norway's oldest standing restaurant. A frequented inn on the "King's" road from Oslo to Bergen, it opened in 1640. Restored in 1987, it is now one of Norway's finest restaurants. Low ceilings, pastel-painted wooden floors, shiny pewter tableware, and the tick-tock of a grandfather clock in the dining room all create the impression that you are walking into 19th-century Scandinavia. Each room has a charm of its own, from the quiet, oblong Doctor's Room to the rustic kitchen with a blazing fire. Perhaps the most innovative menu of the year, which lasts only three days in March, is

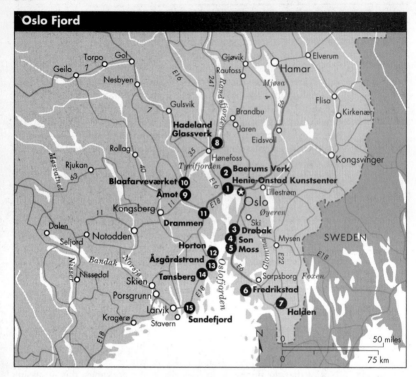

Oslo Fjord

one modeled after the famous meal served in the film *Babette's Feast,*
complete with a faux turtle soup (it is illegal to hunt turtles in Norway), blinis, and quail. ⊠ *Vertshusvn. 10, Brums Verk,* ☎ *67/80–02–
0. AE, DC, MC, V. No lunch.*

EAST OF THE OSLO FJORD

If you've got a weakness for the water and things maritime, getting out
of Oslo to the more savage fjord beaches might be a good idea. The
eastern side of the Oslo Fjord is summer-vacation country for many
Norwegians, who retreat to cabins on the water during July. The towns
have developed facilities to cater to them and brag that they inhabit
the "sunny" side of the fjord.

Many towns along the fjord offer history and culture as well as a place
to bathe. Viking ruins and inscriptions, fortified towns, and bohemian
19th-century artists' colonies provide just a glimpse into the region's
rich past.

Some of the towns mentioned can easily be day trips from Oslo. Roads
can be winding, though, so you might want to devote several days to
exploring the area. Note that ferries shuttle cars and people back and
forth between the archipelago islands and either side of the fjord, so
it is possible to combine this tour with the West of the Oslo Fjord (☞
below) and make a complete circle without backtracking.

Drøbak

❸ *35 km (21 mi) south of Oslo.*

Mention the summer resort town of Drøbak to many Norwegians, and
strangely enough, they'll start talking about Father Christmas. Al-

though there is some question as to where the *Julenisse* (literally, "Christmas elf") came from, Norwegians claim—at least his adopted home—is here in Drøbak.

Norwegian legend says that Julenisse is one of many elves who live in the woods and have magical powers. This Julenisse, who has established his own post office, **Julenissens Posthuset** in Drøbak, responds to nearly 30,000 letters a year from children all over the world, the majority of which come from Japan. ⊠ *Julenissen, 1440 Drøbak.*

The inviting **Tregaardens Julehus** (Wooden Christmas House) dominates the town's central square. Just around the corner from the post office, this 1876 house was once a mission for seafarers unable to reach Oslo because the fjord was frozen over. Now it sells Christmas wares and gifts such as wooden dolls and mice made of cloth—all handmade by Eva Johansen, the store's creator and owner. Spin-offs of this ever-so-authentic Christmas shop include Drøbak's gift of a fir tree to the cities of Berlin and Osaka. ⊠ *1440 Drøbak,* ☎ *64/93–41–78.*

NEED A BREAK? | Back on the main square, stop in **Det Gamle Bageri Ost & Vinstue** (The Old Bakery Wine and Cheese Room, ☎ 64/93–21–05) for some home-brewed smoky-tasting *Rauchbier*, a German specialty. Originally a bakery, this tiny pub serves wine with cheese and fruit plates on heavy wood-slab tables by the central oven.

Lodging

$–$$ 🏨 **Reenskaug Hotel.** The Norwegian author Knut Hamsun frequented this hotel and wrote a book here at the turn of the century. Back then, it was just a wooden house on a dirt road. The 100-year-old hotel's whitewashed exterior complements the quaintness of the town's main road. Inside, the rooms are rather small and nondescript, but they are nonetheless clean. Reasonable summer prices make it worth your while to stay the night in Drøbak. ⊠ *Storgt. 32, 1440 Drøbak,* ☎ *64/93–33–60,* ℻ *64/93–36–66. 29 rooms. Restaurant, bar, nightclub, meeting rooms. AE, MC, V.*

Son

❹ *25 km (15 mi) south of Drøbak.*

You can swim, sail, or sun on the banks of Son (pronounced *soon*), just south of Drøbak. An old fishing and boating village, this resort town has traditionally attracted artists and writers. Artists still flock there, as do city folk in summer. With them comes a rash of activity, which loungers on the immense boulders by the water can hear in the distance.

Count on **Klubben Soon** (☎ 64/95–70–42) for reggae, jazz, house and techno every Saturday afternoon.

Moss

❺ *10 km (6 mi) south of Son.*

Although the area has been inhabited since Viking times, Moss gained borough status in the 18th century and is one of the area's main commercial and shipping centers. This industrial town is also home to the manufacturers of Helly-Hansen sportswear, which is becoming ever-so-popular in the U.S.—you'll find it in sporting goods stores from Duluth, Minnesota to New York City.

OFF THE BEATEN PATH | **GALLERI F15** – A 5-kilometer (3-mile) ride outside Moss, on the island of Jeløy, is an art center set in an old farm. Here you can view the exhibits, which range from photography to Scandinavian crafts, or just stroll the beautiful grounds. ⊠ *Alby Gård,* ☎ *69/27–10–33.* ⌷ *NKr20.* ☉ *June–Sept., Tues.–Sun. 11–7; Oct.–May, Tues.–Sat. 11–5, Sun. 11–7.*

Dining and Lodging

$$$ ✕⌷ **Refsnes Gods.** Refsnes has one of Norway's best kitchens and a wine
★   cellar with some of the oldest bottles of Madeira in the country. Chef Oddmund Haarsaker utilizes the fjords' resources and adds a French touch to traditional Norwegian seafood. The main building dates from 1770, when it was a family estate, but it did not become a hotel until 1938. In the back is a long, tree-lined promenade extending to the shores of the Oslo Fjord. The blue-and-beige rooms are airy and pretty. ⊠ *Box 236, 1502 Moss,* ☎ *69/27–04–11,* ⅨⅩ *69/27–25–42. 60 rooms. Restaurant, pool, sauna, beach, boating, meeting rooms. AE, DC, MC, V.*

Fredrikstad

❻ *34 km (20 mi) south of Moss.*

Norway's oldest fortified city, Fredrikstad lies peacefully at the mouth of the Glomma, the country's longest river. Its bastions and moat date from the 1600s. The **Gamlebyen** (Old Town) has been preserved and has museums, art galleries, cafés, artisans' workshops, antiques shops, and old bookstores.

The **Fredrikstad Museum** documents the town's history. ☎ 69/80–68–65. ⌷ *NKr20.* ☉ *May–Sept., weekdays 11–5, Sun. noon–5.*

Just east of the Fredrikstad town center is **Kongsten Festning** (Kongsten Fort), which mounted 200 cannons and could muster 2,000 men at the peak of its glory in the 16th century. ☎ *69/80–68–65.* ⌷ *Free.* ☉ *May–Sept., 24 hours. Call for guided tour.*

Halden

❼ *30 km (18 mi) south of Fredrikstad.*

Halden is practically at the Swedish border, a good enough reason to fortify the town. Norwegians and Swedes had ongoing border disputes, and the most famous skirmish at Fredriksten fortress resulted in the death of King Karl XII in 1718. Few people realize that slavery existed in Scandinavia, but until 1845 there were up to 200 slaves at Fredriksten, mostly workers incarcerated and sentenced to a lifetime of hard labor for trivial offenses.

Fredriksten Festning (⊠ Fredriksten Fort, ☎ 69/17–35–00), built on a French star-shaped plan in the late 17th century, is perched on the city's highest point. Inside the fort itself is **Fredriksten Kro,** a good, old-fashioned pub with outdoor seating. ☎ *69/17–52–32.* ⌷ *NKr25.* ☉ *Mid-May–mid-Sept., Mon.–Sat. 10–5, Sun. 10–6.*

East of the Oslo Fjord A to Z

Arriving and Departing

BY BOAT

A ferry links Drøbak, on the east side of the fjord, with Hurum, on the west side just north of Horten. Contact Drøbak Turistinformasjon (☞ *below*) for schedule information.

BY BUS

Bus 541 from City Hall to Drøbak affords great glimpses of the fjord (and its bathers). The trip takes an hour, and buses depart roughly every half hour during the week, with reduced service weekends. Bus 117

It helps to be pushy in airports.

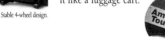

Introducing the revolutionary new TransPorter™ from American Tourister® It's the first suitcase you can push around without a fight. TransPorter's™ exclusive four-wheel design lets you push it in front of you with almost no effort–the wheels take the weight. Or pull it on two wheels if you choose. You can even stack on other bags and use it like a luggage cart.

Stable 4-wheel design.

TransPorter™ is designed like a dresser, with built-in shelves to organize your belongings. Or collapse the shelves and pack it like a traditional suitcase. Inside, there's a suiter feature to help keep suits and dresses from wrinkling. When push comes to shove, you can't beat a TransPorter™ For more information on how you can be this pushy, call 1-800-542-1300.

Shelves collapse on command.

American Tourister®

Making travel less primitive®

links Halden and Fredrikstad eight times a day during the week, with reduced service Saturdays. Contact Nor-Way Bussekspress (☎ 22/17–52–90, FAX 22/17–59–22) for schedules.

BY CAR
Follow Route E18 southeast from Oslo to Route E6. Follow signs to Drøbak and Son. Continue through Moss, following signs to Halden, farther south on E6. The route then takes you north to Sarpsborg, where you can turn left to Fredrikstad.

BY TRAIN
Trains for Halden leave from Oslo S Station and take two hours to make the 136-kilometer (85-mile) trip, with stops in Moss, Fredrikstad, and Sarpsborg.

Contacts and Resources
VISITOR INFORMATION
Drøbak: Drøbak Turistinformasjon (☎ 64/93–50–97). **Fredrikstad:** Fredrikstad Turistkontor (✉ Turistsentret v/Østre Brohode and ✉ 1632 Gamle Fredrikstad, ☎ 69/32–03–30 or 69/32–10–60). **Halden:** Halden Turist Kontor (✉ Storgt. 6, Box 167, 1751 Halden, ☎ 69/17–48–40). **Moss:** Moss Turistkontor (✉ Fleischersgt. 17, 1531 Moss, ☎ 69/25–32–95). **Son:** Son Kystkultursenter, (✉ 1555 Son, ☎ 64/95–89–20).

WEST OF THE OSLO FJORD

Towns lining the western side of the fjord are more industrial on the whole than their neighbors on the eastern side. Still, the western towns have traditionally been some of Norway's oldest and wealthiest, their fortunes derived from whaling and lumbering. Although these activities no longer dominate, their influence is seen in the monuments and in the wood architecture. The area northwest of Oslo draws many visitors to its green, hilly countryside. These once industrial towns are now catering more and more to tourists.

Jevnaker

Follow E16 toward Hønefoss, then follow Rte. 241 to Jevnaker, which is about 70 km (42 mi) northwest of Oslo; it's about 2 hrs driving time.

A day trip to Jevnaker combines a drive along the Tyrifjord, where you can see some of the best fjord views in eastern Norway, with a visit to ❽ a glass factory that has been in operation since 1762. At **Hadeland Glassverk** you can watch artisans blowing glass, or, if you get there early enough, you can blow your own. Both practical table crystal and one-of-a-kind art glass are produced here, which you can buy (first quality and seconds) at the gift shop. The museum and gallery have a collection of 15,000 items, with about 800 on display. Bus 171, marked "Hønefoss," leaves from the university on Karl Johans Gate at seven minutes after the hour. Change in Hønefoss for the Jevnaker bus (no number).✉ *Rte. 241, Postboks 85, 5320 Jevnaker,* ☎ *61/31–10–00.* ☉ *June–Aug., Mon.–Sat. 9–6, Sun. 11–6; Sept.–May, weekdays 9–4, Sat. 10–3, Sun. noon–5.*

Åmot i Modum

❾ *Take Rte. 35 south, along the Tyrifjord. If you are coming from the E18, take Rte. 11 west to Hokksund, and Rte. 35 to Åmot. Then turn onto Rte. 287 to Sigdal. 70 km (45mi) from Oslo.*

The small village of Åmot is famous for its cobalt mines. The blue mineral was used to make dyes for the world's glass and porcelain industries. The **Blaafarveværket** (Cobalt Works) was founded in 1773 to extract cobalt from the Modum mines. Today the complex is a museum and a national park. A permanent collection displays old cobalt-blue glass and porcelain. For children there's a petting farm, and there's a restaurant that serves Norwegian country fare. Up the hill from the art complex is Haugfossen, the highest waterfall in eastern Norway. Outdoor concerts are held on the grounds throughout the summer. The bus to Modum leaves from the university on Karl Johans Gate at 9:45 AM on Tuesday, Thursday, and Saturday. ☎ 32/78–49–00. ☒ *Special exhibitions NKr60; cobalt works free. Guided tours in English.* ☼ *Late May–Sept., daily 10–6.*

Drammen

⓫ *40 km (25 mi) from Oslo; 45 km (27 mi) south of Åmot i Modum.*

Drammen, a timber town and port for 500 years, is an industrial city of 50,000 on the Simoa River at its outlet to a fjord. It was the main harbor for silver exported from the Kongsberg mines. Today cars are imported into Norway through Drammen.

The **Spiralen** (Spiral), Drammen's main attraction, is a corkscrew road tunnel that makes six complete turns before emerging about 600 feet above, on Skansen Ridge. The entrance is behind the hospital by way of a well-marked road. ☒ *Nkr10 parking fee.*

Drammens Museum, a small county museum, is on the grounds of Marienlyst Manor, which dates from 1750. Glass from the Nøstetangen factory, which was in operation between 1741 and 1777, and a collection of rustic painted pieces are on display here. Its new addition looks like a small temple set in the manor garden. ☒ *Konnerudgt. 7,* ☎ *32/83–89–48.* ☒ *NKr30.* ☼ *May–Oct., Tues.–Sat. 11–3, Sun. 11–5; Nov.–Apr., Tues.–Sun. 11–3.*

Dining and Lodging

$$ ✕ **Spiraltoppen Café.** At the top of Bragernes Hill, this café offers excellent views and generous portions of Norwegian food. Try the meatballs with stewed cabbage or the open-face sandwiches. ☒ *Bragernesåsen, Drammen,* ☎ *32/83–78–15. Reservations not accepted. AE, DC, MC, V.*

$$ ▥ **Rica Park.** As with all Rica hotels, the atmosphere is relaxed and button-down and the rooms are comfortable. The nightclub at this hotel in the city center attracts more over-30s than any other one in town. ☒ *Gamle Kirkepl. 3, 3019 Drammen,* ☎ *32/83–82–80,* FAX *32/89–32–07. 103 rooms. 2 restaurants, 2 bars, nightclub. AE, DC, MC, V.*

Horton

⓬ *30 km (17 mi) south of Drammen.*

Off the main route south, the coastal village of Horton has some distinctive museums. The town was once an important naval station and still retains the officers' candidates school.

The **Marinemuseet** (Royal Norwegian Navy Museum), built in 1853 as a munitions warehouse, displays relics from the nation's naval history. Outside is the world's first torpedo boat, from 1872, plus some one-person submarines from World War II. Mistletoe thrives in the trees, but don't pick it: It's protected by law. ☒ *Karl Johans Vern,* ☎ *33/03–*

17–08. ⊠ *Free.* ⊙ *May–Oct., weekdays 10–4, weekends noon–4; rest of yr., weekdays 10–3, Sun. noon–4.*

The **Redningsselskapets Museum** (Museum of the Sea Rescue Association) traces the history of ship-rescue operations. The organization has rescued more than 320,000 people since it was founded more than 100 years ago. ⊠ *Strandpromenaden 8, near Horten Tourist Office,* ☎ *33/04–70–66.* ⊠ *NKr10.* ⊙ *Apr.–Oct., Fri.–Sun. noon–4.*

The **Preus Fotomuseum** houses one of the world's largest photographic collections. Exhibits include a turn-of-the-century photographer's studio and a tiny camera that was strapped to a pigeon for early aerial photography. ⊠ *Langgt. 82,* ☎ *33/04–27–37.* ⊠ *NKr15.* ⊙ *Weekdays 10–4, Sun. noon–4.*

Just beyond Horton, between the road and the sea, lies a Viking grave site, **Borrehaugene,** with five earth and two stone mounds and the 12th-century Borre church.

Åsgårdstrand

⑬ *10 km (6 mi) south of Horton.*

The coastal town of Åsgårdstrand is known as an artists' colony for outdoor painting at the turn of the century. Edvard Munch painted *Girls on the Bridge* here and earned a reputation as a ladies' man. Munch spent seven summers at **Munchs lille hus** (little house), now a museum. ⊠ *Munchsgt.,* ☎ *33/03–17–08 (Horton Tourist Office).* ⊠ *NKr10.* ⊙ *May, Sept., weekends 1–7; Jun.–Aug., Tues.–Sun. 1–7.*

En Route   Travel south from Åsgårdstrand toward Tønsberg and you'll pass **Slagen,** the site where the Oseberg Viking ship, dating from around AD 800 and now on display at Vikingskiphuset in Oslo, was found. Look for a mound where it was buried as you pass Slagen's church.

Tønsberg

⑭ *11 km (6.6 mi) south of Åsgårdstrand.*

According to the sagas, Tønsberg is Norway's oldest settlement, founded in 871. The town's fortunes took a turn for the worse after the Reformation, and the city did not recover until shipping and whaling brought it into prominence in the 18th century. Little remains of Tønsberg's early structures, although the ruins at **Slottsfjellet** (Castle Hill), by the train station, include parts of the city wall, the remains of a church from around 1150, and a 13th-century brick citadel, the **Tønsberghus.** Other medieval remains are below the cathedral and near Storgata 17.

The **Vestfold Fylkesmuseum** (County Museum), north of the railroad station, houses a small Viking ship, several whale skeletons, and some inventions. There's an open-air section, too. ⊠ *Farmannsvn. 30,* ☎ *33/31–29–19.* ⊠ *NKr15.* ⊙ *Mid-May–mid-Sept., Mon.–Sat. 10–5, Sun. noon–5; rest of yr, weekdays 10–2.*

Sandefjord

⑮ *125 km (78 mi) south of Oslo; 25 km (15 mi) south of Tønsberg.*

Once the whaling capital of the world and possibly Norway's wealthiest city at the turn of the century, Sandfjord celebrated its 150th birthday in 1995. Now the whales are gone and all that remains of that trade is a monument to it. Thanks to shipping and other industries, however, the city is still rich and draws many illustrious Norwegians to its beaches, such as film actress Liv Ullmann, who has a cottage here.

Kommandør Christensens Hvalfangstmuseum (Commander Christensen's Whaling Museum) traces the development of the industry from small primitive boats to huge floating factories. An especially arresting display chronicles whaling in the Antarctic. ⊠ *Museumsgt. 39,* ☎ *33/46–32–51.* ⧄ *NKr20.* ⊘ *May–Sept., daily 11–5; Oct.–Apr., Fri.–Sun. noon–4.*

Dining and Lodging

$$–$$$ ✕ **Edgar Ludl's Gourmet.** It took an Austrian chef to show the Nor-
★ wegians that there's more in the sea than cod and salmon. Ludl is a champion of the local cuisine, and specials may include ocean catfish, stuffed sole, a fish roulade, and lobster. Ludl's desserts are equally good, especially the cloudberry marzipan basket. ⊠ *Rådhusgt. 7, Sandefjord,* ☎ *33/46–27–41. AE, DC, MC, V.*

$$–$$$$ ▦ **Rica Park Hotel.** It *looks* formal for a hotel built right on the water in a resort town, but there's no dress code. The decor is 1960s style, but it doesn't seem passé. Ask for one of the newer rooms. ⊠ *Strand-promenaden 9, 3200 Sandefjord,* ☎ *33/46–55–50,* ℻ *33/46–79–00. 174 rooms, 8 suites. 2 restaurants, bar, indoor pool, health club, night-club, convention center. AE, DC, MC, V.*

$–$$$ ▦ **Atlantic Home.** The Atlantic Home was built in 1914, when Sande-fjord was a whaling center. The history of whaling is traced in exhibits in glass cases and in pictures throughout the hotel. There's no restau-rant, but the hotel provides *aftens,* a supper consisting of bread and cold cuts plus hot soup and light beer, as part of the room rate. A cof-feemaker and waffle iron are at your disposal at all times. ⊠ *Jern-banealleen 33, 3201 Sandefjord,* ☎ *33/46–80–00,* ℻ *33/46–80–20. 72 rooms. Lobby lounge, sauna. AE, DC, MC, V.*

West of the Oslo Fjord A to Z

Arriving and Departing

BY BOAT
The most luxurious and scenic way to see the region is by boat: There are guest marinas at just about every port.

BY BUS
Because train service to towns south of Drammen is infrequent, bus travel is the best alternative to cars. Check with **Nor-Way Bussekspress** (☎ 22/17–52–90) for schedules.

BY CAR
Route E18 south from Oslo follows the coast to the towns of this region.

BY TRAIN
Take a suburban train from Nationaltheatret or trains from Oslo S Sta-tion to reach Horten, Tønsberg, and Sandefjord.

Contacts and Resources

VISITOR INFORMATION
Blaafarveværket: (☎ 32/78–49–00). **Drammen:** Drammen Kom-munale Turistinformasjonskontor (⊠ Bragernes Torg 6, 3008 Dram-men, ☎ 32/80–62–10). **Hadeland:** (☎ 61/31–10–00). **Horton and Åsgårdstrand:** Horton Turist Kontor (⊠ Tollbugt. 1a, 3187 Horten, ☎ 33/03–17–08). **Sandefjord:** Sandefjord Reiselivsforening (⊠ Torvet, 3201 Sandfjord, ☎ 33/46–05–90). **Tønsberg:** Tønsberg og Omland Reiselivslag (⊠ Nedre Langgt. 36 B, 3110 Tønsberg, ☎ 33/31–02–20).

THE TELEMARK REGION

Telemark, the interior region of southern Norway, lies in the shadow of the famed beaches and fjords of the coast but doesn't lack majestic scenery. A land of wide-open vistas and deep forests, it's veined with swift-flowing streams and scattered with peaceful lakes—a natural setting so powerful and silent that a few generations ago, trolls were the only reasonable explanation for what lurked in, or for that matter plodded through, the shadows. These legendary creatures, serious Norwegians explain, boast several heads and a couple of noses (used to stir their porridge, of course) and can grow to the size of a village. Fortunately for humans, however, they turn to stone in sunlight.

Telemark was the birthplace of downhill skiing as well as the birthplace of many ancestors to Norwegian-Americans, for the poor farmers of the region were among the first to emigrate to the United States during the 19th century.

Kongsberg

16 *84 km (52 mi) southwest of Oslo.*

Kongsberg, with 20,000 people today, was Norway's silver town for more than 300 years. It was here that silver was discovered in its purest form. King Christian IV saw the town's natural potential when he noticed that a cow's horn had rubbed moss off a stone to expose silver. Thereupon, the Danish builder-king began construction of the town. Thus, Norway's first industrial town, Kongsberg, rose to prominence. The mines are now closed, but the Royal Mint is still going strong.

The **Norsk Bergverksmuseum** (Norwegian Mining Museum), in the old smelting works, documents the development of silver mining and exhibits pure silver, gold, emeralds, and rubies from other Norwegian mines. The **Royal Mint Museum,** in the same building, is a treasure trove for coin collectors, with a nearly complete assemblage of Norwegian coins. Children can pan for silver all summer. The **Kongsberg Ski Museum,** also part of the mining complex, houses exhibits of ancient skis and 23 Olympic and World Championship medals won by Kongsberg skiers. ⊠ *Hyttegt. 3,* ☎ *32/73–32–60.* 🎫 *NKr40.* ☉ *Mid-May–mid-Aug., weekdays 10–6, weekends 10–4; mid–late Aug., daily 10–4; Sept., daily noon–4; Oct.–mid-May, Sun. noon–4. Otherwise, by appointment.*

OFF THE BEATEN PATH

SØLVGRUVENE – In Saggrenda, about 8 kilometers (5 miles) outside Kongsberg toward Notodden, you can visit silver mines. Guided mine tours include a 2.3-kilometer (1.4-mile) ride on the mine train into Kongensgruve (the King's mine) and a ride on the first personnel elevator. The temperature in the mine is about 6°C (43°F) and the tour takes about one hour and 20 minutes, so dress accordingly. ☎ *32/73-32-60.* 🎫 *NKr50.* ☉ *Tours mid-May–June, daily at 11, 12:30, 2; July–mid-Aug., daily at 11, 12:30, 2, 3:30; Sept.–mid-May, Sun. at 2.*

Kongsberg Kirke (Kongsberg Church), finished in 1761, was built during the heyday of the silver mines, with an impressive gilded Baroque altar, organ, and pulpit all on one wall. It seats 3,000. The royal box and the galleries separated the gentry and mine owners from the workers. Organ concerts are given Wednesdays at 6 in summer. ☎ *32/73–19–02.* 🎫 *NKr20.* ☉ *Mid-May–Aug., weekdays 10–noon, Sat. 10–1. Sun. services at 11 with tours afterward until 1:30. Call to confirm times.*

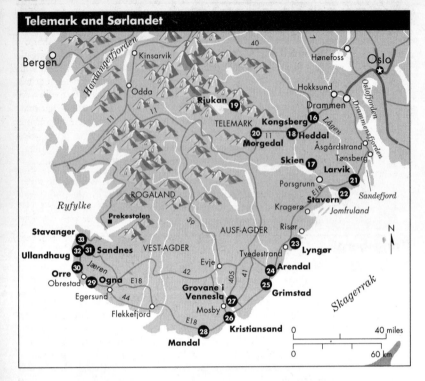

The Arts

Every June jazz fans descend on Kongsberg for its annual **jazz festival.** Contact the tourist office (☞ *below*) for information.

Dining and Lodging

$$ ✕ **Gamle Kongsberg Kro.** This café next to the waterfall at Nybrofossen offers hearty Norwegian dishes at moderate prices. There's a minigolf course nearby. ⊠ *Thornesvn. 4,* ☎ *32/73–16–33,* ☒ *32/73–26–03. DC, MC, V.*

$–$$ 🏠 **Inter Nor Grand Hotel.** A statue of Kongsberg's favorite son, Olympic ski jumper Birger Ruud, stands in the park in front of this modern, centrally located hotel. ⊠ *Kristian Augustsgt. 2, 3600,* ☎ *32/73–20– 29,* ☒ *32/73–41–29. 95 rooms, 2 suites. 2 restaurants, 2 bars, exercise room, indoor pool, nightclub, meeting rooms. AE, DC, MC, V.*

Skien

⑰ *South of Kongsberg on Rtes. 32 and 36.*

Best known as the birthplace of playwright Henrik Ibsen, Skien, with a population of 50,000, is the capital of the Telemark region. Ibsen's home town celebrates its favorite son every August with the **Ibsen-Kultur-festival** (⊠ Skien Tourist Office, Box 192, 3701 Skien, ☎ 35/58– 19–10), which includes concerts as well as drama.

The **Fylkesmuseet** (County Museum), a manor house from 1780, has a collection of Ibsen memorabilia, including his study and bedroom and the "blue salon" from his Oslo flat (other interiors are at the Norsk Folkemuseum in Oslo). Also on display is Telemark-style folk art, including rosemaling and wood carving. ⊠ *Øvregt. 41,* ☎ *35/52–35–*

94. ⊠ NKr20. ☉ *Garden mid–May–Aug., daily 10–8; museum mid–May–Aug., daily 10–6; Sept., Sun. 10–6.*

Venstøp looks just as it did when the Ibsen family lived here from 1835 to 1843. The attic was the inspiration for The Wild Duck. This house, part of Skien's county museum, is 5 kilometers (3 miles) northwest of the city. ☎ 35/52–35–94. ⊠ NKr20. ☉ *House mid–May–Aug., daily 10–8; museum mid–May–Aug., daily 10–6; Sept., Sun. 10–6.*

Dining and Lodging

$$ ✕ **Boden Spiseri.** Boden serves excellent French-influenced Norwegian-style food, such as medallions of reindeer. For dessert, "Gjoegler Boden"—ice cream with rum, raisins, and a touch of ginger—is a delight. ⊠ *Landbrygga 5,* ☎ *35/52–61–70. AE, DC, MC, V. No lunch.*

$–$$ 🏨 **Rainbow Høyers Hotell.** The old-fashioned quality of the exterior, with cornices and pedimented windows, is reflected in the Høyers's lobby, which is an incongruous mixture of old and new. The rooms are modern and light, thanks to the big windows. 🏨 *Kongensgt. 6, 3700,* ☎ *35/52–05–40,* FAX *35/52–26–08. 69 rooms, 1 suite. Restaurant, bar, meeting rooms. AE, DC, MC, V.*

Heddal

⑱ *68 km (42 mi) northwest of Skien and 35 km (20 mi) west of Kongsberg.*

Today Heddal is not much more than a hamlet. It is believed that this area must have been a prosperous one in the Middle Ages, though, because of the size of the town's *stavkirke* (wood church)—85 feet high and 65 feet long.

Heddal Stave Church is Norway's largest. The church dates from the middle of the 12th century and has exceptional stylized animal ornament, along with grotesque human heads, on the portals. ☎ 35/02–08–40. ⊠ NKr15. ☉ *Mid–May–June, Mon.–Sat. 10–5; late June–late Aug., Mon.–Sat. 9–7; late Aug.–mid–Sept., Mon.–Sat. 10–5. Sunday service at 12:30 PM mid–May–mid–Sept.*

En Route   Route 37 northwest from Kongsberg to Rjukan passes the 6,200-foot **Gaustatoppen,** a looming, snow-streaked table of rock popular with hikers.

Rjukan

⑲ *96 km (59 mi) from Heddal.*

The town of Rjukan may not ring a bell, but mention "heavy water," and anyone who lived through World War II or saw the film *The Heroes of Telemark* with Kirk Douglas knows about the sabotage of the "heavy water" factory there, which thwarted German efforts to develop an atomic bomb. Rjukan's history actually began in the decade between 1907 and 1916, when the population grew from a few hundred to 10,000 because of a different kind of "water," hydroelectric power. Norsk Hydro, one of Norway's largest industries, which uses hydroelectric power to manufacture chemicals and fertilizer, was started here.

Heavy water (used in nuclear reactors as a moderator) was produced as a by-product in the manufacture of fertilizer at Vemork, 6 kilometers (4 miles) west of Rjukan along Route 37, where a museum, **Industriarbeidermuseet Vemork,** has been built. Exhibits document both the development of hydroelectric power and the World War II events. Every year on the first Saturday in July, the work of the saboteurs is commemorated, but their 8-kilometer (5-mile) path, starting at Rjukan Fjellstue (mountain lodge) and finishing at the museum, is marked and can be followed at any time. ☎ 35/09–51–53. ☒ NKr40. ☉ May –mid-June, daily 10–4; mid-June–mid-Aug., daily 10–6; mid-Aug.–Sept., weekdays 10–4, weekends 10–6; Oct. and Feb.–Apr., Sat. 10–4.

Rjukan is the site of northern Europe's first cable car, **Krossobanen,** built in 1928 by Hydro to transport people to the top of the mountain, where the sun shines year-round. ☒ NKr20. ☉ Mid-Apr.–mid-Sept. Times vary. Call Rjukan tourist information for details, ☎ 35/09–15–11.

Dining and Lodging

$$ ✕ **Park Hotell.** This small hotel with a traditional family atmosphere is in the center of town. The rooms are prettily decorated in light colors. The restaurant, with the curious name Ammonia, offers a wide selection. ☒ Sam Eydes Gt. 67, 3660, ☎ 35/09–02–88, ☒ 35/09–05–25. 39 rooms. Restaurant, bar, pub, nightclub. AE, DC, MC, V.

$$ ☒ **Gaustablikk Høyfjellshotell.** Built at the foot of Gaustatoppen near Rjukan, this modern timber hotel is a popular ski resort, with nine downhill slopes and 80 kilometers (50 miles) of cross-country trails. In summer, these marked trails are perfect for walks and hikes. ☒ 3660, ☎ 35/09–14–22, ☒ 35/09–19–75. 91 rooms, 14 suites. Restaurant, bar, indoor pool, sauna, exercise room. AE, DC, MC, V.

Morgedal

⑳ 77 km (46 mi) southwest of Rjukan via Åmot.

In the heart of Telemark is Morgedal, the birthplace of modern skiing, thanks to a persistent Sondre Nordheim, who in the 19th century perfected his skis and bindings and practiced jumping from his roof. His innovations included bindings that close behind the heel and skis that narrow in the middle to facilitate turning. In 1868, after revamping his skis and bindings, he took off for a 185-kilometer (115-mile) trek to Oslo just to prove it could be done. A hundred years ago, skiers used one long pole, held diagonally, much like high-wire artists. Eventually the use of two short poles became widespread, although purists feel that the one-pole version is the "authentic" way to ski. Nordheim's traditional Telemark skiing is now the rage in Norway, though the revival was begun in the United States.

The **Bjåland Museum** in Morgedal is named for Olav Bjåland, who was chosen for Amundsen's expedition to Antarctica because he could ski in an absolutely straight line. The museum collections illustrate the development of Telemark skiing. Also on display are Bjåland's streamlined polar sled and his photographs of the expedition. ☒ Opposite Morgedal Turisthotell, ☎ 35/05–42–50 or 35/05–41–56. ☒ NKr50. ☉ Mid-June–mid-Aug., daily 9–7; rest of yr, daily 11–5.

Dalen

The Dalen area is the place to hike, bike, and be outdoors. From Skien you can take boat tours on the Telemark waterways, a combination of canals and natural lakes between Skien and either Dalen or Notodden. The trip to Dalen takes you through Ulefoss, where you can leave the boat and visit the neoclassical Ulefoss Manor, which dates from 1807. For trips to Dalen, call Telemarkreiser, ☎ 35/53–03–00; for Notodden, contact Telemarksbåtene, ☒ 3812 Akkerhaugen, ☎ 35/95–82–11, ☒ 35/95–82–96.

Dining and Lodging

$$$ ✕🏨 **Hotel Dalen.** At the end of the Telemark Canals, Hotel Dalen was restored in 1992 to its original Victorian, "Swiss-style" opulence, complete with dragon carvings, stained-glass windows, and a balcony overlooking the stunning entrance hall. Rooms are relatively small and furnished with plain Norwegian antiques. All meals are provided on request; if you're not a guest, call a day in advance to reserve. You'll be served traditional Norwegian fare and Telemark specialties: porridge, dried mutton, flatbread, and *lefse,* the venerable Norwegian staple. ✉ *3880 Dalen,* ☎ *35/07–70–00,* 𝖥𝖠𝖷 *35/07–70–11. 38 rooms. Breakfast room, lobby lounges, meeting rooms. AE, V. In winter, make advance reservations at Telemarkreiser,* ☎ *35/53–03–00,* 𝖥𝖠𝖷 *35/52–70–07.*

The Telemark Region A to Z

Arriving and Departing

BY BUS

The many bus lines that serve the region are coordinated through **Nor-Way Bussekspress** in Oslo (✉ Bussterminalen, Galleri Oslo, ☎ 22/17–52–90, 𝖥𝖠𝖷 22/17–59–22).

BY CAR

On Route E18 from Oslo, the drive southwest to Kongsberg takes a little more than an hour.

BY TRAIN

The train from Oslo S Station to Kongsberg takes 1 hour and 25 minutes; bus connections to Telemark are available.

Getting Around

BY BUS

Buses in the region rarely run more than twice a day, so get a comprehensive schedule from the tourist office or Nor-Way Bussekspress (☞ Oslo A to Z, *above*) and plan ahead.

BY CAR

Roads in the southern part of the interior region are open and flat. E18 and Routes 11 and 7 are the chief routes of the south.

BY TRAIN

The only train service in the southern part of the region is the Oslo–Stavanger line (via Kristiansand).

Contacts and Resources

VISITOR INFORMATION

Kongsberg (✉ Storgt. 35, ☎ 32/73–50–00); **Notodden** (☎ 35/01–20–22); **Rjukan** (✉ Torget 2, ☎ 35/09–15–11); and **Skien** (✉ Reiselivets Hus, N. Hjellegt. 18, ☎ 35/53–49–80).

SØRLANDET: ALONG THE COAST

Sørlandet, or southern Norway, is a land of wide beaches toasted by the greatest number of sunny days in Norway, waters warmed by the Gulf Stream, and long, fertile tracts of flatland. Not a people to pass up a minute of sunshine, the Norwegians have sprinkled the south with their *hytter* (cabins or cottages) and made it their number one domestic holiday spot. Nonetheless, even at the height of summer, you can sail to a quiet skerry or take a solitary walk through the forest.

Southern Norway is an outdoor paradise, with a mild summer climate and terrain varying from coastal flatland to inland mountains and forests. There's plenty of fish in the rivers and lakes, as well as along the coast. The region is particularly well suited to canoeing, kayaking, rafting, and hiking. Beavers, deer, foxes, and forest birds inhabit the area, so bring binoculars if you like to see them more closely.

The coast bordering the Skagerak, the arm of the North Sea separating Norway and Denmark, is lined with small communities stretching from Oslo as far as Lindesnes, which is at the southernmost tip. Sørlandet towns are often called "pearls on a string," and in the dusk of a summer evening, reflections of the white-painted houses on the water have a silvery translucence.

The two chief cities of Norway's south, Kristiansand on the east coast and Stavanger on the west coast, differ sharply. Kristiansand is a resort town, scenic and relaxed, whereas Stavanger, once a fishing center, is now the hub of the oil industry and Norway's most cosmopolitan city. Stavanger has many more good restaurants than other cities of comparable size, thanks to the influx of both foreigners and money to the city. More than 100 restaurants, bars, and cafés offer everything from Thai, Chinese, and Indian to Italian, French, and, of course, Norwegian cooking. Try the restored warehouse area in the harbor for some of the best restaurants.

Between Kristiansand and Stavanger is the coastal plain of Jæren, dotted with prehistoric burial sites and the setting for the works of some of the country's foremost painters.

Larvik

㉑   *128 km (79 mi) from Oslo; 19 km (12 mi) south of Sandefjord.*

Larvik is the last of the big whaling towns. It's still a port, but now the traffic is made up of passengers to Fredrikshavn, Denmark.

Kong Haakons Kilde (King Haakon's Spring), also called Farris Kilde (Farris Spring), is Norway's only natural source of mineral water. A spa was built here in 1880, but people now drink the water rather than bathe in it. The spring is near the ferry quays. ⊠ *Fjellvn, 3256,* ☎ *33/18–20–00.* ⊡ *Free.* ☉ *Late June–mid-Aug., weekdays.*

The noble Gyldenløve family once owned the large estate, **Herregården,** which dates back to 1677. Inside, the furnishings are masterful examples of trompe l'oeil: Scandinavian nobility had to make do with furniture painted to look like marble or carving rather than the real thing. ⊠ *Herregaardssletta 1, 3257,* ☎ *33/13–04–04.* ⊡ *NKr20.* ☉ *Late June–late Aug., daily noon–5; early Sept.–late May, Sun. noon–5.*

The **Maritime Museum** is in Larvik's former customs house and chronicles the town's seafaring history. There's heavy coverage of Thor Heyerdahl's voyages, with models of *Kon-Tiki* and *Ra II.* ⊡ ☉ *Charges and opening times vary; check with the tourist office.*

OFF THE   **PORSGRUNN PORSELÆNFABRIK ASA** – About 27 kilometers (17 miles)
BEATEN PATH   west of Larvik in Porsgrunn is a porcelain factory where you can take a tour and purchase factory seconds. ⊠ *Porselensgt. 12,* ☎ *35/55–00–40.* ⊡ *NKr10.* ☉ *Tours Aug.–June, weekdays at 10, 11, and 1.*

Dining and Lodging

\$\$ ✕⊡ **Grand.** The rooms are spotless and the service attentive in this large hotel overlooking the fjord. There is a good restaurant in which to sample the local fish soup and smoked-meat platters—especially good for lunch. ⊠ *Storgt. 38–40, 3256,* ☎ *33/18–78–00,* ⅢX *33/18–70–45. 97 rooms. Restaurant, bar, pub, dance club, nightclub. AE, DC, MC, V.*

Stavern

㉒ *8 km (5 mi) south of Larvik.*

A popular sailing center today, Stavern was Norway's main naval station between 1750 and 1850, then called Fredriksvern, named for King Fredrik V.

A fine example of Scandinavian Rococo architecture, **Stavern Church** was built in 1756. Its pews were designed so their backs could be folded down to make beds in case the church had to be used as a field hospital in time of war. ⊠ *On the water east of town,* ☎ *33/19–99–75.* ⊘ *Guided tours by appointment.*

En Route From Stavern to Lyngør, you'll pass through Kragerø, a picturesque town with its own small archipelago. Theodor Kittelsen (1857–1914), famous for his drawings of trolls and illustrations of Norwegian fairy tales, lived in Kragerø, and his birthplace is now a museum. The next pearl ont he string after Kragerø is Risør, which is just of E18 on the coast.

Lyngør

㉓ *18 km (11 mi) south of Risør. To get to Lyngør, follow E18 to the sign for Sørlandsporten (Gateway to the South). Turn off just after the sign and drive 26 km (16 mi) to Lyngørfjorden Marina (☎ 37/16–68–00), where you can take a five-minute watertaxi ride for 80 NKr.*

Hardly changed since the days of sailing ships, Lyngør is idyllic and carless, lined with rows of white-painted houses bearing window boxes filled with pink and red flowers. This island community, on four tiny rocky islands off the coast, is considered by some to be Europe's best-preserved village. In winter the population is 110, but every summer thousands descend upon the village. You'll find white houses all along the southern coast, a tradition that began more than 100 years ago, when Dutch sailors traded white paint for wood. Until that time, only red paint was available in Norway. The only hotel on the island books most of its rooms by the year to large firms, so don't count on staying overnight.

NEED A BREAK? In a historic late-19th-century white house with blue trim, **Den Blå Lanterne** (☎ 37/16–64–80) is Lyngør's only restaurant. Although it's pricey, you can eat as much of the famous fish soup as you like, and there's often live music. It's open May through September.

Arendal

㉔ *33 km (20.5 mi) from Lyngør on E18.*

Picturesque Arendal has more of the tidy white houses that are common to the area. In Tyholmen, the old town, you'll see many of these, as well as some brightly colored well-preserved wooden houses. This is a good town for strolling around. For a more formal tour, ask about the summer walking tours at the tourist office.

OFF THE BEATEN PATH **MERDØGAARD MUSEUM** – On the island of Merdøy, a 30-minute boat ride from Arendal's Langbrygga (long wharf), is an early-18th-century sea captain's home, now a museum. ☎ 37/08-52-43. ⊠ NKr10. ⊘ Late June–mid-Aug., daily 11–5. Guided tours on the hr until 4.

Dining and Lodging

$$ × **Madam Reiersen.** This authentic restaurant on the waterfront serves good food in an informal atmosphere. ⊠ *Nedre Tyholmsvn. 3, 4800,* ☎ *37/02–19–00. AE, DC, MC, V.*

$$ ⊞ **Inter Nor Tyholmen.** This maritime hotel, built in 1988, is in Tyholmen, with the sea at close quarters and a magnificent view of the fjord. The open-air restaurant is great in summer. ⊠ *Teaterpl. 2,* ☎ *37/02–68–00,* 𝔽𝔸𝕏 *37/02–68–01. 60 rooms. 2 restaurants, bar, sauna. AE, DC, MC, V.*

Grimstad

㉕ *50 km (31 mi) south of Arendal.*

Grimstad's glory was in the days of sailing ships—about the same time the 15-year-old Henrik Ibsen worked as an apprentice at the local apothecary shop. Grimstad Apotek is now a part of **Ibsenhuset** (the Ibsen House) and has been preserved with its 1837 interior intact. Ibsen wrote his first play, *Catlina,* here. ⊠ *Henrik Ibsensgt. 14, 4890,* ☎ *37/04–46–53.* ⊡ *NKr25.* ☉ *Mid-Apr.–mid-Sept., Mon.–Sat. 9–5, Sun. 1–5.*

Kristiansand

㉖ *100 km (62 mi) south of Grimstad on E18.*

Kristiansand, with 68,000 inhabitants, is one of Sørlandet's most prosperous cities and the domestic summer-vacation capital of Norway. According to legend, in 1641 King Christian IV marked the four corners of Kristiansand with his walking stick, and within that framework the grid of wide streets was drawn. The center of town, called the **Kvadrat,** still retains the grid, even after numerous fires.

Kristiansand's **Fisketorvet** (fish market) is near the southern corner of the town's grid, right on the sea. **Christiansholm Festning** (fortress) is on a promontory opposite Festningsgata. Completed in 1672, the circular building with 15-foot-thick walls has played more a decorative than a defensive role; it was used once, in 1807, to defend the city against British invasion. Now it contains art exhibits.

The Gothic Revival **cathedral** from 1885 is the third-largest church in Norway. It often hosts summertime concerts in addition to an annual weeklong International Church Music Festival in mid-May (☎ *38/02–13–11* for information) that includes organ, chamber, and gospel music.⊠ *Kirkegt., 4610,* ☎ *38/02–11–88.* ⊡ *Free.* ☉ *June–Aug., daily 9–2.*

A wealthy merchant-shipowner built **Gimle Gård** (Gimle Manor) around 1800 in the Empire style. It displays period furnishings, paintings, silver, and hand-blocked wallpaper. To get there from the city center, head north across the Otra River on Bus 22 or drive to Route E18 and cross the bridge over the Otra to Parkveien. Turn left onto Ryttergangen and drive to Gimleveien, where you'll turn right. ⊠ *Gimlevn. 23, 4630,* ☎ *38/09–02–28.* ⊡ *NKr20.* ☉ *May–Oct., Sun. noon–5.*

The runestone in the cemetery of **Oddernes Kirke** (Oddernes Church) tells that Øyvind, godson of Saint Olav, built this church in 1040 on property he inherited from his father. One of the oldest churches in Norway, it is dedicated to Saint Olav. ⊠ *Oddernesvn, 6430,* ☎ *38/09–01–87 or 38/09–03–60.* ⊡ *Free.* ☉ *May–Aug., Sun.–Fri. 9–2.*

You'll see dwellings and workshops on a reconstructed city street at **Vest-Agder Fylkesmuseum** (County Museum). Here you can visit two *tun*—farm buildings traditionally set in clusters around a common area, which suited the extended families. The museum is 4 kilometers (3 miles) east of Kristiansand on Route E18. ⊠ *Kongsgård, 4631,* ☎ *38/09–02–28.* ☜ *NKr20.* ☉ *Mid-June–mid-Aug., Mon.–Sat. 10–6; late May–mid-Sept., Sun. noon–6; mid-Sept.–mid-May, Sun. noon–5; or by appointment.*

A favorite with hikers and strolling nannies, **Ravnedalen** (Raven Valley) is a lush park that's filled with flowers in springtime. Wear comfortable shoes and you can hike the narrow, winding paths up the hills and climb 200 steps up to a 304-foot lookout. ⊠ *Northwest of town.*

One of Norway's most popular attractions, **Kristiansand Dyrepark** is actually five separate parks, including a water park (bring bathing suits and towels), a forested park, an entertainment park, a fairy-tale park, and a zoo, which contains an enclosure for Scandinavian wolves and Europe's (possibly the world's) largest breeding ground for Bactrian camels. The fairy-tale park, **Kardemomme By** (Cardamom Town), is named for a book by Norwegian illustrator and writer Thorbjørn Egner. His story comes alive here in a precisely replicated village, with actors playing townsfolk, shopkeepers, pirates, and a delightful trio of robbers. Families who are hooked can even stay overnight in one of the village's cozy apartments or nearby cottages (reserve at least a year in advance). The park is 11 kilometers (6 miles) east of town. ⊠ *Kristiansand Dyrepark, 4609 Kardemomme By,* ☎ *38/04–97–00.* ☜ *NKr160 ; includes admission to all parks and rides.* ☉ *Mid-May–mid-Aug., daily 10–6; rest of yr, daily 10–4.*

Dining and Lodging

$$–$$$ ✕ **Sjøhuset.** Built in 1892 as a salt warehouse, this white-trimmed red building has since become a restaurant. The specialty is seafood, appropriately, and the monkfish with Newburg sauce on green fettuccine is colorful and delicious. The interior is furnished with comfortable leather chairs and accented with maritime antiques. ⊠ *Østre Strandgt. 12, 4610,* ☎ *38/02–62–60. AE, DC, MC, V.*

$$ ✕ **Restaurant Bakgården.** At this small and intimate restaurant the menu varies from day to day, but the seafood platter and lamb tenderloin are standard. The staff is especially attentive. ⊠ *Tollbodgt. 5, 4611,* ☎ *38/02–79–55. AE, DC, MC, V. No lunch.*

$ ✕ **Mållaget Kafeteria.** At this cafeteria everything is homemade (except for the gelatin dessert). That includes such dishes as meatballs, brisket of beef with onion sauce, and trout in sour-cream sauce. It's the best deal in town, but it closes right around 6 PM, the time most people think about eating dinner. ⊠ *Gyldenløves Gt. 11, 4611,* ☎ *38/02–22–93. No credit cards.*

$$–$$$ 🏨 **Inter Nor Ernst Park Hotel.** The rooms are decorated with chintz bedspreads and drapes and practical furniture. The corner rooms have a tower nook at one end. On Saturday the atrium restaurant is the local spot for a civilized tea and lovely cakes. ⊠ *Rådhusgt. 2, 4611,* ☎ *38/02–14–00,* 🖷 *38/02–03–07. 112 rooms, 4 suites. Restaurant, 2 bars, nightclub, meeting rooms. AE, DC, MC, V.*

$$ 🏨 **Rainbow Hotel Norge.** This quiet, family hotel in the heart of town has an entrance more modern than that of the Ernst Park, but upstairs the difference is negligible. Here the rooms are furnished in bright colors and dark woods. Get up for breakfast to taste the homemade breads and rolls. ⊠ *Dronningens Gt. 5, 4610,* ☎ *38/02–00–00,* 🖷 *38/02–35–30. 114 rooms. Restaurant, library, meeting rooms. AE, DC, MC, V.*

Outdoor Activities and Sports

BICYCLING

Kristiansand has 70 kilometers (43 miles) of bike trails around the city. The tourist office (☞ Visitor Information *in* Sørlandet A to Z, *below*) can recommend routes and rentals.

FISHING

Just north of Kristiansand there is excellent trout, perch, and eel fishing at Lillesand's **Vestre Grimevann** lake. You can get a permit at any sports store or at the tourist office (☞ Visitor Information *in* Sørlandet A to Z, *below*).

HIKING

In addition to the gardens and steep hills of **Ravnedalen** (☞ *above*), the **Baneheia Forest,** just a 15-minute walk north from the city center, is full of evergreens, small lakes, and paths that are ideal for a lazy walk or a challenging run.

WATER SPORTS

Kuholmen Marina (✉ Roligheden Camping, ☎ 38/09–67–22) rents boats, water skis, and water scooters. **Anker Dykkersenter** (✉ Randesundsgt. 2, Kuholmen, ☎ 38/09–79–09) rents scuba equipment, and **Fun Sport** (✉ Dronningensgt. 59, ☎ 38/02–24–45) rents Windsurfers and holds classes. **Kristiansand Diving Club** (✉ Myrbakken 3, ☎ 38/01–03–32 between 6 PM and 9 PM) has information on local diving.

Combining history and sailing, the magnificent full-rig, square-sail school ship **Sørlandet** (✉ Gravene 2, 4610 Kristiansand, ☎ 38/02–98–90, FAX 38/02–93–34), built in 1927, takes on passengers ranging from senior citizens to college students and younger for two weeks, usually stopping for several days in a northern European port. The price is about NKr7,000.

Grovane i Vennesla

㉗ *20 km (13 mi) north of Kristiansand. Follow Rte. 39 from Kristiansand to Mosby, veer right onto 405, and continue to Grovane.*

At Grovane i Vennesla you will find the **Setesdalsbanen** (Setesdal Railway), a 4.7-kilometer-long (3-mile-long) stretch of narrow-gauge track on which a steam locomotive from 1894 and carriages from the early 1900s run. ✉ *Vennesla Stasjon, 4700,* ☎ *38/15–55–08.* 🎫 *NKr50.* ☉ *Mid-June–Aug., daily at 1:30, Sun. at 11:30, 1:30, and 3.*

Mandal

㉘ *42 km (28 mi) southwest from Kristiansand and 82 km (51 mi) from Evje.*

Mandal is Norway's most southerly town, famous for its historic core of well-preserved wooden houses and its beautiful long beach, Sjøsanden.

Mandal Kirke, built in 1821, is Norway's largest Empire-style wooden church. ☎ *38/26–35–77.* ☉ *Daily 11–2.*

Lindesnes Fyr, Norway's oldest lighthouse, was built on the southernmost point of the country. The old coal-fired light dates from 1822. ☎ *38/25–88–51.* ☉ *Mid-May–mid-Sept., 8 AM–10 PM.*

En Route The road from Mandal climbs and weaves its way through steep, wooded valleys and then descends toward the sea. Here you'll find the small town of Flekkefjord, which is known for its Hollenderbyen (Dutch Town), a historic district with small, white-painted houses lining narrow, winding streets. From Flekkefjord you can take Route E18, which heads inland here, to Stavanger. It is more rewarding, however, to go on the coast road—Route 44. Follow the coast road 40 kilometers (25 miles) past the fishing port of Egersund to Ogna.

Ogna

㉙ *93 km (57 mi) from Flekkefjord on Rte. 42.*

Ogna is known for the stretch of sandy beach that inspired so many Norwegian artists, among them Kitty Kjelland.

Hå Gamle Prestegaard (Old Parsonage), built in the 1780s, is now a cultural center for the area. ▧ *NKr20.* ⊘ *May–mid-Sept., weekdays 11–7, Sat. noon–5, Sun. noon–7; rest of yr, Sat. noon–5, Sun. noon–7.*

Whichever road you choose to continue on out of Ogna, they both head northward along the rich agricultural coastal plain of the **Jæren district.** Flat and stony, it is the largest expanse of level terrain in this mountainous country. The mild climate and the absence of good harbors mean that the population here turned to agriculture, and the miles of stone walls are a testament to their labor.

Ancient monuments in Jæren are still visible, notably the **Hå gravesite** below the Hå parsonage near the Obrestad light. It consists of about 60 mounds, including two star-shaped and one boat-shaped, dating from around AD 500, all marked with stones. Take coastal Route 44.

Outdoor Activities and Sports

BIRD-WATCHING

The **Jærstrendene** in Jæren, from Randabergvika in the north to Ogna in the south, is a protected national park—and a good area for spotting puffins, cormorants, and black guillemots, as well as such waders as dunlins, little stints, and ringed plovers. Some areas of the park are closed to visitors, and it is forbidden to pick flowers or, for that matter, to disturb anything.

FISHING

Three of the 10 best fishing rivers in Norway, the **Ognaelva, Håelva,** and **Figgjo,** are located in Jæren, just south of Stavanger. Fishing licenses, which are sold in grocery stores and gas stations, are required at all of them.

Orre

㉚ *North on Rte. 507 26 km (16 mi) from Ogna.*

Orre is the site of a medieval stone church. It also has one of the few preserved Viking graveyards, dating from the Bronze Age and Iron Age. Near Orre pond, slightly inland, is a bird-watching station.

Dining

$$ ✕ **Time Station.** You'll find this eatery (in fact the only one in Bryne) next to the town's train station. Bryne is just up the road from Orre off Highway 507 and about a 40-minute train ride from Stavanger. Though the meat dishes, such as reindeer, pork and lamb, are tasty, the house specialty is the seafood platter, with salmon, monkfish, ocean catfish, mussels, and ocean crayfish in a beurre blanc sauce. For dessert, try the *krumkake,* a cookie baked on an iron, wafer thin, shaped into a cone, and filled with blackberry cream. ⊠ *Storgt. 346, 4340 Bryne,* ☎ *51/48–22–56. Reservations essential. AE, DC, MC, V. Closed Sun. No lunch weekdays.*

Sandnes

㉛ *25 km (16 mi) south of Stavanger, 52 km (32 mi) north of Orre.*

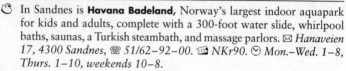 In Sandnes is **Havana Badeland,** Norway's largest indoor aquapark for kids and adults, complete with a 300-foot water slide, whirlpool baths, saunas, a Turkish steambath, and massage parlors. ⊠ *Hanaveien 17, 4300 Sandnes,* ☎ *51/62–92–00.* 🎫 *NKr90.* ☉ *Mon.–Wed. 1–8, Thurs. 1–10, weekends 10–8.*

Ullandhaug

㉜ *15 km (9 mi) west of Sandnes.*

Take your imagination further back in time at Ullandhaug, a reconstruction of an Iron Age farm. Three houses have been built around a central garden, and guides wearing period clothing demonstrate the daily activities of 1,500 years ago, spinning thread on a spindle, weaving, and cooking over an open hearth. ⊠ *Grannesvn.,* ☎ *51/53–41–40.* 🎫 *NKr20.* ☉ *Mid-June–Aug., daily noon–5; early May and mid-Sept., Sun. noon–4.*

You can see the place where what we know as Norway was founded by traveling 1.6 kilometers (1 mile) east on Grannesveien Ullandhaug to the **Harfsfjord.** In 872, in the Battle of Harfsfjord, Harald Hårfagre (Harald the Fair-Haired), the warrior king from the eastern country of Vestfold, finally succeeded in quelling the resistance of local chieftains in Rogaland and was promptly declared king of all Norway. A memorial in the shape of three giant swords plunged halfway into the earth marks the spot.

OFF THE
BEATEN PATH
UTSTEIN KLOSTER (Utstein Monastery) – Originally the palace of Norway's first king, Harald Hårfagre, and later the residence of King Magnus VI, Utstein was used as a monastery from 1265 to 1537, when it reverted to the royal family. One of the best-preserved medieval monuments in Norway, the monastery opened to the public in 1965 and is today used to host classical and jazz concerts on Sunday afternoons during the summer.

After the concert, try the *Får i kål* (mutton, potatoes, and cabbage boiled in a peppery juice, a Norwegian staple) at **Utstein Kloster Vertshus,** approximately 2 kilometers (1 mile) from the monastery along the water's edge. To get to Utstein: Buses depart from Stavanger at 12:15, returning from the monastery at 4:05, Monday through Friday. It's about a half-hour drive from Stavanger. By car, travel north on coastal highway 1, through the world's second-longest undersea car tunnel. There is a toll of NKr75, plus NKr25 per passenger for the tunnel passage. ⊠ *4156 Mosterøy,* ☎ *51/72–46–00.* 🎫 *NKr20.* ☉ *May–mid-Sept., Tues.–Sat. 1–4, Sun. noon–5.*

Stavanger

㉝ *5 km (3 mi) east of Ullandhaug; 198 km (123 mi) from Kristiansand; 6 hrs from Bergen by car and ferry.*

Stavanger has always prospered from the riches of the sea. During the 19th century, huge harvests of brisling and herring established it as the sardine capital of the world. A resident is still called a Siddis, from S(tavanger) plus *iddis,* which means "sardine label," and the city's symbol, fittingly enough, is the key of a sardine can.

During the past two and a half decades, a different product from the sea has been Stavanger's lifeblood—oil. Since its discovery in the late 1960s, North Sea oil has transformed both the economy and the lifestyle of the city. In the early days of drilling, expertise was imported from abroad, chiefly from the United States. Although Norwegians have now taken over most of the projects, foreigners constitute almost a tenth of the inhabitants, making Stavanger the country's most international city. Though the population hovers around 142,000, the city has all the agreeable bustle of one many times its size. However, the city's charm still remains—in the heart of Old Stavanger you can wind down narrow cobblestone streets past small, white houses with many-paned windows and terra-cotta roof tiles.

Stavanger Domkirke (cathedral), a large, well-preserved medieval church, is in the city center next to Breiavatnet, a small pond. Construction was begun in 1125 by Bishop Reinald of Winchester, who was probably assisted by English craftsmen. Largely destroyed by fire in 1272, the church was rebuilt to include a Gothic chancel. The result: Its once elegant lines are now festooned with macabre death symbols and airborne putti. The cathedral often hosts organ recitals. Next to the cathedral is **Kongsgård**, formerly a residence of bishops and kings but now a school and not open to visitors. ▨ *Free.* ☉ *Mid-May–mid-Sept., daily 9–6; rest of yr, Mon.–Sat. 9–2, Sun. 1–8.*

Breidablikk manor house has been perfectly preserved since the '60s and feels as if the owner has only momentarily slipped away. An outstanding example of what the Norwegians call "Swiss-style" architecture, this house was built by a Norwegian shipping magnate. In spite of its foreign label, the house is uniquely Norwegian, inspired by national romanticism. ▨ *Eiganesvn. 40A, 4009,* ☎ *51/52–60–35.* ▨ *NKr20.* ☉ *Mid-June–mid-Aug., daily 11–4; rest of yr, Sun. 11–4.*

Ledaal, the royal family's Stavanger residence, is a stately house built by the Kielland family in 1799. The second-floor library is dedicated to the writer Alexander Kielland, a social critic and satirist. ▨ *Eiganesvn. 45, 4009,* ☎ *51/52–06–18.* ▨ *NKr20.* ☉ *Mid-June–mid-Aug., daily 11–4; rest of yr, Sun. 11–4.*

☙ This fascinating, albeit obscure, museum, the **Norsk Hermetikkmuseum** (Canning Museum), is housed in a former canning factory. Exhibits document the processing of brisling and sardines—the city's most important industry for nearly 100 years, thanks greatly to savvy turn-of-the-century packaging (naturally, the inventor of the sardine-can key was from Stavanger). Tuesdays and Thursdays from mid-June to mid-August, and the first Sunday of the month year-round, the museum holds canning and smoking demonstrations in which visitors are encouraged to participate. Taste tests are free; canned King Oscar sardine purchases in the tiny gift store are voluntary but a must for fish lovers. ▨ *Øvre Strandgt. 88A, 4005,* ☎ *51/53–49–89.* ▨ *NKr20.* ☉ *Mid-June–mid-Aug., daily 11–4; early June and late Aug., Tues.–Fri. 11–3, Sun. 11–4; Sept.–May, Sun. 11–4.*

Along Strandkaien, warehouses face the wharf; the shops, offices, and apartments face the street on the other side. Housed in the only two shipping merchants' houses that remain completely intact is the **Sjøfartsmuseet** (Maritime Museum). Inside, the house is just as it was a century ago, complete with office furniture, files, and posters, while the apartments show the standard of living for the mercantile class at that time. Although signs are only in Norwegian, an English-language guidebook and guided tours outside normal opening hours are available. ▨ *Nedre Strandgt. 17–19, 4005,* ☎ *51/52–59–11.* ▨ *NKr20.* ☉ *Mid-June–mid-Aug., daily 11–4; early June and late Aug., Tues.–Fri. 11–3, Sun. 11–4; Sept.–May, Sun. 11–4.*

You can easily spot the spiky **Valbergtårnet** (▨ Valberget 4, ☎ 51/89–55–01) from any spot on the quay. Built on the highest point of the old city, this tower was a firewatch. Today it is a crafts center, which may not interest you, but it's still worth a visit for the view.

If you are of Norwegian stock you can trace your roots at **Det Norske Utvandresenteret** (Norwegian Emigration Center). Bring along any information you have, especially where your ancestors came from in Norway and when they left the country. The center is on the fourth floor of the brick *Ligningskontoret* (Tax Office) building a few minutes' walk from the harbor. You can make arrangements via fax to have the center do research for you, but the wait for this service is long. ⊠ *Bergjelandsgt. 30, 4012 Stavanger,* ☎ *51/50–12–74,* FAX *51/50–12–90.* ✆ *Free, but each written request costs NKr180.* ۞ *Weekdays 9–3, Sat. 9–1.*

Rogaland Kunstmuseum houses the country's largest collection of works by Lars Hertervig, a Romantic painter who is often considered the country's greatest after Edvard Munch. Other exhibits include Norwegian art from the early 19th century to the present. The museum is near Mosvannet (Moss Lake), which is just off highway E18 at the northern end of downtown. ⊠ *Tjensvoll 6, 4021 Mosvannsparken,* ☎ *51/53–09–00.* ✆ *NKr30.* ۞ *Tues.–Thurs. 10–2 and 6–9, Fri. 10–2, Sat. 11–3, Sun. 11–5.*

☺ **Kongeparken Amusement Park** has a 281-foot-long figure of Gulliver and a lifelike dinosaur exhibit as its main attractions, and plenty of rides. ⊠ *4330 Ålgård,* ☎ *51/61–71–11.* ✆ *NKr110; rides and activities NKr5–NKr20.* ۞ *July, daily 11–5. Other spring and summer hrs vary; call for specific times.*

OFF THE BEATEN PATH	**PREKESTOLEN** (Pulpit Rock) – This huge cube of rock with a vertical drop of 2,000 feet is not a good choice if you suffer from vertigo but is great for a heart-stopping view. You can join a tour to get there (☞ Guided Tours, *below*), or you can do it on your own from June 16 to August 25 by taking the ferry from Fiskepiren across Hildefjorden to Tau. (It takes about 40 minutes from Stavanger.) In summer, a bus runs regularly from the ferry to the parking lot at the Pulpit Rock Lodge. It takes 1½ to 2 hours to walk from the lodge to the rock—the well-marked trail crosses some uneven terrain, so good walking shoes or boots are vital. Food and lodging are near the trail.

Dining and Lodging

$$$$ ✕ **Jans Mat & Vinhus.** The cellar setting is rustic, with old stone walls
★   and robust sideboards providing a nice counterpoint to the refined menu. Saddle of Rogaland county lamb is boned and rolled around a thyme-flavored stuffing, and the fillet is topped with a crunchy mustard crust. For dessert, try the nougat parfait dusted with cocoa. As implied by the restaurant's name (Jan's Food & Winehouse), there's an excellent selection of wines here. ⊠ *Breitorget 4, 4006,* ☎ *51/89–47–73. Reservations essential. Jacket and tie. AE, DC, MC, V. No lunch. Closed Sun.*

$$$ ✕ **Sjøhuset Skagen.** Just a few doors down from N.B. Sørensen's (☞ *below*), this spot is similar in decor, but with a greater variety of food. Try the crepes stuffed with roe of chapelin, onion, and sour cream, and the marinated salmon, Norwegian style, with potatoes in a dill-and-cream sauce. The Brie served with cloudberries marinated in whiskey is excellent. ⊠ *Skagen 16, 4006,* ☎ *51/89–51–80. AE, DC, MC, V.*

$$$ ✕ **Straen Fiskerestaurant.** Right on the quay with two old-fashioned dining rooms, Straen is considered by many the city's best fish restaurant. The three-course meal of the day is always the best value. The house fish soup is excellent. A rock club, a rock café, and a pub are

on the premises. ⊠ *Nedre Strandgt. 15, 4005,* ☎ *51/52–62–30 or 51/52–61–00. AE, DC, MC, V. No lunch. Closed Sun.*

$$ ✕ **City Bistro.** Choose from reindeer medallions with rowanberry jelly, deer fillet with lingonberries and pears, or halibut poached in cream with saffron, garnished with shrimp, crayfish, and mussels at this bistro, where you'll dine at massive oak tables in a turn-of-the-century house. ⊠ *Madlavn. 18–20, 4008,* ☎ *51/53–95–70. Reservations essential. AE, DC, MC, V. No lunch.*

$$ ✕ **Harry Pepper.** This trendy Mexican restaurant has a popular bar. The color schemes are fun, bright, and gaudy, as are the displays of tacky South American souvenirs. ⊠ *Øvre Holmegt. 15, 4006,* ☎ *51/89–39–93. AE, DC, V.*

$-$$ ✕ **N.B. Sørensen's Dampskibsexpedition.** In a restored warehouse
★ decorated with nautical ropes, rustic barrels, and gaslights, this bar and restaurant is right on the quay. The food is Norwegian with a flair. Try the marinated shrimp appetizer and the baked monkfish. The dish of the day, as well as the red house wine, which is always waiting for customers in an N.B. Sørensen's bottle on each table, is one of the better deals in Stavanger. ⊠ *Skagen 26, 4006,* ☎ *51/89–12–70. AE, DC, MC, V.*

$ ✕ **Café Sting.** Right at the foot of the Valbergtårnet, it's a restaurant–gallery–concert hall–meeting place day and night. All food is made in-house and is better than most other inexpensive fare in Norway. There's a skillet dish with crisp fried potatoes and bacon, flavored with leek, and topped with melted cheese and sour cream; and a meat loaf with mashed potatoes and sprinkled with cheese. The chocolate and almond cakes are good, and they serve delicious hot chocolate that will satisfy winter sugar cravings. ⊠ *Valberget. 3, 4006,* ☎ *51/53–24–40. AE, DC, V.*

$$$–$$$$ 🏨 **Reso Atlantic Hotel.** The largest hotel in Stavanger, the Atlantic is just off Breiavatnet in the heart of downtown. The feel is that of an international luxury hotel with several restaurants and the most popular nightclubs in town, but with little local flair. Rooms are immaculate and comfortable, with heavy quilts, thick carpets, and cozy stuffed chairs. 🏨 *Olav V's Gt. 3, 4005 Stavanger,* ☎ *51/52–75–20,* FAX *51/53–48–69. 351 rooms, 5 suites. Restaurant, bar, café, pub, dance club, nightclub, 12 meeting rooms. AE, DC, MC, V.*

$$–$$$ 🏨 **Skagen Brygge.** Housed in three rehabilitated old sea houses, almost all rooms are different here, from modern to old-fashioned maritime, with exposed beams and brick and wood walls; many have harbor views. The hotel has an arrangement with 14 restaurants in the area—they make the reservations and the tab ends up on your hotel bill. 🏨 *Skagenkaien 30, 4006,* ☎ *51/89–41–00,* FAX *51/89–58–83. 106 rooms. Bar, indoor pool, health club, convention center. AE, DC, MC, V.*

$–$$$ 🏨 **Victoria Hotel.** The oldest hotel in Stavanger, it was built at the turn of the century and still retains a clubby, Victorian style, with leather couches, heavy curtains, and dark oil paintings. Rates are significantly lower with Scandinavian Bonuspass in summer and on weekends. Guests receive a 40% to 50% discount at the Trimoteket health club, just behind the hotel. 🏨 *Skansegt. 1, 4006 Stavanger,* ☎ *51/89–60–00,* FAX *51/89–54–10. 107 rooms, 3 suites. 2 restaurants, bar, breakfast room, meeting room. AE, DC, MC, V.*

$–$$ 🏨 **Grand Hotel.** This place on the edge of the town center doesn't aim to be fancy; rooms are comfortable and bright, done in light pastels and white. In summer the rates drop significantly. 🏨 *Klubbgt. 3, Boks 80, 4012,* ☎ *51/53–30–20,* FAX *51/56–19–42. 92 rooms. Bar, breakfast room. AE, DC, MC, V.*

Nightlife and the Arts

NIGHTLIFE

In summer people are out at all hours, and sidewalk restaurants stay open until the sun comes up. Walk along **Skagenkaien** and **Strandkaien** for a choice of pubs and nightclubs. Among media junkies the place for a beer and a bit of CNN is the **Newsman** (⊠ Skagen 14, ☎ 51/53–57–09). **Taket Nattklubb** (⊠ Nedre Strandgt.15, ☎ 51/52–61–00) and **Cobra** at the Atlantic Hotel (⊠ Olav V's Gt. 3, ☎ 51/52–75–20) are for the mid-twenties and above crowd, whereas **Checkpoint Charlie** (⊠ Lars Hertervigs Gt.5, ☎ 51/53–22–45) caters to a younger age group with an image to maintain.

THE ARTS

Stavanger Konserthus (⊠ Concert Hall, Bjergsted, ☎ 51/56–17–16) features local artists and hosts free summertime foyer concerts. Built on an island in the archipelago in the Middle Ages, today **Utstein Kloster** (☞ *above*) is used for its superior acoustics and hosts classical and jazz concerts on some weekday afternoons from June to August.

Outdoor Activities and Sports

BICYCLING

From Stavanger you can take your bike onto the ferry that departs for Finnøy. Spend the day or longer: Weeklong cottage rentals are available from **Finnøy Fjordsenter** (⊠ 4160, Judaberg, ☎ 51/71–26–46, FAX 51/54–17–62). For more information about cottages in the archipelago and maps, contact the Stavanger Tourist Board (☞ Visitor Information in Sørlandet A to Z, *below*). The Ministry of the Environment can also provide information; call its **Bike Project** (⊠ Sandnes Turistinformasjon, Langgt. 8, 4300 Sandnes, ☎ 51/62–52–40).

FISHING

North of Stavanger is the longest salmon river in western Norway, the **Suldalslågen,** made popular 100 years ago by a Scottish aristocrat who built a fishing lodge there. **Lindum** still has cabins and camping facilities, as well as a dining room. Contact the **Lakseslottet Lindum** (⊠ N–4240 Suldalsosen, ☎ 52/79–91–61). The main salmon season is July through September (☞ Water Sports, *below*).

GOLF

The **Stavanger Golfklubb** (⊠ Longebakken 45, 4042 Hafrsfjord, ☎ 51/55–54–31) offers a lush, 18-hole, international-championship course and equipment rental.

HIKING

Stavanger Turistforening (⊠ Postboks 239, 4001 Stavanger, ☎ 51/52–75–66, FAX 51/53–20–44) can plan a hike through the area, particularly in the rolling **Setesdalsheiene** and the thousands of islands and skerries of the **Ryfylke Archipelago.** The tourist board oversees 33 cabins for members (you can join on the spot) for overnighting along the way. Also in the Ryfylke area is a hike up to the **Kjerag,** a sheet of granite mountain that soars 3,555 feet, at the Lysefjord, near Forsand—ideal for thrill seekers.

SKIING

Skiing in Sirdal, 2½ hours from Stavanger, is good from January to April. Special ski buses leave Stavanger on the weekends at 8:30 AM during the season. Especially recommended is Sinnes for its stunning views and non-hair-raising cross-country terrain. Downhill skiing is available at Alsheia on the same bus route. Contact **SOT Reiser** (⊠ Treskeveien 5, 4040 Hafrsfjord, Stavanger, ☎ 51/55–60–66) for transportation information.

WATER SPORTS

Diving is excellent all along the coast—although Norwegian law requires all foreigners to dive with a Norwegian as a way of ensuring that wrecks are left undisturbed. Contact **Dive In** (✉ Madlaveien 5, Stavanger, ☎ 51/52–99–00), which rents equipment and offers a weekend rate.

On the island of **Kvitsøy,** in the archipelago just west of Stavanger, you can rent an apartment, complete with fish-smoking and -freezing facilities, and arrange to use a small sail- or motorboat. Contact **Kvitsøy Maritime Senter** (✉ Box 35, 4090 Kvitsøy, ☎ 51/73–51–88, ℻ 51/73–53–96).

Shopping

Outside of town are a ceramics factory and an outlet store: **Figgjo Ceramics** (✉ Rte. E18, 4333 Figgjo, ☎ 51/67–00–00; 51/67–00–03 after 3:30) was started during World War II, when Norway was occupied by German forces. A museum traces the history of the factory; the seconds shop has discounts of about 50%. **Skjæveland Strikkevarefabrikk** (✉ 4330 Ålgård, ☎ 51/61–85–06) has a huge selection of men's and women's sweaters in both Norwegian patterns and other designs for about NKr200 less than prices found in the shops.

Sørlandet A to Z

Arriving and Departing

BY BOAT

Color Line (✉ Strandkaien, Stavanger, ☎ 51/52–45–45) has four ships weekly on the Stavanger–Newcastle route. High-speed boats to Bergen are operated by **Flaggruten** (☎ 51/89–50–90). There is also a car ferry from Hirtshals, in northern Denmark, that takes about four hours to make the crossing. Another connects Larvik to Frederikshavn, on Denmark's west coast. In Denmark contact **DSB** (☎ 33/14–17–01); in Norway contact **Color Line** (☎ 51/52–45–45, 38/07–88–88 in Kristiansand). **DFDS Seaways** (☎ 22/41–90–90) sails the Kristiansand–Amsterdam route once a week June through September.

BY BUS

Aust-Agder Trafikkselskap (☎ 37/02–65–00), based in Arendal, has two departures daily in each direction for the 5½- to 6-hour journey between Oslo and Kristiansand.

Sørlandsruta (☎ 38/02–43–80), based in Mandal, has two departures in each direction for the 4½-hour trip from Kristiansand (Strandgt. 33) to Stavanger.

For information about both long-distance and local bus services in **Stavanger,** call ☎ 51/56–71–71; the bus terminal is outside the train station. In **Kristiansand,** call ☎ 38/02–43–80.

BY CAR

From Oslo, it is 329 kilometers (203 miles) to Kristiansand and 574 kilometers (352 miles) to Stavanger. Route E18 parallels the coastline but stays slightly inland on the eastern side of the country and farther inland in the western part. Although seldom wider than two lanes, it is easy driving because it is so flat.

BY PLANE

Kristiansand: Kjevik Airport, 16 kilometers (10 miles) outside town, is served by **Braathens SAFE** (☎ 38/00–80–00), with nonstop flights from Oslo, Bergen, and Stavanger, and **SAS** (☎ 81/00–33–00), with nonstop flights to Copenhagen. **MUK Air** serves Aalborg, Denmark; **Agder Fly** serves Göteborg, Sweden, and Billund, Denmark. Tickets on the last two can be booked with Braathen or SAS.

The **airport bus** departs from the Braathens SAFE office (✉ Vestre Strandgate ☎ 94/67–22–42) approximately one hour before every departure and proceeds, via downtown hotels, directly to Kjevik. Tickets cost NKr30.

Stavanger: Sola Airport is 14 kilometers (9 miles) from downtown. **Braathens SAFE** (☎ 51/51–10–00) has nonstop flights from Oslo, Sandefjord, Kristiansand, Haugesund, Bergen, Trondheim, and Newcastle. **SAS** (☎ 51/65–89–00) has nonstop flights from Bergen, Oslo, Copenhagen, Aberdeen, Göteborg, London, and Newcastle. **KLM** (☎ 51/65–10–22) and **British Airways** (☎ 80/03–00–77) have nonstop flights to Stavanger from Billund and London, respectively. **Air UK** (☎ 51/65–26–30) flies nonstop from London.

The **Flybussen** (airport bus) leaves the airport every 15 minutes. It stops at hotels and outside the railroad station in Stavanger. Tickets cost NKr35.

BY TRAIN

The **Sørlandsbanen** leaves Oslo S Station four times daily for the approximately 5-hour journey to Kristiansand and three times daily for the 8½- to 9-hour journey to Stavanger. Two more trains travel the 3½-hour Kristiansand–Stavanger route. Kristiansand's train station is at Vestre Strandgata (☎ 38/07–75–30). For information on trains from Stavanger, call ☎ 51/56–96–00.

Getting Around

BY BUS

Bus connections in Sørlandet are infrequent; the tourist office can provide a comprehensive schedule. Tickets on Stavanger's excellent bus network cost NKr14.

BY CAR

Sørlandet is flat, so it's easy driving throughout. The area around the Kulturhus in the Stavanger city center is closed to car traffic, and one-way traffic is the norm in the rest of the downtown area. Parking is available in numerous marked lots and is free with the **Stavanger Card** (see below).

BY TAXI

All **Kristiansand** taxis are connected with a central dispatching office (☎ 38/03–27–00), as are **Stavanger** taxis (☎ 51/88–41–00). Journeys within the city are charged by the taximeter, otherwise by the kilometer. The initial charge is NKr24 (NKr34 at night), with NKr11 per kilometer during the day and NKr13 at night.

PASSES

Stavanger: The **Stavanger Card,** sold at hotels, post offices, and Stavanger Tourist Information, gives discounts of up to 50% on sightseeing tours, regional and long-distance, buses, car rentals, and other services and attractions. Parking, local buses, and museum admissions are free with the Stavanger Card, which costs NKr110; NKr190; or NKr240 for one, two, or three days, respectively. The **Stavanger Package** includes the Stavanger Card and steeply discounted lodging in some of the leading hotels. For more information call the Stavanger tourist office (☎ 51/89–66–00).

Contacts and Resources

DENTISTS

In Kristiansand, **Skoletannklinikken** (✉ Festningsgt. 40, ☎ 38/02–19–71) is open 7–3. In Stavanger, the tourist office has a list of dentists available for emergencies.

In Kristiansand, **Kvadraturen Legesenter** (⊠ Vestre Strandgt. 32, 4611, ☎ 38/02–66–11) is open 8–4.

EMERGENCIES
Police: ☎ 112. **Fire:** ☎ 111. **Ambulance:** ☎ 113. **Car Rescue:** in Kristiansand, ☎ 38/02–60–00; in Stavanger, ☎ 51/58–29–00.

Hospital Emergency Rooms: In Kristiansand, **Røde Kors** (Red Cross) **Legevakt** (Egsvei, ☎ 38/02–52–20) is open weekdays 4 PM–8 AM and weekends 24 hours. In Stavanger, call **Rogaland Sentralsykehus** (☎ 51/51–80–00).

GUIDED TOURS
Kristiansand: Tours of Kristiansand run summer only. The **City Train** (⊠ Rådhusgt. 11, 4611, ☎ 38/03–05–24) is a 15-minute tour of the center. The M/S *Maarten* (⊠ Pier 6 by Fiskebrygga, ☎ 38/02–60–65) offers two-hour tours of the eastern archipelago and a three-hour tour of the western archipelago early June–late August.

Stavanger: A two-hour bus tour leaves from the marina at **Vågen** daily at 1 between June and August. **Rødne Clipperkontoret** (⊠ Skagenkaien 18, 4006, ☎ 51/89–52–70) offers three different tours, including an eye-popping fjord tour of the Lysefjord and Pulpit Rock. **Rogaland Trafikkselskap** (☎ 51/56–71–71 or 51/52–26–00) does the same, in either high-speed boats or ferries.

LATE-NIGHT PHARMACIES
Elefantapoteket (⊠ Gyldenløvesgt. 13, 4611, Kristiansand, ☎ 38/02–20–12) is open weekdays 8:30–8, Saturday 8:30–6, Sunday 3–6. **Løveapoteket** (⊠ Olav V's Gt. 11, 4005, Stavanger, ☎ 51/52–06–07) is open daily 8 AM–11 PM.

VISITOR INFORMATION
Arendal (SørlandsInfo, ⊠ Arendal Næringsråd, Friholmsgt. 1, 4800, ☎ 37/02–21–93); **Kristiansand** (Tourist Information, ⊠ Dronningensgt. 2, Box 592, 4601, ☎ 38/12–13–14, ℻ 38/02–52–55); **Larvik** (⊠ Storgt. 48, 3250, ☎ 33/13–01–00); **Mandal** (Mandal og Lindesnes Turistkontor, ⊠ Bryggegt., 4500, ☎ 38/26–08–20); and **Stavanger** (Stavanger Kulturhus, ⊠ Sølvberget, ☎ 51/89–66–00).

BERGEN

People from Bergen like to say they do not come from Norway but from Bergen. Enfolded at the crook of seven mountains and fish-boned by seven fjords, Bergen does seém far from the rest of Norway.

Hanseatic merchants from northern Germany settled in Bergen during the 14th century and made it one of their four major overseas trading centers. The surviving Hanseatic buildings on Bryggen (the quay) are neatly topped with triangular cookie-cutter roofs and scrupulously painted red, blue, yellow, and green. A monument in themselves (they are on the UNESCO World Heritage List), they now house boutiques, restaurants, and museums. In the evening, when the harborside is illuminated, these modest buildings, together with the stocky Rosenkrantz Tower and the yachts lining the pier, are reflected in the water—and provide one of the loveliest cityscapes in northern Europe.

During the Hanseatic period, this active port was Norway's capital and largest city. Boats from northern Norway brought dried fish to Bergen to be shipped abroad by the Dutch, English, Scottish, and German merchants who had settled here. By the time the Hansa lost power, the city had an ample supply of wealthy local merchants and shipowners to replace them. For years Bergen was the capital of shipping, and until well into the 19th century, it remained the country's major city.

Culturally Bergen has also had its luminaries, including dramatist Ludvig Holberg, Scandinavia's answer to Molière—whom the Danes claim as their own. Bergensers know better. Norway's musical geniuses Ole Bull and Edvard Grieg also came from the city of the seven hills. Once you've visited Troldhaugen, Grieg's "Hill of Trolls," you'll understand his inspiration. In fact, the city of Bergen has been picked as the EEC's "European Center of Culture" for the year 2000.

About 219,000 people live in the greater metropolitan area now, compared with nearly 500,000 in Oslo. Even though the balance of power has shifted to the capital, Bergen remains a strong commercial force, thanks to shipping and oil, and is a cultural center, with an international music and arts festival every spring. Although it's true that an umbrella and slicker are necessary in this town, the raindrops—actually 219 days per year of them—never obstruct the lovely views.

Exploring Bergen

The heartbeat of Bergen is at Torgalmenningen, the main pedestrian street that runs from the city's central square to the *Fisketorget* (the Fish Market), which sits on the harbor and faces *Bryggen* (the wharf). From here, the rest of the city spreads up the sides of the seven mountains that surround Bergen, with some sights concentrated near the university or a small lake called Lille Lungegårdsvann. Fløyen, the mountain to the east of the harbor, is the most accessible for daytrippers. Before you begin your walking tour, you can take the funicular up to the top of it for a particularly fabulous overview of the city. Bergen is a very walkable city—especially when the sun's shining. If the weather's nice, you may want to take a couple of hours and just wander the streets, exploring the narrow cobblestone alleyways, charming wood houses, and quaint cafés.

Historic Bergen: Bryggen to Fløyen

A GOOD WALK

Start your tour in the center of town at Torget, also called **Fisketorget** ㉞ or Fish Market, where fisherman and farmers deal their goods. Next, walk over to **Bryggen** ㉟, the wharf on the northeast side of Bergen's harbor. The gabled wood warehouses lining the docks mark the site of the city's orginal settlement. Take time to walk the narrow passageways between buildings; shops and galleries are hidden among the wooden facades. Follow the pier to the **Hanseatisk Museum** ㊱ at Finnegården and have a look inside. Afterwards, continue your walk down the wharf, past the historic buildings to the end of the Holmen promontory and to **Bergenhus Festning** ㊲ (Bergenhus Fort), which dates from the 13th century and the nearby **Rosenkrantztårnet** is a 16th-century tower residence. After you've spent some time out here, retrace your steps back to the Radisson SAS Hotel. Beside the hotel is **Bryggens Museum** ㊳, which houses some magnificent archaeological finds. Just behind the museum is the 12th-century church called **Mariakirken** ㊴. Around the back of the church up the small hill is Øvregaten, a street that's the back boundary of Bryggen. Walking down Øvregaten four blocks to **Fløybanen** ㊵, the funicular that runs up and down Fløyen, one of the city's most popular hiking mountains. Don't miss a trip to the top, whether you hike or take the funicular—the view is like no other. At the base of the funicular is Lille Øvregaten. On this street, and in the area of crooked streets and hodge-podge architecture nearby, you'll find most of Bergen's antiques shops. On your left, at the intersection with Kong Oscars Gate is **Bergen Domkirke** ㊶ (Bergen

Bergen

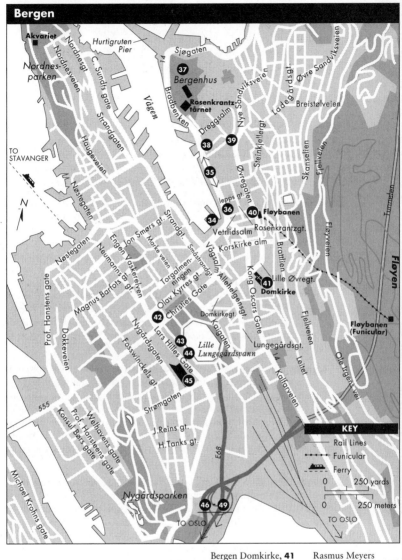

Akvariet
Hurtigruten Pier
Sjøgaten
Nordnes-parken
Nordnesveien
Nordnesgt.
C. Sundts gate
Vågen
Bradbenken
Bergenhus **37**
Rosenkrantz-tårnet
Dreggsalm
Nye Sandviksveien
Øvre Sandviksveien
Ladegårdsgt.
Breistølveien
Skansellen
Fjellveien
38
39
Steinkjellergt.
Strandgaten
Haugeveien
Nøstegaten
35
Øvregaten
TO STAVANGER
N
Nøstegaten
Engen Vaskerelven
Jon Smørs gt.
Strandgt.
Marke veien
Småstrandgt.
Iepps gt.
36
34
Vetrlidsalm
40 Fløybanen
Rosenkrantzgt.
Fløyen
Trangen
Fløyveien
Neumanns gt.
Magnus Barfots gt.
Torgalmen-ningen
Vågsalm
Allehelgensgt.
Korskirke alm
Brattlien
Lille Øvregt.
41
Domkirke
Fløyveien
Prof. Hanstens gate
Dokkeveien
Olav Kyrres gt.
Christies Gate
Domkirkegt.
Kaigaten
Kong Oscars Gate
Fjellveien
Fløybanen (Funicular)
42
Nygårdsgaten
Lars Hilles Gate
Fosswinckels gt.
43
44 Lille Lungegårdsvann
Lungegårdsgt.
Leitet
Kalfarveien
Ole Irgens vei
45
Strømgaten
J.Reins gt.
H.Tanks gt.
Welhavens gate
Prof. Hanstens gate
Konsul Børs gate
555
E68
Michael Krohns gate
Nygårdsparken
46 **49**
TO OSLO

KEY

━━━ Rail Lines
┅┅┅ Funicular
🚢 Ferry

0   250 yards

0   250 meters

TO OSLO

Cathedral). Last, head back to Torgalmenningen in the center of town for a late afternoon snack at one of the the the square's cafés.

TIMING

This tour will take a good portion of a day. Be sure to get to the Fiske-torget early in the morning, as many days it may close as early as 1 or 2. Also, try to plan your trip up Fløyen for a sunny day. Although it may be tough, as Bergen is renowned for rain, you may want to wait a day or two to see if the skies clear up.

SIGHTS TO SEE

41 **Bergen Domkirke (Bergen Cathedral).** This building is constructed in a profusion of styles. The oldest parts, the choir and lower portion of the tower, date from the 13th century. ⊠ *Kong Oscars gt. and Domkirkegt.,* ☎ *55/31–04–70.* ۞ *Weekdays 11–2 in summer only.*

37 **Bergenhus Festning (Bergenhus Fortress).** The buildings here date from the mid-13th century. **Håkonshallen,** a royal ceremonial hall erected during the reign of Håkon Håkonsson between 1247 and 1261, was badly damaged by the explosion of a German ammunition ship in 1944 but was restored by 1961. The nearby **Rosenkrantztårnet** (Rosenkrantz Tower), also damaged in the same explosion, has been extensively re-stored as well. The Danish governor of Bergenhus, Erik Rosenkrantz, built this tower in the 1560s as an official residence and fortification. It is furnished in a formal, austere style. ⊠ *Bergenhus,* ☎ *55/31–60–67.* ⊠ *NKr15.* ۞ *Mid-May–mid-Sept., daily 10–4; rest of yr, daily noon–3, also Thurs. 3–6. Guided tours every hour. Closed during Bergen International Music Festival.*

35 **Bryggen (The Docks, Wharf, or Quays).** A trip to Bergen is not com-plete until you visit Bryggen. One of the most charming walkways in Europe (especially on a sunny day—this town is known for rain, just ask any Bergenser), this row of 14th-century painted wooden build-ings facing the harbor was built by Hansa merchants. The buildings, which are on the UNESCO World Heritage List, are mostly recon-structions, with the oldest dating from 1702. Several fires, the latest in 1955, destroyed the original structures.

38 **Bryggens Museum.** Artifacts found during excavations on Bryggen, in-cluding 12th-century buildings constructed on site from the original foundations, are on display here. The collection provides a good pic-ture of daily life before and during the heyday of the Hansa, down to a two-seater outhouse. ⊠ *Bryggen, 5020,* ☎ *55/31–67–10.* ⊠ *NKr20.* ۞ *May–Aug., daily 10–5; rest of yr, weekdays 11–3, Sat. noon–3, Sun. noon–4.*

34 **Fisketorget (Fish Market).** At the turn of the century, views of this ac-tive and pungent square, with fishermen in Wellington boots and mackintoshes and women in long aprons, were popular postcard sub-jects. Times haven't changed; the marketplace remains just as pic-turesque—bring your camera. ۞ *Mon.–Wed. and Fri. 7–4, Thurs. 7–7, Sat. 7–3.*

OFF THE
BEATEN PATH

AKVARIET (The Aquarium) – Penguins—several kinds, one of which has a platinum feather "hairdo," strangely appropriate in this land of blonds, seem to be the main attraction here. There are also several seals and 50 tanks with a wide variety of fish. The aquarium is on Nordnes Peninsula, a 15-minute walk from the fish market, or take Bus 4. ⊠ *Nordnesparken,* ☎ *55/23-85-53.* ⊠ *NKr45.* ۞ *May–Sept, daily 9–8; rest of yr, daily 10–6. Feeding times: 11, 2, and 6.*

NEED A
BREAK? For an inexpensive snack, try one of the open-face salmon sandwiches sold at the Fish Market. In summer, an array of beautiful, juicy berries is usually available at the adjacent fruit stands. The Norwegian *jordbær* (strawberries) are sure to be some of the best you'll ever have—smaller, but much more flavorful than most American varieties.

40 **Fløybanen (Fløyen Funicular).** The most astonishing view of Bergen is from the top of **Fløyen**, the most popular of the city's seven mountains. A funicular (a cable car that runs on tracks on the ground) takes you to a lookout point 1,050 feet above the sea. Several marked trails lead from Fløyen into the surrounding wooded area, or you can walk back to town on Fjellveien, which is a common Sunday activity for many locals. *NKr30; one-way tickets are half-price.* ☉ *Rides every half hour 7:30 AM–11 PM, Sat. from 8 AM, Sun. from 9 AM. It runs until midnight May–Sept.*

36 **Hanseatisk Museum (Hanseatic Museum).** One of the best-preserved buildings in Bergen, it was the office and home of an affluent German merchant. The apprentices lived upstairs, in boxed-in beds with windows cut into the wall so the tiny cells could be made up from the hall. Although claustrophobic, they retained body heat, practical in these unheated buildings. The 16th-century interior here will give you a feel for the life of a Hanseatic merchant. ✉ *Bryggen,* ☎ *55/31–41–89.* *NKr35; off-season NKr20.* ☉ *June–Aug., daily 9–5; May and Sept., daily 11–2; Oct.–Apr., Sun., Mon., Wed., and Fri. 11–2. Tours in English at 11 and 1 daily. Ticket is also valid for entrance to Schøtstuene, Hanseatic Assembly Rooms.*

39 **Mariakirken (St. Mary's Church).** It began as a Romanesque church in the 12th-century but gained a Gothic choir, richly decorated portals, and a splendid Baroque pulpit, much of it added by the Hanseatic merchants who owned it during the 15th and 16th centuries. Organ recitals are held Tuesday and Thursday mid-June through late August. ✉ *Dreggen, 5020,* ☎ *55/31–59–60.* *NKr10 in summer.* ☉ *Mid-May–early Sept., weekdays 11–4; rest of yr., Tues.–Sun. noon–1:30.*

Rasmus Meyers Allé and Greighallen

A GOOD WALK

From Torgalmenningen, walk to Nordahl Bruns Gate and turn left for the **Vestlandske Kunstindustrimuseum** ㊷, the West Norway Museum of Applied Art. After viewing some of the museum's elaborately crafted works, exit the museum and head for Christies Gate. Follow it along the park and turn left on Rasmus Meyers Allé, which runs along the small lake, Lille Lungegårdsvann, to reach **Stenersens Samling** ㊸, an art museum that has some very impressive holdings, with works by Kandinsky and Klee. Just beyond Stenersens is **Rasmus Meyers Samlinger** ㊹, another museum with equally exciting works, including a large Munch collection. Behind these museums on Lars Hills Gate is **Greighallen** ㊺, Bergen's famous music hall. Although the building's architecture is interesting from street level, try to get a peek of it from the top of Fløyen, where the shape may remind you of a grand piano.

TIMING

All of the museums on this tour are quite small and very near to each other, so you probably won't need more than half a day to complete this tour.

SIGHTS TO SEE

㊺ **Greighallen.** Home of the Bergen Philharmonic Orchestra and stage for the annual International Music Festival, this music hall is a conspicuous slab of glass and concrete, but the acoustics are marvelous.

Built in 1978, the hall was named for the city's famous son, composer Edvard Grieg (1843–1907). ⊠ *Lars Hills Gt. 3A,* ☎ *55/21–61–50.*

44 **Rasmus Meyers Samlinger.** Meyer, a businessman who lived from 1858 to 1916, assembled a superb art collection, with many names that are famous today but were unknown when he acquired them. Here you'll see the best Munch paintings outside Oslo, as well as major works by Scandinavian impressionists. The gallery hosts summertime Grieg concerts. ⊠ *Rasmus Meyers Allé 7,* ☎ *55/56–80–00.* 🎟 *NKr35.* ☉ *Mid-May–mid-Sept., Mon.–Sat. 11–4, Sun. noon–3; rest of yr, Tues.–Sun. noon–3.*

43 **Stenersens Samling.** This is an extremely impressive collection of modern art for a town the size of Bergen. Modern artists represented at this museum include Max Ernst, Paul Klee, Vassily Kandinsky, Pablo Picasso, and Joan Miró, as well as—guess who—Edvard Munch. There is also a large focus here on Norwegian art since the mid-18th century. ⊠ *Rasmus Meyers Allé 3,* ☎ *55/56–80–00.* 🎟 *NKr35.* ☉ *Mid-May–mid-Sept., Mon.–Sat. 11–4, Sun. noon–3; rest of yr, Tues.–Sun. noon–3.*

42 **Vestlandske Kunstindustrimuseum (West Norway Museum of Applied Art).** Seventeenth- and 18th-century Bergen silversmiths were renowned throughout Scandinavia for their heavy, elaborate Baroque designs. Tankards embossed with flower motifs or inlaid with coins form a rich display. ⊠ *Permanenten, Nordahl Bruns Gt. 9,* ☎ *55/32–51–08.* 🎟 *NKr 20.* ☉ *Mid-May–mid-Sept., Tues.–Sun. 11–4; rest of yr, Tues.–Sun. noon–3, Thurs. noon–6 PM.*

Troldhaugen, Fantoft, Lysøen, and Ulriken

A GOOD DRIVE

If you get your fill of Bergen's city life, you can head out for the countryside to four of the area's interesting, but low-key attractions. Follow Route 1 (Nesttun/Voss) out of town about 5 kilometers (3 miles) to **Troldhaugen** ㊻, the villa where Edvard Grieg spent 22 years of his life. After you've spent some time wandering the grounds of Troldhaugen, head for **Lysøen** ㊼, the Victorian dream castle of Norwegian violinist Ole Bull. Getting here is a 30-minute trek by car and ferry, but it's well worth the effort. From Troldhaugen, get back on Route 1 or Route 586 to Fana, over Fanafjell to Sørestraumen. Follow signs to Buena Kai. From here, take the ferry over to Lysøen. After visiting Lysøen, on your way back to Bergen, you can see the **Fantoft Stavkirke** ㊽, which unfortunately was badly damaged in a fire in 1992. It is under reconstruction, though, but may take years to complete. Lastly, end your day with a hike up **Ulriken** ㊾, the tallest of Bergen's seven mountains. If you're too worn out from your day of sightseeing, but still want take in the view from the top, you can always take the Ulriken cable car.

TIMING

Driving time (or bus time) will consume much of your day on this tour. However, the landscape is beautiful, so visiting these sights is a pleasant way to explore Bergen's environs with some direction. You can enjoy the day at a leisurely pace, but note closing times below. Try to take your tour on a Monday or Friday so you can end your day with a "Music on the Mountain" concert at Ulriken.

SIGHTS TO SEE

★ ㊽ **Fantoft Stavkirke (Fantoft Stave Church).** Originally built in the early 12th century in Sognefjord, this ancient wooden stave church was later moved to its present site. Stave churches are unique to Norway, representing a sort of first step, spiritually and architecturally, into Christianity, without complete relinquishment of pagan beliefs. They also parallel Viking ships, as they are built of strips of wood laid edge to edge rather than in log-cabin style. (The church is presently being re-built after a fire, believed to be arson, in 1992.) From *sentral bystasjo-nen* (the main bus station next to the railway station), take any bus leaving from platform 19, 20, or 21. ⊠ *Paradis.* ⊙ *Mid-May–mid-Sept.*

47 **Lysøen.** Ole Bull, not as well known as some of Norway's other cul-tural luminaries, was a virtuoso violinist and patron of visionary di-mension. In 1850, after failing to establish a "New Norwegian Theater" in America, he founded the National Theater in Norway. He then chose the young, unknown playwright Henrik Ibsen to write full-time for the theater and later encouraged and promoted another neophyte—15-year-old Edvard Grieg.

Built in 1873, this villa, complete with an onion dome, gingerbread gables, curved staircase, and cutwork trim just about everywhere, has to be seen to be believed. Inside, the music room is a frenzy of filigree carving, fretwork, braided and twisted columns, and gables with in-tricate openwork in the supports, all done in knotty pine. Bull's de-scendants donated the house to the national preservation trust in 1973. The entrance fee includes a guided tour of the villa.

The ferry, *Ole Bull,* leaves from Buena Kai on the hour Monday–Sat-urday noon–3 and Sunday 11–4; the last ferry leaves Lysøen Mon-day–Saturday at 4, Sunday at 5; return fare is NKr30. By bus, take the "Lysefjordruta" bus from gate 20 at the main bus station to Buena Kai. From here take the *Ole Bull* ferry. Return bus fare is NKr68. ☎ *56/30–90–77.* 🎫 *NKr25.* ⊙ *Mid-May–late Aug., Mon.–Sat. noon–4, Sun. 11–5; Sept., Sun. noon–4.*

46 **Troldhaugen (Troll Hill).** Composer Edvard Grieg began his musical ca-reer under the tutelage of his mother, then went on to study music in Leipzig and Denmark, where he met his future wife, Nina, a Danish soprano. Even in his early compositions, his own unusual chord pro-gressions fused with elements of Norwegian folk music. Norway and its landscape were always an inspiration to Grieg, and nowhere is this more in evidence than at his villa by Nordåsvannet, where he and his wife, Nina, lived for 22 years beginning in about 1885. An enchant-ing white clapboard house with restrained green gingerbread trim, it served as a salon and gathering place for many Scandinavian artists and brims with paintings, prints, and other memorabilia. On Grieg's desk you'll see a small red troll—which, it is said, he religiously bade good night before he went to sleep. The house also contains his Stein-way piano, which is still used for special concerts. Behind the grounds, at the edge of the fjord, you'll find a sheer rock face that was blasted open to provide a burial place for the couple. In 1985 **Troldsalen** (Troll Hall), with seating for 200 people, was built for concerts. Catch a bus from platform 19, 20, or 21 at the bus station, and get off at Hopsbroen, turn right, walk 200 yards, turn left on Troldhaugsveien, and follow the signs for 20 minutes. ☎ *55/91–17–91.* 🎫 *NKr40.* ⊙ *May–Sept., daily 9–5:30; Oct.–Nov. and Apr., Mon.–Sat. 10–2, Sun. 10–4; Feb.–Mar., weekdays 10–2, Sun. 10–4.*

49 **Ulriken Mountain.** Admire summer sunsets from the highest of the seven Bergen mountains—Ulriken—while enjoying free "Music on the Moun-tain" concerts Mondays and Fridays at 7 PM, May through Septem-ber. The Ulriken cable car will transport you up the mountain. You can catch the cable car near Haukeland hospital. It's best reached near the Montana Youth Hostel (Buses 2 or 4). ⊠ *Ulriken 1, 5009 Bergen,* ☎ *55/29–31–60.* ⊙ *The cable car operates 9–9, 10–5 during the win-ter.* 🎫 *NKr50.*

Dining

Among the most characteristic of Bergen dishes is a fresh, perfectly poached whole salmon, served with new potatoes and parsley-butter sauce. To try another typical Bergen repast, without the typical bill, stroll among the stalls at Fisketorvet (the fish market), where you can munch bagsful of pink shrimp, heart-shaped fish cakes, and round buns topped with salmon. Top it off with another local specialty, a *skillings-bolle*, a big cinnamon roll, sometimes with a custard center but most authentic without.

$$$$ ✕ **Lucullus.** Although the decor seems a bit out of kilter—modern art matched with lace doilies and boardroom chairs—the food in this restaurant is always good. This is a good place to splurge on the four-course meal that's offered. ⊠ *Hotel Neptun, Walckendorfsgt. 8,* ☎ *55/90–10–00. Jacket and tie. AE, DC, MC, V. No lunch. Closed Sun.*

$$$–$$$$ ✕ **Finnegaardstuene.** This classic Norwegian restaurant near Bryggen
★ has four small rooms that make for a snug, intimate atmosphere. Some of the timber interior dates from the 18th century. There's a seven-course gourmet menu. The emphasis here is on seafood, although the venison and reindeer are excellent. Traditional Norwegian desserts such as cloudberries and cream are irresistible. ⊠ *Rosenkrantzgt. 6,* ☎ *55/31–36–20. AE, DC, MC, V. Closed Sun.*

$$$ ✕ **To Kokker.** The name means "two cooks," and that's what there are.
★ Ranked among Bergen's best restaurants by many, this spot is on Bryggen, in a 300-year-old building complete with crooked floors. Try the roasted reindeer or the marinated salmon. Desserts use local fruit. ⊠ *Enhjørningsgården,* ☎ *55/32–28–16. Reservations essential. AE, DC, MC, V. No lunch. Closed Sun.*

$$ ✕ **Bryggestuen & Bryggeloftet.** It's always full, upstairs and down. The menu's the same in both places, but only the first floor is authentically old. Poached halibut served with boiled potatoes and cucumber salad, a traditional favorite, is the specialty, but there's also sautéed ocean catfish with mushrooms and shrimp, and grilled lamb fillet. ⊠ *Bryggen 11,* ☎ *55/31–06–30. AE, DC, MC, V.*

$$ ✕ **Munkestuen Café.** With its five tables and red-and-white-check
★ tablecloths, this mom-and-pop place looks more Italian than Norwegian, but locals regard it as a hometown legend—make reservations as soon as you get into town, if not before (they can be booked up to four weeks in advance). Try the monkfish with hollandaise sauce or the fillet of roe deer with morels. ⊠ *Klostergt. 12,* ☎ *55/90–21–49. Reservations essential. AE, DC, MC, V. Closed weekends and 3 wks in July. No lunch.*

$ ✕ **Baker Brun.** This Bergen institution, now in several locations, is great
★ for a quick bite. Try *skillingsbolle,* a roll with cinnamon and sugar, or *skolebrød,* a sweet roll with custard and coconut icing—both are scrumptious. For something less sweet, this bakery serves fresh-baked wheat rolls with Norwegian *hvit ost* (white cheese) and cucumber. ⊠ *Zachariasbryggen,* ☎ *55/31–51–08; Søstergården, Bryggen* ☎ *55/31–65–12.*

$ ✕ **Børs Café.** What began as a beer hall in 1894 is now more of a pub, with hearty homemade food at reasonable prices. The corned beef with potato dumplings is served only on Thursday and Friday; meat cakes with stewed peas and fried flounder plus the usual open-face sandwiches are always on the menu. *Børs* means stock market, and the price of beer fluctuates according to demand. ⊠ *Strandgt. 15,* ☎ *55/32–47–19. Reservations not accepted. No credit cards.*

$ ✕ **Kjøbmandsstuen** and **Augustus.** You can't beat these two cafeterias under the same management for lunch or for cake and coffee in the afternoon. Vegetarians will be impressed by the number of salads and quiches, in addition to pâté and open-faced sandwiches. ⊠ *Kjø-mandsstuen: C. Sundtsgt. 24,* ☎ *55/30–40–00. Augustus: Galleriet,* ☎ *55/32–35–25. AE, DC, MC, V.*

Lodging

From June 20 through August 10, special summer double-room rates are available in 21 Bergen hotels; rooms can only be reserved 48 hours in advance. In the winter, weekend specials are often a fraction of the weekday rates, which are geared toward business travelers. The tourist office (☎ 55/32–14–80) will assist in finding accommodations in hotels, guest houses, or private houses.

$$–$$$ 🏨 **Hotel Admiral.** This dockside warehouse from 1906, right on the
★ water across Vågen from Bryggen, was converted into a hotel in 1987. The building is geometric Art Nouveau, and although the small rooms are ordinary, the larger rooms overlooking the harbor have some of the best nighttime views in town. The harborside restaurant, Emily, has a small but good buffet table. ⊠ *C. Sundts Gt. 9, 5004,* ☎ *55/23–64–00,* 𝔽𝔸𝕏 *55/23–64–64. 143 rooms and 12 suites. Restaurant, bar. AE, DC, MC, V.*

$$–$$$ 🏨 **Hotel Norge.** Other hotels come and go, but the Norge stays. It's an established luxury hotel in the center of town, right by the park. The architecture is standard modern, with large rooms that blend contemporary Scandinavian comfort with traditional warmth. The warm, thick *dyner* (featherbed-like comforters) are so comfy, it's hard to get out of bed in the mornings. ⊠ *Ole Bulls Pl. 4, 5012,* ☎ *55/21–01–00,* 𝔽𝔸𝕏 *55/21–02–99. 348 rooms, 12 suites. 4 restaurants, 2 bars, indoor pool, health club, nightclub, meeting rooms. AE, DC, MC, V.*

$$–$$$ 🏨 **Radisson SAS Hotel.** This popular Bergen hotel opened in 1982 behind the famous buildings at Bryggen on the site of old warehouses. Ravaged by nine fires since 1170, the warehouses have been rebuilt each time in the same style, which SAS has incorporated into the architecture of the hotel. The rooms are rather small but comfortable. ⊠ *Bryggen, 5003,* ☎ *55/54–30–00,* 𝔽𝔸𝕏 *55/32–48–08. 273 rooms, 7 suites. 2 restaurants, bar, pub, indoor pool, sauna, health club, dance club, convention center. AE, DC, MC, V.*

$–$$ 🏨 **Augustin Hotel.** This small but comfortable hotel in the center of town has been restored to its original late–Art Nouveau character. ⊠ *C. Sundts Gt. 22–24, 5004,* ☎ *55/23–00–25,* 𝔽𝔸𝕏 *55/30–40–10. 38 rooms. Meeting rooms. AE, DC, MC, V.*

$–$$ 🏨 **Bryggen Orion.** Facing the harbor in the center of town, the Orion is within walking distance of many of Bergen's most famous sights, including Bryggen and Rosenkrantztårnet. The rooms are decorated in warm, sunny colors. The open fireplace at the bar is cozy in the winter. ⊠ *Bradbenken 3,* ☎ *55/31–80–80,* 𝔽𝔸𝕏 *55/32–94–14. 229 rooms. Restaurant, bar, nightclub. AE, DC, MC, V.*

$–$$ 🏨 **Hotel Park Pension.** Near the university, this small family-run hotel is in a well-kept Victorian building. Both the public rooms and the guest rooms are furnished with antiques. It's a 10-minute walk from downtown. Don't oversleep and miss the simple and delicious Norwegian breakfast—fresh bread, jams, cheeses, and cereal—included in the price. ⊠ *Harald Hårfagres Gt. 35, 5000,* ☎ *55/32–09–60,* 𝔽𝔸𝕏 *55/31–03–34. 21 rooms. Breakfast room. AE, DC, MC, V.*

$ 🏨 **Fantoft Sommerhotell.** This student dorm, 6 kilometers (3½ miles) from downtown, becomes a hotel from May 20 to August 20. Family rooms are available. Accommodation is simple but adequate. Take bus No. 18, 19, or 20 to Fantoft. ⊠ *5036 Fantoft,* ☎ *55/27–60–00,* 𝔽𝔸𝕏 *55/27–60–30. 72 rooms. Restaurant. AE, DC, MC, V.*

Nightlife and the Arts

Nightlife

BARS AND CLUBS

Most nightlife centers on the harbor area. **Zachariasbryggen** is a restaurant and entertainment complex right on the water. **Engelen** (the Angel) at the SAS Royal Hotel attracts a mixed weekend crowd when it blasts hip-hop, funk, and rock. The **Hotel Norge** piano bar and disco are more low-key, with an older crowd. **Dickens** (✉ 8–10 Ole Bulls Pl., ☎ 55/90–07–60), across from the Hotel Norge, is a relaxed meeting place for an afternoon or evening drink. Right next to Dickens is **Losjehavn** (☎ 55/90–08–20), an outdoor patio especially popular in summer. **Wesselstuen**, also on Ole Bull Plads (☎ 55/90–08–20) is a cozy place where you'll find students and the local intelligentsia. **Café Opera** (✉ 24 Engen, ☎ 55/23–03–15) is a sumptuous place to go for a drink or a coffee. It's very comfortable and great for people-watching and whiling away the time. **Banco Rotto** (✉ Vågsalmenningen 16, ☎ 55/32–75–20), in a 19th century bank building, is one of Bergen's most popular watering holes, for young and old alike. The café here—one of the fanciest in town—serves delicious desserts.

Bergen has an active gay community with clubs and planned events. **Homofil Bevegelse** (✉ Gay Movement, Nygårdsgt. 2A, ☎ 55/31–21–39) is open Sunday 2–8 PM. **Café Finken** (✉ Nygårdsgt. 2A, ☎ 55/31–21–39) is open daily until 1 AM.

LIVE MUSIC

Bergensers love jazz, and **Bergen Jazz Festival** (✉ Georgernes Verft 3, 5011 Bergen, ☎ 55/32–09–76) is held here during the third week of August. **Bergen Jazz Forum** (same address) is *the* place, both in winter and summer, when there are nightly jazz concerts. For rock, **Hulen** (the Cave) (✉ Olav Ryesvei 47, ☎ 55/32–32–87) has live music on weekends.

The Arts

Bergen is known for its **Festspillene** (International Music Festival), held each year during the last week of May and the beginning of June. It features famous names in classical music, jazz, ballet, the arts, and theater. Tickets are available from the Festival Office at **Grieghallen** (✉ Lars Hilles Gt. 3, 5015, ☎ 55/21–61–00).

During the summer, twice a week, the **Bjørgvin folk dance group** performs a one-hour program of traditional dances and music from rural Norway at Bryggens Museum. Tickets are sold at the tourist office and at the door. ✉ *Bryggen,* ☎ *55/31–67–10.* ☞ *NKr70. Performances June –Aug., Tues. and Thurs. at 8:30.*

A more extensive program, **Fana Folklore 1997** is an evening of folklore, with traditional wedding food, dances, and folk music, plus a concert, at the 800-year-old Fana Church. The event is now in its 40th season. ✉ *A/S Kunst (Art Association) Torgalmenning 9,* ☎ *55/91–52–40; Fana Folklore, 5047 Fana,* ☎ *55/91–52–40.* ☞ *NKr200 (includes dinner).* ☉ *June–Aug., Mon., Tues., Thurs., and Fri. at 7 pm (for groups 6:45 PM). Return trip back to the city center by 10:30 PM.*

Concerts are held at **Troldhaugen,** home of composer Edvard Grieg (☞ Exploring, *above*), all summer. Tickets are sold at the tourist office or at the door. Performances are given June 26–August 29, Wednesday and Sunday at 7:30, Saturday at 2, and September–October, Sunday at 2.

Outdoor Activities and Sports

Below is a sampling of activities for the Bergen area, but outdoors lovers should be aware that the city is within easy reach of the Hardangervidda, the country's great plateau, which offers limitless outdoor possibilities (☞ Hardangervidda *in* Interior Norway, *below*).

Fishing

The **Bergen Angling Association** (✉ Fosswinckelsgt. 37, ☎ 55/32–11–64) provides information on permits; it's closed in July. Among the many charters in the area, the ***Fiskestrilen*** (☎ 56/33-75–00 or 56/33–87–40) offers evening fishing tours from Glesvaer on the island of Sotra, about an hour's drive from Bergen, where you can catch coal fish, cod, mackerel, or haddock. On the sail home, they'll cook part of the catch.

Hiking

Take the funicular up **Fløyen** (☞ Exploring, *above*), and minutes later you'll be in the midst of a forest. For a simple map of the mountain, ask at the tourist office for the cartoon "Gledeskartet" map, which outlines 1½- to 5-kilometer (1- to 3-mile) hikes. **Mount Ulriken** (☞ Exploring, *above*) is popular with walkers. Maps of the many walking-tour opportunities around Bergen are available from bookstores and from **Bergens Turlag** (touring club; Tverrgata 2–4, 5017 Bergen, ☎ 55/32–22–30), which arranges hikes and maintains cabins for hikers.

In the archipelago west of Bergen, there are many hiking options, ranging from the simple path between Morland and Fjell to the more rugged mountain climb at Haganes. For details, contact the Sund Tourist Office (✉ 5382 Skogsvåg, ☎ 56/33–75–00).

Yachting

The **Bergen Yachting Club** (55/22–65–45) has its harbor at Hjellestad, about a half-hour bus ride from the city bus station. If you want to do more than ogle the boats, however, the 100-year-old Hardanger yacht *Mathilde* (✉ Stiftinga Hardangerjakt, 5600 Kaldestad, ☎ 56/55–22–77), with the world's largest authentic yacht rigging, does both one- and several-day trips, as well as coastal safaris.

Shopping

Shopping Centers

Sundt City (✉ Torgalmenningen 14, ☎ 55/31–80–20) is the closest you'll get to a traditional department store in Norway, with everything from fashion to interior furnishings. However, you'll find better value for your kroner if you shop around for souvenirs and sweaters. **Kløverhuset** (✉ Strandkaien 10, ☎ 55/21–37–90), between Strandgaten and the fish market, has 40 shops under one roof. You'll find outlets for Dale knitwear, souvenirs, leathers, and fur. **Galleriet,** on Torgalmenningen, is the best of the downtown shopping malls. Here you will find Christiana Glasmagasin and more exclusive small shops along with all the chains, like **Hennes & Mauritz** and **Lindex. Bystasjonen,** by the bus terminal, is small but conveniently located for last-minute items.

Specialty Stores

ANTIQUES

There are many antiques shops on **Øvregaten,** and especially around Fløybanen. **Cecilie Antikk** (✉ Kong Oscarsgt. 32, ☎ 55/96–17–53) deals primarily in antique Norwegian glass and ceramics and old and rare books.

GLASS, CERAMICS, PEWTER

Viking Design (✉ Torgalmenning 1, ☎ 55/31–05–20) specializes in pewter—you'll find that some pieces can be picked up quite reasonably. **Tilbords, Bergens Glasmagasin** (⊠ Olav Kyrresgt. 9, ☎ 55/31–69–67) claims to have the town's largest selection of glass and china, both Scandinavian and European designs. **Prydkunst-Hjertholm** (⊠ Olav Kyrresgt. 7, ☎ 55/31–70–27) is the ideal shop for gifts; most everything is of Scandinavian design. You'll find pottery and glassware of the highest quality—much of it from local artisans.

HANDICRAFTS

Husfliden (⊠ Vågsalmenning 3, ☎ 55/31–78–70) caters to all your handicrafts needs, including a department for Norwegian national costumes. Look for the handwoven textiles and hand-carved wood items. **Berle** (⊠ Bryggen 5, ☎ 55/31–73–00) has a huge selection of traditional knitwear and other souvenir items—don't miss the troll cave. Downstairs is an interior-design shop with Scandinavian furniture. There's also an automatic foreign-money exchange machine.

JEWELRY

Theodor Olsens Eftf (⊠ Ole Bulls Pl. 7, ☎ 55/23–18–85) stocks silver jewelry of distinctive Norwegian and Scandinavian design.

Bergen A to Z

Arriving and Departing

BY BOAT

Boats have always been Bergen's lifeline to the world. **Color Line** (⊠ Skuteviksboder 1–2, 5023, ☎ 55/54–86–60) ferries serve Newcastle. Others connect with the Shetland and Faroe islands, Denmark, Scotland, and Iceland. All dock at Skoltegrunnskaien.

Express boats between Bergen and Stavanger run three times daily on weekdays, twice daily on weekends, for the four-hour trip. All arrive and depart from Strandkai Terminalen (☎ 55/23–87–80).

The *Hurtigruten* (⊠ Coastal Express, Veiten 2B, 5012, ☎ 55/23–07–90) departs daily from Frielenes Quay, Dock H, for the 11-day round-trip to Kirkenes in the far north.

BY BUS

The summer-only bus from Oslo to Bergen, **Geiteryggekspressen** (literally, "Goat-Back Express," referring to the tunnel through Geiteryggen Mountain, which looks like a goat's back, between Hol and Aurland) leaves the Nor-Way bus terminal (⊠ Galleri Oslo, ☎ 22/17–52–90) at 8 AM and arrives in Bergen 12½ hours later. Buses also connect Bergen with Trondheim and Ålesund. Western Norway is served by several bus companies, which use the station at Strømgaten 8 (☎ 55/32–67–80).

BY CAR

Bergen is 485 kilometers (300 miles) from Oslo. Route 7 is good almost as far as Eidfjord at the eastern edge of the Hardangerfjord, but then it deteriorates considerably. The ferry along the way, crossing the Hardanger Fjord from Brimnes to Bruravik, runs continually 5 AM to midnight and takes 10 minutes. At Granvin, 12 kilometers (7 miles) farther north, Route 7 joins Route E68, which is an alternative route from Oslo, crossing the Sognefjorden from Refsnes to Gudvangen. From Granvin to Bergen, Route E68 hugs the fjord part of the way, making for spectacular scenery.

Driving from Stavanger to Bergen involves from two to four ferries and a long journey packed with breathtaking scenery. The Stavanger tourist information office can help plan the trip and reserve ferry space.

Flesland Airport is 20 kilometers (12 miles) south of Bergen. **SAS** (☎ 55/99–76–10) and **Braathens SAFE** (☎ 55/23–55–23) are the main domestic carriers. **British Airways** (serviced by Braathens SAFE) and **Lufthansa** (☎ 55/99–82–30) also serve Flesland.

Between the Airport and Downtown: Flesland is a 30-minute bus ride from the center of Bergen at off-peak hours. The **Flybussen** (Airport Bus) departs three times per hour (less frequently on weekends) from the SAS Royal Hotel via Braathens SAFE's office at the Hotel Norge and from the bus station. Tickets cost NKr35.

Driving from Flesland to Bergen is simple, and the road is well marked. Bergen has an electronic toll ring surrounding it, so any vehicle entering the city weekdays between 6 AM and 10 PM has to pay NKr5. There is no toll in the other direction.

A taxi stand is outside the Arrivals exit. The trip into the city costs about NKr200.

BY TRAIN

The **Bergensbanen** has five departures daily, plus an additional one on Sunday, in both directions on the Oslo–Bergen route; it is widely acknowledged as one of the most beautiful train rides in the world. Trains leave from Oslo S Station for the 7½- to 8½-hour journey. For information about trains out of Bergen, call ☎ 55/96–60–50.

Getting Around

The best way to see the small center of Bergen is on foot. Most sights are within walking distance of the marketplace.

BY BUS

Tourist tickets for 48 hours of unlimited travel within the town boundaries cost NKr70, payable on the yellow city buses. All buses serving the Bergen region depart from the central bus station at Strømgaten 8 (☎ 55/32–67–80). Buses between the main post office (Småstrandgt. and Olav Kyrres Gt.) and the railway station are free.

BY CAR

Downtown Bergen is enclosed by an inner ring road. The area within is divided into three zones, which are separated by ONE WAY and DO NOT ENTER signs. To get from one zone to another, return to the ring road and drive to an entry point into the desired zone. It's best to leave your car at a parking garage (the Birkebeiner Senter is on Rosenkrantz Gate, and there is a lot near the train station) and walk. You pay a NKr5 toll every time you drive into the city—but driving out is free.

BY TAXI

Taxi ranks are located in strategic places downtown. All taxis are connected to the central dispatching office (☎ 55/99–77–00) and can be booked in advance (☎ 55/99–77–10).

Contacts and Resources

CHANGING MONEY

Outside normal banking hours, the Tourist Information Office on Bryggen can change money. Post offices exchange money and are open Monday through Wednesday and Friday 8 to 5, Thursday 8 to 6, and Saturday 9 to 2.

DENTISTS

The dental emergency center at Lars Hilles Gate 30 (☎ 55/32–11–20) is open daily 10–11 AM and 7–9 PM.

The outpatient center at Lars Hilles Gate 30 (☎ 55/32–11–20), near Grieghallen, is open 24 hours.

GUIDED TOURS
Bergen is the guided-tour capital of Norway because it is the starting point for most fjord tours. Tickets for all tours are available from the tourist office.

Fjord Tours: Bergen is the much-acclaimed "Gateway to the Fjords," with dozens of fjord-tour possibilities. The following is only meant as a sampling; check with the tourist office (☞ *below*) for additional recommendations. The ambitious all-day **"Norway-in-a-Nutshell"** bus-train-boat tour (you can book through the tourist office) goes through Voss, Flåm, Myrdal, and Gudvangen—truly a breathtaking trip—and is the best way to see a lot in a short amount of time.

Traveling by boat is an advantage because the contrasts between the fjords and mountains are greatest at water level, and the boats are comfortable and stable (the water is practically still), so seasickness is rare. Stops are frequent, and all sights are explained. **Fjord Sightseeing** (☎ 55/31–43–20) offers a four-hour local fjord tour. **Fylkesbaatane** (County Boats) **i Sogn og Fjordane** (☎ 55/32–40–15) has several combination tours. Tickets are sold at the tourist office (☞ *below*) and at the quay. Students receive a 25% discount for most tours.

Orientation Tours: Bergen Guided Tours (☎ 55/28–13–30 or 55/96–55–00) offers four city tours departing from Hotel Norge, including one to Edvard Grieg's home and the Fantoft Stave Church. The excellent **Bryggen Guiding** (1½ hours, June–Aug., ☎ 55/31–67–10) offers a historic tour of the buildings at Bryggen, as well as entrance to Bryggens Museum, the Hanseatic Museum, and Schøtstuene after the tour, conducted by knowledgeable guides. **Bergens-Expressen** (☎ 55/18–10–19), a "train on tires," leaves from Torgalmenningen for a one-hour ride around the center of town, summer only.

LATE-NIGHT PHARMACIES
Apoteket Nordstjernen (☎ 55/31–68–84), by the bus station, is open daily from 7:30 AM to midnight, Sundays from 8:30 AM.

OPENING AND CLOSING TIMES
Most shops are open Monday–Wednesday and Friday 9–5. On Thursday, as well as Friday for some shops, the hours are 9–7. On Saturday shops are open 9–3. The shopping centers are open weekdays 9–8 and Saturdays 9–6.

PASSES
The 24-hour **Bergen Card,** which costs NKr110 (NKr170 for 48 hours), gives free admission to most museums and attractions, and rebates of 25% to 50% off sightseeing, rental cars, and transportation to and from Bergen. It is available at the tourist office and in most hotels.

VISITOR INFORMATION
The **Tourist Information Office** at Bryggen (☎ 55/32–14–80), by the wharf, has brochures and maps and can arrange for accommodations and sightseeing. There is also a currency exchange.

INTERIOR NORWAY: THE HALLINGDAL VALLEY TO HARDANGERFJORD

Norway's interior between Oslo and Bergen is a land of superlatives—the tallest peaks, the biggest national park, and the highest mountain plateau in Europe. There are several varied national parks in this region, and the southern part of Norway's interior, around Hardangervidda, has one of the most popular. It's prime vacation land for wilderness-sports lovers, with fishing, canoeing, rafting, hiking, and horseback riding over the plateau in the summer and skiing, particularly on the slopes of Geilo, in winter.

Hallingdal Valley

120 km (74.5 mi) from Oslo; 92 km (57 mi) from Drammen to Nesbyen.

Route 7 from Drammen winds through the historic Hallingdal Valley, which is lined with small farming communities and ski resorts. Hallingdal is known for its many well-preserved wooden log buildings. **Nesbyen,** a small town in the heart of the valley, has a folk museum as well as many campsites and a youth hostel.

En Route   About 21 kilometers (13 miles) from Nesbyen you'll come across the small community of **Gol.** This town is popular with campers in summer and skiers in winter who throng the mountains to the north and east of Gol during ski season.

Hemsedal

🔟 *35 km (21.5 mi) from Gol.*

Spring, summer, winter, or fall, the valley of Hemsedal, and its surrounding area, is gorgeous. The clear streams, blue lakes, and striking mountains offer hundreds of miles of hiking along with alpine and cross-country trails. In fact, here in Hemsedal, Norwegian World Cup skiers often practice in the top local ski center (☞ Skiing, *below*).

Outdoor Activities and Sports
SKIING

Hemsedal Skisenter (☎ 32/06–22–08): 34 kilometers (21 miles) of alpine slopes, 175 kilometers (108 miles of cross-country trails); 17 ski lifts. The **Vinterlandkortet ski pass** is accepted at all 71 ski slopes in Geilo, Hemsedal, Uvdal, and Ål and is available at ski centers and tourist offices.

Torpo

🔟 *52 km (32 mi) from Hemsedal.*

Driving from Gol to Geilo, you'll pass through the tiny town of Torpo, known for its church, presumably the oldest building in Hallingdal. **Torpo stave church** is believed to have been built in the late 12th century. Its colorful painted ceiling is decorated with scenes from the life of Saint Margaret. ✉ 3579 Torpo. ☉ June–Aug., daily 9:30–5:30.

Geilo

🔟 *35 kilometers (21 miles) west of Torpo; 251 km (155.6 mi) from Oslo; 256 km (159 mi) from Bergen.*

Geilo, population 3,500, is dead-center between Bergen and Oslo. The country's most popular winter resort, it often draws more than a million visitors a year from throughout northern Europe and Scandinavia to its alpine slopes and cross-country trails; many people ski directly from their hotels and cabins. Recently Geilo has become a popular summer destination, with fishing, boating, hiking, and riding—although, admittedly, it still looks like a winter resort minus the snow.

Mountains and Valleys of the Interior

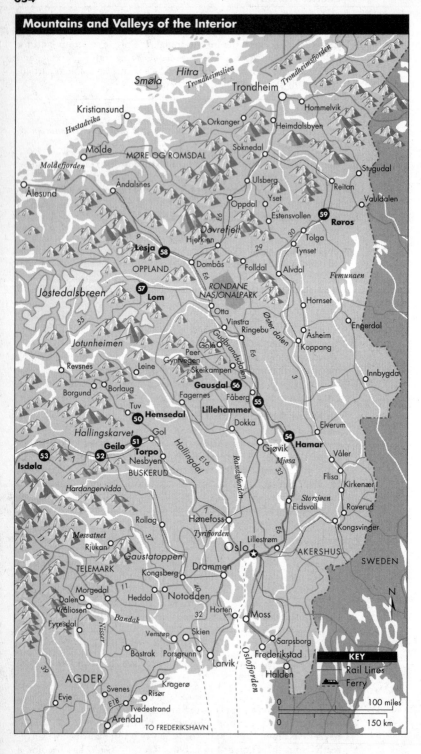

Smøla

Hitra

Trondheimslia

Trondheim

Trondheimsfjorden

Hommelvik

Kristiansund

Hustadvika

Orkanger

Heimdalsbyen

Soknedal

Molde

MØRE OG ROMSDAL

Moldefjorden

Åndalsnes

Ulsberg

Stygudal

Ålesund

Oppdal

Yset

Reitan

Vauldalen

Estensvollen

Dovrefjell

Hjerkinn

Røros

Lesja

Dombås

Folldal

Tolga

OPPLAND

Tynset

Jostedalsbreen

Lom

RONDANE
NASJONALPARK

Alvdal

Femunaen

Otta

Hornset

Jotunheimen

Vinstra

Engerdal

Gola

Ringebu

Åsheim

Revsnes

Peer
Gynt vegen

Østerdalen

Leine

Skeikampen

Koppang

Borgund

Borlaug

Tuv

Gausdal

Fagernes

Faberg

Innbygda

Hemsedal

Lillehammer

Gol

Hallingkarvet

Dokka

Elverum

Geilo

Torpo

Hamar

Isdøla

Nesbyen

Gjøvik

Våler

BUSKERUD

Hallingdal

Randsfjorden

Mjøsa

Flisa

Hardangervidda

Kirkenær I

Rollag

Storsjøen

Roverud

Møsvatnet

Hønefoss

Eidsvoll

Rjukan

Gaustatoppen

Tyrifjorden

Kongsvinger

TELEMARK

Kongsberg

Oslo

Lillestrøm

AKERSHUS

Morgedal

Heddal

Notodden

SWEDEN

Dalen

Horten

Vråliosen

Bandak

Moss

Fyresdal

Nisser

Venstøp

Skien

Sarpsborg

Bostrak

Porsgrunn

Frederikstad

AGDER

Larvik

Halden

Evje

Svenes

Kragerø

Oslofjorden

Risør

Arendal

Tvedestrand

TO FREDERIKSHAVN

N

KEY

Rail Lines

Ferry

100 miles

150 km

Plan ahead if you want to visit at Easter, when Norwegians flock there for a final ski weekend.

On the first Saturday in August, the **Holsdagen** festival presents folk music and a traditional wedding ceremony in the **Hol Stave Church** and **Hol Folkemuseum** (✉ Hol Kommune, Kulturkontoret, 3576 Hol, ☎ 32/08–81–40).

Dining and Lodging

$$$ ✕🏨 **Dr. Holms Hotell.** Truly a place to see and be seen (which means
★ it can be quite a scene), Holms Hotell is among Norway's top resort hotels. Chef Jim Weiss has made the gourmet restaurant (not to be confused with the dining room) worth a special trip. Don't miss the game sausages, which are full of flavor, and the butterscotch pudding with crunchy topping is sensational. An après-ski stop at the bar-lounge is a must. ✉ 3580 Geilo, ☎ 32/09–06–22, FAX 32/09–16–20. 124 rooms. Restaurant, 3 bars, 2 indoor pools, exercise room, hot tub, sauna, meeting rooms. AE, DC, MC, V.

Outdoor Activities and Sports

RAFTING AND CANOEING

In Geilo they've combined rafting and canoeing with skiing, outfitting rubber rafts with a wood rudder and taking off down the slopes for a bracing, if peculiar, swoosh. Contact the tourist board for details. **Flaate Opplevelser** (☎ 61/23–50–00) and **Norwegian Wildlife and Rafting** (☎ 61/23–87–27) also have trips in the Sjoa and Dagali areas.

SKIING

Just to the north, between Bergen and Oslo, is **Geilo Skiheiser** (☎ 32/09–03–33) with 24 kilometers (15 miles) of alpine slopes, 130 kilometers (81 miles) of cross-country trails; 18 lifts; and also a ski-board tunnel. Among the area's other four ski centers, **Vestlia** (☎ 32/09–01–88), west of the Ustedalsfjord, is a good choice for families, as children can play under the guidance of the Troll Klub while their parents ski; **Halstensgård** (☎ 32/09–10–20) and **Slaatta** (☎ 32/09–17–10) have a range of alpine and cross-country trails; and **Havsdalsenteret** (☎ 32/09–17–77) attracts a young crowd to its long alpine slopes. One ski pass gives access to all lifts in all five centers for NKr185. The **Vinterlandkortet ski pass** is accepted at all 71 ski slopes in Geilo, Hemsedal, Uvdal, and Ål and is available at ski centers and tourist offices.

Shopping

Brusletto & Co. (☎ 32/09–02–00), in central Geilo, is a purveyor of high-quality hunting knives with silver-inlaid handles made from burnished metal, walnut, and rosewood. Norwegian men wear these knives, used for hunting and hiking, on their belts—something akin to jewelry.

Hardangervidda

90 km (56 mi) from Geilo to Eidfjord; Rte. 7 is the main road that crosses Hardangervidda.

Geilo is the gateway to Hardangervidda, Europe's largest mountain plateau and Norway's biggest national park—10,000 square kilometers (3,861 square miles) of unique scenery, with the largest herd of wild reindeer in Europe, lakes and streams teeming with trout and char, and home to many birds and animals on the endangered list. It also has rich and varied flora, about 450 different species. Flat in the east and at its center, the plateau is more mountainous in the west.

Hardangervidda's highest peak, **Hardangerjøkulen,** is 1,860 meters above sea level. Touring the plateau, either on horseback or on foot, you can find a trail for any level of proficiency, and along the trails, the Norwegian Touring Association (DNT) has built cabins.

Near **Hardangerjøkulen** (Hardanger Glacier), about an hour's drive north of Geilo, you can take a guided hike to the archaeological digs of 8,000-year-old Stone Age settlements. Contact the Geilo Tourist Office (☎ 32/09–13–00).

En Route   The western settlement of Finse (on the Bergen railroad), about 34 km (21 mi) from Geilo is one of the most frigid places in southern Norway, with snow on the ground as late as August. Here polar explorers Nansen and Scott tested their equipment and the snow scenes in the *Star Wars* movies were filmed. It, too, is a good starting point for tours of Hardangervidda.

If you'd like to try summer skiing, the **Finse Skisenter** (3590 Finse, ☎ 55/52–67–44) is in operation over the summer.

Isdøla

③ *72 km (44 mi) beyond Geilo; 10 km (6 mi) from Finse.*

At the western end of the *vidda* (plateau) is Isdøla, at the junction of the 1-kilometer (0.62-mile, but it seems like 10) road to Fossli and Vøringfossen (Vøring Falls), which has a 464-foot vertical drop. The road down to the valley of Måbødalen was blasted into the mountain early in the century; it has been improved steadily, and now most of the difficult parts are tunneled. Cyclists and hikers can go down the side of the mountain to the base of the falls on the original trail, with 124 swings and 1,300 steps—it takes about 30 minutes—but it's not for amateurs.

At the base of the plateau is the innermost arm of the **Hardangerfjord.** Although it's not as dramatic as some of the other fjords, it is pastoral, with royal-blue water and lush apple orchards.

Interior Norway A to Z

Arriving and Departing

BY TRAIN

The mid-region is served by the Oslo–Bergen line, which is as much an attraction as a means of transportation.

Contacts and Resources

VISITOR INFORMATION

The main tourist offices of the region are in **Geilo** (☎ 32/09–13–00); **Gol** (☎ 32/07–51–15); and **Nesbyen** (☎ 32/07–01–70).

MID-NORWAY: EIDSVOLL TO RØROS

Northward in Norway's midsection, the land turns to rolling hills and leafy forests, and the principal town, Lillehammer, attracts skiers from around the world to its slopes and trails; in 1994 it hosted the Winter Olympics. As you travel north, you'll enter Gubrandsdalen (*dal* means valley), one of the longest and most beautiful valleys in the country. Gudbrandsdalen extends from Lake Mjøsa, north of Oslo, diagonally across the country to Åndalsnes. At the base of the lake is Eidsvoll, where Norway's constitution was signed on May 17, 1814. Most visitors come to the region for the beautiful scenery and outdoor activities. Tourism in this area has increased substantially following the 1994 Winter Olympics.

At the northern end of the region is the copper-mining town of Røros—which is on UNESCO's World Heritage List—a bucolic little town that's changed little over the past 100 years. The tourist board aptly calls the triangle between Oppland and Hedmark counties, south to Lillehammer (and including Peer Gynt country, in Jotunheimen), Troll Park. The otherworldly quality of oblique northern light against wildflower-covered hills has inspired centuries of folk tales as well as artists from Wagner to Ibsen, who was awarded a government grant to scour the land for these very stories. Even today, locals claim he applied for the grant just to have the opportunity to hike the hills.

Hamar

54 *134 km (83 mi) from Oslo; 66 km (41 mi) from Eidsvoll.*

During the Middle Ages, Hamar was the seat of a bishopric; four Romanesque arches, which are part of the cathedral wall, remain the symbol of the city today. Hamar got a new lease on life in 1994 when the **Hamar Olympia Hall** played host to the speed-skating and figure-skating events of the Lillehammer Winter Olympics. The hall, designed to look like an upside-down Viking ship, was built to the highest environmental and construction standards. Contact Hamar Olympia Hall (✉ Åkersvika, 2300 Hamar, ☎ 62/51–02–25) for details on tours and sports facilities.

The **Jernbanemuseet** (Railway Museum) documents the development of rail transportation in Norway, with locomotives and rolling stock on both normal and small-gauge track. Tertittoget, NSB's last steam locomotive, gives rides from mid-May to mid-August. ✉ *Strandvn. 132,* ☎ *62/51–31–60.* ✏ *NKr25.* ☉ *June and Aug., daily 10–4; July, daily 10–6.*

Take a ride on the world's oldest paddleboat, the 130-year-old *Skibladner,* also called the "White Swan of the Mjøsa," which connects the towns along the lake. The schedule is complicated, with only three stops a week in Eidsvoll and Lillehammer but three stops daily three times a week in Gjøvik. Ask for a schedule from the tourist information or the *Skibladner* office. ✉ *Strandgt. 23, 2300 Hamar,* ☎ *62/52–70–85.* ☉ *Late June–mid-Aug. The Skibladner is available for charter late May–late Sept.*

Lillehammer

55 *60 km (37 mi) from Hamar.*

The winter-sports center of Lillehammer has 23,000 inhabitants. In preparation for the 1994 Winter Olympics, this small town built a ski-jumping arena, an ice-hockey hall, a cross-country skiing stadium, and a bobsled and luge track, in addition to other venues and accommodations. However, far-sighted planning kept expansion surprisingly minimal, ensuring that the town was not left in a state of Olympic obsolescence. After the games, which proved hugely successful, many of the structures built to house the foreign media were turned over to the regional college, and one-third of the athletes' quarters were transported to Tromsø to be used as housing.

The **Lillehammer Olympic Information Center** ensures that the memories from the winter of 1994 will be kept alive and that those who weren't there can experience something of the atmosphere of the games. Understandably, considering their achievements (the enthusiastic Norwegians topped the medals count), much attention is given to Norwegian winter sports athletes. There's a boutique with Olympic clothing and souvenirs, and a cafeteria. ✉ *Lillehammer Olympiske Informasjonssenter.*

Elevgt. 19, ☎ *61/27–75–50.* 🖃 *NKr55.* ☉ *Mid-June–mid-Aug.,
Mon.–Sat. 10–8, Sun. noon–8; rest of yr, Mon.–Sat. 10–5, Sun. 11–4.*

Kulturhuset Bankn, a magnificent, century-old bank building, is the main
locale for cultural events. It is decorated with both contemporary and
turn-of-the-century art. Check out the murals on the ceiling of the ceremonial hall. ⊠ *Kirkegt. 41,* ☎ *61/26–68–10.* 🖃 *NKr10.* ☉ *Daily
10–3. Tours by prior arrangement.*

The new **Olympiaparken** (Olympic Park) includes the Lysgårdsbakkene
ski-jumping arena, where the Winter Olympics' opening and closing
ceremonies were held. From the tower you can see the entire town. Also
in the park are **Håkons Hall,** used for ice hockey, and the **Birkebeineren Stadion (ski stadium),** which holds cross-country and biathlon
events. ⊠ *Elvegaten 19,* ☎ *61/26–07–00.* 🖃 *NKr50.*

The winter-sports facilities provide amusement all year round in Lillehammer. You can try the **Downhill and Bobsled simulator** between
Håkons Hall and Kristins Hall in the Olympic Park. It's a five-minute
ride that replicates the sensations of being on a bobsleigh. 🖃 *NKr35.*
☉ *Jan.–late June, daily 11–4; late June–mid-Aug., daily 10–7; late Aug.,
daily 11–4.*

Those over the age of 12 can try the **Bobsleigh on Wheels**—it's the real
thing with wheels instead of blades—at the Lillehammer Bobsleigh and
Luge Stadion. Speeds of 100 kilometers (60 miles) per hour are reached,
so you'll get a distinct impression of what the sport is all about. ☎
61/27–75–50. 🖃 *Arena NKr 15.* ☉ *Daily 8–8.* 🖃 *Wheeled bobsleigh
NKr120.* ☉ *Mid-June–late Aug., noon–8.*

A highlight of Lillehammer's ski year is the **Birkebeineren cross-country ski race,** which commemorates the trek of two warriors whose legs
were wrapped in birchbark (hence *birkebeiner*—birch legs), which
was customary for people who couldn't afford wool or leather leggings.
They raced across the mountains from Lillehammer to Østerdalen in
1205, carrying the 18-month-old prince Håkon Håkonsson away from
his enemies. The race attracts 6,000 entrants annually. Cartoon figures
of Viking children representing Håkon on skis and his aunt Kristin (on
ice skates) were the official mascots for the Olympic games.

Lillehammer claims fame as a cultural center as well. Sigrid Undset, who
won the Nobel Prize in literature in 1928, lived in the town for 30 years.
It is also the site of **Maihaugen,** Norway's oldest (and, according to some,
Scandinavia's largest) open-air museum, founded in 1887. The massive
collection was begun by Anders Sandvik, an itinerant dentist who accepted folksy odds and ends—and eventually entire buildings—from the
people of Gudbransdalen in exchange for repairing their teeth. Eventually Sandvik turned the collection over to the city of Lillehammer, which
provided land for the museum. ⊠ *Maihaugvn 1,* ☎ *61/28–89–00.* 🖃
NKr60. ☉ *June–Aug., daily 9–7; May and Sept., daily 10–5; Oct.–Apr.
2, Tues.–Sun. 11–4. Ticket includes guided tour.*

One of the most important art collections in Norway is housed at the
Lillehammer Bys Malerisamling (Lillehammer Art Museum). In addition to Munch pieces, the gallery has one of the largest collections of
works from the national romantic period. ⊠ *Stortorgt. 2,* ☎ *61/26–
94–44.* 🖃 *NKr30.* ☉ *Tues.–Sun. 11–4, Thurs. 11–8. Tours given
Tues.–Fri. at 1 PM, weekends at noon.*

....

OFF THE   **HUNDERFOSSEN PARK –** This amusement park takes pride in displaying
BEATEN PATH   the world's biggest troll. There's a petting zoo for small children, plenty
🐾   of rides, plus an energy center, with Epcot-influenced exhibits about oil

and gas, and a five-screen theater. The park is 13 kilometers (8 miles) north of Lillehammer. ⊠ *2638 Fåberg,* ☎ *61/27–72–22.* ⬛ *NKr150.* ⊙ *Early June–mid-Aug., daily 10–5.*

Just beyond Hunderfossen Park is **Lilleputthammer,** a miniature version of Lillehammer as it looked at the turn of the century, complete with animated figures in period dress. ⊠ *Øyer Gjestegård, 2636 Øyer,* ☎ *61/27–73–35.* ⬛ *NKr40.* ⊙ *Late June–late Aug., daily 10–7.*

Dining and Lodging

$$–$$$ ✕ **Lundegården Brasserie & Bar.** A piece of the Continent in the middle of Storgata, this restaurant is a haven where guests can enjoy a light snack in the bar area or a full meal. The varied menu offers such dishes as baked salmon with pepper-cream sauce and seasonal vegetables. No detail is overlooked, whether it's the rattan furnishings in the bar or the starched white tablecloths in the dining room. ⊠ *Storgt. 108A,* ☎ *61/26–90–22. Reservations essential. AE, DC, MC, V. No lunch.*

$$–$$$ ✕ **Nikkers Spisested.** The interior of this café and restaurant is light and airy, and the staff is service-minded. The fare is classic Norwegian with cakes, sandwiches, and hot dishes. The restaurant serves lunch specials and à la carte evening meals. ⊠ *Elvegt. 18,* ☎ *61/27–05–56. AE, DC, MC, V.*

$ ✕ **Zeki Grill og Gatekjøkken.** When your purse is empty, everything else is closed, or homesickness overcomes you, come here. A Chicago hot dog costs NKr25. ⊠ *Storgt 83,* ☎ *61/25–85–81.*

$$–$$$ 🏨 **Hammer Home Hotel.** This hotel, a member of the Home Hotel chain, is named for the original Hammer farm, which first opened its doors to guests in 1665. The Hammer Home Hotel, however, opened its doors in August 1991. The rooms are decorated in shades of green with oak furniture, both modern and rustic. Waffles, coffee, light beer, and an evening meal are included in the price. ⊠ *Storgt. 108, 2600,* ☎ *61/26–35–00,* 🖷 *61/26–37–30. 71 rooms. Lobby lounge, sauna, exercise room, meeting rooms. AE, DC, MC, V.*

$$–$$$ 🏨 **Mølla Hotell.** This converted mill houses one of Lillehammer's newer hotels. The intimate reception area on the ground floor gives the feeling of a private home. The bar, Toppen, on the top floor, has a good view of Mjøsa, the town, and the ski-jump arena. Egon, the restaurant, is on three levels linked by stairs that wind down into the basement. Try the fried fillet of catfish with shrimp and capers. ⊠ *Elvegt. 12,* ☎ *61/26–92–94,* 🖷 *61/26–92–95. 58 rooms. Bar, sauna, exercise room. AE, DC, MC, V.*

$$ 🏨 **Gjestehuset Ersgaard.** Dating from the 1500s, originally called Eiriksgård (Eirik's Farm), today this white manor house has all modern facilities but retains its homey atmosphere. The surroundings are beautiful, including views of Lillehammer and Lake Mjøsa, which can be enjoyed from the large terrace. ⊠ *Nordsetervn. 201 (at the Olympic Park),* ☎ *61/25–06–84,* 🖷 *61/25–06–84. 30 rooms, 20. Playground. AE, DC, MC, V.*

$–$$ 🏨 **Birkebeineren Hotel, Motell & Apartments.** Rooms are functional in these central accommodations. ⊠ *Olympiaparken,* ☎ *61/26–47–00,* 🖷 *61/26–47–50. 52 hotel rooms, 35 motel rooms, 40 apartments. Dining room, sauna. AE, DC, MC, V.*

$–$$ 🏨 **Dølaheimen Breiseth Hotell.** This friendly hotel is right beside the railroad station and within walking distance of shops and businesses. The Dølaheimen Kafe serves hearty Norwegian meals. ⊠ *Jernbanegt. 1–5,* ☎ *61/26–95–00,* 🖷 *61/26–95–05. 89 rooms. Bar, brasserie, sauna. AE, DC, MC, V.*

Outdoor Activities and Sports

FISHING

Within the Troll Park, the Gudbrandsdalåen is touted as one of the best-stocked rivers in the country, and the size of Mjøsa trout (locals claim 25 pounds) is legendary. For seasons, permits (you'll need both a national and a local license), and tips, call local tourist boards (☞ Visitor Information *in* Mid-Norway A to Z, *below*).

RAFTING AND CANOEING

The **Sjoa River,** close to Lillehammer, offers some of the most challenging rapids in the country. Contact **Heidal Rafting** (☎ 61/23–60–37).

SKIING

Lillehammer, the 1994 Winter Olympics town, is a major skiing center (20 kilometers [12 miles] of alpine, 400 kilometers [248 miles] of cross-country trails; 7 ski lifts). Within the Lillehammer area, there are five ski centers: **Hafjell** (☎ 61/27–70–78), 10 kilometers (6.3 miles) north, is an Olympic venue with moderately steep slopes; **Kvitfjell** (☎ 61/28–21–05), 50 kilometers (31 miles) north, another Olympic site, has some of the most difficult slopes in the world; **Skei** and **Peer Gynt** (☞ Skiing *in* Gausdal, *below*), 30 kilometers (19 miles) north and 80 kilometers (50 miles) northwest, respectively; and **Galdhøpiggen Sommerskisenter** (☞ Skiing *in* Lom, *below*), 135 kilometers (84 miles) northwest of Lillehammer. One ski-lift ticket, called a **Troll Pass** (☒ NKr175), is good for admission to all the lifts at all five sites.

Gausdal

56 *18 km (11 mi) northwest of Lillehammer.*

The composer of Norway's national anthem and the 1903 Nobel Prize winner in literature, Bjørnstjerne Bjørnson lived at **Aulestad,** in Gausdal, from 1875 until he died in 1910. After his wife, Karoline, died in 1934, their house was opened as a museum. ☒ *2620 Follebu,* ☎ *61/22–03–26.* ☒ *NKr30.* ☉ *Late May–Sept., daily 10–3:30.*

At Gausdal, just north of Lillehammer, you can turn onto the scenic, well-marked **Peer Gynt Vegen** (Peer Gynt Road), named for the real-life person behind Ibsen's character. A feisty fellow, given to tall tales, he is said to have spun yarns about his communing with trolls and riding reindeer backward. As you travel along the rolling hills sprinkled with old farmhouses and rich with views of the mountains of Rondane, Dovrefjell, and Jotunheimen, the road is only slightly narrower and just 3 kilometers (2 miles) longer than the main route. It passes two major resorts, **Skeikampen/Gausdal** and **Golå/Wadahl,** before rejoining E6 at Vinstra. Between Vinstra and Harpefoss, at the Sødorp Church, you can visit Peer Gynt's stone grave and what is said to be his old farm. Although you can walk the grounds, the 15th-century farm is privately owned.

En Route   The E6 highway passes through **Vinstra,** the village of Peer Gynt. The road continues along the great valley of the River Mjøsa, birthplace of Gudbrandsdalsost, a sweet brown goat cheese. The route offers lovely, rolling views of red farmhouses and lush green fields stretching from the valley to the mountainsides.

Dining and Lodging

$$$ ✕☒ **Golå Høyfjellshotell og Hytter.** Tucked away in Peer Gynt terri-
★   tory north of Vinstra, this peaceful hotel is furnished in Norwegian country style. The restaurant has a down-to-earth menu of fresh local fish and game, prepared simply and elegantly. ☒ *2646 Golå,* ☎ *61/29–81–09,* ᴲᴬˣ *61/29–85–40. 42 rooms. Restaurant, pool, downhill skiing, meeting rooms, children's programs. AE, DC, MC, V.*

Outdoor Activities and Sports

HIKING

You can pick up maps and the information-packed **"Peer Gynt"** pamphlet at the tourism office in Vinstra; then hike anywhere along the 50-kilometer (31-mile) circular route, passing Peer's farm, cottages, and monument. Overnighting in cabins or hotels is particularly popular on the Peer Gynt Trail, where you can walk to each of the **Peer Gynt hotels.** (✉ Box 115, N–2647 Hundorp, ☎ 61/29–66–66, FAX 61/29–66–88).

SKIING

Skei (☎ 61/22–85–55), near Gausdal, has both cross-country and alpine trails. **Peer Gynt** (☎ 61/29–85–28) has respectable downhill but is stronger as a cross-country venue. One ski-lift ticket, called a **Troll Pass** (✉ NKr175), is good for admission to lifts at five sites in the area (☞ Skiing *in* Lillehammer, *above*).

Lom

57 *At Otta, Rte. 15 turns off for the 62-km (38-mi) ride to Lom.*

Lom, in the middle of Jotunheimen national park, is a picturesque, rustic town, with log-cabin architecture, a stave church from 1170, and plenty of decorative rosemaling.

Lom Stavkirke (Lom Stave Church), a mixture of old and new construction, is on the main road. The interior, including the pulpit, a large collection of paintings, pews, windows, and the gallery, is Baroque. ☎ 61/21–12–86. ✉ NKr20. ☺ June–Aug., Mon.–Sat. 9–9, Sun. noon–5.

Dining and Lodging

$–$$ ✕🏠 **Fossheim Turisthotell.** Arne Brimi's cooking has made this hotel
★ famous. He's a self-taught champion of the local cuisine and now a household name in Norway; his dishes are based on nature's kitchen, with liberal use of game, wild mushrooms, and berries. Anything with reindeer is a treat in his hands, and his thin, crisp wafers with cloudberry parfait make a lovely dessert. ✉ 2686, ☎ 61/21–10–05, FAX 61/21–15–10. 54 rooms. Restaurant, bar. AE, DC, MC, V.

$ 🏠 **Elveseter Hotell.** About 24 kilometer (15 miles) from Lom in Bøverdalen, this family-owned hotel is like a museum. Imagine a swimming pool in a barn dating from 1579. Every room has a history, and doors and some walls have been painted by local artists. In the public rooms are museum-quality paintings and antiques. There's no place like it. 🏠 2687 Bøverdalen, ☎ 61/21–20–00, FAX 61/25–48–74. 100 rooms. 2 restaurants, bar, indoor pool, meeting rooms. No credit cards. Closed mid-Sept.–mid-May.

Outdoor Activities and Sports

DOGSLEDDING

In **Jotunheimen,** Magnar Aasheim and Kari Steinaug (✉ Sjoa Rafting, ☎ 61/23–87–50, FAX 61/23–87–51) have one of the biggest kennels in Norway, with more than 80 dogs. You can travel as a sled-bound observer or control your own team of four to six dogs, most of which are ridiculously friendly Siberian and Alaskan huskies.

HIKING

In summer you can hike single-file (for safety purposes, in case of calving or cracks) on the ice and explore ice caves on the **Galdhøpiggen** glacier. Call Lom Fjellføring (☎ 61/21–21–42) or the tourist board (☞ *below*).

NATIONAL PARKS

In this region you'll find **Ormtjernkampen,** a virgin spruce forest, and **Jotunheimen,** a rougher area spiked with glaciers, as well as Norway's highest peak, the **Galdhøpiggen.**

SKIING

To the east of the Gudbrandsdalen is the **Troll-løype** (Troll Trail), 250 kilometers (156 miles) of country trails that vein across a vast plateau that's bumped with mountains, including the Dovrefjells to the north. For information, contact the **Otta Tourist Office** (⊠ 2670 Otta, ☎ 61/23–02–44). **Beitostølen** (9 kilometers [5 miles] of downhill slopes, 150 kilometers [93 miles] of cross-country trails; 7 ski lifts), on the southern slopes of the Jotunheim range, has everything from torchlit night skiing to paragliding. **Galdhøpiggen Sommerskisenter** (2686 Bøverdalen, ☎ 61/21–21–42 or 61/21–17–50) sits on a glacier, which makes it great for summer skiing.

Lesja

58 *159 km (99 mi) from Lom.*

Upper Gudbrandsdal has breathtaking scenery. The area around Lesja is trout-fishing country; Lesjaskogvatnet, the lake, has a mouth at either end, so the current changes in the middle. The landscape becomes more dramatic with every mile as jagged rocks loom up from the river, leaving the tiny settlement of **Marstein** without sun for five months of the year.

Outdoor Activities and Sports

MOUNTAIN CLIMBING AND TOURING

From 1932 to 1953, musk ox were transported from Greenland to the Dovrefjell, where about 60 still roam—bring binoculars to see them. For information on safaris, call the **Dombås Tourist Office** (☎ 61/24–14–44).

NATIONAL PARKS

The scrubby, flat, and wide **Rondane** to the southeast of Lesja, and **Dovrefjell,** peaked to the north, have some of the country's steepest mountains and are home to wild musk ox, reindeer, and birds.

Røros

59 *317 km (197 mi) from Lesja; 157 km (97 mi) from Trondheim.*

At the northern end of the Østerdal, the long valley to the east of Gudbrandsdalen, lies Røros, for more than 300 years a one-company town: Practically everyone who lived here was connected with the copper mines. The last mine in the region closed in 1986, but the town has survived thanks to other industries, including tourism, especially after it was placed on UNESCO's World Heritage List.

Røros's main attraction is the **Old Town,** with its 250-year-old workers' cottages, slag dumps, and managers' houses, one of which is now City Hall. Descendants of the man who discovered the first copper ore in Røros still live in the oldest of the nearly 100 protected buildings. The tourist office has 75-minute guided tours of this part of town, starting at the information office and ending at the church. ⊡ *NKr25.* ⊙ *Tours early June and late Aug.–mid-Sept., Mon.–Sat. at 11; late June–mid-Aug., Mon.–Sat. at noon and 3, Sun. at 3; mid-Sept.–May, Sat. at 11.*

The **Røroskirke** (Røros Church), which towers above all the other buildings in the town, is an eight-sided stone structure from 1784, with the mines' symbol on the tower. It can seat 1,600, quite surprising in a town with a population of only 5,000 today. The pulpit looms above the center of the altar, and seats encircle the top perimeter. Two hundred years ago wealthy locals paid for the privilege of sitting there. ☎ 72/41–15–55. ⊡ NKr15. ☉ *Early June and late Aug.–mid-Sept., weekdays 2–4, Sat. 11–1; late June–mid-Aug., Mon.–Sat. 10–5; Oct.–May, Sat. 11–1.*

OFF THE
BEATEN PATH

OLAVSGRUVA (Olaf's Mine) – The guided tour of Olavsgruva, a former copper mine outside of town and now a museum, takes visitors into the depths of the earth, complete with sound-and-light effects. Remember to bring warm clothing and good shoes, as the temperature below ground is about 5°C (41°F) year-round. ⊠ *Rte. 31,* ☎ *72/41–44–50.* ⊡ *NKr35. Guided tours early June and late Aug.–Sept., Mon.–Sat. at 1 and 3, Sun. at noon; late June–mid-Aug., daily at 10:30, noon, 1:30, 3, 4:30, 6; Oct.–May, Sat. at 3.*

The **Rørosmuseet** (Røros Museum), in an old smelting plant, documents the history of the mines, with working models in one-tenth scale demonstrating the methods used in mining. ☎ 72/41–05–00. ⊡ NKr30.

Dining and Lodging

$$–$$$ ✕⊡ **Best Western Bergstadens Hotel.** The lobby is big, but when there's a fire in the stone fireplace it's quite cozy. The main draw here is the dining room: Chef Agnar Risvik sticks to local traditions and products—fish from mountain streams and berries from the nearby forest. ⊠ *Oslovn. 2, 7460,* ☎ *72/41–11–11,* FAX *72/41–01–55. 73 rooms, 2 suites. 2 restaurants, 2 bars, pool, sauna, nightclub, meeting rooms. AE, DC, MC, V.*

Outdoor Activities and Sports

SKIING

At the northern end of the Gubransdalen region, west of Røros, is **Oppdal** (45 kilometers [27 miles] of alpine pistes, 186 kilometers [115 miles] of cross-country trails; 10 ski lifts), a World Cup venue. Like most other areas, it has lighted trails and snow-making equipment.

Mid-Norway: Gudbrandsdal to Horgheim A to Z

Arriving and Departing

BY CAR

The wide, two-lane Route E6 north from Oslo passes through Hamar and Lillehammer. Route 3 follows Østerdalen (the eastern valley) from Oslo. Route 30 at Tynset leads to Røros and E6 on to Trondheim, 156 kilometers (97 miles) farther north.

BY TRAIN

There are good train connections between Oslo and the major interior towns to the north. The region is served by the Oslo-Tondheim line and two other lines.

Getting Around

BY CAR

Roads in the north become increasingly hilly and twisty as the terrain roughens into the central mountains. The northern end of the region is threaded by E16, E6, and Routes 51 and 3. Don't speed: High-tech markers at the roadside, particularly prevalent in the area of Vinstra and Otta, are actually cameras. Exceed the speed limit and you'll receive a ticket in the mail.

Contacts and Resources

VISITOR INFORMATION

Golå (✉ Fjell og Fjord Ferie, DBC–Senteret, ☎ 32/07–45–44); **Hamar** (✉ Vikingskipet, Olympia Hall, ☎ 62/51–02–17 or 62/51–02–25); **Lillehammer** (✉ Lilletorget, ☎ 61/25–92–99); **Lom** (☎ 61/21–12–86); **Øyer** (☎ 61/27–79–50); **Røros** (✉ Peder Hiortsgt. 2, ☎ 72/41–00–00).

THE WEST COAST: FJORD COUNTRY

This fjord-riddled coast, from south of Bergen to Kristiansund, is stippled with islands and grooved with deep barren valleys, with most of the fertile land edging the water. The farther north you travel, the more rugged and wild the landscape. The motionless Sognefjord is the longest inlet, snaking 190 kilometers (110 miles) inland. It is 4,000 feet deep—a depth that often makes it appear black. Some of its sections are so narrow, with rock walls looming on either side, that they look as if they've been sliced from the mountains.

At the top of Sogn og Fjordane county is a succession of fjords referred to as Nordfjord, with Jostedalsbreen, mainland Europe's largest glacier, to the south. Sunnfjord is the coastal area between Nordfjord and Sognefjord, with Florø, the county seat, on an island close to Norway's westernmost point.

The mountains of Møre og Romsdal county are treeless moonscapes of gray rock, stone cliffs that hang out over the water far below. Geirangerfjord is the most spectacular fjord, with a road zigzagging all the way down from the mountaintops to the water beside a famous waterfall.

There is more to the central region than fidgety coasts and peaks. In fact, tourists have been visiting central fjord country ever since the English "discovered" the area some 150 years ago in their search for the ultimate salmon. One of these tourists was Germany's kaiser Wilhelm, who spent every summer except one, from 1890 to 1913, in Molde and helped rebuild Ålesund into one of the most fantastic fits of architectural invention in Scandinavia.

The best way to see the fjord country is to make an almost circular tour—from Oslo to Åndalsnes, out to the coastal towns of Ålesund, Molde, and Kristiansund, then over Trollstigveien to Geiranger, by ferry to Hellesylt, down to Stryn, around Loen and Olden and through the subglacial tunnel to Fjærland, and by ferry to Balestrand, connecting with another ferry down to Flåm, where the railroad connects with Myrdal on the Bergen line (*see* Fjord Tours *in* Bergen A to Z, *above*). Then the trip can either continue on to Bergen or back to Oslo.

While traveling, keep in mind that outside of some roadside snack bars and simple cafeterias, restaurants are few in fjord country. The majority of visitors dine at the hotels, where food is generally abundant and simple. Most feature a cold table at either lunch or dinner.

Åndalsnes

60   *495 km (307 mi) from Bergen; 354 km (219 mi) from Trondheim.*

★   Åndalsnes, an industrial town of 3,000 people, has at least three things going for it: As the last stop on the railroad, it is a gateway to fjord country; Trollstigveien (Trolls' Path); and Trollveggen (Trolls' Wall).

From **Horgheimseidet,** which used to have a gingerbread hotel for elegant tourists—often European royalty—you can view **Trollveggen,** the

Fjord Country

KEY
—— Rail Lines
- - - Ferry

0   150 miles
0   225 km

N

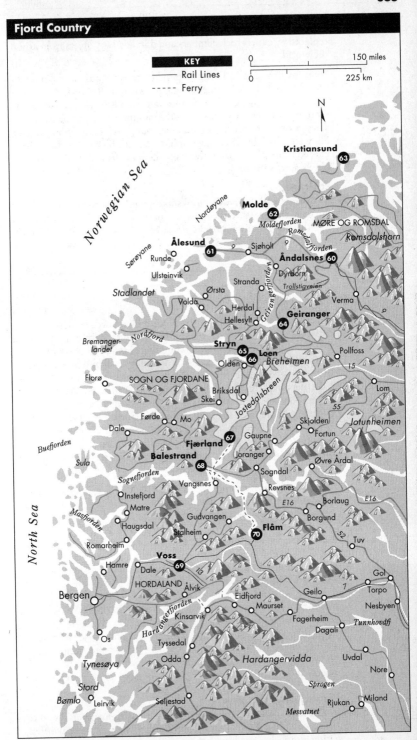

Norwegian Sea

Kristiansund **63**

Molde **62**
Moldefjorden
MØRE OG ROMSDAL
Romsdalshorn

Nordøyane

Ålesund **61**   Sjøholt
Romsdalsfjorden
Åndalsnes **60**

Sørøyane   Runde
Ulsteinvik
Stranda   Dyrdorn
Trollstigveien
Verma

Stadlandet   Ørsta
Volda   Herdal
Hellesylt
Geiranger **64**

Bremanger-landet   *Nordfjord*
Stryn **65**   Loen **66**
Breheimen
Pollfoss

Florø
SOGN OG FJORDANE
Olden
15

Briksdal
Jostedalsbreen
Skei
Lom

Førde   Mo
Dale
Skjolden
Jotunheimen
55

Fjærland **67**   Gaupne
Fortun

Balestrand **68**
Joranger
Øvre Årdal

Vangsnes
Sogndal

Buefjorden
Sula
Sognefjorden
Revsnes
E16
E16

Instefjord
Matre
Gudvangen
E16
Borlaug
Borgund

Masfjorden
Haugsdal
Stalheim
Flåm **70**
52
Tuv

Romarheim
Voss **69**
13
Gol

Hamre   Dale
HORDALAND   Ålvik
Geilo
7
Torpo
Nesbyen

Bergen
Os
Eidfjord
Maurset
Fagerheim
Tunnhovdfj
Dagali

Hardangerfjorden
Kinsarvik
Tyssedal
Hardangervidda
Uvdal
Nore

Tynesøya
Odda
Sprogen

Stord
Bømlo   Leirvik
Seljestad
Møsvatnet
Rjukan   Miland

North Sea

highest sheer rock wall in Europe (3,300 feet). However, the hotel has been a private home for the past 50 years, and the tourists have been replaced by expert rock climbers and daredevil sky divers from around the world.

Trollstigveien, one of Europe's most fantastic roads, starts in Åndalsnes. This road took 100 men 20 summers (from 1916 to 1936) to build, in a constant fight against rock and water. Trollstigveien and Ørneveien (at the Geiranger end) zigzag over the mountains separating two fjords. They're open only during the summer, but there's enough snow for skiing well into July. Trollstigveien has 11 giant hairpin turns, each one blasted from solid rock. Halfway up, the spray from **Stigfoss** (Path Falls) blows across the bridge.

Lodging

$$ 🏨 **Grand Hotel Bellevue.** It looks like a white stucco apartment building from the 1950s. The rooms are spare but adequate, all with a view of either the mountains or the fjord. ⊠ Åndalsgt. 5, 6300, ☎ 71/22–10–11, FAX 71/22–60–38. 90 rooms. 2 restaurants, bar, meeting rooms. DC, MC, V.

Ålesund

⑥ *240 km (150 mi) west of Åndalsnes.*

★ On three islands and between two bright blue fjords is Ålesund, home to 36,000 inhabitants and one of Norway's largest harbors for exporting dried and fresh fish. Nearly 800 buildings in the center of town were destroyed by fire in 1904, said to have been started by a tipped oil lamp. In the rush to shelter the 10,000 homeless victims, Kaiser Wilhelm II led a mercurial rebuilding that married the German Art Nouveau with Viking roots—much of it carried out by an army of young, foreign architects who threw in their own rabid flourishes. Delightfully, nothing has changed. Winding streets are crammed with warehouses topped with turrets, spires, gables, dragonheads, and curlicues, all in a delirious spirit that's best seen while wandering behind the local dock to Kongensgate, the walking street.

You can drive or take a bus (☎ 70/12–41–70) up nearby Aksla Mountain to a vantage point, **Kniven** (the knife), for a splendid view of the city—which absolutely glitters at night.

OFF THE **Runde** – located near Ålesund is Norway's southernmost major bird rock,
BEATEN PATH one of the largest in Europe and a breeding ground for some 130 species, including puffins, gannets, and shags. The island is otherwise known for the "Runde Hoard," 1,300 kilograms of silver and gold coins that were retrieved from a Dutch ship that sank in 1725. A catamaran leaves from Skateflua quay for the 25-minute trip to Hareid, where it connects with a bus for the 50-kilometer (31-mile) trip to Runde. A path leads from the bus stop to the nature reserve. It is also possible to sail around the rock on the yacht *Charming Ruth,* which leaves from Ulsteinvik at 11 on Wednesday and Sunday. Call the Runde tourist office (☞ Visitor Information *in* The West Coast A to Z, *below*) for more information.

Dining and Lodging

$$ ✗ **Fjellstua.** This mountaintop restaurant has tremendous views over the surrounding peaks, islands, and fjords. There are several different eating establishments here, but the main restaurant serves a variety of dishes and homemade desserts. ⊠ *Top of Aksla mountain,* ☎ 70/12–65–82. AE, DC, MC, V. Closed Mar–Nov.

$$ ✕ **Gullix.** The decor is a bit much, with stone walls, plants hanging from the ceiling, musical instruments, and even the odd old-fashioned record player, but you can't fault the food, which ranges from sautéed monkfish garnished with shrimp, mussels, and crayfish to grilled, marinated filet mignon of lamb. ⊠ *Rådstugt. 5B,* ☏ *70/12–05–48. AE, DC, MC, V.*

$$ ✕ **Sjøbua.** Within walking distance of the new hotels, this fish restaurant is typical Ålesund. Pick your own lobster from the large tank. The mixed fish and shellfish platter is the most popular dish on the menu. The lobster soup is excellent, too, but leave room for the raspberry ice cream with nougat sauce. ⊠ *Brunholmgt. 1,* ☏ *70/12–71–00. AE, DC, MC, V. Closed Sun.*

$ ✕ **Brosundet Cafe.** This coffee shop in Hotel Atlantica has its own bak-
★ ery, so there are always homemade bread and rolls. You can order anything from *bløtkake* (cream cake) or the ever-so-popular *nøttekake* (nut cake) to pepper steak. ⊠ *R. Rønnebergsgt. 4,* ☏ *70/12–91–00. Reservations not accepted. AE, DC, MC, V.*

$$ ⊞ **Bryggen Home Hotel.** This hotel is housed in a former turn-of-the-century fish warehouse. The decor in both lobby and guest rooms illustrates the importance of the fishing industry to Ålesund. A light evening buffet is included in the room price, and waffles and coffee are always available. Fishing equipment is available; although Bryggen is on the water, anglers are advised to go farther afield for a better catch. ⊠ *Apotekergt. 1–3, 6021,* ☏ *70/12–64–00,* FAX *70/12–11–80. 65 rooms. Sauna, Turkish bath, fishing, meeting rooms. AE, DC, MC, V.*

$$ ⊞ **Inter Nor Hotel Scandinavie.** The impressive building with towers
★ and arches dates from 1905, while the rooms are modern and beautifully decorated in shades of blues, peaches, and greens with reproduction Biedermeier furniture. Some decorative textiles pay a token tribute to Art Nouveau. ⊠ *Løvenvoldgt. 8, 6002,* ☏ *70/12–31–31,* FAX *70/13–23–70. 65 rooms. Restaurant, bar, pizzeria, meeting rooms. AE, DC, MC, V.*

$$ ⊞ **Scandic Hotel.** This large, postmodern building complex stands next to the Exhibition Hall. Its interior design has a maritime theme. The rooms are spacious. ⊠ *Molovn. 6, 6004,* ☏ *70/12–81–00,* FAX *70/12–92–10. 117 rooms, 6 suites. Restaurant, bar, indoor pool, sauna. AE, DC, MC, V.*

$ ⊞ **Christineborg Turisthotel.** This modern hotel in Runde faces the sea and the bird rocks. It's surprisingly comfortable and civilized, a welcome setting for unwinding. ⊠ *6096, Runde,* ☏ *70/08–59–50,* FAX *70/08–59–72. 31 rooms. Restaurant, bar, fishing boat. MC, V.*

Molde

62 *69 km (43 mi) north of Ålesund on Route 668.*

During World War II the German air force suspected that King Haakon VII was staying in a red house here and bombed every red house in town. These days, Molde is a modern town, after being almost entirely rebuilt, and is known for its yearly jazz festival at the end of July, when big names from around the world gather for a huge jam session. Tickets can be purchased at all post offices in Norway.

Dining and Lodging

$$–$$$ ✕⊞ **Inter Nor Alexandra Molde.** Spisestuen, the restaurant of this
★ premier hotel, is worth a special trip. Kåre Monsås prepares such dishes as pepper-marinated veal fillet. The rooms here, many of which overlook the water, are nondescript but comfortable, with dark-brown wood furniture and textiles in shades of blue. ⊠ *Storgt. 1–7, 6400,*

☎ 71/25–11–33, FAX 71/21–66–35. *150 rooms, 11 suites. 3 restaurants, bar, sauna, indoor pool, exercise room, meeting rooms. AE, DC, MC, V.*

Kristiansund

63   *68 km (42 mi) north of Molde on Route 64.*

This town was spared the destruction of its historic harbor, Vågen, during World War II. Many buildings in Kristiansund—which celebrated its 250th birthday in 1992—are well preserved, including **Woldbrygga,** a cooper's (barrel maker's) workshop from 1875 to 1965, with its original equipment still operational. ⊠ *Dalevn. 17,* ☎ *71/67–15–78.* 🖃 *NKr25.* ⊙ *Tues.–Fri. 10–2, Sun. noon–3.*

Lodging

$$–$$$ 🏨 **Inter Nor Grand.** Practically every Norwegian town has a Grand hotel. This one's primarily a conference hotel, but the rooms are nicer than most others in the chain (certainly much nicer than the lobby), with brass beds and light-wood furniture. ⊠ *Bernstorffstredet 1, 6500,* ☎ *71/67–30–11,* FAX *71/67–23–70. 130 rooms. Restaurant, bar, pub, sauna, exercise room, nightclub, convention center. AE, DC, MC, V.*

Geiranger

64   *85 km (52.5 mi) southwest of Åndalsnes; 413 km (256 mi) from Bergen.*

★   Geiranger is the ultimate fjord, Norway at its most dramatic, with the finest sightseeing in the wildest nature compressed into a relatively small area. The mountains lining the Geiranger Fjord tower 6,600 feet above sea level. The most scenic route to Geiranger is the two-hour drive along Route 63 over Trollstigveien from Åndalsnes (☞ *above*). Once you are there, the Ørneveien (Eagles' Road), down to Geiranger, completed in 1952, with 11 hairpin turns, leads directly to the fjord.

The 16-kilometer-long (10-mile-long), 960-foot-deep Geirangerfjord's best-known attractions are its waterfalls—the Seven Sisters, the Bridal Veil, and the Suitor—and the abandoned farms at **Skageflå** and **Knivsflå,** which are visible (and accessible) only by boat (☞ Guided Tours, *below*). Perhaps the inhabitants left because provisions had to be carried from the boats straight up to Skageflå—a backbreaking 800 feet.

Lodging

$$$ 🏨 **Union Hotel.** This family-owned hotel is more than 100 years old. The old building was torn down, but the present hotel is a tribute to the old style. It is modern and comfortable, with lots of windows facing the view, and light-colored furniture in the rooms, which are relatively large. ⊠ *6216,* ☎ *70/26–30–00,* FAX *70/26–31–61. 155 rooms, 13 suites. Restaurant, bar, indoor pool, steam room, nightclub. AE, DC, MC, V.*

$ 🏨 **Grande Fjord Hotell.** Idyllically set at the edge of the fjord, this small hotel complex has more charm than the big hotels in the area. The rooms are simple but comfortable. ⊠ *6216,* ☎ *70/26–30–90,* FAX *70/26–31–77. 48 rooms, 18 cabins. Restaurant, bar, sauna, fishing, boating. AE, DC, MC, V.*

Stryn

65   *If you continue on to Stryn from Geiranger, take the ferry across the Geiranger Fjord to Hellesylt, a 75-minute ride. It's about 50 km (30 mi) from Hellesylt to Stryn on Rte. 60.*

Stryn, Loen, and Olden, at the eastern end of Nordfjord, were among the first tourist destinations in the region more than 100 years ago. Stryn is famous for its salmon river and summer ski center—**Stryn Sommerskisenter** (✉ 6880 Stryn, ☎ 57/87–19–95).

OFF THE BEATEN PATH
BRIKSDALSBREEN – This is the most accessible arm of the Jostedal glacier. Drive along the mountain road or take a bus (from Olden, Loen, or Stryn) to Briksdal. From here, the glacier is a 45-minute walk from the end of the road, or you can ride there with pony and trap, as tourists did 100 years ago. Local guides lead tours (☞ Guided Tours, *below*) over the safe parts of the glacier. These perennial ice masses are more treacherous than they look, for there's always the danger of calving (breaking off), and deep crevasses are not always visible.

Lodging

$$$ 🏨 **Kong Oscar's Hall.** Mike and Møyfrid Walston have brought back to life a derelict but magnificent hotel from the heyday of the dragon style, 1896, complete with a tower with dragon heads on the eaves. The Great Hall gives new meaning to the word *great,* and the number of royal guests, both present and past, is impressive. ✉ 6880, ☎ FAX 57/87–19–53. 5 suites. Restaurant. No credit cards. Closed Sept.–Apr.

Shopping

Strynefjell Draktverkstad (✉ 6890 Oppstryn, ☎ 57/87–72–20) specializes in stylish knickers, trousers, and skirts made of heavy wool. It's a 10-minute drive east of Stryn on Route 15.

Loen

66 *10 km (6.2 mi) southeast of Stryn.*

Loen and Olden are starting points for expeditions to branches of Europe's largest glacier, Jostedalsbreen. Hovering over the entire inner Nordfjord and Sognefjord regions, this glacier covers 800 square kilometers (309 square miles). In geological time, this 5,000-year-old glacier is relatively young. The ice is in constant motion, crawling as much as 2 kilometers a day in certain places.

OFF THE BEATEN PATH
KJENNDALSBREEN FJELLSTOVE – It's possible to visit the Kjenndal arm of the glacier on the M/B *Kjendal,* which departs from Sande, near Loen. It sails down the 14-kilometer (9-mile) arm of the lake under mountains covered by protruding glacier arms and past Ramnefjell (Ramne Mountain), scarred by rock slides, to Kjenndalsbreen Fjellstove. A bus runs between the Alexandra lodge (☞ *below*) and the glacier.

Dining and Lodging

$$$ ✕🏨 **Alexandra.** The building that houses Alexandra looks more like
★ a huge white hospital than a hotel. More than 100 years ago, English and German tourists stayed here. Even though the original dragon-style building exists only in pictures in the lobby, it is still the most luxurious hotel around. The facilities are first-rate, but the food, prepared by chef Wenche Loen, is the best part—the trout is outstanding. ✉ 6878, ☎ 57/87–76–60, FAX 57/87–77–70. 197 rooms. 2 restaurants, bar, indoor pool, tennis courts, exercise room, boating, nightclub, convention center. AE, DC, MC, V.

Fjærland

67 *From Olden it's 62 km (37 mi) of easy, though not particularly inspiring, terrain to Skei, at the base of Lake Jølster, where the road goes under the glacier for more than 6 km (4 mi) of the journey to Fjærland.*

Fjærland, until 1986, was without road connections altogether. In 1991 the **Norsk Bremuseum** (Norwegian Glacier Museum) opened just north of Fjærland. It has a huge screen on which a film about glacier trekking plays and a fiberglass glacial maze, complete with special effects courtesy of the *Star Wars* movies' set designer. ☎ *57/69–32–88.* ✇ *NKr60.* ☉ *June–Aug., daily 9–7; Apr.–May, Sept., and Oct., daily 10–4.*

<table>
<tr><td>OFF THE
BEATEN PATH</td><td>ASTRUPTUNET – Halfway across the southern shore of Lake Jølster (about a 10-minute detour from the road to Fjærland) is Astruptunet, the farm of artist Nicolai Astrup (1880–1928). The best of his primitive, mystical paintings sell in the $500,000 range, ranking him among the most popular Norwegian artists. His home and studio are in a cluster of small turf-roofed buildings on a steep hill overlooking the lake. ☎ 57/72–67–82 or 57/72–81–05. ✇ NKr50. ☉ July, daily 10–8; late May–June and Aug.–early Sept., Tues.–Sun. 10–5.</td></tr>
</table>

Dining and Lodging

$$–$$$ ✗ 🏨 **Hotel Mundal.** This small, old-fashioned yellow-and-white gingerbread hotel opened in 1891. All rooms are individually and simply decorated. The dining room looks rather dreary, but the food is good. ✉ *5855,* ☎ *57/69–31–01,* ☏ *57/69–31–79. 35 rooms. Restaurant, bar, meeting rooms. No credit cards. Closed in winter.*

Shopping

Audhild Vikens Vevstove (✉ Skei, ☎ 57/72–81–25) specializes in the handicrafts, particularly woven textiles.

Balestrand

68   *30 km (18.6 mi) up the fjord by ferry; 204 km (126 mi) by car to Fjærland.*

By 1997, Fjærland should have road connections with Sogndal, but until then, the only way to travel is by ferry, which stops at both Balestrand and Vangsnes. Balestrand is on the southern bank of **Sognefjord,** one of the longest and deepest fjords in the world, snaking 200 kilometers (136 miles) into the heart of the country. Along its wide banks are some of Norway's best fruit farms, with fertile soil and lush vegetation (the fruit blossoms in May are spectacular). Ferries are the lifeline of the region.

Lodging

$$ 🏨 **Kvikne's Hotel.** This huge, wooden gingerbread house at the edge
★   of the Sognefjord has been a landmark since 1913. It is fjord country's most elaborate old hotel, with rows of open porches and balustrades. The rooms are comfortable—those in the old section have more personality, but the view is the best part. This spot also provides good swimming, hiking, rowing, and fishing. ✉ *5850, Balholm,* ☎ *57/69–11–01,* ☏ *57/69–15–02. 190 rooms. Restaurant, exercise room, fishing, nightclub. AE, DC, MC, V.*

Voss

69   *80 km (50 mi) south of Vangsnes.*

Voss is the birthplace of American football hero Knut Rockne and a good place to stay the night, either in the town itself or 36 kilometers (23 miles) away at Stalheim. The road to Stalheim, an old resort, has 13 hairpin turns in one 1½-kilometer (1-mile) stretch of road that can be almost dizzying—it's 1,800 feet straight down—but well worth the trip for the view. Voss is connected with Oslo and Bergen by train and by roads (some sections are narrow and steep).

Lodging

$$$–$$$$ ⊞ **Stalheim Hotel.** A large, rectangular building, much like other Norwegian resort hotels, the Stalheim has been painted dark red and blends into the scenery better than most other hotels. It has an extensive collection of Norwegian antiques and even its own open-air museum, with 30 houses. ⊠ *5715,* ☎ *56/52–01–22,* ☏ *56/52–00–56. 127 rooms, 3 suites. Restaurant, bar, fishing. AE, DC, MC, V.*

$$ ⊞ **Fleischers Hotel.** The modern addition along the front detracts from the turreted and gabled charm of this old hotel. Inside, the old style has been well maintained, particularly in the restaurant. The rooms in the old section are comfortable and pleasantly old-fashioned; in the rebuilt section (1993) they are modern and inviting. There is also a children's playroom. The motel section has apartments as well. ⊠ *Evangervegen 13, 5700,* ☎ *56/51–11–55,* ☏ *56/51–22–89. 90 rooms, 30 apartments. Restaurant, bar, indoor pool, hot tub, sauna, tennis court, nightclub. AE, DC, MC, V.*

Outdoor Activities and Sports

HIKING

Walks and hikes are especially rewarding in this region, with spectacular mountain and water views everywhere. Be prepared for abrupt weather changes in spring and fall. Voss is a starting point for mountain hikes in Slølsheimen, Vikafjell, and the surrounding mountains. Contact the Voss Tourist Board (☞ *below*) for tips.

RAFTING

For rafting in Dagali or Voss, contact **Dagali-Voss Rafting** (⊠ Dagali Hotel, ☎ 32/09–37–00) for information on organized trips.

SKIING

Voss (40 kilometers [25 miles] of alpine slopes; 1 cable car, 8 ski lifts; 8 illuminated and 2 marked cross-country trails) is an important alpine skiing center in Norway, although it doesn't have the attractions or traditions of some of its resort neighbors to the east. The area includes several schools and interconnecting lifts that will get you from run to run. Call the Voss Tourist Board (☞ *below*) for details.

Flåm

⑦⓿ *131 km (81.2 mi) from Voss.*

One of the most scenic train routes in Europe zooms from Myrdal, high into the mountains and down to the quaint town of Flåm. Flåm's waterfront is swamped with day-trippers who stream off of the train at noon, have lunch in a cafeteria, and sweep out of town at about 3. After they leave, a wonderful stillness descends and Flåm becomes a wonderful place to spend the night.

OFF THE BEATEN PATH   **MYRDAL** – It's possible to ride a ferry from Balestrand to Flåm, from which you can make Norway's most exciting railway journey to Myrdal. Only 20 kilometers (12 miles) long, it takes 40 minutes to travel 2,850 feet up a steep mountain gorge and 53 minutes to go down, with one stop for photos each way. Don't worry about the brakes. The train has five separate systems, any one of which is able to stop it. A masterpiece of engineering, the line includes 20 tunnels. From Flåm it is also an easy drive back to Oslo on E16 along the Lærdal River, one of Norway's most famous salmon streams and King Harald's favorite.

Lodging

$$ ⊞ **Fretheim Hotell.** With the fjord in front and mountains in back, the setting is perfect. The hotel is anonymous, white, and functional. The inside has comfortable lounges and rooms decorated in a Norwegian folk style. ⊠ *5743,* ☎ *57/63–22–00,* FAX *57/63–23–03. 56 rooms, 28 with shared bath. 2 restaurants, bar, fishing. AE, MC, V.

The West Coast A to Z

Arriving and Departing

BY BOAT
The *Hurtigruten* (the coastal steamer) stops at Skansekaia in **Ålesund,** northbound at noon, departing at 3, and stops southbound at midnight, departing at 1. A catamaran runs between Ålesund and Molde at least twice daily.

BY CAR
From Oslo, it is 450 kilometers (295 miles) on Route E6 to Dombås and then Route 9 through Åndalsnes to Ålesund. The well-maintained two-lane road is inland to Åndalsnes and then follows the coastline out to Ålesund.

The 380-kilometer (235-mile) drive from Bergen to Ålesund covers some of the most breathtaking scenery in the world. Roads are narrow two-lane ventures much of the time; passing is difficult, and in summer traffic can be heavy.

BY PLANE
Ålesund's **Vigra Airport** is 15 kilometers (9 miles) from the center of town. **Braathens SAFE** (☎ 70/12–58–00, Ålesund; ☎ 70/18–32–45, Vigra) has nonstop flights from Oslo, Bergen, Trondheim, and Bodø.

Between the Airport and Downtown: It's a 25-minute ride from Vigra to town with Flybussen. Tickets cost NKr50. Buses are scheduled according to flights—they leave the airport about 10 minutes after all arrivals and leave town about 60 or 70 minutes before each each departure.

BY TRAIN
The *Dovrebanen* and *Raumabanen* between Oslo S Station and **Åndalsnes** via Dombås run three times daily in each direction for the 6½-hour ride. At Åndalsnes, buses wait outside the station to pick up passengers for points not served by the train. The 124-kilometer (76-mile) trip to Ålesund takes close to two hours.

Getting Around

BY BOAT
In addition to regular ferries to nearby islands, boats connect Ålesund with other points along the coast. Excursions by boat are available through the tourist office.

BY BUS
Bus routes are extensive. The tourist office has information about do-it-yourself tours by bus to the outlying districts. Three local bus companies serve **Ålesund**; all buses depart from the terminal on Kaiser Wilhelms Gate.

BY CAR
Ferries are a way of life in western Norway, but they are seldom big enough or don't run often enough during the summer, causing built-in delays. Considerable hassle can be eliminated by reserving ahead, as cars with reservations board first.

Contacts and Resources

EMERGENCIES
Hospital Emergency Rooms/Doctors/Dentists: ☎ 70/12–33–48. **Car Rescue:** ☎ 70/14–18–33.

Cruises: The M/S *Geirangerfjord* (☎ 70/26–30–07) offers 105-minute guided minicruises on the Geirangerfjord. Tickets are sold at the dock in Geiranger. ☉ *June–August. Tours at 10, noon, 2, and 5; June 25–Aug. 15, also at 3:30.*

Flying: Firdafly A/S (☎ 57/86–53–88), based in Sandane, has air tours over Jostedalsbreen. Hotel Alexandra in Loen (☞ *above*) arranges group flights. **Mørefly A/S** (☎ 70/18–35–00) runs 20-minute fjord- and mountain-sightseeing trips by helicopter from Ålesund.

Glacier: From Easter through September, **Jostedalen Breførlag** (✉ 5828 Gjerde, ☎ 56/68–32–73) offers glacier tours, from an easy 1½-hour family trip on the Nigard branch (equipment is provided) to advanced glacier courses with rock and ice climbing.

Hiking: Aak Fjellsportsenter (☎ 71/22–64–44) in Åndalsnes specializes in walking tours of the area, from rambling in the hills for beginners and hikers to full-fledged rock climbing, along with rafting on the Rauma River. These are the guys who hang out of helicopters to rescue injured climbers, so they know what they're doing.

Orientation: A 1½-hour guided stroll through Ålesund, concentrating mostly on the Art Nouveau buildings, departs from the tourist information center (Rådhuset) Saturday, Tuesday, and Thursday at 1 PM from June 13 to August 19. ⌨ *NKr45.*

Nordstjernen (✉ Kaiser Wilhelms Gate 22, Ålesund, ☎ 70/12–59–45) is open Wednesday until 6 and Saturday and Sunday from 6 to 8.

Ålesund (✉ Rådhuset, ☎ 70/12–12–02); **Åndalsnes** (✉ Corner Nesgt. and Romsdalsvn., ☎ 71/22–16–22); **Balestrand** (✉ Dockside, ☎ 57/69–12–55); **Flåm** (✉ Railroad station, ☎ 57/63–21–06); **Geiranger** (✉ Dockside, ☎ 70/26–30–99); **Hellesylt** (✉ Dockside, ☎ 70/26–50–52); **Lærdal** (☎ 57/66–65–09); **Molde** (✉ Storgt 1, ☎ 71/21–92–62); **Sogndal** (☎ 57/67–30–83); **Runde** (☎ 70/08–59–96) **Stryn** (☎ 57/87–23–32); **Ulvik** (✉ Dockside, ☎ 56/52–63–60); **Voss** (☎ 56/51–00–51). **Fjord Norway** (☎ 55/31–93–00) in Bergen is a clearinghouse for information on all of western Norway.

TRONDHEIM TO THE NORTH CAPE

The coast of northern Norway fidgets up from Trondheim, scattering thousands of islands and skerries along the way, until it reaches the northernmost point of Europe. Then it continues even farther, straggling above Sweden and Finland to point a finger of land into Russia.

Long and thin, this area covers an astonishing variety of land- and cityscapes, from bustling Trondheim to elegant Tromsø. Some areas, especially when seen from the deck of the mail boats, seem like endless miles of wilderness marked by an occasional dot—a lonely cabin or a herd of reindeer. Views are often exquisite: glaciers, fjords, rocky coasts, and celestial displays of the midnight sun in summer and northern lights (aurora borealis) in winter.

Nordkapp (North Cape) has a character that changes with the seasons. In summer it teems with visitors and tour buses, and in winter, under several feet of snow, it is bleak, subtle, and astonishingly beautiful. It is accessible then only by squealing Snow-Cat snowmobile, a bracing and thoroughly Norwegian adventure.

Keep in mind while traveling, as in the rest of provincial Norway, that most better restaurants are in hotels. If you visit northern Norway be-

Trondheim and the North

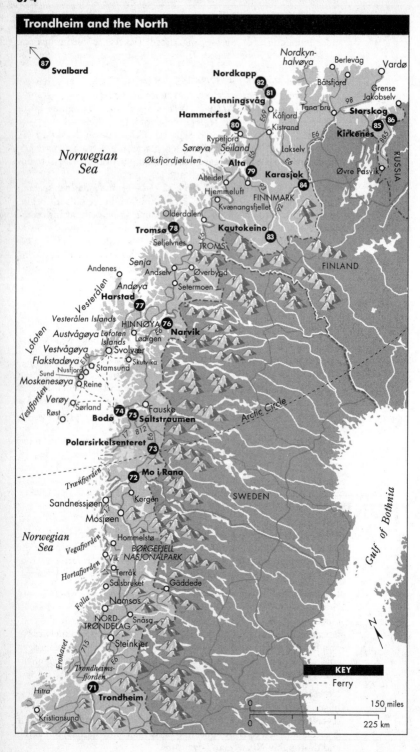

Svalbard

Nordkyn-halvøya
Berlevåg
Vardø
Nordkapp
Båtsfjord
Grense Jakobselv
Honningsvåg
Tana bru
Storskog
Hammerfest
Kåfjord
Kirkenes
Kistrand
Rypefjord
Seiland
Sørøya
Lakselv
Øksfjordjøkulen
Alta
Øvre Pasvik
Alteidet
Karasjok
FINNMARK
Hjemmeluft
Kvænangsfjellet
RUSSIA
Olderdalen
Kautokeino
Tromsø
Seljelnes
TROMS
Senja
Øverbygd
Andenes
Andselv
FINLAND
Vesterålen
Setermoen
Andøya
Harstad
Vesterålen Islands
HINNØYA
Narvik
Austvågøya
Lofoten Islands
Lødigen
Vestvågøya
Svolvær
Flakstadøya
Nusfjord
Stamsund
Skutvika
Sund
Moskenesøya
Reine
Verøy
Sørland
Fauske
Røst
Bodø
Saltstraumen
Arctic Circle
Polarsirkelsenteret
Mo i Rana
Trænfjorden
Korgen
SWEDEN
Sandnessjøen
Mosjøen
Norwegian Sea
Gulf of Bothnia
Vegafjorden
Hommelstø
BØRGEFJELL NASJONALPARK
Vik
Hortafjorden
Terråk
Gäddede
Salsbruket
Namsos
Folla
NORD-TRØNDELAG
Snåsa
Steinkjer
Frohavet
Trondheims-fjorden
Hitra
Trondheim
Kristiansund

Norwegian Sea

E69
E6
E8
98
E6
E6
E6
E6
E10
17
812
17
715
E6

KEY
--- Ferry

0 ———— 150 miles
0 ———— 225 km

N

71 72 73 74 75 76 77 78 79 80 81 82 83 84 85 86 87

tween May and August, try the specialty of *måsegg* and *Mack-øl*, more for curiosity value than for taste. *Måsegg* (seagulls' eggs) are always served hard-boiled and halved in their shells. They're larger than chicken eggs, and they look exotic, with greenish-gray speckled shells and bright orange yolks, but they taste like standard supermarket eggs. *Mack-øl* (similar to pils) is brewed in Tromsø at the world's northernmost brewery.

Trondheim

🟤 *496 km (307.5 mi) north of Oslo; 744 km (461.2 mi) from Bergen.*

Trondheim's original name, Nidaros (still the name of the cathedral), is a composite word referring to the city's location at the mouth of the Nid River. After a savage fire in 1681, the wooden town was rebuilt according to the plan of General Cicignon, a military man from Luxembourg, who also designed Trondheim's fort. The wide streets of the city center are still lined with brightly painted wooden houses and picturesque warehouses.

The Tiffany windows are magnificent at the **Nordenfjeldske Kunstindustrimuseum** (Decorative Arts Museum), which houses one of the finest art collections in Scandinavia. It has superb period rooms from the Renaissance to 1950s Scandinavian modern. ⊠ *Munkegt. 5,* ☎ *73/52– 13–11.* 🎟 *NKr25.* ☉ *Late June–late Aug., Mon.–Sat. 10–8, Sun. noon–5; rest of yr, Mon.–Sat. 10–3, Thurs. 10–7, Sun. noon–4.*

Saint Olav, who formulated a Christian religious code for Norway in 1024 while he was king, was killed in battle against local chieftains at Stiklestad. After he was buried, water sprang from his grave and people began to believe that his nails and hair continued to grow beneath the ground. It is here on the grave of Saint Olav that **Nidaros Domkirke** (Nidaros Cathedral) was built. Following a series of other miracles, the town became a pilgrimage site for the Christians of northern Europe, and Olav was canonized in 1164.

Although construction was begun in 1070, the oldest existing parts of the cathedral date from around 1150. During the Catholic period (ca. 1000–1537) it attracted crowds of pilgrims, but after the Reformation its importance declined and fires destroyed much of it. The crown jewels, which visitors can view, are still kept in the cathedral. Guided tours are offered in English mid-June–mid-August, weekdays at 11, 2, and 4. ⊠ *Kongsgårdsgt. 2,* ☎ *73/52–52–33.* 🎟 *NKr12. Ticket also permits entry to Erkebispegården (☞ below).* ☉ *Mid-June–mid-Aug., weekdays 9–5:30, weekends 9–2; mid-Aug.–mid-Sept., weekdays 9– 3; mid-Sept.–mid-Apr., weekdays noon–2:30, weekends 11:30–2; May–mid-June, weekdays 9–3, weekends 9–2.*

Scandinavia's oldest secular building (actually two buildings connected by a gatehouse) is the **Erkebispegården** (Archbishop's Palace). Dating from around 1160, it was the residence of the archbishop until the Reformation. After that, it was a Danish governor's palace and later a military headquarters.

Within the Erkebispegården is the **Forsvarsmuseet** (Army Museum), with displays of uniforms, swords, and daggers. The **Hjemmefrontmuseet** (Resistance Museum), also there, documents the occupation of Norway during World War II through objects and photographs. *Archbishop's Palace:* ☎ *73/50–12–12.* 🎟 *NKr12. Ticket also permits entry to cathedral.* ☉ *June–Aug., weekdays 9–3, Sat. 9–2, Sun. 12:30–3:30. Army and Resistance museums:* ☎ *73/99–59–97.* 🎟 *NKr5.* ☉ *June–Aug., weekdays 10–3; year-round, weekends 11–3.*

Behind the **Biblioteket** (Library, ✉ Peter Egges Pl. 1) you can see the **remains of St. Olavskirke** (St. Olav's Church). The crypt of another medieval church can be seen inside Trondhjems og Strindens Sparebank (a savings bank at Søndregate 2) during normal banking hours.

Scandinavia's largest wooden building, **Stiftsgården,** was built in 1778 as a private home, the result of a competition between two sisters who were trying to outdo each other with the size of their houses. Today it is the king's official residence in Trondheim. The interior is sparsely furnished. ☎ 73/52–13–11, ✉ NKr30. ☼ June–mid-June, Tues.–Sat. 10–3, Sun. noon–5; late June–mid-Aug., Tues.–Sat. 10–5, Sun. 12–5; late Aug.–May, open one day per month.

Off Munkegate near the water, you can see an immense variety of seafood at **Ravnkloa Fiskehall** (fish market). The **Sjøfartsmuseet** (Maritime Museum), housed in a former prison, displays galleon figureheads, ship models, a harpoon cannon from a whaling boat, and a large collection of seafaring pictures. ✉ Fjordgt. 6A, ☎ 73/52–89–75. ✉ NKr20. ☼ Mon.–Sat. 9–3, Sun. noon–3; closed Sat. in winter.

Trøndelag Folkemuseum has a collection of rustic buildings from the turn of the century, including a dental office and a lace and ribbon maker's workshop. The museum restaurant is from 1739 and serves traditional Norwegian food. ✉ Sverresborg, ☎ 73/53–14–90. ✉ NKr40. ☼ Late May–Aug., daily 11–6, Sept.–Dec., daily noon–4.

OFF THE BEATEN PATH	**RINGVE MUSIC MUSEUM** – For an unusual museum visit, you can take a half-hour ride to Fagerheim and Ringve Gård, the childhood home of the naval hero Admiral Tordenskiold. Guides (music students) demonstrate the instruments on display and tell about their role in the history of music. Concerts are held regularly. ✉ Lade Allé 60, ☎ 73/92–24–11. ✉ NKr50. Guided tours in English late May–June, daily at noon, 2; July–mid-Aug., daily at 11, 12:30, 2:30, 4:30; mid-Aug.–late Aug., daily at 11, 12:30, 3; Sept., daily at noon; Oct.–mid-May, Sun. at 1:30. Tour lasts about 75 min.

Dining and Lodging

Trondheim is known for several dishes, including *surlaks* (pickled salmon), marinated in a sweet-and-sour brine with onions and spices and served with sour cream. A sweet specialty is *tekake* (tea cake), which looks like a thick-crust pizza topped with a lattice pattern of cinnamon and sugar.

$$$ ✕ **Bryggen.** The furnishings are in bleached wood, with dark-blue and
★ red accessories, and the atmosphere is intimate. The menu features reindeer fillet salad with cranberry vinaigrette and herb cream soup with both freshwater and ocean crayfish for appetizers. ✉ Øvre Bakklandet 66, ☎ 73/52–02–30. Reservations essential. AE, DC, MC, V. Closed Sun. No lunch.

$$–$$$ ✕ **Havfruen.** "The Mermaid" has a maritime dining room with an open kitchen at street level; in the cellar, 200-year-old stone walls from the original building frame the setting. Fish soup is the most popular starter; summer main dishes include poached halibut. ✉ Kjøpmannsgt. 7, ☎ 73/53–26–26. AE, DC, MC, V. Closed Sun. No lunch.

$$ ✕ **Hos Magnus.** The price-value ratio is excellent at this old-fashioned, cozy restaurant at Bryggen. The menu ranges from old local-specialty surlaks to modern dishes such as rose of salmon cured and marinated with aquavit brandy. Lamb roulade stuffed with cheese and mushroom sauce is on the menu, and there are ample fish and vegetarian choices, too. ✉ Kjøpmannsgt. 63, ☎ 73/52–41–10. AE, DC, MC, V.

$$ ✕ **Lian.** In the heights above the city, the views here are spectacular. The oldest part of the restaurant dates from 1700, but the round section, from the 1930s, commands the best view. The food is solid, honest, and hearty, with roast beef, reindeer, smoked pork loin, and the old standby, *kjøttkaker* (Norwegian meat cakes). ⊠ *Lianvn.,* ☎ *72/55–90–77. No credit cards. Closed Mon.*

$$ ✕ **Tavern på Sverresborg.** This big, yellow, wooden former ferry-
★ man's house at the Trøndelag Folkemuseum has been an inn since 1739. The food is authentic Norwegian, including meat and fish prepared with old methods—pickled, salted, and dried. Choices include a plate with four different kinds of herring, roast lamb ribs, trout, meat cakes, and rømmegrøt. Homemade oatmeal bread and rolls accompany all dishes. ⊠ *Sverresborg Allé,* ☎ *73/52–09–32. MC, V. No lunch early Sept.–mid-May.*

$ ✕ **De 3 Stuer.** This small bistro chain serves everything homemade, and the daily specials may be fish soufflé, fried fish with sour-cream sauce, split-pea soup with sausage, boiled beef, and lamb stew, all served with dessert and coffee. For lunch there's smørbrød, crescent rolls, salads, and cakes. ⊠ *Trondheim Torg,* ☎ *73/52–92–20;* ⊠ *Gågaten Leuthenhaven,* ☎ *73/52–43–42;* ⊠ *Dronningens Gt. 11,* ☎ *73/52–63–20. Reservations not accepted. No credit cards. Dronningens Gt. closed Sun.*

$$$ 🏨 **Grand Hotel Olav.** Not too many of the impeccably decorated rooms here are similiar—after all, there are 27 different room models. The hotel is part of a complex that contains shops and Olavshallen Concert Hall (home of the Trondheim Philharmonic). ⊠ *Kjøpmannsgt. 48,* ☎ *73/53–53–10,* FAX *73/53–57–20. 106 rooms, 5 no-smoking rooms. 3 restaurants, bar, pub, nightclub, meeting rooms. AE, DC, MC, V.*

$$–$$$$ 🏨 **Prinsen.** Rooms in this hotel in the center of the city are light—monochromatic to the point of being dull. One of the restaurants here, Teatergrillen, serves a good early dinner. ⊠ *Kongensgt. 30, 7002,* ☎ *73/53–06–50,* FAX *73/53–06–44. 85 rooms, 1 suite. 3 restaurants, 3 bars, nightclub. AE, DC, MC, V.*

$$–$$$$ 🏨 **Royal Garden.** The city's showcase hostelry, right on the river, was built in the same style as the old warehouse buildings that line the waterfront, but in glass and concrete instead of wood. This luxury hotel has big rooms with light-wood furniture and predominantly blue textiles. ⊠ *Kjøpmannsgata 73, 7010,* ☎ *73/52–11–00,* FAX *73/53–17–66. 297 rooms, 8 suites. 3 restaurants, bar, indoor pool, exercise room. AE, DC, MC, V.*

$$ 🏨 **Ambassadeur.** You'll see the deep blue waters of the Trondheimsfjord reflect the dramatic and irregular coastline from the roof terrace of this first-rate modern hotel, about 303 feet from the market square. Most rooms in the Ambassadeur have fireplaces, and some have balconies. ⊠ *Elvegt. 18,* ☎ *73/52–70–50,* FAX *73/52–70–52. 34 rooms. Bar. AE, DC, MC, V.*

$–$$ 🏨 **Bakeriet.** The hotel opened in March 1991 in a building built as a
★ bakery in 1863. Few of the rooms look alike, but all are large, with natural wood furniture and beige-and-red-stripe textiles, and stylish in their simplicity. Every room has a VCR and a window thermometer. There's no restaurant, but a hot evening meal is included in the room rate. You can borrow a track suit, and there's free light beer in the lounge by the sauna. ⊠ *Brattørgt. 2, 7011, Trondheim,* ☎ *73/52–52–00,* FAX *73/50–23–30. 98 rooms, 1 suite. Sauna. AE, DC, MC, V.*

$–$$ 🏨 **Trondheim.** If you've always wanted to try mead, the fermented honey drink of the Vikings, do it here—it's produced on the premises. The building is old on the outside, with a curved corner and wrought-iron balconies, but inside it's new. The rooms are big and light, with what is now considered to be classic Scandinavian bentwood furniture. ⊠

Kongensgt. 15, 7013, ☎ *73/50–50–50,* 🅵🅰🆇 *73/51–60–58. 131 rooms. Restaurant, bar, meeting room. AE, DC, MC, V.*

Nightlife

Olavskvartalet is the center of much of the city's nightlife, with a disco, a jazz and blues club, and a bar and beer hall in the cellar. **Monte Cristo** (✉ Prinsensgt.38–40, ☎ 73/52–18–80) has a restaurant, bar, and disco under the same roof and is popular with the mid-twenties and upwards age group. Students and younger people in search of cheap drinks, music, and dancing tend to gravitate toward **Strossa** (✉ Elgeseter Gt. 1, ☎ 73/89–95–10), which is run by students. **Cafe Remis** (✉ Kjoepmannsgt. 12, ☎ 73/52–05–52) is the center for gay nightlife in Trondheim.

Outdoor Activities and Sports

FISHING

The **Nidelven** (Nid River) in Trondheim is one of Norway's best salmon and trout rivers. You can fish right in the city, but, as usual, you'll need a license. Contact the tourist office.

SKIING

Bymarka and **Estenstadmarka,** the wooded areas on the periphery of Trondheim, are popular among cross-country skiers. At **Skistua** (ski lodge) in Bymarka, and at **Vassfjellet** south of the city, there are downhill runs.

En Route Nord Trøndelag, as the land above Trondheim is called, is largely agricultural. Taken on its own, it's beautiful, with farms, mountains, rock formations, and clear blue water, but compared with the rest of Norway, it is subtle, with only an undulating landscape—so many tourists just sleep through it on the night train or fly over it on their way to the North. The first town of any size is Steinkjer, a military base, boot camp for 3,000 Norwegian army recruits every year.

Mo i Rana

 350 km (218 mi) north of Steinkjer.

Mo i Rana (the poetic name means Mo on the Ranafjord) is a center for iron and steel production using ore from nearby mines.

Setergrotta is one of close to 200 caves 26 kilometers (16 miles) northwest of Mo i Rana. Setergrotta, with 7,920 feet of charted underground paths, many narrow passages, natural "chimneys," and an underground river, is for serious spelunkers. The caves are usually open from mid-June to mid-August; however, times vary with conditions. Check with the tourist office (☎ 75/15–06–22, or 75/15–28–87). 🎟 *NKr160 for a two-hour guided tour.*

Grønligrotta, Scandinavia's best-known show cave, even has electric lights. The 20-minute tour goes deep into the limestone cave to the underground river. ☎ 75/16–23–44. 🎟 *NKr50.* ☉ *Mid-June–mid-Aug. Tours daily on the hr 10–7.*

OFF THE BEATEN PATH
SVARTISEN – Glacier fans can hike on the Svartisen—literally Black Ice—the second-largest glacier in Norway, 30 kilometers (19 miles) north of Mo i Rana. **Saltens Dampskibsselskap** (☎ 75/72–10–20) offers seven-hour boat tours from Bodø to the ice cap on Saturdays in summer. The easiest way to get to the glacier is from Mo, 32 kilometers (20 miles) by car to Svartisvatn lake. A boat crosses the lake every hour to within 2½ kilometers (1½ miles) of the Østerdal arm of the glacier. If you plan to get to the glacier on your own, you should inquire at the tourist office about connecting with a guide. Glacier walking is extremely hazardous

and should never be done without a professional guide—even though a glacier may appear fixed and static, it is always changing; there's always the danger of calving and hard-to-spot crevasses.

Polarsikelsenteret

73 *80 km (50 mi) north of Mo i Rana.*

On a bleak stretch of treeless countryside is the Arctic Circle. The Polarsirkelsenteret (Arctic Circle Center), on E6, presents a multiscreen show about Norway. The post office has a special postmark, and you can get your Arctic Circle Certificate stamped. There's also a cafeteria and gift shop. ⊠ *8242 Polarsirkelen,* ☎ *75/16–60–66.* ⌑ *NKr35.* ☉ *May–June, daily 10–8; July–Sept., daily 9 AM–10 PM (Apr., Oct. cafeteria only).*

Bodø

74 *174 km (108 mi) north of the Polarsirkelsenteret.*

Bodø, a modern city of about 37,000 just above the Arctic Circle, is best known as the end station of the Nordlandsbanen railroad and the gateway to the Lofoten Islands and the North. At Bodø the midnight sun is visible from June 2 to July 10. Like many other coastal towns, it began as a small fishing community, but today it is a commercial and administrative center.

Bodø is the best base for boat excursions to the coastal bird colonies on the Væren Islands. Bodø is also site of the **Nordland County Museum,** which depicts the life of the Sami and the regional history of the area, particularly its rich fishing heritage. ⊠ *Prinsengt. 116,* ☎ *75/52–61–28.* ⌑ *Free.* ☉ *Weekdays 9–3, weekends noon–3.*

Dining and Lodging

$$ ✕ **Turisthytta.** This mountaintop lodge is accessible only by car. It's a fine place to have a meal while basking in the midnight sun. There is a good range of dishes, from snacks and open-face sandwiches to fresh fish. ⊠ *Turisthytta,* ☎ *75/58–33–00. No credit cards.*

$$ 🏨 **Diplomat.** This hotel near the harbor is a short walk from the shopping district. The modern rooms are soberly decorated. The restaurant has live entertainment, but the food could be more imaginative. ⊠ *Sjøgt. 23, 8000 Bodø,* ☎ *75/52–70–00,* FAX *75/52–24–60. 104 rooms. 2 restaurants, bar, exercise room, nightclub, convention center. AE, DC, MC, V.*

$$ 🏨 **Norrøna.** This bed-and-breakfast-style establishment is comfortable, with a location just as grand as that of the nearby Grand Royal but at a much more pleasant price. ⊠ *Storgt. 4B,* ☎ *75/52–55–50,* FAX *75/52–33–88. 105 rooms. AE, DC, MC, V.*

$$ 🏨 **SAS Royal.** This grandiose hotel pulses with life and has enough amenities to keep you entertained nearly around the clock. As with all SAS hotels, the rooms have all the amenities, and the service is impeccable. ⊠ *Storgt. 2,* ☎ *75/52–41–00,* FAX *75/52–74–93. 194 rooms. Restaurant, wine bar, sauna, health club, nightclub. AE, DC, MC, V.*

Outdoor Activites and Sports

BIRD-WATCHING

From Moskenes, just north of Å (or from Bodø), you can take a ferry to the bird sanctuaries of **Værøy** and **Røst.** Hundreds of thousands of seabirds inhabit the cliffs of the islands, in particular the eider ducks, favorites of the local population, which build small shelters for their nests. Eventually the down collected from these nests ends up in *dyner* (feather comforters).

Saltstraumen

🔞 *33 km (20 mi) southeast of Bodø on Route 80/17.*

Saltstraumen is a 3-kilometer-long (2-mile-long) and 500-foot-wide section of water between the outer fjord, which joins with the sea, and the inner fjord basin. During high tide, the volume of water rushing through the strait and into the basin is so great that whirlpools form. This is the legendary *malstrøm*—and the strongest one in the world. Sometimes as many as four separate whirlpools can be seen, and the noise made by these "cauldrons" can be both loud and eerie. All that rush of water brings enormous quantities of fish, making the malstrøm a popular fishing spot.

NEED A   **Saltstraumen Hotel** (☎ 75/58–76–85) is practically on top of the mal-
BREAK?   strøm. The restaurant to the left of the entrance serves delicious steamed
             halibut in butter sauce.

Narvik

🔞 *336 km (210 mi) north of Saltstraumen.*

Narvik is more easily reached by rail from Stockholm than from most places in Norway, as it is the end station on the Ofotbanen, the Norwegian railroad that connects with the Swedish railroad's northernmost line. It was originally established as the ice-free port for exporting Swedish iron ore mined around Kiruna.

On May 9, 1940, the German army invaded Norway through Narvik, and German occupying forces stayed for more than five years. After the war, Narvik, which had been leveled by the bombing, was rebuilt. The **Krigsminnemuseet** (War Memorial Museum) documents wartime events with artifacts, models, and pictures. ⊠ *Torget,* ☎ *76/94–44–26.* ⌨ *NKr30.* ⊙ *Mid-June–mid-Sept., Mon.–Sat. 10–10, Sun. 11–5; rest of yr, Mon.–Sat. 11–2.*

Lodging

$$–$$$ 🏨 **Inter Nor Grand Royal.** It looks like an office building from the outside, but inside it is a comfortable top-class hotel, with big, rather formal rooms.⊠ *Kongensgt. 64, 8500 Narvik,* ☎ *76/94–15–00,* FAX *76/94–55–31. 108 rooms. 2 restaurants, 2 bars, sauna, exercise room, nightclub, convention center. AE, DC, MC, V.*

Lofoten Islands

Extending out into the ocean north of Bodø are the Lofoten Islands, a 190-kilometer (118-mile) chain of jagged peaks—mountaintops rising from the bottom of the sea like open jaws. The midnight sun is visible here from May 26 to July 17. In summer the idyll of farms, fjords, and fishing villages makes it a major tourist attraction, whereas in winter the coast facing the Arctic Ocean is one of Europe's stormiest.

Until about 40 years ago, fishing was the only source of income for the area. Cod and haddock were either dried or salted and sold on the Continent. Up to 6,000 boats with 30,000 fishermen would mobilize between January and March for the Lofotfisket, the world's largest cod-fishing event. During the season they fished in open boats and took shelter during stormy nights in *rorbuer,* simple cabins built right on the water. Today many rorbuer have been converted into lodgings, but

Lofotfisket is still an annual tradition. In the summer, crisscrossing wooden racks are densely hung with drying cod while the midnight sun plays on the wooden boats in the harbor.

Svolvær, the main town and administrative center for the villages on Lofoten Islands, is connected with the other islands by express boat and ferry, and by coastal steamer and air to Bodø. It has a thriving summer art colony.

A drive on E10, from Svolvær to the outer tip of Lofoten (130 kilometers [80 miles])—the town with the enigmatic name of **Å**—is an opportunity to see how the islanders really live. Scenic stops include **Nusfjord,** a 19th-century fishing village on the UNESCO list of historic monuments; **Sund,** with its smithy; and **Reine.**

NEED A BREAK? **GAMMELBUA,** in Reine, serves excellent steamed halibut, homemade fish soufflé, and inspired desserts and cakes.

Off the tip of Moskenesøy, the last island with a bridge, is **Moskenesstraumen,** a malstrøm not quite as dramatic as Saltstraumen (☞ *above*) but inspiration to both Jules Verne, who wrote about it in *Journey Beneath the Sea,* and Edgar Allan Poe, who described it in his short story "A Descent into the Maelstrom."

North of the Lofotens are the **Vesterålen Islands,** with more fishing villages and rorbuer, and diverse vegetation.

Dining and Lodging

$$ ✕ **Fiskekrogen.** This quayside restaurant in the fishing village of Henningsvær will prepare your own catch. Chef-owner Otto Asheim's specialties include smoked *gravlaks* (smoking the dill-marinated salmon gives it extra depth of flavor) and sautéed ocean catfish garnished with mussels and shrimp. ⊠ *8330 Henningsvær,* ☎ *76/07–46–52. Reservations essential. DC, MC, V.*

$$–$$$ ⌂ **Nyvågar Rorbu og Aktivitetssenter.** This hotel and recreation complex is a 15-minute drive from the Svolvær airport. Activities are well organized, with fishing-boat tours, eagle safaris, and deep-sea rafting, as well as planned evening entertainment. ⊠ *8310 Kabelvåg, Storvågan,* ☎ *76/07–89–00,* FAX *76/07–89–50. 30 rooms. 2 restaurants, meeting rooms. AE, DC, MC, V.*

$ ⌂ **Henningsvær Rorbuer.** This small group of turn-of-the-century rorbuer, all facing the sea, is just outside the center of Lofoten's most important fishing village. Breakfasts can be ordered from the cafeteria-reception, where there's a fireplace and a TV. Reservations are essential for July. ⊠ *8330 Henningsvær,* ☎ *76/07–46–00,* FAX *76/07–49–10. 15 1- or 2-bedroom rorbuer. Cafeteria, grill, sauna, laundry service. MC, V.*

$ ⌂ **Wulff-Nilsens Rorbuer.** A five-minute drive from Reine, which was named the country's prettiest village by Norwegian travel agents, this neat cluster of red-painted rorbuer is an excellent starting point for fishing excursions and mountain walks. Seagulls nest only yards from the cabins. The rorbuer are rustic but comfortably equipped; they have stoves and refrigerators. ⊠ *Hamnøy, 8390 Reine,* ☎ *76/09–23–20,* FAX *76/09–21–54. 13 1-, 2-, or 3-bedroom rorbuer, 2 without shower. No credit cards.*

Shopping

Lofoten is a mecca for artists and craftspeople, who come for the spectacular scenery and the ever-changing subtle light; a list of galleries and crafts centers, with all locations marked on a map, is available from tourist offices.

Probably the best-known craftsperson in the region is Tor Vegard Mørkved, better known as **Smeden i Sund** (the blacksmith at Sund; ☎ 76/09–36–29). Watch him make wrought-iron cormorants in many sizes, as well as candlesticks and other gift items.

Harstad

(77) *About 121 km (75 mi) from Narvik.*

East of Vesterålen on Hinnøya, Norway's largest island, is Harstad, where the year-round population of 22,000 swells to 42,000 during the annual June cultural festival (the line-up includes concerts, theater, and dance) and its July deep-sea fishing festival.

Dining and Lodging

$$$ ✕ **Røkenes Gård.** The farm was originally homesteaded in AD 400, and the large white wooden building with an intricately carved portal opened in 1750 as a commercial trading house and inn. The ninth generation of descendants restored it, and it is now a cozy restaurant serving regional specialties, such as reindeer gravlaks, and cloudberry parfait. ✉ *9400 Harstad,* ☎ *77/01–74–65. Reservations essential. AE, DC, MC, V. Closed Sun.*

$$–$$$ **Grand Nordic.** It's a brick-red building in the Bauhaus style, with Norwegian 1970s-look leather furniture in the public rooms. Bedrooms, no bigger than necessary, have dark-wood furnishings. The restaurant and conference rooms are lighter and more modern. ✉ *Strandgt. 9, 9400 Harstad,* ☎ *77/06–21–70,* FAX *77/06–77–30. 85 rooms, 3 suites. 2 restaurants, bar, nightclub, convention center. AE, DC, MC, V.*

Tromsø

(78) *318 km (197 mi) northeast of Harstad.*

The midnight sun shines from May 21 to July 23 in Tromsø, the most important city north of the Arctic Circle. At 2,558 square kilometers (987 square miles), Tromsø is Norway's largest city in terms of area, just about the same size as the country of Luxembourg, but home to only 50,000 people. The 13,000 students at the world's northernmost university are one reason the nightlife here is more lively than in many other northern cities.

Certainly the **Ishavskatedralen** (Arctic Cathedral) is the city's best-known structure. A looming peak of 11 descending triangles of concrete and glass, it is meant to evoke the shape of a Sami tent and the iciness of a glacier. Inside, an immense jewel-colored stained-glass window by Norwegian artist Viktor Sparre depicts the Second Coming. ☎ *77/63–76–11.* *NKr10.* *June–Aug., Mon.–Sat. 10–6, Sun. 1:30–6. Times may vary according to church services.*

The **Tromsø Museum,** part of Tromsø University, offers an extensive survey of local history, lifestyles, and nature, with dioramas on Sami culture, arctic hunting practices, and wildlife. Children can listen to animal sounds over earphones, match animals to tales about them, and play with a nearly life-size dinosaur. An open-air museum is on the same grounds. ✉ *Universitetet, Lars Thøringsvei 10,* ☎ *77/64–50–00.* *NKr10.* *June–Aug., daily 9–9; Sept., May, Mon.–Tues. and Thurs.–Fri. 8:30–3:30, Wed. 7 PM–10 PM, Sat. noon–3, Sun. 11–4. At other times, call for hours.*

The **Polarmuseet** (Polar Museum), in an 1830s customs warehouse, documents the history of the polar region, with skis and equipment from Roald Amundsen's expedition to the South Pole and a reconstructed Svalbard hunting station from 1910. ☒ *Søndre Tollbugt. 11b,* ☎ *77/68–43–73.* ☒ *NKr30.* ☼ *Mid-May–mid-June, daily 11–6; mid-June–Aug., daily 11–8; Sept.–mid-May, daily 11–3.*

To get a real sense of Tromsø's northerly immensity and peace, take the **Fjellheisen** (cable car) from behind the cathedral up to the mountains, just a few minutes out of the city center. You'll get a great view of the city from **Storsteinen** (Big Rock), 1,386 feet above sea level. In the late afternoon and on weekends, summer and winter, this is where locals go to ski, picnic, walk their lucky dogs, and admire the view. ☎ *77/63–51–21.* ☒ *NKr 45.* ☼ *Late Apr.–late May, daily 10–5; late May–Sept., daily 10–1:30 AM if it's sunny. At other times, call for hours.*

OFF THE BEATEN PATH

NORDLYSPLANETARIET (the Northern Lights Planetarium) – Here, 112 projectors guarantee a 360-degree view of programs, which include a tour through the northern lights, the midnight sun, and geological history, as well as a film and multimedia show about the city. It's just outside town in Breivika. ☎ *77/67-60-00.* ☒ *NKr50.* ☼ *June–Aug., shows in English daily at noon and 3; Sept.–May call for show times.*

En Route The drive from Tromsø to Alta is mostly on a coastal road. At one point you'll drive along the **Kvænangsfjellet ridge,** where Kautokeino Sami spend the summer in turf huts—you might see a few of their reindeer along the way. Thirteen kilometers (8 miles) west of Alteidet you'll pass by **Øksfjordjøkelen,** the only glacier in Norway that calves into the sea.

Dining and Lodging

$$-$$$ ✕ **Brankos.** Branko and Anne Brit Bartolj serve authentic Croatian, Serbian, and Bosnian dishes here. Try the *cevapcici* (small, spicy meatballs) and *raznici*—accompanied by their own imported wines from the former Yugoslavia, in their art-filled dining room. ☒ *Storgt. 57,* ☎ *77/68–26–73. Reservations essential. AE, DC, MC, V. No lunch.*

$$-$$$ ✕ **Compagniet.** An old wooden trading house from 1837 is now a stylish restaurant serving modern Norwegian food. Chef Anders Blomkvist prepares cream of lobster soup with a dash of brandy and escargot in garlic sauce for starters; main dishes include grilled crayfish and marinated smoked reindeer. ☒ *Sjøgt. 12,* ☎ *77/65–57–21. Reservations essential. AE, DC, MC, V. No lunch in winter.*

$$-$$$ ☷ **Hotel With.** This hotel on the waterfront in the dock area has spacious rooms decorated in shades of gray with the occasional colorful accent. The sauna–relaxation room on the top floor has the best view in town. As part of the Home Hotel chain, Hotel With offers alcohol-free beer, a hot meal, and waffles and coffee at all times, included in the room price. ☒ *Sjøgt. 35–37, 9000,* ☎ *77/68–70–00,* ☒ *77/68–96–16. 76 rooms. Exercise room, meeting rooms. AE, DC, MC, V.*

$$-$$$ ☷ **SAS Royal Hotel.** You'll get splendid views over the Tromsø shoreline at this modern hotel, but standard rooms are tiny, and even the costlier "Royal Club" rooms aren't big enough for real desks and tables, so modular ones have been attached to the walls. ☒ *Sjøgt. 7, 9000,* ☎ *77/60–00–00,* ☒ *77/66–42–60. 193 rooms, 6 suites. Restaurant, bar, nightclub, convention center. AE, DC, MC, V.*

$$ ☷ **Saga.** The central location on a pretty town square and a helpful staff make the Saga a good place to stay. Its restaurant has affordable, hearty meals, and the rooms—though somewhat basic—are quiet and comfortable. ☒ *Richard Withs Pl. 2,* ☎ *77/68–11–80,* ☒ *77/68–23–80. 52 rooms. Restaurant, cafeteria. AE, DC, MC, V.*

$–$$ 🏨 **Polar Hotell.** This no-frills hotel gives good value for the money in winter, when none of the bigger hotels have special rates. Rooms are small, and the orange-brown color scheme is a bit dated, but it's a pleasant, unassuming place. ✉ *Grønnegt. 45, 9000,* ☎ *77/68–64–80,* 𝖥𝖠𝖷 *77/68–91–36. 64 rooms. Restaurant, bar, meeting rooms. AE, DC, MC, V.*

Nightlife

Tromsø brags that it has 10 nightclubs, not bad for a city of 50,000 at the top of the world. **Compagniet** (☞ Dining, *above*) has the classiest nightclub; **Charly's** at the SAS Royal Hotel is also popular. **Boccaccio** (☎ 77/68–49–06) is a good place to go for live bands and attracts a younger crowd. **Dampen** (✉ Kai Gt.1) is more alternative than any other venue in Tromsø in terms of live music and clientele.

Outdoor Activities and Sports

HIKING

In Tromsø there's good hiking in the mountains above the city, reachable by funicular. Other regional possibilities begin anywhere outside the cities (usually only a few minutes away).

SKIING

In Tromsø, the mountains, only eight minutes away by funicular, are a great place to ski. Elsewhere, you'll have to ask specifics from the tourist board. Listen to the weather reports and heed warnings. Blizzards come in quickly over the water; the wind alone can knock a sizable person clear off his or her feet.

Alta

79 *409 km (253 mi) north of Tromsø, 217 km (134 mi) from the North Cape.*

Alta is a major transportation center into Finnmark, the far north of Norway. Most people come just to spend the night before making the final ascent to the North Cape.

OFF THE BEATEN PATH
ALTA MUSEUM – It's worth a trek to Hjemmeluft, southwest of the city, to see four groupings of 2,500- to 6,000-year-old prehistoric rock carvings, the largest in northern Europe. The pictographs, featuring ships, reindeer, and even a man with a bow and arrow, were discovered in 1973 and are included on the UNESCO World Heritage List. The rock carvings form part of the Alta Museum. The museum has displays delineating the history of the area from the Stone Age until today, including its destruction in World War II. ☎ 78/43–53–77. ✆ Summer NKr40; winter NKr30. ☾ May, daily 9–6; early-June–mid-June and mid–late Aug., daily 8–8; mid-June–mid-Aug., daily 8 AM–11 PM; Sept., daily 9–6; Oct.–Apr., weekdays 9–3, weekends 11–4.

Lodging

$$$ 🏨 **SAS Alta Hotell.** This glass-and-white hotel does everything it can to make you forget that you are in a place where it is dark much of the time. Everything is light, from the reflectors on the ceiling of public rooms to the white furniture in the bedrooms. ✉ *Lokkevn. 1, 9500 (Box 1093, 9501),* ☎ *78/43–50–00,* 𝖥𝖠𝖷 *78/43–58–25. 155 rooms. 2 restaurants, 2 bars, lobby lounge, sauna, exercise room, nightclub, meeting rooms. AE, DC, MC, V.*

Outdoor Activities and Sports

DOGSLEDDING

Canyon Huskies (☎ 78/43–33–06), in Alta, arranges all kinds of personalized tours, whether you want to stay in a tent or hotel, and whether you want to drive your team or stay in the sled. Like most Norwegian sled dogs, these are very friendly.

Shopping

Manndalen Husflidslag (☎ 77/71–62–73) at Løkvoll in Manndalen on E6 about 15 kilometers (9 miles) west of Alta is a center for Coastal Sami weaving on vertical looms. Local weavers sell their rugs and wall hangings along with other regional crafts.

Hammerfest

⑧⓪ *145 km (90 mi) north of Alta.*

The world's northernmost town is Hammerfest, an important fishing center. At these latitudes the "most northerlies" become numerous, but certainly the lifestyles here are a testament to determination, especially in winter, when night lasts for months. In 1891 Hammerfest decided to brighten the situation and purchased a generator from Thomas Edison. It was the first city in Europe to have electric street lamps.

Hammerfest is home to the **Royal and Ancient Polar Bear Society.** Don't visit the society if you don't like taxidermic displays. ⊠ *Town Hall Basement.* ⚄ *Free.* ☉ *June–Aug., weekdays 8–8, weekends 10–5.*

Dining and Lodging

$$–$$$ ✕⌷ **Rica Hotel Hammerfest.** The rooms are functional and small, but the furniture is comfortable. There is also an informal pizza pub and a spacious bar. ⊠ *Sørøygt. 15,* ☎ *78/41–13–33,* FAX *78/41–13–11. 88 rooms. Restaurant, bar, pizzeria, sauna, health club, convention center. AE, DC, MC, V.*

$$$ ⌷ **Hammerfest Hotel.** Right on the pleasant Rådhusplassen, this guest house has handsome, harborview rooms for tolerable prices in a town where hotels are expensive. ⊠ *Strandgt. 2–4,* ☎ *78/41–16–22,* FAX *78/41–21–27. 53 rooms. Restaurant, cafeteria, pub, sauna. AE, DC, MC, V.*

Honningsvåg

⑧① *130 km (80.6 mi) from Hammerfest.*

The last village before the Cape, Honningsvåg was completely destroyed at the end of World War II, when the Germans retreated and burned everything they left behind. Only a single wood church, which still survives, was not left in embers. The **Nordkappmuseet** (North Cape Museum), on the third floor of Nordkapphuset (North Cape House), documents the history of the fishing industry in the region as well as the history of tourism at the North Cape. ⊠ *9750 Honningsvåg,* ☎ *78/47–28–33.* ⚄ *NKr15.* ☉ *Mid-June–mid-Aug., Mon.–Sat. 9–8, Sun. 1–8; rest of yr, weekdays 11–4.*

Lodging

$ ⌷ **Hotel Havly.** This simple hotel is cozy and centrally located, with small, spic-and-span rooms and an ample breakfast buffet. Because this is a seamen's hostel, no alcohol is served. ⊠ *9751 Honningsvåg,* ☎ *78/47–29–66,* FAX *78/47–30–10. 35 rooms. Restaurant, meeting rooms. AE, MC, V.*

Outdoor Activities and Sports

BIRD-WATCHING
There are tons of birds in Gjesvær on the east coast of the Honningsvåg. Contact Ola Thomassen (☎ 78/47–57–73) for organized outings.

Nordkapp

③ *34 km (21 mi) from Honningsvåg.*

On your journey to the Nordkapp (North Cape), you'll see an incredible treeless tundra, with crumbling mountains and sparse dwarf plants. Although this area is notoriously crowded in the summer, with endless lines of tour buses, it's completely different from fall through spring, when the snow is yards deep and the sea is frosty gray. Because the roads are closed in winter, the only access is from the tiny fishing village of Skarsvåg via Sno-Cat, a thump-and-bump ride that's as unforgettable as the beautifully bleak view. For winter information, contact North Cape Travel (☎ 78/47–25–99). Knivsjellodden, slightly west and less dramatic than the North Cape, is actually a hair farther north.

The contrast between this near-barren territory and the new **North Cape Hall** is striking. Blasted into the interior of the plateau, the building is housed in a cave and includes a restaurant with incredible views. A tunnel leads past a small chapel to a grotto with a panoramic view of the Arctic Ocean and to the cliff wall itself, passing exhibits that trace the history of the Cape, from Richard Chancellor, an Englishman who drifted around it and named it in 1533, to Oscar II, king of Norway and Sweden, who climbed to the top of the plateau in 1873, and King Chulalongkorn of Siam (now Thailand), who visited the Cape in 1907. Out on the plateau itself, a hollow sculptured globe is illuminated by the midnight sun, which shines from May 11 to August 31. ✉ *9764 Nordkapp*, ☎ *78/47–25–99. Entrance to the hall:* ✇ *NKr150.*

Outdoor Activities and Sports

RAFTING

Deep-sea rafting is a relatively new sport in the area, but one that is as exhilarating as it is beautiful. Among the several tours is a three-hour trip to the North Cape. Call **Nordkapp Safari** (☎ 78/47–27–94).

Trondheim to the North Cape A to Z

Arriving and Departing

BY BOAT

Hurtigruten (the coastal express boat, which calls at 35 ports from Bergen to Kirkenes) stops at Trondheim, southbound at St. Olav's Pier, Quay 16, northbound at Pier 1, Quay 7. Call ☎ 73/52–55–40 for information on Hurtigruten and local ferries.

BY BUS

Buses run only from Oslo to Otta, where they connect with the train to Trondheim. Buses connect Bergen, Molde, Ålesund, and Røros with Trondheim.

Nor-Way Bussekspress (☎ 22/17–52–90) can help you to put together a bus journey to the North. The Express 2000 travels three times a week between Oslo, Kautokeino, Alta, and Hammerfest. The journey, via Sweden, takes 24, 26, and 29 hours, respectively.

BY CAR

Trondheim is about 500 kilometers (310 miles) from Oslo: seven to eight hours of driving. Speed limits are 80 kph (50 mph) much of the way. There are two alternatives, E6 through Gudbrandsdalen or Route 3 through Østerdalen. Roads are decent for the most part but can become thick with campers during midsummer, sometimes making the going slow. It's 727 kilometers (450 miles) from Trondheim to Bodø on Route E6, which goes all the way to Kirkenes. There's a 20NKr toll on E6 just south of Trondheim for travelers in both directions. Cars entering the downtown area must pay a 10NKr toll (6 AM–10 PM).

Trondheim's **Værnes Airport** is 35 kilometers (22 miles) northeast of the city. **SAS** (☎ 74/82–49–22), **Braathens SAFE** (☎ 74/82–32–00), and **Widerøe** (☎ 74/82–49–22) are the main domestic carriers. **SAS** also has one flight between Trondheim and Copenhagen daily, except Sunday, and daily flights to Stockholm.

With the exception of Harstad, all cities in northern Norway are served by airports less than 5 kilometers (3 miles) from the center of town. Tromsø is a crossroads for air traffic between northern and southern Norway and is served by Braathens SAFE, SAS, and Widerøe. SAS flies to eight destinations in northern Norway, including Bodø, Tromsø, Alta, and Kirkenes. Braathens SAFE flies to five destinations, including Bodø and Tromsø. Widerøe specializes in northern Norway and flies to 19 destinations in the region, including Honningsvåg, the airport closest to the North Cape.

The **Dovrebanen** has five departures daily, four on Saturday, in both directions on the Oslo–Trondheim route. Trains leave from Oslo S Station for the seven- to eight-hour journey. Trondheim is the gateway to the North, and two trains run daily in both directions on the 11-hour Trondheim–Bodø route. For information about trains out of Trondheim, call ☎ 73/53–00–10. The **Nordlandsbanen** has two departures daily in each direction on the Bodø–Trondheim route, an 11-hour journey. The **Ofotbanen** has one departure daily in each direction on the Stockholm–Narvik route, a 21-hour journey.

Getting Around

Boat is the ideal transportation in Nordland. The *Hurtigruten* stops twice daily (north and southbound) at 20 ports in northern Norway. It is possible to buy tickets between any harbors right on the boats. **Saltens Dampskibsselskab** (Bodø, ☎ 75/52–10–20) has express boats between Bodø and Hamarøy and Svolvær; **OVDS** (Narvik, ☎ 76/92–37–00) ferries and express boats serve many towns in the region. **TFDS, Troms Fylkes Dampskibsselskap** (Tromsø, ☎ 77/68–60–88) operates various boat services in the region around Tromsø.

Most local buses in **Trondheim** stop at the Munkegata/Dronningens Gate intersection. Some routes end at the bus terminal (✉ Skakkes Gt. 40, ☎ 73/52–44–74). Tickets cost NKr12 and allow free transfer between buses (☎ 73/54–71–00) and streetcars (**Gråkallbanen,** ☎ 72/55–23–55).

North of **Bodø** and **Narvik** (a five-hour bus ride from Bodø), beyond the reach of the railroad, buses go virtually everywhere, but they don't go often. Get a comprehensive bus schedule from a tourist office or travel agent before making plans. Local bus companies include **Saltens Bilruter** (Bodø, ☎ 75/52–50–25), **Ofotens Bilruter** (Narvik, ☎ 76/92–35–00), **Tromsbuss** (Tromsø, ☎ 77/67–02–33), **Tromsøexpressen** (Tromsø, ☎ 77/67–27–87), and **Finnmark Fylkesrederi og Ruteselskap** (FFR, Alta, ☎ 78/43–52–11; Hammerfest, ☎ 78/41–10–00).

The roads aren't a problem in northern Norway—most are quite good, although there are always narrow and winding stretches, especially along fjords. Distances are formidable. Route 17—the *Kystriksvegen* (Coastal Highway) from Namsos to Bodø—is an excellent alternative to E6. Getting to Tromsø and the North Cape involves additional driving on narrower roads off E6. In the northern winter, near-blizzard conditions and icy roads sometimes make it necessary to drive in a convoy. You'll know it when you see it: Towns are cut off from traffic at access roads, and vehicles wait until their numbers are large enough to make the crossing safely.

You can also fly the extensive distances and then rent a car for sightseeing within the area, but book a rental car as far in advance as possible. There's no better way to see the Lofoten and Vesterålen islands than by car. Nordkapp (take the plane to Honningsvåg) is another excursion best made by car.

BY PLANE

Northern Norway has excellent air connections through SAS, Braathens SAFE, and Widerøe (☞ Arriving and Departing by Plane, *above*).

BY TAXI

Taxi stands are located in strategic places in downtown **Trondheim.** All taxis are connected to the central dispatching office (☎ 73/50–50–73). Taxi numbers in other towns are **Harstad** (☎ 77/06–20–50), **Narvik** (☎ 76/94–65–00), and **Tromsø** (☎ 77/68–80–20).

Contacts and Resources

GUIDED TOURS

Tromsø: The tourist information office sells tickets for **City Sightseeing** (Dampskipskaia) and **M/F Karlsøy,** an original Arctic vessel that runs a fishing tour in the waters around Tromsø Island.

Trondheim: The Trondheim Tourist Association offers a number of tours. Tickets are sold at the tourist information office or at the start of the tour.

LATE-NIGHT PHARMACIES

Trondheim: St. Olav Vaktapotek (⊠ Kjøpmannsgt. 65, ☎ 73/52–66–66) is open Monday through Saturday 8:30 AM–midnight and Sunday 10 AM–midnight.

Tromsø: Svaneapoteket (⊠ Fr. Langes Gt. 9, ☎ 77/68–64–24) is open daily 8:30–4 and 6–9.

VISITOR INFORMATION

Trondheim (⊠ Munkegt. 19, 7000, ☎ 73/92–93–94). Other tourist offices in the region are **Alta** (⊠ Finnmark Opplevelser A/S, 9500, ☎ 78/43–54–44); **Bodø** (⊠ Sjøgt. 21, 8006, ☎ 75/52–60–00); **Hammerfest** (⊠ 9600, ☎ 78/41–21–85); **Harstad** (⊠ Torvet 8, 9400, ☎ 77/06–32–35); **Mo i Rana** (⊠ 8600 Mo, ☎ 75/15–04–21); **Narvik** (⊠ Kongensgt. 66, 8500, ☎ 76/94–33–09); **Tromsø** (⊠ Storgt. 61, 9000, ☎ 77/61–00–00); **Vesterålen Reiselivslag** (⊠ 8400 Sortland, ☎ 77/12–15–55); and **Nordkapp** (⊠ Nordkapphuset, Honningsvåg, ☎ 78/47–28–94).

SAMILAND: SVALBARD AND THE FINNISH-RUSSIAN CONNECTION

Everyone has heard of Lapland, but few know its real name, Samiland. The Sami recognize no national boundaries, as their territory stretches from the Kola Peninsula in the Soviet Union through Finland, Sweden, and Norway. These indigenous reindeer herders are a distinct ethnic group, with a language related to Finnish. Although still considered nomadic, they no longer live in tents or huts, except for short periods during the summer, when their animals graze along the coast. They have had to conform to today's lifestyles, but their traditions survive through their language, music (called Joik), art, and handicrafts. Norwegian

Samiland is synonymous with the communities of Kautokeino and colorful Karasjok, capital of the Sami, in Finnmark.

Kautokeino

83 *129 km (80 mi) southeast of Alta.*

Kautokeino is the site of the Sami theater and the Nordic Sami Institute, dedicated to the study of Sami culture. It is a center for Sami handicrafts and education, complete with a school of reindeer herding.

Guovdageainnu (Kautokeino in the Sami language) **Gilisillju,** the local museum, documents the way of life of both the nomadic and the resident Sami of that area prior to World War II, with photographs and artifacts, including costumes, dwellings, and art. ⊠ *9520 Kautokeino,* ☎ *78/45–62–03.* 🎫 *NKr10.* ☉ *Mid-June–mid-Aug., weekdays 9–7, weekends noon–7; mid-Aug.–mid-June, weekdays 9–3.*

The Arts

During Easter, Kautokeino holds its annual **Easter Festival,** including theater, joik (a haunting, ancient form of solo, a cappella song, often in praise of nature), concerts, weddings, and exhibits of traditional crafts. Contact Finnmark Opplevelser (⊠ 9500 Alta, ☎ 78/43–54–44).

From June 15 to August 15, **Beaivváš Sami Theater** (⊠ 9250 Kautokeino, ☎ 78/48–68–11) offers summer programs of traditional Sami folk songs and modern works.

Karasjok

84 Karasjok, on the other side of the Finnmark Plateau, is the seat of the 39-member Sami Parliament and capital of Samiland. It has a typical inland climate, with the accompanying temperature extremes. The best time to come is at Easter, when the communities are celebrating the weddings and baptisms of the year and taking part in reindeer races and other colorful festivities. In summer, when many of the Sami go to the coast with their reindeer, the area is not nearly as interesting.

The **Samid Vuorka-Davvirat** (Sami Collections) are a comprehensive museum of Sami culture, with emphasis on the arts, reindeer herding, and the status of women in the Sami community. ⊠ *Museumsgt. 17,* ☎ *78/46–63–05.* 🎫 *NKr25.* ☉ *Mid-June–mid-Aug., Mon.–Sat. 9–6, Sun. 10–6; late Aug.–Oct., weekdays 9–3, weekends 10–3; Nov.–Mar., weekdays 9–3, weekends noon–3; Apr.–early June, weekdays 9–3, weekends 10–3.*

From late fall to early spring you can go **reindeer sledding.** A Sami guide will take you out on a wooden sled tied to a couple of unwieldy reindeer, and you'll clop through the barren, snow-covered scenery of Finnmark. Wide and relatively flat, the colorless winter landscape is veined by inky alder branches and little else. You'll reach a *lavvu,* a traditional Sami tent, and be invited in to share a meal of boiled reindeer, bread, jam, and strong coffee next to an open alder fire. It's an extraordinary experience. Contact **Karasjok Opplevelser** (☎ 78/46–73–60).

Dining and Lodging

$$$–$$$$
★ ✕🏨 **SAS Karasjok Hotell.** This establishment feels more like a ski chalet than a hotel, with bright rooms, done in warm blues and reds, that are cozy rather than industrial. The lobby is more staid, with a seating arrangement up front. The hotel's wonderful Sami restaurant, Storgammen, serves traditional fare, including reindeer cooked over open fires. ⊠ *Box 38, 9731 Karasjok,* ☎ *78/46–74–00,* 🅵🅰🆇 *78/46–68–02. 56 rooms. Restaurant, bar, saunas, meeting rooms. AE, DC, MC, V.*

Outdoor Activities and Sports

HIKING

In between the Alta and Karasjok areas, the **Finnmarksvidda** has marked trails with overnight possibilities in lodges. Contact the Norske Turist-forening (⊠ Buks 1963 Vika, 0125 Oslo, ☎ 22/83–25–50, FAX 22/83–24–78) and the Finnmark Travel Association (☎ 78/43–54–44).

Shopping

The specialties of the region are Sami crafts, particularly handmade knives. In **Samelandssenter** (☎ 78/46–73–60) is a large collection of shops featuring northern specialties, including **Knivsmed Strømeng** (☎ 78/46–71–05).

Kirkenes

⑧⑤ At its very top, Norway hooks over Finland and touches Russia for 122 kilometers (75 miles). The towns in east Finnmark have a more heterogeneous population than those in the rest of the country. A century ago, during hard times in Finland, many industrious Finns settled in this region, and their descendants keep the language alive there.

A good way to visit this part of Norway is to fly to Kirkenes and then explore the region by car. Only Malta was bombed more than Kirkenes during World War II—virtually everything you see in town has been built within the past 45 years.

In winter this entire region, blanketed by snow and cold, is off the beaten track. As the Norwegians say, there is no bad weather, only bad clothes—so bundle up and explore.

From mid-June to mid-August, the **FFR** (⊠ Hammerfest, ☎ 78/41–10–00) operates visa-free day cruises to Murmansk, Russia, on a high-speed catamaran. Booking is required two weeks in advance.

OFF THE
BEATEN PATH

ST. GEORGS KAPELL – Forty-five kilometers (28 miles) west of Kirkenes is the only Russian-Orthodox chapel in Norway, where the Orthodox Skolt-Sami had their summer encampment. It's a tiny building, and services are held outside, weather permitting.

Lodging

$$–$$$$ ☖ **Rica Arctic Hotel.** Do not confuse this hotel with the Rica Hotel Kirkenes, an older establishment, which ends up costing the same during the summer. Rooms here are spacious and pretty, with white-painted furniture and light print textiles. ⊠ *Kongensgt. 1–3, 9900 Kirkenes*, ☎ *78/99–29–29,* FAX *78/99–11–59. 80 rooms. Restaurant, bar, indoor pool, beauty salon, sauna, exercise room, nightclub, convention center. AE, DC, MC, V.*

Storskog

⑧⑥ *About 60 km (37 mi) from Kirkenes.*

Just east of Kirkenes is Storskog, for many years the only official land crossing of the border between Norway and Russia. The tiny village of **Grense Jakobselv** on the Russian border is where King Oscar II built a chapel right at the border in 1869 as a protest against constant Russian encroachment in the area.

OFF THE
BEATEN PATH

ØVRE PASVIK – The southernmost part of Finnmark, about 118 kilometers 73 miles south of Kirkens, is Øvre Pasvik national park, a narrow tongue of land tucked between Finland and Russia. This subarctic evergreen forest is the western end of Siberia's *taiga* and supports many varieties of flora found only here. The area is surprisingly lush, and in good years all the cloudberries make the swamps shine orange.

Svalbard

87 *640 km (400 mi) north of the North Cape.*

The islands of Svalbard, the largest of which is Spitsbergen, have officially been part of Norway only since 1920. They might have remained wilderness, with only the occasional visitor, if coal had not been discovered late in the 19th century. Today both a Norwegian and a Russian coal company have operations there, and there are two Russian coal miners' communities. The islands offer ample opportunities for ski, dogsled, and snowmobile exploring. The best way to experience Svalbard is by organized tour, as accommodations and travel services on the islands themselves are sparse.

Because Svalbard is so far north, it has four months of continual daylight, from April 21 to August 21. Summers can be lush, with hundreds of varieties of wildflowers. The season is so compressed that buds, full-blown flowers, and seed appear simultaneously on the same plant.

The capital, **Longyearbyen,** is 90 minutes by air from Tromsø (there are no scheduled boats from the mainland to Tromsø). It was named for an American, John Monroe Longyear, who established a mining operation there in 1906. Only three species of land mammal besides humans (polar bears, reindeer, and Arctic foxes) and one species of bird (ptarmigan) have adapted to Svalbard winters, but during the summer months, more than 30 species of bird nest on the steep cliffs of the islands, and white whales, seals, and walruses also come for the season. Do heed warnings about polar bears: They can be a real hazard.

Samiland A to Z

Arriving and Departing

(☞ Trondheim to the North Cape A to Z, *above*).

Getting Around

(☞ Trondheim to the North Cape A to Z, *above*).

Contacts and Resources

GUIDED TOURS

Samiland: Contact **Sami Travel A/S** (⊠ Kautokeino, ☎ 78/48–56–00) for adventure trips to Sami settlements.

Svalbard: Svalbard Polar Travel (⊠ 9170 Longyearbyen, ☎ 79/02–19–71) arranges combination air-sea visits, from 3-day minicruises to 12-day trekking expeditions on the rim of the North Pole. **Spitsbergen Travel** (⊠ 9170 Longyearbyen, ☎ 79/02–24–00) offers specialized "exploring" tours that focus on the plant and animal life of the region.

VISITOR INFORMATION

Karasjok (9730, ☎ 78/46–73–60); **Lofoten** (8300 Svolvær, ☎ 76/07–30–00); and **Svalbard** (9170 Longyearbyen, ☎ 79/02–23–03).

NORWAY A TO Z

Arriving and Departing

Oslo Fornebu Airport is the gateway to Norway for most visitors. Once called a "cafeteria with a landing strip," it has been transformed into a modern airport worthy of a capital city. Other international airports include **Bergen, Kristiansand, Sandefjord, Stavanger,** and **Trondheim.**

By Boat

Only one ferry line serves Norway from the United Kingdom, **Color Line** (⊠ Tyne Commission Quay, North Shields [near Newcastle], LEN29 6EA, ☎ 091/296–1313; ⊠ Skoltegrunnskaien, 5000 Bergen, ☎ 55/32–27–80; or ⊠ 405 Park Ave., New York, NY 10022, ☎ 800/323–7436), which has three departures a week between Bergen, Stavanger, and Newcastle during the summer season (May 22–Sept. 10) and two during the rest of the year. Crossings take about 22 hours. Monday sailings stop first in Stavanger and arrive in Bergen six hours later, whereas the other trips stop first in Bergen.

By Plane

FROM NORTH AMERICA

Scandinavian Airlines (SAS, ☎ 800/221–2350) has daily nonstop flights to Oslo from Newark; daily connections to Oslo via Copenhagen from Chicago, Los Angeles, and Seattle; and twice-weekly connections (also via Copenhagen) from Toronto and Anchorage. During the summer months, **Delta Airlines** (☎ 800/241–4141) has daily nonstop flights from New York to Oslo. **Icelandair** (☎ 800/223–5500) flies from New York and Baltimore to Oslo via Reykjavík.

Flying Time: A nonstop flight from New York to Oslo takes about 7½ hours.

FROM THE UNITED KINGDOM

SAS (☎ 0171/734–4020, FAX 0171/465–0125) flies from Heathrow to Oslo, Stavanger, and Bergen, and from Aberdeen to Stavanger. **Braathens SAFE** (☎ 0129/353–5353) operates flights from Newcastle to Stavanger, Bergen, and Oslo, and from London Gatwick to Oslo. **AirUK** (☎ 0181/745–7321) has several flights weekly from Aberdeen to Stavanger and Bergen. **British Airways** (☎ 0181/897–4000) offers nonstop flights from Heathrow to Bergen, Oslo, and Stavanger. **Aer Lingus** (☎ 01345/01–01–01; in Ireland, 0001/377–777), **Cimber Air** (☎ 01652/688491), **Business Air** (☎ 01382/66345), **Midtfly** (☎ 01224/723357), and **Icelandair** (☎ 0171/388–5599; or 0181/745–7051 at Heathrow Airport) all have flights between Great Britain or Ireland and major Scandinavian cities.

Flying time: A nonstop flight from London to Oslo is about 1¾ hours and about 1½ hours to Stavanger.

By Train

Traveling from Britain to Norway by train is not difficult. The best connection leaves London's Victoria Station (☎ 0171/928–5100) at noon and connects at Dover with a boat to Oostende, Belgium. From Oostende there is a sleeping-car-only connection to Copenhagen that arrives the next morning at 8:25. The train to Oslo leaves at 9:45 AM and arrives at 7:42 PM. A number of special discounted trips are available, including the **InterRail Pass,** which is available for European residents of all ages, and the **EurailPass,** sold in the United States only.

Getting Around

The southern part of Norway can be considered fairly compact—all major cities are about a day's drive from each other (although Trondheim–Stavanger is pushing it). The distances make themselves felt on the way north, where Norway becomes narrower as it inches up to and beyond the Arctic Circle and hooks over Sweden and Finland to touch the Soviet Union. Because distances are so great, it is virtually impossible to visit the entire country from one base.

By Boat

Ferries and passenger ships remain important means of transportation. Along west-coast fjords, car ferries are a way of life. More specialized boat service includes hydrofoil-catamaran trips between Stavanger, Haugesund, and Bergen. There are also fjord cruises out of these cities and others in the north. **Color Line** (⊠ Box 1422, Vika 0115, Oslo, ☎ 22/83–60–10, ℻ 22/83–07–76) is a major carrier in Norwegian waters.

Norway's most renowned boat trip is *Hurtigruten,* or the *Coastal Express,* which departs from Bergen and stops at 36 ports in six days, ending with Kirkenes, near the Russian border, before turning back. Tickets can be purchased for the entire journey or for individual legs. Shore excursions are arranged at all ports. Tickets are available through **Bergen Line travel agents** (⊠ 405 Park Ave., New York, NY 10022, ☎ 800/323–7436), or directly from the companies that run the service: **FFR** (⊠ 9600 Hammerfest, ☎ 78/41–10–00), **OVDS** (⊠ 8501 Narvik, ☎ 76/92–37–00), **Hurtigruten Booking** (⊠ Kjøpmannsgt. 52, 7011 Trondheim, ☎ 73/51–51–20, ℻ 73/51–51–46), and **TFDS** (⊠ 9000 Tromsø, ☎ 77/68–60–88).

By Bus

Every end station of the railroad is supported by a number of bus routes, some of which are operated by NSB, others by local companies. Long-distance buses usually take longer than the railroad, and fares are only slightly lower. Virtually every settlement on the mainland is served by bus, and for anyone with a desire to get off the beaten track, a pay-as-you-go open-ended bus trip is the best way to see Norway.

Most long-distance buses leave from **Bussterminalen** (⊠ Galleri Oslo, Schweigaardsgt., 10, ☎ 22/17–01–66), close to Oslo Central Station. **Nor-Way Bussekspress** (Bussterminalen, ☎ 22/17–52–90, ℻ 22/17–59–22) has more than 40 different bus services, covering 10,000 kilometers (6,200 miles) and 500 destinations, and can arrange any journey. One of its participating services, **Feriebussen** (⊠ Østerdal Billag A/S, 2560 Alvdal, ☎ 62/48–74–00), offers five package tours with English-speaking guides.

By Car

All vehicles registered abroad are required to carry international liability insurance and an international accident report form, which can be obtained from automobile clubs. Collision insurance is recommended. One important rule when driving in Norway: Yield to the vehicle approaching from the right.

Dimmed headlights are mandatory at all times, as is the use of seat belts and children's seats (when appropriate) in both front and rear seats. All cars must carry red reflecting warning triangles to be placed a safe distance from a disabled vehicle. **Norsk Automobil Forbund** (⊠ NAF, ☎ 22/34–16–00 for 24-hour service) patrols main roads and has emergency telephones on mountain roads.

Four-lane highways are the exception and are found only around major cities. Outside of main routes, roads tend to be narrow and sharply twisting, with only token guardrails, and during the summer roads are always crowded. Along the west coast, waits for ferries and passage through tunnels can be significant. Don't expect to cover more than 240 kilometers (150 miles) in a day, especially in fjord country.

Driving is on the right. Norwegian roads are well marked with directional, distance, and informational signs. Some roads, particularly those over mountains, can close for all or part of the winter. If you drive outside major roads in winter, make sure the car is equipped with studded tires for improved traction. Roads are not salted but are left with a hard-packed layer of snow on top of the asphalt. If you're renting, choose a small car with front-wheel drive. Also bring an ice scraper, snow brush, small shovel, and heavy clothes for emergencies. Although the weather along the coast is sunny, a few hours inland, temperatures may be 15° colder, and snowfall is the rule rather than the exception.

The maximum speed limit is 90 kph (55 mph) on major motorways. On other highways, the limit is 80 kph (50 mph). The speed limit in cities and towns is 50 kph (30 mph), and 30 kph (18 mph) in residential areas.

Gas stations are plentiful, and *blyfri bensin* (unleaded gasoline) and diesel fuel are sold virtually everywhere from self-service gas pumps. Those marked *kort* are 24-hour pumps, which take oil-company credit cards or bank cards, either of which is inserted directly into the pump. Gas costs approximately NKr8.50 per liter.

Norway has strict drinking-and-driving laws, and routine roadside checks, especially on Friday and Saturday nights, are common. The legal limit is a blood-alcohol percentage of 0.05%, which corresponds to a glass of wine or a bottle of low-alcohol beer. If you are stopped for a routine check, you may be required to take a breath test. If that result is positive, you must submit to a blood test. No exceptions are made for foreigners, who can lose their licenses on the spot.

Speeding is also punished severely. Most roads are monitored by radar and cameras in gray metal boxes. Signs warning of *Automatisk Trafikkontroll* (Automatic Traffic Monitoring) are posted periodically along appropriate roads. Radar controls are frequent on weekends, especially along major highways. Make sure you double-check all directions and have an up-to-date map before you venture out, because some highway numbers have changed in the past few years, particularly routes beginning with "E." You may come across construction in and around Oslo and other major cities.

By Plane

SAS (☎ 810/03–300) serves most major cities, including Svalbard. **Braathens SAFE** (☎ 67/59–70–00) is the major domestic airline, serving cities throughout the country and along the coast as far north as Tromsø and Svalbard. It also has international routes from Oslo to Billund, Denmark; Malmö, Sweden; and Newcastle, England. **Widerøe** (☎ 22/73–66–00) serves smaller airports (with smaller planes), mostly along the coast, and in northern Norway. **Norsk Air** (☎ 33/46–90–00), a subsidiary of Widerøe, provides similar services in the southern part of the country. **Coast Air** (☎ 52/83–41–10) and **Norlink** (☎ 77/67–57–80), an SAS subsidiary, are commuter systems linking both smaller and larger airports.

A number of special fares are available within Norway year-round, including air passes, family tickets, weekend excursions, and youth (up to the age of 26) and senior (over 67) discounts. Youth fares are cheapest when purchased from the automatic ticket machines at the airport on the day of departure. All Norwegian routes have reduced rates from July through the middle of August, and tickets can be purchased on the spot. SAS offers special **"Jackpot"** fares all year within Norway and Scandinavia, as well as reasonable **"Visit Scandinavia"** fares, which must be purchased in the United States in conjunction with, and at the same time as, an SAS flight to Scandinavia. Braathens SAFE sells a **Visit Norway** pass, which includes the Scandinavian BonusPass. It is available at **Passage Tours of Scandinavia** (☎ 800/548–5960) and **Borton Overseas** (☎ 800/843–0602).

All flights within Scandinavia are no-smoking, as are all airports in Norway, except in designated areas.

By Taxi

Even the smallest villages have some form of taxi service. Towns on the railroad normally have taxi stands just outside the station. All city taxis are connected with a central dispatching office, so there is only one main telephone number, the taxi central. Look in the telephone book under "Taxi" or "Drosje."

By Train

NSB, the Norwegian State Railway System, has five main lines originating from the **Oslo S Station.** Train tickets can be purchased in railway stations or from travel agencies. NSB has its own travel agency in Oslo (⌷ Stortingsgt. 28, ☎ 22/83–88–50). The longest train runs north to Trondheim, then extends onward as far as Fauske and Bodø. The southern line hugs the coast to Stavanger, while the western line crosses some famous scenic territory on the way to Bergen. An eastern line through Kongsvinger to Stockholm links Norway with Sweden, while another southern line through Gothenburg, Sweden, is the main connection with Continental Europe. Narvik, north of Bodø, is the last stop on Sweden's Ofot line, the world's northernmost rail system, which runs from Stockholm via Kiruna. It is possible to take a five-hour bus trip between Bodø and Narvik to connect with the other train.

NSB trains are clean, comfortable, and punctual. Most have special compartments for travelers with disabilities and for families with children under two years of age. First- and second-class tickets are available. Both seat and sleeper reservations are required on express and overnight trains. Prices vary according to one-, two-, or three-bunk cabins. Reserve a few days ahead in the summer, during major holidays, and for Friday and Sunday trains.

Discounted fares include family, senior-citizen (including not-yet-senior spouses), and off-peak "mini" fares, which must be purchased a day in advance. NSB gives student discounts only to foreigners studying at Norwegian institutions.

RAIL PASSES

Norway participates in the following rail programs: **EurailPass** (and its flexipass variations), **Eurail Drive, ScanRail Pass, Scanrail 'n Drive, InterRail,** and **Nordturist Card.** A **Norway Rail Pass** is available for one or two weeks of unlimited rail travel within Norway. The ticket is sold in the United States through **ScanAm** (⌷ 933 Hwy. 23, Pomton Plains, NJ 07444, ☎ 800/545–2204) and in London through **NSB Travel** (⌷ 21–24 Cockspur St., London SW1Y 5DA, ☎ 0171/930–6666). Prices are about $180/£124 for one week in second class; $243/£167 for two weeks in second class, with first-class rail passes approximately 30% higher. Low-season prices are offered October through April. Rail passes do not guarantee that you will get seats on the trains you want to ride, and seat reservations are sometimes required, particularly on express trains. You will also need reservations for overnight sleeping accommodations.

Contacts and Resources

Language

Norwegian has three additional vowels: æ, ø, and å. Æ is pronounced as a short "a." The ø, sometimes printed as *oe*, is the same as ö in German and Swedish, pronounced very much like a short "u." The å is a contraction of the archaic "aa" and sounds like long "o." These three letters appear at the end of alphabetical listings.

There are two officially sanctioned Norwegian languages, Bokmål and Nynorsk. Bokmål is used by 84% of the population and is the main written form of Norwegian, the language of books, as the first half of its name indicates. Nynorsk, which translates as "new Norwegian," is actually a compilation of older dialect forms from rural Norway, which evolved during the national romantic period around the turn of this century. All Norwegians are required to study both languages, and 25% of all state (NRK) television and radio broadcasting is required to be in Nynorsk. Every Norwegian also receives at least seven years of English instruction, starting in the second grade.

The Sami (incorrectly called Lapp) people have their own language, which is distantly related to Finnish.

Lodging

For camping information and a list of sites, contact local tourist offices or the **Norwegian Automobile Federation** (⊠ Storgt. 2, 0155, Oslo 1, ☎ 22/34–14–00). For a list of vandrerhjem in Norway, contact **Norske Vandrerhjem** (⊠ Dronningensgt. 26, 0154 Oslo, ☎ 22/42–14–10, FAX 22/42–44–76) *See also* Lodging *in* Pleasures and Pastimes at the beginning of this chapter.

Mail

The letter rate for Norway is NKr3.50, NKr4 for the other Nordic countries, NKr4.50 for Europe, and NKr5.50 for outside Europe for a letter weighing up to 20g (¾ ounce).

Money and Expenses

The unit of currency in Norway is the *krone* (plural: *kroner*), which translates as "crown," written officially as NOK. Price tags are seldom marked this way, but instead read "Kr" followed by the amount, such as Kr10. (In this book, the Norwegian krone is abbreviated NKr.) One krone is divided into 100 øre, and coins of 10 and 50 øre, 1, 5, 10, and 20 kroner are in circulation, although 10 øre are no longer in production. Bills are issued in denominations of 50, 100, 200, 500, and 1,000 kroner. In summer 1996, the exchange rate was NKr6.56 to U.S.$1, NKr9.87 to £1, and NKr4.81 to C$1. These rates fluctuate, so be sure to check them when planning a trip.

SAMPLE PRICES

Cup of coffee, from NKr12 in a cafeteria to NKr25 or more in a restaurant; a 20-pack of cigarettes, NKr50; a half-liter of beer, NKr30–NKr50; the smallest hot dog (with bun plus *lompe*—a flat Norwegian potato bread—mustard, ketchup, and fried onions) at a convenience store, NKr15; cheapest bottle of wine from a government store, NKr60; the same bottle at a restaurant, NKr120–NKr200; urban transit fare in Oslo, NKr15; soft drink, from NKr20 in a cafeteria to NKr35 in a better restaurant; one adult movie ticket, NKr45; shrimp or roast beef sandwich at a cafeteria, NKr40; 1.6-kilometer (1-mile) taxi ride, NKr30–NKr50 depending upon time of day.

Value-added tax, VAT for short but called *moms* all over Scandinavia, is a hefty 23% on all services and purchases except books; it is included in the prices of goods. All purchases of consumer goods totaling more than NKr300 (approximately $45) for export by nonresidents are eligible for value-added tax refunds.

Shops subscribing to "Norway Tax-Free Shopping" provide customers with vouchers, which they must present together with their purchases upon departure in order to receive an on-the-spot refund of 16.25% of the tax.

Shops that do not subscribe to this program have slightly more detailed forms, which must be presented to the Norwegian Customs Office along with the goods to obtain a refund by mail. This refund is closer to the actual amount of the tax.

It's essential to have both the forms and the goods available for inspection upon departure. Make sure the appropriate stamps are on the voucher or other forms before leaving the country.

Outdoor Activities and Sports

Norway is a sports lover's paradise. Outdoor sports have always been popular, while indoor facilities have been built nationwide. Close to 100 recreational and competitive sports are recognized in Norway, each with its own national association, 57 of which are affiliated with the **Norges Idrettsforbund** (Norwegian Confederation of Sports) (⊠ Hauger Skolevei 1, 1351 Rud, ☎ 67/15–46–00). The tourist board's Norway brochure, which lists sporting- and active-holiday resources and contacts, is a more helpful starting point for visitors.

BICYCLING

Most cities have marked bike and ski routes and paths. Bicycling on country roads away from traffic is a favorite national pastime, but as most routes are hilly, this demands good physical condition. All cyclists are required to wear protective helmets and use lights at night. You can rent a bike and get local maps through any local tourist board.

Den Norske Turistforening (DNT, ⊠ Box 1963 Vika, 0125 Oslo 1, ☎ 22/83–25–50, FAX 22/83–24–78) provides inexpensive lodging for cyclists planning overnight trips. You can also contact the helpful **Syklistenes Landsforening** (⊠ Maridalsvn. 60, 0458 Oslo 4, ☎ 22/71–92–93) for general information and maps, as well as the latest weather conditions.

BIRD-WATCHING

Northern Norway contains some of northern Europe's largest bird sanctuaries and teems with fantastic numbers of seabirds, including cormorants, razorbills, auks, guillemots, eider ducks, puffins, and even eagles. For organized tours, contact **Borton Overseas** (☎ 800/843–0602) or the Norwegian Tourist Board.

CANOEING

There are plenty of lakes and streams for canoeing in Norway, as well as rental facilities. Contact **Norges Padlerforbund** (⊠ Hauger Skolevei 1, 1351 Bærum, ☎ 67/15–46–00) for a list of rental companies and regional canoeing centers.

DIVING

Diving is very well organized and popular in Norway, especially on the west coast. There are few restrictions regarding sites—special permission is required to dive in a harbor, and diving near army installations is restricted. Contact **Norges Dykkforbund** (✉ Hauger Skolevei 1, 1351 Baerum, ☎ 67/15–46–00) for a list of diving centers.

FISHING

To fish, you'll have to buy an annual fishing tax card at the post office and a local license from the sporting-goods store nearest the fishing site. Live bait is prohibited, and imported tackle must be disinfected before use.

PARAGLIDING AND HANG GLIDING

The mountains and hills of Norway provide excellent take-off spots. However, winds and weather conspire to make conditions unpredictable. For details on local clubs, regulations, and equipment rental, contact **Norsk Aeroklubb** (✉ Moellesvingen 2, 0854 Oslo, ☎ 22/93–03–00).

RAFTING

Rafting excursions are offered throughout Norway. For more information, contact **Flåteopplevelser** (✉ Postboks 227, 2051 Jessheim, ☎ 63/97–29–04) or **Norwegian Wildlife and Rafting** (✉ 2254 Lundersæter, ☎ 62/82–97–24).

SAILING

Contact **Norges Seilforbund** (✉ Hauger Skolevei 1, 1351 Bærum, ☎ 67/56–85–75) about facilities around the country.

SKIING

The **Skiforeningen** (✉ Kongevn. 5, 0390 Oslo 3, ☎ 22/92–32–00) provides national snow-condition reports.

SPORTS FOR PEOPLE WITH DISABILITIES

Norway encouraged active participation in sports for people with disabilities long before it became popular elsewhere and has many Special Olympics medal winners. **Beitostølen Helsesportsenter** (✉ 2953 Beitostølen, ☎ 61/34–12–00) has sports facilities for the blind and other physically challenged people as well as training programs for instructors. Sports offered include skiing, hiking, running, and horseback riding.

Opening and Closing Times

Banks are open weekdays 8 to 3:30, Thursday until 5. Most shops are open 9 or 10 to 5 weekdays, Thursday until 7, Saturday 9 to 2, and are closed Sunday. Some large shopping centers are open until 8 weekdays and 6 on Saturdays. Supermarkets are open until 8 or 10 weekdays and until 6 on Saturdays. During the summer, most shops close weekdays at 4 and at 1 on Saturday; banks open at 8:15 and close at 3, with a Thursday closing at 5. Most post offices are open weekdays 8 to 5, Saturday 9 to 2. In small towns, post offices are often closed on Saturdays.

Telephones

The telephone system in Norway is modern and efficient; international direct service is available throughout the country. Phone numbers consist of eight digits throughout the country; there are no area codes.

Public telephones are of two types. Push-button phones, which accept NKr1, 5, and 10 coins (and some of the newer phones, which accept NKr20 coins), are easy to use: Lift the receiver, listen for the dial tone, insert the coins, dial the number, and wait for a connection. The digital screen at the top of the box indicates the amount of money in your "account."

Older rotary telephones sometimes have a grooved slope at the top for NKr1 coins, allowing them to drop into the phone as needed. Place several in the slope, lift the receiver, listen for the dial tone, dial the number, and wait for a connection. When the call is connected, the telephone will emit a series of beeps, allowing coins to drop into the telephone.

Both types of telephones have warning signals (short pips) indicating that the purchased time is almost over.

INTERNATIONAL CALLS
Dial the international access code, 00, then the country code, and number. All telephone books list country code numbers, including the United States and Canada (1), Great Britain (44), and Australia (61). Norway's code is 47. For operator-assisted calls, dial 117 for national calls and 115 for international calls. All international operators speak English.

LOCAL CALLS
Local calls cost NKr2 or NKr3 from a pay phone and about NKr3 from hotel phones.

LONG-DISTANCE CALLS
All eight digits are required when dialing in Norway, both for local and long-distance calls. Rates vary according to distance and time of day. Toll-free numbers beginning with "800" or "810" are also becoming more common, although this is mostly among large corporations.

OPERATOR INFORMATION
Dial 180 for information for Norway and the other Scandinavian countries, 181 for other international telephone numbers.

Tipping
Tipping is kept to a minimum in Norway because service charges are added to most bills. It is, however, handy to have a supply of NKr5 or 10 coins for less formal service. Tip only in local currency.

Airport and railroad porters (if you can find them) have fixed rates per bag, so they will tell you how much they should be paid. Tips to doormen vary according to the type of bag and the distance carried—NKr5–NKr10 each, with similar tips for porters carrying bags to the room. Room service usually has a service charge included already, so tipping is discretionary.

Round off a taxi fare to the next round digit, or tip anywhere from NKr5 to NKr10, a little more if the driver has been particularly helpful with luggage.

All restaurants include a service charge, ranging from 12% to 15%, in the bill. It is customary to add an additional 5% for exceptional service, but it is not obligatory. Maître d's are not tipped, and coat checks have flat rates, ranging from NKr5 to NKr10 per person.

Visitor Information
Norwegian Tourist Board, 655 3rd Ave., New York, NY 10017, ☎ 212/949–2333, ⨎ 212/983–5260.

Norwegian Tourist Board, 5 Lower Regent St., London SW1Y 4LX, ☎ 0171/839–6255, ⨎ 0171/839–4180.

6 Sweden ✓

The Kingdom of Crystal, the Swedish Riviera, Dalarna and the Folklore District, Norrland and Norbotten—these evocative names conjure up the vividly distinct regions of Scandinavia's largest country. In the south, red-painted wooden farmhouses line the shores of pristine, sun-dappled lakes. In the north, untamed rivers cut through isolated moorland, and glacier-topped mountains neighbor vast forests of pine, spruce, and birch.

By Chris
Mosey

Updated by
Kathryn
Sampson

SWEDEN REQUIRES THE VISITOR to travel far, in terms of both distance and attitude. Approximately the size of California, Sweden reaches as far north as the Arctic fringes of Europe, where glacier-topped mountains and thousands of acres of pine, spruce, and birch forests are broken here and there by wild rivers, countless pristine lakes, and desolate moorland. In the more populated south, roads meander through mile after mile of softly undulating countryside, skirting lakes and passing small villages with their ubiquitous sharp-pointed church spires. Here, the lush forests that dominate Sweden's northern landscape have largely fallen to the plow.

Once the dominant power of the region, Sweden has traditionally looked mostly inward, seeking to find its own, Nordic solutions. During the cold war, it tried with considerable success to steer its famous "Middle Way" between the two superpowers, both economically and politically. Its citizens were in effect benignly subjected to a giant social experiment aimed at creating a perfectly just society, one that adopted the best aspects of both socialism and capitalism.

In the late 1980s, as it slipped into the worst economic recession since the 1930s, Sweden made adjustments that lessened the role of its all-embracing welfare state in the lives of its citizens. Although fragile, the conservative coalition, which defeated the long-incumbent Social Democrats in the fall of 1991, attempted to make further cutbacks in welfare spending as the country faced one of the largest budget deficits in Europe. In a kind of nostalgic backlash, the populace voted the Social Democrats back into power in 1994, hoping to recapture the party's policy of cradle-to-grave protection, but the world economy hasn't cooperated: The budget deficit problem remains as difficult as ever. At the same time, an influx of immigrants is reshaping what was once a homogeneous society. As a result, the mostly blond, blue-eyed Swedes may now be more open to the outside world than at any other time in their history. Indeed, another major change was Sweden's decision to join the European Union (EU) as of January 1995, a move that represents a radical break with its traditional independent stance on international issues.

The country possesses stunning natural assets. In the forests, moose, deer, bears, and lynx roam, coexisting with the whine of power saws and the rumble of automatic logging machines as mankind exploits a natural resource that remains the country's economic backbone. Fish abound in sparkling lakes and tumbling rivers, sea eagles and ospreys soar over myriad pine-clad islands in the archipelagoes off the east and west coasts.

The country is Europe's fourth largest, 173,731 square miles in area, and its population of 8.7 million is thinly spread. If, like Greta Garbo, one of its most famous exports, you want to be alone, you've come to the right place. A law called *Allemansrätt* guarantees public access to the countryside; NO TRESPASSING signs are seldom seen.

Sweden stretches 977 miles from the barren Arctic north to the fertile plains of the south. Contrasts abound, but they are neatly tied together by a superbly efficient infrastructure, embracing air, road, and rail. You can catch salmon in the far north and, thanks to the excellent domestic air network, have it cooked by the chef of your luxury hotel in Stockholm later the same day.

Sweden

The seasons contrast savagely: Sweden is usually warm and exceedingly light in the summer, then cold and dark in the winter. The sea may freeze, and in the north, iron railway lines may snap.

Sweden is also an arresting mixture of ancient and modern. The countryside is dotted with runic stones recalling its Viking past: trade beginning in the 8th century eastward to Kiev and as far south as Constantinople and the Mediterranean, expansion to the British Isles in the 9th through the 11th century, and settlement in Normandy in the 10th century. Small timbered farmhouses and maypoles around which villagers still dance at Midsummer in their traditional costumes evoke both the pagan early history and the more recent agrarian culture.

Many of the country's cities are sci-fi modern, their shop windows filled with the latest in consumer goods and fashions, but Swedes are reluctant urbanites: Their hearts and souls are in the forests and the archipelagoes, and there they faithfully retreat in the summer and on weekends to take their holidays, pick berries, or just listen to the silence. The skills of the wood-carver, the weaver, the leatherworker, and the glassblower are all highly prized. Similarly, Swedish humor is earthy and slapstick. Despite the praise lavished abroad on introspective dramatic artists such as August Strindberg and Ingmar Bergman, it is the simple trouser-dropping farce that will fill Stockholm's theaters, the scatological joke that will get the most laughs.

Again, despite the international musical success of the Swedish rock groups Ace of Base, Roxette, and Abba, the domestic penchant is more often for the good, old-fashioned dance band. Gray-haired men in pastel sweaters playing saxophones are more common on TV than heavy-metal rockers. Strangely, in ultramodern concert halls and discos, it is possible to step back in time to the 1950s, if not the 1940s.

Despite the much-publicized sexual liberation of Swedes, the joys of hearth and home are most prized in what remains in many ways an extremely conservative society. Conformity, not liberty, is the real key to the Swedish character: The good of the collective has always come before that of the individual, and this is why socialism had such a strong appeal here.

At the same time, Swedes remain devoted royalists and patriots, avidly following the fortunes of King Carl XVI Gustaf, Queen Silvia, and their children in the media, and raising the blue-and-yellow national flag each morning on the flagpoles of their country cottages. Few nations, in fact, make as much of an effort to preserve and defend their natural heritage. It is sometimes difficult in cities such as Stockholm, Göteborg, or Malmö to realize that you are in an urban area. Right in the center of Stockholm, thanks to a cleanup program in the 1970s, you can fish for salmon or go for a swim. In Göteborg's busy harbor, you can sit aboard a ship bound for the archipelago and watch fish jump out of the water; in Malmö hares hop around in the downtown parks. It is this pristine quality of life that can make a visit to Sweden a step out of time, a relaxing break from the modern world.

Pleasures and Pastimes

Beaches

Beaches in Sweden range from wide, sandy strands to steep, rocky shores, from oceanfront to lakefront, from highly developed resorts to remote nature preserves. The area most favored for the standard sunbathing and wave-frolicking vacation is known as the Swedish Riviera, on the coast south of Göteborg.

Camping

As soon as the winter frost abates, the Swedes migrate en masse to the country, with camping and sports gear in tow. Of the 760 registered campsites nationwide, many are offer fishing, boating, or canoeing, and about 200 remain open in winter for skiing and skating. Many campsites also offer accommodations in log cabins at various prices, and some have special facilities for guests with disabilities.

Dining

The nation's standard home-cooked meal is basically peasant fare—sausages, potatoes, and other hearty foods to ward off the winter cold. However, it has also produced the *smörgåsbord*, a generous and artfully arranged buffet featuring both hot and cold dishes. You start with herring, then eat your way through salads, vegetable dishes, meats, cheeses, and breads, winding up with a slice of *tårta* (cake) or some fruit. Fish—fresh, smoked, or pickled—is a Swedish specialty; herring and salmon both come in myriad traditional and new preparations.

In August look for *kräftor* (crayfish), which are boiled with dill, salt, and sugar, then cooled overnight. Swedes eat them with hot buttered toast, caraway seeds, and schnapps or beer. Later in the season comes an exotic assortment of mushrooms and wild berries. Regional specialties include *spettekaka,* a cake of eggs and sugar made in Skåne, and *Gotlandsflundror,* a smoked flat fish from the island of Gotland. In Norrland, specialties include *surströmming* (fermented herring), *palt* (a stuffed dumpling), *mandelpotatis* (almond-shape potatoes), and *tunnbröd* (thin bread made from barley flour) eaten with butter, potatoes, and elk meat, or fermented herring. Trout and salmon are common, as are various cuts of elk and reindeer. But to the foreign palate, the most acceptable of Norrland's culinary specialties is undoubtedly *löjrom*, pinkish caviar from a species of Baltic herring, which is eaten with chopped onions and sour cream, and the various desserts made from the cloudberries that thrive here.

Husmanskost (home-cooking) recipes are often served in restaurants as a *dagens rätt* (daily special). Examples are *pyttipanna* (literally, "bits in the pan"—beef and potato hash topped with a fried egg), *Janssons frestelse* ("Jansson's Temptation"—gratin of potatoes with anchovy), or pea soup with pancakes, a traditional meal on Thursday.

Sweden is known for its coffee. Jealous Danes theorize that foreigners like their coffee weak and therefore prefer Swedish varieties; Swedes say it just tastes better.

The hotel breakfast is often a well-stocked smörgåsbord-style buffet. Lunches are markedly less expensive than dinner. Even in Stockholm, it is still possible to eat the *dagens rätt* between 11:30 AM and 2 PM for less than SKr50, with bread, salad, a light beer, and a cup of coffee.

Dinner is a different matter entirely. An indifferent steak and potatoes can set you back SKr160, and a bottle of mediocre wine with the meal will cost at least that much again. Dinner for two with wine in one of the better Stockholm restaurants could easily cost SKr600 or more.

Swedes are conservative in dress; in keeping with their egalitarian impulses, they avoid flash and dazzle and tend to invest in low-profile, durable materials. In the more expensive restaurants, you'll see men in dark suits and artistic ties and women wearing simple but flattering dresses and suits in a range of earth tones. Even in pubs and discos at the other end of the price scale, people favor neutral colors, unstructured designs, and a minimum of jewelry.

CATEGORY	COST*
$$$$	over SKr500
$$$	SKr250–SKr500
$$	SKr120–SKr250
$	under SKr120

per person for a two-course meal, including service charge and tax but not wine

Fishing

The sight of a fisherman landing a fat, sparkling salmon from the quay in the middle of downtown Stockholm is not unusual. Beyond Stockholm, the country is laced with streams and lakes full of fish, and there's excellent deep-sea fishing off the coast.

Lodging

Service in a Swedish hotel, in any price range, is unfailingly courteous and efficient. There are accommodations of great charm and beauty to be found, usually on the expensive side, but the advantages of location held by less luxurious establishments shouldn't be overlooked. The woodland setting of a camper's *stuga* may be just as desirable and memorable as the gilded antiques of a downtown hotel.

In summer many discounts, special passes, and summer packages are available. Your travel agent or the Swedish Travel and Tourism Council (in New York) will have full details, but some of the better buys are as follows: The Reso hotel chain offers a 5% discount on second, third, and fourth nights, with the fifth night free; summer rates (June 21– Aug. 13) are reduced by as much as 50%. The Scandic Hotel Summer Check plan enables you to pay for accommodations in advance with checks costing SKr550 each for one night in a double room; with a supplementary PlusCheck, which costs SKr120, you can stay in one of their city-center hotels. Sweden Hotel's Scandinavian Bonus Pass costs SKr160 and gives discounts of 15% to 50% from May 15 to September 24 and on weekends year-round. In mid-1993 the government reduced the tax on hotels and domestic travel services from 21% to 12%, a welcome change for visitors.

Vandrarhem (youth hostels), also scrupulously clean and well run, are more expensive than elsewhere in Europe. The Swedish Touring Association (STF) has 280 hostels nationwide, most with four- to six-bed family rooms and 80 with running hot and cold water in the rooms. They are open to anyone regardless of age. Prices range from SKr60 to SKr90 per night for members of STF or organizations affiliated with the International Youth Hostel Federation. Nonmembers are charged an additional SKr35 per night. STF publishes an annual hostel handbook.

CATEGORY	COST*
$$$$	over SKr1,300
$$$	SKr1,000–SKr1,300
$$	SKr750–SKr1,000
$	under SKr750

All prices are for a standard double room, including breakfast and tax.

Sailing

Deep at heart, modern Swedes are still seafaring Vikings. Sweden's cultural dependence on boats runs so deep that at Christmas, the leading department store sells gift packages of large black candles made with creosote, to provide the comforting scent of dock and hull repairs for when sailors can't be on their boats—which is most of the year. When they can, though, they're everywhere, in the archipelago, on the lakes and rivers, out at sea; and on long summer days, even nine-to-five office workers dash from desk to dock to get in a few hours of sailing before dark. Boating opportunities for visitors are plentiful, from hourly rentals to chartered cruises, in anything from kayaks to motor launches to huge luxury ferry liners.

Tennis

When Björn Borg began to win Wimbledon with almost monotonous regularity, Sweden became a force in world tennis. As such, the country is filled with indoor and outdoor courts, and major competitions take place regularly. One of the most unusual is the annual Donald Duck Cup, in Båstad, for children ages 11 to 15: Ever since the young Bjorn Borg won a Donald Duck trophy, the tournament has attracted thousands of youngsters who hope to imitate his success.

Exploring Sweden

Sweden consists of 24 counties. In the southeast is Stockholm, the capital and largest city. The industrial seaport city of Göteborg and the neighboring west coastal counties of Bohuslän and Halland (the so-called Swedish Riviera) form another region, along with Värmland on the Norwegian border. The southernmost part of Sweden, a lovely mix of farmland, forests and châteaus, includes Skåne, Småland, Blekinge, Västergötland, Östergötland, and the island of Öland. Dalarna, the country's heartland, is centered on Lake Siljan and the town of Mora; this is where Swedish folklore and traditions are most visible. The northern half of Sweden, called Norrland and including the counties of Lappland and Norrbotten, is a great expanse consisting mostly of mountains and wilderness; here the hardy Sami herd reindeer and hardy tourists come to see the midnight sun.

Numbers in the text correspond to numbers in the margin and on the maps.

Great Itineraries

Sampling all of Sweden's far-flung variety is best suited to a traveler with either no time constraints or an exceedingly generous purse. However, a few representative stops can make even a short visit worthwhile.

IF YOU HAVE 3 DAYS

Spend two days in ⊞ **Stockholm** ①–㉙; one of these days may be spent on a boat trip into the archipelago or into Lake Mälaren. Take the third day either to visit ⊞ **Göteborg** ㊱–㊼ by high-speed train, or to fly to **Mora** ㉙, in the heart of Sweden's folklore country.

IF YOU HAVE 5 DAYS

Start with two days in ⊞ **Stockholm** ①–㉙; add a third day for a side trip to **Uppsala** ㉟. On day four, fly to ⊞ **Mora** ㉙ in Dalarna and rent a car for a drive around Lake Siljan. On day five, fly to ⊞ **Göteborg** ㊱–㊼.

IF YOU HAVE 10 DAYS

This itinerary can be accomplished easily by publbic transportation. Start with three days in ⊞ **Stockholm** ①–㉙; on day four, take the high-speed train to ⊞ **Göteborg** ㊱–㊼ and stay two nights; on day six, take the train to ⊞ **Kalmar** ㉓ via **Växjö** ㉔. From Kalmar, catch the ferry to **Gotland** ㉞ and then back to Stockholm. Spend day nine either taking the bus or train to ⊞ **Mora** ㉙ or flying to ⊞ **Kiruna** ㉒. Return to Stockholm on day ten.

When to Tour Sweden

The official tourist season—which means generally when hotel rates go down and museum and castle doors open up—runs from mid-May through early August. This is Sweden's balmiest time of year; summer days are sunny and warm, and nights refreshingly cool. (Summer is also mosquito season, especially in the north, but also as far south as Mora.) The colors of autumn fade out as early as September, when the rainy season begins. Winter comes in October and stays through March, often longer, but winter days can be magnificent when the snow is fresh and the sky is a brilliant Nordic blue. April brings spring, and by the middle of June the whole country goes mad for Midsummer Day.

STOCKHOLM

Set at the point where the waters of Mälaren (Lake Mälar) rush into the Baltic, Stockholm is one of Europe's most beautiful capitals. Nearly 1.6 million people now live in the greater Stockholm area, yet it remains a quiet, almost pastoral city.

Built on 14 small islands among open bays and narrow channels, Stockholm is a handsome, civilized city filled with parks, squares, and airy boulevards, yet it is also a bustling, modern metropolis. Glass-and-steel skyscrapers abound, but you are never more than five minutes' walk from twisting medieval streets and waterside walkways.

The first written mention of Stockholm dates from 1252, when a powerful regent named Birger Jarl built a fortified castle and city here. King Gustav Vasa took it over in 1523, and King Gustavus Adolphus made it the heart of an empire a century later.

During the Thirty Years' War (1618–48), Sweden gained importance as a Baltic trading state, and Stockholm grew commensurately. But by the beginning of the 18th century, Swedish influence had begun to wane and Stockholm's development had slowed. It did not revive until the Industrial Revolution, when the hub of the city moved north from the Old Town area.

Nowadays most Stockholmers live in high-rise suburbs that dot the pine forests and by lakesides around the capital, linked to it by a highly efficient infrastructure of roads, railways, and one of the safest subway systems in the world. Air pollution is minimal, and the city streets are relatively clean and safe.

Exploring Stockholm

Although Stockholm is built on a group of islands adjoining the mainland, the waterways between them are so narrow, and the bridges so smoothly integrated, that the city really does feel more or less continuous. The island of Gamla Stan (Old Town) and its smaller neighbors, Riddarholmen and Helgeandsholmen, lie pretty much at the center of town. South of Gamla Stan, Södermalm spreads over a wide area, where the many art galleries and bars attest to a slightly bohemian edge. North of Gamla Stan is Norrmalm, the financial and business heart of the city. West of Norrmalm is the island of Kungsholmen, site of Stadshuset (City Hall) and most of the city government offices. East of Norrmalm is Östermalm, an old residential neighborhood where many of the embassies and consulates are located. Finally, between Östermalm and Södermalm lies the island of Djurgården, once a royal game preserve, now the site of lovely parks and museums such as Skansen, the open-air cultural heritage park.

Modern Stockholm

The area bounded by Stadshuset, Hötorget, Stureplan, and Dramaten is essentially Stockholm's downtown, where the city comes closest to feeling like a bustling metropolis. Shopping, nightlife, business, traffic, dining, festivals—all are at their most intense in this part of town.

A GOOD WALK

Start at the redbrick **Stadshuset** ① (City Hall), a powerful symbol of Stockholm and among the most impressive pieces of modern architecture in Europe. Cross the bridge to Klara Mälarstrand and follow the waterfront to Drottninggatan, a pedestrian street that will take you north to the hub of the city, **Sergels Torg** ②. **Kulturhuset** ③ (House of Culture) is the imposing building on the southern side of Sergels Torg that houses a library, theater, exhibition center, and restaurant. Continuing north on Drottninggatan, you'll come out at **Hötorget** ④ (Hay Market), where you'll find colorful fruit and vegetable stands, the PUB department store, and Konserthuset (Concert House; ☞ Nightlife and the Arts, *below*). The intersection of Kungsgatan and Sveavägen, at the corner of Konserthuset, is one of the busiest pedestrian crossroads in town, with an atmosphere resembling (though on a much smaller scale) New York's Times Square.

Head north up Sveavägen for a brief detour to see the spot where Prime Minister Olof Palme was assassinated in 1986. A plaque has been laid on the righthand side of the street, just before the intersection with Olof Palmes Gata; his grave is in Adolf Fredrik's Churchyard, a few blocks farther on. Then continue north along Sveavägen, and turn left up Tegnérgatan to find **Strindbergsmuseet Museet Blå Tornet** ⑤ (Strindberg Museum, Blue Tower), the house where playwright August Strindberg lived from 1908 to 1912. Return to Hötorget by way of Drottninggatan.

Next, walk east down Kungsgatan, one of Stockholm's main shopping streets, to Stureplan, where you'll find Sturegallerian, an elegant indoor shopping precinct. A short detour north on Birger Jarlsgatan will allow a visit to **Moderna Museet** (Museum of Modern Art); this location is only temporary, however, as the museum will take up its old residence on Skeppsholmen in February of 1998. South along Birger Jarlsgatan, a street named for the nobleman generally credited with founding Stockholm around 1252, there are still more interesting shops and restaurants. When you reach Nybroplan, linger for a look at the grand **Kungliga Dramatiska Teatern** ⑥ (Royal Dramatic Theater).

Heading west up Hamngatan, stop in at **Hallwylska Museet** ⑦ (Hallwyl Museum) for a tour of the private collection of Countess von Hallwyl's treasures. Continue along Hamngatan to **Kungsträdgården** ⑧, a park since 1562 but previously the royal kitchen garden. There are many outdoor cafés and restaurants here, and usually public concerts and events in the summer. At the northwest corner of the park you will find Sverigehuset (Sweden House; ☞ Visitor Information *in* Stockholm A to Z, *below*), with its excellent tourist center, and, on the opposite side of Hamngatan, the NK department store.

TIMING

Allow about 3 ½ hours for the walk, plus an hour each for guided tours of Stadshuset and Hallwylska Museet.

SIGHTS TO SEE

❼ **Hallwylska Museet.** This private turn-of-the-century palace with imposing wood-panel rooms houses a collection of furniture, paintings, and musical instruments in a bewildering mélange of styles assembled by Countess von Hallwyl, who left it to the state on her death. ⊠ *Hamngatan 4*, ☎ *08/666–4499.* 🎫 *SKr50.* ☉ *Guided tours only. Tours in English July and Aug., daily at 1; Sept.–June, Sun. at 1.*

❹ **Hötorget.** Once the city's hay market, this is now a popular gathering place with an excellent outdoor fruit and vegetable market in the center. Also in the square are the Konserthuset, the PUB department store, and a multiscreen cinema.

NEED A
BREAK? Go underground at Hötorget to check out **Hötorgshallen,** an old-fashioned food market with relatively inexpensive restaurants, or take a window table at Konditoriet, (☎ 08/217001), a café inside PUB to enjoy the view of the market.

❸ **Kulturhuset.** The Culture House offers an array of exhibitions, from drawings by Michelangelo to costumes by Fellini. ⊠ *Sergels Torg 3,* ☎ *08/700–0100* FAX *08/700–0144.*

❻ **Kungliga Dramatiska Teatern.** Locally known as Dramaten, the Royal Dramatic Theater is housed in a grand but appealing building with gilded statuary that looks out over the city harbor. Here occasional productions by Ingmar Bergman, the country's leading director, provoke the imagination.

☙ ❽ **Kungsträdgården.** Stockholm's centerpiece park, once the royal kitchen garden, now hosts most of the city's major festivals. Attractions include a playground, an ice-skating rink in winter, and numerous cafés and restaurants.

Moderna Museet. Until the end of 1997, the Museum of Modern Art will be housed in an old streetcar station; in February, 1998, the museum will reopen in its original location on Skeppsholmen. The excellent collection includes works by Picasso, Kandinsky, Dali, Brancusi, and other international artists, as well as significant Swedish painters and sculptors. There is also an extensive section on photography. 1997:⊠ *Birger Jarlsgatan 57,* ☎ *08/666–4250,* FAX *08/611–8311.* 🎟 *SKr50.* ☉ *Tues.–Thu. noon–7, Fri.–Sun. noon–5.* 1998:⊠ *Skeppsholmen,* ☎ *08/666–4250,* ☉ *to be announced.* 🎟 *SKr50.*

❷ **Sergels Torg.** This square in the center of Stockholm was named for Johan Tobias Sergel (1740–1814), one of Sweden's greatest sculptors. Sergels Torg's traffic circle is dominated by modern, functional buildings and a large, sunken pedestrian square with subterranean connections to the rest of the neighborhood.

★ ❶ **Stadshuset.** The architect Rangnar Östberg, one of the founders of the National Romantic movement, completed Stockholm's City Hall in 1923. As headquarters of the city council, the building is functional but also ornate: Its immense Blue Hall is the venue for the Nobel Prize dinner, Stockholm's principal social event, each December. A trip to the top of the 348-foot tower, most of which can be achieved by elevator, is rewarded by a breathtaking panorama of the city and Riddarfjärden. ⊠ *Hantverkargatan 1,* ☎ *08/785–9074.* 🎟 *SKr30.* ☉ *Guided tours only, daily 10–4:30. Tours in English, Oct.–Apr., daily 10 and noon; May and Sept., daily 10, noon, and 2, June–Aug. daily 10, 11, noon, and 2.*

NEED A
BREAK? After climbing the Stadshuset tower, relax on its fine grass terraces, which lead down to the bay, or perhaps have lunch in **Stadshuskällaren** (the City Hall Cellar, ☎ 08/650-5454), whose kitchen prepares the annual Nobel banquet. You can also head a few blocks down Hantverkargatan to find several good small restaurants.

❺ **Strindbergsmuseet Blå Tornet.** (Strindberg Museum, Blue Tower.) Hidden away over a grocery store, this museum is dedicated to Sweden's most important author and dramatist (1849–1912). This was actually August Strindberg's home from 1908 until his death, and the interior has been expertly reconstructed with authentic furnishings and other objects (including one of his pens). It also has a library, a printing press, and a picture archives, and it is the site of literary, musical, and the-

410

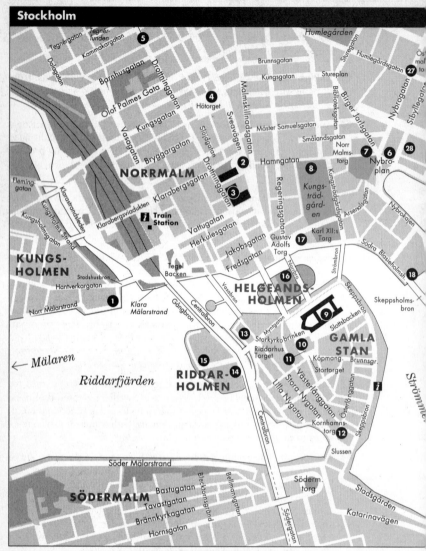

Biologiska Museet, **25**
Gröna Lund, **22**
Hallwylska Museet, **7**
Historiska Museet, **26**
Hötorget, **4**
Järntorget, **12**
Kaknästornet, **29**
Kulturhuset, **3**
Kungliga Dramatiska
Teatern, **6**

Kungliga Slottet, **9**
Kungsträdgården, **8**
Musikmuseet, **28**
National Museet, **18**
Nordiska Museet, **21**
Operan, **17**
Östasiatiska
Museet, **19**
Östermalmstorg, **27**
Riddarholmskyrkan, **14**
Riddarhuset, **13**

Riksdagshuset, **16**
Sergels Torg, **2**
Skansen, **23**
Stadshuset, **1**
Storkyrkan, **10**
Stortorget, **11**
Strindbergsmuseet Blå
Tornet, **5**
Svea Hovrätt, **15**
Vasa Museet, **20**
Waldemarsudde, **24**

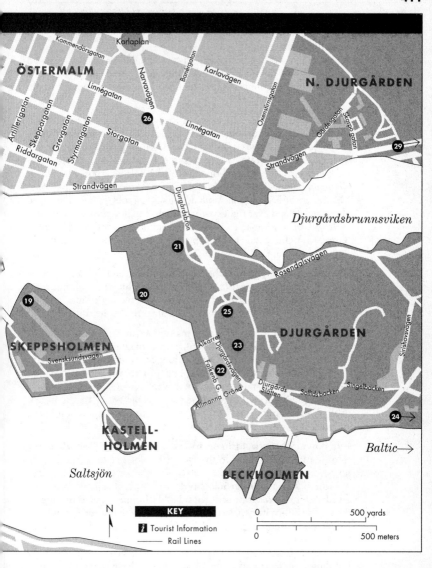

ÖSTERMALM

Kommendörsgatan

Karlaplan

Narvavägen

Banérgatan

Karlavägen

N. DJURGÅRDEN

Linnégatan

Oxenstirnsgatan

Gärdesgatan

Storpo gatan

26

Linnégatan

Artillerigatan

Skeppargatan

Grevgatan

Styrmangatan

Riddargatan

Storgatan

Strandvägen

29

Strandvägen

Djurgårdsbron

Djurgårdsbrunnsviken

21

Rosendalsvägen

20

25

19

Alkärret

Djurgårdsvägen

23

DJURGÅRDEN

Sirishovvägen

SKEPPSHOLMEN

Svensksundsvägen

Falkenb G.

22

Djurgårds Slätten

Sollidsbacken

Singelbacken

Allmänna Gränd

24

KASTELL-
HOLMEN

BECKHOLMEN

Baltic→

Saltsjön

N

KEY

🛈 Tourist Information
— Rail Lines

0   500 yards

0   500 meters

atrical events. ✉ *Drottninggatan 85,* ☎ *08/411–5354.* 🎟 *SKr25.* ☉
Tues. 11–7, Wed.–Fri. 11–4, weekends noon–4.

Gamla Stan

Gamla Stan (Old Town) sits on a cluster of small islands between two
of Stockholm's main islands and is the site of the medieval city. The
narrow, twisting cobbled streets are lined with superbly preserved old
buildings.

A GOOD WALK

Start at the waterfront edge of Kungsträdgården and cross Strömsbron
to the **Kungliga Slottet** ⑨ (Royal Palace), where guided tours give visitors a view of the State Apartments, the Royal Armory, and the Treasury. Here you can get a good view of the Baltic harbor, with the *af
Chapman* sailing-ship youth hostel and the Grand Hotel and National
Museum in the background. Walk up the sloping cobblestone drive called
Slottsbacken and bear right past the Obelisk to find the main entrance
to the palace. Stockholm's 15th-century Gothic cathedral, **Storkyrkan** ⑩
(Great Church), stands at the top of Slottsbacken, but its entrance is
at the other end, on Trångsund.

Following Källargränd from the Obelisk or Trångsund from Storkyrkan,
you will reach **Stortorget** ⑪ (Great Square), which is small but mar-
velously atmospheric, fronted by magnificent old merchants' houses.
The **Stockholms Fondbörs** (Stock Exchange) fronts the square.

Walk down Svartmangatan past many ancient buildings, including
the Tyska Kyrkan (German Church), with its magnificent oxidized copper spire and airy interior. Continue along Svartmangatan, take a right
on Tyska Stallplan to Prästgatan, and just to your left you'll find
Mårten Trotzigs Gränd, a picturesque, lamplit alley stairway that leads
downhill to **Järntorget** ⑫. From here you can take Västerlånggatan back
north across Gamla Stan, checking out the pricey fashion boutiques,
galleries, and souvenir shops along the way.

Cut down Storkyrkobrinken to the 17th-century **Riddarhuset** ⑬
(House of Nobles), built in the Dutch Baroque style. A short walk
takes you over Riddarholmsbron to Riddarholmen (Island of Knights),
on which stands **Riddarholmskyrkan** ⑭, the burial place for 17
Swedish kings over four centuries. Riddarholmen is also the site of
the white 17th-century palace that houses the **Svea Hovrätt** ⑮ (Swedish
High Court). Returning across Riddarhusbron, take Myntgatan back
toward the palace and turn left at Mynttorget to cross the bridge and
pass through the refurbished stone **Riksdagshuset** ⑯ (Parliament
Building) on Helgeandsholmen (Holy Ghost Island). Another short
bridge puts you on Drottninggatan; take a right onto Fredsgatan to
Gustav Adolfs Torg.

Operan ⑰ (Opera House) occupies the waterfront between Gustav Adolfs
Torg and Kungsträdgården. A little farther along on Strömgatan, a host
of tour boats docks in front of the stately Grand Hotel, where Nobel
laureates are accommodated each year. Pass the Grand and visit the
National Museet ⑱, Sweden's National Gallery of Art; then cross the
footbridge to the idyllic island of Skeppsholmen, where you'll find the
beautifully situated **Östasiatiska Museet** ⑲ (Museum of Far Eastern Antiquities), with a fine collection of Buddhist art.

The adjoining island, Kastellholmen, is a pleasant place for a stroll,
especially on a summer evening, with fine views of Gamla Stan's
seafront across the Baltic harbor and of Djurgården's lighted parks.

Rail Europe: can take you _to_ Scandinavia by train, or _through_ Scandinavia by car!

For the independent spirit who wants to travel the highways and byways of Scandinavia, _Rail Europe_ offers the Scanrail Pass which allows you to explore 4 of the Nordic countries. Choose unlimited rail travel, combination rail with car travel, and get free or discounted passage on many luxurious ferries.

Scanrail Pass

Travel on the national rail networks of Denmark, Finland, Norway and Sweden. Three pass durations to choose from: any 5 days unlimited train travel in a 15 day period or any 10 days in 1 month or 1 month unlimited train travel.

Scanrail 'n Drive

For the utmost in flexibility to explore cities, country sides, villages and hamlets, combine our rail and car travel. Travel any 8 days out of 15; 5 days train travel _plus_ 3 days car rental.

Scanrail 55+ Pass

A Scanrail Pass especially designed for travelers aged 55 and up. Enjoy all the benefits of the Scanrail Pass including all the travel bonuses at a reduced rate.

Also Available...

Finnrail Pass

Historic cities, unspoiled forests and thousands of fresh water lakes... you can visit the southern coastal cities, travel east to the Russian border, or as far north as the Arctic Circle.

Norway Railpass

Experience all of the sights that Norway has to offer. This country of contrast with mountains, valleys, forests, and fjords, can be seen up close, by train, with the Norway Railpass.

US: 1-800 - 4-EURAIL
Canada: 1-800 - 361- RAIL

Visit us at:
http://www.raileurope.com

Ca# 17550.20

Your ticket to all of Scandinavia.

It's easy with the Visit Scandinavia Air Pass. Just fly SAS round-trip across the Atlantic to Scandinavia and these special passes are yours – starting at only $80. With an Air Pass in hand, you can fly SAS to one of a number of destinations within Scandinavia and Finland.

Purchase up to six Air Passes. Use them for flights between Denmark, Norway and Sweden, and on flights between Sweden and Finland. They're even good for flights within Sweden and Norway. So see more of the land for less with a Visit Scandinavia Air Pass. Contact your travel agent or SAS at 800-221-2350.

Easy as SAS.

TIMING

Allow 3 hours for the walk, plus as much as 2 hours to tour the various parts of the palace. The National Museum and the Far Eastern Museum may take up to an hour each.

SIGHTS TO SEE

⑫ **Järntorget.** So named for its original use as an iron and copper marketplace, the Iron Square was also a venue for public executions. ✉ *Gamla Stan, at the intersection of Västerlånggatan and Österlånggatan.*

NEED A BREAK?
There are coffeehouses and pubs all along Västerlånggatan; where it crosses Stora Gråmunkegränd, you can stop for coffee and a pastry in the **Grå Munken** (Gray Monk) coffeehouse (✉ Västerlångatan 18, no phone).

OFF THE BEATEN PATH
STOCKHOLMS LEKSAKMUSEET – In Södermalm, Stockholm's Toy Museum has a collection of toys and dolls from all over the world, as well as a children's theater with clowns, magicians, storytellers, and puppet shows. The museum is near the Mariatorget subway station, two stops south of Gamla Stan. ✉ *Mariatorget 1, Södermalm,* ☎ *08/641–6100.* ▨ *SKr30.* ⊙ *Tues.–Fri. 10–4, weekends noon–4.*

★ ⑨ **Kungliga Slottet.** Watch the changing of the guard in the curved terrace entrance of this magnificent granite edifice designed by Nicodemus Tessin and completed in 1760. View the palace's fine furnishings and Gobelin tapestries on a tour of the **Representationsvän** (State Apartments, ☎ 08/402–6130) or survey the crown jewels, which are no longer used in this self-consciously egalitarian country, in the **Skattkammaren** (Treasury, ☎ 08/402–6130). The Livrustkammaren (Royal Armory, ☎ 08/666–4475) has an outstanding collection of weaponry, coaches, and royal regalia. Entrances to the Treasury and Armory are on the Slottsbacken side of the palace. ✉ *Gamla Stan,* ▨ *State Apartments SKr45, Treasury SKr40, Royal Armory SKr45.* ⊙ *State Apartments and Treasury, June–Aug., daily 10–4; Sept.–May, Tues.–Sun., noon–3. Armory, May–Aug., daily 11–4; Sept.–Apr., Tues.–Sun. 11–4.*

⑱ **National Museet.** The National Gallery of Art has a fine collection of old masters, including some of Rembrandt's major works. ✉ *Södra Blasieholmshamnen,* ☎ *08/666–4250.* ▨ *SKr40 (free Fri. mid-May–mid-Oct.).* ⊙ *Wed. and Fri.–Sun. 11–5, Tues. and Thurs. 11–8 (closes some Tuesdays at 5 mid-May–mid-Oct.).*

⑰ **Operan.** The baroque Opera House, which holds productions of both opera and ballet, is almost more famous for its restaurants and bars than for its theater. It has been one of Stockholm's magnets for artistic and literary socializing since the first Operakällaren restaurant opened on the site in 1787. ✉ *Gustav Adolfs Torg,* ☎ *08/248240,* FAX *08/411–0242.*

⑭ **Riddarholmskyrkan.** Riddarholm Church is a Greyfriars monastery dating from 1270; the second-oldest structure in Stockholm, it has been the burial place for 17 Swedish kings for more than four centuries. The most famous figures interred within are King Gustavus Adolphus, hero of the Thirty Years' War, and the warrior king Karl XII, renowned for his daring invasion of Russia, who died in Norway in 1718. The latest king to be put to rest here was Gustav V, in 1950. The various rulers' sarcophagi, usually embellished with their monograms, are visible in the small chapels given over to the various dynasties. The red-brick structure, distinguished by its delicate iron fretwork spire, is rarely used for services. ✉ *Riddarholmen, Gamla Stan.,* ☎ *08/402–*

6130. ☜ SKr20. ☉ June–Aug., daily noon–4; May and Sept., Wed. and weekends noon–3.

⑬ Riddarhuset. Before the abolition of the aristocracy early in the 20th century, the House of Nobles was the gathering place for the First Estate of the realm. Hanging from its walls are 2,325 escutcheons, representing all the former noble families of Sweden. Because of the building's excellent acoustic properties, Riddarhuset is often used for concerts. ⊠ *Riddarhustorget,* ☎ *08/100857.* ☜ *SKr20.* ☉ *Weekdays 11:30–12:30.*

Stockholms Fondbörs. The Swedish Academy meets at the Stock Exchange every year to decide the winner of the Nobel Prize for Literature. The Stock Exchange itself is computerized and rather quiet. There are no tours in English, but there is a film about the Stock Exchange in Swedish. ⊠ *Källargränd 2,* ☎ *08/613–8892. Group tours by appointment.*

⑮ Svea Hovrätt. The Swedish High Court commands a prime site on the island of Riddarholmen: Its quiet and restful quayside is an excellent place to end an afternoon's sightseeing. Sit by the water's edge, watching the boats on Riddarfjärden (Bay of Knights) and, beyond it, Lake Mälar. From here you can see the lake, the magnificent arches of Västerbron (West Bridge) in the distance, the southern heights, and above all the imposing profile of the City Hall, which appears almost to be floating on the water. At the quay you may see one of the Göta Canal ships.

⑯ Riksdagshuset. The Parliament Building opened in 1905 and was renovated in 1983. The marble entrance hall is particularly impressive. ⊠ *Riksgatan 3A,* ☎ *08/786–4000.* ☜ *Free.* ☉ *Tours in English late June–late Aug., weekdays 2:30 and 2; Sept.–June, weekends 1:30.*

⑩ Storkyrkan. Swedish kings were crowned in the 15th-century Great Church until 1907. Today, its main attractions are a dramatic wooden statue of Saint George slaying the dragon, carved by Bernt Notke of Lübeck in 1489, and the *Parhelion,* a painting of Stockholm dating from 1520, the oldest in existence. ⊠ *Trångsund 1,* ☎ *08/723–3000.*

⑪ Stortorget. Here in Gamla Stan's Great Square in 1520, the Danish king Christian II ordered a massacre of Swedish noblemen, paving the way for a national revolt against foreign rule and the founding of Sweden as a sovereign state under King Gustav Vasa, who ruled from 1523 to 1560. One legend holds that if it rains heavily enough on the anniversary of the massacre, the old stones still run red.

⑲ Östasiatiska Museet. The Museum of Far Eastern Antiquities has a fascinating collection of Chinese and Japanese Buddhist sculptures and artifacts. ⊠ *Skeppsholmen,* ☎ *08/666–4250,* ﹃℻ *08/611–2845.* ☜ *SKr40. ☉ Tues. noon–8, Wed.–Sun. noon–5.*

Djurgården and Skansen

Djurgården is Stockholm's pleasure island: On it you will find the outdoor museum Skansen, the Gröna Lund amusement park, and the *Vasa,* a 17th-century warship raised from the bottom of the harbor in 1961, as well as other delights.

A GOOD WALK

You can approach Djurgården from the water aboard the small ferries that leave from Slussen at the southern end of Gamla Stan or from Nybrokajen (New Bridge Quay) in front of the Kungliga Dramatiska Teater. Alternatively, starting at the theater, stroll down the Strandvägen quayside, taking in the magnificent old sailing ships permanently anchored here and the fine views over the harbor, and then cross

Djurgårdsbron (Djurgården Bridge) to the island. As you turn immediately to the right, your first port of call should be the **Vasa Museet** ⑳, which dramatically displays a splendid 17th-century warship. Return to the main street, Djurgårdsvägen, to find the entrance to the **Nordiska Museet** ㉑ (Nordic Museum), worth a quick visit for an insight into Swedish folklore.

Continue on Djurgårdsvägen to the amusement park **Gröna Lund** ㉒, a popular amusement park where Stockholmers of all ages come to play. Beyond the park, cross Djurgårdsvägen to **Skansen** ㉓, the world's first open-air museum and a must for any visitor to Stockholm.

From Skansen, continue following Djurgårdsvägen to Prins Eugens Väg, and follow signs to **Waldemarsudde** ㉔, the beautiful turn-of-the-century home of the painter Prince Eugen. On the way back to Djurgårdsbron, follow the small street called Hazeliusbacken to the charmingly archaic **Biologiska Museet** ㉕ (Biological Museum) before heading back into town.

TIMING

Allow half a day for this tour, unless you're planning to turn it into a full day's event with lengthy visits to Skansen and Gröna Land. The Vasa Museum deserves 2 hours, and the Nordiska and Biologiska museums can be seen in an hour combined. Waldemarsudde requires another ½ hour.

SIGHTS TO SEE

㉕ **Biologiska Museet.** The Biological Museum, in the shadow of Skansen, has a collection of stuffed animals in various simulated environments. ✉ *Hazeliusporten,* ☎ *08/442–8215.* 🎫 *SKr20.* ☉ *Apr.–Sept., daily 10–4; Oct.–Mar., Tues.–Sun. 10–3.*

NEED A BREAK?	On Hazeliusbacken, the Cirkus Theater (✉ Djurgårdsslätten, ☎ 08/660-8-81) and Hasselbacken Hotel (✉ Hazeliusbacken 20, ☎ 08/670-5000) both have excellent terrace cafés.

㉒ **Gröna Lund.** On a smaller scale than Copenhagen's Tivoli and Göteborg's Liseberg, the amusement park at Gröna Lund is a clean, well-organized pleasure garden with a wide range of rides, attractions and restaurants. ✉ *Allmänna Gränd 9,* ☎ *08/670–7600,* 📠 *08/670–7699.* 🎫 *SKr35 daytime, SKr40 evening, not including coupons or passes for rides.* ☉ *Late Apr.–early Sept. Call ahead for prices and hours, as they are subject to frequent change.*

㉑ **Nordiska Museet.** In this splendid late-Victorian structure you'll find peasant costumes from every region of the country and exhibits on the Sami (pronounced *sah*-mee; Lapps)—formerly seminomadic reindeer herders who inhabit the far north. Families with children should visit the delightful "village-life" play area on the ground floor. ✉ *Djurgårdsvägen 6–16,* ☎ *08/666–4600,* 📠 *08/666–4580,* 🎫 *SKr50.* ☉ *Tues.–Sun. 11–5.*

㉓ **Skansen.** The world's first open-air museum, Skansen was founded by philologist and ethnographer Artur Hazelius (who is also buried here) in 1891 to preserve traditional Swedish architecture, including farmhouses, windmills, barns, a working glassblower's hut, and churches, brought from all parts of the country. Not only is Skansen a delightful trip out of time in the center of a modern city, it also provides an easily assimilated insight into the life and culture of Sweden's various regions. In addition, the park has a zoo, a children's circus, a carnival area, an aquarium, a theater, and cafés. ✉ *Djurgårdsslätten 49–51,* ☎ *08/442–8000,* 📠 *08/442–8282.* 🎫 *Sept.–Apr., SKr30 weekdays,*

SKr40 weekends; May–Aug., SKr50. ☉ Sept.–Apr., daily 9–5; May–Aug., daily 9–10.

NEED A
BREAK?

For a snack with a view during your visit to Skansen, try the **Solliden Restaurant** (☎ 08/660–1055) near the front of the park, overlooking the city. The cozy **Bredablick Tower Café** (☎ 08/663–4778) is at the back of Skansen, next to the children's circus. There are also a number of open-air snack bars and cafés in the park. Gröna Lund has four different restaurants.

★ ⑳ **Vasa Museet.** The *Vasa*, a warship that sank on its maiden voyage in 1628, was forgotten for three centuries, located in 1956, and raised from the seabed in 1961. Its hull was found to be largely intact, because the Baltic's brackish waters do not support worms that eat ships' timbers. Now largely restored to her former, if brief, glory, the man-of-war resides in a handsome new museum. ⊠ *Galärvarvet, Djurgården,* ☎ *08/666–4800.* ⊡ *SKr45. ☉ Thurs.–Tues. 10–5, Wed. 10–8. Tours in English every hr in summer; Aug.–May, weekdays 12:30 and 2:30, weekends 10:30, 12:30, 2:30, and 4:30.*

㉔ **Waldemarsudde.** This estate, Djurgården's gem, was bequeathed to the Swedish people by Prince Eugen at his death in 1947 and maintains an important collection of Nordic paintings from 1880 to 1940, in addition to the prince's own works. ⊠ *Prins Eugens väg 6,* ☎ *08/662– 1833.* ℻ *08/667–7459* ⊡ *SKr40. ☉ June–Aug., Wed. and Fri.–Sun. 11–5, Tues. and Thurs. 7 am–9 pm; Sept.–May, Tue.–Sun. 11–4.*

Östermalm and Kaknästornet

Marked by waterfront rows of Renaissance-era buildings with palatial rooftops and ornamentation, Östermalm is a quieter, more residential section of central Stockholm, its elegant streets lined with museums and fine shopping. On Strandvägen, the boulevard that follows the harbor's edge from the busy downtown area to the staid diplomatic quarter, you can choose one of the three routes: the waterside walk, with its splendid views of the city harbor, busy with tour boats and sailboats; the inside walk that skirts upscale shops and exclusive restaurants; or the tree-shaded paths down the middle, where you'll meet the occasional horseback rider, very properly attired in helmet, jacket, and high polished boots.

A GOOD WALK

Walk east from the Kungliga Dramatiska Teatern along Strandvägen. At Djurgårdsbron, stop to admire the ornate little bridge, then turn left and head up Narvavägen to the **Historiska Museet** ㉖ (Museum of National Antiquities), which houses important collections of Viking gold and silver treasures. Cross Narvavägen at Oscars Kyrka before heading up the street to Karlaplan, a pleasant, circular park with a fountain; go across or around the park to find Karlavägen, a long boulevard lined with small shops and galleries. At Sibyllegatan, turn left and proceed to **Östermalmstorg** ㉗, where you'll find Saluhall, an excellent indoor food market. Continue down Sibyllegatan to the **Musikmuseet** ㉘ (Music Museum), installed in the city's oldest industrial building. Then go on to Nybroplan, where you can catch the 69 bus going east to **Kaknästornet** ㉙ for a spectacular view of Stockholm from the tallest tower in Scandinavia.

TIMING

This tour requires no more than a half day. You'll want to spend ½ to 1 hour in each of the museums; the bus ride from Nybroplan to Kaknästornet takes about 15 minutes, and the tower merits another ½ hour.

SIGHTS TO SEE

26 Historiska Museet. Viking treasures are the main draw here, but well-presented changing exhibitions also cover various periods of Swedish history, and an excellent shop sells books and gifts. ⊠ *Narvavägen 13–17,* ☎ *08/783–9400,* FAX *08/667–6578.* ⚏ *SKr55.* ⊙ *Tues.–Sun. 11–5, Thurs. 11–8.*

NEED A
BREAK?

The bistro **Cassi** (⊠ Narvavägen 30, just off Karlaplan) is just right for a great coffee and a quick snack. The indoor mall at **Fältöversten** on Karlaplan has several coffee shops and fast-food eateries.

OFF THE
BEATEN PATH

MILLESGÅRDEN – This gallery and sculpture garden are dedicated to the former owner of the property, the American-Swedish sculptor Carl Milles (1875–1955). On display are Milles' own works as well as his private collection. The setting is exquisite: The sculptures top columns on terraces in a magical garden high above the harbor and the city. Millesgården can be reached easily via subway to Ropsten, where you catch the Lidingö train and get off at Herserud, the second stop. The trip takes about 30 minutes. ⊠ *Carl Milles väg 2, Lidingö,* ☎ *08/731–5060,* FAX *08/767–0902.* ⚏ *SKr40.* ⊙ *May–Sept., daily 10–5; Oct.–Apr., Tues.–Sun. noon–4.*

29 Kaknästornet The 511-foot radio and television tower, completed in 1967, is the highest building in Scandinavia. Here you can eat a meal in a restaurant 426 feet above the ground and enjoy panoramic views of the city and the archipelago. ⊠ *Mörkakroken, off Djurgårdsbrunsvägen,* ☎ *08/667–8030,* FAX *08/667–8507.* ⚏ *SKr20.* ⊙ *Apr.–Aug., daily 9 AM–10 PM; Sept.–May, daily 10–9.*

28 Musikmuseet. The Music Museum presents a history of music and instruments in its displays. Children are invited to touch and play some of the instruments, and a motion-sensitive "Sound Room" allows visitors to produce musical effects simply by gesturing and moving around. ⊠ *Sibyllegatan 2,* ☎ *08/666–4530.* ⚏ *SKr30.* ⊙ *Tues.–Sun. 11–4.*

27 Östermalmstorg. This market square and its neighboring streets represent the old, established side of Stockholm. **Saluhall** is more like a collection of boutiques than an indoor food market; the fish displays can be especially intriguing. At the other end of the square, **Hedvig Eleonora Kyrka**, a church with characteristically Swedish faux-marble painting throughout its wooden interior, is the site of frequent lunchtime concerts during spring and summer.

NEED A
BREAK?

The little restaurants inside **Saluhall** offer everything from a take-out coffee to a sit-down meal.

Dining

Restaurant prices have recently declined, and a greater selection of less expensive restaurants have appeared on the scene. Even the higher-priced restaurants in Stockholm have kept their prices down. One factor has been the decrease in the value-added tax on restaurant food from 25% to 21%. Among Swedish dishes, the best bets are fish, particularly salmon, and the smörgåsbord buffet, which is usually a good value. Many restaurants close for either July or August, and most close on Christmas and New Year's Day. It is advisable to telephone first to make sure the restaurant is open. Reservations are usually necessary on weekends.

$$$$ ✕ **Grands Franska Matsalen.** From this classic French restaurant in the Grand Hotel, you can enjoy an inspiring view of the Old Town and the Royal Palace across the inner harbor waters. The food is equally inspiring, prepared by Sweden's Chef of the Year for 1989, Roland Persson. The menu changes five times a year, but the emphasis is always on Swedish ingredients, which are used to create such dishes as medallions of deer with shiitake mushrooms in wild-berry cream sauce. The thickness of the carpet and opulence of the decor are equal to the thickness of the patrons' wallets. ⊠ *Grand Hotel, Södra Blasieholmshamnen 8,* ☎ *08/679–3584. Reservations required. Jacket required. AE, DC, MC, V.*

$$$$ ✕ **Operakällaren.** Stockholm's best-known restaurant is magnificently situated in the Opera House at the end of Kungsträdgården. Operakällaren opened in 1787 and has a predictably snobbish atmosphere: Resting on its laurels, the restaurant is more a Swedish institution than a great gastronomic experience. Deep Oriental carpeting, shiny polished brass, and handsome carved-wood chairs and tables fill the room; the crystal chandeliers are said to be Sweden's finest, and the high windows on the south side give fine views of the Royal Palace. The restaurant is famed for its smörgåsbord, available from early June, with seasonal variations, through Christmas. Top selections include pickled herring, rollmops (rolled herring), reindeer and elk in season, and ice cream with cloudberry (yellow blackberry) sauce. In summer, the veranda opens for service as the Operabryggan Café, facing Kungsträdgården and the waterfront. ⊠ *Operahuset, Jakobs Torg 2,* ☎ *08/676–5801. Reservations required. Jacket and tie. AE, DC, MC, V. Main dining room closed in July.*

$$$$ ✕ **Paul & Norbert.** This quaint, romantic restaurant is rustic but re-
★   fined; It's on the city's most elegant avenue, overlooking one of its most picturesque bays. French-style preparations include indigenous wild game dishes such as reindeer, elk, partridge, and grouse; the fish dishes are also noted. ⊠ *Strandvägen 9,* ☎ *08/663–8183. Reservations required. AE, DC, MC, V. Closed weekends.*

$$$$ ✕ **Ulriksdals Wärdshus.** Lunchtime smörgåsbord is the calling card at
★   this beautifully situated country inn, built in 1868. The inn is in the park of an 18th-century palace, with a traditional interior overlooking orchards and a peaceful lake; guests even stand and sing the Swedish national anthem as the flag is lowered each evening. This restaurant is arguably the single most expensive in Stockholm, but the impeccable service and outstanding cuisine make it worthwhile. ⊠ *Ulriksdals Slottspark, Solna,* ☎ *08/850815,* FAX *08/850858. Reservations required. Jacket required. AE, DC, MC, V. No dinner Sun.*

$$$ ✕ **De Fyras Krog.** The name, "Inn of the Four Estates," is a reference to the four social classes originally represented in the Swedish Riksdag—Nobility, Clergy, Burghers and Peasants. The decor carries out the theme, with rococo furnishings, church pews, an upper gallery, and a stone-flagged cellar dining room to represent the four lifestyles. Completely rebuilt in 1995, De Fyras Krog offers a menu of Swedish regional specialties and an intimate atmosphere. ⊠ *Järntorgsgatan 5,* ☎ *08/240347. AE, DC, MC, V. Closed Sun.*

$$$ ✕ **Den Gyldene Freden.** Sweden's most famous old tavern, Freden opened for business in 1722. Every Thursday, the Swedish Academy, whose members choose the winner of the Nobel Prize in Literature, meets here in a private room on the second floor. The haunt of bards and barristers, artists and ad people, Freden could probably serve sawdust and still be popular, but the food and staff are worthy of the restaurant's hallowed reputation. The cuisine has a Swedish orientation, but Continental influences are spicing up the menu. Season permitting, try the oven-baked fillets of turbot served with chanterelles and crèpes;

the gray hen fried with spruce twigs and dried fruit is another good selection. The menu changes regularly, and the friendly staff will gladly make recommendations. ⊠ *Österlånggatan 51,* ☏ *08/249760. AE, DC, MC, V. No lunch. Closed Sun.*

$$$ ✕ **Edsbacka Krog.** In 1626, Edsbacka, just outside town, became Stockholm's first licensed inn. Its exposed roughhewn beams, plaster walls, and open fireplaces still give it the feel of a country inn for the gentry. The Continental Swedish cuisine is reliably superb. The owner, Christer Lindström, is an award-winning chef; his tarragon chicken with winter vegetables is worth the occasional long wait. ⊠ *Sollentunavägen 220, Sollentuna,* ☏ *08/963300. AE, DC, MC, V. No dinner Mon. No lunch Sat. Closed Sun.*

$$$ ✕ **Gåsen.** This is a classic Östermalm restaurant: very classy, cozy, and costly. The Swedish-French menu is excellent, including such dishes as smoked breast of goose with apple chutney, grilled turbot with fresh beetroot and spinach, and Arctic raspberry ice cream with blue curaçao sauce. The service is usually impeccable. ⊠ *Karlavägen 28,* ☏ *08/611–0269. Jacket and tie. AE, DC, MC, V. Closed weekends May–Aug., Sun. Sept.–Apr., and July.*

$$$ ✕ **Greitz.** Home-style Swedish cuisine is served in this classy and comfortable restaurant. Try the *Sotare* (grilled Baltic herring with parsley and butter) or perch and salmon roe with sautéed white beets. The decor is revamped café style, with the once-stained wood paneling around the room painted burgundy red. ⊠ *Vasagatan 50,* ☏ *08/234820. AE, DC, MC, V. Closed Sun. and July.*

$$$ ✕ **Källaren Aurora.** Extremely elegant, if a little staid, this Old Town cellar restaurant is set in a beautiful 17th-century house. Its largely foreign clientele enjoys top-quality Swedish and international cuisines served in intimate small rooms. Try charcoal-grilled spiced salmon, veal Parmesan, or orange-basted halibut fillet. ⊠ *Munkbron 11,* ☏ *08/219359. AE, DC, MC, V. No lunch.*

$$$ ✕ **KB.** The most urbane of Stockholm's quality restaurants serves Swedish country fare, painstakingly prepared. The middle-aged waitresses are familiar in the best sense, and the patrons are among the city's most relaxed. There are soft, fitted benches around the smallish dining room, and there's another, more casual dining room in the bar next door, where you might try the excellent *mejramkorv* (marjoram sausage). Chef Örjan Klein offers low-cal, low-fat dishes in the modern tradition—with visible homage to France. Try the rack of lamb with artichoke sauce and leek-and-morel coulis, or the Swedish freshwater crayfish in season. ⊠ *Smålandsgatan 7,* ☏ *08/679–6032. AE, DC, MC, V. No lunch Sat. Closed Sun. and late June–early Aug.*

$$$ ✕ **Stallmästaregården.** A historic old inn with an attractive courtyard and garden, Stallmästaregården is in the Haga Park, just north of Norrtull, about 15 minutes by car or bus from the city center. The fine summer meals are served in the courtyard overlooking the waters of Brunnsviken. Specialties include *Anka Roti,* charcoal-grilled duck kebab. ⊠ *Norrtull, near Haga,* ☏ *08/610–1300. AE, DC, MC, V. Closed Sun. and Christmas–New Year's.*

$$$ ✕ **Wedholms Fisk.** Noted for its fresh seafood dishes, Wedholms is ap-
★ propriately situated by a bay in the center of Stockholm, on Berzelii Park. High ceilings, large windows, and tasteful modern paintings from the owner's personal collection create a spacious, sophisticated atmosphere. The traditional Swedish cuisine, which consists almost exclusively of seafood, is simple but outstanding. Try the poached sole in lobster-and-champagne sauce or the Pilgrim mussels Provençale. ⊠ *Nybrokajen 17,* ☏ *08/611–7874. AE, DC, MC, V. Closed Sun. and July.*

420

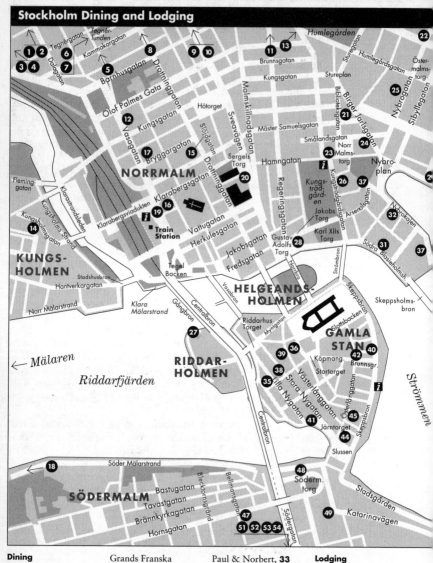

Dining

Bakfickan, **28**
Butler's, **4**
Cassi, **34**
Clas på Hörnet, **10**
De Fyras Krog, **44**
Den Gyldene
Freden, **45**
Diana, **42**
Edsbacka Krog, **9**
Gåsen, **13**

Grands Franska
Matsalen, **31**
Greitz, **12**
Hannas Krog, **52**
Källaren Aurora, **35**
KB, **24**
Nils Emil, **54**
Open Gate, **51**
Operakällaren, **28**
Örtagården, **25**

Paul & Norbert, **33**
Prinsen, **21**
Rolfs Kök, **7**
Söders Hjärta, **47**
Stallmästare-
gården, **8**
Tranan, **1**
Ulriksdals
Wärdshus, **3**
Wasahof, **2**
Wedholms Fisk, **37**

Lodging

af Chapman, **43**
Alexandra, **53**
Amaranten, **14**
Anno 1647, **49**
Bema, **5**
Berns, **26**
Birger Jarl, **11**
Bosön, **30**
Central Hotel, **17**
City, **15**
Clas på Hörnet, **10**

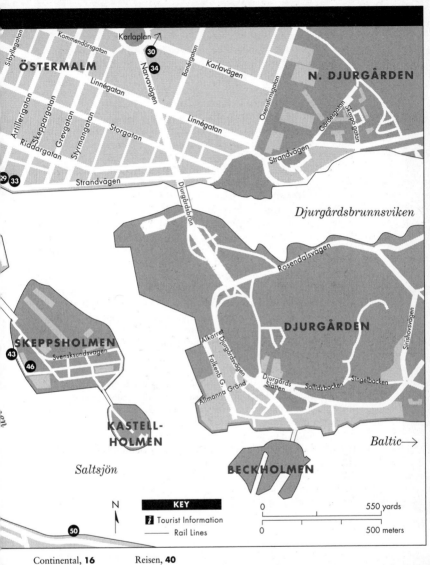

ÖSTERMALM

N. DJURGÅRDEN

Karlaplan

Kommendörsgatan

Sibyllegatan
Artillerigatan
Skeppargatan
Grevgatan
Styrmangatan
Riddargatan

Linnégatan
Narvavägen
Banérgatan
Karlavägen
Oxenstiernsgatan
Gärdesgatan
Storpsgatan

Storgatan

Linnégatan

Strandvägen

Strandvägen

Djurgårdsbron

Djurgårdsbrunnsviken

Rosendalsvägen

DJURGÅRDEN

Sirishovsvägen

SKEPPSHOLMEN

Svensksundsvägen

Alkärret
Djurgårdsvägen
Falkenb G.
Allmänna Gränd

Djurgårds
Slätten
Solfids backen
Singelbacken

KASTELL-
HOLMEN

Saltsjön

BECKHOLMEN

Baltic→

KEY

ℹ️ Tourist Information
— Rail Lines

N

| 0 | | 550 yards |
| 0 | | 500 meters |

$$ ⚔ **Bakfickan.** The name, which means "hip pocket," is appropriate, as
★ this restaurant is tucked around the back of the Opera House complex.
It's a less expensive alternative to the nearby Operakällaren and is par-
ticularly popular at lunchtime, offering Swedish home cooking and a
range of daily specials. Counter and table service are available. ⊠ *Op-
erahuset, Jakobs Torg 2,* ☎ *08/207745. AE, DC, MC, V. Closed Sun.*

$$ ⚔ **Butler's.** The menu is short but dependable, specializing in eclectic
lamb dishes from southern Europe. Try the fillet of lamb with Provençale
black salsify or the entrecôte with herb cream. The checkered tablecloths
and French bistro chairs lend a Continental atmosphere. Butler's is noisy
but very trendy for lunch. ⊠ *Rörstrandsgatan 11,* ☎ *08/321823. Reservations required. AE, DC, MC, V. No lunch weekends.*

$$ ⚔ **Cassi.** This downtown restaurant, with an espresso bar dominating
the front room, specializes in French bistro–style cuisine at reasonable
prices. ⊠ *Narvavägen 30,* ☎ *08/661–7461. DC, MC, V. Closed Sat.*

$$ ⚔ **Diana.** This atmospheric Gamla Stan cellar dates from the Middle
Ages. The menu draws on the best indigenous products from the
Swedish forest and shoreline. In summer customers may be predomi-
nantly foreign or businesspeople from the provinces. ⊠ *Brunnsgränd
2,* ☎ *08/107310. AE, DC, MC, V. Closed Sun.*

$$ ⚔ **Hannas Krog.** What started out as an interesting neighborhood
spot has become one of Södermalm's trendiest restaurants. Guests are
serenaded at 10 minutes before the hour by a mooing cow that emerges
from the cuckoo clock just inside the door. Ranging from Caribbean
shrimp specialties to Provençale lamb dishes, the food is good, if a bit
pricey. Service is consistent with the restaurant's crowded and relaxed
atmosphere. ⊠ *Skånegatan 80,* ☎ *08/643–8225. Reservations re-
quired. AE, DC, MC, V. No lunch weekends and July.*

$$ ⚔ **Nils Emil.** This bustling restaurant in Södermalm is known for deli-
★ cious Swedish cuisine and generous helpings at reasonable prices; try
the *Kåldomar* (ground beef wrapped in cabbage) or the Baltic herring.
The restaurant attracts members of the royal family on a regular basis.
The paintings of personable owner-chef Nils Emil's island birthplace in
the Stockholm archipelago are by a well-known Swedish artist, Gustav
Rudberg. ⊠ *Folkungagatan 122,* ☎ *08/640–7209. Reservations required.
Jacket and tie. AE, DC, MC, V. No lunch Sat. Closed July.*

$$ ⚔ **Prinsen.** Established in 1897, this lively restaurant has remained an
unpretentious, unchanging presence in a fashionable area given to
overtrendiness—one reason for Prinsen's popularity with the city's
writers, musicians, and artists. The food—primarily robust, if plain,
Swedish and French fare—is served by attentive waiters negotiating nar-
row aisles and crowded booths. ⊠ *Mäster Samuelsgatan 4,* ☎ *08/611–
1331. AE, DC, MC, V. No lunch Sun.*

$$ ⚔ **Rolfs Kök.** Small and modern, Rolfs combines an informal atmosphere with excellent Swedish-French cuisine, serving three meals a day
at reasonable prices. The lamb is usually a good bet, as are the stir-
fried Asian dishes. ⊠ *Tegnérgatan 41,* ☎ *08/101696. AE, DC, MC,
V. No lunch weekends.*

$$ ⚔ **Söders Hjärta.** Conveniently located on Södermalm, just across
from a floodlit church, this bistro is not far from the Slussen subway
station. Sample Swedish home-style cooking in the dining room, and
then move over to the adjacent large bar, which is cheerful and friendly.
⊠ *Bellmansgatan 22,* ☎ *08/640–1462. AE, DC, MC, V. No lunch Sun.*

$$ ⚔ **Tranan.** A young, yuppie crowd frequents Tranan for its bar, which
often has live music, and for its unpretentious restaurant. The stark
walls and checkered floor are from Tranan's days as a workingman's
beer parlor. Chef Joakim Haglund prepares traditional Swedish cuisine. ⊠ *Karlbergsvägen 14,* ☎ *08/300765. AE, DC, MC, V.*

$$ ✕ **Wasahof.** Popular with newspaper reporters, copywriters, and ad-
★ vertising types, Wasahof is noted for its friendly, bistrolike atmosphere.
Often packed and smoky on weekday nights, it offers a tasty menu once
you squeeze past the crowded bar. Specialties include oysters and crab.
⊠ *Dalagatan 46,* ☎ *08/323440. AE, DC, MC, V. No lunch.*

$ ✕ **Open Gate.** Near the Slussen locks, on the south side of Stockholm
Harbor, this popular, trendy trattoria is part art deco, part Italian—
and attracts a youngish crowd. Pasta dishes are the specialty. ⊠ *Hög-
bergsgatan 40,* ☎ *08/643–9776. AE, DC, MC, V. Closed Sun.*

$ ✕ **Örtagården.** This is a truly delightful vegetarian, no-smoking restau-
★ rant above the Östermalmstorg food market. It offers an attractive buf-
fet of soups, salads, hot dishes, and homemade bread—not to mention
the SKr5 bottomless cup of coffee—in a turn-of-the-century atmosphere.
⊠ *Nybrogatan 31,* ☎ *08/662–1728. AE, MC, V.*

Lodging

In spite of the prohibitively expensive reputation of Stockholm's ho-
tels, great deals can be found during the summer, when prices are sub-
stantially lower and numerous discounts are available. More than 50
hotels offer the "Stockholm Package," providing accommodations for
one night, breakfast, and a Key to Stockholm card, which gives free
admission to museums and travel on public transport. Costs run from
SKr360 to SKr760. Details are available from travel agents, tourist bu-
reaus, **Stockholm Information Service** (⊠ Box 7542, S–103 93 Stock-
holm, ☎ 08/789–2400, ☒ 08/789–2450), or **Hotellcentralen** (⊠
Centralstation, S–111 20 Stockholm, ☎ 08/240880, ☒ 08/7918666).
All rooms in the hotels reviewed are equipped with shower or bath un-
less otherwise noted.

$$$$ 🏨 **Berns.** In a successful attempt to distinguish itself from the rest of
the crowd, the 132-year-old Berns opted for an art deco look in its 1989
renovation. Indirect lighting, modern Italian furniture, and expensive
marble, granite, and wood inlays now dominate the decor of the pub-
lic areas and guest rooms. You can breakfast in the Red Room, im-
mortalized by August Strindberg's novel of the same name: This was
one of his haunts. Rates include the use of a nearby fitness center with
a pool. ⊠ *Näckströmsgatan 8, S–111 47,* ☎ *08/614–0700,* ☒ *08/611–
5175. 64 rooms, 3 suites. Restaurant, bar, no-smoking rooms, meet-
ing room. AE, DC, MC, V.*

$$$$ 🏨 **Continental.** Located in the city center across from the train station,
the Continental is a reliable hotel that's especially popular with Amer-
ican guests. First opened in 1966, it was renovated in 1992. Rooms
are equipped with minibar, trouser press, and satellite television. An
extravagant Scandinavian buffet is served in the Gustavian breakfast
rooms. ⊠ *Klara Vattugränd 4, S–101 22,* ☎ *08/244020,* ☒ *08/411–
3695. 268 rooms. Restaurant, bar, no-smoking rooms, sauna, meet-
ing rooms. AE, DC, MC, V.*

$$$$ 🏨 **Diplomat.** Within easy walking distance of Djurgården, this elegant
hotel is less flashy than most in its price range. The building is a turn-
of-the-century town house that housed foreign embassies in the 1930s
and was converted into a hotel in 1966. Rooms have thick carpeting
and high ceilings; those in the front, facing the water, have magnifi-
cent views over Stockholm Harbor. A calm and dignified atmosphere
compensates for the sometimes slow service. ⊠ *Strandvägen 7C, S–104
40,* ☎ *08/663–5800,* ☒ *08/783–6634. 133 rooms. Restaurant, bar,
no-smoking rooms, sauna, meeting room. AE, DC, MC, V.*

$$$$ 🏨 **Grand.** The city's showpiece hotel is an 1874 landmark on the quay-
side at Blasieholmen, just across the water from the Royal Palace. Vis-

iting political dignitaries, Nobel Prize winners, and movie stars come to enjoy the gracious Old World atmosphere, which extends to the comfortable, well-furnished rooms. One of the hotel's nicest features is a glassed-in veranda overlooking the harbor, where an excellent smörgåsbord buffet is served. Guests have access to the Sturebadet Health Spa nearby. ⊠ *Södra Blasieholmshamnen 8, Box 16424, S–103 27,* ☎ *08/679–3500,* FAX *08/611–8686. 319 rooms, 20 suites. 2 restaurants, bar, no-smoking rooms, sauna, shops, meeting rooms. AE, DC, MC, V.*

$$$$ ⚄ **Lady Hamilton.** As charming, desirable, and airily elegant as its name-
★ sake, the Lady Hamilton opened in 1980 as a modern hotel inside a 15th-century building. It's so close to the Royal Palace in Gamla Stan that some rooms afford a view of the changing of the guard. Swedish antiques accent the light, natural-toned decor in all the guest rooms and common areas. Romney's "Bacchae" portrait of Lady Hamilton hangs in the foyer, where a large, smiling figurehead from an old ship supports the ceiling. The breakfast room, furnished with captain's chairs, looks out onto the lively cobblestone street, while the subterranean sauna rooms, in whitewashed stone, provide a secluded fireplace and a chance to take a dip in the building's original, medieval well. ⊠ *Storkyrkobrinken 5, S–111 28,* ☎ *08/234680,* FAX *08/411–1148. 34 rooms. Bar, breakfast room, no-smoking rooms, sauna, meeting room. AE, DC, MC, V.*

$$$$ ⚄ **Lord Nelson.** The owners of the Lady Hamilton and the Victory run this small hotel with a nautical atmosphere right in the middle of the Old Town. Space is at a premium—the rooms are little more than cabins—but service is excellent. Noise from merrymakers in the pedestrian street outside can be a problem during the summer. ⊠ *Västerlånggatan 22, S–111 29,* ☎ *08/232390,* FAX *08/101089. 31 rooms. Café, no-smoking rooms, sauna, meeting room. AE, DC, MC, V.*

$$$$ ⚄ **Reisen.** This 17th-century hotel on the waterfront in Gamla Stan has been in operation since 1819. It has a fine restaurant, a grill, tea and coffee service in the library, and what is reputed to be the best piano bar in town. The swimming pool is built under the medieval arches of the foundation. ⊠ *Skeppsbron 12–14, S–111 30,* ☎ *08/223260,* FAX *08/201559. 114 rooms. 2 restaurants, bar, no-smoking floor, indoor pool, sauna, meeting rooms. AE, DC, MC, V.*

$$$$ ⚄ **Royal Viking (Radisson SAS).** In 1984, what was slated as a convenient store site only yards from Central Station became the Royal Viking hotel—whose best quality, appropriately enough, is convenience, both in location and service. Guest rooms lack nothing except space. They have attractive natural textiles and artwork, sturdy writing desks, minibars, separate seating areas, and plush robes in the large bathrooms. Triple-glazed windows and plenty of insulation keep traffic noise to a minimum, but check whether the current bar pianist is the exuberant type before taking a room on the atrium. The large atrium lobby is spacious, and the split-level lounge is elegant. There is a business-class SAS check-in counter in the lobby. ⊠ *Vasagatan 1, S–101 24,* ☎ *08/141000 or 800/448–8355,* FAX *08/108180. 319 rooms. Restaurant, bar, no-smoking rooms, indoor pool, sauna, convention center. AE, MC, V.*

$$$$ ⚄ **Scandic Crown.** Working with what appears to be a dubious location (perched on a tunnel above a six-lane highway), the Scandic Crown has pulled a rabbit out of a hat. The hotel was built in 1988 on special cushions; you know the highway is there, but it intrudes only minimally, mainly in view. The intriguing labyrinth of levels, separate buildings, and corridors is filled with such unique details as a rounded stairway lighted from between the steps. The guest rooms are exquisitely designed and decorated in modern style, with plenty of stainless steel and polished wood inlay to accent the maroon color scheme. Note-

worthy is the Couronne d'Or, a French eatery, and a cellar with wines dating to 1650 where winetasting is available. The hotel is at Slussen, easily accessible from downtown. ⊠ *Guldgränd 8, S–104 65,* ☎ *08/702–2500,* FAX *08/642–8358. 264 rooms. 2 restaurants, piano bar, no-smoking rooms, indoor pool, beauty salon, sauna, meeting rooms. AE, DC, MC, V.*

$$$$ ▦ **Sergel Plaza.** This stainless-steel-paneled high-rise has a welcoming lobby, with cane chairs in a pleasantly skylit seating area. Well-lit rooms are practical but lack the luxury feel the price tag might lead you to expect. The decor is almost disappointing, with run-of-the-mill furnishings and too many grays. The location is central, right on the main pedestrian mall, but most windows view only office buildings. A few rooms are high up, with a view of the inner-city rooftops and beyond. ⊠ *Brunkebergstorg 9, S–103 27,* ☎ *08/226600,* FAX *08/215070. 406 rooms. Restaurant, bar, no-smoking rooms, sauna, shops, convention center. AE, DC, MC, V.*

$$$$ ▦ **Stockholm.** This Sweden Hotels property occupies the upper floors of a downtown office building. It has a mainly modern decor, offset by traditional Swedish furnishings that help create a friendly atmosphere. The hotel is basic, clean, and efficient, a good spot for those who want to spend their waking hours shopping, sightseeing, or on business. Breakfast is included in the room rate, but you can also order room service from McDonald's, in the same building, almost around-the-clock. ⊠ *Normalmstorg 1, S–111 46,* ☎ *08/678–1320,* FAX *08/611–2103. 92 rooms. Restaurant, bar, no-smoking rooms, meeting room. AE, DC, MC, V.*

$$$$ ▦ **Strand (Radisson SAS).** This Old World yellow-brick hotel, built in 1912 for the Stockholm Olympics, has since been completely and tastefully modernized. The waterside location is right across from the Royal Dramatic Theater. No two of its rooms are the same, but all are furnished with antiques and have such rustic touches as flowers painted on woodwork and furniture. The Piazza is an indoor restaurant with an outdoor feel to it: Italian cuisine is the specialty, and the wine list is superb. An SAS check-in counter for business-class travelers adjoins the main reception area. ⊠ *Nybrokajen 9, Box 163 96, S–103 27,* ☎ *08/678–7800,* FAX *08/611–2436. 148 rooms. Restaurant, no-smoking rooms, sauna, meeting rooms. AE, DC, MC, V.*

$$$$ ▦ **Victory.** Slightly larger than its brother and sister hotels, the Lord Nelson and Lady Hamilton, this extremely atmospheric Old Town building dates from 1640. Decor is nautical, with items from the HMS *Victory* and Swedish antiques. Each room is named after a 19th-century sea captain. The noted Lejontornet restaurant boasts an extensive wine cellar. ⊠ *Lilla Nygatan 5, S–111 28,* ☎ *08/143090,* FAX *08/202177. 48 rooms. Restaurant, bar, bistro, no-smoking floor, 2 saunas, meeting rooms. AE, DC, MC, V.*

$$$ ▦ **Amaranten.** A little out of the way, on the island of Kungsholmen, this large, modern hotel is, however, just a few minutes' walk from Stockholm's central train station. Rooms are contemporary, with minibar, sofa, and satellite television with complimentary movie channels. Fifty rooms have air-conditioning and soundproofing available for an extra charge. Guests enjoy a brasserie and a piano bar. ⊠ *Kungsholmsgatan 31, Box 8054, S–104 20,* ☎ *08/654–1060,* FAX *08/652–6248. 410 rooms. Restaurant, piano bar, no-smoking rooms, pool, sauna, meeting rooms. AE, DC, MC, V.*

$$$ ▦ **Anno 1647.** The name is the date the building was erected. A small,
★   pleasant, friendly hotel on Södermalm, it is three stops on the subway from the city center. Rooms vary in shape, but all have original, well-worn pine floors, with 17th-century-style funishings. There's no elevator in this four-story building. ⊠ *Mariagränd 3, S–116 41,* ☎

08/644–0480, ℻ 08/643–3700. *42 rooms, 30 with bath. Snack bar.*
AE, DC, MC, V.

$$$ 🏨 **Birger Jarl.** A short bus ride from the city center, and half a block from
the temporary Museum of Modern Art, this contemporary, conserva-
tive, thickly carpeted venue attracts business travelers, catered confer-
ences, and tourists requiring unfussy comforts. Breakfast is an extensive
buffet just off the lobby, but room service is also available. Rooms are
not large but are well furnished and have nice touches, such as heated
towel racks in the bathrooms; all double rooms have bathtubs. Four fam-
ily-style rooms have extra floor space and sofa beds. ⊠ *Tulegatan 8, S–104
32,* ☎ *08/151020,* ℻ *08/673–7366. 225 rooms. Coffee shop, no-smok-
ing rooms, sauna, meeting rooms. AE, DC, MC, V.*

$$$ 🏨 **Central Hotel.** Less than 300 yards from the Central Station, this
practical hotel was constructed in 1989. Rooms are small and face a
pleasant, quiet courtyard; bathrooms have a shower only. ⊠ *Vasagatan
38, S–101 20,* ☎ *08/220840,* ℻ *08/247573. 93 rooms. No-smoking
rooms, meeting rooms. AE, DC, MC, V.*

$$$ 🏨 **City.** A large, modern-style hotel built in the 1940s but completely ren-
ovated in 1984, the City is near the city center and Hötorget market. It
is owned by the Salvation Army, so alcohol is not served. Breakfast is
served in the atrium restaurant Winter Garden. ⊠ *Slöjdgatan 7, S–111
81,* ☎ *08/723–7200,* ℻ *08/723–7209. 293 rooms with bath. Restau-
rant, no-smoking rooms, sauna, meeting rooms. AE, DC, MC, V.*

$$$ 🏨 **Clas på Hörnet.** This may be the most exclusive—and smallest—hotel
★ in town: 10 rooms (8 doubles) in an 18th-century inn converted into
a small hotel in 1982. The rooms, comfortably furnished with period
antiques, go quickly. The restaurant is worth visiting even if you don't
spend the night: Its old-fashioned dining room is tucked away on the
ground floor of a restored 1739 inn; its Swedish and Continental menu
includes outstanding *strömming* (Baltic herring) and cloudberry mousse
cake. ⊠ *Surbrunnsgatan 20, S–113 48,* ☎ *08/165130,* ℻ *08/612–5315.
10 rooms. AE, DC, MC, V. Closed July. Restaurant* ☎ *08/165136,* ℻
*08/612–5315. Reservations required. Jacket and tie. AE, DC, MC, V.
Closed July and Christmas–New Year's.*

$$$ 🏨 **Gamla Stan.** This quiet, cozy hotel is tucked away in one of Old
Town's 17th-century houses. Each of its 51 rooms is uniquely deco-
rated. ⊠ *Lilla Nygatan 25,* ☎ *08/244450,* ℻ *08/216483. 51 rooms.
No-smoking floor, meeting rooms. AE, DC, MC, V.*

$$$ 🏨 **Mornington.** A quiet, modern Best Western hotel that prides itself
on a friendly atmosphere, the Mornington is within easy walking dis-
tance of Stureplan and downtown shopping areas and particularly
handy to Östermalmstorg, with its food hall. Rooms tend to be small;
decor is standard Best Western style. ⊠ *Nybrogatan 53, S–102 44,* ☎
08/663–1240, ℻ *08/662–2179. 140 rooms. Restaurant, bar, no-smoking rooms, sauna, steam rooms, meeting rooms. AE, DC, MC, V.*

$$$ 🏨 **Tegnérlunden.** A quiet city park fronts this modern hotel, a 10-minute
walk from the downtown hub of Sergels Torg, with the shops of
Sveavägen along the way. Although the rooms are small and sparely
furnished, they are clean and well maintained. The lobby is bright with
marble, brass, and greenery, as is the sunny rooftop breakfast room.
⊠ *Tegnérlunden 8, S–113 59,* ☎ *08/349780,* ℻ *08/327818. 103
rooms. Breakfast room, no-smoking rooms, sauna, meeting room.
AE, DC, MC, V.*

$$ 🏨 **Alexandra.** Although it is in the Södermalm area, to the south of
the Old Town, this small, modern hotel is only five minutes by sub-
way from the city center. A new floor was added in 1990. ⊠ *Magnus
Ladulåsgatan 42, S–118 27,* ☎ *08/840320,* ℻ *08/720–5353. 75
rooms, 6 2-room suites. Breakfast rooms, no-smoking rooms, sauna.
AE, DC, MC, V.*

$$ 🏨 **Mälardrottningen.** One of the more unusual establishments in Stockholm, Mälardrottningen, a Sweden Hotels property, was once Barbara Hutton's yacht. Since 1982, it has been a quaint and pleasant hotel, with a crew as service-conscious as any in Stockholm. Tied up on the freshwater side of Gamla Stan, it is minutes from everything. The small suites are suitably decorated in a navy-blue and maroon nautical theme. Some of the below-deck cabins are a bit stuffy, but in summer you can take your meals out on deck. Its chief assets are novelty and absence of traffic noise. ⊠ *Riddarholmen 4, S–111 28,* ☎ *08/243600 or 800/448–8355,* 𝔽𝔸𝕏 *08/243676. 59 cabins. Restaurant, bar, grill, nosmoking rooms, sauna, meeting rooms. AE, DC, MC, V.*

$ 🏨 **Bema.** This small hotel has a reasonably central location, on the ground floor of an apartment block near Tegnérlunden. Room decor is Swedish modern, with beechwood furniture. One four-bed family room is available. Breakfast is served in your room. ⊠ *Upplandsgatan 13, S–111 23,* ☎ *08/232675,* 𝔽𝔸𝕏 *08/205338. 12 rooms. AE, DC, MC, V.*

$ 🏨 *Gustav af Klint.* A "hotel ship" moored at Stadsgården quay, near Slussen subway station, the *Gustav af Klint* is divided into two sections—a hotel and a hostel. The hostel section has 18 4-bunk cabins and 10 2-bunk cabins; a 14-bunk dormitory is also available from May through mid-September. The hotel section has 4 single-bunk and 3 2-bunk cabins at SKr380 and SKr480 respectively, with bedsheets and breakfast included. The hostel rates are SKr120 per person in a 4-bunk room, and SKr 140 per person in a 2-bunk room; these do not include bedsheets or breakfast. All guests share common bathrooms and showers. There is a cafeteria and a restaurant, and you can dine on deck in summer. ⊠ *Stadsgårdskajen 153, S–116 45,* ☎ *08/640–4077,* 𝔽𝔸𝕏 *08/640–6416. 7 hotel cabins, 28 hostel cabins, 28 dormitory beds. AE, MC, V.*

Youth Hostels

Don't be put off by the "youth" bit: There's actually no age limit. The standards of cleanliness, comfort, and facilities offered are usually extremely high.

🏨 *af Chapman.* This circa-1888 sailing ship is permanently moored in Stockholm Harbor, just across from the Royal Palace; it is a landmark in its own right. Book early—the place is so popular in summer that finding a bed may prove difficult. Breakfast (SKr45) is not included in the room rate; there are no kitchen facilities. ⊠ *Västra Brobänken, Skeppsholmen S–111 49,* ☎ *08/679–5015,* 𝔽𝔸𝕏 *08/6119875. 136 beds, 2- to 6-bed cabins. Café June–Aug. DC, MC, V. Closed Christmas–Mar.*

🏨 **Bosön.** Out of the way on the island of Lidingö, this hostel is part of the Bosön Sports Institute, a national training center pleasantly situated close to the water. You can rent canoes on the grounds and go out for a paddle. Breakfast is included in the room rate. There are laundry facilities and a kitchen for guest use. ⊠ *Bosön, S–181 47 Lidingö,* ☎ *08/605–6600,* 𝔽𝔸𝕏 *08/767–1644. 70 beds. Cafeteria, sauna, coin laundry. MC, V.*

🏨 **Långholmen.** This former prison, built in 1724, was converted into a combined hotel and hostel in 1989. The hotel rooms are made available as additional hostel rooms in the summertime. Rooms are small and windows are nearly nonexistent—you *are* in a prison—but that hasn't stopped travelers from flocking here. Each room has two to five beds, and all but 10 have bathrooms with shower. The hostel is on the island of Långholmen, which has popular bathing beaches and a Prison Museum. The Inn, next door, serves Swedish home cooking, the Jail Pub offers light snacks, and a garden restaurant operates in the summertime. ⊠ *Långholmen, Box 9116, S–102 72,* ☎ *08/668–0510.*

June–Sept.: 254 beds. Sept.–May: 26 beds. Cafeteria, restaurant, sauna, beach, coin laundry. AE, DC, MC, V.

🔟 **Skeppsholmen.** A former craftsman's workshop in a pleasant and quiet part of the island was converted into a hostel for the overflow from the *af Chapman,* an anchor's throw away. Breakfast (SKr45) is not included in the room rate. ✉ *Skeppsholmen, S–111 49,* ☎ *08/679–5017,* 𝔽𝔸𝕏 *08/611–7155. 155 beds, 2- to 6-bed rooms. DC, MC, V.*

Camping

Camping in the Stockholm area costs SKr65–SKr130 per night. Try any of the following sites: **Bromma** (✉ Ängby Camping, S–161 55 Bromma, ☎ 08/370420, 𝔽𝔸𝕏 08/378226), **Skärholmen** (✉ Bredäng Camping, S–127 31 Skärholmen, ☎ 08/977071, 𝔽𝔸𝕏 08/708–7262), **Sollentuna** (✉ Rösjöbadens Camping, S–191 56 Sollentuna, ☎ 08/962184, 𝔽𝔸𝕏 08/929295).

Nightlife and the Arts

The hub of Stockholm's nightlife is Kungsträdgården, where several popular bars and discos line the western edge of the park. On weekends these spots are often packed with tourists and locals. Be forewarned: Many establishments will post and enforce a minimum age requirement, which could be anywhere from 18 to 30, depending on the clientele they wish to serve.

Bars

If you prefer exploring areas not entirely swamped by crowds, you will find a bar-hopping visit to Södermalm rewarding. Start at **Mosebacke Etablissement** (✉ Mosebacke Torg 3, ☎ 08/641–9020), a combined indoor theater and outdoor café with a spectacular view of the city. Wander along Götagatan with its lively bars and head for the **Pelikan Restaurant** (✉ Blekingegatan 40, ☎ 08/743–0695), a former beer hall and now an unpretentious but well-priced restaurant and bar. The trendy **Hannas Krog** (✉ Skånegatan 80, ☎ 08/643–8225) restaurant has a bar in the cellar with low lights, little furnishing, loud music, and a black-clad 20-something crowd.

Piano bars are part of the Stockholm scene. Try the **Anglais Bar** on weekends at the Hotel Anglais (✉ Humlegårdsgatan 23, ☎ 08/614–1600) or the **Clipper Club** at the Hotel Reisen (✉ Skeppsbron 12–14, ☎ 08/223260).

Irish pubs have recently become very popular among the happy-hour crowds, with **Limerick** (✉ Tegnérgatan 10, ☎ 08/673–4398), **Dubliner** (✉ Smålandsgatan 8, ☎ 08/679–7707), and **Bagpiper's Inn** (✉ Rörstrandsgatan 21, ☎ 08/311855) currently leading the pack.

Hus 1 (Huset) (✉ Sveavägen 57, ☎ 08/315533) has a restaurant, café, bookshop, and disco, run by gays for gays.

Cabaret

Stockholm's biggest nightclub, **Börsen** (✉ Jakobsgatan 6, ☎ 08/787–8500), offers high-quality international cabaret shows. Another popular spot is the **Cabaret Club** (✉ Barnhusgatan 12, ☎ 08/411–0608), at which reservations are advised. Drag shows are the main attraction at **Studion** (✉ St. Eriksplan 4, ☎ 08/344454).

Casinos

Many hotels and bars have a roulette table and sometimes blackjack, operating according to Swedish rules aimed at restricting the amount you can lose. The **Monte Carlo** (☎ 08/411–0025), at the corner of Kungsgatan and Sveavägen, offers roulette and blackjack 11:30 AM–5 AM daily;

there is food service and a bar, with a disco on weekends. Clientele tends to be on the rough side.

Classical Music

Free concerts are held in **Kungsträdgården** every summer—for details, contact the tourist office or check *Stockholm This Week*. International orchestras often visit **Konserthuset** (⊠ Hötorget 8, ☎ 08/102110), the main concert hall. The **Music at the Palace** series (☎ 08/102247, ℻ 08/215911) runs June through August. Off-season, there are weekly concerts by Sweden's Radio Symphony Orchestra at **Berwaldhallen** (Berwald Concert Hall) (⊠ Strandvägen 69, ☎ 08/784–1800, ℻ 08/663–1514).

Dancing

Café Opera (⊠ Operahuset, ☎ 08/411–0026), at the waterfront end of Kungsträgården, is a popular meeting place for young and old alike. It has the longest bar in town, plus dining and roulette, and dancing after midnight; the kitchen offers a night menu until 2:30 AM. **Daily's Bar** (☎ 08/215655), a glitzy disco at the other end of Kungsträdgården, near Sweden House, has a restaurant and is open until 3 AM. **King Creole** (⊠ Kungsgatan 18, ☎ 08/244700) offers big-band dance music alternating with rock. **Berns' Salonger** (⊠ Berzelii Park, ☎ 08/614–0550), an elegant restaurant and bar in a renovated period building with a large balcony facing the Royal Dramatic Theater, turns into a lively disco at night. **Sture Compagniet** (⊠ Sturegatan 4, ☎ 08/611–7800) is a complex of bars, food service, and dance areas on three levels inside the Sture Gallerian shopping mall. **Gino** (⊠ Birger Jarlsgatan 27, ☎ 08/791–7120) offers live rock and pop music performances, with plenty of dance space and a good bar. **Penny Lane** (⊠ Birger Jarlsgatan 29, ☎ 08/201411) is a soft-disco nightclub specifically for 30- or even 40-something patrons. **Mälarsalen** (⊠ Torkel Knutssonsgatan 2, ☎ 08/658–1300) caters to the jitterbug and fox-trot crowd in Södermalm.

Film

Cinemas are listed in the Yellow Pages under *Biografer*; you can also find the current shows in the local evening papers, although a specific movie might be hard to spot with its Swedish title. (Foreign movies are not dubbed.) Bear in mind that most, if not all, cinemas take reservations over the phone, and shows often sell out well ahead of time. Most cinemas are part of the SF chain (☎ 08/840500), including the 14-screen **Filmstaden Sergel,** installed at Hötorget in 1995. The best-quality cinema in town is the **Grand** (⊠ Sveavägen 45, ☎ 08/4112400). The cinema at **Filmhuset** (⊠ Borgvägen 5, ☎ 08/665–1100), headquarters of the Swedish Film Institute, usually has a good program but requires a membership fee of SKr70. **FolketsHusBio** (The People's Cinema) (⊠ Sturegatan 10–12, Sundbyberg, ☎ 08/281490) is a leftover from more idealistic times, showing films that don't get general release.

Jazz Clubs

The best venue is **Fasching** (⊠ Kungsgatan 63, ☎ 08/216267), close to the city center and featuring international and local bands. **Stampen** (⊠ Stora Nygatan 5, ☎ 08/205793), an overpriced but atmospheric club in the Old Town, offers traditional jazz nightly. The bar at the **Lydmar Hotel** (⊠ Sturegatan 10, ☎ 08/223160), known as the film festival's favorite watering hole, presents live jazz.

Opera

In 1755, Queen Lovisa Ulrika began introducing opera to her subjects; since then, the country has produced such names as Jenny Lind, Jussi Björling, and Birgit Nilsson. **Operan** (The Royal Opera House, ⊠ Jakobs Torg 2, ☎ 08/248240), dating from 1898, continues Sweden's operatic tradition. **Folkoperan** (⊠ Hornsgatan 72, ☎ 08/616–0750), a lively, modern company with its headquarters in Södermalm, features "opera in the round"—riding roughshod over traditional methods of presentation and interpretation of the classics, generally to scintillating effect.

Rock Clubs

Berns' (⊠ Berzelii Park, ☎ 08/614–0720), near the Royal Dramatic Theater, offers a choice of entertainment and dining in several different rooms. **Gino** (⊠ Birger Jarlsgatan 27, ☎ 08/791–7120) serves a trendy crowd on one of Stockholm's busier streets. **Lido** (⊠ Hornsgatan 92, subway: Zinkensdamm; ☎ 08/668–2333) is on Södermalm. **Krogen Tre Backar** (⊠ Tegnérgatan 12–14, ☎ 08/673–4400) can be found just off Sveavgen.

Theater

Kungliga Dramatiska Teatern (or Dramaten: the Royal Dramatic Theater, ⊠ Nybroplan, ☎ 08/667–0680) sometimes stages productions of international interest, in Swedish, of course. Productions by the English Theatre Company and the American Drama Group Europe are occasionally staged at **Södra Teatern** in Södermalm (⊠ Mosebacke Torg 1, ☎ 08/644–9900).

Outdoor Activities and Sports

Beaches

The best bathing places in central Stockholm are on the island of Långholmen and at Rålambshov at the end of Norr Mälarstrand. Both are grassy or rocky lakeside hideaways. Topless sunbathing is virtually de rigueur.

Bicycling

Stockholm is well supplied with bicycle routes, and except during peak traveling times, bikes may be taken aboard commuter trains for excursions to the suburbs. The average rental cost is SKr80 a day. **Cykelfrämjandet** (⊠ Torsgatan 31, Box 6027, S-102 31, ☎ 08/321680, FAX 08/310305), a local bicyclists' association, publishes an English-language guide to cycling trips. Bicycles may be rented from **Cykel & Mopeduthyrning** (⊠ Strandvägen at Kajplats 24, ☎ 08/660–7959). **Skepp & Hoj**—pronounced "ship ahoy"—(⊠ Galärvarvsvägen 2, ☎ 08/660–5757) is another rental option.

Fitness Centers

Fitness is a Swedish obsession. **Friskis & Svettis** (⊠ St. Eriksgatan 54, 100 28 Stockholm, ☎ 08/654–4414, FAX 08/654–3909) is a legendary local gym chain specializing in aerobics. There are branches all over the Stockholm area. Monday through Thursday at 6 PM, from the end of May into late August, it hosts free summer sessions in Rålambshovsparken. The **Atalanta Sports Club** (⊠ St. Eriksgatan 34, ☎ 08/650–6625, FAX 08/651–6650) was expanded in early 1996 and has both women's and mixed gym facilities for a SKr90 entry fee. For a relatively inexpensive massage (around SKr70), try **Axelsons Gymnastiska Institut** (⊠ Gästrikegatan 10–12, ☎ 08/165360).

Golf

There are numerous golf courses around Stockholm; contact **Stockholms Golfförbund** (⊠ Solkraftsvägen 25, 135 70 Stockholm, ☎ 08/742–6940, FAX 08/742–6920) for information. Try **Lidingö Golfklubb** (⊠ Kyttingevägen 2, Lidingö, ☎ 08/731–7900, FAX 08/765–5479) or **Djursholms Golfklubb** (⊠ Hagbandsvägen 1, Djursholm, ☎ 08/755–1477, FAX 08/755–5932), each about a 20-minute drive from the center of town.

Jogging

Numerous parks with footpaths dot the central city area, among them Haga Park (which also has canoe rentals), Djurgården, and Liljans Skogen. A very pleasant public path follows the waterfront across from Djurgården, going east from Djurgårdsbron past some of Stockholm's finest old mansions and the wide-open spaces of Ladugårdsgärdet.

Skiing

A new center called the **Discover Sweden Shop,** in the Sweden House (⊠ Kungsträdgården, Stockholm, ☎ 08/789–2000), has information on skiing and other sport and leisure activities and will advise on necessary equipment.

Spectator Sports

There are two main sports stadiums in Stockholm, featuring soccer in summer and ice hockey in winter. **Globen** (⊠ Box 10055, S–121 27, Globentorget 2, ☎ 08/725–1000), at 281 feet said to be the world's tallest spherical building, has its own subway station, just across the water from Södermalm; the Stockholm Open Tennis Tournament is held here each November. North of town there is **Råsunda Stadion** (⊠ Box 1216, Solnavägen 51, S–171 23 Solna, ☎ 08/735–0935).

Swimming

In the center of town, **Centralbadet** (⊠ Drottninggatan 88, ☎ 08/242403) has an extra-large pool, a whirlpool, steambath, and sauna. **Sturebadet** (⊠ Sturegallerian, ☎ 08/679–6700) offers aquatic aerobics and a sauna.

Tennis

There are many tennis courts in and around Stockholm. **Kungliga Tennishallen** (Royal Tennis Hall, ⊠ Lidingövägen 75, ☎ 08/459–1500, ℻ 08/664–3888) is where former champion Björn Borg plays. Another good venue is **Tennisstadion** (⊠ Fiskartorpsvägen 20, ☎ 08/215454, ℻ 08/207345).

Shopping

The three main department stores are in the central city area, as are the Gallerian and Sturegallerian shopping malls. However, there are interesting boutiques and galleries in Västerlånggatan, the main street of the Old Town, and some excellent handicrafts and art shops line the raised sidewalk at the start of Hornsgatan in Södermalm. Drottninggatan, Birger Jarlsgatan, and Hamngatan also offer some of the city's best shopping.

Department Stores

Sweden's leading department store, **NK** (the initials, pronounced enn-*koh,* stand for *Nordiska Kompaniet*), is at Hamngatan 18–20, across the street from Kungsträdgården (☎ 08/762–8000). The **Åhléns** department store (☎ 08/676–6000) is only on Hamngatan at Klarabergsgatan 50. Greta Garbo used to work at **PUB** (the initials of founder Paul U. Bergström)—at Drottninggatan 63, next to Hötorget—but she probably wouldn't recognize it today: Since its renovation in 1995, the store has become really a mall, with 42 independent boutiques. Garbo fans should visit the small exhibit on level H2, with an array of photographs beginning with her employee ID card.

Specialty Stores

ANTIQUES

There are three principal local auction houses. Perhaps the finest is **Lilla Bukowski** (⊠ Strandvägen 7, ☎ 08/614–0800), in its elegant quarters on the waterfront. **Auktions Kompaniet** (⊠ Regeringsgatan 47, ☎

08/235700) is next to NK downtown. **Stockholms Auktionsverk** (⊠ Jakobsgatan 10, ☎ 08/453–6700) is under the Gallerian shopping center.

BOOKS

Hemlins (⊠ Västerlånggatan 6, in the Old Town, ☎ 08/106180) carries foreign titles and antique books.

CLOTHING FOR MEN

For suits and evening suits for both sale and rental, **Hans Allde** (⊠ Birger Jarlsgatan 58, ☎ 08/207191) provides good, old-fashioned service. For shirts, try **La Chemise** (⊠ Smålandsgatan 11, ☎ 08/611–1494).

CLOTHING FOR WOMEN

There are many boutiques in **Biblioteksgatan** and **Västerlånggatan** in Gamla Stan. A shop that specializes in lingerie but carries fashionable clothes as well is **Twilfit** (⊠ Nybrogatan 11, ☎ 08/662–3817; Gallerian, ☎ 08/216996; and Gamla Brogatan 36–38, ☎ 08/201954). **Hennes & Mauritz** (⊠ Hamngatan 22; Drottninggatan 53 and 56; Sergelgatan 1 and 22; and Sergels Torg 12; all ☎ 08/796–5500) is one of the few Swedish-owned clothing stores to have achieved international success. **Polarn & Pyret** carries high-quality Swedish children's and women's clothing (⊠ Hamngatan 10, ☎ 08/411–4140; Gallerian, ☎ 08/411–2247; Drottninggatan 29, ☎ 08/106790).

CRYSTAL

Nordiska Kristall (⊠ Kungsgatan 9, ☎ 08/104372), near Sturegallerian, has a small gallery of one-of-a-kind art glass pieces. **Svenskt Glas** (⊠ Birger Jarlsgatan 8, ☎ 08/679–7909) is near the Royal Dramatic Theater. The **Crystal Art Center** (⊠ Tegelbacken 4, ☎ 08/217169), near Central Station, has a great selection of smaller glass items. **NK** (☞ Department Stores, *below*) carries a good, representative line of Swedish glassworks in its Swedish Shop downstairs.

HANDICRAFTS

Swedish handicrafts from all over the country are available at **Svensk Hemslöjd** (⊠ Sveavägen 44, ☎ 08/232115). Though prices are high at **Svenskt Hantwerk** (⊠ Kungsgatan 55, ☎ 08/214726), so is the quality. For elegant home furnishings and timeless fabrics, Stockholmers tend to favor **Svenskt Tenn** (⊠ Strandvägen 5A, ☎ 08/6701600), best known for its selection of designer Josef Franck's furniture and fabrics.

Street Markets

Hötorget is this site of a **flower and fruit market** every day. A **flea market** (*loppmarknad*) takes place daily in the shopping center of the suburb of Skärholmen. The best streets for bric-a-brac and **antiques** are Odengatan and Roslagsgatan (Odenplan subway station).

Stockholm A to Z

Arriving and Departing

BY BUS

Buses arrive at Cityterminalen, across from the central railway station. **Swebus** (☎ 08/279000) is the principal bus company, offering intercity service all over Sweden.

BY CAR

You will approach the city by either the E20 or E18 highway from the west, or the E4 from the north or south. The roads are clearly marked and well sanded and plowed during winter. Signs for downtown read CENTRUM.

BY PLANE

Initially opened in 1960 solely for international flights, Stockholm's **Arlanda Airport** now also contains a domestic terminal. Arlanda is 41 kilometers (26 miles) from the center of Stockholm and is linked to it by freeway.

Between the Airport and City Center. Buses leave both the international and domestic terminals every 10 to 15 minutes from 6:30 AM to 11 PM and run to the city terminal (Cityterminalen) at Klarabergsviadukten, next to the central railway station. The trip costs SKr50. For more information, call ☎ 08/600–1000.

If you find a **taxi** with a large SKr300 sign on the back or side window, or ask for *fast pris* (fixed price), the fare will be SKr300. A bus-taxi combination package is available (☎ 08/670–1010). The bus lets you off by the taxi stand at Cityterminalen and you present your receipt to the taxi driver, who takes you to your final destination. The cost is SKr140 if your destination is within city limits, SKr200 to go anywhere in the Stockholm area. SAS operates a shared limousine to any point in central Stockholm for SKr274 per person; the counter is in the arrivals hall, just past customs. If two or more people travel to the same address together in a limousine, only one pays the full rate; the others pay SKr130. For information and bookings, call ☎ 08/797–3700.

BY TRAIN

All trains arrive at Stockholm's Central Station (Vasagatan, ☎ 08/762–2000) in downtown Stockholm. From here regular commuter trains serve the suburbs, and an underground walkway leads to the central subway station.

Getting Around

The most effective way to get around the city is to purchase a **Stockholmskortet** (Key to Stockholm card). Besides giving unlimited transportation on city subway, bus, and rail services, it offers free admission to 60 museums and several sightseeing trips. The card costs SKr175 for 24 hours, SKr350 for two days, and SKr525 for three days. It is available from the tourist center at Sweden House on Hamngatan, from the Hotellcentralen accommodations bureau at Central Station, and from the tourist center at Kaknäs Tower.

BY BOAT

Waxholmsbolaget (Waxholm Ferries; ☎ 08/679–5830) offers the **Båtluffarkortet,** a discount pass for its extensive commuter network of archipelago boats; the price is SKr250 for 16 days of unlimited travel.

The **Strömma Canal Company** (☎ 08/233375) operates a fleet of archipelago boats, some of which provide excellent sightseeing tours and excursions.

BY BUS AND SUBWAY

Stockholm has an excellent bus and subway network. Subway stations are marked by a blue-on-white T (short for *Tunnelbanan,* or subway). The subway covers more than 60 route miles, and trains run frequently between 5 AM and 2 AM. There are also several night buses. Maps and timetables for all city transportation networks are available from the SL information desks at Sergels Torg, Central Station, and Slussen. Information is also available by phone (☎ 08/600–1000).

Tickets may be bought on buses or at the subway barrier. The minimum fare is SKr13. It is cheaper to buy a **discount coupon** from one of the many Pressbyrån newsstands. The standard discount coupon (**Rabattkupong**) valid for both subway and buses costs SKr85 and is good for a fixed number of trips (approximately 10) within the greater

Stockholm area during an unlimited period of time. If you plan to travel within the greater Stockholm area extensively during a 24-hour period, you can purchase an SKr54 pass; an SKr107 pass will allow for 72 hours of travel. The 24-hour pass includes the ferries between Djurgården, Nybroplan, and Slussen; the 72-hour pass also entitles the holder to admission to Skansen, Gröna Lund, and Kaknäs Tower. People under 18 or over 65 pay a reduced price on these passes.

BY CAR

Driving in Stockholm is often deliberately frustrated by city planners, who impose many restrictions in order to keep traffic down. Get a good city map, called a **Trafikkarta,** available at most service stations for around SKr62; the map legend and parking laws are helpfully translated to English.

BY PLANE

Gotland. Sixteen flights a day arrive in Gotland's airport from Stockholm. For information, call SAS (☎ 020/727000).

BY TAXI

Stockholm's taxi service is efficient but overpriced. To order a cab from one of the taxi companies, telephone **Taxi Stockholm** (☎ 08/150000), **Taxi 020** (☎ 020/850400), or **Taxikurir** (☎ 08/300000). **Taxi Stockholm** has an immediate charge of SKr23 whether you hail a cab or order one by telephone. A trip of 10 kilometers (6 miles) costs SKr93 between 6 AM and 7 PM, SKr103 at night, and SKr110 on weekends. If you call a cab, ask the dispatcher to quote you a *fast pris,* which is usually lower than the meter fare.

Contacts and Resources

CAR RENTALS

Rental cars are readily available in Sweden and relatively inexpensive. Because of the availability and efficiency of public transport, there is little point in using a car within the city limits. However, if you are traveling elsewhere in Sweden, roads are uncongested and well marked, but gasoline is expensive (SKr8 per liter at press time). All major car-rental firms are represented, including **Avis** (⊠ Ringvägen 90, ☎ 08/ 644–9980) and **Hertz** (⊠ Vasagatan 2224, ☎ 08/240720).

DOCTORS AND DENTISTS

There is a 24-hour national health-service emergency number (☎ 08/ 644–9200) and private care via City Hälsocentral (☎ 08/206990).

The emergency dental clinic is at Sankt Erik's Hospital (☎ 08/654– 1117, 8 AM–9 PM; ☎ 08/644–9200, 9 PM–8 AM).

EMBASSIES AND CONSULATES

U.S. Embassy (⊠ Strandvägen 101, ☎ 08/783–5300). **Canadian Embassy** (⊠ Tegelbacken 4, ☎ 08/613–9900). **U.K. Embassy** (⊠ Skarpögatan 6–8, ☎ 08/671–9000).

EMERGENCIES

Dial ☎ 112 for emergencies—this covers police, fire, ambulance, and medical help, as well as sea and air rescue services.

ENGLISH-LANGUAGE BOOKSTORES

Nearly all bookshops stock English-language books. For newspapers and magazines, try one of the newsstands at Central Station or the **Press Center** (⊠ Gallerian shopping center, Hamngatan, ☎ 08/723–0191). **Hedengren's** (⊠ Sturegallerian shopping complex, ☎ 08/611–5132) has one of the best English-book selections. **Akademibokhandeln** (⊠ Mäster Samuelsgatan 32, near the city center, ☎ 08/613–6100) is another good bet.

A bus tour in English and Swedish covering all the main points of interest leaves each day at 9:45 AM from the tourist center at Sweden House (⊠ Hamngatan 27, Box 7542, S–103 93 Stockholm, ☎ 08/789–2490); it costs SKr230. Other, more comprehensive tours, taking in museums, the Old Town, and City Hall, are also available at the tourist center.

Strömma Kanalbolaget and **Stockholm Sightseeing** (⊠ Skeppsbron 22, ☎ 08/233375) run a variety of boat and bus sightseeing tours of Stockholm. Boats leave from the quays outside the Royal Dramatic Theater, the Grand Hotel, and City Hall.

City Sightseeing (☎ 08/411–7023 or 08/240470) runs several tours, including the "Romantic Stockholm" tour of the Cathedral and City Hall; the "Royal Stockholm" tour, which features visits to the Royal Palace and the Treasury; and the "Old Town Walkabout," which strolls through Gamla Stan in just over one hour.

Individual city guides may be hired from Stockholm Information Service's **Guide Centralen** (⊠ Sweden House, Hamngatan 27, Box 7542, S–103 93 Stockholm, ☎ 08/789–2496, FAX 08/789–2496), but be sure to book well in advance.

C. W. Scheele (⊠ Klarabergsgatan 64, ☎ 08/218934) is open around-the-clock.

For a complete listing, see the Yellow Pages under *Resor-Resebyråer*.

American Express is at Birger Jarlsgatan 1 (☎ 08/679–5200, FAX 08/611–6214). **SJ**, the state railway company, has its main ticket office at Central Station (⊠ Vasagatan 1, ☎ 020/757575). For air travel, contact **SAS** (⊠ Klarabergsviadukten 72, accessible from Central Station, ☎ 020/727000).

The free publication *Stockholm This Week* is available at most hotels and tourist centers. The Friday editions of the daily newspapers *Dagens Nyheter* and *Svenska Dagbladet* carry current listings of events, films, restaurants, and museums (in Swedish). *City Nytt,* a large newsprint magazine, carries the latest write-ups of Stockholm's nightlife and current events; though it's also in Swedish, it's easy to decipher.

Stockholm Information Service, the main tourist office for the region, is in the center of the city at **Sweden House** (⊠ Hamngatan 27, Box 7542, S–103 93 Stockholm, ☎ 08/789–2490). Open every day, it provides information on current events, sightseeing, one-day tours, maps, and books. Bookings can be made for tours and tickets obtained for public events.

SIDE TRIPS FROM STOCKHOLM

Surrounding Stockholm is a network of small, historic islands, most of them crowned with castles straight out of a storybook world. Set aside a day for a trip to any of these; half the pleasure of an island outing is a leisurely boat trip to get there. (However, the castles can all be reached by alternative overland routes, if you prefer the bus or train.) Farther afield is the island of Gotland, whose medieval festival, Viking remains, and wilderness reserves will take you back in time. The cathedral town of Uppsala is another popular day-trip from Stockholm, its quiet atmosphere providing an enlightening contrast to the mood of the city.

Drottningholm★

③⓪ *½ mi (1 km) west of Stockholm.*

Occupying an island in Mälaren (Sweden's third-largest lake) some 45 minutes from Stockholm's center, **Drottningholms Slott** (Queen's Island Castle) is a miniature Versailles dating from the 17th century. The royal family once used this property only as a summer residence, but, tiring of the immensity of the Royal Palace back in town, they moved permanently to one wing of Drottningholm in the 1970s. Today it remains one of the most delightful of European palaces, embracing all that was best in the art of living practiced by mid-18th-century royalty. The interiors are from the 17th, 18th, and 19th centuries, and most are open to the public. ⊠ *Drottningholm,* ☏ *08/759–0310.* ⌨ *SKr30.* ☉ *May–Aug., daily 11–4:30; Sept., weekdays 1–3:30, weekends noon–3:30.*

The lakeside gardens of Drottningholms Slott are its most beautiful asset, containing **Drottningholms Slottsteater** (Court Theater), the only complete theater to survive from the 18th century anywhere in the world. Built by Queen Lovisa Ulrika in 1766 as a wedding present for her son Gustav III, the theater fell into disuse after his assassination at a masked ball in 1792 (dramatized in Verdi's opera *Un Ballo in Maschera*). In 1922 the theater was rediscovered; there is now a small theater museum here as well. To obtain tickets for a performance, book well in advance; the season runs from late May to early September (box office ☏ 08/660–8225). A word of caution: The seats are extremely hard—take a cushion. ⊠ *Drottningholm,* ☏ *08/759–0406.* ⌨ *SKr40.* ☉ *May–Aug., daily noon–4:30; Sept., daily 1–3:30. Guided tours in English at 12:30, 1:30, 2:30, 3:30, and 4:30. Closed for 10 days beginning of July.*

Drottningholm A to Z

Boats bound for Drottningholms Slott leave from Klara Mälarstrand, a quay close to City Hall. Call **Strömma Kanalbolaget** (☏ 08/233375) for schedules and fares.

Mariefred

③① *63 km (39 mi) southwest of Stockholm.*

The most delightful way to experience the true vastness of Mälaren, Sweden's third-largest lake, is the trip to Mariefred—an idyllic little town of mostly timber houses—aboard the coal-fired steamer of the same name, built in 1903 and still going strong.

Mariefred's principal attraction is **Gripsholm Slott.** First built in 1540, the castle contains fine Renaissance interiors, a superbly atmospheric theater commissioned in 1781 by the ill-fated Gustav III, and Sweden's royal portrait collection. ☏ *0159/10194.* ⌨ *SKr40.* ☉ *Guided tours only. Oct.–Mar., weekends noon–3; Apr. and Sept., Tues.–Sun. 10–3; May–June and Aug., daily 10–4; July, daily 9–5.*

Mariefred A to Z

ARRIVING AND DEPARTING

The **S.S. *Mariefred*** departs from Klara Mälarstrand, near Stockholm's City Hall. The journey takes 3½ hours each way, and there is a restaurant on board. You can also travel by narrow-gauge steam railway from Mariefred to a junction on the main line to Stockholm, returning to the capital by ordinary train. Contact the Mariefred Tourist Office for details. S.S. *Mariefred,* ☏ 08/669–8850. ⌨ *SKr160 round-trip.* ☉ *Departures at 10 AM: May, weekends only; mid-June–late Aug., Tues.–Sun. Return trip departs from Mariefred at 4:30.*

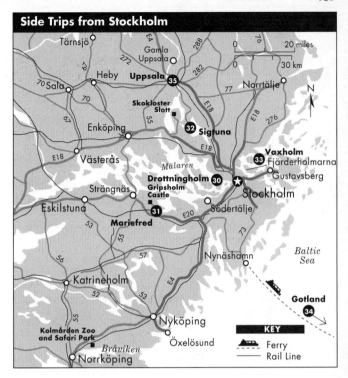

Side Trips from Stockholm

VISITOR INFORMATION
The Mariefred tourist office (☎ 0159/29790) is open only in the summer; the rest of the year, call Mälarturism (☎ 0152/29690) for information on all of Lake Mälaren.

Sigtuna

32 *48 km (30 mi) northwest of Stockholm.*

A picturesque, restful town on a northern arm of Lake Mälar, Sigtuna was the principal trading post of the Svea, the tribe that settled Sweden after the last Ice Age; its Viking history is still apparent in the many runic stones preserved all over town. After it was sacked by Estonian pirates, its merchants founded Stockholm sometime in the 13th century. Little remains of Sigtuna's former glory, beyond parts of the principal church. The town hall dates from the 18th century, the main part of town from the early 1800s, and there are two houses said to date from the 15th century.

About 20 kilometers (12 miles) northeast of Sigtuna and accessible by the same ferry boat is **Skokloster Slott,** an exquisite Baroque castle. Commissioned in 1654 by a celebrated Swedish soldier, Field Marshal Carl Gustav Wrangel, the castle is furnished with the spoils of Wrangel's successful campaigns in Europe in the 17th century. The castle can be reached by boat from Sigtuna (Strömma Kanalbolaget, ☎ 08/233375). ⊠ *Bålsta,* ☎ *018/386077.* 🎫 *SKr40.* ☉ *Daily noon–6.*

Sigtuna A to Z

From June to mid-August Sigtuna can be reached by boat from the quay near City Hall (Strömma Kanalbolaget, ☎ 08/233375); round-trip fare is SKr140. Another option is to take a commuter train from Stockholm's Central Station to Märsta, where you change to Bus 570 or 575.

Vaxholm and the Archipelago

③③ *32 km (20 mi) northeast of Stockholm.*

Skärgården (the archipelago) is Stockholm's greatest natural asset: More than 25,000 islands and skerries, many uninhabited, spread across an almost tideless sea of clean, clear water. To sail lazily among these islands aboard an old steamboat on a summer's night is a timeless delight.

For the tourist with limited time, one of the simplest ways to get a taste of the archipelago is the one-hour ferry trip to Vaxholm, an extremely pleasant, though sometimes crowded, mainland seaside town of small, red-painted wooden houses. Here, a fortress guarding what was formerly the main sea route into Stockholm now houses a small museum, **Vaxholms Kastell Museum,** showing the defense of Stockholm over the centuries. You have to take a small boat from the town landing, in front of the Tourist Bureau, over to the castle. ☎ 08/541–72157. ⌑ *SKr50, including boat fare.* ⊙ *Mid-May–Aug., daily noon–4. Group admission at other times by arrangement.*

An even quicker trip into the archipelago is the 20-minute ferry ride to **Fjäderholmarna** (the Feather Islands), a group of four secluded islands. After 50 years as a military zone, the islands were opened to the public in the early 1980s. Today they are crammed with arts-and-crafts-studios, shops, an aquarium, a small petting farm, a boat museum, a large cafeteria, an ingenious "shipwreck" playground, and even a smoked-fish shop.

For an in-depth tour of the archipelago, seek out the **Blidösund.** A coal-fired steamboat built in 1911 that has remained in almost continuous regular service, it is now run by a small group of enthusiasts who take parties of around 250 merrymakers on evening music-and-dinner cruises. The *Blidösund* leaves from a berth close to the Royal Palace in Stockholm. S.S. *Blidösund, Skeppsbron,* ☎ 08/411–7113, ℻ 08/202186. ⌑ *SKr120. Departures early May–late Sept., Mon.–Thurs. 7 PM (returns at 10:45).*

Among the finest of the archipelago steamboats is the **Saltsjön,** which leaves from Nybrokajen, close to the Strand Hotel. Tuesday through Thursday evenings you can take a jazz-and-dinner cruise for SKr120; Fridays, pay SKr175 to go to Utö, an attractive island known for its bike paths, bakery, and restaurant. In December, there are three daily Julbord cruises, serving a Christmas smörgåsbord. ⊠ *Saltsjön, Strömma Kanalbolaget, Skeppsbron 22,* ☎ 08/233375. *Departures July–early Aug. and Dec.*

Dining

$$$ ✕ **Fjäderholmarnas Krog.** A crackling fire on the hearth in the bar area welcomes the sailors who frequent this place. Lacking your own sailboat, you can time your dinner to end before the last ferry returns to the mainland. The food here is self-consciously Swedish: fresh, light, and beautifully presented; the service is professional, and the ambience relaxed. It's a great choice for a quiet, special night out in Stockholm. ⊠ *Fjäderholmarna,* ☎ 08/718–3355, ℻ 08/716–3989. ⊙ *Daily, noon–midnight; closed Oct.–April. AE, DC, MC, V.*

$ ✕ **Gröna Caféet.** A grassy garden terrace and an appealing selection of fresh open sandwiches on hearty brown bread make this small, old-fashioned Vaxholm café a hit. It's on Rådhusgatan, by the town square. ⊠ *Rådhusgatan 26,* ☎ 08/541–31510. *No credit cards.*

Vaxholm and the Archipelago A to Z

The **Vaxholms Tyristbyrå** (Vaxholm Tourist Bureau) is in a large kiosk at the bus terminal, adjacent to the marina and ferry landing. ⊠ *Söderhamnen, 185 83 Vaxholm,* ☎ 08/541–31480.

Regular ferry services to the archipelago depart from Strömkajen, the quayside in front of the Grand Hotel. Cruises on a variety of boats leave from the harbor in front of the Royal Palace or from Nybrokajen, across the road from the Royal Dramatic Theater.

Ferries to the Feather Islands run almost constantly all day long in the summer (Apr. 29–Sept. 17), from Slussen, Strömkajen, and Nybroplan. ⊠ *Strömma Canal Co.,* ☎ *08/233375; Waxholmsbolaget,* ☎ *08/679–5830; Fjäderholmarna information,* ☎ *08/718–0100.*

Gotland

 85 km (53 mi) southwest of Stockholm.

Gotland is Sweden's main holiday island, a place of wide, sandy beaches and wild cliff formations called *raukar.* Measuring 125 kilometers (78 miles) in length and 52 kilometers (32 miles) across at its widest point, the island is characterized by verdant sheep-farming country, as well as glades in which 35 different varieties of wild orchids thrive, attracting botanists from all over the world.

Gotland was first inhabited around 5000 BC and by the time of the Roman Iron Age had become a leading Baltic trading center. Germans arrived later and built most of its churches in the 13th century. They established close trading links with the Hanseatic League in Lübeck. The Danes followed, and it was not until 1645 that Gotland finally became part of Sweden.

Gotland's capital, **Visby,** is a delightful, hilly town of about 20,000 people in which medieval houses, ruined fortifications, and churches blend with cobbled lanes of fairy-tale cottages, their facades covered with roses that to bloom even in November because the climate is so gentle.

In its heyday Visby was protected by a wall, of which 3 kilometers (2 miles) survive today, along with 44 towers and numerous gateways. It is considered the best-preserved medieval city wall in Europe after that of Carcassonne in southern France. The north gate provides the best vantage point for an overall view of the wall.

Visby's cathedral, **St. Maria Kyrka,** is the only one of the town's 13 medieval churches that is still intact and in use.

Near the harbor is the **Gamla Apoteket** (Old Apothecary), a late-medieval four-story merchant's house. ⊠ *Strandgatan 28,* ☎ *0498/212889.* ☞ *Free.* ☉ *Daily 9–5.*

Burmeisterska Huset, the home of the Burmeister, or principal German merchant, offers exhibitions and artisans. Call the tourist office in Visby (☎ *0498/201700*) to arrange for viewing. ⊠ *Strandgatan 9, no phone.* ☞ *Free.*

Fornsalen (the Fornsal Museum) contains examples of medieval artwork, hoards of silver from Viking times, and impressive picture stones that predate the Viking runic stones. ⊠ *Mellangatan 19, S–62156,* ☎ *0498/247010.* ☞ *SKr30.* ☉ *Mid-May–Sept., daily 11–6; rest of yr, Tues.–Sun. noon–4.*

The stalactite caves at **Lummelunda,** about 18 kilometers (11 miles) north of Visby on the coastal road, are unique in this part of the world and are worth visiting. A pleasant stop along the way to Lummelunda is the **Krusmyntagården** (☎ *0498/70153*), a garden with more than 200 herbs, 8 kilometers (5 miles) north of Visby.

There are approximately 100 old churches on the island that are still in use today, dating from Gotland's great commercial era. **Barlingbo,** from the 13th century, has vault paintings, stained-glass windows, and a remarkable 12th-century font. The exquisite **Dalhem** was constructed about 1200. **Gothem,** built during the 13th century, has a notable series of paintings of that period. **Grötlingbo** is a 14th-century church with stone sculpture and stained glass (note the 12th-century reliefs on the facade). **Tingstäde** is a mix of six building periods from 1169 to 1300. The massive ruins of a Cistercian monastery founded in 1164 are now called the **Roma Kloster Kyrka** (Roma Cloister Church). **Öja,** a medieval church decorated with paintings, houses a famous holy rood from the late 13th century.

Curious rock formations dot the coasts of Gotland, and two **bird refuges,** Stora and **Lilla Karlsö,** stand off the coast south of Visby. The bird population consists mainly of guillemots, which look like penguins. Visits to these refuges are permitted only in the company of a recognized guide. ⊠ *Stora Karlsö,* ☎ *0498/241113; Lilla Karlsö,* ☎ *0498/ 241139.* ☎ *SKr 170 for guided tour.* ☉ *Daily, May–Aug.*

Dining

$$ ✕ **Gutekällaren.** Despite the name, which means cellar in Swedish, this restaurant is located above ground in a building that dates from the 12th century. The menu is Mediterranean. ⊠ *Stora Torget 3,* ☎ *0498/ 210043. DC, MC.*

$$ ✕ **Lindgården.** This atmospheric restaurant specializes in both local dishes and French cuisine. ⊠ *Strandgatan 26,* ☎ *0498/218700. Reservations required. AE, DC, MC, V. No lunch weekends.* ☉ *Sun. in summer only.*

Nightlife and the Arts

Medeltidsveckan (Medieval Week), celebrated in Visby during early August, is a city-wide festival marking the invasion of the prosperous island by the Danish king Valdemar on July 22, 1361. Beginning with Valdemar's grand entrance parade, events include jousting, an open-air market on Strandgatan, and a variety of street-heater performances re-creating the period.

Outdoor Activities and Sports

Bicycles, tents, and camping equipment can be rented from **Gotlands Cykeluthyrning** (⊠ Skeppsbron 8, ☎ 0498/214133).

Gotlandsleden is a 200-kilometer (120-mile) bicycle route around the island; contact the tourist office for details.

Gotland A to Z

ARRIVING AND DEPARTING

Car ferries sail from Nynäshamn, a small port on the Baltic an hour by car or rail from Stockholm; commuter trains leave regularly from Stockholm's Central Station for Nynäshamn. Ferries depart at 11:30 PM year-round. From June through mid-August there's an additional ferry at 12:30 PM. A fast ferry operates from mid-April until mid-September, departing three times a day. The regular ferry takes about five hours; the fast ferry takes 2½ hours. Boats also leave from Oskarshamn, farther down the Swedish coast and closer to Gotland by about an hour. *Gotland City Travel,* ⊠ *Kungsgatan 57,* ☎ *08/236170 or 08/233180 (a recording); Nynäshamn,* ☎ *08/5206400; Visby,* ☎ *0498/247065.*

GUIDED TOURS

Guided tours of the island and Visby, the capital, are available in English by arrangement with the tourist office.

VISITOR INFORMATION

The main tourist office is **Gotlands Turistservice** (☎ 0498/206000, FAX 0498/249059), at Österport in Visby. You can also contact **Gotland City**

AB in Stockholm for lodging (☎ 08/233180) or ferry reservations (☎ 08/236170).

Uppsala

 67 km (41 mi) north of Stockholm.

Sweden's principal university town vies for that position with Lund in the south of the country. August Strindberg, the nation's leading dramatist, studied here—and by all accounts hated the place. Ingmar Bergman, his modern heir, was born here. It is a historic site where pagan (and extremely gory) Viking ceremonies persisted into the 11th century. Uppsala University, one of the oldest and most highly respected institutions in Europe, was established here in 1477 by Archbishop Jakob Ulfson. As late as the 16th century, nationwide *tings* (early parliaments) were convened here. Today it is a quiet home for about 170,000 people, built along the banks of Fyris River, a pleasant jumble of old buildings dominated by its cathedral, which dates from the early 13th century.

Ideally you should start your visit with a trip to **Gamla Uppsala** (Old Uppsala), 5 kilometers (3 miles) north of the town. Here under three huge mounds lie the graves of the first Swedish kings—Aun, Egil, and Adils—of the 6th-century Ynglinga dynasty. Close by in pagan times was a sacred grove containing a legendary oak from whose branches animal and human sacrifices were hung. By the 10th century, Christianity had eliminated such practices. A small church, which was the seat of Sweden's first archbishop, was built on the site of a former pagan temple. Today the archbishopric is in Uppsala itself, and the church, **Gamla Uppsala Kyrka,** is largely for the benefit of tourists.

A small open-air museum in Gamla Uppsala, **Disagården,** features old farm buildings, most of them from the 19th century. 🎫 *Free.* ☉ *June–Aug., daily 9–5.*

NEED A BREAK? You can drink mead brewed from a 14th-century recipe at the **Odinsborg Restaurant** (☎ 018/323525), near the burial mounds of Gamla Uppsala.

Back in Uppsala, your first visit should be to **Uppsala Domkyrka** (Uppsala Cathedral), whose twin towers—at 362 feet the same height as the length of the nave—dominate the city. Work on the cathedral began in the early 13th century; it was consecrated in 1435 and restored between 1885 and 1893. Still the seat of Sweden's archbishop, the cathedral is also the site of the tomb of Gustav Vasa, the king who established Sweden's independence in the 16th century. Inside is a silver casket containing the bones of Saint Erik, Sweden's patron saint. 🎫 *Free.* ☉ *Daily 8–6.* The **Domkyrka Museet** in the north tower has handicrafts, church vestments, and church vessels on display. 🎫 *SKr10.* ☉ *May–Aug., daily 9–5; rest of yr, Sun. 12:30–3.*

Work on **Uppsala Slott** (Uppsala Castle) was started in the 1540s by Gustav Vasa, who intended it to symbolize the dominance of the monarchy over the church. It was completed under Queen Christina nearly a century later. Students gather here every April 30 to celebrate the Feast of Valborg and optimistically greet the arrival of spring. 🎫 *Castle SKr30.* ☉ *Guided tours of castle mid-Apr.–Sept., daily at 11 and 2 (additional tours late June–mid-Aug., weekends at 10 and 3).*

In the excavated Uppsala Slott ruins, the **Vasa Vignettes,** scenes from the 16th century, are portrayed with effigies, costumes, light, and sound effects. 🎫 *SKr30* ☉ *Mid-Apr.–Aug., daily 11–4 (10–5 on weekends in Sept.).*

One of Uppsala's most famous sons, Carl von Linné, also known as Linnaeus, was a professor of botany at the university during the 1740s and created the Latin nomenclature system for plants and animals. The **Linné Museum** is dedicated to his life and works. ✉ *Svartbäcksgatan 27,* ☎ *018/136540.* 🎫 *SKr10.* ☉ *Late May and early Sept., weekends noon–4; June–Aug., Tues.–Sun. 1–4.*

The botanical treasures of Linné's old garden have been resuscitated and are now on view in **Linnéträdgården.** The garden's orangery houses a pleasant cafeteria and is used for concerts and cultural events. ✉ *Svartbäcksgatan 27,* ☎ *018/109490.* 🎫 *SKr10.* ☉ *May–Aug., daily 9–9; rest of yr, daily 9–7.*

Uppsala Universitetet (Uppsala University, ☎ 018/182500), founded in 1477, is known for its **Carolina Rediviva** (university library), which contains a copy of every book published in Sweden, in addition to a large collection of foreign literature. One of its most interesting exhibits is the *Codex Argentus,* a Bible written in the 6th century.

Completed in 1625, the **Gustavianum,** which served as the university's main building for two centuries, is easy to spot by its remarkable copper cupola, now green with age. The building houses the ancient anatomical theater where lectures on human anatomy and public dissections took place. The Victoria Museum of Egyptian Antiquities and the Museums for Classical and Nordic Archeology are also in the building. ✉ *Akademigatan 3,* ☎ *018/182500.* 🎫 *SKr20 (SKr10 to anatomical theater only).* ☉ *June–Aug., daily 11–3. Anatomical Theater only, Sept.–May, weekends noon–3.*

Dining

$$$ ✕ **Domtrappkällaren.** In a 14th-century cellar near the cathedral, Domtrappkällaren serves excellent French and Swedish cuisines. Game is the specialty, and the salmon and reindeer are delectable. ✉ *Sankt Eriksgränd 15,* ☎ *018/130955,* 🆑 *018/101740. Reservations required. AE, DC, MC, V.*

Uppsala A to Z

GUIDED TOURS

You can explore Uppsala easily by yourself, but English-language guided group tours can be arranged through the tourist office; the guide service number there is ☎ 018/274818.

VISITOR INFORMATION

The main tourist office (☎ 018/117500 or 018/274800) is at Fyris Torg 8, in the center of town; in summer a small tourist information office is also open at Uppsala Castle (☎ 018/554566).

GÖTEBORG

If you arrive in Göteborg (Gothenburg) by car, don't drive straight through the city in your haste to reach your coastal vacation spot; it is well worth spending a day or two exploring this attractive port. A quayside jungle of cranes and warehouses attests to the city's industrial might, yet within 10 minutes' walk of the waterfront is an elegant, modern city of broad avenues, green parks, and gardens. This is not to slight the harbor: it comprises 22 kilometers (14 miles) of quays with warehouses and sheds covering more than 1.5 million square feet and spread along both banks of the Göta Älv (river), making Göteborg Scandinavia's largest port. The harbor is also the home of Scandinavia's largest corporation, the automobile manufacturer Volvo (which means "I roll" in Latin), as well as of the roller-bearing manufacturer SKF and the world-renowned Hasselblad camera company.

Historically, Göteborg owes its existence to the sea. Tenth-century Vikings sailed from its shores, and a settlement was founded here in the 11th century. Not until 1621, however, did King Gustav II Adolf grant Göteborg a charter in order to establish a free-trade port on the model of others already thriving on the Continent. The west-coast harbor would also allow Swedish shipping to avoid Danish tolls exacted for passing through Öresund, the stretch of water separating the two countries. Foreigners were recruited to make these visions real: The Dutch were its builders—hence the canals that thread the city—and many Scotsmen worked and settled here, though they have left little trace.

Today Göteborg resists its second-city status by being a leader in terms of attractions and civic structures: The Scandinavium was until recently Europe's largest indoor arena; the Ullevi Stadium stages some of the Nordic area's most important concerts and sporting events; Nordstan is one of Europe's largest indoor shopping malls; and Liseberg, Scandinavia's largest amusement park in area, attracts some 2.5 million visitors a year. Over the Göta River is Älvsborgsbron, at 3,060 feet the longest suspension bridge in Sweden, while under a southwestern suburb runs the Gnistäng Tunnel, which at 62 feet claims the odd distinction of being the world's widest tunnel cut through rock for motor vehicles.

Exploring Göteborg

Göteborg is an easy city to explore: Most of the major attractions are within walking distance of one another, and the streetcar network is excellent—in summer you can take a sightseeing trip on an open-air streetcar. The heart of Göteborg is Avenyn (the Avenue; actually Kungsportsavenyn, but over the years shortened to simply Avenyn), a 60-foot-wide, tree-lined boulevard that bisects the center of the city in a south–north direction, linking its cultural heart, Götaplatsen, at the southern end, with the main commercial area, now dominated by the modern Nordstan shopping center. Beyond lies the waterfront, busy with all the traffic of the port, as well as some of Göteborg's newer cultural developments.

Cultural Göteborg

A pleasant stroll will take the visitor from Götaplatsen's modern architecture down the Avenyn and across both canals to finish at the State Museum building.

A GOOD WALK

Start your tour in **Götaplatsen** ㊱, a square dominated by a statue of Poseidon. Behind the statue stands the **Konstmuseet** (Art Museum), flanked by the **Konserthuset** (Concert Hall) and the **Stadsteatern** (Municipal Theater), three contemporary buildings in which the city celebrates its important contribution to Swedish cultural life. Also in Götaplatsen, the Stadsbiblioteket (Municipal Library) boasts a collection of more than 550,000 books, many in English.

From Götaplatsen, stroll downhill past the cafés and restaurants along **Avenyn** (Kungsportavenyn), to the intersection with Vasagatan. A short way to the left down Vasagatan, at the junction with Teatergatan, you can visit the **Röhsska Museet** ㊲ (Museum of Arts and Crafts), the country's only museum of Swedish design.

Continue down Vasagatan to Folkhögskolan, Göteborg Universitet (Göteborg University), and, if the weather's good, to the neighboring Vasa Park. Turn right to go north on Viktoriagatan, cross the canal, and then make an immediate left to visit one of the city's most peculiar attractions, **Feske Körkan** ㊳, an archaic spelling of *Fisk Kyrkan*, the Fish Church. It resembles a place of worship but is actually an indoor fish market.

Following this you may feel inspired to visit the city's principal place of worship, **Domkyrkan** ㊴ (Göteborg Cathedral). To get here from Feske Körkan, follow the canal eastward until you come to Västra Hamngatan; then head north about four blocks to the church. Next, continue northward on Västra Hamngatan to the junction with Norra Hamngatan, where you'll find the **Stadsmuseet** ㊵ (City Museum), housed in the 18th-century Swedish East India Company.

TIMING
Depending on how much time you want to spend in each museum, this walk may take anywhere from an hour to the better part of a day.

SIGHTS TO SEE

★ **Avenyn.** Kungsportsavenyn resembles the Champs-Elysées in Paris; it's a pretty boulevard whose broad sidewalks are lined with elegant shops, cafés, and restaurants. The street slopes gently up from the canal at Kungsportsplats and ends at Poseidon's fountain in Götaplatsen.

㊴ **Domkyrkan.** The cathedral, in neoclassic yellow brick, dates from 1802; though it's not particularly attractive from the outside, the interior is impressive. ✉ *Kungsgatan 20,* ☎ *031/130479.* ☺ *Weekdays 8–5, Sat. 8–3, Sun. 10–3.*

㊳ **Feske Körkan.** Built in 1872, this covered fish market is nicknamed the Fish Church because of its Gothic-style architectural details. ✉ *Fisktorget-Rosenlundsgatan.*

OFF THE
BEATEN PATH   **FISKHAMNEN –** An excellent view of **Älvsborgsbron** (Älvsborg Bridge), the longest suspension bridge in Sweden, is available from Fiskhamnen, the Fish Docks west of Stigbergstorget. Built in 1967, the bridge stretches 3,060 feet across the river and is built so high that ocean liners can pass beneath. The government is considering plans to turn this part of the harbor into a scenic walkway with parks and cafés. Also look toward the sea to the large container harbors, Skarvikshamnen, Skandiahamnen (where boats depart for England), and Torshamnen, which bring most of the cargo and passengers to the city today.

★ ㊱ **Götaplatsen.** The cultural center of Göteborg was built in 1923 in celebration of the city's 300th anniversary. In the center is the Swedish-American sculptor Carl Milles' fountain statue of Poseidon choking an enormous shark.

OFF THE
BEATEN PATH   **LISEBERG NÖJESPARK –** Göteborg proudly claims Scandinavia's largest amusement park. The city's pride is well earned: Liseberg is one of the best-run, most efficient parks in the world. In addition to a wide selection of carnival rides, Liseberg also has numerous restaurants and theaters, all set amid beautifully tended gardens. It's about a 30-minute walk from the city center or a ten-minute ride by bus or tram; in summer a vintage open streetcar makes frequent runs to Liseberg from Brunnsparken in the middle of town. ✉ *Örgrytevägen,* ☎ *031/400100.* ⚞ *SKr35.* ☺ *Late Apr.–June and late Aug., daily 3–11; July–mid-Aug., daily noon–11; Sept., Sat. 1–11, Sun. noon–8.*

Konstmuseet. After an extensive renovation, the Art Museum re-opened in January 1996 with a new, more accessible entrance and expanded facilities; one of these is the Hasselblad Center, devoted to progress in the art of photography. The museum continues to display an impressive collection of the works of leading Scandinavian painters and sculp-

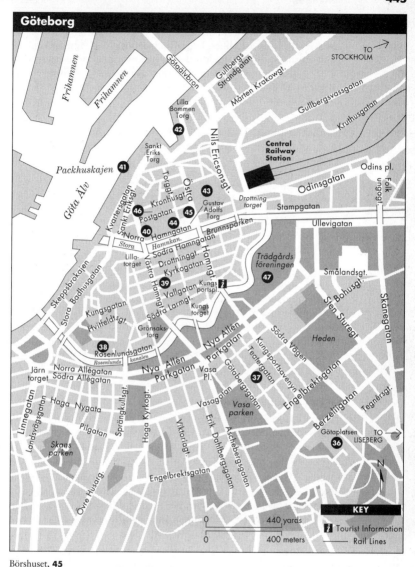

Göteborg

Börshuset, **45**

Domkyrkan, **39**

Feske Körkan, **38**

Götaplatsen, **36**

Kronhuset, **46**

Maritima
Centrum, **42**

Nordstan, **43**

Rådhuset, **44**

Röhsska Museet, **37**

Stadsmuseet, **40**

Utkiken, **41**

Trädgarn, **47**

tors, encapsulating some of the moody introspection of the artistic community in this part of the world. Among the artists represented are Swedes such as Carl Milles, Johan Tobias Sergel, the Impressionist Anders Zorn, the Victorian idealist Carl Larsson, and Prince Eugen. The 19th- and 20th-century French art collection is the best in Sweden, and there's also a small collection of old masters. ⊠ *Götaplatsen, S–412 56,* ☎ *031/612980,* ℻ *031/184119.* ⊡ *SKr35.* ⊙ *Weekdays 11–4 (Wed. until 9), weekends 11–5. Closed Mon. Sept.–May.*

㊲ **Röhsska Museet.** The Museum of Arts and Crafts features fine collections of furniture, books and manuscripts, tapestries, and pottery. ⊠ *Vasagatan 37–39, Box 53178, S–400 15,* ☎ *031/613850,* ℻ *031/ 184692.* ⊡ *SKr35.* ⊙ *Weekends noon–5; May–mid-June, weekdays noon–4; mid-June–Aug., weekdays noon–6, Tues. noon–9; Apr. and Sept., Tues. noon–9, Wed.–Fri. noon–4.*

㊵ **Stadsmuseet.** Once the warehouse and auction rooms of the Swedish East India Company, a major trading firm founded in 1731, this palatial structure dates from 1750. Today it contains exhibits on the Swedish west coast, with a focus on Göteborg's nautical and trading past. One interesting exhibit deals with the East India Company and its ship the *Göteborg*, which in 1745, returning from China, sank just outside the city while members of the crew's families watched from shore. ⊠ *Norra Hamngatan 12, S–411 14,* ☎ *031/612770,* ℻ *031/774–0358.* ⊡ *SKr30.* ⊙ *Weekdays noon–6, weekends 11–4. Closed Mon. Sept.–Apr.*

| NEED A BREAK? | In the cellar of Stadsmuseet, the **Ostindiska Huset Krog & Kafé** (☎ 031/135750) re-creates an 18th-century atmosphere. The *dagenslunch,* priced at SKr50, is available from 11:30 to 2. |

Commercial Göteborg

Explore Göteborg's portside character, both historic and modern, at the waterfront development near the center of town, where an array of markets and boutiques may keep you busy for hours.

A GOOD WALK

Begin at the harborside square known as Lilla Bomen, where the **Utkiken** ㊶ (Lookout Tower) offers a bird's-eye view of the city and harbor. The waterfront development here includes the training ship **Viking,** the Opera House, and the **Maritima Centrum** ㊷ (Marine Center), whose collection of sea vessels is open to the public.

From Lilla Bomen Torg, take the pedestrian bridge across the highway to **Nordstan** ㊸, the vast indoor shopping mall. Leave the mall at the opposite end, which puts you at Brunnsparken, the hub of the city's streetcar network. Turn right and cross the street to Gustav Adolfs Torg, the city's official center, dominated by **Rådhuset** ㊹, the City Hall. On the north side of the square is the **Börshuset** ㊺ (Stock Exchange), built in 1849.

Head north from the square along Östra Hamngatan and turn left onto Postgatan to visit **Kronhuset** ㊻ (Crown House), the city's oldest secular building, dating from 1643. The **Kronhusbodarna** are carefully restored turn-of-the-century shops and handicrafts boutiques that surround the entrance to Kronhuset.

Return to Gustaf Adolfs Torg and follow Östra Hamngatan south across the Stora Hamnkanal to Kungsportsplats, where the **Saluhall** (Market Hall) has stood since 1888. A number of pedestrian-only shopping streets branch out through this neighborhood on either side of Östra Hamngatan.

Crossing the bridge over Rosenlunds Kanalen from Kungsportsplats brings you onto Kungsportsavenyn and the entrance to **Trädgarn** ㊼, short for Trädgårdsföreningen (Horticultural Park), Göteborg's finest public garden.

TIMING

The walk itself will take no more than an hour but allow extra time if you plan on shopping at Nordstan.

SIGHTS TO SEE

㊺ **Börshuset.** Completed in 1849, the former Stock Exchange building houses city administrative offices as well as facilities for large banquets. ✉ *Gustaf Adolfs Torg 5.*

Kronhusbodarna. Glassblowing and watchmaking are among the handicrafts offered in the Historical Shopping Center adjoining Kronhuset; there is also a nice, old-fashioned café. ✉ *Kronhusgatan 1D* ⊘ *Closed Sun.*

㊻ **Kronhuset.** The city's oldest secular building, dating from 1643, was originally the city's armory. In 1660 Sweden's Parliament met here to arrange the succession for King Karl X Gustav, who died suddenly while visiting the city. ✉ *Postgatan 6–8,* ☎ *031/711–7377.* ✍ *SKr20.* ⊘ *Weekends 11–4.*

㊷ **Maritima Centrum.** Here modern naval vessels, including a destroyer, submarines, a lightship, a cargo vessel, and various tugboats, provide insight into Göteborg's historic role as a major port. ✉ *Packhuskajen, S–411 04,* ☎ *031/101035 or 031/101290 for a recording in English.* ✍ *SKr45.* ⊘ *Mar.–Apr., daily 10–4; May–June, daily 10–6; July and Aug., daily 10–9; Sept.–Nov., daily 10–4.*

㊸ **Nordstan.** Sweden's largest indoor shopping mall includes a huge parking garage, a 24-hour pharmacy, a post office, several restaurants, entertainment for children, the department store Åhlens, and a tourist information kiosk. ✉ *Entrances on Köpmansgatan, Nils Ericsonsgatan, Kanaltorgsgatan, and Östra Hamngatan.*

㊹ **Rådhuset.** Though the Town Hall dates from 1672, when it was designed by Nicodemus Tessin Senior, its controversial modern extension by Swedish architect Gunnar Asplund is only from 1937. ✉ *Gustaf Adolfs Torg 1.*

㊼ **Trädgarn.** Trädgårdsföreningen comprises beautiful open green space, a Rose Garden, a Butterfly House, and a Palm House.

㊶ **Utkiken.** This red-and-white-striped skyscraper towers 282 feet above the waterfront, offering an unparalleled view of the city and skyscrapers. ✉ *Lilla Bomen.* ✍ *SKr25.* ⊘ *May–Aug., daily 11–7; Oct.–Apr., weekends 11–4.*

OFF THE BEATEN PATH

GASVERKSKAJEN – For a good tour of the docks, head east from Lilla Bomen about 1.5 kilometers (1 mile) along the riverside to the Gas Works Quay, just off Gullbergsstrandgatan. Today this is the headquarters of a local boating association, its brightly colored pleasure craft contrasting with the old-fashioned working barges either anchored or being repaired at Ringön, just across the river.

NYA ELFSBORGS FÄSTNING – Boats leave regularly from Lilla Bomen to the Elfsborg Fortress, which was built in 1670 on a harbor island to protect the city from attack. ✉ *Börjessons, Lilla Bommen, kajskul 205, Box 31084, S–400 32,* ☎ *031/800750,* ℻ *031/154395.* ✍ *SKr65.* ⊘ *Early May–Aug. daily and Sept. weekends, 6 departures per day.*

Viking. This four-masted schooner, built in 1907, was among the last of Sweden's sailing cargo ships. In February 1995 the Hotel and Restaurant School of Goteborg opened a hotel and restaurant inside the ship. Visitors are welcome. ⊠ *Lilla Bommen.* ☎ *031/635800.* 🎫 *SKr25.*

Dining

You can eat well in Göteborg, but you must expect to pay dearly for the privilege. Fish dishes are the best bet here. Check to make sure restaurants are open first, as many close for a month in summer.

$$$ ✕ **Belle Avenue.** A dramatic tribute to the power of interior decoration, this plush, wood-paneled restaurant entered from the modern lobby of the SAS Park Avenue is another world. The chef is an expert at creating gourmet dishes out of fresh local fish and shellfish. ⊠ *Kungsport-savenyn 36–38,* ☎ *031/176520. Reservations required. No lunch weekends or July. AE, DC, MC, V.*

$$$ ✕ **Chablis.** Long popular in Göteborg, this is an excellent fish restaurant. ⊠ *Aschebergsgatan 22,* ☎ *031/203545,* 🖷 *031/208201. AE, DC, MC, V. No lunch. Closed 3 wks in July.*

$$$ ✕ **A Hereford Beefstouw.** Probably as close as you come to an American steak house in Sweden, this restaurant has gained popularity in a town dominated by fish restaurants. Diners' beef selections are cooked by chefs at grills in the center of the three dining rooms (one of which is set aside for nonsmokers). The rustic atmosphere is heightened by thick wooden tables, pine floors, and landscape paintings. ⊠ *Linné-gatan 5,* ☎ *031/775–0441,* 🖷 *031/775–0060. AE, DC, MC, V. No lunch weekends or July.*

$$$ ✕ **The Place.** Possibly Göteborg's finest dining establishment, the Place
★ offers a warm, intimate atmosphere created by terra-cotta ceilings, pastel-yellow walls, and white linen tablecloths. A wide selection of exotic dishes, from smoked breast of pigeon to beef tartare with caviar, are prepared with quality ingredients. This is also the home of one of the best wine cellars in Sweden, with Mouton Rothschild wines dating from 1904. An outdoor terrace is open during summer. ⊠ *Arkiv-gatan 7,* ☎ *031/160333,* 🖷 *031/167854. Reservations required. AE, DC, MC, V.*

$$$ ✕ **Räkan.** This informal and popular place makes the most of an unusual gimmick: The tables are arranged around a long tank, and if you order shrimp, the house specialty, they arrive at your table in radio-controlled boats you navigate yourself. ⊠ *Lorensbergsgatan 16,* ☎ *031/169839,* 🖷 *031/186418. Reservations required. AE, DC, MC, V. No lunch weekends.*

$$$ ✕ **Sjömagasinet.** Seafood is the obvious specialty at this waterfront restaurant. Situated in a 200-year-old renovated shipping warehouse, the dining room has views of the harbor and suspension bridge. An outdoor terrace opens up in summer. ⊠ *Klippans Kulturreservat,* ☎ *031/246510,* 🖷 *031/245539. Reservations required. AE, DC, MC, V.*

$$ ✕ **Fiskekrogen.** Its name means Fish Inn, and it has more than 30 fish and seafood dishes to choose from. Lunches are particularly good, and the location is just across the canal from Stadsmuseet. ⊠ *Lilla Torget 1,* ☎ *31/711–2184. AE, DC, MC, V. Closed Sun.*

$$ ✕ **Weise.** The Weise family still owns and runs the restaurant its German ancestors opened in 1893. Although it moved to the present location in 1993 in order to offer outdoor dining in summer, the owners brought along all the original furniture and accessories, including a work made just for Herr Weise by Albert Angstöm, one of Sweden's leading painters. Lunch is Swedish *husmanskost,* (home cooking) but dinner is a more Continental menu. ⊠ *Linnégatan 54,* ☎ **FAX** *031/426014. AE, MC, V.*

$ ✕ **Amanda Boman.** This little restaurant in one corner of the market hall at Kungsportsplats keeps early hours, so unless you eat an afternoon dinner, plan on lunch instead. The cuisine is primarily Swedish, including fish soup and gravlax (marinated salmon). ⊠ *Saluhallen,* ☎ *031/137676. AE, DC, MC, V. Closed Sun.*

$ ✕ **Gabriel.** A buffet of fresh shellfish and the fish dish of the day draw crowds to this restaurant on a balcony above the fish hall. You can eat lunch and watch all the trading. ⊠ *Feske Körkan,* ☎ *031/139051. AE, DC, MC, V. No dinner. Closed Sun. and Mon.*

Lodging

$$$$ ▥ **Park Avenue (Radisson SAS).** Though a 1991 renovation failed to give this modern luxury hotel the ambience it so sorely lacks, all the facilities are in place, including an SAS check-in counter. The well-equipped rooms are decorated in earth tones and have good views of the city. ⊠ *Kungsportsavenyn 36–38, Box 53233, S–400 16,* ☎ *031/176520,* **FAX** *031/169568. 318 rooms. 2 restaurants, bar, 2 no-smoking floors, indoor pool, sauna, meeting room. AE, DC, MC, V.*

$$$$ ▥ **Sheraton Hotel and Towers.** Opened in 1986 across Drottningtorget from the picturesque central train station, the Sheraton Hotel and Towers is Göteborg's most modern and spectacular international-style hotel. The attractive atrium lobby holds two restaurants: Frascati, which serves international cuisine, and the Atrium, a piano bar with a light menu. Rooms are large and luxurious and decorated in pastels. Guests receive a 20% discount at the well-appointed health club on the premises. ⊠ *Södra Hamngatan 59–65, S–401 24,* ☎ *031/806000,* FAX *031/159888. 344 rooms. Restaurant, piano bar, no-smoking rooms, beauty salon, health club, shops, casino, convention center, travel services. AE, DC, MC, V.*

$$$ ▥ **Eggers.** Dating from 1859, Best Western's Eggers has more Old World
★ character than any other hotel in the city. It is a minute's walk from the train station and was probably the last port of call in Sweden for many emigrants to the United States. Rooms vary in size, and all are beautifully appointed, often with antiques. Only breakfast is served. ⊠ *Drottningtorget, Box 323, S–401 25,* ☎ *031/806070,* FAX *031/154243. 65 rooms. No-smoking rooms, meeting rooms. AE, DC, MC, V.*

$$$ ▥ **Europa.** Large and comfortable, this hotel is part of the Nordstan
★ mall complex, very close to the central train station. ⊠ *Köpmansgatan 38, S–401 24,* ☎ *031/801280,* FAX *031/154755. 475 rooms, 5 suites. Restaurant, piano bar, no-smoking floors, indoor pool, sauna, conference center, parking. AE, DC, MC, V.*

$$$ ▥ **Liseberg Heden.** Not far from the famous Liseberg Amusement Park, Liseberg Heden is a popular, family hotel. Rooms are modern and are done in light colors; most have wood floors, and all have satellite television, minibar, and a large desk. Perks include a sauna and a gourmet restaurant. ⊠ *Sten Sturegatan, S–411 38,* ☎ *031/200280,* FAX *031/165283. 160 rooms. Restaurant, no-smoking rooms, sauna, meeting rooms. AE, DC, MC, V.*

$$$ ▥ **Opalen.** If you are attending an event at the Scandinavium stadium, or if you have children and are heading for the Liseberg Amusement Park, this Reso hotel is ideally located. Rooms are bright and modern. ⊠ *Engelbrektsgatan 73, Box 5106, S–402 23,* ☎ *031/810300,* FAX *031/187622. 241 rooms. Restaurant, bar, 2 no-smoking floors, sauna. AE, DC, MC, V.*

$$$ ▥ **Panorama.** Within reach of all downtown attractions, this Best Western hotel nevertheless manages to provide a quiet, relaxing atmo-

sphere. ⊠ *Eklandagatan 51–53, Box 24037, S–400 22,* ☎ *031/810880,* FAX *031/814237. 339 rooms. Restaurant, no-smoking floors, hot tub, sauna, nightclub, meeting rooms, free parking. AE, DC, MC, V.*

$$$ 🏨 **Riverton.** Convenient for people arriving in the city by ferry, this hotel is close to the European terminals and overlooks the harbor. Built in 1985, it has a glossy marble floor and reflective ceiling in the lobby; rooms are decorated with abstract-pattern textiles and whimsical prints. ⊠ *Stora Badhusgatan 26, S–411 21,* ☎ *031/101200,* FAX *031/130866. 190 rooms. Restaurant, bar, no-smoking rooms, hot tub, sauna, meeting rooms, free parking. AE, DC, MC, V.*

$$$ 🏨 **Royal.** Göteborg's oldest hotel, built in 1852, is small, family owned,
★   and traditional. Rooms, most with new parquet floors, are individually decorated with reproductions of elegant Swedish traditional furniture. It's in the city center a few blocks from the central train station. ⊠ *Drottninggatan 67, S–411 07,* ☎ *031/806100,* FAX *031/156246. 82 rooms. Breakfast room, no-smoking floor. AE, DC, MC, V.*

$$$ 🏨 **Rubinen.** The central location on Avenyn is a plus, but this Reso hotel can be noisy during the summer. ⊠ *Kungsportsavenyn 24, Box 53097, S–400 14,* ☎ *031/810800,* FAX *031/167586. 185 rooms. Restaurant, bar, no-smoking rooms, meeting rooms. AE, DC, MC, V.*

$ 🏨 **Ostkupans Vandrarhem.** Situated in a modern apartment block, this hostel is 5 kilometers (3 miles) from the train station. Rooms are contemporary, with Swedish-designed furnishings. Breakfast (SKr40) is not included in the rates. ⊠ *Mejerigatan 2, S–412 76,* ☎ *031/401050,* FAX *031/401151. 250 beds, 6- to 8-bed apartments. MC, V. Closed Sept.–May.*

$ 🏨 **Partille Vandrarhem.** This hostel is in a pleasant old house 15 kilometers (9 miles) outside the city, next to a lake for swimming. You can order meals or prepare them yourself in the guest kitchen. ⊠ *Landvettervägen, Box 214, S–433 24, Partille,* ☎ *031/446501,* ☎FAX *031/446163. 120 beds, 2- to 6-bed rooms.*

Camping

⚠ There are campsites at **Uddevalla** (Hafstens Camping, ☎ 0522/644117), **Göteborg** (Kärralund, ☎ 031/840200, FAX 031/840500), and **Askim** (Askim Strand, ☎ 031/286261, FAX 031/681335).

Nightlife and the Arts

Konserthuset is the home of the highly acclaimed Göteborg Symphony Orchestra. A mural by Sweden's Prince Eugene is among the works of art in the lobby. ⊠ *Götaplatsen, S–412 56,* ☎ *031/167000,* FAX *031/681335.*

Operan, home of the Göteborg's opera company, was completed in 1994 and incorporates a 1,250-seat auditorium with a glassed-in dining area overlooking the harbor. ⊠ *Packhuskajen,* ☎ *031/131300.*

Stadsteatern has a good reputation in Sweden. The vast majority of its productions are in Swedish. ⊠ *Götaplatsen, Box 5094, S–402 22,* ☎ *031/819960 for tickets, 031/778–6600 for information.*

Outdoor Activities and Sports

Beaches

There are several excellent local beaches. The two most popular (though visitors are unlikely to find them crowded) are Näset and Askim.

Fishing

Mackerel fishing is popular here. Among the boats that take expeditions into the archipelago is the M.S. *Daisy,* which leaves from Hjuvik on the Hisingen side of the Göta River (☎ 031/963018 or mobile phone 010/235–8017).

Shopping

Department Stores

The local branch of **NK,** Sweden's leading department store, is at Östra Hamngatan 42 (☎ 031/107000). **Åhléns** is in the Nordstan mall (☎ 031/800200).

Specialty Stores

ANTIQUES

Antikhallarna (Antiques Halls, ✉ Västra Hamngatan 6, ☎ 031/711–1324) claim to be the largest of their kind in Scandinavia. You'll find Sweden's leading auction house, **Bukowskis,** on Avenyn (✉ Kungsportsavenyn 43, ☎ 031/200360).

CLOTHING FOR MEN

Ströms (✉ Kungsgatan 27–29, ☎ 031/177100) has occupied its street-corner location two generations; the clothing selection is of high quality and good taste. The fashions at **Gillblads** (✉ Kungsgatan 44, ☎ 031/108846) suit a younger, somewhat trendier customer.

CLOTHING FOR WOMEN

For furs, try **Andreassons** (✉ Kungsportsavenyn 22, ☎ 031/168330, and Södra Hamngatan 49, ☎ 031/155535). **Gillblads** (✉ Kungsgatan 44, ☎ 031/108846) has the most current fashions. **Ströms** (✉ Kungsgatan 27–29, ☎ 031/177100) offers clothing of high quality and mildly conservative style. **Hennes & Mauritz** (✉ Kungsgatan 55–57, ☎ 031/711–0011) sells clothes roughly comparable to the standard choices at Sears or Marks & Spencer.

HANDICRAFTS

The most atmospheric settings for the purchase of Swedish handicrafts and glassware are in the various shops in **Kronhusbodarna.** Excellent examples of local handicrafts can also be bought at **Bohusslöjden** (✉ Kungsportsavenyn 25, ☎ 031/160072).

Göteborg A to Z

Arriving and Departing

BY BUS

All buses arrive in the downtown area. The principal company is **Swebus** (☎ 031/103285).

BY CAR

You can approach Göteborg on either the E20 or the E4 highway from Stockholm (495 kilometers [307 miles]) and the east, or on the E6/E20 coastal highway from the south (Malmö is 290 kilometers [180 miles] away). Markings are excellent, and roads are well sanded and plowed in winter.

BY PLANE

The airport, **Landvetter** (☎ 031/941100), is approximately 26 kilometers (16 miles) from the city center. Among the airlines operating from it are SAS (☎ 031/942000 or 020/727000), British Airways (☎ 020/781144), **Air France** (☎ 031/941180), and Lufthansa (☎ 031/941325 or 020/228800).

Between the Airport and City Center. Landvetter is linked to Göteborg by freeway. Buses leave Landvetter every 15 to 30 minutes and arrive 30 minutes later at Nils Ericsonsplatsen by the central train station, with stops at Lisebergsstationen, Korsvägen, the SAS Park Avenue

Hotel, and Kungsportsplatsen; weekend schedules include some non-stop departures. The price of the trip is SKr50. For more information, call **GL** (Göteborg Bus and Tram) at ☎ 031/801235.

A **taxi** to the city center should cost no more than SKr220. A shared **SAS limousine** for up to four people to the same address costs SKr199 (SAS Limousine Service, ☎ 031/942424).

There is regular service from Stockholm, taking a little over 4½ hours, as well as frequent high-speed (X2000) train service, which takes about 3 hours. All trains arrive at the central train station (☎ 031/805000) in Drottningtorget, downtown Göteborg. For schedules, call **SJ** (☎ 031/104445 or 020/757575). Streetcars and buses leave from here for the suburbs, but the hub for all streetcar traffic is a block down Norra Hamngatan, at Brunnsparken.

Getting Around

BY BOAT

Traveling the entire length of the Göta Canal by passenger boat to Stockholm takes four or six days. For details, contact the **Göta Canal Steamship Company** (✉ Hotellplatsen 2, Box 272, S–401 24, Göteborg, ☎ 031/806315, FAX 031/158311; N. Riddarholshamnen 5, S–111 28, Stockholm, ☎ 08/202728).

For information on sailing your own boat on the Göta Canal, contact AB Göta Kanalbolaget (☎ 0141/53510).

BY BUS AND TRAM

Göteborg has an excellent transit service, called Stadstrafiken; pick up a brochure in English at a TidPunkten office (✉ Drottningtorget, Brunnsparken, Nils Ericsonsplatsen, and Folkungabron, ☎ 031/801235), which explains the various discount passes and procedures.

The best bet for the tourist, however, is the **Göteborg Card,** which covers free use of public transport, various sightseeing trips, and admission to Liseberg and local museums, among other benefits. The card costs SKr125 for one day, SKr225 for two days, and SKr275 for three days; there are lower rates for children under 18 from mid-June to mid-September. You can buy the Göteborg Card as well as regular tram and bus passes at Pressbyrån shops, camping sites, and the tourist information offices.

BY CAR

Avis has offices at the airport (☎ 031/946030) and the central railway station (☎ 031/805780). **Hertz** is at Spannmålsgatan 16 (☎ 031/803730).

BY TAXI

To order a taxi, telephone **Taxi Göteborg** at ☎ 031/650000; for advance bookings, call ☎ 031/500504.

Contacts and Resources

DOCTORS AND DENTISTS

Dial ☎ 031/703–1500 day or night for information on medical services. Emergencies are handled by the **Sahlgrenska Hospital** (☎ 031/601000), **Östrasjukhuset** (☎ 031/374000), and **Mölndalssjukhuset** (☎ 031/861000). There is a private medical service at City Akuten weekdays 8–6 (✉ Drottninggatan 45, ☎ 031/101010). There is a 24-hour children's emergency service at Östrasjukhuset as well.

The national dental-service emergency number is ☎ 031/807800; the private dental-service emergency number is ☎ 031/800500. Both are available 8 AM–9 PM only; for emergencies after hours, call ☎ 031/703–1500.

EMBASSIES AND CONSULATES
U.K. Consulate: Götgatan 15, ☎ 031/151327.

EMERGENCIES

Dial ☎ 112.

ENGLISH-LANGUAGE BOOKSTORES

Nearly all bookshops stock English-language books. The broadest selection is at **Eckersteins Akademibokhandeln** (✉ Södra Larmgatan 11, ☎ 031/171100).

GUIDED TOURS

A 90-minute bus tour and a two-hour combination boat-and-bus tour of the chief points of interest leave from outside the main tourist office at Kungsportsplatsen every day from mid-May through August and on Saturdays in April, September, and October. Call the tourist office (☎ 031/100740) for the schedule.

For a view of the city from the water and an expert commentary on its sights and history in English and German, take one of the **Paddan** sightseeing boats. *Paddan* means "toad" in Swedish, an apt commentary on the vessels' squat appearance. The boats pass under 20 bridges and take in both the canals and part of the Göta River. ✉ *Kungsportsbron,* ☎ *031/133000.* 🎫 *SKr60.* ☺ *Late Apr.–late June and mid-Aug.–early Sept., daily 10–5; late June–mid-Aug., daily 10–9; early Sept.–Oct. 1, daily noon–3.*

LATE-NIGHT PHARMACY

Vasen (✉ Götgatan 12, ☎ 031/804410), in the Nordstan shopping mall, is open 24 hours.

TRAVEL AGENCIES

The **Ticket Travel Agency** is at Östra Hamngatan 35 (☎ 031/176860). **STF** has a travel agency at Drottningtorget 6 (✉ Box 305, S–401 24, ☎ 031/150930, 🖷 031/155995). For other travel agencies see the Yellow Pages under *Resor-Resebyråer.*

VISITOR INFORMATION

The main tourist office is **Göteborg's Turistbyrå** (✉ Kungsportsplatsen 2, S–411 10 Göteborg, ☎ 031/100740, 🖷 031/132184). There are also offices at the Nordstan shopping center (✉ Nordstadstorget, S–411 05 Göteborg, ☎ 031/150705) and in front of the central train station at Drottningtorget.

A free visitor's guide called *Göteborgarn* is available in English during the summer; you can pick it up at tourist offices, shopping centers and some restaurants, and on the streetcars.

The Friday edition of the principal morning newspaper, *Göteborgs Posten,* includes a weekly supplement titled "Aveny"—it's in Swedish but is reasonably easy to decipher.

SIDE TRIPS FROM GÖTEBORG

Göteborg is a pleasantly relaxed place from which to explore the west coast of Sweden, where wide, unspoiled beaches and a majestic rocky coastline alternate with timbered fishing villages. From here you can set out on the Göta Canal, Sweden's "blue ribbon," down which barges once sailed laden with exports and imports but which today provides a picturesque water journey through the Swedish countryside.

Bohuslän

This coastal region north of Göteborg, with its indented, rocky coastline, provides a foretaste of Norway's fjords farther north. It was from these rugged shores that the 9th-and 10th-century Vikings sailed southward on their epic voyages. Today small towns and attractive fishing villages nestle among the distinctively rounded granite rocks and the thousands of skerries and islands that form Sweden's western archipelago, best described by Prince Vilhelm, brother of the late King Gustav V, as "an archipelago formed of gneiss and granite and water that eternally stretches foamy arms after life." The ideal way to explore the area is by drifting slowly north of Göteborg, taking full advantage of the uncluttered beaches and small, picturesque fishing villages. Painters and sailors haunt the region in summer.

Kungälv

48 *15 km (9 mi) north of Göteborg.*

Strategically placed at the confluence of the two arms of the Göta River, Kungälv was an important battle grounds in ancient times. Though today it is something of a bedroom suburb for Göteborg, the town still has several ancient sights, including a white wooden church dating from 1679, with an unusual Baroque interior.

For a sense of Kungälv's military past, visit **Bohus Fästning,** a ruined fortress built by the Norwegians in 1308 where many battles between Swedish, Norwegian, and Danish armies took place. ⊠ *Kungalv.* ☎ *0303/99200.* ☞ *SKr15.* ☉ *May–June and Aug., daily 10–7; July, daily 10–8; Sept., weekends 11–5.*

The local **tourist office** is at Fästningsholmen (☎ 0303/99200).

OUTDOOR ACTIVITIES AND SPORTS
There is excellent **deep-sea fishing** for mackerel from Skärhamn on the island of Tjörn, which can be reached by road bridge from Stenungsund.

Uddevalla

49 *64 km (40 mi) north of Kungälv; 79 km (49 mi) north of Göteborg.*

This former shipbuilding town at the head of a picturesque fjord is best known for a battle in which heavy rains doused musketeers' matches, effectively ending hostilities. The local **tourist office** is at Kampenhof (☎ 0522/511787).

En Route **Lysekil,** off the E6 highway on a promontory at the head of the Gullmarn Fjord, has been one of Sweden's most popular summer resorts since the 19th century. It specializes in boat excursions to neighboring islands and deep-sea fishing trips. The best bathing is at Pinnevik Cove. A little to the north lies the Sotenäs Peninsula and the attractive island of **Smögen,** which can be reached by road bridge. It is locally renowned for its shrimp.

Before the E6 highway reaches Strömstad, stop at **Tanumshede** to see Europe's largest single collection of Bronze Age rock carvings at **Vitlycke.** They cover 673 square feet of rock and depict battles, hunting, and fishing. The carvings are close to the main road and are well marked.

Strömstad

50 *90 km (56 mi) northwest of Uddvalla; 169 km (105 mi) north of Göteborg.*

This popular Swedish resort claims to have more summer sunshine than any other town north of the Alps. Formerly Norwegian, it has been the site of many battles between warring Danes, Norwegians, and

Side Trips from Göteborg

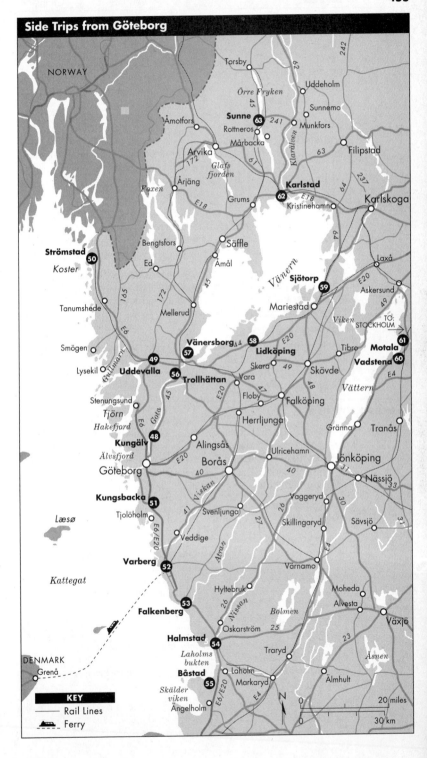

NORWAY

Torsby

Örre Fryken

Uddeholm

Sunnemo

Åmotfors

Sunne 63

Rottneros

Munkfors

Mårbacka

Arvika

Filipstad

Glafs
fjorden

Årjäng

Foxen

Karlstad

Grums

62

Kristinehamn

Katlskoga

Bengtsfors

Säffle

Strömstad 50

Koster

Ed

Åmål

Vänern

Laxå

Sjötorp 59

Askersund

Tanumshede

Mellerud

Mariestad

Viken

TO:
STOCKHOLM

Smögen

Vänersborg 58

Motala 61

57

Lidköping

Tibro

Vadstena 60

Lysekil

Uddevalla 49

56

Skara

Skövde

Stenungsund

Trollhättan

Vara

Vättern

Tjörn

Floby

Falköping

Hakefjord

Herrljunga

Kungälv 48

Alingsås

Gränna

Tranås

Älvsfjord

Ulricehamn

Jönköping

Göteborg

Borås

Nässjö

Kungsbacka 51

Vaggeryd

Tjolöholm

Svenljunga

Skillingaryd

Sävsjö

Laesø

Veddige

Varberg 52

Värnamo

Kattegat

Hyltebruk

Moheda

Falkenberg 53

Oskarström

Bolmen

Alvesta

Växjö

Halmstad 54

Traryd

DENMARK

Laholms
bukten

Åsnen

Grenå

Båstad 55

Laholm

Älmhult

Skälder
viken

Markaryd

Ängelholm

N

0   20 miles

0   30 km

KEY
— Rail Lines
Ferry

Swedes. A short trip over the Norwegian border takes you to Halden, where Sweden's warrior king, Karl XII, died in 1718. The local **tourist office** is at Tullhuset, Norra Hamnen (☎ 0526/13025).

KOSTER ISLANDS – There are regular ferry boats from Strömstad to the Koster Islands, a favorite holiday spot, with uncluttered beaches and trips to catch prawn and lobster.

Bohuslän A to Z

ARRIVING AND DEPARTING

Buses leave from behind the central train station in Göteborg (bus lines: GL, ☎ 031/801235, and Bohustrafiken, ☎ 0522/14030). The trip to Strömstad takes two to three hours.

GETTING AROUND

By Car. The best way to explore Bohuslän is by car. The E6 highway runs the length of the coast from Göteborg north to Strömstad, close to the Norwegian border, and for campers there are numerous well-equipped and uncluttered camping places along the coast's entire length.

By Train. There is regular service along the coast between all the major towns of Bohuslän. The trip from Göteborg to Strömstad takes about two hours, and there are several trains each day. For schedules, call **SJ** (✉ Göteborg, ☎ 031/103000 or 020/757575).

VISITOR INFORMATION

The principal tourist office for the region is **Göteborg Turistbyrå** (☞ Göteborg A to Z, *above*). In addition to the local tourist offices in the towns on this tour, try **Kungshamn** (✉ Hamngatan 6, ☎ 0523/37150). **Öckerö** (✉ Stranden 2, ☎ 031/965080) is another local office.

Swedish Riviera

The coastal region south of Göteborg, locally dubbed the Swedish Riviera, is the closest that mainland Sweden comes to having a resort area. Fine beaches abound, and there are plenty of opportunities for many sporting activities. The region stretches down to Båstad in the country's southernmost province, Skåne.

Kungsbacka

51 *25 km (15 mi) south of Göteborg.*

This bedroom suburb of Göteborg holds a market on the first Thursday of every month. The **tourist office** is at Storgatan 41 (☎ 0300/34595).

FJÄRÅS – A break in a high ridge, the Fjärås Crack offers a fine view of the coast. On the slopes of the ridge are Iron Age and Viking graves.

En Route At **Tjolöholm,** 12 kilometers (7 miles) down the E6/E20 highway from Kungsbacka, you'll encounter Tjolöholms Slott (Tjolöholm Castle), a manor house built by a Scotsman at the beginning of this century in mock English Tudor style. ✉ S–430 33 Fjärås, ☎ 0300/44200. ⌧ SKr40. ☼ Mid-June–mid-Aug., daily 11–4; Apr.–May and Sept., weekends 11–4; Oct., Sun. 11–4.

Near Tjolöholm is the tiny 18th-century village of **Äskhult,** the site of an open-air museum, the Gamla By. ☎ 0300/42159. ⌧ SKr10. ☼ May–Aug., daily 10–6; Sept., weekends 10–6.

Varberg

52 *40 km (25 mi) south of Kungsbacka; 65 km (40 mi) south of Göteborg.*

Varberg is a busy port with connections to Grenå in Denmark and some good beaches. It is best known for a suit of medieval clothing preserved in the museum in the 13th-century **Varbergs Fästning** (Varberg Fortress). The suit belonged to a man who was murdered and thrown into a peat bog. The peat preserved his body, and his clothes are the only suit of ordinary medieval clothing in existence. The museum also contains a silver bullet said to be the one that killed Karl XII. ☎ 0340/18520. ☒ SKr10. ☉ *Weekdays 10–4, weekends noon–4. Hourly guided tours mid-June–mid-Aug., daily 10–7; May–mid-June and mid-Aug.–Sept., Sun. 10–7.*

Varberg's **tourist office** is at Brunnsparken (☎ 0340/88770).

Falkenberg

53 *29 km (19 mi) south of Varberg; 94 km (59 mi) south of Göteborg.*

With fine beaches and salmon fishing in the Ätran River, Falkenberg is one of Sweden's most attractive resorts. Its Gamla Stan (Old Town) is full of narrow, cobblestone streets and quaint old wooden houses. Here you'll find **Törngren's,** a pottery shop, probably the oldest still operating in Scandinavia, owned and run by the seventh generation of the founding family. ☒ *Krukmakaregatan 4. Shop (☎ 0346/16920) open normal business hours. Pottery (☎ 0346/10354) may be visited by prior arrangement.*

Falkenberg's **tourist office** is at Stortorget, ☎ 0346/17410.

Halmstad

54 *40 km (25 mi) south of Falkenberg; 143 km (88 mi) south of Göteborg.*

With a population of 50,000, Halmstad is the largest seaside resort on the west coast. The Norreport town gate, all that remains of the town's original fortifications, dates from 1605. The modern Town Hall has interior decorations by the so-called Halmstad Group of painters, formed here in 1929. A 14th-century church in the main square contains fragments of medieval murals and a 17th-century pulpit. The local **tourist office** is at Lilla Torg (☎ 035/109345).

Båstad

55 *35 km (22 mi) south of Halmstad; 178 km (110 mi) south of Göteborg.*

In the southernmost province of Skåne, Båstad is the most fashionable resort in Sweden, where ambassadors and local captains of industry have their summer houses. Aside from this, it is best known for its tennis. In addition to the **Båstad Open,** a Grand Prix tournament in late summer, there is the annual **Donald Duck Cup** in July for children ages 11 to 15; it was the very first trophy won by Björn Borg, who later took the Wimbledon men's singles title an unprecedented five times in a row. Spurred on by Borg and other Swedish champions, such as Stefan Edberg and Mats Wilander, thousands of youngsters take part in the Donald Duck Cup each year. For details, contact the **Svenska Tennisförbundet** (Swedish Tennis Association) (Lidingövägen 75, Stockholm, ☎ 08/667–9770).

The local **tourist office** is at Stortorget 1 (☎ 0431/75045).

NEED A BREAK? **Norrviken Gardens** (☎ 0431/69040), 3 kilometers (2 miles) northwest of Båstad, are beautifully laid out in different styles, with a restaurant, a shop, and a pottery studio. ☒ *SKr35. ☉ Early June–mid-Aug., daily 10–6; late Aug.–May, daily 10:30–5.*

Swedish Riviera A to Z

ARRIVING AND DEPARTING

By Bus. Buses leave from behind Göteborg's central train station.

By Car. Simply follow the E6/E20 highway south from Göteborg. It parallels the coast.

By Train. Regular train service connects the Göteborg central station with all major towns. Contact **SJ** (⊠ Göteborg, ☎ 031/103000 or 020/757575).

VISITOR INFORMATION

In addition to the tourist offices listed in each town, there is an office at **Laholm** (⊠ Rådhuset, ☎ 0430/15216 or 0430/15450).

Göta Canal

Stretching 614 kilometers (380 miles) between Stockholm and Göteborg, the Göta Canal is actually a series of interconnected canals, rivers, lakes, and even a stretch of sea. Bishop Hans Brask of Linköping in the 16th century was the first to suggest the idea; in 1718, King Karl XII ordered the canal to be built, but work was abandoned when he was killed in battle the same year. Not until 1810 was the idea again taken up in earnest. The driving force was a Swedish nobleman, Count Baltzar Bogislaus von Platen (1766–1829), and his motive was commercial. Von Platen saw in the canal a way of beating Danish tolls on shipping that passed through the Öresund and of enhancing the importance of Göteborg by linking the port with Stockholm on the east coast. At a time when Swedish fortunes were at a low ebb, the canal was also envisaged as a means of reestablishing faith in the future and boosting national morale.

The building of the canal took 22 years and involved a total of 58,000 men. The linking of the various stretches of water required 87 kilometers (54 miles) of man-made cuts through soil and rock, the building of 58 locks, 47 bridges, 27 culverts, and 3 dry docks. Unfortunately, the canal never achieved the financial success hoped for by von Platen. By 1857 the Danes had removed shipping tolls, and in the following decade the linking of Göteborg with Stockholm by rail effectively ended the canal's commercial potential. The canal did come into its own as a 20th-century tourist attraction, however.

Drifting lazily down this lovely series of waterways, across the enormous lakes, Vänern and Vättern, through a microcosm of all that is best about Sweden—abundant fresh air; clear, clean water; pristine nature; well-tended farmland—it is difficult to conceive of the canal's industrial origins. A bicycle path runs parallel to the canal, offering another means of touring the country.

En Route The trip from Göteborg takes you first along the Göta Älv (river), a wide waterway that 10,000 years ago, when the ice cap melted, was a great fjord. Some 30 minutes into the voyage the boat passes below a rocky escarpment, topped by the remains of **Bohus Fästning** (Bohus Castle), distinguished by two round towers known as Father's Hat and Mother's Bonnet. It dates from the 14th century and was once the mightiest fortress in western Scandinavia, commanding the confluence of the Göta and Nordre rivers. It was strengthened and enlarged in the 16th century and successfully survived 14 sieges. From 1678 onward, the castle began to lose its strategic and military importance and fell into decay, until 1838, when King Karl XIV passed by on a river journey, admired the old fortress, and ordered its preservation.

Just north of Kungälv along the Göta Canal, you'll come to the quiet village of **Lödöse,** once a major trading settlement and a predecessor of Göteborg. From here, the countryside becomes wilder, with pines and oaks clustered thickly on either bank between cliffs of lichen-clad granite.

Trollhättan

56 *70 km (43 mi) north of Göteborg.*

In this pleasant industrial town of about 50,000 inhabitants, a spectacular waterfall was in 1906 rechanneled to become Sweden's first hydroelectric plant. In most years, on specific days the waters are allowed to follow their natural course, a fall of 106 feet in six torrents. This is a sight that is well worth seeing. The other main point of interest is the area between what were the falls and the series of locks that allowed the canal to bypass them. Here are disused locks from 1800 and 1844 and a strange Ice Age grotto where members of the Swedish royal family have carved their names since the 18th century. Trollhättan also has a fine, wide marketplace and pleasant waterside parks.

En Route Soon after leaving Trollhättan, the Göta Canal route takes you past Hunneberg and Halleberg, two strange, flat-topped hills, both more than 500 feet high; the woods surrounding them are extraordinarily rich in elk, legend, and Viking burial mounds. It then proceeds through **Karls Grav,** the oldest part of the canal, begun early in the 17th century; its purpose was to bypass the Ronnum Falls on the Göta River, which have been harnessed to a hydroelectric project.

Vänersborg

57 *15 km (9 mi) north of Trollhättan; 85 km (53 mi) north of Göteborg.*

Eventually, the canal enters **Vänern,** Sweden's largest and Europe's third-largest lake: 3,424 square kilometers (2,123 square miles) of water, 145 kilometers (90 miles) long and 81 kilometers (50 miles) wide at one point.

At the southern tip of the lake is Vänersborg, a town of about 30,000 inhabitants that was founded in the mid-17th century. The church and the governor's residence date from the 18th century, but the rest of the town was destroyed by fire in 1834. Vänersborg is distinguished by its fine lakeside park, the trees of which act as a windbreak for the gusts that sweep in from Vänern.

Lidköping

58 *55 km (34 mi) east of Värnersberg; 140 km (87 mi) northeast of Göteborg.*

On an inlet at the southernmost point of Vänern's eastern arm lies the town of Lidköping, which received its charter in 1446 and is said to have the largest town square in Sweden.

OFF THE
BEATEN PATH

LÄCKÖ SLOTT – Lying 24 kilometers (15 miles) to the north of Lidköping, on an island off the point dividing the eastern arm of Vänern from the western, is Läckö Castle, one of Sweden's finest 17th-century Renaissance palaces. Its 250 rooms were once the home of Magnus Gabriel de la Gardie, a great favorite of Queen Christina. Only the Royal Palace in Stockholm is larger. In 1681 Karl XI, to curtail the power of the nobility, confiscated it, and in 1830 all its furnishings were auctioned. Many of them have since been restored to the palace.

En Route On a peninsula to the east of Lidköping, the landscape is dominated
by the great hill of **Kinnekulle,** towering 900 feet above the lake. The
hill is rich in colorful vegetation and wildlife and was a favorite hike
for the botanist Linnaeus.

Sjötorp

 *67 km (42 mi) northeast of Lidköping; 207 km (128 mi) northeast of
Göteborg.*

At the lakeside port of Sjötorp, the Göta Canal proper begins: a cut
through earth and granite with a series of locks raising the steamer to
Lanthöjden, at 304 feet above sea level the highest point on the canal.
The boat next enters the narrow, twisting lakes of Viken and Botten-
sjön and continues to Forsvik through the canal's oldest lock, built in
1813. It then sails out into **Vättern,** Sweden's second-largest lake,
nearly 129 kilometers (80 miles) from north to south and 31 kilometers (19 miles) across at its widest point. Its waters are so clear that in
some parts the bottom is visible at a depth of 50 feet. The lake is subject to sudden storms that can whip its normally placid waters into a
choppy maelstrom.

Vadstena

 249 km (154 mi) northeast of Göteborg (via Jönköping).

This little-known historic gem of a town grew up around the monastery
founded by Saint Birgitta, or Bridget (1303–73), who wrote in her *Revelations* that she had a vision of Christ in which he revealed the rules
of the religious order she went on to establish. These rules seem to have
been a precursor for the Swedish ideal of sexual equality, with both
nuns and monks sharing a common church. Her order spread rapidly
after her death, and at one time there were 80 Bridgetine monasteries
in Europe. Little remains of the Vadstena monastery, however; in 1545
King Gustav Vasa ordered its demolition, and its stones were used to
build **Vadstena Slott** (Vadstena Castle), the huge fortress dominating
the lake. Swedish royalty held court here until 1715. It then fell into
decay and was used as a granary. Today it houses part of the National
Archives and is also the site of an annual summer opera festival. ☎
0143/15123. ✆ SKr30. ☉ *Mid-May–June and late Aug., daily noon–4;
July–mid-Aug., daily 11–4. Guided tours mid-May–mid-Aug. at 12:30
and 1:30, late Aug. also at 2:30.*

Vadstena Kyrka is also worth visiting. The triptych altarpiece on the
south wall features Saint Birgitta presenting her book of revelations
to a group of kneeling cardinals. There is also a fine wood carving of
the Madonna and Child from 1500.

Vadstena's **tourist office** is at Rådhustorget (☎ 0143/15125).

Lodging

$$ 🏨 **Kungs-Starby Wärdshus.** This functional guest house, reached via
Route 50, adjoins a renovated manor house and restaurant, surrounded
by a park on the outskirts of town. ⌧ *S–592 01 Vadstena,* ☎ *0143/
75100,* ℻ *0143/75170. 61 rooms. Restaurant, no-smoking rooms, pool,
sauna, meeting rooms. AE, DC, MC, V.*

$$ 🏨 **Vadstena Klosterhotel.** This hotel is housed in Sweden's oldest secular building, parts of which date from the 13th century. Rooms are
modern and well appointed, and there are three comfortable lounges.
⌧ *Klosterområdet, off Lasarettsgatan, S–592 30 Vadstena,* ☎ *0143/
11530,* ℻ *0143/13648. 29 rooms. Restaurant, no-smoking rooms, meeting rooms. AE, DC, MC, V.*

Motala

61 *13 km (8 mi) north of Vadstena; 262 km (162 (mi) northwest of Göteborg.*

Before reaching Stockholm, the canal passes through Motala, where Baltzar von Platen is buried close to the canal. He had envisaged the establishment of four new towns along the waterway, but only Motala fulfilled his dream. He designed the town himself, and his statue is in the main square.

En Route At Borenshult a series of locks take the boat down to **Boren,** a lake in the province of Östergötland. On the southern shore of the next lake, Roxen, lies the city of **Linköping,** capital of the province and home of Saab, the aircraft and automotive company. Once out of the lake, you follow a new stretch of canal past the sleepy town of **Söderköping.** A few miles east, at the hamlet of Mem, the canal's last lock lowers the boat into Slätbaken, a Baltic fjord presided over by the ruins of the ancient **Stegeborg Fortress.** The boat then steams north along the coastline until it enters **Mälaren** through the Södertälje Canal and finally anchors in the capital at Riddarholmen.

Motala A to Z

Bohusturist in Uddevalla (⊠ Skansgatan 3, ☎ 0522/14055) is a regional tourist office. **Västergötlands Turiströd** is another regional tourist office, in Skövde (⊠ Kyrkogatan 11, ☎ 0500/418050). There's a local tourist office in **Karlsborg** (⊠ N. Kanalgatan 2, ☎ 0505/17350).

Värmland

Close to the Norwegian border on the north shores of Vänern, this province is rich in folklore. It was also the home of Alfred Nobel and the birthplace of other famous Swedes, among them the Nobel Prize–winning novelist Selma Lagerlöf, the poet Gustaf Fröding, former prime minister Tage Erlander, and present-day opera star Håkan Hagegård. Värmland's forested, lake-dotted landscape attracts artists seeking refuge and Swedes on holiday.

Karlstad

62 *255 km (158 mi) northeast of Göteborg.*

Värmland's principal city (population 74,000) is situated on Klaraälven (the Klara River) at the point where it empties into Vänern. Founded in 1684, when it was known as Tingvalla, the city was totally rebuilt after a fire in 1865. Its name was later changed to honor King Karl IX—Karlstad, meaning Karl's Town. In **Stortorget,** the main square, there is a statue of Karl IX by the local sculptor Christian Eriksson.

The **Värmlands Museum** has rooms dedicated to both Eriksson and the poet Fröding. ⊠ *Sandgrun, Box 335, S-651 08, Karlstad,* ☎ *054/211419.* ☺ *SKr20.* ☺ *Thurs.–Tues. noon–4, Wed. noon–8.*

The **Marieberg Skogspark** (Marieberg Forest Park) is worth visiting. A delight for the whole family, the park has restaurants and an outdoor theater. ☺ *Early June–late Aug., Thurs.–Tues. 11–5, Wed. 11–8; late Aug.–early June, Tues.–Sun. noon–4, Wed. noon–8.*

Karlstad is the site of the **Emigrant Registret** (Emigrant Registry), which maintains detailed records of the Swedes' emigration to America. Visitors of Swedish extraction can trace their ancestors at the center's research facility. ⊠ *Norra Strandgatan 4, Box 331, S-651 08, Karlstad,* ☎ *054/159272.* ☺ *Free.* ☺ *May–Sept., daily 8–4; rest of yr, Tues.–Sun. 8–4:30, Mon. 8–7.*

DINING AND LODGING

$$$ ✕ **Inn Alstern.** Overlooking Lake Alstern, this elegant restaurant offers Swedish and Continental cuisine, with fish dishes as the specialty. ⊠ *Morgonvägen 4,* ☎ *054/834900. Reservations advised. AE, MC, V.*

$$$ 🏨 **Stadshotellet.** On the banks of Klarälven (Klara River), this hotel built in 1870 is steeped in tradition. All of the rooms are decorated differently, some in modern Swedish style, others evoking their original look. You can dine at the gourmet Matsalon or in the more casual atmosphere of the Cafeet Statt. ⊠ *Kungsgatan 22, S–651 08,* ☎ *054/ 215220,* FAX *054/188211. 143 rooms. Restaurant, pub, no-smoking rooms, sauna, nightclub, meeting rooms. AE, DC, MC, V.*

$$ 🏨 **Gösta Berling.** In the center of town, this small hotel, named for the hero of the Selma Lagerlöf novel, offers nondescript common rooms but inviting, plushly carpeted guest rooms. ⊠ *Drottninggatan 1, S–652 24,* ☎ *054/150190,* FAX *054/154826. 66 rooms. No-smoking rooms, sauna, meeting rooms. AE, DC, MC, V.*

KARLSTAD A TO Z

There is regular service to Karlstad from Stockholm and Göteborg on **SJ** (Göteborg, ☎ 031/103000 or 020/757575).

Karlstad's **tourist office** is at Carlstad Conference Center (☎ 054/ 149055).

En Route Värmland is, above all, a rural experience. Drive along the **Klaräalven,** through the beautiful Fryken Valley, to Ransater, where author Erik Gustaf Geijer was born in 1783 and where Erlander, the former prime minister, also grew up. The rural idyll ends in **Munkfors,** where some of the best-quality steel in Europe is manufactured.

OFF THE BEATEN PATH **SUNNEMO AND UDDEHOLM** – Ten kilometers (6 miles) north of Munkfors, the little village of **Sunnemo** offers a beautiful wooden church. At the northern end of Lake Råda, the town of **Uddeholm** is home of the Uddeholm Corporation, which produces iron and steel, forestry products, and chemicals.

Sunne

63 *63 km (39 mi) north of Karlstad; 318 km (197 mi) northeast of Göteborg.*

Straddling the long, narrow Fryken Lake, Sunne is best known as a jumping-off point for Mårbacka, a stone's throw southeast. Here the estate where Nobel Prize winner Selma Lagerlöf was born in 1858 has been kept much as she left it at the time of her death in 1940; it can be seen by guided tour. ⊠ *Östra Ämtervik, S–686 26 Sunne,* ☎ *0565/ 31027.* 🎟 *SKr40.* ☉ *Mid-May–June and Aug.–early Sept., daily 10– 5, tours every hr; July, daily 9:30–5, tours every half-hr.*

Sunne Turistbyrå (the tourist office) is at Mejerigatan 2 (☎ 0565/13530).

OFF THE BEATEN PATH On the western shore of Fryken Lake, 5 kilometers (½ mile) south of Sunne, you'll find **Rottneros Herrgårds Park** (Rottneros Manor), the inspiration for Ekeby, the fictional estate in Lagerlöf's *Gösta Berlings Saga* (*The Tale of Gösta Berling*). The house is privately owned, but visitors are invited to admire its park, with its fine collection of Scandinavian sculpture—including works by Carl Milles, Norwegian artist Gustav Vigeland, and Wäinö Aaltonen of Finland. The entrance fee covers both the sculpture park and the Nils Holgerssons Adventure Park, an elaborate playground for children. ⊠ *S–686 02 Rottneros,* ☎ *0565/60295.* 🎟 *SKr50.* ☉ *Mid-May–early*

*June and late Aug., weekdays 10–4, weekends 10–6; June, weekdays
10–5, weekends 10–6; July–Aug., daily 10–6.*

Värmland A to Z

ARRIVING AND DEPARTING

By Car. From Stockholm, follow E18 west; from Göteborg, take Route
45 north to E18.

VISITOR INFORMATION

In addition to the local tourist offices listed above, the regional tourist
office is **Värmlands Turistbyrå** (⊠ Tage Erlandergatan 10, Karlstad, ☎
054/102160).

THE SOUTH AND
THE KINGDOM OF CRYSTAL

Southern Sweden is a world of its own, clearly distinguished from the
rest of the country by its geography, culture, and history. Skåne (pronounced *skoh*-neh), the southernmost province, is known as the granary of Sweden. It is a comparatively small province of beautifully fertile
plains, sand beaches, thriving farms, medieval churches, and summer
resorts. These gently rolling hills and fields are broken every few miles
by lovely castles, chronologically and architecturally diverse, that have
given this part of Sweden the name Château Country; often they are
surrounded by beautiful grounds and moats. A significant number of
the estates have remained in the hands of the original families and are
still inhabited.

The two other southern provinces, Blekinge and Halland, are also fertile and rolling and edged by seashores. Historically, these three
provinces are distinct from the rest of Sweden: They were the last to
be incorporated into the country, having been ruled by Denmark until
1658. They retain the influences of the Continental culture in their
architecture, language, and cuisine, viewing the rest of Sweden—especially Stockholm—with some disdain. Skåne even has its own independence movement, and the dialect here is so akin to Danish that
many Swedes from other parts of the country have trouble understanding it.

Småland, to the north, is larger than the other provinces, with a harsh
countryside of stone and woods, the so-called Kingdom of Crystal. It
is an area of small glassblowing firms, such as Kosta Boda and Orrefors, that are world-renowned for the quality of their products. In
addition to visiting these works (and perhaps finding some bargains),
the traveler forms an insight into a poorer, harsher way of life that led
thousands of peasants to emigrate from Småland to the United States
in search of a better life. Those who stayed behind developed a reputation for their inventiveness in setting up small industries to circum-
vent the region's traditional poverty and are also notorious for being
extremely careful—if not downright mean—with money.

Our itinerary follows the coast from the western city of Helsingborg
around the southern loop and up the eastern shore, making a side trip
to the Baltic island province of Öland before heading inland to finish
at Växjo. The entire route can be followed by train, with the exception of Öland and most of the glassworks in Småland—the Orrefors
factory is the only one on the railway line. It's easy to continue your
trip in any direction from Växjö, as it lies at a main crossroads for both
highways and railway lines.

The South and the Kingdom of Crystal

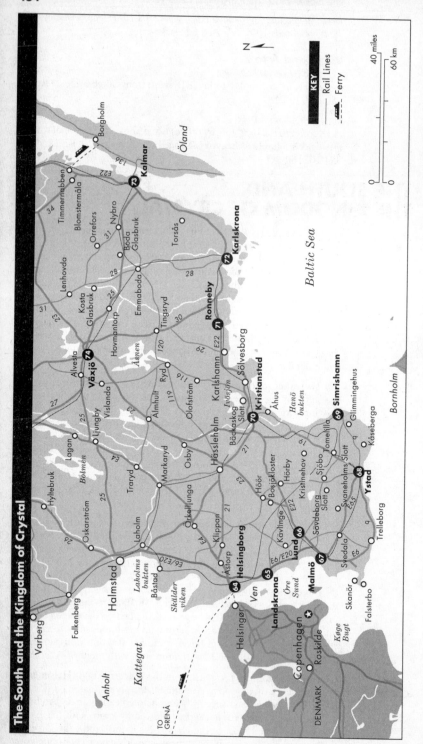

KEY
Rail Lines
Ferry

40 miles
60 km

N

Kattegat

Anholt

Varberg
Falkenberg
Halmstad
Hyltebruk
Oskarström
Laholm
Båstad
Laholms
bukten
Skälder
viken

Bolmen

Lagan
Ljungby
Vislanda
Traryd
Markaryd
Örkelljunga
Klippan
Åstorp
Helsingborg 63
Landskrona 64
Ven
Öre
Sund
Malmö 67
Skanör
Falsterbo
Trelleborg
Svedala

Helsingør
Copenhagen
Roskilde
Köge
Bugt
DENMARK
TO GRENÅ

Hässleholm
Osby
Höör
Hörby
Kävlinge
Lund 66
Sjöbo
Svaneholms Slott
Sövdeborg
Slott
Krageholm
Svedala

Växjö 74
Alvesta
Hovmantorp
Ryd
Almhult
Olofström
Bäckaskog
Slott
Bosjökloster
Ivösjön
Karlshamn
Sölvesborg
Kristianstad 70
Åhus
Kivik
Hanö
bukten
Simrishamn 69
Glimmingehus
Kåseberga
Ystad 68
Tomelilla
Kr’nehov
Sölvesborg

Lenhovda
Kosta
Glasbruk
Emmaboda
Tingsryd
Åsnem

Timmernabben
Blomstermåla
Orrefors
Nybro
Boda
Glasbruk
Torsås
Kalmar 73
Karlskrona 72
Ronneby 71

Borgholm
Öland

Baltic Sea

Bornholm

31
34
28
25
31
27
25
25
23
23
30
29
28
120
119
116
E4
E6/E20
E4
21
21
23
E65
E22
E22
136
136

Helsingborg

🟢 *221 km (137 mi) south of Göteborg; 186 km (115 mi) southwest of Växjö; 64 km (40 mi) north of Malmö.*

Helsingborg (still sometimes spelled the old way, Hälsingborg), with a population of 108,000, seems to the first-time visitor little more than a nondescript ferry terminal (it has connections to Denmark, Norway, and Germany). Actually, it has a rich history, having first been mentioned in 10th-century sagas and since been the site of many battles between the Danes and the Swedes. Together with its twin town, Helsingör (Elsinore in William Shakespeare's *Hamlet*), across the Öresund, it controlled shipping traffic in and out of the Baltic for centuries. Helsingborg was officially incorporated into Sweden in 1658 and totally destroyed in a battle with the Danes in 1710. It was then rebuilt, and Jean-Baptiste Bernadotte, founder of the present Swedish royal dynasty, landed here in 1810.

The Helsingborg **Stadshuset** (Town Hall) has a small museum of exhibits on the city and the region. ✉ *Södra Storgatan 31,* ☎ *042/105963.* 🎫 *SKr10.* ⊙ *May–Aug., Tues.–Sun. noon–5; rest of yr, Tues.–Sun. noon–4.*

All that remains of Helsingborg's castle is **Kärnan** (the Keep). The surviving center tower, built to provide living quarters and defend the medieval castle, is the most remarkable relic of its kind in the north. The interior is divided into several floors, where there are a chapel, a kitchen, and other medieval fittings. It stands in a park and offers fine views over the Öresund from the top. ✉ *Slottshagen,* ☎ *042/105991.* 🎫 *SKr10.* ⊙ *June–Aug., daily 10–7; Apr.–May and Sept., daily 9–4; Oct.–Mar., daily 10–2.*

Sofiero Slott (Sofiero Castle), 5 kilometers (3 miles) outside the town, was, until very recently, a royal summer residence. It opened to the public for the first time in May 1995. Built in 1865 in the Dutch Renaissance style, it has a fine park designed by Crown Princess Margareta. ✉ *Sofierovägen (on the road to Laröd),* ☎ *042/137400.* 🎫 *SKr25.* ⊙ *May–mid-Sept., daily 10–6; guided tours only. Park open year-round.*

The local **tourist office** is at Knutpunkten (☎ 042/120310).

Dining and Lodging

$$$ ✕🏨 **Grand Hotel.** The dining room of one of Sweden's oldest hotels
★ has a longstanding reputation for excellence, with a good selection of wines at reasonable prices. Antiques and fresh flowers fill the hotel, and the well-equipped guest rooms have a TV, VCR, hair dryer, and trouser press. The hotel is conveniently close to the railway station and ferry terminals. ✉ *Stortorget 8–12, S–251 11,* ☎ *042/120170,* 🅵🅰🆇 *042/118833. 115 rooms. Restaurant, bar, no-smoking rooms, sauna, meeting rooms. AE, DC, MC, V.*

$ 🏨 **Villa Thalassa.** This youth hostel has fine views over Öresund. One large building contains 140 bunks in two-, four-, and six-bunk rooms. There are also 12 cottages near the water, each with two bedrooms (with double bed and bunkbed), bathroom with shower, and kitchen. The SKr40 breakfast is not included. ✉ *Dag Hammarskjölds väg, S-254 33,* ☎ *042/210384,* 🅵🅰🆇 *042/128792. 145 beds, 4- to 6-bed rooms (in winter 2-bed rooms also available). Meeting rooms. No credit cards.*

Landskrona

🟢 *26 km (16 mi) south of Helsingborg (via E6/E20); 41 km (25 mi) north of Malmö; 204 km (126 mi) southwest of Växjö.*

The 17th-century Dutch-style fortifications of Landskrona are among the best preserved of their kind in Europe. Though it appears to be just another modern town, Landskrona actually dates from 1413, when it received its charter. In 1888, author Selma Lagerlöf worked at Landskrona's elementary school, where she began her novel *Gösta Berlings Saga*.

Landskrona's **Citadellet** (castle) was built under orders of the Danish king Christian III in 1549 and is all that remains of the original town, which was razed in 1747 on orders of the Swedish Parliament to make way for extended fortifications. The new town was then built on land reclaimed from the sea. ⊠ *Slottsgatan*, ☎ *0418/16980*. ⊡ *SKr20*. ☉ *Early June–late Aug., daily 11–4.*

The local **tourist office** is at Rådhusgatan 3 (☎ 0418/16980).

OFF THE
BEATEN PATH

VEN – From Landskrona Harbor there are regular 25-minute boat trips to the island of Ven (⊡ SKr60 roundtrip; ☉ departures every 90 minutes 6 AM–9 PM). The Danish astronomer Tycho Brahe conducted his pioneering research here from 1576 to 1597. The foundations of his Renaissance castle, **Uranienborg**, can be visited, as can Stjärneborg, his reconstructed observatory. The small **Tycho Brahe Museet** is dedicated to Brahe and his work. ⊠ *Landsvägen, Ven*, ☎ *0418/79557*. ⊡ *SKr10*. ☉ *May–Sept., daily 10–4:30.*

Outdoor Activities and Sports

Three kilometers (2 miles) north of Landskrona lies the **Borstahusen recreation area** (⊠ 261 61 Landskrona, ☎ 0418/10837), with long stretches of beach, a marina, and a holiday village with 74 summer chalets.

Ven is ideal for **camping;** check with the local tourist office (⊠ Landsvägen 2, ☎ 0418/72420) or the Landskrona tourist office (⊠ Rådhusgatan 3, ☎ 0418/16980). There are special paths across Ven for **bicycling;** rentals are available at Bäckviken, the small harbor.

Lund

 34 km (21 mi) southeast of Landskrona (via E6/E20 and Route 16); 25 km (16 mi) northeast of Malmö; 183 km (113 mi) southwest of Växjö.

One of the oldest towns in Europe, Lund was founded in 990. In 1103 Lund became the religious capital of Scandinavia and at one time had 27 churches and 8 monasteries—until King Christian III of Denmark ordered most of them razed to use their stones for the construction of Malmöhus Castle in Malmö. Lund lost its importance until 1666, when its university was established. It is now one of Sweden's two chief university towns and one of the nicest of Swedish towns, having managed to preserve its historic character.

Lund's monumental gray stone Romanesque **cathedral** is the oldest in Scandinavia, consecrated in 1145. Its crypt features 23 finely carved pillars, but its main attraction is an astrological clock, *Horologum Mirabile Lundense* (the miraculous Lund clock), dating from 1380 and restored in 1923. It depicts an amazing pageant of knights jousting on horseback, trumpets blowing a medieval fanfare, and the Magi walking in procession past the Virgin and Child as the organ plays *In Dulci Jubilo*. The clock plays at noon and 3 PM on weekdays and at 1 and 3 PM on Sunday.

One block east of the cathedral is the **Botaniska Trädgården** (Botanical Gardens), which contains 7,500 specimens of plants from all over the world—very pleasant on a summer's day. ⊠ *Östra Vallgatan 20,*

☎ 046/222–7320. ☜ *Free.* ☉ *Gardens daily 6* AM*–8* PM*; greenhouses noon–3.*

Esaias Tegnér, the Swedish poet, lived from 1813 to 1826 in a little house immediately behind the cathedral. The house has since been turned into the **Tegnér Museet,** providing insight into his life and works. ⊠ *Gråbrödersgatan,* ☎ *046/691319.* ☜ *SKr10.* ☉ *First Sun. each month noon–3.*

On the southern side of the main square is **Drottens Kyrkoruin** (the Church Ruins of Drotten), an "underground" museum of Lund's middle ages in the cellar of a modern five-story building. The foundations of three Catholic churches are here: The first and oldest was built of wood in approximately AD 1000. It was torn down to make room for one of stone built in about 1100; this was replaced by a second stone church built around 1300. ⊠ *Kattensund 6,* ☎ *046/141328.* ☜ *SKr10.* ☉ *Tues.–Fri. and Sun. noon–4, Sat. 10–2.*

NEED A BREAK? Drop by **Stortorgets Bar & Restaurant** (⊠ Stortorget, ☎ 046/139290) in the center of town, a great place to watch and meet locals.

☾ **Kulturen** (the Museum of Cultural History) is both an outdoor and an indoor museum, including 20 old cottages, farms, and manor houses from southern Sweden plus an excellent collection of ceramics, textiles, weapons, and furniture. ⊠ *Karolinsplats,* ☎ *046/350400.* ☜ *SKr30.* ☉ *May–Sept., Fri.–Wed. 11–5, Thurs. 11–9; rest of yr, Tues.–Sun. noon–4.*

Lund's **tourist office** is at Kyrkogatan 11 (☎ 046/355040).

Dining and Lodging

$$ ✕ **Fiskaregatan.** In April and October (no fixed date) head chef Lars Fogelholm, backed by an excellent staff, prepares a "gourmet evening" with 10 courses—interrupted by a stroll around town at the halfway stage. A specialty is stuffed breast of pheasant. ⊠ *Lilla Fiskaregatan 11,* ☎ *046/151620. AE, DC, MC, V.*

$$$ ☷ **Djingis Khan.** This English colonial–style Best Western hotel is in a quiet part of town. ⊠ *Margarethevägen 7, S–222 40,* ☎ *046/140060,* FAX *046/143626. 55 rooms. No-smoking rooms, hot tub, sauna, exercise room, bicycles, meeting rooms. AE, DC, MC, V. Closed July.*

$$$ ☷ **Grand.** This elegant red-stone hotel is in the heart of the city, close to the railway station in a pleasant square. Renovated rooms have vintage turn-of-the-century decor and charm. The elegant restaurant offers an alternate vegetarian menu. ⊠ *Bantorget 1, S–221 04,* ☎ *046/2117010,* FAX *046/147301. 80 rooms. Restaurant, no-smoking rooms, hot tub, meeting rooms. AE, DC, MC, V.*

$$$ ☷ **Hotel Lundia.** Only 330 feet from the train station, Hotel Lundia is ideally situated for those who want to be within walking distance of the city center. Built in 1968, the modern, four-story square building has transparent glass walls on the ground floor. Rooms are decorated with Scandinavian fabrics and lithographs. ⊠ *Knut den Stores torg 2, Box 1136, S–221 04,* ☎ *046/124140,* FAX *046/141995. 97 rooms. Restaurant, no-smoking rooms, nightclub, meeting rooms. AE, DC, MC, V.*

$$ ☷ **Concordia.** This center-city Sweden Hotel property is in an elegant former home built in 1890. A 1990 renovation gave the rooms a modern and clean, if somewhat colorless, look. ⊠ *Stålbrogatan 1, S–222 24,* ☎ *046/135050,* FAX *046/137422. 49 rooms. No-smoking rooms, sauna, meeting rooms. AE, DC, MC, V.*

$ 🚉 **STF Vandrarhem Tåget.** So named because of its proximity to the train station (*tåget* means "train"), this youth hostel faces a park in central Lund. ⊠ *Bjerredsparken, Vävareg. 22, S–222 37 Lund,* ☎ *046/ 142820. 108 beds. No credit cards.*

OFF THE BEATEN PATH	**BOSJÖKLOSTER –** About 30 kilometers (19 miles) northeast of Lund via E22 and Route 23, Bosjökloster is an 11th-century, white Gothic castle with lovely grounds on Ringsjön, the second-largest lake in southern Skåne. The castle's original owner donated the estate to the church, which turned it over to the Benedictine order of nuns. They founded a convent school for the daughters of Scandinavian nobility, no longer in existence, and built the convent church with its tower made of sandstone. The 300-acre castle grounds, with a 1,000-year-old oak tree, a network of pathways, a children's park, a rose garden, and an indoor-outdoor restaurant, are ideal for picnics. ⊠ *Höör,* ☎ *0413/25048.* 🎫 *SKr35.* ☉ *Castle grounds May–Oct., daily 8–8. Restaurant and exhibition halls May–Sept., Tues.–Sun. 10–6.*

Malmö

🔞 *25 km (16 mi) southwest of Lund (via E22); 198 km (123 mi) southwest of Växjö.*

Malmö is very different from Lund. Capital of the province of Skåne, with a population of about 250,000, this is Sweden's third-largest city.

The city's castle, **Malmöhus,** completed in 1542, was for many years used as a prison (James Bothwell, husband of Mary, Queen of Scots, was one of its notable inmates). Today it houses a variety of museums, including the City Museum, the Museum of Natural History, and the Art Museum with a collection of Nordic art. Across the street you will find the Science and Technology Museum, the Maritime Museum, and a toy museum. ⊠ *Malmöhusvägen,* ☎ *040/341000.* 🎫 *SKr40.* ☉ *June–Aug., daily 10–4; rest of yr, Tues.–Sun. noon–4.*

⊙ On the far side of the castle grounds from Malmöhus, **Aq-va-kul** is a water park that offers a wide variety of bathing experiences for children and their parents, from water slides to bubble baths. ⊠ *Regementsgatan 24,* ☎ *040/300540.* 🎫 *SKr55 adults.* ☉ *Weekdays 9–9, weekends 9–6; Mon. and Wed. evening adult sessions 7–9:30.*

There's a clutch of tiny red-painted shacks called the **Fiskehodderna** (Fish Shacks), adjoining a dock where the fishing boats come in every morning to unload their catch. The piers, dock, and huts were restored in 1991 and are now a government-protected district. You can buy fresh fish directly from the fishermen Tuesday through Saturday mornings.

In Gamla Staden, the Old Town, look for the **St. Petri Church** on Kalendegatan; dating from the 14th century, it is an impressive example of the Baltic Gothic style, with its distinctive stepped gables. Inside there is a fine Renaissance altar.

Rådhuset (Town Hall), dating from 1546, dominates Stortorget, a huge, cobbled market square in Gamla Staden, and makes an impressive spectacle when illuminated at night. In the center of the square stands an equestrian statue of Karl X, the king who united this part of the country with Sweden in 1658. Off the southeast corner of Stortorget is Lilla Torg, an attractive small cobblestone square surrounded by restored buildings from the 17th and 18th centuries.

The **Museum of Sport** occupies **Baltiska Hallen** next to Malmö Stadium. It traces the history of sports, including soccer and wrestling, from antiquity to the present. ☎ *040/342688.* ☜ *Free.* ☉ *Weekdays 8–4.*

Also downtown, the **Rooseum,** in a turn-of-the-century brick building that was once a power plant, is one of Sweden's most outstanding art museums, with exhibitions of contemporary art and a quality selection of Nordic art. ⊠ *Gasverksgatan 22,* ☎ *040/121716.* ☜ *SKr30.* ☉ *Tues.–Sun. 11–5. Guided tours weekends at 2.*

Malmö's **tourist office** is at Skeppsbron at the Central Station (☎ 040/ 300150).

Dining and Lodging

$$$ ✕ **Årstiderna.** Marie and Wilhelm Pieplow's restaurant (the name means
★ "The Seasons" in Swedish) has a pleasant, intimate atmosphere. It is known for large portions and a good, medium-price wine list. ⊠ *Grynbodsgatan 9,* ☎ *040/230910. AE, DC, MC, V. Closed Sun. and July.*

$$$ ✕ **Johan P.** This extremely popular restaurant specializes in seafood and shellfish prepared in Swedish and Continental styles. White walls and crisp white tablecloths give it an elegant air, which contrasts with the generally casual dress of the customers. An outdoor section opens during the summer. ⊠ *Saluhallen, Lilla Torg,* ☎ *040/971818. AE, DC, MC, V. Closed Sun.*

$$$ ✕ **Kockska Krogen.** In the cellar of a 16th-century house, one of the few in Malmö, this popular restaurant serves internationally influenced Swedish food, such as Dover sole with lobster and chestnuts. Glassware, cutlery, and decor are calculated to re-create a 16th-century atmosphere. ⊠ *Stortorget,* ☎ *040/70320. AE, DC, MC, V.*

$$ ✕ **Anno 1900.** Here is a curiosity: a charming little restaurant located in a former working-class area of Malmö. It is a popular local luncheon place with a cheerful outdoor garden terrace for summer eating. ⊠ *Norra Bulltoftavägen 7,* ☎ *040/184747. Reservations required. AE, MC, V.*

$$ ✕ **B & B.** It stands for *Butik och Bar* (Bar Shop) because of its location in the market hall in central Malmö. There's always good home cooking, and sometimes even entertainment at the piano. The restaurant is extremely popular with a young crowd on weekday nights. ⊠ *Saluhallen, Lilla Torg,* ☎ *040/127120. AE, DC, MC, V.*

$$ ✕ **La Mélisse.** This friendly little restaurant usually gives extremely good value. The special menu, *Kvartersmenyn,* is an excellent bet, with a three-course prix fixe for SKr175. ⊠ *Foreningsgatan 37,* ☎ *040/116816. Reservations advised. AE, DC, MC, V.*

$$ ✕ **Valvet.** Centrally located in the St. Jörgen hotel, this restaurant was expanded in 1992. Although the wine list has been deemphasized, the restaurant still offers good Swedish cuisine with a French accent and excels at grilled meats and fish. ⊠ *Stora Nygatan 35,* ☎ *040/77300. AE, DC, MC, V. Closed Sun. and mid-June–mid-Aug.*

$$$$ ⌂ **Mäster Johan Hotel.** The unpretentious exterior of this Best West-
★ ern hotel disguises a plush and meticulously crafted interior. The 1990 top-to-bottom redesign of a 19th-century building, with the focal point an Italianate atrium breakfast room, is unusually personal in tone for a chain hotel. The rooms are impressive, with exposed Dutch brick walls, recessed lighting, oak floors, Oriental carpets, and French cherrywood furnishings. ⊠ *Mäster Johansgatan 13, S–211 22,* ☎ *040/71560,* ℻ *040/127242. 68 rooms. Breakfast room, no-smoking rooms, room service, sauna, meeting rooms. AE, DC, MC, V.*

$$$$ ⌂ **Radisson SAS Hotel.** Only a five-minute walk from the train station, this modern luxury hotel has rooms decorated in several styles: Scandinavian, Asian, and Italian. There are even special rooms for guests with pets. Service is impeccable. The restaurant serves Scandinavian and Continental cuisine, and there's a cafeteria for quick meals. ⊠ *Östergatan 10, S–211 25,* ☎ *040/239200,* FAX *040/112840. 221 rooms. Restaurant, no-smoking rooms, sauna, exercise room, meeting rooms. AE, DC, MC, V.*

$$$$ 🏨 **Sheraton.** Ultramodern, in steel and glass, the Sheraton opened in 1989. It's the city's only skyscraper—at a modest 20 floors—and it provides excellent views all the way to Copenhagen on a clear day. Rooms are standard Sheraton style. The hotel is connected to the Triangeln shopping center. ⊠ *Triangeln 2, S–200 10,* ☎ *040/74000,* FAX *040/ 232020. 214 rooms. Restaurant, bar, no-smoking rooms, sauna, exercise room, meeting rooms. AE, DC, MC, V.*

$$ 🏨 **Baltzar.** A turn-of-the-century house in central Malmö was converted
★   in 1920 into a small, comfortable hotel. Rooms are modern, with thick carpets. ⊠ *Södergatan 20, S–211 34,* ☎ *040/72005,* FAX *040/ 236375. 41 rooms. No-smoking rooms. AE, DC, MC, V.*

$ 🏨 **Prize Hotel.** In the newly renovated Malmö Harbor area, this low-overhead, minimal-service hotel has small but comfortable rooms equipped with satellite TV, telephone, and radio. The large front entrance and lobby atrium are inventively created out of a narrow strip of empty space between two buildings. Though the hotel doesn't add a surcharge to the telephone bill, it also doesn't include the SKr55 breakfast in the room rate: You get exactly what you pay for. ⊠ *Carlsgatan 10C, S–211 20,* ☎ *040/112511,* FAX *040/112310. 109 rooms. Breakfast room. AE, DC, MC, V.*

OFF THE   **FALSTERBRO AND SKANÖR –** On a tiny peninsula 32 kilometers (20
BEATEN PATH   miles) from Mälmö, at the country's southwesternmost corner, are the idyllic towns of Falsterbo and Skanör, both popular summer resorts. Ornithologists gather at Falsterbo every fall to watch the spectacular migration of hundreds of raptors.

En Route   One of Skåne's outstanding Renaissance strongholds, **Svaneholms Slott** lies 30 kilometers (19 miles) east of Malmö, on E65. First built in 1530 and rebuilt in 1694, the castle today features a museum occupying four floors with sections on the nobility and the peasants. On the grounds are a noted restaurant (Gästgiveri, ☎ 0411/40540), walking paths, and a lake for fishing and rowing. ⊠ *Skurup,* ☎ *0411/40012.* 🎫 *SKr25.* ☺ *May–Aug., Tues.–Sun. 11–5; Sept.–mid-Oct., Wed.–Sun. 11–4.*

OFF THE   **TORUP SLOTT –** Built around 1550 near a beautiful beech forest, Torup
BEATEN PATH   Castle is a great example of the classic, square fortified stronghold. From Malmö, drive 10 kilometers (6 miles) southeast on E65, then head north for another 6 kilometers (3.5 miles) to Torup. ⊠ *Torup.* 🎫 *SKr25.* ☺ *May–Jun., weekends 1–4:30. Group tours available at other times through Malmö Turistbyrå,* ☎ *040–341270.*

Malmö A to Z

Visitors can purchase the **Malmökortet** (Malmö Card), which entitles the holder to, among other benefits, free admission or discounts to most museums, concert halls, nightclubs, theaters, and many shops and restaurants. In June and August, a one-day card costs SKr100, a two-day card costs SKr125, and a three-day card costs SKr150; prices are higher the rest of the year. The cards are available at the tourist office in Malmö.

Ystad

68 *64 km (40 mi) southeast of Malmö (via E65); 205 km (127 mi) southwest of Växjö.*

Ystad was a smuggling center during the Napoleonic Wars and has preserved its medieval character with winding, narrow streets and hundreds of half-timber houses from four or five different centuries. The principal ancient monument is **St. Maria Kyrka,** begun shortly after 1220 as a basilica in the Romanesque style but with later additions. The local **tourist office** is at St. Knuts Torg (☎ 0411/77681).

OFF THE BEATEN PATH

SÖVDEBORG SLOTT – Twenty-one kilometers (13 miles) north of Ystad on Route 13, Sövdeborg Slott (Sövdeborg Castle) is open for tours booked in advance by groups of at least 10. Built in the 16th century and restored in the mid-1840s, the castle, now a private home, consists of three two-story brick buildings and a four-story-high crenellated corner tower. The main attraction is the Stensal (Stone Hall), with its impressive stuccowork ceiling. ⊠ *Sjöbo,* ☎ *0416/16012.* ☞ *SKr50.*

En Route Eighteen kilometers (11 miles) east of Ystad, on the coastal road off of Route 9, is the charming fishing village of Kåseberga. On the hill behind it stand the impressive **Ales stenar** (Ale's stones), an intriguing 251-foot arrangement of 58 Viking stones in the shape of a ship. The stones are still something of a puzzle to anthropologists.

About 28 kilometers (17 miles) east of Ystad and 10 kilometers (6 miles) southwest of Simrishamn just off Route 9, **Glimmingehus** (Glimminge House) is Scandinavia's best-preserved medieval stronghold. Built between 1499 and 1505 to defend the region against invaders, the late-Gothic castle was lived in only briefly. The walls are 8 feet thick at the base, tapering to 6½ feet at the top of the 85-foot-high building. On the grounds are a small museum and a theater. There are concerts and lectures throughout the summer and a medieval festival at the end of August. ⊠ *Hammenhög,* ☎ *0414/32089.* ☞ *SKr30.* ☉ *Apr. and Sept., daily 10–4; May–Aug., daily 9–6; Oct., weekends 11–4.*

Simrishamn

69 *41 km (25 mi) east of Ystad (via Route 9); 105 km (65 mi) east of Malmö; 190 km (118 mi) south of Växjö.*

This bustling fishing village of 25,000 swells to many times that number during the summer. Built in the mid-1100s, the town has cobblestone streets lined with tiny brick houses covered with white stucco. The medieval St. Nicolai's Church, which dominates the town's skyline, was once a landmark for local sailors. Inside are models of sailing ships.

The **Frasses Musik Museum** contains an eclectic collection of music oddities, such as self-playing barrel organs, antique accordions, children's gramophones, and the world's most complete collection of Edison phonographs. ⊠ *Peder Mörksvägen 5,* ☎ *0414/14520.* ☞ *SKr10.* ☉ *Early June–late Aug., Sun. 2–6; July, Sun.–Wed. 2–6.*

En Route If you're in the area between July 1 and mid-August, you might want to stop off at **Kristinehov**—a castle about 8 kilometers (5 miles) west of Brösarp and 35 kilometers (22 miles) north of Simrishamn, via Route 9—where a summer wine festival is presented by a local Swedish wine producer (Åkersson & Sons, ☎ 0417/26215). Known as the pink castle, Kristinehov was built in 1740 by Countess Christina Piper in the late Caroline style. Although closed to the public since 1989, the castle is occasionally used for rock concerts and other summer programs. Check with the **Kristianstad tourist office** (⊠ Stora Torg, ☎ 044/121988) for the schedule.

Kristianstad

⑩ *73 km (45 mi) north of Simrishamn (via Routes 9/19 and E22); 95 km (59 mi) northeast of Malmö (via E22); 126 km (78 mi) south of Växjö.*

Kristianstad was founded by Danish king Christian IV in 1614 as a fortified town to keep the Swedes at bay. Its former ramparts and moats are today wide, tree-lined boulevards. **Holy Trinity Church,** consecrated in 1628, is an excellent example of so-called Christian IV–style architecture.

En Route About 17 kilometers (11 miles) east of Kristianstad is **Bäckaskog Slott** (Bäckaskog Castle), located on a strip of land between two lakes, just north of the E22 highway. Originally founded as a monastery by a French religious order in the 13th century, it was turned into a fortified castle by Danish noblemen during the 16th century and later appropriated by the Swedish government and used as a residence for the cavalry. The castle was a favorite of the Swedish royalty until 1900. ⊠ *Fjälkinge,* ☎ *044/53250.* ⊡ *SKr20.* ☉ *May 15–Aug. 15, daily 10–6; open off-season to groups by appointment.*

Ronneby

⑪ *86 km (53 mi) east of Kristianstad (via E22); 181 km (122 mi) northeast of Malmö; 86 km (53 mi) south of Växjö.*

The spa town of Ronneby has a picturesque waterfall and rapids called **Djupadal,** where a river runs through a cleft in the rock just 5 feet wide but 50 feet deep. There are boat trips on the river each summer. The local **tourist office** is at Kallingevägen 3 (☎ 0457/17650).

Karlskrona

⑫ *111 km (69 mi) east of Kristianstad (via E22); 201 km (125 mi) northeast of Malmö; 107 km (66 mi) southeast of Växjö.*

A small city built on the mainland and five nearby islands, Karlskrona achieved great notoriety in 1981, when a Soviet submarine ran aground a short distance from its naval base. The town dates from 1679, when it was laid out in the Baroque style on the orders of Karl XI. In 1790 it was severely damaged by fire.

The **Admiralitetskyrkan** (Admiralty Church) is Sweden's oldest wooden church. Two other churches, **Holy Trinity** and **Frederiks,** were designed by the 17th-century architect Nicodemus Tessin.

The **Marinmuseum** (Naval Museum), dating from 1752, is one of the oldest museums in Sweden. ⊠ *Admiralitetsslatten,* ☎ *0455/84000.* ⊡ *SKr10.* ☉ *June and Aug., daily 10–4; July, daily 10–6; Sept.–May, daily noon–4.*

The local **tourist office** is at Borgnästoregatan 68 (☎ 0455/83490).

Kalmar

⑬ *91 km (56 mi) north of Karlskrona (via E22); 292 km (191 mi) northeast of Malmö; 109 km (68 mi) east of Växjö.*

The attractive coastal town of Kalmar, opposite the Baltic island of Öland, is dominated by the imposing **Kalmar Slott,** Sweden's best-preserved Renaissance castle, part of which dates from the 12th century. The living rooms, chapel, and dungeon can be visited. ⊠ *Slottsvägen,* ☎ *0480/*

56450. ✉ *SKr40.* ☉ *Mid-June–mid-Aug., Mon.–Sat. 10–6, Sun. noon–6; Apr.–mid-June and mid-Aug.–Oct., weekdays 10–4, weekends noon–4; Sept.–Mar., Sun. 1–3.*

The **Kalmar Läns Museum** (Kalmar District Museum), which has good archaeological and ethnographic collections, contains the remains of the royal ship *Kronan,* which sank in 1676. Consisting primarily of cannons, wood sculptures, and old coins, they were raised from the seabed in 1980. Another exhibit focuses on Jenny Nystrom, a painter famous for popularizing the *tomte,* a rustic Christmas elf. ✉ *Skeppsbrogatan 51,* ☎ *0480/15350.* ✉ *SKr30.* ☉ *Mid-June–mid-Aug., Mon.–Sat. 10–6, Sun. noon–6; rest of yr, Mon.–Tues., Thurs.–Fri. 10–4, Wed. 10–8, weekends noon–4.*

Kalmar's **tourist office** is at Larmgatan 6 (☎ 0480/15350).

Dining and Lodging

$$ ✕⊞ **Stadshotellet.** Located in the city center, Best Western's Stadshotellet is a fairly large hotel with traditional English decor. The main building dates from 1907. Guest rooms are freshly decorated and have hair dryers and radios, among other amenities. There's also a fine restaurant. ✉ *Stortorget 14, S–392 32,* ☎ *0480/15180,* 🆎 *0480/15847. 140 rooms. Restaurant, bar, no-smoking rooms, hot tub, sauna, meeting rooms. AE, DC, MC, V.*

$$$ ⊞ **Slottshotellet.** Occupying a gracious old house on a quiet street, Slottshotellet faces a waterfront park, a few minutes' walk from both the train station and Kalmar Castle. Guest rooms are charmingly individual, with carved-wood bedsteads, old-fashioned chandeliers, pretty wallpaper, wooden floors, and antique furniture. The bathrooms are spotlessly clean. Only breakfast is served year-round, but in summer, full restaurant service is offered on the terrace. ✉ *Slottsvägen 7, S–392 33,* ☎ *0480/88260,* 🆎 *0480/88266. 36 rooms with shower. No-smoking rooms, sauna, meeting room. AE, DC, V.*

Öland

8 km (5 mi) east of Kalmar (via the Ölandsbron bridge).

Linked to the mainland by one of the longest bridges in Europe (6 kilometers [4 miles]), Öland is a limestone plateau 139 kilometers (86 miles) long and 37 kilometers (23 miles) at its widest point. First settled some 4,000 years ago, the island is fringed with fine sandy beaches and is dotted with old windmills and such archaeological remains as the massive stone walls of the 6th-century **Gråborg Fortress,** the 5th-century fortified village of **Eketorp,** and the medieval **Borgholm Castle.** In spring and fall, Öland is a way station for hundreds of species of migrating birds.

The royal family has a summer home at **Solliden** on the outskirts of Borgholm, the principal town, 25 kilometers (16 miles) north of the bridge via Route 136.

Dining and Lodging

$$ ✕⊞ **Halltorps Gästgiveri.** This manor house from the 17th century has modernized duplex rooms decorated in Swedish landscape tones and an excellent restaurant. ✉ *S–387 92 Borgholm,* ☎ *0485/85000,* 🆎 *0485/85001. 35 rooms. Restaurant, no-smoking rooms, 2 saunas, meeting rooms. AE, DC, MC, V.*

OFF THE
BEATEN PATH
COASTAL TOWNS – On the mainland coast opposite Öland, along E22, numerous picturesque seaside towns dot the coastline, such as **Pata-**

holm, with its cobblestone main square, and **Timmernabben,** which is famous for its caramel factory and from which the Borgholm-bound car ferries depart. Miles of clean, attractive, and easily accessible—if windy—beaches line this strip of the coast.

The Kingdom of Crystal

Stretching roughly 109 km (89 mi) between Kalmar and Växjo.

Scattered among the rocky woodlands of Småland province are isolated villages whose names are synonymous with quality in crystal glassware. In the streets of Kosta, Orrefors, Boda, and Strömbergshyttan, red-painted cottages surround the actual factories, which resemble large barns. The region is the home of 16 major glassworks, and visitors may see glass being blown and crystal being etched by skilled craftspeople. *Hyttsil* evenings are also arranged, a revival of an old tradition in which Baltic herring (*sil*) is cooked in the glass furnaces of the *hytt* (literally "hut," but meaning the works). Most glassworks also have shops selling seconds at a discount, and the larger establishments have restrooms and cafeterias.

Fifteen kilometers (9 miles) north of Route 25 on Route 28 is **Kosta Glasburk,** the oldest works, dating from 1742 and named for its founders, Anders Koskull and Georg Bogislaus Stael von Holstein, two former generals. Faced with a dearth of local talent, they initially imported glassblowers from Bohemia. The Kosta works pioneered the production of crystal (to qualify for that label, glass must contain at least 24% lead oxide). On weekends from early May through August, and on weekdays in July, you can watch glassmaking demonstrations. To get to Kosta from Kalmar, drive 49 kilometers (30 miles) west on Route 25, then 14 kilometers (9 miles) north on Route 28. ☎ *0478/ 34500.* ☉ *Weekdays 9–6, Sat. 10–4, Sun. noon–4; late June–early Aug., Sat. 9–4, Sun. 11–4.*

On Route 31, about 18 kilometers (25 miles) east of Kosta, is **Orrefors,** one of the best known of the glass companies. Orrefors came on the scene late—in 1898—but set particularly high artistic standards. The skilled workers in Orrefors dance a slow, delicate minuet as they carry the pieces of red-hot glass back and forth, passing them on rods from hand to hand, blowing and shaping them. The basic procedures and tools are ancient, and the finished product is the result of unusual teamwork, from designer to craftsman to finisher. One of Orrefors's special attractions is a magnificent display of pieces made during the past century; younger visitors will probably be more interested in the cafeteria and playground. ☎ *0481/34000.* ☉ *Aug.–May, weekdays 8–3; June and July, weekdays 8–3, Sat. 10–3, Sun. 11–3.*

Boda Glasbruk, part of the Kosta Boda Company, is just off Route 25, 42 kilometers (26 miles) west of Kalmar. ☎ *0481/24030.* ☉ *Daily 8–3.*

Växjö

⓴ *109 km (68 mi) northwest of Kalmar (via Rte. 25); 198 km (123 mi) northeast of Malmö; 228 km (141 mi) southeast of Göteborg; 446 km (277 mi) southwest of Stockholm.*

Some 10,000 Americans visit this town every year, for it was from this area that their Swedish ancestors set sail in the 19th century. On the second Sunday in August, Växjö celebrates "Minnesota Day": Swedes and Swedish-Americans come together to commemorate their common heritage with American-style square dancing and other festivities. The **Ut-vandrarnas Hus** (Emigrants' House) in the town center tells the story of the migration, when more than a million Swedes—one quarter of the population—departed for the promised land. The museum exhibits provide a vivid sense of the rigorous journey, and an archive room and research center allow American visitors to trace their ancestry. ⊠ *Museum Park, Box 201, S–351 04,* ☏ *0470/20120,* ℻ *0470/39416.* ☉ *Sept.–May, weekdays 9–4; June–Aug., weekdays 9–5, Sat. 11–3, Sun. 1–5.*

The **Småland Museum** has the largest glass collection in northern Europe; it was reopened in summer 1996 after extensive renovation. ⊠ *Södra Jarnvägsgatan 2, S–351 04,* ☏ *0470/45145.* ▦ *SKr30*

Växjö's **tourist office** is at Kronobergsgatan 8 (☏ 0470/41410).

OFF THE
BEATEN PATH **KRONOBERGS SLOTT** – About 5 kilometers (3 miles) north of Växjö, this 14th-century castle ruin lies on the edge of the Helgasjön (Holy Lake). The Småland guerrilla fighter Nils Dacke used the castle as a base in his attacks against the Danish occupiers during the mid-1500s; now it's an idyllic destination. In summer, you can eat waffles from the café under the shade of birch trees or take a lunch or sightseeing cruise around the lake on the toylike *Thor,* Sweden's oldest steamboat. *Castle,* ☏ *0470/ 45145. Boat tours,* ☏ *0470/63000. Tours offered late June–late Aug.* ▦ *Lunch cruise SKr250; 2½-hr canal trip to Årby SKr100; 1-hr around-the-lake trip SKr75.*

Dining and Lodging

$$$ ✕🎴 **Hotel Statt.** Now a Best Western hotel, this conveniently located, traditional property is popular with tour groups. The building dates from 1853, but the rooms themselves are modern. The hotel has a cozy Irish pub and two restaurants. ⊠ *Kungsgatan 6, S-351 04,* ☏ *0470/13400,* ℻ *0470/44837. 130 rooms. 2 restaurants, pub, no-smoking rooms, sauna, exercise room, meeting rooms. AE, DC, MC, V.*

$ 🎴 **Esplanad.** In the center of town, the Esplanad is a small family hotel offering basic amenities. 🎴 *Norra Esplanaden 21A, S-351 04,* ☏ *0470/ 22580,* ℻ *0470/26226. 27 rooms. No-smoking rooms. MC, V.*

The South and the Kingdom of Crystal A to Z

Arriving and Departing

BY BOAT

The most common form of arrival in southern Sweden is by boat. Several regular services run from Copenhagen to Malmö, including Hovercrafts that make the trip in less than an hour, and a bus-ferry service from Copenhagen Station, which also goes to Lund. There are also regular ferry connections to Denmark, Germany, and Poland from such ports as Malmö, Helsingborg, Landskrona, Trelleborg, and Ystad. **Stena Line** (⊠ Kungsgatan 12–14, Stockholm, ☏ 08/141475; Danmarksterminalen, Göteborg, ☏ 031/858000) is one of the major Swedish carriers.

Day-trippers can pick up tickets at Malmö Harbor and catch one of the hourly Copenhagen-bound Hovercrafts operated by the following ferry lines: **Flygbåtarna** (☏ 040/103930), **Pilen** (☏ 040/234411), and **Shopping Linje** (☏ 040/110099). **SFL Skandlines** (☏ 040/362000) runs the only car-ferry service between Dragör, Denmark, and Limhamn, Sweden, a town that adjoins Malmö's southern edge.

A special 48-hour *Öresund Runt* (Around Öresund) pass is available from the Malmö Tourist Office: at SKr149, the ticket covers a train from Malmö to Helsingborg, a ferry to Helsingør, a train to Copenhagen, and a ferry back to Malmö. A similar ticket includes a car ferry crossing between Dragoør and Limhamn one way and Helsingborg and Helsingoør the other way; it costs SKr495.

Malmö is 620 kilometers (384 miles) from Stockholm. Take the E4 freeway to Helsingborg, then the E6/E20 to Malmö and Lund. From Göteborg, take the E6/E20.

Malmö's airport, **Sturup** (☎ 040/613–1100), was opened in 1972. Sturup is approximately 30 kilometers (19 miles) from Malmö and 25 kilometers (16 miles) from Lund. Its only international destination is Amsterdam, served by KLM. Domestic Swedish airlines—SAS and Malmö Aviation—use the Stockholm airports for connections with other domestic destinations, especially SAS, which also makes international connections via Stockholm's Arlanda. The airlines represented include **SAS** (☎ 040/357200 or 020/727000), **KLM** (☎ 040/500530), and **Malmö Aviation** (☎ 040/502900).

SAS offers discounts on trips to Malmö year-round; ask for the "Jackpot" discount package (SKr1,108). Hertz car rentals are available for SKr600 a day on weekends (less during the summer) if you book an SAS flight. For more information, contact SAS (S–161 87 Stockholm, ☎ 020/727000).

Between the Airport and City Center. Buses for Malmö and Lund meet all flights at the Sturup Airport. The price of the trip is SKr55 to either destination. For more information on bus schedules, routes, and fares, call ☎ 020/616161 or the airport at ☎ 040/613–1100.

A **taxi** from the airport to Malmö or Lund costs about SKr200. For SAS **limousine service,** call ☎ 040/500600.

There is regular service from Stockholm to Helsingborg, Lund, and Malmö. The journey takes about 6½ hours. All three railway stations are centrally located.

Getting Around
Roads are extremely well marked and maintained. Traveling around the coast counterclockwise from Helsingborg, you take the E6/E20 to Landskrona, Malmö and Lund, then the E6/E22 to Trelleborg; Route 9 follows the south coast from there to Simrishamn and north until just before Kristianstad, where you pick up E22 all the way through Karlshamn, Ronneby, Karlskrona, and up the east coast to Kalmar. From Kalmar, Route 25 goes fairly directly west through Växjö to Halmstad, on the west coast between Helsingborg and Göteborg.

The major towns of the south are all connected by rail.

Contacts and Resources
For travelers from Denmark who want to rent a car as soon as they arrive, several rental companies have locations at Malmö Harbor, including **Avis** (☎ 040/77830), **Hertz** (☎ 040/74955), and **Europcar/InterRent** (☎ 040/71640).

As elsewhere in Sweden, call ☎ 112 for emergencies.

VISITOR INFORMATION
Skånes Turistråd, the Skåne Tourist Council, is at Skiffervägen 38, Lund (☎ 046/124350). For visitors to Småland, there's a local tourist office in **Jönköping** (✉ Västra Storgatan 18A, ☎ 036/199570) in addition to those listed in the individual towns above.

DALARNA: THE FOLKLORE DISTRICT

Dalarna is considered to be the most typically Swedish of all the country's 24 provinces, a place of forests, mountains, and red-painted wooden farmhouses and cottages by the shores of pristine, sun-dappled lakes. It is the favorite site for midsummer celebrations, in which Swedes don folk costumes and dance to fiddle and accordion music around maypoles garlanded with wildflowers.

Dalarna played a key role in the history of the nation. It was from here that Gustav Vasa recruited the army that freed the country from Danish domination during the 16th century.

The region is also important artistically, both for its tradition of naive religious decoration and for producing two of the nation's best-loved painters, Anders Zorn (1860–1920) and Carl Larsson (1853–1915), and one of its favorite poets, the melancholy, mystical Dan Andersson, who sought inspiration in the remote camps of the old charcoal burners deep in the forest.

As for dining and lodging, do not expect too much in Dalarna. Traditionally, visitors to the area—many from elsewhere in Scandinavia or from Germany—make use either of the region's many well-equipped campsites or of *stugbyar* (small villages of log cabins, with cooking facilities), usually set near lakesides or in forest clearings.

Our itinerary circles Lake Siljan, the largest of the 6,000 lakes in the province and the center of Dalarna's folklore, then crosses east to the coastal town of Gävle. The main points can all be reached by train, except for the southern side of Lake Siljan.

En Route On the route from Stockholm to Dalarna, 158 kilometers (98 miles) from Stockholm and just south of Avesta on Route 70, stands the world's biggest *Dalahäst* (Dala horse), 13 meters (43 feet) tall. The bright orange-red painted monument marks a modern roadside rest stop with a spacious cafeteria and a well-appointed tourist information center.

Falun

⑦⑤ *224 km (139 mi) northwest of Stockholm (via E18 and Rte. 70).*

Falun is the traditional capital of Dalarna, though in recent years the nondescript railway town of Borlänge has grown in importance. Falun's history has always been very much bound to its copper mine. This has been worked since 1230 by Stora Kopparbergs Bergslags AB (today just *Stora*), which claims to be the oldest limited company in the world. Its greatest period of prosperity was the 17th century, when it financed Sweden's "Age of Greatness," and the country became the dominant Baltic power. In 1650, Stora produced a record 3,067 tons of copper; probably as a result of such rapid extraction, 37 years later its mine shafts caved in. Fortunately, the accident was on Midsummer's Day, when most of the miners were off duty, and as a result no one was killed. Today the major part of the mine is an enormous hole in the ground that has become Falun's principal tourist attraction, with its own museum, **Stora Museum.** ☎ *023/711475.* ✇ *Mine SKr55; museum free*

Dalarna

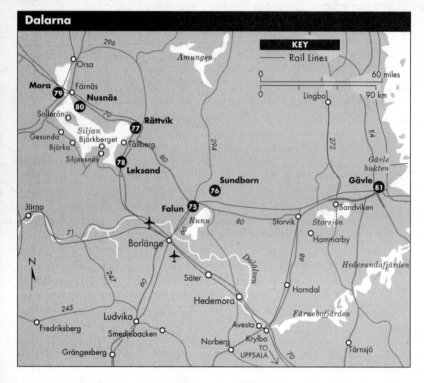

with mine tour. ⊙ *Mine May–Aug., daily 10–4:30; Sept.–mid-Nov., Mar.–Apr., weekends 12:30–4:30. Museum May–Aug., daily 10–4:30; rest of yr, daily 12:30–4:30.*

Lodging

$$$ 🏨 **Bergmästaren.** This small, cozy hotel in the town center is built in
★   traditional Dalarna style and filled with antique furnishings. Some rooms share bathrooms. ✉ *Bergskolegränd 7, S–791 26,* ☎ *023/63600,* FAX *023/22524. 88 rooms. Restaurant, no-smoking rooms, hot tub, sauna, meeting room. AE, DC, MC, V.*

$$$ 🏨 **Grand.** Now part of the First Hotel chain, this conventional, modern hotel is close to the town center. The bright rooms are decorated with Chippendale-style furnishings, and most have a minibar. ✉ *Trotzgatan 9–11, S–791 71,* ☎ *023/18700,* FAX *023/14143. 183 rooms. Restaurant, bar, no-smoking rooms, indoor pool, sauna, exercise room, convention center, parking. AE, DC, MC, V.*

$$$ 🏨 **Scandic.** This ultramodern, Legolike high-rise hotel is located in the expanded Lugnet sports and recreation center outside Falun, where the 1993 World Skiing Championships took place. The comfortable, standard rooms have good views. ✉ *Svärdsjögatan 51, S–791 31 Falun,* ☎ *023/221 60,* FAX *023/12845. 135 rooms. Restaurant, pub, snack bar, no-smoking rooms, indoor pool, sauna, meeting rooms, parking. AE, DC, MC, V.*

$$ 🏨 **Falun.** Rolf Carlsson runs this small, friendly but bland-looking hotel just 1,300 feet from the railway station. Twelve rooms have shared baths and are offered at a lower rate. The front desk closes at 9 PM. ✉ *Centrumhuset, Trotzgatan 16, S–791 30,* ☎ *023/29180,* FAX *023/13006. 27 rooms. No-smoking rooms, meeting rooms. AE, DC, MC, V.*

$ 🏨 **Birgittagården.** This small hotel, 8 kilometers (5 miles) out of town, run by the religious order Stiftelsen Dalarnas Birgitta Systrar (the Dalarna Sisters of Birgitta), is smoke-free, alcohol-free, and set in a fine park. There are no telephones or televisions in the rooms. It is open year-round. ⊠ *Uddnäsvägen, S–791 46,* ☎ *023/32147,* 𝔽𝔸𝕏 *023/32471. 25 rooms. No-smoking rooms, meeting rooms. No credit cards.*

Falun A to Z

Falun's **tourist office** (⊠ Stora Torget, ☎ 023/83637) can arrange for English-speaking guides to Falun and the region around Lake Siljan. The guides cost about SKr850.

Sundborn

🕖 *10 km (6 mi) northeast of Falun (off Rte. 80).*

In this small village you can visit **Carl Larsson Gården,** the lakeside home of the Swedish artist Carl Larsson. Larsson was an excellent drafts-man who painted scenes from his family's busy, domestic life. The house itself was creatively painted and decorated by Larsson's wife, Karin, who was also trained as an artist. Their home's turn-of-the-century fittings and furnishings have been carefully preserved; their great-grand-children still use the house on occasion. ☎ *023/60053 in summer, 023/60069 in winter.* 🖼 *SKr55; guided tours only (can be a 2-hr wait in summer).* ⊙ *May–Sept., daily 10–5; rest of yr, Tues. 11. Off-sea-son visits by advance reservation.*

Rättvik

🕖 *48 km (30 mi) northeast of Falun (via Rte. 80).*

Rättvik is a pleasant town of timbered houses on the eastern tip of Lake Siljan, which is surrounded by wooded slopes. A center for local folk-lore, the town has several shops that sell handmade articles and pro-duce from the surrounding region. Contact the **tourist office** (⊠ Railway Station House, ☎ 0248/70200) for details.

Every year in June, hundreds of people wearing traditional costumes arrive in longboats to attend midsummer services at the town's 14th-century church, **Rättvik Kyrka,** which stands on a promontory stretch-ing into the lake. Its interior contains some fine examples of local naive religious art.

The open-air museum **Rättvik Gammalgård** gives the visitor an idea of the peasant lifestyles of bygone days. Tours in English can be ar-ranged through the Rättvik tourist office. 🖼 *Free; guided tour SKr10.* ⊙ *Mid-June–mid-Aug., daily 11–6; tours at 1 and 2:30.*

Leksand

🕖 *18 km (11 mi) south of Rättvik (via Rte. 70); 66 km (41 mi) north-east of Falun (via Rättvik).*

Thousands of tourists converge on Leksand in June each year for the Midsummer celebrations; they also come in July for *Himlaspelet* (*The Play of the Way That Leads to Heaven*), a traditional musical with an all-local cast, staged outdoors near the town's church. It is easy to get seats for this; ask the local tourist office for details.

Leksand is also an excellent vantage point from which to watch the "church-boat" races on Siljan. These vessels are claimed to be successors to the Viking longboats and were traditionally used to take peasants from outlying regions to church on Sunday. On Midsummer Eve, the longboats, crewed by people in folk costumes, skim the lake. Consult the **tourist office** (⊠ Norsgatan, ☎ 0247/80300) for dates and times.

In the hills around Leksand and elsewhere near Siljan you will find the *fäbodar,* small settlements in the forest where cattle were taken to graze during the summer. Less idyllic memories of bygone days are conjured up by **Käringberget,** a 720-foot-high mountain north of town where alleged witches were burned to death during the 17th century.

En Route From Leksand, drive the small road toward Mora along the southern shores of Siljan, passing through the small communities of Siljansnäs and Björka before stopping at **Gesunda,** a pleasant little village at the foot of a mountain (with a chairlift) from which there are unbeatable views over the lake.

Near Gesunda, **Tomteland** (Santaland) somewhat unconvincingly claims to be the home of Santa Claus, or Father Christmas. Toys are for sale at Santa's workshop and kiosks. There are rides in horse-drawn carriages in summer and sleighs in winter. ⊠ *Gesundaberget, S–792 90, Sollerön,* ☎ *0250/29000.* ⌨ *SKr95.* ☉ *Mid-June–late Aug., daily 10– 5; July, daily 10–6; Dec.–early Jan., call for daily schedule.*

The large island of **Sollerön** is connected to the mainland at Gesunda by bridge, from which there are fine views of the mountains surrounding Siljan. Several excellent bathing places and an interesting Viking gravesite are also here. The church here dates from 1775.

Mora

⑲ *50 km (31 mi) northwest of Leksand; 83 km (51 mi) northwest of Falun (via Rte. 70).*

To get to this pleasant and relaxed lakeside town of 20,000, you can take Route 70 directly from Rättvik along the northern shore of Lake Silja, or follow the lake's southern shore through Leksand and Gesunda to get a good sense of Dalarna.

Mora is best known as the finishing point for the world's longest cross-country ski race, the *Vasalopp,* which begins 90 kilometers (53 miles) away at Sälen, a ski resort close to the Norwegian border. The race commemorates a fundamental piece of Swedish history: the successful attempt by Gustav Vasa in 1521 to rally local peasants to the cause of ridding Sweden of Danish occupation. Vasa, only 21 years old, had fled the capital and described to the Mora locals in graphic detail a massacre of Swedish noblemen ordered by the Danish king Christian in Stockholm's Stortorget. Unfortunately, no one believed him and the dispirited Vasa was forced to abandon his attempts at insurrection and take off on either skis or snowshoes for Norway, where he hoped to evade Christian and go into exile. Just after he left, confirmation reached Mora of the Stockholm bloodbath, and the peasants, already discontented with Danish rule, relented, sending two skiers after Vasa to tell him they would join his cause. The two men caught up with the young nobleman at Sälen. They returned with him to Mora, where an army was recruited. Vasa marched south, defeated the Danes, and became king and the founder of modern Sweden. The commemmorative race, held on the first Sunday in March, attracts thousands of competitors from all over the world. There is a spectacular mass start at Sälen before the field thins out. The finish is eagerly awaited in Mora, though in recent years the number of spectators has fallen, thanks to the often frigid temperatures and the fact that the race is now usually televised live. You can get a comfortable glimpse of the race's history in the **Vasaloppsmuseet,** new in 1995, with its collection of past ski gear and photos, news clippings, and a short film. ⊠ *Vasagatan,* ☎ *0250/39225.* ☒ *SKr30.* ☉ *Mid-May–Aug., daily 10–6; rest of yr, daily 11–5.*

Mora is also known as the home of Anders Zorn (1860–1920), Sweden's leading Impressionist painter, who lived in Stockholm and Paris before returning to his roots here, painting the local scenes for which he is now famous. His former private residence, a large, sumptuous house designed with great originality and taste by the painter himself, has retained the same exquisite furnishings, paintings, and decor it had when he lived there with his wife. The garden, also a Zorn creation, is open to the public. Next door, the **Zorn Museet** (Zorn Museum), built 19 years after the painter's death, contains many of his best works. ⊠ *Vasagatan 36,* ☎ *0250/16560.* ☒ *Museum SKr 25; home SKr 30.* ☉ *Museum mid-May–mid-Sept., Mon.–Sat. 9–5, Sun. 11–5; rest of yr, Mon.–Sat. 10–5, Sun. 1–5. Home: Guided tours only, mid-May–mid-Sept., Mon.–Sat. 10–4, Sun. 11–4; rest of yr, Mon.–Sat. 12:30–4, Sun. 1–4.*

On the south side of town you'll find **Zorns Gammalgård,** a fine collection of old wooden houses from local farms, brought here and donated to Mora by Anders Zorn. One of them was converted in 1995 into the **Textil Kammare,** the first exhibit of Zorn's collection of textiles and period clothing. ⊠ *Yvradsvägen,* ☎ *0250/10454 (summer only).* ☒ *SKr20.* ☉ *June–Aug., daily 11–5.*

Mora's **tourist office** is at Ångbåtskajn (☎ 0250/26550).

Lodging

$$ 🏨 **Kung Gästa.** This modern, reasonably sized hotel is 2 kilometers (1 mile) from the center of town and only 330 feet from the Mora train station. ⊠ *Kristeneberg, S–792 32,* ☎ *0250/15070,* 🖷 *0250/17078. 47 rooms. Restaurant, no-smoking rooms, indoor pool, sauna, exercise room, meeting rooms. AE, DC, MC, V.*

$$ 🏨 **Mora.** A pleasant little hotel, situated in the center of town, 5 kilometers (3 miles) from the airport, the Mora is part of the Best Western chain. Its comfortable rooms are brightly decorated and have minibars and radios. ⊠ *Strandgatan 12, S–792 01,* ☎ *0250/71750,* 🖷 *0250/18981. 138 rooms. Restaurant, bar, no-smoking rooms, indoor pool, sauna, meeting rooms. AE, DC, MC, V.*

$$ 🏨 **Siljan.** Part of the Sweden Hotel group, this small, modern hotel affords views over the lake. Rooms are standard, with radio, television, and wall-to-wall carpeting; most are single rooms with sofa beds. ⊠ *Moragatan 6, S–792 22,* ☎ *0250/13000,* 🖷 *0250/13098. 45 rooms. Restaurant, bar, no-smoking floor, sauna, exercise room, dance club, meeting room. AE, DC, MC, V.*

$ 🏨 **Moraparken.** This modern hotel sits in a park by the banks of the Dala River, not far from the center of town. ⊠ *Parkgarten 1, S–792 25,* ☎ *0250/17800,* 🖷 *0250/18583. 75 rooms. Restaurant, no-smoking rooms, sauna, convention center. AE, DC, MC, V.*

Outdoor Activities and Sports

Dalarna's principal ski resort is **Sälen,** starting point for the Vasalopp, about 80 kilometers (50 miles) west of Mora.

Nusnäs

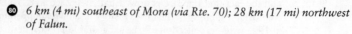

80 *6 km (4 mi) southeast of Mora (via Rte. 70); 28 km (17 mi) northwest of Falun.*

The lakeside village of Nusnäs is where the small, brightly red-painted wooden Dala horses are made. These were originally carved by the peasants of Dalarna as toys for their children, but their popularity rapidly spread with the advent of tourism in the 20th century. Mass production of the little horses started at Nusnäs in 1928. In 1939 they achieved international popularity after being shown at the New York World's Fair, and since then they have become a Swedish symbol—today some of the smaller versions available in Stockholm's tourist shops are even made in East Asia. At Nusnäs you can watch the genuine article being made, now with the aid of modern machinery but still painted by hand. Naturally you'll be able to buy some to take home; shops are open every day except Sunday.

Gävle

81 *176 km (109 mi) east of Mora (via Rtes. 70 and 80); 92 km (57 mi) east of Falun (via Rte. 80).*

The port town of Gävle achieved dubious renown at the time of the Chernobyl nuclear accident in 1986 by briefly becoming the most radioactive place in Europe. A freak storm dumped extralarge amounts of fallout from the Soviet Union on the town. For a while farmers had to burn newly harvested hay and keep their cattle inside. However, the scare soon passed and today one can visit the town in perfect safety. Gävle is worth visiting for two relatively new museums.

The **Joe Hill Museet** (Joe Hill Museum), dedicated to the Swedish emigrant who went on to become America's first well-known protest singer and union organizer, is located in Hill's former home in the oldest section of Gävle. Once a poor, working-class district, ironically this is now the most picturesque and highly sought-after residential part of town, with art studios and handicrafts workshops nearby. The museum, which is furnished in the same style as when Hill lived there, contains very few of his possessions but does display his prison letters. The house itself bears witness to the poor conditions that forced so many Swedes to emigrate to the United States (an estimated 850,000 between 1840 and 1900). Hill, whose original Swedish name was Joel Hägglund, became a founder of the International Workers of the World and was executed for the murder of a Salt Lake City grocer in 1914, but he maintained his innocence right up to the end. ✉ *Nedre Bergsgatan 28,* ☎ *026/613425.* 🎫 *Free.* ⊗ *June–Aug., daily 11–3.*

The **Skogsmuseet Silvanum** (Silvanum Forestry Museum) is on the west end of town, by the river. Silvanum, which is Latin for "The Forest," was inaugurated in 1961; it was the first such museum in the world and remains the largest. The museum provides an in-depth picture of the forestry industry in Sweden, still the backbone of the country's industrial wealth: Trees cover more than 50% of the Sweden's surface area, and forest products account for 20% of national exports. Silvanum includes a forest botanical park and an arboretum that contain examples of every tree and bush growing in Sweden. ✉ *Kungsbäcksvägen 32,* ☎ *026/614100.* 🎫 *Free.* ⊗ *Tues., Thurs.–Fri. 10–4, Wed. 10–9, weekends 1–5.*

Dalarna A to Z

Arriving and Departing

BY BUS

Swebus/Vasatrafik runs tour buses to the area from Stockholm on weekends (☎ 020/656565).

BY CAR

From Stockholm, take E18 to Enköping and follow Route 70 northwest. From Göteborg, take E20 to Örebro and Route 60 north from there.

BY PLANE

Dalarna is served by two airports: Dala at Borlänge and Mora Airport. There are 11 flights daily from Stockholm to **Dala Airport** (☎ 0243/55100). **Mora Airport** is served by Holmström Air (☎ 0250/30175), with 5 flights daily from Stockholm Monday through Friday, fewer on weekends.

Between the Airport and Town. Dala Airport is 8 kilometers (5 miles) from Borlänge, where there are half-hourly bus connections on weekdays to Falun, 26 kilometers (17 miles) away. Mora Airport is 6 kilometers (4 miles) from town.

The 601 **bus** runs every half hour from Dala Airport to Borlänge. The price of the trip is SKr12. There are no buses from Mora Airport.

A **taxi** from Dala Airport to Borlänge costs around SKr90, to Falun approximately SKr200. A taxi into Mora from Mora Airport costs SKr84. Taxis are best ordered in advance through your travel agent or when you make an airline reservation. The Dala–Falun taxi service can also be booked by calling ☎ 0243/229290.

BY TRAIN

There is regular daily train service from Stockholm to both Mora (☎ 0250/94515) and Falun (☎ 023/54210).

Contacts and Resources

CAR RENTALS

Avis has offices in Borlänge (☎ 0243/87080) and Mora (☎ 0250/16711). **Hertz** has offices in Falun (☎ 023/58872) and Mora (☎ 0250/28800). **Europcar/InterRent** has its office in Borlänge (☎ 0243/19050).

DOCTORS AND DENTISTS

Call **Falun Hospital** (☎ 023/82000) or **Mora Hospital** (☎ 0250/25000). There is a 24-hour medical advisory service at ☎ 023/82900.

EMERGENCIES

For emergencies, dial ☎ 112.

LATE-NIGHT PHARMACIES

There are no late-night pharmacies in the area, but doctors called to emergencies can supply medication. **Vasen** pharmacy in Falun (⊠ Åsgatan, ☎ 023/20000) is open until 7 PM weekdays.

VISITOR INFORMATION

In addition to the tourist offices listed in individual towns above, there are offices at **Ludvika** (⊠ Sporthallen, ☎ 0240/86050) and **Sälen** (⊠ Sälen Centrum, ☎ 0280/20250).

NORRLAND AND NORBOTTEN

The north of Sweden, Norrland, is a place of wide-open spaces where the silence is almost audible. Golden eagles soar above snowcapped crags; huge salmon fight their way up wild, tumbling rivers; rare orchids bloom in Arctic heathland; and wild rhododendrons splash the land with color.

In the summer the sun shines at midnight above the Arctic Circle. In the winter it hardly shines at all. The weather changes with bewildering rapidity. A June day can dawn sunny and bright; then the skies may darken and the temperature drop to around zero as a snow squall blows in. Just as suddenly, the sun comes out again and the temperature starts to rise.

Here live the once-nomadic Lapps, or Sami (Same) as they prefer to be known, generally smaller and darker than Swedes, with high cheekbones and slightly slanting eyes. They carefully guard what remains of their identity, while doing their best to inform the public of their culture. Many of the 17,000 Sami who live in Sweden still earn their living herding reindeer, but as open space shrinks, the younger generation is turning in greater numbers toward the attractions of the cities. Often the Sami exhibit a sad resignation to the gradual disappearance of their way of life as the modern world makes incursions. This is best expressed in one of their folk poems: "Our memory, the memory of us vanishes/We forget and we are forgotten."

Yet there is a growing struggle, especially among younger Sami, to maintain their identity, and, thanks to their traditional closeness to nature, they are now finding allies in Sweden's Green movement. They refer to the north of Scandinavia as *Sapmi,* their spiritual and physical home, making no allowance for the different countries that now rule it.

Nearly all Swedish Sami now live in ordinary houses, having abandoned the *kåta* (Lapp wigwam), and some even herd their reindeer with helicopters. Efforts are now being made to protect and preserve their language, which is totally unlike Swedish and bears far greater resemblance to Finnish. The language reflects their closeness to nature. The word *goadnil,* for example, means "a quiet part of the river, free of current, near the bank or beside a rock."

Nowadays many Sami depend on the tourist industry for their living, selling their artifacts, such as expertly carved bone-handled knives, wooden cups and bowls, bark bags, silver jewelry, and leather straps embroidered with pewter thread.

The land that the Sami inhabit is vast. Norrland stretches 1,000 kilometers (620 miles) from south to north, making up more than half of Sweden; its size is comparable to that of Britain. On the west there are mountain ranges, to the east a wild and rocky coastline, and in between boundless forests and moorland. Its towns are often little more than a group of houses along a street, built around a local industry such as mining, forestry, or hydropower utilities. However, thanks to Sweden's excellent transportation infrastructure, Norrland and the northernmost region of Norbotten are no longer inaccessible and even travelers with a limited time schedule can to get at least a taste of the area. Its wild spaces are ideal for open-air holidays. Hiking, climbing, canoeing, river rafting, and fishing are all popular in summer, skiing, skating, and dogsledding in winter.

A word of warning: In summer mosquitoes are a constant nuisance, even worse than in other parts of Sweden, so be sure to bring plenty of repellent. Fall is perhaps the best season to visit Norrland. Roads are well maintained, but watch out for *gupp* (holes) following thaws. Highways are generally traffic-free, but keep an eye out for the occasional reindeer.

Dining and lodging are on the primitive side in this region. Standards of cuisine and service are not nearly as high as prices—but hotels are usually exceptionally clean and staffs scrupulously honest. Accommodations are limited, but the various local tourist offices can supply details of bed-and-breakfasts and holiday villages equipped with housekeeping cabins. The area is also rich in campsites—but with the highly unpredictable climate, this may appeal only to the very hardy.

Norbotten is best discovered from a base in Kiruna, located in the center of the alpine region that has been described as Europe's last wilderness. You can tour south and west to the mountains and national parks, east and south to Sami villages, and farther south still to Baltic coastal settlements.

Kiruna

🔵 *1,239 km (768 mi) north of Stockholm.*

About 145 kilometers (90 miles) north of the Arctic Circle, and 1,670 feet above sea level, Kiruna is the most northerly city in Sweden. Although its inhabitants number only around 26,000, Kiruna is Sweden's largest city, in that it spreads over the equivalent of half the area of Switzerland; indeed, until an Australian community took the claim, Kiruna was often called "the world's biggest city." With 20,000 square kilometers within the municipal limits, Kiruna boasts that it could accommodate the entire world population with 4 square meters of space per person.

Kiruna lies at the eastern end of Lake Luossajärvi, spread over a wide area between two mountains, Luossavaara and Kirunavaara, that are largely composed of iron ore—its raison d'être. Here is the world's largest underground iron mine, with reserves estimated at 500 million tons. Automated mining technology has largely replaced the traditional miner in the Kirunavaara underground mines, which are some 500 kilometers (310 miles) long. Of the city's 26,000 inhabitants, an estimated fifth are Finnish immigrants who came to work in the mine.

The city was established in 1890 as a mining town, but true prosperity came only with the building of the railway to the Baltic port of Luleå and the northern Norwegian port of Narvik in 1902.

Like most of Norrland, Kiruna is full of remarkable contrasts, from the seemingly pitch-black, months-long winter to the summer, when the sun never sets and it is actually possible to play round-the-clock golf for 50 days at a stretch. Here, too, the ancient Sami culture exists side by side with the high-tech culture of cutting-edge satellite research. In recent years the city has diversified its economy and now supports the Esrange Space Range, about 40 kilometers (24 miles) east, which sends rockets and balloons to probe the upper reaches of the earth's atmosphere, and the Swedish Institute of Space Physics, which has pioneered the investigation of the phenomenon of the northern lights. The city received a boost in 1984 with the opening of Nordkalottvägen, a 170-kilometer-long (105-mile-long) road to Narvik.

One of Kiruna's few buildings of interest is **Kiruna Kyrka** (Kiruna Church), on Gruvvägen, near the center of the city. It was built in 1921, its inspiration a blending of a Sami kåta with a Swedish stave church. The altarpiece is by Prince Eugen (1863–1947), Sweden's painter prince.

Kiruna's **tourist office** is at Folkets Hus (☎ 0980/18880).

Lodging

$$$ 🏨 **Ferrum.** Part of the Reso Hotels chain, this late-1960s-vintage hotel is situated near the railway station. Rooms have wall-to-wall carpeting and modern, standard furniture. ✉ *Lars Janssonsgatan, Box 22, S–981 21,* ☎ *0980/18600,* 📠 *0980/14505. 169 rooms. 2 restaurants,*

Norbotten

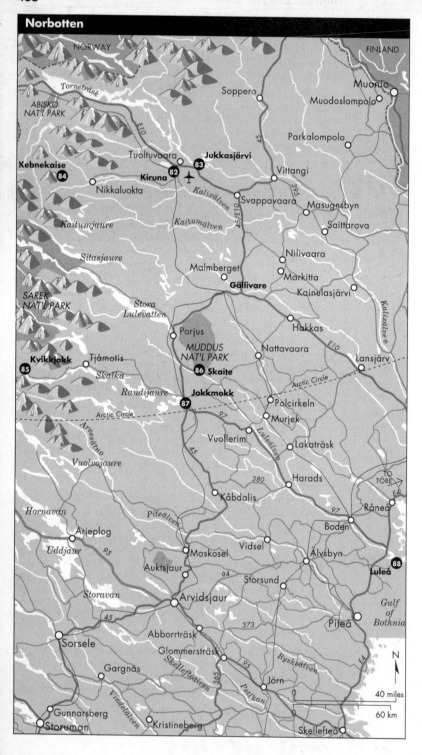

bar, no-smoking rooms, sauna, exercise room, dance club, meeting rooms. AE, DC, MC, V.

$$ ⊞ **Kebne och Kaisa.** These twin modern hotels are close to the railway station and the airport bus stop. Rooms are blandly decorated but modern and comfortable. The restaurant is one of the best in Kiruna; it's open for breakfast and dinner. ⊠ *Konduktörsgatan 7, S–981 34,* ☎ *0980/12380,* FAX *0980/82111. 54 rooms. Restaurant, no-smoking rooms, sauna. AE, DC, MC, V.*

$ ⊞ **Fyra Vindar.** Dating from 1903, this small hotel has the advantage of being close to the railway station. ⊠ *Bangårdsvägen 9, S–981 34,* ☎ *0980/12050. 18 rooms. Restaurant, no-smoking rooms. DC, MC, V.*

$ ⊞ **STF Vandrarhem.** Formerly a hospital for the aged, this modernized, 1926 building now serves as a youth hostel. It faces a large park near the railway station. ⊠ *Skyttegatan 16A, S–981 34,* ☎ *0980/17195 or 0980/12784. 35 2- to 5-bed rooms. Closed mid-Aug.–mid-June. No credit cards.*

En Route Driving south from Kiruna toward Muddus National Park, you'll pass several small former mining villages before coming into the **Kalixälv** (Kalix River) valley, where the countryside becomes more settled, with small farms and fertile meadows replacing the wilder northern landscape.

Jukkasjärvi

83 *16 km (10 mi) east of Kiruna.*

The history of Jukkasjärvi, a Sami village by the shores of the fast-flowing Torneälven (Torne River), dates from 1543, when a market was recorded here. There is a wooden church from the 17th century and a small open-air museum that gives a feeling of Sami life in times gone by.

Here, if you are gastronomically adventuresome, you may sample one of the most unusual of Sami delicacies: *kaffeost,* a cup of thick black coffee with small lumps of goat cheese. After the cheese marinates in the coffee, you fish it out with a spoon and consume it, then drink the coffee. Another challenging local activity is riding the rapids of the Torne River in an inflatable boat. In winter Jukkasjärvi also offers dogsled rides and snowmobile safaris.

Dining and Lodging

$$$ ✕⊞ **Ice Hotel.** At the peak of winter, tourists are drawn by the annual construction of the world's largest igloo, which opens for business as a hotel from December through April, after which it melts away. Made of snow, ice, and sheet metal, the Ice Hotel offers rooms for 40 guests, who spend the night in specially insulated sleeping bags on top of layers of reindeer skins and spruce boughs. The bar is called In the Rocks, and colored electric lights are employed to liven up the solid ice walls. Breakfast is served in the sauna, with a view of the (nonelectric) northern lights. The entire hotel is designated nonsmoking, as it takes only a few puffs to tarnish the snow-white interiors. ⊠ *Marknadsvägen 63, S–981 91 Jukkasjärvi,* ☎ *0980/21190,* FAX *0980/21406. 40 beds (1 bridal suite). Restaurant, bar, sauna, cross-country skiing, snowmobiling, chapel, meeting rooms. AE, DC, MC, V. Closed May–Nov.*

$ ✕⊞ **Jukkasjärvi Wärdshus och Hembygdsgård.** The restaurant spe-
★ cializes in Norrland cuisine and is the lifework of its manager, Yngve Bergqvist. The manor has one large honeymoon suite with wood floors and antique furniture; there are 45 cabins around it, 30 with bathroom, kitchen, and two bedrooms with bunk beds. Fifteen called "camping cabins" are simple shelters that share the use of a common house with toilets, showers, sauna, kitchen, and washing machine. Breakfast is not included. River-rafting and canoeing trips can be arranged. ⊠

Jukkasjärvi, Marknadsvägen 63, S–981 91, ☎ *0980/21190,* 🅵🅰🅷 *0980/21406. 1 suite, 45 cabins. Restaurant, sauna, meeting rooms. AE, DC, MC, V.*

Kebnekaise

84   *85 km (53 mi) west of Kiruna.*

At 7,000 feet above sea level, Kebnekaise is Sweden's highest mountain, but you'll need to be in good physical shape just to get to it. From Kiruna you travel about 66 kilometers (41 miles) west to the Sami village of Nikkaluokta. (There are two buses a day from Kiruna in the summer.) From Nikkaluokta it is a hike of 19 kilometers (12 miles) to the Fjällstationen (mountain station) at the foot of Kebnekaise, though you can take a boat 5 kilometers (3 miles) across Lake Ladtjojaure. Kebnekaise itself is easy to climb in good weather; mountaineering equipment is not necessary. If you feel up to more walking, the track continues past the Kebnekaise Fjällstationen to become part of what is known as Kungsleden (the King's Path), a 500-kilometer (310-mile) trail through the mountains and Abisko National Park to Riksgränsen on the Norwegian border.

Lodging

$ 🏠 **Kebnekaise Fjällstation.** This rustic, wooden mountain station consists of seven separate buildings. Choose between the main building, with its heavy wood beams, wood floors, and wood bunk beds—five per room—and the newer annex, where more modern rooms each contain two or four beds. All guests share the use of a service house, with toilets, men's and women's showers, and sauna. The facility is 19 kilometers (12 miles) from Nikkaloukta and can be reached by footpath, a combination of boat and hiking, or helicopter. Guided mountain tours are available. ✉ *S–981 29 Kiruna,* ☎ *0980/55042,* 🅵🅰🅷 *0980/55048. (Contact Abisko tourist office off-season,* ✉ *S–980 24 Abisko,* ☎ *0980/40200). 200 beds. Restaurant, bar, sauna. AE, V. Closed mid-Aug.–mid-Mar.*

Outdoor Activities and Sports

All the regional tourist offices can supply details of skiing holidays, but never forget the extreme temperatures and weather conditions. For the really adventuresome, the Kebnekaise mountain station offers combined skiing and climbing weeks at SKr3,475. It also offers weeklong combined dogsledding, skiing, and climbing holidays on the mountains, which vary in price from SKr3,995 to SKr4,995. Because of the extreme cold and the danger involved, be sure to have proper equipment. Consult the mountain station well in advance for advice (☎ 0980/55000).

Kvikkjokk and Sarek National Park

85   *310 km (192 mi) southwest of Kiruna (via Rte. 45).*

Sarek is Sweden's largest high mountain area and was molded by the last Ice Age. It totals 487,000 acres, a small portion of which is forest, bogland, and waterways. The remainder is bare mountain. The park has 90 peaks some 6,000 feet above sea level. The mountains have been sculpted by glaciers, of which there are about 100 in the park.

The Rapaätno River, which drains the park, runs through the lovely, desolate Rapadalen (Rapa Valley). There is a surprising variety of landscape, luxuriant green meadows contrasting with the snowy peaks of the mountains. Animals here include elk, bears, wolverines, lynx, ermines, hare, Arctic foxes, red foxes, and mountain lemmings. Birdlife includes ptarmigan, willow grouse, teal, wigeon, tufted ducks, bluethroat, and warblers. Golden eagles, rough-legged buzzards, and merlins have been spotted here as well.

Visiting Sarek demands a good knowledge of mountains and a familiarity with the outdoors. The park can be dangerous in winter because of avalanches and snowstorms. However, in summer, despite its unpredictable, often inhospitable climate, the attracts large numbers of experienced hikers. At Kvikkjokk, hikers can choose between a trail through the Tarradalen (Tarra Valley), which divides the Sarek from the Padjelanta National Park to the west, or part of the Kungsleden trail, which crosses about 15 kilometers (9 miles) of Sarek's southeastern corner.

Skaite and Muddus National Park

86 *192 km (110 mi) south of Kiruna south of Kiruna (via E10 and Rte. 45).*

Established in 1942, Muddus Park is less mountainous and spectacular than Sarek, its 121,770 acres comprising mainly virgin coniferous forest, some of whose trees may be up to 600 years old. The park's 3,680 acres of water are composed primarily of two huge lakes at the center of the park and the Muddusjåkkå River, which tumbles spectacularly through a gorge with 330-foot-high sheer rock walls and includes a 140-foot-high waterfall. The highest point of Muddus is Sör-Stubba mountain, 2,158 feet above sea level. From Skaite, where you enter the park, a series of well-marked trails begins. There are four well-equipped overnight communal rest huts and two tourist cabins. The park shelters bears, elk, lynx, wolverines, moose, ermines, weasels, otters, and many bird species. A popular pastime is picking cloudberries in autumn.

The nearest **tourist office** is in the nearby town of Gällivare (✉ Storgatan 16, ☎ 0970/16660).

Jokkmokk

87 *205 km (127 mi) south of Kiruna (via E10 and Rte. 45).*

Jokkmokk is an important center of Sami culture. Each February it is the scene of the region's largest market, nowadays an odd event featuring everything from stalls selling frozen reindeer meat to Sami handcrafted wooden utensils.

Jokkmokk makes perhaps the best base in Norrland for the outdoor vacationer. The village has three campsites and is surrounded by wilderness. The local tourist office sells fishing permits, which cost SKr50 for 24 hours, SKr100 for 3 days, SKr 150 for 1 week, and SKr300 for the entire year. The office can also supply lists of camping and housekeeping cabins.

The local **tourist office** is at Stortorget 4 (☎ 0971/12140 or 0971/17257).

Lodging

$$$ ⊞ **Hotel Jokkmokk.** A modern hotel of this level of luxury seems incongruous in this remote region but is welcome nevertheless. Rooms are carpeted, and six of them are designated as "Ladies' Rooms," meaning they are all pastels and florals. The hotel is in the center of town but can arrange dogsled rides and helicopter trips to the Sarek and Muddus national parks, and there is excellent fishing nearby. ✉ *Solgatan 45, S–962 23, ☎ 0971/55320, ℻ 0971/55625. 75 rooms. Restaurant, no-smoking rooms, indoor pool, sauna, meeting rooms. AE, DC, MC, V.*

$ ▦ **Gästis.** This small hotel in central Jokkmokk was opened in 1915. Rooms are standard, with television, shower, and either carpeted or vinyl floors. ✉ *Herrevägen 1, S–962 31,* ☎ *0971/10012,* ℻ *0971/10044. 30 rooms. Restaurant, no-smoking rooms, sauna, meeting rooms. AE, DC, MC, V.*

$ ▦ **Jokkmokks Turistcenter.** This complex is in a pleasant forest area, near Luleälven, 3 kilometers (2 miles) from the railway station. Rooms have bunk beds, a small table, and chairs; showers, toilets, and a common cooking area are in the hall. ✉ *Box 75, S–962 22,* ☎ *0971/12370,* ℻ *0971/12476. 26 rooms, 84 cabins. 4 outdoor pools, sauna, meeting rooms. MC, V.*

En Route   One hundred thirty kilometers (81 miles) southeast of Jokkmokk on Route 97 is Boden, the nation's largest garrison town; it dates from 1809, when Sweden lost Finland to Russia and feared an invasion of its own territory. The **Garnisonsmuseet** (Garrison Museum), contains exhibits from Swedish military history, with an extensive collection of weapons and uniforms. ✉ *Garnisonsmuseet, Sveavägen 10, Boden,* ☎ *0921/68399.* ▦ *Free.* ☉ *Mid-June–late Aug., Tues.–Sat. 11–4, Sun. 1–4.*

Luleå

88   *340 km (211 mi) southeast of Kiruna (via E10 and E4).*

The most northerly major town in Sweden, Luleå is an important port at the top of the Gulf of Bothnia, at the mouth of the Luleälv (Lule River). The town was some 10 kilometers (6 miles) farther inland when it was first granted its charter in 1621, but by 1649 trade had grown so much that it was moved closer to the sea. The development of Kiruna and the iron trade is linked, by means of a railway, with the fortunes of Luleå, where a steelworks was set up in the 1940s. Like its fellow port towns (Piteå, Skellefteå, Umeå, and Sundsvall) farther south, Luleå is a very modern and nondescript city, but it has some reasonable hotels. It also boasts a beautiful archipelago of hundreds of islands.

The **Norrbottens Museet** (Norbotten Museum) has one of the best collections of Sami ethnography in the world. ✉ *Hermelinsparken 2,* ☎ *0920/220355.* ▦ *Free.* ☉ *Mid-June–mid-Aug., Thurs.–Tues. (previously said daily) 10–6, Wed. 10–8.*

Luleå's **tourist office** is at Kulturcentrum Ebeneser (☎ 0920/293500).

Dining and Lodging

$$$ ✕▦ **Arctic.** Right in the center of town, the Arctic is renowned locally for its restaurant. ✉ *Sandviksgatan 80, S–972 34,* ☎ *0920/10980,* ℻ *0920/60980. 94 rooms. Restaurant, no-smoking rooms, hot tub, sauna, meeting rooms. AE, DC, MC, V.*

$$$$ ▦ **Luleå Hotel (Radisson SAS).** As you might expect of an SAS hotel, this one is large, modern, and centrally situated. Each floor has a different decor: Choose between the third floor, done in blue tones; the second floor, decorated in Eznglish colonial style, with ceiling fans and dried flowers; and the ground floor, with art deco decor. ✉ *Storgatan 17, S–971 28,* ☎ *0920/94000,* ℻ *0920/88222. 216 rooms. Restaurant, no-smoking rooms, indoor pool, sauna, exercise room, nightclub, meeting rooms. AE, DC, MC, V.*

$$$$ ▦ **Luleå Stads Hotell.** This large, centrally located Best Western hotel has nightly, sometimes rowdy dancing. Rooms are spacious and carpeted, with turn-of-the-century furnishings (the building dates back to 1901). ✉ *Storgatan 15, S–972 32,* ☎ *0920/67000,* ℻ *0920/67092.*

135 rooms, 3 suites. Restaurant, café, no-smoking rooms, sauna, dance club, meeting rooms. AE, DC, MC, V.

$$$ ⌂ **Scandic.** This hotel, located on Lake Sjö, has an extremely pleasant location and is also 2 kilometers (1 mile) from the railway station. ✉ *Banvägen 3, S–973 46,* ☎ *0920/228360,* FAX *0920/69472. 157 rooms. Restaurant, no-smoking rooms, indoor pool, sauna, exercise room, meeting rooms. AE, DC, MC, V.*

$$ ⌂ **Amber.** A particularly fine old building, listed on the historic register, houses this hotel close to the railway station. Rooms are modern, with plush carpeting, minibars, and satellite television. ✉ *Stationsgatan 67, S–972 34,* ☎ *0920/10200,* FAX *0920/87906. 16 rooms. No-smoking rooms. AE, DC, MC, V.*

$$ ⌂ **Aveny.** Rooms are of varying sizes and colors, but all are spotless and fresh. It's close to the railway station. ✉ *Hermelinsgatan 10, S–973 46,* ☎ *0920/221820,* FAX *0920/220122. 24 rooms. No-smoking rooms. AE, DC, MC, V.*

Norrland and Norbotten A to Z

Arriving and Departing

BY PLANE
There are two nonstop SAS flights a day from Stockholm to **Kiruna Airport** (☎ 0980/12410) and three additional flights via Luleå. Check SAS (☎ 0980/83100) for specific times.

Between the Airport and Town: It is 5 kilometers (3 miles) from the airport to the center of Kiruna. In summer, **buses** connect with the flights from Stockholm. The fare is about SKr40. A **taxi** from the airport to the center of Kiruna costs SKr67; book through the airline or by calling ☎ 0980/12020.

BY TRAIN
The best and cheapest way to get to Kiruna is to take the evening sleeper from Stockholm on a Tuesday, Wednesday, or Saturday, when the fare is reduced to SKr554 single. The regular one-way price is SKr645 plus SKr85 for the couchette, double for return. You'll arrive at around lunchtime the next day.

Getting Around
Since public transportation is nonexistent in this part of the country, having a car can save the traveler a great deal of time. The few roads are well built and maintained, although spring thaws can present unexpected potholes. Keep in mind that habitations are very few and far between in this wilderness region.

CAR RENTALS
In Kiruna **Avis** has a branch in the Hotel Ferrum (☎ 0980/13080). **Hertz** is at Industrivägen 5 (☎ 0980/19000). **Europcar/InterRent** is at Växlaregatan 20 (☎ 0980/14365).

Contacts and Resources

DOCTORS AND DENTISTS
You can call **Kiruna Health Center** (✉ Thulegatan 29, ☎ 0980/73000), the medical advisory service in **Luleå** (☎ 0920/71400), or the **Jokkmokk Health Center** (✉ Lappstavägen 9, ☎ 0971/44444).

EMERGENCIES
For emergencies dial ☎ 112.

GUIDED TOURS
Local tourist offices have information on guided tours. For tours of Sami villages and holy places, contact the **Swedish Same Association** (✉ Brogatan 5, S–90325, Umeå, ☎ 090/141180). **Same Lans Resor**

(✉ c/o Rental Line I Jokkmok, Hermelinsgatan 20, 962 33, Jokkmok, ☎ 0971/10606) arranges tours to points of interest in Lappland.

There are no late-night pharmacies in Norbotten, but doctors called to emergencies can supply medicines. The pharmacy at the Gallerian shopping center in Kiruna (✉ Föreningsgatan 6, ☎ 0980/18775) is open weekdays 9:30–6 and Saturdays 9:30–1.

Norrbottens Turistråd (✉ Stationsgatan 69, Luleå, ☎ 0920/94070) covers the entire area.

SWEDEN A TO Z

Arriving and Departing

By Car and Ferry

There are excellent links between Harwich and Göteborg and Newcastle and Göteborg aboard **Scandinavian Seaways** ferries (✉ Scandinavian Seaways, DFDS Ltd., Scandinavia House, Parkeston Quay, Harwich, Essex, CO12 4QG, England, ☎ 01255/240–240). An alternate approach is through Denmark, using ferry crossings to Malmö or Helsingborg.

By Plane

Stockholm's Arlanda Airport and Göteborg's Landvetter Airport are served by SAS (☎ 800/221–2350 in the U.S., ☎ 0171/734–4020 in the U.K.), British Airways (☎ 0181/897–4000 in the U.K.), American, TWA, and other major international airlines.

By Train

From London, the **British Rail European Travel Center** (✉ Victoria Station, London, ☎ 0171/834–2345) can be helpful in arranging connections to Sweden's SJ (Statens Järnvägar).

Getting Around

By Boat

An excellent way of seeing Sweden is from the many ferry boats that ply the archipelagoes and main lakes. In Stockholm, visitors should buy a special *båtluffarkort*. This gives unlimited travel on the white archipelago ferry boats for a 16-day period and is available at ferry ticket offices.

Highly popular four-day cruises are available on the Göta Canal, which makes use of rivers, lakes, and, on its last lap, the Baltic Sea. This lovely waterway, which links Göteborg on the west coast with Stockholm on the east, has a total of 65 locks, and you travel on fine old steamers, some of which date almost from the canal's opening in 1832. The oldest and most desirable is the *Juno,* built in 1874. Prices start at SKr5,700 for a bed in a double cabin. For more information, contact the **Göta Canal Steamship Company** (✉ Box 272, S–401 24 Göteborg, ☎ 031/806315, ℻ 031/158311).

By Bus

There is excellent bus service between all major towns and cities. Consult the Yellow Pages under *Bussresearrangörer* for the telephone numbers of the companies concerned. Recommended are the services offered to different parts of Sweden from Stockholm by **Swebus** (✉ Cityterminalen, Klarabergsviadukten 72, ☎ 020/640640).

By Car

Sweden has an excellent highway network of more than 80,000 kilometers (50,000 miles). The fastest routes are those with numbers prefixed with an *E* (for "European"), some of which are the equivalent of American highways or British motorways. All main and secondary roads are well surfaced, but some minor roads, particularly in the north, are gravel. If you plan on extensive road touring, consider buying the *Vägatlas över Sverige,* a detailed road atlas published by the Mötormännens Riksförbund, available at bookstores for around SKr240.

RULES OF THE ROAD

Drive on the right, and, no matter where you sit in a car, seat belts are mandatory. You must also have at least low-beam headlights on at all times. Signs indicate five basic speed limits, ranging from 30 kph (19 mph) in school or playground areas to 110 kph (69 mph) on long stretches of *E* roads.

BREAKDOWNS

The **Larmtjänst** organization, run by a confederation of Swedish insurance companies, provides a 24-hour breakdown service. Its phone numbers are listed in all telephone books. A toll-free emergency number, ☎ 020/ 910040, is also available.

GASOLINE

Sweden has some of the highest gasoline rates in Europe, about SKr 7.85 per liter. Lead-free gasoline is readily available. Gas stations are self-service: Pumps marked SEDEL are automatic and accept SKr20 and SKr100 bills; pumps marked KASSA are paid for at the cashier; the KONTO pumps are for customers with Swedish gas credit cards.

PARKING

Parking meters and, increasingly, timed ticket machines, operate in larger towns, usually between 8 AM and 6 PM. The fee varies from about SKr4 to SKr20 per hour. Parking garages in urban areas are mostly automated, often with machines that accept credit cards; LEDIGT on a garage sign means space is available.

By Plane

All major cities and towns are linked with regular flights by **Scandinavian Airlines System (SAS).** Most Swedish airports are located a long way from city centers but are served by fast and efficient bus services. SAS also operates a limousine service at leading airports. For more information, contact SAS (☎ 797–4175).

By Train

Statens Järnvägar, or SJ, the state railway company, has a highly efficient network of comfortable, electric rains. On nearly all long-distance routes there are buffet cars and, on overnight trips, sleeping cars and couchettes in both first and second class. Seat reservations are advisable, and on some trains—indicated with *R, IN,* or *IC* on the timetable—they are compulsory. An extra fee of SKr15 is charged to reserve a seat on a trip of less than 150 kilometers (93 miles); on longer trips there is no extra charge. Reservations can be made right up to departure time (☎ 020/757575). The high-speed X2000 train has been introduced on several routes; the Stockholm–Göteborg run takes just under three hours. Travelers under 19 travel at half-fare. Up to two children under 12 may travel free if accompanied by an adult. For more information, contact SJ (✉ Central Station, Vasagatan 1, ☎ 08/762–2000 or 020/757575).

For SKr150 you can buy a **Reslustkort,** which gets you 50% reductions on *röda avgångar* ("Red," or off-peak, departures).

The **ScanRail Pass** allows unlimited travel in Scandinavia. Two versions of the pass are available in Sweden, for unlimited 21-day travel and for 5 travel days within a 15-day period. The 21-day pass costs SKr3,000 first-class and SKr2,250 second-class for adults over 25, SKr2,250 first-class and SKr1,700 second-class for ages 12–25, and SKr1,500 first-class and SKr1,125 second-class for children 4–11. The 5-day pass runs SKr1,850 first-class and SKr1,550 second-class for adults over 25, SKr1,400 first-class and SKr1,150 second-class for ages 12–25, and SKr925 first-class and SKr775 second-class for children 4–11. Children under 4 travel free (a small fee is charged if seats are reserved for them).

The **Eurail and InterRail** passes are both valid in Sweden. SJ also organizes reduced-cost package trips in conjunction with local tourist offices. Details are available at any railway station or from SJ (☞ *above*).

Contacts and Resources

Camping
There are 760 registered campsites nationwide, many located close to uncrowded bathing places and with fishing, boating, or canoeing; they may also offer bicycle rentals. Prices range from SKr60 to SKr110 per 24-hour period. Many campsites also offer accommodations in log cabins at various prices, depending on the facilities offered, and some have special facilities for guests with disabilities. Most are open between June and September, but about 200 remain open in winter for skiing and skating enthusiasts. **Sveriges Campingvärdarnas Riksförbund** (SCR, ⊠ Box 255, S–451 17 Uddevalla, ☎ 0522/39345, FAX 0522/33849), the Swedish Campsite Owners' Association, publishes, in English, an abbreviated list of sites; contact the office for a free copy.

Car Rentals
Major car-rental companies such as Avis, Hertz, Europcar/InterRent, Bonus, Budget, and OK have facilities in all major towns and cities as well as at airports. It is worth shopping around for special rates. The various service-station companies also offer car rentals, including Shell, Statoil, Texaco, and Q8. See the Yellow Pages under *Biluthyrning* for telephone numbers and addresses.

Emergencies
Anywhere in Sweden, dial ☎ 112 for emergency assistance.

Guided Tours

EuroCruises (⊠ Box 30925, New York, NY 10011, ☎ 212/691–2099) offers cruises to Sweden from Amsterdam, Helsinki, St. Petersburg, Newcastle, North Cape, Tallinn, and Turku. **Scandinavian Seaways** (⊠ Crown Place, Suite 212, 6499 N.W. 9th Ave., Ft. Lauderdale, FL 33309, ☎ 800/533–3755, and Parkeston Quay, Harwich, England, ☎ 0255/240–240) offers overnight crossings to Sweden from England and Holland.

Cole Travel Service Inc. (⊠ 310 W. State St., Geneva, IL 60134, ☎ 312/232–4450) can arrange bed-and-breakfast holidays at 200 hotels, inns, and guest houses at 130 locations in Sweden. **Scantours Inc.** (⊠ 1535 6th St., Suite 205, Santa Monica, CA 90401, ☎ 213/451–0911) can prepare independent packages, escorted tours, and group travel.

Scandinavian American World Tours, Inc. (⌧ 795 Franklin Ave., Franklin Lakes, NJ 07417, ☏ 201/891–6641) offers deluxe, first-class, and escorted tours. **Bennett Tours** (⌧ 270 Madison Ave., New York, NY 10016, ☏ 800/221–2420) offers tours of Scandinavia. **Watling Sweden** (⌧ 91–93, Cranbrook Rd., Ilford, Essex, England, ☏ 0181/553–3883) offers chalet holidays for the family. **Swedish Chalets** (⌧ 28 Hillcrest Rd., Orpington, Kent, BR6 9AW, England, ☏ 689/24958) is another chalet-holiday agency. **Star Tour of Scandinavia** (⌧ 209 Edgware Rd., London W2 1ES, ☏ 0171/706–2520) offers low-cost charter flights from the United Kingdom. **Scanscape Holidays** (⌧ Hillgate House, 13 Hillgate St., London W8 7SP, ☏ 0171/221–3244) is another charter-flight agency based in Britain. **Anglers World** (⌧ 46 Knifesmith Gate, Chesterfield, Derbyshire, England, ☏ 246/221717) runs holidays for fishing enthusiasts in Sweden.

Language

Swedish is closely related to Danish and Norwegian. After "z," the Swedish alphabet has three extra letters, "å," "ä," and "ö," something to bear in mind when using the phone book. Another oddity in the phone book is that *v* and *w* are interchangeable; Wittström, for example, comes before Vittviks, not after. Most Swedes speak English.

Mail

Postcards and letters up to 20 grams can be mailed for SKr6 to destinations within Europe, SKr7.50 to the United States and the rest of the world.

Money and Expenses

The unit of currency is the krona (plural kronor), which is divided into 100 öre and is written as SKr. The 10-öre coin was phased out in 1991, leaving only the 50-öre, SKr1, and SKr5 coins. These have recently been joined by an SKr10 coin. Bank notes are at present SKr20, 50, 100, 500, and 1,000. At press time (winter 1996), the exchange rate was SKr6.19 to the dollar, SKr10.27 to the pound, and SKr4.6 to the Canadian dollar.

BANK CARDS

The 1,000 or so blue **Bankomat** cash dispensers nationwide have been adapted to take some foreign cards, including MasterCard and bank cards linked to the Cirrus network. For more information, contact Bankomat Centralen, ☏ 08/7257240, or your local bank. There are American Express cash and traveler's check dispensers at Arlanda, Stockholm's international airport, and outside the American Express office at Birger Jarlsgatan 1, Stockholm. American Express also has a Swedish toll-free number (☏ 020/793211) that connects you with a customer service representative in the U.S.

SAMPLE PRICES

Some sample prices: cup of coffee, SKr15–20; a beer, SKr30–SKr45; mineral water, SKr10–SKr20; cheese roll, SKr20–40; pepper steak, à la carte, SKr120–SKr160; cheeseburger, SKr40; pizza, starting at SKr40.

TAXES

All hotel, restaurant, and departure taxes and VAT (called *moms* all over Scandinavia) are automatically included in prices. VAT is 25%; non-EU residents can obtain a 15% refund on goods of SKr 200 or more. In order to receive your refund at any of the 15,000 stores that participate in the tax-free program, you'll be asked to fill out a form and show your passport. The form can then be turned in at any airport or ferry customs desk. Keep all your receipts and tags; occasionally, customs authorities ask to see your purchases, so pack them where they will be accessible.

TIPPING

In addition to the 12% value-added tax, most hotels usually include a service charge of 15%; it is not necessary to tip unless you have received extra services. Similarly, a service charge of 13% is usually included in restaurant bills. It is a custom, however, to leave small change when buying drinks. Taxi drivers and hairdressers expect a tip of about 10%.

Opening and Closing Times

Banks are open weekdays 9:30 AM to 3 PM, but some stay open until 5:30 on most days. The bank at Arlanda Airport is open every day with extended hours, and the Forex and Valuta Specialisten currency-exchange offices also have extended hours.

The opening times for museums vary widely, but most are open from 10 AM to 4 PM weekdays and over the weekend but are closed on Monday. Consult the guide in *På Stan,* the entertainment supplement published in *Dagens Nyheter's* Friday edition, or *Stockholm This Week.*

Shops are generally open weekdays from 9 AM, 9:30 AM, or 10 AM until 6 PM and Saturday from 9 AM to 1 or 4 PM. Most of the large department stores stay open later in the evenings, and some open on Sunday. Several supermarkets open on Sunday, and there are a number of late-night food shops.

Outdoor Activities and Sports

BICYCLING

Rental costs average around SKr80 per day. Tourist offices and **Svenska Turistförening** (STF; the Swedish Touring Association) (✉ Kungsgatan 2, Box 25, S101 20 Stockholm, ☎ 08/4632100, FAX 08/201332) have information about cycling package holidays that include bike rentals, overnight accommodations, and meals. The bicycling organization, **Cykelfrämjandet** (✉ Torsgatan 31, Box 6027, S–102 31 Stockholm, ☎ 08/321680, FAX 08/310503), publishes a free English-language guide to cycling trips.

BOATING AND SAILING

STF, in cooperation with Telia (Sweden's PTT—Postal, Telephone, and Telegraph authority), publishes an annual guide in Swedish to all the country's marinas. It is available from **Telemedia** (☎ 08/6341700) or in your nearest Telebutik. The **Swedish Canoeing Association** (Svenska Kanotförbundet, ✉ *Skeppsbron 11, 611 35 Nyköping,* ☎ *0155/69508) publishes a similar booklet for canoeists.*

GOLFING

Sweden has 365 golf clubs; you can even play by the light of the midnight sun at Boden in the far north. The **Swedish Golfing Association** (Svenska Golfförbundet, ✉ *Box 84, S–182 11 Danderyd,* ☎ 08/622–1500, FAX *08/7558439) publishes an annual guide in Swedish; it costs around SKr80, including postage.*

SKIING

There are plenty of both downhill and cross-country facilities. The best-known resorts are in the country's western mountains: Åre in the north, with 29 lifts; Idre Fjäll, to the south of Åre, offering accommodations for 10,000; and Sälen in the folklore region of Dalarna. You can ski through May at Riksgränsen in the far north.

TENNIS

Contact the **Swedish Tennis Association** (Svenska Tennisförbundet, ⊠ *Lidingövägen 75, Box 27915, S–115 94 Stockholm,* ☎ *08/667–9770,* FAX *08/664–6606).*

Telephones

Post offices do not have telephone facilities, but there are plenty of pay phones, and long-distance calls can be made from special telegraph offices called *Telebutik,* or marked "Tele." You can also purchase a **Telefonkort** (telephone card) from a Telebutik, Pressbyrån (large blue-and-yellow newsstands), or hospital for SKr30, SKr50, or SKr95, which works out to be cheaper if you're making numerous domestic calls. Most of the pay phones in downtown Stockholm and Göteborg take only these cards, so it's a good idea to carry one.

INTERNATIONAL CALLS

The foreign dialing code is 009, followed by the country code, then the number you require. Sweden's country code is 46. The **AT&T USA Direct** access code is 020–795–611. The **MCI call-USA** access code is 020–795–922.

LOCAL CALLS

Public phones are of three types: One takes SKr1 and SKr5 coins; another takes only credit cards; and the last, most common type, takes only the prepaid Telefonkort. A local call costs a minimum of SKr2. For calls outside the locality, dial the area code.

OPERATORS AND INFORMATION

For international calls, the operator assistance number is ☎ 0018; directory assistance is ☎ 07977. Within Sweden, dial ☎ 90130 for operator assistance and ☎ 07975 for directory assistance.

Visitor Information

Swedish Travel and Tourism Council (Britain), ⊠ 73 Welbeck St., London W15 8AN, ☎ 0171/935–9784, FAX 0171/935–5853.

Swedish Travel and Tourism Council (U.S.), ⊠ 655 3rd Ave., 18th Floor, New York, NY 10017, ☎ 212/949–2333, FAX 212/697–0835.

DANISH VOCABULARY

	English	Danish	Pronunciation

Basics

	English	Danish	Pronunciation
Yes/no	Ja/nej	yah/nie
Thank you	Tak	tak
You're welcome	Selv tak	**sell** tak
Excuse me (to apologize)	Undskyld	**unsk**-ul
Hello	Hej	hi
Goodbye	Farvel	fa-**vel**
Today	I dag	ee **day**
Tomorrow	I morgen	ee **morn**
Yesterday	I går	ee **gore**
Morning	Morgen	**more**-n
Afternoon	Eftermiddag	**ef-tah**-mid-day
Night	Nat	nat

Numbers

1	een/eet	een/eet
2	to	toe
3	tre	tre
4	fire	fear
5	fem	fem
6	seks	sex
7	syv	syoo
8	otte	**oh**-te
9	ni	nee
10	ti	tee

Days of the Week

Monday	mandag	man-day
Tuesday	tirsdag	**tears**-day
Wednesday	onsdag	**ons**-day
Thursday	torsdag	**trs**-day
Friday	fredag	**free**-day
Saturday	lørdag	**lore**-day
Sunday	søndag	**soo**(n)-day

Useful Phrases

Do you speak English?	Taler du engelsk	te-ler doo in-galsk
I don't speak . . .	Jeg taler ikke Dansk	yi tal-ler **ick** Dansk
I don't understand.	Jeg forstår ikke	yi fahr-store **ick**
I don't know.	Det ved jeg ikke	deh **ved** yi ick
I am American/British.	Jeg er amerikansk/britisk	yi ehr a-mehr-i-**kansk**/ bri-**tisk**
I am sick.	Jeg er syg	yi ehr **syoo**
Please call a doctor.	Kan du ringe til en læge?	can **doo** rin-geh til en lay-eh

Do you have a vacant room?	Har du et værelse?	har **doo** eet va(l)r-sa
How much does it cost?	Hvad koster det?	va cos-ta **deh**
It's too expensive.	Det er for dyrt	deh ehr **fohr** dyrt
Beautiful	Smukt	smukt
Help!	Hjælp	yelp
Stop!	Stop	stop
How do I get to . . .	Hvordan kommer jeg til?	vore-**dan** kom-mer yi til
. . . the train station?	banegarden	**ban** eh-gore-en
. . . the post office?	postkontoret	**post**-kon-toh-raht
. . . the tourist office?	turistkonoret	too-**reest**-kon-tor-et
. . . the hospital?	hospitalet	hos-peet-**tal**-et
Does this bus go to . . . ?	Går denne bus til?	**goh** den-na boos til
Where is the W.C.?	Hvor er toilettet	vor **ehr** toi-le(tt)-et
On the left	Til venstre	til **ven**-strah
On the right	Till højre	til **hoy**-ah
Straight ahead	Lige ud	**lee** u(l)

Dining Out

Please bring me . . .	Må jeg få	mo yi foh
menu	menu	me-**nu**
fork	gaffel	gaf-**fel**
knife	kniv	kan-**ew**
spoon	ske	skee
napkin	serviet	serv-**eet**
bread	brød	brood
butter	smør	smoor
milk	mælk	malk
pepper	peber	**pee**-wer
salt	salt	selt
sugar	sukker	**su**-kar
water/bottled water	vand	van
The check, please.	Må jeg bede om regningen	mo yi bi(d) om **ri**-ning

FINNISH VOCABULARY

English	Finnish	Pronunciation
Basics		
Yes/no	Kyllä/Ei	kue-la/ee
Please	Olkaa hyvä	**ol**-kah **hue**-va
Thank you very much.	Kiitoksia paljon	**kee**-tohk-syah **pahl**-yon
You're welcome.	Olkaa hyvä	**ol**-kah **hue**-va

Excuse me.	Anteeksi	**ahn**-teek-see
(to get by someone)	Suokaa	**soo**-oh-kah
(to apologize)	anteeksi	**ahn**-teek-see
Hello	Hyvää päivää	**hue**-va **paee**-va
	terve	**tehr**-veh
Goodbye	Näkemiin	**na**-keh-meen
Today	Tänään	**ta**-naan
Tomorrow	Huomenna	**hoo**-oh-men-nah
Yesterday	Eilen	**ee**-len
Morning	Aamu	**ah**-moo
Afternoon	Iltapäivä	**eel**-tah-**pay**-va
Night	Yö	**eu**-euh

Numbers

1	Yksi	uek-see
2	Kaksi	**kahk**-see
3	Kolme	**kohl**-meh
4	Neljä	**nel**-ya
5	Viisi	**vee**-see
6	Kuusi	**koo**-see
7	Seitsemän	**sate**-seh-man
8	Kahdeksan	**kah**-dek-sahn
9	Yhdeksän	**uef**-dek-san
10	Kymmenen	**kue**-meh-nen

Days of the Week

Monday	maanantai	mah-nahn-tie
Tuesday	tiistai	**tees**-tie
Wednesday	keskiviikko	**kes**-kee-veek-koh
Thursday	torstai	**tohrs**-tie
Friday	perjantai	**pehr**-yahn-tie
Saturday	lauantai	**loo**-ahn-tie
Sunday	sunnuntai	**soon**-noon-tie

Useful Phrases

Do you speak English?	Puhutteko englantia?	poo-hoot-teh-koh ehng-lahn-tee-ah
I don't speak . . .	En puhu suomea . . .	ehn **poo**-hoo **soo**-oh-mee-ah
I don't understand.	En ymmärrä.	ehn **eum**-mar-ra
I don't know.	En tiedä.	ehn **tee**-eh-da
I am American/ British.	Minä olen amerikkalainen/ englantilainen.	**mee**-na **oh**-len **ah**-mehr-ee-kah-lie-nehn/**ehn**-glahn-tee-lie-nehn
I am sick.	Olen sairas.	**oh**-len **sigh**-rahs
Please call a doctor.	Haluan kutsua lääkärin.	**hah**-loo-ahn **koot**-soo-ah **lay**-ka-reen
Do you have a vacant room?	Onko teillä vapaata huonetta?	**ohn**-koh **teel**-la **vah**-pah-tah **hoo**-oh-neht-tah?

How much does it cost?	Paljonko tämä maksaa?	**pahl**-yohn-koh **ta**-ma **mahk**-sah
It's too expensive.	Se on liian kallis.	**say** ohn **lee**-ahn **kah**-lees
Beautiful	Kaunis	**kow**-nees
Help!	Auttakaa!	**ow**-tah-kah
Stop!	Seis!/ Pysähtykää!	say(s) **peu**-sa-teu-kay
How do I get to . . .	Voitteko sanoa miten pääsen . . .	**voy**-tay-koh **sah**-noh-ah **mee**-ten **pay**-sen
. . . the train station	asema (. . . pääsen asemalle?)	**ah**-say-mah (**pay**-sen **ah**-say-mah-lay)
. . . the post office?	posti (. . . paasen postiin?)	**pohs**-tee (**pay**-sen **pohs**-teen)
. . . the tourist office?	matkatoimisto (. . . pääsen matkatoimistoon?)	**maht**-kah-**toy**-mees-toh (**pay**-sen **maht**-kah-**toy**-mees-tohn)
. . . the hospital?	sairaala (. . . pääsen sairaalaan?)	**sigh**-rah-lah (**pay**-sen **sigh**-rah-lahn)
Does this bus go to . . . ?	Kulkeeko tämä bussi-n	**kool**-kay-koh **ta**-ma **boo**-see-n?
Where is the W.C.?	Missä on W.C.?	**mee**-sa ohn **ves**-sah
On the left	Vasemmalle	**vah**-say-mahl-lay
On the right	Oikealle	**ohy**-kay-ah-lay
Straight ahead	Suoraan eteenpäin	**swoh**-rahn **eh**-tayn-pa-een

Dining Out

Please bring me . . .	Tuokaa minulle . . .	too-oh-kah mee-new
menu	ruokalista	**roo**-oh-kah-lees-tah
fork	haarukka	**hahr**-oo-kah
knife	veitsi	**vayt**-see
spoon	lusikka	**loo**-see-kah
napkin	lautasliina	**low**-tahs-lee-nah
bread	leipä	**lay**-pa
butter	voi	**voh**(ee)
milk	maito	**my**-toh
pepper	pippuri	**pee**-poor-ee
salt	suola	**soo**-oh-lah
sugar	sokeri	**soh**-ker-ee
water/bottled water	vesi/ kivennäisvesi	**veh**-see/**kee**-ven-eyes-veh-see
The check, please.	Lasku, olkaa hyvä/Saanko maksaa	**lahs**-kew, **ohl**-kah **heu**-va/**sahn**-koh **mahk**-sah

ICELANDIC VOCABULARY

English	Icelandic	Pronunciation
Basics		
Yes/no	já/nei	yow/nay
Thank you very much.	kærar akkir takk	**kie**-rahr **thah**-kihr **ta**hkk
You're welcome.	Ekkert a-akka	**ehk**-kehrt ath **thah**-ka
Excuse me. (to get by someone)	Afsakid	**ahf**-sah-kith(e)
(to apologize)	Fyrirgefi	**feer**-ee-geh-vith(e)
Hello	Góan dag	goh-than **dahgh**
Goodbye	bless	bless
Today	í dag	**ee dahgh**
Tomorrow	á morgun	ow **mohr**-gun
Yesterday	í gær	ee **gah-eer**
Morning	morgun	**mohr**-gun
Afternoon	eftirmidagur	**ehf**-teer-mihth-dahg-ur
Night	nótt	noht
Numbers		
1	einn	ehnn
2	tveir	**tveh**-eer
3	Prír	threer
4	fjórir	**fyohr**-eer
5	fimm	fehm
6	sex	sex
7	sjö	sy-uh
8	átta	**owt**-tah
9	níu	**nee**-uh
10	tíu	**tee**-uh
Days of the Week		
Monday	mánudagur	mown-ah-dah-gur
Tuesday	ðriðjudagur	**thrithe**-yoo-dah-gur
Wednesday	miðvikudagur	**meethe**-veek-uh dah-gur
Thursday	fimmtudagur	**feem**-too-dah-gur
Friday	föstudagur	**fuhs**-too-dah-gur
Saturday	laugardagur	**loy**-gahr-dah-gur
Sunday	sunnudagur	**soon**-noo-dah-gur
Useful Phrases		
Do you speak English?	Talar ðú ensku?	tah-lahr thoo ehn-skoo
I don't speak Icelandic	Ég tala ekki islensku . . .	**yeh** tah-lah **ehk**-keh **ees**-lehn-skoo
I don't understand.	Ég skil ekki	yeh **skeel ehk**-keh

I don't know.	Ég veit ekki	yeh **vayt ehk**-keh
I am American/British.	Ég er ameriskur/breskur	yeh ehr **ah**-mehr eeskur/brehs-koor
I am sick.	Ég er veik(ur)	yeh ehr vehk(oor)
Please call a doctor.	Viltu hringja í lækni, takk	veel-too **hreeng**-yah ee **lahk**-nee **tah**-kk
Do you have a vacant room?	Átt þú laust herbergi	owt thoo laysht **hehr**-behr-ghee
How much does it cost?	Hvað kostar Það	kvathe kohs-tahr thathe
It's too expensive.	Það er of dýrt	thahthe ehr ohf deert
Beautiful	Fallegur/t	**fahl**-lehg-oor
Help!	Hjálp	hyalp
Stop!	Stopp	stohp
How do I get to . . .	Hvernig kemst ég	**kvehr**-neeg kehmst **yehg**
. . . the post office?	á pósthúsi	ow pohst-hoos-ihthe
. . . the tourist office?	á feramálará	ow **fehr**-tha-mow-lahr-owthe
. . . the hospital?	á spitalan	ow **spee**-tah-lahn
Does this bus go to . . . ?	Fer Þessi vagn	fehr **thehs**-see **vakn**
Where is the W.C.?	hvar er salerni	kvahr ehr sahl-ehr-nihthe
On the left	til vinstri	teel **veen**-stree
On the right	til hægri	teel **hie**-ree
Straight ahead	beint áfram	baynt **ow**-frahm

Dining Out

Please bring me . . .	get ég fengi	geht yehg fehn-gihthe
menu	matseðil	**maht**-seh-theel
fork	gaffal	**gah**-fahl(t)
knife	hnif	hneef
spoon	skeið	skaythe
napkin	servetta	sehr-**veht**-tah
bread	brauð	braythe
butter	smjör	smyoor
milk	mjólk	myoolk
pepper	pipar	**pay**-pahr
salt	salt	sahlt
sugar	sykur	**say**-koor
water/bottled water	vatn	vahtn
The check, please.	reikninginn	takk **rehk**-nihn-ghihn

NORWEGIAN VOCABULARY

	English	Norwegian	Pronunciation
Basics			
	Yes/no	Ja/nei	yah/nay
	Please	Vær så snill	**vehr** soh snihl
	Thank you very much.	Tusen takk	**tews**-sehn tahk
	You're welcome.	Vær så god	**vehr** soh goo
	Excuse me.	Unnskyld	**ewn**-shewl
	Hello	God dag	goo **dahg**
	Goodbye	Adjø	ah-**dyur**
	Today	i dag	ee **dahg**
	Tomorrow	i morgen	ee **moh**-ern
	Yesterday	i går	ee **gohr**
	Morning	morgen	**moh**-ern
	Afternoon	ettermiddag	**eh-terr**-mid-dahg
	Night	natt	naht
Numbers			
	1	en	ehn
	2	to	too
	3	tre	treh
	4	fire	**feer**-eh
	5	fem	fehm
	6	seks	sehks
	7	syv, sju	shew
	8	åtte	**oh**-teh
	9	ni	nee
	10	ti	tee
Days of the Week			
	Monday	mandag	mahn-dahg
	Tuesday	tirsdag	**teesh**-dahg
	Wednesday	onsdag	**oonss**-dahg
	Thursday	torsdag	**tohsh**-dahg
	Friday	fredag	**fray**-dahg
	Saturday	lørdag	**loor**-dahg
	Sunday	søndag	**suhn**-dahg
Useful Phrases			
	Do you speak English?	Snakker De engelsk?	snahk-kerr dee ehng-ehlsk
	I don't speak Norwegian.	Jeg snakker ikke norsk.	yay **snahk**-kerr **ik**-keh nohrshk
	I don't understand.	Jeg forstår ikke.	yay fosh-**tawr** **ik**-keh
	I don't know.	Jeg vet ikke.	yay veht **ik**-keh
	I am American/British.	Jeg er amerikansk/engelsk.	yay ehr ah-mehr-ee-kahnsk/ehng-ehlsk
	I am sick.	Jeg er dårlig.	yay ehr **dohr**-lee

Please call a doctor.	Vær så snill og ring etter en lege.	vehr soh snihl oh ring **eht**-ehr ehn **lay**-geh
Do you have vacant room?	Har du et rom som er ledig?	yay vil **yehr**-neh hah eht room
How much does it cost?	Hva koster det?	vah **koss**-terr deh
It's too expensive.	Det er for dyrt.	deh ehr for **deert**
Beautiful	vakker	**vah**-kehr
Help!	Hjelp!	yehlp
Stop!	Stopp!	stop
How do I get to . . .	Hvor er	voor ehr
. . . the train station?	jernbanestasjonen	yehrn-bahn-eh sta-**shoon**-ern
. . . the post office?	posthuset	**pohsst**-hewss
. . . the tourist office?	turistkontoret	tew-**reest**-koon-toor-er
. . . the hospital?	sykehuset	**see**-keh-hoo-seh
Does this bus go to . . . ?	Går denne bussen til . . . ?	gohr **den**-nah boos teel
Where is the W.C.?	Hvor er toalettene?	voor ehr too-ah-**leht**-te-ne
On the left	Til venstre	teel **vehn**-streh
On the right	Til høyre	teel **hooy**-reh
Straight ahead	Rett fram	reht **frahm**

Dining Out

menu	meny	meh-new
fork	gaffel	gahff-erl
knife	kniv	kneev
spoon	skje	shay
napkin	serviett	ssehr-vyeht
bread	brød	brur
butter	smør	smurr
milk	melk	mehlk
pepper	pepper	pehp-per
salt	salt	sahlt
sugar	sukker	sook-kerr
water/bottled water	vann	vahn
The check, please.	Jeg vil gjerne betale.	yay vil **yehr**-neh beh-**tah**-leh

SWEDISH VOCABULARY

English	Swedish	Pronunciation

Basics

| Yes/no | Ja/nej | yah/nay |
| Please | Var snäll; Var vänlig | vahr snehll vahr vehn-leeg |

Thank you very much.	Tack så **mee**-keh	tahk soh mycket.
You're welcome.	Var så god.	vahr shoh **goo**
Excuse me. (to get by someone)	Ursäkta.	oor-**shehk**-tah
(to apologize)	Förlåt.	fur-**loht**
Hello	God dag	goo **dahg**
Goodbye	Adjö	ah-**yoo**
Today	I dag	ee **dahg**
Tomorrow	I morgon	ee **mor**-ron
Yesterday	I går	ee **gohr**
Morning	Morgon	**mohr**-on
Afternoon	Eftermiddag	**ehf**-ter-meed-dahg
Night	Natt	naht

Numbers

1	ett	eht
2	två	tvoh
3	tre	tree
4	fyra	fee-rah
5	fem	fem
6	sex	sex
7	sju	shoo
8	åtta	oht-tah
9	nio	nee
10	tio	tee

Days of the Week

Monday	måndag	mohn-dahg
Tuesday	tisdag	tees-dahg
Wednesday	onsdag	ohns-dahg
Thursday	torsdag	tohrs-dahg
Friday	fredag	freh-dahg
Saturday	lördag	luhr-dahg
Sunday	söndag	sohn-dahg

Useful Phrases

Do you speak English?	Talar ni engelska?	tah-lahr nee ehng-ehl-skah
I don't speak . . .	Jag talar inte svenska . . .	yah tah-lahr **een**-teh **sven**-skah
I don't understand.	Jag förstår inte.	yah fuhr-**stohr** **een**-teh
I don't know.	Jag vet inte.	yah **veht een**-teh
I am American/ British.	Jag är amerikan/ engelsman.	yah ay ah-mehr-ee-**kahn**/ **ehng**-ehls-mahn
I am sick.	Jag är sjuk.	yah ay **shyook**
Please call a doctor.	Jag vill skicka efter en läkare.	yah veel **shee**-kah **ehf**-tehr ehn **lay**-kah-reh

Do you have a vacant room?	Har Ni något rum ledigt?	hahr nee noh-goht **room leh**-deekt
How much does it cost?	Vad kostar det?/ Hur mycket kostar det?	vah **kohs**-tahr deh/hor **mee**-keh **kohs**-tahr deh
It's too expensive.	Den är för dyr.	dehn ay foor **deer**
Beautiful	Vacker	**vah**-kehr
Help!	Hjälp	yehlp
Stop!	Stopp, stanna	stop, **stahn**-nah
How do I get to . . .	Kan Ni visa mig vägen till	kahn nee **vee**-sah may **vay**-gehn teel
. . . the train station?	stationen	stah-**shoh**-nehn
. . . the post office?	posten	**pohs**-tehn
. . . the tourist office?	en resebyrå	ehn-**reh**-seh-**bee**-roh
. . . the hospital?	sjukhuset	**shyook**-hoo-seht
Does this bus go to . . . ?	Går den här bussen	gohr dehn hehr **boo**-sehn
till?	teel	
Where is the W.C.?	Var är toilett/ toaletten	vahr ay twah-**leht**
On the left	Till vänster	teel **vehn**-stur
On the right	Till höger	teel **huh**-gur
Straight ahead	Rakt fram	rahkt **frahm**

Dining Out

Please bring me . . .	Var snäll och hämta åt mig	vahr snehl oh hehm-tah oht may
menu	matsedeln	maht-seh-dehln
fork	en gaffel	ehn gahf-fehl
knife	en kniv	ehn kneev
spoon	en sked	ehn shehd
napkin	en servett	ehn sehr-veht
bread	bröd	bruh(d)
butter	smör	smuhr
milk	mjölk	myoolk
pepper	peppar	pehp-pahr
salt	salt	sahlt
sugar	socker	soh-kehr
water	vatten	vaht-n
The check, please.	Får jag be om notan?	fohr yah beh ohm **noh**-tahn

508

INDEX

Note: For entries beginning with the Icelandic letter Þ (pronounced "th" as in *thin*), see under T.

Index

NOTES

NOTES

NOTES

CNN✈
Airport Network

Your
Window
To The
World
While You're
On The
Road

Keep in touch when you're traveling. Before you take off, tune in to CNN Airport Network. Now available in major airports across America, CNN Airport Network provides nonstop news, sports, business, weather and lifestyle programming. Both domestic and international. All piloted by the top-flight global resources of CNN. All up-to-the minute reporting. And just for travelers, CNN Airport Network features two daily Fodor's specials. "Travel Fact" provides enlightening, useful travel trivia, while "What's Happening" covers upcoming events in major cities worldwide. So why be bored waiting to board? TIME FLIES WHEN YOU'RE WATCHING THE WORLD THROUGH THE WINDOW OF CNN AIRPORT NETWORK!

WHEREVER YOU TRAVEL, *H*ELP IS NEVER FAR AWAY.

From planning your trip to providing travel assistance along the way, American Express® Travel Service Offices are always there to help.

Scandinavia

American Express Travel Service
Amagertorv 18 (Stroget)
Copenhagen, Denmark
3/312-2301

Area Travel Agency Limited (R)
Helsinki-Vantaa Airport
International Terminal
Helsinki, Finland
0/818-3438

Area Travel Agency Limited Helsinki (R)
Tallinnanaukio 6
Helsinki, Finland
0/33 60 55

Urval-Utsyn Travel Ltd. (R)
Radhustorg 3
Akureyri, Iceland
46/25 000

Urval-Utsyn Travel Ltd. (R)
Lagmuli 4
Reykjavik, Iceland
5/69 93 00

American Express Limited
Mariboesgt 13
Oslo, Norway
2/298-3700

American Express Travel Service
Birger Jarlsgatan 1
Stockholm, Sweden
8/679-5200

Nyman & Schultz American Express
Sky City Arlanda Airport
Stockholm-Arlanda, Sweden
771/79 00 25

Travel

http://www.americanexpress.com/travel

American Express Travel Service Offices are found in central locations throughout Scandinavia.